THE NEW LAW OF TORTS

DANUTA MENDELSON

OXFORD
UNIVERSITY PRESS

253 Normanby Road, South Melbourne, Victoria 3205, Australia

Oxford University Press is a department of the University of Oxford. It furthers the University's objective of excellence in research, scholarship, and education by publishing worldwide in

Oxford New York

Auckland Cape Town Dar es Salaam Hong Kong Karachi
Kuala Lumpur Madrid Melbourne Mexico City Nairobi
New Delhi Shanghai Taipei Toronto

With offices in

Argentina Austria Brazil Chile Czech Republic France Greece
Guatemala Hungary Italy Japan Poland Portugal Singapore
South Korea Switzerland Thailand Turkey Ukraine Vietnam

OXFORD is a trade mark of Oxford University Press in the UK and in certain other countries

Copyright © Danuta Mendelson 2007
First published 2007
Reprinted 2007

Reproduction and communication for educational purposes
The Australian Copyright Act 1968 (the Act) allows a maximum of one chapter or 10% of the pages of this work, whichever is the greater, to be reproduced and/or communicated by any educational institution for its educational purposes provided that the educational institution (or the body that administers it) has given a remuneration notice to Copyright Agency Limited (CAL) under the Act.

For details of the CAL licence for educational institutions contact:

Copyright Agency Limited
Level 19, 157 Liverpool Street
Sydney NSW 2000
Telephone: (02) 9394 7600
Facsimile: (02) 9394 7601
E-mail: info@copyright.com.au

Reproduction and communication for other purposes
Except as permitted under the Act (for example a fair dealing for the purposes of study, research, criticism or review) no part of this book may be reproduced, stored in a retrieval system, communicated or transmitted in any form or by any means without prior written permission. All inquiries should be made to the publisher at the address above.

National Library of Australia
Cataloguing-in-Publication data:

> Mendelson, Danuta.
> The new law of torts.
>
> Includes index.
> ISBN 9780195553567.
>
> ISBN 0 19 555356 X.
>
> 1. Torts—Australia. I. Title.
>
> 346.9403

Edited by Trischa Baker
Text design by Patrick Cannon
Cover design by Mason Design
Typeset by Cannon Typesettting, Melbourne
Proofread by Natasha Broadstock
Indexed by Puddingburn Publishing Services
Printed in Hong Kong by Sheck Wah Tong Printing Press Ltd

Contents

Preface	x
Table of Cases	xiii
Table of Statues	xxxvi

Part I
INTRODUCTION   1

1 Introduction to the Law of Torts and Historical Overview   3
Introduction   3
Definition and classification of torts   4
Historical origins of the law of torts   9
Torts reforms of 2002–03   19
Further reading   26

2 The Law of Compensation and Damages   27
Introduction   27
History of compensation in the law of torts   29
Nature of compensation in the law of torts   31
Classification of damages   38
Damages for gratuitous services and attendant care   53
Assessment of damages   58
Further reading   67

3 Survival Actions and Wrongful Death; Statutory Compensation Schemes   68
Introduction   68
Survival of causes of action   68

	Statutory compensation schemes	77
	Further reading	88

Part II
INTENTIONAL TORTS — 89
Actions *in personam* and actions *in rem* — 89

4 Trespass to the Person (Battery, Assault and False Imprisonment) — 91
- Introduction — 91
- Historical origins of the tort of trespass to the person — 91
- The tort of battery — 95
- The tort of assault — 99
- Negligent trespass — 104
- The tort of false imprisonment — 105
- Further reading — 113

5 Trespass to Land — 114
- Introduction — 114
- Trespass to land: history and rationale — 114
- Elements of the tort of trespass to land — 117
- Trespass beneath and above the surface of the land — 121
- Damages — 123
- Limitations of the tort of trespass to land — 124
- Tort of trespass to land and the right to privacy in Australia — 125
- Further reading — 127

6 Miscellaneous Intentional Torts of Action on the Case — 128
- History — 128
- Action on the case for intentional infliction of physical harm — 129
- Cause of action for intentional infliction of nervous shock — 130
- Malicious prosecution — 135
- Tort of collateral abuse of process — 139
- Misfeasance in public office — 143
- Torts of breach of confidence and misuse of private information — 152
- Further reading — 156

7	**Deceit and Injurious Falsehood**	**157**
	Introduction	157
	Deceit	158
	Injurious falsehood	166
8	**Torts of Intentional Interference with Goods**	**171**
	Introduction	171
	Trespass to goods (chattels)	173
	Detinue	178
	Conversion	182
	Special action on the case for intentional damage to goods	201
	'Spoliation': intentional or negligent destruction of evidence	202
	Further reading	203
9	**Defences to Intentional Torts**	**204**
	Introduction	204
	The concept of fault in intentional torts	204
	Consent in intentional torts	205
	Exceptions to battery	218
	Defence of self-defence and defence of others	223
	Defence of insanity	225
	Statutory defences of legal authority	226
	Defences to false imprisonment	227
	Exceptions and defences to trespass to land	229
	Defence of limitation of actions	231
	Mistake	232
	Further reading	233

Part III
THE TORT OF NEGLIGENCE — 235
Introduction — 235

10	**Negligence: Duty of Care**	**241**
	Introduction	241
	Liability of landlords and occupiers	256
	Duty to the unborn	263
	Further reading	269

11 Breach of Duty of Care — 270

Introduction — 270
Retrospective nature of the inquiry — 271
General breach principles — 272
Social utility — 284
Time for assessing the risk — 285
Individual responsibility and community standards — 287
Relevance of the obvious nature of the risk — 289
Public authorities — 298
Industry standards — 306
Professional standards — 307
Standard of care: the reasonable person — 314
The nature of inference in law — 320
'Slipping' cases — 322
Further reading — 324

12 Causation and *Res Ipsa Loquitur* — 325

Introduction — 325
General common law rules for attributing legal liability — 327
Statutory definition of legal causation — 334
Tests for attributing legal liability in exceptional cases of 'evidential gaps' — 337
Statutory approach to 'evidential gaps' — 351
Attributing legal liability in cases of failure to advise — 354
Statutory approaches to hindsight bias — 361
Novus actus interveniens — 363
Attribution of liability for unrelated subsequent events — 368
Attribution of liability for property damage — 370
Further reading — 374

13 Remoteness of Damage — 375

Introduction — 375
The meaning of 'reasonable foreseeability' — 375
The concept of remoteness of damage — 377
The test for remoteness of damage — 380
Further reading — 385

Part IIIA
PARTICULAR CATEGORIES OF CASE 387
Introduction 387

14 Pure Nonfeasance (Pure Omissions) 393
Historical introduction: acts and omissions 393
Pure nonfeasance and the common law 394
Liability of public authorities for omissions at common law 397
Liability of highway authorities 411
Entities vested with regulation-making power 413
Further reading 414

15 Mental Harm: Liability for Negligently Occasioned Pure Psychiatric Injury 415
Introduction 415
Evolution of liability for negligently occasioned pure psychiatric injury 421
Codification of the law of psychiatric injury in Australia 437
Statutory paradigm for recovery of damages for negligently caused mental harm 437
Further reading 443

16 Pure Economic Loss 445
Negligently occasioned pure economic loss 445
Negligent misstatement 450
Pure economic loss caused through negligent physical conduct 465
Further reading 472

17 Defences to negligence 473
Introduction 473
Historical background 475
Contributory negligence 478
Voluntary assumption of risk 503
Further reading 525

Part IV
STRICT-LIABILITY TORTS — 527

18 Private Nuisance — 529
Introduction — 529
Legal species of nuisance — 530
Definition of the tort of private nuisance — 534
Interference with the use and enjoyment of property rights — 536
Activities that offend sensibilities of neighbouring occupiers — 545
Title to sue — 549
Who may be sued? — 550
Remedies — 554
Defences — 556
Further reading — 559

19 Breach of Statutory Duty — 560
Historical introduction — 560
Nature of private action for breach of statutory duty — 562
Elements of the action for breach of statutory duty — 565
Defences — 573
Further reading — 577

20 Establishing Defamation — 578
Introduction — 578
Libel and slander — 581
Cause of action for publication of defamatory matter — 582
Elements of the cause of action — 585
Element 1: The matter conveys a defamatory imputation or imputations — 586
Element 2: The matter identifies, or is capable of identifying, the plaintiff as the person defamed — 598
Element 3: The matter has been published by the defendant to at least one person other than the plaintiff — 601
Procedural matters — 606
Non-litigious means of resolving disputes — 609
Further reading — 609

21	**Defences and Remedies in Defamation Law**	**610**
	Introduction	610
	Justification	610
	Honest opinion (fair comment)	616
	Absolute privilege	623
	Public documents	626
	Reports of proceedings of public concern	627
	Common law qualified privilege	629
	Statutory qualified privilege	644
	Triviality	648
	Remedies	648
	Further reading	651
22	**Vicarious Liability and Non-Delegable Duty of Care: Types of Liability**	**652**
	Introduction	652
	Vicarious liability	653
	Independent contractors	663
	Non-delegable duty of care	665
	Solidary and proportionate liability	674
	Further reading	681
	Index	*682*

Preface

During the period 2002–06, each Australian jurisdiction enacted legislation, referred to as the Torts reforms, which codified large parts of the law of damages, the substantive law of negligence, the law of defamation, and other important aspects of torts' jurisprudence. This book presents the post–Torts reform landscape of the law of torts. It provides a detailed comparative analysis of the reform legislation in each Australian jurisdiction, pointing out similarities and differences between the common law and the new legislative tort regimes in various Australian jurisdictions. The examination of the major areas of tort law includes intentional interference with the person (battery, assault, and false imprisonment), trespass to land, malicious prosecution, abuse of process, and misfeasance in public office, conversion, detinue and trespass to goods, deceit and injurious falsehood as well as nuisance, breach of statutory duty, and the principles governing vicarious and concurrent liability. There is an extended discussion of the tort of negligence with its three major categories of case (omissions, mental harm, and pure economic loss), and defamation.

This book is intended to convey an appreciation of the new law of torts in the context of its historical development. The underlying theme that runs through the book is the question whether foundational principles and policies of torts law reflect the social and moral values of modern Australian society. Ulpian (193–235 CE), the great Roman jurist, said (at *Justinian's Digest* 1.1.10.1), that 'the main principles which a just [legal] system should seek to implement, [are] in particular the duty not to harm others and the duty to render each his due'. Is the law of torts just? This question is left for you, the reader, to answer.

THE OVERVIEW OF THE BOOK

From its beginnings, the common law of torts was characterised by conceptual flexibility that has enabled it to continually transform itself, expand, and redefine its purposes. Over many centuries the fundamental concepts of fault and compensation have been adapted to suit and reflect the values and expectations of society as it evolved from agrarian feudalism, based on a system of land tenures and villeinage (serfdom), to the modern post-industrial polity based on universal franchise and espousing such notions as virtual property. The law of torts thus can be discussed from many perspectives, including history, philosophy, economics, sociology, politics, feminism, comparative law, and minority and Aboriginal studies, to name but a few. My approach is essentially chronological. The book does not aim to provide a comprehensive analysis of the history of the law of torts. Rather, it locates the post-reform law in its historical context by tracing sequentially the evolution of the most important areas of torts law, discussing the history of each tort and, where appropriate, its elements. The main focus is on common law torts; however, statutory torts such as breach of statutory duty are included.

As noted above the characteristic of the common law of torts is its dynamism. It builds, not necessarily in a systematic manner, on the already existing body of laws, both legislative and judge-made. The recent history of the law of torts may give an impression of its jurisprudence being out of control—prone to sudden changes and shifts. Chronology provides an intellectual framework for ascertaining the development of doctrines and principles that explain why certain causes of action have particular elements, requirements and limitations.

The book is divided into four parts. It begins with a brief explanation of the nature and history of the law of torts, followed by an analysis of the law of damages, in particular, the nature of compensation, and methods of obtaining redress for civil wrongs. The law of damages is discussed at the outset because the notion of compensation is fundamental to the theory and practice of torts law.

Part II concentrates on the generic tort of trespass, one of the earliest writs issued by the Chancery, and its species. Some tortious causes of action tend to form distinct conceptual clusters—for example, trespass to goods, detinue and conversion. The genus of the action on the case is initially explored through examination of various intentional torts on the case (intentional infliction of physical injury or nervous shock; malicious prosecution; abuse of process; misfeasance in public office; deceit; injurious falsehood).

Part III focuses on the most prominent species of action on the case: negligence. The elements of negligence—duty of care, breach of duty of care, causation, and remoteness of damage—as well as defences to negligence, and special categories of case omissions, pure mental harm, and pure economic loss are examined in depth.

Part IV presents an analysis of the tort of nuisance, which though of ancient provenance, has been substantially modified; the relatively modern cause of action for breach of statutory duty, and defamation, which has been codified only recently. The final chapter is devoted to a critical consideration of the strict liability regimes: vicarious liability and non-delegable duty of care, as well as solidary and proportionate liability.

The book examines seminal cases determined by the High Court of Australia and, where relevant, the House of Lords. However, some interesting appellate cases are also discussed in some detail, for I agree with Kirby J's observation in *Woolcock St Invest v CDG Pty Ltd* (2004) 216 CLR 515, at [123], that:

> the one lesson that has emerged from recent Australian cases about the law of negligence is that the facts and the evidence, taken as a whole, are critical for the resolution of the issues presented by the tort. It is out of the detail of the facts that the 'salient features' and pertinent factors will emerge that help the decision-maker to decide whether a duty of care exists, whether it has been breached and, if so, whether that breach caused the plaintiff's damage.

One could add that Kirby J's comments are equally applicable to all torts, and that the importance of facts is twofold: they are critical to the process of judicial decision-making, while reminding us that the law is not an abstract science, it is about people. The facts of each case recount a story, which has invariably blighted the life of the plaintiff, and often that of the defendant.

I am grateful to Sharon Erbacher for contributing the important chapters on Defamation, Deceit and Injurious Falsehood. I also wish to thank Professor Mirko Bagaric, Head of the Deakin University School of Law for his support, and the Faculty of Business and Law for granting me a Research Semester to write this book. The critique and comments provided by anonymous Oxford University Press reviewers were of great assistance. Trischa Baker, the editor for Oxford University Press burnished the manuscript to make the text elegant and clear, while Katie Ridsdale, the publishing editor, provided amiable and tactful support.

The friendship, consideration and wonderful counsel of my husband, George Mendelson, have been invaluable. I am indebted to my colleagues, the many torts scholars and members of the judiciary whose writings have helped me to appreciate, and, hopefully, elucidate the breath, depth, and intricacy of the modern Australian torts law. Writing this book was a fascinating voyage of intellectual discovery for me, and I hope that you, the reader, shall find it equally interesting.

In memory of my wonderful parents,
Chaim and Sabina Wachenhauser

Table of Cases

As you progress through this book you will encounter a great number of cases. Not all of these cases are equally important. In decreasing order of importance, for the purposes of this subject, cases fall into the following categories:

- Cases that establish, explain or illustrate legal principles. You will be asked questions about these cases and you must be very familiar with them.
- Cases that are digested for you in the text. You should know the propositions of law for which these cases are cited.
- Cases that are merely referred to in the text as authority for a proposition of law under discussion. It is not essential that you study these cases.

To assist your revision, all cases referred to in the book are listed here. All High Court of Australia decisions since 1947 are also available on the website of the Australian Legal Information Institute (http:\\austlii.law.uts.edu.au). Please note that citations to unreported Australian cases decided after 1997 are cited in media neutral form.

The following casebooks are available in Australia:

- Luntz H & Hambly D, *Torts Cases and Commentary*, Butterworths, Sydney, 1995
- Morison WL & Sappideen C, *Torts: Commentary and Materials*, 8th ed, Law Book Co., Sydney, 1993
- Swanton, JP, McDonald B, Anderson R, *Cases on Torts*, 2nd ed, Federation Press, Leichhardt, NSW, 1994

A (Children) (Conjoined Twins: Surgical Separation) [2001] 2 WLR 480; [2000] 4 All ER 961   220
Ackerley v Parkinson (1815) 3 M & S 411; 105 ER 665   143
Adam v Ward [1917] AC 309   629, 631, 633
Adamson v Motor Vehicle Insurance Trust (1957) 58 WALR 56   318
Agar v Hyde; Agar v Worsley (2000) 201 CLR 552   395, 413
Airedale NHS Trust v Bland [1993] AC 789; 1 All ER 821   209
Akerhielm v De Mare (1959) AC 789   162, 163
Alati v Kruger (1955) 94 CLR 216   165
Albrighton v Royal Prince Alfred Hospital [1980] 2 NSWLR 542   258
Alcock v Chief Constable [1992] 1 AC 310; [1991] 3 WLR 1057; 4 All ER 907   425
Aldred v Benton (1610) 9 Co Rep 57   543
Aldridge v Booth (1988) 80 ALR 1   215
Alexander v NE Rwy (1865) 6 B&S 340   612
Allcorp Cleaning Services Pty Ltd v Fairweather [1998] NSWSC 291   323
Allen v Tasmania Police [2004] TASSC 30   549
Allen v Tobias (1958) 98 CLR 367   202
Allianz Australia Insurance Ltd v General Cologne Re Australia Ltd (2003) 57 NSWLR 321   333
Allianz Australia Insurance Ltd v GSF Australia Pty [2005] HCA 26   326, 332, 333, 337, 572
Alphacell Ltd v Woodward [1972] AC 824   326
Amalgamated Television Services Pty Ltd v Marsden (1998) 43 NSWLR 158   593
Anchor Products Ltd v Hedges (1966) 115 CLR 493   372
Andar Transport Pty Ltd v Brambles Ltd (2004) 78 ALJR 907; [2004] HCA 28   574, 575, 577
Anderson v Mirror Newspapers Ltd (1986) 6 NSWLR 99   591
Anderson v Nationwide News Pty Ltd (2001) 3 VR 619   613, 620
Anderson v Nationwide News Pty Ltd (No 2) (2001) 3 VR 639   619
Andreae v Selfridge & Co Ltd [1938] Ch 1; [1937] 3 All ER 255   546
Andrews v Grand and Toy Alberta Ltd (1978) 83 DLR (3d) 452   48
Animal Liberation (Vic) Inc v Gasser [1991] 1 VR 51   548, 549, 550
Annetts v Australian Stations Pty Ltd (2000) 23 WAR 35   428
Annetts v Australian Stations Pty Ltd (2002) *see* Tame v New South Wales; Annetts v Australian Stations Pty Ltd
Anns v Merton London Borough Council [1978] AC 728   389, 399
Anon (c 1310) YB 2 & 3 Edw II   180
Ansell v Waterhouse (1817) 2 Chit RI   244, 245
Arbrath v North Eastern Railway Co (1883) 11 QBD 440   138
Archer v Brown [1984] 2 All ER 251   166
Argy v Blunts and Lane Cove Real Estate Pty Ltd (1990) 26 FCR 112   158
Armory v Delamirie (1722) 1 Stra 505   189, 202
Arscott v The Coal Authority [2004] EWCA (Civ) 892 (CA)   539
Ashby v White (1703) 2 Ld Raym 938; 1 Smith's Leading Cases (13th ed) 253   38, 143
Astley v Austrust Ltd (1999) 197 CLR 1   459, 483, 484, 575, 577
Attorney-General v Guardian Newspapers Ltd (No 2) [1990] 1 AC 109   154, 155
Attorney-General v Stone (1895) 12 TLR 76   552
Attorney-General v Tod Heatley [1897] 1 Ch 560   532
Attorney-General (Qld) (Ex Rel Kerr) v T (1983) 46 ALR 275; 1 Qd R 404; 8 Fam LR 875   263
Attorney-General's Reference (No 6 of 1980) [1981] QB 715; 73 Cr App R 63   216
Augustus v Gosset [1996] 3 SCR 268   76
Austin v Commissioner of Police of the Metropolis [2005] EWHC 480 (QBD)   39
Austin v Dowling (1870) LR 5 CP 534   110
Austin v Mirror Newspapers Ltd [1986] AC 299   640, 646
Australian Broadcasting Corporation v Comalco Ltd (1986) 12 FCR 510   583, 592, 593, 618, 621, 622, 629, 630, 631, 649
Australian Broadcasting Corporation v Lenah Game Meats Pty Ltd (2001) 208 CLR 199   126, 579
Australian Broadcasting Corporation v Waterhouse (1991) 25 NSWLR 519   607
Australian Capital Schools Authority v El Sheik [2000] FCA 931   667
Australian Consolidated Press Ltd v Ettingshausen (unreported, NSWCA, 13 October 1993)   125
Australian Consolidated Press v Uren (1967) 117 CLR 221   42
Australian Guarantee Corporation Ltd v Commissioners of State Bank of Victoria [1989] ATR 80-229; [1989] VR 617   197, 201, 483

Australian Institute of Management v Rossi [2004] WASCA 302   80
Australian Safeway Stores Pty Ltd v Zaluzna (1987) 162 CLR 479; 69 ALR 615; 61 ALJR 180   258, 671
Australian Traineeship System v Wafta [2004] NSWCA 230   297
Autodesk Inc v Yee (1996) 68 FCR 391   186

B v Marinovich (1999) NTSC 127   43
B (A Minor) (Wardship Medical Treatment), Re [1981] 1 WLR 1421   212
Baby A, Re [1999] NSWCA 787   212
Backwell v AAA (1997) 1 VR 182   43
Baker v Willoughby [1970] AC 467; [1969] 3 AllER 1528   368
Ballina Shire Council v Ringland (1994) 33 NSWLR 680   584
Balmain New Ferry Co v Robertson (1906) 4 CLR 379   107
Baltic Shipping Company v Dillon (1993) 176 CLR 344   138
Baltimore City Pass R Co v Kemp 61 Md 74; 48 Am Rep 134 (1884)   381
Bamford v Turnley (1862) 3 B & S 62 (Ex Ch);121 ER 27; [1861-73] All ER 706   536, 537, 546
Banque Bruxelles Lambert SA v Eagle Star Insurance Co Ltd [1997] AC 191 (HL)   354, 357
Barbaro v Amalgamated Television Services Pty Ltd (1985) 1 NSWLR 30   646
Barker v Sands & Madougall Co Ltd (1890) 16 VLR 719   136
Barker v The Queen (1983) 163 CLR 338; 57 ALJR 426; 47 ALR 1   119
Barnes v Commonwealth (1937) 37 SR(NSW) 511   427
Barrett v Associated Newspapers Ltd (1907) 23 TLR 666   166
Barton v Armstrong [1969] 2 NSWR 451   103
Barwon Spinners Pty Ltd v Podolak [2005] VSCA 33   79
Battista v Cooper (1976) 14 SASR 225   133
Bazley v Curry [1999] 2 SCR 534   659
Beach Club Port Douglas Pty Ltd v Page [2005] QCA 475   141
Beitzel v Crabb [1992] 2 VR 121   624
Bendeich, Re (No 2) (1994) 53 FCR 422   513
Bendix Mintex Pty Ltd v Barnes (1997) 42 NSWLR 307   348
Benjamin v Currie [1958] VR 259   77
Bennett v Minister of Community Welfare (1992) 176 CLR 408; 107 ALR 617; 66 ALJR 550   240, 326, 329, 340, 347
Benning v Wong (1969) 122 CLR 249; [1970] ALR 585; 43 ALJR 467   557, 671
Berkoff v Burchill [1996] 4 All ER 1008   597
The Bernina (No 2); Mills v Armstrong (1887) 12 PD 58   479
Bernstein of Leigh (Baron) v Skyviews & General Ltd [1978] 1 QB 478   122
Berrigan Shire Council v Ballerini [2005] VSCA 159   249, 292
Berryman v Joslyn; Wentworth Shire Council v Joslyn [2001] NSWCA 95   459, 493
Berryman v Joslyn; Wentworth Shire Council v Joslyn [2004] NSWCA 121   493
Berryman v Joslyn; Wentworth Shire Council v Joslyn (2) [2004] NSWCA 239   494
Betts v Whittingslowe (1945) 71 CLR 637   339, 571
Bieletski v Obadiak (1921) 61 DLR 494; affd (1922) 65 DLR 627   134
Bik v Mirror Newspapers Ltd [1979] 2 NSWLR 679   592
Birchmeier v Rockdale Municipal Council (1935) 51 WN (NSW) 201   138
Bird v Holbrook (1828) 4 Bing 628; 130 ER 911   129, 130
Bird v Jones (1845) 7 QB 742; 115 ER 663   107
Birkett v Director General of Family & Community Services (unreported, NSWSC, Bryson J, 3 February 1994)   213
Bjelke-Peterson v Warburton [1987] 2 Qd R 465   587, 600
Blake v Midland Rly Co (1852) 21 LJ QB 233; 18 QB 93; 118 ER 35   74, 236, 415
Blakeley v Shortal's Estate 20 NW 2d 28 (1945)   133
Blatch v Archer [(1774) 1 Cowp 63; 98 ER 969   58
Blundell v Musgrave (1956) 96 CLR 73   30
Blyth v Birmingham Waterworks Co (1856) 11 Exch 781   245, 270
Board of Management of Royal Perth Hospital v Frost (unreported WAFC 26 February 1997 BC9700642)   350
Bolam v Friern Hospital Management Committee (1957) 1 WLR 582   308
Bolitho v City and Hackney Health Authority [1997] UKHL 46; [1998] AC 232   308, 309

Bolton, Re; Ex parte Beane (1987) 162 CLR 514   105
Bolton v Stone [1951] AC 850; [1951] 1 All ER 1078   275, 279, 281, 284
Bone v Seale [1975] 1 WLR 797; 1 All ER 787   543
Bonello (by his tutor Bonello) v Lotzof (unreported, NSWSC, Grove J, 23 September 1997)   357
Bonnard v Perryman [1891] 2 Ch 269   651
Bonnington Castings Ltd v Wardlaw [1956] AC 613; [1956] 1 All ER 615   337, 338, 339, 341, 436, 573
Boothman v Canada (TD) [1993] 3 FC 381   134
Boroondara City Council v Cattanach [2004] VSCA 139   302, 303
Boson v Sandford (1691) 91 ER 382   654
Bourhill (or Hay) v Young [1943] 1 AC 92   254, 423, 426, 427
Bourke v Butterfield and Lewis Ltd (1926) 38 CLR 354; 27 ST(NSW) 339   575
Bowman v Secular Society Ltd [1917] AC 406   30
Boyd v Mirror Newspapers Limited [1980] 2 NSWLR 449   597
Boyded Industries Pty Ltd v Canuto [2004] NSWCA   288, 297
Boyle v State Rail Authority (NSW) [1997] NSWDDT 3; (1997) 14 NSWCCR 374   676
Bradshaw v McEwans Pty Ltd (unreported, HCA, 1951)   321
Brady v Girvan Bros Pty Ltd (1986) 7 NSWLR 241   323
Brainton v Pinn (1290)   654
Brander v Ryan and Messenger Press Pty Ltd [2000] SASC 446   597
Breen v Williams (1996) 186 CLR 71   155
Bridge v Grand Junction Railway Company (1838) 3 M & W 244   478, 479
Briginshaw v Briginshaw (1938) 60 CLR 336   34
British American Tobacco Australia Services Ltd v McCabe [2002] VSCA 197   202
British Fame (Owners) v Macgregor (Owners) [1943] AC 197   502
British Railways Board v Herrington [1972] AC 877   256
British Steel Plc v Simmons [2004] UKHL 20   381
British Transport Commission v Gourley [1956] AC 185, [1955] 3 All ER 796   30
Broadmoor Special Hospital Authority v Robinson [2000] 1 WLR 1590   155
Broder v Saillard [1876] 2 Ch D 692   537
Brodie v Singleton Shire Council; Ghantous v Hawkesbury City Council (2001) 206 CLR 512   240, 291, 301, 302, 304, 323, 391, 399, 403, 411, 412, 531, 533, 534, 577
Brooks v Commissioner of Police [2005] 1 WLR 1495   391
Broome v Cassell & Co Ltd [1972] AC 1027; [1972] 1 All ER 801   39, 42
Bruce v Dyer (1966) 58 DLR (2d) 211   101
Bryan v Maloney (1995) 182 CLR 609   447, 463, 469, 470
Buckle v Bayswater Road Board (1936) 57 CLR 259; 13 LGR 130; 10 ALJ 378   412
Bunyan v Jordan (1936) 36 SR(NSW) 350   427
Bunyan v Jordan (1937) 57 CLR 1; 10 ALJ 465; 37 SR(NSW) 119   133, 427
Burchett v Kane [1980] 2 NSWLR 266   629
Burke v New South Wales [2004] NSWSC 725   442
Burnett v British Waterways Board [1972] 1 WLR 1329   507
Burnett v British Waterways Board [1973] 1 WLR 700   503, 505, 507
Burnicle v Cutelli [1982] 2 NSWLR 26   54
Burnie Port Authority v General Jones Pty Ltd (1994) 179 CLR 520   280, 390, 468, 556, 557, 666, 669–72
Bus v Sydney City Council (1989) 167 CLR 78; 85 ALR 577   240
Butcher v Lachlan Elder Realty Pty Ltd (2004) 218 CLR 592   460
Butler v Simmonds Crowley & Galvin [1999] QCA 475; [2000] 2 Qd R 2   141, 142
Butterfield v Forrester (1809) 11 East 60; 103 ER 926   245, 478, 479
Byrne v Australian Airlines Ltd (1995) 185 CLR 410; 131 ALR 422; 69 ALJR 797   560, 561, 562, 563, 568
Byrne v Boadle (1863) 2 H&C 722; 159 ER 299   371
Byrne v Dean [1937] 1 KB 818   595
The Bywell Castle [1879] 4 PD 219 (CA)   501

Cabassi v Vila (1940) 64 CLR 130   624
Cairns v John Fairfax & Sons Ltd (1983) 2 NSWLR 708   591, 595
Caledonian Collieries Ltd v Speirs (1957) 97 CLR 202; 57 SR(NSW) 513; 31 ALJ 132   279, 282, 283

Caltex Oil (Aust) v The Dredge Willemstad (1976) 136 CLR 529; 11 ALR 227   389, 465, 466, 467
Cambridge Water Co Ltd v Eastern Counties Leather PLC [1994] 2 AC 264; 1 All ER 53   538, 539
Campbell v Mirror Group Newspapers Ltd [2004] AC 457   153
Campbelltown City Council v Mackay (1989) 15 NSWLR 501   425, 426
Campbelltown Golf Club Ltd v Winton [1998] NSWSC 257 (23 June 1998)   542
Camporese v Parton (1983) 150 DLR (3d) 208   631
Candelwood Navigation Corp v Mitsui Osk Lines (The Mineral Transporter) [1986] AC 1   467
Cannon v Tahche (2002) 5 VR 317   146, 147, 150
Canterbury Bankstown Rugby League Football Club Ltd v Rogers (1993) Aust Tort Reports 81-246   94, 216, 662
Caparo Industries PLC v Dickman [1990] 2 AC 605; 1 All ER 568   389, 390, 391
Carey v Population Services Int'l, 431 US 678 (1977)   152
Carleton v Australian Broadcasting Corporation (2002) 172 FLR 398   593, 594, 603
Carlyon v Lovering (1857) 1 H & N 784; 156 ER 1417   559
Carrett v Smallpage (1808) 9 East 330   151
Carrey v ACP Publishing Pty Ltd [1999] 1 VR 875   613
Carrier v Bonham [2001] QCA 234   132, 133, 318
Carslogie Steamship Co Ltd v Royal Norwegian Government [1952] AC 292; [1951] 2 Lloyd Rep 441   370
Carson v John Fairfax & Sons Ltd (1993) 178 CLR 44   94, 649
Cartwright v McLaine and Long Pty Ltd (1979) 143 CLR 549   550
Casley-Smith v FS Evans & Sons Pty Ltd [No 5] [1989] Aust Torts Reports 68,351   552
Cassidy v Daily Mirror Newspapers Ltd (1929) 2 KB 331   590, 591
Caswell v Powell Duffryn Associated Collieries Ltd [1940] AC 152   485, 575
Caterson v Commissioner for Railways (NSW) (1973) 128 CLR 99; 47 ALJR 249   364, 501
Cattanach v Melchior (2003) 215 CLR 1   264–8
Catterton v Secretary of State for India [1895] 2 QB 189   625
Cattle v Stockton Waterworks (1875) LR 10 QB 453   445, 447, 448
Cavalier v Pope [1906] AC 428   256, 257
Cedars-Sinai Medical Center v Superior Court of Los Angeles County 954 P 2d 511 (1998)   202
Chadwick v British Railways Board [1967] 1 WLR 912; 2 All ER 945   424
Chakravarti v Advertiser Newspapers Ltd (1998) 193 CLR 519   578, 581, 582, 586, 587, 589, 593, 594, 650
Challen v The McLeod Country Golf Club [2004] QCA 358   551
Champagne View Pty Ltd v Shearwater Resort Management Pty Ltd (unreported, VSC, Gillard J, 25 May 2000)   542
Chandley v Roberts [2005] VSCA 273   490
Chapman v Hearse (1961) 106 CLR 112; [1962] ALR 379   252, 253, 376
Chappel v Hart (unreported, NSWCA, No 40438/94, 24 December 1996)   355, 357, 358, 359
Chappel v Hart (1998) 195 CLR 232   240, 287, 331, 332, 341, 347, 348, 350, 354–62, 365
Chappell v Mirror Newspapers Ltd (1984) Aust Torts Rep 80-691   650
Charleston v News Group Newspapers Ltd [1995] 2 AC 65   592, 593
Chatterton v Gerson [1981] 1 QB 432; [1981] 1 All ER 257   206
Cheater v Cater [1918] 1 KB 247   256
Cherneskey v Armadale Publishers Ltd (1978) 90 DLR (3d) 321   621
Chester v Waverley Municipal Council (1940) 62 CLR 1   422–3
Chief Constable of Thames Valley Police v Hepburn [2002] EWCA Civ 1841   102
Chomentowski v Red Garter Restaurant (1970) 92 WN (NSW) 1070   262
Christie v Bridgestone Australia Pty Ltd (1983) 33 SASR 177   482
Church of Scientology v Woodward (1982) 154 CLR 25   125
City Motors (1933) Pty Ltd v Southern Aerial Service Pty Ltd (1961) 106 CLR 477   199
City of Richmond v Scantelbury [1991] 2 VR 38   554
Clarey v Principal & Council of Women's College (1953) 90 CLR 170   556
Clark v Canada (TD) [1994] 3 FC 323   134
Clarke v Burton [1994] 2 Tas SR 370   111
Clarke v Coleambally Ski Club Inc [2004] NSWCA 376   290, 511
Close v Steel Company of Wales Ltd [1962] AC 367   572
CLT v Connon (2000) 77 SASR 449   407
Club Italia (Geelong) Inc v Ritchie [2001] VSCA 180   261

CMLAS Pty Ltd v Producers & Citizens Co-operative Assurance Co *see* Colonial Mutual Life Assurance Society Ltd v Producers & Citizens Co-operative Assurance Co of Australia Ltd
Cocks v Sheppard (1979) 25 ALR 325   487
Coco v AN Clark (Engineers) Ltd [1969] RPC 41   155
Coco v The Queen (1994) 179 CLR 427; [1994] Aust Torts Reports 81-270   229, 230, 564
Coggs v Barnard (1703) 2 Ld Raym 909   171
Cohen, Re [1953] Ch 88   189
Cohen v Daily Telegraph Ltd [1968] 1 WLR 916   618
Cole v Sth Tweed Heads Rugby Club (2004) 217 CLR 469   247, 252, 270, 273, 287, 288, 504
Cole v Turner (1704) 6 Mod 149; Holt KB 1083; 90 ER 958   95
Collins v Wilcock [1984] 1 WLR 1172   95, 217
Colonial Mutual Life Assurance Society Ltd v Producers & Citizens Co-operative Assurance Co of Australia Ltd (1931) 46 CLR 41   656, 657, 664
Commercial Banking Co of Sydney Ltd v RH Brown & Co (1972) 126 CLR 337   163
Commissioner for Railways v Halley (1978) 20 ALR 409   485, 486
Commissioner for Railways v Ruprecht (1979) 142 CLR 563   487
Commissioner of Main Roads v Jones (2005) 214 ALR 249; [2005] HCA 27   271, 285, 286, 300, 301, 305
Commonwealth v Introvigne (1982) 150 CLR 258   667
Commonwealth v McLean (1996) 41 NSWLR 398   384, 427, 498
Commonwealth v Verwayen (1990) 170 CLR 394   231
Commonwealth Life Assurance Society Ltd v Brain (1935) 53 CLR 343   137, 138
CompuServe Inc v Cyber Promotions, Inc, 962 F Supp 1015, 1022 (SD Ohio 1997)   127, 185
Connolly v Sunday Time Publishing Co Ltd (1908) 7 CLR 263   39
Conservation Council of SA Inc v Chapman (2003) 87 SASR 62   638, 639, 643, 644
Consolidated Trust Co Ltd v Browne (1948) 49 SR (NSW) 86   585, 599, 602
Cook v Cook (1986) 162 CLR 376; 68 ALR 353   240, 316, 317
Cooper v Chitty (1756) 1 Burr 20   183
Corbertt v Pallas [1995] ATR 81-329; 86 LGERA 312   536, 558
Corlett v Mifsud [2004] QSC 35   50
Cornfoot v Fowke (1840) 6 M&W 358; 151 ER 450   163
Cornwall v Rowan (2004) 90 SASR 269; [2004] SASC 384   145, 148, 149, 628, 629, 639, 644
Coultas v Victorian Railway Commissioners (1886) 12 VLR 895   421, 423, 424
Cowan v Milbourn [1867] LR 2 Ex 230   30
Coward v Wellington (1836) 7 Car & P 531; 173 ER 234   633
Cowell v Corrective Services Commission (1988) 13 NSWLR 714   228
Cowell v Rosehill Racecourse Co Ltd (1937) 56 CLR 605; 11 ALJ 33   120, 121
Cox v Bath (No 3) (1893) 14 LR (NSW) 263; 9 WN(NSW) 171   231
Cox v Journeaux No 2 (1935) 52 CLR 713   140
Coyle or Brown v John Watson Ltd [1915] AC 1   325
Coyne v Citizen Finance Ltd (1991) 172 CLR 211   611, 649
Criminal Injuries Compensation Act 1983, In the matter of an application under [2004] ACTSC 60   84
Crimmins v Stevedoring Industry Finance Committee (1999) 200 CLR 1   304, 390, 391, 403, 407–9, 563
Crofter Hand Woven Harris Tweed v Veitch [1942] AC 435   31
Crosthwaite v Pietila [1999] VSCA (unreported, VCA, 11 August 1999)   257
Crowther v Australian Guarantee Corp Ltd [1985] ATR 80-709   179
Cruise and Kidman v Express Newspaper plc [1998] QB 931   613
CSR Ltd v Eddy [2005] HCA 64   54, 57, 58
Cubbon v Roads and Traffic Authority of NSW [2004] NSWCA 326   435
Cullen v Morris (1819) 2 Stark 577; 171 ER 741   143
Curmi v McLennan [1993] ATR 81-254; [1994] 1 VR 513   316, 367
Curwen v Yan Yean Land Co Ltd (1891) 17 VLR 745   160
Czatyrko v Edith Cowan University [2005] HCA 14   278, 486, 668

D v East Berkshire Community Health NHS Trust [2005] 2 AC 373   391
D (A Minor), Re [1976] Fam 185   212
D & L Caterers Ltd v D'Ajou [1945] KB 210   582

Da Costa v Cockburn Salvage & Trading Pty Ltd (1970) 124 CLR 192   485
Dalton v Angus (1881) 6 AC 740   536, 666
Dalton v Skuthorpe (unreported, NSWSC, McLelland J, 17 November 1994)   213
Darker v Chief Constable of the West Midlands Police [2000] 3 WLR 747   146
Darling Island Stevedoring and Lighterage Co Ltd v Long (1957) 97 CLR 36; 31 ALR 208   129, 567
Davies v Adelaide Chemical and Fertilizer Co Ltd (1946) 74 CLR 541   576
Davies v Bennison [1927] 22 Tas LR 52   121
Davies v Mann (1842) 10 M & W 546; 152 ER 588   479
Davies v Taylor [1974] AC 207   34
Davis v Bromley Corporation [1908] 1 KB 170   143
Dawson Bloodstock Agency Pty Ltd v Mirror Newspapers Ltd [1979] 1 NSWLR 16   596
De Jager v Payneham & Magill Lodges Hall Inc (1984) 36 SASR 498   553
De Reus v Gray [2003] VSCA 84   45
De Sales v Ingrilli [2002] HCA 52   75
Deasy Investments Pty Ltd v Monrest Pty Ltd [1996] QCA 466 (22 November 1996)   550
Deatons Pty Ltd v Flew (1949) 79 CLR 370; 50 SR (NSW) 50; 23 ALJ 522   661
Dennis v Ministry of Defence [2003] EWHC 793 (QB)   544, 556
Derbyshire County Council v Times Newspapers [1993] AC 534   584
Derrick v Cheung (2001) 181 ALR 301   271, 279, 286
Derry v Peek (1889) 14 App Cas 337   159, 161, 162, 446, 450
Devries v Australian National Railways Commission (1993) 177 CLR 472   360
Diamond v Simpson (No 1) [2003] NSWCA 67   21
Dillon v Legg 68 Cal 2d 728; 441 P 2d 912 (Cal 1968)   246
Dingle v Associated Newspapers Ltd [1961] 2 QB 162   675
Director General, New South Wales Department of Community Services v Y [1999] NSWSC 644   212
Director General of the Department of Community Services v 'BB' [1999] NSWSC 1169   213
Dobson (Litigation Guardian of) v Dobson (1999) 174 DLR (4th) 1; [1999] 2 SCR 753   263
Doherty v Liverpool District Council (1991) 22 NSWLR 284   36
Dollar Sweets Pty Ltd v Federated Confectioners Association of Australia [1986] VR 383   547, 548
Domachuk v Feiner (unreported, NSWCA, 28 November 1996)   543
Donnelly v Joyce [1974] QB 454   31
Donoghue v Stevenson [1932] AC 562; All ER 1   250, 251, 253, 255, 363, 378, 387, 388, 393, 394, 416, 465
Dooley v Cammell Laird & Co [1951] 1 Lloyd's Rep 27   424
D'Orta-Ekenaike v Victoria Legal Aid [2005] HCA 12   249, 392, 411, 624
Dorset Yacht Co Ltd v Home Office [1970] AC 1004   261, 262, 400, 663
Doubleday v Kelly [2005] NSWCA 151   273, 281, 294, 499
Doughty v Cassidy [2004] QSC 366   63
Douglas v Hello! Ltd [2001] 2 WLR 992; [2001] 2 All ER 289   125
Dovuro Pty Ltd v Wilkins (2003) 215 CLR 317   319, 468
Dow Jones & Co Inc v Gutnick (2002) 210 CLR 575   580, 607
Dowell v General Steam Navigation Co (1855) 5 E & B 195   478, 479
Dowling v Colonial Mutual Life Assurance Society Ltd (1915) 20 CLR 509   140
Doyle v Olby (Ironmongers) Ltd [1969] 2 QB 158   165
Drewe v Coulton (1787) 1 East 563n; 102 ER 217   143
Dulieu v White & Sons [1901] 2 KB 669   382
Dunford Publicity Studios Ltd v News Media Ownership Ltd [1971] NZLR 961   631
Dungog Shire Council v Babbage [2004] NSWCA 160   305
Dunlop v Woollahra Municipal Council [1982] AC 158   143, 145

E v Australian Red Cross (1991) 31 FCR 299   284
EAM Burns v National Bank of New Zealand Ltd [2003] NZCA 232   203
Earl Spencer and Countess Spencer v the United Kingdom (1998) 25 EHRR CD 105   125
eBay, Inc v Bidder's Edge 100 F Supp 2d 1058 (ND Cal 2000)   127, 175, 177, 185
Edgington v Fizmaurice (1885) 29 Ch D 459   160
Egan v State Transport Authority (1982) 31 SASR 481   181
Eisenstadt v Baird, 405 US 438 (1972)   152

Elguzouli-Daf v Commissioner of Police of the Metropolis [1995] QB 335   148
Elliott v Bickerstaff (1999) 48 NSWLR 214   673
Emmens v Pottle (1885) 16 QBD 354   604
Encev v Encev (unreported, VSC, Ashley J, 24 November 1997)   384
Endean v Canadian Red Cross Society (1998) 42 OR (3d) 391   203
Entick v Carrington (1765) 2 Wils KB 275, 95 ER 807   116, 125
Environment Agency v Empress Car Co (Arbertillery) Ltd [1999] 2 AC 22   331, 333, 335
Esanda Finance Corporation Limited v Peat Marwick Hungerfords (1997) 188 CLR 159   453, 454, 462
Etna v Arif [1999] VR 353   513
Ettingshausen v Australian Consolidated Press Ltd (1991) 23 NSWLR 443   579, 592, 597
Everitt v Martin [1952] NZLR 298   174, 177
Evers v Bennett (1982) 31 SASR 228   487
Evitt v Price (1827) 1 Sim 483; 57 ER 659   154

F v R (1983) 33 SASR 189   209
F v West Berkshire HA [1990] 2 AC 1   218
Fabre v Arenales (1992) 27 NSWLR 437   520
Fagan v Metropolitan Police Commissioner [1969] 1 QB 439   98
FAI General Insurance Co Ltd v Lucre (2000) 32 MVR 540   426
Fairchild v Glenhaven Funeral Services [2002] UKHL 22; [2003] 1 AC 32   327, 336, 338, 341–4, 347–9, 351, 353, 354
Fallas v Mourlas [2006] NSWCA 32   512
Fangrove Pty Ltd v Todd Group Holdings Pty Ltd [1999] 2 Qd R 236   470
Farquhar v Bottom [1980] 2 NSWLR 380   593
Farrington v Thomson & Bridgland [1959] VR 286   145
Faulkner v Keffalinos (1970) 45 ALJR 80   370
Favell v Queensland Newspapers Pty Ltd [2005] HCA 52   586, 587, 589, 612
Felk Industries Pty Ltd v Mallet [2005] NSWCA 111   259
Fennell v Robson Excavations Pty Ltd [1977] 2 NSWLR 486   552
Feo v Pioneer Concrete (Vic) Pty Ltd [1999] VSCA 180   582
Fetter v Beal (1701) 1 Ld Raym 339; 91 ER 1122   35, 36
Fine Art Society v Union Bank of London Ltd (1886) 17 QBD 705   197
Fisher v Prince (1762) 97 ER 876   16
Fitch v Hyde-Cates (1982) 150 CLR 482   70
Fitzgerald v Penn (1954) 91 CLR 268   514
Fletcher v Rylands *see* Rylands v Fletcher
Flewster v Royale (1808) 1 Camp 187   109
Flower v Adam (1810) 127 ER 1098   325
Flower & Hart v White Industries (Qld) Pty Ltd (1999) 87 FCR 134   142
Flower & Hart v White Industries (Qld) Pty Ltd (2001) 109 FCR 280; [2001] FCA 370   142
Fontaine v British Columbia (Official Administrator) [1998] 1 SCR 424   371
Fontin v Katapodis (1962) 108 CLR 177   223
Ford v Andrews (1916) 21 CLR 317   202
Fouldes v Willoughby (1841) 8 M&W 540, 151 ER 1153   184, 185, 186
Fox v Percy (2003) 77 ALJR 989   11
Franklin v South Eastern Railway Co (1858) 3 H & N 211; 157 ER 448   74
Franklin v Victorian Railways Commissioners (1959) 101 CLR 197   372
Fraser v State Transport Authority (1985) 39 SASR 57   262
Freeman v Home Office (No 2) [1984] QB 524   218, 504
Froom v Butcher [1976] QB 286; [1975] 3 All ER 520; 3 WLR 379   491
Frost v Chief Constable of the South Yorkshire Police *see* White (or Frost) v Chief Constable of the South Yorkshire Police

Gala v Preston (1991) 172 CLR 243   521
Galashiels Gas Co Ltd v O'Donnell [1949] AC 275; [1949] 1 All ER 319   571
Gardiner v John Fairfax & Sons Pty Ltd (1942) 42 SR (NSW) 171   618, 619, 621
Garrett v Attorney-General [1997] 2 NZLR 332   146, 150

Gartner v Kidman (1962) 108 CLR 12   535
Gates v City Mutual Life Assurance Society Ltd (1986) 160 CLR 1   165
Gatward v Alley (1940) 40 SR (NSW) 174   186
Gavalas v Singh [2001] VSCA 23 (22 March 2001, unreported, BC200101238)   350
Gazzard v Hutchesson (1995) Aust Torts Reps 81-337   554, 556
Gee v Treece, Ill App (27 April 2006)   350
Genay v Norris, 1 SCL (1 Bay) 6 (1784)   41
General & Financial Facilities v Cooks Cars [1963] 2 All ER 1   179
General Steel Industries Inc v Commissioner for Railways (NSW) (1965) 112 CLR 125   140
Gerard v Hope [1965] Tas SR 15   111
Gerick v Municipality of Peterborough [1984] Aust Torts Reports 80-605   400
Ghani v Jones (1970) 1 QB 693   189, 216
Ghantous v Hawkesbury City Council *see* Brodie v Singleton Shire Council; Ghantous v Hawkesbury City Council
Gibbons v Duffell (1932) 47 CLR 520   623, 624, 625
Gibbons v Pepper (1695) 1 Ld Raym 38; 2 Salk 637; 91 ER 922   243
Gibbs v Rea [1998] 3 WLR 72   138
Gifford v Strang Patrick Stevedoring Pty Ltd [2003] HCA 33   419, 433, 434
Gilchrist v Estate of the Late Sara Alexander Taylor [2004] NSWCA 476   36, 38
Giller v Procopets [2004] VSC 113   134
Gillespie v Commonwealth (1991) 105 FLR 196   424
Gillick v West Norfolk and Wisbech Area Health Authority [1986] AC 112; [1985] 3 All ER 402   211
Gillies v Saddington [2004] NSWCA 110   283, 290
Given v Holland (Holdings) Pty Ltd (1977) 15 ALR 439   160
Glasgow Corporation v Muir [1943] AC 448   488
Glinski v McIver [1962] AC 726   138
Godfrey v Demon Internet Ltd [1999] 4 All ER 342   605
Goldman v Hargrave (1966) 115 CLR 458 (in the Privy Council, [1967] 1 AC 645)   258, 282, 534, 553
Goldsborough v John Fairfax & Sons Ltd (1934) 34 SR (NSW) 524   617, 619
Goldsmith v Sperrings Ltd [1977] 2 All ER 566   603
Gomes v Metroform Pty Ltd [2005] NSWCA 171   259
Gordon v Tamworth Jockey Club Inc [2003] NSWCA 82   661
Gorham v British Telecommunications plc [2000] 1 WLR 2129   456
Gorris v Scott (1874) LR 9 Ex 125   572
Gould v Vaggelas (1985) 157 CLR 215   164
Government Insurance Office of NSW v Fredrichberg (1968) 118 CLR 403   372
Gowan v Hardy (unreported, CA 40531/89, 8 November 1991)   515
Graham v Baker (1961) 106 CLR 340; [1962] ALR 331   30, 67
Graham v Voight (1989) ATR 80-296   199, 200
Graham Barclay Oysters Pty Ltd v Ryan (2002) 211 CLR 540   252, 304, 399, 400, 403, 409–11, 571
Grainger v Hill (1834) 132 ER 769   139, 140, 141, 142
Gray v Dight (1677) 2 Show 144   136
Gray v Motor Accident Commission (1998) 196 CLR 1   28, 42, 43, 91
Great Western Railway Company v London and County Banking Company [1901] AC 414   197
Greater Shepparton Council v Davis [2004] VSCA 140   303
Greenland v Chaplin (1850) 5 Ex 243   377
Greenwood v Commonwealth of Australia [1975] VR 859 (FC)   658
Gregg v Scott [2005] UKHL 2   343, 348, 350, 354
Greig v Greig [1966] VR 376   123
Griffin v Coles Myer Ltd [1991] ATR 81-109; [1992] 2 Qd R 478   323
Griffiths v Kerkemeyer (1977) 139 CLR 161; 15 ALR 387; 51 ALJR 792   30, 31, 46, 53, 481
Grincelis v House (2000) 201 CLR 321; 173 ALR 564; 74 ALJR 1247   53
Griswold v Connecticut, 381 US 479 (1965)   152
Grundemann v Georgeson [1996] Aust Torts Rep 63-500   620
Guidera v Government Insurance Office (NSW) [1990] ATR 81-040; MVR 423   491
Gumbleton v Grafton (1600) Cro Eliz 781, 78 ER 1011   183

Haber v Walker [1963] VR 339   73, 74, 328, 363
Hales' Case (c 1560)   529
Hall-Gibbs Mercantile Agency Ltd v Dun (1910) 12 CLR 84   167, 596
Halliday v Nevill (1984) 155 CLR 1; 57 ALR 331; 59 ALJR 124   125, 226, 227, 231
Halsey v Esso Petroleum Co Ltd [1961] 2 All ER 145; [1961] 1 WLR 683   538, 540, 541
Hargrave v Goldman (1963) 110 CLR 40; 37 ALJR 277   394, 397, 532, 534, 550
Harman v Tappenden (1801) 1 East 555; 102 ER 214   143
Harper v Ashtons Circus Pty Ltd [1972] 2 NSWLR 395   483
Harriton v Stephens [2002] NSWSC 461 (12 June 2002)   264
Harriton v Stephens [2006] HCA 15   268
Harriton v Stephens; Waller v James; Waller v Hoolahan (2004) 59 NSWLR 694   269
Hart v Herron [1984] Aust Torts Reports 80-201 (NSWSC)   113, 206, 219
Hastings Council v Giese [2003] NSWCA 178   302
Haukyns v Broune (1477) Trin 17 Edw IV, fo 3 pl 2   119
Havenaar v Havenaar [1982] 1 NSWLR 626   427
Hawke v Tamworth Newspapers [1983] 1 NSWLR 699   594, 616, 617, 618, 620, 621
Hawkins v Clayton Utz (1988) 164 CLR 539   454, 458, 460
Hazell v Parramatta City Council [1968] 1 NSWR 165   227
HC Buckman & Son Pty Limited v Flannagan (1974) 133 CLR 422   575
Healing (Sales) Pty Ltd v Inglis Electrix Pty Ltd (1969) 121 CLR 584   181
Heaven v Pender (1883) 11 QBD 502   250
Hedley Byrne v Heller & Partners [1964] 1 AC 465   450, 451, 452, 455, 460, 465, 466
Henjo Investments Pty Ltd v Collins Marrickville Pty Ltd (No 2) (1989) 40 FCR 76   165
Henry v TVW Enterprises (1990) Aust Torts Rep 81-031   593, 599, 602
Henry Berry & Co Pty Ltd v Rushton [1937] Q St R 109   177
Henville v Walker (2001) 206 CLR 459   339, 464, 572
Henwood v Municipal Tramways Trust (SA) (1938) 60 CLR 438   524
Hepburn v TCN Channel 9 Pty Ltd [1983] 2 NSWLR 682   594
Herald & Weekly Times Ltd v Popovic [2003] VSCA 161   582, 612, 613, 616, 619, 622, 630, 635,
    636, 639, 640, 646
Herd v Weardle Steel, Coal and Coke Co Ltd [1915] AC 67   112
Herskovits v Group Health Coop 99 Wash 2d 609, 664 P 2d 474 (1983)   350
Hill v Chief Constable of West Yorkshire [1989] AC 53   263
Hill v Van Erp (1997) 188 CLR 159; 142 ALR 687   390, 391, 403, 449, 453–6, 459, 460, 462, 463
Hinz v Berry [1970] 2 QB 40   419
Hird v Gibson [1974] Qd R 14   384
Hocking v Matthews (1670) 1 Vent 86   136
Hole v Sittingbourne and Sheerness Railway Co (1861) 6 H & N 488   666
Holland v Tarlinton (1989) 10 MVR 129   520
Hollins v Fowler (1874) LR 7 HL 757; [1874-80] All ER 118   192, 197
Hollis v Vabu Pty Ltd (2001) 207 CLR 21   654, 655, 659, 664, 665
Holloway v McFeeters (1956) 94 CLR 470   321
Holmes v Amerex Rent-a-Car 710 A 2d 846, 854 (1998)   202
Holmes v Jones (1907) 4 CLR 1692   164
Holmes v Mather [1875] LR 10 Ex 261; [1874-80] All ER 345   244
Home Office v Dorset Yacht Club [1970] AC 1004   388
Hooper v Rogers [1975] Ch 43   550
Hore-Lacy v David Syme & Co Ltd [1998] VSC 96   613
Horkin v North Melbourne Football Club Social Club [1983] 1 VR 153   483
Horrocks v Lowe [1975] AC 30   641
Hotson v East Berkshire Area Health Authority [1987] 1 AC 750   59, 344–5, 348
Hough v London Express Newspaper Ltd [1940] 2 KB 502   591
Houghland v R Low (Luxury) Coaches Ltd [1962] 1 QB 694   181
Howard E Perry & Co Ltd v British Rlys Board [1980] 1 WLR 1375   180, 193
Howard v Howard (1885) 2 WN (NSW) 5   601
Howden v 'Truth' & 'Sportsman' Ltd (1937) 58 CLR 416   611
Howe v Lees (1910) 11 CLR 361   631
Huckle v Money (1763) 2 Wils 205; 95 ER 768   40, 41, 105
Huet v Lawrence [1948] Q St R 168   231

Hughes v Lord Advocate [1963] AC 837; 1 All ER 705   380, 384
Hulton & Co v Jones (1910) AC 20   599
Humberstone v Northern Timber Mills (1949) 79 CLR 389; 23 ALJ 584; [1950] VLR 44   663
Hunter v Canary Wharf Ltd [1997] AC 655   134, 135, 535, 544, 545, 549, 550
Husher v Husher (1999) 197 CLR 138   64
Hutchins v Maughan [1947] VLR 131   176
Huth v Huth [1915] 3 KB 32   602

I de S et Uxor v W de S (1348), YB, 22 Edw III, f 99, pl 60   99
Imperial Chemical Industries Ltd v Shatwell [1965] AC 656   507, 508, 577
Innes v Wylie (1844) 1 Car & K 257   101
Insurance Commissioner v Joyce (1948) 77 CLR 39   506
Ira S Bushey & Sons Inc v United States 398 F 2d 167 (1968)   655
Irving v Penguin Books Ltd [2000] EWHC QB 115   615
Irving v Penguin Books Ltd [2001] EWCA Civ 1197   615
Isaack v Clark (1614) 2 Bulst 306, 80 ER 1143   183
Isaacs & Sons Ltd v Cook [1925] 2 KB 391   625

J Lyons & Sons v Wilkins (1899) 1 Ch 255   547
Jackson v Harrison (1978) 138 CLR 438   521
Jaensch v Coffey (1983) 155 CLR 549   236, 239, 389, 417, 424–7, 442, 443, 466
James v Commonwealth (1939) 62 CLR 339   146
Jamieson v The Queen (1993) 177 CLR 574; 67 ALJR 793   33
Janvier v Sweeney [1919] 2 KB 316   131
JD (FC) v East Berkshire Community Health NHS Trust [2005] 2 AC 373   391
Jobling v Associated Dairies Ltd [1982] 1 AC 794   369
John Fairfax Pty Ltd v Attorney-General (NSW) (2000) 181 ALR 694   637, 638
John Fairfax Publications Pty Ltd v Blake (2001) 53 NSWLR 541   614, 615
John Fairfax Publications Pty Ltd v O'Shane [2005] NSWCA 164   638, 640, 646
John Fairfax Publications Pty Ltd v Rivkin (2003) 201 ALR 77   587, 591, 593, 603, 612
John Jones & Sons Ltd v Financial Times Ltd (1909) 25 TLR 677   626
John Pfeiffer Pty Ltd v Canny (1981) 148 CLR 218   573
John Pfeiffer Pty Ltd v Rogerson (2000) 203 CLR 503   19, 26
Johnson v Pickering [1907] 2 KB 437   189
Johnson v Weedman, 5 Ill 495 (1843)   184, 185
Jolley v Sutton London BC [2000] 1 WLR 1082   284, 380
Jones v Bartlett (2000) 205 CLR 166   257, 258, 259, 359, 672
Jones v Dumbrell [1981] VR 1990   161
Jones v Dunkel (1959) 101 CLR 298   321
Jones v Fairfax (1986) 4 NSWLR 466   628
Jones v Hart (1698) 2 Salk 441, 91 ER 382   654
Jones v Livox Quarries Ltd [1952] 2 QB 608; TLR 1377   490
Jones v Powell (1629) Palm 536; Hutton 135   541
Jones v Skelton (1963) 63 SR (NSW) 644   586, 606
Jones v Skelton [1964] NSWR 485   586
Jones v Swansea City Council [1990] 1 WLR 54   143
Joslyn v Berryman (2003) 214 CLR 552   488, 489, 492, 493, 496, 499, 503

Kalokerinos v Burnett (unreported, NSWCA, 1 November 1995)   487
Kaplan v Go Daddy Group Group Inc [2005] NSWSC 636   168, 170
Karahalios v National Federation of Federal Employees Local 1263 489 US 527 (1989)   563
Kars v Kars (1996) 187 CLR 354; 141 ALR 37   53
Kavanagh v Akhtar (1998) 45 NSWLR 588   341, 365, 367, 383, 440
Kavanagh v Gudge 7 Man & G 316; 135 ER 132   206
Kaye v Robertson [1991] FSR 62   124
Kebewar Pty Ltd v Harkin (1987) 9 NSWLR 738   535, 536, 569
Kelly v Bega Valley County Council (unreported, NSWCA, 13 September 1982)   500
Kelly v Partington (1833) 4 B&Ad 700; 110 ER 619   633
Kemp v Sober (1851) 1 Sim(NS) 517, at 520; 61 ER 200   139

Kemsley v Foot [1952] AC 345   617, 618
Kent v Scattini [1961] WAR 74   508
Khashoggi v IPC Magazines Ltd [1986] 3 All ER 577   613, 651
Khorasandjian v Bush [1993] QB 727; 3 All ER 669; 3 WLR 476   135, 549, 550, 556
Kimber v Press Association Ltd [1893] 1 QB 65   627
Kinaston v Moor (1626) Cro Car 89; 79 ER 678   183
Kine v Selwell (1838) 3 M&W 297   633
Kirk v Gregory (1876) 1 Ex D 55; 45 LJQB 186   174, 178
Knupfler v London Express [1944] AC 116   600
Kocis v SE Dickens Pty Ltd (t/as Coles New World Supermarket) [1996] ATR 81-382   322, 323
Koehler v Cerebos (Australia) Ltd (2005) 214 ALR 355   274, 430, 431, 434
Kondis v State Transport Authority (1984) 154 CLR 672   240, 664, 666, 667
Konskier v B Goodman Ltd [1928] 1 KB 421; [1927] All ER 187   120
The Koursk (1924) 131 LTR 700; [1924] All ER 168 (CA); P 140   675
Kraemers v Attorney-General (Tas) [1966] Tas SR 113   559
Krahe v TCN Channel Nine Pty Ltd (1986) 4 NSWLR 536   594
Krakowski v Eurolynx Properties Ltd (1995) 130 ALR 1   160, 162, 163, 464
Kremen v Cohen 337 F3d 1024 (2003)   175
Krivoshev v Royal Society for the Prevention of Cruelty to Animals Inc [2005] NSWCA 76   227
Kuddus v Chief Constable of Leicestershire Constabulary [2002] 2 AC 122   42
Kurrie v Azouri (1998) 28 MVR 406   49
Kuwait Airways Corpn v Iraqi Airways Co (Nos 4 and 5) [2002] 2 AC 883   333

L Shaddock & Ass Pty Ltd v Parramatta City Council (1980-81) 150 CLR 225   453, 455, 456, 460, 463
Lake v Transport Accident Commission [1998] 1 VR 616   52
Lamb v Camden Council [1981] QB 625   536
Lamb v Cotogno (1987) 164 CLR 1; 74 ALR 188   40
Lane v Cotton (1701) 11 Mod 12, 88 ER 853   654
Lange v Australian Broadcasting Corporation (1997) 189 CLR 520   411, 578, 630–40, 643
Lawlor v Alton (1873) 9 Ir R CL 160   151
Lawrence v Kempsey Shire Council [1995] ATR 81-344   557, 558
Laws v Australian Broadcasting Tribunal (1990) 170 CLR 70   33
Le Lievre v Gould [1893] 1 QB 491   446
Leahy v Beaumont (1981) 27 SASR 290   318
Leakey v National Trust for Places of Historic Interest or Natural Beauty [1980] QB 485   553, 554
Leame v Bray (1803) 3 East 593; 102 ER 724   29
Lee v Wilson (1934) 51 CLR 276   598, 599
Leichhardt Council v Serratore [2005] NSWCA 406   303
Lemoto v Able Technical Pty Ltd [2005] NSWCA 153   53
Lepore v State of New South Wales [2001] NSWCA 112   673
Lester-Travers v City of Frankston [1970] VR 2   542, 558
L'Estrange v Graucob [1934] 2 KB 394   516
Letang v Cooper [1965] 1 QB 232   104, 503
Levi v Colgate-Palmolive Pty Ltd (1941) 41 SR(NSW) 48   427
Lewis v Daily Telegraph [1964] AC 234   586, 587, 591
Liftronic Pty Limited v Unver (2001) 179 ALR 321   486, 503
Lincoln J v Transport Accident Commission [2002] VCAT 300 (26 April 2002)   52
Lippiatt v South Gloucestershire Council [2000] QB 51 (CA)   552
Lister v Hesley Hall Ltd [2002] 1 AC 215   659
Little v Law Institute of Victoria [1990] VR 257   136
Littler v Liverpool Corporation [1986] 2 All ER 343   302
Livingstone v Rawyards Coal Co [1880] 5 AC 25   30
LJP Investments Pty Ltd v Howard Chia Investments Pty Ltd (No 2) [1991] ATR 81-069   122
LJP Investments Pty Ltd v Howard Chia Investments Pty Ltd (No 3) (1990) 24 NSWLR 499; [1991] ATR 81-070   122
Lloyd v David Syme & Co Ltd (1985) 3 NSWLR 728   618
Lloyd v Osborne (1899) 20 LR (NSW) 19   179
Locher v Turner [1995] Aust Torts Reps 81-336   350

Lois Austin, Geoffrey Saxby v Commissioner of Police of the Metropolis [2005] EWHC 480 (QBD) 39
London Artists Ltd v Littler [1969] 2 QB 375   618, 619
London Association for Protection of Trade v Greenlands Ltd [1916] 2 AC 15   630
London Borough of Southwark v Mills [1999] 3 WLR 939; [1999] 4 All ER 449   552
Lord Mounteagle v Countess of Worcester (1554) 2 Dyer 121a, 73 ER 265   183
Lord Petre v Heneage (1701) 12 Mod Rep 519   187
Loveday v Sun Newspapers Ltd (1938) 59 CLR 503   206
Loving v Virginia, 388 US 1 (1967)   152
Lowns v Woods [1996] Aust Torts Reps 81-376   309
Luxton v Vines (1952) 85 CLR 352   321
Lynch v Knight (1861) 9 HLC 577; 11 ER 854   384
Lynch v Lynch (1991) 25 NSWLR 411   263
Lynch v Nurdin (1841) 1 QB 29; 113 ER 1041   499
Lyttleton Times Co Ltd v Warners Ltd [1907] AC 476 (PC); [1904-7] All ER 20   556

Mabo v Queensland (1991-92) 175 CLR 1   18
Macallister v Stevenson *see* Donoghue v Stevenson
Macarthur Districts Motor Cycle Sportsmen Inc v Ardizzone [2004] NSWCA 145   286
McCormick v John Fairfax & Sons Ltd (1989) 16 NSWLR 485   600
McCoy Constructions Pty Ltd v Aleko Dabrowski [2000] QSC 385   548
McDonald v Coles Myer Ltd (t/as K-Mart Chatswood) [1995] ATR 81-361   107
McFarlane v Tayside Health Board [2000] 2 AC 59   267
McGhee v National Coal Board [1973] 1 WLR 1   338–43, 346, 347, 354
McGrath (Infants), Re [1983] 1 Ch D 143   212
McHale v Watson (1964) 111 CLR 384   204, 205
McHale v Watson (1966) 115 CLR 199; 39 ALJR 459   205, 315, 499
McKellar v Container Terminal Management Services Ltd (1999) 165 ALR 409   148
McKinnon Industries v Walker [1951] 3 DLR 577   540
McLean v Tedman (1984) 155 CLR 306   284, 485, 486
Macleay Pty Ltd v Moore [1991] Aust Torts Reports 81-151   519
McLoughlin v O'Brian [1983] 1 AC 410   245, 388, 425
MacPherson v Brown (1975) 12 SASR 184   100
Macpherson v Buick Motor Co 217 NY 382; 111Ne 1050 (1916)   250
McPherson v Whitfield [1995] QCA 62 (unreported, 15 March 1995)   514
Magill v Magill (2005) Aust Torts Reports 81-783   158
Mahony v J Kruschich (Demolitions) Pty Ltd (1985) 156 CLR 522   31, 236, 366–8, 385
Maisel v Financial Times Ltd [1915] 3 KB 336   612
Mako v Land [1956] NZLR 624   658
Malec v JC Hutton Pty Ltd (1990) CLR 638   34, 58–61, 64, 65, 344, 416
Malette v Shulman (1990) 67 DLR 4th 321   208
Mallet v McMonagle [1970] AC 166   59
Manley v Alexander [2005] HCA 79   288, 295, 296
Mann v O'Neill (1997) 191 CLR 204   623, 624, 625
Mann v The Medicine Group (1992) 38 FCR 400   600
March v E & M H Stramare Pty Ltd (1991) 171 CLR 506   328, 330, 331, 333, 363, 365, 376, 481, 501, 503
Marchant v Finney (unreported, NSWSC, Waddell C, 10 July 1992)   213
Marcq v Christie Manson & Woods Ltd (Trading As Christie's) [2004] QB 286   196
Marfani & Co Ltd v Midland Bank Ltd [1968] 1 WLR 956; [1968] 2 All ER 573   175, 197
Marion's Case *see* Secretary, Department of Health and Community Services (NT) v JWB and SMB
Marshall v Whittaker's Building Supply Co (1963) 109 CLR 210   664
Martin v Watson [1996] AC 74   137
Martin v Western District of the Australasian Coal and Shale Employees' Federation Workers' Industrial Union of Australia (Mining Department) (1934) 34 SR (NSW) 593   564
Matthew v Ollerton [1962] Comb 218; 90 ER 438   216
Mayfair Ltd v Pears [1986] NZLJ 459   123
Mears v London & South Western Rly Co (1862) 11 CB (NS) 850   201
Medlin v State Government Insurance Commission (1995) 182 CLR 1   64, 240, 364

Mendelssohn v Normand Ltd [1970] 1 QB 177   517
Mercer v Commissioner for Road Transport & Tramways (NSW) (1936) 56 CLR 580   306
Meyer v Nebraska, 262 US 390 (1923)   152
Microsoft Corporation v Auschina Polaris Pty Ltd (1997) 71 FCR 231   198
Middendorp Electric Co Pty Ltd v Sonneveld [2001] VSC 312   582, 595, 650
Milk Bottles Recovery v Camillo [1948] VLR 344   193
Miller v Jackson [1973] QB 966   541
Millington v Wilkie t/as Max Wilkie Plumbing Services [2005] NSWCA 45   575
Ming Kuei Property Investments Pty Ltd v Hampson (1994) 126 ALR 313; [1995] 2 Qd R 251   180
Minister Administering the Environmental Planning & Assessment Act 1979 v San Sebastian Pty Ltd (1983) 2 NSWLR 268   343, 376, 467
Minister for Health v AS [2004] WASC 286   212, 214
Mirror Newspapers Ltd v Fitzpatrick [1984] 1 NSWLR 643   591
Mirror Newspapers Ltd v Harrison (1982) 149 CLR   586, 589, 612
Mirror Newspapers Ltd v World Hosts Pty Ltd (1979) 141 CLR 632   167, 596, 599
Mitchell v John Heine & Son Ltd (1938) 38 SR NSW 466   138
Mitchell v University of Wollongong [2004] HCA Trans 181   297
Mitchil v Alestree (1676) 1 Vent 195; 3 Keb 650   242, 254
Moch Co Inc v Rensselaer Water Co (1928) 247 NY 160   446
Modbury Triangle Shopping Centre Pty Ltd v Anzil (2001) 205 CLR 254   258, 260, 262, 359, 391, 661
Monsanto v Tilly [2000] Env LR 313   223
Montana Hotels v Fasson (1986) 69 ALR 258; 61 ALJR 282   550
Moore v Queensland [2005] QCA 299   351
Moorgate Mercantile Co Ltd v Finch & Read [1962] 1 QB 701; 3 WLR 110   193
Moorgate Tobacco Co Ltd v Philip Morris Ltd (No 2) (1984) 156 CLR 414   154
Morgan v John Fairfax & Sons Ltd [No 2] (1991) 23 NSWLR 374   646
Morgan v Lingen (1863) 8 LT (ICS) 800   598
Morgan v Pearson (1979) 22 SASR 5   285
Morgan v Tame (2000) 49 NSWLR 21   428
Morgans v Launchbury [1973] AC 127   658
Morison v London County & Westminster Bank Ltd [1914] 3 KB 356   197
Morosi v Mirror Newspapers Ltd [1977] 2 NSWLR 749   648
Morris v KLM Royal Dutch Airlines [2002] 2 AC 628   417, 420
Morris v Marsden [1952] 1 All ER 925; WN 188   225
Morris v Robinson (1824) 3 B & C 196; 107 ER 706   184
Motor Vehicle Insurance Trust v Wilson [1976] WAR 175   481
Mount Isa Mines Ltd v Pusey (1971) 125 CLR 383   132, 236, 253, 419, 420, 423–4, 427, 432, 433, 436, 443
Mouse's Case (1609) 12 Co Rep 63; 77 ER 1341   223
Mowlds v Fergusson (1940) 64 CLR 206   629, 632, 633
Moyne Shire Council v Pearce [2004] VSCA 246   302
Mulholland v Mitchell [1971] AC 666   35
Mulligan v Coffs Harbour City Council [2005] HCA 63   258, 278, 281, 283, 288, 291, 292, 299, 300, 305
Mummery v Irvings Pty Ltd (1956) 96 CLR 99   372, 373
Municipal Tramways Trust v Ashby [1951] SASR 61   501
Munro v Southern Dairies Ltd [1955] VLR 332   543
Murley Bros v Grove (1882) 46 JP 360   531
Murphy v Plasterers Society [1949] SASR 98   587, 594
Murphy v Stone-Wallwork (Charlton) Ltd [1969] 1 WLR 1023   35
Murray v McMurchy [1949] 2 DLR 442   207, 219
Murray v Minister of Defence [1988] 1 WLR 692   105, 113
Musca v Astle Corp Pty Ltd (1988) 80 ALR 251   158, 166
Mutch v Sleeman (1928) 29 SR (NSW) 125   613, 615
Mutual Life and Citizens' Assurance Co Ltd v Evatt (1968) 122 CLR 556   452, 453, 456
Mutual Life and Citizens' Assurance Co Ltd v Evatt [1971] AC 793   453, 463
Myer Stores Ltd v Jovanovic [2004] VSC 478   200
Myer Stores v Soo [1991] 2 VR 597; ATR 81-077   107–10, 112, 113

Nader v Urban Transit Authority of NSW (1985) 2 NSWLR 501   382, 384, 427, 440
Nagle v Chulov [2001] NSWSC 9   646
Nagle v Rottnest Island Authority (1993) 177 CLR 423   240, 288, 296, 300, 404
National Crime Authority v Flack (1998) ALR 501   188
National Mutual Life Association of Australasia Ltd v GTV Corporation Pty Ltd (1989) VR 747   651
Navenby v Lassels and Stanford (1367) KB 27/428, m 73   654
Naxakis v Western General Hospital (1999) 197 CLR 269   240, 309, 310, 350
Naxakis v Western & General Hospital [1999] VSC 389   309
Neill v Fallon [1995] ATR 81-321   516
Neindorf v Junkovic [2005] HCA 75   239, 240, 256, 259, 271, 285, 286, 288
Nelson v Nelson [1923] QSR 37   180
Nettleship v Weston [1971] 2 QB 691   314, 503
New South Wales v Bujdoso [2005] HCA 76   275, 410–11
New South Wales v Burton [2006] NSWCA 12   351
New South Wales v Godfrey & Godfrey [2004] NSWCA 113   262
New South Wales v Knight [2002] NSWCA 392   104
New South Wales v Lepore; Samin v Queensland; Rich v Queensland (2003) 212 CLR 511   93, 280, 652, 655, 659, 660, 666, 667, 672
New South Wales v Riley [2003] NSWCA 208   227
New South Wales v Seedsman [2000] NSWCA 119   424
Newcastle City Council v McShane [2004] NSWCA 425   302
Newcastle City Council v Shortland Management Services (2003) 57 NSWLR 173   535, 545
Nguyen v Nguyen (1990) 169 CLR 245   53
Nicholls v F Austin (Leyton) Ltd [1946] AC 493   572
Nicholson v Atlas Steel Foundry and Engingeering Co Ltd [1957] 1 WLR 613   339
Nickells v Melbourne Corporation (1938) 59 CLR 219   118
Nicol v Allyacht Spars Pty Ltd [1987] 2 Qd R 212; ATR 80-127   573, 574, 575, 577
Nominal Defendant v Gardikiotis (1996) 186 CLR 49   36, 363
Norris v Sibberas [1990] VR 161   460–2
Northern Sandblasting Pty Ltd v Harris (1997) 188 CLR 313   240, 257, 664, 668, 672
Northern Territory v Mengel (1995) 185 CLR 307   143–51, 563

Oakley v Lyster [1931] 1 KB 148; [1930] All ER 234   186, 188, 192, 195
O'Brien v Cunard Steamship Co 28 NE 266 (Mass Sup Jud Ct) (1891)   217
O'Brien v Smolonogov (1983) 53 ALR 107   158
O'Connor v SP Bray Ltd (1937) 56 CLR 464   563, 566, 568
O'Dwyer v Leo Buring Pty Ltd [1966] WAR 67   307
Ogle v Barnes (1799) 8 TR 188; 101 ER 1338   244
Onus v Alcoa of Australia Ltd (1981) 149 CLR 27   569
The Ophelia [1916] 2 AC 206   202
Orion Pet Products v RSPCA (2002) 120 FCR 191   616, 618, 639
O'Shea v Sullivan (1994) Aust Torts Reports 81-273   487
Overseas Tankship (UK) Ltd v Miller Steamship Co Ltd (The Wagon Mound (No 2)) [1967] 1 AC 617; ALR 97; 3 WLR 498   274, 379, 531, 539
Overseas Tankship (UK) Ltd v Morts Dock & Engineering Co Ltd (The Wagon Mound (No 1)) [1961] AC 388   377–9, 380
Owners <Dash> Strata Plan 156 v Gray [2004] NSWCA 304   49

P Perl (Exporters) Ltd v Camden London Borough Council [1984] QB 342   395
Pacific Carriers Ltd v BNP Paribas (2004) 78 ALJR 1045; 208 ALR 213   515
Paff v Speed (1961) 105 CLR 549   46
Page v Smith [1996] 1 AC 155   425
Palmer Bruyn & Parker Pty Ltd v Parsons (2001) 218 CLR 366   158, 165, 168–70
Palsgraf v Long Island Railroad Co 248 NY 339; 162 NE 99 (1928)   253, 353, 423
Pan Australian Credits (SA) Pty Ltd v Kolim Pty Ltd (1981) 27 SASR 353   175
Papatonakis v Australian Telecommunications Commission (1985) 156 CLR 7   320
Pargiter v Alexander (1995) 5 Tas R 158; [1995] ATR 81-349   178
Paris v Stepney Borough Council [1951] AC 367   280

Parker v British Airways Board [1982] 1 QB 1004   190
Parker v Commonwealth [1965] 112 CLR 295   75
Parkinson v Kuehnast [1996] FCA 1145   64
Parkinson v St James and Seacroft University Hospital NHS Trust [2002] QB 266   268
Parsons v Randwick Muncipal Council [2003] NSWCA 171   302
Parsons v The Queen (1999) 195 CLR 619   197
Partridge v Equity Trustees Executors and Agency Co Ltd (1947) 75 CLR 149   175
Pasley v Freeman (1789) 3 TR 51   158, 159
Pasmore v Oswaldtwistle Urban Council [1898] AC 387   564
Paton v British Pregnancy Advisory Services Trustees [1979] 1 QB 276   263
Patterson v McGinlay [1991] 55 SASR 258; ATR 81-087   285
Paulsen v Gundersen 218 Wis 578, 260 NW 448 (1935)   207
Peek v Gurney (1873) LR 6 HL 377   163
Penfolds Wines Pty Ltd v Elliott (1946) 74 CLR 204   172–5, 187, 188, 194, 201
Pennington v Norris (1956) 96 CLR 10   484, 502
Penrith City Council v Parks [2004] NSWCA 201   64
Percario v Kordysz [1990] 54 SASR 259   50
Performance Cars v Abraham (1962) 1 QB 33; [1961] 3 All ER 413   371
Perkins v NSW Aboriginal Land Council (unreported, NSWSC, Badgery-Parker J, 15 August 1997)   648
Perpetual Trustees & National Executors of Tasmania Ltd v Perkins [1989] ATR 80-295   187, 192, 195
Perre v Apand Pty Ltd (1999) 198 CLR 180   390, 391, 448, 449, 454, 462, 467, 468
Pervan v North Queensland Newspaper Co Ltd (1993) 178 CLR 309   617, 618, 620, 621
Peterson v Advertiser Newspapers (1995) 54 SASR 152   616, 618, 619, 620, 621
Petrie v Dowling [1989] Aust Torts Reports 80-263   425
Phelps v Kemsley (1942) 168 LT 18   633
Philips v Philips [1878] 4 QBD 127   33
Philips v William Whiteley Ltd [1938] 1 All ER 566   320
Phillips v Britannia Hygienic Laundry Co Ltd [1923] 2 KB 832; All ER 127   566
Pickard v Smith (1861) 10 CB (NS) 470; 142 ER 535   666
Piening v Wanless (1968) 117 CLR 498   372
Pierce v Society of Sisters, 268 US 510 (1925)   152
Piro v W Foster & Co Ltd (1943) 68 CLR 313; 17 ALJ 268   571, 575
Pitman Training Ltd v Nominet UK [1997] EWHC Ch 367   140
Pitt v Yalden (1767) 4 Burr 2060; 98 ER 74   243
Pitt Son & Badgery Ltd v Proulefco (1984) 153 CLR 644   262
Plaintiff S157/2002 v Commonwealth (2003) 211 CLR 476   564
Platt v Nutt (1988) 12 NSWLR 213   97, 206
Plenty v Dillon (1991) 171 CLR 635; 98 ALR 353; 65 ALJR 231   114, 117, 122, 125, 206, 229
Plenty v Dillon & Will (unreported, SASC 6372, Kelly J, 19 September 1997)   123, 124
Podrebersek v Australian Iron & Steel Pty Ltd (1985) 59 ALR 529; 59 ALJR 492   486, 502
Poggi v Scott 167 Cal 372; 139 P 815 (1914)   193
Polemis and Fyrness Withy & Co Ltd, Re [1921] 3 KB 560; 8 Ll LR 351   378, 379
Police v Greaves [1964] NZLR 295   103
Pollard v Ensor [1969] SASR 57   487
Pollard v Photographic Co (1888) 40 ChD 345   154
Polly Peck plc v Trelford [1986] QB 1000   613, 614
Powell v Gelston [1916] 2 KB 615   602
Powtney v Walton (1597) YLS MS G R29.9, fo 239v; abridged in HLS MS 2069, fo 277; 1 Rolle Abr 10 line 1   242
PQ v Australian Red Cross Society & Ors [1992] 1 VR 19   271
Prast v Town of Cottesloe (2000) 22 WAR 474   287, 299
Priestly v Fowler (1837) 3 M&W 1; 150 ER 1030   475, 477, 667
Prince v Massachusetts, 321 US 158 (1944)   152
Prince Albert v Strange (1849) 2 De Gex & Sm 652; 64 ER 293   154
Progress Properties Ltd v Craft (1976) 135 CLR 651; 12 ALR 59; 51 ALJR 184   524, 567
Public Transport Corporation v Sartori [1997] 1 VR 168   262
Public Trustee v Sutherland Shire Council (1992) Aust Torts Reports 81-149   36

Pullman v Walter Hill & Co [1891] 1 QB 185   601, 602
Pyrenees Shire Council v Day (1998) 192 CLR 330   304, 391, 395, 397, 403, 404–7, 468, 562, 568

Quilty v Windsor (1999) SLT 346   595
Quin v Greenock Tramways [1926] SC 544   415

R v Bishop [1975] QB 274   595
R v Brown [1993] 2 WLR 556   216
R v De'Zilwa (2002) 5 VR 408   513
R v Garrett (1988) 50 SASR 392   109
R v Governor of Brockhill Prison; Ex parte Evans (No 2) [2000] 3 WLR 843   229
R v Hall (1671) 1 Vent 169   531
R v Howe (1958) 100 CLR 448   223
R v Ireland [1997] QB 114   102
R v Leusenkamp (2003) 40 MVR 108   513
R v Manchester City Magistrates' Court; Ex part Davies [1989] 1 QB 631   111
R v Waltham Forest Justices; Ex parte Solanke [1986] QB 983   111
R v Whitbread (unreported, VSC, Appeal Division, 14 March 1995)   418, 419
R v Williams [1923] 1 KB 340   215
Rabay v Bristow [2005] NSWCA 199   259
Raciti v Hughes (1995) 7 BPR 14,837   546
Radford v Ward (1990) 11 MVR 509   514
Radio 2UE Sydney Pty Ltd v Parker (1992) 29 NSWLR 448   616, 617, 618
Radley v London and North Western Railway Company 1 App Cas 754   479
Ragnelli v David Jones (Adelaide) Pty Ltd (2004) 90 SASR 233   324
Rahemtulla v Vanfed Credit Union [1984] 3 WWR 296   134
Railtrack plc v Wandsworth London Borough Council, The Times, 2 August 2001; [2001] EWCA
    Civ 1236   532
Rajski v Carson (1988) 15 NSWLR 84   606
Random House Australia Pty Ltd v Abbott (1999) 94 FCR 296   578, 586, 587, 588, 594, 595, 600,
    649, 650
Randwick City Council v Muzic [2006] NSWCA 66   507
Ratcliffe v Evans [1892] 2 QB 524   166, 169
Rawlinson v Rice [1997] 2 NZLR 651   150
Reader's Digest Services Pty Ltd v Lamb (1982) CLR 500   587, 594
Reardon v Bonutti Orthopaedic Services Ltd 316 Ill App 3d 699; 737 NE 2d 309 (2000)   350
Rees v Darlington Memorial Hospital NHS Trust [2004] 1 AC 3   267
Reeves v Commissioner of Police [2000] 1 AC 360   247, 256, 365, 400
Register.com Inc v Verio Inc 356 F 3d 393 (2d Cir NY 2004)   176
Renouf v Federal Capital Press of Australia Pty Ltd (1977) 17 ACTR 35   621
Reynolds v Clarke (1725) 1 Stra 634, 2 Ld Raym 1399; 93 ER 747   128, 133
RH Willis & Son v British Car Auctions Ltd [1978] 1 WLR 438   192
Rich v Queensland *see* New South Wales v Lepore; Samin v Queensland; Rich v Queensland
Richmond Valley Council v Standing [2002] NSWCA 359   302
Richards v Mills (2003) 27 WAR 200   481, 491
Rickards v Lothian [1913] AC 263; [1911-13] All ER 71   368
Riddick v Thames Board Mills [1977] QB 893   601
Rigby v Hewitt (1850) 5 Ex 240   377
Rivkin v Amalgamated Television Services Pty Ltd [2001] NSWSC 432   595, 612
Roach v Yates [1938] 1 KB 256   31
Roads and Traffic Authority v McGregor [2005] NSWCA 388   303
Roads and Traffic Authority of NSW v McGuinness [2002] NSWCA 210   302
Robbins v Jones (1863) 15 CB (NS) 221   256
Roberts v Bass (2002) 212 CLR 1   168, 621, 631, 635, 640–4
Roberts v Ramsbottom [1980] 1 WLR 823; 1 All ER 7   317
Robertson v Belson [1905] VLR 555   161
Robin v Tupman & Anor [1993] 15 EG 145; 1 EGLR 169   559
Robinson v Balmain New Ferry Co Ltd [1910] AC 295   107
Robinson v Harman (1848) 1 Exch 850   30

Roe v Minister of Health [1954] 2 QB 66; 2 All ER 131; 2 WLR 915 (CA)   285, 286, 377
Roe v Wade 410 US 113 (1973)   152
Rofe v Smith Newspapers (1924) 25 SR (NSW) 4   611
Rogers v Nationwide News Ltd 216 CLR 327   628, 629, 646, 647, 649, 650
Rogers v Whitaker (1992) 175 CLR 479   206, 207, 209, 240, 287, 309, 310, 311–3, 319, 355, 357, 369, 465, 647
Roggenkamp v Bennett (1950) 80 CLR 292   505, 514
Romeo v Conservation Commission (NT) (1998) 192 CLR 431   259, 276–8, 279, 282, 287–9, 292, 298, 299, 304, 305, 406
Rookes v Barnard (1964) AC 1129   41
Rootes v Shelton (1967) 116 CLR 383   507, 509
Rosenberg v Percival (2001) 205 CLR 434   286, 287, 350, 358–62, 426, 463, 510
Royal Alexandra Hospital v J [2005] NSWSC 465   212
Royal Alexandra Hospital v Joseph [2005] NSWSC 422   212
Ruddock v Taylor [2003] NSWCA 262   106, 112
Ruddock v Taylor [2005] HCA 42   106, 152
Rufo v Hosking [2004] NSWCA 391 (1 November 2004)   350, 351
Ruhani v Director of Police [2005] HCA 42   19, 105, 106
Russell v Palmer (1767) 2 Wils 325   243
Ryan v Fildes [1938] 3 All ER 517   93
Ryan v Great Lakes Council *see* Graham Barclay Oysters Pty Ltd v Ryan
Ryde City Council v Saleh [2004] NSWCA 219   302
Ryde-Parramatta Golf Club (unreported, NSWSC, Helsham CJ, 23 February 1978)   542
Rylands v Fletcher (1866) LR 1 Ex 265; affirmed at (1868) LR 3 HL   539, 666, 669

Sadler & State of Victoria v Madigan [1998] VSCA 53   108
Sainsbury v Great Southern Energy Pty Ltd [2000] NSWSC 479   499
St George's Health Care Trust v S [1999] Fam 26   210
Salahuddin v Alaji 232 F3d 305; 2000 US App (2000)   563
Saltman Engineering Co Ltd v Campbell Engineering Co Ltd [1948] 65 RPC 203   155
Samin v Queensland *see* New South Wales v Lepore; Samin v Queensland; Rich v Queensland
Samson v Aitchison (1960) 103 CLR 215   658
San Sebastian Properties Pty Ltd v Minister Administering the Environment Planning & Assessment Act 1979 (1986) 162 CLR 341   450, 458, 460, 464
Sanders v Snell (1998) 196 CLR 329   144
Sanders v Snell (2003) 130 FCR 149; [2003] FCAFC 150   144, 145, 148–51
Saville v Roberts (1698) 1 Ld Raym 374   136, 137
Scanlon v American Cigarette Company (Overseas) Pty Ltd (No 3) [1987] VR 289   506, 514
Scarsbrook v Mason [1961] 3 All ER 767   658
Schellenberg v Tunnel Holdings Pty Ltd (2000) 200 CLR 121   371, 372, 373
Schemmell v Pomeroy (1989) 50 SASR 450   185
Schindler Lifts Australia Pty Ltd v Debelak (1989) 89 ALR 275   168
Schloendorff v Society of New York Hospital 105 NE 92 (1914)   208
Schmidt v Argent [2003] QCA 507   44, 46
Scott v Davis (2000) 204 CLR 333   280, 658, 666
Scott v London & St Katherine Docks Co (1865) 3 H & C 596; [1861-73] All ER 246 (Ex Ch)   371
Scott v Shephard (1773) 2 Wm Bl 892; 3 Wils 403; [1558-1774] All ER 295   98, 176
Seager v Copydex Ltd [1967] 1 WLR 923   154, 184
Seas Sapfor v Electricity Trust of South Australia (unreported SASC FC, 9 August 1996)   472
Secretary, Department of Health and Community Services (NT) v JWB and SMB (Marion's Case) (1992) 175 CLR 218   96, 97, 206, 209, 211, 213, 216, 217, 218
Secretary, Department of Natural Resources & Energy v Harper [2000] VSCA 36   298
Sedleigh-Denfield v O'Callaghan [1940] AC 880   551
Selecta Homes and Building Co Pty Ltd v Advertiser-Weekend Publishing Co Pty Ltd (2001) 79 SASR 451   603
Semayne's Case (1604) 5 Co Rep 91a; 77 ER 194; [1558-1774] All ER 62   115, 116, 124, 229
Sendil's Case (1585) 7 Co Rep 6a   115
Sghendo v Mann [2000] SADC 154   50

Shaddock (L) & Ass Pty Ltd v Parramatta City Council (1980-81) 150 CLR 225   453, 455, 456, 460, 463
Shapiro v La Morta (1923) 40 TLR 201   168
Sheldrick v Abery (1793) 1 Esp 55; 170 ER 278   174
Shepton v Dogge (No 1) (1442) CP 40/725, m 49 (Pas 1442)   158
Shipard v Motor Accident Commission (1997) 70 SASR 240   426
Shipton v Dogge (No 2) (1442) Doige's Case   158
Sibley v Kais (1967) 118 CLR 424   488, 490
Sibley v Milutinovic [1990] Aust Torts Rep 81-013   206
Sid Ross Agency Pty Ltd v Actors and Announcers Equity Association of Australia [1971] 1 NSWLR 760   547
Sidaway v Governors of Bethlem Royal Hospital (1985) AC 871   207, 308
Silkin v Beaverbrook Newspapers Ltd [1958] All ER 516   620
Sim v Stretch (1936) 52 TLR 669   586
Simpson v Diamond [2001] NSWSC 925   20
Simpson v Thompson (1877) 3 AC 279   446
Sims v Wran [1984] 1 NSWLR 317   603
Singh v Commonwealth of Australia [2004] HCA 43   564
Skinner v Oklahoma, 316 US 535 (1942)   152
Slater v Baker (1767) 2 Wils KB 359   243
Slater v Swann [1730] 2 Stra 872; 93 ER 906   174
Smedley v Smedley (1984) Tas R 49   491
Smith v Broken Hill Pty Co Ltd (1957) 97 CLR 337   485
Smith v Chadwick (1884) 9 App Cas 187   162
Smith v Charles Baker & Sons [1891] AC 325   504, 508
Smith v Howard Johnson Company 615 NE 2d 1037, 1038 (1993)   202
Smith v Jenkins (1970) 119 CLR 397   520, 521
Smith v Leech Brain & Co Ltd [1962] 2 QB 405   382
Smith v Leurs (1945) 70 CLR 256   261, 315, 316, 395, 663
Smith v London and South Western Railway Company (1870) LR 6 CP 14   378
Smith v O'Brien [1862] 1 W & W (L) 386   111
Smith v Retirement Benefits Fund Investment Trust [1994] ATR 81-286   373
Smith v Scott [1973] Ch 314   552
Smith v Selwyn [1914] 3 KB 98   94
Smith v Superior Court 198 Cal Rptr (Ct App 1984)   202
Smith v Tabain [1985] ATR 80-716   320
Smith New Court Securities Ltd v Scrimgeour Vickers [1997] AC 254   165
Smith's Newspapers Ltd v Becker (1932) 47 CLR 279   632
Smithson v Garth (1691) 3 Lev 324; 83 ER 711   674
Soblusky v Egan (1960) 103 CLR 215   658
Soffos v Eaton 80 US App DC 306; 152 F 2d 682 (1945 CA DC)   141
Sony Music Entertainment (Australia) Ltd v University of Tasmania (No 1) (2003) 129 FCR 472   186
Sorrell v Smith [1925] AC 700; [1925] All ER Rep 1   101
Sotelo v DirectRevenue, LLC 384 F Supp 2d 1219 (Ill 2005)   185
South Australia v Johnson (1982) 42 ALR 161   165
South Staffordshire Water Co v Sharman [1896] 2 QB 44   191
South Tweed Heads Rugby League Football Club Ltd v Cole (2002) 55 NSWLR 113   247
Southwark London Borough Council v Tanner [2001] AC 1   537, 541
Sovar v Henry Lane Pty Ltd (1967) 116 CLR 397   562, 564, 565, 566
Spartan Steel & Alloys Ltd v Martin & Co (Contractors) [1973] QB 27; 3 WLR 502; 3 All ER 557   448, 449
Spasic v Imperial Tobacco Ltd (1998) 42 OR (3d) 391   203
Spautz v Butterworth (1996) 41 NSWLR 1   110, 111
Spautz v Dempsey [1984] 1 NSWLR 449   111
Spicer v Coppins (1991) 56 SASR 175   514
Spring v Guardian Assurance plc [1995] 2 AC 296   453, 457
Stand Electric and Engineering Co Ltd v Brisford Entertainments Ltd [1952] 2 QB 246   181
Standard Chartered Bank v Pakistan National Shipping Co [2000] 3 WLR 1692   480
Standard Chartered Bank v Pakistan National Shipping Co (Nos 2 & 4) [2002] 3 WLR 1547   166

Stanley v Powell [1891] 1 QB 86; [1886-90] All ER 314   177, 387
State v Brown 364 A 2d 186 (1976)   216
State Bank of New South Wales Ltd v Currabubula Holdings Pty Ltd [2001] NSWCA 47   601
State Government Insurance Commission v Fiorenti; Worthley v Fiorenti [1991] SASC 2897   49
State Government Insurance Commission v Trigwell (1979) 142 CLR 617   18
State of New South Wales *see* New South Wales
State Rubbish Collectors Assoc v Siliznoff 240 P 2d 282 (1952)   134
Steel and Morris v McDonald's Corporation [1999] EWCA Civ 1144   584, 594
Stephens v Avery [1988] 2 All ER 477   154
Stephens v West Australian Newspapers Ltd (1994) 182 CLR 211   627, 630–2
Stern v Piper [1997] QB 123   612
Stevens v Brodribb Sawmills Co Pty (1986) 160 CLR 16; 63 ALR 513   664, 665
Stoakes v Brydges [1958] QWN 5   546
Stockwell v State of Victoria [2001] VSC 497   550, 553, 555
Stovin v Wise [1996] AC 923   389, 390, 394, 396, 399, 400, 403
Stuart v Bell [1891] 2 QB 341   629, 633
Sturch v Willmott [1997] 2 Qd R 310   57
Sturgess v Bridgman (1879) 11 Ch D 852 (CA)   559
Sullivan v Gordon (1999) 47 NSWLR 319   57
Sullivan v Micallef (1994) Aust Torts Reps 81-308   350
Sullivan v Moody; Thompson v Connon (2001) 207 CLR 562   152, 248, 390–2, 398, 426, 428, 433, 457
Suncorp Insurance and Finance Ltd v Blakeney (1993) 18 MVR 361   514
Sungravure Pty Ltd v Meani (1964) 110 CLR 24   484
Sungravure Pty Ltd v Middle East Airlines Airliban SAL (1975) 134 CLR 1   167, 596, 598
Sutherland Shire Council v Heyman (1985) 157 CLR 424   240, 389, 390, 395, 398, 400–4, 406, 466, 469, 470, 562, 569
Swain v Waverley Municipal Council [2005] HCA 4   246, 255, 274, 291, 300
Swan v Williams (Demolition) Pty Ltd (1987) 9 NSWLR 172; [1987] Aust Torts Reports 80-104   426
Sweeney v Boylan Nominees Pty Ltd [2006] HCA 19   656, 657
Swimsure (Laboratories) Pty Ltd v McDonald [1979] 2 NSWLR 796   167, 170
Switzerland Australia Health Fund Pty Ltd v Shaw (1988) 81 ALR 111   634
Symes v Mahon [1922] SASR 447   108, 109

T v T [1988] 2 WLR 189; 1 All ER 613   207
Taggart v Rose [1975] WAR 41   481
Tahche v Cannon [2003] HCA Trans 524   146, 147
Tame v New South Wales; Annetts v Australian Stations Pty Ltd (2002) 211 CLR 317   240, 248, 251, 255, 274, 419, 428–33, 435, 436, 439, 441, 442
Tampion v Anderson [1973] VR 715   146, 147
Tarleton v Fisher (1781) 2 Douglas 671   130
Taylor v Nesfield (1854) 3 El & Bl 724; 118 ER 1312   143
TC by his tutor Sabatino v New South Wales [2001] NSWCA 380   348
TCN Channel Nine Pty Ltd v Anning [2002] NSWCA 82   124
Telegraph Newspaper Co Ltd v Beford (1934) 50 CLR 632   630
Telnikov v Matusevitch [1992] 2 AC 343   621
Temple Community Hospital v Superior Court of Los Angeles County 976 P 2d 223 (1999)   202
Tenant v Goldwin (1704) 2 Ld Raym 1089; 3 Ld Raym 324; 6 Mod Rep 311   536
Tepko Pty Limited v Water Board (2001) 206 CLR 1   455, 457, 460
Teubner v Humble (1963) 108 CLR 491   27
Thatcher v Charles (1960-61) 104 CLR 57   47
Theaker v Richardson [1962] 1 WLR 151   602
Theofel v Farey-Jones, 359 F3d 1066, 2003 US App (9th Cir Cal 2004)   127
Theophanous v Herald & Weekly Times Ltd (1994) 182 CLR 104   636, 638, 649
Thompson v Australian Capital Television (1996) 186 CLR 574; 141 ALR 1; 71 ALJR 131   605, 674, 675
Thompson v Commissioner of Police of the Metropolis [1998] QB 498
Thompson v Stanhope (1774) Amb 737; 27 ER 476   154

Thompson v Woolworths (Qld) Pty Ltd [2005] HCA Trans 7   245
Thompson v Woolworths (Qld) Pty Ltd [2005] HCA 19   259, 281, 288, 291, 489
Thompson-Schwab v Costaki [1956] 1 WLR 335   545, 552
Thorley v Lord Kerry (1812) 4 Taunt 355   594
Three Rivers District Council v Bank of England (No 3) [2003] 2 AC 1   143, 145, 148–51
Thrifty-Tel Inc v Bezenek 54 Cal Rptr 2d 468 (Cal Ct App 1996)   127, 176
Timbs v Shoalhaven City Council [2004] NSWCA 81   404
Timbu Kolian v The Queen (1968) 119 CLR 47   326
TJ Larkins & Sons v Chelmer & Anor [1965] Qd R 68   159
TNT Management Pty Ltd v Brooks (1979) 23 ALR 345   321
Todorovic v Waller (1981) 150 CLR 402   65
Toll (FGCT) Pty Ltd v Alphapharm Pty Ltd (2004) 219 CLR 165   515
Tomlinson v Congleton Borough Council [2004] 1 AC 46   255, 260, 284
Toogood v Spyring (1834) 1 CM&R 181   629, 630, 632
Torette Howe Pty Ltd v Berkman (1940) 62 CLR 637   536, 550
Touche Ross & Co v Redington Trustee 442 US 560 (1979)   563
Tozer v Child (1857) 7 El & Bl 377; 119 ER 1286   143
Traian v Ware [1957] VR 200   230
Transport Accident Commission v Lincoln [2003] VSCA 67   52
Travel Compensation Fund v Robert Tambree t/as R Tambree and Associates [2005] HCA 69   332,
    333, 334, 564, 572
Traztand Pty Ltd v Government Insurance Office of New South Wales (1984) 2 NSWLR 598   601
Trobridge v Hardy (1955) 94 CLR 147   105
Trustees of the Roman Catholic Church, Bathurst v Koffman [1996] Aust Torts Reports 81, 399   262
Tuberville v Savage (1669) 1 Mod 3   103
Tuberville v Stampe (1697) 1 Ld Raym 264; 92 ER 944   654
Tucker v Tucker [1956] SASR 297   315
Tuff v Warman (1858) 5 CBNS 573   478, 479
Turner v Sterling (1671) 2 Vent 25; 86 ER 287   143

Ultramares Corporation v Touche 255 NY 170; 174 NE 441 (1931)   446, 447
University of Wollongong v Mitchell [2003] NSWCA 94   297
Uren v John Fairfax & Sons Pty Ltd (1966) 117 CLR 118   39, 650, 651

Vairy v Wyong Shire Council [2005] HCA 62   256, 271, 272, 274, 278, 281, 285, 286, 291, 292,
    299, 300, 305
Vallance v The Queen (1961) 108 CLR 56   226
Van Gervan v Fenton (1992) 175 CLR 327; 109 ALR 284   53, 56
Varawa v Howard Smith Co Ltd (1911) 13 CLR 35   141
Varnas v Peake [2001] SASC 330 (23 October 2001)   50
Venning v Chin (1974) 10 SASR 299   105, 204, 483
Victims Compensation Fund Corporation v Brown [2003] HCA 54   84
Victims Compensation Fund Corporation v GM [2004] NSWCA 185   84
Victoria Park Racing and Recreation Grounds Co Ltd v Taylor (1937) 58 CLR 479   125
Victorian Railway Commissioners v Coultas (1888) 13 AL 222   422
Victorian WorkCover Authority v Carrier Air Conditioning Pty Ltd [2006] VSCA 63   486
Victorian WorkCover Authority v Syrad [2004] VSCA 234   52
Viet Hong Lieng v Harold Delvers [2002] NSWCA 170   322
Vignoli v Sydney Harbour Casino [1999] NSWSC 1113   112
Vine v Waltham Forest London Borough Council [2000] 1 WLR 2383   516
Vitale v Bednall [2000] WASC 207   600
Vizetelly v Mudie's Select Library [1900] 2 QB 170   604
Voli v Ingleswood Shire Council (1963) 110 CLR 74   668
Von Bruhl v Victorian WorkCover Authority (unreported, Vic CC, Lewis J, 31 January 2003)   52
Voss v Suncorp-Metway Ltd [2003] QCA 252   197
Vyner v Waldenberg Brothers Ltd [1946] KB 50   339

W v Essex County Council [2000] 2 WLR 601   425
W (a Minor) (Inherent Jurisdiction: Consent to Treatment), Re [1992] 3 WLR 7758   207

Wagner v International Railway Co 232 NY 176 (1921)   253
Wainwright v Home Office [2003] UKHL 53   132, 153
Waldon v Marshall (1370) YB Mich 43 Edw III, f 33, pl 38   241
Walker v Adelaide City Corporation [2004] SASC 98   536, 557
Walker v Northumberland County Council [1995] 1 All ER 737   424
Wall v Brim 138 F 2d 478 (5th Circ, 1943)   207
Waller v James; Waller v Hoolahan [2006] HCA 16   268
Walsh v Ervin [1952] VLR 361; [1952] ALR 650   531
The Walter D Wallet [1893] P 202   136
Wason v Walter (1968) LR 4 QB 73   627, 630
Waterhouse v Broadcasting Station 2GB Pty Ltd (1985) 1 NSWLR 58   628, 650
Waterways Authority v Mathews [2003] NSWCA 330   290, 297, 298
Watt v Bretag (1981) 27 SASR 301   487
Watt v Hertfordshire County Council (1954) 2 All ER 368; 1 WLR 835   285
Watt v Rama [1972] VR 353   263
Waugh v James K Allan Ltd [1964] SC (HL) 102   318
Waugh v Kippen (1986) 160 CLR 156; 64 ALR 195   566
Waverley Council v Ferreira [2005] NSWCA 418   274
Waverley Municipal Council v Lodge (2001) 117 LGERA 447   297, 298
Weaver v Ward (1616) Hob 134; 80 ER 284   29, 225
Weld-Blundell v Stephens [1920] AC 956   325
Wenhak v Morgan (1880) 20 QBD 637   601
Wenman v Ash (1853) 13 CB 536   601
Western Australia v Watson [1990] WAR 248   385
Whelan v John Fairfax Publications Pty Ltd [2002] NSWSC 1028   613
Whisprun Pty Ltd v Dixon [2003] HCA 48   11
White (or Frost) v Chief Constable of South Yorkshire Police [1999] 2 AC 455   425, 436
White v Jameson (1874) 18 LR Eq 303   551, 552
White v Jones [1995] 2 AC 207   456
White v Mellin [1895] AC 154   168
White Buffalo Ventures LLC v Univ of Texas 420 F 3d 366 (SD Ohio 2005), certiorari denied 126 S Ct 1039, 163 L Ed 2d 856 (US 2006)   175, 185
Whitehorn v The Queen (1983) 152 CLR 657   147
Whitfield v McPherson (1995) 21 MVR 18
Whittlesea City Council v Merie [2005] VSCA 199   303
Wilkes v Wood (1763) Lofft 1; 98 ER 489   40, 116
Wilkinson v Downton [1897] 2 QB 57   4, 131, 132, 133, 148, 416, 427
Wilkinson v Joyceman [1985] 1 Qd R 567   507
Wilkinson v Law Courts Limited [2001] NSWCA 196   258
Williams v Milotin (1957) 97 CLR 465   104
Williams v Spautz (1992) 174 CLR 509   94, 140, 141, 142
Wilsher v Essex Area Health Authority [1988] 1 AC 1074; 2 WLR 557   314, 338, 340, 345–7, 348
Wilson v New South Wales Land and Housing Corporation (unreported, NSWSC, Harrison M, 18 March 1998) 1998 NSW LEXIS 477   550
Wilson v Peisley (1975) 50 ALJR 207   385
Wilsons and Clyde Coal Co v English [1938] AC 57   667
Wilton v Commonwealth Trading Bank of Australia (1973) 10 SASR 299   483
Winterbottom v Wright (1842) 10 M & W 109   244
Woadson v Nawton (1727), 2 Stra 777; 93 ER 842   177
Wood v Manley (1839) 11 AD & E 34; 113 ER 325   206
Woodrow v Commonwealth of Australia (1993) 45 FCR 52   427
Woods v Lowns (1995) 36 NSWLR 344   309
Woods v Multi-Sport Holdings Pty Ltd (2002) 208 CLR 460   287, 288, 290, 291, 292, 297, 306, 307, 486
Woodward v Porteous [1971] Tas SR 386   491
Woolcock St Investments [2002] Aust Torts Reports 81-660   470, 471
Woolcock St Invest v CDG Pty Ltd (2004) 216 CLR 515   17, 19, 447, 454, 462, 467, 470
Woollahra Municipal Council v Sved (1996) 40 NSWLR 101   470
Woolworths Ltd v Crotty (1942) 66 CLR 603   73

Woolworths Ltd v Lawlor [2004] NSWCA 209   56
Wright v Ramscot (1668) 1 Wms Saund 84; 85 ER 93   174
Wynbergen v Hoyts Corporation Pty Ltd (1997) 149 ALR 25   481, 502, 503
Wynn v NSW Insurance Ministerial Corporation (1995) 184 CLR 485   61, 64, 65, 66, 67
Wyong Shire Council v Shirt (1980) 146 CLR 40   274, 275, 276, 283, 306, 410, 412, 469
Wysse v Andrewe (1531) KB 27/1081   182

X (Minors) v Bedfordshire County Council [1995] 2 AC 633   248, 398, 560, 561, 570, 571
XL Petroleum (NSW) Pty Ltd v Caltex Oil (Australia) Pty Ltd (1985) 155 CLR 448   42, 675, 676

York Bros (Trading) Pty Ltd v Commissioner of Main Roads [1983] 1 NSWLR 391   557
Youssoupoff v Metro-Goldwyn Mayer Pictures Ltd (1934) 50 TLR 581   598
Yu Ge by her tutor Tao Ge v River Island Clothing Pty Ltd [2002] NSWSC 28; (2002) Aust Torts Reports 81-638   38

Zanker v Vartzokas (1988) 34 A Crim R 11; appealed (1989) 44 A Crim R 243; 51 SASR 277   100, 101
Zumpano v Montagnese (1997) 2 VR 525   470
Zuvela v Cosmarnan Concrete Pty Ltd (1996) 140 ALR 227; 71 ALJR 29   461

Table of Statutes

Commonwealth

Acts Interpretation Act 1901
    s 15AB   563
ASIC Act 2001
    s 12GF   678
Audit Reform Disclosure Act 2004   677
Australia Act 1986   19
Australian Federal Police Act 1979
    s 64B   663
    s 64B(1)   663
    s 64B(2)   663
    s 64B(3)   43
Commonwealth Constitution
    s 51(ix)   228
    s 51(xx)   123
    s 122   24
Commonwealth Motor Vehicles (Liability) Act 1959
    s 5   658
Commonwealth Volunteers Protection Act 2003   23, 222, 249
    s 4(2)   222
    s 6(2)   222
Copyright Act 1968
    s 116(1)   186
Corporations Act 2001
    s 1041I   678
Damage by Aircraft Act 1999   122
    s 9   123
    s 10   122
    s 11   122
Family Law Act 1975
    s 63F   211
Judiciary Act 1903   18
Migration Act 1958
    s 189   106
National Occupational Health and Safety Commission Act 1985   668
Navigation Act 1912
    s 59a   667
Occupational Health and Safety (Commonwealth Employment) Act 1991   668
    s 79   566
Privacy Act 1988   156
Quarantine Act 1908
    s 2B   228
Safety, Rehabilitation and Compensation Act 1988   25, 78, 79
    s 4   79
    s 4(1)(b)   79
    s 6   79
    s 6A   79
Seafarers Rehabilitation and Compensation Act 1992   25, 79
    s 3   79
    s 9   79
    s 39(7)   50
Sex Discrimination Act 1984
    s 28   215
Social Security Act 1991
    s 94(1)   50
Social Security and Veterans' Affairs Act 1988
    s 6   79
    s 94(1)   50
Stevedoring Industry Act 1956
    s 8   407
Taxation Laws Amendment (Structured Settlements and Structured Orders) Act 2002   37
Therapeutic Goods Administration Act 1989   309
Trade Practices Act 1974   21, 24, 519
    s 45D(1)   549
    s 52   157, 158, 160, 332, 464
    s 53   464
    s 60   549
    s 68   517
    s 68B   22, 517, 518
    s 74   517, 518
    s 74(1)   517
    s 74(2)   517

s 80 549
s 82 157, 549, 678
s 87 157
s 87D 32
s 87M 48
ss 87P–87S 48, 438
s 87U 62
s 87V(1)(a) 63
s 87W(2)(a) 55
s 87W(2)(b) 55
s 87W(2)(d) 55
s 87W(2)(e) 55
s 87W(3) 55
s 87ZB(1) 42
Trade Practices Amendment (Liability for Recreational Services) Act 2002 517, 518
Trade Practices Amendment (Personal Injuries and Death) Act (No 2) 2004 55

Australian Capital Territory

Civil Law (Wrongs) Act 2002 24, 47
  Ch 7A 677
  Ch 8 23, 533
  Ch 9 580
  Pt 3.2 22
  Pt 4.4 22, 23
  s 5 23, 219, 248
  s 5(1) 221
  s 5(2)(b) 221
  s 6 23
  s 7(2)(iii) 25
  s 8(1) 222, 249
  s 8(2) 222
  s 15(2) 68
  s 16 70, 71
  s 16(2) 70
  s 16(3)(c) 70
  s 18 71
  s 19 483
  s 24 23
  s 25(1) 72
  s 25(3) 72
  s 26 75
  s 28(1) 72
  s 32 241, 418
  s 33 422
  s 34(1) 438
  s 34(2) 441
  s 34(4) 439
  s 35(1) 438
  s 35(2) 438
  s 36 423, 443
  s 38 23
  s 39 23
  s 40 335
  s 41(2) 25
  s 42 286, 314
  s 43 272
  s 43(1)(b) 275
  s 43(2) 276, 440
  s 43(3) 439
  s 44(a) 282
  s 44(b) 283
  s 45 440
  s 45(1) 335
  s 45(2) 352
  s 46 348
  s 47 482
  s 92 496
  s 94 25, 261
  s 95(1)(b) 496
  s 95(2)(a) 495
  s 96 498
  s 96(5) 498
  s 97 498
  s 97(1) 498
  s 98 62, 75
  s 98(3)(a) 63
  s 99 48
  s 100 58, 76
  s 101(1) 482, 483
  s 102(1) 482
  s 102(1)(a) 483
  s 102(1)(b) 502
  s 102(2) 483, 577
  s 107B(1)(a) 678, 680
  s 107B(3)(a) 677
  s 107B(3)(b) 677
  s 107B(6) 678
  s 107D(1) 678
  s 107E(1) 680
  s 107F(1) 678
  s 107F(2)(a) 679
  s 107K 679
  s 109(3) 32
  s 110 282, 304
  s 111(2) 570
  s 112 414
  s 113 303, 413
  s 114 411
  s 127 611
  s 141 231
  s 168 260
  ss 180–185 52
  s 189 53
Criminal Injuries Compensation Act 1983 84
Crimes Act 1900
  s 34A 548
  s 35 135
Domestic Animals Act 2000
  s 109 530
Health Records (Privacy and Access) Act 1997 156
Law Reform (Miscellaneous Provisions) Act 1955 480
  s 5 43

s 21   667
s 24(1)   423
s 29   257, 260
Law Reform (Miscellaneous Provisions)
    (Amendment) Act 1991
    s 3   260
Limitation Act 1985
    s Pt 3   232
    s 11(1)   201
    s 16   72
    s 16B   232
    s 16B(2)   69
    s 21B   608
    s 36(4)   231
Medical Treatment Act 1994
    s 6   209
Mental Health (Treatment and Care) Act 1994
    s 25   228
    s 36G   228
    s 38   228
Occupational Health and Safety Act 1989   668
    s 95   566
Police Offences (Amendment) Act 1991   663
Residential Tenancies Act 1997
    s 67   672
    s 68   672
Supreme Court Act 1933
    s 22   606
Transplantation and Anatomy Act 1978
    Pt 2, Div 5   214
Victims of Crime Act 1994
    Dict   85
Victims of Crime (Financial Assistance) Act
    1983
    s 2   85
    s 10   84
    s 10(e)   86
    s 10(f)   86
    s 17(1)(a)   86
    s 19   84
    s 53   85
    s 54   85
    s 56   85
    s 57   85
    s 58   85
Workers' Compensation Act 1951   25
    s 6(1)   79
    s 118(2)   79

New South Wales

Children (Care and Protection) Act 1987
    s 20A   213
Children and Young Persons (Care and
    Protection) Act 1998
    s 174   214
    s 174(1)   213
Civil Liability Act 2002   24, 47

Pt 1A, Div 4   22
Pt 1A, Div 5   260
Pt 1A, Div 6   22
Pt 1A, Div 8   22
Pt 2   23
Pt 2, Div 7   23
Pt 3   22, 423
Pt 4   677
Pt 5   23, 533
Pt 8   23, 219, 248
Pt 8A   249
Pt 9   23, 222, 249
s 3B(1)   437
s 3B(1)(a)   28, 205
s 3B(1)(b)   25, 353
s 3B(1)(c)   25, 353, 437
s 3B(1)(d)   25
s 3B(1)(e)   25
s 3B(1)(f)   25
s 5   241, 335
s 5B   272
s 5B(1)   275
s 5B(2)   276, 440
s 5B(3)   439
s 5C(a)   282
s 5C(b)   283
s 5D   440
s 5D(1)   334
s 5D(2)   352
s 5D(3)   361
s 5E   348
s 5F   293, 295, 509, 513
s 5G   293
s 5G(2)   510
s 5H   294
s 5H(2)(c)   510
s 5I   286
ss 5K-5N   22
s 5K   294, 512, 518
s 5L   22, 294, 513
s 5L(1)   512
s 5L(2)   512
s 5N   518
s 5O   309
s 5O(1)   310
s 5O(2)   310
s 5O(3)   310
s 5O(4)   310
s 5P   309, 313
s 5Q   673
s 5Q(1)   653
s 5R   488
s 5R(2)(a)   499
s 5R(2)(b)   489
s 5S   482
s 5T   77
s 11   32
s 12(2)   75
s 12(3)   63, 66

s 13(1) 64
s 14 66
s 14(2)(b) 76
s 15(1) 55
s 15(2)(a) 55
s 15(2)(b) 55
s 15(2)(c) 55
s 15(4) 55
s 16 48, 438
s 16(2) 48
s 16(3) 48
s 21 28, 42
s 26C 48
s 26E 62
s 27 418
s 29 422
s 30 442
s 30(2)(b) 442
s 31 438
s 32(1) 438
s 32(2) 441
s 32(4) 439
s 33 438
s 34(1)(a) 677, 678, 680
s 34(1)(b) 678
s 34(1A) 678
s 34(2) 678
s 34A(1)(a) 680
s 34A(1)(b) 680
s 35(1) 678
s 35(3)(a) 679
s 39 679
s 42 282, 304
s 43(2) 570
s 43A(3) 305
s 44 414
s 45 303, 413
s 45(1) 413
s 45(2) 413
s 46 411
s 49 296, 495
s 50 286, 295
s 50(1) 496
s 50(3) 495
s 50(5) 496
s 51 224
s 52 224
s 52(3) 224
s 53 25, 224
s 54 25, 522
s 54(2) 522
s 54A 225
s 56 221
s 58(2)(a) 221
s 58(2)(b) 221
s 58(3) 221
ss 62–66 222
s 70 267
s 71 266

s 71(2) 267
Civil Liability Amendment (Personal Responsibility) Act 2002 22, 423
Compensation to Relatives Act 1847
  s 3(1) 73
  s 3(3)(a)-(c) 75
  s 4(1) 72
  s 5 72
Construction Safety Regulations 1912
  reg 73(2) 575
  reg 80 575
  reg 141 575
Crimes Act 1900
  s 352 227
  s 437 83
  s 545B 548
  s 562AB 135
Damage by Aircraft Act 1952
  s 2 122
Damages (Infants and Persons of Unsound Mind) Act 1929 38
Defamation Act 1974 579
  s 8A 584
  s 15 611
  s 16 615
  s 22 581, 640, 646
  s 22(1)(c) 647
  s 64A 649
Defamation Act 2005 (uniform law)
  Pt 3, Div 1 609
  s 4 611
  s 5 626, 628
  s 6 585
  s 7 582
  s 8 582
  s 9 584, 585
  s 9(3) 584
  s 20 609
  s 21 606
  s 21(3) 606
  s 22(5) 606
  s 24 610, 616
  s 24(2) 648
  s 25 611
  s 26 613, 614
  s 27 623, 624, 625, 627
  s 27(2)(c) 624
  s 27(2)(d) 624
  s 28 626, 627
  s 28(2) 626
  s 28(3) 626
  s 28(4) 626
  s 29 627, 631
  s 29(2) 628
  s 29(3) 628
  s 29(4) 628
  s 30 640, 644–8
  s 30(3)(j) 646
  s 30(4) 648

s 31   616, 621, 623
s 31(3)   622
s 31(4)   622
s 31(5)   622
s 32   605, 606
s 32(2)   605
s 32(3)   605
s 32(3)(g)   605
s 33   582, 648
s 34   649
s 35   650
s 35(2)   651
s 36   651
s 37   651
s 38   609, 650
s 38(2)   650
s 47   608
s 48   608
Sch 1   623
Sch 2   626, 627
Sch 3   628
District Court Act 1973
s 55   493
Dust Diseases Tribunal Act 1989
ss 12A–12D   70
Fair Trading Act 1987
s 42   332
Health Care Liability Act 2001   23
Health Records and Information Privacy Act 2002   156
Law Reform (Miscellaneous Provisions) Act 1944   435
s 2   68
s 2(2)(a)(i)   71
s 2(2)(a)(ii)   70
s 2(2)(b)   70
s 2(2)(d)   70
s 2(5)   71
s 3   422, 423
s 4   423
Law Reform (Miscellaneous Provisions) Act 1946
s 5(1)   435
Law Reform (Miscellaneous Provisions) Act 1965   480
s 8   483
s 9   576
s 9(1)   482
s 9(1)(b)   502
s 9(2)   483
s 10   80
Legal Practitioners Act 1987
ss 198C–198I   52
Legal Profession Act 1987
Div 5C   53
Limitation Act 1969
s 14(1)(b)   201
s 14B   608
s 18A(2)   232

s 19   231
s 50A   72
s 50C   232
s 50C(1)(a)   69
s 50C(1)(b)   69
s 50C(3)   69
s 50E   232
s 56A   608
Local Government Act 1919   401, 456
Local Government Act 1993
s 569   260
Meat Industry Act 1978
s 59F   260
Mental Health Act 1990
Pt II, Div 1   228
s 8   228
Minors (Property and Contracts) Act 1970   520
Motor Accidents Act 1988   236, 332, 493
s 74   492, 494
s 76   492, 506
s 81A   43
Motor Accidents Amendment Act 1995   332
Motor Accidents Compensation Act 1999   69, 82
s 3B   82
s 144   43
Motor Accidents (Lifetime Care and Support) Act 2006   82
s 7(3)   83
Occupational Health and Safety Act 1983   668
s 22   566
Partnership Act 1892
s 10   658
Police Act 1990
s 212   663
s 213   663
Pure Foods Act 1908-44   172, 194
Rural Lands Protection Act 1989
s 66   260
Scaffolding and Lifts Regulations 1912
reg 139(7)   568
Terrorism (Police Powers) Amendment (Preventative Detention) Act 2005   229
Victims Rights Act 1996
s 5   416
Victims Support and Rehabilitation Act 1996
s 8   85
s 9   85
s 18   84
s 18(1)(a)   86
s 19   84
s 20(1)   84
s 21   86
s 43   84, 85
Sch 1, cl 5(a)   84, 416
WorkCover Legislation Amendment Act 1996
Sch 1, item 1.3   78
Workers Compensation Act 1926
s 65   667

Workers Compensation Act 1987   25, 332
   s 4   79
   s 9A   79
   s 10(1)   79
   s 151AA   667
   s 151H   50
   s 151O   506
Workplace Injury Management and Workers Compensation Act 1998   49, 51

Northern Territory

Compensation (Fatal Injuries) Act 1974
   s 7(1)   73
   s 8   72
   s 10   415
   s 10(2)   72
   s 10(3)(e)(iii)   77
   s 10(3)(f)   77
   s 10(4)   75
   s 11(1)   77
Consumer Affairs and Fair Trading Act 1996 (as in force in 2005)
   s 68A   22, 518
   s 68A(3)   518
Crimes (Victims Assistance) Act 1989
   s 9(1)   86
   s 9(1)(e)   86
   s 9(1)(f)   86
   s 13   84
   s 21   85
   s 22   85
Criminal Code
   s 155   253
   s 189   548
Defamation Act 1938   580
Emergency Medical Operations Act 1992   220
   s 3   214
Juries Act 1962
   s 7(1)   606
Law Reform (Miscellaneous Provisions) Act 1956   480
   s 5(2)   68
   s 6   70
   s 6(b)   70
   s 6(c)(ii)   70
   s 7(1)(a)   69
   s 9   71
   s 16(1)   576
   s 22   667
   s 24(1)   422
   s 25   423, 437, 443
Law Reform (Miscellaneous Provisions) Act 2001
   s 6   43
   s 6(a)   71
   s 7(1)(b)   69
   s 7(2)   69
   s 10A   261
   s 12(1)(b)   201
   s 15(1)   483
   s 16(1)   482
   s 16(2)   483
Limitation Act 1981
   s 12(1)(b)   232
   s 17   72
   s 44   231
Mental Health and Related Services Act
   Pt 3   228
   Pt 6   228
Motor Accidents (Compensation) Act 1979   81, 236
   s 5(1)   81
   s 7   82
   ss 13–19   82
   s 17(1)(c)   82
Motor Accidents (Compensation) Rates of Benefit Regulations 1984   236
Natural Death Act 1988
   s 4   209
Personal Injuries (Liabilities and Damages) Act 2003   24
   Pt 3   22
   Pt 4, Div 6   23
   s 3   496
   s 4(3)   25
   s 4(3)(c)   25, 353
   s 7   23, 222, 249
   s 7(1)   222
   s 7(2)(a)   222
   s 7(2)(b)   222
   s 8   23, 219, 248
   s 8(1)   221
   s 8(2)   221
   s 8(3)   221
   s 9   261
   s 10   261
   s 14   295
   s 14(2)(a)   495
   s 14(2)(b)   496
   s 15(1)   498
   s 15(2)   498
   s 16   497
   s 16(1)(b)   502
   s 17   497
   s 18   62
   s 19   28, 42
   s 20   62, 75
   ss 22–28   50, 438
   s 22   66
   s 22(2)(b)   76
   s 23   55
   s 23(1)(a)   55
   s 23(1)(b)   55
   s 23(2)   55
   s 24   23
   s 24(a)   47

xlii *Table of Statutes*

s 27   23
s 27(1)(a)   48
Personal Injuries (Liabilities and Damages)
   Regulations 2003
   reg 3   25
Police Administration Act 1978
   s 148C(1)   663
   s 148C(3)   663
   s 65(2)   663
   s 163(3)   43
Proportionate Liability Act 2005   677
   s 3   677
   s 4(2)(a)   678, 680
   s 4(2)(b)   678
   s 6(1)   678
   s 7   680
   s 8   678
   s 13(1)(a)   678
   s 13(1)(b)   678
   s 13(2)   679
   s 14   679
Tenancy Act 1996
   s 55(1)   672
Work Health Act 1986   25, 79, 668
   s 3   79
   s 3(1)   79
   s 4   79
   s 34   566
Work Health Act 2005   25

Queensland

Building Act 1975   471
Civil Liability Act 2003   24, 47
   Ch 2, Pt 1, Div 3   22
   Ch 2, Pt 1, Div 4   22, 260
   Ch 2, Pt 1, Div 6   22
   Ch 2, Pt 2   677
   Ch 2, Pt 3   222, 249
   Ch 2, Pt 3, Div 2   23
   Ch 3, Pt 3   23, 533
   Ch 3, Pt 4   23
   s 1   22
   ss 3–16   22
   s 5(a)   25
   s 5(b)   25, 353
   s 5(c)   25, 353
   s 5(d)   25
   s 5(1)   28, 42
   s 5(2)   28, 42
   s 9   272
   s 9(1)   275
   s 9(2)   276
   s 10(1)(a)   282
   s 10(1)(b)   283, 502
   s 11(1)   334, 335
   s 11(2)   353
   s 11(3)   361

   s 12   348
   s 13   293, 509
   s 13(5)   509
   s 14   293
   s 14(1)   511
   s 14(2)   510
   s 15   294
   s 15(1)(c)   510
   s 16   286
   s 18   294, 512
   s 19   22, 294
   s 19(1)   512
   s 19(2)   512
   s 21   22, 312
   s 22   22, 286, 309
   s 22(1)   310
   s 22(2)   310
   s 22(3)   310
   s 22(4)   310
   s 23   488, 499
   s 23(2)(b)   489
   s 24   482
   s 25   23
   s 26   23, 222
   s 27   222
   s 28(1)(a)   678, 680
   s 28(1)(b)   678
   s 28(2)   678
   s 28(3)(a)   677
   s 28(3)(b)   677
   s 30(1)   678
   s 31(1)   678
   s 31(3)   679
   s 32F   680
   s 32I   679
   s 32I(d)   679
   ss 34–37   23
   s 35   282, 304
   s 36   570
   s 37   303, 413
   ss 40–44   222
   s 45   522
   s 45(1)   25
   s 45(2)   522
   s 46   296, 495
   s 47   295, 496
   s 47(3)(a)   495
   s 47(3)(b)   496
   s 47(4)   497
   s 48(1)   498
   s 48(3)   498
   s 48(4)   498
   s 48(5)   498
   s 49(2)   498
   s 49A   266
   s 49B   266
   s 52   28, 42
   s 52(2)   28, 205
   s 54   62

s 54(1)   75
s 54(2)   75
s 57   66
s 57(1)   76
s 57(2)   76
s 59(1)(a)   55
s 59(1)(b)   55
s 59(1)(c)   55
s 59(3)   57
s 59(4)   55
s 61   50, 438
s 61(1)   50
s 61(1)(b)   50
s 62   48, 50, 438
s 79   249
Sch 2, Dict   496
Sch 2, s 8   62, 63
Civil Liability Regulation 2003   23
Criminal Code Act 1899
   s 277   120
   s 359B   135
   s 534   548
Criminal Offence Victims Act 1995
   s 5   85
   s 19(1)(c)   86
   s 22   84, 85
   s 25   84
   Sch 1   86
Defamation Act 1889   579
   s 15   611
Defamation Act 2005 see Defamation Act 2005 (NSW)
Fair Trading Act 1989
   s 38   680
Health Regulation 1996
   reg 14   260
Health Services Act 1991
   s 62A   156
Invasion of Privacy Act 1971
   s 43   230
Law Reform Act 1995
   Pt 6   23
   s 3   667
   s 5   483
   s 10(1)   482
   s 10(2)   483
Law Reform (Abolition of the Rule of Common Employment) Act 1951   667
Law Reform (Tortfeasors Contribution, Contributory Negligence and Division of Chattels) Act 1952   480
Law Reform (Contributory Negligence) Act 2001
   s 5   576
Limitation of Actions Act 1974
   s 10(1)(a)   201
   s 11   69, 72, 232
   s 29   232
   s 30   69

s 31(2)   231
s 32   69
Mental Health Act 2000
   s 25   228
   s 34   228
   s 36   228
   s 39   228
   s 40   228
   s 114   228
   s 185   228
Motor Accidents Insurance Act 1994
   s 55   43
Personal Injuries Proceedings Act 2002   24
   s 6(3)(b)   353
   s 56   52
Police Service Administration Act 1990
   s 5.15(a)   663
   s 10.5(1)   663
   s 10.5(1A)   663
   s 10.5(2)   43, 45, 663
   s 10.6(1)   663
Residential Tenancies Act 1994
   s 103   672
Rural Lands Protection Act 1985
   s 149   260
Succession Act 1981
   s 15(1)   455
   s 66   69
   s 66(1)   68
   s 66(2)   70
   s 66(2)(b)   71
   s 66(2)(c)   70
   s 66(2)(d)(ii)   70
   s 66(4)   71
Supreme Court Act 1995
   s 18(1)   72
   s 19   72
Supreme Court of Queensland Act 1991
   s 17   73
   s 23   75
Terrorism (Preventative Detention) Act 2005   229
Transplantation and Anatomy Act 1979
   s 20   214
WorkCover Queensland Act 1996
   s 319   43
Workers' Compensation Act 1990
   s 2(1)   79
Workers Rehabilitation and Compensation Act 1986   25
Workplace Health and Safety Act 1989   668

South Australia

Civil Liability Act 1936   24, 47
   Div 3   122
   Div 5   533
   Pt 2   580

Pt 4 260
Pt 7 22
s 3 25, 62, 66, 75, 241, 418, 483, 484
s 23 73
s 24(3) 72
s 25 72
s 28 76, 415
s 29 76, 415
s 30 77
s 31 286, 314
s 32 272
s 32(1) 275
s 32(2) 276
s 34(1) 335
s 34(2) 351
s 35 348
s 36 293, 509
s 37 22, 293, 511
s 37(1) 510
s 37(2) 510
s 37(3) 511
s 38 22, 294
s 38(2)(c) 510
s 39 286
s 40 286, 309, 319, 320
s 41 22, 286, 309
s 41(1) 310
s 41(2) 310
s 41(3) 310
s 41(4) 310
s 42 23, 303, 413
s 43 28, 205
s 43(1) 25, 523
s 43(2) 523
s 43(4) 25
s 43(4)(a)(i) 25
s 43(4)(c) 523
s 44(1) 488
s 45 77
s 46 295
s 46(1)(a) 495
s 46(2)(b) 496
s 46(3) 497
s 46(4) 497
s 47(1) 498
s 47(1)(c) 496
s 47(2) 498
s 47(4) 498
s 47(5) 498
s 47(6) 498
s 48(1) 497
s 48(2) 496
s 49 498
s 52 438
s 52(1) 49, 50
s 52(2) 49, 50
s 52(2)(c)(ii) 50
s 52(3) 49
s 53(1) 442

s 53(2) 438
s 53(3) 438
s 54(2) 75
s 54(3) 75
s 55 66
s 58 55
s 58(2) 55
s 58(3) 56
s 59 659, 663
s 67(1) 266
s 67(2) 266
s 67(3) 266
s 73 135
s 74 219, 248
s 74(2) 221
s 74(4)(b) 221
Community Welfare Act 1972
  s 91(1)(b) 398
Consent to Medical Treatment and Palliative
  Care Act 1995 220
  s 4 208
  s 6 209, 213
  s 7 209
  s 12 213
  s 13(5) 214
Criminal Law Consolidation Act 1935
  s 15B 224
  s 15C(2) 224
  s 19AA 135, 548
Defamation Act 2005 606, 623
  s 4 611
  s 6 585
  s 7 582
  s 8 582
  s 9 584, 585
  s 23 611
  s 24 613
  s 25 623
  s 27 627
  s 28 644
  s 29 616
  s 30 605
Industrial Code 1920-36
  s 321 571
Juries Act 1927
  s 5 606
Juvenile Courts Act 1971 117
Law Reform (Contributory Negligence and
  Apportionment of Liability) Act 2001 677
  Pt 3 677
  s 3 576, 678
  s 3(1) 653
  s 3(2) 677, 678, 680
  s 3(2)(a) 680
  s 3(3) 679
  s 7(1) 483
  s 7(2) 482
  s 7(2)(b) 502
  s 8 679

s 8(4)   678, 680, 681
s 8(6)   679
s 11   678
Law Reform (Ipp Recommendations) Bill 2003   22
   s 8   335
Limitation of Actions Act 1936
   s 35   104
   s 35(c)   201
   s 36   104, 232
   s 37   608
   s 45   232
   s 45A   232
   s 48   231
Listening and Surveillance Devices Regulations 2003   126
Local Government Act 1934
   s 703   260
Medical Practice Act 2004
   s 81   135
Mental Health Act 1993
   Pt IV   228
Minors Contracts (Miscellaneous Provisions) Act 1979   520
Motor Vehicles Act 1959
   s 113A   43
Occupational Health and Safety and Welfare Act 1986   668
Police Act 1998
   s 65(1)   663
   s 65(2)   663
Police Regulations 1999
   Pt 12   192
Racial Vilification Act 1996   135
Recreational Services (Limitation of Liability) Act 2002   22, 519
   s 3   518
Residential Tenancies Act 1997
   s 65   672
   s 68   672
Survival of Causes of Action Act 1940
   s 2(2)   68
   s 3(1)   70
   s 3(1)(a)(iv)   70
   s 3(1)(b)   71
   s 3(2)   70
   s 4(a)   69
   s 4(b)   69
   s 6(1)   71
Terrorism (Preventative Detention) Act 2005   229
Victims of Crime Act 2001
   s 4   85
   s 12   83
   s 17   85
   s 17(2)   86
   s 17(4)   86
   s 20   84, 86
   s 28   85

Volunteers Protection Act 2001   23, 222, 249
   s 4   222
Workers Rehabilitation and Compensation Act 1986   25, 79
   s 30(2)(a)   79
   s 30A   79
Wrongs Act 1936
   Pt 2A   23
   Div 13   23
   s 3A   335
   s 17D   257
   s 17E   257
   s 27A   575
   s 28   422
   s 30   667
   s 35A(4)   506
Wrongs (Limitation and Damages for Personal Injury) Amendment Act 2002
   s 24B   23

Tasmania

Administration and Probate Act 1935
   s 27   583
   s 27(2)   68
   s 27(3)   43
   s 27(3)(a)   71
   s 27(3)(b)   70
   s 27(3)(c)(iii)   70
   s 27(5)(a)   69
   s 27(5)(b)   69
   s 27(9)   71
Civil Liability Act 2002   24, 47
   Pt 2, Div 7   22
   Pt 5   23
   Pt 6, Div 4   22
   Pt 6, Div 5   22, 260
   Pt 6, Div 6   22
   Pt 7   23
   Pt 8   22
   Pt 9   23, 533
   Pt 9A   677
   Pt 10   23, 222, 249
   s 3B(1)   437
   s 3B(1)(a)   28, 205
   s 3B(1)(b)   25, 353, 437
   s 3B(2)   25
   s 3B(3)   25
   s 3B(4)   25
   s 5   295
   s 5(1)   494, 495, 496
   s 5(2)   497
   s 5(3)   497
   s 5(4)   496
   s 5(6)   496
   s 6   25
   s 6(1)   522
   s 11   272

s 11(1) 275
s 11(2) 276, 440
s 11(3) 282, 439
s 12(a) 283
s 13 440
s 13(1) 334, 335
s 13(2) 353
s 13(3) 361
s 14 348
s 15 293, 509
s 16 293
s 16(1) 511
s 16(2) 510
s 17 294
s 17(c) 510
s 19 294, 512
s 20 22, 294
s 20(1) 512
s 20(2) 512
s 21 313
s 22 286
s 22(1) 310
s 22(2) 310
s 22(3) 310
s 22(4) 310
s 23(1) 488
s 26(1) 62, 63, 75
s 26(2) 63
s 27 52, 438
s 28 48
s 28C 55
s 29 418
s 31 422
s 32 442
s 32(3) 442
s 33 438
s 34(1) 438
s 34(2) 441
s 34(4) 439
s 35 438
s 38 282, 304
s 40 570
s 41 414
s 42 303, 413
s 43 411
s 43A(1)(a) 677, 678, 680
s 43A(1)(b) 678
s 43A(2) 678
s 43A(5)(a) 680
s 43A(5)(b) 680
s 43A(9) 678
s 43B(1) 678
s 43B(3)(a) 679
s 43G 679
s 47(2) 222
s 47(3) 222
s 47(4) 222
Criminal Code Act 1924
  s 9(3) 94

s 179 130
s 192 135, 548, 549
Criminal Injuries Compensation Act 1976
  Pt 3 86
  s 4(1)(a) 85
  s 4(3)(a) 86
  s 4(3)(d) 86
  s 4(5) 85
  s 4(6) 86
  s 6 84
  s 9 84, 85
  s 16 86
Damage by Aircraft Act 1963 122
Defamation Act 1957 579
  s 15 611
Defamation Act 2005 *see* Defamation Act 2005 (NSW)
Electricity Supply Industry Act 1995
  s 43 260
Employers' Liability Act 1943
  s 5 667
Fatal Accidents Act 1934
  s 4 73
  s 5 72
  s 6(1) 72
  s 10(1)(a) 75
  s 10(1)(b) 75
  s 10(1)(d) 75
Fire Service Act 1979
  s 59 260
Human Tissue Act 1985
  s 21 214
Industrial Safety, Health and Welfare Act 1977 668
Limitations Act 1974
  Pt III 232
  s 4(1)(a) 201
  s 5A 72, 232
  s 5A(3) 232
  s 5A(5) 231
Local Government Act 1993
  s 245 260
  s 249 260
Mental Health Act 1996
  s 24 228
  s 35 228
  s 39 228
  s 83E 228
  s 83F 228
  s 88 228
Minors Contracts Act 1988 520
Motor Accidents (Liabilities and Compensation) Act 1973 55, 81, 236
  s 4 81
  s 14 81
  s 23 81
  Sch 2 81
Noxious Weeds Act 1964
  s 18 260

Police Service Act 2003
    s 84(1) 663
    s 84(2) 663
Terrorism (Preventative Detention) Act 2005
  229
Tortfeasors and Contributory Negligence Act 1954
    s 2(c) 576
    s 4 480
Workers Compensation Act 1988
    s 3(1) 79
Workers Rehabilitation and Compensation Act 1988 25
    s 25(1)(b) 79
Wrongs Act 1954
    s 4 482
    s 4(1) 77, 502
    s 4(1)(a) 483
    s 4(4) 77

Victoria

Accident Compensation Act 1985 25, 474
    s 5(1) 79
    s 83 79
    s 91 50
    s 93B(5) 51
    s 134AA 43
    s 134AB 79
    s 134AB(16) 79
    s 134AB(17) 79
    s 134AB(22)(c) 43
    s 134A 43
    s 135A(7)(c) 43
Accident Compensation (Work Cover Insurance) Act 1993 474
Administration and Probate Act 1958
    s 29(1) 68, 407
    s 29(2) 70
    s 29(2)(a) 71
    s 29(2)(b) 70
    s 29(2)(c)(iii) 70
    s 29(2A) 70
    s 29(3) 69
    s 29(3)(a) 69
    s 29(3A) 69
    s 29(5) 71
Building Act 1993
    Pt 7 530
Building Regulations 1994 530
Crimes Act 1958
    s 21A 135, 549
    s 318(2)(b) 513
    s 320 530
Criminal Injuries Compensation Act 1972 84
Defamation Act 2005 see Defamation Act 2005 (NSW)

Domestic (Feral and Nuisance) Animals Act 1994
    s 32 530, 567
    s 32(1) 530
    s 32(2) 530
    s 32(3) 531
Domestic (Feral and Nuisance) Animals Regulations 2005 531
Employers and Employees Act 1958
    s 34 667
Environment Protection Act 1970
    s 65A 530
Environment Protection (Residential Noise) Regulations 1997 530
Extractive Industries Development Act 1995
    s 51 260
Fair Trading Act 1999 519
    s 11 464
    s 13 464
Fair Trading (Recreational Services) Regulations 2004
    reg 5 518
Goods Act 1958
    s 97A 22
Guardianship and Administration Board Act 1986 210
Health Act 1958
    Pt III 530
    s 119(a) 226
    s 120A 226
    s 120AC 226
    s 121 226
    s 123 228
    s 124 228
    s 125 228
Health Records Act 2001 156
Human Tissue Act 1982
    s 24 214
Infertility (Medical Procedures) Act 1984
    s 6 263
Limitation of Actions Act 1958
    s 6 201
    s 23A 231
    s 27 201
    s 27D 232
    s 27E 232
    s 27I 232
    s 27J 232
Local Government Act 1958 405
    s 695(1A) 405
Local Government Act 1989
    s 111 530
    Sch 1 530
    Sch 10 530
Marine Act 1988
    s 38 530
Medical Treatment Act 1988 208, 209, 220
    s 5 209
    s 5B 210

Melbourne City Link Act 1995
   s 32D 121
   s 33 121
   s 34A 121
Mental Health Act 1986
   Pt IV 228
   s 7(7) 228
   s 8 228
   s 9 228
   s 9A 228
   s 9B 228
   s 10 228
   s 12 228
   s 12(1A) 228
   s 12C 228
Mental Health Regulations 1998
   reg 6 228
   reg 6A 228
Mineral Resources Development Act 1990
   s 115 260
Occupational Health and Safety Act 1985 668
   s 28 566
Partnership Act 1958
   s 14 658
Petroleum Act 1998
   s 127 260
Police Regulation Act 1958
   s 123(1) 663
   s 123(2) 663
Pollution of Waters by Oil and Noxious Substances Act 1986 530
Residential Tenancies Act 1997
   s 60 530
   s 65 672
   s 68 672
Road Management Act 2004
   Pt 6 533
   s 102 303, 413
Sentencing Act 1991
   s 86 530
Summary Offences Act 1966
   Pt V 530
   Pt VI 530
   Pt VII 530
   Pt VIII 530
   s 4 530
   s 5 530
   s 7 530
   s 8 530
   s 48A 530
   ss 62–65A 530
Supreme Court Act 1986
   s 41 94
Surveillance Devices Act 1999
   s 3 126
   s 7 126
Transport Accident Act 1986 25, 80, 236, 474
   s 6(1) 81
   s 38 79

   s 60(1A) 81
   s 93 43
   s 93(1) 81
   s 93(2) 80
   s 93(3) 80
   s 93(4) 80
   s 93(4)(b) 51
   s 93(7)(a) 81
   s 93(7)(b) 81
   s 93(8) 81
   s 93(9) 81
   s 93(10)(c) 81
   s 93(11) 81
   s 93(12A) 81
   s 93(17) 80
Victims of Crime Assistance Act 1996
   Pt II 85
   s 8 84
   s 8(2)(a) 86
   s 8A 84
   s 10 84
   s 10A 84
   s 12 84
   s 13 84
   s 15 86
   s 51 85
Water Industry Act 1994
   s 23 260
Wrongs Act 1958 24, 51, 328, 580
   Pt IIA 494
   Pt IV 122
   Pt IVAA 677
   Pt VB 23
   Pt VC 23
   Pt VIA 23, 219, 248
   Pt VIB 249
   Pt IX 22, 23, 222, 249
   Pt X 335
   Pt XII 533
   s 3 335
   s 14A(1) 257
   s 14B 260
   s 14B(fa) 494
   s 14B(fb) 261, 494
   s 14B(3) 257
   s 14B(4) 257
   s 14G 22, 295, 520
   s 14G(2) 494
   s 14G(2)(a) 497
   s 14G(2)(b) 25
   s 16 73
   s 17 72
   s 19(1) 75
   s 19A 76
   s 19A(b) 57
   s 19B(1) 76
   s 20 72
   s 23 422
   s 24AF(1)(a) 678, 680

s 24AF(1)(b) 678
s 24AF(2) 678
s 24AG 677
s 24AH(1) 678
s 24AI(1) 678
s 24AM 680
s 24AN 679
s 24AP 679
s 24AP(d) 28, 42, 679
s 25(1) 483
s 25(1A) 483
s 26(1) 482
s 26(1)(b) 502
s 26(4) 77
s 28B 32
s 28C(2) 28, 205
s 28C(2)(d) 25
s 28F(1)(b) 75
s 28F(1)(a) 62
s 28F(3)(a) 63
s 28H 48
s 28I 66
s 28I(1)(b) 76
s 28IA(1)(a) 55
s 28IA(1)(b) 55
s 28IA(2) 55
s 28IB 55
s 28ID 57
s 28IF(2)(a) 25
s 28IF(2)(b) 25
s 28LB 50, 51, 438
s 28LC 50
s 28LC(2)(b) 25
s 28LE 50, 438
s 28LF 50, 438
s 28LG 51
s 28LH 51, 52
s 28LI 51
s 28LJ 51
s 28LK 51
s 28LL 51, 52
s 28LZH 51
s 28LZI 52
s 28LZI(1) 51
s 28LZN 51
s 28LZO 52
s 28M 37
s 31A 221
s 31B(1) 221
s 31B(2) 221
s 31B(3) 219
s 36(c) 22
s 38 222
s 43 241
s 45(1)(e) 353
s 45(1)(f) 353
s 48 272
s 48(2) 276, 440
s 48(3) 275, 439

s 49(b) 282, 283
s 50 297
s 51 440
s 51(1) 335
s 51(2) 352
s 51(3) 362
s 52 348
s 53 22, 293, 363, 509
s 53(5) 509
s 54 22, 293, 317
s 54(1) 511
s 54(2) 511
s 55 286, 287
s 57 309
s 58 286, 309, 314, 319, 320
s 59 22, 286, 309
s 59(1) 310
s 59(2) 310
s 59(3) 310
s 59(4) 310
s 59(5) 310
s 59(6) 310
s 60 22, 309, 313
s 61 673
s 61(1) 653
s 62 22, 488, 499
s 62(2)(b) 489
s 63 22, 482
s 67 418
s 69 22
s 69(1) 437
s 69(1)(f) 437
s 72(1) 438, 439
s 72(2) 441
s 72(3) 439
ss 73–75 22
s 73(2) 442
s 73(2)(b) 442
s 75 438
ss 79–85 22
s 83 282, 304
s 84 570
s 84(3) 570
s 84(4) 571
s 85 411, 569
Wrongs and Other Acts (Law of Negligence) Act 2003 47
Wrongs (Contributory Negligence) Act 1951 480

Western Australia

Civil Liability Act 2002 24, 47
    Pt 1A, Div 4 22, 260
    Pt 1A, Div 5 22
    Pt 1B 22
    Pt 1C 23
    Pt 1D 23, 219, 248

Table of Statutes

Pt 2, Div 2 23
Pt 2, Div 4 23
Pt 3 677
s 3 32
s 3A(1) 25, 28, 205, 437
s 3A(4) 353
s 5AA 411
s 5AD(1) 221
s 5AE 221
s 5AI(1)(a) 677, 678, 680
s 5AI(1)(b) 678
s 5AJ(4) 678
s 5AJA(1)(a) 680
s 5AJA(1)(b) 680
s 5AK(1) 678
s 5AK(3)(a) 679
s 5AO 679
s 5B 272
s 5B(1) 275
s 5B(2) 440
s 5B(3) 439
s 5C 440
s 5C(1) 335
s 5C(2) 352
s 5C(3) 361
s 5C(3)(b) 361
s 5D 348
s 5E 294, 512, 518
s 5F 293, 509
s 5H 22, 294
s 5H(1) 512
s 5H(2) 512
s 5I 22
s 5J 518
s 5K 488, 499
s 5K(2)(b) 489
s 5K(2) 484
s 5L 295
s 5L(2) 496
s 5L(3) 495
s 5L(4) 496
s 5N 293
s 5N(2) 510
s 5O 294
s 5O(2) 510
s 5P 286
s 5PA 310
s 5PB(1) 310
s 5PB(3) 310
s 5PB(4) 310
s 5PB(5) 310
s 5PB(6) 313
s 5Q 418
s 5S(1) 438
s 5S(2) 441
s 5S(4) 439
s 5T 438
ss 5W–5Z 23
s 5W 282, 304

s 5X 305, 570
s 5Z 303, 413, 533
s 6(4) 353
s 7 28, 42
s 9 52, 438
s 10 52, 438
s 11(1) 62, 75
s 11(3) 62
s 12(3) 55
s 12(5) 55
s 12(6) 55
s 12(7) 55
s 13(1) 55
Criminal Code 1913
    Ch 35 580
    s 338D 548
    s 338E 135
Criminal Code Amendment (Racist Harassment And Incitement to Racist Hatred) Act 1990 135
Criminal Injuries Compensation Act 2003
    s 6(3) 86
    s 10 85
    s 13 83
    s 14 83
    s 16 83
    s 17 83
    s 21 85
    ss 31–34 84
    s 35(2) 87
    s 35(3) 87
    s 36 87
    s 43 85
    s 68 85
    s 69 85
Criminal and Found Property Disposal Bill 2005 192
Damage by Aircraft Act 1964
    s 5 122
Defamation Act 2005 *see* Defamation Act 2005 (NSW)
Fatal Accidents Act 1959 86
    s 4 73
    s 5(2) 75
    s 6(2) 72
    s 7(1) 72
Health Act 1911
    s 369 260
Human Tissue and Transplant Act 1982
    s 21 214
Law Reform (Common Employment) Act 1951
    s 3 667
Law Reform (Contributory Negligence and Tortfeasors' Contribution) Act 1947
    s 3 576
    s 4 481
    s 4(1) 77, 481, 482, 502
    s 4(1)(a) 483

s 4(2) 77
s 4(3) 483
Law Reform (Miscellaneous Provisions) Act 1941
   s 4(1) 68
   s 4(2) 70
   s 4(2)(a) 71
   s 4(2)(b) 70
   s 4(2)(ca) 70
   s 4(2)(e) 70
   s 4(2a) 70
   s 4(3)(a) 69
   s 4(3)(b) 69
   s 4(5) 71
Limitation Act 1935
   s 38 608
   s 38(1)(c)(iv) 201
   s 38A 232
   s 40 232
Limitation Act 2005
   s 14 231
   s 16 231
Mental Health Act 1996
   s 12 228
   s 26 228
   s 43 228
Motor Vehicle (Third Party Insurance) Act 1943 25
Occupational Safety and Health Act 1984 668
Occupiers' Liability Act 1985 260
   s 4 257
   s 5 257
   s 9 257
Police Act 1892
   s 137(3) 663
   s 137(6) 663
   s 137(5) 663
Residential Tenancies Act 1987
   s 42(1) 672
Surveillance Devices Act 1998 126
Terrorism (Preventative Detention) Bill 2005 229
Volunteers (Protection from Liability) Act 2002 23, 222, 249
   s 6(2) 222
   s 6(3) 222
   s 6(4) 222
Workers' Compensation and Rehabilitation Act 1981 25
   s 5(1) 79
   s 19 79
Workers' Compensation and Injury Management Act 1981 25

United Kingdom

Australia Courts Act 1828 9 Geo IV c 83
   s 24 18

Common Law Procedure Act 1852 15 & 16 Vict, c 76
   s 49 183
   Sch B 44 206
Commonwealth of Australia Constitution Act 1900 18, 24
Courts Act 1971 13
Criminal Injuries Compensation Act 1995 84
Criminal Justice Act 1988 84
Defamation Act 1952
   s 5 615
Directors' Liability Act 1890 446
Employers' Liability Act 1880 477
Fatal Accidents Act 1976
   s 1A 415
Fatal Accidents Act (Lord Campbell's Act) (1846) 9 & 10 Vict, c 93 71, 73
Fires Prevention (Metropolis) Act 1774 14 Geo 111 c 78 669
Grinding of Metals (Miscellaneous Industries) Regulations 1925
   reg 1 573
Highways (Miscellaneous Provisions) Act 1961
   s 1(1) 412
Law of Property Act 1922 115
Law Reform (Contributory Negligence) Act 1945 245
   s 1 480, 482
Law Reform (Miscellaneous Provisions) Act 1934 68
Law Reform (Personal Injuries) Act 1948
   s 1 667
Mental Capacity Act 2005 209
   s 25 210
Northern Ireland (Emergency Provisions) Act 1978
   s 14 105
Protection from Harassment Act 1997 135
Quo Warranto 1290 Stat 18 Ed I 40
Railway and Land Traffic Carriers' Act 1854 17 & 18 Vict c 31 245
Railway Regulation Act 1840 3 & 4 Vict c 97
   s 3 235
Statute of Conspirators Stat 21 Ed I 135
Statute of Glouster 1278 Stat 6 Ed I 40
Statute of Labourers 23 Edw III, m 87 d 560
Statute of Westminster II, In Consimili Casu 1285 Stat 1 13 Edw I c 24 529
Statute of Winchester 1285 Stat 13 Ed I 40
Statute of Military Tenures (Tenures Abolition Act) 1660 115
Supreme Court of Judicature Act 1873 36 & 37 Vict, c 66 13
Treasure Act 1996 192
Torts (Interference with Goods) Act 1977 178
Workmen's Compensation Act 1897 60 & 61 Vict, c 37 78, 477, 667

Other

Accident Compensation Act 1972 (NZ) 84
Accident Insurance Law 1884 (Germany) 78
  21 78
Child Support Recovery Act 1992 (US)
  s 228 563
Civil Liability Act 1961 (Ireland)
  s 49 415
Contributory Negligence Act 1947 (NZ) 480
Criminal Injuries Compensation Act 1963 (NZ) 83
Emergency Rent Act (US) 141
Restatement (Second) of Torts (1965) (US)
  s 217(b) 174
  s 218(b) 174
  s 222A 182
  s 320 411
Stored Communications Act 2003 (US) 127

Part I

INTRODUCTION

Part I provides a historical and conceptual background to the law of compensation. Chapter 1 discusses the definition of a 'tort' and classification of torts. It provides a concise account of the historical origins of the common law courts and the early evolution of the law of torts and civil forensic processes, culminating in the 2002–03 Torts reforms. Chapter 2 examines historical sources of compensation in the law of torts, and explains the nature of compensation, classification and assessment of damages. Chapter 3 focuses on other important aspects of the law of compensation: survival of actions, actions for wrongful death, and statutory compensation schemes.

Introduction to the Law of Torts and Historical Overview

INTRODUCTION

Chapter 1 is divided into three parts. The first part introduces the definition of 'tort' and classification of torts, the second focuses on the short history and evolution of the law of torts, and the third provides the background to, and overview of, the 2002–03 Torts reforms.

The notion of common law, as used in this book, refers to the single national customary law which in the late medieval period displaced the local and baronial law in England and was later supplemented by Equity, though Equity remained separately administered through the Court of Chancery until the Judicature reforms of 1873–75. Based on a system of judge-made precedent, the common law has no organised or unified theory of law except for the normative standards of the rule of law, which encompasses such fundamental principles as:

- the powers exercised by government and its officials must have a legitimate foundation, and they must be legally authorised;
- the law should conform to certain minimum standards of fairness and justice, both substantive and procedural.

Thus, the law affecting individual liberty ought to be reasonably certain and predictable; a person ought not to be deprived of his or her liberty, status, or other substantial interest without having been given the opportunity of a fair hearing before an impartial tribunal.

DEFINITION AND CLASSIFICATION OF TORTS

What is a tort?

In Latin the word 'tortus' means twisted or crooked. In Old French it came to denote wrong or harm. This meaning was adopted by English common law, where it signifies an actionable, wrongful act, other than breach of contract, done intentionally, negligently, or in circumstances involving strict liability (ie where the plaintiff need not prove negligence or fault on the part of the defendant). Professor Winfield declared in his *Law of Torts* that, 'all injuries done to another person are torts, unless there is some justification recognised by law'.[1]

The High Court of Australia in *John Pfeiffer Pty Ltd v Rogerson* (2000) 203 CLR 503, at 519, noted that:

> the term 'tort' is used ... to denote not merely civil wrongs known to the common law but also acts or omissions which by statute are rendered wrongful in the sense that a civil action lies to recover damages occasioned thereby.

Most relationships arising out of social intercourse and professional endeavour are governed by the law of torts. Each tort relates to a particular interest or interests that the law regards as worthy of protection. For example, the law regards as worthy of safeguarding our interest in personal liberty; in unimpaired reputation; in physical, emotional and economic integrity. Economic integrity refers to the right to security of our property, and the right to exploit it within the limits of the law.

A defendant's conduct will be deemed wrongful where a failure to act in accordance with normative standards of behaviour occasions an injury to the plaintiff's interests. For instance, it is a normative standard of civilised society that one person may not interfere with another's body without the latter's consent or lawful justification.

Legally recognised wrongs that have specific names are called 'nominate torts'. By contrast, innominate torts are known by the names of cases that first legally recognised the wrong involved, for example the tort of *Wilkinson v Downton* [1897] 2 QB 57. Thus, the law of torts comprises a miscellaneous group of civil wrongs, other than breach of contractual terms, which afford a remedy in the form of damages to a person who has sustained an injury as a result.

Remedies

Litigation—or arbitration, or mediation—is a means of obtaining a legal remedy. Unlike criminal law, which aims to punish the wrongdoer, the main object of torts law is to obtain damages for loss suffered as a result of the tortious conduct. The

---

1. Winfield PH, *Law of Torts*, 4th edn, Sweet & Maxwell Ltd, London, 1948, p 13.

economic theory of the law of torts suggests that the social function of an award of damages is loss-spreading. Indeed, the central concern of the law of compensation is not the question of absolute right or wrong, but who should bear responsibility for the injured party's loss: the injured person or the wrongdoer?

Compensation in the form of damages may not be automatic upon the plaintiff proving wrongful conduct. Before the loss is shifted onto the defendant, the plaintiff must show not only that the injury-causing conduct was legally recognised as wrong, but also that the injury itself was of a kind recognised by the law of torts, and that it was not too remote.

In other cases, the person will not be compensated if the alleged injury is outside the interests recognised and protected by the law of torts. The law of torts thus differentiates between various interests for which individuals may claim protection against injury or loss by others. Historically, the common law has been more ready to safeguard against intentional deprivation of liberty or trespassory injury to body, property, honour or reputation, than to safeguard against injury to feelings or damage to economic interests through unintentional acts. The law of torts also has another function: that of deterrence. This aspect of the law of torts will be discussed in Chapter 2 under punitive damages.

The law provides for various remedies for conduct which may amount to a tort, a breach of contract, or a breach of trust. There are also non-judicial remedies, such as the self-help remedy of abatement of nuisance, the privilege of recaption of chattels, and alternative dispute resolution (ADR), either through the adversarial process of arbitration or through the non-adversarial process of conciliation and mediation. Judicial remedies include compensation through damages, punishment, restitution, and coercive relief by way of injunction and specific performance. Restitutionary remedies are different from compensation in the form of damages, in that they are based on rectifying the gain to the defendant.[2] Other remedies will be discussed in the context of specific torts.

Classification of torts

Broadly speaking, at present the law of torts in Australia protects the following interests:

- The right to physical integrity—the immunity of the body from direct and indirect injury, and preservation and furtherance of bodily health—is protected by the torts of battery and negligence.

---

2. Tilbury M, Noone M & Krecher B, *Remedies: Commentary and Materials*, The Law Book Company Ltd, Sydney, 1993, p 69.

- The right to freedom from serious and unreasonable interference with mental integrity—mental poise and comfort—is protected by the torts of assault, action on the case for intentional infliction of nervous shock (the tort of *Wilkinson v Downton*), liability for negligently inflicted nervous shock, defamation, and nuisance.
- Our right to privacy is relatively modern, and has received scant protection at common law. However, as society ascribes to it more value, it is possible either that a new tort protecting privacy will be recognised or that existing torts will be expanded to encompass aspects of the right to privacy.
- Our legal interest in freedom of movement—the right of personal liberty to lawfully choose where to be and which way to go—is protected by the tort of false imprisonment.
- Our right to use land, light, air, running water, the sea, and the shore of the sea is to some degree safeguarded by the torts of trespass to land, private nuisance, public nuisance and, sometimes, the tort of negligence.
- The rights to free belief and opinion, religious and political, are partly protected through the torts of malicious prosecution, false imprisonment and defamation.
- Our right to free social and commercial exchange without economic or physical duress is protected by means of such torts as interference with contractual relations, conspiracy, duress, and the tort of collateral abuse of process. The tort of misfeasance in public office protects against intentional misuse of power by public officers.
- Our rights of property—corporeal property, including the right of gift and bequest, and intellectual property, such as patents and copyrights—are partially protected through such torts as conversion, detinue, trespass to goods, passing off, misrepresentation, and injurious falsehood.

To sum up, this book covers the following torts:

- trespass to person (battery, assault, and false imprisonment);
- trespass to land;
- action on the case for intentional infliction of physical harm;
- action on the case for intentional infliction of nervous shock;
- malicious prosecution;
- collateral abuse of power;
- misfeasance in public office;
- trespass to goods;
- detinue;
- conversion;
- negligence including:
    - non-delegable duty of care
    - omissions

- pure economic loss
- nervous shock: liability for negligently occasioned pure psychiatric injury
• defamation;
• deceit and injurious falsehood;
• nuisance; and
• breach of statutory duty.

Priority is given to the study of the tort of negligence because of its comparative importance.

The table below sets out nominate torts categorised by area of impact.

Table 1.1 Nominate torts categorised by area of impact

Intentional torts

Trespass	Indirect intentional torts	Tortious communications	Economic torts
Battery	Action on the case for intentional infliction of physical injury	Defamation	Interference with contractual relations
Assault		Slander	Conspiracy
False imprisonment	Action on the case for the intentional infliction of nervous shock	Libel	Unfair competition
Trespass to land			Duress
	Misfeasance in public office		Passing off
	Deceit		Misrepresentation
	Malicious prosecution		Injurious falsehood
	Collateral abuse of process		Conversion
			Detinue

Unintentional torts

Negligence
Breach of statutory duty

Miscellaneous torts

Private nuisance
Liability for animals

The law of torts can be divided into three main taxonomic categories: trespass, action on the case, and statutory torts.

The common law tort species of the genus of trespass can be diagrammatically summarised in the following way.

8 *Part I: Introduction*

Figure 1.1 Trespass

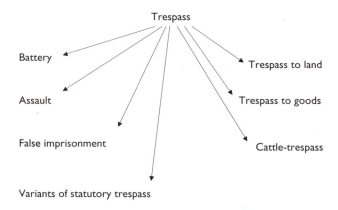

The tort of negligence is one of the species of action on the case. Its place within the context of the law of torts can be expressed in the diagrammatic form shown below.

Figure 1.2 Action on the case

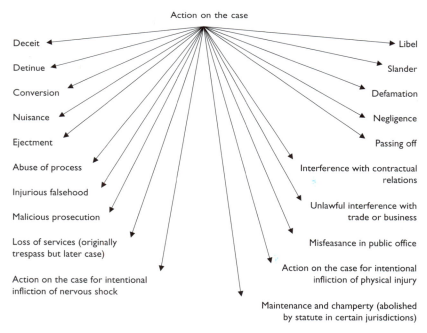

A statutory tort is a breach of statutory duty.

HISTORICAL ORIGINS OF THE LAW OF TORTS

Origins of customary law of torts

The etymology of the word 'law' is not derived directly from the Latin *lex*, but from the Old Norse *lagu* (something 'laid down' or fixed), and Old North German *lagh*. The Romans ruled most of Britain for 400 years. Yet the withdrawal of Roman military and civil administration from Britain in 410 was followed by a rapid collapse of the physical, administrative and cultural infrastructure of the British Roman towns and provinces. Within some thirty years, the knowledge of Latin, and hence the Roman law, became a rarity. The illiterate Germanic tribes—Angle, Saxon, and Jute—settled most of the country through conquest and migration and created a network of tribal, hereditary kingships. The Anglo-Saxons, as they came to be called, introduced their own customary laws, which were modified after the Viking Danish conquered eastern England in the ninth century and imposed 'Danelaw'.

Germanic laws (Salic) of the Anglo-Saxons and Danes recognised conduct that we would today consider wrong or tortious, but they dealt with it in terms of 'folk-rights'. These were unwritten customs developed by a particular locality or tribe. In some localities, for example, wronged persons were expected to personally pursue the wrongdoer. If the wrongdoer was caught 'hand-having' or 'back-bearing' (ie 'red-handed'), the victim was allowed to execute the wrongdoer on the spot.[3] Thus, the *Northumberland Assize Rolls* for 1255 record how a certain 'foreigner', Gilbert of Niddesdale, met a hermit on the moors of Northumberland. Gilbert 'beat him and wounded him and left him half dead, and stole his garments and one penny, and fled away'. When Gilbert was caught, the hermit asked for his stolen penny. However, he was told that by the custom of the county, in order to recover his stolen goods, he must behead the thief with his own hands. Determined to regain his penny, the hermit did so.[4] The custom referred to was blood feud under the law of vengeance.

In Anglo-Saxon England, customary laws of private vengeance and solidarity of kindreds in feuds (the family feud was known as *faida*), were long-standing and widespread. They were based upon a highly sensitised understanding of family honour and loyalty combined with encouragement to immediate retaliation. The law of vengeance was generally invoked for murder, adultery, violation or rape of a married woman, violation of the dead, aggravated robbery, or, importantly, any insult to the family honour.[5] It was open to all ranks among the Germanic,

---

3. Houge AR, *Origins of the Common Law*, Liberty Press, Indianapolis, 1966, p 16.
4. Coulton GG, 'Some Problems in Medieval Historiography', The Raleigh Lecture on History (1932) 17 *Proceedings of the British Academy*, 17–18. For a full record of the case, see: (1891) *Surtees Society*, 70, quoted by Houge AR, *Origins of the Common Law*, Liberty Press, Indianapolis, 1966, p 16.
5. Duels of honour—private combat in the form of consensual revenge for the perceived injury to the participants' honour and reputation—were probably the best-known vestiges of the law of vengeance.

English, and Frankish people of the early Middle Ages, and for centuries the royal authority—before and after the Norman invasion—as well as the Church, struggled to suppress it. Thus, the code of Æthelberht, the king of Wessex (d 865), contains elaborate tariffs of fines for breach of the peace. The preservation of peace would be the mainspring of the law of trespass.

The institution of ordeals

Forensic procedures of customary law were based upon a premise that law was not 'made' or 'created', but instead the law was 'declared' by those familiar with the custom of a certain territory. Customary laws approved by use carried the greatest authority. The wise men of each community were familiar with procedures for settling disputes by imposition of physical tests, known as 'ordeals'. Ordeals were meant to invoke the miraculous intervention of God in settling human disputes. In an ordeal of hot iron, a piece of iron would be placed in the fire and then handed to the suspect, who had to carry the red-hot iron, weighing between 500 g and 1.5 kg, over a distance of between three and nine paces. Sometimes, the suspect had to walk barefoot over nine red-hot ploughshares. The suspect's hands or feet were inspected by the priest three days later; if the burn had festered, God was taken to have decided against the party. The ordeal by hot water followed a similar procedure. Failure of the test meant not only the loss of the suit, but also a conviction for perjury. Ordeals were abolished as part of the canon law by the Fourth Lateran Council in 1215, but persisted in common law for a number of centuries.

The administration of the oath or 'wager of law' was also governed by custom. With the court's consent, either of the parties could be required to swear to the truth of their case on the holy evangels. The custom required that the party swearing the oath bring a number of compurgators or 'oath-helpers', usually kinsmen or peers who also swore the oath, to back up the assertions. If pronounced in the correct manner, the oaths were considered as proof. There was always a danger that the party who had more money to bribe the greatest number of witnesses would win. The Frankish Queen Fredegond (d 597) persuaded three bishops and 300 nobles to swear that the infant prince was actually begotten by her deceased husband.[6] Nevertheless, the 'wager of law' persisted until 1833.

The oaths and ordeals were intended to preclude human judgment on the merits of the case. The Normans introduced the judicial combat called ordeal by battle both upon accusations of felony (an ancient form of a law suit known as 'appeal') and on an equally ancient writ of right for the recovery of land.[7]

---

6. Gregory of Tours, *History of the Franks* (Dalton OM, trans), Vol 2, Oxford University Press, Oxford, 1927, pp 334–335; quoted by Riedel CF, *Crime and Punishment in the French Romances*, AMS Press Inc, New York, 1966, p 33.
7. Seipp DJ, 'Symposium: the Distinction between Crime and Tort in the Early Common Law' (1996) 76 *Boston University Law Review* 59–87.

Where, by reason of age or physical incapacity, a party could not fight, or if the party were a woman or an ecclesiastic, a substitute—usually a kinsman or a hired champion—could fight the combat. The first recorded refusal of trial by battle in an action for trespass dates back to 1304.[8] According to William Blackstone, the last trial by battle allowed in a civil suit was during the reign of Queen Elizabeth I.[9]

Traditionally, the adversarial civil litigation process is considered to be essentially a fact-finding endeavour in the sense that it is a trial of the strength of each side's advocacy and ability to adduce the most credible evidence in support of its pleas and allegations. In his book *The Judge*,[10] Lord Devlin observed that 'the centrepiece of the adversary system is the oral trial and everything that goes before it is a preparation for the battlefield.' The presumption is that 'the best way of getting at the truth is to have each party dig for the facts that help it; between them they will bring all to light.' Lord Devlin's reference to 'battlefield' aptly characterises the nature of cross-examination of witnesses in the open court which aims to expose dissimulation, concealment, and fraud—and which often leaves deep emotional scars.

More recently, however, Kirby J in a dissenting judgment in *Whisprun Pty Ltd v Dixon* [2003] HCA 48 at [117]–[118] noted that the function of the trial judge is intellectually more complex:

> With respect, the joint reasons in this Court, and the reasons of the primary judge, appear to approach that function as if the judge were the successor to the adjudicator of the combat of knights of old—in a kind of public tournament between parties. In my view, we have travelled some distance since those times. The modern civil trial process is a more rational undertaking. It is based upon a close analysis of the relevant evidence, evaluated by a competent decision-maker who is obliged, if a judge, to give reasons which explain the decision arrived at … The law has advanced since the days when truth was distinguished from falsehood at trial by battle and ordeal or by their modern equivalent—conclusive judicial assessment based on impression and on necessarily limited evidence.[11]

His Honour (at [120]) went on to define the function of the trial judge in a civil trial thus:

> the ultimate duty of the decision-maker in an Australian court [is] to decide a case according to law and the substantial justice of the matter proved in the evidence, not as some kind of sport or contest wholly reliant on the way the case was presented by a party.

---

8. YB 32; see also: 33 Edw I (RS) 318, 320.
9. *Commentaries on the Laws of England, A Facsimile of the First Edition of 1768*, Vol 3, Clarendon Press, Oxford; photographically reprinted by The University of Chicago Press, Chicago & London, 1979, pp 336–341.
10. Oxford University Press, Oxford, 1981, pp 54, 60.
11. Kirby J referred to: Holdsworth, *A History of English Law*, 7th edn, Methuen, London, 1956, Vol 1, pp 308–312 and *Fox v Percy* (2003) 77 ALJR 989 at 995 ([30]–[31]); 197 ALR 201 at 209–10.

The courts

At the time of the Norman Conquest, England was divided into counties and hundreds (administrative subdivision of counties sufficient to sustain 100 families). Customary laws administered in shire-moots, hundreds, and county courts were very diverse, and in many ways incapable of adapting to social and political change. With the growth of the feudal system and its institutions of overlordship and vassalage, traditional communal courts based upon customary law gave way to the seignorial (baronial) courts.

Following the Norman Conquest in 1066, William the Conqueror (r 1066–87) began the process of administrative and judicial centralisation in England by organising the judiciary and regulating criminal and evidentiary law. The royal courts, known as *curiae regis*, were created as part of the efforts by Henry II (r 1154–89) to establish legal institutions capable of maintaining social order. Initially, royal justice was dispensed by the King. He exercised judicial powers personally, or through appointed surrogates—earls, bishops, abbots and royal counsellors—in his council, the *Curia Regis*.[12] This court came to be known as *coram rege* (before the king) or the Court of King's Bench.

The beginnings of the modern law of torts are generally traced to the twelfth century when, under Henry II, royal courts were vested with jurisdiction to protect peaceable possession of land. The Court of Exchequer (or Exchequer of Pleas) was the first court to be established as a separate royal court. Originally it dealt with revenue cases, but later became the main court of Equity as well as having limited jurisdiction to hear civil cases.[13] The Court of Common Pleas was the central royal court that sat at Westminster. The Court of Common Pleas had jurisdiction throughout England for most civil actions (real and personal) at first instance, particularly those where the breach of peace was involved, as well as all actions relating to land under the feudal system.

From 1179, in any case concerning property rights the defendant could choose between trial by jury in the royal courts and trial by battle in the baronial courts. Trial by jury has its origins in the Republican Rome of 149 BCE, when jurors (*iudices*) were selected from a standing list to a permanent tribunal investigating charges of extortion. The cases were determined by majority vote.[14] However, the direct predecessor of the English jury system was the French royal *inquisition* established under Charlemagne. The jury, arraigned from free men who came from the locality where the dispute arose, was entrusted with the task of resolving

---

12. Crawford J, *Australian Courts of Law*, Oxford University Press, Melbourne, 1986, p 9.
13. The Court of Common Pleas had sole jurisdiction over real actions.
14. Mousourakis G, *The Historical and Institutional Context of Roman Law*, Ashgate, Aldershot, 2003, p 224.

questions of fact. The jury thus replaced ordeals, and in particular, the judicial duel, as the means of proof in civil matters.[15]

In medieval times, travelling was slow and dangerous, and it was very inconvenient for the jurors to have to come to Westminster. Henry II's royal sessions, the Assize of Clarendon (1166) and the Assize of Northampton (1176), established the system of circuit judges[16] who travelled throughout the country during four 'law terms'.[17] Their rounds were organised in 1328 into a fixed pattern of six circuits. These remained virtually unchanged in England until 1971. In Australia, as in England, senior judges of the Supreme Court and County or District Court in each jurisdiction, as well as judges of the Federal Court and the High Court, still go 'on circuit'.

From the beginning of the fourteenth century, civil cases were generally tried by summoning the juries to the Court of Common Pleas at Westminster or to the Court of King's Bench, unless (*nisi prius*) the judges had earlier visited the locality to hear the juries' verdict. Judges would then bring the verdict back to the court in which the case had begun, for it to be formally recorded.[18] And thus the fourth of the royal courts, the Court of Nisi Prius, came to be established. The Court of Nisi Prius was a court of first instance composed of a judge and jury.

The royal courts operated in parallel with the old customary courts. Local courts and old feudal (baronial) courts were not dismantled; however, plaintiffs were given a choice of redress either through the local courts or the royal courts.

The writ system

From the twelfth century, an action in the royal courts was usually commenced by a royal writ issued from Chancery. Writs were collected and catalogued in the Registry of Writs for the use of clerks and attorneys.[19] Chancery was also known as *officina brevium* ('the writ-shop'), because then, as today, the plaintiff had to pay for a writ. It was through the royal writ system that the foundations of the common law became established.[20]

---

15. van Caenegem RC, *An Historical Introduction to Private Law*, Cambridge University Press, Cambridge, 1988, pp 26, 107.
16. *Courts Act 1971* (UK).
17. Since the twelfth century, the Court of Common Pleas and other courts heard cases almost continuously during four distinct periods of the year, known as the law terms: Michaelmas term (autumn); Hilary term (winter); Easter term (spring); and Trinity term (summer). The *Supreme Court of Judicature Act 1873* 36 & 37 Vict c 66 abolished the legal terms and replaced them with court 'sittings', at times which correspond to the old 'terms'. See: *Historical Note on the Legal Terms* at <http://www.newsquarechambers.co.uk/calculators/termdatecalculator.htm historicalnote> (accessed on 11 August 2005).
18. Baker JH, *An Introduction to English History*, 2nd edn, Butterworths, London, 1981.
19. Hogue AR, *Origins of the Common Law*, Liberty Press, Indianapolis, 1966, pp 14–15, 208–209.
20. Although the writ has been regarded as a prerequisite of proceedings at common law, some early actions were begun by bill. See: Kiralfy AK, *The Action on the Case*, Sweet & Maxwell, London, 1951, p 231.

A 'writ', also called 'formula', was an order issued by the court in the sovereign's name under the Great Seal, addressed to the sheriff of the county in which the cause of action arose, or in which the defendant resided, commanding the sheriff to cause the defendant to appear in the King's Court on a certain day to answer the complaint. Only free men (women had no standing to sue in their own right) had the right to turn directly to the royal jurisdiction. Villeins and serfs had no right of redress in the royal courts.[21]

The writ system was founded on the principle that the plaintiff must inform the defendant about the facts upon which the plaintiff's grievance is based and about the remedy sought. Every writ would contain a precise and succinct formula founded on some principle of law giving the plaintiff a legal right of action. The plaintiff's pleadings included facts that brought the case within the relevant legal principle.

Writs had specific names, which reflected the particular cause of action. For instance the writ of *Covenant* was used to secure enforcement of an agreement; the writ of *Debt* to collect certain moneys lent; *Replevin* was applicable when a plaintiff tried to recover personal property or chattels illegally taken; and *Scienter* ('*scienter retinuit*') applied to owners and keepers of dangerous animals; they were strictly liable for any injury occasioned by the animal. The fault lay in keeping the animal with knowledge of the danger. The writ of *Assumpsit* (late Latin for undertaking) was issued to enforce parol agreements or informal contracts whereby the defendant 'took upon himself' (*assumpsit super se*) to do something, but did it so badly that the plaintiff suffered damage.[22] The writ of *Assumpsit* would eventually evolve in the sixteenth century into the *special assumpsit* for misfeance—an undertaking that was badly executed to the detriment of the plaintiff—and the *indebitatus assumpsit*—an action for nonfeasance in the sense of contractual non-performance.[23]

Some of the early causes of actions were edicts or enactments made at the royal sessions and directed at the judges and officials of Chancery's Register of Writs. They were also referred to as 'assizes'.[24] Today, all tortious actions are initiated by writs of summons.

The courts had the final word on the suitability of the chosen writ: if it did not fit the facts of the case, it was quashed. In accordance with the maxim 'no writ, no remedy', the plaintiff would be left without legal relief. The plaintiff could accept the ruling or petition the King and his Privy Council for a new remedy.

---

21. van Caenegem RC, *An Historical Introduction to Private Law*, Cambridge University Press, Cambridge, 1988, p 100.
22. Baker JH, *An Introduction to English History*, 2nd edn, Butterworths, London, 1981, p 274.
23. For a discussion, see: Ibbetson DJ, *A Historical Introduction to the Law of Obligations*, Oxford University Press, Oxford, 1999, pp 130–151.
24. Hogue AR, *Origins of the Common Law*, Liberty Press, Indianapolis, 1966, p 255. For instance a possessory assize of *Novel Disseisin* created in 1166 by the Assize of Clarendon provided a remedy to a dispossessed freeholder.

The origins of the doctrine of precedent

In the royal courts, royal judges declared what the law was. By the end of the twelfth century, laymen specialising in law began to be appointed as professional judges. Their status as the King's surrogates gave these professional jurists the power to interpret, articulate, and enforce the law. The practices and traditions of customary law guided judges of the early royal courts. But the new professional judiciary was also influenced by the *ius commune*. This combination of Roman law, canon law and customary law was taught at the universities of Padua, Bologna, Pavia, Montpellier, Sorbonne, Oxford, and Cambridge. Roman and canon law are both based on a system of casuistry, whereby in determining the question of right and wrong in relation to a particular conduct—or an issue of conscience—the judge applies general principles of 'right conduct'. These would evolve into normative standards, against which the conduct of the alleged wrongdoer would be measured. However, in early medieval England, the common law and its rules were not codified and had no systematic theoretical underpinnings. Consequently, in order to discern the relevant general principle, the judges would look to previous decisions that dealt with a similar issue. Indeed, the major difference between the functionaries of the customary and baronial courts and the royal judiciary was that the latter respected the principle that like cases should be judged in like fashion. To aid memory, records of facts, arguments and determinations made in the royal courts were written on parchment.

One medieval judge of the Court of King's Bench (*regis coram*), Henry Bracton (c 1200–68), examined and, in his *Note Book*, transcribed from the manuscripts of the old royal plea rolls, some 2000 cases which he believed were the best sources of authority. Bracton used cases decided in the first twenty-four years of the reign of Henry III (r 1216–72), from rolls held at De Banco and Coram Rege courts as well as the Eyres of Martin of Pateshull.[25] Some of these cases were utilised in the treatise known as the *De Legibus et Consuetudinibus Angliæ* (Laws and Customs of England).[26] According to modern research, most of the material in *De Legibus et Consuetudinibus Angliæ* was written by others during the 1220s and 1230s. It was then edited and partially updated from the late 1230s to the 1250s, and was greatly influenced by the institutions of *ius commune*.[27] Bracton was probably the last owner of the original manuscript and the last author to supplement the treatise.

It was in *De Legibus* that the principle of precedent was formulated in the following way:

> If any new and unwonted circumstances ... shall arise, then if anything analogous has happened before, let the case be adjudged in like manner, since it is a good

---

25. Houge AR, *Origins of the Common Law*, Liberty Press, Indianapolis, 1966, pp 200–201.
26. Bracton H, *De Legibus et Consuetudinibus Angliæ*, probably written between 1240 and 1256.
27. See Bracton H, *On the Laws and Customs of England* (Thorne SE, trans), William S Hein & Co, Buffalo, New York, Vol 1, 1997, pp XXXVI–XL.

opportunity for proceeding from like to like. (*Si tamen similia evenerint per simile iudicentur, cum bona sit occasio a similibus procedere ad similia.*)[28]

English law thus became a body of recorded rules enforced by the State through the royal courts. By the end of the reign of Henry II, the process of developing a *single* national customary law, common to the entire kingdom, in contrast to the collection of diverse laws administered through local and baronial courts, was well advanced.[29] Though the phrase 'common law' denotes judge-made law, historically it meant the law administered through the royal courts based on principles common throughout the realm. Since medieval times, the law of torts in England evolved almost entirely through case law.

In the 1280s, the first Year Books containing reports of cases heard in the Royal Courts began to appear. Written in Law French, they were originally disseminated as manuscripts, and then between 1481 and 1535 in printed form. They were written by mainly anonymous lawyers for those practicing at the bar. Rather than recording the final determination, they tended to focus on procedural rules, points of law, legal arguments and reasons for a particular adjudication.[30] The Year Books were precursors of law reports by named reporters who concentrated on recording judicial decisions.

Although initially judicial decisions per se did not have normative force as a source of law,[31] judges would examine a line of cases to distil the correct principle, which would be followed unless good reasons existed for bypassing or reversing it. In *Fisher v Prince* (1762) 97 ER 876 at 876, Lord Mansfield was to comment: 'the reason and spirit of cases make law; not the letter of particular precedents.'[32]

Finally, the system of forms of actions enabled the law to develop in response to the values and needs of the English society at various stages of its development. The obverse of the writ system's flexibility was lack of conceptual coherence, in so far as these writs constituted a straggle of theories that relied upon or blended diverse categories of law. Though torts diverged from the 'public wrongs' of crime in the sixteenth century, it was only in the eighteenth century that William Blackstone, in his *Commentaries on the Laws of England*,[33] expressly separated contract (*assumpsit*) from 'private wrongs' (torts) when he wrote:

---

28. Bracton, *De Regibus*, fol 1b, quoted in Houge AR, *Origins of the Common Law*, Liberty Press, Indianapolis, 1966, p 200.
29. van Caenegem RC, *An Historical Introduction to Private Law*, Cambridge University Press, Cambridge, 1988, p 35.
30. Windeyer WJV, Lectures on Legal History, The Law Book Company, Sydney, 1957, p 148.
31. Berman HJ & Reid CJ, Jr, 'The Transformation of English Legal Science: From Hale to Blackstone' (1996) 45 *Emory Law Journal* 437 at 445.
32. For a further discussion, see: Berman HJ & Reid CJ, Jr, 'The Transformation of English Legal Science: From Hale to Blackstone' (1996) 45 *Emory Law Journal* 437 at 449.
33. *Commentaries on the Laws of England, A Facsimile of the First Edition of 1768*, Vol 3, Clarendon Press, Oxford; photographically reprinted by The University of Chicago Press, Chicago & London, 1979, 117.

Personal actions are such whereby a man claims a debt, or personal duty, or damages in lieu thereof; and likewise whereby a man claims a satisfaction in damages for some injury done to his person or property. The former are said to be founded in contracts, the latter upon torts or wrongs ... Of the former nature are all actions upon debt or promises; of the latter all actions for trespasses, nusances [sic], assaults, defamatory words, and the like. [emphasis in original]

Throughout the nineteenth and twentieth centuries, the common law refined the system of precedent. McHugh J in *Woolcock St Invest v CDG Pty Ltd* (2004) 216 CLR 515, at [59]–[61], explained the constituent elements of this system thus:

[59] The common law distinguishes between the holding of a case, the rule of the case and its *ratio decidendi*. The holding of a case is the decision of the court on the precise point in issue—for the plaintiff or the defendant. The rule of the case is the principle for which the case stands—although sometimes judges describe the rule of the case as its holding. The *ratio decidendi* of the case is the general rule of law that the court propounded as its reason for the decision.

[60] Under the common law system of adjudication, the *ratio decidendi* of the case binds courts that are lower in the judicial hierarchy than the court deciding the case. Moreover, even courts of co-ordinate authority or higher in the judicial hierarchy will ordinarily refuse to apply the *ratio decidendi* of a case only when they are convinced that it is wrong.

[61] Prima facie, the *ratio decidendi* and the rule of the case are identical. However, if later courts read down the rule of the case, they may treat the proclaimed *ratio decidendi* as too broad, too narrow or inapplicable. Later courts may treat the material facts of the case as standing for a narrower or different rule from that formulated by the court that decided the case. Consequently, it may take a series of later cases before the rule of a particular case becomes settled. ... If later courts take the view that the rule of a case was different from its stated *ratio decidendi*, they may dismiss the stated *ratio* as a mere dictum or qualify it to accord with the rule of the case as now perceived.

Thus, the major characteristic of common law is its constant change. Over the centuries, common law judges have incidentally developed whole new branches of law in the course of deciding specific cases. Their responses have traditionally focused upon the protection of individual rights rather than furthering abstract legal principles of social justice. Generally, in their deliberations, they were influenced by legal reasons provided by judges who had determined similar issues before them, and the normative standards of the rule of law.

Reception of English torts law in Australia

On 26 January 1788 Governor Arthur Phillip, under commission from the British Government, brought a party of sailors, soldiers and convict prisoners to eastern Australia, named New South Wales by James Cook in 1770, and took possession of the land in the name of His Majesty King George III. In a settled colony,[34] as Australia was supposed to be, the English colonists brought with them 'so much of the English law as [was] applicable to their own situation and the condition of the infant colony',[35] which at this time was described as a 'desert uninhabited country'. From the strictly legal point of view, it was through the enactment of the *Australia Courts Act 1828* 9 Geo IV c 83, s 24 that on 25 July 1828 the common law, the rules of equity, and statutes then in force in England, except as locally altered, became formally applicable in New South Wales and other colonies.[36] Until well into the second part of the nineteenth century, judges—mostly free settlers—were appointed to the colonial Supreme Courts by the British Government.

Naturally, when determining torts cases, nineteenth-century Australian judges followed English precedents. Homogeneity in the development of common law principles was ensured through appeals to the Judicial Committee of the Privy Council, which was created in 1833 exclusively to hear appeals from courts in the then Colonies and Dominions of the British Empire.[37] The need for uniformity, certainty, and predictability of law led to the development of the doctrine of *stare decisis*[38] whereby the *ratio decidendi* in a particular case, rather than a line of cases, became binding upon a court in a later similar case.

When the Commonwealth of Australia came into existence on 1 January 1901, Australian Colonies, which continued as States, retained their common law jurisdictions. However, one of the aims of the Founding Fathers was to ensure a reasonable degree of uniformity of common law among the States (and later, Territories) of the Federation. To this end, Part III of the Commonwealth Constitution[39] created the High Court of Australia as the Court of Appeal from

---

34. The international law of the eighteenth century recognised three effective ways of acquiring sovereignty: by conquest, cession, or occupation (settlement) of a territory that did not have a settled population.
35. This was because, for the purposes of the common law, the colonists were regarded as if living under the law of England. The law was not amenable to alteration by exercise of prerogative. Blackstone W, *Commentaries on the Laws of England, A Facsimile of the First Edition of 1765*, Vol 1, Clarendon Press, Oxford; photographically reprinted by The University of Chicago Press, Chicago & London, 1979, p 107; *State Government Insurance Commission v Trigwell* (1979) 142 CLR 617 at 625, 634; *Mabo v Queensland* (1991–1992) 175 CLR 1 at 35.
36. The courts were composed almost entirely of free settlers, and adopted standard practices of the English courts. Colonial legislation was reviewable by the Privy Council, as were colonial court decisions involving more than £3000.
37. Colonial legislation was also reviewable by the Privy Council.
38. Short for *stare decisis et non quieta movere*, variously translated as 'stand by the thing decided and do not disturb the calm', and 'to stand by the decisions and not to disturb settled points'.
39. *Commonwealth of Australia Constitution Act 1900* (UK). The High Court itself was established by the *Judiciary Act 1903* (Cth).

all State Supreme Courts, whether exercising federal or purely State or Territory jurisdiction.[40] Moreover, its common law determinations on cases appealed from any jurisdiction were binding on all Australian courts.[41] The object was to create a single system of jurisprudence comprising the Constitution, federal, State, and Territory laws, and the common law of Australia.[42] For, as Gleeson CJ, Gaudron, McHugh, Gummow, and Hayne JJ said in *John Pfeiffer Pty Ltd v Rogerson* (2000) 203 CLR 503 at 518:

> because there is a single common law of Australia there will be no difference in the parties' rights or obligations on that account, no matter where in Australia those rights or obligations are litigated.

Indeed, over the past century, the High Court has moulded and developed a relatively uniform Australian common law of torts.[43] In the 1980s, the system of *stare decisis* came to be regarded as too rigid, and was tacitly abandoned in favour of the system described by McHugh J in *Woolcock St Invest v CDG Pty Ltd* (2004) 216 CLR 515 (above). In *Ruhani v Director of Police* [2005] HCA 42, Kirby J noted (at [196]) that 'in matters of ordinary public and private law, judges of this [High] Court normally submit to the considered exposition of the law as stated by the majority.' In other words, until overturned, it is the majority's opinion that states the valid law. The problem for lower-instance courts, legal practitioners and law students arises when the seven Justices of the High Court unanimously agree on the outcome of the case (for the claimant/appellant or for the respondent) but each, in a separate judgment, provides a different *ratio decidendi*.

TORTS REFORMS OF 2002–03

Background to reforms

The partial codification of the law of torts, carried out to a lesser or greater extent by all Australian jurisdictions over four years (2002–06), can best be compared to the English Judicature reforms of 1875–78,[44] which unified legal and equitable jurisdictions and included significant procedural and substantive law reforms.

---

40. The *Australia Act 1986* (Cth) abolished all appeals to the Judicial Committee of the Privy Council from the State Supreme Courts.
41. Crawford J, *Australian Courts of Law*, Oxford University Press, Melbourne, 1986, p 160.
42. *John Pfeiffer Pty Ltd v Rogerson* (2000) 203 CLR 503 at 534 [66], per Gleeson CJ, Gaudron, McHugh, Gummow, and Hayne JJ.
43. Jurisdictional variations were mainly due to legislative actions; historically, the areas of the law of torts regulated by statute included defamation, occupiers' liability and contributory negligence.
44. Polden P, 'Mingling the Waters: Personalities, Politics and the Making of the Supreme Court of Judicature' (2002) 61 *Cambridge Law Journal* 575–611; Lobban M, 'Preparing for Fusion: Reforming the Nineteenth-century Court of Chancery. Parts I and II' (2004) 22 *Law and History Review* 389–427, 565–599.

In order to properly comprehend Australian post-reform law, one needs to understand the background to the reforms. The immediate trigger for the legislative action was the public liability insurance crisis of 2001–02. During this period, community groups, businesses, public authorities, medical practitioners, and other professionals experienced difficulty in obtaining public liability and professional indemnity coverage at reasonable premiums. Several factors contributed to the problems of availability and level of insurance. These included the terrorist attacks of 11 September 2001, the global slump in share prices, and the collapse of the HIH insurance group in August 2001, which affected some 30 000 individuals, community groups, home owners, businesses, public authorities, volunteers, medical practitioners, and other holders of professional indemnity.[45] Many were unable to obtain replacement policies at reasonable premiums. The HIH collapse was essentially due to incompetence and mismanagement rather than wholesale fraud and embezzlement,[46] but the insurance industry blamed high levels of litigation for its difficulties.[47]

Indeed, there was a community perception that personal injury litigation increased dramatically in the last two decades of the twentieth century, that the law of negligence as applied in the courts was 'unclear and unpredictable', that 'it has become too easy for plaintiffs in personal injury cases to establish liability for negligence', and that 'damages awards in personal injuries cases have been too high'.[48]

One of the cases credited with precipitating the insurance crisis was *Simpson v Diamond* [2001] NSWSC 925,[49] in which the trial judge awarded A$14 202 042 to Calandre Simpson, who was born in 1979 and suffered from athetoid cerebral palsy. It was held that Calandre's condition was caused by Dr Diamond, who attempted five times to deliver her with forceps before performing a caesarean section.[50]

---

45. *Final Report of the HIH Royal Commission* <http://www.hihroyalcom.gov.au/finalreport/>.
46. *Final Report of the HIH Royal Commission* <http://www.hihroyalcom.gov.au/finalreport/>.
47. Some of the blame was justified, for the Australian Law Reform Commission Report (1995, No 75) on *Costs Shifting—Who Pays for Litigation* (at [3.20]) noted that insurance companies are major participants in litigation as defendants in personal injury and property damage claims. In 1995 these categories of claim constituted about 50 per cent of District and Supreme Court civil litigation in New South Wales, with a similar pattern evident in other States and Territories. Available on Austlii.edu.au.
48. Ipp D, Cane P, Sheldon D and Macintosh I, *Review of the Law of Negligence Report* (*Ipp Report*) at [3.5]. The Second Report, incorporating the First Report, was released on 10 October 2002: see <http://www.revofneg.treasury.gov.au/content/reports.asp>.
49. For a detailed analysis of the case and damages awarded, see: Luntz H, 'Damages in Medical Litigation in New South Wales' (2005) 12 *Journal of Law and Medicine* 280.
50. In 2006 Gibson CS, MacLennan AH, Goldwater PN, Haan EA, Priest K & Dekker GA published a study on 'Neurotropic Viruses and Cerebral Palsy: Population-based Case-control Study' (2006) 332 *British Medical Journal* 76–80, which shows that there is a significant association between the presence of neurotropic viral nucleic acids in the blood of newborns and the subsequent diagnosis of cerebral palsy. According to the study, the risk of cerebral palsy is nearly doubled with an in-utero exposure to herpes group B viruses; though it may require other factors, such as genetic susceptibility to infection and inherited thrombophilia or, *inter alia*, growth restriction or prematurity—for the brain damage and

Dr Diamond was indemnified by United Medical Protection Ltd. Although two years later the New South Wales Court of Appeal reduced the original quantum of damages to $10 998 692 (*Diamond v Simpson (No 1)* [2003] NSWCA 67), on 3 May 2002 United Medical Protection Ltd, Australasian Medical Insurance Ltd, and MDU Australia Insurance Co Pty Ltd went into provisional liquidation citing the Simpson damages payout as the main factor. In the event, the majority of medical practitioners in New South Wales and Queensland found themselves without medical indemnity insurance.[51] The uninsured doctors threatened that they would cease to see private patients. In a country with a fee-for-service medical system, this would have led to a health care crisis.[52] Medical practitioners in all jurisdictions, particularly those practising in such high-risk areas as obstetrics and neurosurgery, were also making decisions to prematurely retire from practice or to move to areas less prone to claims for damages.[53]

The immediate response to the general insurance and professional indemnity crisis by the federal and State governments was to commission two reports. At the request of the Australian Health Ministers Advisory Council, the Victorian Law Reform Commissioner, Professor Marcia Neave,[54] produced a report titled *Responding to the Medical Indemnity Crisis: An Integrated Reform Package*,[55] which recommended *inter alia* capping damages; improving courts' usage of expert witnesses; changes to limitation of action periods; thresholds for compensable injuries; and the institution of structured settlements. She also recommended that apologies following 'adverse events' caused by medical treatment, rather than the patient's underlying condition, should not be regarded as an admission of fault.

On 30 May 2002, at a Ministerial Meeting on Public Liability, ministers from the Commonwealth, State and Territory governments jointly agreed to appoint a panel to examine and review the law of negligence, including its interaction with the *Trade Practices Act 1974*. The panel was chaired by the Honourable Justice David Andrew Ipp, at the time, an Acting Judge of Appeal, Court of Appeal,

---

subsequent cerebral palsy to occur. None of these factors seems to be associated with the conduct of delivery, negligent or otherwise.

51. At the time, 32 000 doctors, constituting approximately 60 per cent of the nationwide market were insured with the UMP: Webster A, 'Australian Doctors Down Tools', *BBC News* (30 April 2002) available at <http://news.bbc.co.uk/1/hi/world/asia-pacific/1959303.stm> (accessed on 27 December 2004). In 2001, St Paul International Insurance Co Ltd (UK), the major underwriter of medical defence organisations, withdrew from the Australian market.
52. For a further discussion, see: Masada ST, 'Australia's "Most Extreme Case": A New Alternative For US Medical Malpractice Liability Reform' (2004) 13 *Pacific Rim Law & Policy Journal* 163.
53. Apparently, in April 2002, the typical annual premium for a neurosurgeon or obstetrician was A$100 000: Webster A, 'Australian Doctors Down Tools', *BBC News* (April 30, 2002), available at <http://news.bbc.co.uk/1/hi/world/asia-pacific/1959303.stm> (accessed on 27 December 2004); cf Luntz H, 'Medical Indemnity and Tort Law Reform' (2003) *Journal of Law and Medicine* 1–9.
54. <http://www.ahic.org.au/events/meeting_dates.html>.
55. Neave M, *Responding to the Medical Indemnity Crisis: An Integrated Reform Package*, 18 September 2002, available at <http://www.health.act.gov.au/c/health?a=da&did=10011741&pid=1054039339> (accessed on 1 February 2005).

Supreme Court of New South Wales, also a Justice of the Supreme Court of Western Australia, and included Peter Cane, Professor of Law in the Research School of Social Sciences at the Australian National University; Dr Don Sheldon, Medical Practitioner and the Chairman of the Council of Procedural Specialists; and Mr Ian Macintosh, Mayor of Bathurst City Council in New South Wales, and the Chairman of the NSW Country Mayors' Association. The Panel consulted widely with lawyers, doctors, professional and voluntary organisations, insurance companies, community associations, and other interested parties. Its report, titled *Review of the Law of Negligence Report* and known as the *Ipp Report*,[56] recommended partial codification of, and far-ranging changes to, the law of negligence and the law of damages, to be contained in a single statute to be enacted in each jurisdiction. Among the recommended changes were:

- altered tests for foreseeability of a risk of harm and duty to take precautions with regard to obvious risks;[57]
- modification of tests for standard of care for professionals;[58]
- introduction of more stringent rules relating to contributory negligence[59] and voluntary assumption of risk;[60]
- waivers of liability in relation to recreational activities;[61]
- statutory restrictions on circumstances in which damages for pure mental harm can be awarded;[62]

---

56. <http://www.revofneg.treasury.gov.au/content/reports.asp>.
57. *Civil Liability (Personal Responsibility) Act 2002* (NSW), Pt 1A, Div 4 (obvious risks), s 5L, hereinafter referred to as *Civil Liability Act 2002* (NSW) *Wrongs Act 2003* (Vic), ss 53, 54 (obvious risks); *Civil Liability Act 2003* (Qld), Ch 2, Pt I, Div 3 (obvious and inherent risks), ss 19, 21 (medical duty to warn of all risks); *Civil Liability Act 2002* (WA), Pt 1A, Div 4; *Civil Liability Act 1936* (SA), Pt 6, Div 3; *Civil Liability Act 2002* (Tas), Pt 6, Div 4 and s 20.
58. *Civil Liability Act 2002* (NSW), Div 6; *Wrongs Act 2003* (Vic), ss 59–60, 69; *Civil Liability Act 2003* (Qld), ss 21, 22; *Civil Liability Act 1936* (SA), Pt 6, Div 4; *Civil Liability Act 2002* (Tas), Pt 6, Div 6.
59. *Civil Liability Act 2002* (NSW), Pt 1, Div 8; *Civil Law (Wrongs) Act 2002* (ACT), Pt 4.4; *Personal Injuries (Liabilities and Damages) Act 2003* (NT), Pt 3; *Wrongs Act 1958* (Vic), ss 62–63, 14G; *Civil Liability Act 2003* (Qld), Ch 2, Pt 1, Div 6; *Civil Liability Act 2002* (WA), Pt 1A, Div 5; *Civil Liability Act 1936* (SA), Pt 7; *Civil Liability Act 2002* (Tas), Pt 2, Div 7; *Wrongs Act 1954* (Tas), s 4.
60. *Civil Liability Act 2002* (NSW), Div 4; *Wrongs Act 1958* (Vic), s 54; *Civil Liability Act 2003* (Qld), ss 13–16; *Civil Liability Act 2002* (WA), Pt 1A, Div 6; *Civil Liability Act 1936* (SA), ss 37, 38; *Civil Liability Act 2002* (Tas), Pt 6, Div 4.
61. *Trade Practices Act 1974* (Cth), s 68B; *Civil Liability Act 2002* (NSW), ss 5K–5N; *Wrongs Act 1958* (Vic), Pt IX, s 36(c); *Goods Act 1958* (Vic), s 97A; *Civil Liability Act 2003* (Qld), Ch 2, Pt 1, Div 4; *Civil Liability Act 2002* (WA), Pt 1A, Div 4, ss 5H, 5I; *Recreational Services (Limitation of Liability) Act 2002* (SA); *Civil Liability Act 2002* (Tas), Pt 6, Div 5; *Consumer Affairs and Fair Trading (Amendment) Act 2003* (NT), s 68A.
62. *Civil Liability Act 2002* (NSW), Pt 3; *Wrongs Act 2003* (Vic), ss 73–75; *Civil Liability Act 2002* (WA), Pt 1B; *Civil Liability Act 1936* (SA), s 53; *Civil Liability Act 2002* (Tas), Pt 8; *Civil Law (Wrongs) Act 2002* (ACT), Pt 3.2.

- imposition of caps on damages for personal injury claims (past and future economic and non-economic loss);[63]
- introduction of structured settlements;[64]
- exclusion of civil liability for wrongful acts and omissions when done in good faith by good samaritans and volunteers;[65] and
- provision of a statutory policy defence for public authorities.[66]

The new statutory principles are applicable to any claim for damages for personal injury or death resulting from negligence, regardless of whether the claim is brought in tort, contract, equity, or under a statute or any other cause of action.[67] In this sense, the Australian law of damages for personal injury is moving towards the civil law concept of the law of obligations. At the same time, the new statutory regime involves primarily the law of negligence, thus highlighting the distinction between intentional fault-based torts and non-intentional fault-based torts (see Chapter 2, for further discussion of this point).

The process of implementation

Encouraged by community groups, professional organisations, and insurance companies, in 2002–03 each Australian legislature participated in implementing a series of reforms to the substantive law of negligence and to the law of damages for negligently occasioned injury. Whereas common law principles and doctrines of negligence were codified with some alterations, the changes to the law of damages were much more substantive. The legislature did not intend the new statutory provisions to form an 'exclusive' source of law; rather, the intention was to modify

---

63. *Civil Liability Act 2002* (NSW), Pt 2; *Health Care Liability Act 2001* (NSW); *Wrongs Act 1958* (Vic), Pt VB; *Civil Liability Act 2003* (Qld), Ch 3, Pt 3; *Civil Liability Regulation 2003* (Qld); *Civil Liability Act 2002* (WA), Pt 2, Div 2; *Wrongs (Limitation and Damages for Personal Injury) Amendment Act 2002* (SA), s 24B; *Wrongs Act 1936* (SA), Pt 2A; *Civil Liability Act 2002* (Tas), Pt 7; *Civil Law (Wrongs) Act 2002* (ACT), ss 38, 39; *Personal Injuries (Liabilities and Damages) Act 2003* (NT), ss 24, 27.
64. *Civil Liability Act 2003* (Qld), Ch 3, Pt 4; *Wrongs Act 1958* (Vic), Pt VC; *Civil Liability Act 2002* (WA), Pt 2, Div 4; *Personal Injuries (Liabilities and Damages) Act 2003* (NT), Pt 4, Div 6; *Civil Law (Wrongs) Act 2002* (ACT), Ch 4, Pt 4.4; *Civil Liability Act 2002* (NSW), Pt 2, Div 7; *Civil Liability Act 2002* (Tas), Pt 5.
65. *Personal Injuries (Liabilities and Damages) Act 2003* (NT), ss 7, 8; *Civil Law (Wrongs) Act 2002* (ACT), ss 5, 6; *Wrongs Act 1936* (SA), Div 13; *Volunteers Protection Act 2001* (SA); *Civil Liability Amendment Act 2003* (WA), Pt 1D; *Volunteers (Protection from Liability) Act 2002* (WA); *Law Reform Act 1995* (Qld), Pt 6 (protects doctors and nurses in circumstances of emergency); *Civil Liability Act 2003* (Qld), Pt 3, Div 2; ss 25, 26 (exempt emergency service agencies in circumstances of emergency); *Wrongs Act 1958* (Vic), Pts VIA, IX; *Civil Liability Act 2002* (NSW), Pts 8, 9; *Civil Liability Act 2002* (Tas), Pt X (volunteer protection); *Commonwealth Volunteers Protection Act 2002* (Cth).
66. *Civil Liability Amendment (Personal Responsibility) Act 2002* (NSW), Pt 5 (Sch 1 [5]); *Wrongs Act 2003* (Vic), ss 79–85; *Civil Liability Act 2003* (Qld), ss 34–37; *Civil Liability Act 2002* (WA), Pt 1C, ss 5W–5Z; *Civil Liability Act 2002* (Tas), Pt 9; *Civil Law (Wrongs) Act 2002* (ACT), Ch 8.
67. *Ipp Report* <http://www.revofneg.treasury.gov.au/content/reports.asp> at [2.1]–[2.3].

and supplement the existing common law regime.[68] Nevertheless, not only the law of negligence, but the law of torts in general, has been profoundly changed.

The *Ipp Report* recommended that a similar single statute be enacted by each Australian jurisdiction. However, Australia is a federation comprising six States and two Territories. Under the Commonwealth Constitution,[69] the legislative power to administer and regulate the common law, including torts and contract law, is vested in State and Territory Parliaments. The Federal government can only exercise powers conferred upon it by the Federal Constitution or by referral from the States under special constitutional arrangements. Since the States were not asked to cede the relevant powers to the Federal Parliament (and did not volunteer to do so), the Commonwealth lacked legislative power to validly enact a Torts Reform statute that would bind the States.[70] Consequently, each jurisdiction has enacted its own distinct statutory code of tortious liability. Although several existing common law principles have been statutorily entrenched across all States and Territories, other rules were legislatively modified or significantly changed in some jurisdictions but not in others. Moreover, while the wording of certain legislative provisions has been replicated in all or most Australian jurisdictions, there are marked differences in the drafting of others. As a result, despite the commonality of features, the common law of negligence, which until 2002 was relatively uniform throughout Australia, is fragmenting into eight discrete systems.[71]

This means that in cases where in issue is an interpretation or an approach to a particular reform provision, the opinion of the High Court will bind the courts of the originating jurisdiction. As a general rule, jurisdictions that have identical or corresponding legislative provisions will also be bound. However, since no two reform statutes are identical, in non-originating jurisdictions, judges who disagree with the High Court's approach will be able to distinguish the decision on the basis of the particular legislative context. Moreover, unless, while interpreting a particular reform provision, the High Court takes the opportunity to declare a general principle of law, jurisdictions which do not have the same, or a very similar, provision will not be bound. High Court decisions concerning common law not directly modified by the reform legislation will bind all jurisdictions, except where a specific State or Territory legislation provides otherwise. Strictly speaking, the

---

68. Hon Mr Carr, Second Reading Speech, *Civil Liability Amendment (Personal Responsibility) Bill*, New South Wales Legislative Assembly, *Hansard*, 23 October 2002.
69. *Commonwealth of Australia Constitution Act 1900* (UK).
70. Under s 122 of the Commonwealth Constitution, the Federal Parliament has plenary powers to make laws for the Territories to the extent and on the terms which it thinks fit. The Commonwealth, however, chose not to exercise these powers in the area of torts reform.
71. *Civil Liability Act 2002* (NSW); *Personal Injuries Proceedings Act 2002* (Qld); *Civil Liability Act 2003* (Qld); *Civil Law (Wrongs) Act 2002* (ACT); *Civil Liability Act 1936* (SA); *Civil Liability Act 2002* (Tas); *Civil Liability Act 2002* (WA); *Volunteers (Protection from Liability) Act 2002* (WA); *Wrongs Act 1958* (Vic); *Personal Injuries (Liabilities and Damages) Act 2003* (NT); *Trade Practices Act 1974* (Cth) as amended.

Australian doctrines of precedent and *stare decisis* operated in the same way under the pre-reform regime; the difference now is in the scale and diversity of statutes and provisions.

Scope of the reforms

As a general rule, work-related injuries covered by various workers compensation schemes,[72] personal injuries that fall within the purview of transport accident compensation schemes,[73] and injuries caused by tobacco products, or dust-related disease, are excluded from the scope of the legislation.[74] Some jurisdictions have introduced a statutory defence of 'illegal activity', which may diminish or prevent the award of damages;[75] others preclude compensation for injury or death sustained while the claimant was engaged in conduct constituting a serious offence.[76] Although the diverse pre-existing statutory compensation schemes[77] that exist in each Australian jurisdiction were not directly affected by the Torts reforms, they have influenced the choice of reform models.

Coincidentally with partial codification of negligence and damages law, long-mooted reforms of defamation law were undertaken. The new defamation provisions, unlike the statutory changes to damages and negligence laws, are mostly homogeneous throughout Australia.

---

72. *Civil Liability Act 2002* (Tas), s 3B(3) and (4); *Civil Liability Act 2002* (WA), s 3A(1); *Wrongs Act 1958* (Vic), s 28C(2)(d); *Civil Liability Act 1936* (SA), s 3; *Civil Liability Act 2003* (Qld), s 5(a) and (b); *Civil Liability Act 2002* (NSW), s 3B(1)(f); *Civil Law (Wrongs) Act 2002* (ACT), s 41(2); *Personal Injuries Act 2003* (NT), s 4(3).
73. *Personal Injuries (Liabilities and Damages) Regulations 2003* (NT), s 3; *Civil Liability Act 2002* (Tas), s 3B(2); *Civil Law (Wrongs) Act 2002* (ACT), s 7(2)(iii); *Civil Liability Act 2002* (NSW), s 3B(1)(d) and (e); *Wrongs Act 1958* (Vic), s 28LC(2)(b); *Civil Liability Act 2002* (WA), s 3A(1). The *Civil Liability Act 1936* (SA), s 43(4)(a)(i), excludes liability in certain cases involving criminal conduct 'arising from a motor accident (whether caused intentionally or unintentionally)'.
74. *Civil Liability Act 2002* (Tas), s 3B(1)(b); *Civil Liability Act 2002* (NSW), s 3B(1)(b) and (c); *Civil Liability Act 2002* (WA), s 3A(1); *Wrongs Act 1958* (Vic), s 28IF(2)(a) and (b); *Civil Liability Act 2003* (Qld), s 5(c) and (d); *Personal Injuries (Liabilities and damages) Act 2003* (NT), s 4(3)(c). South Australia does not provide for this kind of exclusion.
75. *Wrongs Act 1958* (Vic), s 14G(2)(b); depending on interpretation, *Civil Liability Act 2002* (WA), s 3A(1).
76. *Civil Liability Act 2002* (Tas), s 6 (recovery by criminals); *Civil Liability Act 2002* (NSW), ss 53, 54; *Civil Liability Act 2003* (Qld), s 45(1); *Civil Law (Wrongs) Act* (ACT), s 94 (an indictable offence); depending on interpretation, *Civil Liability Act 2002* (WA), s 3A(1). In South Australia, under the *Civil Liability Act 1936* (SA), s 43(1) and (4), the court has to be, *inter alia*, 'satisfied beyond reasonable doubt that the accident occurred while the injured person was engaged in conduct constituting an indictable offence.'
77. For example: *Safety, Rehabilitation and Compensation Act 1988* (Cth); *Seafarer's Rehabilitation and Compensation Act 1992* (Cth); *Workers' Compensation Act 1951* (ACT); *Workers Compensation Act 1987* (NSW); *Accident Compensation Act 1985* (Vic); *Transport Accident Act 1986* (Vic); *Workers' Compensation and Rehabilitation Act 2003* (Qld); *Workers Rehabilitation and Compensation Act 1986* (SA); *Workers' Compensation and Rehabilitation Act 1981* (WA); *Workers Rehabilitation and Compensation Act 1988* (Tas); *Motor Vehicle (Third Party Insurance) Act 1943* (WA); *Workers' Compensation and Injury Management Act 1981* (WA); *Work Health Act 2005* (NT).

The post-reform fragmentation of the law of torts has important implications for the choice of laws. In *John Pfeiffer Pty Ltd v Rogerson* (2000) 203 CLR 503, Gleeson CJ, Gaudron, McHugh, Gummow, and Hayne JJ, in a joint judgment (at 544), determined that *lex loci delicti*, the law of the place of the tort, 'should be applied by courts in Australia as the law governing all questions of substance to be determined in a proceeding arising from an intranational tort.' Moreover, 'laws that bear upon the existence, extent or enforceability of remedies, rights and obligations should be characterised as substantive and not as procedural laws'. This means that, as a general rule, the laws governing compensation are those of the State or Territory in which the tort was committed. For example, under the *lex loci delicti* doctrine, if a vehicle collision between two Queensland drivers takes place in Western Australia, a Queensland court hearing the case will have to apply not its own laws, but those of Western Australia. It follows that the lawyers must understand the law of torts governing every jurisdiction within the Australian federation.

At the time of writing, relatively few post-reform cases have reached the appellate courts, and these are mainly from New South Wales, which was the first Australian jurisdiction to implement the reforms. Hence, many cases discussed in the book are from New South Wales, and they may not reflect the interpretative approach that will be adopted by courts in other Australian jurisdictions.

FURTHER READING

Baker JH, *An Introduction to English Legal History*, 2nd edn, Butterworths, London, 1981.

Brand, P, *Observing and Recording the Medieval Bar and Bench at Work*, Selden Society, London, 1999.

Capua JV, 'Feudal and Royal Justice in Thirteenth-century England: The Forms and Impact of Royal Review' (1983) 27 *The American Journal of Legal History* 54–84.

Ibbetson DJ, *A Historical Introduction to the Law of Obligations*, Oxford University Press, Oxford, 1999.

Luntz H, *Assessment of Damages for Personal Injury and Death*, 4th edn, LexisNexis Butterworths, 2002.

Mendelson D, 'Australian Tort Law Reform: Statutory Causation and the Common Law' (2004) 11 *Journal of Law and Medicine* 492–510.

Pound, R, 'Interests of Personality' (1915) 28, *Harvard Law Review* 343–65.

Summerson HRT, 'The Structure of Law Enforcement in Thirteenth-century England' (1979) 23 *The American Journal of Legal History* 313–327.

Trindade F & Cane P, *The Law of Torts in Australia*, 2nd edn, Oxford University Press, Melbourne, 1993, Ch 1.

Tilbury M, Noone M & Krecher B, *Remedies: Commentary and Materials*, The Law Book Company Ltd, Sydney, 1993, pp 46–66.

van Caenegem RC, *An Historical Introduction to Private Law*, Cambridge University Press, Cambridge, 1988.

The Law of Compensation and Damages

INTRODUCTION

Compensation is the *raison d'être* of the law of torts. In his *Commentaries on the Laws of England*, William Blackstone[1] divided wrongs into private wrongs and public wrongs. He suggested that private wrongs involve 'an infringement or privation of the private or civil rights belonging to individuals, considered as individuals', whereas public wrongs are based on 'a breach and violation of public rights and duties, which affect the whole community.' The main aim of the law of torts is to settle disputes between private persons, and to compensate for harm sustained as a result of the private wrong. Today, the tortfeasor is compelled to pay fair compensation (*Teubner v Humble* (1963) 108 CLR 491 at 505, per Windeyer J) for

> past and future economic loss suffered by the plaintiff as a result of the injury, and any needs created by the wrongful conduct that would not otherwise exist, and pain and suffering.

The law of compensation is governed by statute and common law. When implementing the 2002–03 Torts Reforms, the Federal Parliament and the parliaments of each State and Territory enacted sets of rules and principles that differ from jurisdiction to jurisdiction. This means we have nine jurisdictional paradigms regulating different aspects of compensation, as well as common law, governing principles of assessment and damages for intentional wrongs.

The new statutory principles are applicable to any claim for damages for personal injury or death, as well as property damage or economic loss resulting from negligence, regardless of whether the claim is brought in tort, contract, equity, under a statute, or any other cause of action.[2] In this sense, the Australian law of damages

---

1. A Facsimile of the First Edition of 1768, Vol 3, Clarendon Press, Oxford; photographically reprinted by The University of Chicago Press, Chicago & London, 1979, p 2.
2. *Ipp Report* <http://www.revofneg.treasury.gov.au/content/reports.asp> at [2.1]–[2.3].

for unintentionally caused loss is moving towards the civil law (derived from Roman law) concept of the law of obligations. At the same time, except in the Australian Capital Territory and, partly, South Australia,[3] awards where the fault concerned is an intentional act that is done with intent to cause death or injury or concerns sexual assault or other sexual misconduct[4] are excluded from the operation of the statutory provisions, including damages. Thus, the distinction between such intentional fault-based torts as trespass to the person, trespass to land, false imprisonment, action on the case for intentional infliction of physical harm or nervous shock, malicious prosecution, conversion, and the like, and non-intentional fault-based torts such as negligence, has acquired a new importance in the law of damages.

Intentional wrongs continue to be governed by common law, which means that a person claiming for intentionally caused injury can sue without having to reach a statutory threshold (discussed below) and that, if the claim is successful, damages will not be capped. Moreover, punitive, exemplary, and aggravated damages, which in some jurisdictions have been abolished for negligently occasioned personal injury,[5] remain available for intentional torts (see below: Aggravated and exemplary damages).

In view of statutory limitations imposed on recovery of damages for negligence, certain statements by the High Court will need to be re-assessed. One of the statements in need of reconsideration is the observation by Gleeson CJ, McHugh, Gummow, and Hayne JJ in *Gray v Motor Accident Commission* (1998) 196 CLR 1, at 9, that:

> there can be cases, framed in negligence, in which the defendant can be shown to have acted consciously in contumelious disregard of the rights of the plaintiff or persons in the position of the plaintiff. Cases of an employer's failure to provide a safe system of work for employees in which it is demonstrated that the employer, well knowing of an extreme danger thus created, persisted in employing the unsafe system might, perhaps, be of that latter kind.

Where there is an overlap between intentional and negligent conduct (negligent in the sense of breach of duty of care) in the post-reform environment, a legal

---

3. The *Civil Liability Act 1936* (SA), s 43, which excludes liability for criminal conduct, applies where damages are claimed for personal injury '(i) arising from a motor accident (whether caused intentionally or unintentionally); or (ii) arising from an accident caused wholly or in part (a) by negligence; or (b) by some other unintentional tort on the part of a person other than the injured person; or (c) by breach of a contractual duty of care.'
4. *Wrongs Act 1958* (Vic), s 28C(2); *Civil Liability Act 2002* (Tas), s 3B(1)(a); *Civil Liability Act 2002* (NSW), s 3B(1)(a); *Civil Liability Act 2003* (Qld), s 52(2); *Civil Liability Act 2002* (WA), s 3A(1).
5. *Personal Injuries Act 2003* (NT), s 19; *Civil Liability Act 2003* (Qld), s 5(1) and (2), s 52; *Civil Liability Act 2002* (NSW), s 21; *Wrongs Act 1958* (Vic), s 24AP(d). The *Civil Liability Act 2002* (WA), s 7, provides that no awards are allowed except according to the Division, which seems to indirectly exclude punitive and aggravated damages. The Australian Capital Territory, South Australia and Tasmania do not appear to address this issue.

adviser may need to consider whether the facts of the case would support an action for intentional torts, as well as, or instead of, negligence. The law of damages is thus a constant reference point for torts lawyers: it forms and informs their ultimate advice.

At the same time, the law of damages is very complex; revisiting this part of the book after familiarisation with the substantive law of torts is recommended.

The following discussion of the law of damages will involve examination of:

- the nature of compensation for wrongfully occasioned loss and injury;
- classification of damages obtainable in actions for compensation in tort; and
- general rules governing assessment of damages.

HISTORY OF COMPENSATION IN THE LAW OF TORTS

Evolution of liability

Early medieval England was governed by customary law, according to which the defendant was liable for all the harm inflicted upon another, irrespective of whether this was done intentionally, negligently or accidentally. As the common law developed, the courts began to hold the wrongdoer strictly liable, unless, in the words of *Weaver v Ward* (1616) Hob 134; 80 ER 284, he could show that accident was inevitable—'judged utterly without his fault'. In *Leame v Bray* (1803) 3 East 593; 102 ER 724, at 727, Grose J held that every voluntary trespassory conduct would expose the defendant to prima facie liability even 'though it happens accidentally or by misfortune'. However, strict liability only attached if the plaintiff proved that the damage was caused by an act that fell within the scope of a form of action recognised by Chancery, and not by some other type of act.

Thus, the medieval principle of civil liability was based on strict liability for the damage to the plaintiff's interests. Strict liability for damage was an inducement to forgo the right to take revenge. For, by the thirteenth century, the Bractonian treatise reported that, homicide excluded, a victim of a wrong could choose to proceed criminally for punishment, or civilly for damages.[6] In the later medieval period, perhaps by analogy with the sale of church indulgences, the courts would award damages 'for the benefit of the wrongdoer's soul rather than of the victim's pocket', on the basis that 'the conscience of the wrongdoer must be purged by making restitution'.[7] Such terms as 'soul' and 'conscience' are religious concepts, and we still tend to associate 'wrong' with morality. It has taken a long time for the

---

6. Seipp DJ, 'Symposium: the Distinction between Crime and Tort in the Early Common Law' (1996) 76 *Boston UL Rev* 59–87 at 81.
7. Williams G, 'The Aims of the Law of Tort' (1951) 137 *Current Legal Problems* 143.

common law to develop secular jurisprudence.[8] Lord Goddard in *British Transport Commission v Gourley* [1956] AC 185, at 206, pointed out that despite the use of such words as 'wrongs' and 'wrongdoers', which connote moral opprobrium, the law of torts generally does not regard compensation either as a reward or as a punishment. Traditionally, once the court found that the defendant infringed a legal right of another, the former would owe 'the compensation for that right in the same way as any other civil debt.'[9]

Eventually, in the first part of the nineteenth century, the judiciary crystallised the concept of compensatory damages in terms of putting the claimant into as good a position as if no wrong had occurred, measured by the loss he or she had suffered.[10] Lord Blackburn in *Livingstone v Rawyards Coal Co* [1880] 5 AC 25 observed (at 39) that an award of a lump sum was:

> believed, so far as money can, [to] put the injured person in the same position as he or she would have been in if the wrong had not been committed.

This is known as the principle of *restitutio in integrum*. However, Lord Blackburn's statement has been interpreted to mean that, in an action for damages for personal injuries, apart from general damages,[11] plaintiffs could recover damages only where their disabilities had been, may, or may be, productive of financial loss in relation to loss of earning capacity.[12]

In Australia, the rule was articulated in 1956, when in *Blundell v Musgrave* (1956) 96 CLR 73, the High Court was asked to determine whether the tortfeasor should be liable for hospital and ambulance expenses stemming from an accident. The expenses had been charged by the employer, the Navy Department of the Commonwealth, to the injured claimant's pay account, but the employer had a statutory discretion to waive them. The High Court held that the costs or value of the services in an action for damages for personal injuries could not be recovered

---

8. For example, it was only in *Bowman v Secular Society Ltd* [1917] AC 406 that the House of Lords held that a bequest for the promotion of agnostic teaching was not contrary to good morals, overruling a longstanding judicial precedent in *Cowan v Milbourn* [1867] LR 2 Ex 230, at 234, that denial of the teachings of Christianity was a 'violation of the first principle of the law'.
9. Munkman J, *Damages for Personal Injuries and Death*, Butterworths, London, 1985, p 6.
10. *Robinson v Harman* (1848) 1 Exch 850 at 855.
11. The term 'general damages' has different meanings in different contexts. Frequently, it refers to compensation for past and future 'pain and suffering', involving both physical pain as well as any psychiatric condition caused by the injury or emotional distress consequent upon the knowledge that the injury has caused a disability or disfigurement, and limitations imposed by the disability on future enjoyment of life.
12. *Graham v Baker* (1961) 106 CLR 340 at 347. In *Griffiths v Kerkemeyer* (1977) 139 CLR 161, at 166, Gibbs CJ adopted the *Graham v Barker* principle, stating: 'In my opinion, in cases of this kind ... the plaintiff is entitled to damages only to the extent that the need thus created is or may be productive of financial loss.' Gibbs CJ, however, was in the minority on this point.

unless the claimant could establish that there was, or would be, a legal obligation to pay or refund them.[13]

When assessing damages, the judges sometimes took into consideration the needs for nursing or other services created by the injury.[14] However, it was in *Griffiths v Kerkemeyer* (1977) 139 CLR 161 that the High Court adopted Windeyer J's idea that plaintiffs can recover damages for loss as manifested by the needs created by the wrongful injury or death, and extended it to cover a need for services provided on voluntary basis.[15]

NATURE OF COMPENSATION IN THE LAW OF TORTS

Definition of damages and compensation

Viscount Simon in *Crofter Hand Woven Harris Tweed v Veitch* [1942] AC 435 at 442 observed that 'injury' is limited to actionable wrong, while 'damage', in contrast with injury, means loss or harm occurring in fact, whether actionable as an injury or not. The term 'damages' refers to pecuniary compensation for an injury (actionable wrong). In *Mahony v J Kruschich (Demolitions) Pty Ltd* (1985) 156 CLR 522 at 527 [4], the High Court in a joint judgment explained the difference between 'damage' and 'damages' for the purposes of action in negligence as follows:

> In negligence, 'damage' is what the plaintiff suffers as the foreseeable consequence of the tortfeasor's act or omission. Where a tortfeasor's negligent act or omission causes personal injury, 'damage' includes both the injury itself and other foreseeable consequences suffered by the plaintiff. The distinction between 'damage' and 'damages' is significant. Damages are awarded as compensation for each item or aspect of the damage suffered by a plaintiff, so that a single sum is awarded in respect of all the foreseeable consequences of the defendant's tortious act or omission.

---

13. The full court agreed on this principle. McTiernan, Williams, Webb, and Taylor JJ in a joint judgment found on the facts of the case that the legal obligation existed, whereas Dixon CJ and Fullagar J found that it did not.
14. For example, in *Roach v Yates* [1938] 1 KB 256 damages were awarded for loss of wages foregone by the wife and sister-in-law of the injured plaintiff (they had to give up their paid employment to look after him).
15. In *Griffiths v Kerkemeyer*, the High Court of Australia followed the English Court of Appeal decision in *Donnelly v Joyce* [1974] QB 454. For further discussion, see: Mendelson D, 'Jurisprudential Legerdemain: Damages for Gratuitous Services and Attendant Care' (2005) *Journal of Law and Medicine* 402–412.

In the Torts Reform legislation, the phrase, 'personal injury damages' has been statutorily defined as 'damages that relate to the death of or injury to a person caused by the fault of another person'.[16]

Terminology

In personal injury litigation, damages are meant to compensate the injured person for the disability suffered as a result of the defendant's wrongful conduct.

Disability and impairment

The term 'disability' has a different meaning in law from 'impairment' and they should not be used interchangeably. The World Health Organization, in its *International Classification of Impairments, Disabilities, and Handicaps* (Geneva, 1980), defined the term 'impairment' as 'any loss or abnormality of psychological, physiological, or anatomical structure or function.' Therefore, the assessment or rating of impairment is a medical responsibility.

The term 'disability' refers to the harmful consequences and effects resulting from impairment that affect a person's ability to perform normal human activities. For example, let us suppose that you have always wanted to be an air force pilot. While in your last year of training, you suffered a permanent injury to your eyesight through another's negligence. Because of your impaired vision you were told that you would never be able to drive a car, let alone fly an aircraft again. The determination of your *disability*, which is the function of the assessing tribunal, will involve a review not only of medical factors, but also legal, psychological, social, and vocational considerations.[17] The level of disability is one of the most important factors in the assessment of the quantum of damages for past and future pain and suffering, loss of enjoyment of life, and loss of earning capacity.

Rights and duties in the law of compensation

The discourse on rights and duties in law can take place at many levels. In discussing compensation for tortious injury, these terms signify two different levels of analysis. At the first level, rights and duties refer to interests protected by the law of torts as discussed in Chapter 1. When the right is thus recognised, others are under a corresponding obligation or duty not to infringe that right. These are called primary rights and obligations. For example, I have a legally protected right

---

16. *Wrongs Act 1958* (Vic), s 28B; see also: *Civil Law (Wrongs) Act 2002* (ACT), s 109(3); *Civil Liability Act 2002* (NSW), s 11; *Civil Liability Act 2002* (WA), s 3; *Trade Practices Act 1974* (Cth), s 87D.
17. Mendelson G, 'The Rating of Psychiatric Impairment in Forensic Practice: A Review' (1991) 25 *Australian and New Zealand Journal of Psychiatry* 84–94.

to physical integrity. Correspondingly, others are obligated not to infringe my right by crashing into me.

If this legal obligation is breached and my right is infringed without legal justification, I have a cause of action, which could result in an award of damages, and, in turn, create a fresh set of rights and obligations: namely, the right to enforce the duty to pay judicially determined compensation.[18] Ernest Weinrib described these 'secondary rights and obligations' thus:

> Just as the plaintiff's right constitutes the subject matter of the defendant's duty, so the wrongful interference with the right entails the duty to repair. Thus, tort law places the defendant under the obligation to restore the plaintiff, in so far as possible, to the position the plaintiff would have been in had the wrong not been committed.[19]

Common law process of obtaining personal injury compensation

It is part and parcel of the accepted process of settlement of industrial and legal disputes, including personal injury claims, for both sides to make ambit claims in anticipation of the final, more moderate settlement. The claimant is often encouraged by friends, family, and solicitors not to belittle the symptoms of the injury and its adverse consequences. The respondents (employers, occupiers, landlords, motorists, persons providing professional or skilled services, private individuals and insurance companies) try their utmost to find ways of reducing liability.

In approximately 95 per cent of cases, this bargaining process will lead to an out-of-court settlement. However, if the settlement is not forthcoming, the parties will serve each other with pleadings. The traditional function of pleadings has been defined as 'written identification and communication of the extent of the plaintiff's claim'.[20] In *Laws v Australian Broadcasting Tribunal* (1990) 170 CLR 70 at 85, Mason CJ and Brennan J wrote that specifically, pleadings are the written statements of each party in which they identify the issues of fact. These issues will arise for determination at the trial, unless the defendant admits liability in relation to them beforehand. In other words, only the facts stated in the pleadings that are denied by the opposite side will have to be proved and ultimately submitted for judicial decision. Pleadings also determine the range of evidence the parties may need to adduce at the trial and the extent of discoverable documents and available

---

18. Tilbury M, Noone M & Krecher B, *Remedies, Commentary and Materials*, The Law Book Company Ltd, Sydney, 1993, p 1.
19. Weinrib E, 'The Gains and Losses of Corrective Justice' (1994) 44 *Duke Law Journal* 277 at 295.
20. *Philips v Philips* (1878) 4 QBD 127 at 139; *Jamieson v The Queen* (1993) 67 ALJR 793 at 579, cited in *Laws v Australian Broadcasting Tribunal* (1990) 170 CLR 70 at 85.

interrogatories. They thus define the limits within which each party's case will be confined.[21]

It is worth noting that an adversary system under common law is not designed to 'ferret out the truth' in any absolute sense. Rather, the common law has always focused on the question whether the burden of proving allegations has been discharged. Damages follow if the plaintiff succeeds in this task.

The nature of proof in civil cases

The term 'the standard of proof' refers to the required degree of persuasion for the fact-finder to find a fact. Unlike criminal trials, where the Crown has to prove its case beyond reasonable doubt, in civil litigation, according to Dixon J (as he then was) in *Briginshaw v Briginshaw* (1938) 60 CLR 336, at 361–2, the standard of persuasion (proof) is one of 'the reasonable satisfaction which … may, not must, be based on a preponderance of probability'.

In the case of *Davies v Taylor* [1974] AC 207, at 219, Lord Simon described the notion of 'balance of probabilities' in mathematical terms. His Lordship suggested that the concept involves the plaintiff having 'the burden of showing odds of at least 51 to 49 that such-and-such has taken place or will do so.' In *Malec v JC Hutton Pty Ltd* (1990) 169 CLR 638, at 642–3, Deane, Gaudron and McHugh J in a joint judgment explained the legal consequences flowing from the probability test:

> A common law court determines on the balance of probabilities whether an event has occurred. If the probability of the event having occurred is greater than it not having occurred, the occurrence of the event is treated as certain; if the probability of it having occurred is less than it having not occurred, it is treated as not having occurred.

This means that where the party bearing the onus of proof can only show that the probability of the event having occurred was 50 per cent, it will be treated as not having occurred, and the onus will not be discharged.

However, in *Briginshaw v Briginshaw* (1938) 60 CLR 336, at 361–2, Dixon J (as he then was) warned:

> when the law requires proof of any fact, the Tribunal must feel an actual persuasion of its occurrence or existence before it can be found. It cannot be found as a result of a mere mechanical comparison of probabilities independent of any belief in its reality.

---

21. Colbran M, 'Pleadings, Principles and Practice', *Court Forms, Precedents and Pleading: Victoria*, Vol 2, Butterworths, Sydney, ¶54,021.

The 'once for all' rule

Under common law, compensation in the form of damages is awarded unconditionally, as a lump sum, usually in the currency of the country in which the case was tried. Once the plaintiff has recovered damages for the wrongful injury, as a general rule, he or she will not be allowed to bring another action based on the same facts, even if the injury develops into a much more serious condition than it appeared at the time of trial. This is known as the 'once for all' rule, which was established in 1699 in the gruesome case of *Fetter v Beal* (1701) 91 ER 1122. In that case, the plaintiff sued in battery claiming that the defendant broke his skull. The defendant was found liable, and ordered to pay £11 in damages. Eight years later, the plaintiff, having recovered damages, brought a second action, because a portion of his skull had to be removed by trepanning (a surgical operation removing part of bone of the skull with a cylindrical saw, a trepan). The defendant successfully demurred.[22] Holt CJ (at 1123) simply stated that the rule was settled, and that if 'this matter' (presumably the additional damage) had been raised in earlier evidence, as a probable consequence of the battery, the plaintiff would have recovered damages for it. Conversely, once fixed, damages are not decreased on the basis that subsequently the claimant miraculously recovered or died soon after the verdict.

In *Murphy v Stone-Wallwork (Charlton) Ltd* (1969) 1 WLR 1023, Lord Pearce (at 1027) justified the 'once for all' rule on the grounds that it prevents the possibility of unending litigation. His Lordship expressed the rule in the following terms:

> If later the plaintiff suffers greater loss from an accident than was anticipated at the trial, he cannot come back for more. Nor can the defendant come back if the loss is less than was anticipated.

The 'once for all' rule probably works to the advantage of the defendant, because it either delays compensation if the plaintiff waits to discover the extent of the injury before going to trial, or the compensation may be less than warranted by the harm suffered. In serious injury cases, the court is compelled to predict economic, social, and political changes in the distant future. If sufficient consideration is given to these factors in cases of plaintiffs who have suffered catastrophic injury (brain damage, quadriplegia, paraplegia, etc), resulting awards of damages tend to be regarded as shockingly generous, even when, from a long-term perspective, they merely tend to keep the plaintiffs' standard of living just above the poverty line.

Generally, the 'once for all' rule applies to all common law actions in tort, though under the doctrine in *Mulholland v Mitchell* [1971] AC 666, at 680 (per Lord Wilberforce), in exceptional cases Courts of Appeal have the power to reassess

---

22. Demurrer is a challenge on the basis of insufficiency of pleading. It may include denial of the allegations, denial of the statement, exception or objection to a pleading.

damages. Moreover, in cases for continuing nuisance, successive actions can be brought for every fresh injury.

Lump sum awards and structured settlements

Until the Torts reforms of 2002–03, plaintiffs were awarded damages in a lump sum. McHugh J, in the case of *Nominal Defendant v Gardikiotis* (1996) 186 CLR 49 at 60 explained the traditional role of a court in awarding common law damages in the following way:

> Except in those cases where the plaintiff is under a legal disability, a court has no interest in what happens to the plaintiff's damages. It has a duty to assess fair compensation for all the effects, physical, mental and financial, that the defendant's negligence has had on the plaintiff. But at common law, compensation is given on a one-off basis; there are no periodic payments of compensation. The court awards a single sum and enters judgment. Its role is then finished. To the inadequate extent that monetary compensation can compensate for the effects of personal injury, a court has done its duty when it makes its award of damages. What the plaintiff does with the verdict moneys is a matter entirely for the plaintiff.

The *Fetter v Beal* case above, which entrenched the 'once for all' lump sum rule, also illustrated its shortcomings in relation to the predictability of the ultimate injury. In *Fetter v Beal* the plaintiff's injury was much more severe than originally anticipated. However, there have also been cases where plaintiffs died soon after obtaining very large sums in damages. For example, in *Gilchrist and Ors v The Estate of the Late Sara Alexander Taylor* [2004] NSWCA 476, twelve-year-old Sara sustained an injury when she was hit in the head by a golf ball struck by her brother in 1987. On the same day, she was treated and operated on at the Wagga Wagga Base Hospital. Nevertheless, Sara was left with a significant neurological deficit and suffered from frequent severe epileptic seizures and spontaneous uncontrolled grande mal epileptic seizures. She sued the hospital and individual doctors in negligence. The claim was settled, without admission of liability, in the sum of $2.5 million plus costs on 20 December 2002. Sara died on 21 January 2003. The application by the defendants for a reduction in damages that would otherwise be payable was refused, on the basis that counsel for the respondent negotiating the settlement should have included a clause providing for the possibility of early death.[23]

The 'once for all' rule is also problematic when compensation awards are very large: nowadays they often exceed half a million dollars. In *Nominal Defendant v Gardikiotis* (1996) 186 CLR 49, counsel (unsuccessfully) argued that the rule should be modified because many injured plaintiffs do not have the skills to manage

---

23. See also: *Doherty v Liverpool District Council* (1991) 22 NSWLR 284; *Public Trustee v Sutherland Shire Council* (1992) Aust Torts Reports 81–149.

their compensation awards in a manner that would provide them with a secure source of income for the rest of their lives. In their joint judgment, Brennan CJ, Dawson, Toohey, and Gaudron JJ (at 52) stated that:

> it is contrary to common sense to speak of the accident causing a need for assistance in managing the fund constituted by her [the plaintiff's] verdict moneys in circumstances where her intellectual abilities are not in any way impaired.

Yet there have been many tragic stories of parents gambling away their injured children's compensation awards, and of awards mismanaged by claimants, their families, or fraudulent financial advisers.[24] Follow-up studies of successful plaintiffs have revealed that it is rare for lump sum awards to sustain them at a reasonable level of comfort on a long-term basis.[25] Professor Harold Luntz has noted that curial attempts to protect plaintiffs from dissipating their compensation awards, either through incompetence or bad luck, and thus prevent them from becoming a burden on social security, may be considered paternalistic. However, he points out that: 'since the funds for the payment of damages are mostly made available through compulsory insurance, the State has an obligation to see that the funds are used to meet the needs for which they were created'.[26]

Structured settlement agreements

One way to remedy at least the management issue of large compensation awards is to invest the lump sum in a guaranteed annuity fund. Yet until the enactment of the *Taxation Laws Amendment (Structured Settlements and Structured Orders) Act 2002* (Cth), there were financial disincentives for settlements other than by way of a lump sum. For although the lump sum itself was not taxable, with few exceptions, income earned on investment of the lump sum was. Following the Torts reforms, annuities are exempted from income tax as are certain deferred lump sums paid under structured settlements to seriously injured people.

Once the taxation impediment was removed, all jurisdictions enacted legislation enabling the parties to litigation to enter into a 'structured settlement' agreement, whereby the defendant is required to pay all or part of plaintiff's damages in the form of periodic payments funded by an annuity or other agreed means rather than in a single lump sum (for example, the *Wrongs Act 1958* (Vic), s 28M). The court first calculates damages as a lump sum according to the ordinary rules for assessment of damages. Some or all of that lump sum is then used to buy an annuity that would generate income out of which payments will be made to the plaintiff

---

24. For examples and discussion see: Luntz H, *Assessment of Damages for Personal Injury and Death*, 4th edn, LexisNexis Butterworths, Sydney, 2002, pp 26–27.
25. Ibid p 26.
26. Ibid p 26.

from time to time, according to an agreed schedule.²⁷ The reform provisions only partially remedy the problem of long-term financial management of the awards, for courts are not empowered to require the parties to enter into a structured settlement against their wishes.

The question arises whether the 'once for all' rule, including structured settlements, is the best method of safeguarding long-term socio-economic, emotional, and health interests of catastrophically injured claimants.

Compromise of a claim

Statutory structured settlement agreements are different from settlements arrived at by compromise of a claim. At common law, the parties are free to negotiate and reach an agreement regarding a claim at any time through formal or informal discussions, exchange of letters, mediation, arbitration, etc, before proceedings are instituted. A settlement, in the sense of compromise, can also be reached in or out of court at any stage during the hearing of an action, but before the final judgment. The terms of settlement or compromise are usually expressed in a consent order (sometimes known as a 'rule of court'), which is a signed order of the court, and has the same force as a judgment. In cases where infants or persons with impaired mental capacity are involved, the court must approve every out-of-court settlement, to ensure that the amount and terms are sufficiently beneficial to the claimant.²⁸ Many out-of-court settlements in personal injury cases are reached with a respondent who does not admit any liability. This was the case in *Gilchrist and Ors v The Estate of the Late Sara Alexander Taylor* [2004] NSWCA 476.

CLASSIFICATION OF DAMAGES

Nominal damages and contemptuous damages

Nominal damages are awarded when the plaintiff's legal right has been infringed, in cases where the tort is actionable *per se*, ie, without proof of damage. Holt CJ, in the case of *Ashby v White* (1703) 2 Ld Raym 938 at 955, referring to intentional torts (in particular, battery and assault), stated that 'If a man gives another a cuff on the ear, though it cost him nothing, not so much as a little diachylon [plaster], yet he shall have his action, for it is a personal injury.' Depending on the circumstances of the case, nominal damages can range from small to substantial.²⁹ An award of even

---

27. For example, at present the Master of the Supreme Court of Victoria administers the award money on behalf of some 5100 injured children and disabled people.
28. See, for example: *Damages (Infants and Persons of Unsound Mind) Act 1929* (NSW); *Yu Ge by her tutor Tao Ge v River Island Clothing Pty Ltd & Ors* [2002] NSWSC 28; (2002) Aust Torts Reports 81–638.
29. Winfield PH, *Law of Torts*, 4th edn, Sweet & Maxwell Limited, London, 1948, p 146.

a relatively small sum in nominal damages to the plaintiff means that the defendant has to pay the costs of the action. However, where the jury awards the plaintiff a derisory amount—'no more than the lowest coin of the realm'—thus indicating the court's low opinion of the plaintiff's bare legal claim, the court has discretion to deprive the plaintiff of costs.[30] These derisory awards are known as 'contemptuous damages'.[31] Nowadays, pursuing technically viable but otherwise unmeritorious claims is also discouraged by legislation.

Aggravated (compensatory) and exemplary (punitive) damages

The customary law did not differentiate between public and private law, and this has influenced the modern law of compensation for, historically, another function of the law of torts—like that of criminal law—is to deter wrongful conduct. A civil court may pursue this goal through the award of exemplary (punitive) damages.[32]

In *Broome v Cassell & Co Ltd* [1972] AC 1027 at 1085, a case of libel, the House of Lords defined aggravated damages as a hybrid between compensatory and punitive damages. In *Uren v John Fairfax & Sons Pty Ltd* (1966) 117 CLR 118, a case involving defamation, Windeyer J (at 149) described the distinction between aggravated and punitive damages thus:

> aggravated damages are given to compensate the plaintiff when the harm done to him by a wrongful act was aggravated by the manner in which the act was done: exemplary damages, on the other hand, are intended to punish the defendant, and presumably to serve one or more of the objects of punishment—moral retribution or deterrence.

Aggravated damages are awarded where the defendant's wrong has been committed in a 'high handed, malicious, insulting or oppressive way'. Where the plaintiff suffers more than the loss compensable under compensatory damages, aggravated damages may be awarded, for example for humiliation and emotional distress.

---

30. *Connolly v Sunday Time Publishing Co Ltd* (1908) 7 CLR 263. See also: Luntz H, *Assessment of Damages for Personal Injury and Death*, 4th edn, LexisNexis Butterworths, Sydney 2002, p 93.
31. *Connolly v Sunday Time Publishing Co Ltd* (1908) 7 CLR 263. The English case of *Lois Austin, Geoffrey Saxby v Commissioner of Police of the Metropolis* [2005] EWHC 480 (QBD), which involved a political May Day march involving some 3000 people who had deliberately given no notice to the police that they intended to gather in Oxford Circus, provides another example. In *Lois Austin*, the organisers, including Ms Austin, refused to cooperate with the police in any way at all. To prevent personal injuries or death, and damage to property, the police cordoned off the streets around Oxford Circus. Ms Austin brought an action for false imprisonment. Tugendhat J rejected her claim, adding that if she were successful, he would have made an award of £5.
32. The United Kingdom Law Commission, *Aggravated, Exemplary and Restitutionary Damages*, Consultation Paper No 132, HMSO, 1993, p 2.

Unlike aggravated damages, punitive damages do not compensate the victim for his or her injury; rather, until recently, they were defined as private fines levied by civil juries to punish reprehensible conduct and to deter its future occurrence. Punitive damages are a vestige of the customary law of vengeance, in particular, the custom of 'deadly feud'. Under Saxon laws, if damages, known as *wergild* or *wergeld* (blood money) were not paid to the relatives of a slain man, his kinsmen could lawfully take up arms against the murderer and, in 'a Profession of an irreconcilable Hatred, till a Person is revenged even by Death of his Enemy, exact vengeance upon him'.[33] Apart from having to pay damages to the kin of the killed or injured person, defendants were also liable to pay an 'amercement', a civil fine, to the King's Treasury.[34] Under early common law, successful actions for forcible trespass, which were tried in a court of record, led to liability for damages to the plaintiff and a fine.

Edward I (r 1272–1307) enacted a series of statutes,[35] which codified medieval English Law, and attempted to protect the feudal system of vassalage, by providing that the disseissee could recover double or treble fines against alienee tenants. However, according to Sir Edward Coke (5 Co Rep 49), in actions where no force, fraud or deceit was alleged, no fine was imposed. Today, as the High Court of Australia pointed out in *Lamb v Cotogno* (1987) 164 CLR 1 at 9:

> it is an aspect of exemplary damages that they serve to assuage any urge for revenge felt by the victim and to discourage any temptation to engage in self-help likely to endanger peace.

With the development of civil jurisdiction and the separation of trespassory torts from their criminal law origins, these fines, now called punitive damages (also known as vindictive or exemplary damages), were awarded in the civil courts only in certain exceptional circumstances. The term 'exemplary damages' was first employed in 1763 in the cases of *Wilkes v Wood* (1763) 98 ER 489 (CP) and its companion, *Huckle v Money* (1763) 2 Wils 205; 95 ER 768. In *Wilkes v Wood* the plaintiff, John Wilkes, published an article critical of the speech made at the opening of Parliament by George III (r 1760–1820) in *The North Briton* newspaper (23 April, 1763, no 45). Lord Halifax, Secretary to the King, issued a 'general' arrest warrant authorising a search of Wilkes' house. In his address to the jury, Charles Pratt, 1st Earl Camden, the Chief Justice of the Court of Common Pleas, pointed out (at 498) that no offenders' names were specified in the warrant, giving

---

33. Stat 43 Ed I c 13, 1601; quoted in Jacob G, *New Law Dictionary*, 7th edn, Henry Lintot, Savoy, 1756, under *Wergild*.
34. Pollock F & Maitland FW, *The History of the English Law*, 2nd edn, Cambridge University Press, Cambridge, 1923, pp 513–515.
35. Known as the *Statute of Glouster 1278* Stat 6 Ed I, the *Statute of Winchester 1285* Stat 13 Ed I and *Quo Warranto 1290* Stat 18 Ed I.

the King's messengers (officers) a discretionary power to search 'wherever their suspicions may chance to fall'.[36] The Chief Justice then explained (at 499) that:

> a jury have it in their power to give damages for more than the injury received. Damages are designed not only as a satisfaction to the injured person, but likewise as a punishment to the guilty, to deter from any such proceeding for the future, and as a proof of the detestation of the jury to the action itself.

The jury found the general warrant to be invalid, and awarded Wilkes £1000 in damages.

While they were searching Wilkes' house, the officers arrested one of his printers, and kept him for six hours. The agents of King George treated him with 'beef-steaks and beer'. Nevertheless, he sued (*Huckle v Money*) for false imprisonment and trespass, and was awarded 300 guineas in exemplary damages because, as the court said (at 207, 769), 'to enter a man's house by virtue of a nameless warrant, in order to procure evidence, is worse than the Spanish Inquisition ... it [is] a most daring public attack made upon the liberty of the subject.' In both cases, the courts made it clear that exemplary damages were awarded because of the arbitrary and outrageous use of executive power against private citizens.

Later, exemplary damages were also awarded for other particularly reprehensible intentional wrongs. For example, in *Genay v Norris* (1784) 1 SCL (1 Bay) 6, the South Carolina Supreme Court awarded 'vindictive damages' against a physician who used his professional knowledge to cause injury. He proposed, after settling a quarrel with the plaintiff, that they drink a reconciliation toast. The defendant then secretly spiked the plaintiff's wine glass with a large dose of cantharides, thus causing him 'extreme and excruciating pain'.

In *Rookes v Barnard* [1964] AC 1129, while considering the tort of intimidation, the House of Lords considered exemplary damages to be an anomaly in a modern common law system. Lord Devlin (at 1226) stated that there were only three categories of case that could provide:

> a practical justification for admitting into the civil law a principle which ought logically to belong to the criminal.

The first category of case included oppressive, arbitrary or unconstitutional acts of government servants, whereas the second involved circumstances where 'a defendant with a cynical disregard for a plaintiff's rights has calculated that money to be made out of his wrongdoing will probably exceed the damages at risk' (at 1226).[37] The third category of case was the one in which exemplary damages

---

36. The defendants claimed that the 'general warrant' gave them the right to break open escrutores (writing tables), and seize papers, with no duty to make an inventory of the things thus taken away.
37. In the second category of case, the purpose of exemplary damages is to 'to teach a wrongdoer that tort does not pay.' See: *Rookes v Barnard* [1964] AC 1129 at 1227.

were expressly authorised by statute. In *Kuddus v Chief Constable of Leicestershire Constabulary* [2002] 2 AC 122, the court held that the determining criterion for the award of exemplary damages is whether the tortious action of a public official was oppressive, arbitrary or unconstitutional, rather than a specific cause of action.

The Australian High Court rejected this restrictive approach in *Australian Consolidated Press Ltd v Uren* (1967) 117 CLR 118.[38] In *XL Petroleum (NSW) Pty Ltd v Caltex Oil (Australia) Pty Ltd* (1985) 155 CLR 448, a case involving trespass to land, Brennan J (at 471) stated that:

> an award of exemplary damages is intended to punish the defendant for conduct showing a conscious and contumelious disregard for the plaintiff's rights and to deter him from committing like conduct again ...

However, apart from a plea for moderation,[39] the High Court of Australia has not provided any further guidelines for assessment of exemplary damages.

Following the Torts Reforms, the *Trade Practices Act 1974* (Cth), s 87ZB(1), prohibits awards of exemplary damages or aggravated damages in respect of death or personal injury. Punitive and aggravated damages, which in some jurisdictions have been abolished for negligently occasioned personal injury,[40] remain available for common law intentional torts and for injuries and death resulting from smoking or other use of tobacco products.

The most recent major pre-reform case in which the High Court discussed exemplary damages was *Gray v Motor Accident Commission* (1998) 196 CLR 1. Mr Gray, the plaintiff, then aged sixteen, was walking across a street with a group of Aboriginal youths in an Adelaide suburb when he was struck by a motor car deliberately driven at him by Bransden, the defendant. Under compulsory third-party insurance in South Australia, the statutory motor vehicle insurer was liable for the driver's actions. Subsequently, Bransden was convicted of intentionally causing grievous bodily harm, and was sentenced to seven years' imprisonment. The sentencing judge found that Bransden acted maliciously. Mr Gray was awarded compensatory damages for personal injury, but the trial judge dismissed his claim for exemplary damages on the basis that Bransden had already been punished by a criminal court.

---

38. Affirmed by the Privy Council in *Australian Consolidated Press Ltd v Uren* (1967) 117 CLR 221.
39. In *XL Petroleum*, Gibbs CJ agreed with the statements of Lord Hailsham of St Marylebone LC in *Broome v Cassell & Co* (1972) AC 1027, at 1081, who enjoined judges to make sure in their direction that the jury is fully aware of the danger of an excessive award.
40. *Personal Injuries Act 2003* (NT), s 19; *Civil Liability Act 2003* (Qld), ss 5(1) and (2), 52; *Civil Liability Act 2002* (NSW), s 21. The *Trade Practices 1974* (Cth), s 87ZB(1), prohibits awards of exemplary damages or aggravated damages in respect of death or personal injury. The *Civil Liability Act 2002* (WA), s 7, provides that no awards are allowed except according to the Division, which seems to indirectly exclude punitive and aggravated damages. The Australian Capital Territory, South Australia and Tasmania do not appear to address this issue. In Victoria, punitive damages are available under proportionate liability (*Wrongs Act 1958* (Vic), s 24AP(d)).

The actions of Bransden were intentional; however, the action was pursued as a claim for damages for negligence. This led the High Court (at [20]) to observe that although the action in *Gray* was framed in negligence, it was 'conducted at trial as if it were a claim in trespass' and that the case was one of a deliberate wrongdoing. Consequently, in principle, punitive damages could have been awarded. Nevertheless, the court (at [97]) decided not to disturb the decision on the ground that trial judges have discretion whether or not to award exemplary damages. According to Kirby J, since the object of awarding exemplary damages is to punish the wrongdoer in 'an emphatic and a public way', the court should take into consideration the fact that this was already done by criminal conviction, or that conviction is likely to follow.

The holding of the majority of the High Court in *Gray* that exemplary damages can only be awarded in a case of negligence where there was 'conscious wrongdoing by the defendant' may have overcome two Victorian cases from the mid-1990s where exemplary damages were awarded for professional malpractice (*B v Marinovich* (1999) NTSC 127; *Backwell v AAA* (1997) 1 VR 182).

In New South Wales, Western Australia, Queensland and the Northern Territory, the High Court's decision in *Gray v Motor Accident Commission* [1998] HCA 70; (1998) 73 ALJR 45 is applicable to intentional torts but not negligence.

Award of punitive damages is prohibited under the New South Wales and Victorian motor vehicle accident regimes.[41] They are not available against motor vehicle insurers in Queensland and South Australia.[42] In these jurisdictions, however, where the court is of the view that the defendant's conduct was sufficiently reprehensible, exemplary damages may be awarded against him or her personally.

Under the Commonwealth, Queensland, Northern Territory, Australian Capital Territory, and Tasmanian legislation, the Crown is not liable to pay exemplary damages for the conduct of police officers,[43] though the officers found liable can be personally punished in this manner. Finally, aggravated or exemplary damages cannot be recovered in personal injury proceedings against a deceased estate in the Australian Capital Territory, Northern Territory, or Tasmania.[44]

Thus, in a number of jurisdictions the applicability of aggravated and punitive damages tends to be confined to intentional torts such as false imprisonment, battery, assault, misfeasance in public office, trespass to land and the like. In the

---

41. *Motor Accidents Compensation Act 1999* (NSW), s 144; *Motor Accidents Act 1988* (NSW), s 81A; *Transport Accident Act 1986* (Vic), s 93; *Accident Compensation Act 1985* (Vic), s 135A(7)(c) and, for post-20 October 1999, ss 134AA, 134AB(22)(c), 134A.
42. *Motor Accidents Insurance Act 1994* (Qld), s 55 as amended; *WorkCover Queensland Act 1996* (Qld), s 319; *Motor Vehicles Act 1959* (SA), s 113A.
43. *Australian Federal Police Act 1979* (Cth), s 64B(3); *Police Service Administration Act 1990* (Qld), s 10.5(2); *Police Administration Act 1978* (NT), s 163(3); *Law Reform (Miscellaneous Provisions) Act 1955* (ACT), s 5; *Administration and Probate Act 1935* (Tas), s 27(3); *Law Reform (Miscellaneous Provisions) Act 1956* (NT), s 6.
44. *Law Reform (Miscellaneous Provisions) Act 1955* (ACT), s 5; *Administration and Probate Act 1935* (Tas), s 27(3); *Law Reform (Miscellaneous Provisions) Act 1956* (NT), s 6.

context of these wrongs, aggravated and exemplary damages are an important affirmation of the rule of law and civil rights.

For example, the case of *Schmidt v Argent and Ors* [2003] QCA 507 involved infringement of fundamental rights to personal freedom and dignity. Helena Schmidt, a resident of Ipswich, was walking with her baby on 30 December 1998 when she was stopped by a police officer who, while inquiring into some unrelated matter, asked her to provide her address and date of birth. A computer check at the police station revealed that she had outstanding warrants for non-payment of two fines totalling $696. Acting on this information, in the early afternoon of the same day, at least five police officers went to Ms Schmidt's house. Ms Schmidt was at home with her two young children. Police officers told Ms Schmidt that they had warrants to arrest her, yet they did not have a copy of any warrant, and did not know what the warrants related to. Nevertheless, they searched the property and located a hydroponic system for growing cannabis, belonging to her partner.

When told that she was under arrest, Ms Schmidt asked a female police officer if she could be left with her children and allowed to come in to the police station the next day. Her request was refused. She was told that she had fifteen minutes to make arrangements for the children or the police would involve Family Services. The stress of the arrest brought on a panic attack, and the plaintiff experienced elevated heart rate, sweating, shaking and vomiting. It was a hot day, and she was wearing a rather skimpy 'teddy' outfit, but was not allowed to change into a pair of jeans or put on shoes. With the local children, including her daughter's school friends gathered to watch, skimpily dressed and totally humiliated, Ms Schmidt was led in handcuffs to the paddy wagon.

At the Ipswich police station the duty officer searched the computer for details of the warrants. In error he extracted details of four other warrants outstanding for unpaid traffic fines in relation to another woman with a similar name. The particulars of the incorrect warrants were entered in the Watchhouse Custody Register. Ms Schmidt was strip-searched and made to squat and 'duck walk' while naked. Before the search she was not informed that she would be strip-searched or the reason for this humiliating procedure. Some forms were brought to her. Greatly distressed, she signed the forms without reading them. No warrant was read to her nor was she told details of any warrants. She was detained in a cell in full view of male prisoners. Eventually her partner was able to provide her with a shirt.

In the early hours of the morning of 31 December 1998 Ms Schmidt was transported to the Brisbane watchhouse. She was again handcuffed, and placed in the back of a police van with a number of male prisoners. At the Brisbane watchhouse a female officer tried for some thirty minutes to remove the ring Ms Schmidt was wearing, resulting in the finger becoming red and painfully swollen. The attempt to remove the ring only ceased when Ms Schmidt said that she would sue if her finger was dislocated. She was then strip-searched again and given a prison tracksuit to wear.

The overnight detention caused Ms Schmidt more distress in relation to her children. The police told her on the way to the Brisbane watchhouse that she would not be able to stay with the baby if he were hospitalised. Despite several requests, she was not able to telephone the children until about 10 am on 31 December. She then learned that the baby had being crying almost constantly since she had left him. Ms Schmidt was released from the Brisbane watchhouse at about lunchtime on 31 December 1998. On the train journey home she looked at the paperwork that the police had given her and noticed for the first time that it related to fines imposed on another woman with a similar, but not identical name, and a different date of birth.

The episode had a serious deleterious effect on the mental well-being of Ms Schmidt. She was diagnosed as suffering from chronic adjustment disorder, and became reclusive, avoiding crowds, her children's school friends and other parents.

Following a trial by jury for false imprisonment, battery and assault, a judgment was entered in favour of Ms Schmidt against the arresting officer in the sum of $65 000, including $20 000 in aggravated damages and $35 000 in exemplary damages; against the officer who conducted the strip-search at the Brisbane watchhouse in the sum of $40 000, including $10 000 for aggravated damages and $20 000 for exemplary damages; and against the State of Queensland in the sum of $80 000, including $60 000 for aggravated damages. Under the *Police Service Administration Act 1990*, s 10.5(2), the State of Queensland is not liable for exemplary damages for torts committed by police officers, which means that plaintiffs may find it very difficult to collect exemplary damages from the defendant police officers. Apart from the punitive and aggravated damages, the court awarded Ms Schmidt special damages of $8600. The defendants' appeal was dismissed with costs.[45]

Compensatory damages

Compensation for wrongfully inflicted loss, damage or injury may, and often does, include consolatory damages, in the sense that they are awarded to console the claimant for emotional harm ('pain and suffering') occasioned by the wrongdoer. In cases of detinue and conversion, the court may also order the defendant to restore something, such as an *objet d'art* or an heirloom, of which the owner has

---

45. In *De Reus & Ors v Gray* [2003] VSCA 84, the jury found that a strip-search of Mrs Gray in the corridor of the police station was an unnecessary and unauthorised use of power, which was calculated to humiliate the claimant and cause her distress and embarrassment (she was arrested in relation to unpaid parking fines). The jury award against the State of Victoria in favour of the plaintiff for $337 000 with $3370 by way of damages in the nature of interest, was reduced by the Victorian Court of Appeal (Winneke P, Ormiston and Charles JJA) to $135 000, which comprised $75 000 by way of punitive damages and $65 000 for compensatory damages including aggravated damages.

been deprived. A not-infrequent remedy for the tort of nuisance is an injunction, whereby the court issues an order prohibiting a party from doing or continuing to do a certain activity productive of, or threatening to result in, nuisance.

Special and general damages

Special damages

There is virtually no substantive distinction between special damages[46] and general damages.[47] Traditionally, the term 'special damages' refers to compensation for expenditure actually incurred. Fullagar J in *Paff v Speed* (1961) CLR 549 at 558–9, observed that special damages are assessed only up to the date of the verdict, and must be capable of accurate quantification. They generally include fees paid or payable for ambulance, hospital, medications, medical, psychiatric, surgical, nursing, and physiotherapy services and the like, and other expenses directly attributable to the consequences of the wrongful conduct, as well as loss of income or loss of support. Under statutory reforms, compensation for past gratuitous services is now quantifiable, and thus would be included within special damages.

In *Schmidt v Argent and Ors* [2003] QCA 507, when the court assessed Ms Schmidt's special damages at $8600, the sum would have included the Brisbane to Ipswich train ticket, expenditure she incurred through medical and hospital bills, and loss of income up to the time of trial. Though unspecified, Ms Schmidt's compensation probably included approximately $40 000 in compensatory damages for loss of amenities (see below) due to her psychiatric injury.

General damages

Some torts—for instance, battery, assault, false imprisonment, and libel—are actionable *per se*, which means that the plaintiff may be awarded 'damages at large' without the need to prove that any actual loss has been sustained. These damages compensate the claimant for infringement of his or her dignitary interests (sense of dignity, honour and decorum). General damages, both for intentional and for non-intentional torts, include non-economic loss or non-pecuniary loss (pain and suffering), compensation for estimated future needs, and the loss of future earning capacity. The reforms have profoundly affected the law of general damages for negligently occasioned personal injury.

---

46. In New South Wales 'special damages' are often referred to as 'out-of-pocket expenses'.
47. See: *Griffiths v Kerkemeyer* (1977) 139 CLR 161 at 179, per Stephen J; discussed by Harold Luntz in *Assessment of Damages for Personal Injury and Death*, 4th edn, LexisNexis Butterworths, Sydney, 2002, p 64.

Though all jurisdictions have statutorily changed many aspects of the common law of damages, only the Northern Territory's *Personal Injuries (Liability and Damages) Act 2003*, s 24(a), actually states that the purpose of the legislation is:

> to abolish common law principles relating to the assessment and awarding of damages for pain and suffering, loss of amenities of life, loss of expectation of life or disfigurement.[48]

Non-economic loss

Damages for pain and suffering

Under the Torts reform legislation, non-economic loss is defined as including pain and suffering; loss of amenities of life; disfigurement; and loss of enjoyment of life. Damages for non-economic loss for past and future pain and suffering may involve physical pain as well as psychological and psychiatric sequelae of the injury. This includes any recognised psychiatric condition caused by the injury, as well as the anguish one suffers upon disability or disfigurement caused by the injury, and the knowledge that one's ability to enjoy life in future is limited by the physical or mental disability.

The idea of providing wrongfully injured persons with an amount of money to comfort or console them goes back to early German customary law, and was adopted in Europe some 300 years ago. In relation to disfigurement, compensation was originally provided only to women, on the basis that for them, beauty was a matter of vital importance—it facilitated prospect of marriage and hence material security.[49] The court has to consider psychological and psychiatric expert opinion presented by the parties, but final determination regarding the diminution in quality of life is based on the judge's or the jury's own instinctive understanding of the evidence. Indeed, given that they are subjective, and, to use Windeyer J's phrase in *Thatcher v Charles* (1960–61) 104 CLR 57 at 71–2, 'dealing in incommensurables', damages for pain and suffering do not provide compensation for quantifiable losses. In *Thatcher v Charles*, Windeyer J referred to them as 'consolatory' (at 71–2), which

---

48. See also: *Civil Law (Wrongs) Act* (ACT)—'An Act to consolidate and reform the statute law relating to wrongs, and for other purposes'; *Civil Liability Act 2002* (NSW)—'An Act to make provision in relation to the recovery of damages for death or personal injury caused by the fault of a person ...'; *Civil Liability Act 2003* (Qld)—'An Act to reform the law of civil liability for negligent acts ...'; *Civil Liability Act 1936* (SA)—'An Act to consolidate certain Acts relating to wrongs'; *Civil Liability Act 2002* (Tas)—'An Act to effect civil liability reforms'; *Wrongs and Other Acts (Law of Negligence) Act 2003* (Vic)—the main purposes of this Act are to amend the *Wrongs Act 1958* in relation to (i) negligence, (ii) contributory negligence, (iii) mental harm, (iv) the liability of public authorities, and (v) damages for injury or death; *Civil Liability Act 2002* (WA)—'An Act relating to various aspects of civil liability, to restrict advertising legal services relating to personal injury, to restrict touting, and for related purposes'.
49. Zimmermann R, *The Law of Obligations*, Clarendon Press, Oxford, 1996, pp 1026–1027.

is a more accurate description. Dickson J in the Canadian case of *Andrews v Grand and Toy Alberta Limited* (1978) 83 DLR (3d) 452 at 475–6 observed that:

> There is no medium of exchange for happiness. There is no market for expectation of life. The monetary evaluation of non-pecuniary losses is a philosophical and policy exercise more than a legal or logical one. The award must be fair and reasonable, fairness being gauged by earlier decisions; but the award must also of necessity be arbitrary or conventional. No money can provide true restitution. Money can provide for proper care …

The subjective nature of damages for pain and suffering has meant that historically, similar claims tended to attract damages which were at great variance with one another. The *Review of the Law of Negligence Report*[50] (the *Ipp Report* at [13.49]), having observed that: 'pain is pain whether it is endured in Darwin, Townsville, Burnie or Sydney', recommended that pain and suffering damages be capped on a national basis at the same level. However, statutory caps on the maximum amount that the plaintiff can receive for this head of damages differ in each jurisdiction. The Commonwealth has adopted the *Ipp Report*'s recommendation of a $250 000 limit as has Queensland;[51] while New South Wales and the Northern Territory have set the limits at $350 000.[52] Victoria has the highest cap, at $371 380.[53] Tasmania and the Australian Capital Territory have no cap on general damages for pain and suffering; however, their respective courts, like those in other jurisdictions, 'may refer to earlier decisions of that or other courts for the purpose of establishing the appropriate award in the proceedings'.[54]

Thresholds for non-economic damages

Eight jurisdictions also enacted statutory thresholds, which claimants have to meet before they can obtain damages for non-economic loss. The Commonwealth *Trade Practices Act 1974*, ss 87P–87S, and the *Civil Liability Act 2002* (NSW), s 16, specify that 'No damages may be awarded to a claimant for non-economic loss unless the severity of the non-economic loss is at least 15 per cent of a most extreme case'. Damages for non-economic loss are to be awarded on a proportionate basis in accordance with the statutory table in s 16(3) of the New South Wales Act, which sets out percentages of loss relative to a most extreme case and the corresponding statutory percentage of the maximum award. The amount payable is determined by

---

50. <http://www.revofneg.treasury.gov.au/content/reports.asp>
51. *Trade Practices Act 1974* (Cth) s 87 (indexed according to the Consumer Price Index under a formula contained in s 87M); *Civil Liability Act 2003* (Qld), s 62 (does not provide for indexation).
52. *Civil Liability Act 2002* (NSW), s 16(2); *Personal Injuries (Liabilities and Damages) Act 2003* (NT), s 27(1)(a).
53. This amount is to be indexed according to inflation: *Wrongs Act 1958* (Vic), s 28H.
54. *Civil Liability Act 2002* (Tas), s 28; *Civil Law (Wrongs) Act 2002* (ACT), s 99.

multiplying the maximum amount that may be awarded in a most extreme case by the percentage set out in the table.[55] The statutory scheme, with its percentages and arithmetical calculations, provides an appearance of a scientific approach; however, the numbers the court ultimately arrives at are highly influenced by an emotional response to the claimants' demeanour and their story of suffering. Subjective and idiosyncratic exercise of judicial discretion when determining the percentage of non-economic loss relative to the most extreme case tends to result in arbitrary awards. Long before the enactment of the *Civil Liability Act* in 2002, Sheppard AJA in *Kurrie v Azouri* (1998) 28 MVR 406, at 413–14,[56] noting that 'cases of quadriplegia, perhaps some serious cases of paraplegia, cases of serious brain damage and, perhaps, some cases of extremely serious scarring and disfigurement caused, especially to young children, by scalding or burning' would fall within the category of the most extreme cases, warned that:

> it would be very dangerous for judges exercising the discretion provided for in the section to look at the second column [amount payable as a percentage of the maximum award] before considering the first [percentage of loss relative to the most extreme case]. The second column should only be considered after a clear conclusion has been reached in relation to the first unaided by any consideration of the amounts which will be yielded by the application of the second column to the percentage selected under the first.[57]

South Australia has an initial threshold for general damages of at least seven days' impairment or medical expenses incurred of $2750 (indexed in accordance with the Consumer Price Index).[58] Once this threshold is reached, in South Australia under *Civil Liability Act 1936* (SA), s 52(2), the court has to proceed in four steps. First, it has to determine the threshold question of whether the claimant has established, on the balance of probabilities, that his or her injury resulted in non-economic loss in terms of (a) pain and suffering; (b) loss of amenities of life; (c) loss of expectation of life; or (d) disfigurement.[59] Once satisfied that the claimant's non-economic loss is

---

55. Under the *Civil Liability Act 2002* (NSW), s 26C, 'offenders in custody' (prison inmates, periodic detainees, home detainees or persons performing a community service order) who have been injured by negligence of a 'protected defendant' (the Crown, government departments and public health organisations and their employees, and other persons exercising official functions with respect to offenders in custody) cannot be awarded any damages (whether for economic or non-economic loss) unless the injury results in the death of the offender or in a degree of permanent impairment of the offender that is at least 15 per cent. The degree of impairment is to be assessed in the same way as it is under the *Workplace Injury Management and Workers Compensation Act 1998* (NSW).
56. Cited with approval by Sheller JA in *Owners—Strata Plan 156 v Gray* [2004] NSWCA 304 at [38].
57. *Kurrie v Azouri* (1998) 28 MVR 406 at 414.
58. *Civil Liability Act 1936* (SA), ss 52(1), 3 'prescribed minimum'.
59. Unless the court is so satisfied, it cannot award any damages for non-economic loss. See: *State Government Insurance Commission and Squire v Fiorenti; Worthley v Fiorenti* [1991] SASC 2897 at [2], per Legoe J.

compensable, the court will assess its level of severity,[60] which might be significant, moderate,[61] etc. The court will then allocate the value of the claimant's injury by comparing it 'with the most serious and the least serious non-economic loss which anyone could suffer'[62]—on a value scale of 0 to 60.[63] In Queensland, under the *Civil Liability Act 2003* (Qld), ss 61 and 62, a similar four-step process applies, on a scale running from 0 to 100.[64] Provisions in both jurisdictions assume that the gravest conceivable kind of injury would attract the highest value.[65] Monetary damages for non-economic loss are calculated by application of a statutory mathematical formula. For example in *Corlett v Mifsud* [2004] QSC 35, Mrs Corlett, at the age of eighteen, sustained a 'whiplash' style injury to her neck, which resulted in constant neck pain and headaches as well as periodic pain in her mid- or lower thoracic spine. It was accepted that the symptoms were likely to be permanent, and the trial judge attributed a value of 15 to the non-economic loss on the scale of 60. Section 52(2)(c)(ii) of the *Civil Liability Act 1936* (SA) provides that if the value is between 11 and 20 inclusive, the court should add 'to $11 500 an amount calculated by multiplying the number by which the scale value exceeds 10 by $2300'. This means that a scale value of 15 would attract $23 000.

Claimants in Victoria[66] and the Northern Territory[67] have to establish a minimum statutory level of permanent impairment defined as 'significant injury' before being eligible for pain and suffering damages. The requirement of permanent impairment excludes compensation for transient bruising and hurt.[68] With the exception of intentional torts, sexual assault or sexual misconduct, the threshold of 'significant injury' applies to all claims for non-economic loss, including breach of contract or any other cause of action.[69] The model of 'significant injury' is not new—for more than a decade, some compensation statutes,[70] and motor accident

---

60. *Percario v Kordysz* [1990] 54 SASR 259 at 260, per King CJ. His Honour did not spell out or define the 'well-known principles'. However, King CJ's phrase has been referred to in subsequent judgments as a self-explanatory authority; see: *Sghendo v Mann* [2000] SADC 154.
61. *Sghendo v Mann* [2000] SADC 154; *Varnas v Peake* [2001] SASC 330 (23 October 2001) at [20].
62. Ibid.
63. *Civil Liability Act 1936* (SA), s 52(2).
64. *Civil Liability Act 2003* (Qld), s 61(1).
65. *Civil Liability Act 1936* (SA), s 52(2); *Civil Liability Act 2003* (Qld), s 61(1)(b).
66. *Wrongs Act 1958* (Vic), ss 28LB, 28LE, 28LF.
67. *Personal Injuries (Liabilities and Damages) Act 2003* (NT), Div 4, ss 22–28.
68. The *Civil Liability Act 1936* (SA), s 52(1), specifies that to be compensable the injury need not be permanent, however, damages may only be awarded for non-economic loss if: '(a) the injured person's ability to lead a normal life was significantly impaired by the injury for a period of at least 7 days; or (b) medical expenses of at least the prescribed minimum have been reasonably incurred in connection with the injury.'
69. By virtue of the *Wrongs Act 1958* (Vic), s 28LC, with the exception of intentional torts, sexual assault or sexual misconduct, the threshold of 'significant injury' applies to all claims for non-economic loss including breach of contract or any other cause of action.
70. For example: *Seafarers Rehabilitation and Compensation Act 1992* (Cth), s 39(7); *Social Security Act 1991* (Cth), 94(1); *Workers Compensation Act 1987* (NSW), s 151H; *Accident Compensation Act 1985* (Vic), s 91. For an illuminating discussion of conceptual confusion between impairment and disability

compensation schemes[71] have included thresholds based on levels of permanent impairment as a prerequisite to statutory compensation. In the *Wrongs Act 1958* (Vic), 'significant injury' is defined as greater than 5 per cent permanent physical impairment as assessed by an approved medical practitioner.[72] Section 28LH of the *Wrongs Act 1958* stipulates that the assessment must be made in accordance with the AMA Guides.[73] Each party can appeal to a medical panel, which has power to determine (under Division 5) whether the degree of impairment satisfies the threshold level.

To pass the threshold for psychiatric significant injury, a claimant must be assessed as having permanent psychiatric impairment of more than 10 per cent by an approved psychiatrist.[74] Secondary psychiatric or psychological impairment cannot be included in the assessment of degree of impairment.[75]

There is a provision for binaural loss of hearing of more than 5 per cent.[76] The loss of a foetus, or loss of a breast, as well as 'psychological or psychiatric injury arising from the loss of a child due to an injury to the mother or the foetus or the child before, during or immediately after the birth' come within the definition of 'serious injury'.[77] An injury will automatically be considered significant if the parties agree to waive assessment, or if a court determines it likely that the injury would have been assessed as significant in cases where the claimant has died or death is imminent.[78] As a general rule, both the parties and the court must accept the medical panel's determination as to whether the requisite degree of permanent impairment exists.[79] Moreover, s 28LZI(1) provides that:

> No appeal on the merits may be made to a court from an assessment or determination of a Medical Panel under this Division [Division 5—Procedure of Medical Panel].

---

in federal and State legislation, see: Mendelson G, 'Survey of Methods for the Rating of Psychiatric Impairment in Australia' (2004) 11 *Journal of Law and Medicine* 446–482.

71. The *Motor Accidents Compensation Act 1999* (NSW), s 131, provides that: 'no damages may be awarded for non-economic loss unless the degree of permanent impairment of the injured person as a result of the injury caused by the motor accident is greater than 10 per cent.' See also: *Workplace Injury Management and Workers Compensation Act 1998* (NSW).
72. *Wrongs Act 1958* (Vic), ss 28LB, 28LH.
73. As defined in *Wrongs Act 1958* (Vic), s 28LG.
74. *Wrongs Act 1958* (Vic), ss 28LB, 28LI.
75. *Wrongs Act 1958* (Vic), s 28LJ: '*Regard not to be had to secondary psychiatric or psychological impairment*: In assessing a degree of impairment of a person under this Part, regard *must not* be had to any psychiatric or psychological injury, impairment or symptoms arising as a consequence of, or secondary to, a physical injury.'
76. *Wrongs Act 1958* (Vic), s 28LK.
77. In the *Accident Compensation Act 1985* (Vic), 93B(5), and *Transport Accident Act 1986* (Vic), s 93(4)(b), 'serious injury' is defined as an impairment of 30 per cent or more, which gives the claimant a right to sue for damages at common law.
78. *Wrongs Act 1958* (Vic), s 28LZN. Only impairments arising out of one incident to be assessed. These impairments must be assessed together, and impairments resulting from those injuries are to be combined using the tables in the AMA Guides or the methods prescribed for the purposes of this Part (s 28LL). Impairments from unrelated injuries or causes are to be disregarded in making an assessment (s 28LL).
79. *Wrongs Act 1958* (Vic), s 28LZH.

This provision, together with the ouster of the inherent jurisdiction of the Supreme Court of Victoria to review the decision of a medical panel,[80] is presumably intended to preclude judges from substituting their own 'diagnosis' of the injury and level of impairment.[81]

Although neither party can appeal on the merits of a medical panel's determination,[82] each can appeal on points of law, particularly in relation to the non-adherence to the detailed provisions regulating impairment assessments. Grounds for appeal could therefore include failure to use the prescribed methods and instruments[83] for conducting independent examinations,[84] or failure by the Panel to include all impairments resulting from one incident in its assessment.[85]

Tasmania and Western Australia have 'deductible thresholds', which are graded between the minimum threshold of $4000 (Tasmania)[86] or $12 000 (Western Australia).[87] In Western Australia, claims for general damages must exceed $12 000 before payments can be made, and a plaintiff whose damages for non-economic loss fall between $12 000 and $20 000 will receive a percentage thereof indexed to a statutory formula.[88] The Australian Capital Territory does not impose monetary thresholds on damages; however, it imposes a statutory maximum on amounts for legal services payable in cases where damages recovered on a claim for personal injury damages is $50 000 or less.[89] Moreover, undertaking a claim for damages or a defence of the claim that has no reasonable prospect of success may lead the court

---

80. *Wrongs Act 1958* (Vic), s 28LZO.
81. For an example of a judge seeking 'to redefine migraine headaches as a brain disorder in themselves', see: *Lincoln J v Transport Accident Commission* [2002] VCAT 300 (26 April 2002, Strong J). Strong J's interpretation of the AMA Guides and his approach to the assessment of the relative impairment ratings were criticised by the Court of Appeal in *Transport Accident Commission v Lincoln* [2003] VSCA 67, at [18]–[20], [29].
82. *Wrongs Act 1958* (Vic), s 28LZI.
83. Per s 28LH, *Wrongs Act 1958* (Vic): the AMA Guides, as well as the Minister's operational guidelines for the use of the AMA Guides or methods. On the interpretation of the AMA Guides, see: *Lake v Transport Accident Commission* [1998] 1 VR 616 at 626 and *Transport Accident Commission v Lincoln* [2003] VSCA 67.
84. *Von Bruhl v Victorian WorkCover Authority* (unreported, County Court of Victoria, Lewis J, 31 January 2003), cited in *Victorian WorkCover Authority v Syrad* [2004] VSCA 234 at [28], regarding a medical practitioner, who in assessing hearing loss, proceeded by reference to the AMA Guides, instead of the guidelines provided by the National Acoustic Laboratory.
85. In accordance with the *Wrongs Act 1958* (Vic), s 28LL.
86. *Civil Liability Act 2002* (Tas), s 27.
87. *Civil Liability Act 2002* (WA), ss 9, 10.
88. Stanhope J, Second Reading Speech, *Civil Liability Bill*, Legislative Assembly of Western Australia, *Hansard*, 11 December 2003, Week 14, p 5212.
89. *Civil Law (Wrongs) Act 2002* (ACT), ss 180–185. New South Wales and Queensland have also introduced limits on legal costs in small claims. The *Legal Practitioners Act 1987* (NSW), Div 5B, ss 198C–198I, provide that for claims less than $100 000, legal costs can only be charged up to $10 000 or 20 per cent of the amount recovered, whichever is the greater. The *Personal Injuries Proceedings Act 2002* (Qld), s 56, limits payment of costs in cases involving damages awards of not more than $50 000.

to direct that the lawyer should pay or repay to the client all or part of the costs that the client has been ordered to pay to another party.[90]

Assessment of loss manifested by the needs created by the injury

Future pecuniary needs include future expenses of rehabilitation, medical, nursing, or psychological services, pharmaceutical expenses, domestic services and attendant care.

DAMAGES FOR GRATUITOUS SERVICES AND ATTENDANT CARE

In Australia, damages for gratuitous services and attendant care are often referred to as the *Griffiths v Kerkemeyer* head of damages.[91] In *Griffiths v Kerkemeyer* (1977) 139 CLR 161, the plaintiff, who was rendered a quadriplegic by the defendant's negligence, recovered damages that included past and future nursing and other services provided gratuitously by his fiancée and family. The High Court determined that plaintiffs can recover damages for loss manifested by the needs created by the wrongful injury. It is irrelevant whether these services are provided gratuitously or, indeed, whether the provider of these services happens to be the tortfeasor, as in *Kars v Kars* (1996) 187 CLR 354.

In *Van Gervan v Fenton* (1992) 175 CLR 327, the High Court determined that even where the domestic services were provided gratuitously, the quantum of damages should be measured by reference to the market value of like services. Under the gratuitous damages doctrine, once damages are awarded, the claimant is under no legal obligation to reimburse the altruistic carers for their services.[92] In *Grincelis v House* (2000) 210 CLR 321, the majority of the High Court determined that when assessing damages for the past gratuitous services, the court should add interest at the rate of 12 per cent 'to take account of inflation'.

In separate dissenting judgments, Kirby and Callinan JJ pointed out the incongruity and artificiality of this approach. Kirby J (at 333 [29]–[30]) wrote:

> the very essence of the entitlement is that the services in question have been provided gratuitously; that the services are not usually donated for reasons of profit-making; that the amount recovered by the plaintiff is not legally repayable to

---

90. *Civil Law (Wrongs) Act 2002* (ACT), s 189; for a judicial critique of the *Legal Profession Act 1987* (NSW), Div 5C, see: *Lemoto v Able Technical Pty Ltd & 2 Ors* [2005] NSWCA 153.
91. See: Mendelson D, 'Jurisprudential Legerdemain: Damages for Gratuitous Services and Attendant Care' (2005) 12 *Journal of Law and Medicine* 402–412.
92. *Nguyen v Nguyen* (1990) 169 CLR 245 at 262–3; *Kars v Kars* (1996) 187 CLR 354 at 372.

those who provided the services; and that nobody has actually been out of pocket in money terms at all. ... To add interest upon a sum of money so derived takes logic almost to snapping point. It requires an extension of presuppositions that oblige a court, asked to adopt this course, to pause and ask where logic, in the form of 'basic legal principles', has taken the law.

In *CSR Limited v Eddy* [2005] HCA 64 at [39], Gleeson CJ, Gummow and Heydon JJ (Callinan J specifically agreeing) stated in a joint judgment that:

> It is a general principle of the law relating to the recovery of damages for negligently inflicted personal injury that if the negligence has caused financial loss, it is recoverable as special damages, and if it has caused non-financial loss, that loss is recoverable as a component of an award of general damages.[93]

According to their Honours at [30]:

> So far as *Griffiths v Kerkemeyer* permits plaintiffs to recover the costs of nursing and home care services which are to be paid for, it accords with these principles. So far as it permits recovery of those costs even though the services may never be supplied or may never be paid for, it is not only exceptional, but anomalous.[94]

McHugh J at [91] expressed the problem thus:

> As a matter of principle, *Griffiths v Kerkemeyer* damages are an anomaly. There is no reason in principle why the inability of an injured person to meet his or her needs should be regarded as a special case, no reason why that inability should be distinguished from incapacities such as restriction of use or movement or the pursuit of social, sporting or business activities. Incapacities falling into the latter categories are compensated under the head of general damages. They are compensated in the same way as pain and suffering under the general head of the loss of enjoyment of life. They are not given a special award of damages. In principle, neither should incapacity resulting in the need for services, except in respect of liabilities incurred up to the date of verdict.

Statutory reforms

The High Court's critique of *Griffiths v Kerkemeyer* damages has come too late. During the 2002–03 reforms, in most jurisdictions, tests and requirements governing compensation for gratuitous services were codified. The Commonwealth,

---

93. Their Honours referred to *Burnicle v Cutelli* [1982] 2 NSWLR 26 at 28, per Reynolds JA.
94. This head of damages 'can produce very large awards—some think disproportionately large compared to the sums payable under traditional heads of loss': *CSR Limited v Eddy* [2005] HCA 64 at [26], per Gleeson CJ, Gummow and Heydon JJ.

New South Wales, Victoria, the Northern Territory and Queensland stipulate that damages for gratuitous services[95] are not to be awarded:

- unless 'the services are necessary';[96] or 'there is (or was) a reasonable need for the services to be provided';[97] and
- unless the need for the services arose solely out of the injury in relation to which damages are awarded;[98] and
- if the services are provided, or are to be provided for less than six hours per week, and for less than 6 months.[99]

As a general rule, under the Commonwealth *Trade Practices* legislation, in New South Wales, Victoria, the Northern Territory, Western Australia, and Tasmania,[100] damages for gratuitous services are subject to a maximum of forty hours a week and a maximum hourly rate of one fortieth of average weekly earnings in the relevant jurisdiction.[101] Western Australia excludes any services that would have been provided in any event, and has a monetary threshold of $5000, adjusted for annual inflation, with calculation of damages over the monetary threshold tied to weekly earnings.[102] South Australia's *Civil Liability Act 1936* (SA), s 58, which regulates damages for gratuitous services, is ambiguous. It suggests that persons other than 'a parent, spouse or child' can only recover 'reasonable out-of-pocket expenses', though the legislation does not provide any thresholds or limits upon such expenses. In relation to 'a parent, spouse or child of the injured person', there is no mention of out-of-pocket expenses; however, the cap of 4.25 times average weekly earnings is set for gratuitous service,[103] though the court may award damages in excess of this

---

95. In some jurisdictions gratuitous services are defined as 'attendant care services', which refer to '(a) services of a domestic nature; (b) services relating to nursing; (c) services that aim to alleviate the consequences of an injury.' See, for example: *Civil Liability Act 2002* (NSW), s 15(1).
96. *Civil Liability Act 2003* (Qld), s 59(1)(a). Section 59(4) also provides that: 'In assessing damages for gratuitous services, a court must take into account—(a) any offsetting benefit the service provider obtains through providing the services; and (b) periods for which the injured person has not required or is not likely to require the services because the injured person has been or is likely to be cared for in a hospital or other institution.'
97. *Civil Liability Act 2002* (NSW), s 15(2)(a); *Personal Injuries Act 2003* (NT), s 23(1)(a); *Wrongs Act 1958* (Vic), s 28IA(1)(a); *Trade Practices Amendment (Personal Injuries and Death) Act (No 2) 2004* (Cth), s 87W(2)(a).
98. *Civil Liability Act 2003* (Qld), s 59(1)(b); *Civil Liability Act 2002* (NSW), s 15(2)(b); *Personal Injuries Act 2003* (NT), s 23(1)(b); *Wrongs Act 1958* (Vic), s 28IA(1)(b); *Trade Practices Amendment (Personal Injuries and Death) Act (No 2) 2004* (Cth), s 87W(2)(b).
99. *Civil Liability Act 2003* (Qld), s 59(1)(c); *Civil Liability Act 2002* (NSW), s 15(2)(c); *Personal Injuries Act 2003* (NT), s 23(2); *Wrongs Act 1958* (Vic), s 28IA(2); *Trade Practices Amendment (Personal Injuries and Death) Act (No 2) 2004* (Cth), s 87W(2)(d) and (e).
100. In Tasmania awards for gratuitous services do not apply to claims under the *Motor Accidents (Liabilities and Compensation) Act 1973* (Tas): *Civil Liability Act 2002* (Tas) s 28C.
101. *Trade Practices Amendment (Personal Injuries and Death) Act (No 2) 2004* (Cth), s 87W(3); *Civil Liability Act 2002* (NSW), s 15(4); *Wrongs Act 1958* (Vic), s 28IB; *Personal Injuries Act 2003* (NT), s 23; *Civil Liability Act 2002* (WA), ss 12(5), (6) and (7).
102. *Civil Liability Act 2002* (WA), ss 12(3), 13(1).
103. *Civil Liability Act 1936* (SA), s 58(2).

limit.[104] The Australian Capital Territory is governed by common law in relation to awards of damages for gratuitous care provided to the plaintiff.

How will the court determine whether or not the need for gratuitous services has arisen solely because of the injury occasioned by the defendant?

This question was discussed in *Woolworths Ltd v Lawlor* [2004] NSWCA 209, which involved Mrs Lawlor, then aged fifty-six, who while on leave from work fell on a moving walkway in a shopping complex. The accident was due to the defendants' negligence. Mrs Lawlor 'suffered aggravations of pre-existing degenerative conditions in both her neck and her lower back', which left her 'with continuing symptoms of some significance'. The court found that as a result of these aggravations, Mrs Lawlor 'suffered a major interference in her general amenity of life', which made her resort frequently to anti-inflammatory and pain-killing medication. Nevertheless, at the end of her leave she returned to work as a court officer in the Attorney-General's Department with no loss of income resulting from her injuries. She was, however, unable to fully resume her previously very active community involvement. Mrs Lawlor's damages for non-economic loss were assessed at 30 per cent ($93 000) of a most extreme case, and she was awarded $126 453.60 for past and future domestic assistance.

Using a hypothetical example of a claimant with a pre-existing condition who required assistance of five hours per week before the accident, and fifteen hours of post-accident gratuitous care, Beazley JA (Hodgson and Tobias JJA concurring), interpreted s 15(2)(b) as allowing for an award of ten hours for gratuitous attendant care services because the need for those ten hours had arisen 'solely because of the injury to which the damages relate' (at [28]).[105]

Her Honour effectively adopted the approach of Deane and Dawson JJ in *Van Gervan v Fenton* (1992) 175 CLR 327 at 350, who in their dissenting judgment canvassed the argument that, in assessing the value of gratuitous services, 'it is proper to have regard to the fact that where the services are provided by gratuitous carers in their own home, to the extent that they were providing some domestic services before the plaintiff suffered the injury, the need for which the plaintiff should be compensated relates only to those services that were not previously provided by the carer.' The court needs to make a comparison between provision of gratuitous services before and after the accident. This will involve an inquiry into the reasons for, and the nature of gratuitous services, and the length of time such services were provided to the claimant before the accident, and then clearly

---

104. Under the *Civil Liability Act 1936* (SA), s 58(3), if the court is satisfied that: '(a) the gratuitous services are reasonably required by the injured person; and (b) it would be necessary, if the services were not provided gratuitously by a parent, spouse or child of the injured person to engage another person to provide the services for remuneration', then the damages awarded are not to reflect a rate of remuneration for the person providing the services in excess of State average weekly earnings.
105. Somewhat puzzlingly, Beazley JA added: 'This construction derives directly from the definition of "injury" which includes "impairment of a person's physical or mental condition".'

delineate them in pre- and post-accident terms. It also would be helpful to develop a definition of 'need' for the purposes of gratuitous services or devise a legal test for assessing it. Statutory thresholds merely measure its 'quantity' in terms of hours, to be translated into hourly or weekly rates.

Loss of capacity to provide care for others

An obverse of *Griffiths v Kerkemeyer* damages is the head of damages for loss of capacity to provide gratuitous personal or domestic services for another person, known in Australia as *Sullivan v Gordon* damages. In *Sullivan v Gordon* (1999) 47 NSWLR 319, the New South Wales Court of Appeal awarded damages to the claimant, who suffered frontal lobe brain damage as a result of a motor car accident, for her incapacity to take care of her children.

This head of damage was challenged in *CSR Limited v Eddy* [2005] HCA 64. In *Eddy*, due to the defendants' admitted negligence, Mr Thompson contracted mesothelioma, of which he died in 2003. At the trial he was awarded $465 899.49 including $165 480 for his loss of capacity to care for his disabled wife, including care that would be needed after his death (*Sullivan v Gordon* damages). In the High Court, Gleeson CJ, Gummow and Heydon JJ (at [68], Callinan J specifically agreeing at [121]) determined that 'all the Australian cases supporting *Sullivan v Gordon* as a principle of Australian common law should be overruled'.

McHugh J concurred, noting (at [113]) that 'if the law of damages is to retain its coherence, overruling *Sullivan v Gordon* is a necessity.'

Thus, at common law the *Sullivan v Gordon* head of damages no longer exists; instead, damages for loss of capacity to care for others are to be awarded under general damages (loss of amenity and pain and suffering). However, Queensland and Victoria have enacted a restricted version of the *Sullivan v Gordon* head of damages.[106] In Queensland, s 59(3) of the *Civil Liability Act 2003* (Qld) was enacted on the assumption that at common law, as set out in *Sturch v Willmott* [1997] 2 Qd R 310, damages were available for services provided by the injured person. This case was overruled by the High Court, together with *Sullivan v Gordon*, in *CSR Limited v Eddy*. However, their Honours noted (at [51]) that the incorrect assumption of the Queensland legislature about the common law rule does not render the provision 'unworkable'. In Victoria, the *Wrongs Act 1958* (Vic), s 28ID(b), requires claimants to establish either that they actually were providing support and care before the injury occurred or that there was 'a reasonable expectation that, but for the injury, of the deceased, the gratuitous care would have been provided to the dependants.'[107]

---

106. *Civil Liability Act* (Qld), s 59(3): 'Damages are not to be awarded for gratuitous services replacing services provided by an injured person, or that would have been provided by the injured person if the injury had not been suffered, for others outside the injured person's household.'
107. See also: *Wrongs Act 1958* (Vic) s 19A(b), which applies to wrongful death actions.

The *Civil Law (Wrongs) Act 2002* (ACT), s 100, predates the Australian common law *Sullivan v Gordon* head of damages.[108] It allows the plaintiff to recover damages for loss of capacity to perform gratuitous domestic services that he or she previously rendered, or might have been reasonably expected to render to others.

ASSESSMENT OF DAMAGES

Assessing damages for past and future or potential events

Before the court can embark on an assessment of damages for future economic loss, it has to determine which, if any, future or potential events in the life of the injured claimant will be productive of such loss.

In torts litigation, the adversarial process is designed to enable the court to determine whether it believes the story as told by the plaintiff or the defendant. The story contains allegations, the truth of which each side has to establish or refute on the balance of probabilities. As Lord Mansfield in *Blatch v Artcher* (1774) 1 Cowp 63, at 65; 98 ER 969, at 970, observed, in common law courts:

> all evidence is to be weighted according to the proof which it was in the power of one side to have produced, and in the power of the other to have contradicted.

Establishing allegations of past events and their present consequences can be achieved by way of witness and expert evidence. But how does one establish possible future events and their economic consequences?

This question was discussed by the High Court in *Malec v JC Hutton Pty Ltd* (1990) 169 CLR 638. The plaintiff, Mr Malec, worked as labourer in the defendant's meat works between 1972 and 1980. The trial judge found that sometime between 1975 and 1977, as a result of the employer's negligence, Mr Malec contracted acute brucellosis (an infectious disease acquired from animals), which lasted until June 1983. Acute brucellosis is characterised by fever, sweating, weakness and aching. Mr Malec sued his employer in negligence. He claimed that as a consequence of brucellosis he developed:

1   A psychiatric illness ('a neurotic decomposition') diagnosed in 1979. It was held that the plaintiff's damages should be assessed on the basis that his neurotic condition at the time of the trial was caused by depression induced by acute brucellosis. However, it was also determined that the plaintiff's personality predisposed him to a 'neurotic condition' as the consequence of his back pain. The psychiatric condition had rendered Mr Malec unable to continue his employment at age forty-four, and made him unemployable by the

---

108.   See: *CSR Limited v Eddy* [2005] HCA 64 at [53].

time of verdict (September 1987) when he was forty-nine; it also necessitated the need for special care and attention provided by his wife.

2   A painful back condition from which he began to suffer in 1982. Apparently, brucellosis can result in the development of a degenerative spinal condition. However, the trial judge determined that Mr Malec's back condition was *not* a consequence of contracting brucellosis, and therefore was *not* connected with the defendant's negligence.

The defendant-employer argued that Mr Malec's back condition *might* have rendered him unemployable by the age of forty-four even if he had not contracted brucellosis. Moreover, since it was also established that Mr Malec's personality made it 'likely that the development of symptoms from his deteriorating back condition would have produced a similar neurotic condition even if he had never contracted the brucellosis', the employer argued that there was also a chance that the plaintiff would have become unemployable after 1982. Consequently, according to the defence counsel, damages for the pain and suffering occasioned by the depressive illness, which he developed as a result of brucellosis, should be awarded only for the period 1979–82, and no award should be made for care and attention provided by his wife.

In its analysis of events in relation to which the damages are assessed, Brennan and Dawson JJ (at 640) distinguished between past (until the time of trial) and future events. Whether or not a past event has allegedly occurred is determined on the balance of probabilities:

> The fact that the plaintiff did not work is a matter of history, and facts of that kind are ascertained for the purposes of civil litigation on the balance of probabilities: if the court attains the required degree of satisfaction as to the occurrence of an historical fact, that fact is accepted as having occurred.

This means that 'in respect of events which have or have not occurred, damages are assessed on an all or nothing approach'.[109] Thus, under the all or nothing rule, if the party to litigation can to show on the balance of probabilities that it was more probable than not (51 per cent) that a certain past event had or had not occurred, the court will treat it as certainty for the purposes both of liability and of compensation (quantum of damages). Mr Malec could show on the balance of probabilities that he did contract brucellosis, and the court treated the occurrence of this event as a certainty. He also proved that, at the date of the trial (May 1987), due to a psychiatric condition caused by the defendant's negligence, he was unemployable for the rest of his life. Therefore, 'subject to an allowance for the

---

109. *Malec v JC Hutton Pty Ltd* (1990) 169 CLR 638 at 643. See also: Lord Ackner in *Hotson v East Berkshire Area Health Authority* [1987] 1 AC 750, at 792: 'In determining what happened in the past the court decides on the balance of probabilities. Anything that is more probable than not is treated as certainty'. His lordship cited *Mallet v McMonagle* [1970] AC 166 at 176, per Lord Diplock.

ordinary vicissitudes of life', he was entitled to compensation for economic loss suffered after May 1987. Conversely, Mr Malec was unable to show on the balance of probabilities that his painful spine was due to brucellosis, so the employer was not deemed liable for any compensation with regard to it.

How did the court determine the issue of future events in which to base its assessment of future economic loss? According to Deane, Gaudron, and McHugh JJ (at 642–3):

> The future may be predicted and the hypothetical may be conjectured. But the questions as to the future or hypothetical effect of physical injury or degeneration are not commonly susceptible of scientific demonstration or proof. If the law is to take account of future or hypothetical events in assessing damages, it can only do so in terms of the degree of probability of those events occurring. The probability may be very high—99.9 per cent—or very low—0.1 per cent. But unless the chance is so low as to be regarded as speculative—say less than 1 per cent—or so high as to be practically certain—say over 99 per cent—the court will take that chance in assessing the damages. Where proof is necessarily unattainable, it would be unfair to treat as certain a prediction which has a 51 per cent probability of occurring. Thus, the court assesses the degree of probability that an event would have occurred, or might occur, and adjusts its award of damages to reflect the degree of probability. The adjustment may increase or decrease the amount of damages otherwise to be awarded.

Brennan and Dawson JJ (at 640), in a joint judgment, criticised assessment of damages in terms of percentages on the ground that 'damages founded on hypothetical evaluations defy precise calculation.' Their Honours also objected (at 640) to the use of the term 'probability' to describe the possibility of occurrence of a situation when the possibility is minimal.

In *Malec*'s case, the relevance of future events had to do with the finding of the likelihood ('a more than 50 per cent chance') that by May 1987, due to his back problems, thus independently of the defendant's negligence, Mr Malec would have been suffering from a similar neurotic condition to the one for which he claimed damages for pain and suffering. The High Court determined that in respect of such a future hypothetical event, it was impossible to conclude 'that it was 100 per cent certain that the plaintiff's back condition and consequent unemployability would have precipitated a similar neurotic condition'. The defence plea of an alternative cause for Mr Malec's neurotic condition was *not* a certainty. Hence, whatever the precise prospect that the plaintiff would have developed a similar psychiatric condition, he was entitled to damages for pain and suffering on the basis that his psychiatric condition was a direct result of the defendant's negligence. Those damages, however, had to be reduced (discounted) to take account of the chance that factors unconnected with the defendant's negligence, such as the painful condition of the spine, might have inevitably brought about the onset of a similar psychiatric condition. The quantum of damages for the care and attention provided by Mr Malec's wife was reduced for the same reason.

Malec v JC Hutton Pty Ltd is a very important case in which the High Court elucidated the distinction between the approach to assessment of damages for past events and their consequences: an 'all or nothing' determination according to the standard of the balance of probabilities on the one hand, and events that might have occurred but were not established to the satisfaction of the court and future events on the other. These latter—hypothetical—events are not included in the initial assessment of the quantum of damages. They only become relevant once factual causation has been established on the balance of probabilities. The quantum of damages will be reduced or increased to take account of the hypothetical events, unless the chance of their occurring 'is so low as to be regarded as speculative' (under one per cent).

In *Malec*, their Honours did not heed the dictum of the great classical rhetorician, Quintilian (*Justitutio Oratoria* 8.2.24), 'One should aim not at being possible to understand but at being impossible to misunderstand.'

For example, in a relatively short judgment of some 3200 words, the word 'chance' appears at least eighteen times in different semantic permutations. This imprecise use of language has given rise to novel doctrines, each claiming *Malec* as precedent, no matter how inexplicit that support is. The most important of these doctrines is the 'buffer' head of damages (see below) and the 'loss of chance' doctrine of causation (see Chapter 12).

Assessment of loss of earning capacity

Loss of earning capacity is calculated by looking at the injured person's net pay per week, multiplying that sum by 52 to find the yearly amount, then multiplying the yearly amount by the number of years the injured person is likely to lose, in employment terms. From this aggregate sum of total lost earnings due to loss of earning capacity, such costs of self-maintenance as clothing, grooming, tools and equipment, travelling expenses, books, computers and computer software are deducted. The reason for these deductions is that if you do not have the capacity to work in the job or profession that necessitated the outgoings, you save yourself the expenditure on these items.

There is also a discount for future contingencies.

The case of *Wynn v NSW Insurance Ministerial Corporation* (1995) 184 CLR 485 can serve as an example of the way in which courts assess damages for loss of earning capacity. The plaintiff, Mrs Wynn, commenced work with American Express in 1981, was promoted to a managerial position in 1985, and was made manager of authorisations in 1986.

In that year (1986), at the age of thirty, she was injured in a motor vehicle accident. The accident seriously aggravated a pre-existing condition, occasioned by a previous car accident (1972) in which her cervical spine was injured. That injury was successfully treated in 1974, with the affected area being stabilised by a bone graft.

Mrs Wynn continued with her work after the 1986 accident, and was promoted in October 1987 to the position of Director of Customer Services, one step below Vice-President. In 1992, this position attracted a salary package of $75 556 net per year, or $1453 net per week. However, as a result of her deteriorating physical condition, in 1988 she ceased work with American Express, and began to work part-time in the family business.

Her earning capacity thus diminished, her net weekly loss at the date of hearing was assessed at $1013 per week, after a deduction of $440 to reflect the fact that she was working part-time. The trial judge found that Mrs Wynn would have expected to work for some twenty-three years for American Express before retiring at the age of sixty. According to the trial judge, having worked her way to the position of Director of Customer Services, it was unlikely that Mrs Wynn would have retired by reason of marriage or motherhood. Calculation of $1013 per week until the age of sixty (23.75 years) produced an amount of $743 137. From that sum deductions and discounts would be made.

Following the Torts reforms, apart from South Australia, where damages for loss of earning capacity are set at $2.2 million (adjusted for inflation),[110] New South Wales, Victoria, Queensland, the Australian Capital Territory, the Northern Territory, and Western Australia[111] have adopted a statutory regime whereby the maximum amount for damages per week for:

(a) past pecuniary loss due to loss of earnings or the deprivation or impairment of earning capacity (up to the date of trial);
(b) future pecuniary loss due to the deprivation or impairment of earning capacity; or
(c) the loss of expectation of financial support,

cannot exceed three times the 'average weekly earnings' in a particular jurisdiction as assessed by the Australian Statistician for the year or the quarter preceding the time of the trial.[112] The Commonwealth caps damages for economic loss at twice the amount of average weekly earnings.[113] The refererence is to the 'plaintiff's gross

---

110. *Civil Liability Act 1936* (SA), s 3.
111. *Wrongs Act 1958* (Vic), s 28F(1)(a); *Personal Injuries Act 2003* (NT), s 20; *Civil Liability Act 2002* (NSW), s 26E; *Civil Liability Act 2003* (Qld), s 54; *Civil Liability Act 2002* (WA), s 11(1); *Civil Law (Wrongs) Act 2002* (ACT), s 98. Section 26(1) limits damages for loss of income to 4.25 times average weekly earnings.
112. Except in Queensland, where the amount is to be 'averaged over the last 4 quarters for which the statistician's report is available': *Civil Liability Act 2003* (Qld), Sch 2, s 8.
113. *Trade Practices Act 1974* (Cth), s 87U.

weekly earnings.'[114] Variations in the actual amounts will be considerable for the definition of 'average weekly earnings' differs from jurisdiction to jurisdiction.[115] Thus, the *Civil Liability Act 2002* (NSW) s 12(3), the *Wrongs Act 1958* (Vic) s 28F(3)(a) and the *Trade Practices Amendment Act 2004* (Cth) s 87V(1)(a) define 'average weekly earnings' in terms of 'the average weekly total earnings of all employees'. The *Civil Liability Act 2003* (Qld), Schedule 2, s 8 and the *Personal Injuries Act 2003* (NT), s 18, as well as the *Civil Liability Act 2002* (Tas), s 26(2), use the formulation of 'full-time adult ordinary time earnings', while the *Civil Liability Act 2002* (WA), s 11(3), refers to 'the average weekly total earnings of full-time adult employees in Western Australia for the quarter ending most recently before the date of the award'.

In Queensland the maximum amount to be awarded for economic loss in a personal injury claim is three times the average weekly earnings per week as defined in Schedule 2 of the principal Act: *Civil Liability Act 2003* (Qld), Schedule 2, s 8.[116] Additionally, the calculation is not to be affected by the level of earning capacity retained.

The most generous is the *Civil Law (Wrongs) Act 2002* (ACT), s 983(a), which specifies the average weekly 'all males total earnings' seasonally adjusted for the Australian Capital Territory. Differences in formulation of average weekly earnings will affect the ultimate quantum of damages available in each jurisdiction. For example, in February 2004, the Australian Statistician's assessments for Australia were as follows:

- full-time adult ordinary time earnings for males: $1000.70 (all employees: $947.80);
- full-time adult total earnings for males: $1064.00 (all employees: $993.90); and
- all employees total earnings for males: $900.10 (all employees: $754.30).

Presumably, differences in formulations of average earnings as determinants of the ultimate quantum of damages reflect the desire of legislators to ensure a degree of uniformity throughout Australia in personal injury compensation payouts. This approach has not been entirely successful. For example, the average weekly earnings in Queensland and Tasmania for the December 2004 quarter as assessed by the Australian Statistician were $728.80, and $696.90 respectively. In New South Wales and Victoria they were assessed at $803.80 and $783.80 respectively for the same quarter. However, the average weekly ordinary time earnings of full-time

---

114. Trade Practices Act 1974 (Cth), s 87U(d).
115. I am grateful to Professor Harold Luntz for bringing this issue to my attention.
116. The calculation of economic loss is not to be affected by the level of earning capacity retained by the claimant. The legislation was amended in 2005 to overturn the method of calculating economic loss used by the Queensland Supreme Court in *Doughty v Cassidy* [2004] QSC 366.

equivalents for Queensland and Tasmania were $904.30 and $880.30 respectively, which is well above the New South Wales and Victorian average weekly earnings.

The *Civil Liability Act 2002* (NSW) imposes additional limitations on damages for future economic loss. By virtue of s 13(1) the claimant has the onus of showing: 'that the assumptions about future earning capacity or other events on which the award is to be based accord with the claimant's most likely future circumstances but for the injury'. In *Penrith City Council v Parks* [2004] NSWCA 201, the New South Wales Court of Appeal has interpreted this provision as grounded in the common law rule[117] that requires claimants to establish future pecuniary loss by comparing the economic benefit derived 'from exercising earning capacity before injury and the economic benefit from exercising earning capacity after injury'.[118]

The doctrine of 'buffer' damages

Damages for future loss of earning capacity are assessed on the hypothesis that if the plaintiff had not been tortiously injured, she or he would be able to earn a particular amount of money. Brennan and Dawson JJ in *Malec v JC Hutton Pty Ltd* (1990) 169 CLR 638 at 639, noted that assessing such future hypothetical loss of earning capacity 'involves an evaluation of possibilities … [and] the court must speculate to some extent'. This is so even in the case of plaintiffs like Mrs Wynn, who have had a steady working history before the accident. The assessment of future loss of earning capacity verges on a guess and conjecture in cases where claimants did not have an established pattern of work prior to the accident, and thus cannot establish diminution of economic benefits derived from the exercise of their earning capacity subsequent to the injury. There are also cases where the injured claimant's future earning capacity is contingent on an outcome of surgical or medical procedures aimed at correcting or ameliorating the injury. In such cases, judges tend to award 'buffer' damages that reflect a chance that the contingent loss in the future may or may not occur. Thus, in *Parkinson v Kuehnast* [1996] FCA 1145 at [27], Gallop J observed that the assessment of 'buffer damages for a chance of loss of earning capacity is made not 'by arithmetical calculation but by intuition'.

Discounting for future contingencies and 'the vicissitudes of life'

In its assessment, the court has to consider medical opinions which, as in *Malec*'s case, may be contradictory in their evaluation of the plaintiff's present and future medical or psychiatric impairment, and his or her prognosis and capacity to obtain

---

117. *Medlin v State Government Insurance Commission* (1995) 182 CLR 1 at 4; *Husher v Husher* (1999) 197 CLR 138 at 143.
118. *Penrith City Council v Parks* [2004] NSWCA 201 at [3].

employment. The court also has to predict the nature of that person's future employment, the level of remuneration, the vagaries of inflation decades into the future, and political developments that may impact on the economy, and consider other contingencies that may influence the ultimate amount to be awarded.

Future contingencies, also called 'vicissitudes of life', may be adverse or positive. Adverse contingencies include sickness, accident, unemployment, and industrial disputes. Predisposition to physical or psychological ill health is considered a negative or adverse contingency, as is taking time off work because of maternity leave; looking after one's loved ones; travelling; or study. Advancement and increased earnings by the plaintiff fall into the category of positive contingencies.

When assessing damages, the court considers the likely impact of these contingencies, both negative and positive, on the injured person's earning capacity subjectively, by focusing on the particular plaintiff, not by reference to the workforce generally (*Wynn* at 497). In *Wynn*'s case, the trial judge discounted the amount of $743 137 for future economic loss by 5 per cent to take account both of adverse and of positive future contingencies, resulting in a final award sum of $705 980. This quantum was varied by the High Court of Australia, which determined that the appropriate discount for maternity leave and the possible effects of the condition brought about by the 1972 accident, balanced against the prospect of further advancement, should be 12.5 per cent (at 500).

When assessing Mr Malec's damages, the court took into account the plaintiff's medical condition (painful back), which was unconnected with the defendant's negligence but might have resulted in similar consequences to those 'precipitated by brucellosis'.

In *Malec*, the damages were discounted because (1) some symptoms from which he suffered at the time of trial were referable to the condition of the lumbar and cervical regions of his spine which was unrelated to brucellosis; and (2) his vulnerable personality made him predisposed to the onset of psychiatric disability as a result of the occurrence of some other event, whether at work or elsewhere.

Statutory discount rate for lump sum damages

The court expects the plaintiff to invest the lump sum compensation and receive a stream of income from the investment. To ensure that the plaintiff does not receive too much, the sum of the expected total future losses and expenses is reduced by using a 'discount rate' in order to calculate its present value. It seems that the statutory discount does not differentiate between lump sum awards and structured settlements.

At common law, the High Court in *Todorovic v Waller* (1981) 150 CLR 402 imposed a 3 per cent discount rate on the present value of the future pecuniary loss component of the damages award. Presumably, this lower rate of discount will continue to apply to lump sums awarded for personal injury occasioned by intentional conduct, as well as in those jurisdictions that do not have statutory discount rates. New South Wales, Victoria, Queensland, the Northern Territory and South Australia have imposed a discount rate of 5 per cent on awards for future pecuniary loss.[119] In Western Australia, the discount rate is determined by Order of the Governor (at present it is 6 per cent), and in Tasmania the rate is 7 per cent.

The process is as follows: the original lump sum for future economic loss is first discounted by, let us say, 12 per cent for vicissitudes of life and future contingencies. This—now smaller—sum is then discounted by 5 per cent to arrive at the actual sum the claimant will receive.

For example, let us assume that Mrs Wynn was injured in 2003, and her damages were being assessed in February 2005. In Mrs Wynn's case, the applicable provision would be the *Civil Liability Act 2002* (NSW), s 12(3), which now governs award of damages for future economic loss due to the deprivation or impairment of earning capacity. In calculating the total for future economic loss, the court would have to disregard any amount by which Mrs Wynn's gross weekly earnings would have exceeded an amount that is three times the amount of average weekly earnings at the date of the award. In 2004, Mrs Wynn's earning capacity would probably have been at the level of $4846 per week. If, as a result of the injury, her earning capacity was reduced to $1846, that would mean her total capacity lost was $3000 per week. The court would then reduce the amount of $3000 by 12 per cent (to $2640) for negative and positive contingencies, as was done in the actual case. This sum would be further reduced by the statutory 5 per cent, leaving the total of $2518. The statutory limit of three times 'average weekly total earnings of all employees' in New South Wales for the December 2004 quarter was $2411.40. Consequently, in calculating Mrs Wynn's future loss of earning capacity until the age of sixty, the court would have to use the sum of $2411.40 rather than $2518 as the base (disregarding $106.60 per week).

Discounting damages for 'outgoings'

In *Wynn v NSW Insurance Ministerial Corporation* (1995) 184 CLR 485 at 495, the majority of the High Court of Australia observed that since compensation in tort is paid for the impairment of earning capacity that may be productive of financial loss, 'outgoings which are deducted for the purpose of calculating economic loss are those which are necessarily incurred in or in connection with the employment or undertaking by which earning capacity is realised.' The court asks whether the particular item of expenditure is or would be necessary to undertaking the plaintiff's employment. If it is found to be necessary, its cost will be deducted from the assessment of future economic loss.

---

119. *Civil Liability Act 2002* (NSW), s 14; *Civil Liability Act 2003* (Qld), s 57; *Wrongs Act 1958* (Vic), s 28I; *Personal Injuries (Liabilities and Damages) Act 2003* (NT), s 22; *Civil Liability Act 1936* (SA), ss 55, 3.

In *Wynn*'s case the court found that Mrs Wynn would have continued to work until the age of retirement. Since she was of child-bearing age, the question arose whether the cost of domestic and child-minding help that she would incur should be deducted from her damages for future economic loss. Relying on *Graham v Baker* (1961) 106 CLR 340 (at 347), the majority of the High Court determined that 'necessary outgoings' include transport costs, tools and equipment, but not domestic help. The majority stressed that 'there is simply no basis for treating domestic help as necessary for the realisation of earning capacity.' Likewise, the cost of child care should be regarded as one of the various costs associated with having children, and not as a necessary prerequisite for the realisation of earning capacity (at 496). Consequently, neither expenses relating to domestic help nor child care should be deducted when the quantum for loss of earning capacity is being calculated.

FURTHER READING

American Bar Association, Special Commission on the Tort Liability Systems: *Towards a Jurisprudence of Injury: The Continuing Creation of a System of Substantive Justice in American Tort Law*, 1984.

Horsburgh B, 'Redefining the Family: Recognising the Altruistic Caretaker and the Importance of Relational Needs' (1992) 25 *University of Michigan Journal of Law* 423.

Luntz H, *Assessment of Damages for Personal Injury and Death*, 4th edn, LexisNexis Butterworths, Sydney, 2002.

Luntz, H, *Assessment of Damages for Personal Injury and Death: General Principles*, LexisNexis, Sydney, 2006.

Mendelson D, 'The Case of *Backwell v AAA*: Negligence—a Compensatory Remedy or an Instrument of Vengeance?' (1996) 4 *Journal of Law and Medicine* 112.

Mendelson D, 'Jurisprudential Legerdemain: Damages for Gratuitous Services and Attendant Care' (2005) 12 *Journal of Law and Medicine* 402–412.

Milsom SFS, *Historical Foundations of the Common Law*, 2nd edn, Butterworths, London, Boston, 1981, Ch 11.

Nicholson LA, 'Hedonic Damages in Wrongful Death and Survival Actions: The Impact of Alzheimer's Disease' (1994) 2 *Elder Law Journal* 249.

Tilbury M & Luntz H, 'Punitive Damages in Australian Law' (1995) 17 *Loyola International & Comparative Law Journal* 769.

Tilbury M, 'Reconstructing Damages' [2003] 27 *Melbourne University Law Review* 697.

Winfield PH, 'Myth of Absolute Liability' (1926) 42 *Law Quarterly Review* 37.

3 Survival Actions and Wrongful Death; Statutory Compensation Schemes

INTRODUCTION

Chapter 3 examines two statutory causes of action, namely survival of causes of action and wrongful death (*Lord Campbell's Act*) action, as well as various statutory compensation schemes. The two causes of action were specifically created to cure a mischief in the common law of compensation. They present another aspect of the law of torts and the nature of compensation, with which this Part of the book is concerned.

SURVIVAL OF CAUSES OF ACTION

A person injured by the tortious conduct of another can sue for damages. But what happens when either the plaintiff or the defendant dies before action in tort is commenced?

The old rule that remedies for actions in tort lapsed upon the death of either party was first abrogated in England by the *Law Reform (Miscellaneous Provisions) Act 1934* (UK). Today, in all Australian jurisdictions most tortious causes of action survive the death of either party. The exceptions are seduction and defamation which, apart from in Tasmania,[1] do not survive the death of either party.

---

1. While the *Administration and Probate Act 1935* (Tas), s 27(2), extinguishes the right of action for seduction, there is no mention of defamation. The *Survival of Causes of Action Act 1940* (SA), s 2(2); *Administration and Probate Act 1958* (Vic), s 29(1); *Succession Act 1981* (Qld), s 66(1); and *Civil Law (Wrongs) Act 2002* (ACT), s 15(2), provide that causes of action in defamation do not survive the death of either party. The *Law Reform (Miscellaneous Provisions) Act 1941* (WA), s 4(1); *Law Reform (Miscellaneous Provisions) Act 1956* (NT), s 5(2); and *Law Reform (Miscellaneous Provisions) Act 1944* (NSW), s 2, provide that causes of action for defamation or seduction will not survive the death of either party.

Defendants

In general, if the defendant dies, the action will survive where proceedings were commenced before death and there is no defence barring the claim.[2] Where no proceedings were commenced before the defendant's death, the survival of action will depend on whether the cause of action arose not earlier than six months before the defendant's death (in South Australia),[3] or twelve months (in Western Australia, Tasmania and the Northern Territory).[4] In Victoria, under the *Administration and Probate Act 1958*, s 29(3) and (3A), the action has to be commenced within 'the period within which those proceedings might have been commenced against him had he lived', namely, three years, though the court has the discretion to vary the limit. New South Wales, Queensland and the Australian Capital Territory have similar limitations periods.[5]

The proceedings are generally brought against the defendant's estate, except in Queensland, where actions may also be brought against the defendant's beneficiaries (*Succession Act 1981* (Qld), s 66). The *Limitation of Actions Act 1974* (Qld), s 11, imposes a three-year limit on all actions for personal injury and death, although s 32 of this Act provides that the beneficiaries of a surviving action may apply to the court to have the limitation period extended by one year. The court will extend the period if it can be shown that 'a material fact of a decisive character relating to the right of action was not within the means of knowledge of the deceased person or the applicant until a date after the expiration of the limitation period'.[6]

Plaintiffs

Under the survival of actions rule, the estate of the deceased plaintiff may proceed with a cause of action the deceased would have had if she or he had lived. This rule applies in cases where the defendant's wrongful conduct caused the plaintiff's injury and death, and in cases where the plaintiff had an action against the defendant for personal injury but died before trial from unrelated causes.

---

2. *Administration and Probate Act 1958* (Vic), s 29(3)(a); *Survival of Causes of Action Act 1940* (SA), s 4(a); *Law Reform (Miscellaneous Provisions) Act 1941* (WA), s 4(3)(a); *Administration and Probate Act 1935* (Tas), s 27(5)(a); *Law Reform (Miscellaneous Provisions) Act 1956* (NT), s 7(1)(a).
3. *Survival of Causes of Action Act 1940* (SA), s 4(b).
4. *Law Reform (Miscellaneous Provisions) Act 1941* (WA), s 4(3)(b); *Administration and Probate Act 1935* (Tas), s 27(5)(b). However, the court in the Northern Territory can waive the twelve months limit: *Law Reform (Miscellaneous Provisions) Act 2001* (as in force in 2004) (NT), s 7(1)(b) and (2).
5. *Limitation Act 1985* (ACT), s 16B(2). Under the *Limitation Act 1969* (NSW), s 50C(1)(a) and (b), where the action is for compensation for an injury caused by an act or omission committed after 2002, and is not brought under the *Motor Accidents Compensation Act 1999* (NSW), actions are not maintainable after whichever period finishes first: (i) three years from when the injury was discoverable by the plaintiff, or (ii) twelve years from when the act or omission occurred. By virtue of the *Limitation Act 1969* (NSW), s 50C(3), the twelve-year limitation period runs from the death of the deceased.
6. See *Limitation of Actions Act 1974* (Qld), s 30, for a definition of 'material facts'.

The estate may sue for the loss of the deceased person's earning capacity and other pecuniary losses such as medical, hospital and nursing expenses, in the period between the injury and death, as well as funeral expenses. Subject to statutory thresholds and caps (see Chapter 2), damages for the value of voluntary services for the period between injury and death are generally available, except in the Australian Capital Territory, where the *Civil Law (Wrongs) Act 2002*, s 16(3)(c), excludes damages for loss of capacity to perform domestic services. In all jurisdictions damages are restricted to the actual loss that follows from the breach of a promise to marry.[7]

When assessing damages in survivor actions, the courts in all jurisdictions have to exclude the future probable earnings of the deceased, and the loss of his or her earning capacity that relates to any period after the death.[8] The exclusionary legislation was enacted to overcome the case of *Fitch v Hyde-Cates* (1982) 150 CLR 482, in which the High Court held that damages were recoverable for loss of capacity to earn in relation to the years during which the deceased would have worked had he or she not died.

Moreover, with some exceptions relating to dust diseases, in a survivor action, damages for pain and suffering, or for any bodily or mental harm, or for the curtailment of expectation of life, are excluded.[9] In Victoria (under the *Administration and Probate Act 1958* (Vic), s 29(2A)) and New South Wales (under the *Dust Diseases Tribunal Act 1989* (NSW), ss 12A–12D), the estate can recover damages for pain and suffering as well as loss of expectation of life where the deceased who is the subject of the claim was suffering from a dust-related condition and where proceedings were commenced before the death of that person.[10]

---

7. *Succession Act 1981* (Qld), s 66(2)(c); *Law Reform (Miscellaneous Provisions) Act 1941* (WA), s 4(2)(b); *Law Reform (Miscellaneous Provisions) Act 1956* (NT), s 6(b); *Administration and Probate Act 1958* (Vic), s 29(2)(b); *Administration and Probate Act 1935* (Tas), s 27(3)(b); *Law Reform (Miscellaneous Provisions) Act 1944* (NSW), s 2(2)(b)
8. *Law Reform (Miscellaneous Provisions) Act 1944* (NSW), s 2(2)(a)(ii); *Administration and Probate Act 1958* (Vic), s 29(2)(c)(iii); *Administration and Probate Act 1935* (Tas), s 27(3)(c)(iii); *Succession Act 1981* (Qld), s 66(2)(d)(ii); *Survival of Causes of Action Act 1940* (SA), s 3(1)(a)(iv); *Law Reform (Miscellaneous Provisions) Act 1941* (WA), s 4(2)(e); *Law Reform (Miscellaneous Provisions) Act 2001* (as in force in 2004) (NT), s 6(c)(iii); *Civil Law (Wrongs) Act 2002* (ACT), s 16.
9. *Law Reform (Miscellaneous Provisions) Act 1944* (NSW), s 2(2)(d); *Survival of Causes of Action 1940* (SA), s 3(1); *Civil (Wrongs) Act 2002* (ACT), s 16(2); *Administration and Probate Act 1958* (Vic), s 29(2); *Succession Act 1981* (Qld), s 66(2); *Law Reform (Miscellaneous Provisions) Act 1956* (NT), s 6; *Law Reform (Miscellaneous Provisions) Act 1941* (WA), s 4(2).
10. The *Law Reform (Miscellaneous Provisions) Act 1941* (WA), s 4(2a), allows the estate of a person whose death was caused by a latent injury following from the inhalation of asbestos to recover damages for pain and suffering, loss occasioned by any mental or physical harm and for curtailment of expectation of life, provided the action had been brought by the deceased before his or her death and was pending at time of death. Furthermore, under s 4(2)(ca) pecuniary damages for asbestos-related injuries are limited to $120 000. The *Survival of Causes of Action Act 1940* (SA), s 3(2), provides that if a person commences an action in respect of a dust-related condition and dies as a result of the dust-related condition before the matter has been finally determined, his or her estate can recover damages for pain and suffering, loss occasioned by any mental or physical harm and for curtailment of expectation of life. Tasmania, the Northern Territory, the Australian Capital Territory and Queensland do not have special provisions governing actions for dust-related injuries.

In actions which survive the death of the plaintiff, exemplary damages are excluded.[11]

The causes of actions that survive the death of a plaintiff or defendant are simply a posthumous continuation of the causes of action that the deceased would have had to establish or defend before his or her death. This means that all elements of the action will have to be established or defended by the estate. If, for example, the defendant's estate successfully pleads the defence of contributory negligence, the estate's damages will be reduced in proportion to the degree of plaintiff's responsibility for the harm in issue.

The survival of causes of action legislation was enacted for the benefit of the estates of the deceased persons; consequently it is distinct from and independent of the statutory action for wrongful death, which confers a statutory right on the dependants of deceased persons to sue the defendant for loss of reasonable expectation of pecuniary support.[12]

Wrongful death

History

In continental European countries since the seventeenth century, the wife and children of a wrongfully killed man have been able to obtain compensation for the loss of support resulting from the death of the breadwinner.[13] However, in England and its colonies, until the *Fatal Accidents Act 1846* (Eng) 9 & 10 Vict, c 93, known as *Lord Campbell's Act*, remedies for actions in tort died with the wronged person.

The legislation created a statutory cause of action for the benefit of the immediate dependants or family members of a person wrongfully killed, in cases where the deceased would have been entitled to maintain an action and recover damages in respect of the wrongful conduct. The Australian Colonies enacted similar statutes to *Lord Campbell's Act*, though each jurisdiction's wording differed slightly. In general, the deceased's personal representative may bring an action on behalf of dependants after the grant of probate, or action can be initiated by the dependants or family

---

11. *Law Reform (Miscellaneous Provisions) Act 1944* (NSW), s 2(2)(a)(i); *Administration and Probate Act 1958* (Vic), s 29(2)(a); *Succession Act 1981* (Qld), s 66(2)(b); *Survival of Causes of Action Act 1940* (SA), s 3(1)(b); *Law Reform (Miscellaneous Provisions) Act 1941* (WA), s 4(2)(a); *Administration and Probate Act 1935* (Tas), s 27(3)(a); *Law Reform (Miscellaneous Provisions) Act 2001* (as in force in 2004) (NT), s 6(a); *Civil Law (Wrongs) Act 2002* (ACT), s 16.
12. The rights of survivors are in addition to and not in derogation of any rights they hold as dependants in respect of wrongful death: *Law Reform (Miscellaneous Provisions) Act 1956* (NT), s 9; *Administration and Probate Act 1935* (Tas), s 27(9); *Survival of Causes of Action Act 1940* (SA), s 6(1); *Succession Act 1981* (Qld), s 66(4); *Administration and Probate Act 1958* (Vic), s 29(5); *Civil Wrongs Act 2002* (ACT), s 18; *Law Reform (Miscellaneous Provisions) Act 1941* (WA), s 4(5); *Law Reform (Miscellaneous Provisions) Act 1944* (NSW), s 2(5)
13. Zimmermann R, *The Law of Obligations*, Clarendon Press, Oxford, 1996, p 1025.

members themselves. As McHugh J observed in *Woolcock Street Investments Pty Ltd v CDG Pty Ltd* [2004] HCA 16 (at [47]), the *Lord Campbell's Act* cause of action—and its Australian equivalents—is exceptional, in so far as it allows the dependants to recover 'pure' economic loss in a derivative action based on a breach of a duty owed by the defendant to a person who was tortiously injured or killed.

The legislation provides that as a general rule, not more than one action, on behalf of all claimants, shall lie for and in respect of the same subject-matter complained of. Since damages are calculated by reference to the needs created by the wrongful injury or death,[14] the net amount recovered in damages is to be divided among the dependants in 'such shares' as the court determines.[15]

Limitation provisions for commencement of actions for wrongful death vary. The *Civil Liability Act 1936* (SA), s 25, the *Limitation Act 1981* (as in force in 2000) (NT), s 17, and the *Limitation of Actions Act 1974* (Qld), s 11, impose a three-year limitation period, from the date on which the cause of action arose, for all actions brought for compensation resulting from the death of deceased. In Victoria, under the *Wrongs Act 1958*, s 20, the claimants can commence the action for wrongful death within six years after the death of the deceased person, or within six years from the time they first know that the deceased person's death was caused by an injury in the form of a disease or disorder, where the deceased person did not know before he or she died: (a) that he or she had suffered the injury; or (b) that the injury was caused by the act or omission of some person. The *Limitation Act 1985* (ACT), s 16, provides that any cause of action for wrongful death is not maintainable after whichever period expires later: (i) six years from the time when the wrongful conduct occurred; or (ii) three years from the day of death of deceased. The *Limitation Act 1974* (Tas), s 5A, and the *Limitation Act 1969* (NSW), s 50A, effectively impose a three-year limitation period, running from the earliest of the following times: (i) when the cause of death was discoverable by the personal representative of deceased; (ii) when the personal representative was appointed if he she knew or ought to have known the date of discoverability; or (iii) when the personal representative knew or ought to have known of the date of discoverability if he or she acquired that knowledge after being appointed—up to a maximum of twelve years after the time of death.

---

14. *Wrongs Act 1958* (Vic), s 20; *Compensation (Fatal Injuries) Act 1974* (NT), s 8; *Civil Liability Act 1936* (SA), s 25; *Compensation to Relatives Act 1874* (NSW), s 5; *Supreme Court Act 1995* (Qld), s 19; *Fatal Accidents Act 1934* (Tas), s 6(1); *Fatal Accidents Act 1959* (WA), s 7(1); *Civil Law (Wrongs) Act 2002* (ACT), s 28(1).
15. *Wrongs Act 1958* (Vic), s 17; *Compensation (Fatal Injuries) Act 1974* (NT), s 10(2); *Civil Liability Act 1936* (SA), s 24(3); *Compensation to Relatives Act 1847* (NSW), s 4(1); *Fatal Accidents Act 1934* (Tas), s 5; *Fatal Accidents Act 1959* (WA), s 6(2); *Supreme Court Act 1995* (Qld), s 18(1); *Civil Law (Wrongs) Act 2002* (ACT), s 25(1) and (3).

The scope of the legislation

Section 16 of the *Wrongs Act 1958* (Vic) reads:

> Whensoever the death of a person is caused by a wrongful act neglect or default and the act neglect or default is such as would (if death had not ensued) have entitled the party injured to maintain an action and recover damages in respect thereof, then and in every such case the person who would have been liable if death had not ensued shall be liable to an action for damages notwithstanding the death of the person injured.[16]

In most cases, 'a wrongful act neglect or default' will be a tort such as negligence, trespass to the person (assault, battery), breach of statutory duty, or nuisance. However, the defendant's conduct need not amount to negligence or any actionable tort, but may instead be a breach of contract or breach of fiduciary duty, for example. The wide operation of *Lord's Campbell's Act* was established in *Woolworths Ltd v Crotty* (1942) 66 CLR 603. In this case, the parents sued Woolworths Ltd, for pecuniary loss occasioned to them by the death of their son. Their daughter had purchased an electric globe which was defective in that the solder by which the wiring was fixed into the plug had been allowed to run and make contact with the brass cover of the plug. Consequently, her brother was electrocuted when he used the globe: once its plug was in use, the brasswork and anything with which it came in contact became electrified. The plaintiffs alleged that Woolworths Ltd was in breach of an implied condition in the contract of sale, namely that the globe was reasonably fit for the purpose for which it was required.

Requirements

The requirements for establishing a claim of wrongful death under the legislation are set out below.

Causation

In all jurisdictions claimants must establish a legal nexus between the defendant's wrongful conduct and the death, showing that the deceased's death was caused by some act, neglect, or default of the defendant.

In *Haber v Walker* [1963] VR 339, the deceased suffered severe brain damage in a motor car collision caused by the defendant. He developed clinical depression,

---

16. See also: *Compensation (Fatal Injuries) Act 1974* (NT), s 7(1); *Civil Liability Act 1936* (SA), s 23; *Compensation to Relatives Act 1847* (NSW), s 3(1); *Fatal Accidents Act 1934* (Tas), s 4; *Fatal Accidents Act 1959* (WA), s 4; *Supreme Court of Queensland Act 1991* (Qld), s 17; *Civil Law (Wrongs) Act 2002* (ACT), s 24.

and committed suicide some eighteen months after the accident. In determining whether the deceased's death had been caused by 'some act, neglect or default of the defendant', Lowe and Smith JJ (at 349 and 355 respectively) interpreted this requirement as relating strictly to causation (either directly caused or 'materially' contributed to by the defendant), without the limitation that the death be reasonably foreseeable.

Deceased's right of action

The claimants must demonstrate the deceased's right to bring and maintain an action for compensation. The representatives or dependants of the deceased person must show that:

(a) had she or he lived, the deceased would have brought an action in relation to the injury; and
(b) the deceased could have recovered damages in such action.

The claimants must show that complete defences such as the limitation of actions (the claim that the action was time-barred), voluntary assumption of risk by the deceased, exclusionary clauses, statutory provisions relating to dangerous recreational activities or criminal conduct would not have defeated the deceased's action (see Chapters 11 and 17).

Foreseeable loss

Claimants must show that as a result of the victim's death they suffered a foreseeable loss (*Haber v Walker* [1963] VR 339). In all jurisdictions apart from South Australia and the Northern Territory, recovery for wrongful death by dependants is restricted to pecuniary losses. Claimants have to show that they had a reasonable expectation of pecuniary support arising from a personal relationship with the deceased (*Franklin v South Eastern Railway Co* (1858) 157 ER 448 at 449, per Pollock CB). In *Blake v Midland Railway Co* (1852) 21 LJ QB 233, Mrs Blake brought an action against the Midland Railway Company under *Lord Campbell's Act* for damages for loss of dependency and for pain and suffering occasioned by the death of her husband, who was accidentally killed through the admitted negligence of the defendant railway company. The court decided (at 237–8) that the Act intended to restrict compensation to only those types of injuries 'of which a pecuniary estimate could be made'. The award of general damages in the form of *solatium* for mental suffering of the claimants was rejected on the grounds that:

> if a jury were to proceed to estimate the relative degree of mental anguish of a widow and twelve children from the death of the father of a family, a serious danger might arise of damages being given to the ruin of the defendants.

South Australia and the Northern Territory have provisions for *solatium*, which allows the relatives of a wrongly injured or killed person to claim compensation for emotional suffering as distinct from financial loss or physical suffering (see '*Solatium*' below; also see Chapter 15 for a discussion of damages for pure mental harm).

Assessment of damages

The assessment of damages is based on the claimant's reasonable expectation of benefit had the deceased lived. In calculating pecuniary damages, the court will consider the deceased's earnings prior to his or her death. This amount is then multiplied by the number of years that would have been left until the deceased's retirement, taking into account positive and negative contingencies, including prospects of promotion, ill health, possibility of retrenchment, early retirement, etc (*Parker v Commonwealth* [1965] 112 CLR 295). These contingencies do not include remarriage or domestic partnership or prospect of remarriage or domestic partnership. In *De Sales v Ingrilli* [2002] HCA 52, the High Court held that courts should not be making a separate reduction to a former spouse or partner in a wrongful death action on the basis of their marriage or partnership prospects (a greater deduction used to be made for claimants who were physically attractive).

Pecuniary loss: loss of earning capacity

In Victoria (under the *Wrongs Act 1958*, s 28F(1)(b)), when calculating damages for future economic loss due to the deprivation of earning capacity, 'the court is to disregard the amount (if any) by which the claimant's gross weekly earnings would (but for the death or injury) have exceeded an amount that is 3 times the amount of average weekly earnings at the date of the award'.[17]

At the same time, legislation in all jurisdictions provides that such collateral benefits as contracts of assurance or insurance, superannuation benefits, pension benefits and gratuities are not to be taken into account in the assessment of damages for wrongful death.[18]

---

17. *Civil Liability Act 2002* (NSW), s 12(2); *Personal Injuries (Liabilities and Damages) Act 2003* (NT), s 20; *Civil Liability Act 2002* (WA), s 11(1); *Civil Liability Act 2003* (Qld), s 54(1) and (2); *Civil Law (Wrongs) Act 2002* (ACT), s 98. The *Civil Liability Act 2002* (Tas), s 26(1), provides for 4.25 times the earning of the adult average weekly earnings as last published by the ABS; the *Civil Liability Act 1936* (SA), ss 3, 54(2) and (3), provides that any award for loss of earning capacity must not exceed the *'prescribed maximum'* which is $2.2 million, plus CPI from 2002.
18. *Wrongs Act 1958* (Vic), s 19(1); *Compensation (Fatal Injuries) Act 1974* (NT), s 10(4); *Civil Liability Act 1936* (SA), s 24(2aa); *Compensation to Relatives Act 1847* (NSW), s 3(3)(a)–(c); *Fatal Accidents Act 1934* (Tas), s 10(1)(a), (b) and (d); *Fatal Accidents Act 1959* (WA), s 5(2); *Supreme Court of Queensland Act 1991* (Qld), s 23; *Civil (Wrongs) Act 2002* (ACT), s 26.

Some jurisdictions have introduced limits on damages for loss of gratuitous services provided by the deceased to his or her dependants.[19] The claimants must satisfy the court that the deceased provided them with gratuitous services and care for at least six hours per week over at least six consecutive months before the death (or the injury that caused the death), and that there was a reasonable expectation that but for the death, such services would have been provided for at least six hours per week over at least six consecutive months. Under the *Wrongs Act 1958* (Vic), s 19B (1), where the court is satisfied that, but for the death, the deceased person would have provided gratuitous care to his or her dependants for not less than forty hours per week, the amount of damages that may be awarded in respect of the loss of that care must not exceed the average weekly earnings as estimated by the Australian Statistician for Victoria. In cases where the gratuitous services would have been provided for less than forty hours per week, the amount of damages that may be awarded for the loss of that care must not exceed the amount calculated at an hourly rate of one-fortieth of the average weekly earnings.[20]

In some jurisdictions, in the absence of statutory provisions to the contrary, a discount rate of 5 per cent is to be applied to damages for future economic loss, including damages for gratuitous services and care.[21]

Reasonable funeral expenses of the deceased person that are incurred by a person for whose benefit the action is brought are recoverable in all jurisdictions except Victoria and Queensland.

Solatium

In civil law, the family and others who fall into the category of 'secondary victims' (in French, *victimes par ricochet*) have always been entitled to compensation for damages resulting from wrongful death of a loved person under the law of *solatium*.[22] In 1936, South Australia introduced statutory provisions (now the *Civil Liability Act 1936* (SA), ss 28, 29), which grant the court discretion to award a specified payment of *solatium* for non-pecuniary loss suffered by the parents ($3000), spouse, or putative spouse ($4200), of the deceased. The award of *solatium* is to be made in addition to, not in derogation of, any other rights conferred on the

---

19. *Wrongs Act 1958* (Vic), s 19A; but see: *Civil Law (Wrongs) Act 2002* (ACT), s 100.
20. *Wrongs Act 1958* (Vic), s 19B(1).
21. *Wrongs Act 1958* (Vic), s 28I(1)(b); *Civil Liability Act 2003* (Qld), s 57(1) and (2); *Personal Injuries (Liabilities and Damages) Act 2003* (NT), s 22(2)(b); *Civil Liability Act 2002* (NSW), s 14(2)(b).
22. In Canada, under the law of Quebec (*Civil Code of Lower Canada*, Art 1053, 1056), for example, damages for *solatium doloris* include 'all extrapatrimonial damage, both immediate grief and the loss of future moral support resulting from the death of a loved one'. The criteria for assessment of damages under this head include: circumstances of the death; age of the deceased; age of the parent; nature and quality of the relationship between the deceased and the parent; personality of the parent and his or her ability to manage the emotional consequences of the death; effect of the death on the parent's life, in light, *inter alia*, of the presence of other children or the possibility of having other children. See: *Augustus v Gosset* [1996] 3 SCR 268.

parent, husband or wife by the *Civil Liability Act*.[23] In the Northern Territory the *Compensation (Fatal Injuries) Act 1974* (NT), s 10(f), provides for an unliquidated sum for *solatium*, and s 10(3)(e)(iii) of the same Act allows infant children to recover damages for loss of care and guidance.

Contributory negligence

In the majority of jurisdictions, finding that the deceased was guilty of a contributory negligence to his or her own death will result in a reduction of damages that claimants under the wrongful death action can recover.[24]

In Victoria, the *Wrongs Act 1958* (Vic), s 26(4), provides that contributory negligence by the deceased does not operate to reduce damages under wrongful death actions. For example, a wife dies in a collision as a result partly of her contributory negligence and partly of the wrong of the other driver. If the husband brings an action as a dependant, his damages will not be reduced by reason of the deceased wife's contributory negligence. At the same time, in Victoria, the contributory negligence of the claimant will reduce his or her damages. Thus, in *Benjamin v Currie* [1958] VR 259, the claimant was a driver of a motor car which collided with another vehicle. His wife, who was a passenger, died in the collision. The jury found that the claimant–driver's own negligence contributed 20 per cent to the collision. Consequently, the husband's damages under the wrongful death action were reduced by 20 per cent.

STATUTORY COMPENSATION SCHEMES

Statutory compensation schemes for personal injury and death

Australia does not have a uniform compensation scheme for personal injury and death. Instead, each State and Territory, as well as the Commonwealth, has a discrete statutory compensation scheme covering various fields of activity. For example, New South Wales has a compulsory sporting injuries insurance scheme that is not replicated in other jurisdictions.

There exists a conceptual difference between benefits paid under statutory compensation schemes and damages obtained under the common law. Depending on jurisdiction, a person seriously injured in a road accident may be entitled either to sue for damages in tort, or to claim benefit under the appropriate statutory

---

23. *Civil Liability Act 1936* (SA), s 30.
24. *Compensation (Fatal Injuries) Act 1974* (NT), s 11(1); *Civil Liability Act 1936* (SA), s 45; *Law Reform (Contributory Negligence and Tortfeasors' Contribution) Act 1947* (WA), s 4(1) and (2); *Wrongs Act 1954* (Tas), s 4(1) and (4); *Civil Liability Act 2002* (NSW), s 5T.

scheme. In a tort action, there would be two parties to the suit: the injured plaintiff and the defendant injurer or the insurance company subrogated to the rights of the defendant. A defendant who is found liable will be ordered to pay damages. These damages will be calculated by reference to the harm suffered by the plaintiff and the needs created as a result of the interaction—through the road accident—between the injured and the injurer.

By contrast, if an injured person chooses to claim under the statutory scheme, the benefit will be paid from a fund rather than being paid by the individual who caused the injury. The injured person is paid not because, having examined the interaction between the two parties, the court has vindicated his or her personal right to compensation from the tortfeasor; rather, providing they fit within statutory requirements, injured claimants will be paid because as a result of the accident they have certain financial needs, which the state has decided to meet. The law of statutory benefits is not based on the private law's notion of correlativity, but on the public law principle that the State should look after those who cannot look after themselves.

Workers' compensation

The German *Accident Insurance Law 1884*[25] was the first compulsory 'no-fault' accident insurance scheme for injury or death suffered by workers. It was copied in the English *Workmen's Compensation Act 1897* 60 & 61 Vict c 37 which, in turn, served as a model in Australia. However, until 1946 the English scheme was not compulsory.

Today, all private employers in Australia, unless they are self-insurers, must obtain workers' compensation insurance that provides compensation in respect of injury or death attributable to employment. Commonwealth public servants are covered by the *Safety, Rehabilitation and Compensation Act 1988* (Cth). As a general rule, compensation entitlements under statutory schemes are not available where injury or death is deliberately self-inflicted, or is attributable to serious and wilful misconduct.

All Australian workers' compensation schemes are 'no-fault',[26] but some schemes allow injured workers to choose between suing at common law or claiming statutory compensation, providing their injury meets the prescribed statutory threshold, which in Victoria for example is a 'serious injury'—ie an impairment assessed under the AMA Guides, as being of more than 30 per cent of the whole

---

25. *Unfallversicherungsgesetz (Accident Insurance Law)*, v 6.6.1884 (RGBl s 21).
26. This means that workers are eligible to receive full statutory benefits even if they contributed in some way to the incident, provided that their actions were not the result of 'serious or willful misconduct'; see for example: *WorkCover Legislation Amendment Act 1996* (NSW), Sch 1, item 1.3.

body.[27] Other legislatures, including the Commonwealth,[28] South Australia,[29] and the Northern Territory,[30] abrogated most rights to sue at common law for persons injured in the course of work.

Under the workers' compensation schemes, benefits will be payable by the employer when the following five preconditions are satisfied:

1. The claimant is an employee or an independent contractor covered by the scheme.
2. The claimant must show that he or she has suffered an injury,[31] a disability or a disease.[32]
3. The particular injury has the required connection with the employment, in the sense that it arose 'out of or in the course of employment,'[33] in the sense that the 'employment was a substantial contributing factor to the injury'.[34]
4. The injury has resulted in a circumstance such as death, or incapacity to work, or a permanent physical impairment for which the statute provides compensation.[35] In the case of a worker's death, compensation is payable to or for the benefit of specified dependants.

---

27. *Accident Compensation Act 1985* (Vic), s 134AB(16). By virtue of s 134AB(17), if a worker establishes that the injury is a serious injury by reference only to consequences of pain and suffering, the worker is entitled in any common law proceeding to 'recover damages for pain and suffering only'. For a detailed discussion of s 134AB, see: *Barwon Spinners Pty Ltd v Podolak* [2005] VSCA 33.
28. *Safety, Rehabilitation and Compensation Act 1988* (Cth)—common law rights abolished from December 1988; *Seafarers Rehabilitation and Compensation Act 1992* (Cth)—common law rights to compensation abolished from June 1993.
29. *Workers Rehabilitation and Compensation Act 1986* (SA)—common law rights against employers abolished for injuries occurring after December 1992.
30. *Work Health Act 1986* (NT)—common law rights against employers or fellow workers abolished for injuries suffered after January 1987.
31. *Safety Rehabilitation and Compensation Act 1988* (Cth), s 4; *Workers' Compensation Act 1951* (ACT), s 6(1); *Work Health Act 1986* (NT), s 3; *Workers' Compensation Act 1987* (NSW), s 4; *Accident Compensation Act 1985* (Vic), s 5(1); *Workers' Compensation Act 1990* (Qld), s 2 (1); *Workers' Compensation Act 1988* (Tas), s 3(1).
32. The *Seafarers Rehabilitation and Compensation Act 1992* (Cth), s 3; *Workers' Compensation Act 1951* (ACT), s 6(1); *Work Health Act 1986* (NT), s 3(1); *Workers' Rehabilitation and Compensation Act 1986* (SA), s 3(1); *Workers' Compensation Act 1988* (Tas), s 3(1); *Accident Compensation Act 1985* (Vic), s 5(1); and *Workers' Compensation and Rehabilitation Act 1981* (WA), s 5(1), define 'disease' as including any physical or mental ailment, disorder, defect or morbid condition, whether of sudden or gradual development.
33. *Workers' Compensation Act 1987* (NSW), s 10(1), relating to journey claims; *Work Health Act 1986* (NT), s 4; *Accident Compensation Act 1985* (Vic), s 83; *Workers' Compensation and Rehabilitation Act 1981* (WA), s 19; *Transport Accident Act 1986* (Vic), s 38; *Safety, Rehabilitation and Compensation Act 1988* (Cth), ss 4(1)(b), 6, 6A; *Seafarers Rehabilitation and Compensation Act 1992* (Cth), s 9; *Social Security and Veterans' Affairs Act 1988* (Cth), s 6; *Workers Rehabilitation and Compensation Act 1988* (Tas), s 25(1)(b); *Workers Rehabilitation and Compensation Act 1986* (SA), s 30(2)(a). The interpretation of the phrase 'out of or in the course of employment' has generated a great volume of jurisprudence.
34. For example: *Workers' Compensation Act 1987* (NSW), s 9A; *Workers Compensation Act 1951* (ACT), s 118(2); *Safety, Rehabilitation and Compensation Act 1988* (Cth), s 4; *Workers Rehabilitation and Compensation Act 1986* (SA) s 30A.
35. Mills CP, 'Workers' Compensation', in *Halsbury's Laws of Australia*, Butterworths, Sydney, 1994, ¶450–65, pp 863, 938.

5   The application of the doctrine of contributory negligence is governed by legislation.[36]

The major problem facing injured workers claiming compensation under workers' compensation schemes is the changing nature of the labour market. The work that used to be done by employees is now frequently outsourced. As a result, many people have become self-employed subcontractors, or independent contractors using labour-hire companies.[37] Each workers' compensation scheme has a different definition of who is a 'worker' or 'eligible person' entitled to make claims. Some definitions are sufficiently broad to include subcontractors, independent contractors, and the like; others are narrow, and may thus exclude from 'no-fault' compensation a significant segment of the workforce.

Motor accident compensation

Victoria, Tasmania and the Northern Territory have 'no-fault' transport and motor accident schemes.

In Victoria, the *Transport Accident Act 1986* provides compensation for loss through personal injury or death resulting from transport (bicycle, train, and tram accidents are included within the ambit of the scheme), or motor vehicle (motor cycle and trail bike as well as motor car) accidents, regardless of fault. Under the Act, benefits in respect of loss of earnings and medical and associated expenses are provided to all persons injured in 'transport accidents', defined as incidents 'directly caused by the driving of' a motor vehicle, train, or tram. To obtain benefits, claimants have to establish a causal relationship between their use of transport and the injury suffered.

To sue for damages at common law, the claimants have to be assessed as having suffered 'serious injury'—a disability of 30 per cent or greater[38]—resulting in:

(a) serious long-term impairment or loss of a body function; or
(b) permanent serious disfigurement; or
(c) severe long-term mental or severe long-term behavioural disturbance or disorder; or
(d) loss of a foetus.[39]

However, by virtue of the *Transport Accident Act 1986* (Vic), s 93(4), even persons whose degree of impairment was assessed at less than 30 per cent may still bring proceedings for the recovery of damages at common law if either the

---

36. *Law Reform (Miscellaneous Provisions) Amendment Act 2000* (NSW), s 10: Workers compensation and contributory negligence.
37. See for example: *Australian Institute of Management v Rossi* [2004] WASCA 302.
38. *Transport Accident Act 1986* (Vic), s 93(2), (3).
39. *Transport Accident Act 1986* (Vic), s 93(17).

Transport Accident Commission issues a certificate that it is satisfied that the injury is a serious injury; or a court, on the application of the person, gives leave to bring the proceedings.

Under the *Transport Accident Act 1986* (Vic), s 93(7)(a), damages for pecuniary loss may only be awarded if they are assessed in excess of $30 520, and they cannot exceed $686 840; while damages for pain and suffering may only be awarded if they are assessed to exceed $30 520, and they cannot exceed $305 250: s 93(7)(b). In either case, the amount which can be awarded is the amount assessed or the maximum, whichever is the lesser amount, as reduced first under s 93(11), in relation to compensation entitlements, and second in respect of the person's responsibility for the injury (contributory negligence). Damages for gratuitous services and care are excluded by virtue of the *Transport Accident Act 1986* (Vic), s 93(10)(c), as are damages for pecuniary loss suffered in the first eighteen months following the accident. There are restrictions on damages for medical and associated expenses (ss 60(1A), 93(1)). A person may recover damages not exceeding $500 000 under Part III of the *Wrongs Act 1958* (Vic) in respect of the death of a person as a result of a transport accident (*Transport Accident Act 1986* (Vic), s 93(8) and (9)). Again, damages in respect of services in the nature of housekeeping or the care of a child which would have been provided by the deceased are excluded (s 93(12A)). Under s 6(1), a maximum of $1500 may be awarded for reasonable costs of family counselling services provided to family members by a medical practitioner or a registered psychologist in respect of a death resulting from the accident, if these costs are incurred in Australia.

The Tasmanian *Motor Accidents (Liabilities and Compensation) Act 1973* 'no-fault' compensation scheme provides for scheduled benefits payable in cases where a Tasmanian resident dies or suffers bodily injury as a result of an accident occurring in Tasmania or involving a vehicle registered in Tasmania. The Motor Accidents Insurance Board, which is the statutory third-party insurer for registered vehicles (*Motor Accidents (Liabilities and Compensation) Act 1973*, s 4), has two functions. It determines the right of a claimant to a benefit—including medical and funeral expenses, for death and for disability—and its amount (*Motor Accidents (Liabilities and Compensation) Act 1973*, s 23; *Motor Accidents (Liabilities and Compensation) Regulations 1980*, Sch 2). Since the Tasmanian scheme does not abrogate the right to common law damages, the Motor Accidents Insurance Board is liable to indemnify a person owning or using a motor vehicle or his or her legal representatives for common law liability incurred for the death or bodily injury of another in Tasmania (*Motor Accidents (Liabilities and Compensation) Act 1973*, s 14).

The *Motor Accidents (Compensation) Act 1979* (NT) provides a 'no-fault' accident compensation scheme, and abrogates common law damages (*Motor Accidents (Compensation) Act 1979*, s 5(1)). The Act imposes residence requirements on claimants, but allows claims by those who suffer injury or death from an accident 'that occurred in the Territory or in or from a Territory motor vehicle' (*Motor

Accidents (Compensation) Act 1979, s 7). The Act provides for compensation for loss of earning capacity, loss of a limb, or other permanent impairment assessed 'as a percentage of the whole person equal to not less than 5 per cent.'[40] Other statutory benefits include compensation for reasonable medical and rehabilitation expenses, reimbursement of costs for alterations to houses, motor vehicles and other equipment (ss 13–19).

In New South Wales, the Motor Accidents (Lifetime Care and Support) Bill 2006 establishes a hybrid statutory compensation scheme for persons (participants) who suffered catastrophic injuries occasioned by motor accidents where no-one is considered to have been at fault—either a blameless or an inevitable accident, as where a person is injured because a driver experiences an unforseen illness or medical condition that results in a loss of control over the vehicle.[41] The new scheme extends provision of benefits available under the *Motor Accidents Compensation Act 1999* (NSW), which limits statutory compensation to persons who suffered injury in an accident caused by the fault of another driver.

The scheme sets geographical limits—it applies only in respect of injuries resulting from motor accidents occurring in New South Wales, in circumstances where at least one of the vehicles involved in the accident was covered by motor accident insurance within the meaning of s 3B of the *Motor Accidents Compensation Act 1999* (NSW).

Under the scheme, the Lifetime Care and Support Authority (LCSA) is empowered to pay for 'the treatment and care needs of the participant as they relate to the motor accident injury in respect of which the person is a participant and as are reasonable and necessary in the circumstances'. According to the Bill, the LCSA may pay for specified expenses (the medical and dental treatment, ambulance transportation, rehabilitation, respite care, attendant care services, aids, appliances, artificial members, eyes and teeth, and home and transport modification) either on an ongoing basis, or 'by the payment to the participant of an amount to cover those expenses over a fixed period pursuant to an agreement between the LCSA and the participant'.

The participants in the scheme will have to establish that their motor accident injury satisfies the eligibility criteria set out in guidelines issued by the LCSA. The eligibility criteria are yet to be drafted, but according to the Second Reading Speech, the scheme is intended to cover spinal cord injuries which result in permanent neurological deficits; or serious traumatic brain injuries resulting in a more than one week duration of post-traumatic amnesia; or significant impacts to the head; or

---

40. *Motor Accidents (Compensation) Act 1979* (NT), s 17(1)(c).
41. John Watkins (Member for Ryde, Deputy Premier, and Minister for Transport), Second Reading Speech, *Motor Accidents Compensation Bill* NSW Legislative Assembly *Hansard*, 9 March 2006, at 23; available at <http://research.lawlex.com.au/> (accessed on 17 March 2006).

cerebral insults. Injuries that may result in a need for lifetime support, such as severe burns or bilateral amputations, will also fall within LCSA guidelines.[42]

By virtue of the *Motor Accidents (Lifetime Care and Support) Act 2006* (NSW), s 7(3), 'a person will not be eligible to participate in the Scheme if the person has been awarded common law damages for their treatment and care needs, and participation in the Scheme will disentitle a person to recover damages for their treatment and care needs.' However, those wishing to obtain compensation for loss of earning capacity and pain and suffering will have to sue for damages at common law.

Criminal injuries compensation

Crimes of violence happen in every community. The problem faced by injured victims of violent crimes is that perpetrators might not be found, and those who are either known to the victim or apprehended often do not have any assets (or if they are members of the family, have assets in common with the victim). Consequently, in the past, legislation enabling the court to direct that certain amounts of money be paid out of the property of the convicted offender 'to any aggrieved person, by way of compensation for injury, or loss', sustained through, or by reason of, such offence[43] was of limited utility. In some jurisdictions the Crown can make an application for restitution or compensation on behalf of a victim in criminal proceedings.[44] There are many cases, particularly of rape, where the Crown is unable to prosecute or prove the accused's guilt beyond reasonable doubt, and even more cases where the perpetrator of violent injury is never prosecuted.[45]

The idea that prevention of criminal violence is essentially a communal responsibility, and therefore both the punishment of the offender and compensation to his or her victims falls within the scope of communal obligations, goes back to the ancient Babylonian, Greek, Jewish, and Germanic law.[46] However, it was only in the second half of the twentieth century that common law countries developed criminal injuries compensation schemes whereby eligible victims of crime are paid out of a special statutory fund.

New Zealand was the first jurisdiction to enact legislation, the *Criminal Injuries Compensation Act 1963* (NZ), which provided a state-funded restitution and

---

42. Injuries will be assessed using the functional independence measure (FIM), whereby the injured person must also score 5 or less on such functions as self-care, mobility, locomotion, communication, social interaction and cognitive function. A FIM rating of 1 indicates that the person requires total assistance and a rating of 7 would indicate that they are completely independent. A rating of 5 or less on an index item indicates that the person requires some supervision to perform the task. A paediatric version of FIM will be used for assessing children's brain injury.
43. Now repealed: *Crimes Act 1900* (NSW), s 437.
44. See for example: *Victims of Crime Act 2001* (SA), s 12.
45. See *Criminal Injuries Compensation Act 2003* (WA), ss 13, 14, 16, 17.
46. Freckelton I, *Criminal Injuries Compensation: Law, Practice and Policy*, LBC Information Services, Sydney, 2001, pp 12–14.

compensation scheme for victims of crime. However, this Act was subsumed under the *Accident Compensation Act 1972* (NZ), with the result that certain specific rights it created for victims of crime, including compensation for pain and suffering, gave way to general entitlements under the national 'no-fault' accident scheme.[47]

The United Kingdom operated a non-statutory scheme for compensating those who suffered personal injury or death directly attributable to a 'crime of violence'[48] for over two decades before enacting the *Criminal Justice Act 1988* (UK), superseded by *Criminal Injuries Compensation Act 1995* (UK).

In Australia, the *Criminal Injuries Compensation Act 1972* (Vic) was the first statutory scheme to enable victims of crime to recover compensation for personal injury. It served as a model for other jurisdictions; however, in the 1990s this area of law underwent profound alterations relating to limitations on and schedules setting maximum amounts payable for compensable injuries, imposing caps on compensation[49] and introducing thresholds for eligibility.[50] For example, the *Victims Support and Rehabilitation Act 1996* (NSW), Schedule 1, cl 5(a), provides that compensation for nervous shock: 'is payable only if the symptoms and disability persist for more than 6 weeks …'. In *Victims Compensation Fund Corporation v Brown & Ors* [2003] HCA 54, Mr Brown, the applicant, answered a knock at his front door. He was violently attacked, and during a lengthy struggle he was punched, kicked and stabbed in the stomach area with a broken bottle. The attack was witnessed by Mr Brown's companion. The assailant was later convicted of malicious wounding. Mr Brown and the witness were unsuccessful in claiming statutory compensation because the court found that although each had 'symptoms' of shock which persisted for six weeks, neither could establish a 'disability'.[51]

An award of statutory compensation does not affect a person's right to commence or maintain common law proceedings.[52] In Western Australia, for example, the claimant may be required to enforce other remedies available either in tort or

---

47. Ibid, p 22.
48. Ibid, p 18.
49. *Victims Support and Rehabilitation Act 1996* (NSW), ss 18, 19; *Crimes (Victims Assistance) Act 1989* (NT), s 13; *Victims of Crime Act 2001* (SA), s 20; *Criminal Injuries Compensation Act 1976* (Tas), s 6; *Victims of Crime Assistance Act 1996* (Vic), ss 8, 8A, 10, 10A, 12, 13; *Criminal Injuries Compensation Act 2003* (WA), ss 31–34; *Victims of Crime (Financial Assistance) Act 1983* (ACT), ss 10, 19; *Criminal Offence Victims Act 1995* (Qld), s 25. See also: *In the matter of an application under the Criminal Injuries Compensation Act 1983* [2004] ACTSC 60.
50. The *Victims Support and Rehabilitation Act 1996* (NSW), s 20(1), has a $2400 monetary threshold for recovery.
51. In *Victims Compensation Fund Corporation v GM & 5 Ors* [2004] NSWCA 185 at [136], the New South Wales Court of Appeal determined that for the purposes of the *Victims Support and Rehabilitation Act 1996* (NSW), 'bodily harm' was only established if there was hurt or injury calculated to interfere with the health or comfort of the victim and that the hurt or injury need not be permanent, but must be more than merely transient and trifling.
52. *Victims Support and Rehabilitation Act 1996* (NSW), s 43; *Criminal Offence Victims Act 1995* (Qld), s 22; *Criminal Injuries Compensation Act 1976* (Tas), s 9.

under contract of insurance.[53] However, to the extent of any payment made by it, the State is subrogated, to all the rights and remedies the injured person has at common law, for the injury against anyone responsible for the injury.[54]

In general, under the legislative schemes, the victims of crime are defined as persons:

> who suffered harm from a violation of the State's criminal laws (a) because a crime is committed that involves violence committed against the person in a direct way; or (b) because the person is a member of the immediate family of, or is a dependant of, a victim mentioned in paragraph (a); or (c) because the person has directly suffered the harm in intervening to help a victim mentioned in paragraph (a).[55]

The Tasmanian *Criminal Injuries Compensation Act 1976*, s 4(1)(a), specifies that: 'Compensation may be awarded under this Act where a person is killed or suffers injury—(a) as a result of the act or omission of another that constitutes an offence or would have constituted an offence, but for the fact that that other had not attained a specified age, or was insane, or had other grounds of excuse or justification at law for his act or omission'. Other jurisdictions categorise eligible applicants or claimants as 'primary', 'immediate',[56] 'secondary' and/or 'related'[57] victims.[58]

In general, statutory compensation can be awarded for:

- prescribed injuries received by the victim;
- compensation for financial loss (actual expenses, loss of earnings, and in certain cases, loss of personal effects), incurred by the victim as a direct result of any such compensable injury. The *Criminal Injuries Compensation Act 1976*

---

53. *Criminal Injuries Compensation Act 2003* (WA), s 21.
54. In other words, the State can recover the payments made to the claimant, if he or she is awarded common law compensation for the same injury: *Victims Support and Rehabilitation, 1996* (NSW), s 43; *Criminal Offence Victims Act 1995* (Qld), s 22; see also: *Victims of Crime Assistance Act 1996* (Vic), s 51; *Criminal Injuries Compensation Act 1976* (Tas), s 9; *Criminal Injuries Compensation Act 2003* (WA), ss 43, 68, 69; *Crimes (Victims Assistance) Act 1982* (NT), ss 21, 22; *Victims of Crime Act 2001* (SA), s 28; *Victims of Crime (Financial Assistance) Act 1983* (ACT), ss 53, 54, 56, 57, 58.
55. *Criminal Offence Victims Act 1995* (Qld), s 5.
56. The *Victims of Crime Act 2001* (SA), ss 4, 17, specify that the claimant must be: '(a) an immediate victim of the offence; and [that] (b) at least one of the following conditions is satisfied: (i) the offence involved the use of violence or a threat of violence against the person or a member of the person's immediate family; (ii) the offence created a reasonable apprehension of imminent harm to the person or a member of the person's immediate family; (iii) the offence is a sexual offence; (iv) the offence caused death or physical injury.'
57. *Victims of Crime (Financial Assistance) Act 1983* (ACT), s 2; *Victims of Crime Act 1994* (ACT), Dictionary; *Victims Support and Rehabilitation Act 1996* (NSW), ss 8, 9; *Victims of Crime Assistance Act 1996* (Vic), Pt II.
58. The *Criminal Injuries Compensation Act 1976* (Tas), s 4(5), allows compensation: 'to any person responsible for the maintenance of the victim who has suffered pecuniary loss as a result of the injury or death; and in a case where the compensation is payable in respect of the death of the victim, to or for the benefit of any one or more of his dependants or, if there are no such dependants, to any person who has incurred expenses as a result of the victim's death.' See also: *Criminal Injuries Compensation Act 2003* (WA), s 10.

(Tas), s 4(6), allows the court (Commissioner) to award compensation to 'any person suffering loss by reason of the destruction of, or the damage to, the property';[59] and
- funeral expenses associated with the burial of the primary victim.[60]

There is no general pattern with respect to compensation for pain and suffering. Tasmanian legislation provides compensation for pain and suffering of the victim arising from the injury.[61] Likewise, in the Northern Territory, the court may provide assistance in respect of pain and suffering and mental distress, but damages for grief are excluded.[62] In contrast, the South Australian *Victims of Crime Act 2001*, ss 17(2) and 20, specifically provide that statutory compensation is available for grief suffered in consequence of the commission of a homicide to a spouse of the deceased victim (not exceeding $4200), or—where the deceased victim was a child—a parent of the deceased victim (not exceeding $3000). In the Australian Capital Territory, under the *Victims of Crime (Financial Assistance) Act 1983*, s 10(e), an amount not exceeding $50 000 can be awarded for pain and suffering if the victim is a police officer, ambulance officer or firefighter, and the criminal injury was sustained in the course of the exercise of his or her functions. Primary victims who sustained criminal injury as a result of a violent sexual offence are eligible for 'special assistance by way of reasonable compensation for pain and suffering in an amount of no more than $50 000' (s 10(f)). New South Wales and Victoria have abolished damages for pain and suffering, and instead have payments for approved counselling services.[63]

In the Queensland *Criminal Offence Victims Act 1995*, the Compensation Table contained in Schedule 1 provides for minor (2 to 10 per cent), moderate (10 to 20 per cent) and severe (20 to 34 per cent) nervous shock as a percentage of the

---

59. The *Criminal Injuries Compensation Act 1976* (Tas), Pt 3, s 16, empowers the court '(a) to make restraining orders that the property of a defendant is not to be disposed of, or otherwise dealt with, by any person except in such manner and in such circumstances, if any, as are specified in the order; and (b) if the judge is satisfied that circumstances require it—that the Public Trustee or another person specified in the order is to take control of that property.'
60. *Victims of Crime Assistance Act 1996* (Vic), s 15; *Victims of Crime Act 2001* (SA), s 17(4); *Criminal Offence Victims Act 1995* (Qld), s 19(1)(c); see also: *Crimes (Victims Assistance) Act 1982* (NT), s 9(1) (compensation can be gained for 'expenses actually incurred as a result of the injury suffered by, or the death of, the victim'); *Criminal Injuries Compensation Act 1976* (Tas), s 4(3)(a) (compensation can be gained for 'expenses actually incurred as a result of the injury or death'); *Victims Support and Rehabilitation Act 1996* (NSW), s 18(1)(a) (compensation can be gained for 'actual expenses' resulting from the crime); *Criminal Injuries Compensation Act 2003* (WA), s 6(3) (compensation can be gained for 'loss' for which 'damages could be awarded to the relative under the *Fatal Accidents Act 1959* if the death of the victim [was] caused by the wrongful act, neglect or default of another'); *Victims of Crime (Financial Assistance) Act 1983* (ACT), s 17(1)(a) (compensation can be gained for 'the expense reasonably incurred by or on behalf of the related victim as a consequence of the primary victim's criminal injury and death').
61. *Criminal Injuries Compensation Act 1976* (Tas), s 4(3)(d).
62. *Crimes (Victims Assistance) Act 1989* (NT), s 9(e) and (f).
63. *Victims Support and Rehabilitation Act 1996* (NSW), s 21; *Victims of Crime Assistance Act 1996* (Vic), s 8(2)(a).

prescribed maximum amount (scheme maximum). Western Australia has very comprehensive provisions governing compensability of injury by way of 'mental and nervous shock'. However, under s 35(2) of the *Criminal Injuries Compensation Act 2003* (WA): 'compensation award for mental and nervous shock suffered by a victim as a consequence of the commission of an offence, or for any loss in respect of such shock' cannot be made unless the assessor is satisfied:

(a) that the victim also suffered bodily harm or became pregnant as a consequence of the commission of the offence;
(b) that the victim was the person against whom, or against whose property, the offence was committed;
(c) that a person other than the victim died or suffered injury as a consequence of the offence and the victim was personally present when or immediately after the offence was committed;
(d) that immediately before the offence was committed the victim was the parent or step-parent of a person who died as a consequence of the commission of the offence; or
(e) that immediately before the offence was committed the victim:
  (i) was a close relative of a person who suffered injury or died as a consequence of the commission of the offence; and
  (ii) was living with that person.

At the same time, assessors 'must not make a compensation award in favour of a close relative of the person for mental and nervous shock suffered by the close relative as a result of the death or injury' unless they are satisfied (a) that a person died or was injured as a consequence of the commission of an offence; and (b) that the death occurred or the injury was suffered when the person was committing a separate offence.[64] Moreover, by virtue of s 36:

An assessor must not make a compensation award in favour of a victim, or a close relative of a deceased victim, if the assessor is of the opinion (a) that there is a relationship or connection between the person who committed the offence and the victim or close relative; and (b) that by reason of the relationship or connection any money paid under the award is likely to benefit or advantage the person who committed the offence.

This provision seems to be applicable to all compensatory awards under the *Criminal Injuries Compensation Act 2003* (WA).

---

64. *Criminal Injuries Compensation Act 2003* (WA), s 35(3).

FURTHER READING

Luntz H, *Assessment of Damages for Personal Injury and Death, General Principles*, LexixNexis, Sydney, 2006.

Freckelton I, *Criminal Injuries Compensation: Law, Practice and Policy*, LBC Information Services, Sydney, 2001.

Kleeberg JM, 'From Strict Liability to Workers' Compensation: The Prussian Railroad Law, the German Liability Act, and the Introduction of Bismarck's Accident Insurance in Germany, 1838–84' (2003) 36 *New York University Journal of International Law and Policy* 53.

Mendelson D, 'Jurisprudential Legerdemain: Damages for Gratuitous Services and Attendant Care' (2005) 12 *Journal of Law and Medicine* 402–412.

Mendelson G, 'Survey of methods for the rating of psychiatric impairment in Australia' (2004) 11 *Journal of Law and Medicine* 446–81.

Mendelson G, 'Outcome-related compensation: in search of a new paradigm' in Halligan PW, Bass C, Oakley DA (eds), *Malingering and Illness Deception*. Oxford: Oxford University Press, 2003, at 220–231.

Part II

INTENTIONAL TORTS

This part of the book introduces you to the tort of trespass with its three species: trespass to the person (battery, assault and false imprisonment); trespass to land; and torts involving intentional interference with goods. There is also a discussion of action on the case for the intentional infliction of physical harm, action on the case for the intentional infliction of nervous shock, malicious prosecution, the tort of collateral abuse of process, misfeasance in public office, and the tort of breach of confidence.

Intentional torts form the oldest part of the law of torts. Trespassory torts lie at the very foundation of the common law. They safeguard from infringement by others, including the State, the legal rights of individuals to personal, physical and proprietary integrity. The rules and principles that govern intentional torts were created to serve the needs of a feudal, agricultural society. Yet because intentional torts involve the most fundamental social relationships between people—to each and every individual, in the community—their universality has both shaped and reflected the ever-evolving notion of a civil society. Common law jurisprudence has created a rich and varied tapestry of intentional causes of action.

ACTIONS *IN PERSONAM* AND ACTIONS *IN REM*

In all countries whose legal systems are substantially derived from Roman law, civil actions in tort are divided into actions *in personam* (personal actions) and actions *in rem* (real actions). Personal actions or personal claims are so called not because the litigation is between persons (it always is), but because the gist of the legal relationship is one that concerns legal interests in personal autonomy between persons.

In Roman law, for culpability to arise there had to be actual damage or harm. At common law, a person may be at fault not only through causing actual (material) personal or economic damage but also through intentional and direct action infringing legal rights of another person with or without causing actual injury. The latter kind of culpability is characteristic of trespass.

In Roman law, actions *in rem* were based on the concept of ownership of the *res* (thing or land), and the actions protecting ownership were regarded as part of the law of property.[1] The common law, however, has developed the concept of possession, which vests the possessor of a thing or land with certain legal rights over it. Nevertheless, both in Roman and in Anglo-Australian common law, actions *in rem* differ from actions *in personam* because the gist of these claims is the legal relationship that exists between a person and a thing. The question in actions *in rem* is: who is the true owner of and or has better possessory rights to the *res*?[2] At the same time, at common law, actions relating to possessory rights form part of the law of torts rather than the law of property.

This Part examines actions *in personam* such as trespass to the person (Chapter 4); miscellaneous actions on the case for intentional infliction of harm (Chapter 6); deceit and injurious falsehood (Chapter 7); *actions in rem*, in particular, trespass to land (Chapter 5); and torts of intentional interference with goods (Chapter 8); as well as defences to intentional torts (Chapter 9).

---

1. Milton JRL, 'The Law of Neighbours in South Africa' (1969) *Acta Juridica* 123 at 134.
2. Metzger E (ed), *A Companion to Justinian's Institutes*, Cornell University Press, Ithaca, New York, 1998, p 218.

Trespass to the Person (Battery, Assault and False Imprisonment)

INTRODUCTION

'Trespass' is a generic term encompassing all wrongful direct and intentional interference with the person, his or her land and chattels (goods). Although 'assault' is a separate tort with its own set of elements, it is often, mistakenly, used as an appellation for the tort of battery.

In the second part of the twentieth century, the tort of negligence was the preferred cause of action even where on the facts, an intentional tort, such as battery or assault, was more apposite (for example *Gray v Motor Accident Commission* (1998) 196 CLR 1 discussed in Chapter 2). There was a strong, if misguided, conception that there were too many torts, and that as many of them as possible should be incorporated into or subsumed under the tort of negligence. However, following the limitations imposed by the Torts Reform legislation on recovery of damages for negligence (discussed in Chapter 2), it will be prudent to sue in trespass rather than negligence in cases where a claim for injury sounds in both.

This chapter examines the generic tort of trespass to the person, and its species: torts of battery, assault, and false imprisonment.

HISTORICAL ORIGINS OF THE TORT OF TRESPASS TO THE PERSON

Historical overview

The concept of early medieval kingship incorporated the notion of *'parens patriae'*, whereby kings were considered to be guardians of individual and social interests of all kinds, including that of internal and external peace of the realm.[1] If the particular social interest was deemed worthy of royal protection, Chancery would issue a writ, which imposed a duty upon individuals to safeguard that interest; its breach could be prosecuted through the royal courts. Thus, in the thirteenth century the law began to enforce duties imposed on individuals to secure interests in freedom from violence and direct injury. These interests became individual legal rights. When Chancery commenced to issue writs of trespass in 1252, its primary purpose was to replace the customary laws of self-redress and vengeance with the public machinery of legal process manifested by criminal prosecution, and compensation through an award of damages.[2] The writ of trespass allowed for trial by jury, though defendants were permitted to demand trial by battle.[3] The objective behind the original writ of trespass known as *vi et armis et contra pacem Domini Regis* (with force and arms and contrary to the King's peace) was punishment of offenders against the royal peace. The action in trespass was based on the principle that, through the misuse of force (*vi et armis*), the wrongdoer was at fault. The fault (Latin *dolus* or *culpa*) in trespass, and torts generally, is acting in a way, or doing something, that the law does not permit. The damage in trespass lay in the breach of peace (*contra pacem*).

Initially forcible trespass was interpreted literally—there had to be a breach of peace by way of force of arms. However, it soon came to mean any direct and intentional invasion of the plaintiff's rights which might lead to instant retaliation or vengeance, and hence to breach of the peace.

Conceptual basis of trespass to the person

The allegation of breach of the royal peace had important implications. To begin with, the allegation in the pleadings of offence against the royal peace meant that the culprit–defendant had to appear before the royal courts. This was a clever way of removing a significant portion of jurisdiction from customary and baronial courts. In terms of substantive law, the allegation of breach of peace determined the issue of fault.

It also meant that action in trespass to the person did not require proof of actual damage. This was because the use of force involved a breach of the royal peace and thus was in itself wrongful; therefore personal damage was not a necessary element of liability. Later on, when the civil tort of trespass developed separately, it did so without losing its criminal law characteristic of being primarily an offence against the royal or public peace. As late as 1694, a defendant found liable in a civil action

---

1. Pound R, 'Interests of Personality', in *Harvard Law Review*, Vol 28, No 4, 1915, pp 343–365.
2. Posner RA, *Law and Literature: A Misunderstood Relation*, Harvard University Press, Cambridge, 1988, p 27.
3. Bracton, H, *On the Laws and Customs of England*, (Thorne SE, William S Hein and Co, Inc, trans and revd), Buffalo, New York, 1997, Vol 3, p 341.

for trespass, besides having to pay damages to the injured plaintiff, also had to pay a fine to the Crown.[4]

Since the rationale behind the writ of trespass was to prevent conduct that would lead to immediate retaliation, the law was not interested in the *intentions* of the defendant, but rather in the *causal sequence* of events. The fault was held to be an unlawful conduct leading to the breach, or threatened breach, of the royal peace. This meant that, originally, trespass would apply to all direct injuries, even those not intended by the defendant.

In fact, until the development of action on the case in the middle of the fourteenth century, there was no remedy for indirect injuries. Modern law has almost completely abandoned the classification of injuries as direct or indirect, and instead looks at whether the injury was caused by intentional or negligent conduct of the wrongdoer.

Fault, for the purposes of the modern law of trespass, involves intending to do, and then doing, something the law regards as wrongful, for example touching a person without his or her permission. It also includes reckless or deliberate intent to perform the act resulting in direct contact. For example, while reversing out of the driveway, a driver notices in the rear vision mirror a toddler running across the driveway. Nevertheless, the driver allows the car to roll back so that it eventually touches the toddler. The fault of effecting contact with the body of the toddler with the wheel of the car without consent or legal justification will be imputed to the driver.

However, it is arguable that if the toddler's father runs after her into the driveway, retrieves the frightened but otherwise unharmed child, and gives her a smack while pointing to the driveway and saying 'No, no, Claire must not run into driveways', his conduct, though technically trespassory, will be excused on the basis of 'reasonable chastisement'.[5]

Today, the tort of trespass to the person guards not only the right of individuals to physical integrity, but also any interference with their person that is offensive to a reasonable sense of honour and dignity. Therefore, trespass requires no proof of actual damage or physical injury. The direct and intentional invasion of the plaintiff's rights is regarded as a wrong in itself.

The nature of damages for trespass to the person

In trespass, the tortfeasor is liable for all the damage directly traceable—in the sense of flowing 'naturally'—from the trespassory act. For example, when a person suffers physical or psychiatric harm as a result of wrongful interference with his or

---

4. Fleming JG, *The Law of Torts*, 9th edn, The Law Book Company Ltd, Sydney, 1998, p 21.
5. Reasonable chastisement, as against unreasonable, inappropriate or excessive chastisement, is still a defence to battery and assault: *New South Wales v Lepore; Samin v Queensland; Rich v Queensland* [2003] HCA 4 at [12], [78], [79] and [132]; see also: *Ryan v Fildes* [1938] 3 All ER 517.

her body, the defendant may be ordered to pay compensatory damages as well as nominal damages. In addition, aggravated damages may be awarded in recognition that the tort of trespass protects from injury to honour and dignity. At the same time, according to *Carson v John Fairfax & Sons Ltd* (1992) 67 ALJR 634 (at 646), in torts generally, be they false imprisonment, battery, negligence or defamation, 'any award of aggravated damages must be confined to what is truly compensation for the relevant harm and must not include any element of punitive damages'.

In some instances, the court will impose exemplary or punitive damages if the tortious conduct in question was particularly oppressive, arbitrary and unconscionable. For example, in *Canterbury Bankstown Rugby League Football Club Ltd v Rogers; Bugden v Rogers*,[6] in a match played between two professional rugby clubs, Rogers' jaw was broken when he was struck on the face by Bugden's forearm. Bugden played for the opposing club, Canterbury Bankstown. The court determined that Bugden struck Rogers' face deliberately and with intention to hurt him.[7] Rogers was awarded aggravated damages in addition to compensatory damages because the effect of Bugden's wrongful actions was public humiliation of Rogers as a professional footballer.

The court also awarded exemplary damages to punish Bugden for actions which were intended to hurt Rogers and which carried with them a possibility of killing. Such intentional and illegitimate conduct on the part of players was something, which in the opinion of the court, '*should be clearly recognised and clearly deterred*' [emphasis provided].[8]

Should victims of serious battery and assault have a choice of taking action for damages in civil courts before the matter is prosecuted in criminal courts?

The rule known as 'the felonious tort rule', which used to preclude a plaintiff who was a victim of a criminal offence committed by the defendant from obtaining compensation in the civil courts 'unless the defendant [had] been prosecuted or a reasonable excuse [had] been shewn for his not having been prosecuted' (*Smith v Selwyn* [1914] 3 KB 98 at 102), has been abolished by statute in Victoria and Tasmania.[9] In *Williams v Spautz* (1992) 174 CLR 509 at 545, Deane J observed that modern courts tend to treat this common law rule as 'archaic'. Deane J's comment would suggest that persons who have been victims of such criminal offences as rape, beatings and serious assault, having reported the offence to the police, should consider suing their attackers for damages in a private action, before the defendants dissipate most or all their assets on a criminal defence.

---

6. (1993) Aust Torts Reports ¶81–246.
7. Ibid at 62,543.
8. Ibid at 62,546.
9. *Supreme Court Act 1986* (Vic), s 41; *Criminal Code Act 1924* (Tas), s 9(3). In the United Kingdom the rule was abolished by the House of Lords in *Rose v Ford* [1937] AC 826.

THE TORT OF BATTERY

Definition

The tort of battery has been defined as wrongful conduct that directly and intentionally or negligently brings about harmful or offensive contact with the person of another.[10]

The tort of battery was considered in the case of *Collins v Wilcock* [1984] 1 WLR 1172, which involved a police officer, Tracey Wilcock, who attempted to question Alexis Collins whom she suspected of soliciting clients. Soliciting was illegal under the relevant Local Government Act. When Collins shrugged her shoulders and began to walk away, Wilcock followed her, taking hold of Collins in order to restrain her. The suspect scratched the officer's arm, and was then arrested. Collins was charged and convicted of assaulting the police officer in execution of her duty. Collins appealed. The appeal was allowed on the ground that the officer had gone beyond the scope of her duty in detaining Collins without informing her why she was being arrested. This meant that Wilcock had no legal justification for holding Collins' arm in an effort to restrain her, and therefore committed a battery. In his judgment, Goff LJ (at 1176–1178) stated that the fundamental principle underlying the tort of battery is:

> that every person's body is inviolate. It has long been established that any touching of another person, however slight, may amount to battery. So Holt CJ held in *Cole v Turner* (1704) 6 Mod 149 that 'the least touching of another in anger is a battery'. The breadth of the principle reflects the fundamental nature of the interest protected.

Today, anger or hostility is not an element of the cause of action for battery; however, Holt CJ's point about 'the least touching' is still valid. In the second part of the eighteenth century, Sir William Blackstone extended the scope of battery to all nonconsensual contacts by eliminating the requirement of violence. In his *Commentaries on the Laws of England*, Blackstone wrote:

> the law cannot draw the line between different degrees of violence, and therefore totally prohibits the first and lowest stage of it: every man's person being sacred, and no other having a right to meddle with it, in any the slightest manner.[11]

The first clause of Blackstone's statement deals with a principle common to all major systems of law (including the Roman law, the Jewish law known as the Halacha, the Moslem law known as the Shariah), that generally, where the law cannot draw the line between degrees of a conduct which is morally and socially

---

10. Luntz H & Hambly P, *Torts: Cases and Commentary*, Butterworths, Sydney, 1995, p 649.
11. *A Facsimile of the First Edition of 1768*, Clarendon Press, Oxford; photographically reprinted by The University of Chicago Press, Chicago & London, 1979, Vol 3, 1979, p 120.

repugnant, it will prohibit the first and the lowest 'stage', or manifestation, of it. For Blackstone, the rationale of the prohibition of all nonconsensual contacts lay in the sacredness or inviolability of the human person. He argued that because 'Life is the immediate gift of God, a right inherent by nature in every individual',[12] there exists an absolute right to personal security, vested in each person: 'the right of personal security consists in a person's legal and uninterrupted enjoyment of his life, his limbs, his body, his health, and his reputation.'[13]

As an inviolate legal right, the principle of sacredness of the human person is operative in both the public and the private spheres. In public law, it has been interpreted as the State interest in preservation of human life. The protection of life remains a primary function of criminal law, and underlies the State's interest in preventing suicide. The principle also lies at the core of the jurisprudential argument against capital punishment. In private law, the principle is manifested through the tort of battery. Goff LJ observed that the tort of battery protects not only against physical injury but also against any form of physical molestation.

In *Secretary, Department of Health and Community Services (NT) v JWB and SMB* (1992) 175 CLR 218, known as *Marion's Case*, the issue was who could validly consent to sterilisation of a severely intellectually impaired young woman. Brennan J (at 236) commented thus on Blackstone's explanation:

> Blackstone's reason for the rule which forbids any form of molestation, namely that 'man's person [is] sacred' points to the value which underlines and informs the law: each person has a unique dignity which the law respects and which it will protect ... The law will protect equally the dignity of the hale and hearty and the dignity of the weak and lame; of the frail baby and of the intellectually disabled.

Today, the tort of trespass to the person protects the right of an adult person with full mental capacity to be free of uninvited physical contact, including medical treatment. In *Marion's Case*, McHugh J (at 309–310) defined the modern tort of battery thus:

> the common law respects and preserves the autonomy of adult persons of sound mind with respect to their bodies. By doing so, the common law accepts that a person has rights of control and self-determination in respect of his or her body which other persons must respect. Those rights can only be altered with the consent of the person concerned. Thus, the legal requirement of consent to bodily interference protects the autonomy and dignity of the individual and limits the power of others to interfere with that person's body.[14]

---

12. Ibid, Vol 1, pp 125, 129–130.
13. Ibid, Vol 3, pp 119–120.
14. In *Marion's Case*, McHugh J was a dissentient; however his Honour's approach has not been challenged.

Elements of battery

In *Marion's Case*, McHugh J (at 311) in an *obiter dictum* said that to establish battery the plaintiff has to show that:

- a direct act of the defendant made or had the effect of causing contact with the body of another; and
- the direct act was intentional or reckless.

Consent to the contact may make the act lawful, but, if there is no evidence on the issue of consent, the tort is made out. It is the defendant who has the burden of proving consent (for further discussion of the defence of consent see Chapter 9).[15]

Therefore the following elements must be present to constitute battery:

- intentional conduct;
- positive and affirmative action directly resulting in contact with the person of another; and
- voluntary act.

Intention for the purposes of battery

The *intention* goes only into the commission of the *act* of contact. Thus, Glanville Williams in his seminal *The Sanctity of Life and the Criminal Law* wrote: 'To the eye of common sense a result that is foreseen as certain, as a consequence of what is done, is in exactly the same position as a result that is intended.'[16] For instance, two boys sitting on an embankment above a motorway decided to amuse themselves by throwing stones at passing cars. A stone penetrated the roof of one of the cars and injured the driver. The plea that the boys did not intend to injure the driver would not be accepted in battery, because it could be shown that the boys intended the act of throwing the stone, and the driver could show that contact with his body was substantially certain to follow from such conduct.

Positive and affirmative action

The conduct of the defendant must be positive and affirmative, not passive. For instance, standing 'like a wall' in the path of a running child and letting a child crash into you will not amount to battery. However, positive and affirmative action may be imputed where intention to make contact has been formed, even if the intention is not coincidental with the original act—it is sufficient if, once it is

---

15. *Platt v Nutt* (1988) 12 NSWLR 213.
16. Williams G, *The Sanctity of Life and the Criminal Law*, Alfred Knopf, New York, 1970, p 203.

formed, the intention continues as part of it. For example, in *Fagan v Metropolitan Police Commissioner* [1969] 1 QB 439, the defendant accidentally brought a car to rest on a policeman's foot. He then ignored several requests to move the wheel off the plaintiff's foot, before turning on the ignition and driving off. The intention to commit battery was imputed to the defendant from the moment he became aware of his wheel resting on the policeman's foot.

Direct act resulting in contact with the person of another

Generally, contact must form part of the defendant's action.

The defendant's act must be direct in the sense that contact follows so immediately upon the act that it may be termed part of that act. However, the actual physical contact with the person of another need not be immediate, in the sense that physical touching of the plaintiff's body can take a form of throwing or propelling an object at him or her. Providing that the same object makes contact—touches— the body of the victim, the tort of battery will be made out.

Scott v Shepherd (1773) 2 Wm Bl 892

At a fair, the defendant, Shepherd, threw a lighted squib made of gunpowder from the street into the marketplace where it landed on the stall of Yates, who sold gingerbread. Willis, who was close by, instantly picked it up and, to prevent an injury to himself, threw the squib across the marketplace onto the stall of Ryal, who also sold gingerbread. Ryal, in order to save his goods, at once lifted the still lighted squib and threw it to another part of the marketplace, where it struck the plaintiff, Scott, in the face, exploded, and blinded him in one eye. Scott sued Shepherd for damages in trespass. Three out of four judges in the Court of the Common Pleas found battery to the plaintiff. According to the majority, Shepherd's act of throwing the lighted squib into the market place was unlawful, it was in breach of the peace and statute. Given that the object they were forced to handle was an explosive (as against a stone, for example), Willis and Ryal acted under a compulsive necessity for their own safety and preservation, and *not* as free agents. Their actions thus did not break the chain of directness. Sir William Blackstone, who was then a judge in the Court of Common Pleas, dissented, saying that Scott's injury was consequential, and therefore should sound in action on the case. Nevertheless, the majority opinion still stands.

Voluntary act

The act causing the contact must be voluntary. Where a person in an epileptic fit stretches out his arm and thereby hits the plaintiff, such act will not be deemed voluntary, and battery will not be made out. Similarly, if a person picks up another person and throws her at the plaintiff, the liability in battery will be attributed solely to the thrower.

The question arises whether intention, in the sense of motive, matters for the purposes of battery, or for that matter any species of trespass to the person.

The answer to this question is 'no'. The motive for the direct contact is irrelevant. Any intentional act, no matter how benevolently motivated, may constitute battery when it directly interferes with the plaintiff's body: for example, lifesaving surgery against the wishes of a competent and adult patient constitutes battery, unless the defendant can establish statutory justification.

Knowledge of the contact

Another question which arises in relation to battery is whether the other party's knowledge of the contact is necessary for liability in battery.

The plaintiff need not be aware of the unlawful contact at the time of the incident, but will have to show evidence of the contact, such as bruising, or evidence of those who have seen the contact take place. For instance, a girl may not know that, without her prior consent, the defendant has kissed her while she was asleep. However, if witnesses can testify that the act took place, she will have an action in battery against the defendant.

Conversely, the defendant need not know that the contact has actually taken place to incur liability in battery. An example is where the defendant, while attempting to shoot a duck, misses the bird but injures another duck shooter of whose existence he had no knowledge.

THE TORT OF ASSAULT

Brief history of the tort of assault

The tort of assault is a sibling to the tort of battery, in the sense that the two torts are often, though not always, committed in close succession. In the fourteenth century, the Chancery officials and the courts recognised that conduct which directly threatens an imminent harmful physical contact with another can provoke retaliation just as effectively as the actual use of physical force. If the retaliation is physical, it will inevitably result in the breach of peace as illustrated in the first scene of Shakespeare's *Romeo and Juliet*. It was also recognised that directly threatening, intentional, and outrageous conduct may have an immediate emotional effect on the victim even in the absence of physical contact.

The tort of assault goes back to 1348, when in the case of *I de S et Uxor v W de S* (1348) YB 22 Edw III f 99, pl 60, the defendant threw a hatchet at a tavern keeper's wife, narrowly missing her. He was found liable for assault, and had to pay compensation for the fright he had caused. Ever since then, the tort of assault has extended protection to a person's right to be free of emotional disturbance brought about by intentional threats of physical violence.

The tort of assault allows an action for damages, not for any material harm, but for a purely transient emotional reaction to the defendant's conduct. Percy H Winfield and Arthur L Goodhart, in their article on trespass and negligence,[17] argue that compensation for injury suffered has never been the primary aim of the tort of trespass to the person. It is the act of trespass—any form of conduct that may provoke an imminent danger of retaliation, and the consequent breach of the King's peace—which constitutes the wrong for which the remedy is granted. Any emotional or physical injury suffered may extend the quantum of damages, but apart from apprehension, physical or emotional injury is not an essential element of the cause of action.

Definition of assault

The tort of assault is brought for intentional (and, possibly, also for negligent) threats which create in another person an apprehension of imminent harmful or offensive contact.

Assault tends to be followed by battery. However, when battery is committed from behind, without warning, or upon a sleeping or unconscious person, it is possible to have battery without assault. Conversely, it is possible to have assault without battery, where the threat to inflict unlawful force creates reasonable apprehension, but is not actually carried out. For example, in *Zanker v Vartzokas* (1988) 34 A Crim R 11, a young woman missed a lift from her sister while she was making a phone call from a phone booth. The defendant, who was sitting on a nearby bench, offered to give her a lift in his van. After some hesitation she agreed, and asked him to follow her sister's car. Once they were driving, he offered her money for sex. She rejected the offer, and when he persisted, she demanded that he stop the vehicle to let her out. He then accelerated and told her that he was going to take her to his mate's house, and that the mate would 'really fix her up'. Even though the vehicle was travelling at 60 kilometres per hour, the woman was so frightened that she opened the door and leapt out on to the roadside. She was hurt, but apparently the injuries were not very serious. She sued the defendant for assault.

In determining whether the threats made by the defendant created in the plaintiff an apprehension of an immediate or imminent physical violence, the trial judge followed the reasoning of Zelling J in the case *of MacPherson v Brown* (1975) 12 SASR 184. According to Zelling J, in cases where a person who is being threatened with physical harm is unlawfully confined by the defendant, the threat

---

17. 'Trespass and Negligence' (1933) 49 *The Law Quarterly Review* 359.

can operate 'immediately on the victim's mind' and 'in a continuing way', which will last as long as the unlawful imprisonment continues. In *Zanker*, the woman was 'in the captive position of a mouse to which a playful cat poses a continuing threat of injury or death at the time to be decided by the cat.'

The elements of the tort of assault

A threat of itself is merely an expression of a proposed action, and as such, is legally 'neutral'. According to Lord Dunedin in *Sorrell v Smith* [1925] AC 700; All ER Rep 1, whether the threat is actionable will depend on whether the proposed action is legal or tortious. Only if the threat involves an intimation of an illegal—tortious—act will a person have the right to sue.

Apprehension of impending contact

It is the reasonable apprehension of the impending contact which constitutes the gist of the tort of assault.

Although the plaintiff must *know* of the possible contact and expect it, he or she need not *fear* the contact; apprehension is not the same as fear. The contact apprehended must be of an immediate and harmful or offensive nature.

Apprehension must be reasonable

The plaintiff's apprehension of imminent contact must be reasonable. It will be deemed reasonable if the defendant has the apparent ability to carry out the threat immediately. In that situation, the defendant will be liable in assault, even if a third party prevents the threat from being carried out.

Victim's state of mind

Because the remedy focuses upon the victim's state of mind, it is the reasonable belief of the plaintiff in the threat posed that matters, not whether the defendant intended to carry it out, or had the actual—as opposed to apparent—means to follow up the threat:

> There need be no actual intention or power to use violence, for it is enough if the plaintiff on reasonable grounds believes that he is in danger of it.[18]

---

18. *Bruce v Dyer* (1966) 58 DLR (2d) 211 at 216, per Ferguson J, citing Salmond JW, *Law of Torts: A Treatise on the English Law of Liability for Civil Injuries*, 8th edition, Sweet & Maxwell, London; Carswell, Toronto, p 373, who in turn rephrased Denman CJ's statement in *Innes v Wylie* (1844) 1 Car & K 257 at 262.

In this sense the test is subjective; however, the element of objectivity is introduced through the requirement that apprehension be reasonable in the circumstances.

Thus if, on a hot summer afternoon, a four-year-old girl points a plastic water-pistol at me and threatens to shoot me, I will find it difficult to prove that I had a reasonable apprehension of an imminent harmful or offensive contact with my body. Although the elements of directness and of immediate contact through the medium of a spray of water will be satisfied, the necessary requirement that the contact be harmful or offensive will be missing. In these circumstances my assertion of apprehension would not be regarded as reasonable.

However, where a person late at night in a deserted street exaggerates the apparent ability to carry out a threat immediately by pointing a replica of a gun or an unloaded gun while demanding money, he or she will be liable if the victim has reasonable grounds for believing the pistol was real, or loaded.

Direct physical threat

The threat must be a direct physical threat. It may be conveyed by act alone, by an act coupled with threatening words, or by words alone.

Words are not necessary for an assault if the act clearly places the plaintiff in a reasonable apprehension of imminent, harmful physical contact. For instance, in *Chief Constable of Thames Valley Police v Hepburn* [2002] EWCA Civ 1841, police raided a public house pursuant to a warrant, which authorised constables to enter and search 'for the following articles or persons: drugs and related paraphernalia'. Upon entering the premises, PC Hargreaves shouted 'Police—warrant—get down', but the plaintiff, who was eating his supper at the time, made to leave. PC Hargreaves barred his way with a long baton held out at waist level. A fracas involving the police and the plaintiff followed. Having affirmed that the warrant as issued did not include the power to stop and search persons who happened to be on the premises so as to prevent such persons from leaving the premises, Sedley LJ held [at 17] that:

> While it is not an assault simply to get in someone's way, it is a technical assault to obstruct them in circumstances which make it clear that if they go on they will be stopped forcibly. PC Hargreaves' stance, holding out his baton to stop Mr Hepburn leaving, was a textbook example of the latter.[19]

An example of an assault by way of an act coupled with words is when someone wearing a balaclava enters a bank, and, pointing a pistol at the teller, demands money.

Given the right circumstances, silence can be just a threatening as words. Thus in *R v Ireland* [1997] QB 114, Ireland admitted making more than fourteen

---

19. The plaintiff was awarded £4100 damages for assault and false imprisonment.

telephone calls within an hour to a woman and remaining silent when she answered; he phoned two other women in the same manner. Each of the women suffered psychological harm, such as palpitations, difficulty in breathing, cold sweats, anxiety, inability to sleep, dizziness and stress. Swinton Thomas LJ (at 122), speaking for the court, held that all elements of assault were present: the phone calls were intentional acts; by using a telephone Ireland put himself in immediate contact with the victims; and in the circumstances in which these constant telephone calls were made, followed by silence, they were 'just as capable of being terrifying to the victims as if actual threats had been made'.[20]

The threat of bodily violence must be direct and imminent. Therefore assault will be nullified if the defendant dispels the immediacy of that threat. The often-quoted example is that of *Tuberville v Savage* (1669) 1 Mod 3, in which Tuberville laid his hand upon his sword and said, 'If it were not assize time, I would not take such language from you'. The court held (at 3) that the act was threatening, and could have amounted to an assault but for 'the declaration that he would not assault him, the judges being in town'.

Conditional threats

Assault can be carried out through conditional threats. However, the law distinguishes between:

- threats of lawful force; and
- threats of unlawful force.

In the first category the threatening party provides a warning or suggests that unless the party addressed ceases to act unlawfully, legal force will be used to effect the cessation. For example, a lawful occupier may lawfully threaten a trespasser that unless he or she leaves the premises immediately, the occupier will resort to the use of proportionate force.

The case of *Police v Greaves* [1964] NZLR 295 is an illustration of the second category of conditional threat. In that case a constable, who had gone into the defendant's home in response to a call for help, was threatened by him with a carving knife. The defendant said: 'Don't you bloody move. You come a step closer and you will get this straight through your guts.'

The court held that the defendant's words constituted assault because they threatened imminent and direct violence unless the plaintiff desisted from lawful acts in the course of his police duties.

A conditional threat will also constitute assault where the defendant makes it clear that no bodily contact will ensue if the plaintiff obeys the unlawful instructions:

---

20. Swinton Thomas LJ was referring to Taylor J's judgment in *Barton v Armstrong* [1969] 2 NSWR 451.

'I won't stab you with this syringe full of contaminated blood if you hand over your wallet.'

Threats of tortious actions may sometimes constitute the tort of intimidation where a trader is compelled to discontinue the lawful conduct of trade under a threat of personal violence.

Alarming words

There are at least two kinds of alarming statements which may amount to tortious conduct:

1   Statements which indicate that the defendant will use physical force to cause imminent harmful or offensive contact with the plaintiff's body. For instance, 'I am going to detonate a bomb inside the boot of the car you are driving' or 'I'll shoot you', will constitute an assault if the defendant has the apparent means to carry out the threat immediately.
2   Statements such as 'Your mother is dead' or 'The theatre is on fire!', which are intended to cause harm, and do in fact produce some effect on the plaintiff of the kind intended, will be actionable under action on the case for intentional infliction of nervous shock, rather than assault.

NEGLIGENT TRESPASS

In England, *Letang v Cooper* [1965] 1 QB 232 abolished an old cause of action known as negligent trespass. The High Court's joint judgment in *Williams v Milotin* (1957) 97 CLR 465 is regarded as an authority for the continued existence of this cause of action in Australia (see *State of New South Wales v Knight* [2002] NSWCA 392). *Williams v Milotin* involved interpretation of the now repealed *Limitation of Actions Act 1936–48* (SA), s 35, providing for a six year limitation period for *inter alia* 'actions which would formerly have been brought in the form of actions called trespass on the case', and s 36, providing for a three year limitation period for trespass. The High Court determined that the young boy who was 'immediately or directly hit' by a negligently driven motor truck while he was cycling along a street, could sue, by his next friend, under s 35. Their Honours commented (at 474):

> When you speak of a cause of action you mean the essential ingredients in the title to the right which it is proposed to enforce. The essential ingredients in an action of negligence for personal injuries include the special or particular damage—it is the gist of the action—and the want of due care. Trespass to the person includes neither. But it does include direct violation of the protection which the law throws round the person. It is true that in the absence of intention of some kind or want of due care, a violation occurring in the course of traffic in a thoroughfare is not actionable as a trespass.

The last sentence of this paragraph has been interpreted as implying that collisions involving motor vehicles off the highway may fall within the cause of action for negligent trespass (*Venning v Chin* (1974) 10 SASR 299 at 307).

THE TORT OF FALSE IMPRISONMENT

Brief history of the tort of false imprisonment

The tort of false (unlawful) imprisonment is yet another species of trespass to the person. The tort originated as part of the writ of trespass; therefore it usually pertains to the intentional restriction on freedom of movement of the plaintiff, but may also apply to negligent or careless false imprisonment. The fault lay in any prohibited conduct, with damage being an actual or threatened breach of the royal peace. In the opening scenes of Shakespeare's *Romeo and Juliet*, a fight ensues between the followers of the Montagues and those of the Capulets after the latter deliberately block the Montagues from entering the public square in Verona. Apparently, already in 1348, wrongful restraint in a public street was held to constitute false imprisonment.

Today, the emphasis is placed on the infringement of liberty of the individual rather than breach of peace. The significance attached by the common law to the liberty interests protected by the tort of false imprisonment may be gauged by the fact that *Huckle v Money* (1763) 2 Wils KB 205; 95 ER 768, which was one of the earliest reported cases of punitive damages, involved false imprisonment. Fullagar J in *Trobridge v Hardy* (1955) 94 CLR 147 (at 152) said that the right to be free from interference with one's person and liberty is one of the 'most elementary and important of all common law rights'.[21]

The tort of false imprisonment protects several rights: our right to personal liberty; the immunity of our will from coercion; our right to free motion and locomotion (freedom of movement) in the sense of free choice and judgement as to what we can lawfully do; as well as our right to an uninterrupted lawful passage on the public highway.

As a species of trespass, false imprisonment is actionable *per se*, and the claimant does not need to establish actual damage. *Murray v Minister of Defence* [1988] 1 WLR 692 concerned the arrest of the plaintiff who was suspected of collecting money for the purchase of arms for the IRA in her house. The plaintiff claimed to have been falsely imprisoned between 7 am and 7.30 am—ie from the time that the soldiers first entered her house till the time she was actually told that she was under arrest. Lord Griffith said that the circumstances of the arrest were governed by s 14 of the *Northern Ireland (Emergency Provisions) Act 1978*, which laid

---

21. See also: *Re Bolton; Ex parte Beane* (1987) 162 CLR 514 at 523, 528; *Ruhani v Director of Police* [2005] HCA 43 at [63].

down rules for anti-terrorist operations, and by reasonable precautions which had to be employed in such cases. However, His Lordship also pointed out (at 703) that as a general rule:

> The law attaches supreme importance to the liberty of the individual and if he suffers a wrongful interference with that liberty it should remain actionable even without proof of special damage.

Definition of the tort of false imprisonment

The tort of false imprisonment involves a direct and intentional or careless, or bona fide in the sense of acting under misapprehension of the law, total confinement of the plaintiff within an area fixed by the defendant, without legal justification or statutory authority. There has to be an intention to detain.

Burden of proof in the tort of false imprisonment

The tort of false imprisonment is a tort of strict liability. The plaintiff does not have to prove fault on the part of the defendant. The burden of proof is on the defendant to prove legal justification such as statutory authority. The executive arm of government (the ministers) is not in a special position in this regard, and must establish that its officers had lawful authority to detain.[22] In *Ruddock v Taylor* [2005] HCA 48, the plaintiff, Taylor, was a holder of a Permanent Transitional Visa. In 1996, he was convicted of eight sexual offences against children and given a jail term. In 1999 his visa was cancelled, which meant that upon release from jail Taylor was declared an 'unlawful non-citizen' and detained for periods of 161 days and 155 days respectively. He sued the Commonwealth of Australia for false imprisonment. Gleeson CJ, Gummow, Hayne, and Heydon JJ found that Taylor's detention was lawful under s 189 of the *Migration Act 1958* (Cth). The provision, when read in its context, authorised the detention of those whom the officer knew or suspected to be unlawful non-citizens (at [26]–[27]).[23]

Elements of the tort of false imprisonment

To establish a cause of action for false imprisonment the plaintiff has to establish the following elements:

- total restraint of plaintiff's liberty; and
- that the restrain is directly, intentionally and voluntarily effected by the defendant.

We shall deal with each element in turn.

---

22. *Ruddock v Taylor* [2003] NSWCA 262 at [3], per Spigelman CJ (Ipp JA agreeing).
23. See also: *Ruhani v Director of Police* [2005] HCA 43.

Restraint of liberty must be total

The tort distinguishes between total and partial restraint. The restraint of liberty is not total where there are reasonable means of escape. The principle that a partial obstruction of the plaintiff's will is not sufficient was first enunciated in the case of *Bird v Jones* (1845) 7 QB 742, which said (at 744), that that false imprisonment is a total restraint of the liberty of the person, for however short a time, and not a partial obstruction of the person's will, whatever inconvenience it may bring him or her.

Means of escape will not be considered 'reasonable' if:

- the only way of escape is dangerous, for instance, jumping from a first-floor window, or into the water;
- the plaintiff does not know of the way out and it is not apparent (for example, if the way out is through a concealed trapdoor);
- the plaintiff reasonably believes that any attempt to escape would involve a risk of public embarrassment, or the use of physical force by the defendant.

In the absence of statutory authority, it is unlawful to enforce a civil claim against another by imprisoning that person without due process of law. However, reasonableness is, or should be, the overarching test for all actions in tort. For example, in the classic case of *Balmain New Ferry Co v Robertson* (1906) 4 CLR 379,[24] Mr Robertson intended to take a ferry to Balmain in Sydney. The notice posted near the turnstile at the entrance to the wharf required any person passing through in either direction to put in a penny, whether or not he had travelled on a ferry. Mr Robertson paid the penny to enter, but once inside, he changed his mind, when he found that the next boat would not depart for twenty minutes. He demanded to be allowed to exit without having to pay the second penny, but his request was refused. He unsuccessfully sued for false imprisonment. The case was dismissed on the grounds that he was aware of and bound by the terms imposed by the defendants with regard to entrance to and exit from their property.

Myer Stores & Ors v Soo (1991) 2 VR 597[25]

On 31 July 1985, the Myer city store security camera video recorded a person stealing a crystal jug. Evans, the Myer security officer, reported the crime to a police officer, Barrett, who came over to the store. Barrett, Evans, and an unidentified salesperson watched the video. When on 8 August 1985 Mr Soo Lin Seng entered the hi-fi department, the same unidentified salesperson informed Evans that the shoplifter captured on the videotape was at the store.

Evans then pointed out Mr Soo as the shoplifter to two uniformed policemen, Mann and Sterling, whose duties included dealing with shoplifting in the city. They

---

24. Affirmed by *Robinson v Balmain New Ferry Co Ltd* [1910] AC 295.
25. See also: *McDonald v Coles Myer Ltd (t/as 'K-Mart Chatswood')* (1995) Aust Torts Reps ¶81–361.

approached Mr Soo and told him that a few days before a security video camera had recorded a male person matching his description stealing an item from another section of the store. Mr Soo protested, but followed Evans, Mann, and Sterling to the security room 'to sort things out'. There he produced his name and address, as well as proofs of purchase, and after an hour was allowed to go. Nevertheless, Barrett asked for and obtained from a magistrate a search warrant to enter and search Mr Soo's house 'during the daylight hours' on 16 August 1985. The police entered the Soo family house at 5.30 pm and fruitlessly searched the premises for 50 minutes. By the time they left, it was dark outside. On the following day, Mr Soo was interviewed by Barrett and two other policemen at the Russell Street police station. Mr Soo attended the interview voluntarily, but he mentioned that he wished to leave at 1 pm. The interview, however, continued until 1.20 pm, when Barrett took Mr Soo to the section sergeant and stated that Mr Soo was innocent and exonerated.

The Victorian Supreme Court of Appeal held that Myer was liable for falsely imprisoning Mr Soo on two occasions: (1) on 8 August 1985, when Evans, Mann, and Sterling, having spoken to Mr Soo, escorted him to the security office; and (2) when he was interviewed for an hour in the security office. Although Evans did not enter the security room in which Mr Soo was wrongfully restrained, he was found liable for false imprisonment on the grounds that he participated in the restraint of the claimant's liberty by providing the room and maintaining an interest in the investigation.[26]

Restraint by psychological coercion

The defendant may wrongfully effect a total restraint of the plaintiff by psychological coercion. For instance, it will be a false imprisonment where the defendant indicates that, if the plaintiff does not comply with his request, force will be brought to bear; in this situation, psychological coercion alone will be sufficient for total restraint. However, unlawful restraint can also be effected through the victim's fear of embarrassment. In *Myer Stores & Ors v Soo*, despite explaining on the spot that he was the wrong suspect, Mr Soo was psychologically compelled to follow Evans and the two policemen down from the second floor into the security office located on the first floor because he feared the embarrassment of an arrest in a public space.

The case of *Symes v Mahon* [1922] SASR 447 is a classic illustration of false imprisonment by psychological coercion. In that case the plaintiff was a married man who lived and worked as a teacher in the Adelaide Hills. The defendant police officer mistakenly believed that an arrest warrant had been issued against the

---

26. See also: *Sadler & State of Victoria v Madigan* [1998] VSCA 53 involving false imprisonment of the claimant at the police station.

plaintiff in Adelaide for failing to maintain an extramarital child and its mother. He visited the plaintiff at his home, and in spite of the latter's denials, the defendant required him to come to Adelaide the next day. The following morning, they met at the train station and travelled in different compartments. On arrival at Adelaide, although a police vehicle was waiting for them at the station, they decided to walk. On the way, the plaintiff checked into a hotel where he left his luggage. They then took a tram to the police station, where the mistake was discovered. The defendant said: 'I am very sorry, but don't forget I told you all along that you were not under arrest.' The plaintiff replied 'Yes, you told me when I was getting on the electric car [tram] that I was not under arrest.'

The court held that the policeman was liable for false imprisonment from the time the plaintiff met the defendant at the station in the Adelaide Hills, for there was evidence 'of complete submission by him to the control of the other party' (at 453).

Place of restraint

Does the tort of false imprisonment require the plaintiff to be confined to some defined physical place?

As *Symes v Mahon* shows, a fixed space is not necessary. The essential question is whether the plaintiff submitted himself to the defendant's will, reasonably thinking that he had no reasonable means of escape.[27] In the case of *Symes v Mahon*, the plaintiff obviously thought that if he refused to go with the policeman, or tried to escape, he would immediately be arrested.

Can the plaintiff be unlawfully restrained in his or her own home?

In *Myer Stores & Ors v Soo*, the court found that Mr Soo was not falsely imprisoned in his home because even in winter 5.30 to 6.20 pm is within the scope of 'daylight hours' as specified by the magistrate on the search warrant. However, a police search that continued until 9 pm, would have been outside the 'daylight hours' authorisation of the warrant, and thus the presence of the police at Mr Soo's home would amount both to false imprisonment (an occupier of premises would be loath to leave them while a search is being carried out), and to trespass to land.

Direct act of restraint

A plaintiff who has been totally restrained by a third party must also establish that the defendant directly caused or actively promoted the imprisonment.

The defendant may effect the plaintiff's false imprisonment personally, or through the agency of a third party. This rule was established in *Flewster v Royale* (1808) 1 Camp 187. In this case, the defendant, a jilted fiancée, gave the name

---

27. *R v Garrett* (1988) 50 SASR 392 at 405: the will of a person may be overborne by the threats of immediate physical force to the safety of another person.

of the plaintiff to the press gang, saying that he was fit and eligible to serve in the King's navy. He was seized and held on board a ship. In fact, he was exempted from the impress-law, whereby certain young men were forced to serve in the King's navy or army. The court held that the defendant was liable for false imprisonment. Lord Ellenborough (at 187) explained the principle of directness as pertaining to the tort of false imprisonment:

> There was clearly trespass here in seizing the plaintiff, and the defendant therefore was a trespasser in procuring it to be done ... If the defendant in this case had said that she believed the plaintiff was liable to be impressed, leaving it to the officer of the press-gang to make necessary inquires, and to act as he should think most advisable ... she would not have been amenable in this action. But she took upon herself positively to aver that he was compellable to serve in a king's ship, and she must therefore answer for the consequences.

In *Myer Stores & Ors v Soo*, the court held that the cause of action for false imprisonment against Barrett and Evans (Myer Stores) was not established in relation to the search of Mr Soo's home on 16 August 1985. It was carried into effect following the administrative decision of the magistrate to issue a warrant on the basis of the application by Barrett. Barrett, in turn, asked for a warrant upon receiving a message from Mann and Sterling, which contained Mr Soo's name and address, but no directions or advice on a possible course of action. It was the magistrate's discretionary decision to grant the search warrant. Therefore, the element of directness was missing.

It should be noted, however, that where a person makes false statements to the police, and the police—as ministerial officers of the law—acting on these allegations, but at their own initiative, arrest the plaintiff, the author of the false charges will not be liable in trespass for false imprisonment. In the case of *Austin v Dowling* (1870) LR 5 CP 534, the court held that the person's act of merely laying charges or signing the charge sheet will not amount to false imprisonment, unless that person knows that the plaintiff's arrest would proceed as the immediate consequence of signing the charge sheet.

Can a magistrate or a judge be liable for false imprisonment by issuing an order to search or to detain, which is later successfully challenged as invalid?

In *Spautz v Butterworth* (1996) 41 NSWLR 1, Dr Spautz laid a criminal defamation charge against a professor of the University of Newcastle, which was dismissed. He was ordered to pay costs of $5000 within three months or in default serve 200 days' imprisonment with hard labour. Dr Spautz did not pay the amount owing and Butterworth J, then a magistrate, issued a warrant of committal in respect of the costs order. Dr Spautz was arrested, and spent fifty-six days in jail before being released on bail pending proceedings to declare his imprisonment illegal. The court found that the issue and execution of the warrant of committal for the failure by Dr Spautz to pay costs under a costs order lacked statutory authorisation, and directed that it be quashed.[28] Dr Spautz then sued for damages for false imprisonment. The Court of Appeal held that since in this particular instance, the punishment by way of imprisonment was not assigned by law for non-payment of the sum Dr Spautz was ordered to be paid, his incarceration amounted to false imprisonment. The court also rejected the defence proposition that by failing to pay the costs Dr Spautz consented to his own incarceration; he was awarded a sum of $75 000.

Clarke J, who delivered the leading judgment in *Spautz v Butterworth*, stated that statutory provisions in every Australian jurisdiction afford protection to the judiciary 'in circumstances where they have jurisdiction to impose a term of imprisonment, but because of a procedural irregularity they act outside their jurisdiction so that the imprisonment was unlawful,'[29] providing that the punishment is no greater than that assigned by law.[30] However, the judiciary has no protection from a suit for false imprisonment in cases where there is no power to order imprisonment of the plaintiff either for an offence of which the plaintiff was convicted or for non-payment of the sum ordered to be paid.[31]

The defendant's conduct must be voluntary

Voluntary conduct in the context of false imprisonment implies absence of coercion operating on the defendant. For instance, an armed robber orders a bank employee to open an underground safe vault, hand over its contents, and then lock all his fellow employees inside the vault. The employee will not be liable for false imprisonment because he was not in a position to exercise discretion as to whether or not to effect the restraint of the co-workers.

Other aspects of the tort

Defendant's failure to act

As a general rule, trespassory conduct has to be positive. However, false imprisonment is probably an exception.

What is the position of the defendant in cases where the plaintiff voluntarily enters a confined space belonging to the defendant, then decides he wants out,

---

28. *Spautz v Dempsey* [1984] 1 NSWLR 449.
29. *Spautz v Butterworth* (1996) 41 NSWLR 1 at 18.
30. *R v Waltham Forest Justices; Ex parte Solanke* [1986] QB 983; *Smith v O'Brien* [1862] 1 W & W (L) 386. Where, as a result of a clerical mistake, the punishment is greater than that assigned by law, damages may be awarded: *Gerard v Hope* [1965] Tas SR 15.
31. *Clarke v Burton* [1994] 3 Tas SR 370; *R v Manchester City Magistrates' Court; Ex parte Davies* [1989] 1 QB 631; *Spautz v Butterworth* (1996) 41 NSWLR 1.

but the defendant refuses to let him go? In other words, can a refusal to act by the defendant constitute false imprisonment?

Excluding special circumstances where the release of a person is impractical (as when a passenger on an aeroplane flying across the Pacific Ocean suffers a panic attack and wants to leave the plane), or where the detention is legally justified, the defendant's refusal to accede to the request to be released will probably be regarded as false imprisonment. This is because the courts of today would hardly tolerate the idea that contractual consent to deprivation of liberty, once given, cannot be revoked. Neither would the courts tolerate an imprisonment by a creditor of a debtor in order to compel him to pay his debt. This may be so even in the case where the debtor-plaintiff wrongly thinks that the sum is not owed.

There is an old House of Lords case of *Herd v Weardle Steel, Coal and Coke Co Ltd* [1915] AC 67, where an employee miner in the defendant's coal mine was lowered to the bottom of the mine at the start of his shift. He and the other miners were ordered to do certain work, which they refused, claiming it was unsafe. Although their shift did not finish until 4 pm, at 11 am they requested to be taken to the surface in the lift; this was the only way out. The employer ordered them not to use the lift until 1.30 pm. Under the oral contracts of employment, and under the Coal Mines Regulation Acts (UK) of the time, the miners were not entitled to be raised to the surface until the end of their shift, and the plaintiff lost his action for false imprisonment. A contemporary court would decide this matter in a different way.

Motive and malice

Motive for the intention to detain is not an element of the tort:

> in the absence of some statutory provision, if a defendant wrongfully imprisons a plaintiff he is guilty of the tort, no matter how innocent, ignorant or even idealistic he may be.[32]

Evidence of malice, in the sense of ill-will or 'unreasoning prejudice', will be considered when damages are assessed. Thus, in *Myer Stores & Ors v Soo*, the actions of Evans were not premeditated and were not malicious *per se*; but his persistence in suspecting Mr Soo despite such conduct being 'completely unsupportable by circumstantial evidence' (at 600), evidenced 'unreasoning prejudice' of which the law disapproves. The court awarded Mr Soo aggravated damages.[33]

---

32. *Ruddock v Taylor* [2003] NSWCA 262 at [73], per Meagher JA.
33. See also: *Vignoli v Sydney Harbour Casino* [1999] NSWSC 1113.

Knowledge of false imprisonment

Knowledge is not an essential requirement of false imprisonment. In *Myer Stores & Ors v Soo* O'Brien J of the Supreme Court of Victoria followed the House of Lords ruling in *Murray v Ministry of Defence* [1988] 1 WLR 692 (at 701), holding that the victim need not be aware of the fact of the denial of liberty. However, knowledge of unlawful restraint may be relevant to the issue of quantum of damages. In *Hart v Herron* [1984] Aust Torts Reports ¶80–201 (NSW Supreme Court), the jury found that the plaintiff was falsely imprisoned after being detained and given *deep sleep* therapy treatment to which he did not consent; this was so, even though he had no recollection of the imprisonment.

FURTHER READING

Fordham M, 'False Imprisonment in Good Faith' (2000) 8 *Tort Law Review* 53.

Mendelson D, 'The Historical Evolution and Modern Implications of the Concepts of Consent To, and Refusal Of, Medical Treatment in the Context of the Law of Trespass' (1996) 17 *Journal of Legal Medicine* 1–71.

Owen, DG, *Philosophical Foundations of Tort Law*, Clarendon Press, Oxford, 1996.

Seipp DJ, 'Symposium: The Distinction between Crime and Tort in the Early Common Law' (1996) 76 *Boston University Law Review* 59–87.

Trindade F & Cane P, *The Law of Torts in Australia*, 3rd edn, Oxford University Press, Melbourne, 1999, pp 42–50.

Young PW, *The Law of Consent*, The Law Book Company, Sydney, 1986.

5 Trespass to Land

INTRODUCTION

In *Plenty v Dillon & Ors* (1991) 171 CLR 635, the High Court of Australia defined trespass to land as any intentional direct interference with land in the possession of another, without some lawful justification or the occupier's consent (express or implied). An aggrieved occupier is entitled to have his or her right of property vindicated by a substantial award of damages.

The tort of trespass to land protects actual possession as such, while the old action on the case for ejectment, now called 'the action for possession of land', has traditionally protected the owner's right to immediate possession. Title to land has been protected in equity and through legislation. This chapter focuses on the tort of trespass to land.

TRESPASS TO LAND: HISTORY AND RATIONALE

History

Following the Norman conquest in 1066, the Normans introduced the feudal system under which only the Crown could own the land. Consequently, all land in England was regarded as being owned by William I. The King's subjects held land through a system of tenures either directly from the Crown as tenants-in-chief, or indirectly, when tenants-in-chief sub-granted parcels of land to their own vassals and tenants (who could then sub-grant their portions to others). The process was known as *subinfeudation*. Those who held the land through subinfeudation had to perform certain services for their immediate superior, who was called their *mesne lord*.[1] Some

---

1. These services included *knight service* (duty to render military service for a specified number of days each year); *frankalmoign* (services of religious character); and *socage* (rendering of agricultural services, or other specified services, including payment of money).

tenures were free and involved *socage* (freeholds); however, apart from freeholds, much of the land in medieval England was held under unfree tenure, known as copyhold, whereby the tenant (*villein*) was required to give any type of labour required by the lord of the manor. The distinction was important in law, because the ownership of copyhold tenure was enforceable only in the court of the lord of the manor and not through the royal courts.

The royal courts began to safeguard the interests of those who had free tenure in land long before legal protection was extended to the interest in bodily integrity. Between 1164 and 1179, Henry II enacted statutes protecting the *seisin*—possession of a freehold estate in land. Originally, trespass to land (*quare clausum fregit*) was aimed against acts of intentional aggression in forcible breach of the King's peace. Trespass to land was based on the doctrine that no man need answer for his free tenement without the royal writ. Subsequently, the writ of trespass was also used to settle boundary disputes, and to prevent the acquisition of easements by prescriptive use.

The feudal system with its emphasis on tenures ended when the Long Parliament of the Cromwellian Commonwealth enacted *The Statute of Military Tenures (Tenures Abolition Act)* of 1660. This statute reduced all tenures in England to socage (freehold) and copyhold. Copyhold tenure was converted into socage by the *Law of Property Act 1922* (UK).

The modern principles underlying trespass to land originated in the political and jurisprudential theories which underlay the struggle of the Parliament of England and the common law judiciary against Stuart absolutism. Thus, in the famous *Semayne's Case* (1604) 5 Co Rep at 91a; [1558–1774] All ER Rep 62, Sir Edward Coke (at 63) said:

> the house of everyone is to him as his castle and fortress as well for his defence against injury and violence as for his repose.

By identifying the rights of every subject of the realm in his own house, Coke was referring to the medieval theory of the sovereignty of law whereby the King accepted a general responsibility to maintain the laws of the realm. Under the doctrine of trespass to land, the King could not, on his own initiative, curtail the right to property through unlawful seizure (*Sendil's case* (1585) 7 Co Rep 6a).[2]

In the wake of the English Civil War, political theories of personal liberty and proprietary freedom propounded by John Locke in his *The Second Treatise of Government* (1688)[3] and by Thomas Hobbes in *Leviathan* (1651), were based upon the notion of self-ownership. According to William S Holdsworth's *A History of English Law*,[4] they became, in the course of the eighteenth century, a 'deep-seated

---

2. Hogue AR, *Origins of the Common Law*, Liberty Press, Indianapolis, 1966, p 160.
3. Laslett P (ed), Cambridge University Press, Cambridge, 1970, 5.27.
4. Methuen & Co Ltd, London, 1938, Vol 10, p 658.

popular feeling in favour of liberty' at the expense of the power of the State. In 1762, articles critical of King George III and the government were published in a weekly paper called *The Monitor* or *British Freeholder*. The government considered them seditious and the Secretary of State, Lord Halifax, issued general warrants (warrants framed in very general terms) to search the premises and arrest a number of people concerned with their publication. Amongst them was John Entic, a clerk in the printery that published the paper.[5] His house was searched for four hours, though he was not arrested. He sued for trespass to land one of the King's messengers, Nathan Carrington who, together with three others, executed the search. The case, *Entick v Carrington* (1765) 95 ER 807, was tried in the Court of Common Pleas at Westminster Hall before Lord Camden CJ, who held that the warrants were unlawful, which meant that the search amounted to trespass to land.

In *Entick v Carrington* Lord Camden CJ affirmed the rule in *Semayne's Case* that a property owner has an absolute right to refuse entry to anyone, including the Crown and its representatives, unless they can show legal justification. Reflecting the notion that the law should extend protection of the individual vis-à-vis the State, Lord Camden CJ said (at 817):

> by the laws of England, every invasion of private property, be it ever so minute, is a trespass. No man can set his foot upon my ground without my license, but he is liable to an action, though the damage be nothing, which is proved by every declaration in trespass, where the defendant is called upon to answer for bruising the grass and even treading upon the soil. If he admits the fact, he is bound to show by way of justification, that some positive law has empowered or excused him.

His Lordship extended Blackstone's prohibition against the smallest degree of violent conduct in relation to the sanctity of life and person[6] to 'sanctity' of property when he stated:

> Our law holds the property of every man so sacred that no man can set foot upon his neighbour's close without his leave.

Today, a number of statutes confer the power to enter land without consent. However, the common law presumption remains that, in the absence of express provision to the contrary, the legislature does not intend to authorise what would otherwise be tortious conduct.

---

5. John Entic was an associate of John Wilkes, of *Wilkes v Wood* (1763) Lofft 1; 98 ER 489, discussed in Chapter 2.
6. Namely: 'the law cannot draw the line between different degrees of violence, and therefore totally prohibits the first and the lowest stage of it; every man's person being sacred, and no other having a right to meddle with it, in any the slightest manner.' Blackstone W, *Commentaries on the Laws of England*, A Facsimile of the First Edition 1768, Vol 3, Clarendon Press, Oxford; photographically reprinted by The University of Chicago Press, Chicago & London, 1979, p 120.

Plenty v Dillon & Ors (1991) 171 CLR 635

Two police officers went to Mr Plenty's farm on 5 December 1978 in order to serve a summons on his daughter and notices on Mr and Mrs Plenty. The summons and the notices were issued pursuant to the provisions of the *Juvenile Courts Act 1971* (SA). In earlier statements and correspondence, Mr Plenty had made it plain that, if the summons was to be served, it had to be served by post. The officers, therefore, entered the farm without any express or implied consent of the occupier. Mr Plenty, who was sitting in a car in his garage, refused to accept the summons and the notices, so Officer Dillon placed them on the car seat. As the officers were leaving the farm, Plenty attempted to strike Dillon with a piece of wood. After a struggle, he was arrested. He was subsequently convicted of assaulting an officer in the execution of his duty. However, the conviction was quashed after the High Court determined that in the circumstances, since the two policemen were trespassers from the time they entered Plenty's land, Dillon did not act in the 'execution of his duty'.

According to Gaudron and McHugh JJ (at 654), the law relating to trespass to land protects the occupier of land from an unlawful invasion, and is actionable *per se*, without material damage, because:

> If the courts of Common Law do not uphold the rights of individuals by granting effective remedies, they invite anarchy, for nothing breeds social disorder as quickly as the sense of injustice which is apt to be generated by the unlawful invasion of a person's rights, particularly when the invader is a government official.

Gaudron and McHugh JJ further stated (at 647):

> The policy of the law is to protect the possession of property and the privacy and security of its occupier.

ELEMENTS OF THE TORT OF TRESPASS TO LAND

Direct interference with the plaintiff's land

To establish the tort of trespass, there has to be evidence of *direct* interference with the plaintiff's land. The trespasser must have directly and voluntarily intended the act of interference, but the wrongdoer need not be aware of the trespass. The plaintiff does not have to prove that the defendant had acted negligently or carelessly, or that he or she intended trespass. The defendant has the burden of proving lawful justification or the occupier's consent (explicit or implied) to the entry onto the land.

There are, broadly, six ways in which trespassory conduct may be committed:

- Where there is no authority to enter at all, entering will be trespassory.
- No public official, police constable or citizen has any right at Common Law to enter a dwelling-house merely because he or she suspects something is wrong.
- Unlawful entry onto the land may include erection of a building
- Where an authority to enter exists, but for a specific purpose only, entry for some other purpose will be trespassory.
- Where a person has entered under licence but refuses to leave, after the licence is withdrawn and after being given reasonable opportunity to leave, such refusal to leave will be trespassory.
- A person also commits trespass if he or she enters, propels an object such as a ball or an arrow, a substance (for example spraying water by hose across another's land), or a third person onto the plaintiff's land, without lawful authority or consent.

Landlords

The right of the lessee to peaceful possession of land is protected by trespass to land. Although landlords may have the right to manage the property, to sell or financially encumber it, etc, for the duration of a valid lease they have neither possession not the immediate right to possession of the leased land. Consequently, liability in trespass to land at the suit of the tenant will lay against them for coming on the land without consent or legal justification.

Therefore, a landlord who, without authorisation, enters a house under a valid lease to a tenant, and removes a window from the house, commits trespass to land; however, no liability in trespass will attach to a landlord who cuts off the gas and electricity to the validly tenanted house. In the second case, the element of directness will be missing because cutting off supply of electricity and gas is not regarded as direct interference with another's possessory rights in land (that, however, could be a breach of residential tenancy legislation).

Voluntary and affirmative nature of the defendant's conduct

The defendant will be liable in trespass only if his or her conduct, as well as being intentional and direct, is also voluntary and affirmative. In *Nickells v Melbourne Corporation* (1938) 59 CLR 219 the Melbourne Corporation's employee drove a wide horse-drawn garbage cart up a narrow lane which was flanked by glass shop windows. The size of the cart was such that in order to turn at the end of the lane, the cart had to be brought to within twelve or fifteen inches of one of the windows.

While turning, the horse became startled and backed the cart through the window, breaking it and damaging the goods on show. Dixon J (as he then was) observed (at 225):

> involuntary trespass to land is not always an actionable wrong. Just as in trespass to the person and in trespass to goods it has come to be the law that an unintentional injury to or interference with another's person or property on the part of the user of a highway is not actionable in the absence of negligence, so, if, in the course of any reasonable use of a public way, a man unintentionally damages neighbouring premises, the law does not hold him liable as a trespasser unless he has been guilty of negligence.

The doctrine of trespass *ab initio*

The doctrine of trespass *ab initio* appears to have been an established concept already in the fifteenth century. For in the case of *Haukyns v Broune* (1476–83) Trin 17 Edw IV, fo 3 pl 2,[7] Sulyard, Serjeant at Law (the highest ranking barrister), discussed an example of a man who having distrained the plaintiff's horse, sells or kills it. He then commented that 'this subsequent conduct shows the taking to have been a trespass *ab initio*'.[8]

According to this doctrine, the defendant will be deemed to have committed a trespass if he or she enters with lawful authority on official business (not by way of plaintiff's invitation), but later abuses that authority by committing a tortious act such as battery or assault. The defendant's entry will then be treated retroactively as a trespass. However, in the case of *Barker v The Queen* (1983) 47 ALR 1 at 21, Brennan and Deane JJ expressed doubts as to whether the doctrine of trespass *ab initio* is still applicable today. Professor Fleming in *The Law of Torts*[9] suggested that the doctrine is 'justifiable at best' as a constitutional safeguard against abuse by officials acting under governmental authority. Whatever the situation might have been in the twentieth century, the legislative response to political events at the beginning of the second millennium—particularly the rise of terrorism—has included an expansion in statutory grants of surveillance and entry on land. Consequently, it is important to retain, and possibly even expand, the trespass *ab initio* to safeguard rights of occupiers against invasion by persons acting under statutory authorisation. In some cases, the authority to come onto the land may be nullified by evidence of *ultra vires* intent, if it amounts to an abuse of power.

---

7. Baker JH & Milsom SFC, *Sources of English Legal History: Private Law to 1750*, Butterworths, London, 1986, p 630.
8. For examples of trespass *ab initio* in the eighteenth century, see: Oldham J, *English Common Law in the Age of Mansfield*, The University of North Carolina Press, Chapel Hill & London, 2004, p 295.
9. Fleming JG, *The Law of Torts*, 9th edn, The Law Book Company Ltd, Sydney, 1998, p 42.

Continuing trespass

In *Konskier v B Goodman Ltd* [1928] 1 KB 421, the defendant builders left rubbish on the roof of the house they renovated. The court held that the failure to remove it constituted a continuing trespass.

Possessory interests and standing to sue for trespass to land

Only a person with a possessory interest in the land affected has standing to sue for trespass to land. Persons who have the required possessory interest include house owners; landowners; grantees of a legal or equitable interest in land such as easements or profits a prendre (rights to catch rabbits, cut timber, fisheries, etc); and tenants in possession.

Lodgers, invitees to dinner, and persons with an admission ticket are allowed entry on the land as 'mere licensees'. Their licence to be on the land is a purely personal right, it is not a right *in rem*. They cannot sue for trespass to land, because their licence does not confer on them any proprietary rights or rights in possession, and is revocable at the will of the licensor. The licensee can sue the licensor for damages in contract but not in trespass to land. This is not to say that licensees may never sue in tort—they can, for instance, in appropriate circumstances, sue for false imprisonment or battery or negligence.

In the case of *Cowell v Rosehill Racecourse* (1937) 56 CLR 605, the plaintiff bought an entry ticket to a racecourse meeting. The defendant revoked his consent to the plaintiff remaining at the racecourse, and when the plaintiff refused to leave the land, he was forcibly removed from it. The plaintiff sued in assault. The defendant claimed that trespass by the plaintiff justified what might otherwise be assault.

The court held that the plaintiff was a mere licensee. Buying a ticket for an entertainment is a mere contractual transaction, without any grant of an interest in the land and is revocable at will. It is a mere permission to do what would otherwise be an invasion of the licensor's rights.[10]

Adverse possessors

Exclusive possessors of land without title but with the acquiescence of the owner to their presence are deemed to have been in possession ever since their right of entry began to accrue. They thus acquire the right to an immediate possession and can sue a stranger in trespass to land.

The following question needs to be asked before a determination can be made regarding the plaintiff's *locus standi* (the right to bring an action): Was the plaintiff

---

10. See also: *Criminal Code Act 1899* (Qld), s 277.

a grantee of a legal or equitable right in land, or was the person a mere contractual or social licensee without any proprietary interest in the land? If the person is a licensee, once the license (the permission to remain on the land) is terminated, any further continuance of the stay on the land becomes unauthorised, that is, trespassory. Nonetheless, the licensee does not become a trespasser until:

- notice of termination of the license is received; and
- after the lapse of reasonable time required to leave the land and remove any property brought in under the license.

At that point, if the trespasser then refuses to leave, he or she can be forcibly removed as a trespasser, as was the case in *Cowell v Rosehill Racecourse*. Any force must be reasonable in the circumstances. If the force used in ejecting a trespasser is disproportionate, he or she can sue in assault, battery, and false imprisonment.

TRESPASS BENEATH AND ABOVE THE SURFACE OF THE LAND

Interest in exclusive possession of land extends both below and above the surface.

Below the surface of the land

Entry underneath the surface at any depth is trespass, unless mining rights have been granted, or the State or Territory government has legislated to abrogate this principle.[11] Thus, unless consented to, or authorised by legislation, extracting minerals, laying sewer or drainage pipes, pouring water or other fluids under the plaintiff's property constitutes trespass.

Above the surface of the land

Air space above the surface is the dominion of the owner only to the extent normally necessary for the proper enjoyment of the surface.

In Australia, the rule in relation to trespass above the surface of land was established by the Tasmanian case of *Davies v Bennison* [1927] Tas LR 52. The defendant, while in his own yard, fired a bullet from a rifle, aimed at the plaintiff's cat sitting on a roof of a shed in the plaintiff's yard. The defendant killed the cat. The court held that any intrusion above the land at the height of rooftops is a direct interference with the owner's dominion, and is, in principle, a trespass. The test of trespass to air space is whether the nature and height of the intrusion interferes with ordinary usage of the land.

---

11. *Melbourne City Link Act 1995* (Vic), ss 32D, 33, 34A.

Projecting objects

Trespass to air space includes a direct invasion by such artificial projections as swinging cranes, advertising signs, electric cables and overhanging walls. It is actionable *per se* and warrants a mandatory injunction to compel the removal of the artificial projections. For instance, in *LJP Investments Pty Ltd v Howard Chia Investments (No 2)* [1991] Aust Torts Reports ¶81–069, the plaintiff obtained an injunction for the removal of scaffolding, which directly encroached upon its property from the adjoining property of the defendant.[12]

Aircraft

In the English case of *Bernstein of Leigh (Baron) v Skyviews and General Ltd* [1978] 1 QB 478, the defendants took aerial photos of the plaintiff's property and his country house for publication in an unauthorised book. The English Court of Appeal determined that the plaintiff could not succeed in an action for trespass to land because:

- the aircraft flying at an allowed height did not interfere with the plaintiff's use of land and, consequently, did not infringe his rights to the airspace; and
- since the mere taking of photos is not wrongful, taking photos flying at an allowed height did not constitute trespass.

Every jurisdiction in Australia and elsewhere allows the privilege of an 'innocent passage' of an aircraft (see below). However, the defendants' action could hardly be considered 'innocent'; it was exploitative, and invasive of privacy. The defendants used 'the advantage of all that science now offers in the use of airspace' to invade another person's privacy of his home for monetary gain. The case did not address the need for adequate balance between private ownership and the public interest.

The High Court of Australia, if presented with a similar set of facts, would probably determine the case taking into consideration the ambit and the purposes of the tort of trespass to land explicated in *Plenty v Dillon & Ors*.

Remedies

Remedies for trespass to land include injunctions to prevent actual or threatened encroachment on the property, and damages.

Liability for loss or damage caused by aircraft is regulated by statute.[13] For example, the *Damage by Aircraft Act 1999* (Cth) applies to acts, omissions, matters

---

12. See also: *LJP Investments Pty Ltd v Howard Chia Investments (No 3)* [1991] Aust Torts Reports ¶81–070.
13. *Civil Liability Act 1936* (SA), Div 3; *Damage by Aircraft Act 1964* (WA), s 5; *Damage by Aircraft Act 1952* (NSW), s 2; *Damage by Aircraft Act 1963* (Tas); *Wrongs Act 1958* (Vic), Pt IV; *Damage by Aircraft Act 1999* (Cth), ss 10, 11.

and things within Australian territory. The Act applies to Commonwealth aircraft (but not to a Defence Force aircraft); aircraft owned by a foreign corporation or a trading or financial corporation (within the meaning of s 51(xx) of the Commonwealth Constitution); aircraft (including foreign aircraft) engaged in international air navigation; or air navigation in relation to trade and commerce with other countries and among the States; or air navigation conducted by a foreign corporation or a trading or financial corporation (within the meaning of s 51(xx) of the Constitution); or air navigation to or from, or within, the Territories; or landing at, or taking off from, a place acquired by the Commonwealth for public purposes. By virtue of s 9, the Act extends to all external territories.

DAMAGES

Nominal damages

Nominal damages are awarded in vindication of a landowner's right to exclude a trespasser from the property, regardless of absence of personal injury, damage to property, or financial loss. In addition, compensatory damages will be awarded where the trespass caused actual damage to the land or buildings on the land.

Compensatory damages

Traditionally, the defendant has been held liable for all the 'reasonable and natural' consequences of trespass, whether foreseeable or not. However, in *Mayfair v Pears* [1986] NZLJ 459, a New Zealand court held that the defendant should be only liable for the foreseeable consequences of trespass. In this case, a car parked without permission unexpectedly caught fire and did unforeseeable damage to the garage.

In *Plenty v Dillon & Will* (unreported, SASC 6372, Kelly J, 19 September 1997), Mr Plenty was awarded $100 000 in compensatory damages for a depressive illness he developed as a result of the incident, in particular, his conviction for 'assault', which, according to the court, was a major cause for the termination of his church membership.

Aggravated damages

Aggravated damages may be awarded to compensate for injury to feelings caused by tortious conduct that was particularly officious, abusive, insulting or humiliating. Thus, in the case of *Greig v Greig* [1966] VR 376, the defendant, who was the plaintiff's brother, secretly entered the plaintiff's flat and installed a microphone in the lounge-room chimney to record conversations of his brother's housekeeper, whom the defendant regarded as an 'adventuress' and not a fit person to look after his brother's children. Despite the defendant's sincerity in seeking to disabuse his brother of his misconceived infatuation with the housekeeper, Gillard J (at 38) deplored that 'anybody should have his privacy invaded', and awarded damages of £100 sterling 'as a solatium to his injured feelings.'

In the more recent case of *TCN Channel Nine Pty Ltd v Anning* [2002] NSWCA 82, the court found TCN Channel 9 Pty Ltd liable for trespass to Mr Anning's land. The trespass was committed by a reporter and cameramen of 'A Current Affair', a program produced by TCN Channel 9 Pty Ltd, who entered Mr Anning's rural property 'with cameras rolling' and confronted him about the thousands of tyres he had collected. Mr Anning told them to leave and they did so, but then broadcast the segments filmed on the property on 'A Current Affair'. The Court of Appeal held that while there is an implied licence to enter land through an unlocked gate to ask the occupier for permission to film, there is no implied licence to enter while filming for the purpose of broadcasting the images of the confrontation to the public at large. Moreover, in this case, the cameramen filmed other parts of the property. Mr Anning was awarded $25 000 in general damages to vindicate his right to exclusive occupation, and $25 000 in aggravated damages for hurt to feelings, humiliation, and affront to dignity.

Exemplary damages

Exemplary damages may be awarded where tortious conduct was so outrageous as to deserve the inclusion of a punitive element in the assessment of damages. In *Plenty v Dillon & Will*, the judge awarded Mr Plenty $5000 in exemplary damages.

LIMITATIONS OF THE TORT OF TRESPASS TO LAND

As noted above, according to Sir Edward Coke, in *Semayne's Case* (1604) 5 Co Rep 91a, the tort of trespass to land is based on the principle that 'the house of everyone is to him as his castle and fortress as well for his defence against injury and violence as for his repose'. Does this principle indicate that the ambit of trespass to land is wide enough to provide a general remedy for violation of privacy?

There are a number of substantive law reasons why the tort of trespass to land is incapable of protecting privacy in general. The primary reason is that an action for trespass to land is limited to protecting proprietary interests in land. Therefore the action is not available to residents of caravans or houseboats. They may have an action for trespass to goods; however, trespass to goods does not protect privacy. Likewise, proceedings for trespass to land can be instituted only by an occupier entitled to exclusive possession of the land. House guests, hospital patients, students occupying rooms in university residences, and lodgers in boarding houses do not have standing to bring such action. For example, in *Kaye v Robertson* [1991]

FSR 62, Mr Kaye, the plaintiff, a 'television celebrity' was treated in a hospital for catastrophic brain injuries. A newspaper reporter and photographer invaded the plaintiff's hospital room, ignoring notices pinned on the door of Mr Kaye's room, which listed persons allowed to visit him. They purported to interview him and took photographs, despite the fact that he was incapable of providing a valid consent to being either photographed or interviewed. Publication of the interview was restrained by interlocutory injunction on the ground that it was arguably a malicious falsehood to represent that the plaintiff had consented to it. However, the plaintiff could not rely on the law of trespass to land for a remedy because he had no proprietary interest in the hospital room.

The tort cannot protect the personal privacy of an individual against lawful intrusions on land. According to *Halliday v Nevill* (1984) 155 CLR 1, consent is generally implied to any bona fide person, to the extent of entry along a garden path to the front door, and to ring the door bell or knock, unless express contrary notice is given, as happened in *Plenty v Dillon*. Moreover, although under the common law there are very few exceptions where entry is permitted without the occupier's consent, there are hundreds of State and Commonwealth statutory provisions conferring such power on their officers to enter land.[14] For example, officers of electricity and gas distributors, and of water boards, are authorised, pursuant to their respective Acts, to enter any land for the purpose of carrying out their functions.

TORT OF TRESPASS TO LAND AND THE RIGHT TO PRIVACY IN AUSTRALIA

Developments in protection of the interest in personal privacy have been hampered by Lord Camden CJ's statement in *Entick v Carrington* (1765) 95 ER 807 at 817, that the 'eye cannot by the law of England be guilty of trespass'. In accordance with this maxim, the English and Australian courts—in contrast to United States jurisprudence—have traditionally refused to regard optical surveillance of private property as tortious.[15]

In Australia, *Victoria Park Racing and Recreation Grounds Co Ltd v Taylor* (1937) 58 CLR 479 has been interpreted as precluding the existence of a cause of action for invasion of privacy.[16] However in *Australian Broadcasting Corporation*

---

14. Australian Law Reform Commission, *Privacy*, Report No 22, 1993, at [152]. Quoted in Handley RP, 'Trespass to Land as a Remedy for Unlawful Intrusion on Privacy' (1988) 62 *The Australian Law Journal* 216–222 at 221.
15. But see: *Douglas v Hello! Ltd* [2001] 2 WLR 992; 2 All ER 289; *Earl Spencer and Countess Spencer v the United Kingdom* [1998] 25 EHRR CD 105.
16. *Church of Scientology v Woodward* (1982) 154 CLR 25 at 68, per Murphy J; *Australian Consolidated Press Ltd v Ettingshausen* (unreported, Court of Appeal of New South Wales, 13 October 1993) at 15, per Kirby J).

v Lenah Game Meats Pty Ltd (*Lenah*) [2001] HCA 63, the High Court, without declaring the existence of an actionable wrong of invasion of privacy, determined that neither policy nor precedent would impede the incorporation of such a tort into the Australian common law. *Lenah* involved trespass to the premises of Lenah Game Meats' abattoir by unknown persons who made an unauthorised, ten-minute long videotape of its processing operations. The operations included the stunning and killing of possums, which Lenah was licensed to carry out. Animal Liberation Ltd sent the videotape to the Australian Broadcasting Corporation (ABC). Lenah, to protect the goodwill of its business against the damage that would follow upon the screening of the videotape by the ABC, sought mandatory injunctions. The majority (Gleeson CJ, Gaudron, Gummow, Kirby, and Hayne JJ) refused to grant injunctive relief on the ground that Lenah's business operations, though carried out on a private land, did not have the character of a 'private act'. As Gummow and Hayne JJ put it (at [79]), the sensitivity of the plaintiff was merely 'that of the pocket book', and therefore distinct from 'the situation where an individual is subjected to unwanted intrusion into his or her personal life and seeks to protect seclusion from surveillance and to prevent the communication or publication of the fruits of such surveillance.'

A number of Australian jurisdictions have enacted legislation that regulates the use of listening devices for monitoring and recording of private conversations, optical surveillance devices to record private activities, and tracking devices in respect of the location of persons and objects. The legislation provides limited protection for unlawful use of surveillance devices. For example, in Victoria, s 7 of the *Surveillance Devices Act 1999* (Vic)[17] makes it a criminal offence to use optical surveillance devices to observe and record private activities;[18] to use listening devices to listen to and record private conversations, or to use tracking devices to track people and objects, without the express or implied consent of each party to the activity. However, such surveillance can be undertaken:

- under a warrant or an emergency authorisation
- under 'a law of the Commonwealth'
- if it falls within the performance of duties as a law enforcement officer
- if it is authorised by an occupier of the premises
- if there is a reasonable necessity 'for the protection of any person's lawful interests.

---

17. See also: *Surveillance Devices Act 1998* (WA); Listening and Surveillance Devices Regulations 2003 No 207 (SA).
18. The *Surveillance Devices Act 1999* (Vic), s 3, defines 'private activity' as 'an activity carried on in circumstances that may reasonably be taken to indicate that the parties to it desire it to be observed only by themselves, but does not include (a) an activity carried on outside a building; or (b) an activity carried on in any circumstances in which the parties to it ought reasonably to expect that it may be observed by someone else.'

In the United States, the courts are extending common law remedies for wrongful intentional interference with electronic networks, unauthorized access to web sites, and use of web site information without license or permission, by analogy with trespass to land and trespass to chattels[19] (see Chapter 8). Thus, in eBay, Inc v Bidder's Edge 100 F Supp 2d 1058 (ND Cal 2000), Whyte J of the United States District Court for the Northern District of California granted a preliminary injunction to eBay, an internet-based auction trading site, to prevent the defendant, an internet-based auction aggregation site, from accessing the plaintiff's computer system by use of any automated querying program without eBay's written authorisation. His Honour (at 1067) reasoned that:

> If eBay were a brick and mortar auction house with limited seating capacity, eBay would appear to be entitled to reserve those seats for potential bidders, to refuse entrance to individuals (or robots) with no intention of bidding on any of the items, and to seek preliminary injunctive relief against non-customer trespassers eBay was physically unable to exclude.

Likewise in Theofel v Farey-Jones, 359 F3d 1066, 2003 US App (9th Cir Cal 2004), Kozinski J speaking for the Court (at 1073), used an analogy with trespass, which protects those who rent space from a commercial storage facility to hold sensitive documents, when interpreting provisions of the *Stored Communications Act*, 18 USCS (2003). These provisions were designed to protect users whose digital communications are in electronic storage with an Internet service provider or other electronic communications facility against intentional unauthorised access. The court held that permission to access a stored digital communication 'does not constitute valid authorisation if it would not defeat a trespass claim in analogous circumstances'.

FURTHER READING

Butler D, 'A Tort of Invasion of Privacy in Australia?' (2005) 29 *Melbourne University Law Rev* 339.
Fleming JG, *The Law of Torts*, 9th edn, The Law Book Company, Sydney, 1998.
Hogue AR, *Origins of the Common Law*, Liberty Press, Indianapolis, 1966.
Ibbetson D, *A Historical Introduction to the Law of Obligations*, Oxford University Press, Oxford, 1999.
Kearney D, 'Network Effects and the Emerging Doctrine of Cybertrespass' (2005) 23 *Yale Law & Policy Review* 313.
Motooka WM, 'Can the Eye Be Guilty of a Trespass? Protecting Noncommercial Restricted Websites after Konop v. Hawaiian Airlines' (2004) 37 *UC Davis L Rev* 869.

---

19. See also: Thrifty-Tel, Inc v Bezenek, 54 Cal Rptr 2d 468 (Cal Ct App 1996); Compuserve Inc v Cyber Promotions, Inc, 962 F. Supp 1015 (SD Ohio 1997); Ebay, Inc v Bidder's Edge (2000) 100 F Supp 2d 1058 (ND Cal 2000).

6 Miscellaneous Intentional Torts of Action on the Case

The following discussion involves seven distinct and discrete intentional torts, each of which is a species of action on the case.

HISTORY

Action on the case for intentional infliction of indirect physical harm or nervous shock stands midway between intentional torts such as trespass and unintentional torts such as negligence. All the torts that have been examined so far have directness and immediacy as their essential elements. The writ of trespass *simpliciter* was limited—and still is—to injuries which were *direct* and *immediate*. Fortescue J in *Reynolds v Clarke* (1725) 1 Stra 634, at 635, explained:

> If a man throws a log into the highway, and in that act it hits me, I may maintain trespass because it is an immediate wrong; but if as it lies there I tumble over it, and receive an injury, I must bring an action upon the case; because it is only prejudicial in consequence.

As the common law developed, it became clear that a remedy was needed for indirect intentional injuries. However, by the end of the thirteenth century, Chancery had restricted the granting of writs to those already on its registers. According to Bracton, new writs could only be secured for a 'like case falling under the same law and requiring a like remedy.'[1] A clause known as *in consimili casu* (in similar case), authorised the plaintiff to petition Parliament for creation of a new writ analogous to an existing form of action, should the Chancery clerks and the 'wise men' of the realm fail to grant the necessary writ. Nevertheless, relatively few new writs were issued from that time on, although some old writs were adapted to meet special circumstances of a new case.

---

1. Bracton H, *On the Laws and Customs of England* (Thorne SE, tran), William S Hein & Co, Buffalo, New York, Vol 2, 1997, p 21.

Eventually, the concept of a 'wrong' was redefined so as to include not only the fault of breaching the royal peace, but also fault by infliction of damage upon the plaintiff's person, land, or chattels. This led Chancery, in 1367, to issue a new writ for action on the case which came to be used as a remedy for non-forceful and indirect injuries. However, to obtain a remedy the plaintiff had to explain how he had suffered damage; that is, the plaintiff had to state his 'special' case (*sur le Cas*).

Consequently, the plaintiff pleading general trespass would recite the two counts: *vi et armis* (with force of arms) and *contra pacem* (against the peace), and then proceed with a fairly concise declaration that the defendant beat and wounded him at such and such a time and place. It was for the defendant to disprove the claim.

The plaintiff pleading special trespass would omit the first counts of *vi et armis* and *contra pacem*, but specify in greater detail the facts on which he hoped to persuade the court to give him a remedy on the writ *sur le Cas*. The burden of proof was on the plaintiff.

The presence or absence of the two counts identified the forms of action as 'trespass' or 'case'. In general, as Kitto J noted in *Darling Island Stevedoring and Lighterage Co Ltd v Long* (1957) 97 CLR 36, at 64:

> The old action of trespass was confined to instances of the direct application of force. An indirect application of force would support only an action of trespass on the case.

ACTION ON THE CASE FOR INTENTIONAL INFLICTION OF PHYSICAL HARM

Definition of the tort

A person will be liable for damages in an action on the case for indirect intentional acts that are calculated to cause harm, and do in fact produce some effect of the kind intended. In *Bird v Holbrook* (1828) 4 Bing 628, the defendant Holbrook grew tulips in a walled garden. To protect his valuable bulbs (in 1800 a common price for a single tulip bulb was fifteen guineas),[2] Holbrook placed a spring gun in the garden. It was set to go off when a person entered the tulip beds. The sixteen-year-old plaintiff was asked to retrieve a peahen that had strayed into the tulip garden. As he jumped the wall into the garden, his foot came in contact with the wires attached to the gun, so that it discharged into the plaintiff's leg, injuring him. At the Court of Common Pleas, Best CJ held that the defendant was liable in an action on the case for damages for an indirect intentional act, which caused the harm of the kind that was intended.

---

2. MacKay C, *Memoirs of Extraordinary Popular Delusions* (1841), edited by Tobias, A under the title: *Extraordinary Popular Delusions and the Madness of Crowds*, Crown, New York, 1980, p 101.

Elements of the tort

Intention

By definition, in intentional torts on the case, wrongful intention is an essential element of action. Lord Mansfield, in *Tarleton v Fisher* (1781) 2 Douglas 671 at 673, commented that:

> in trespass, innocence of intention is no excuse: in case, the whole turns upon it'.

Thus, in an action on the case for injury to the person, the plaintiff has to show that the defendant's indirect intentional act was 'for the express purpose of doing injury.

In action on the case for intentional injury to the person, 'intention' means either:

(i) that the defendant intended to do the harm which materialised; or
(ii) that he or she knew that the injury was certain or substantially certain to follow from the conduct.

Thus, the nature of intention for the purposes of action on the case for intentional injury differs from intention for purposes of trespass: the latter is limited to the commission of the act that is substantially certain to result in a direct unauthorised physical contact, whether or not such contact was in fact intended.

For the purposes of action on the case for intentional infliction of physical harm, intention to harm will be imputed in cases where the defendant sets up a situation fraught with risk of harm to others and fails to provide notice of such risk.

Requirement of damage

According to *Bird v Holbrook* (at 628), the intended harm must have materialised: 'he who sets spring guns, without notice, is guilty of an inhuman act, and ... if injurious consequences ensue, he is liable to yield redress to the sufferer'.[3] The plaintiff must show that he or she suffered harm of the kind that was intended by the defendant.

CAUSE OF ACTION FOR INTENTIONAL INFLICTION OF NERVOUS SHOCK

Definition

A cause of action for indirect intentional injury to the person can also arise by way of a statement intended to cause the plaintiff nervous shock. The term 'nervous

---

3. In Tasmania, setting mantraps is a criminal offence under the *Criminal Code Act* 1924, s 179.

shock' is now a legal term of art denoting damage in the form of psychiatric illness that is not consequent on physical injury or physical contact.[4]

Wilkinson v Downton [1897] 2 QB 57

Wilkinson v Downton was the first case in which the common law recognised that intentional statements can cause damage to the psychological health of the victim (torts of slander and defamation have safeguarded damage to reputation for a long time).

In this case, the defendant Downton, a customer at the Albion public house, told Mrs Wilkinson, the plaintiff, that her husband, the landlord of the Albion, who had gone to the races earlier that day, 'was smashed up in an accident and that he was lying at The Elms at Leytonstone with both legs broken' (at 58). The story was false and meant to be a practical joke; Mr Wilkinson returned safely by train later that evening. However, the effect of Downton's story on Mrs Wilkinson was 'a violent shock to her nervous system, producing vomiting and other more serious and permanent physical consequences at one time threatening her reason and entailing weeks of suffering and incapacity' (at 58).

The defendant admitted that he intended to give the plaintiff a shock, though not of the intensity and seriousness she in fact suffered. The jury awarded Mrs Wilkinson £100 for nervous shock, but the defence claimed that she did not have a good cause of action. Wright J determined that Downton was liable in an action on the case because his conduct was so plainly calculated to produce some effect of the kind which was produced, namely nervous shock, that the intention to produce it ought to be imputed to him. Noting that 'the effect was produced on a person proved to be in an ordinary state of health and mind', Wright J concluded (at 58):

> It is difficult to imagine that such a statement, made suddenly and with apparent seriousness, could fail to produce grave effects under the circumstances upon any but an exceptionally indifferent person, and therefore an intention to produce such an effect must be imputed, and it is no answer in law to say that more harm was done than was anticipated, for that is commonly the case with all wrongs.

The principles enunciated in *Wilkinson v Downton* were reaffirmed by the Court of Appeal in *Janvier v Sweeney* [1919] 2 KB 316. In that case, during the First World War (1914–18), the defendants, two private detectives, pretended to be military policemen. They wanted Miss Janvier, a French citizen, to hand over to them certain letters which were in the possession of her employers. To this end, they falsely alleged that Miss Janvier was wanted by military authorities for corresponding with her fiancé, whom they accused of being a German spy. The

---

4. Mendelson D, *Interfaces of Medicine and Law: The History of Liability for Negligently Caused Psychiatric Injury (Nervous Shock)*, Ashgate International, Aldershot, 1998.

shock of the accusations, together with the fear for her fiancé's safety, caused Miss Janvier to suffer a severe psychosomatic illness. Miss Janvier successfully sued for intentional infliction of nervous shock. Bankes LJ (at 322) stated that 'terror wrongfully induced and inducing physical mischief gives a cause of action'.

In *Carrier v Bonham* [2001] QCA 234, the defendant, Bonham, a schizophrenia sufferer, having absconded from a psychiatric hospital, attempted to commit suicide by jumping in front of a bus driven by the plaintiff, Carrier. The plaintiff was unable to stop the bus, and as a result Bonham sustained physical injury. However, the experience of the collision also had an injurious impact on Carrier, who developed adjustment disorder. Subsequently, he was compelled to give up bus driving, thus sustaining both personal injury and economic loss. The Queensland Court of Appeal (McMurdo P, McPherson JA, and Moynihan J) determined that Bonham was liable in action on the case for intentional infliction of nervous shock.

In England, Lord Hoffmann in *Wainwright v Home Office* [2003] UKHL 53, having discussed *Wilkinson v Downton*, commented (at [41]) that *Wilkinson v Downton* does not have a 'leading role in the modern law'. However, in Australia, following negligence reforms that have imposed liability thresholds and caps, the *Wilkinson v Downton* cause of action will be of greater importance than previously.

Elements of the tort

In an action on the case for intentional infliction of nervous shock, the plaintiff has to establish:

- *intention*: that the defendant made a statement intended to cause shock to the plaintiff; and
- *damage*: that he or she suffered damage of the kind intended by the defendant.

Intention

The test of liability for intentional infliction of harm focuses upon the intention of the defendant's conduct. The truth or falsity of the defendant's statement or conduct has no relevance. Liability can arise from a true statement if it was intended, or could reasonably be said to have been intended, to cause physical or nervous shock (psychiatric illness) to the plaintiff. This, however, does not mean that reasonable people need to worry about tortious liability when communicating distressing news. As Windeyer J pointed out in *Mount Isa Mines Ltd v Pusey* (1971) 125 CLR 383, at 407:

> There is no duty in law to break bad news gently or to do nothing which creates bad news ... unless there be an intention to cause a nervous shock.

Where there is evidence that the defendant, by committing suicide in the plaintiff's house, intended to 'shock' or distress the plaintiff, and the plaintiff suffers psychiatric injury as a result, then the defendant's estate will be liable in an action on the case for damages for nervous shock. This was the case in *Blakeley v Shortal's Estate* 20 NW 2d 28 (1945). Conversely, the defendant will be liable to the plaintiff for intentional infliction of nervous shock if he or she fakes suicide in the plaintiff's house, and the latter suffers nervous shock as a result.

In *Carrier v Bonham* [2001] QCA 234, McMurdo P noted (at [12]) that the term 'calculated', in the context of the intention required for liability under *Wilkinson v Downton*, should be interpreted as meaning 'likely to have that effect' rather than 'intending to have that effect'.

Bunyan v Jordan (1937) 57 CLR 1

In *Bunyan v Jordan* the High Court of Australia affirmed the principle that the tort is available in Australia if the defendant intentionally makes a statement intended to cause nervous shock and succeeds in doing so. In *Bunyan v Jordan*, Miss Bunyan observed her employer, the defendant Jordan—who was drunk at the time—handling a loaded revolver. She also overheard him saying to another employee that he intended to shoot himself or someone else. Having fired a pistol shot in another building, the defendant returned to his office and proceeded to tear up one-pound notes, shouting that he would not live until the morning. A doctor was called, though from the reports it is not clear whether he attended Miss Bunyan or the defendant. Miss Bunyan suffered symptoms of neurasthenia, as a result of which she was unable to work for three months. Miss Bunyan sued her employer for nervous shock.

The High Court decided that intention to cause emotional distress alone was insufficient. The intentional words must be uttered directly to the plaintiff, or at least in his or her presence. Since Jordan neither uttered the threats in Miss Bunyan's presence nor intended to cause her personally any distress, the plaintiff had no cause of action. The High Court's insistence the statement should be targeted at the harmed individual and uttered in his or her presence is inconsistent with the theory of action on the case, which since the eighteenth century has provided remedy for consequential wrongs.[5] This aspect of *Bunyan v Jordan* was criticised by the South Australian Full Court of the Supreme Court in *Battista v Cooper* (1976) 14 SASR 225.

Canadian courts have never insisted on the requirement that the intentional harmful statements be directed at and uttered in the plaintiff's presence. Thus, in

---

5. *Reynolds v Clarke* (1725) 1 Stra 634 at 635.

Bieletski v Obadiak (1921) 61 DLR 494; affd (1922) 65 DLR 627, the plaintiff recovered damages after she suffered nervous shock upon hearing a false rumour, originated by the defendant, that her son had hanged himself. In Canada, claimants have also successfully sued their employers for intentional infliction of nervous shock in the workplace. Some wrongful actions resulting in nervous shock to the plaintiff have involved false accusations of theft and dismissal;[6] highly discriminatory conduct by co-workers and superior officers;[7] conduct aimed at controlling and dominating the claimant by exploiting his or her sensitivities; making derogatory comments in order to humiliate the claimant; and taking actions which were known to engender extreme emotional reactions.[8]

The nature of injury

In Australia, unless consequent upon an infringement of a legal right or physical injury, so-called 'purely mental distress'—such as mere fright, grief, fear, anxiety horror, shame, anger, embarrassment, and humiliation—will not sound in damages. For example, in *Giller v Procopets* [2004] VSC 113, the defendant distributed a video cassette showing sexual activity between the parties, as a result of which the plaintiff felt distressed and humiliated. Her claim failed because the mental harm she suffered did not amount to psychiatric illness. In *Hunter v Canary Wharf Ltd* [1997] AC 655, at 707, however, Lord Hoffmann made the following observation:

> I see no reason why a tort of intention should be subject to the rule which excludes compensation for mere distress, inconvenience or discomfort in actions based on negligence ... The policy considerations are quite different.

Indeed, in some jurisdictions of the United States, the courts have created a tort of outrage that does not require physical damage or lasting emotional disturbance in cases where the defendant, by outrageous conduct of no social utility, has upset the plaintiff's emotional and mental tranquillity.[9]

Intentional harassment

Although the common law does not recognise a general tort of harassment, acts of harassment may constitute other torts, such as private nuisance, and, when the harassing conduct involves threats of imminent violence, also assault and an action on the case.

---

6. *Rahemtulla v Vanfed Credit Union* [1984] 3 WWR 296 (BCSC).
7. *Clark v Canada (TD)* [1994] 3 FC 323.
8. *Boothman v Canada (TD)* [1993] 3 FC 381.
9. See, for example: *State Rubbish Collectors Assoc v Silinzoff* 240 P 2d 282 (1952).

In the English case of *Khorasandjian v Bush* [1993] QB 727, the Court of Appeal held that harassment which results in physical or psychiatric harm may be actionable under the tort of *Wilkinson v Downton*. The defendant, a twenty-one-year-old man, had met the plaintiff, a sixteen-year-old girl, at a snooker club in 1990. They became friends. However, in late 1991, their friendship broke down and the plaintiff told the defendant she did not wish to see him again. Unable to accept this, the defendant began to harass the plaintiff, threatening her with violence. He also pestered her with telephone calls at her parents' and grandmother's house. The plaintiff was granted an interim injunction restraining the defendant from molesting, harassing, or otherwise interfering with her, and from coming within 200 yards of her parents' home or any other address at which she might reside. The Court of Appeal upheld the injunction. Eventually, he was sent to prison for threatening to kill her.

In the *Khorasandjian* case, the plaintiff did not seek damages. However, the Court of Appeal observed that had the requisite injury in the form of a recognised psychiatric condition been pleaded and established, the plaintiff would have been able to recover damages. The House of Lords, in *Hunter v Canary Wharf Ltd; Hunter v London Docklands Corp* [1997] AC 655, overruled *Khorasandjian* on the issue of standing to sue in nuisance, while leaving the issue of the tort of harassment open. The *Protection from Harassment Act 1997* (UK) placed the law of harassment in England on a statutory basis. In Australia, Khorasandjian's conduct would be classified as stalking, which is a criminal offence.[10]

MALICIOUS PROSECUTION

History

According to William Holdsworth's *A History of English Law*,[11] the tort of malicious prosecution developed in the sixteenth and seventeenth centuries from an action on the case founded upon the common law writ of conspiracy. This action, in turn, was derived from a statutory writ of conspiracy dating back to the reign of Edward I. The *Statute of Conspirators* (1293) 21 Ed I, allowed an action against persons who conspired to procure a false indictment (wrongly setting the criminal law in motion). It was actionable as a species of trespass on the case, and punishable as a crime.[12]

---

10. *Criminal Code 1913* (WA), s 338E; *Criminal Code Act 1899* (Qld), s 395B; *Crimes Act 1900* (ACT), s 35; *Crimes Act 1900* (NSW), s 562AB; *Criminal Law Consolidation Act 1935* (SA), s 19AA; *Criminal Code Act 1924* (Tas), s 192; *Crimes Act 1958* (Vic), s 21A. Protection from sexual harassment is embodied in equal opportunity and anti-discrimination codes. See also: protection against racially motivated harassment: *Criminal Code Amendment (Racist Harassment And Incitement to Racist Hatred) Act 1990* (WA); *Racial Vilification Act 1996* (SA); and 'victimisation: *Civil Liability Act 1936* (SA), s 73; *Medical Practice Act 2004* (SA), s 81 (which specifically refers to 'victimisation' as a tort)
11. Holdsworth W, *A History of English Law*, Methuen & Co Ltd, Vol 8, 1973, p 385.
12. Winfield P, 'The Writ of Conspiracy' (1917) 23 *LQR* 28.

Today, the tort of malicious prosecution protects personal liberty and reputation by providing an avenue of redress to the citizen hurt by abuse of power. Unlike the tort of false imprisonment, actual deprivation of a plaintiff's liberty is not an essential element of this cause of action.

Principles and elements of malicious prosecution

The tort of malicious prosecution seeks to balance two competing principles: the notion that every person should have the right to bring wrongdoers to justice on the one hand, and the right of individuals to be free from baseless prosecution on the other. Malicious prosecution is an action on the case, therefore the plaintiff must show damage. In the case of *Saville v Roberts* (1698) 1 Ld Raym 374, Holt CJ (at 378) defined the requirements for the tort, stressing that the plaintiff must establish damage in one of the following three forms: risk to reputation; risk to personal security; or risk to security of property.

Risk to reputation in the sense of 'damage to his fair fame'

Criminal proceedings are considered sufficient damage because they involve accusation of illegal conduct, which if wrongful, is defamatory. In the United States, malicious prosecution can apply in cases where the defendant filed or prosecuted the underlying civil action. Historically, until *Little v Law Institute of Victoria* [1990] VR 257, apart from bankruptcy, insolvency, and winding-up proceedings against a company,[13] English and Australian courts have been reluctant to extend the tort of malicious prosecution to cover other wrongful civil proceedings.[14] However, according to Professor Fleming:

> there is nothing in the history of the action nor any pronouncement of binding authority to suggest that the action is confined to criminal proceedings.[15]

Indeed, maliciously instigated malpractice proceedings can ruin the reputation, and hence the livelihood of any professional person.

Risk to personal security

This category of damage was described by Hale CJ in *Saville v Roberts* (1698) 1 Ld Raym 374 at 378, as arising 'when a man is put in danger to lose his life, limb or

---

13. Historically, the courts also allowed damages for malicious procurement of excommunication by an ecclesiastical court: *Hocking v Matthews* (1670) 1 Vent 86; *Gray v Dight* (1677) 2 Show 144; and for malicious arrest of a ship: *The Walter D Wallet* [1893] P 202.
14. In *Barker v Sands & Madougall Co Ltd* (1890) 16 VLR 719, the court held that loss of reputation by adverse publicity due to a writ for recovery of debt was not within the requisite damage.
15. Fleming JG, *The Law of Torts*, 9th edn, The Law Book Company Ltd, Sydney, 1998, p 675.

liberty'. The risk to personal security can arise, for example, in high-profile cases where a person is charged with a crime or tort that society considers particularly reprehensible, and the media encourages populist feelings of outrage.

Risk to security of property

A person can sustain damage to property when 'forced to expend his money in necessary charges to acquit himself of the crime of which he is accused' (*Saville v Roberts* at 381). This phrase has been interpreted as disallowing the actual costs of defending criminal prosecution; however, loss of income, loss of leases, having to move accommodation, and travelling expenses may constitute sufficient damage.

Once damage is established, the plaintiff has to prove the following:

1. Institution, adopting or continuing of criminal proceedings by the defendant. This may include provision of information by an informant to a public prosecuting authority with malice and knowing the information to be false (*Commonwealth Life Assurance Society Ltd v Brain* (1935) 53 CLR 343; *Martin v Watson* [1996] AC 74).

2. Termination of those proceedings in the plaintiff's favour, if from their nature they were capable of so terminating (this may include quashing of the conviction).

The plaintiff must then establish two fault elements: instrumentality and malice.

1. The defendant must have been actively instrumental in the institution of the proceedings without reasonable or probable cause of action

Whether the defendant was actively instrumental in the institution of the proceedings is a question of law. Supplying incriminating or suspicion-raising information to the police, on which they eventually decide to prosecute, is not sufficient unless such information has a self-executing effect that compels prosecution, leaving the police with no discretion. For example, In *Martin v Watson* [1996] 1 AC 74 the defendant in an action for malicious prosecution made a complaint to the police that the plaintiff had indecently exposed himself to her, whereupon the plaintiff was charged by the police. The House of Lords held that the defendant was liable to be sued for malicious prosecution on the grounds that where a complainant has falsely and maliciously given a police officer information indicating that a person is guilty of an offence, and the facts relating to the alleged offence were solely within the complainant's knowledge, so that the police officer could not have exercised any independent discretion, then the complainant could properly be said to have been instrumental in setting the prosecution in motion.

Whether the defendant actually believed that the plaintiff was guilty of an offence or had committed a tort is a question of fact (*Commonwealth Life Assurance*

Society Ltd v Brain (1935) 53 CLR 343). In the past, Australian jurisprudence has concentrated on the question whether the defendant had reasonable and probable cause for prosecuting the plaintiff. For example, in *Mitchell v John Heine & Son Ltd* (1938) 38 SR NSW 466, Jordan CJ (at 469) stated:

> (1) The prosecutor must believe that the accused is probably guilty of the offence. (2) This belief must be founded upon information in the possession of the prosecutor pointing to such guilt, not upon mere imagination or surmise. (3) The information, whether it consists of things observed by the prosecutor himself, or things told to him by others, must be believed by him to be true. (4) This belief must be based upon reasonable grounds. (5) The information possessed by the prosecutor and reasonably believed by him to be true, must be such as would justify a man of ordinary prudence and caution in believing that the accused is probably guilty.

In *Glinski v McIver* [1962] AC 726, Lord Denning (at 758) discussed the nature of the requisite belief:

> In the first place, the word 'guilty' is apt to be misleading. It suggests that, in order to have reasonable and probable cause, a man who brings a prosecution, be he a police officer or a private individual, must, at his peril, believe in the guilt of the accused. That he must be sure of it, as a jury must, before they convict, whereas in truth he has only to be satisfied that there is a proper case to lay before the court, or in the words of Lord Mansfield, that there is a probable cause to bring the [accused] 'to a fair and impartial trial'.[16]

2. The defendant must have had malicious intent or a primary purpose other than that of carrying the law into effect

The commencement of a prosecution without reasonable and probable cause is evidence from which malice may be inferred.[17] However, unless the element of malice (wrongful or sinister motive actuated by spite, ill-will or vengeance, or by self-gain), is satisfied, the plaintiff will fail, even where the proceedings were brought without reasonable and probable cause.

Damages

In *Baltic Shipping Company v Dillon* (1993) 176 CLR 344, Mason CJ (at [32]) stated that damages could be recovered by a plaintiff for anxiety, disappointment

---

16. See also: *Birchmeier v Rockdale Municipal Council* (1935) 51 WN (NSW) 201 at 202, per Jordan CJ.
17. *Arbrath v North Eastern Railway Co* (1883) 11 QBD 440; *Gibbs v Rea* [1998] 3 WLR 72 at 80: malice covers not only spite and ill will but also improper motive.

or distress when those feelings were the consequence of assault, false imprisonment, malicious prosecution and defamation.[18]

TORT OF COLLATERAL ABUSE OF PROCESS

History

The cause of action for abusing judicial process for an 'ulterior purpose' was first enunciated in *Grainger v Hill* (1838) 132 ER 769, the case in which the defendant mortgagees of a vessel had the owner, Grainger, arrested, ostensibly for non-payment of a mortgage debt that was not yet due. Their object was to compel Grainger to hand over the register of the vessel, to which they had no right, and without which the ship—the mortgagees' security—could not sail. Grainger sued the defendants in a special action on the case. The court declared that the action was not for malicious prosecution or malicious arrest, rather, it was a distinct and independent action for abuse of process, and awarded Grainger damages for the loss of the voyages that he could not undertake without the register. Tindall CJ (at 773) stated that Grainger's complaint was 'that the process of the law has been abused, to effect an object not within the scope of the process'.

Tindall CJ then noted that 'the action is not for maliciously putting process in force, but for maliciously abusing the process of the Court' (at 773). His Honour distinguished the new cause of action from the tort of malicious prosecution in the following way (at 773):

> it is immaterial whether the suit which that process commenced has been determined or not, or whether or not it was founded on reasonable and probable cause.

The abuse of process was not the commencement of proceedings for the debt which the defendants knew was not yet due, but the commencement of the proceedings with the wholly ulterior purpose of extorting the register. According to Bosanquet J (at 774):

> This is not an action for a malicious arrest or prosecution, or for maliciously doing that which the law allows to be done: the process was enforced for an ulterior purpose; to obtain property by duress to which the Defendants had no right. The action is not for maliciously putting process in force, but for maliciously abusing the process of the Court.

---

18. His Honour was discussing Lord Cranworth V-C's statement in *Kemp v Sober* (1851) 1 Sim (NS) 517 at 520; 61 ER 200 at 201.

The nature of the tort

Thus, the tort of collateral abuse of process protects the court process from abuse by requiring that parties to litigation do not institute or maintain proceedings in order to 'to effect an object not within the scope of the process' (*Grainger v Hill* at 773).[19]

For the purposes of the tort, 'process' encompasses not only court proceedings and procedures but also all processes incidental to litigation, such as discovery, subpoenas, and bankruptcy proceedings.[20]

The party alleging collateral abuse of process has to establish that the defendant either deliberately instituted proceedings or intentionally misused existing proceedings for an ulterior motive, seeking a collateral advantage (object) beyond what the law or the legal process offers.

For example, in *Williams v Spautz* (1992) 174 CLR 509, Dr Spautz used proceedings for criminal defamation against academics and members of the Newcastle University Council as a means of securing his reinstatement. The High Court found that although he might have had an arguable case in criminal defamation, Dr Spautz instituted the proceedings not to vindicate his legal right, but for an ulterior, and therefore, improper, purpose: reinstatement. Mason CJ, Dawson, Toohey, and McHugh JJ said (at 522) that where the proceedings are used as an instrument of oppression, the court has the power to prevent the abuse of process even if the instigator has a prima facie case.

It is unclear whether, in Australia, damage is an essential element of the tort of collateral abuse of process.[21] However, in the great majority of cases, the claimant alleging collateral abuse of process would have suffered not only litigation costs occasioned through the abuse, but also economic loss such as loss of profits, emotional distress, possibly injury to dignity and reputation or even, in some cases, physical harm.

Elements of action for abuse of process

Abuse of proceedings

Threats to sue are not sufficient to support the tort of collateral abuse of process (*Pitman Training Ltd v Nominet UK* [1997] EWHC Ch 367). For the tort to arise,

---

19. Action on the case for collateral abuse of process is distinct from the plea of abuse of process, in which defendants seek an exercise of the inherent jurisdiction of the court to stay actions that are frivolous and vexatious and an abuse of process. In order to succeed, the defendants must demonstrate 'that the case of the plaintiff is so clearly untenable that it cannot possibly succeed': *General Steel Industries Inc v Commissioner for Railways (NSW)* (1965) 112 CLR 125 at 129, per Barwick CJ. See also: *Cox v Journeaux No 2* (1935) 52 CLR 713 at 720, per Dixon J.
20. *Dowling v The Colonial Mutual Life Assurance Society Ltd* (1915) 20 CLR 509.
21. In the United States, out of the fifty-one jurisdictions which recognise the tort of collateral abuse of process, seventeen require damages as an element of the tort: Utermohle JJ, 'Look What They've Done to My Tort, Ma: The Unfortunate Demise of "Abuse of Process" in Maryland' (2002) 32 *U Balt L Rev* 1.

proceedings must be instituted. In *Williams v Spautz* the High Court commented (at 528) that this is especially so:

> when the party commencing the proceedings has previously threatened that, unless the other party complies with some improper demand the first party has made, such as payment of an alleged debt, criminal proceedings will be commenced and prosecuted to a conviction. In such a case, the very commencement of the proceedings amounts to use of them for an improper purpose.

Unlike malicious prosecution, the gist of which is a lawsuit that was initiated without cause, under the *Grainger v Hill* doctrine, the gist of abuse of process is not that the proceedings—civil or criminal—instigated by the defendant were without foundation, but that their purpose was predominantly other than that for which they were designed.[22] Plaintiffs therefore do *not* have to show that the proceedings were resolved in their favour.[23] For example, in an American case, *Soffos v Eaton*, 80 US App DC 306; 152 F 2d 682 (1945 CA DC), Soffos had a long-term lease on a house owned by Eaton. When the United States entered the Second World War, the rent payable by Soffos was reduced by 10 per cent under the *Emergency Rent Act*. Eaton then instigated four successive suits against Soffos, each being a pretext to recover possession of the house. Each was unsuccessful. Soffos then sued Eaton for abuse of process, claiming damages for the expense of defending the suits, injury to reputation (one of the suits had involved charges of disorderly behaviour and nuisance), and mental anguish caused by threatened loss of a home. The Court of Appeal for the District of Columbia granted the relief, stating (at 683) that 'one who twice sues another maliciously and without probable cause is responsible to him in damages' for abuse of process.

In some cases, deliberate misuse of the tools of litigation such as motions to adjourn, subpoenas, or discovery, when filed for improper purpose—as an 'instrument of oppression'—may also constitute the tort of abuse of process.

Intention and manifestation of improper purpose

The nature of intention for the purposes of the tort was thus defined by Brennan J in *Williams v Spautz* at 537:

> I would hold that an abuse of process occurs when the only substantial intention of a plaintiff is to obtain an advantage or other benefit, to impose a burden or to

---

22. In Queensland, the claimant also has to show that an improper act was involved in the prosecution of the proceedings: *Beach Club Port Douglas Pty Ltd v Page* [2005] QCA 475 at [14]; see also: *Butler v Simmonds Crowley & Galvin* [2000] 2 Qd R 2.
23. In *Varawa v Howard Smith Co Ltd* (1911) 13 CLR 35 the High Court insisted that the claimant has to establish the want of reasonable and probable cause, which confused the tort of malicious prosecution with the tort of collateral abuse of process.

create a situation that is not reasonably related to a verdict that might be returned or an order that might be made in the proceeding.

His Honour noted (at 537) that:

> Substantiality is a matter of degree, ascertained by reference to the intention attributed to the plaintiff in all the circumstances of the case. At the end of the day, the court must determine, by reference to the intention attributed to the plaintiff, not merely whether the collateral purpose of the proceeding outweighs any legitimate purpose but whether the plaintiff entertained any substantial intention that the proceeding should achieve a legitimate purpose.

Consequently, according to Brennan J, the test of intention to abuse the process of law is subjective.

However, reprehensible motive or malice for instigation of the proceedings may not provide sufficient evidence to establish the tort (*Williams v Spautz* at 529, 534–5). The intention—in the sense of 'ulterior objective'—for the litigation, prosecution, or prolongation of the proceedings has to be identified. While improper purpose is an element of the tort, it is not yet conclusively settled in Australia whether evidence of improper purpose by such overt acts as threats, extortion,[24] letters involving improper demands, or commercial duress need to be established independently of the proceedings.[25]

For example, in *Flower & Hart v White Industries (Qld) Pty Ltd* (1999) 87 FCR 134, the defendant Flower & Hart, a firm of solicitors, advised its client in writing to institute and continue proceedings, including a baseless allegation of fraud. The correspondence between the defendant solicitors and counsel indicated that the purpose of the litigation was not to vindicate any right that the client might have, but to put White Industries under pressure and thus reduce the amount payable to White Industries under a building contract. The court held that this amounted to an abuse of process because of the illegitimate purpose for which the proceedings were instituted. Further, the court found that the manner in which Flower & Hart conducted the proceedings, and the obstructionist and delaying conduct in which it indulged, exacerbated the abuse of process. In doing so, Flower & Hart as solicitors breached the duty they owed to the court, warranting a costs order against the firm.[26]

If a claimant alleges deliberate misuse of the tools of litigation, he or she must explain how, exactly, the improper objective of the other party's litigation tactics outweighs any legitimate purpose that they might otherwise have.

---

24. *Grainger v Hill* (1834) 132 ER 769.
25. *Butler v Simmonds Crowley & Galvin* [1999] QCA 475, at [38], considered that evidence of an 'overt act' in addition to proceedings is an essential element of the tort.
26. On the issue of costs and interest, see: *Flower & Hart v White Industries (Qld) Pty Ltd* [2001] FCA 370.

MISFEASANCE IN PUBLIC OFFICE

Definition

Misfeasance in public office was defined by Deane J, in *Northern Territory v Mengel* (1995) 185 CLR 307 (at 370), as a tort involving invalid or unauthorised acts by public officers in the purported discharge of their public duty, which has the effect of causing loss or harm to the claimant. His Honour noted that the critical element of the tort is malice.

History

The origins of the tort of misfeasance in public office have been traced to *Turner v Sterling* (1671) 2 Vent 25; 86 ER 287, but the best-known early case is *Ashby v White* (1703) 1 Smith's Leading Cases (13th edn) 253; 2 Ld Raym 938, where the court found that an elector, who was wilfully denied a right to vote by a returning officer, could sue the officer in misfeasance in public office.[27] The nineteenth century saw a number of cases in which judges in the lower instance courts were sued for malicious acts within their jurisdiction.[28] Although in *Davis v Bromley Corporation* [1908] 1 KB 170, the English Court of Appeal 'denied the existence of the tort', the Privy Council in *Dunlop v Woollahra Municipal Council* [1982] AC 158 (at 172) described the tort as 'well established'.

Rationale of the tort of misfeasance in public office

Nourse LJ, in *Jones v Swansea City Council* [1990] 1 WLR 54 (at 85F), observed that the rationale of the tort is that in a legal system based on the rule of law, executive or administrative power 'may be exercised only for the public good', and not for ulterior and improper purposes. In England, the most exhaustive analysis of different aspects of the tort was undertaken by the House of Lords on 18 May 2000 and 22 March 2002 respectively, and the decision was reported as *Three Rivers District Council & Ors v Governor and Company of the Bank of England (No 3)* [2003] 2 AC 1 (*Three Rivers Case*). The claimants applied to the House of Lords to determine the correct test for misfeasance in public office in order to consider whether the facts they alleged were capable of meeting that test. Their Lordships held that the plaintiffs in a class action could sue the Bank of England for misfeasance in public office in performance of its public duty to supervise the

---

27. See also: *Drewe v Coulton* (1787) 1 East 563n; 102 ER 217; *Tozer v Child* (1857) 7 El & Bl 377; 119 ER 1286; *Cullen v Morris* (1819) 2 Stark 577; 171 ER 741.
28. *Ackerley v Parkinson* (1815) 3 M & s 411; 105 ER 665; *Harman v Tappenden* (1801) 1 East 555; 102 ER 214; *Taylor v Nesfield* (1854) 3 El & Bl 724; 118 ER 1312, cited in the *Three Rivers Case* at 191, per Lord Steyn.

banking operations of a commercial bank, the Saudi Arabian Bank of Credit and Commerce International, in which they held deposits. The Saudi Arabian bank's collapse was due to fraud perpetrated at a senior level of its hierarchy. The plaintiffs alleged that the loss was caused by the Bank of England wrongly granting the bank a licence, or wrongly failing to revoke the licence.

The High Court of Australia discussed the nature and the elements of the tort of misfeasance in public office in *Northern Territory v Mengel* (1995) 185 CLR 307 (*Mengel*) and *Sanders v Snell* (1998) 196 CLR 329 (*Sanders*). In *Mengel*, the plaintiffs were cattle farmers who owned two stations. A campaign to eradicate bovine brucellosis was carried out by the Northern Territory's Department of Primary Industry and Fisheries. The brucellosis-free status of the plaintiffs' cattle was previously confirmed; however, the Department's officials ordered that the movement of those cattle be restrained so tests could be administered. Restrictions were imposed at a time when the plaintiffs intended to sell the herd. Part of the plaintiffs' herd perished during the period of testing, and by the time the restrictions were lifted—after the tests established that the herds were free from the disease— cattle market prices were significantly lower. The officers believed they were acting in accordance with their statutory powers in ordering the constraint of movement, as did the plaintiffs, who believed that non-compliance with the restrictions would expose them to criminal liability. In fact, the movement restriction regulations did not apply to the plaintiffs' cattle.

The High Court (Mason CJ, Dawson, Toohey, Gaudron, and McHugh JJ in a joint judgment; Brennan and Deane JJ delivering separate judgments), proceeded on the basis that the tort requires an act which the public official knows is beyond power and which involves the foreseeable risk of harm. The plaintiffs' action failed.

The case of *Sanders* involved a dismissal of an executive officer, Snell, employed on a contract basis by the Norfolk Island Government Tourist Bureau. The dismissal was effected by Sanders, the Norfolk Island Minister for Immigration and Tourism. Sanders directed the Tourist Bureau to terminate Snell's employment following a spot audit instigated by him. When the Tourist Bureau chair expressed concerns about the accuracy of the audit report, and suggested that Snell, in the interests of natural justice, should be given an opportunity to tell his side of the story, Sanders revoked the appointments of the six-member board of the Tourist Bureau, and appointed a new board. He then directed the new board to terminate Snell's contract, which was done on the following day. The Full Federal Court held that the tort of misfeasance in public office against Sanders was made out, but the High Court (Gleeson CJ, Gaudron, Kirby, and Hayne JJ), in a joint judgment, upheld Snell's appeal and ordered a retrial. When the case was retried, at first instance the defendant was found liable; however, the Full Court of the Federal Court in *Sanders v Snell* [2003] FCAFC 150 upheld Sanders' appeal.

Elements of the tort

Broadly,[29] to establish the tort, it has to be shown that:

1. the defendant was a public officer;
2. the defendant performed/exercised an invalid or unauthorised act in the purported discharge of his or her public duties (exercise of power as a public officer);
3. the defendant had the requisite state of mind (malice):
   (a) targeted malice—a specific intention to injure a person or persons; or
   (b) knowledge that he or she had no power to do the act complained of and that it would probably injure the plaintiff; this was said to involve 'bad faith' in as much as the public officer did not have an honest belief that the act was lawful or showed reckless indifference or deliberate blindness to the invalidity or lack of power and the likely injury (*Cornwall & Ors v Rowan* [2004] SASC 384 at [212]);
4. the plaintiff has sufficient interest to found a legal standing to sue;
5. damage: the act had caused loss to the plaintiff[30]

Public officers

In *Mengel*, Brennan J stated that the tort provides a remedy for intentional misuse of power by public officers: that is, persons who take reward from any source for a discharge of public duty.

The requirement of a reward restricts the ambit of liability, and thus differs from the traditional definition of 'public office' provided by Professor Winfield,[31] who defined 'public office' in the context of a discussion of the tort of usurpation of public office or interference with the discharge of it 'a post the occupation of which involves the discharge of duties towards community or some section of it, whether the occupier of the post is or is not remunerated'. According to Lord Steyn in the *Three Rivers Case* (at 191), in England, the institution of a 'public office' for the purpose of the tort may include a local authority exercising private-law functions as a landlord.

---

29. Deane J in *Northern Territory of Australia v Mengel* (1996) 185 CLR 307, at 370, adopted the paradigm of the tort as defined by Lord Diplock in *Dunlop v Woollahra Municipal Council* [1982] AC 158 at 172. See also: Lord Steyn in *Three Rivers District Council v Bank of England (No 3)* [2003] 2 AC 1; *Sanders v Snell* [2003] FCAFC 150.
30. In *Farrington v Thomson & Bridgland* [1959] VR 286, the plaintiff was ordered to close a hotel and cease serving alcohol by the defendants who knew they did not have the power to give such an order.
31. Winfield P, *A Text-Book of the Law of Tort*, 4th edn, Sweet & Maxwell Ltd, London, 1948, p 628.

Unless public officers act under a *de facto* authority, they are personally liable for misfeasance in public office.[32] The position of public officers is thus analogous to professional private practitioners.

Exercise of power by police officers would invariably fall within the scope of the tort.[33] For example, in *Darker & Ors v Chief Constable of the West Midlands Police* [2001] 1 AC 435, the plaintiffs were indicted on counts alleging conspiracy to import cannabis resin and on a count alleging conspiracy to forge American Express travellers' cheques. They were charged following an undercover operation conducted by members of the police. During the trial, the Crown failed to comply with the judge's orders for disclosure. The trial judge then held that the police had been significantly at fault in the disclosure process, and directed that the charges be permanently stayed on the ground of abuse of process. The House of Lords determined that the plaintiffs could sue for misfeasance in public office committed by police officers under the direction and control of the chief constable. According to Lord Hope of Craighead (at 448):

> The rule of law requires that the police must act within the law when they are enforcing the law or are investigating allegations of criminal conduct. It also requires that those who complain that the police have acted outside the law in the performance of those functions, as in cases alleging unlawful arrest or trespass, should have access to a court for a remedy.

The judiciary and persons in equivalent positions, such as royal commissioners, presidents of boards of inquiry, etc, are public officers, though they may be protected by statutory grants of immunity. In *Cannon v Tahche* (2002) 5 VR 317, at [28], the Victorian Court of Appeal stated that 'although the tort [of misfeasance in public office] is ordinarily concerned with executive or administrative powers, it seems that it also operates in respect of the exercise of a judicial power; at least in certain contexts'.[34]

Do barristers and solicitors come within the definition of 'public officers'? The answer depends on whether or not they are deemed to hold public office, or if they do hold such an office, the nature of the particular public duty in question. For example, in *Tampion v Anderson* [1973] VR 715,[35] the full Court of the Supreme Court of Victoria (Smith, Pape, and Crockett JJ), held that counsel—a member of the Victorian Bar who had been briefed to assist the Board of Inquiry into Scientology—was not a 'public officer' for the purposes of the tort, even though his fees were provided from public revenue. The reason was that counsel had no

---

32. *Northern Territory of Australia v Mengel* (1996) 185 CLR 307 at 347; *James v Commonwealth* (1939) 62 CLR 339 at 359–360, per Dixon, J.
33. *Garrett v Attorney-General* [1997] 2 NZLR 332.
34. The High Court refused application for special leave to appeal: *Tahche v Cannon & Ors* [2003] HCA Trans 524.
35. Affirming McInerney J, at first instance, reported at [1973] VR 321.

statutory powers with respect to the inquiry, and was not answerable to members of the public for the performance or non-performance of his duty.

Again, in *Cannon v Tahche* (2002) 5 VR 317, similar claims of misfeasance in public office were dismissed. Robert Tahche's retrial for a 'revenge rape' of Sammia Abboud had been the subject of a *nolle prosequi* by the Director of Public Prosecutions on the grounds that the conviction would be unsafe in view of evidence that Abboud had also laid a complaint against Tahche's cousin, Charlie Tahche, which turned out to be false. Robert Tahche then claimed that the prosecuting barrister and the instructing solicitor in the original revenge rape trial committed misfeasance in public office because at the time they were aware of Abboud's allegations against Charlie, yet failed to disclose them to him. Winneke P, Charles, and Chernov JJA followed *Tampion* and determined that in relation to disclosure of information, prosecuting counsel's public duty is owed to the court, not the client. In denying Tahche's application for the special leave to appeal to the High Court,[36] Gleeson CJ affirmed the conclusion of the Court of Appeal that the duties owed by the barrister and solicitor were not 'directly enforceable at the suit of the accused or anyone else by prerogative writ, judicial order or action for damages.'[37] Duties of disclosure and calling of witnesses, are owed to the court: 'the relevant sanction for their breach is the making of orders at the trial of the accused or on appeal to prevent or remedy any miscarriage of justice resulting from breach of duty.'

An invalid or unauthorised act

In *Mengel* (at 347), Mason CJ, Dawson, Toohey, Gaudron, and McHugh JJ determined, in their joint judgment, that the defendant must be a 'public official' who acted:

> with an intention to cause harm to the plaintiff (or the class of which the plaintiff is a member) or had knowingly acted in excess of his or her power (*ultra vires*) in a way calculated in the ordinary course to cause harm.

Acts constituting the relevant misfeasance comprise all acts and omissions that the public official knows are beyond power, including conduct that is invalid for want of procedural fairness. However, in *Mengel*, Brennan J (at 358) said that the tort requires more than mere negligence:

> the tort of misfeasance in public office is not concerned with the imposition of duties of care. It is concerned with conduct which is properly to be characterised as an abuse of office and with the results of that conduct. Causation of damage is relevant; foreseeability of damage is not.

Whether a defendant has acted honestly or dishonestly is a question of fact.

---

36. *Tahche v Cannon & Ors* [2003] HCA Trans 524.
37. Gleeson CJ referred to *Whitehorn v The Queen* (1983) 152 CLR 657 at 665, per Deane J.

Intention

The essence of the tort is an abuse of power;[38] but the unauthorised or invalid act or omission must have been intentional. According to the joint judgment in *Mengel* (at 347), although the tort guards against exercise of invalid or unauthorised power by public officers, 'the principle suggests' that it 'is a counterpart to, and should be confined in the same way as, those torts which impose liability on private individuals for the intentional infliction of harm'.

It is unclear whether this passage makes a general point that misfeasance in public office as species of action on the case for harm occasioned by intentional conduct is part of private law, and thus should not include interpolations from public law, or whether this tort should be 'confined' so as not to include the trespassory concept of intention. Be that as it may, in relation to the requirement of intention, their Honours (at 347) determined that misfeasance in public office includes 'acts which are calculated in the ordinary course to cause harm, as in *Wilkinson v Downton* [1897] 2 QB 57', and that:

> It may be that analogy with the torts which impose liability on private individuals for the intentional infliction of harm would dictate the conclusion that, provided there is damage, liability for misfeasance in public office should rest on intentional infliction of harm, in the sense that is the actuating motive, or on an act which the public officer knows is beyond power and which is calculated in the ordinary course to cause harm.

Malice: knowledge and recklessness

In the *Three Rivers Case*, the House of Lords distinguished between three forms of liability for misfeasance in public office based on malice: targeted malice; untargeted malice; and recklessness.

Targeted malice

Targeted malice by a public officer involves conduct specifically intended to injure a person or persons (*Three Rivers Case* at 191, per Lord Steyn; *Mengel* at 347; *Sanders* at 503). In 'targeted malice', the intention to inflict harm must be shown to be 'the actuating motive' for the exercise of the power *(McKellar v Container Terminal Management Services Ltd* (1999) 165 ALR 409). In this form of the tort, malice or bad faith stems from the exercise of public power for an improper or ulterior motive, which means that the power was exercised unlawfully (*Cornwall & Ors v Rowan* [2004] SASC 384 at [212]).

---

38. *Elguzouli-Daf v Commissioner of Police of the Metropolis* [1995] QB 335 at 347b, per Steyn LJ; *Northern Territory of Australia v Mengel* (1996) 185 CLR 307, particularly Brennan J's judgment.

For example, in *Cornwall & Ors v Rowan* [2004] SASC 384, Dr Cornwall, the South Australian Minister for Health and Community Welfare, was found guilty of misfeasance in public office by acting maliciously towards the plaintiff, Mrs Rowan. Dr Cornwall, in the exercise of his public duties as the responsible minister, targeted the plaintiff by directing publication of a report that he knew to contain unsubstantiated allegations against the plaintiff, without affording her procedural fairness. He published the report with intention to cause harm to the plaintiff by publicly discrediting her, at the same time as he decided to withdraw funding from a women's shelter she ran. His actions caused loss or harm to Mrs Rowan. The plaintiff was awarded $25 000 in exemplary damages specifically for misfeasance in public office 'to mark the disapproval of Dr Cornwall's abuse of his position, to punish him for his outrageous conduct and to deter others from like conduct'.[39]

Untargeted malice

In the *Three Rivers Case*, Lord Steyn (at 191) said that the second form of malice in the tort of misfeasance in public office involves untargeted malice. The claimant has to demonstrate that the public officer was acing in bad faith because he or she did not have an honest belief that the act was lawful, that is:

> where a public officer acts knowing that he has no power to do the act complained of and that the act will probably injure the plaintiff. It involves bad faith inasmuch as the public officer does not have an honest belief that his act is lawful.

The concepts of 'honest belief' and 'bad faith' are rather abstruse, and the courts also refer to the defendant officer having 'actual knowledge' of the lack of power and likely harm, or manifesting 'reckless indifference' to the absence of the power (*Three Rivers Case*; *Sanders v Snell* [2003] FCAFC 150). In *Mengel*, the High Court held that the claimants did not demonstrate the element of untargeted malice on the part of Department's officials. Likewise, the *Sanders* decision suggests that, at least in Australia, the second form of malice—based on reckless indifference to the absence of power and giving rise to want of procedural fairness, is difficult to establish. In *Sanders*, the High Court (at 349) found that although two other officers had advised Sanders that he should give Snell 'natural justice', neither of them: 'was a lawyer and neither of them pretended to give legal advice to the appellant'. Their Honours pointed out that these officers counselled the Minister to give Snell a fair chance to put his side of the story because they thought that was the fair thing to do, not because they thought giving a hearing was necessary as a matter of law. In the

---

39. *Cornwall & Ors v Rowan* [2004] SASC 384 at [722]. Mrs Rowan was awarded a total of $305 425.10.

view of the majority, the fact that Sanders had been given advice but chose to ignore it 'did not amount to the appellant knowing that he was acting beyond power'.[40]

According to the High Court, the claimant must establish that the officer had *actual knowledge* of the lack of power, or was recklessly indifferent to the presence or absence of the power. This, it would appear, can only be accomplished by demonstrating that the defendant was in possession of professional legal advice on the limitations of his or her power. In both *Mengel* and *Sanders*, the High Court held that the respective claimants did not demonstrate the element of untargeted malice on the part of the public officers.

Recklessness

The element of malice is satisfied by reckless indifference to the exercise of the power, as when the official's exercise of power in the performance of the relevant duty lacks honesty and thus makes the act an abuse of power, or where public officials recklessly disregard the means of ascertaining the extent of their power (*Garrett v Attorney-General* [1997] 2 NZLR 332; *Rawlinson v Rice* [1997] 2 NZLR 651). In the *Three Rivers Case*, Lord Hope of Craighead (at 252) defined recklessness necessary for the purposes of the tort thus:

> Recklessness is demonstrated where it is shown that the public officer was aware of a serious risk of loss due to an act or omission on his part which was unlawful but chose deliberately to disregard that risk. That is sufficient to establish that he did not have an honest belief in the lawfulness of the conduct which, to his knowledge, gave rise to that risk. Recklessness about the consequences, in the sense of not caring whether the consequences happen or not, will satisfy the test. In this context there is no additional element of dishonesty or bad faith that requires to be satisfied.

Malice may also be present when the harm is occasioned by a public official who recklessly ignores 'the means of ascertaining the existence of a contract, and acts in its breach' (*Northern Territory v Mengel* (1995) 185 CLR 307 at 347).

Locus standi (having standing to sue)

The plaintiff must establish that he or she is a member of the public to whom the defendant owed a duty to exercise the power legitimately: namely, only in the public interest and not for an ulterior purpose (*Cannon v Tahche* (2002) 5 VR 317 at [28]).

---

40. The High Court ordered that there be a new trial on the issue of the plaintiff's claim alleging misfeasance in public office.

Causation and damage

Lord Steyn, in the *Three Rivers Case*, emphasised (at 194) that damage is an essential element of the tort, and plaintiffs must establish that the defendant's conduct caused them to suffer damage, which may include consequential economic loss. Causation is a question of fact.

Remoteness of damage

In the *Three Rivers Case* the House of Lords preferred the test of remoteness based on the defendant's knowledge that the decision would probably damage the plaintiff. According to Lord Steyn (at 196):

> a plaintiff must establish not only that the defendant acted in the knowledge that the act was beyond his powers but also in the knowledge that his act would probably injure the plaintiff or person of a class of which the plaintiff was a member.

However, in *Mengel*, Brennan J (at 358) did not consider foreseeability of damage relevant.

Policy considerations

The High Court majority in *Sanders v Snell* stressed (at 503) that the tort has to balance two competing public interests: on the one hand, an interest in not deterring 'officials from exercising powers conferred on them when their exercise would be for the public good', and on the other hand, an interest in ensuring that persons affected by an abuse of public power be compensated. The decision tips the balance in favour of protecting public officials.

In *Mengel* (at 345), the High Court commented that the boundaries of the tort of misfeasance in public office remain uncertain. One could add that following the decision in *Sanders v Snell*, the boundaries, at least in relation to untargeted malice, have been drawn so narrowly as to make misfeasance in public office a theoretical rather than a practical remedy. In 1948, Professor Winfield[41] noted that there are two cases, *Carrett v Smallpage* (1808) 9 East 330 and *Lawlor v Alton* (1873) 9 Ir R CL 160, in which the courts recognised the existence of an old tort that protects persons lawfully entitled to a public office against an usurpation of that office or interference with the discharge of it. Conceivably, in the future, a person in Snell's position could sue someone like Sanders under this tort.

The approach of the majority of the High Court in *Sanders* is surprising, for the object of the tort is to compensate individuals for harm occasioned by officials acting in the knowledge that what they are doing is unlawful. As a general rule, ignorance of the law is not a defence to a claim in tort. By deciding that absence

---

41. *A Text-Book of the Law of Tort*, 4th edn, Sweet & Maxwell Ltd, London, 1948, p 628.

of professional legal advice may shield the defendant from liability, even where the refusal to do the 'the fair thing' also amounts to an abuse of power, the High Court has created an exception not only to this particular tort, but to the whole notion of what constitutes 'knowledge' for the purposes of the law of torts. In so far as such an exception is contrary to the doctrine of the coherence of the fundamental principles of the law (*Sullivan v Moody; Thompson v Connon* (2001) 207 CLR 562), the better view is that it should not be followed.

In *Ruddock v Taylor* [2005] HCA 48, the claimant's Permanent Transitional Visa was twice cancelled unlawfully, and he was twice detained by the Department of Immigration. He sued the minister, Mr Ruddock, the then Minister for Immigration and Multicultural Affairs who had made the two decisions to cancel his visa, and the Commonwealth, for false imprisonment. Gleeson CJ, Gummow, Hayne, and Heydon JJ in a joint judgment found no false imprisonment, but commented (at [28]) that in relation to the lawfulness of the minister's exercise of power, 'if it were suggested that the Minister had exercised power where the Minister knew or ought to have known that what was done was beyond power an action may lie for the tort of misfeasance in public office. But that has never been the respondent's case in this matter.'

TORTS OF BREACH OF CONFIDENCE AND MISUSE OF PRIVATE INFORMATION

Confidentiality and privacy are quite different concepts, with separate histories and contexts. The concept of confidentiality, classically attached to interpersonal communications, defines rights and obligations of the two parties to a relationship. Privacy relates less to interpersonal communications and more to the scope and limits of individual autonomy.[42]

Whereas the legal concept of confidentiality reflects notions of trust embedded in the Judeo-Christian moral and ethical heritage, the concept of privacy—in the sense of a personal privilege to exclude others—is based on a social and legal distinction between intimate and public domains.[43] The modern notion of privacy can be traced to the rise of economic and social hegemony of the bourgeoisie in

---

42. Ortiz DR, 'Privacy, Autonomy, and Consent' (1989) 12 *Harv J L & Pub Pol'y* 91 at 91–92.
43. Thus, there is no express right to privacy in the United States Constitution, though the United States Supreme Court, in a series of cases, found an implied constitution right to privacy, and applied it in such diverse areas as *child rearing and education* (*Pierce v Society of Sisters*, 268 US 510 (1925); *Meyer v Nebraska*, 262 US 390 (1923)); *family relationships* (*Prince v Massachusetts*, 321 US 158 (1944)); *procreation* (*Skinner v Oklahoma*, 316 US 535 (1942)); *Carey v Population Servs Int'l*, 431 US 678 (1977)); *marriage* (*Loving v Virginia*, 388 US 1 (1967)); *contraception* (*Griswold v Connecticut*, 381 US 479 (1965)); see also: *Eisenstadt v Baird*, 405 US 438 (1972)); and *the right of a woman to decide whether or not to beget or bear a child* (*Carey v Population Servs Int'l*, 431 US 678 (1977); see also: *Roe v Wade*, 410 US 113 (1973); Buchanan GS, 'The Right to Privacy: Past, Present, and Future' (1989) 16 *Ohio N U L Rev* 403; Warren SD & Brandeis LD, 'The Right to Privacy' (1890) 4 *Harvard Law Review* 193.

the nineteenth century,[44] with its emphasis on personal independence and a general right or liberty of individuals to have their private lives protected from public scrutiny. In 1890, young Samuel D Warren and Louis D Brandeis published 'The Right to Privacy' in the *Harvard Law Review*.[45] It became the classic exposition of the right to privacy in the context of common law.

In relation to personal information, the right to privacy has been defined as protecting 'data which relates to and identifies an individual and which, it can be assumed, the individual would prefer not to be made available to unauthorised persons or for unauthorised purposes.'[46] In England, the House of Lords decided in *Wainwright v Home Office* [2003] 3 WLR 1137 that there is no general tort of invasion of privacy; instead, in *Campbell v MGN Limited* [2004] UKHL 22; AC 457, it expanded the ambit of the action for breach of confidence.

In *Campbell*, the plaintiff, Naomi Campbell, a thirty-year-old celebrity fashion model who was a drug and alcohol addict, sued the English *Daily Mirror* newspaper for publishing a photograph which:

> showed her in the street on the doorstep of a building [where Narcotics Anonymous meetings were held] as the central figure in a small group. She was being embraced by two people whose faces had been pixelated. Standing on the pavement was a board advertising a named café. The article did not name the venue of the meeting, but anyone who knew the district well would be able to identify the place shown in the photograph. (at [5], per Lord Nicholls of Birkenhead)

Traditionally, the claimant in an action for breach of confidence had some kind of prior relationship with the alleged wrongdoer. However, in *Campbell*, the House of Lords, by a majority of three to two (Lord Hope of Craighead, Baroness Hale of Richmond, Lord Carswell; Lord Nicholls of Birkenhead and Lord Hoffmann dissenting), extended the operation of the tort of breach of confidence to encompass publication of private information by persons who were not in a pre-existing relationship with the plaintiff where it causes harm and is not outweighed by public interest or freedom of expression values.

History

In English law, protection of confidentiality had formed part of Chancery's equitable jurisdiction since the sixteenth century.[47] However, it was in the late eighteenth and

---

44. Until the nineteenth century, privacy as a social and legal construct was nebulous. Social, economic and sanitary conditions excluded any possibility of privacy for the rural and urban poor, whereas royalty and the nobility, for dynastic reasons, choose not to avail themselves of it
45. Warren SD & Brandeis LD, 'The Right to Privacy' (1890) 4 *Harvard Law Review* 193, available at <http://www.swiss.ai.mit.edu/classes/6.805/articles/privacy/Privacy_brand_warr2.html>.
46. Hughes G, *Data Protection in Australia*, The Law Book Company Limited, Sydney, 1991, p 1.
47. Maitland FW, *Equity (Two Courses of Lectures)*, Cambridge University Press, 1910, p 7.

early nineteenth centuries that the obligation of confidence as a legally enforceable right (outside of contract) began to evolve.[48] The case of *Prince Albert v Strange* (1849) 2 De Gex & Sm 652; 64 ER 293, affirmed on appeal (1849) 1 Mac & G 25, was the first in which breach of confidence was conceptualised as an actionable infringement of an interest in privacy. The Court of Equity granted an injunction to restrain the defendant from publishing a catalogue containing descriptions of private etchings made by the Prince Albert of members of the royal family at home. The court held (at 44–45) that impressions of the etchings had come into the hands of the defendants 'surreptitiously or improperly'; they may have been provided by the printer to whom the Prince had entrusted them, or through the Prince's own acquaintances.[49]

Thus, the doctrinal underpinnings of breach of confidence lie in equity.[50] In 1981, the United Kingdom Law Commission Report on *Breach of Confidence*[51] suggested that confidential information should be considered as property, and recommended a new statutory tort of breach of confidence. Although the United Kingdom Parliament did not act on this recommendation, liability both in equity and in tort for breach of confidence seems to be well established.[52] In *Campbell v MGN Limited* [2004] AC 457, Lord Nicholls of Birkenhead observed (at [13]) that: 'the breach of confidence label harks back to the time when the cause of action was based on improper use of information disclosed by one person to another in confidence'. His Lordship then (at [14]) explained the modern status of action for breach of confidence thus:

> This cause of action has now firmly shaken off the limiting constraint of the need for an initial confidential relationship. In doing so it has changed its nature. In this country this development was recognised clearly in the judgment of Lord Goff of Chieveley in *Attorney-General v Guardian Newspapers Ltd (No 2)* [1990] 1 AC 109, 281. Now the law imposes a 'duty of confidence' whenever a person receives information he knows or ought to know is fairly and reasonably to be regarded as confidential.

Noting that 'even this formulation is awkward', Lord Nicholls of Birkenhead pointed out (at [14]) that the expansion of the original tort from one where a

---

48. *Thompson v Stanhope* (1774) Amb 737; 27 ER 476; *Evitt v Price* (1827) 1 Sim 483; 57 ER 659. For further discussion see: Gurry F, *Breach of Confidence*, Clarendon Press, Oxford, 1984.
49. The privacy aspect of the action for breach of confidence was also emphasised in *Pollard v Photographic Co* (1888) 40 ChD 345, which involved the unauthorised publication of the plaintiff's photographic portrait, which she had commission for herself, on Christmas cards.
50. *Moorgate Tobacco Co Ltd v Philip Morris Ltd (No 2)* (1984) 156 CLR 414 at 437–38; *Seager v Copydex Ltd* [1967] 1 WLR 923 at 931, per Lord Denning MR; see also: *Stephens v Avery & Ors* [1988] 2 All ER 477 at 482, per Sir Nicholas Browne-Wilkinson.
51. United Kingdom Law Commission, *Breach of Confidence*, Report No 110 (Cmnd 8388), 1981, London HMSO.
52. Reid BC, *Confidentiality and the Law*, Waterlow Publishers, London, 1986, p 184.

particular duty of confidence arose from a particular relationship to a tort imposing general duty has changed the very nature of this cause of action:

> The continuing use of the phrase 'duty of confidence' and the description of the information as 'confidential' is not altogether comfortable. Information about an individual's private life would not, in ordinary usage, be called 'confidential'. The more natural description today is that such information is private. The essence of the tort is better encapsulated now as misuse of private information.

In Australia, although most cases relating to breach of confidence involve unauthorised disclosure of commercial information, in *Breen v Williams* (1996) 186 CLR 71, at 128, Gummow J observed that the subject-matter of confidential information:

> is not confined to trade secrets.[53] It extends to information as to the personal affairs and private life of the plaintiff, and in that sense may be protective of privacy.

Requirements

Whether in equity or at common law, action for breach of confidence has to be brought by the affected party,[54] and he or she must persuade the court that the public interest in maintaining confidence outweighs any countervailing public interest favouring disclosure.[55]

Since the tort of breach of confidence is an action on the case, the claimant has to show damage. In *Coco v AN Clark (Engineers) Ltd*,[56] Megarry J included the requirement of detriment, but suggested that it should be interpreted broadly.[57] While in equity breach of confidence is actionable *per se*,[58] there would need to

---

53. His Honour referred to *Saltman Engineering Co Ltd v Campbell Engineering Co Ltd* [1948] 65 RPC 203.
54. In *Broadmoor Special Hospital Authority & Anor v Robinson* [2000] 1 WLR 1590, the English Court of Appeal refused to grant an injunction to restrain a convicted patient in a special hospital from delivering and distributing a book, which identified other patients and detailed their offences. The court held that the Broadmoor Authority could not bring proceedings to protect other patients' rights to privacy or confidence or to prevent distress to the victims' families unless the conduct complained of interfered with the performance of the Authority's duties. To protect their confidences, proceedings would have had to be instituted by or on behalf of patient-confiders.
55. *Attorney-General v Guardian Newspapers (No 2)* [1990] 1 AC 109 at 282.
56. *Coco v AN Clark (Engineers) Ltd* [1969] RPC 41 at 48.
57. The issue of the requirement of detriment as an essential element of the action is not finally settled: see *Attorney-General v Guardian Newspapers (No 2)* [1990] 1 AC 109 at 255E, per Lord Keith of Kinkel; at 270D, per Lord Griffiths; at 281H, per Lord Goff.
58. See: Lord Keith in *Attorney General v Guardian Newspapers (No 2)* [1990] 1AC 109, at 256A: 'Further, as a general rule, it is in the public interest that confidences should be respected, and the encouragement of such respect may in itself constitute a sufficient ground for recognising and enforcing the obligation of confidence even where the confider can point to no specific detriment to himself.'

be very strong policy reasons for dispensing with the requirement of damage in tortious breach of confidence.

In Australia, collection and disclosure of personal information is protected through legislation, including the *Privacy Act 1988* (Cth), the *Health Records (Privacy and Access) Act 1997* (ACT), the *Health Records Act 2001* (Vic), the *Health Records and Information Privacy Act 2002* (NSW), and the *Health Services Act 1991* (Qld), s 62A.

FURTHER READING

Dix EJ, 'The Origins of the Action of Trespass on the Case' (1937) 46 *The Yale Law Journal* 1142–1176.

Intentional infliction of nervous shock

Magnusson R, 'Recovery for Mental Distress in Tort, with Special References to Harmful Words and Statements' (1994) 2 *Torts Law Journal* 126.
Mendelson D, *Interfaces of Medicine and Law: The History of Liability for Negligently Caused Psychiatric Injury (Nervous Shock)*, Ashgate International, Aldershot, 1998.
Mendelson D, 'The Defendants' Liability for Negligently Caused Nervous Shock in Australia—Quo Vadis?' (1992) 18 *Monash Law Review* 16–70.
Mullany N & Handford P, *Tort Liability for Psychiatric Damage*, The Law Book Company, Sydney, 1993, pp 283–297.

Malicious prosecution, collateral abuse of process, misfeasance in public office, breach of confidence

Fleming JG, *The Law of Torts*, 9th edn, The Law Book Company, Sydney, 1998, Ch 27.
Balkin RP & Davis JLR, *Law of Torts*, 2nd edn, Butterworths, Sydney, 1996, Ch 25.
Trindade F & Cane P, *The Law of Torts in Australia*, Oxford University Press, Melbourne, 1999, pp 82–100.
Cockburn T & Thomas M, 'Personal Liability of Public Officers in the Tort of Misfeasance in Public Office—Part 1' (2001) 9 *Torts Law Journal* 80.
Gurry F, *Breach of Confidence*, Clarendon Press, Oxford, 1984.
Reid BC, *Confidentiality and the Law*, Waterlow Publishers, London, 1986.
Warren SD & Brandeis LD, 'The Right to Privacy' (1890) 4 *Harvard Law Review* 193.

Deceit and Injurious Falsehood*

INTRODUCTION

The tortious actions of deceit and injurious falsehood[1] impose liability for knowingly false statements causing loss to the plaintiff. In the case of deceit, liability is imposed for a false and fraudulent representation directed to the plaintiff that induces the plaintiff to act in reliance on the statement to his or her loss. In the case of injurious falsehood, liability arises where the defendant has maliciously made to third parties a false representation concerning the plaintiff's goods or services that induces the third parties to act in reliance on the statement, causing loss to the plaintiff.

The following discussion of the actions of deceit and injurious falsehood will be comparatively brief, due to the fact that these torts have now largely been superseded by s 52 of the *Trade Practices Act 1974* (Cth) and its equivalents in the State and Territory Fair Trading legislation. Section 52 contains a statutory prohibition on misleading or deceptive conduct or conduct that is likely to mislead or deceive. Liability under s 52 is strict, and not dependent on proof of malice or knowledge of falsity, as required by the common law torts. Furthermore, the range of remedies contained in ss 82 and 87 of the *Trade Practices Act* for a contravention of s 52 are more extensive than those available at common law, conferring, for example, a power to order corrective advertising. For these reasons, s 52 has rendered the common law torts of deceit and injurious falsehood redundant to a degree.

---

*   This chapter was written by Sharon Erbacher.
1. Sir John Salmond, in his *The Law of Torts, a Treatise on the English Law of Liability for Civil Injuries*, Stevens & Haynes, London, 1907 at [149], is credited with coining the name of this cause of action. It has also been called slander of goods, disparagement of title, trade label, interference with prospective advantage, etc. See: Prosser WL, 'Injurious Falsehood: The Basis of Liability' (1959) 58 (3) *Columbia Law Review* 425.

Notwithstanding the above, it could be advantageous for a plaintiff to proceed under the common law torts rather than under s 52 in some circumstances. First, knowledge of falsity or proof of malice) is a requirement of the torts, so the plaintiff might well be entitled to claim aggravated or exemplary damages. In *Musca v Astle Corp Pty Ltd* (1988) 80 ALR 251, at 263–8, the High Court determined that those damages were not available for claims under the *Trade Practices Act*. Second, s 52 is only applicable where the conduct in question occurred 'in trade or commerce'. A misrepresentation made in a non-commercial context, such as a misrepresentation by a private vendor of a residential home or other private asset, is not conduct in trade or commerce, and therefore s 52 is not applicable.[2] In that circumstance, the plaintiff will need to rely on such common law causes of action as either deceit or negligent misstatement. Although the conduct underlying an injurious falsehood claim would normally occur in the course of trade or business, making s 52 available in the alternative, this will not always be the case. Thus, a letter written by a local councillor to other members of the council, intended as an in-house joke, would arguably not have been conduct in trade or commerce,[3] rendering s 52 inapplicable. *Magill v Magill* (2005) Aust Torts Reports ¶81–783, which, at the time of writing, had been granted special leave to appeal to the High Court from the decision of the Court of Appeal of the Supreme Court of Victoria, will determine whether the tort of deceit applies within a matrimonial situation.

DECEIT

Introduction

The tort of deceit is committed where the defendant fraudulently makes a false representation to the plaintiff with the intention that the plaintiff should rely on that representation, and the plaintiff does in fact rely on the false representation and suffers loss as a result. The writ of deceit goes back to 1201. In the fifteenth century, action on the case for deceit safeguarded people from being tricked into purchases they would not have otherwise made.[4] In 1534, Anthony Fitzherbert (1470–1538), a Judge of the Common Pleas in the reign of Henry VIII, wrote that 'this writ lieth properly where one man doth anything in the name of another, by which the other person is damnified and deceived'.[5] However, *Pasley v Freeman* (1789) 3 TR 51

---

2. *O'Brien v Smolonogov* (1983) 53 ALR 107; *Argy v Blunts and Lane Cove Real Estate Pty Ltd* (1990) 26 FCR 112.
3. *Palmer Bruyn & Parker Pty Ltd v Parsons* (2001) 218 CLR.
4. *Shepton v Dogge (no 1)* (1442) CP 40/725, m 49 (Pas 1442); *Shipton v Dogge (no 2)* (1442) (*Doige's Case*) [different spellings refer to the same case] reproduced and discussed in Baker JH & Milsom SFC, *Sources of English Legal History; Private law to 1750*, Butterworths, London, 1986, pp 390–395.
5. Fitzherbert A, *Natura Brevium*, 9th edn, 1794, at 95E; cited by Professor Winfield in *Law of Tort*, 4th edn Sweet & Maxwell Ltd, London, 1948, p 374.

was the first case on record to establish this cause of action as an independent tort. In *Pasley v Freeman*, the plaintiff recovered damages from the defendant, who had assured him that a buyer wishing to purchase sixteen bags of cochineal at £2600—a fortune in the eighteenth century—could be given credit for the purchase. The plaintiff acted on this assurance and lost the money. The defendant knew that his assurance was totally false. Buller J (at 56) stated that:

> The foundation of this action is fraud and deceit in the defendant and damage to the plaintiffs … Fraud without damage, or damage without fraud, gives no cause of action.

One hundred years later, Lord Herschell in *Derry v Peek* (1889) 14 App Cas 337 enunciated the main requirements of the tort. According to his Lordship, negligent misstatement is not sufficient; it must be proven that the defendant acted fraudulently in the sense that he or she knew the statement was false, or did not believe it to be true, or was reckless as to whether the statement was true or false.

An action for deceit is available only if the plaintiff who has suffered the loss is a person to whom the representation was directed and who was induced to rely on the false representation. Where the loss suffered by the plaintiff was attributable to a false representation made to a *third party* who was induced to rely on that representation, the appropriate cause of action is in injurious falsehood.[6] To illustrate: assume the plaintiff misses out on a job opportunity because of intentional false misrepresentations contained in a reference provided by a former employer. In this circumstance, any cause of action rests in injurious falsehood rather than deceit, as the plaintiff's loss resulted from the reliance by the prospective employer on the false reference, not from his or her own reliance on the false reference.

Elements of the tort of deceit

The tort of deceit comprises four elements:

1. the defendant made a false representation to the plaintiff;
2. the defendant made the representation fraudulently—ie knowing the statement to be false, or having no belief in its truth, or being recklessly indifferent to its truth or falsity;
3. the defendant intended the plaintiff to believe in and rely on the false representation; and
4. the plaintiff was induced to rely on the representation and as a result suffered economic loss.

These elements are considered in turn.

---

6. *TJ Larkins & Sons v Chelmer Holdings & Anor* [1965] Qd R 68.

False representation

There must be a representation to the plaintiff, and the representation must be false. Regarding the first of these requirements, a representation will generally amount to a statement—oral or written—but conduct might also convey a representation in some circumstances. Thus, the display of a motor vehicle showing a particular odometer reading is a representation that the vehicle has travelled the distance indicated.[7] The representation must be one as to fact; however in this regard it has famously been said by Bowen LJ in *Edgington v Fizmaurice* (1885) 29 Ch D 459, at 483, that 'The state of a man's mind is as much a fact as the state of his digestion'. A statement of opinion, belief or intention implies as a fact that the defendant honestly holds the opinion or belief, or honestly intends to act in the way represented. It follows that a statement of opinion, belief, or intention that the defendant does not honestly hold or does not honestly intend to fulfil will potentially give rise to liability in deceit.

The non-disclosure by the defendant of a material fact will not ordinarily amount to a representation. The general principle is *caveat emptor*, or in other words, 'let the buyer beware'. The onus is on the plaintiff to investigate all matters relevant to the transaction at hand, and the defendant is not liable for failing to disclose matters, even where the defendant knows that those matters would be critical to the plaintiff's decision whether or not to proceed with the transaction. It is only in exceptional circumstances that silence or non-disclosure will amount to a false representation at common law. The main exceptional circumstances are where there is a partial disclosure; where a statement is true when made but subsequently becomes false; and where a statement is believed to be true when made but is later found to be false.

(a) Partial disclosure. A defendant who has partially disclosed certain facts will be liable where the partial disclosure creates a deception. As Higginbotham CJ said in *Curwen v Yan Yean Land Co Limited* (1891) 17 VLR 745 (at 751):

> concealment of a fact may cause the true representation of another fact to be misleading, and may thus become a substantive misrepresentation ... A true representation, coupled with concealment, thus [becomes] a positive misrepresentation calculated to deceive.

This statement of principle was referred to with approval by the High Court in *Krakowski v Eurolynx Properties Ltd* (1995) 130 ALR 1, at [20]. The prospective purchasers of shop premises commenced proceedings in deceit, and under s 52 of the *Trade Practices Act*, on the basis of statements made by the vendor during the purchase negotiations to the effect that the premises were leased at an annual

---

7. *Given v Holland (Holdings) Pty Ltd* (1977) 15 ALR 439.

rental of $156 000. The defendant vendor did not disclose the existence of a collateral agreement with the lessee containing a number of incentives, such as a three-month rent-free period and payment of twelve months' rental to the lessee. The High Court held that, by failing to disclose the existence of the collateral agreement, the defendant had falsely represented that the lease agreement constituted the full agreement with the lessee and that the rent of $156 000 was the true rent being paid by the lessee. The court acted on the basis that this was not in fact a case of non-disclosure, but of a positive misrepresentation that the lease agreement contained the whole agreement between the defendants and the lessees. It was irrelevant that the defendant had not made an actual statement to the effect that the lease was the exhaustive contractual arrangement with the lessee, as the way the defendant and its agents had conducted the transaction represented that this was the case.

(b) Subsequent change of circumstances. A defendant is liable in deceit for failing to disclose that a stated fact, true at the time of the statement, had become false prior to the plaintiff acting in reliance on it. This principle is illustrated by *Jones v Dumbrell* [1981] VR 199. The defendant represented to the plaintiffs, shareholders in a company, that he wished to purchase their shares in order to continue to operate the business as a family concern. The plaintiffs sold their shares to the defendant at less than their full value on the basis of these representations. Subsequent to the representations, but before the share transaction was finalised, the defendant changed his mind and decided to purchase the shares in order to resell them to third parties for a profit, but did not disclose this change of mind to the plaintiffs. The defendant was found liable in deceit. The court held that a representation of fact will ordinarily be taken as continuing up until the moment that the transaction is concluded. A representor who becomes aware that a fact as represented has become false is under an obligation to disclose that change of circumstances to the recipients of the representation. On the facts, the defendant had acted fraudulently by his conduct in completing the negotiations without disclosing his change of mind, and with the intention that his initial representation should continue to operate on the minds of the plaintiffs and consequently to deceive them.

(c) Subsequent discovery of the falsity of the representation. A person who makes a representation believing it to be true, but who discovers it to be false prior to the recipient acting in reliance on it, will be liable in deceit if he or she fails to disclose this new knowledge (*Robertson v Belson* [1905] VLR 555).

The defendant made the representation fraudulently

As Lord Herschell emphasised in *Derry v Peek* (1889) 14 App Cas 337 (at 374):

> Fraud is proved when it is shown that a false representation has been made (1) knowingly, (2) without belief in its truth, or (3) recklessly careless whether it be true or false.

Negligence—even gross negligence—is not equivalent to fraud,[8] unless the plaintiff has deliberately shut his or her eyes to the facts or has deliberately refrained from investigating the truth of the matters. A mere failure by the defendant to take reasonable steps to verify the accuracy of the representations will not be actionable in deceit (although might be actionable as a negligent misstatement). It was for this reason that the action for deceit failed in *Derry v Peek*. In that case, representations by the directors of a company that the company had the right to use steam power for their trams, while false, were not fraudulent. The directors honestly believed they did have such a right, and therefore, although they had acted negligently, they had not acted fraudulently. In contrast, the majority of the court in *Krakowski* found that the defendant vendor, Eurolynx Properties Ltd, acted with fraud in not disclosing the existence of a collateral agreement to the plaintiff purchasers. The defendant and its agents knew that Mr and Mrs Krakowski were buying the property in the belief that the rental as shown in the lease agreement represented the commercial rent that the premises would yield and that there was no other agreement that would reduce the true amount of the rent. The defendant knew this to be false, and therefore had acted fraudulently.

Provided the defendant had the requisite state of mind, his or her motive in deceiving the plaintiff is irrelevant. A defendant who knowingly or recklessly makes a false statement is liable in deceit, even where the defendant believed that he or she was acting in the best interests of the plaintiff. As Lord Herschell observed in *Derry v Peek* (at 374), the necessary requirement is that the defendant intended to *deceive* the plaintiff, not that the defendant intended to *injure* the plaintiff.

Where a representation is ambiguous and could be understood in different ways by different people, the test is whether the defendant did not honestly believe in the truth of the representation in the sense in which the defendant intended it to be understood. This principle was confirmed by the High Court in *Krakowski*. The court held that the plaintiff must prove that the defendant had no honest belief in the truth of the representation giving it the meaning as intended by the defendant. Their Honours (at [29]) endorsed the following statement by the Privy Council in *Akerhielm v De Mare* (1959) AC 789 at 805–6:

> the question is not whether the defendant in any given case honestly believed the representation to be true in the sense assigned to it by the court on an objective consideration of its truth or falsity, but whether he honestly believed the representation to be true in the sense in which he understood it albeit erroneously when it was made.

This general proposition will not apply where the meaning placed by the defendant on the representation was not one which would be conveyed to any

---

8. *Smith v Chadwick* (1884) 9 App Cas 187 at 201.

reasonable person. In that circumstance, it might be possible to draw the conclusion that the defendant did not honestly understand the representation to bear the claimed meaning.[9]

The defendant intended that the plaintiff would rely on the representation

The plaintiff must prove that the defendant intended both to make the representation, and that the plaintiff would act on the basis of the representation. If the representation was made unconsciously or by mistake (for example due to a printing error in a document) the defendant will not be liable in deceit (though will perhaps be liable in negligence). Likewise, a principal who does not authorise an agent to make a particular representation will not be personally liable in fraud if the representation is in fact made by the agent, even though the principal knows the facts which make the representation false.[10]

The defendant must not only intend the representation to be made, but also must intend for it to be made to the *plaintiff* and for the *plaintiff* to act upon it. In other words, the defendant is liable only to the persons whom it intended should act upon the representation. So in *Peek v Gurney* (1873) LR 6 HL 377 the House of Lords held that a person who purchased shares on the stock market could not sue the directors of the company in deceit in relation to false representations in the company's prospectus. The prospectus was intended only for original shareholders or persons invited to become allottees of shares, and not for persons who bought shares on the stock market. However, it is not necessary to show that the defendant made the representation directly to the plaintiff; it is sufficient that that the defendant intended it to be passed on to the plaintiff, or that the defendant made the representation to a class of persons of whom the plaintiff was a member, so that the plaintiff was *one of the persons* who was intended to act on it. These principles were established by the High Court in *Commercial Banking Co of Sydney Ltd v RH Brown & Co* (1972) 126 CLR 337. The plaintiffs were a firm of woolgrowers who sold their clip on the sheep's back to a dealer, Wool Exporters Pty Ltd. When the time to deliver the wool was approaching, the plaintiffs heard rumours that the purchasers were in financial difficulties and were in doubt about whether or not they should deliver the wool. They requested their bank, the Bank of New South Wales, to make enquiries about the financial standing of the purchasers. The Bank of New South Wales made enquiries with the defendant bank, where the purchaser was a customer. The defendant bank responded that 'the company has always met its engagements, is trading satisfactorily and we consider that it would be safe for its trade engagements generally'. There was a disclaimer clause stating that the opinion was 'confidential and for your private use and without responsibility of the defendant bank or its officers'.

---

9. *Akerhielm v De Mare* (1959) AC 789; *Krakowski v Eurolynx Properties Ltd* (1995) 130 ALR 1 at [29].
10. *Cornfoot v Fowke* (1840) 6 M&W 358; 151 ER 450.

The Bank of New South Wales advised the plaintiffs of the opinion and the disclaimer. The plaintiffs delivered the wool but did not receive payment from the purchasers. The trial judge found that the opinion as to the purchasers' solvency was not honestly held by the defendant bank and that it had falsely represented the purchasers' financial position. The trial judge also found that the defendant bank knew that the enquiry by the Bank of New South Wales was made on behalf of a customers likely to enter into business dealings with the purchasers, and knew that its opinion was likely to be relied on by those customers. The main issue before the High Court was whether in these circumstances the representation could be said to have been directed to the plaintiffs. The court (Menzies and Gibbs JJ writing the main judgments) confirmed that the representation must be made to the plaintiff or to a class of persons including the plaintiff to induce them to act upon it. It was not necessary, however, that the representation should have been made to the plaintiff in person; it was enough that it was made to another person with the intention that it should be acted on by the plaintiff. On the facts, it was open to the trial judge to find that the defendant bank had provided the information with the intention that it be passed on to the customers on behalf of whom the request for information was made. The court rejected the defendant's argument that the disclaimer clause demonstrated that the opinion was to be used only by the bank itself, and that although it might be used as the basis of their opinion, it was not intended that it should be communicated to the customers. The evidence showed that the defendant bank knew that the Bank of New South Wales was not relying on the advice for its own purposes, but that it was being sought on behalf of customers of the bank proposing to deal with Wool Exporters. In that circumstance, the words in the disclaimer clause could not be conclusive. Gibbs J (at 350) held that it should not be accepted that:

> a man who fraudulently gives false information to A, with the intention that B will act upon it, can avoid responsibility by telling A that the info is for his use only. In my opinion the question whether a representation was made to one person, with the intention that another should act on it, is simply one of fact. The circumstance that the document containing the representation included the statement that it was for the private use of the person to whom it was addressed is relevant, but is only one of the circumstances of the case, all of which would have to be considered. It is not conclusive.

The plaintiff was induced to rely on the representation and as a result suffered economic loss

The plaintiff must establish that he or she was induced to rely on the representation to his or her detriment. In *Gould v Vaggelas* (1985) 157 CLR 215, at 236, Wilson J cited with approval Isaacs J's statement in *Holmes v Jones* (1907) 4 CLR 1692, at 1706, that:

The plaintiffs have the onus of proving that the representations they complain of were material, and that they were induced to act upon them.

Consequently, the false representation need not be the *sole* reason for the plaintiff acting to his or her detriment; it is sufficient that the fraudulent misrepresentation was a materially contributing factor to the plaintiff's decision to act. However, the action will fail where there is no causal relationship between the representation and the claimed loss, as where the representation was corrected before the relevant transaction was entered into (*Alati v Kruger* (1955) 94 CLR 216).

Remedies

The plaintiff is entitled to damages for all causally related losses (*State of South Australia v Johnson* (1982) 42 ALR 161). For instance, in *Doyle v Olby (Ironmongers) Ltd* [1969] 2 QB 158, the plaintiff bought an ironmongers' business from the defendants after being shown accounts for the preceding three years which showed considerable annual profits. He was also told that all the trade was over-the-counter. He soon found out that the turnover had been misrepresented, and that half the trade had in fact been obtained by one of the defendants acting as part-time travelling salesman. The English Court of Appeal determined that the plaintiff had been tricked into buying a business that he would otherwise not have purchased, and should be awarded his overall loss up to his final disposal of the business, less any benefits he had received. Thus, where the deception has caused the plaintiff to purchase a business, the plaintiff is entitled to the difference between the price paid for the business and its real value at that time, as well as compensation for any consequential losses, such as losses incurred in running the business.

It is currently uncertain whether the plaintiff must prove that the defendant could reasonably foresee the loss that occurred. In *Gates v City Mutual Life Assurance Society Ltd* (1986) 160 CLR 1, at 12, Mason, Wilson, and Dawson JJ stated that in an action for deceit a plaintiff is entitled 'to all the consequential loss directly flowing from his reliance on the representation, at least if the loss is foreseeable'.[11] However, the English courts have adopted a contrary view,[12] and in *Palmer Bruyn & Parker Pty Ltd v Parsons* (2001) 218 CLR 366, at [63ff], Gummow J has argued that the English approach is to be preferred. His Honour noted (at [66]) that 'the law with respect to intentional torts had developed satisfactory means of limiting a defendant's liability, without the need to resort to that notion', ie reasonable foreseeability.

---

11. Followed in *Henjo Investments Pty Ltd v Collins Marrickville Pty Ltd (No 2)* (1989) 40 FCR 76 at 92.
12. *Doyle v Olby (Ironmongers) Ltd* [1969] 2 QB 158 at 176; *Smith New Court Securities Ltd v Scrimgeour Vickers* [1997] AC 254 at 265, 281.

Aggravated damages are available to compensate the plaintiff for insult and humiliation experienced as a result of the deception (*Archer v Brown* [1984] 2 All ER 251). Exemplary damages are available where the deception was committed in a particularly calculated and callous fashion (*Musca v Astle Corp Pty Ltd* (1988) 80 ALR 251).

The plaintiff's damages will not be reduced for contributory negligence, for example because the plaintiff did not take reasonable steps to verify the accuracy of the representations (*Standard Chartered Bank v Pakistan National Shipping Co (Nos 2 & 4)* [2002] 3 WLR 1547). This represents a procedural advantage of deceit over the action in negligent misstatement, as the apportionment legislation will apply to the latter action to reduce the careless plaintiff's damages.

INJURIOUS FALSEHOOD

Introduction

The tort of injurious falsehood is an action on the case for special damage resulting from false and malicious statements made to a third party about the plaintiff's goods, property or business. Its origins lie in the sixteenth-century action on the case for 'slander of title' or 'disparagement of title'. The allegation was that the defendant cast aspersions on the plaintiff's ownership of land, as a result of which the plaintiff was unable to sell or lease the land. This action was always regarded as distinct from defamation, for there was no need to show injury to the plaintiff's personal character. The commonest forms of the tort involved claims for specific damage mainly, but not necessarily, resulting from interference with business.[13] For example, in *Barrett v Associated Newspapers Ltd* (1907) 23 TLR 666, the plaintiff sued over a false claim by the defendants that his house was haunted. In the nineteenth century the action was expanded to encompass false statements about goods.

The classic case of *Ratcliffe v Evans* [1892] 2 QB 524 concerned a plaintiff who had for many years carried on a business as an engineer and boiler-maker under the name of 'Ratcliffe & Sons'. The defendant published in his newspaper *County Herald*, a false statement 'purposely made about the manufactures of the plaintiff', which was intended to, and did in fact, cause him loss of business. Bowen LJ at 527–8 defined the tort of injurious falsehood in the following terms:

> [that] an action will lie for written or oral falsehoods, not actionable per se nor even defamatory, where they are maliciously published, where they are calculated in the ordinary course of things to produce, and where they do produce, actual

---

13. Prosser WL, 'Injurious Falsehood: The Basis of Liability', (1959) 58 (3) *Columbia Law Review* 425.

damage, is established law. Such an action is not one of libel or of slander, but an action on the case for damage wilfully and intentionally done without just occasion or excuse, analogous to an action for slander of title. To support it, actual damage must be shewn, for it is an action which only lies in respect of such damage as has actually occurred.

This statement of the tort was adopted by the High Court of Australia in *Hall-Gibbs Mercantile Agency Ltd v Dun* (1910) 12 CLR 84 and reiterated in *Sungravure Pty Ltd v Middle East Airlines Airliban SAL* (1975) 134 CLR 1.

Distinction between injurious falsehood and defamation

The tort of defamation (see Chapters 20 and 21) is also concerned with false statements concerning the plaintiff. Although the same factual claim might support an action both in defamation and in injurious falsehood—as where the statement denigrates the quality of the goods or services provided by the plaintiff—there is an important point of distinction between the two torts. To establish defamation of a professional or business reputation it is essential to prove that the statement disparaged that reputation[14] In contrast, it is sufficient for the purposes of injurious falsehood that the statement regarding the plaintiff's business is false; it is not a necessary requirement that the statement denigrate the business. For example, it is not defamatory to state falsely that the plaintiff's business has been acquired by another company and has ceased to trade (*Hall-Gibbs Mercantile Agency Ltd v Dun* (1910) 12 CLR 84), or that it has gone into bankruptcy, at least where there is no suggestion that this had occurred because of poor business skills (*Mirror Newspapers Ltd v World Hosts Pty Ltd* (1979) 141 CLR 632, at 638–9). However, these statements are potentially actionable as an injurious falsehood. Thus, in *Ratcliffe v Evans* [1892] 2 QB 524, the court accepted that the false article about the demise of the plaintiff's business, although not disparaging of the business, was made with malice and caused financial damage.

There are two further points of distinction between the two torts. First, the tort of defamation is concerned with protecting personal reputation as well as commercial and professional reputation, whereas the tort of injurious falsehood is only concerned with the latter. Second, proof of actual damage is an essential requirement of the tort of injurious falsehood;[15] however, at least since the enactment of the uniform defamation laws, it has not been necessary to prove special damage to establish an action in defamation.

---

14. Previous statutory provisions in Queensland and Tasmania included in the definition of defamatory matter statements that are likely to injure the plaintiffs in their business. These provisions have now been repealed following the enactment of the uniform defamation laws.
15. *Swimsure (Laboratories) Pty Ltd v McDonald* [1979] 2 NSWLR 796.

Elements of injurious falsehood

According to *Palmer Bruyn & Parker Pty Ltd v Parsons* (2001) 218 CLR 366, which adopted earlier authorities, three preconditions must be met to establish the tort:

1. a false statement made about the plaintiff's goods, business or profession;
2. malice by the defendant; and
3. actual damage to the plaintiff's business or profession caused by the malicious statement.

False statement about the plaintiff's goods, business or profession

Unlike the tort of deceit, where the wrong consists of false statements made to the plaintiff which induce the plaintiff to act, resulting in loss, the tort of injurious falsehood is concerned with false statements made *about* the plaintiff's goods or business, to third parties, which induce *third parties* to act, resulting in loss to the plaintiff.[16] Typically, the false statement consists of a representation to the customers about the plaintiff's business that induces the customers to take their business elsewhere.

In establishing falsity the plaintiff is not confined to the literal meaning of the words published, but can rely on inferences or imputations conveyed by the words.[17]

The statements were motivated by malice

The plaintiff must prove not only that the statement was false, but also that it was motivated by malice. It is the element of malice that causes the most difficulty for courts, at least in part because there is no clear statement of what amounts to malice in this context. Malice is proven where the defendant was motivated to make the statement for a collateral, dishonest or improper motive, such as a personal hatred of the plaintiff.[18] Also, following the High Court decision in *Roberts v Bass* (2002) 212 CLR 1, it would appear that knowledge of the falsity of the statements, or recklessness as to their truth or falsity, will be almost conclusive proof of malice.[19] Although that case was decided in a different context (the defamation defence of qualified privilege), the principles enunciated there will no doubt be influential

---

16. *Palmer Bruyn & Parker Pty Ltd v Parsons* (2001) 218 CLR 366 at [59], per Gummow J.
17. Ibid at [34], [157]; *Kaplan v Go Daddy Group Group Inc* [2005] NSWSC 636 at [29].
18. See the discussion of malice by Callinan J in: *Palmer Bruyn & Parker Pty Ltd v Parsons* (2001) 218 CLR 366 at [192]–[194].
19. See also: *White v Mellin* [1895] AC 154 at 160; *Shapiro v La Morta* (1923) 40 TLR 201 at 203; *Schindler Lifts Australia Pty Ltd v Debelak* (1989) 89 ALR 275 at 291.

in defining the concept of malice in other areas of torts law such as injurious falsehood.

The malicious statements caused actual damage to the plaintiff's business or profession

As stated in *Ratcliffe v Evans* [1892] 2 QB 524 (at 528), proof of actual damage to the plaintiff's business or profession is an essential element of injurious falsehood. The plaintiff must also prove a causal link between the falsehood and the damage suffered, either on the basis that the defendant intended the harm that materialised, or that it was the 'natural and probable consequence' of the falsehood. These principles were laid down by the High Court in *Palmer Bruyn & Parker Pty Ltd v Parsons* (2001) 218 CLR 366. The plaintiff was a consultant company that assisted other companies with the preparation of development and zoning applications. At the relevant time it had a consultancy contract with McDonald's Australia Ltd with respect to a proposed redevelopment and rezoning of land in Newcastle for a McDonald's restaurant. The plaintiff commenced proceedings against the defendant for injurious falsehood on the basis of a forged letter sent by the defendant to members of the Australian Labor Party Caucus of the Newcastle City Council. The letter purported to be from a Mr McNaughton, an employee of the plaintiff, and referred to the development application before the Council. The letter contained absurd threats and inducements, such as an offer of a free supply of items from the McDonald's menu, and was clearly not meant to be taken seriously. A newspaper circulating in the Newcastle area subsequently published an article stating that police were investigating a bogus letter sent to ALP councillors purportedly from Mr McNaughton. McDonald's decided to cancel the plaintiff's consultancy after learning of the bogus letter through the newspaper article, apparently because it did not want to be involved in any matter that might cause bad publicity for it. There was no evidence that McDonald's employees had seen the letter. The action for injurious falsehood failed on the basis that the publication of the letter was not the cause of the plaintiff's loss. The defendant had not published the letter with the intention of causing the plaintiff to lose its consultancy, but rather to influence the prospects of the success of the McDonald's development application. Furthermore, the loss of the consultancy could not be said to be the 'natural and probable consequence' of the publication of the letter. The circumstances of the publication of the letter showed that it was only intended to be read by a small number of councillors as an in-house joke; it was not intended for general publication. Furthermore, the terms of the newspaper article were very different from that of the letter. The article did not convey that the original letter was merely intended as a joke, but implied starker allegations. It could not be said that the publication of the article, in terms which failed to convey the form of ridicule in the original letter, was a natural and probable result of the publication of the letter.

Remedies

A successful plaintiff will be entitled to compensatory damages for causally related losses, as well as aggravated and exemplary damages in appropriate circumstances. In *Palmer Bruyn*, Gleeson CJ (at [13]) and Gummow J (at [63]-[80]), agreed that the better view is that it is not necessary for the plaintiff to establish that the defendant could reasonably foresee the kind of harm that occurred. It is sufficient that the defendant intended the harm, or that it was the natural and probable consequence of the defendant's falsehood.

The plaintiff will be awarded an interlocutory injunction to prevent the publication or repetition of the statements where the plaintiff can establish that there is a serious question to be tried. Despite the requirement that the plaintiff must suffer actual loss, an injunction can lie to restrain the commission of the tort to prevent such loss occurring.[20] Such cases as *Swimsure Laboratories Pty Ltd v McDonald* [1979] 2 NSWLR 796, at 802, and *Kaplan v Go Daddy Group* [2005] NSWSC 636, at [27], suggest that the reluctance of the courts to award an interlocutory injunction on defamatory acts in order not to unduly infringe freedom of speech has not been applied to the area of injurious falsehood.

FURTHER READING

Prosser WL, 'Injurious Falsehood: The Basis for Liability', (1959) 59 Columbia Law Review 425.

Rosey, 'The Ambidextrous Lawyer: Conflict of Interest and the Medieval and Early Modern Legal Profession', (2000) 7 The University of Chicago Law School Roundtable 137.

---

20. *Swimsure Laboratories Pty Ltd v McDonald* [1979] 2 NSWLR 796 at 802; *Kaplan v Go Daddy Group* [2005] NSWSC 636 at [27].

Torts of Intentional Interference with Goods

INTRODUCTION

The term 'chattel' comes from Old French, which in turn adopted it from the Latin word *cato* (head). The terms 'goods' and 'chattels' will be used interchangeably in this chapter.

This chapter discusses four torts that safeguard our right to possession of personal property free from intentional wrongful interference: trespass to goods (chattels), detinue, conversion, and special action on the case for damage to goods. Their scope overlaps, and, in many instances the same facts will give raise to two or more torts. However, each action has its own set of elements with well-settled jurisprudence.

The system of bailment

Under the system of bailment, the owner of a chattel (bailor) can transfer the physical possession of it to another person (bailee) on the basis that the bailor retains the ownership of the property: the bailee becomes the custodian of the chattel, and takes care of it for the duration of the bailment. This kind of transfer differs from a gift or sale. In *Coggs v Barnard* (1703) 2 Ld Raym 909,[1] John Coggs successfully sued William Barnard, who gratuitously undertook to stave and carry several casks of brandy belonging to Coggs from one cellar and lay them down again in another cellar. Barnard was so negligent in staving them that 150 gallons of brandy were spilled on the ground and lost. Holt CJ identified six types of bailments:

---

1. Reproduced in Baker JH & Milsom SFC, *Sources of English Legal History* Butterworths, London 1986 pp 370–377.

1. bailment for the bailor's benefit, in the form of gratuitous custody by the bailee of the bailor's goods (*depositum*);
2. bailment for the benefit of the bailee in the form of gratuitous loan of goods by the bailor to the bailee (*commodatum*);
3. bailment for hire, whereby the bailee pays the bailor for use of goods (*locatio*);
4. bailment in the form of a pledge, whereby goods are pawned by the bailor as pledge for repayment of debt (*vadium*);
5. bailment for the purposes of carriage, for which the bailor pays the bailee (postal services); and
6. gratuitous bailment for the purpose of carriage.

Liability of bailor and bailee depends on the nature of the bailment. However, in each case, during the term of bailment, the bailor's property interest in the chattel is based on ownership, whereas the bailee's property interest is grounded in possession.

Penfolds Wines Pty Ltd v Elliott (1946) 74 CLR 204

Penfolds Wines Pty Ltd v Elliott provides an excellent analysis of the tort of intentional interference with chattels. Penfolds Wines Pty Ltd, the plaintiff, made wine and sold it in bottles. It retained ownership of the bottles, which were embossed with a statement informing the vendors of their products and customers that: 'This bottle is the property of Penfolds Wines Ltd.' It did so to indicate that the property in the bottles did not pass to buyers of Penfolds wine and brandy, but that the bottles were merely lent. The defendant, Elliott, was a hotelkeeper who knew that property in the bottles was retained by Penfolds and that only the content of the bottles were being sold. The action arose out of a visit to Elliott's hotel by a customs officer, Mr Moon, who was an honorary authorised inspector under the *Pure Foods Act 1908–44* (NSW). The officer also happened to be an employee of an 'organisation interested in the protection of the property in branded bottles', of which Penfolds was a member. Mr Moon obtained from Elliott some bulk wine in two branded Penfolds bottles. The price he was asked to pay was for the wine alone.[2]

Penfolds alleged that Elliott, without its consent, was receiving and collecting its branded bottles from his customers, and then using them as receptacles to sell non-Penfolds bulk wine to customers who wished to purchase such wine. The plaintiffs claimed that Elliott's conduct amounted to special action on the case, trespass to goods, and conversion.

---

2. There was a controversy as to whether what took place between the defendant and the inspector was really a voluntary sale or a 'surrender' of the filled bottles in the pursuance of the *Pure Foods Act*. The trial judge found against a sale and the majority in the High Court accepted this finding.

Elliott admitted that he did sell bulk wine in small quantities to a few customers who brought their own containers, including branded Penfolds bottles, and usually left them with him to be filled. But he claimed that there was never any confusion as to the identity of the bottles. The trial judge accepted that the defendant always knew which bottles belonged to which customer. Elliott also admitted that the two bottles delivered to Mr Moon were brought to his hotel by his brother to be filled with wine other than the Penfolds wine. Elliott insisted, however, that his customers paid only for the liquid, not the bottles.

Penfolds did not take Elliott all the way to the High Court simply to establish that the hotelkeeper had converted two mass-manufactured bottles of minimal value. The litigation, just like Penfolds' support of the 'organisation interested in the protection of the property in branded bottles', was motivated by the desire to destroy the bulk wine trade, which the big wine and spirit companies regarded as competition. The practical effect of the injunction to restrain Elliott from 'placing any other liquor in any of the bottles' would have been to constrain the trade in bulk wine by forcing publicans to use only unbranded receptacles. However, granting the injunction would also potentially make a tortfeasor of any parent at a school fair who sold homemade barley water or raspberry cordial in Penfolds-branded bottles to raise money for the class gymnastic team. The High Court (Starke, Dixon, and McTiernan JJ; Latham CJ and Williams J dissenting) refused to grant the injunction restraining Elliott from using any of its branded bottles in an unauthorised manner.[3]

References to the *Penfolds Wines* case will be made throughout this chapter.

TRESPASS TO GOODS (CHATTELS)

Definition

Historically, this cause of action was known as 'trespass to chattels'; however in the 1980s, in an effort to make legal language more comprehensible, it was changed to 'trespass to goods'. Trespass to goods protects the person in possession of, or with the right to possession of, a chattel from having it intentionally interfered with by wrongful damage or appropriation.

According to Stroud Francis C Milsom,[4] the original form writ of *trespass de bonis asportatis* (Latin: 'of goods carried away') was first issued in 1220. This writ safeguarded those in possession of goods against wrongful asportation, in the sense

---

3. Starke and McTiernan JJ, having found conversion, refused to grant an injunction on the ground that Elliott's wrongful dealing with Penfolds' bottles happened rarely and casually. Their Honours determined that Penfolds should be left to its remedies at common law. Dixon J found that the facts proved did not disclose the commission of any tort by Elliott in relation to the Penfolds bottles.
4. *Studies in the History of the Common Law*, The Hambeldon Press, London, 1995, p 18.

of carrying off the goods out of possession of another. Milsom provides an example of a writ from 1255 alleging that the defendant took animals from a servant who was on the way to the market.

In such cases as *Wright v Ramscot* (1668) 1 Wms Saund 108; 85 ER 93 and *Sheldrick v Abery* (1793) 1 Esp 55; 170 ER 278, the action for trespass to chattels was extended to include cases where the goods were destroyed or damaged but not taken—as where animals were killed or beaten. Eventually, the tort would encompass any direct, intentional, harmful and non-consensual contact with a chattel in the possession of another.

The nature of damage for the purposes of trespass to chattels

There has been controversy about what constitutes 'actual damage' for the purposes of trespass to chattels. In the United States, by virtue of the Restatement (Second) of Torts § 217(b); § 218(b) (1965), trespass to goods involves intentional 'using or intermeddling with a chattel in the possession of another, with the result that 'the chattel is impaired as to its condition, quality, or value'. Likewise, in *Everitt v Martin* [1953] NZLR 298 (at 302–3), a New Zealand court suggested that, unlike trespass to the person and trespass to land, the law does not consider the dignitary interest in the inviolability of chattels as sufficiently important to require legal redress. Therefore, mere touching of an object—without any actual damage—may not attract even nominal damages.[5] However, Francis Trindade and Peter Cane in *The Law of Torts in Australia*[6] argue that there are good policy reasons for making non-consensual contact with objects actionable where such conduct causes potential damage, humiliation and distress—as in allowing museums and galleries to sue for unauthorised touching of exhibits, or giving relatives an action for trespass in cases of interference with corpses through unauthorised autopsies.

At the same time, any unauthorised use of the goods which amounts to deprivation of possession will be regarded as sufficient actual damage, provided other elements of the tort are satisfied.[7] Indeed, loss of possession, even for a brief interval, may amount to damage at law. For example, if the defendant takes a $10 bill from the plaintiff's purse and returns it thereafter upon request, the loss of possession is sufficient to satisfy the requirement of damage. Likewise, moving goods without permission, or making unauthorised use of a chattel for a significant period, will amount to actionable damage.

---

5. See also: *Slater v Swann* [1730] 2 Stra 872; 93 ER 906.
6. 3rd edn, Oxford University Press, Melbourne, 1999, p 136.
7. *Kirk v Gregory* (1876) 1 Ex D 55; *Penfolds Wines v Elliott* (1946) 74 CLR 204.

Elements of trespass to goods

Locus standi (possession)

In order to sue for trespass to chattels, the plaintiff must be in actual possession, be entitled to immediate possession upon demand, or be in constructive possession. For example, a person is in actual or constructive possession of a chattel and has standing to sue if one of the four volumes of Blackstone's *Commentaries on the Laws of England*, which she is carrying up the stairs, falls down: she is in actual possession of the three volumes, and has constructive possession of the fourth. She can sue a passer-by who wrongfully interferes with her possession of the fourth volume by picking it up and walking away. Trespass to goods will also lie against anyone who snatches one of the remaining volumes out of her hand. Other examples include bailors with an immediate right to retake the possession of goods:

(a) employers in constructive possession, whose employees had custody—actual possession—of the goods on the employer's behalf at the time of the wrong (*Marfani & Co Ltd v Midland Bank Ltd* [1968] 1 WLR 956);
(b) principals in relation to wrongful interference with their goods in the actual possession of an agent;
(c) trustees—if custody of the goods is with the beneficiary;
(d) owners of the franchise in shipwrecks, who can sue in trespass for interference with the wrecks;
(e) administrators and executors of an estate, who may sue for trespass committed between the date of death and grant of probate (*Partridge v Equity Trustees Executors and Agency Co Ltd* (1947) 75 CLR 149);
(f) mortgagees after default (*Pan Australian Credits (SA) Pty Ltd v Kolim Pty Ltd* (1981) 27 SASR 353); and
(g) owners of computer systems, websites, domain names, etc (*Ebay Inc v Bidder's Edge* 100 F Supp 2d 1058 (ND Cal 2000); *Kremen v Cohen* 337 F3d 1024 (2003).[8]

In *Penfolds Wines Pty Ltd v Elliott*, Dixon J (as he then was) explained (at 225) that in relation to the two specific Penfolds bottles, Elliott did not infringe anyone's possessory rights because his brother delivered the specific bottles in question to him. At the time he filled these particular bottles, Elliott was in possession of them. This was also true in the case of any other customer who requested that bulk wine be poured into a Penfolds-branded bottle.

---

8. In *White Buffalo Ventures LLC v Univ of Texas* 420 F 3d 366 (2005) (United States Supreme Court certiorari denied by *White Buffalo Ventures LLC v Univ of Texas* US 9 Jan, 2006), the United States Court of Appeals for the Fifth Circuit followed the *ratio decidendi* in *Ebay, Inc v Bidder's Edge* 100 F Supp 2d 1058 (ND Cal 2000), and refused to grant an injunction sought by the plaintiff, an online dating service provider that targeted students at the University of Texas, to enjoin the university from blocking its email servers from receiving bulk commercial emails sent to students.

If the bottles had been out of Elliott's possession—in the possession of some other person—and, if he then took them against that person's will and filled them with wine, his actions would have amounted to trespass, because the movement of the bottles and the use of them as receptacles would have been *trespass de bonis asportatis*: an invasion of the possessory rights of the second person. However, in this case, Penfolds, as bailor, was out of possession of the bottles (though it had a right to possession). As Dixon J put it, not without sarcasm aimed at Penfolds' legal advisers (at 227):

> it is difficult to see how there can be a forcible and immediate injury *vi et armis* to a mere legal right; and there are some parts of the law of trespass and theft which are inexplicable on such a view.

According to his Honour (at 227):

> It is submitted that the correct view is that the right to possession, as a title for maintaining trespass, is merely a right in one person to sue for a trespass done to another's possession; that this right exists whenever the person whose actual possession was violated held as a servant, agent or bailee under a revocable bailment for or under or on behalf of the person having the right to possession.

Thus, the majority (Dixon, Starke, and McTiernan JJ) held that Penfolds had no standing to sue in trespass.

Direct interference

The defendant's interference must be direct and result in an immediate contact with the goods of the plaintiff. The contact, however, need not be personal. For example, the plaintiff's chattel may be damaged by the defendant throwing a stone at it; or the defendant may throw a bait to a dog, as happened in *Hutchins v Maughan* [1947] VLR 131, but not lay the bait. Interference will be regarded as direct where the defendant, without consent or legal justification, sails a yacht belonging to someone else; releases fish from a fish farm belonging to another; or throws a stone at a vehicle denting its door.

However, the notion of directness will also encompass the *Scott v Shephard* (1773) 2 Wm B1 892 situation, whereby the initial wrongful intentional act sets in motion an unbroken chain of continuing consequences. For example, accessing another person's computers by transmission of electronic signals,[9] or robot programs such as automated software programs performing multiple successive queries[10] constitutes direct interference.

---

9. *Thrifty-Tel Inc v Bezenek*, 54 Cal Rptr 2d 468 (Cal Ct App 1996) at 473.
10. *Register com Inc v Verio Inc*, 356 F 3d 393 (2d Cir NY 2004).

Wrongful intention

Wrongful intention, recklessness or conscious carelessness is necessary for recovery, but as in the case of all torts derived from the old writ of trespass, the 'intent' is limited to the intention to commit the act of interference, and requires no wrongful motive.[11]

The act must be voluntary

The interference must be voluntary. The action of a person who breaks a porcelain statuette in the course of an epileptic fit will not be considered 'voluntary'.

Defence of *jus tertii* (the right of a third person)

The plea of *jus tertii* asserts that the plaintiff had no right to possession because that right is vested in a third party. In general, *jus tertii* cannot be pleaded as a defence in cases where the plaintiff has actual or constructive possession.[12] Further, defendants cannot rely on the *jus tertii* defence if they wrongfully took the goods out of actual or constructive possession of the plaintiff, even if they later return them to the true owner. In such cases, according to *Woadson v Nawton* (1727) 2 Stra 777; 93 ER 842, unless the defendant acted under the authority of the person rightfully entitled to possession, the plaintiff can sue them for trespass to goods.

Mistake

It is no defence that the defendant mistakenly believed either that he or she owned the goods in question, or had the owner's permission to move them.

Measure of damages

If the chattel is restored to the plaintiff in a damaged state, the measure of trespassory damages is either the extent of depreciation in value, or the reasonable cost of repairs necessitated by the trespassory conduct. In relation to electronic trespass, damages can be obtained for loss of data, reduced or impired system performance, or system unavailability (*Ebay Inc v Bidder's Edge*, 100 F Supp 2d 1058 (ND Cal 2000) at 1066).

---

11. *Stanley v Powell* [1891] 1 Q B 86; *Everitt v Martin* [1953] NZLR 298.
12. *Henry Berry & Co v Rushton* [1937] St R Qd 109.

A plaintiff permanently deprived of goods in his or her possession can recover their full value. Nominal damages may be awarded where there is asportation but no actual damage.[13]

DETINUE

The origins and definition of the tort of detinue

Detinue, like trespass, is one of the oldest writs.[14] Between the thirteenth and fifteenth centuries the theory of action for detinue underwent a number of permutations; however, the tort tended to be based on bailment and involve a request by the bailor for re-delivery of bailed goods. Thus, the writ of detinue commanded the sheriff to order the defendant to yield up to the plaintiff the chattels which were unjustly kept from him (detained). So, the gist of the tort of detinue is deprivation of possession by wrongful detention—it protects the person in possession of, or with the right to possession of, a chattel from having it wrongfully detained.

The cause of action in detinue arises when the defendant fails to deliver the goods upon the request of a plaintiff entitled to immediate possession. The defendant must have had the goods in his or her possession at some stage, though not necessarily at the time of the demand. It is a continuing cause of action, accruing at the date of the wrongful refusal to deliver the goods and continuing until the delivery of the goods, or judgment in the action for detinue.

A common law action in replevin (procedure for provisional recovery of goods taken out of the plaintiff's possession) is also available to plaintiffs in cases where entitlement to goods as between defendant and plaintiff is in question. The plaintiff can obtain from the court an order for delivery of the goods as interim relief until the court determines entitlement. The plaintiff has to deposit security with the court in case entitlement is decided against him or her, resulting in return of the goods.[15]

Lawful detention

Merely being in possession of another's goods without permission is not a tort. Where the goods are acquired lawfully, their detention—in the absence of some manifestation of intent to either keep them adversely, or in defiance of the true

---

13. *Kirk v Gregory* [1876] 1 Ex D 55, affirmed in *Pargiter v Alexander* (1995) 5 Tas R 158; [1995] Aust Torts Reps ¶81–349.
14. In the United Kingdom, detinue was abolished by the *Torts (Interference with Goods) Act 1977*. Instead, the action of conversion is now substituted in all English cases in which detinue would formerly have been available.
15. Trindade F & Cane P, *The Law of Torts in Australia*, 3rd edn, Oxford University Press, Melbourne, 1999, p 160.

owner's rights—is not a wrong. For example, Diplock LJ observed in *General & Financial Facilities v Cooks Cars* [1963] 2 All ER, that a finder of a chattel who does not know the identity of the true owner will not commit detinue by merely keeping the chattel for safe custody. Likewise, it is legitimate for the holder of goods to take time to enquire into the plaintiff's title, providing the holder has no actual or imputed information about the plaintiff's rightful claim. Once the claim is verified, the holder will ordinarily be expected to do no more than simply permit the owner to come and get the goods.

Elements of detinue

Locus standi (possession)

The plaintiff need only prove an immediate right to possession; he or she need not prove ownership of the goods.

Demand

To establish detinue, the plaintiff must prove that he or she has demanded the return of the chattel and that the defendant has refused to comply. In cases where the defendant is under a contractual obligation to deliver the goods, the demand, when it is made, must contain specific instructions about the time and place of required delivery. For example, in the case of *Lloyd v Osborne* (1899) 20 LR (NSW) 19, the plaintiff's solicitor wrote a letter of demand, which required the defendant to deliver certain sheep branded 'F' or 'FG' 'at once' to the plaintiff or her agent. The defendant did nothing. The court held that the demand was not specific enough because it lacked details such as the place of delivery and the name of the agent.

However, once the judgment for delivery is obtained, defendants cannot remain inactive: they must deliver the goods, or if they are in possession of some bulky material, they must indicate to the plaintiff the manner, time and place of collection. Plaintiffs may come and remove the goods personally.

In the following situations the requirement of detailed demand may be dispensed with:

(a) where the defendant's possession is unlawfully acquired;
(b) where the defendant has wrongfully disposed of the goods; and
(c) where the defendant has demonstrated intent not to deliver. Thus, in *Crowther v AGC Ltd* (1985) Aust Torts Reports ¶80–709 (at 69,102), King CJ noted that it is not 'an immutable rule that there must be a demand for and a refusal of the return of goods, before an action in detinue or conversion will lie. A man may demonstrate that he intends not to deliver up the goods come what may. If that intent is proved, absence of demand will not defeat the plaintiff's claim.'

Refusal

Refusal to deliver the goods may amount both to detinue and to conversion. The refusal must be categorical and unqualified, expressing or implying an assertion of dominion inconsistent with the plaintiff's rights.

Qualified refusal

The elements of either tort will not be made out if a defendant who lawfully obtained possession makes a qualified refusal to deliver them with reasonable and legitimate reasons for refusal; as where prudence requires the defendant to enquire into the rights of the plaintiff–claimant. For example, in *Ming Kuei Property Investments Pty Ltd v Hampson & Ors* (1994) 126 ALR 313, a customs official required a proof of identity before handing over a shipment. However, the basis or motive for a qualified refusal must be reasonable. Thus, in the case of *Howard E Perry v Brit Rlys Board* [1980] 1 WLR 1375; 2 All ER 579, the fear of union retaliation was not regarded as a sufficiently reasonable basis for refusal to deliver the plaintiff's goods. The English Court of Appeal held that the refusal amounted to detinue and conversion. At the same time, *Nelson v Nelson* [1923] QSR 37 suggests that a mere omission to reply to a letter of demand may not of itself be considered a refusal.

Bailment

From medieval times, the writ of detinue would lie against bailees who refused the plaintiff's demand to give up possession of goods that the plaintiff had previously entrusted to them. For example, in *Anon* (*c* 1310) YB 2 & 3 Edw II,[16] the plaintiff complained to the Court of Common Pleas that the defendant wrongfully 'detained and did not deliver up' 10 sheep to the value of thirty shillings. The plaintiff bailed the sheep 'to pasture on such a day and to keep from Michaelmas until such day; on which he came and demanded them and could not have them.'

The bailee's duty to deliver is a continuing one. The plaintiff can make a demand for possession even where the plaintiff knows that the defendant's inability to deliver is due to the prior act of conversion which is no longer actionable. The bailor–plaintiff can still sue in detinue upon the bailee's failure to deliver. This is because in detinue, it is immaterial whether the bailee's inability to deliver is due to a prior intentional act of wrongful disposition, or to the mere negligence resulting in the loss of goods—the bailee will be liable unless he or she proves that there was no fault involved.

---

16. Reproduced in Baker JH & Milsom SFC, *Sources of English Legal History: Private Law to 1750*, Butterworths, London, 1986, p 265.

In an English case, *Houghland v R Low (Luxury) Coaches Ltd* [1962] 1 QB 694, the plaintiff proved that she had delivered her suitcase to the bus driver at the start of a tour. At one stage of the journey, the bus failed to start, and a relief bus had to be summoned. The first bus was left unattended until the second bus arrived. At this point the passengers, under the supervision of the driver, transferred the luggage of the party. It transpired that the plaintiff's suitcase was missing and it was never found. The Court of Appeal held that the defendant bus company could only avoid liability in detinue by proving what in fact had happened to the suitcase and showing that it was without fault in respect of the disappearance. However, since it could not explain the loss, it was liable in detinue.

Measure of damages

Specific restitution and compensatory damages

Since the main objective of the plaintiff suing in detinue is to obtain specific restitution of the detained chattel, particularly heirlooms, unique and valuable objects, it was suggested in the past that the action should be categorised as one *in rem*. However, detinue is now regarded as a tort, and the Supreme Courts in all Australian jurisdictions have the power to order the delivery up of the goods in question (specific restitution) as well as the power to award damages for their wrongful detention. Where the chattel is restored to the plaintiff, the measure of damages for detention includes compensation for any damage to the goods, and for losses suffered by the plaintiff due to deprivation of the chattel. Where the defendant is unable to return the chattel to the plaintiff, or where the object in question is regarded as an ordinary article of commerce—and thus not suitable for an order of specific restitution—compensatory damages will be awarded, in the amount of value of the goods at the time of judgment.

In cases where the plaintiff hires out the chattel to users in the course of business, the normal measure of damages for lost hire fees due to detention will be the market rate at which it could have been hired.[17] Reasonable costs of replacement hire fees incurred by having to hire a replacement chattel during wrongful detention would be recoverable on the same basis.

Exemplary damages

Exemplary damages are also available for unlawful seizure and detention (*Healing (Sales) Pty Ltd v Inglis Electrix Pty Ltd* (1969) 121 CLR 584). In *Egan v State Transport Authority* (1982) 31 SASR 481, the South Australian Railway Authority terminated a contract with the plaintiff on the grounds that tests it conducted

---

17. *Stand Electric and Engineering Co Ltd v Brisford Entertainments Ltd* [1952] 2 QB 246 at 252, 253–4.

allegedly indicated that the concrete used by the plaintiff was below the required standard. Asserting its right under a term of contract, it therefore seized the plaintiff's plant and materials. The plaintiff sued for detinue and conversion of his equipment. The court awarded exemplary damages in detinue, but not conversion, because of 'sloppy' methods used by the defendant to establish the plaintiff's breach of contract, the overbearing and peremptory exercise of contractual powers, and the underhand manner of termination, which provided the defendant with financial advantages, but had a traumatic effect on the plaintiff.

CONVERSION

Definition

Conversion protects the person in possession of a chattel (including rights contained or evidenced in documents, and negotiable instruments), or with a right of possession, from having the chattel wrongfully interfered with by wrongful dealing, exploitation or disposal through use, alteration, sale, or destruction. In the United States, the *Second Restatement of the Law of Torts* defines conversion as 'an intentional exercise of dominion or control over a chattel which so seriously interferes with the right of another to control it that the actor may justly be required to pay the other full value of the chattel.'[18]

Origins and evolution of the tort of conversion

The original writs of trespass to goods and detinue were encumbered by ancient procedural rules, including the wager of law. For example, if P gave D bailment for term of a horse, and D refused to return it, P could sue D in detinue. However, it was possible for D to defeat P's claim by asserting some right to the horse and then waging his law.[19] D would win the suit if, having chosen the oath wager, he brought a higher number of 'oath-helpers' to back up his claim. P was thus left without a remedy, since trespass would not lie, as P could not establish that D took the horse 'unlawfully and by violence'.

In the sixteenth century, a new species of action on the case called 'trover' (from Old French *trover*, 'to find') was devised to fill the legal lacunae left by detinue and trespass to goods. In one of the early cases, *Wysse v Andrewe* (1531) KB 27/1081,[20] Wysse alleged he had lost a purse which Andrewe found, and that the latter refused to return it. Andrewe then 'feloniously sold them [the contents of the

---

18. American Law Institute Publishers, St Paul, Minnesota, 1965, §222A.
19. Windeyer WJV, *Lectures on Legal History*, 2nd edn, The Law Book Company Ltd, Sydney, 1957, pp 109–110.
20. Reproduced in Baker JH & Milsom SFC, *Sources of English Legal History: Private Law to 1750*, Butterworths, London, 1986, p 531.

purse] and converted the proceeds'. Andrewe pleaded that he bought the goods in London, but the jury did not believe him and found for Wysse.

In the centuries that followed, the old tort of detinue went into abeyance and was only reintroduced in its modern form after the wager of law was abolished by statute in 1833. Trover was also preferred to trespass to goods. There were two major reasons for the popularity of the writ of trover. First, it avoided wager of law, and second, its pleading enabled plaintiffs to claim deprivation of their property in a chattel.[21] Trover was originally based on a form of pleadings whereby the plaintiff claimed he lost his goods, which were found by the defendant, who instead of returning them, used them himself, or disposed of them to someone else. The defendant was not permitted to deny the allegation of losing and finding; the only issues to be litigated were those of the plaintiff's right to possession and the conversion itself.

Tortious conduct need not include fault on the part of the defendant. The bailor can sue in conversion even where the loss occurs without the fault of a bailee (as in robbery). The absence of fault means that the tort is one of strict liability.

Lord Mansfield in *Cooper v Chitty* (1756) 1 Burr 20, at 31, pointed out that trover was a substantive remedy 'to recover the value of personal chattels wrongly converted by another for his own use'. However, the form of action involving allegation of loss and finding was a legal fiction.[22] Modern jurisprudence has emphasised the tortious conduct fundamental to trover by renaming it 'conversion'. The term 'conversion' itself is not new. It was part of the standard formula in pleadings for trover whereby the plaintiff alleged that he was possessed of certain goods, that he casually lost them, that the defendant found them, and did not return them, but instead 'converted them for his own use'.[23]

Trespass to goods and trover: the concepts of possession and title

In the eighteenth century, trespass to goods and trover came to be regarded as alternative remedies for the same wrong. In *Cooper v Chitty* (1756) 1 Burr 20, at 31, Lord Mansfield noted that: 'whenever trespass for taking goods will lie, that is, where they are taken wrongfully, trover will lie'. Lord Chief Baron Gilbert, a contemporary of Mansfield, provided the following example of how this doctrine worked:

---

21. *Gumbleton v Grafton* (1600) Cro Eliz 781; 78 ER 1011; *Isaack v Clark* (1614) 2 Bulst 306; 80 ER 1143; *Kinaston v Moore* (1626) Cro Car 89; 79 ER 678.
22. The formula alleging the loss and finding was statutorily abolished by the *Common Law Procedure Act 1852* 15 & 16 Vict, c 76, s 49: Windeyer WJV, *Lectures on Legal History*, 2nd edn, The Law Book Co, Sydney, 1957, p 111.
23. *Lord Mounteagle v Countess of Worcester* (1554) 2 Dyer 121a; 73 ER 265, reproduced in Baker JH & Milsom SFC, *Sources of English Legal History: Private Law to 1750*, Butterworths, London, 1986, pp 531–533.

> If a man take my Horse and ride him, and re-deliver him to me again, I may have an Action of Trover against him notwithstanding the Re-delivery, for he had him in his Possession and did convert him to his Use.[24]

There have always been, however, significant differences between these two actions. The essence of trespass is possession, but the gist of trover is title to the goods. Consequently, the prerequisite to an action in trespass is wrongful taking of goods from another's possession, but wrongful taking is *not* an element of trover (conversion). Moreover, under trespass, the plaintiff remained the owner; thus when the chattel was returned by the defendant, the plaintiff had to accept it. The plaintiff's recovery was limited to damages sustained through the loss of possession or harm to the chattel, which were usually less than the value of the chattel.

Since the tort of trover safeguards title to goods, in cases of sufficiently serious interference, the defendant is deemed to have appropriated the plaintiff's title. In a successful action in trover, the court effectively compels the defendant to buy the chattel at a forced sale. The plaintiff therefore can refuse to accept the chattel when it is tendered back. Instead, the plaintiff can sue for the full value of the chattel. Once damages are paid in full, the title of the chattel passes to the defendant, and the plaintiff has nothing more to do with it; although mere entry of judgment, without satisfaction, does not affect the title (*Morris v Robinson* (1824) 3 B & C 196 [107] ER 706; *Seager v Copydex Ltd* [No 2] [1969] 1 WLR 809).

In the 1840s, the courts began to reconsider Lord Mansfield's approach to trover and trespass. The first case was that of *Fouldes v Willoughby* (1841) 8 M & W 540; 151 ER 1153, in which the plaintiff, having paid an appropriate fare, boarded a ferry with two horses. He apparently behaved in such a disorderly fashion that the ferryman refused to carry him across the river. When the plaintiff refused to disembark, the defendant led the two horses off the boat and onto the shore. The plaintiff still refused to leave the boat, and was taken across the river. The horses were subsequently sold when the plaintiff refused to pay for their upkeep. The plaintiff sued in conversion. The court found there was no conversion. Lord Abinger CB (at 544–5) explained:

> a simple asportation of a chattel, without any intention of making any further use of it, although it may be a sufficient foundation for an action of trespass, is not sufficient to establish conversion.

By merely leading the horses off the ferry, the defendant did not interfere with the plaintiff's title to the horses in the sense of asserting a 'general right of dominion' over the horses.

About the same time, in the New World, a young lawyer named Abraham Lincoln successfully argued against conversion in the case of *Johnson v Weedman*

---

24. Lord Chief Baron Gilbert, *The Law of Evidence*, 5th edn, Joseph Crukshank, London; Philadelphia, 1788, p 260. In the eighteenth century, re-delivery would only be an evidence in mitigation of damage. Id.

5 Ill 495 (1843), in which a horse was left with the defendant to be agisted and fed. On one occasion the defendant rode on it for fifteen miles. The court held that there was no conversion, because the ride did not constitute a sufficiently serious invasion of the owner's rights. *Fouldes* and *Weedman* established, in their respective jurisdictions, that the tort of conversion is a remedy for major interferences with the chattel, or with the plaintiff's rights in it resulting in serious damage, loss, or destruction. Trespass remains a remedy for minor interferences, where the damage is not sufficiently serious or important to amount to conversion.

When deciding whether the tortious conduct amounts to trespass or conversion, the court will consider:

- the extent and duration of the defendant's exercise of control over the chattel;
- the defendant's intent to assert a right inconsistent with the plaintiff's title;
- the defendant's good faith or bad intentions;
- the harm done to the chattel; and
- the expense and inconvenience caused to the plaintiff.

Thus in *Schemmell v Pomeroy* (1989) 50 SASR 450, the court held that an accident, which resulted in an extensive damage to the plaintiff's car in the course of a 'joy ride' by the defendant, transformed an initial trespass to goods into conversion.

More recently, trespass to chattels has been held to encompass unauthorised digital contacts with the plaintiff's personal property such as computer systems. In Ebay, Inc v Bidder's Edge 100 F Supp 2d 1058 (ND Cal 2000), Whyte J stated (at 1066) that a plaintiff who claims either damages or injunctive relief for 'electronic' or 'digital' trespass must establish that: (1) defendant intentionally and without authorisation interfered with plaintiff's possessory interest in the computer system; and (2) defendant's unauthorised use resulted in damage to plaintiff.

The nature of the requisite damage was discussed in Sotelo v DirectRevenue, LLC 384 F Supp 2d 1219 (Ill 2005). Mr Soleto in a class action alleged that DirectRevenue, deceptively installed spyware on 12 thousands computers, allowing it to deliver targeted pop-up advertisements, which, *inter alia*, have the effect of obscuring the web page a user is viewing. Gettleman J denied the defendant's motion to dismiss the claim for trespass to chattels. His honour opined (at 1230) that interferences which 'cause computers to slow down, take up the bandwidth of the user's Internet connection, incur increased Internet-use charges, deplete a computer's memory, utilise pixels and screen-space on monitors, require more energy because slowed computers must be kept on for longer, and reduce a user's productivity while increasing their frustration' are sufficient to sustain an action for trespass to chattels, as opposed to an action for conversion.[25]

---

25. See also: CompuServe Inc v Cyber Promotions, Inc, 962 F Supp 1015, 1022 (SD Ohio 1997), and White Buffalo Ventures, LLC v Univ of Texas, 420 F 3d 366 (5th Cir Tex 2005); *writ of certiorari denied* 126 S Ct 1039, 163 L Ed 2d 856 (US 2006).

Plaintiff's title

In general, at the time of conversion, the plaintiff must be the true owner in actual possession, or entitled to immediate possession of the chattel. In the case of *Gatward v Alley* (1940) 40 SR (NSW) 174, Jordan CJ (at 180) explained:

> de facto possession is prima facie evidence of ownership, and also of itself creates a legal right to possess which is enforceable against anyone who cannot prove that he has a superior right to possess; any person who interferes with this legal right, without being able to prove a superior right, is therefore a wrongdoer.

The case of *Oakley v Lyster* [1931] 1 KB 148 provides a good illustration of the notion of possessory title. In that case, the plaintiff, at the end of the First World War, had a contract for clearing land that had been used as an aerodrome. Under the terms of the contract, he obtained 8000 tons of hard-core and tar macadam. He rented a site on which he deposited these substances. While there were still some 4000 tons of the hard-core and tar macadam on the site, and during the plaintiff's tenancy, the defendant bought the freehold of the site. The defendant mistakenly asserted an immediate right to occupancy of the site rented by the plaintiff, and ownership of 'the stuff'. At his direction, his employees carted away a small quantity of these materials. The defendant's solicitors advised the plaintiff that the hard-core and tar macadam belonged to their client, and that the plaintiff had no right to remove any of it. The plaintiff sued in conversion. The Court of Appeal determined that the defendant was not entitled to occupancy until expiry of the plaintiff's tenancy, and that the plaintiff had an immediate right to possession of the hard-core and tar macadam. Since the defendant, who was not the owner of the 'stuff', had asserted dominion over it by carting some of it away and prevented the plaintiff from removing the rest, he was liable in conversion and had to pay the plaintiff for its full value.

Owners of copyright, including computer programs, sound and visual recordings may bring action for conversion and detinue under s 116(1) of the *Copyright Act 1968* (Cth).[26] Though according to Burchett J in *Autodesk Inc & Ors v Yee & Anor* (1996) 68 FCR 391, at 396, under the statutory regime, the copyright owner is not the owner of the copy, rather a fictional ownership is imposed 'so as to give rise to the rights in conversion or detention which that ownership would bring'.

Possession

Mere taking of possession is not sufficient to constitute conversion—there must be a 'major' interference with plaintiff's title. For instance, in *Fouldes v Willoughby* (1841) 8 M & W 540, 151 ER 1153, putting the plaintiff's horses ashore was not

---

26. *Sony Music Entertainment (Australia) Ltd v University of Tasmania (No 1)* (2003) 129 FCR 472 at [28].

conversion because the defendant's possession was only momentary; no damage was done; and far from disputing the owner's title, the defendant emphasised that he did not want the horses.

However, although mere possession, for however long, does not constitute conversion, even temporary possession may be 'major' interference with the true owner's title. This rule was established in *Lord Petre v Heneage* (1701) 12 Mod Rep 519, where Holt CJ determined that the wife of the executor of the late Lord Petre, who took and wore a pearl necklace belonging to the estate, was liable in conversion.

In *Penfolds Wines* Latham CJ, Williams, Starke, and McTiernan JJ found that a conversion had occurred because of unauthorised use and transfer of possession of Penfold bottles by Elliott to his customers. According to the majority, Elliott's use and transfer of the Penfolds bottles manifested intent to exercise dominion over them. Dixon J, in dissent, stated that mere use of the chattel in an unauthorised manner, or transfer of its possession, does not amount to conversion unless it affects the bailor's immediate right to possession.

Plaintiff's possessory rights

To sue in conversion, the plaintiff needs mere possessory rights. The plaintiff must show possession at law, but not possession in fact.

Perpetual Trustees & National Executors of Tasmania v Perkins & Ors (1989) Aust Torts Reports ¶80–295, heard before the Tasmanian Supreme Court, illustrates the nature of possessory title held by a gratuitous bailor. It all began at the turn of the twentieth century, when John and Emmely Perkins had their portraits painted by a well-known colonial artist, Benjamin Duterrau. They hung the portraits in their family home. When their grandson Allan died in 1951, he bequeathed the portraits to his wife Nora, who in turn bequeathed them to their three daughters. In 1967, the three sisters moved out of the old family home. Since there was not enough room for the portraits in their new house, the sisters gave them to their brother Bill on a 'long loan'. In 1975 Bill, as bailee, transferred the possession of the portraits to another brother, David. At no time did the sisters indicate that the portraits were a gift to either brother. In 1979 and 1980, David told his son, Tim, that the portraits would belong to him one day. After David's death in 1984, the Art Gallery of South Australia bought the portrait of Emmely Perkins from David's widow and Tim for $55 000. Tim then attempted to sell the portrait of John Perkins in New South Wales, but at this point the sisters' solicitors intervened.

In 1985 and 1987 the sisters made written demands of the Board of the Art Gallery of South Australia and David's widow respectively for the return of the portraits. These demands were not complied with, so the plaintiffs sued in conversion and detinue. In issue was ownership: were the sisters owners of the portraits?

The defendants argued that David had asserted ownership in 1980, and that the plaintiffs' claim was time-barred. The court disagreed, and held that the sisters as bailors retained possessory title to the portraits throughout. This was because the portraits were bequeathed to them by their mother on the understanding they would remain in the family. The evidence demonstrated that ownership had vested in the sisters. The indefinite loan to Bill was a gratuitous bailment revocable at will. Consequently, the sisters retained the right to the return of the portraits on demand, and their possessory title was never extinguished. Since title did not pass to Bill, his subsequent transfer of the portraits to David, David's widow, and then to Tim could not give these persons any possessory rights greater than the gratuitous bailment enjoyed by Bill. Therefore, the sisters' right to immediate possession gave them sufficient title to bring the actions in conversion and detinue. The Supreme Court ordered specific restitution—the delivery of the two portraits to the sisters.

Likewise in *Penfolds Wines*, the claimant could show possession at law because by branding its bottles, 'This bottle is the property of Penfolds Wines Ltd', it never relinquished the claim to the ownership of the bottles and thus remained in constructive possession. The title to each branded bottle remained with Penfolds.

However, a bailee with possessory right is not precluded from suing in conversion a person who, without a better right to possession, has nevertheless wrongly interfered with the chattel and asserted a title (dominion) over it.

Physical possession

The defendant need not be in physical possession of goods to deny the plaintiff's title. In *Oakley v Lyster* (1931) 1 KB 148, the defendant argued he never had possession of the hard-core and tar macadam, and thus could not be liable in conversion. However, as Greer LJ of the Court of Appeal pointed out (at 155) that the defendant had asserted possession of these substances 'by saying to all the world that no one should have [them] without his permission.'

Denial of ownership and possessory rights

Sometimes, denial of ownership will not extinguish the claimant's possessory rights. Thus, in *National Crime Authority v Flack* (1998) ALR 501, police officers searched Mrs Flack's rented house under warrant, which was based on suspicion that Mrs Flack's son had been involved in drug-related offences. They discovered a locked briefcase containing $433 000 in cash. At the time, Mrs Flack said that she was unaware of the presence of the briefcase in her home, and manifested shock and horror when confronted with the presence of the goods. She said that she would not have countenanced the presence of the briefcase full of money had she known of it. Later, the court by majority would interpret these exclamations as expressions of surprise and anxiety, not as disclaimers of possession. The police took the goods away to help in the investigation of the son's activities, however, no prosecutions were launched against the son.

At common law, an article seized under warrant cannot be kept for any longer than is reasonably necessary for police to complete their investigations or to preserve it for evidence at the forthcoming trial.[27] Neither at common law nor under statute is there a general power of the State to forfeit goods simply because they appear 'suspicious'. Mrs Flack, therefore, brought proceedings against the Chairperson of the National Crime Authority and the Commonwealth for the return the briefcase and cash.

The court held that since Mrs Flack was the tenant of an ordinary residential house, she had possession in law of those premises. In the circumstances, that fact was sufficient to establish the requisite manifestation of intention to possess all chattels on the premises. When confronted with the goods, Mrs Flack did not deny possession, though she denied prior knowledge, and therefore, implicitly, ownership. However, the court distinguished between possessory rights and ownership. You may have a possessory right as an occupier even where the article in question has been hidden or deliberately placed on the premises (*Johnson v Pickering* [1907] 2 KB 437 at 444–5; *Re Cohen* [1953] Ch 88). Consequently, since the statutory rights of the National Crime Authority and the Commonwealth to retain possession under the warrant had expired, and they could show no legal right to possession of the briefcase that was equal to or greater than that of Mrs Flack, the order for the return of the goods to her was upheld.

Finders

Finders of chattels generally acquire good title to them against all but the rightful owners. This principle was established early in the eighteenth century in *Armory v Delamirie* (1722) 1 Stra 505; 93 ER 664, in which a chimney-sweep boy found a jewel and took it to Paul de Lamerie (1688–1751), a well-known goldsmith of the time, 'to know what it was'. The boy gave the jewel to the goldsmith's apprentice, who, under pretence of weighing it, extracted the stones from their setting and called to the master 'to let him know it came to three half-pence'. The master offered the money to the boy, who refused it. He was given back the socket without the stones. He sued the goldsmith. In the court of *nisi prius*, Sir John Pratt CJ (at 505) ruled that the boy, as finder, acquired possessory title in the jewel, which was not impaired by temporarily entrusting the custody of the jewel to the defendant. The evidence established that the value of the stone which would fit the socket was that of 'the finest water'. Consequently, unless the defendant produced the jewel, the jury 'should presume the strongest against him and make the value of the best jewels

---

27. *Ghani v Jones* [1970] 1 QB 693 at 709.

the measure of their damages: which they accordingly did'. The boy could also have claimed in detinue, and, had the jewel been snatched from his hand, in trespass.

In *Parker v British Airways Board* [1982] QB 1004, the English Court of Appeal discussed the law of finders at some length. The plaintiff, while waiting for his plane in the international executive lounge at Heathrow Airport, found a gold bracelet lying on the floor. Possibly pressed for time, he handed the bracelet to an anonymous official of the defendants, British Airways Board, rather than the police. He also gave the official a note of his name and address asking that the bracelet be returned to him if it was not claimed by the owner. The official in turn handed the bracelet to the British Airways lost property department. The owner never claimed the bracelet; however, instead returning it to the plaintiff, the defendants sold it and kept the proceeds of £850. When the plaintiff discovered what had happened, he sued for conversion and was awarded £850 in damages and £50 in interest.[28] In his judgment, Donaldson LJ (at 1017) defined the major principles relating to the rights and obligations of finders in the following way:

1   The finder of a chattel acquires no rights over it unless (a) it has been abandoned or lost and (b) he takes it into his care and control.
2   A finder of a chattel who takes it into his care and control, whilst not acquiring any absolute property or ownership in the chattel, acquires a right to keep it against all but the true owner or those in a position to claim through the true owner (or one who can assert a prior right to keep the chattel which was subsisting at the time) when the finder took the chattel into his care and control.
3   A person having a finder's rights has an obligation to take such measures as in all the circumstances are reasonable to acquaint the true owner of the finding and present whereabouts of the chattel and to care for it meanwhile.

The general principle is that the person who finds abandoned or lost goods on premises open to the public will acquire an interest which is sufficient to sustain an action in conversion in preference to the owner or occupier of the shop, club lounge, etc. However, the finder must not be an employee or an agent who acquires the custody of the goods by reason of his or her employment. Lord Donaldson (at 1017) formulated the rule thus:

Unless otherwise agreed, any servant or agent who finds a chattel in the course of his employment or agency and not wholly incidentally or collaterally thereto and who takes it into his care and control does so on behalf of his employer or principal who acquires a finder's rights to the exclusion of those of the actual finder.

---

28. In the United Kingdom detinue has been abolished by statute. However, if the *Parker* case were litigated in Australia, the plaintiff would also have sued in detinue.

What are the possessory rights of the occupier of land and/or buildings where property found was attached to the land or premises? According to Donaldson LJ (at 1017–18):

1. An occupier of land has rights superior to those of a finder over chattels in or attached to that land and an occupier of a building has similar rights in respect of chattels attached to that building, whether in either case the occupier is aware of the presence of the chattel. An example provided by Donaldson LJ was the case of *South Staffordshire Water Co v Sharman* [1896] 2 QB 44, where the defendant was employed by the occupier of land to remove mud from the bottom of a pond. He found two gold rings embedded in the mud. The Court of Appeal held that the plaintiff occupier was held to be entitled to the rings.
2. Occupiers of a building will have rights superior to those of a finder over chattels not attached to the walls, etc, if, before the chattel was found, they had manifested an intention to exercise control over the building and the things which may be upon it or in it.
3. Occupiers are under an obligation to take such measures as in all the circumstances are reasonable to ensure that lost chattels are found and, upon their being found, whether by them or by a third party, to acquaint the true owner of the finding and to care for the chattels meanwhile.

What is the position of finders who come across an abandoned or lost chattel as a result of trespass to land? The finder of the goods is less likely to acquire an interest in them if he finds them as a result of trespass to land. This is because the person vis-à-vis whom he is a trespasser has a better title. The fundamental basis of this proposition is public policy that wrongdoers should not benefit from their wrongdoing. Likewise, the finder of a chattel acquires very limited rights over it if he or she takes it into his care and control with dishonest intent.

Crown's treasure trove exception

Proprietary prerogatives of the Crown include entitlement to treasure trove.[29] Historically, the term 'treasure trove' referred to gold and silver coins deliberately hidden by an unknown person. If found on Crown land, be it State or Commonwealth, such objects belong by law to the Crown. Nowadays, the Crown tends to lay claim to money in banknotes as well as other objects.[30] This happened when a person found $200 000 in the rubbish bin of a railway station in Melbourne. The finder (later joined by another who also found a similar amount of money at the same station) asserted title to the money, but handed it over to police for the matter to resolved by the court. At the trial, the Crown elected not to defend its title.

---

29. Evatt HV, *The Royal Prerogative*, The Law Book Company Ltd, Sydney, 1987, pp 30–31.
30. Toohey J, 'Jubilant Jamie and the Elephant Egg: Acquisition of Title by Finding' (1998) 6 *Australian Property Law Journal* 117 at 117.

Some jurisdictions have introduced legislation to create a legislative regime to regulate found property and property seized during criminal investigations.[31] These regulations would include procedures for determining the ownership of certain property; conditions for return of property seized during a criminal investigation; and an offence of unlawfully dealing with seized property knowing it to be seized property.[32]

The character of the defendant's conduct

Conversion can result only from conduct intended to affect title to the chattel through wrongful interference, which means the defendant must intentionally or recklessly deal with the goods in some way.

Intent to exercise inconsistent dominion

Intent for the purposes of conversion must involve intent to exercise dominion or control over the goods which is inconsistent with the plaintiff's title. This means that a purchaser of stolen goods—unless purchased on the market overt—or auctioneers who sell stolen goods in the utmost good faith, become converters because their acts constitute interference with the plaintiff's control of his or her property. According to *RH Willis & Son v British Car Auctions* [1978] 1 WLR 438, an auctioneer who honestly and reasonably, but wrongly, believes the vendor has good title to goods put up for sale, is liable to the true owner for conversion. For, as Cleasby B pointed out in *Hollins v Fowler* (1874) LR 7; QB 639 at 633:

> The foundation for the action of conversion rests neither in the knowledge nor the intent of the defendant. It rests upon the unwarranted interference by the defendant with the dominion over the property of the plaintiff from which injury to the latter results. Therefore neither good nor bad faith, neither care nor negligence, neither knowledge nor ignorance, are of the gist of the action.

On further appeal to the House of Lords (1874) LR 7; HL 758, Blackburn J (at 766) qualified this rule by stating that 'From the nature of the action, as explained by Lord Mansfield [in *Cooper v Chitty* 1 Burr 20], it follows that it must be an interference with the property which would not, as against the true owner, be justified, or at least excused, in one who came lawfully into the possession of the goods.'

Mistaken or reckless intent

The required intent need not be conscious wrongdoing. The defendant can be liable for acting in ignorance, or under an innocent mistake. This was the case in *Oakley v*

---

31. For example, *Police Regulations 1999* (SA) Pt 12; Criminal and Found Property Disposal Bill 2005 (WA).
32. In the United Kingdom this area of the law is governed by the *Treasure Act 1996* (UK).

Lyster and *Perpetual Trustees & National Executors of Tasmania v Perkins*, discussed above. In *Poggi v Scott* (1914) 167 Cal 372; 139 P 815, the defendant, on moving into a new house, found the plaintiff's barrels of wine left in the cellar for storage. Assuming that they were abandoned, the defendant sold them as junk. He was held liable for conversion.

Where defendants deal with another person's property in a manner fraught with serious risk of loss, intention in the form of recklessness will be imputed to them. For example, in *Moorgate Mercantile v Finch & Read* (1962) 1 QB 701, the defendant used the plaintiff's car to smuggle Swiss watches. He was caught, and customs officers confiscated the car. The plaintiff, a finance company, successfully sued the defendant in conversion.

The term 'wrongful dealing'

Many kinds of conduct amount to wrongful dealing with the goods. Among them are:

(a) intentional or reckless destruction of goods;
(b) changing the nature or character of the goods, for example:
   – pouring water into wine
   – breaking the seal on a document
   – taking things out of packaging
   – breaking up the bulk
   – making grapes into wine, flour into bread, etc;
(c) unqualified refusal to deliver after demand (withholding possession);
(d) qualified refusal where the qualification is not reasonable, as in *Howard E Perry & Co Ltd v British Rly Board* (1980) 1 WLR 1375, where defendant–carriers, without asserting title to the plaintiffs' steel they held in their depot, failed to provide the plaintiffs with the delivery date, because of the fear of union reprisals;
(e) unauthorised permanent transfer or disposal of goods, whether by sale and delivery, or by a mistaken delivery to a wrong person; mere sale without delivery is not conversion, because it does not affect either possession or title; thus, disposal of goods by sale or gift must include delivery, because the 'wrongful dealing' is in the delivery; and
(f) serious misuse of another's chattels involving obvious defiance of the owner's rights; in the days of glass milk bottles, in the case of *Milk Bottles Recovery v Camillo* (1948) VLR 344, a milkman was found liable in conversion for using another's bottles when delivering milk to his customers; the court regarded his conduct as serious interference because of the high risk of breakage.

Conversely, casual and harmless misuse without assertion of title will not be a sufficiently serious dealing for the purposes of conversion. Likewise, unauthorised movement of the chattel, without other interference, may amount to trespass to goods, but not conversion. This is particularly so if there is no intent to assume further control over the chattel, or to deprive the owner of it, and the interference is brief and otherwise harmless.

The judicial views may differ on whether the particular dealing amounted to an obvious defiance of the owner's right or a harmless misuse without assertion of title. For example, in *Penfolds Wines*, Latham CJ, Williams, Starke, and McTiernan JJ found that there was wrongful dealing by Elliott in relation to the transaction between Elliott and Mr Moon. According to Latham CJ (at 219):

> In the present case there was not, in my opinion, a mere removal of the bottles received from the defendant's brother independently of any claim over them in favour of the defendant or anyone else. There was a handling of the bottles, an actual user of them, for the purposes of the defendant's trade—for containing and disposing of the defendant's wine and for the use of the defendant's customer, his brother. Such dealing with the bottles, under a claim of right so to deal with them (a claim in which the defendant still persists) was inconsistent with the dominion of the owner of the bottles and was a conversion.

Latham CJ thus did not accept the trial judge's finding that the transaction involving Mr Moon was a forced surrender of the bottles filled with bulk wine; his Honour considered the transaction to be a sale, and determined (at 219) that:

> the defendant delivered the bottles to Moon in return for eight shillings, a sum which he evidently kept for himself. He dealt with the bottles (as well as with their contents) as being a person entitled to dispose of them to Moon, that is as owner, and I can see no reason for holding that such a disposition was not a conversion of the bottles.

Dixon J (as he then was), in dissent on this issue, accepted the finding of fact that the delivery of the two bottles to the inspector under the *Pure Foods Act* was not a sale because (at 229):

> On the side of the inspector, he was obtaining them for the appellants, and, on the side of the respondent, he was giving them over to an official who demanded them in order to examine the wine. There was no conversion, and indeed, having regard to the inspector's employment to act for the appellants, the transaction could not amount to an actual wrong to property.

Consequently, Dixon J reasoned (at 229) that since:

> the essence of conversion is a dealing with a chattel in a manner repugnant to the immediate right of possession of the person who has the property or special property in the chattel. ... damage to the chattel is not conversion, nor is use, nor is a transfer of possession otherwise than for the purpose of affecting the immediate right to possession, nor is it always conversion to lose the goods beyond

hope of recovery. An intent to do that which would deprive 'the true owner' of his immediate right to possession or impair it may be said to form the essential ground of the tort.

Elliott's conduct in supplying wine to customers who brought bottles to receive it did not involve taking to himself the property in the bottles or depriving Penfolds of the property, nor of asserting any title in them and denying it to the plaintiffs. His re-delivery of the bottles to the customers who left them could not amount to a conversion because, 'though involving a transfer of possession, its purpose was not to confer any right over the property in the bottles, but merely to return or restore them to the person who had left them there to be filled.' Moreover (at 229):

> To fill the bottles with wine at the request of the person who brought them could not in itself be a conversion. It was not a use of the bottles involving any exercise of dominion over them, however transitory.

On this interpretation, the essential elements of the tort of conversion were lacking because there was no act of ownership: Elliott did not use the bottles on the footing that he was their owner or that Penfolds had no title to the bottles. Dixon J noted that even if at times a wrong bottle was returned to the person who left one for filling, it is doubtful whether that would amount to conversion, considering the purpose and the nature of the transaction.

Positive misfeasance

The tort of conversion requires that the defendant must intentionally or recklessly deal with the goods in some way. Bare oral assertion of ownership without any dealing with the goods is insufficient to constitute conversion. If, in *Oakley v Lyster*, the defendant had merely denied the owner's right to the hard-core and tar macadam, he would not have been liable in conversion—though he would be liable in detinue. Conversion lay because he asserted title by using some of the material himself, and because he stopped the plaintiff from removing it.

A refusal to deliver, or a positive misfeasance, such as sale and delivery or gift and delivery, though it need not involve dishonesty by the defendant, will be regarded as conversion. In *Perpetual Trustees and National Executors of Tasmania v Perkins*, when David originally told his son Tim the portraits would become his, he did so without handing them over. Consequently, he did not commit conversion at the time. It was only after David's death, when his widow and Tim sold and delivered one of the portraits to the National Gallery of South Australia, that the act of conversion took place.

Do agents who receive goods from someone who is their apparent owner, and later returns them to him, owe any duty to their true owner to investigate title in the absence of anything to put him on inquiry?

This was the question posed in *Marcq v Christie Manson & Woods Ltd (Trading As Christie's)* [2004] QB 286. Mr Marcq was the owner of an oil painting by a Dutch master, Jan Steen, which was stolen from his house in 1979 and registered as stolen on the Art Loss Register. In 1997, the defendant, Christie's auction house, took possession of the painting from a prospective seller, Mr Schuenemann, who instructed them to sell it at auction on the terms of their conditions of business. Under that contract they catalogued and advertised the painting, offering it for sale at a public auction of old masters. The painting remained unsold and was returned by the defendants to Mr Schuenemann. Mr Marcq was unsuccessful in his action against Christie's claiming damages in conversion and bailment. The Court of Appeal (at 302) held that:

> an auctioneer who receives goods from their apparent owner and simply redelivers them to him when they are unsold is not liable in conversion provided he has acted in good faith and without knowledge of any adverse claim to them.

In coming to this conclusion, the Court of Appeal (at 302) distinguished between intention to deal and actual wrongful dealing:

> The auctioneer intends to sell and if he does so will incur liability if he delivers the goods to the buyer. But his intention does not make him liable; it is what he *does* in relation to the goods which determines liability. Mere receipt of the goods does not amount to conversion.

In receiving the painting from Mr Schuenemann and redelivering it to him as its apparent owner, the auctioneer 'has only acted ministerially', ie in accordance with the contract between the parties, the terms of which did not interfere with the title to the painting; Christie's did not receive the painting as a pledge. The court found that Christie's merely changed the position of the painting and not the property in it.[33]

Of course, Christie's would have been liable in conversion to the true owner if, having accepted the painting for sale in good faith and without notice of its true ownership, it sold and delivered the painting to a buyer, since that would involve interfering with the title or ownership of the painting. Incidentally, the Court of Appeal also noted that the picture had been registered as stolen on the Art Loss Register since 1979. This meant that if Mr Marcq had sued Christie's in negligence rather than conversion, the defendant would have had to explain why it—as an international auctioneer—did not exercise the reasonable care expected of their profession by consulting the Register to discover the true owner.

---

33. *Marcq v Christie Manson & Woods Ltd (Trading As Christie's)* [2004] QB 286 at 302..

What may be converted?

The subject of conversion was first determined through a fiction of 'losing and finding'. Any tangible chattel could be lost and found and thus could be converted. Since land was obviously incapable of getting lost, no trover would lie for dispossession or withholding of real property. Sand, gravel, timber, crops ('emblements'), and fixtures, which were regarded as a part of the land, became personal property once severed from the land, and trover could be brought for their removal. Money as currency could not be lost and found, therefore was not capable of being converted. However, coins or banknotes with distinguishing characteristics could be regarded as personal property and litigated upon in trover.

Likewise, since intangible rights were not considered capable of being lost or found, no action in trover lay for their conversion. But from the mid-nineteenth century, courts recognised that trover may lay for conversion of such negotiable documents as promissory notes, cheques, bonds, bills of lading, and stock certificates.[34] By the mid-twentieth century, conversion of tangible paper documents or plastic cards was also regarded as conversion of the intangible rights vested in them. Such 'goods' would include title deeds, mortgage documents, insurance policies, savings bank passbooks, credit cards, tax receipts, and account books. In *Marfani & Co Ltd v Midland Bank Ltd* [1968] 2 All ER 573, at 578, Diplock LJ expressed the rule in the following terms:

> At common law one's duty to one's neighbour who is the owner, or entitled to possession, of any goods is to refrain from doing any voluntary act in relation to his goods which is a usurpation of his proprietary or possessory rights in them. Subject to some exceptions … it matters not that the doer of the act of usurpation did not know, and could not by the exercise of any reasonable care have known, of his neighbour's interest in the goods. This duty is absolute; he acts at his peril. A banker's business, of its very nature, exposes him daily to this peril. … If the customer is not entitled to the cheque which he delivers to his banker for collection, the banker, however, innocent and careful he might have been, would at common law be liable to the true owner of the cheque for the amount of which he receives payment, either as damages for conversion or under the cognate cause of action, based historically on assumpsit, for money had and received.

In the case of *Australian Guarantee Corp v Commissioners of the State Bank of Victoria* (1989) Aust Torts Reports ¶80–229, two swindlers persuaded the plaintiff, the Australian Guarantee Corporation (AGC), to hand over to them, as brokers,

---

34. *Hollins v Fowler* (1875) LR 7 HL 757; *The Fine Art Society v The Union Bank of London Ltd* (1886) 17 QBD 705; *The Great Western Railway Company v The London and County Banking Company* [1901] AC 414; *Morison v London County & Westminster Bank Ltd* [1914] 3 KB 356; *Marfani & Co Ltd v Midland Bank Ltd* [1968] 1 WLR 956; *Parsons v The Queen* (1999) 195 CLR 619; *Voss & Anor v Suncorp-Metway Ltd & Ors* [2003] QCA 252.

six cheques payable to a third party. They then deposited the cheques in their own account with the State Bank of Victoria. The Bank credited the six cheques, even though they were drawn in the name of the third party payee, bore his full address and were crossed 'not negotiable credit bank a/c payee only'. Ormiston J found the State Bank of Victoria liable for conversion of the six AGC cheques amounting to $250 000.

In relation to copyright, it has been noted that although copyright is intangible property, infringing copies are tangible.[35]

Developments in electronic commerce have meant that the intangible rights can be converted through manipulation of electronic data. New technologies, for example keylogging software, and 'sniffer-type' hardware devices, have enabled criminals to discover customer account numbers, passwords and other sensitive information through the tracking of buttons pressed on computer keyboards. Reports of millions of dollars being stolen through unauthorised electronic transfers from individual bank accounts are commonplace.[36] In relation to its customers, a bank is strictly liable in conversion for any unauthorised transfer of funds—whether criminal or mistaken—from their accounts. There are few, if any, reported cases relating to electronic conversion of funds, because conscious of their liability and anxious to avoid exposure, when alerted to unauthorised electronic fund transfers, banks tend to replace the missing funds without customers having to resort to litigation.

Bailment for use

In general, violation of the terms of bailment exposes the bailee to strict liability for any damage to the chattel. However, mere use contrary to the terms of bailment will not constitute conversion, for example, where:

- the bailee uses the goods in an unauthorised way but does not damage them;
- the goods sustain light damage;
- transfer of possession does not affect the bailor's immediate right to possession; and
- goods are lost, but there is a reasonable hope of recovery.

However, where the departure from the terms of bailment is so serious as to amount to denial of the bailor's title, it will be regarded as conversion. This will occur where the bailee destroys, sells, or pledges the goods in question, denies the bailor's title to them, or refuses to re-deliver.

---

35. *Microsoft Corporation & Anor v Auschina Polaris Pty Ltd* (1997) 71 FCR 231 at 247, per Lindgren J.
36. Bleeding Edge, 'More Dangers in Online Banking' 26 July 2006, available at <http://www.bleedingedge.com.au/blog/> (accessed 29 July 2006); see also: Warren P & Streeter M, 'Stealing the Limelight: Global Gangs are Infiltrating our Computers, Which Could Threaten the Success of the Internet', Guardian Unlimited Online, 17 March 2005, available at <http://www.guardian.co.uk/online/story/0,3605,1438851,00.html> (accessed on 22 March 2005).

A contract of bailment for term—for instance, a hire-purchase contract—may provide that any breach of special contractual terms by the bailee will terminate the bailment. Such breach may not amount to conversion, but it will entitle the bailor to an immediate right of possession.

A bailor is regarded as a reversionary owner if, under the contract of bailment, he or she will be entitled to possession only after the expiry of the bailment. In *City Motors v Southern Aerial Service* (1961) 106 CLR 477, Kitto J observed (at 486) that such a person can be liable in conversion if he or she dispossesses the bailee during the subsistence of the term of a bailment which is not determinable at will.[37] Moreover, under common law, a reversionary owner cannot sue in conversion during the subsistence of the bailment. The reversionary owner lacks the right to immediate possession, unless the goods were bailed for a special purpose, yet dealt with in a manner inconsistent with that purpose. Thus, if the bailee sells the goods or subleases them in breach of the bailment contract, the bailor is entitled to terminate contract, gaining an immediate right to possession. The reversionary owner as bailor can then commence proceedings for conversion against the bailee. Very clear contractual or statutory language can, however, displace this rule.

Measure of damages

Conversion forces an involuntary purchase on the converter, and allows recovery of special loss suffered as a result of conversion. The full value of the chattel is assessed at the time of conversion.

Where the value of the goods has risen between the time of conversion and the trial, the plaintiff is entitled to recover the increased value, if the goods cannot be returned. For instance, in *Graham v Voight* (1989) Aust Torts Reports ¶80–296, the plaintiff, Graham, was boarding at Voight's house when in 1985 he fell some two weeks behind in his board payments and was told to leave the house immediately. He did so, but he left some of his property behind, including nine stamp albums with stamps valued at $43 000. When in 1986 Graham called on Voight to collect his goods, the defendant claimed that she handed them over to an unknown 'agent' of the plaintiff. Graham successfully sued in conversion. Damages were awarded on the basis of the valuation of stamps as well as a 3 per cent interest.

General damages for conversion can be awarded where it was foreseeable that the plaintiff would suffer anguish or anxiety caused by the loss of or serious

---

37. Southern Aerial Service Co purchased a truck on hire-purchase terms from City Motors. As part of the deal, it provided an old truck as a trade-in to cover a substantial part of the price. The trade-in truck broke down after it had gone into the possession of City Motors and the new vehicle had gone into the possession of the purchaser, but before the finance company formally accepted the hiring agreement. The finance company refused to provide the balance of the price, but Southern Aerial Service Co tendered cash and a cheque instead. City Motors refused the tender and repossessed the new truck. The High Court held that Southern Aerial Service Co could sue in detinue.

damage to the goods. In *Graham v Voight*, the plaintiff was awarded general damages for the loss of the albums, which represented a lifelong hobby, and distress thereby occasioned on the basis that they were 'plainly foreseeable'.

The court will also consider the purpose for which the converted goods would have been used by the owner when determining the measure of damages. For example, in *Myer Stores Limited v Jovanovic* [2004] VSC 478, the plaintiff, Ms Jovanovic, a professional photographer, through her agent entered into agreement with Myer in 1995, whereby she supplied Myer with three identical portfolios of forty-four prints to be used by Myer/Grace Bros solely for display and exhibition purposes. All copyright pertaining to the photographs remained with the artist, though 'reasonable reproduction for purposes of publicising the "exhibition"' was permitted. The agreement further provided that when no longer required, one set of photographs was to be donated to a public gallery or museum, while the remaining sets were to be disposed of in consultation with the photographer. The court found that the agreement was one of bailment, not sale, even though at the time, $12 000 was paid by Myer to Ms Jovanovic. Instead of donating a set to the museum or gallery, and consulting with the plaintiff about the rest, in 2000 Myer disposed of all but forty photographs to its employees. In 2002, a letter demanding the return of the photographs was sent to Myer by Ms Jovanovic's solicitors, but none of the photographs were returned. Ms Jovanovic was successful in her action in detinue and conversion. The plaintiff claimed that had the photographs been returned to her, rather than selling, she would have donated them to a gallery or a museum, with the purpose of receiving a benefit by way of publicity and prestige. Consequently, Balmford J (at [36]) determined that in this case, the measure of damages should not be the market value of the photographs, but 'the value of the prestige to be attached to having the photographs in museums or galleries.'

The courts have discretionary power to order specific restitution in cases of heirlooms or other goods of special significance to the plaintiff. If the defendant improves the chattel, the plaintiff must pay for the betterment; however, damages will be awarded where repairs are needed due to the defendant's fault. Specific restitution will not be granted where the defendant has mistakenly changed the nature of the converted material—for example, making a necklace out of a gold ingot—or where a winery makes wine out of grapes that, technically, it does not own. In such cases, the defendant will acquire a better claim to possession than the owner of the raw material. The latter will only be able to claim damages for the value of the ingot or the grapes.

Consequential damages in the form of lost profits, hire expenses, etc, will be awarded for conversion, providing they are not too remote. However, pure economic loss, like a loss of contract with third parties of which the defendant had no notice, is not compensable.

Exemplary damages can be awarded for conversion.

Contributory negligence is not a defence to the tort of conversion in Victoria (*Australian Guarantee Corporation Ltd v Commissioners of the State Bank of Victoria* [1989] VR 617 at 638, per Ormiston J).

SPECIAL ACTION ON THE CASE FOR INTENTIONAL DAMAGE TO GOODS

Special action on the case remedies intentional damage sustained by a plaintiff who is out of possession. It does *not* require the plaintiff to have immediate right to possession. Before the emergence of the tort of negligence, this was the only action available to a bailor where the chattel had been damaged while held for a term of bailment, or until fulfilment of a condition. Since the foundation of the action on the case is damage, permanent damage to the chattel must have occurred, in the sense that the harm would enure to the reversionary owner. For example, in *Mears v The London & South Western Rly Co* (1862) 11 CB (NS) 850, an owner–plaintiff let a barge to a third party for a term which had not expired when the defendant dropped a boiler, badly damaging the barge. The court held the bailor could sue the defendant for negligently or intentionally causing permanent damage to the barge.

In *Penfolds Wines*, the court held that special action on the case was inappropriate. Elliott did no permanent damage to the plaintiff's bottles: he simply cleaned them before pouring in the wine, albeit non-Penfolds wine. When the customer consumed the wine with which the bottle had been replenished, the bottle resumed its former condition.

Limitation of actions

As a general rule, limitation of actions legislation in all jurisdictions except the Northern Territory, prevents plaintiffs from bringing an action in conversion or wrongful detention of a chattel (detinue) more than six years from the accrual of the cause of action in respect of the original conversion or detention.[38] However, concealment of conversion may prevent the limitation period of six years commencing.

---

38. A six-year limitation period is provided under the following: *Limitation Act 1985* (ACT), s 11(1); *Limitation Act 1969* (NSW), s 14(1)(b); *Limitation of Actions Act 1974* (Qld), s 10(1)(a); *Limitation of Actions Act 1936* (SA), s 35(c); *Limitation Act 1974* (Tas), s 4(1)(a); *Limitation of Actions Act 1958* (Vic), s 6, s 27; *Limitation Act 1935* (WA), s 38(1)(c)(iv). Under the *Limitation Act 1981* (NT), s 12(1)(b), the limit is three years.

'SPOLIATION': INTENTIONAL OR NEGLIGENT DESTRUCTION OF EVIDENCE

In *Armory v Delamirie* (1722) 1 Str 505, Pratt CJ's direction to the jury (at 505) regarding 'the strongest possible presumption' against the jeweller, who failed to produce the original jewel for valuation, was based on the maxim *omnia praesummuntur contra spoliatorem* (all things presumed against the destroyer). Pratt CJ used the concept of spoliation or destruction of evidence as a procedural rule of evidence in relation to the assessment of damages. In *The Ophelia* [1916] 2 AC 206, *The Ophelia*, a German auxiliary military hospital ship, was seized by the British navy under suspicion of spying during the First World War. Her captain admitted that when the ship was about to be searched he ordered the Morse signal book, the stock book of signal lights, and other records to be thrown overboard. The evidence showed that *The Ophelia* was adapted and used as a signalling ship for military purposes. The vessel was condemned by the English court as lawful prize on the ground that she had forfeited the right to the protection to which military hospital ships are entitled under the Hague Convention No X. On appeal to the Privy Council, their Lordships concluded that the intentional spoliation of evidence by the captain gave rise to an evidentiary presumption that his evidence could not be relied upon. The procedural remedy of evidentiary presumption that the destroyed evidence would have been unfavourable to the destroyer, be that the plaintiff or the defendant, was adopted by the High Court of Australia in *Ford v Andrews* (1916) 21 CLR 317, at 324, and *Allen v Tobias* (1958) 98 CLR 367.

In the United States, *Smith v Superior Court* 198 Cal Rptr (Ct App 1984) was the first to establish an independent tort of 'spoliation of evidence', which was said to safeguard the interest of the parties to a civil litigation in preservation of evidentiary material against an unreasonable interference with it. The *Smith* decision was overruled as unsustainable in *Cedars-Sinai Medical Center v Superior Court of Los Angeles County* 954 P 2d 511 (1998) and *Temple Community Hospital v Superior Court of Los Angeles County* 976 P 2d 223 (1999).

In other United States jurisdictions, two causes of action for spoliation have been recognised: (1) intentional spoliation involving destruction and concealment of documents (*Smith v Howard Johnson Company* 615 NE 2d 1037 at 1038 (1993)); and (2) negligent or reckless spoliation (*Holmes v Amerex Rent-a-Car* 710 A 2d 846 at 854 (1998)). The tort is essentially based on the doctrine of loss of chance—had all evidence been available to the plaintiff, he or she would have had a better chance to successfully establish the case. Given that, by definition, the probity of the missing evidence is impossible to assess, the court may just as well consult a crystal ball in estimating the nature and the value of that lost chance.

The tort of spoliation was rejected by the Victorian Court of Appeal in *British American Tobacco Australia Services Ltd v McCabe* [2002] VSCA 197. Likewise, following a detailed discussion of principle and policy, the Court of Appeal of New Zealand in *EAM Burns v The National Bank of New Zealand Ltd & Ors* [2003] NZCA 232 determined that an independent tort of spoliation, whether negligent or intentional, should not be recognised in New Zealand.[39]

FURTHER READING

Ames B, 'History of Trover' (1898) 11 *Harvard Law Review* 374.
Balkin RP & Davis JL, *Law of Torts*, 2nd edn, Butterworths, Sydney, 1996, pp 63–114.
Jones C, 'The Spoliation Doctrine and Expert Evidence in Civil Trials' (1998) 32 *The University of British Columbia Law Review* 293–315.
Kern BJ, 'Whacking, Joyriding and War-Driving: Roaming Use of Wi-Fi and the Law' (2004) 21 *Santa Clara Computer & High Technology Law Journal* 101.
Wilson EM, 'The Alabama Supreme Court Sidesteps a Definitive Ruling in *Christian v Kenneth Chandler Construction Co*: Should Alabama Adopt the Independent Tort of Spoliation?' (1996) 47 *Alabama Law Review* 971.

---

39. The tort of spoliation was also rejected by Canadian courts in *Endean v Canadian Red Cross Society* (1998) 157 DLR (4th) 465 and, less emphatically, in *Spasic v Imperial Tobacco Ltd* (1998) 42 OR (3d) 391.

9 Defences to Intentional Torts

INTRODUCTION

As a general rule, in intentional torts, including trespass and action on the case for intentional harm, once the cause of action is established, defendants are responsible for damage flowing directly and naturally from their wrongful conduct.

In the seventeenth century, Matthew Hale (1609–76) in his *Pleas of the Crown*, published posthumously in 1736–39 (T Payne, London, 1800, vol 1, ¶15, p 213), considered that infancy, mental disability, chance, ignorance, civil subjection, compulsion, necessity, and fear did not ordinarily excuse a person from civil liability because 'such a recompense is not by way of penalty, but a satisfaction for damage done to the party.' Nevertheless, in the course of the past two centuries, common law and the legislature developed several defences and exceptions to intentional torts. This chapter examines the major ones, including the question of who has the burden of proof in establishing trespass.

THE CONCEPT OF FAULT IN INTENTIONAL TORTS

The High Court of Australia is yet to conclusively establish whether it is the plaintiff or the defendant who has to establish fault in trespass to the person. Discussions of the issue by Windeyer J in *McHale v Watson* (1964) 111 CLR 384, at 388, opined that with regard to fault in trespass, 'it is for the defendant … to prove an absence of intent and negligence on his part'.[1] As noted in Chapters 1 and 2, since the 2002–03 Torts reforms, the issue of fault in intentional torts has acquired greater significance because, apart from the Australian Capital Territory and, partly, South

---

1. See also: Bray CJ in *Venning v Chin* (1974) 10 SASR 299.

Australia,[2] all jurisdictions provide that legislative limitations in relation to damages. However, thresholds do not apply to wrongs 'where the fault concerned is an intentional act that is done with intent to cause death or injury, or that is sexual assault or other sexual misconduct'.[3]

The leading case on the issue of fault in trespass to the person is *McHale v Watson* (1964) 111 CLR 384. In that case, in January 1957, the plaintiff, nine-year-old Susan McHale, two other girls, and Barry Watson aged twelve, were playing a variation of the hide-and-seek game. Windeyer J found that at the end of the game, Barry threw a steel welding rod, about six inches in length and with a sharpened end, at a corner post of a wooden ornamental tree guard. The object either missed the post or hit it and glanced off and struck Susan, who was standing in front of Barry, less than five feet away. It pierced her right eye.

Susan, through her next friend, sued in trespass to the person and in negligence, alleging that Barry either threw the object directly at her (trespass), or in her direction (negligence). In relation to trespass, Windeyer J discussed the onus of proving the issue of fault. His Honour concluded (at 389) that it was Barry as the defendant who had to prove an absence of fault in terms of intent and negligence on his part.

Windeyer J found the defendant not liable, stating (at 396) that 'Barry Watson did not throw the so-called dart with intent that it hit Susan McHale'. His Honour also determined (at 397) that Barry was 'not negligent in a legal sense' when he hit the post because the risk of the harm to Susan could not reasonably have been foreseen by a boy of twelve. Susan appealed to the full bench of the High Court on the issue of negligence, but the majority dismissed the appeal (*McHale v Watson* (1966) 115 CLR 199).

CONSENT IN INTENTIONAL TORTS

If it is accepted that lack of consent is the gist of trespass, then valid consent will be deemed a complete defence. The common law has always looked with disfavour at non-consensual conduct, though originally consent was seen less as an expression of a personal right to autonomy than as a factor in the enforcement of the peace of the realm. Although there has never been any doubt that in trespass to land, the burden of proving consent rests with the defendant, the question whether consent in trespass to the person should be regarded as a defence, with the defendant bearing

---

2. The *Civil Liability Act 1936* (SA), s 43, excludes liability for criminal conduct, and applies where damages are claimed for personal injury (i) arising from a motor accident (whether caused intentionally or unintentionally); or (ii) arising from an accident caused wholly or in part (a) by negligence; or (b) by some other unintentional tort on the part of a person other than the injured person; or (c) by breach of a contractual duty of care.
3. *Wrongs Act 1958* (Vic), s 28C(2); *Civil Liability Act 2002* (Tas), s 3B(1)(a); *Civil Liability Act 2002* (NSW), s 3B(1)(a); *Civil Liability Act 2003* (Qld), s 52(2); *Civil Liability Act 2002* (WA), s 3A(1).

the onus of proving consent, or as an element of the cause of action—with the result that the plaintiff must show absence of consent—is yet to be settled definitively by the High Court of Australia.

McHugh J, who admittedly was the dissentient in *Secretary, Department of Health & Community Services (NT) v JWB and SMB (Marion's Case)* (1992) 175 CLR 218, discussed the relevant authorities in the following way (at 310–11):

> Notwithstanding the English view, I think that the onus is on the defendant to prove consent. Consent is a claim of 'leave and licence'. Such a claim must be pleaded and proved by the defendant in an action for trespass to land (*Kavanagh v Gudge* 7 Man & G 316 [135 ER 132]; *Wood v Manley* (1839) 11 AD & E 34 [113 ER 325]; *Plenty v Dillon* (1991) 171 CLR 635 at 647). It must be pleaded in a defamation action when the defendant claims that the plaintiff consented to the publication (See *Loveday v Sun Newspapers Ltd* (1938) 59 CLR 503 at 525). The *Common Law Procedure Act 1852* (15 & 16 Vict c 76) (Sch B 44) also required any 'defence' of leave and licence to be pleaded and proved. However, those who contend that the plaintiff must negative consent in an action for trespass to the person deny that consent is a matter of leave and licence. They contend that lack of consent is an essential element of the action for trespass to a person.

His Honour disagreed with the notion that consent is an element of trespass to the person, and defined this cause of action thus:

> The essential element of the tort is an intentional or reckless, direct act of the defendant which makes or has the effect of causing contact with the body of the plaintiff. Consent may make the act lawful, but, if there is no evidence on the issue, the tort is made out. The contrary view is inconsistent with a person's right of bodily integrity. Other persons do not have the right to interfere with an individual's body unless he or she proves lack of consent to the interference.

In *Sibley v Milutinovic* [1990] Aust Torts Reports ¶81–013, Miles CJ said that consent was a defence with the burden of proof resting upon the defendant. To establish absence of wrongful intent, the defendant must prove that the plaintiff consented to the interference. A similar approach was taken by Fisher J of the New South Wales Supreme Court in *Hart v Heron* (1980) Aust Torts Reports ¶80-201, and the majority of the New South Wales Court of Appeal in *Platt v Nutt* (1988) 12 NSWLR 213, though with a notable dissent by Kirby P.

The question arises as to whether consent will always be regarded as valid for the purposes of the cause of action in trespass.

Consent of adults to medical procedures

The English case *Chatterton v Gerson* [1981] 1 QB 432, at 443, is the authority, adopted in Australia by the High Court in *Rogers v Whitaker* (1992) 175 CLR 479, for the rule that in order to give 'real' or *valid consent* for the purposes of battery, the person needs to be informed in broad terms of the nature of the physical contact, its site, its general purpose, and any major risks associated with it.

In the English case of *In re W (a Minor) (Medical Treatment: Court's Jurisdiction)* [1992] 3 WLR 758, at 765, Lord Donaldson of Lymington MR provided a most insightful explanation of the importance and purpose of consent to medical treatment:

> [consent] has two purposes, one clinical and the other legal. The clinical purpose stems from the fact that in many instances the co-operation of the patient and the patient's faith or at least confidence in the efficacy of the treatment is a major factor contributing to the treatment's success. Failure to obtain such consent will not only deprive the patient and the medical staff of this advantage, but will usually make it much more difficult to administer the treatment ... The legal purpose is quite different. It is to provide those concerned in the treatment with a defence to a criminal charge of assault or battery or a civil claim for damages for trespass to the person. It does not, however, provide them with any defence to a claim that they negligently advised a particular treatment or negligently carried it out.

Consent to treatment, and its obverse—the refusal of treatment—are critical factors in good clinical practice and will materially affect the patient's future physical and mental condition. Furthermore, as Lord Donaldson pointed out, a patient's decision to consent to or to refuse medical treatment has important legal implications for the treating doctor.

Courts in the United States, Canada, the United Kingdom, and Australia have upheld the rule that unless emergency circumstances apply, any medical or surgical procedure that goes beyond the scope of a patient's express consent is trespass, even where there was no evidence of explicit prohibition.[4] In the absence of consent, legal justification (necessity), or statutory authorisation (infectious disease and mental health legislation), a medical practitioner who administers treatment to a patient is liable for damages in trespass to the person. Wood J observed in *T v T* [1988] 2 WLR 189, at 203, that this rule applies even when the medical procedure will benefit the patient:

> The incision made by the surgeon's scalpel need not be and probably is most unlikely to be hostile, but unless a defence of justification is established it must ... fall within a definition of a trespass to the person.

In *Rogers v Whitaker* (1992) 175 CLR 479, the High Court followed the majority of the House of Lords in the case of *Sidaway v Governors of Bethlem Royal*

---

4. *Paulsen v Gundersen* 218 Wis 578, 260 NW 448 (1935); *Wall v Brim* 138 F 2d 478 (5th Circ, 1943); *Murray v McMurchy* [1949] 2 DLR 442; *T v T* [1988] 2 WLR 189; *Rogers v Whitaker* (1992) 175 CLR 479.

Hospital [1985] AC 871 in rejecting the American doctrine of informed consent in the context of negligence. Their Honours (at 490) noted that the expression 'the patient's right of self-determination' is 'perhaps, suitable to cases where the issue is whether a person has agreed to the general surgical procedure or treatment ...'.

In Victoria, trespassory aspects of medical treatment have been codified under the *Medical Treatment Act 1988* (Vic).

Right to refuse lifesaving treatment

The right to refuse lifesaving or life-sustaining medical treatment is commonly referred to as the 'right to die' doctrine. It is a relatively novel legal interest. The case which is most often invoked as a precedent for this doctrine, *Schloendorff v Society of New York Hospital* 105 NE 92 (1914), did not involve life-and-death choices. The case concerned the defendant hospital's liability for torts committed by surgeons using its facilities: in particular, a surgeon who removed a fibroid tumour in circumstances where the patient had consented to an abdominal examination under anaesthesia, but had specifically requested 'no operation'. In the course of his judgment, Cardozo J stated (at 93) that 'every human being of adult years and sound mind has a right to determine what shall be done with his own body'. This statement has been interpreted as standing for the principle of inviolability of individual decisions regarding one's body.

In the 1980s, the principle of self-determination was extended to include the right to a death-choice, which manifests itself as refusal of life-sustaining or lifesaving treatment. The phrase 'lifesaving treatment' refers to therapies such as antibiotics, blood transfusions, organ transplants, and cardiopulmonary resuscitation, designed to cure or stabilise a life-threatening but potentially reversible medical condition. Lifesaving treatment may also include therapies undertaken from time to time to arrest or stabilise symptoms of incurable chronic conditions (for example, treatment administered to persons suffering from diabetes, chronic renal failure, chronic hepatitis, or chronic lymphatic leukaemia). The concept of 'life-sustaining treatment' involves a constant, rather than intermittent, application of such medical devices as mechanical ventilators, catheters, or feeding tubes, to keep alive patients whose life cannot be sustained without them. The *Consent to Medical Treatment and Palliative Care Act 1995* (SA), s 4, statutorily defines 'life-sustaining measures' as 'medical treatment that supplants or maintains the operation of vital bodily functions that are temporarily or permanently incapable of independent operation, and includes assisted ventilation, artificial nutrition and hydration and cardiopulmonary resuscitation.'

The person's legal right to make a death-choice was succinctly expressed by Robins J of the Ontario Court of Appeal in *Malette v Shulman* (1990) 67 DLR 4th 321, at 328:

A competent adult is generally entitled to reject a specific treatment or all treatment, or to select an alternate form of treatment, even if the decision may entail risks as serious as death and may appear mistaken in the eyes of the medical profession or of the community. Regardless of the doctor's opinion, it is the patient who has the final say on whether to undergo the treatment.

In *Rogers v Whitaker* (1992) 175 CLR 479 (FC), at 487, the joint judgment adopted the statement of King CJ in *F v R* (1983) 33 SASR 189, at 193, that 'a person is entitled to make his own decisions about his life'. While in the USA, the right to refuse life-saving and life-sustaining treatment has constitutional as well as common law foundations,[5] in Australia, Canada and England the law is primarily grounded in common law battery.[6] Thus, Lord Mustill in *Airedale NHS Trust v Bland* [1993] AC 789, at 891, expressed this rule in the following terms:

> If the patient is capable of making a decision on whether to permit treatment and decides not to permit it his choice must be obeyed, even if on any objective view it is contrary to his best interests. A doctor has no right to proceed in the face of objection, even if it is plain to all, including the patient, that adverse consequences and even death will or may ensue.

According to the High Court in *Marion's Case* (1992) 175 CLR 218, competent adults are presumed to have a right to voluntarily choose whether or not to consent to any medical intervention, including lifesaving or life-sustaining treatment.[7] This common law right of an adult person of sound mind to refuse any medical treatment is reinforced by statute in Victoria,[8] South Australia,[9] the Northern Territory,[10] and the Australian Capital Territory.[11] Statutory provisions

---

5. Mendelson D, 'Historical Evolution and Modern Implications of the Concepts of Consent to, and Refusal of, Medical Treatment in the Context of the Law of Trespass' (1996) 17 *Journal of Legal Medicine* 1–71.
6. Mendelson D, 'Legal Aspects of Euthanasia', in Smith R, *Health Care Crime and Regulatory Control*, Australian Institute of Criminology, Hawkins Press, Sydney, 1998, pp 149–166.
7. For a wider discussion, see: Mendelson D & Jost TS, 'A Comparative Study of the Law of Palliative Care and End-of-life Treatment' (2003) 31 *Journal of Law, Medicine and Ethics* 130–143. See also: *Mental Capacity Act 2005* (UK).
8. *Medical Treatment Act 1988* (Vic), s 5. In all Australian jurisdictions, patients have the common law right to refuse palliative care. Agents (and guardians) appointed under the *Medical Treatment Act 1988* (Vic) have the power to refuse medical treatment but not palliative care: Ashby M & Mendelson D, '*Gardner; Re BWV*: Victorian Supreme Court Makes Landmark Australian Ruling on Tube Feeding' (2004) 181(8) *Medical Journal of Australia* 442–445, at <http://www.mja.com.au/public/issues/181_08_181004/ash10074_fm.html>.
9. The *Consent to Medical Treatment and Palliative Care Act 1995* (SA) allows persons over sixteen to decide whether or not to undergo medical treatment (s 6); and persons over eighteen to make anticipatory decisions, in case of incompetence, about medical treatment related to the terminal phase of a terminal illness, or a persistent vegetative state (s 7).
10. The *Natural Death Act 1988* (NT), s 4, allows adult 'terminally ill' patients to refuse the undertaking or continuing of 'extraordinary measures' that prolong life.
11. *Medical Treatment Act 1994* (ACT), s 6.

also enable adults of sound mind to appoint an agent, or an alternate agent,[12] who can refuse medical treatment—including continuing administration of life support systems—on behalf of the patient after he or she becomes incompetent.[13]

Refusal of consent to treatment and the welfare of viable foetus

The issue of right to refuse medical treatment becomes more complex when a pregnant woman refuses or withdraws consent to medical treatment as a result of which not only her life, but also the life of a viable foetus, is placed in danger. In the United Kingdom, in *St George's Healthcare NHS Trust v S* [1999] Fam 26, the plaintiff, S, was thirty-six weeks' pregnant and had not previously sought antenatal care. She was diagnosed as suffering from pre-eclampsia (a toxaemia with acute elevation of blood pressure) and oedema (accumulation of fluid in tissues); if not treated, pre-eclampsia will develop into full eclampsia, leading to convulsions, severe brain damage, and coma. S was advised of the need for bed rest followed by an induced delivery, without which her life and that of her unborn child would be in peril. S understood the risks but refused to consent to any treatment, wishing 'to allow nature to "take its course," without intervention'. According to the report, 'she wanted to go to Wales, where her baby would be born in a barn. When it was pointed out that her baby might die she responded that she was not interested in the pregnancy or the baby.' The hospital authorities applied *ex parte* to a judge in chambers who granted a declaration that allowed the doctors to carry out a caesarean section without the consent of S. She delivered a healthy baby girl. Afterwards, S appealed to the English Court of Appeal, which held that pregnant women have the right to refuse treatment even where the treatment is intended to benefit the unborn child. This is because, although pregnancy increases the personal responsibilities of a woman, it does not diminish her entitlement to decide whether to undergo medical treatment. According to the Court of Appeal, an unborn child is not a separate person from its mother and its need for medical assistance does not prevail over the mother's right not to be forced to submit to an invasion of her body against her will. This is so whether or not the mother's own life, or that of her unborn child, depends on it.[14] It is uncertain whether the Australian courts will follow the English approach.

---

12. *Medical Treatment Act 1988* (Vic), s 5B. Guardians appointed under the *Guardianship and Administration Board Act 1986* (Vic) are granted the same powers to refuse medical treatment on behalf of the represented persons as agents appointed under an enduring power of attorney.
13. At common law a person of sound mind has the right to appoint another person to manage his or her affairs; however the power of attorney lapses after the donor becomes legally incompetent.
14. This rule might have to be re-interpreted in light of the *Mental Capacity Act 2005* (UK), s 25.

Consent of minors and incompetent persons

The High Court in *Marion's Case* (1992) 175 CLR 218, at 235, noted that there are three main sources of parental power, including the power to consent to medical treatment of the child, where the parent is also a guardian of a child of a marriage: the common law, the State or Territory legislation, and s 63F of the *Family Law Act 1975* (Cth), which states that subject to the order of a competent court, each parent of a child under eighteen years is a guardian of the child. Parents generally provide consent to medical treatment for very young children. The High Court observed (at 240) that the overriding criterion to be applied in the exercise of parental authority on behalf of a child is the welfare of the child objectively assessed, in accordance with the best interests standard.

Since parental rights are derived from parental duty and exist only so long as they are needed for the protection of the person and property of the child, the High Court in *Marion's Case* concluded that parental power to consent to medical treatment on behalf of a child diminishes relatively to the growth of a child's capacities and maturity. To provide valid consent, the child has to understand the nature of the treatment and its consequences, as well as the concept of consent. In *Marion's Case*, the High Court majority stated (at 239):

> it cannot be presumed that an intellectually disabled child is, by virtue of his or her disability, incapable of giving consent to treatment. The capacity of a child to give informed consent to medical treatment depends on the rate of development of each individual.

Thus, in Australia, there is no fixed age for a valid consent. The High Court referred to Lord Frazer's explanation of the principle in *Gillick v West Norfolk and Wisbech Area Health Authority* [1985] 3 All ER 402, at 409,[15] who said:

> Providing the patient, a boy or girl, is capable of understanding what is proposed, and of expressing her or his own wishes, I see no reason for holding that he or she lacks the capacity to express them validly and effectively and to authorise a medical man [or woman] to make the examination and give the treatment which he [or she] advises.

Parental consent or refusal of treatment will only prevail if it accords with the best interests of the child. Medical practitioners who witness, or even merely suspect, the presence of duress may request the Supreme Court under its inherent *parens patriae* jurisdiction,[16] the Family Court or a guardianship board to intervene in the interests of the child.

---

15. The *Gillick* case involved the question of whether a sixteen-year-old girl could validly consent to medical treatment, involving a prescription of the contraceptive pill.
16. Under the common law doctrine of *parens patriae*, the sovereign's responsibility to look after the welfare of children and those of unsound mind forms part of the inherent jurisdiction of the State Supreme Courts and the Family Court.

The law treats differently a child who, having understood the nature and consequences of the proposed treatment, consents to it, and a minor who has a capacity to consent but refuses lifesaving treatment. Thus, in *Minister for Health v AS & Anor* [2004] WASC 286, a fifteen-year-old boy, L, was diagnosed with a treatable abdominal lymphoma. L signed a form, which stated that he: 'withholds his consent to and forbids under any circumstances the administration of blood or blood products'. L and his parents were Jehovah's Witnesses. Pulling J (at [20]), referring to *Director General, New South Wales Department of Community Services v Y* [1999] NSWSC 644 at [99]–[103]) determined that where the child refuses medical treatment, particularly lifesaving treatment, his or her decision, 'while relevant and important does not prevent the court [under its *parens patriae* jurisdiction] from authorising medical treatment' where the best interest of the child so requires.

In L's case, Pulling J found (at [23]) that the boy's wishes were governed by his religious belief which 'led him to reject the expert medical advice that was available to him'. His Honour emphasised (at [21]) that:

> The guiding principle upon which the exercise of the *parens patriae* jurisdiction is based is that the welfare of the child is paramount. Protection of the child should be elevated above all other interests, although those other interests are not completely disregarded (*Re D (A Minor)* [1976] Fam 185; *Re Baby A* [1999] NSWCA 787 at [20]) ... The welfare of the child encompasses the child's physical wellbeing (*Re McGrath (Infants)* [1983] 1 Ch D 143 at 148). Where faced with the stark reality that the child will die if lifesaving treatment is not performed which has a good prospect of a long-term cure, it is beyond doubt that it is in the child's best interests to receive that treatment (*Re B (A Minor) (Wardship Medical Treatment)* [1981] 1 WLR 1421 at 1424).

As a general rule, legal adulthood begins at the age of eighteen. Consequently, under the *parens patriae* jurisdiction, superior courts and the Family Court can make orders for minors over the age of sixteen who refuse lifesaving medical treatment. For instance, in *Royal Alexandra Hospital v Joseph & Ors* [2005] NSWSC 422; *Royal Alexandra Hospital v J & Ors* [2005] NSWSC 465, sixteen-year-old Joseph and his family were Jehovah's Witnesses. When Joseph was diagnosed with acute lymphoblastic leukaemia in 2005, he refused transfusion of blood or blood products. The evidence established ([2005] NSWSC 465, at [25]) that unless Joseph received immediate transfusions of packed cells and platelets he would suffer spontaneous cerebral haemorrhage, or stroke, which is frequently fatal. Without transfusions, Joseph was also at risk of spontaneous bleeding within other organs, which presented a serious risk to his health. While acknowledging Joseph's spiritual anguish, Einstein J (as did Gzell J at an earlier hearing) determined (at [50]) that:

> Notwithstanding that he is over sixteen years old and that his wishes must be given serious consideration, in law he is still a child. What must guide the Court is its consideration of his best interests.

The exception to the minority rule is in South Australia, where the *Consent to Medical Treatment and Palliative Care Act 1995* (SA), s 6, specifically enables children 'of or over 16 years of age' to make decisions about their own medical treatment as validly and effectively as adults. In contrast, under s 12, a consenting younger child may make such decisions if:

> the medical practitioner who is to administer the treatment is of the opinion that the child is capable of understanding the nature, consequences and risks of the treatment and that the treatment is in the best interest of the child's health and well-being.

The physician's opinion has to be 'supported by the written opinion of at least one other medical practitioner who personally examines the child before the treatment is commenced'.

In New South Wales, according to s 174(1) of the *Children and Young Persons (Care and Protection) Act 1998* (NSW):

> A medical practitioner may carry out medical treatment on a child or young person without the consent of:
> (a) the child or young person, or
> (b) a parent of the child or young person, if the medical practitioner is of the opinion that it is necessary, as a matter of urgency, to carry out the treatment on the child or young person in order to save his or her life of to prevent serious damage to his or her health.

In *Birkett v Director General of Family & Community Services* (unreported, SC NSW, Bryson J, 3 February 1994), Bryson J said that for the purposes of the *Children (Care and Protection) Act 1987* (NSW), s 20A (the wording of which is identical to s 174(1) of the *Children and Young Persons (Care and Protection) Act 1998*), the test of necessity is based on the contemporaneous opinion of the attending medical practitioner, rather than 'objective facts' as determined retrospectively by the court.[17] However, in certain circumstances, the court can make orders under its *parens patriae* jurisdiction allowing doctors to institute a non-consensual treatment regime aimed at preventing the child's condition becoming life-threatening (s 174(1) applies to urgent lifesaving interventions).[18]

In *Marion's Case*, the High Court determined that in relation to mentally incompetent children, procedures for 'non-therapeutic' purposes must be authorised by the Family Court or a guardianship board. *Marion's Case* itself concerned the question whether family in consultation with doctors could provide valid consent to

---

17. For further judicial interpretation of the *Children (Care and Protection) Act 1987* (NSW), s 20A, see: *Dalton v Skuthorpe* (unreported, SC NSW, McLelland J, 17 November 1994) and *Marchant v Finney* (unreported, SC NSW, Waddell C, 10 July 1992).
18. *Director General of the Department of Community Services v 'BB'* [1999] NSWSC 1169 (19 November 1999) at [21] and [29].

sterilisation of their incompetent child, where such procedure was carried out not for the purpose of treating some malfunction or disease, but to prevent her or him from becoming a parent. According to the majority judgment (at ¶49), in cases of sterilisation of incompetent minors for 'non-therapeutic' purposes:

> Court authorisation is required, first, because of the significant risk of making the wrong decision ... about what are the best interests of a child who cannot consent, and secondly, because the consequences of a wrong decision are particularly grave.

Since the rule refers to children, it is unclear whether it applies to all incompetent patients. Moreover, the scope of the 'non-therapeutic' medical treatment needs to be further defined. For example, does discontinuation of life-sustaining treatment fall within the legal definition of 'non-therapeutic' interventions?[19]

Consent to blood transfusion for a child

In the majority of cases, minors who refuse lifesaving treatment do so on religious grounds. All Australian jurisdictions have provisions[20] that empower medical personnel to transfuse minors without the consent of any person who is legally entitled to authorise the blood transfusion if a request for consent has been refused, or where the parent or guardian cannot be found after reasonable search, and at least two doctors have agreed that the transfusion is essential (or 'reasonable and proper treatment') to save the minor's life. In South Australia, s 13(5) of the *Consent to Medical Treatment and Palliative Care Act 1995* provides for the best interests of the child's health and well-being to be the governing test, where parents of guardians refuse consent to treatment, including blood transfusion.

In *Minister for Health v AS & Anor* [2004] WASC 286, Pulling J noted (at [24]) that if the situation were reached where L was likely to die, then s 21 of the *Human Tissue and Transplant Act* 1982 (WA) would apply. This provision would allow a medical practitioner to perform a blood transfusion upon a child without the consent of any person legally entitled to authorise it, if:

(a) such person—
  (i) fails or refuses to so authorize the blood transfusion when requested to do so; or

---

19. For a further discussion of this issue, see: Ashby M & Mendelson D, '*Gardner; Re BWV*: Victorian Supreme Court Makes Landmark Australian Ruling on Tube Feeding' (2004) 181(8) *The Medical Journal of Australia* 442–445, at <http://www.mja.com.au/public/issues/181_08_181004/ash10074_fm.html>.
20. *Human Tissue Act 1982* (Vic), s 24; *Children and Young Persons (Care and Protection) Act 1998* (NSW), s 174; *Transplantation and Anatomy Act 1979* (Qld), s 20; *Consent to Medical Treatment and Palliative Care Act 1995* (SA), s 13(5); *Human Tissue and Transplant Act 1982* (WA), s 21; *Human Tissue Act 1985* (Tas), s 21; *Emergency Medical Operations Act 1992* (NT), s 3; *Transplantation and Anatomy Act 1978* (ACT), Pt 2, Div 5.

(ii) cannot be found after such search and enquiry as is reasonably practicable in the circumstances of the case

and

(b) the medical practitioner and another medical practitioner agree—
   (i) as to the condition from which the child is suffering
   (ii) that the blood transfusion is a reasonable and proper treatment for that condition; and
   (iii) that without a blood transfusion the child is likely to die

and

(c) the medical practitioner who performs the blood transfusion on the child
   (i) has had previous experience in performing blood transfusions; and
   (ii) has, before commencing the transfusion, assured himself that the blood to be transfused is suitable for the child.

The nature of consent: fraud and duress

A plaintiff's consent obtained by fraud or duress will not be regarded as valid consent, and will not make trespassory (intentional) acts lawful.

Fraud

In *R v Williams* [1923] 1 KB 340, the defendant persuaded the plaintiff that she needed a 'special' surgical procedure in the form of sexual intercourse to improve her voice. The court held that the fraud induced a misapprehension as to the actual nature of the act—the plaintiff thought that what the defendant did was a surgical procedure, not a sexual act. Therefore the defendant could not show that the plaintiff validly consented to intercourse.

Duress

In *Aldridge v Booth* (1988) 80 ALR 1, the plaintiff was employed at 'The Tasty Morsel' cake shop in Stafford. When she started the job she was nineteen, and had been unemployed for one year. She agreed to acts of sexual intercourse with her employer, Mr Booth, under economic duress, namely the fear of losing her first full-time job. Spender J observed that these were non-consensual acts, with the employer exploiting the young woman's particular vulnerability as to job security. His conduct amounted to sexual harassment under s 28 of the *Sex Discrimination Act 1984* (Cth).

In general, in cases of apparent power imbalance, such as between a lawyer and client, school or university teacher and student, doctor and patient, banker and client, creditor and debtor, the court may well regard acts of sexual intercourse as lacking valid consent by the weaker party.

Mere acquiescence rather than genuine consent may also be the case in other situations involving imbalance of power between the parties. In *Ghani v Jones* (1970) 1 QB 693, at 705, Lord Denning MR explained the difference:

> The second thing to notice is that the police officers kept the passport and letter without the consent of the holders. Mr Leonard suggested that they took them with consent. This is a little far-fetched. Here were two police officers asking a Pakistani for the passport of himself and his wife. Of course he handed them to them. It would look bad for him if he did not. He bowed to their authority.

Sadomasochistic practices

In *Matthew v Ollerton* [1692] Comb 218; 90 ER 438 the court said 'If a man license another to beat him, such license is void as it is against the peace'. Even though there is nothing in this statement to suggest it covers consensual acts performed in private, where breach of the peace may not easily arise, the majority of the High Court, in *Marion's Case*, has taken it to mean (at 309) that 'a person cannot consent to the infliction of grievous bodily harm without "good reason".' The phrase 'good reason' refers to the judgment of Lord Lane in *Attorney-General's Reference (No 6 of 1980)* [1981] 1 QB 715, at 719, who wrote that: 'It was not in the public interest that people should try to cause or should cause each other bodily harm for no good reason.'

The case that gave rise to the Attorney-General's Reference concerned two youths who, following a quarrel, agreed to resolve their difference in a fist fight outside a pub, as a result of which one of them suffered a nosebleed, and the other a black eye. The public interest principle was subsequently approved by the majority of the House of Lords in the case of *R v Brown* [1993] 2 WLR 556, which held that consent to serious injuries consequent upon sado-masochistic practices was ineffective as a shield against criminal responsibility.

In *State v Brown* 364 A 2d 27 (1976), a husband was charged with an offence of 'atrocious assault and battery'. The United States Superior Court of New Jersey refused to regard as valid the consent of a wife to being beaten by her husband 'with his hands and other objects' if she got drunk. The court reasoned (at 31–2) that to allow such a defence would seriously threaten the dignity, peace, health, and security of society.

Implied consent

In *Canterbury Bankstown Rugby League Football Club Ltd v Rogers; Bugden v Rogers* [1993] Aust Torts Reports ¶81–246, it was held that Rugby League players gave their consent to being struck by the opposing players in the chest and shoulders because that was proper under Rugby League rules; but consent would not extend to being struck on the head, since such tackles were contrary to the rules. Under the doctrine of implied consent, which is based on the maxim *qui tacet, consetire vedetur* (he who is silent consents), by participation, players are taken to have indicated consent to those contacts with the body within the rules of the game. The doctrine of implied consent operates where the person by actions indicates consent. For example, in *O'Brien v Cunard SS Co* 28 NE 266 (1891) (Mass Sup Jud Ct), the court held that the motion of a person holding up her arm to be vaccinated implied a valid assent to an injection.

Exigencies of everyday life

If William Blackstone's precept that the slightest non-consensual touching constitutes battery were to be interpreted literally, we all would be liable for battery, for it is impossible to function in our society without some non-consensual touching. To avert such possibility, the law has developed the doctrine of ordinary exigencies of life, which was thus explained by Robert Goff LJ in *Collins v Wilcock* [1984] 1 WLR 1172, at 1178:

> Generally speaking consent is a defence to battery; and most of the physical contacts of ordinary life are not actionable because they are impliedly consented to by all who move in society and so expose themselves to the risk of bodily contact. So nobody can complain of the jostling which is inevitable from his presence in, for example, a supermarket, an underground station or a busy street; nor can a person who attends a party complain if his hand is seized in friendship, or even if his back is, within reason, slapped.

The majority in the *Marion's Case* (at 233) adopted Goff LJ's doctrine of the 'exigencies of everyday life', and also noted that 'the absence of consent is irrelevant in a lawful arrest or in circumstances which amount to self-defence' (discussed below). All other acts that fall outside the ambit of reasonable and generally acceptable conduct constitute a *prima facie* cases of battery to which a common law defence or other justification must be raised.

The plea of *volenti non fit injuria*

The plea of consent is different from the defence based on the maxim that is today known as *volenti non fit injuria* (no wrong is done to the one who consents),[21] loosely derived from Roman law.[22] Bracton (*c* 1200–68) interpreted this maxim as *cum volenti at scienti non fiat iniuria* (with consent and knowledge no injury is done).

---

21. The spelling of the Latin word 'iniuria' as 'injuria' is the accepted common law form of medieval Latin.
22. Ingman T, 'A History of the Defence of *Volenti Non Fit Injuria*' (1981) 26 *Juridical Review* 1.

Though the word *scienti* was later eliminated, knowledge of the risk of injury being consented to has remained an element of the *volenti* defence, which is based upon the principle that a person should have the right to waive his or her legal rights. Donaldson MR, in *Freeman v Home Office (No 2)* [1984] QB 524 (CA), at 557, pointed out that the maxim of *volenti non fit injuria* provides a bar to enforcing a cause of action—it does not negative the cause of action itself. Whereas traditionally, the concept of consent has been applicable to immediate contacts, the plea of *volenti* is used mainly in cases of consent to negligent failure to prevent or minimise the risk that has resulted in the injury to the claimant. The concept of voluntary assumption of risk will also be discussed in the context of defences to negligence.

EXCEPTIONS TO BATTERY

Defence of necessity

A successful defence of necessity is a complete defence to any trespassory conduct: battery, assault, trespass to land, false imprisonment, or trespass to goods. In *Marion's Case*, McHugh J observed:

> Consent is not necessary ... where a surgical procedure or medical treatment must be performed in an emergency and the patient does not have the capacity to consent and no legally authorized representative is available to give consent on his or her behalf.[23]

One of the major cases that discussed the defence of necessity was *In Re F v West Berkshire HA* [1990] 2 AC 1. It involved a thirty-six-year-old mentally handicapped woman, F, who resided as a voluntary in-patient in a mental hospital and who had the mental age of a small child. She formed a sexual relationship with a male patient. The hospital staff and F's mother considered that she would be unable to cope with the effects of pregnancy and giving birth. Apart from sterilisation, all other forms of contraception were found unsuitable. Since it was considered undesirable to further curtail F's limited freedom of movement in order to prevent sexual activity, the House of Lords held that sterilisation was in her best interests.

As a general rule, for the defence of necessity to succeed, the person who has *prima facie* committed a trespass must prove: (1) reasonable necessity for the trespassory action; (2) 'duress of circumstances'; and (3) that he or she did not create the situation of imminent peril. These prerequisites will be discussed in turn.

It must be reasonably necessary to do the act in respect of which the action was brought, to preserve life and health, or protect the property from a situation of imminent danger or harm. Convenience, usefulness or taking advantage of

---

23. *Secretary, Department of Health and Community Services (NT) v JWB and SMB (Marion's Case)* (1992) 175 CLR 218 at 310.

the circumstances are not sufficient. In *Murray v McMurchy* [1949] 2 DLR 442, the defendant–surgeon, who was unable to deliver a child by forceps on two attempts, decided to perform a caesarean section on the plaintiff. The plaintiff was anesthetised. At the request of the surgeon, the plaintiff's husband signed the permission for the operation and any other surgical procedure found necessary by the attending medical practitioner. In the course of the operation, the surgeon discovered the presence in the wall of the uterus of ten fibroid tumours, including one that was the size of a small orange. The tumours were not, at the time of operation, dangerous to the plaintiff's health. After consultation with his assistant, the surgeon tied the fallopian tubes of the patient to prevent her from undergoing the hazards of a second pregnancy. The Supreme Court of British Columbia held that without the consent of the patient, the surgeon was not authorised to take the additional step of sterilisation at the time of performing the caesarean section to forestall the possibility of some future hazard. Hence, even if the medical practitioner considers it convenient and desirable to undertake an invasive medical procedure in order to prevent some possible future—as against imminent—danger, it is still for the patient to decide whether to have a given extra procedure or not.[24]

Moreover, since consent is always limited to the particular act or procedure that has been described and discussed by the medical practitioner, and does not extend to other procedures unless these additional procedures can be justified on the grounds of necessity. The fact that the doctor mistakenly believes that she has the consent of the patient does not make the defence of consent applicable. A person who had consented to having his right knee reconstructed, but instead had an operation upon his left knee, could obtain damages for battery.

Under the doctrine of 'duress of circumstances', the situation must involve 'an urgent situation of imminent peril.' A sincere but mistaken belief that a situation of urgency and peril existed is not sufficient. Jurisdictions that have enacted 'good samaritan' legislation[25] have modified the common law, in so far as the legislation provides statutory protection from civil liability for those who act 'honestly and without recklessness in assisting' a person who 'is apparently injured or at risk of being injured'. The adverb 'apparently' suggests that an apparent as against 'real' need for assistance is sufficient to trigger the immunity.

Under common law the defence of necessity does not apply in circumstances where the defendant created or contributed to the occasion of emergency through his or her intentional conduct, negligence or intention. While all other jurisdictions have codified this rule, Victoria (*Wrongs Act 1958* (Vic), s 31B(3)) exempts from liability in any civil proceeding individuals who had caused the emergency or

---

24. See also: *Hart v Herron & Anor* [1984] Aust Torts Reports ¶80–201.
25. *Civil Liability Act 2002* (NSW), Pt 8; *Civil Liability (Wrongs) Act 2002* (ACT), s 5; *Civil Liability Act 1936* (SA), s 74; *Wrongs Act 1958* (Vic), Pt VIA; *Civil Liability Act 2002* (WA), s 1D; *Personal Injuries Act 2003* (NT), s 8.

accident 'by an act or omission', providing they fulfil the statutory criteria for rendering assistance (discussed below).

At the same time, in Victoria, even in circumstances of necessity, a medical practitioner who is aware of the existence of a valid Refusal of Treatment Certificate executed under the *Medical Treatment Act 1988* (Vic) by a patient who has become incompetent is prohibited by legislation from undertaking lifesaving medical treatment, provided the refusal of treatment certificate covers the patient's present condition. The Northern Territory and South Australia have specific legislation covering the administration of emergency treatment.[26]

In England, Ward and Brooke LJJ of the Court of Appeal in *A (Children) (Conjoined Twins: Surgical Separation)* [2001] Fam 147; 2 WLR 480 developed a variant of the defence of others that applies in strictly medical setting to certain medical procedures aimed at preserving one life at the cost of another in circumstances where, without such intervention, the death of both will inevitably occur. The case concerned a surgical separation of conjoined twins, which would save the life of one of the twins, while causing the death of the other.[27] If no operation was performed, both were likely to die within a very short period of time. The Court of Appeal held that the following elements of the defence of necessity were satisfied: (a) the act was required to avoid inevitable and irreparable evil; (b) no more would be done than was reasonably necessary for the purpose to be achieved; and (c) the evil to be inflicted was not disproportionate to the evil avoided.

Although this defence was framed in the context of criminal law, excusing what would otherwise be criminal conduct in relation to an innocent victim, it would be equally applicable to civil proceedings to justify action, which otherwise would be trespassory or negligent, for example, where the twins' parents[28] wished to sue the medical personnel for damages either on behalf of the surviving twin for battery, or for negligently occasioned nervous shock (see Chapter 15).

Statutory defences under 'good samaritan' and volunteers legislation

Good samaritans

Since the 1980s, when Australian society became progressively more litigious, many people were deterred from coming to succour those in need of assistance for

---

26. *Emergency Medical Operations Act 1973* (NT); *Consent to Medical Treatment and Palliative Care Act 1995* (SA).
27. M had severe brain abnormalities, no lung tissue and no properly functioning heart. The blood supply keeping M alive emanated from J who was in all other essential respects functioning and developing normally.
28. In *A (Children) (Conjoined Twins: Surgical Separation)* [2001] Fam 147; 2 WLR 480, parents of the conjoined twins appealed against the ruling granting the medical personnel authority to proceed with the elective separation.

fear of being sued. In 2002–03, six States and Territories enacted 'good samaritan' legislation to exempt from personal civil liability those who assist, succour or take care of a person in apparent need of emergency assistance, where they expect no money or other financial reward. The wording differs from jurisdiction to jurisdiction; however, the provisions cover members of the general public who seek to assist others in this way, as well as off-duty medical and health care professionals, emergency workers, and others whose actions are outside the scope of their authorised statutory duties.[29] As a general rule, statutory immunity does not cover any act or omission that occurs prior to the good samaritan activities.

To come within the scope of immunity, the good samaritan's acts or omission must be 'made honestly' (the Australian Capital Territory),[30] or in 'good faith' (South Australia, New South Wales, Western Australia, the Northern Territory, Victoria);[31] 'without recklessness' (the Australian Capital Territory, the Northern Territory, South Australia, Western Australia);[32] and his or her 'capacity to exercise appropriate care and skill at the relevant time' (New South Wales)[33] must not be 'significantly impaired' by alcohol or other recreational drugs (the Australian Capital Territory, South Australia, New South Wales, Western Australia, the Northern Territory).[34] Victoria is the sole jurisdiction that lacks the recklessness and impairment safeguards. Consequently, no action will lie against a drunk and reckless good samaritan who in good faith has caused a 'pre-natal injury; psychological or psychiatric injury; disease; aggravation, acceleration or recurrence of an injury or disease' (*Wrongs Act 1958* (Vic), s 31A) to a hapless person 'apparently at risk of death or injury, or … apparently injured' (*Wrongs Act 1958* (Vic), s 31B(1)). The meaning of such expressions as 'good faith' (conceptually part of insurance law), and 'significant impairment' (central to the law of damages) will have to be judicially defined in the context of the good samaritan provisions, as will the scope of these provisions.

The *Civil Liability Act 2002* (NSW), s 58(3), contains a specific provision that no protection from personal liability is conferred 'on a person in respect of any act or omission done or made while the person is impersonating a health care or emergency services worker or a police officer or is otherwise falsely representing

---

29. Persons who provide advice by telephone or other means of communication to a person at the scene of an emergency or accident also fall within the category of 'good samaritans'.
30. *Civil Law (Wrongs) Act 2002* (ACT), s 5(1).
31. *Civil Liability Act 1936* (SA), s 74(2); *Civil Liability Act 2002* (NSW), s 56; *Civil Liability Act 2002* (WA), s 5AD(1); *Personal Injuries (Liabilities and Damages) Act 2003* (NT), s 8(1); *Wrongs Act 1958* (Vic), s 31B(2).
32. *Civil Law (Wrongs) Act 2002* (ACT), s 5(1); *Civil Liability 1936* (SA), s 74(2); *Civil Liability Act 2002* (WA), s 5AD(1); *Personal Injuries (Liabilities and Damages) Act 2003* (NT), s 8(2).
33. The *Civil Liability Act 2002* (NSW), s 58(2)(b), excludes immunity from good samaritans who 'failed to exercise reasonable care and skill in connection with the act or omission.'
34. *Civil Law (Wrongs) Act 2002* (ACT), s 5(2)(b); *Civil Liability Act 1936* (SA), s 74(4)(b); *Civil Liability Act 2002* (NSW), s 58(2)(a) (whether or not consumed as medication); *Civil Liability Act 2002* (WA), s 5AE; *Personal Injuries (Liabilities and Damages) Act 2003* (NT), s 8(3) (intoxication).

that the person has skills or expertise in connection with the rendering of emergency assistance.'

In Queensland, the *Civil Liability Act 2003* (Qld), ss 26 and 27, confers protection from civil liability on persons and entities 'performing duties to enhance public safety ... in the course of rendering first aid or other aid or assistance to a person in distress'. The first aid or assistance must be 'in good faith and without reckless disregard for the safety of the person in distress or someone else' and must be given in circumstances of emergency.

Volunteers

In 2000–02, many voluntary organisations were unable to insure their members against liability in tort. Legislation, relatively uniform, in all Australian jurisdictions, including the Commonwealth, was enacted to remedy this situation.[35] Provided they act in good faith, volunteers do not incur personal civil liability for acts and omissions done in the course of community work organised by a community organisation, or as an office holder of a community organisation.[36] Volunteers are generally defined as persons who receive no remuneration for the work, or are remunerated for the work but within limits prescribed by regulation, or are reimbursed for reasonable expenses.

Statutory protection does not apply to conduct and work done outside the scope of voluntary work organised by community organisation or contrary to instructions; nor to wrongful acts and omissions due to impairment through alcohol and drugs, or injuries caused by driving a motor vehicle; nor to defamation.[37] Volunteers who are required to have personal liability insurance also tend to fall outside statutory immunity.

In all jurisdictions, legislation precludes a community organisation from entering into an arrangement that would entitle it to seek an indemnity from a volunteer in respect of a liability of the community organisation arising out of the conduct of the volunteer.

---

35. *Wrongs Act 1958* (Vic), Pt IX; *Civil Liability Act 2002* (NSW), Pt 9; *Civil Liability Act 2003* (Qld), Ch 2, Pt III (also includes exemption for food donations); *Civil Liability Act 2002* (Tas), Pt 10; *Volunteers Protection Act 2001* (SA); *Volunteers (Protection from Liability) Act 2002* (WA); *Personal Injuries (Liabilities and Damages) Act 2003* (NT), s 7; *Civil Law (Wrongs) Act 2002* (ACT), s 8(1); *Commonwealth Volunteers Protection Act 2003* (Cth).
36. The *Commonwealth Volunteers Protection Act 2003* (Cth), s 4(2), refers to 'an individual [who] does work for the Commonwealth or a Commonwealth authority on a voluntary basis'.
37. *Commonwealth Volunteers Protection Act 2003* (Cth), s 6(2); *Civil Law (Wrongs) Act 2002* (ACT), s 8(2); *Civil Liability Act 2002* (NSW), ss 62–66; *Civil Liability Act 2002* (Tas), s 47(2), (3) and (4); *Volunteers (Protection from Liability) Act 2002* (WA), ss 6(2), (3), (4); *Civil liability Act 2003* (Qld), ss 40–44; the *Personal Injuries (Liabilities and Damages) Act 2003* (NT), s 7(1), requires that the act be done 'without recklessness'; s 7(2) excludes (a) acts outside the scope of authority or contrary to the instructions of the community organisation; or (b) intoxication; *Volunteers Protection Act 2001* (SA), s 4, Exceptions; *Wrongs Act 1958* (Vic), s 38.

Defence of property

In *Mouse's Case* (1609) 12 Co Rep 63, a barge on the Thames was imperilled by tempest. In order to save the lives of the passengers, Mouse, who was a passenger, jettisoned a casket belonging to the plaintiff, so as to lighten the barge. The court held that in such a case of necessity, it was lawful for Mouse to jettison the casket to safeguard the lives of the passengers, and the plaintiff had to bear the loss himself. In later cases, this defence has been interpreted very narrowly.[38]

Under common law, the defendant does not have to succeed in saving the life or property of another. Nor does the defendant have to prove that injury or destruction would have occurred but for the interference.

DEFENCE OF SELF-DEFENCE AND DEFENCE OF OTHERS

The courts regard an act in self-defence as an instinctive reflex, usually with very little time for rational analysis of measures to be taken. The onus is on the person pleading self-defence to show the act was *reasonably* necessary and proportionate to the perceived threat. For example in *Fontin v Katapodis* (1962) 108 CLR 177, Katapodis hit Fontin with a T-square (a wooden measuring stick about 1.25 metres long with a short cross piece at one end): once on the arm and once on the shoulder. When Katapodis raised the T-square to hit Fontin again, Fontin called to another person standing nearby for help, then picked up an offcut of louvre glass thirty-eight centimetres long and five to eight centimetres wide and threw it at Katapodis' face. The glass piece hit and seriously injured the hand of Katapodis, which he had raised to fend off the missile. The court determined (at 181–2) that in the circumstances, it 'was out of all reasonable proportion to the emergency confronting Fontin' to throw such a very dangerous weapon as the piece of glass at Katapodis in order to protect his right of personal safety. Owen J also observed (at 186) that, as a general rule:

> the fact that a means of escape was open to a person who claims to have been defending himself against attack is not a decisive factor in considering whether he has acted reasonably (*Reg v Howe* (1958) 100 CLR 448, at 471) and the weight to be attached to such a circumstance will necessarily vary according to the circumstances.

In this case, the trial judge found that instead of throwing the piece of glass at Katapodis, Fontin could easily have moved away from him and thus avoided further blows from the T-square.

---

38. For a discussion, see: *Monsanto v Tilly & Ors* [2000] Env LR 313.

In some jurisdictions, the principle of reasonable proportionality in self-defence has been statutorily modified. For example, in South Australia, the *Criminal Law Consolidation Act 1935* (SA), s 15B, codifies the common law by stating: that 'the defendant's conduct be (objectively) reasonably proportionate to the threat that the defendant genuinely believed to exist does not imply that the force used by the defendant cannot exceed the force used against him or her.' However, s 15C(2) dispenses with the requirement of reasonable proportionality in cases of 'an innocent defence against home invasion'.

Sections 51 and 52 of the *Civil Liability Act 2002* (NSW) relating to self-defence are very extensive. They both reflect and modify the common law. They grant immunity from civil liability 'of any kind for personal injury damages or damage to property' for acts of self-defence, if according to s 52:

(1) ... the conduct to which the person was responding was unlawful, or would have been unlawful if the other person carrying out the conduct to which the person responds had not been suffering from a mental illness at the time of the conduct.

(2) A person carries out conduct in self-defence if and only if the person believes the conduct is necessary to:
  (a) defend himself or herself or another person, or
  (b) prevent or terminate the unlawful deprivation of his or her liberty or the liberty of another person, or
  (c) protect property from unlawful taking, destruction, damage or interference, or
  (d) prevent criminal trespass to any land or premises or to remove a person committing any such criminal trespass.

Generally, for statutory immunity from liability to operate, the conduct must be a reasonable response in the circumstances as the person perceives them. Moreover, by virtue of s 52(3), statutory protection is excluded:

if the person uses force that involves the intentional or reckless infliction of death only:
  (a) to protect property, or
  (b) to prevent criminal trespass or to remove a person committing criminal trespass.

However, s 53 provides that the s 52 protection may extend to a person whose conduct in self-defence was not a reasonable response in the circumstances as he or she perceived them, but the court is satisfied that these circumstances were 'exceptional', and 'a failure to award damages would be harsh and unjust'. If the court decides to award damages in such cases, these cannot include damages for non-economic loss.

DEFENCE OF INSANITY

In *Weaver v Ward* (1617) Hob 134; 80 ER 284,[39] during military exercises, Ward fired his musket, wounding Weaver. Weaver sued in trespass for assault and battery, and Ward pleaded that the wounding was accidental and against his will. Hobart CJ and Winch J (Warburton J dissenting) held that the plea was bad. In the course of the judgment, their Honours opined that:

> felony must be done *animo felonico*; yet in trespass, which tends only to give damages according to hurt or loss, it is not so. And therefore if a lunatic hurt a man he shall be answerable in trespass.

Likewise, Sir Matthew Hale (1609–76) in his *Pleas of the Crown* (T Payne, London, 1800), Chapter 2, while discussing defences to criminal offences, wrote (p 16) that persons acting under 'incapacity of defect of will' including 'dementia' are 'ordinarily' not excused:

> from civil actions to have a pecuniary recompense for injuries done, as trespasses, batteries, woundings, because such a recompense is not by way of penalty, but a satisfaction for damage done to the party.

In *Morris v Marsden* (1952) 1 All ER 925, a civil action for damages, Sable J held (at 928) that liability will attach to a voluntary and intentional act of the defendant who knew the nature and quality of his act even though he did not realise that his act was wrong, for:

> knowledge of wrongdoing is an immaterial ... and... where there is the capacity to know the nature and quality of the act, albeit that the mind directing the hand that did the wrong was diseased, that suffices.

Sable J also noted that a person who committed trespass to the person in a condition of complete automatism would not be liable because of the lack of the necessary intention. As a general rule, the onus of proving insanity is on the party alleging it.

In New South Wales, s 54A of the *Civil Liability Act 2002* limits damages for loss that results from a serious offence committed by mentally ill person by excluding damages for non-economic loss and loss of earnings.

---

39. Reproduced in Baker JH & Milsom SFC, *Sources of English History; Private Law to 1750*, Butterworths, London, 1986, pp 331–333. The judgment went on to say that: 'And therefore no man shall be excused of a trespass (for it is in the nature of excuse, and not justification *prout ei bene licuit*) except it may be adjudged utterly without his fault'.

STATUTORY DEFENCES OF LEGAL AUTHORITY

Involuntary and non-voluntary medical treatment

Non-voluntary treatment is based on the doctrine of necessity and is a major common law exception to the rule that there must be an express consent to medical treatment. *Involuntary* treatment implies treatment against a legally competent patient's express wishes, and is governed by legislation. The determination whether to carry out non-voluntary and involuntary treatment involves a balance between the personal interest in autonomy as against the interests of life, safety, or welfare of the person himself or herself, or of a third party, and the community at large.[40]

For example, in relation to non-voluntary treatment, under s 120A of the *Health Act 1958* (Vic), where it is 'necessary in the interest of rapid diagnosis and treatment for any of those involved', a test for certain infectious diseases may be carried out on people who are unable to consent because they are unconscious, or have died, or for some other reason. The prescribed tests also can be carried out on persons whose lack of capacity to consent is only temporary,[41] and who have a guardian with the capacity to consent to such a test.

In respect to involuntary treatment, s 121 of the *Health Act 1958* (Vic) provides that in certain strictly defined cases, the authorised officer (secretary to the Department of Health and Human Services) may make an order in writing for a person to undergo an appropriate test, treatment and detention, if the secretary:

> reasonably believes that a person has an infectious disease or has been exposed to an infectious disease in circumstances where a person is reasonably likely to contract the disease; and if infected with that infectious disease, the person is likely to transmit that disease; and there is a serious risk to public health.

Lawful arrest

In a number of Australian jurisdictions, the common law of citizen's arrest has been entirely replaced by statute. However, speaking in relation to the Tasmanian *Criminal Code,* Windeyer J pointed out in *Vallance v The Queen* (1961) 108 CLR 56, at 76, that since these statutes adopted common law terminology, they are as if 'written on a palimpsest, with the old writing still discernible behind'; hence they should be interpreted in the light of established common law principles.

In *Halliday v Nevill* (1984) 155 CLR 1, the High Court developed the concept of implied licence to enter another's property through an open driveway. This

---

40. Mason J & McCall Smith R, *Law and Medical Ethics*, 4th edn, Butterworths, London, 1994, pp 219–220. See also: *Health Act 1958* (Vic), s 119(a).
41. The *Health Act 1958* (Vic), s 120AC, provides for post-test or authorisation counselling of persons who have regained capacity to consent.

may include entering the driveway for the purpose of effecting arrest. In *Halliday*, two policemen walked down an open driveway and arrested Halliday, who was attempting to reverse a car into the street while disqualified from driving. The officers did not seek the permission of the owner of the premises before entering and making the arrest. While being escorted towards the police car, Halliday broke away and ran across the street to his own home. The officers pursued him into the house, a scuffle ensued, and he was overcome. Gibbs CJ, Mason, Wilson, and Deane JJ determined that since the driveway from which Halliday attempted to reverse his car was open, the officers had an implied licence from the owner of the premises to be on the driveway, and accordingly the arrest was lawful and so was the police custody of him. Once he escaped from the lawful custody, the officers had the right to pursue him into his home and subdue him under the rule that a police officer may use a force that is 'not disproportionate' to effect or assist in effecting a lawful arrest. An essential prerequisite to a lawful arrest without a warrant is that the arrestee must be 'found committing an offence'—caught in *flagrante delicto*.[42] In this case, Halliday was committing the offence of escaping from lawful custody.

The concept of an offence giving rise to an arrest without warrant tends to be strictly interpreted. For example, although a failure to provide name and address to a police officer may constitute an offence, Isaacs J in *Hazell v Parramatta City Council* [1968] 1 NSWR 165 held that it is not a proper use of police powers to arrest a person for refusing to provide his or her name and address, where the requesting officer already knows it.

A person being arrested without warrant must be informed by the arresting officer of the true ground on which he or she is being arrested. This common law principle has been codified in the *Crimes Act 1900* (NSW), s 352. For example, in *State of New South Wales v Riley* [2003] NSWCA 208, the court determined that police officers were liable *inter alia* for false imprisonment when they arrested the plaintiff, Mr Riley. Acting on information that gunshots had been heard in his house, the police searched his car without a warrant. Even though the search revealed no firearm on Mr Riley or in the car, he was arrested, without being told why.

DEFENCES TO FALSE IMPRISONMENT

The defendant must establish on the balance of probabilities that there was either no imprisonment, or that imprisonment was lawfully justified at common law or by statute. False imprisonment is nullified by valid consent, and by statutory or common law powers of arrest.

---

42. *Hazell v Parramatta City Council* [1968] 1 NSWR 165; *Krivoshev & Anor v Royal Society for the Prevention of Cruelty to Animals Inc & Ors* [2005] NSWCA 76 at [24], per Young CJ in Eq.

228 *Part II: Intentional Torts*

The Commonwealth, all States, and the Territories have legislation permitting involuntary medical examination, detention, and treatment of people with infectious diseases presenting a threat to public health. At the federal level, the power to legislate resides in the Commonwealth under s 51(ix) of the *Commonwealth Constitution* (quarantine). Under the *Quarantine Act 1908* (Cth) s 2B, the Governor-General, if 'satisfied that an epidemic caused by a quarantinable disease or quarantinable pest or danger of such an epidemic exists in a part of the Commonwealth' may, by proclamation, 'declare the existence in that part of the Commonwealth of that epidemic or of the danger of that epidemic'. The States also have very wide powers of quarantine. Thus, typically, the *Health Act 1958* (Vic), s 123, grants the Governor in Council power to proclaim emergency for the purpose of stopping, limiting or preventing the spread of an infectious disease. By virtue of s 124, once the Governor in Council has made a proclamation under s 123, the Secretary may make an order which could include all or any of the following provisions:

(a) that persons of a specified class may be prevented from entering or leaving the proclaimed area;

(b) that persons of a specified class may be arrested without warrant and detained in the proclaimed area;

(c) that land, buildings or things in the proclaimed area may be seized—
  (i) to be used in connection with stopping, limiting or preventing the spread of infectious diseases; or
  (ii) to be disinfected; or
  (iii) to be damaged or destroyed if the land, building or thing is contributing to the spread of infection;[43]

(d) any other provisions required to ensure that the order is carried into effect.

Mental Health Acts in all jurisdictions also provide for involuntary certification of psychiatric patients.[44]

Incarceration of persons under a jail sentence is governed by statute in every jurisdiction. Prisoners who are detained for longer than their legal term can successfully sue for false imprisonment because misapprehension of the law by the authorities is not a defence. For example, in *Cowell v Corrective Services Commission* (1988) 13 NSWLR 714, the plaintiff's entitlement to remissions had been calculated, to his detriment, in accordance with a court decision that had subsequently been overruled. Although, at the time, those responsible for the calculation acted in good faith, complying with the law as they understood it, the New South Wales

---

43. The *Health Act 1958* (Vic), s 125, provides for compensation 'for seizure of land, building or thing'.
44. *Mental Health Act 1986* (Vic), ss 7(7), 8, 9, 9A; 9B, 10, 12, 12(1A), 12C, Pt IV; *Mental Health Regulations 1998* (Vic), Reg 6, Reg 6A; *Mental Health (Treatment and Care) Act 1994* (ACT), ss 25, 36G, 38; *Mental Health Act 1990* (NSW), s 8, Pt II, Div 1; *Mental Health and Related Services Act* (NT), Pt 3 and Pt 6; *Mental Health Act 2000* (Qld), ss 25, 34, 36, 39, 40, 114, 185; *Mental Health Act 1993* (SA), Pt IV; *Mental Health Act 1996* (Tas), ss 24, 35, 39, 83E, 83F, 88; *Mental Health Act 1996* (WA), ss 12, 26, 43.

Court of Appeal held that the Commission could be liable for unlawful imprisonment. Likewise, in *R v Governor of Brockhill Prison; Ex parte Evans (No 2)* [2000] 3 WLR 843, the House of Lords held that a detention of a prisoner amounted to a false imprisonment—even though the governor of the prison was acting in good faith when he interpreted the law, which appeared to have been settled by precedent, but subsequently turned out to have been wrong.

The concept of preventive detention orders under anti-terrorism legislation—now being enacted in every Australian jurisdiction[45]—is yet another statutory exception to common law false imprisonment.

EXCEPTIONS AND DEFENCES TO TRESPASS TO LAND

As a general rule, under both common law and statute, officers of the Crown are empowered to forcibly enter private land if they hold a warrant for an arrest, and if their request for the door to be opened has been refused. However, under the third resolution of *Semayne's Case* (1604) 77 ER 194 (discussed in Chapter 5), the warrant must involve a case where the sovereign is a party to the action—that is, in criminal matters that are pleas of the Crown (proceedings upon indictment, presentment, or information *ex officio*).

Offences punishable summarily are proceedings between subject and subject. Since the Crown is not a party to prosecution of offences that are punishable summarily, servers of such summonses have no right to enter the premises without consent. Likewise, according to *Plenty v Dillon & Ors* (1991) 171 CLR 635, service of a summons in relation to a civil matter is a matter between subject and subject. The object of serving a summons is to notify the defendants of the charges against them and to give them an opportunity to defend the charges. Whether the defendants accept the writ and appear in answer to the summons is a matter entirely for them. If they do not accept the writ and appear in answer to the summons, then an adverse judgment will be entered. Therefore, the failure to serve a summons is not regarded as a matter in which the Crown—through the administration of justice—is involved.

A number of statutes confer power to enter land without the occupier's consent, but the common law presumption is that, in the absence of express provision to the contrary, the legislature does not intend to authorise what would otherwise be tortious conduct. For example, in *Coco v The Queen* (1994) 179 CLR 427, Santo Antonio Coco was convicted of an offence of offering to bribe Commonwealth officers. Much of the evidence was obtained through listening devices installed

---

45. *Terrorism (Police Powers) Amendment (Preventative Detention) Act 2005* (NSW); *Terrorism (Preventative Detention) Act 2005* (Qld); *Terrorism (Preventative Detention) Act 2005* (SA); *Terrorism (Preventative Detention) Act 2005* (Tas); Terrorism (Preventative Detention) Bill 2005 (WA).

on his premises by two federal police officers impersonating telephone repairmen. Their purported authority was under s 43 of the *Invasion of Privacy Act 1971* (Qld), which provided that 'the use of any listening device by a member of the police force acting in the performance of his duty if he has been authorised in writing to use a listening device by the Commissioner ... under and in accordance with an approval in writing given by a judge of the Supreme Court' would not constitute an offence under the Act. On appeal, the High Court found that s 43 did not contain express words conferring power upon the Supreme Court's judge to authorise conduct that would otherwise be tortious. In particular, the word 'use', in relation to listening devices, was too narrow to extend to entry onto premises. The majority in *Coco* (at 436) said:

> The presence of general words is insufficient to authorise interference with the basic immunities which are the foundation of our freedom; to constitute authorisation express words are required.

Under common law, the following defences to trespass to land are available: trespass in defence of property; re-entry on land; abatement by self-help; the privilege of recaption of chattels.

Trespass in defence of property

A person who comes onto land without consent and thus interferes with another's exclusive possession of it can be ejected. Such a person must be given a reasonable time to leave voluntarily, and no more force than necessary may be used.

Re-entry on land

The common law allowed a person entitled to exclusive possession of land to come onto the land and eject a person who is no longer entitled to be there, without incurring tortious liability, if he or she uses no more force than is necessary. This exception is nowadays regulated by statute.

Abatement by self-help

A person with the right of abatement of nuisance (removal of nuisance will be discussed in Chapter 18) can enter the defendant's land to put an end to a nuisance without incurring liability in trespass. The modern courts, however, do not favour the remedy of abatement in preference to legal action. Therefore, strong reasons will be required to justify the use of this remedy when it involves entering upon another's land. Martin J, in *Traian v Ware* [1957] VR 200, at 207, stated that the onus of proving and justifying abatement is on the trespasser.

The privilege of recaption of chattels

Persons deprived of their goods can recover them immediately, and without recourse to law, by entering upon the land of the person who has deprived them of possession in exercise of the right of recaption of chattels.[46]

Where the chattel came onto the land by accident, as where a fruit falls onto a neighbour's land—and the owner of the land has not been actively responsible for the chattel, or fruit, being on his or her land—an owner may enter the land to retrieve it, but must not use any force. Also, where a car has been stolen, taken for a joyride and then dumped in someone else's yard, the owner will have the privilege of entry into the yard to retake his or her car.

In *Halliday v Nevill* (1984) 155 CLR 1, the majority reaffirmed the existence of the privilege of recaption of chattels, and also described, without specifically naming it, the defence of exigencies of life in relation to trespass to land—as where a parent enters another person's land brings back a toddler who has run onto it.

The claim of recaption of chattels is a complete defence to the action for trespass to land (*Cox v Bath (No 3)* (1893) 14 LR (NSW) 263; *Huet v Lawrence* [1948] Q St R 168).

In some jurisdictions, the defence to action for trespass to land has been codified. For example, s 141 of the *Civil Law (Wrongs) Act 2002* (ACT) provides:

> It is a defence to an action for trespass to land if the defendant establishes that—
>
> (a) the defendant does not claim any interest in the land; and
>
> (b) the trespass was because of negligence or was not intentional; and
>
> (c) the defendant made a reasonable offer to make amends to the plaintiff before the action was brought.

DEFENCE OF LIMITATION OF ACTIONS

Statutes of Limitation in every Australian jurisdiction prescribe a specified period within which proceedings for torts claims must commence. The defendant has the right to defeat a claim brought outside the statutory limitation period (*Commonwealth of Australia v Verwayen* (1990) 170 CLR 394). In some jurisdictions, however, the court can exercise its discretion to extend the period of limitation in relation to personal injury claims, having regard to the circumstances of a particular case.[47]

---

46. See: Blackstone W, *Commentaries on the Laws of England*, A Facsimile of the First Edition of 1768, Vol 3, Clarendon Press, Oxford; photographically reprinted by The University of Chicago Press, Chicago & London, 1979, pp 2–3.
47. *Limitation of Actions Act 1958* (Vic), s 23A and Div 3; *Limitation of Actions Act 1974–81* (Qld), s 31(2); *Limitation of Actions Act 1936* (SA), s 48; *Limitation Act 1969* (NSW), s 19; *Limitation Act 2005* (WA), ss 14, 16; *Limitation Act 1974* (Tas), s 5A(5), s 26; *Limitation Act 1981* (NT), s 44; *Limitation Act 1985* (ACT), s 36(4).

In all Australian jurisdictions, actions for personal injuries have to be commenced within three years from the date on which the cause of action accrued or the 'date of discoverability' (the date when the plaintiff knew or ought to have known injury had occurred), the cause of which is attributable to the defendant and the injury is significant enough to warrant proceedings.[48]

Some statutes, for example the *Limitation of Actions Act 1958* (Vic), s 27D, specify that personal injury actions:

> shall not be brought after the expiration of whichever of the following periods is the first to expire—
> (a) the period of 3 years from the date on which the cause of action is discoverable by the plaintiff
> (b) the period of 12 years from the date of the act or omission alleged to have resulted in the death or personal injury with which the action is concerned.[49]

A number of jurisdictions provide for statutory extension of the limitation period for personal injury claimants who are under disability,[50] and for children.[51]

MISTAKE

Mistake either of fact or law is no defence to intentional torts: if a defendant intends to shoot A but instead shoots B, who is wearing A's distinctive clothing, the defendant is liable for the direct contact he intended. There is one exception to this rule: mistaken self-defence. If a defendant erroneously, but reasonably, believes the plaintiff is about to attack him, and consequently uses force to defend himself, there will be no liability, providing the defendant used no more force than he reasonably believed necessary.

---

48. *Limitation of Actions Act 1936* (SA), s 36; *Limitation of Actions Act 1974* (Qld), s 11; *Limitation Act 1985* (ACT), s 16B; *Limitation Act 1981* (NT), s 12(1)(b); *Limitation Act 1969* (NSW), ss 18A(2), 50C; *Limitation of Actions Act 1958* (Vic), ss 27D, 27E; *Limitation Act 1974* (Tas), s 5A; *Limitation Act 1935* (WA), s 38A (injuries due to inhalation of asbestos and other latent injuries).
49. See also: *Limitation Act 1969* (NSW), s 50C (the '12 year long-stop limitation period'); *Limitation Act 1974* (Tas), s 5A(3) (damages for negligence, nuisance or breach of duty in relation to personal injury).
50. *Limitation Act 1985* (ACT), Pt 3; *Limitation of Actions Act 1936* (SA), s 45; *Limitation Act 1974* (Tas), Pt III; *Limitation of Actions Act 1958* (Vic), ss 27E, 27J; *Limitation of Actions Act 1974* (Qld), s 29; *Limitation Act 1935* (WA), s 40; *Limitation Act 1969* (NSW), s 50E.
51. *Limitation Act 1985* (ACT), Pt 3; *Limitation of Actions Act 1936* (SA), s 45A; *Limitation Act 1969* (NSW), s 50E; *Limitation of Actions Act 1957* (Vic), s 27I.

FURTHER READING

Annas G, 'Nancy Cruzan and the Right to Die' (1990) 323 *New England Journal of Medicine* 670.

Brock DW & Wartman SA, 'When Competent Patients Make Irrational Choices' (1990) 322 *New England Journal of Medicine* 1595.

Bursztajn HJ, Harding HP, Gutheil TG & Brodsky A, 'Beyond Cognition: The Role of Disordered Affective States in Impairing Competence to Consent to Treatment' (1991) 19 *Bulletin of the American Academy of Psychiatry and Law* 383.

Foley K, 'The Relationship of Pain and Symptom Management to Patient Requests for a Physician-assisted Suicide' (1991) 6 *Journal of Pain Symptom Management* 289.

Freckelton I, 'Masochism, Self-mutilation, and the Limbs of Consent' (1994) 2 *Journal of Law and Medicine* 47.

Kissane DW, Street A & Nitschke P, 'Seven Deaths in Darwin: Case Studies under the *Rights of the Terminally Ill Act*, Northern Territory, Australia' (1998) 352 *Lancet* 1087.

McLean K, 'Children and Competence to Consent: *Gillick* Guiding Medical Treatment in New Zealand' [2000] *Victoria University of Wellington Law Review* 31.

Mendelson D, 'Historical Evolution and Modern Implications of the Concepts of Consent to, and Refusal of, Medical Treatment in the Context of the Law of Trespass' (1996) 17 *The Journal of Legal Medicine* 1.

Mendelson D, 'Jurisprudential Aspects of Withdrawal of Life Support Systems from Incompetent Patients in Australia' (1995) 69 *Australian Law Journal* 259.

Mendelson D, 'Medico-legal Aspects of the "Right to Die" Legislation in Australia' (1993) 19 *Melbourne University Law Review* 112.

Mendelson D, 'Palliative Care, Assisted Suicide or Euthanasia? Toward a Common Discourse in the Terminology of Treatments at the End of Life' (1999) 7(5) *Progress in Palliative Care* 230.

Miller FH, 'Denial of Health Care and Informed Consent in English and American Law' (1992) 18 *American Journal of Law and Medicine* 37.

Stewart C, 'Advanced Directives, the Right to Die and the Common Law: Recent Problems with Blood Transfusions' (1999) *Melbourne University Law Review* 6.

Sullivan MD & Youngner SJ, 'Depression, Competence, and the Right to Refuse Medical Treatment' (1994) 157 *American Journal of Psychiatry* 971.

Yeo S, 'Accepted Inherent Risks Among Sporting Participants' (2001) 9 *The Torts Law Review* 114.

Part III

THE TORT OF NEGLIGENCE

INTRODUCTION

The advent of railways in the early 1830s, which brought in its wake an unprecedented toll of accidental injuries and death, provided the impetus for the development of negligence as a separate tort. According to the 1857 Annual Report of the English Board of Trade, out of nearly 140 million passengers who traveled on United Kingdom's railways in that year, 236 were killed, and 738 injured 'from causes beyond their own control.'[1] No statistics were collated for casualties among the railway employees,[2] and members of the general public who died or were injured in railway collisions and accidents.[3] Today, what we euphemistically call the 'road

---

1. Moore A, *A Hand-Book of Railway Law*, W H Smith & Son, London, 1859, p xxxii.
2. Under the *Railway Regulation Act 1840* 3 & 4 Vict c 97, s 3 (UK), the companies were supposed to provide data to the Railway Department of the Board of Trade relating to 'accidents which shall have occurred ... attended with personal injury.' This data, however, was notoriously incomplete: Bartrip PWS & Burman SB, *The Wounded Soldiers of Industry 1833–1897*, Clarendon Press, Oxford, 1983, pp 40–43. A set of figures compiled by the *Railway Service Gazette* for 1872–73 showed that 1387 servants of the Lancashire and Yorkshire Railway Company were injured, and 54 died in railway accidents during that period.
3. The casualties suffered by the general public were very high indeed, because although railway companies were granted a privilege to bisect districts, cross thoroughfares, and intersect the course of footpaths, until the 1860s they were not compelled by law to make such level crossings safe: Anonymous, 'Railway Crossings,' *The Law Times*, 28 September 1867, pp 369–370.

toll' still accounts for a disproportionately large percentage of deaths and injury in our society.[4]

The rationale for the tort of negligence is two-fold: (1) to enable those wrongfully injured through the negligent conduct of others to obtain compensation from the injurers; and (2) to impose standards based on a duty to avoid creating risks which may result in an injury to another. If there is no way of avoiding a particular risk or of predicting whether or not it will materialise, then the risk ought to be disclosed to those who may be harmed by it.

The tort of negligence is a species of action on the case, consequently, plaintiffs carry the burden of proof with respect to all facts in issue, and all the substantive requirements. They must tilt the balance of probabilities in their favour.

Likewise, as for all other species of the action on the case genus, the threshold requirement for liability in negligence is damage.

Compensable damage for purposes of negligence

The cause in negligence will not accrue unless and until the plaintiff has incurred damage. In *Mahony v Kruschich (Demolitions) Pty Ltd* (1985) 156 CLR 522, at 527, the High Court in a joint judgment stated:

> In negligence, 'damage' is what the plaintiff suffers as the foreseeable consequence of the tortfeasor's act or omission. Where a tortfeasor's negligent act or omission causes personal injury, 'damage' includes both the injury itself and other foreseeable consequences suffered by the plaintiff.

The injury, however, has to be of a kind regarded as compensable in law. According to Deane J in *Jaensch v Coffey* (1983–84) 155 CLR 549, at 587:

> It is now settled law in this country that there is a distinction, for the purposes of the law of negligence, between mere grief or sorrow which does not sound in damages, and forms of psychoneurosis and mental illness (which lawyers imprecisely termed 'nervous shock') which may [sound in damages].[5]

Unless accompanied by physical injury or a recognised psychiatric condition or illness, distressing but 'transient' emotions such as sorrow, anguish or anxiety are not classified as 'nervous shock' (nowadays referred to as 'mental harm'), and therefore are not compensable. Moreover, every State and Territory has imposed statutory

---

4. In some States, statutory no-fault compensation schemes have greatly reduced common law litigation in respect of injuries caused by motor vehicle collisions: *Motor Accident Act 1988* (NSW); *Transport Accident Act 1986* (Vic); *Motor Accidents (Liabilities and Compensation) Act 1973* (Tas); *Motor Accidents (Compensation) Act 1979* (NT); *Motor Accidents (Compensation) Rates of Benefit Regulations 1984* (NT).
5. Deane J reaffirmed the rule established in *Blake v Midland Railway Co* (1852) 21 LJ QB 233. See also the statements of Windeyer J in: *Mount Isa Mines Ltd v Pusey* (1971) 125 CLR 383 at 394.

threshold requirements in respect of compensable injuries. These thresholds were discussed in Chapter 2.

Paradigm of the cause of action in negligence

Liability for negligent conduct presented a complex jurisprudential conundrum to the nineteenth century judiciary. It is still awaiting a satisfactory resolution. Liability for negligence goes to the very core of the purpose and function of the law and the notion of what is just. Aristotle in his *Nicomachean Ethics*[6] distinguished between distributive and corrective justice. According to Aristotle, distributive justice is 'exercised in the distribution of honour, wealth, and other divisible assets of the community, which can be allotted to its members in equal or unequal shares'.[7] Although this concept has been interpreted in different ways by various legal theorists, there appears to be a consensus of opinion that 'distributive justice' is akin to 'legislative justice' manifested through statutory enactments dealing with provision of benefits or imposition of burdens 'in patterns and proportions that we can accept as fair or rational having regard to the subject-matter'.[8] Consequently, decisions made on the basis of distributive justice are open to criticism that the judges who made them have strayed into the province of the legislature.[9] Indeed, under the liberal democracy system of governance, the legislatures have the power to modify or abrogate any judicial decision which they, as popularly elected representatives of the people, consider to be inimical or unfair to the general welfare of the community.

In contrast, according to Aristotle, corrective justice is a 'judicial justice' whereby the judge has the power to correct or put right something that has gone wrong, and thus to restore the equilibrium where the just balance in a bipolar relationship[10] has been disturbed:

> the law looks only at the character of the injury, treating the parties as equal, it asks whether one is in the wrong and the other is being wronged, and whether one inflicted injury and the other has received it. Since this kind of injustice lies in inequality, the judge endeavours to equalise it; also in cases where one man has received and the other has inflicted a wound, or one has killed and the other has been killed, in these cases the suffering and the action have been equally divided, but the judge endeavours to make them equal by means of the penalty, taking away the gain.[11]

---

6. Aristotle, *Nicomachean Ethics*, (Ross WD, trans), in McKeon R (ed), *Basic Works of Aristotle*, Random House, New York, 1941.
7. Ibid at 5.2.12.
8. Kelly JM, *A Short History of Western Legal Thought*, Clarendon Press, Oxford, 1994, p 26.
9. See Lord Hoffmann in: *White v Chief Constable of South Yorkshire Police* [1999] 2 AC 455 at 511.
10. A phrase used by Weinrib EJ, 'The Gains and Losses of Corrective Justice' (1994) 44 *Duke LJ* 27 7–297 at 277.
11. *Nicomachean Ethics*, 5.4.3. Aristotle adds that the term 'gain' also applies as to: 'the person who inflicts a wound and "loss" to the sufferer; at all events when the suffering has been estimated, the one is called loss and the other gain'.

Technically, the tort of negligence, like other tortious remedies, is a quintessential embodiment of the concept of correlative justice—it restores the equilibrium, through an award of compensation, within the individual bipolar relationship of the injured plaintiff and the defendant. However, unlike intentional torts, negligence imposes liability for unintentionally occasioned injuries, and particularly in an industrial and post-industrial environment, has a very broad reach.

It became clear as early as the nineteenth century that if the judges made compensation for negligently occasioned injury too readily available or too high, manufacturers and service providers, being found liable, would be forced into bankruptcy; or—once third party insurance was introduced—subject to prohibitive insurance premiums. The judiciary was aware that such developments could engender anxiety about introducing innovative, but untried and thus risky, procedures, machinery, and techniques. At least in theory, making laws, which influence the course of social, intellectual and economic development of the community, are the prerogative of democratically elected Parliaments whose domain is distributive justice.

Given these considerations, the balance between the objective of corrective justice to compensate those physically injured by the wrongful conduct of others, and the need to refrain from imposing too heavy a burden of liability on wrongdoers whose fault often would involve a momentary want of care or forethought, tended to fall in favour of the latter. As a result, the common law paradigm of negligence is composed of progressive barriers to compensation in the form of elements that constitute this cause of action.

The following elements of the cause of action in negligence must be established by plaintiffs, on the balance of probabilities, before they can obtain damages:

1. *Duty of care*: The plaintiff has to establish a legal right to sue the particular defendant.
2. *Breach of duty*: Negligence is a fault-based cause of action, and fault lies in failure to exercise reasonable care (falling below the standard of care expected of a reasonable person in the position of the defendant).
3. *Causation*: As a general rule, plaintiffs have to establish a factual connection between the defendant's particular breach of duty of care and their injury (cause in fact). They then have to persuade the court that the defendant should bear legal liability for the injury (legal causation).
4. *Remoteness of damage*: The plaintiff must show that the kind of injury caused by the defendant was reasonably foreseeable.

If the plaintiff fails to prove any one of the four requirements, the action in negligence will fail.

Defences may be raised and pleaded by the defendant. The defence of illegality and the defence based upon the maxim *volenti non fit injuria* (voluntary assumption of the risk of being negligently injured without legal recourse) tend to be argued by the defendant as threshold issues affecting existence of duty of care. The *Limitation of Actions* legislation is also argued at the outset, because if valid, it extinguishes the plaintiff's cause of action. Once the plaintiff has established his or her case, the burden of proof shifts to the defendant to plead and establish the defence of contributory negligence.

In relation to the elements of the tort of negligence, Gleeson CJ in *Neindorf v Junkovic* [2005] HCA 75, at [50], observed:

> it is neither possible nor desirable to attempt to consider the duty of care issue independently of the breach element or, indeed, the other elements relevant to a decision on liability for negligence. The questions that the successive stages of negligence doctrine pose are not entirely free standing. They are interrelated. Negligence is a unified concept. Its subdivision into issues is adapted for convenience and to promote consistency of approach and accurate analysis. The parts should not divert attention from the whole.

In the twentieth century, it became apparent that the modern law of torts is too complex a system to be explained, determined, or delimited by the single concept of corrective justice.[12] As often as not, judges determining private law cases also have to consider the relevant statutory torts, legislative compensation schemes, limits or extensions of tortious duties and liabilities provided for by the Parliament, and other manifestations of distributive justice. In *Neindorf v Junkovic* [2005] HCA 75,[13] Kirby J (at [42]) reiterated that 'it is the duty of Australian courts to start their analysis of the legal liability of parties affected not with the pre-existing common law but with the statutory prescription'—for, his Honour explained, 'where Parliament has spoken, it is a mistake to start with common law authority.'

This jurisprudential principle will be of pivotal importance when the High Court begins to determine cases subsequent to the Torts Reform legislation.

One of the major factors that served as a trigger for Torts Reform was strictly jurisprudential. The judicial process of altering the checks and balances within the paradigm of negligence—designed to broaden the scope of the tort—began in the early 1980s. Some changes were long overdue; in particular, the loosening of barriers to recovery of damages for pure nervous shock (mental harm),[14] the

---

12. Professor Tony Honoré in 'The Morality of Tort Law—Questions and Answers', in Owen DG, *Philosophical Foundations of Tort Law*, Clarendon Press, Oxford, 1997, pp 73–99, at p 85 has pointed out that the Aristotelian notion of corrective justice of itself cannot account for such restitutionary remedies as unjust enrichment, where the defendant did not do any damage though the plaintiff has sustained harm. Nor can the Aristotelian definition of corrective justice alone justify the concept of vicarious liability.
13. Mrs Neindorf, the defendant held a 'garage sale', which was open to the public, in the driveway of her house. The claimant sustained injury when she entered the premises and tripped on the uneven surface of the driveway. Gleeson CJ, Hayne, Callinan, and Heydon JJ found no breach of duty of care; Kirby J dissented.
14. *Jaensch v Coffey* (1983) 155 CLR 549.

imposition of non-delegable duty of care on employers for safe system of work,[15] and a less-restrictive approach to omissions and pure economic loss.[16] However, the courts went much further, and during the period of two decades, they extended the classes of defendants (for example, public authorities, including highway authorities, became liable for nonfeasance),[17] as well as their scope of liability. The courts did so either by modifying or by failing to clearly define the legal tests for duty, breach,[18] causation,[19] and remoteness of damage.[20]

According to calculations done by Professor Luntz,[21] in the fifty-five personal injury torts actions determined by the High Court during the thirteen-year period of Sir Anthony Mason's Chief Justiceship (1987–99), the law found for the plaintiff in 69 per cent of cases and for defendants in 29 per cent, with 2 per cent of cases falling into an 'unclear, or dispute between defendants' category. With few exceptions, all causes of action involved negligence.

The volume of negligence cases determined by the High Court between 2000 and 2005 grew dramatically, and between 2003 and 2005, there was also some attempt by the High Court to constrain the imperial march of negligence.[22] Their Honours heard sixty-three cases, of which 37 per cent were determined in favour of the plaintiff, and 58 per cent in favour of defendants (5 per cent of cases were categorised as 'unclear, or dispute between defendants').

Professor Luntz's statistics do not reflect cases governed by the Torts Reform legislation, which was enacted between 2002 and 2004 and which, in a classic exercise of distributive justice, tilted the checks and balances within the paradigm of negligence yet again.

By introducing statutory thresholds to and caps on compensation, as well as exemptions from liability, the Torts Reform legislation modified the scope of duty of care in negligence.[23] However, the major principles underpinning the concept of duty of care are still governed by common law.

---

15. *Kondis v State Transport Authority* (1984) 154 CLR 672.
16. *Sutherland Shire Council v Heyman* (1985) 157 CLR 424.
17. *Brodie v Singleton Shire Council; Ghantous v Hawkesbury City Council* (2001) 206 CLR 512.
18. *Bus v Sydney City Council* (1989) 167 CLR 78; *Bennett v Minister of Community Welfare* (1992) 176 CLR 408; *Nagle v Rottnest Island Authority* (1993) 177 CLR 423; *Northern Sandblasting Pty Ltd v Harris* (1997) 188 CLR 313; *Tame v New South Wales* (2002) 211 CLR 317.
19. *Cook v Cook* (1986) 162 CLR 376; *Rogers v Whitaker* (1992) 175 CLR 479; *Chappel v Hart* (1998) 195 CLR 232; *Naxakis v Western General Hospital* (1999) 197 CLR 269.
20. *Medlin v State Government Insurance Commission* (1995) 182 CLR 1.
21. Professor Harold Luntz, personal communication, 21 December 2005; Luntz H, 'An Alternative to Tort Law Reform', Paper presented at the Law Society of South Australia's Personal Injury Law Conference, Adelaide, March 2006.
22. See Kirby J's judgment in: *Neindorf v Junkovic* [2005] HCA 75.
23. The reform legislation defines duty of care in terms of standard of duty. Therefore, the relevant provisions will be examined in Chapter 11.

Negligence: Duty of Care 10

INTRODUCTION

A short history of negligence

This chapter will briefly deal with the evolution of the tort of negligence and its first element—the duty of care.

For the purposes of civil liability, negligence has been statutorily defined as 'failure to exercise reasonable care and skill',[1] including 'a breach of a tortious, contractual or statutory duty of care'.[2] However, duty of care as a legal theory became a part of the common law long before the tort of negligence was crystallised.

In the middle of the fourteenth century, the concept of a legal duty of care entered the common law in the form of the 'common custom of the realm', which was imposed upon innkeepers, common carriers, smiths, surgeons, taverners, vintners, and butchers. These medieval tradesmen and professionals could be made strictly liable in an action on the case if, as a result of want of care, skill or honesty, persons transacting with them suffered damage.

Civil liability based upon negligence was unknown to the medieval common law, although it underlay the development of actions on the case, in which the damage flowing from the act was the gist of the action. For instance, in the fourteenth-century case of *Waldon v Marshall* (1370) YB Mich 43 Edw III, f 33, pl 38,[3] the plaintiff brought an action on the case against a horse doctor for negligently killing a horse he had undertaken to cure:

---

1. *Civil Liability Act 2002* (ACT), s 32; *Civil Liability Act 2002* (NSW), s 5; *Civil Liability Act 1936* (SA), s 3; *Wrongs Act 1958* (Vic), s 43.
2. *Civil Liability Act 1936* (SA), s 3.
3. Reproduced in Dix EJ, 'The Origins of the Action of Trespass on the Case' (1937) 46 *The Yale Law Journal* 1142–1176 at 1155.

Belknap [for plaintiff] ... and this action is brought because you worked your cure so negligently that the horse died, wherefore it is reasonable that we maintain this special writ according to the case, ... for we have no other writ.

Kirton [for the defendant]. You may have a writ of trespass, that he killed your horse generally.

Belknap. A general writ we could not have had, because the horse was not killed by force, but died by *default* of his cure.

... And then the writ was adjudged good [emphasis added].

Counsel clearly distinguished between wrongful killing of the horse by direct force (*trespass vi et armis*), and wrongful killing of the horse by negligence ('default of his cure'). Thus, liability on the case lay if, having undertaken to do something for another (*assumpsit*), the person did it so badly that the other was damaged. But the liability was based upon conduct which, by reason of prior undertaking, was regarded 'by the common custom of the realm' as wrongful. This kind of action on the case continued to develop throughout the fifteenth century.

In the sixteenth century, plaintiffs suing under the writ of *assumpsit* would allege incompetent or negligent misperformance (misfeasance) rather than non-performance (nonfeasance) of an undertaking.[4] Slowly, the courts began to distinguish between tortious performance—of a contractual or a gratuitous undertaking—and breach of contract, which required proof of consideration. Thus, in *Powtney v Walton* (1597) YLS MS G R29.9, fo 239v; abridged in HLS MS 2069, fo 277; 1 Rolle Abr 10 line 1, the defendant Walton 'took upon himself to cure' Powtney's sick horse. Walton apparently was not paid for his curative efforts, which resulted in the horse's death. Fenner and Clench JJ determined that absence of consideration was not fatal to Powtney's suit, because the gist of his cause of action was the defendant's negligence, not the *assumpsit*.

In *Powtney v Walton*, the undertaking created a relationship between the parties, which existed prior to the act of negligence. The first reported case in which negligently occasioned injury was held recoverable despite absence of prior relationship between the parties was the seventeenth-century case of *Mitchil v Alestree* (1676) 1 Vent 195; 3 Keb 650. Alestree's servant, Scrivener, while breaking in horses at Lincoln's Inn Fields, a popular London fairground, lost control of the beasts, with the result that Mitchil was kicked by them. In his first action, Mitchil alleged Alestree negligently permitted his horses to injure him.

This was a novel kind of allegation of liability, since it did not include a plea either of *trespass vi et armis* nor of any prior relationship between the parties, other than that brought about by the injury. Hale CJ ruled that there was no evidence

---

4. Baker J, *The Oxford History of the Laws of England*, Vol VI, Oxford University Press, Oxford, 2003, pp 756–758.

of want of care in controlling the untamed horses: Alestree's servant, Scrivener, was not negligent at the time the horses ran down poor Mitchil. On the contrary, apparently Scrivener tried very hard to hold them back.

Mitchil then brought a second action: a writ on the case alleging that the defendants acted 'improvide and incaute', without due consideration for the unsuitability for breaking horses in the vicinity of a marketplace 'where people are always going to and fro about their business'. Negligence was not mentioned. This time the court held (1 Vent 295) that it was Alestree's fault, 'to bring a wild horse into such a place where mischief might probably be done, by reason of the concourse of people.'

This action succeeded, even though there was no allegation of force of arms, prior undertaking, or *scienter*.[5] Negligence, as we understand it today, was the essence of the decision. The defendant set in motion a chain of events, in the form of bringing unruly horses to a fairground, which he was thereafter unable to control. Percy H Winfield and Arthur L Goodhart, in their seminal article, 'Trespass and Negligence',[6] noted that Alestree's liability in negligence was due to his carelessness in allowing his servant to create this dangerous situation. Likewise, in *Gibbons v Pepper* (1695) 1 Ld Raym 38; 91 ER 922, the defendant caused a collision when he lost control over a wagon. His conduct was classified as neglect actionable on the case.

Thus, at the beginning of the eighteenth century, there were two kinds of actions on the case involving allegation of negligence:

- actions on the case for harm-causing misfeasance through carelessness or negligence; and
- actions on the case for harm caused by want of care under 'the custom of the realm' theory of law.

As the century progressed, the courts would focus on the elements that were common to these two kinds of actions. Duty of care was expanded to cover not only surgeons and apothecaries (*Slater v Baker* (1767) 2 Wils KB 359), but also attorneys, who it was alleged fell below the required professional standard of competence. In *Russell v Palmer* (1767) 2 Wils 325, Wilmont J, having ascertained through expert testimony the construction and practice of a particular procedural rule that this construction was 'universally known by the city attorneys', held that the defendant attorney was grossly negligent, and hence liable for loss occasioned by his failure to comply with the rule.[7] In the same year, in *Pitt v Yalden* (1767) 4 Burr 2060; 98 Eng Rep 74, Lord Mansfield, the Chief Justice of the King's Bench, reaffirmed the principle that attorneys, like surgeons, were under a legal duty of

---

5. Under the writ of *scienter* ('*scienter retinuit*'), owners and keepers of dangerous animals were strictly liable. The fault lay in keeping the animal with knowledge of the danger.
6. (1993) 49 *The Law Quarterly Review* 359–378.
7. For a discussion, see: Oldham J, *English Common Law in the Age of Mansfield*, The University of North Carolina Press, Chapel Hill & London, 2004, p 280.

care to perform their professional obligations without negligence, and could be held liable for breach of this duty.[8]

During the reign of George III, the courts also began to accept a new category of actions on the case for 'injuries arising from negligence or folly'. Thus, Lord Bathurst in a legal practitioners' manual called *An Institute of Law Relative to Trials at Nisi Prius* (expanded by Francis Buller as *Introduction to the Law Relative to Trials at Nisi Prius*, H Woodfall and W Strahan, London, 1772, p 25), wrote:

> Every man ought to take reasonable care that he does not injure his neighbour; therefore whenever man receives hurt through default of another, though the same were not wilful, yet if it be occasioned by negligence or folly, the law gives him an action to recover damages for injury sustained ... However, it is proper in such cases to prove that the injury was such as would probably follow from the act done.

In *Ogle v Barnes* (1799) 8 TR 188; 101 ER 1338, the plaintiff successfully sued the defendant in action on the case for so negligently positioning his vessel upon the river that 'wind and tide' pushed it into the plaintiff's boat. In these cases, the courts distinguished between careless creation of the risk and careless control of the situation once the risk has materialised. This was a novel way of determining liability because, rather than examining who did what once the risk eventuated, the law imposed a duty not to create foreseeable risks of injury to others in the first place.[9] Subsequently, in *Ansell v Waterhouse* (1817) 2 Chit R 1, a case that concerned the plaintiff's wife, who was injured while a passenger in a common stagecoach, Bayley J was able to state:

> actions on the case lie for recovery of damages for consequential wrongs, accruing from misfeasance or nonfeasance, from negligence or wilful conduct of the party sued, in doing or omitting to do something, contrary to the duty which the law casts upon him [the common carrier] in a particular case.

However, the law rarely progresses in a linear fashion. For example, in *Winterbottom v Wright* (1842) 10 M & W 109, the court determined that the plaintiff who was injured when, due to the manufacturer's negligence, the carriage in which he was travelling as a passenger broke down, could not sue the manufacturer. The court found that the plaintiff was a stranger to the manufacturer (he did not order the carriage), and was not a party to the contract of sale. The passenger could not

---

8. Ibid. Lord Mansfield observed, however (at 2061), that attorneys should not be liable 'for every error or mistake'.
9. However, old notions die hard. More than 200 years later, Bramwell B in *Holmes v Mather* [1875] LR 10 Ex 261 refused recovery to a plaintiff injured when the defendant tested his wild horses on the street and lost control when they were startled by a dog. As a result, the defendant's carriage crushed the plaintiff. Bramwell B refused to award damages stating that the defendant did his utmost to restrain the horses after they ran away. The learned judge ignored as irrelevant the defendant's original decision to test horses on the street.

sue the driver or his master, because it was shown that the driver took all the care due in the circumstances.

Between 1760 and 1830, the development of steam engine, and such technical innovations as conversion of coal to coke and gas-making led to new methods of industrial production, including the factory system, rapid urbanisation and exponential growth in the use of road, canal and (after 1830) railway transport. There was a parallel exponential growth in the rate of industrial and transport accidents. As noted above, the railways became the greatest source of injury and accidental death in England and elsewhere. Initially, the courts adopted the approach of *Ansell v Waterhouse*, enabling injured passengers to sue the railway companies, which were classified as common carriers,[10] either in action on the case for negligence, or in contract.[11] As common carriers, the railway companies were responsible for any physical injury to the passengers that occurred as a direct result of their negligence. In England and in the United States, passenger carriers of all kinds were held to a standard of utmost care and, providing there was no contributory negligence on the part of the claimant,[12] were often found liable for damages in an action on the case. However, this approach was unsustainable and by the middle of the nineteenth century, the courts began to apply the standard of reasonable care (*Blyth v Birmingham Waterworks* (1856) 11 Exch 781).

Concept of reasonableness and the definition of 'duty of care'

Reasonableness is the touchstone of the law of negligence. The law obligates us to take *reasonable* care to guard against the 'not insignificant' risk of harm that is *reasonably* foreseeable. Reasonable foresight, in turn, is generally defined as a foresight of a reasonable person who adheres to the minimum standards required in a civilised society. The notion of what is 'reasonable' will vary, depending on the set of circumstances and their temporal, social and cultural context. In *McLoughlin v O'Brian* (1983) 1 AC 410, at 420, Lord Wilberforce observed that 'reasonable' is an adjective used to express moral judgments about what is just and fair. More recently, Mr Walker, SC, appearing before the High Court in *Thompson v Woolworths (Qld) Pty Ltd* [2005] HCA Trans 7,[13] suggested that for the purposes of the law of negligence,

---

10. *Railway and Land Traffic Carriers' Act (An Act for the Better Regulation of the Traffic on Railways and Canals) 1854*, 17 & 18 Vict c 31 (UK).
11. For a discussion, see: Mendelson D, 'English Medical Experts and the Claims for Shock Occasioned by Railway Collisions in the 1860s: Issues of Law and Ethics and Medicine' (2002) 25 *International Journal of Law and Psychiatry* 303–329.
12. From the 1809 case of *Butterfield v Forrester* (1809) 11 East 60; 103 ER 926 until modified by the *Law Reform (Contributory Negligence) Act 1945* (UK) (followed in other common law jurisdictions later), a successful plea of contributory negligence had the effect of defeating the plaintiff's recovery entirely.
13. Available at http://www.austlii.edu.au/cgi-bin/disp.pl/au/other/HCATrans/2005/7.html?query=Thompson%20v%20Woolworths (accessed on 31 July 2006).

the adjective 'reasonable' also implies 'value judgments, including matters of social, utility and amenity and personal liberties'. In *Swain v Waverley Municipal Council* [2005] HCA 4, at [5], Gleeson CJ, discussing the centrality of reasonableness in the legal formulation of both the duty and the standard of care, noted that the notion of reasonableness in negligence is primarily an acknowledgment of the fact that:

> Life is risky. People do not expect, and are not entitled to expect, to live in a risk-free environment. The measure of careful behaviour is reasonableness, not elimination of risk. Where people are subject to a duty of care, they are to some extent their neighbours' keepers, but they are not their neighbours' insurers.

What do lawyers mean when they refer to the 'duty of care' in negligence? In *Prosser and Keeton on Torts*,[14] the authors defined duty of care in negligence as 'an obligation, to which the law will give recognition and effect, to conform to a particular standard of conduct, towards another.'

In *Dillon v Legg* 441 P 2d 912 at 916 (Cal 1968), the California Supreme Court quoted William L Prosser's *Law of Torts*,[15] statement that the duty of care:

> is not sacrosanct in itself, but only an expression of the sum total of those considerations of policy which lead the law to say that the particular plaintiff is entitled to protection.

In other words, the referential point in duty of care is the legal right. Duties—be they religious, moral, social, or customary—are inherent in any conduct that affects others. However, judicial determination designates only some of these as legal duties.

The scope of the duty of care and the principle of personal responsibility

In a number of cases handed down in 2004 and 2005, several Justices of the High Court have qualified the defendants' scope of the duty by the principle of personal responsibility. For instance, the statement of Gleeson CJ in *Swain v Waverley Municipal Council* [2005] HCA 4, at [5], that 'where people are subject to a duty of care, they are to some extent their neighbours' keepers' is a reference to Lord Atkin's distinction between the duty of care arising from the notion of legal neighbourhood and duties arising from the notion of moral neighbourhood as represented in the Gospel parable of the Good Samaritan. The allusion to the question posed by Cain[16] links both notional neighbourhoods through the ethical

---

14. Keeton WP, Dobbs DB, Keeton RE & Owen DC, *Prosser and Keeton on Torts*, 5th edn, West Publishing Co, 1984, St Paul, Minnesota, p 356.
15. Prosser WL, *Law of Torts*, 3rd edn, West Publishing Co, St Paul, Minnesota, 1964, p 353.
16. 'And the Lord said unto Cain, where is Abel thy brother? And he said, I know not: Am I my brother's keeper?'. Genesis iv.9.

principle of personal responsibility, which is fundamental to the imposition of any duty of care. The limitation on the scope of the legal duty—'to some extent'—stems from the fact that personal responsibility is not confined only to those who are subject to a duty of care; it applies equally to the persons who are the objects of the duty, unless they are minors, physically or psychiatrically impaired adults, or persons acting under duress.

The relationship between duty of care and the responsibility of adults for their own conduct was discussed in *Cole v Sth Tweed Heads Rugby Club* (2004) 217 CLR 469. The trial judge found that Mrs Cole, 'a healthy woman of mature age', 'voluntarily and in full possession of her faculties, embarked on a drinking spree' at the licensed premises of the Rugby Club between 10 am and 3 pm (when her request for more alcohol was refused by the Club). At about 5.30 pm, the Club manager asked her to leave the Club; he offered her the use of the Club's courtesy bus, or to call her a taxi. Mrs Cole rejected those offers and left the premises on foot in the company of two apparently sober men, who said that they would 'look after her'. Mrs Cole suffered serious injuries when she was struck by a motor vehicle while walking in an intoxicated state (her alcohol level was 0.238 g per 100 mL), along a public road at 6.20 pm, some 100 metres from the Club. She sued the Club in negligence;[17] however, her claims that that the Club was under a duty of care to cease supplying her with liquor at a time when a reasonable person would have known she was intoxicated, and to ensure that she travelled from the Club safely, were unsuccessful.[18]

According to the majority, a duty to provide care of the nature claimed by Mrs Cole would impose on the Club the duty to restrain or prevent her from engaging in voluntary behaviour. Gleeson CJ (at [14]) rejected such an extension of the scope of the duty of care on the ground that it would infringe the principle of autonomy. His Honour cited the following statement of Lord Hope of Craighead in *Reeves v Commissioner of Police of the Metropolis* ([2000] 1 AC 360 at 379–80): 'On the whole people are entitled to act as they please, even if this will inevitably lead to their own death or injury', noting that 'this principle gives effect to a value of the law that respects personal autonomy'. Likewise, Callinan J (at [130]) specifically endorsed as correct the statement of Heydon JA (as he then was) in the New South Wales Court of Appeal,[19] who held that:

> if the tort of negligence were extended as far as the [appellant] submitted, it would 'subvert many other principles of law, and statutory provisions, which strike a balance of rights and obligations, duties and freedoms'.

---

17. Mrs Cole was unsuccessful in her action against the motor car driver.
18. Gleeson CJ, Gummow, Hayne, and Callinan JJ held that if the Club owed a duty of care, it had been discharged by the offer of transport. McHugh and Kirby JJ dissented.
19. *South Tweed Heads Rugby League Football Club Ltd v Cole* (2002) 55 NSWLR 113 at 1156, [4]–[7].

Since the court, as a matter of a matter of public or legal policy, can impose a duty to avoid creating certain risks that may result in an injury to another, it can equally waive or displace this duty on the grounds of policy considerations. Early in the twentieth century, Professor Winfield, in his article, 'Public Policy and the English Common Law' (1928) 42 *Harvard Law Review* 76, at 92, wrote that public interest or public policy is 'a principle of judicial legislation or interpretation founded on the current needs of the community'.

For example, in *Sullivan v Moody; Thompson v Connon* (2001) 207 CLR 562 the plaintiffs were fathers who sued doctors, social workers, hospitals, and departmental officers for pure nervous shock and consequential personal and financial loss as a result of being informed that they were accused of sexually abusing their children. The High Court found that the defendants involved in investigating and reporting upon allegations of child sexual abuse did not owe the plaintiffs a duty of care.[20] According to Gleeson CJ, Gaudron, McHugh, Hayne, and Callinan JJ in a joint judgment (at [42]):

> A defendant will only be liable, in negligence, for failure to take reasonable care to prevent a certain kind of foreseeable harm to a plaintiff, in circumstances where the law imposes a duty to take such care.

Their Honours added (at [60]), that:

> People may be subject to a number of duties provided they are not irreconcilable ... But if a suggested duty of care would give rise to inconsistent obligations, that would ordinarily be a reason for denying that a duty exists.

In *Tame v New South Wales* (2002) 211 CLR 317, Gummow and Kirby JJ at [231] stated that the police officer's duty to investigate the conduct in question is grounded 'in the statutory framework and anterior common law by which the relevant police service is established and maintained'; consequently, it is 'unlikely' that police officer would owe a duty of care to a person whose conduct is under investigation. Hayne J at [298], went further, stating that:

> Police officers investigating possible contravention of the law do not owe a common law duty to take reasonable care to prevent psychiatric injury to those whose conduct they are investigating. Their duties lie elsewhere and to find a duty of care to those whom they investigate would conflict with those other duties.

Thus, as a general rule, police officers have immunity from suit in negligence when acting in an investigative role. In another example, the public interest in encouraging altruistic conduct in our community underpins the good samaritan,[21]

---

20. See also: *X (Minors) v Bedfordshire County Council* [1995] 2 AC 633.
21. The legislation does not capitalise this term: *Civil Liability Act 2002* (NSW), Pt 8; *Civil Liability (Wrongs) Act 2002* (ACT), s 5; *Civil Liability Act 1936* (SA), s 74; *Wrongs Act 1958* (Vic), Pt VIA; *Civil Liability Act 2002* (WA), s 1D; *Personal Injuries Act 2003* (NT), s 8.

food donors,[22] and volunteers[23] legislation, which exempts from liability acts or omissions of persons who voluntarily, in good faith, while sober and not affected by drugs, render aid in an emergency. However, it is rather more difficult to discern any credible public interest in the decision of the majority (Gleeson CJ, Gummow, Hayne, and Heydon JJ) of the High Court in *D'Orta-Ekenaike v Victoria Legal Aid* [2005] HCA 12, which reaffirmed the rule that at common law barristers cannot be sued by their clients for negligence in the conduct of a case in court, or in work out of court, that leads to a decision affecting the conduct of a case in court.[24]

Given the inherent uncertainty of a policy-based approach to determining the existence of duty, 'it is ... not surprising that the problem of duty is as broad as the whole law of negligence, and that no universal test for it ever has been formulated.'[25] This comment by the authors of *Prosser and Keeton on Torts* is as true today as it was in 1984, when it was written. Indeed, in *Berrigan Shire Council v Ballerini & Anor* [2005] VSCA 159, Callaway JA observed (at [8]):

> the imposition of general duties of care in negligence has no sure foundation in legal principle. It involves trade-offs and value judgments that may have been better left to the legislature ... The search for a principle is worse than looking for a needle in a haystack. The needle is not there.

Evolution of the requirement of a duty of care

In intentional torts, the question is who did what to whom, in the sense of invading the other party's legal rights without legal justification. In negligence, the question is whether the defendant failed to take precautions to prevent a foreseeable risk of harm in circumstances where a reasonable person in his or her position would have taken those precautions.

To establish a legal right to sue the particular defendant, the plaintiff has to show:

- the defendant was under a duty to exercise reasonable care and skill because his or her conduct involved a foreseeable risk of injury or harm to others; and
- the plaintiff was within the class of persons to whom that duty was owed.

---

22. *Wrongs Act 1958* (Vic), Pt VIB; *Civil Liability Act 2003* (Qld), s 79; *Civil Liability Act 2002* (NSW), Pt 8A.
23. *Wrongs Act 1958* (Vic), Pt IX; *Civil liability Act 2002* (NSW), Pt 9; *Civil liability Act 2003* (Qld), Pt III (also includes exemption for food donations); *Civil Liability Act 2002* (Tas), Pt 10; *Volunteers Protection Act 2001* (SA); *Volunteers (Protection from Liability) Act 2002* (WA); *Personal Injuries (Liabilities and Damages) Act 2003* (NT), s 7; *Civil Law (Wrongs) Act 2002* (ACT), s 8(1); *Commonwealth Volunteers Protection Act 2003* (Cth).
24. Defences of voluntary assumption of risk and joint illegal enterprise also effectively exclude duty of care.
25. Keeton WP, Dobbs DB, Keeton RE & Owen DC, *Prosser and Keeton on Torts*, 5th edn, West Publishing Co, St Paul, Minnesota, 1984, pp 357–358.

The notion of reasonable foreseeability as a legal standard for the duty of care developed over a number of decades in the nineteenth and early twentieth centuries. The dissenting judgment of Brett MR in *Heaven v Pender* (1883) 11 QBD 503 is generally considered as the conceptual springboard for this development. The case concerned a dock owner who supplied defective rope for a staging that enabled vessels using his dock to be painted. The plaintiff worked as a ship-painter under an employer who had a contract with the ship-owner to paint his ship in dock. When the painter tried to use the stage, the rope broke and the stage fell, injuring the plaintiff. He sued the dock owner, but the trial judge ruled that the dock owner did not owe him a duty of care. In the Court of Appeal, Cotton LJ determined (at 516–17) that the dock owner was under a duty to take reasonable care in relation to the appliances, which at the time were provided by him for the immediate use in the dock:

> were in a fit state to be used—that is, in such a state as not to expose those who might use them for repair of the ship to any danger and risk not necessarily incident to the service in which they were employed.

This was a very narrowly constructed principle of liability. Brett MR (at 509) reflected Francis Buller's formulation of 1772 in his judgment:

> whenever one person is by circumstances placed in such a position with regard to another that every one of ordinary sense who did think would at once recognize that if he did not use ordinary care and skill in his own conduct with regard to those circumstances he would cause danger of injury to the person or property of the other, a duty arises to use ordinary care and skill to avoid such danger.

The majority of the Court of Appeal rejected this test of duty as too wide. However, in the seminal case of *Macpherson v Buick Motor Company* 217 NY 382; 111 NE 1050 (1916), Cardozo J mentioned Brett MR's judgment, when he articulated the principle that a manufacturer of inherently dangerous goods that are defective can be liable in negligence if the defect caused a reasonably foreseeable injury to a foreseeable third person—the ultimate purchaser. Lord Atkin also referred to the opinion of Brett MR when in *Donoghue v Stevenson* [1932] AC 562, at 599, he found that:

> A manufacturer of products which he sells in such a form as to show that he intends them to reach the ultimate consumer in the form in which they left him with no reasonable possibility of intermediate examination, and with the knowledge that the absence of reasonable care in the preparation or putting up of the products will result in an injury to the consumer's life or property, owes a duty to the consumer to take that reasonable care.

The case concerned the plaintiff ('pursuer'), Mrs May Donoghue, née Macallister, who in August 1928 went to Wellmeadow Cafe in Paisley, Scotland, and ordered an ice-cream float. She was served a bottle of ginger beer bearing the name of D Stevenson. She drank a glass of the ginger beer, and when it was refilled, out came the remains of a decomposed snail. The bottle was made of opaque glass; therefore the snail could not be detected until most of the contents had been consumed. Mrs Donoghue successfully sued the manufacturer for severe gastroenteritis and nervous shock, which she suffered as a result of drinking the contaminated fluid.

Mrs Donoghue was successful because she was able to establish that a legal relationship existed between the defendant's failure to take reasonable care in bottling the ginger beer and the consumers of his product, of whom she was one. In other words, he should have reasonably foreseen that unless he took reasonable care in conducting his business, she was within a class of persons (in this case consumers), who may be injured as a result of his negligent conduct. The reasonable contemplation or foresight defines the defendant's legal responsibility. Thus, to establish the existence of a duty of care, the plaintiff must show that he or she was within the range of the defendant's 'legal neighbourhood' as established through reasonable foresight. It is this principle that has made the case of *Macallister* (or *Donoghue*) *v Stevenson*[26] the jurisprudential cornerstone of the modern tort of negligence in Anglo–Australian law. According to Lord Atkin (at 580):

> The liability for negligence, whether you style it such or treat it as in other systems as a species of 'culpa,' [fault] is no doubt based upon a general public sentiment of moral wrongdoing for which the offender must pay ... Who, then, in law is my neighbour? The answer seems to be—persons who are so closely and directly affected by my act that I ought reasonably to have them in contemplation as being so affected when I am directing my mind to the acts or omissions which are called in question.

Today, in cases both of physical and of psychiatric injury (see: *Tame v New South Wales* (2002) 211 CLR 317), reasonable foresight of risk of harm creates a relationship of legal neighbourhood or proximity. The notion of 'nearness or closeness' does not require either physical or temporal propinquity between the wrongful conduct and the plaintiff's harm, but extends beyond the limitations of time and space as long as there is an uninterrupted chain of events between the defendant's negligence and the plaintiff's injury.

General limitations of duty of care

Apart from policy considerations, duty of care is generally limited by:

- reasonable foreseeability of the plaintiff as a person or class to whom the duty is owed;

---

26. In Scotland, maiden names are used in court reports.

- reasonable foreseeability of not an insignificant risk to a reasonably foreseeable plaintiff or class; and
- the nature of the foreseeable risk.

Reasonable foreseeability of the plaintiff as a person or class to whom the duty is owed

To create a relationship of legal neighbourhood, or legal proximity, which gives rise to the duty of care, the plaintiff must show that he or she was a reasonably foreseeable member of the class to whom the duty of care is owed. However, a mere finding of the existence of a general duty of care is not sufficient for its imposition. To determine the question whether the defendant owed the plaintiff a legally enforceable duty of care, the court has to consider not only its existence at an abstract level as between the parties *qua* parties, but in relation to the actual facts of the case.[27] For, as Gummow and Hayne JJ stated in *Cole Sth Tweed Heads Rugby Club* (at [82]), 'the duty that must be found to have been broken is a duty to take reasonable care to avoid what *did* happen, not to avoid "damage" in some abstract and unformed sense.' [emphasis in original]

The question the court asks is whether, in the particular circumstances, the likelihood of risk eventuating to the plaintiff, or a class of people including the plaintiff, was foreseeable. For example, in *Chapman v Hearse* (1961) 106 CLR 112, on a dark and rainy September night in 1958, Chapman negligently collided with another vehicle. On impact, his car door swung open and he was thrown onto the road. Soon after the accident, another motorist, Dr Cherry, saw Chapman lying on the roadway. He stopped his vehicle and went to Chapman's assistance. While Dr Cherry was attending the unconscious Chapman, another car, driven by Hearse, struck Dr Cherry and caused him injuries of which he later died. Hearse did not see Dr Cherry until it was too late, but claimed that Dr Cherry contributed to his own injuries and subsequent death because he failed to see Hearse's car. The High Court found that Hearse failed to prove on the balance of probabilities that Dr Cherry, having seen the approaching car, did not make some attempt, unseen by Hearse, to attract the latter's attention, in order to protect Chapman.

Dr Cherry's estate sued Chapman. The question was whether Chapman owed the deceased a duty of care even though Dr Cherry was actually injured by Hearse. The High Court (at 121) held that it was not necessary for the plaintiff to show that the *precise manner* in which his injuries were sustained was reasonably foreseeable. It was sufficient if injury to a class of persons was reasonably foreseeable. In this case, it was reasonably foreseeable that as a result of Chapman's original negligence, injury might occur to rescuers, a class to which Dr Cherry belonged.

---

27. *Cole v Sth Tweed Heads Rugby Club* (2004) 217 CLR 469 at [1], per Gleeson CJ; at [56], Gummow and Hayne JJ, citing McHugh J in *Graham Barclay Oysters Pty Ltd v Ryan* (2002) 211 CLR 540 at [106].

Rescuers

The High Court in *Chapman v Hearse* adopted Cardozo J's doctrine in *Wagner v International Railway Co* 232 NY 176 (1921) that tortfeasors who create conditions of emergency are liable to a person who comes to the rescue, even if the rescuer is injured by the negligent conduct of others.[28]

Another leading Australian case on the law of rescue is *Mount Isa Mines Ltd v Pusey* (1971) 125 CLR 383, which involved an engineer, Mr Pusey, who worked in the defendant's powerhouse. On the day of the accident, two electricians were severely burned by an electric arc while testing a switchboard. When Mr Pusey heard the noise of the explosion, he went to the upper floor, where he assisted one of the injured electricians by carrying him to an ambulance. Mr Pusey later developed a psychiatric disorder, and was awarded damages from his employer. In both cases, the High Court found that a duty was owed to the rescuers. The duty of care owed to rescuers is grounded in policy that rescue should be encouraged.

The common law does not impose a general duty to rescue third parties; for such duty to arise, there must exist either an antecedent duty based on a pre-existing relationship between the parties, or a specified legal obligation. The Northern Territory is the only Australian jurisdiction that imposes such a duty. Section 155 of the *Criminal Code* (NT) provides that: 'any person who, being able to provide rescue, resuscitation, medical treatment, first aid or succour of any kind to a person urgently in need of it and whose life may be endangered if it is not provided, callously fails to do so is guilty of a crime and is liable to imprisonment for 7 years.'

The unforeseeable plaintiff

In what circumstances could it be said that a defendant could not reasonably have foreseen the injured plaintiff either as an individual or as a member of a class? This question focuses on an important characteristic of the duty of care.

In the American case of *Palsgraf v Long Island Railroad Co* 162 NE 99 (1928), which was decided before *Donoghue v Stevenson*, Cardozo CJ said that the fact that the defendant owes a duty of care not to injure one person does not mean that the duty of care is owed equally to another. The reasonable foreseeability of harm test establishing duty of care must be applied separately to each particular plaintiff who suffers harm as a result of the defendant's conduct.

The *Palsgraf* case involved an incident at a train station where a man who was carrying a parcel jumped aboard an already moving train, but seemed unsteady. The guard on the car, who thought the passenger might fall out, reached forward to help him, while another guard on the platform pushed him from behind. The shoving and pushing dislodged the package, containing fireworks, which fell upon

---

28. For a discussion, see: Mendelson D, '*Quo Iure*? Defendants' Liability to Rescuers in the Tort of Negligence' (2001) 9 *Torts Law Review* 130–163.

the rails. The force of the resulting explosion threw down some heavy brass scales at the other end of the platform. The falling scales struck a bystander, the plaintiff, causing her injuries. She sued the rail company in negligence.

Cardozo CJ (at 101) pointed out that:

> Negligence is not a tort unless it results in a commission of a wrong, and a commission of a wrong imports a violation of ... the right to be protected against interference with one's bodily security ... One who seeks redress at law does not make out a cause of action by showing without more that there has been damage to his person. If the harm is not wilful, he must show that the act as to him had the possibilities of danger so many and so apparent as to entitle him to be protected against the doing of it though the harm was unintended ... The victim does not sue derivatively, or by right of subrogation, to vindicate an interest invaded in the person of another ... he sues for breach of a duty owing to himself.

In his judgment, Cardozo CJ at 100, echoed the judgment of Hale CJ in *Mitchil v Alestree* when he described liability in negligence based on the careless release of destructive force which the defendant will be unable to control:

> This does not mean, of course, that one who launches a destructive force is always relieved of liability, if the force, though known to be destructive, pursues an unexpected path.

Thus, although the concept of duty is notional, it is not totally speculative or at large. There are limits to the required foresight—the defendant must be shown to have owed a duty to the particular plaintiff.

For example, in the case of *Bourhill v Young* [1943] AC 92 (HL), Young was a motorcyclist who, by his careless driving, caused an accident in which he was killed. The plaintiff, Mrs Bourhill, who had just alighted from a tram across the road, heard the noise of the collision; having crossed the road to inspect what happened, she saw blood on the road. She suffered nervous shock, as a result of which she miscarried. The House of Lords decided that Young could not have foreseen either the risk of physical injury or the risk of nervous shock to the plaintiff, who was standing behind the tram when the collision occurred. He was in breach of his duty of care to numerous others in the vicinity of his driving, but her physical position put the plaintiff outside the ambit of reasonable foreseeability. Lord Macmillan (at 105) opined that:

> if ... the appellant has a cause of action, it is because of a wrong to herself. She cannot build on a wrong to someone else. Her interest, which was her own bodily security, was of a different order from the interest of the owner of the car [that struck the plaintiff].[29]

---

29. For a discussion of this issue, see: Goodhart AL, 'The Shock Cases and the Area of Risk' (1953) 16 *The Modern Law Review* 17.

Reasonable foreseeability of a not insignificant risk of injury to others

Lord Atkin's general test of duty of care is based upon the concept of the sphere of risk that surrounds every kind of activity; the court determines the foreseeable extent of that sphere. For example if, due to the negligence of a train driver, the train derails and its passengers are injured, the railway company will be vicariously liable for the train driver's breach of duty. The railway company's duty of care extends to the rescuers who are injured in the process of rescue; it may also encompass close relatives of the injured or killed passengers, as well as those who suffer mental harm as a result of being present at the scene and witnessing the disaster (see Chapter 15). Thus, at the stage of assessing the existence and extent of the duty, the defendant's activities are viewed not in the concrete circumstances of the harmful event, but at a higher level of abstraction to determine what kinds of people were prospectively put at risk when those activities were undertaken. The legal analysis therefore concerns 'a notional relationship between the defendant and an unidentified group of people within the sphere of risk'[30] rather than a personal relationship between the plaintiff and the defendant. McHugh J, in *Swain v Waverley Municipal Council* [2005] HCA 4 (at [79]), emphasised that 'reasonable foreseeability in the law of negligence is not a simple question of the likelihood that an event will occur and cause harm. It is not a mere question of fact or prediction'. Rather, according to his Honour, the notion of reasonable foreseeability as is a 'fact–value complex',[31] in so far as:

> Inherent in the notion of 'reasonable foreseeability' are questions of fairness, policy, practicality, proportion, expense, and justice.

Consequently, McHugh J noted, the practice of mechanically equating reasonable foreseeability with physical possibility is incorrect.

The nature of the foreseeable risk

In *Donoghue v Stevenson* the bottle was opaque. Mrs Donoghue might not have succeeded if the bottle had been made of clear glass and the remains of the snail were visible. In *Tomlinson v Congleton Borough Council* [2004] 1 AC 46, Lord Hoffman determined that a duty to protect against reasonable risks may not extend to 'obvious risks'. According to his Lordship (at [46]):

> A duty to protect against obvious risks or self-inflicted harm exists only in cases in which there is no genuine and informed choice, or in the case of employees, or some lack of capacity, such as the inability of children to recognise danger (*British*

---

30. Davies M, 'The End of the Affair: Duty of Care and Liability Insurance' (1989) 9 *Legal Studies* 69.
31. His Honour referred to Stone J, *Precedent and Law*, Butterworths, Sydney, 1985, p 256; *Tame v New South Wales* (2002) 211 CLR 317 at 355 [105], per McHugh J.

Railways Board v Herrington [1972] AC 877) or the despair of prisoners which may lead them to inflict injury on themselves (*Reeves v Commissioner of Police* [2000] 1 AC 360).

However, in *Vairy v Wyong Shire Council* [2005] HCA 62, McHugh J (at [40]) commented that this proposition does not accurately represent 'the common law of Australia'. In *Neindorf v Junkovic* [2005] HCA 75, Kirby J (at [73]) rejected the notion that 'occupiers, with responsibilities for the safety of premises can totally ignore those responsibilities because of the alleged obviousness of the risk to entrants'. Neither of these cases was determined by reference to the Torts reform legislation, which has imposed limitations on the duty of care in relation to obvious risks. The concept of 'obvious risk' will be further examined in Chapter 11.

LIABILITY OF LANDLORDS AND OCCUPIERS

Landlords' liability

Under the law of property, the leasing of land to a tenant is regarded as being in the nature of a sale of premises for a term. This is because, when a landlord leases land to a tenant, the lessee acquires an interest in the land for the term of the lease. As a general rule, the lessor surrenders both the possession and the control of the land to the lessee, retaining only a revisionary interest.[32] The contractual nature of a lease had important consequences with regard to tortious liability, for there was no implied covenant by landlords that land or unfurnished residential premises let by them were fit for habitation. If they were let in a dangerous or dilapidated condition then, barring express contract, unless the landlords had acted fraudulently, they were not liable for injuries that arose from the defective state of land or premises. The reason was provided by Erle CJ in *Robbins v Jones* (1863) 15 CB (NS) 221, at 240:

> A landlord who lets a house in a dangerous state is not liable to the tenant's customers or guests for accidents happening during the term; for, fraud apart, there is no law against letting a tumble-down house.

This dictum was repeated by Lord Macnaghten in *Cavalier v Pope* [1906] AC 428, at 430. Consequently, the contractual doctrine of *caveat emptor* was traditionally applied to lessees, and, as in *Cheater v Cater* [1918] 1 KB 247, at 252–6, the tenant was expected to inspect the land before agreeing to the lease, or be left to take it as he found it.

---

32. Kecton WP (Gen Ed), Dobbs DB, Keeton RE, Owen DG, *Prosser and Keeton on Torts*, 5th edn, West Publishing Co, St Paul, Minnesota, 1984, p 434.

In *Cavalier v Pope*, a landlord of a dilapidated house contracted with the tenant to repair a defective floor, but failed to do so.[33] The tenant's wife was injured as a consequence. The House of Lords held that the landlord was not liable in contract because the wife was not a party to the contract. There was no liability in tort because no legal duty existed with respect to a ruinous house.

The Australian Capital Territory is the only jurisdiction in Australia where the rule in *Cavalier v Pope* has been abolished outright by s 29 of the *Law Reform (Miscellaneous Provisions) Act 1955* (ACT).[34] Western Australia, Victoria, and South Australia have also enacted provisions limiting landlords' immunity from liability in tort for defective premises.[35] The relevant provisions contain codified criteria for determining whether the duty of care has been discharged.[36] However, by implication, the statutory regime is confined to circumstances where the landlord has actual control over the premises before commencement of the tenancy.

In *Northern Sandblasting Pty Ltd v Harris* (1997) 188 CLR 313, the High Court decided that *Cavalier v Pope* should not be followed in Australia. Thus, landlords of defective or dangerous residential premises owe a duty of care to the tenants and their households. The existence of this duty was reaffirmed and defined in *Jones v Bartlett* (2000) 205 CLR 166, which concerned a claim against the landlord for injuries sustained by the tenants' son, who inadvertently walked through a glass door at the premises. The High Court determined that landlords should only be considered occupiers if they had control of the premises before the commencement of the tenancy.[37] Gummow and Hayne JJ observed (at [170]) that this would exclude cases in which the landlord had never had control, either de facto, in the case of consecutive tenancies, or de jure, in the case where a landlord assumes ownership after the tenant has gone into possession. In their position as landlords they must arrange for an assessment of premises for known or apparent dangerous defects.

If they fail to do so, and an accident—one that can be traced to the negligent failure to assess and remove dangerous defects—happens once the premises have been let, they will be liable as occupiers. Unless specific terms of the lease provide otherwise, as soon as tenants assume exclusive possession of premises, they acquire the status of occupiers, and the landlords lose their control over the premises.

---

33. When *Cavalier v Pope* was before the Court of Appeal, Mathew LJ in a dissenting judgment held that the fraudulently made representation by the landlord could provide the tenant's wife with an action for misrepresentation.
34. 'Rule in *Cavalier v Pope* abolished. A lessor of premises is not exempt from owing a duty of care to persons on those premises by reason only that the lessor is not the occupier of those premises.'
35. *Occupiers' Liability Act 1985* (WA), ss 4, 5, 9; *Wrongs Act 1958* (Vic), ss 14A(1), 14B(3); *Wrongs Act 1936* (SA), s 17D. See also: *Crosthwaite v Pietila* [1999] VSCA 110 (unreported, Victorian Court of Appeal, Tadgell, Phillips, and Batt JJA, 11 August 1999).
36. *Wrongs Act 1958* (Vic), s 14B(4); *Wrongs Act 1936* (SA), s 17E.
37. Gleeson CJ at [50], and Gaudron J at [82]–[83]; Gummow and Hayne JJ at [170].

The duty to take care then substantially shifts from the landlord to the occupier. Gummow and Hayne JJ noted (at [184]) that the requirement of inspection does not involve the engagement of experts in 'electrical wiring, and glass fabrication and installations, where such risks of defects could be, in the nature of things, seen as a possibility'. The High Court emphasised that where the premises are constructed in accordance with the standards prevailing at the time and adequately maintained, the landlord's duty of care is to put and keep the premises in safe repair, and does not extend to a guarantee of absolute safety.[38] However, Gummow and Hayne JJ (at [197]) observed that landlords have a duty of care to third parties in relation to the presence of dangerous defects:

> arising not merely from occupation and possession of premises, but from the letting out of premises as safe for purposes for which they were not safe. What must be involved is a dangerous defect of which the landlord knew or ought to have known.

Occupiers' liability

Historically, an occupier's duty of care depended upon which category of person entered the land: invitee, licensee or trespasser. Since the High Court's decision in *Australian Safeway Stores Pty Ltd v Zaluzna* (1987) 162 CLR 479; 69 ALR 615, occupiers' liability towards all entrants is governed by the principles of the ordinary common law duty to take care, based on reasonable foreseeability of a real risk of injury.[39]

According to *Goldman v Hargrave* (1966) 115 CLR 458 and *Modbury Triangle Shopping Centre Pty Ltd v Anzil* (2000) 205 CLR 254, at [17] and [102], as a general rule, the duty for the purposes of occupiers' liability in negligence with regard to the physical state or condition of the premises arises from the occupiers' power to control who enters and remains on the land, and their power to control the state or condition of the land. They also are in a better position than an entrant to know the physical state of the premises.

However, it appears that the major determining factor, both for the existence of occupiers' duty of care and for its content, is not the status of those who enter the land (invitees, lawful entrants and trespassers), but the status of the land (public or private) and its use (commercial, recreational or private).

In *Mulligan v Coffs Harbour City Council* [2005] HCA 63, Mr Mulligan was diving into Coffs Creek when his head struck a sandform, breaking his neck. He

---

38. *Jones v Bartlett*, Gleeson CJ at [22]–[23]; Gaudron J at [92]–[93]; Gummow and Hayne JJ at [171], [192]–[193]; Kirby J at [251]–[252]; Callinan J at [289].
39. See also: *Albrighton v Royal Prince Alfred Hospital* (1980) 2 NSWLR 542; *Wilkinson v Law Courts Limited* [2001] NSWCA 196.

unsuccessfully sued the Coffs Harbour City Council, as the occupier of the channel, for failure to erect signs warning about the risk of diving in the creek. The High Court unanimously dismissed his appeal. McHugh J (at [18]) noted[40] that the nature of a duty of care owed to entrants on public land:

> is a duty owed to them as a class, and not to each of them as individuals, and is not to be measured by reference to the personal characteristics of individual members of that class.

In contradistinction, a duty of care owed to entrants on private land may extend to each person individually, and may be measured by 'the personal characteristics of that individual member'. Thus, in *Thompson v Woolworths (Q'land) Pty Limited* [2005] HCA 19, Gleeson CJ, McHugh, Kirby, Hayne, and Heydon JJ, in a joint judgment, determined that the defendant–occupier was liable in negligence for failing to establish systems and procedures that took account of the plaintiff's small stature.[41] The plaintiff, while making a delivery of bread to the defendant supermarket, decided to move a big rubbish bin out of the way of her van. She suffered some injury to her back, which aggravated a pre-existing painful condition. The male witnesses in the case gave evidence of moving the bins without suffering any harm (at [8]). Their Honours distinguished cases like *Thompson v Woolworths*, where private occupiers of land used it for strictly commercial purposes, and occupiers of private households, noting:

> There are ... no risk-free dwelling houses. The community's standards of reasonable behaviour do not require householders to eliminate all risks from their premises, or to place a notice at the front door warning entrants of all the dangers that await them if they fail to take care for their own safety.[42]

This approach was adopted in *Neindorf v Junkovic* [2005] HCA 75, a case that involved an occupier of a private land—albeit on occasion used for commercial purposes. Mrs Neindorf, the defendant, held a garage sale in the driveway of her house. The sale was open to the public, and the claimant sustained injury when she tripped on the uneven surface of the driveway.[43] Gleeson CJ pointed out (at [4]):

> Very few occupiers keep their land in perfect repair. People are permitted to occupy, and some people can only afford to occupy, premises that are in a state of some disrepair. Legislative and regulatory incursions upon the general

---

40. His Honour referred to *Romeo v Conservation Commission (NT)* (1998) 192 CLR 431.
41. *Thompson v Woolworths (Q'land) Pty Limited* [2005] HCA 19 has been distinguished in: *Felk Industries Pty Ltd v Mallet* [2005] NSWCA 111; *Gomes v Metroform Pty Ltd* [2005] NSWCA 171; *Rabay v Bristow* [2005] NSWCA 199.
42. The court thus endorsed the approach expressed in *Jones v Bartlett* (2000) 205 CLR 166 at [23]. For a somewhat tenuous interpretation of this passage, see: Kirby J (at [87]) in *Neindorf v Junkovic* [2005] HCA 75.
43. Gleeson CJ, Hayne, Callinan, and Heydon JJ found no breach of duty of care; Kirby J dissented.

proposition that a landowner may use land as the landowner sees fit, extensive as they have been, have never gone to the point of requiring people to remove all potential hazards from their land. It would not be possible to comply with such a requirement.

In relation to occupiers' duty of care on land used for recreational purposes, Lord Hoffmann in *Tomlinson v Congleton Borough Council* [2004] 1 AC 46, at [47], approached the issue as one of striking the balance between imposing a duty to guard against risks involved in recreational and other activities on the one hand, and the right to individual autonomy on the other. Tomlinson sustained a serious injury when he dived into the shallow water at the edge of a lake and struck his head on the bottom. Swimming in the lake was prohibited, and the Congleton Borough Council had erected notices and distributed leaflets warning of the dangers of swimming in the lake. The House of Lords held that the Council was not liable. Lord Hoffmann observed (at [45]) that 'it will be extremely rare for an occupier of land to be under a duty to prevent people from taking risks which are inherent in the activities they freely choose to undertake upon the land.'

In New South Wales, Tasmania, Western Australia, and Queensland, legislation limits occupiers' duty of care in relation to recreational activities.[44] However, there are many different statutory provisions, in every jurisdiction, which govern liability of occupiers.[45]

Occupiers' liability for criminal conduct of third parties

The courts have to determine the existence and scope of the duty of care not only in relation to risky physical characteristics of the land, but also in relation to risk-creating persons who enter it with or without permission.

In *Modbury Triangle Shopping Centre Pty Ltd v Anzil* (2001) 205 CLR 254, Gleeson CJ, Gaudron, Hayne, and Callinan JJ (Kirby J dissenting) held that the duty of the owners of the Modbury Triangle Shopping Centre, as occupiers, did not extend to taking reasonable care to prevent physical injury to the plaintiff resulting

---

44. *Civil Liability Act 2002* (NSW), Div 5; *Civil Liability Act 2002* (Tas), Div 5; *Civil Liability Act 2002* (WA), Div 4; *Civil Liability Act 2003* (Qld), Div 4. In these jurisdictions, the legislation creates a distinction between 'recreational' and 'dangerous recreational' activities.
45. For example: *Civil Law (Wrongs) Act 2002* (ACT), s 168; *Civil Liability Act 1936* (SA), Pt 4; *Law Reform (Miscellaneous Provisions) Act 1955* (ACT), s 29; *Law Reform (Miscellaneous Provisions) (Amendment) Act 1991* (ACT), s 3; *Health Act 1911* (WA), s 369; *Occupiers' Liability Act 1985* (WA); *Local Government Act 1993* (NSW), s 569; *Meat Industry Act 1978* (NSW), s 59F; *Rural Lands Protection Act 1989* (NSW), s 66; *Health Regulation 1996* (Qld), s 14; *Rural Lands Protection Act 1985* (Qld), s 149; *Extractive Industries Development Act 1995* (Vic), s 51; *Mineral Resources Development Act 1990* (Vic), s 115; *Petroleum Act 1998* (Vic), s 127; *Water Industry Act 1994* (Vic), s 23; *Wrongs Act 1958* (Vic), s 14B; *Local Government Act 1934* (SA), s 703; *Civil Liability Act 1936* (SA), Pt IV; *Electricity Supply Industry Act 1995* (Tas), s 43; *Fire Service Act 1979* (Tas), s 59; *Local Government Act 1993* (Tas), ss 245, 249; *Noxious Weeds Act 1964* (Tas), s 18.

from the criminal behaviour of third parties on their land. The plaintiff was attacked by three unidentified men when, at 10.30 pm, he went to his car, which was parked at the car park belonging to the shopping centre. The plaintiff was an employee of a video store that leased premises from the Modbury Triangle Shopping Centre. The video store operated until 10 pm, and lights at the car park were automatically switched off at that time. According to the High Court, landlords are not liable for criminal acts of third parties over whom they have no control, but who come onto the premises.

However, occupiers may have a duty to take reasonable steps to hinder or prevent criminal conduct of third persons they know are on the premises, if the latter pose a risk to other lawful entrants. For example, in *Club Italia (Geelong) Inc v Ritchie* [2001] VSCA 180, the Club Italia manager knew that some inebriated guests were behaving very aggressively at a debutante ball. He made no attempt to warn two police officers about the danger of the drunken patrons when they were called to quell the disturbance. The officers were savagely assaulted by one of the guests, who (at [35]):

> was allowed to misbehave, out of control, when he should have been kept under control by the Club, which had invited him on to its premises and allowed him to remain there for the purposes of its business ...

The Club, as the occupier, was found liable for the criminal acts of the patrons on their premises, whom it failed to control, even though it had the means or opportunity to do so.

In some jurisdictions, the legislation specifically excludes the common law duty of care of occupiers and owners of private or commercial premises to persons who are entering or have entered such premises either with the intention to commit, or who have committed therein, an offence punishable by imprisonment.[46]

Duty to control third parties

As a general rule, no duty is imposed upon one person or an institution to control another individual to prevent the latter doing damage to a third party. In *Smith v Leurs* (1945) 70 CLR 256, at 262, Dixon J (as he then was) said that it was exceptional 'to find in the law a duty to control another's actions to prevent harm to strangers'. The law will impose a duty to control another's actions only in cases where there exists a special relationship between the person who has the power to control and the person under control. Special relationships of this kind have been found to exist between prison or other custodial authorities and the inmate;[47]

---

46. *Law Reform (Miscellaneous Provisions) Act 2001* (NT), s 10A; *Personal Injuries Act 2003* (NT), s 9, s 10; See also: *Wrongs Act 1958* (Vic), s 14B(fb); *Civil Law (Wrongs) Act 2002* (ACT), s 94.
47. *Dorset Yacht Co v Home Office* [1970] AC 1004 at 1038.

employer and employee;[48] school and pupil;[49] and bailor and bailee.[50] They may also include parents and children, for it is incumbent upon a parent who maintains control over a young child to take reasonable steps to avoid the risk that the child's conduct may expose others to unreasonable danger.

In *Modbury Triangle Shopping Centre Pty Ltd v Anzil* (2000) 176 ALR 411, the High Court decided that the scope of an occupier's duty of care does not extend to safeguarding lawful entrants from injuries caused by criminal acts of third parties. The majority (Gleeson CJ, Gaudron, Hayne, and Callinan JJ) pointed out that other than in exceptional circumstances, or in the context of a special relationship between the parties, the common law does not impose any liability for omissions to take positive steps to protect another from a third party's criminal acts.

Are prison authorities liable for injuries occasioned by jail escapees? In *State of New South Wales v Godfrey & Godfrey* [2004] NSWCA 113, a prisoner escaped from prison in July 1990. In October 1990 he entered a newsagency, pointed a shotgun at the plaintiff shop assistant, screamed that if she moved 'she would get it', and demanded money. The plaintiff, who was twenty-three weeks pregnant, suffered nervous shock which, according to medical evidence, precipitated parturition eight days after the robbery. Her son suffered disabilities brought about by his premature birth. The newsagency was a very long distance from the prison. Spigelman CJ (Sheller and McColl JJA agreeing) determined that the prison authorities did not owe the plaintiff and her son a duty of care because: 'There is no authority which recognises a duty of care to the public at large, beyond the immediate vicinity of the jail from which an escape occurred' (at [31]). This doctrine was articulated in *Dorset Yacht Co Limited v Home Office* [1970] AC 1004, in which Lord Diplock (at 1070) commented:

> The risk of sustaining damage from the tortious acts of criminals is shared by the public at large. It has never been recognised at common law as giving rise to any cause of action against anyone but the criminal himself. It would seem arbitrary and therefore unjust to single out for the special privilege of being able to recover compensation from the authorities responsible for the prevention of crime a person whose property was damaged by the incautious act of a criminal merely because the damage to him happened to be caused by a criminal who had escaped from custody before completion of his sentence instead of by one who had been lawfully released or who had been put on probation or given a suspended sentence or who had never been previously apprehended at all.

---

48. *Chomentowski v Red Garter Restaurant Ltd* (1970) 92 WN (NSW) 1070; *Public Transport Corporation v Sartori* [1997] 1 VR 168; *Fraser v State Transport Authority* (1985) 39 SASR 57.
49. *Trustees of the Roman Catholic Church for the Diocese of Bathurst v Koffman* [1996] Aust Torts Reports ¶81,399.
50. *Pitt Son & Badgery Ltd v Proulefco* (1984) 153 CLR 644.

Spigelman CJ also discussed (at [52]) the problem of imposing duty of care in cases where it is impossible to predict the likelihood of the risk that an escapee prisoner would re-offend, and the location and the nature of such offence. According to his Honour:

> A factor of considerable significance in the present case is the extent and indeterminate nature of the liability that may arise in the case of an escapee. Where or when such a person may commit further offences cannot be determined. Nor can the nature of the offences be identified in advance.[51]

DUTY TO THE UNBORN

In general, the foetus—while still a foetus—does not have any rights or standing in law.[52] In *Attorney-General for the State of Queensland (Ex Rel Kerr) v T* (1983) 46 ALR 275, Gibbs CJ at 277 quoted with approval the statement of Sir George Baker P in *Paton v BPAS Trustees* [1979] 1 QB 276, at 279, that 'a foetus has no right of its own until it is born and has a separate existence from its mother'.

This does not mean that a duty of care may not be owed to someone who is not yet born. In *Watt v Rama* [1972] VR 353, the Victorian Supreme Court decided that a child who was born handicapped, as a result of injuries sustained by his mother in a motor car collision while she was pregnant, could sue the negligent driver of the other vehicle. In the case of *Lynch v Lynch* (1991) 25 NSWLR 411, the New South Wales Court of Appeal held that a mother owed a duty of care not to cause injury to her own foetus, at least where she is covered by compulsory insurance that will indemnify her for liability. In *Lynch* the child was born disabled as a result of injuries sustained by the pregnant mother when she lost control of a truck she was driving and crashed into a bank.

In contrast, in *Dobson (Litigation Guardian of) v Dobson* (1999) 174 DLR (4th) 1, [1999] 2 SCR 753, Cory J of the Supreme Court of Canada (Lamer C.J. C, L'Heureux-Dubé, Gonthier, Iacobucci and Binnie JJ concurring) ruled that a woman who admitted negligence in causing a vehicular collision, which resulted in serious prenatal injuries to her foetus, was not liable in tort for damages to her child. The court distinguished between a child's action for prenatal negligence against a third-party tortfeasor, on the one hand, and against his or her mother, on the other. The Supreme Court advanced the following arguments in support of its decision:

---

51. See also: *Hill v Chief Constable of West Yorkshire* [1989] AC 53.
52. I say 'in general', because the prohibition in s 6 of the *Infertility (Medical Procedures) Act 1984* (Vic), on research and experimentation on embryos following syngamy, clearly extends to foetuses as well.

1   The actions of a pregnant woman, including driving, are inextricably linked to her familial role, her working life, and her rights of privacy, bodily integrity, and autonomous decision-making.
2   Recognition of maternal liability for prenatal injuries in tort would involve severe psychological consequences for the relationship between mother and child, the family and society in general.
3   The imposition of the legal duty would necessitate an articulation of a standard of conduct for a 'reasonable pregnant woman'. Such a rule might raise the spectre of tort liability for lifestyle choices, and undermine the privacy and autonomy rights of women.
4   From the gender equality point of view, since only females can become pregnant, the courts should be hesitant to impose additional legal burdens upon pregnant women.
5   There is a general principle of immunity from tortious liability of mothers for prenatal injuries occasioned to the foetus. A rule based on a strictly defined motor vehicle exception to delineate the scope of maternal tort liability would amount to sanctioning a legal solution based solely on access to insurance.

Liability for 'wrongful life'

Recovery of damages from medical practitioners for so-called 'wrongful life', either by the child—whether born healthy or impaired[53]—or by the parents, is a very controversial issue. Judgments on these issues cannot be disentangled from one's moral, philosophical, ideological, and religious beliefs. The late John Fleming commented:

> Negligent failures of contraception, voluntary sterilisation or abortion or failures to diagnose genetic defects have raised the question of liability by physicians, pharmacists and even parents for an unwanted birth. Such claims have particular poignancy where the unwanted child was born, as feared, with congenital defects. Even so, the critical distinction from the foregoing cases remains that here the defendant has not caused the infant's injury but merely failed to prevent its birth. To hold a physician responsible for possibly lifetime support of the child may well strike one as a disproportionate sanction for his fault.[54]

In *Cattanach v Melchior* (2003) 215 CLR 1, Mr and Mrs Melchior sued Dr Cattanach, an obstetrician and gynaecologist who had performed a tubal ligation upon Mrs Melchior in 1992. Previously, Mrs Melchior told Dr Cattanach that her right ovary and her right fallopian tube had been removed in 1967. When Dr Cattanach performed the tubal ligation, the right fallopian tube was obscured by

---

53. *Harriton v Stephens* [2002] NSWSC 461 (12 June 2002) New South Wales Supreme Court.
54. Fleming J, *The Law of Torts*, 9th edn, The Law Bok Company Ltd, Sydney, 1998, p 184.

bowel adhesions resulting from the 1967 surgery; the clinical picture thus appeared to confirm what the patient told him. He therefore attached a clip only to the left fallopian tube. However, contrary to the information provided by Mrs Melchior, her right fallopian tube had not been removed. She gave birth to a healthy son in 1997.

In the words of Gleeson CJ (at [12]), Dr Cattanach was found liable in negligence for having 'too readily and uncritically accepted his patient's assertion that her right fallopian tube had been removed ... he should have advised her to have that specifically investigated, and ... should have warned her that, if she was wrong about that, there was a risk that she might conceive.' Mr and Mrs Melchior claimed that Dr Cattanach's negligence had caused them to become the parents of an unintended child and thereby suffer loss and damage. McHugh, Gummow, Kirby, and Callinan JJ (Gleeson CJ, Hayne and Heydon JJ dissenting) determined that a court can require the doctor to bear the cost of raising and maintaining until the age of eighteen years the child born as a consequence of medical negligence. The majority held further that the benefits received from the birth of a healthy child are not legally relevant to the head of damage that compensates for the cost of raising and maintaining the child.

In dissent, Gleeson CJ noted (at [6]) that 'the value of human life, which is universal and beyond measurement, is not to be confused with the joys of parenthood, which are distributed unevenly'. Heydon J (at [347]) stated that a birth of a healthy child should not be characterised as a 'loss' because:

> since the law assumes that human life has unique value and brings into existence corresponding duties of a unique kind, the impact of a new life in a family is incapable of estimation in money terms. Secondly, the award of damages to which the majority reasoning leads would have the result, entirely alien to the assumptions and goals of the legal system, of encouraging parents to exaggerate the abilities of their children, the customs of their families or the troubles of their children. It would encourage parental misrepresentation of the parent-child relationship, and create an odious spectacle. Thirdly, the majority reasoning tends to generate litigation about children capable of causing the children distress and injury if they hear about it.[55]

Hayne J (at [208]) asked:

How are the damages allowed for bringing up a child to be assessed? Unless the motives of the parent are taken into account, does it mean that if wealthy parents want, and are able, to spend large sums in the care and education of a

---

55. Heydon J was referring to the majority of the Court of Appeal of Queensland ([2001] QCA 246) which awarded Mr and Mrs Melchior damages of $105 249.33 for maintenance of their unwanted child. His Honour's points, however, were also directed at the majority decision of the High Court, which affirmed the award.

child, the negligent doctor should bear all of those costs regardless of the capacity of the parents to bear them? Should recovery be limited to the costs of some hypothetical average amount outlaid in bringing up a child? Again, it would be difficult to justify a rule under which the extent of the liability of a careless doctor did not depend upon the particular damages shown to have been suffered by the plaintiff. Why should the damages to be allowed to a plaintiff be limited to some standardised amount?

The High Court's decision in *Cattanach v Melchior* was legislatively overcome by the Parliaments of Queensland, South Australia, and New South Wales. In Queensland, by virtue of *Civil Liability Act 2003* (Qld), s 49A, courts cannot award damages for economic loss arising out of the costs ordinarily associated with rearing or maintaining a child where 'following a procedure to effect the sterilisation of an individual [tubal ligation and vasectomy], the individual gives birth to, or fathers, a child because of the breach of duty of a person in advising about, or performing, the procedure'.[56]

In South Australia, under the *Civil Liability Act 1936* (SA), s 67(1), 'no damages are to be awarded to cover the ordinary costs of raising a child'. Section 67(2) specifies that 'ordinary costs of raising a child' include 'all costs associated with the child's care, upbringing, education and advancement in life except, in the case of a child who is mentally or physically disabled, any amount by which those costs would reasonably exceed what would be incurred if the child were not disabled'. The exclusions and limitations apply (s 67(3)) to actions for negligence resulting in 'the unintended conception of a child'; or 'failure of an attempted abortion'; or 'the birth of a child from a pregnancy that would have been aborted but for the negligence'; or actions 'for innocent misrepresentation resulting in (i) the unintended conception of a child; or the birth of a child from a pregnancy that would have been aborted but for the misrepresentation'. The s 67(1) exclusion also applies to: 'an action for damages for breach of a statutory or implied warranty of merchantable quality, or fitness for purpose, in a case where a child is conceived as a result of the failure of a contraceptive device.'

In New South Wales, the operation of s 71 of the *Civil Liability Act 2002* (NSW) is much wider. It provides:

(1) In any proceedings involving a claim for the birth of a child ..., the court cannot award damages for economic loss for:
 (a) the costs associated with rearing or maintaining the child that the claimant has incurred or will incur in the future, or

---

56. The *Civil Liability Act 2003* (Qld), s 49B, precludes damages for economic loss arising out of the costs ordinarily associated with rearing or maintaining a child in cases of failed contraceptive procedure or contraceptive advice.

(b) any loss of earnings by the claimant while the claimant rears or maintains the child.

(2) Subsection (1)(a) does not preclude the recovery of any additional costs associated with rearing or maintaining a child who suffers from a disability that arise by reason of the disability.

Section 70 specifies that the claim for damages in civil proceedings for the birth of a child can be made in tort, in contract, under statute or otherwise—which suggests that the scope of liability extends not only to medical and allied health care practitioners, pharmaceutical companies, assisted reproduction clinics, and hospitals, but also to partners who have negligently failed to take precautions before having sex. It is also unclear whether claimants suing for 'costs associated with rearing or maintaining a child who suffers from a disability that arise by reason of the disability' will need to show both causation and that a child born with disabilities was a reasonably foreseeable result of the particular pregnancy and childbirth, or whether the mere event of 'the birth of a child' will activate recovery of damages under s 71(2). Presumably, the latter interpretation will be rejected on the grounds that it would impose an absolute liability on the defendants.

In other Australian jurisdictions, *Cattanach v Melchior* is the ruling precedent, although it may be subject to statutory restrictions that govern recovery of personal damages for negligence. Significantly, while the nature of the *Cattanach v Melchior* award is clear—namely the cost of raising and maintaining the (unwanted) child—it is difficult to identify the precise nature of the duty of care and causation that underpin this head of damages.

In the United Kingdom, the House of Lords (Lord Bingham of Cornhill, Lord Nicholls of Birkenhead, Lord Steyn, Lord Hope of Craighead, Lord Hutton, Lord Millett, and Lord Scott of Foscote) in *Rees v Darlington Memorial Hospital NHS Trust* [2004] 1 AC 3, unanimously refused to follow *Cattanach v Melchior*. Instead, their Lordships adhered to the House of Lords majority decision in *McFarlane v Tayside Health Board* [2000] 2 AC 59, which held that following negligence related to the vasectomy operation carried out on the father, the mother, who gave birth to a healthy, normal child was only entitled to general damages for pain and suffering, and the inconvenience of pregnancy and childbirth, together with associated special damages. The House of Lords determined that damages for the costs of rearing a healthy child were not recoverable in an action for wrongful birth. Likewise in *Rees*, the majority (Lord Bingham of Cornhill, Lord Nicholls of Birkenhead, Lord Millett, and Lord Scott of Foscote) held it was impossible to quantify the benefits of parenthood and inappropriate to regard a child solely as a financial liability. Therefore, considerations of what was fair, just, and reasonable, and principles of distributive justice, precluded an award of damages against a doctor or health authority in respect of the costs of bringing up a normal healthy child. Nevertheless, the mother was entitled to damages relating to the pregnancy and birth, and to an additional award of £15 000 as judicial acknowledgment that she was a victim of a legal wrong which had denied her the opportunity to live in the way she had planned.

In *Harriton v Stephens* [2006] HCA 15 and *Waller v James*; *Waller v Hoolahan* [2006] HCA 16 the High Court determined that life is not capable of constituting a legally cognisable injury. The claimants, Alexia Harriton and Keeden Waller respectively, were born with severe congenital disabilities. In Keeden Waller's case, the disability was caused by a genetically transmitted paternal anti-thrombin 3 deficiency blood disorder, known as 'AT3' (a propensity of the blood of the affected individual to clot in the arteries and veins). Alexia Harriton's disabilities were a consequence of exposure to the rubella virus *in utero*; her mother had contracted rubella in the first trimester of pregnancy. The claimants, suing by their tutors, did not plead that the defendant medical practitioners brought about or caused their disabilities, for it was not the doctors' fault that Alexia was injured by the rubella infection of her mother,[57] or that Keeden inherited his father's blood-clotting disorder.[58] Rather, it was a novel claim that the doctors should be liable in negligence to Keeden and Alexia for the damage of being born ('life with disabilities').[59] The claimants contended that if the doctors had advised the parents about the medical risks—of a life with disabilities—the parents of Keeden would not have proceeded with in vitro fertilisation, thus precluding his conception, and Alexia's mother would have lawfully terminated her pregnancy, thus ensuring that she would not have been born.

The High Court (Gleeson CJ, Gummow, Hayne, Callinan, Heydon and Crennan JJ; Kirby J dissenting) held that neither claimant was entitled to damages upon the basis that he or she 'should never have been born'. According to Crennan J (at [251]), with whom Gleeson CJ, Gummow and Heydon JJ concurred:

> Because damage constitutes the gist of an action in negligence, a plaintiff needs to prove actual damage or loss and a court must be able to apprehend and evaluate the damage, that is the loss, deprivation or detriment caused by the alleged breach of duty. Inherent in that principle is the requirement that a plaintiff is left worse off as a result of the negligence complained about, which can be established by the comparison of a plaintiff's damage or loss caused by the negligent conduct, with the plaintiff's circumstances absent the negligent conduct.

---

57. In *Harriton v Stephens* [2006] HCA 15 at [244], per Crennan J.
58. *Waller v James*; *Waller v Hoolahan* [2006] HCA 16 at [84], per Crennan J.
59. In *Harriton v Stephens* [2006] HCA 15 at [223], Crennan J noted that the term 'wrongful life' has been internationally accepted as denoting a claim by children for 'life with disabilities' in contradistinction to 'wrongful birth' claims by parents for the costs of raising a child, whether healthy (*Cattanach v Melchior* (2003) 215 CLR 1) or disabled (*Parkinson v St James and Seacroft University Hospital NHS Trust* [2002] QB 266), whose unplanned birth occurs as a result of medical negligence.

Her Honour, as well as all other members of the majority, agreed with Spigelman CJ of the New South Wales Court of Appeal who, at the appeal stage,[60] pointed out that on the facts as pleaded, had the defendants performed their duties without negligence, neither claimant would exist:

> In such a case, in order to constitute damage which is legally cognizable, ie which gives rise to a right to compensation, it must be established that non-existence is preferable to life with the disabilities *to the child*. Unless that is so, there is, in my opinion, no 'damage', of the character which constitutes the gist of an action in negligence, for purposes of an action *by the child*.

Crennan J (at [252]) found that 'a comparison between a life with disabilities and non-existence, for the purposes of proving actual damage and having a trier of fact apprehend the nature of the damage caused, is impossible'.[61] Consequently, since the claimants did not suffer what the law should recognise as 'damage', they had no cause of action in negligence.

FURTHER READING

Dietrich J, 'Liability in Negligence for Harm resulting from Third Parties' Criminal Acts: *Modbury Triangle Shopping Centre Pty Ltd v Anzil*' (2001) 9 *Torts Law Journal* 152.

Fleming JG, *The Law of Torts*, 9th edn, The Law Book Company, Sydney, 1998, Ch 6.

Mendelson D, '*Jones v Bartlett*: Landlords' Liability to Tenants and Members of Their Household in Negligence' (2001) 6 *Deakin University Law Review* 174–184.

Scott R, 'Maternal Duties Towards Unborn? Soundings from the Law of Torts' (2000) 8 *Medical Law Review* 1–68.

Trindade F & Cane P, *The Law of Torts in Australia*, 3rd edn, Oxford University Press, Melbourne, 1999, Ch 10.

Yeo S, 'Am I my Child's Keeper? Parental Liability in Negligence' (1998) 12 *Australian Journal of Family Law* 150.

---

60. *Harriton (by her tutor) v Stephens; Waller (by his tutor) v James & Anor; Waller (by his tutor) v Hoolahan* (2004) 59 NSWLR 694 at [43].
61. Hayne J specifically concurred at [170]; see also Callinan J at [205]: 'To seek to compare, for the purpose of assessing damages, non-existence with the state of existence is impossible.'

11 Breach of Duty of Care*

INTRODUCTION

Negligence is a fault-based tort. Once the plaintiff has established the existence of a duty of care, he or she must then show, on the balance of probabilities, that the defendant was at fault. Unlike trespass, where the fault lies in the infringement of a right to personal integrity and freedom without legal justification, in negligence the fault (*culpa* in Latin) lies in breach of a duty of care. The notion of breach of duty of care can be traced to the early declarations in the writ of *covenant* alleging, under *assumpsit super se* ('took upon himself'), that whereas the defendant undertook and promised to do work competently, skilfully and carefully, he did the work incompetently, unskilfully and negligently. The concept of fault in negligence has both legal and moral implications.[1]

A defendant breaches the duty of care owed to the plaintiff by failing to take reasonable steps to avoid a risk of injury to the plaintiff that was reasonably foreseeable. As Baron Alderson put it in *Blyth v Birmingham Waterworks* (1856) 11 Exch 781, at 782:

> Negligence is the omission to do something which a reasonable man, guided upon those considerations which ordinarily regulate the conduct of human affairs, would do, or doing something which a prudent and reasonable man would not do.

The tort of negligence has a dual role. Its object is not only compensation, but also regulation. The rationale of the tort of negligence is regulatory in nature—it identifies the 'content of the duty of care' in the sense of the acceptable standard of conduct in a given situation by reference to the touchstone of reasonableness. As Kirby J pointed out in *Cole v South Tweed Heads Rugby League Football Club Ltd* [2004] HCA 29 (at [91]):

---

* This chapter was jointly written by Danuta Mendelson and Sharon Erbacher.
1. For a discussion of the nature of fault, see: Honoré T, *Responsibility and Fault*, Hart Publishing, Oxford, 1999.

The law of tort exists not only to provide remedies for injured persons where that is fair and reasonable and consonant with legal principle. It also exists to set standards in society, to regulate wholly self-interested conduct and, so far as the law of negligence is concerned, to require the individual to act carefully in relation to a person who, in law, is a neighbour.

In view of its regulatory aim, it is not surprising that the reasonable standard of care for the purposes of the law of negligence is objective and normative. This means that the legal question is what *ought* to have been done in the circumstances, not what *is* done in similar circumstances by most people—or even by all people. Thus, fault will be imputed to persons who, while under a duty of care, could have observed the normative standard of care that the duty imposed upon them, but failed to do so. Inherent in the notion is a moral opprobrium that attaches to anyone who has failed to measure up to the standard.

As a general rule, the defendant cannot plead the inadequacy of his or her actual resources as being relevant to the legal determination of the breach of the required standard, for unless warned, third parties have the right to assume that a reasonable person in the defendant's position would have had adequate resources to conduct the enterprise in which he or she was engaged.[2] This rule is subject to the common law and statutory exception that applies to public authorities (discussed below).

RETROSPECTIVE NATURE OF THE INQUIRY

In torts, occurrences of past events are invariably analysed in retrospect; consequently, there is always a risk that people who have caused an injury may appear negligent, even if in fact they took reasonable care, as they undersood it at the time. The legal standard of foresight is a synonym for prudence in the sense of the capacity for judging in advance the probable results of one's actions. The approach of the courts in the last decades of the twentieth century, which equated the requirement of foresight with prescience in the sense of knowledge of actions or events before they occur, was unrealistic and unfair. Reasonable people may fail to recognise or overlook a foreseeable risk of injury, which, once it materialises, necessarily becomes the focus of special attention. Yet, as Gleeson CJ noted in *Commissioner of Main Roads v Jones* [2005] HCA 27, at [5], if it was only one risk among many, there may have been no reason, at the time of the accident, to single it out.[3] This 'distorting effect of litigious hindsight'[4] is often reinforced by sympathy for the injured plaintiff. In *Derrick v Cheung* (2001) 181 ALR 301, the High Court commented on the

---

2. *PQ v Australian Red Cross Society & Ors* [1992] 1 VR 19.
3. See also: *Vairy v Wyong Shire Council* [2005] HCA 62 at [126ff], per Hayne J; *Neindorf v Junkovic* [2005] HCA 75 at [94], per Hayne J.
4. *Commissioner of Main Roads v Jones* [2005] HCA 27 at [5] per Gleeson CJ.

'hindsight bias' with regards to expected standards. In that case, the defendant was travelling on a busy inner suburban road, within the line of traffic, at between 40 and 50 kilometres per hour, even though the specified speed limit was 60 kilometres per hour. A toddler, twenty-one months old, suddenly emerged from between two parked vehicles into the path of her car. The defendant braked and swerved to the right in order to avoid the child. Unfortunately, her vehicle skidded and made a collision unavoidable. The child suffered severe and permanent brain injury. The trial judge and the majority of the New South Wales Court of Appeal found that the motorist was negligent, driving at an 'excessive speed', because evidence established that had she been driving at 20 or 30 kilometres per hour, she would have been able to stop instantly. On appeal, the High Court held that there was no basis upon which any finding of negligence could be made. In a joint judgment, Gleeson CJ, Gaudron, Kirby, Hayne, and Callinan JJ (at [13]) commented that:

> Few occurrences in human affairs, in retrospect, can be said to have been, in absolute terms, inevitable. Different conduct on the part of those involved in them almost always would have produced a different result. But the possibility of a different result is not the issue and does not represent the proper test for negligence. That test remains whether the plaintiff has proved that the defendant, who owed a duty of care, has not acted in accordance with reasonable care.

In other words, although the judgment about breach of duty must inevitably take place after the event has occurred, it should not be made with the benefit of hindsight. In *Vairy v Wyong Shire Council* [2005] HCA 62, Hayne J commented (at [124]) that the enquiry into breach, although made after the event, must seek to answer whether a reasonable person at the time of the accident would have responded differently to avoid the risk of injury taking into account the range of risks involved in the activity. One of the possible answers to that inquiry must be 'no'.[5]

GENERAL BREACH PRINCIPLES

General breach of duty principles have been enacted in legislation in each Australian jurisdiction save for the Northern Territory. The provisions uniformly specify three preconditions to negligence liability:[6]

(1) A person is not negligent in failing to take precautions against a risk of harm unless—

---

5. *Vairy v Wyong Shire Council* [2005] HCA 62 at [124], per Hayne J.
6. *Civil Law (Wrongs) Act 2002* (ACT), s 43; *Civil Liability Act 2002* (NSW), s 5B; *Civil Liability Act 2003* (Qld), s 11; *Civil Liability Act 1936* (SA), s 32; *Civil Liability Act 2002* (Tas), s 11; *Wrongs Act 1958* (Vic), s 48; *Civil Liability Act 2002* (WA), s 5B.

(a) the risk was foreseeable (that is, it is a risk of which the person knew or ought to have known); and

(b) the risk was not insignificant; and

(c) in the circumstances, a reasonable person in the person's position would have taken those precautions.

These tests are not alternatives; each of the three requirements must be satisfied before negligence liability can be imposed. The tests of foreseeability (paragraph (a)) and reasonableness (paragraph (c)) reflect the pre-reform common law position. The requirement in paragraph (b) that the risk be 'not insignificant' introduces a new test that does not have a common law equivalent. Moreover, under the codified tort of negligence in all jurisdictions other than the Territories, the defendants' response to the risk is predicated by the nature of the foreseeable risk. Legislation distinguishes between three kinds of risk: 'real' in the sense of 'not an insignificant risk'; an 'obvious risk' and an 'inherent risk'. Obvious and inherent risks are subject to specific statutory rules (discussed below, and in Chapter 17).

The three elements of the general breach of duty inquiry will be discussed in turn.

Reasonable foreseeability

Legislation in each of the jurisdictions adopts the previous common law position that the risk of harm must be reasonably foreseeable. Defendants are not expected to exercise due care *unless* they should reasonably have known that if they were not careful, a compensable harm to person or property might eventuate. It is not necessary that the defendant could foresee the precise manner in which the injury was inflicted; it is enough that the injury and its infliction were reasonably foreseeable in a general way.[7] In *Doubleday v Kelly* [2005] NSWCA 151, the plaintiff, Bianca, was seven years old when she stayed overnight at the home of her five-year-old friend, Lucy, the defendants' daughter. The girls woke up at about 6 am the next morning and, while the rest of the family was still sleeping, put on roller skates and attempted to skate on the trampoline in the yard of the house. Bianca had never been on a trampoline before and thought that the top of it was a hard surface on which she might be able to skate. She climbed onto the trampoline, rolled backwards, and then fell off, injuring her right hand. Bianca sued the defendants in negligence on the basis that they should have turned the trampoline on its side, or completely over, so that she could not use it unsupervised. The defendants argued that it was not reasonably foreseeable that the plaintiff would attempt to roller skate on the trampoline. The New South Wales Court of Appeal (Bryson JA; Young CJ and Hunt AJA agreeing) accepted that it was not specifically reasonably

---

7. *Cole v South Tweed Heads Rugby League Football Club Ltd* [2004] HCA 29 at [32], per McHugh J.

foreseeable that the plaintiff would climb on the trampoline so as to roller skate on the surface. Nevertheless, this did not absolve the defendants of liability as it was generally foreseeable that the girls might go onto the trampoline unsupervised. In fact, it was seen specifically as a possibility by one of the defendants, and she had warned the two girls the night before not to go onto the trampoline unsupervised. Bryson JA (at [11]) stated the relevant principle as follows:

> The actual events as they happened are not the circumstances to which considerations of foreseeability of risk is applied; what is to be considered is foresight in more general terms of risk of injury.[8]
>
> Where the defendant knew of the risk in question (for example, because a similar accident had occurred previously), the defendant must be taken to have foreseen the risk. Where the defendant did not have actual knowledge of the risk, the question will be whether the defendant as a reasonable person 'ought to have known' of the risk. Before the reforms, the test of foreseeability as established in *Overseas Tankship (UK) Ltd v The Miller Steamship Co Pty Ltd* (*The Wagon Mound No 2*) [1967] AC 617 and *Wyong Shire Council v Shirt* (1980) 146 CLR 40 was very broad: a risk of injury was reasonably foreseeable (and therefore ought to have been known by the reasonable defendant) unless it was a 'far-fetched or fanciful' possibility.[9] This was so even where a risk of injury had a very small chance of occurrence.

The test of foreseeability, which has been taken to embrace risks that are quite unlikely to occur, is open to criticism for being too undemanding and inadequate as a filter of negligence liability.[10] In *Swain v Waverley Municipal Council* [2005] HCA 4, McHugh J (at [80]) opined that if the common law of negligence is to survive it must set 'its face against the principles expounded in *The Wagon Mound (No 2)* and the cases that have faithfully followed it'.

'Not insignificant' risk of harm

The Torts reform legislation in each jurisdiction other than the Northern Territory has introduced the requirement that the risk of harm, in addition to being foreseeable, must be 'not insignificant'. This new requirement was adopted on the recommendation of the 2002 *Review of the Law of Negligence Report* (the *Ipp Report*). After a review of the reasonable foreseeability principles, the *Ipp Report* concluded

---

8. This principle was specifically adopted by Ipp JA (Spigelman CJ and Tobias JA agreeing) in *Waverley Council v Ferreira* [2005] NSWCA 418 at [42].
9. *Overseas Tankship (UK) Ltd v The Miller Steamship Co Pty Ltd* (*The Wagon Mound No 2*) [1967] AC 617; *Wyong Shire Council v Shirt* (1980) 146 CLR 40.
10. *Tame v New South Wales* [2002] 211 CLR 317 at [96]–[104], per McHugh J, with whom Callinan J agreed at [331]; *Koehler v Cerebos (Australia) Ltd* (2005) 214 ALR 355 at [54]; *Vairy v Wyong Shire Council* [2005] HCA 62 at [213], per Callinan and Heydon JJ.

that the 'far-fetched or fanciful' threshold was too low, and that it should be replaced with a threshold test requiring a higher degree of probability of harm.[11] The *Ipp Report* suggested that the requirement should be that the risk is 'not insignificant'. This phrase was intended to indicate a risk that is of higher probability than is indicated by the phrase 'not far-fetched or fanciful', but of a lower probability than what might be termed a 'substantial' or 'significant' risk. It follows that a 'not insignificant' risk falls somewhere between a 'far-fetched or fanciful' risk and a 'significant' risk.

A foreseeable risk that is very unlikely to occur might be considered to be an 'insignificant' risk which the defendant can reasonably ignore. *Bolton v Stone* [1951] AC 850, discussed below, illustrates how a risk that the cricket ball would fly over the fence and hit a person standing outside the ground was considered to be of sufficiently low probability to be classified as insignificant.

The meaning given in the *Ipp Report* to the phrase 'insignificant risk' has been embodied in legislation in Victoria. For instance, s 48(3) of the *Wrongs Act 1958* (Vic) which provides:

(a) *insignificant risks* include, but are not limited to, risks that are far-fetched or fanciful; and
(b) risks that are *not insignificant* are all risks other than insignificant risks and include, but are not limited to, significant risks.[12] (original emphasis)

Calculus of negligence factors

If the risk of harm is reasonably foreseeable and 'not insignificant', it is then necessary to ask whether, taking into account all the circumstances, the defendant responded to the risk of harm in the way that a reasonable person would. In *New South Wales v Bujdoso* [2005] HCA 76, Gleeson CJ, Gummow, Kirby, Hayne, Callinan, and Heydon JJ, in a joint judgment (at [51]), reiterated the principle that defendants are not required to *guarantee* that the plaintiff will not be harmed because of the occurrence of the foreseeable risk, but they must respond to the risk, taking *reasonable care* in doing so.

At common law, the High Court in *Wyong Shire Council v Shirt* (1980) 146 CLR 40[13] identified four considerations to be weighed in determining the

---

11. *Ipp Report*, paras 7.14, 7.15.
12. Very similar provisions are contained in the *Civil Liability Act 2003* (Qld), s 9(1); *Civil Liability Act 2002* (NSW), s 5B(1); *Civil Liability Act 1936* (SA), s 32(1); *Civil Liability Act 2002* (WA), s 5B(1); *Civil Liability Act 2002* (Tas), s 11(1); *Civil Law (Wrongs) Act 2002* (ACT), s 43(1)(b).
13. In this case, Mr Shirt, who was an inexperienced water skier, decided to swim in a lake under the control of Wyong Shire Council. He saw a sign facing the shoreline of the lake bearing the words 'Deep Water'. He understood the sign to mean that the water immediately beyond the sign was deep, whereas in fact the depth was only three feet six inches: the only deep water was in a channel situated in front of the sign. Mr Shirt suffered quadriplegic paralysis as a result of striking his head on the bottom of the lake.

reasonableness of the defendant's response: the probability of the risk occurring; the magnitude of harm; the expense, difficulty and inconvenience of adopting precautions; and the social utility of the defendant's conduct. These considerations, called the 'calculus of negligence', have now been embodied in statute in each Australian jurisdiction other than the Northern Territory.[14] Although the statutory wording is somewhat different from that used in *Wyong Shire Council v Shirt*, the provisions are generally intended to reflect the common law.[15] The statutory provisions uniformly specify that:

> In determining whether a reasonable person would have taken precautions against a risk of harm, the court is to consider the following (among other relevant things)—
> (a) the probability that the harm would occur if care were not taken; and
> (b) the likely seriousness of the harm; and
> (c) the burden of taking precautions to avoid the risk of harm; and
> (d) the social utility of the activity that creates the risk of harm.

None of these four factors will of itself be determinative of liability; the courts balance them against each other in order to decide whether the defendant should have taken additional precautions to avoid the risk of injury. Thus, a defendant might be justified in ignoring a risk that could potentially cause very serious harm to the plaintiff where the probability of the risk of injury was very small and it would have been prohibitively expensive or difficult to avoid the risk. Likewise, a defendant might not act unreasonably in doing nothing in response to a risk with a high probability of occurrence but which would only be likely to cause minor injury, yet difficult or costly to avoid. Conversely, a defendant who ignores a risk that has a high probability of occurrence and of causing serious harm might be found to have acted negligently by failing to take relatively practicable and inexpensive steps to prevent that risk, unless such failure was justified on grounds of social utility (see 'Social utility', below).

The High Court decision in *Romeo v Conservation Commission of the Northern Territory* (1998) 192 CLR 431 provides a good illustration of the application of the negligence calculus to determine liability. The fifteen-year-old plaintiff, Nadia Romeo, went with a friend, Jacinta Hay, to a beach party at a nature reserve at Dripstone Cliffs in Darwin. The two girls bought a 750 ml bottle of Bundaberg Rum and some Coca-Cola on the way. They met their friends in a car park of the Dripstone Cliffs Park, the perimeter of which consisted of a low log fence. Each consumed approximately 150 ml of rum during the evening prior to the

---

14. *Civil Liability Act 2003* (Qld), s 9(2); *Civil Liability Act 2002* (NSW), s 5B(2); *Civil Liability Act 1936* (SA), s 32(2); *Civil Law (Wrongs) Act 2002* (ACT), s 43(2); *Civil Liability Act 2002* (WA), s 5B(2); *Civil Liability Act 2002* (Tas), s 11(2); *Wrongs Act 1958* (Vic).
15. *Ipp Report*, para 7.17.

accident, which occurred sometime after 11.45 pm, when they wandered off from the party, and fell six metres from the top of the Dripstone Cliffs onto the beach below. Neither could recall the circumstances of their fall. Nadia suffered serious spinal injuries causing high-level paraplegia. She claimed damages against the Conservation Commission of the Northern Territory, a public authority charged with management and control of the nature reserve, the Dripstone Cliffs, and the beach. The case was conducted on the basis that the authority should have created a barrier or provided illumination of the cliff, which was about two kilometres in length. Alternatively, it should have erected warning signs near the car park fence warning of the dangers of the cliff.

The majority (Brennan CJ, Toohey, Gummow, and Kirby JJ) held that the public authority, by virtue of the functions (powers) vested in it, owed a duty of care to persons entering the reserve to take reasonable care to avoid reasonably foreseeable risks of injury to such persons. Furthermore, the public authority could reasonably foresee that an entrant might occasionally fall over the cliff. However, the failure of the public authority to erect a barrier and provide illumination of the edge of the cliff, or to warn of the dangers of the cliff, did not amount to a breach of duty of care. Toohey and Gummow JJ emphasised that the authority was not required to guarantee, by whatever means, that entrants would not suffer injury by falling over the cliff. It was only required to do what was reasonable in the circumstances to prevent such an accident occurring. Although the risk that someone would fall off the cliff was reasonably foreseeable by the public authority, that risk existed only in the case of someone who ignored the obvious danger, and therefore the probability of this kind of accident was very low. Nor were special precautions required at the particular spot where the girls fell: the cliff top was an obvious part of the cliff, and 'not a viewing point except in the sense that visitors used the car park in order to watch sunsets from their cars' (at [53]). In those circumstances, the authority's duty of care did not extend taking steps advocated by the plaintiff in order to prevent the foreseeable risk of a fall. Kirby J likewise emphasised that the dangers presented by the cliff were obvious, and could have been avoided by the exercise of reasonable care by entrants to the area. Furthermore, in determining whether the authority owed a duty to the plaintiff to erect a barrier, the court should not focus exclusively on the car park area of the cliffs. An accident of the kind that occurred in *Romeo* might have occurred at any other cliff area in every similar reserve under the control of a public authority to which members of the public had access. Yet, the resources of public authorities are limited and the allocation of resources to the fencing of promontories in natural reserves would divert them from other operational priorities. Moreover, according to his Honour (at [132]):

> The proposition that such precautions were necessary to arrest the passage of an inattentive young woman affected by alcohol is simply not reasonable. The perceived magnitude of risk, the remote possibility that an accident would

occur, the expense, difficulty and inconvenience of alleviating conduct and the other proper priorities of the Commission confirm the conclusion that breach of the Commission's duty of care to the appellant was not established. The Commission's failure to provide protection against the risk that occurred was not unreasonable.

The High Court has often emphasised that the calculus of negligence should not be applied as an inflexible formula; it is not a mathematical or mechanical exercise but a judgment.[16] Ultimately, the conclusion whether the defendant has acted reasonably is to be determined in all of the circumstances, and represents an application of community standards of reasonable behaviour.[17] Thus, the standard of care imposed by the court may vary in accordance with the judicial interpretation of the social and cultural expectations of society at a given time. For example, in *Czatyrko v Edith Cowan University* [2005] HCA 14, Gleeson CJ, McHugh, Hayne, Callinan and Heydon JJ held (at [12]) that the standard of care of the employer to provide a safe system of work includes taking reasonable care to avoid 'a real risk of an injury' to employees who may be thoughtless, careless or inadvertent in their performance of a task in a workplace, 'by devising a method of operation for the performance of the task that eliminates the risk, or by the provision of adequate safeguards'. This is particularly so if the employees are engaged in repetitive work. In *Czatyrko*, the plaintiff was injured when he stepped backward and fell from the truck he was instructed to load. While re-organising the load, Mr Czatyrko assumed that a mobile platform, which enabled workers to get onto and down from the truck, was up. In fact, a fellow employee had lowered the platform without letting the plaintiff know. According to the High Court (at [13]), the risk that the employee 'would attempt to step backwards on to the platform in the belief that it was raised, without checking whether this was the case, was plainly foreseeable', and easily preventable, for example by introducing a warning beeper as and when the platform was being lowered.

The statutory provisions laying down the general breach principles explicitly recognise that the calculus factors are not the only relevant factors to be considered; all relevant circumstances must be taken into account in determining the reasonableness of the defendant's conduct. One overarching principle that has assumed importance in recent times is the obligation of persons injured to take reasonable care for their own safety (discussed below under the heading 'Individual responsibility and community standards').

It is with this principle in mind that individual calculus of negligence factors will be discussed.

---

16. See: *Vairy v Wyong Shire Council* [2005] HCA 62 at [155], per Hayne J (Gummow J relevantly agreeing); *Mulligan v Coffs Harbour* [2005] HCA 63 at [3], per Gleeson CJ and Kirby J.
17. *Mulligan v Coffs Harbour* [2005] HCA 63 at [3], per Gleeson CJ and Kirby J.

Probability of harm

A defendant might be justified in ignoring a risk of harm that—although foreseeable—is very small, even where the resultant harm is likely to be quite severe. This will be particularly so if the only precautions that could be taken to avert the injury are particularly expensive or inconvenient. In *Bolton v Stone* [1951] AC 850, a country cricket club was established in 1864. In 1910, a road was constructed off one end of the cricket club's grounds, and a housing estate was built. In 1947, the plaintiff, while standing outside her house, was injured by a ball hit out of the ground during the match. There was evidence that in more than thirty years balls had very rarely been hit out of the ground. The House of Lords held that although there was a possibility that residents living near the ground would be injured by a cricket ball, the chance of an accident of this kind actually happening was 'extremely small'. The cricket club had not breached its duty of care to adjoining residents as the risk was of negligible proportions, yet the action to eliminate it would involve great expense and inconvenience. The precautions suggested by the plaintiff of moving the wickets a few steps further away from the road end, or the heightening of the fencing, would have had little or no effect in averting the peril. The only practical means by which the possibility of danger could have been avoided would have been to stop playing cricket on the ground altogether, which would have deprived the local community of a valuable sporting activity. However, Lord Reid emphasised that he would have reached a different conclusion had he thought the risk was other than extremely small.

The decision of the High Court in *Romeo v Conservation Commission of the Northern Territory*, discussed above, was also a case where the very low probability of the harm occurring was an important factor in concluding that it was not unreasonable for the defendant to do nothing in response to the foreseeable risk. Likewise, in *Derrick v Cheung* [2001] HCA 48, the High Court pointed out that it was unreasonable to make motorists drive at a speed of less than 40 kilometres per hour on busy metropolitan roads in order to avoid a foreseeable, but unlikely, risk that an unattended toddler would dart in front of a vehicle.

Seriousness of the harm

The seriousness of the possible harm that could be sustained if the foreseeable risk materialises is always taken into consideration in determining the reasonableness of the defendant's response. The precautionary measures reasonably expected of the defendant will vary according to the likely severity of the resultant injury. In *Caledonian Collieries Ltd v Speirs* (1957) 97 CLR 202, the plaintiff's husband was killed when struck by runaway freight train carriages at a level crossing on a busy highway. The railway line was a private line owned and operated by the defendants. The defendants had built the junction and the level crossing at which the accident occurred. The plaintiff argued that the defendants should have installed catch-points on the line to deflect runaway carriages (perhaps derailing them). The defendants argued that installation of catch-points was a drastic measure, because these devices had to be changed manually, leading to delays on the line, and causing significant economic loss. Their Honours disagreed, and held (at 223 [14]), that given the density of population, and the busy traffic using the crossing, 'there was only one way, so far as the evidence suggested, in which it was possible to ensure that the danger to road traffic from runaway rolling-stock on the line might be effectually averted, and that was by installing a set of catch-points.' Moreover (at 225 [16]):

> when the danger to be guarded against is of the order of a level crossing collision, it may well be that drastic measures are within the limits of reasonable care.

In *Burnie Port Authority v General Jones Pty Ltd* (1994) 179 CLR 520, at 554, the High Court went further:

> In the case of dangerous substances or activities, a reasonably prudent person would exercise a higher degree of care. Indeed, depending upon the magnitude of the danger, the standard of reasonable care may involve a degree of diligence so stringent as to amount practically to a guarantee of safety.

Standard of care requiring 'a degree of diligence so stringent as to amount practically to a guarantee of safety' effectively imposes upon the defendant strict liability. However, Gleeson CJ (at [33]) and Gummow J (at [250]) in *Scott v Davis* (2000) 204 CLR 333, and Gummow and Hayne JJ (at [266]) in *New South Wales v Lepore; Samin v Queensland; Rich v Queensland* (2003) 212 CLR 511, expressed reservations about interpolating notions of strict liability into the law of negligence.

Defendant's knowledge of plaintiff's vulnerability

Defendants might also be required to adopt special precautionary measures where they know, or ought to know, that the particular plaintiff will suffer greater injury than would a 'normal' person exposed to the risk. This is so even though the probability of the risk materialising is no greater for that person than any other. In *Paris v Stepney Borough Council* [1951] AC 367, the plaintiff was employed by the defendant as a fitter's mate on the maintenance and repair of council vehicles. The defendant knew that the plaintiff was practically blind in the left eye. While working, a fragment of metal lodged in the plaintiff's right eye, as a consequence of which he became entirely blind. The plaintiff successfully established negligence based on the failure by the employer to provide a safe system of work and, in particular, the failure to provide him with protective goggles. The House of Lords recognised that the probability of an accident of this kind occurring was no greater in the plaintiff's case than it was in the case of fellow full-sighted workers. Nevertheless, the reasonable, prudent defendant would be influenced, not only by the lesser or greater probability of an accident occurring, but also by the gravity of the consequences if the accident did occur. If an employer knows of circumstances that mean a particular employee is likely to suffer a more serious injury than fellow workers from the happening of a given event, this must be taken into consideration in assessing the nature of the employer's obligation to that employee.

The burden of taking precautions to avoid the risk of harm

The plaintiff must establish that it was reasonably practicable for the defendant to take precautions to avoid the foreseeable risk of harm. Before a court can arrive at a conclusion of negligence, the plaintiff must identify the precautions the defendant should have taken, and then show that the burden of expense, difficulty, and inconvenience involved was not unreasonable. If the precautions to avoid the risk are onerous, the defendant may not be required to adopt them. This will be especially so where the probability of the risk materialising was quite low. Thus, in *Bolton v Stone*, one of the factors militating against a finding of negligence was that the cricket club could only have effectively prevented a similar accident occurring if it ceased playing cricket at the ground. Other precautions, such as moving the pitch or increasing the height of the fence, would not have been effective.

In contrast, in *Doubleday v Kelly* [2005] NSWCA 151 (discussed above), once the defendants admitted they were aware of risks to young children playing on the trampoline without supervision, the New South Wales Court of Appeal held that the defendants should have taken the precaution either of placing it on its side or of turning it over with the legs folded up.

Ultimately, however, a determination of breach in a particular case is governed by an application of community standards of reasonable behaviour,[18] and the mere fact that the harm could have been avoided easily and inexpensively does not of itself give rise to liability in negligence. For instance, Gleeson CJ and Kirby J have indicated, in *Vairy v Wyong Shire Council* [2005] HCA 62 (at [8]), that the obligation of a public authority to warn of the risks of engaging in a risky recreational activity, such as diving into water of unknown depth, is not to be determined by comparing the (insignificant) cost of a warning sign with the seriousness of the harm likely to result. The obligations of the authority will be influenced by a range of other factors, such as the obviousness of the danger, the expectation that persons will take reasonable care for their own safety, and the diffuse range of risks naturally involved in recreational pursuits.[19]

---

18. *Thompson v Woolworths (Q'land) Pty Ltd* [2005] HCA 19; *Mulligan v Coffs Harbour* [2005] HCA 63 at [3], per Gleeson CJ and Kirby J.
19. See also: Hayne J at [128].

The High Court has emphasised, particularly in the context of claims against public authorities, that in determining the reasonableness of the defendant's conduct the court should not isolate the particular risk that occurred and ignore the cost to the authority of alleviating other risks of harm for which the authority is responsible. As noted above, in *Romeo v Conservation Commission (NT)* the majority considered that it would be inappropriate to ignore the fact that an imposition of the duty to fence one particular cliff area, would involve an unreasonably onerous implication requiring the authority to fence off *all* cliff tops under its control in the Northern Territory to prevent similar hazards (of someone falling off). This approach has now been codified in five jurisdictions, which provide that 'the burden of taking precautions to avoid a risk of harm includes the burden of taking precautions to avoid similar risks of harm for which the person may be responsible'.[20]

Any assessment of whether a public authority has breached its duty of care must take into account the limited resources available to a public authority.[21] It might not in the circumstances be reasonable to require the defendant to expend resources to alleviate the particular risk where this would necessarily divert resources from other matters of 'equal or possibly greater priority' (Kirby J in *Romeo* at [129]). At the same time, the resources available to private defendants will not generally be taken into account, as defendants who choose to engage in an activity should ensure that they possess the resources to do so in a safe manner. It will be different, however, if the hazard is thrust upon the defendant—as where a tree growing on the defendant's land is hit by lightening and set on fire. In determining whether the defendant acted reasonably in preventing the spread of the fire to an adjoining property, account should be taken of the resources (physical or material) available to the defendant (*Goldman v Hargrave* [1967] AC 645).

Relevance of the subsequent adoption of safer precautions

The adoption by the defendant after the accident of a precaution that would prevent a recurrence of the risk will not of itself conclusively determine liability or amount to an admission that the pre-accident precautions were negligent (*Caledonian Collieries Ltd v Spiers* (1957) 97 CLR 202). If it were otherwise, defendants might be reluctant to adopt a new safety precaution, fearing that the new precaution would be used in evidence against them by the plaintiff.

This common law proposition is now embodied in legislation in most jurisdictions. For example, s 49(c) of the Victorian *Wrongs Act* 1958 provides:

---

20. *Wrongs Act 1958* (Vic), s 49(b); *Civil Law (Wrongs) Act 2002* (ACT), s 44(a); *Civil Liability Act 2002* (NSW), s 5C(a); *Civil Liability Act 2003* (Qld), s 10(a); *Civil Liability Act 2002* (Tas), s 11(3).
21. *Civil Law (Wrongs) Act 2002* (ACT), s 110; *Civil Liability Act 2002* (NSW), s 42; *Civil Liability Act 2003* (Qld), s 35; *Civil Liability Act 2002* (Tas), s 38; *Wrongs Act 1958* (Vic), s 83; *Civil Liability Act 2002* (WA), s 5W.

the subsequent taking of action that would (had the action been taken earlier) have avoided a risk of harm does not of itself give rise to or affect liability in respect of the risk and does not of itself constitute an admission of liability in connection with the risk.

The operation of this principle is illustrated by *Gillies v Saddington* [2004] NSWCA 110. The plaintiff slipped when walking down the steep driveway of the defendant's home. The fact that the defendant had applied a non-slip surface coating shortly after the plaintiff's fall, although demonstrating that it could have been done earlier, was a natural reaction to an injury suffered by a friend, and did not weigh heavily as something the defendant was under a duty of care to do.

In *Mulligan v Coffs Harbour City Council* [2005] HCA 63, Mr Mulligan, without checking the depth of the water, dived forward into a channel that formed part of a creek. His head struck a bedform (sand dune), breaking his neck. Sand dunes are a well-known and natural phenomenon, found in tidal estuaries around the world. Gummow J noted (at [39]) that after Mr Mulligan's trial at first instance, the Coffs Harbour City Council erected four signs displaying pictorial devices accompanied by warnings 'Submerged Objects', 'Dangerous Current', 'Slippery Rocks' and 'No Lifeguard or Lifesaving Service here Today'. His Honour commented that the 'later placement of signs may have been a relevant part of the *Wyong Shire Council v Shirt* calculus' (in relation to practicability), but not to whether there was a prior duty to provide the warning sinage. The fact that the defendant adopted safer precautions or erected warnings after the event may be used as evidence that those precautions could practicably have been adopted before the accident, but will not, of itself, determine the question of breach.[22]

Onus of proof

The onus is on the plaintiff to prove that it was reasonable for the defendant to adopt the proposed precautions. This principle has now been adopted by legislation in Victoria, the Australian Capital Territory, New South Wales, Tasmania, and Queensland. The relevant statutory provisions direct that:

> the fact that a risk of harm could have been avoided by doing something in a different way does not of itself give rise to or affect liability for the way in which the thing was done.[23]

---

22. In *Caledonian Collieries Ltd v Speirs*, the defendant had installed catch-points on its line within a fortnight of the accident. Although the plaintiff could not use this action as an admission by the defendant that reasonable care in the management of the line required the provision of catch-points, at the time of the trial (some four years later) there was no evidence that they had caused practical difficulties.
23. *Wrongs Act 1958* (Vic), s 49(b); *Civil Law (Wrongs) Act 2002* (ACT), s 44(b); *Civil Liability Act 2002* (NSW), s 5C(b); *Civil Liability Act 2003* (Qld), s 10(b); *Civil Liability Act 2002* (Tas), s 12(a).

This indicates that the burden of proof remains on the plaintiff throughout. In other words, the mere fact that the plaintiff can establish that there was an alternative way of doing something will not of itself be determinative; the plaintiff then has to show that the proposed precautions would not be burdensome.

These provisions overcome the High Court's decision in *McLean v Tedman* (1984) 155 CLR 306, which applied in cases involving an employer–employee relationship. In that case, it was held that once the plaintiff employee demonstrated that an alternative safer system of work, which would have obviated the risk of the relevant injury, could have been implemented, the burden of proof shifted to the defendant employer to establish that the implementation of such alternative system was impractical. Pursuant to the statutory provisions, it is for the plaintiff to prove that the method used by the defendant was an unreasonable response to the foreseeable risk in all the circumstances, including the existence of the different method.

SOCIAL UTILITY

In balancing the elements of the calculus of negligence the court may also take into account policy considerations. The court might have to balance the risk to the plaintiff against the end which might be achieved by not taking all possible precautions: injured claimants may go uncompensated under the theory that in certain circumstances, the overall benefit to the community of the defendant's acts or omissions is such that it outweights the harm caused to an individual. For example, in *E v Australian Red Cross* (1991) 31 FCR 299, a claim against the Red Cross Blood Bank by a plaintiff who contracted AIDS when he was given an HIV-infected blood transfusion was rejected, partly on the basis of the public benefit of the service provided by the Red Cross and the significant problems that would have arisen if a blood shortage were to arise from having to discard untested blood.[24] Likewise, in *Bolton v Stone* [1951] AC 850, the House of Lords found that the cricket club's activity, which was lawful and socially useful, would have to cease if the club was obligated to remove the risk to persons outside its grounds of being hit by a cricket ball. In contrast, in *Tomlinson v Congleton Borough Council* [2003] UKHL 47, Lord Hoffmann (at [36]) commented that in *Jolley v Sutton BC* [2000] 1 WLR 1082, the defendant council ought to have removed a derelict abandoned cabin cruiser from the grounds of its housing estate 'whether it created a risk of injury or not'. There was no social utility in allowing the abandoned wreck to remain on the council's property. The rotten planking of the boat gave way, and it collapsed on fourteen-year-old Justin Jolley, rendering the youngster paraplegic. The council was found liable for the injury, 'which, though foreseeable, was not particularly likely'.

---

24. The case pre-dated the availability of blood tests for HIV antibodies in 1985.

There are some circumstances, in which the emergency services may be justified in taking some risks in saving life and limb.[25] However, this principle cannot be extended too far. In cases involving emergency vehicles such as police cars, ambulances, and fire-engines, the applicable test is whether the defendant has exercised reasonable care having regard to all the circumstances. The courts have noted that although drivers of emergency vehicles must be free to perform their services without too readily being found guilty of negligence, there is no point in killing people in the course of a journey designed to save the lives or property of others.[26]

TIME FOR ASSESSING THE RISK

The reasonableness of the defendant must be assessed by the standard of the reasonable person acting *in the circumstances of the time*. Although it is inevitable that the judgment about breach of duty will take place after the event has occurred, the inquiry about what would have been reasonable and practicable must not be taken in hindsight.[27] Lord Denning's judgment in *Roe v Minister of Health* [1954] 2 QB 66 illustrates this principle. In that case, two men underwent an operation for a minor ailment on the same day in 1947. Each was given a spinal anaesthetic by the visiting specialist. Following their respective operations, each became paralysed from the waist down. They sued the hospital in negligence. Evidence established that, in an effort to prevent contamination of the ampoules containing the anaesthetic, hospital anaesthetists decided to keep the ampoules in a jar of disinfectant (phenol). Unfortunately, the medical practitioners did not know that phenol could seep through cracks in the ampoules that were so fine they could not be detected by the naked eye. Such seepage did in fact occur, and when phenol-contaminated anaesthetic was injected into the spines of the plaintiffs, it corroded all nerves controlling the lower parts of their bodies. The plaintiffs alleged that the medical practitioners were negligent by failing to colour the phenol with a deep dye which would then have alerted them to any contamination of the anaesthetic. However their claim was rejected by the English Court of Appeal. Denning LJ (at 83) held that, at the time of the incident, the doctors could not have been reasonably expected to know that there would be undetectable cracks in the ampoules. The courts needed to be cautious in judging the defendant's actions with the benefit of hindsight after the event: 'we must not look at the 1947 accident with 1954 spectacles'.

---

25. See, for example: *Watt v Hertfordshire County Council* (1954) 1 WLR 835.
26. See, for example: *Morgan v Pearson* (1979) 22 SASR 5; *Patterson v McGinlay* [1991] Aust Torts Reports ¶81–087.
27. See in particular: *Commissioner of Main Roads v Jones* (2005) 215 ALR 418 at [5], per Gleeson CJ; *Vairy v Wyong Shire Council* [2005] HCA 62 at [126ff], per Hayne J; *Neindorf v Junkovic* [2005] HCA 75 at [94], per Hayne J.

As noted above, since 2001, the High Court of Australia has emphasised in a number of cases that the inquiry into the breach of duty must be prospective.[28] The principles from *Roe v Minister of Health* are embodied in legislation in the Australian Capital Territory and South Australia, where it is provided that the standard of care required of the defendant is that of a reasonable person in the defendant's position who was in possession of all information that the defendant had or ought reasonably to have had at the relevant time.[29] Moreover, in New South Wales, Queensland, South Australia, Tasmania, and Victoria,[30] legislation confirms that the liability of a professional for the provision of a professional service is to be judged by peer professional opinion at the time of the service. South Australia and Victoria also provide that the standard of care to be expected of persons holding out as possessing a particular skill has to be determined by reference to (a) what could reasonably be expected of a person possessing that skill; and (b) the relevant circumstances as at the date of the alleged negligence and not a later date. [31]

Inherent risks

Apart from the Australian Capital Territory, the Northern Territory, and Tasmania, all other jurisdictions have enacted legislation dealing with 'inherent' risks. Section 55 of the *Wrongs Act 1958* (Vic) is representative of these provisions:[32]

(1) A person is not liable in negligence for harm suffered by another person as a result of the materialisation of an inherent risk.
(2) An inherent risk is a risk of something occurring that cannot be avoided by the exercise of reasonable care.
(3) This section does not operate to exclude liability in connection with a duty to warn of a risk.

This provision and its equivalents reinforce the principle that the defendant should not be liable in circumstances where the risk cannot be removed by the exercise of reasonable care. Conversely, the defendant will be liable where reasonableness required that the defendant take steps to reduce or eliminate the inherent risk. In *Macarthur Districts Motor Cycle Sportsmen Inc v Ardizzone* [2004] NSWCA 145, the plaintiff, who was twelve years old at the time of the incident, sustained personal injury while participating in a motor cross race. The track and the event

---

28. *Rosenberg v Percival* [2001] HCA 18; *Derrick v Cheung* [2001] HCA 48; *Commissioner of Main Roads v Jones* (2005) 215 ALR 418 at [5], per Gleeson CJ; *Vairy v Wyong Shire Council* [2005] HCA 62 at [124]–[130], per Hayne J; *Neindorf v Junkovic* [2005] HCA 75 at [94], per Hayne J.
29. *Civil Law (Wrongs) Act 2002* (ACT), s 42; *Civil Liability Act 1936* (SA), s 31.
30. *Civil Liability Act 2002* (NSW), s 50; *Civil Liability Act 2003* (Qld), s 22; *Civil Liability Act 1936* (SA), s 41; *Civil Liability Act 2002* (Tas), s 22; *Wrongs Act 1958* (Vic), s 59.
31. *Civil Liability Act 1936* (SA), s 40; *Wrongs Act 1958* (Vic), s 58.
32. See also: *Civil Liability Act 2002* (NSW), s 5I; *Civil Liability Act 2003* (Qld), s 16; *Civil Liability Act 1936* (SA), s 39; *Civil Liability Act 2002* (WA), s 5P.

were controlled by the defendants. The plaintiff suffered the injury when he fell after attempting to take a jump, and was then struck by a following motorcycle. The plaintiff argued that there was an insufficient number of marshals to ensure the safety of the riders on the track. The plaintiff conceded that the sport of motor cross was inherently risky, and that the risk of falling from the motorcycle and being hit by another competitor was an inherent risk of engaging in that sport. Nevertheless, the New South Wales Court of Appeal found that the defendants had breached their duty of care by failing to position a marshal at the jump where the plaintiff fell to warn oncoming riders of falls. The provision of marshals, in adequate numbers and at appropriate stations, would not remove all the risks inherent in the sport, but would tend to operate to reduce or eliminate risks from being realised, and to protect participants against injury.

Section 55 and its equivalents do not affect any obligation of the defendant to provide a *warning* of an inherent risk. Thus, a defendant might be liable for failing to warn of an inherent risk where the circumstances reasonably required that a warning be given. For example, a medical practitioner will not be liable merely because the patient suffers a complication or side-effect of an operation if the particular complication or side-effect could not be avoided by the exercise of reasonable care. However, depending on the significance of the risk, the medical practitioner might be liable for failing to warn of the possibility that that complication or side-effect might occur. Accordingly, a number of medical negligence cases have been conducted not on the basis that the medical practitioner performed the operation negligently, but on the basis that the medical practitioner was negligent in failing to warn of the relevant risk.[33] Likewise, it has been said that one of the inherent risks of swimming in the ocean is being 'dumped' by a wave.[34] The public authority that manages that beach area has no control over the natural forces that determine wave size and therefore will not be liable merely by virtue of the fact that a person was injured when dumped by a wave. Consequently, the focus of the litigation will ordinarily be whether the public authority should reasonably have warned of the risks, especially where the waves are unusually large.

INDIVIDUAL RESPONSIBILITY AND COMMUNITY STANDARDS

The central question in any negligence case is whether it is reasonable to impose upon the defendant the duty contended by the plaintiff.[35] This judgment has to

---

33. See, for example: *Rogers v Whitaker* (1992) 175 CLR 479; *Chappel v Hart* (1998) 195 CLR 232; *Rosenberg v Percival* (2001) 205 CLR 434.
34. For example: *Prast v Town of Cottesloe* (2000) 22 WAR 475.
35. See, for example: *Romeo v Conservation Commission (NT)* (1998) 192 CLR 431 at [128], per Kirby J; *Woods v Multi-Sport Holdings Pty Ltd* (2002) 208 CLR 460 at [39], per Gleeson CJ; *Cole v South Tweed Heads Rugby League Football Club Limited* [2004] HCA 29 at [18], per Gleeson CJ.

be made by considering all the circumstances of the case, not merely by a rigid application of the calculus of negligence. For as Gleeson CJ and Kirby J declared in *Mulligan v Coffs Harbour* [2005] HCA 63 (at [3]):

> This Court recently said, in *Thompson v Woolworths (Q'land) Pty Ltd*, that reasonableness may require no response to a foreseeable risk, and pointed out that householders do not ordinarily place notices at their front doors warning entrants of all the dangers that await them if they fail to take reasonable care for their own safety. *That observation was not the product of a calculus; it was simply a statement about community standards of reasonable behaviour.* [emphasis added]

Indeed, in a series of cases the High Court has emphasised that notions of individual choice and responsibility are factors to be taken into account in determining the reasonableness of the defendant's conduct. Such decisions as *Romeo v Conservation Commission (NT)* (1998) 192 CLR 431; *Woods v Multi-Sport Holdings Pty Ltd* (2002) 208 CLR 460; *Cole v South Tweed Heads Rugby League Football Club Ltd* [2004] HCA 29;[36] and *Neindorf v Junkovic* [2005] HCA 75 demonstrate a deliberate shift away from the previous position—which protected claimants against their own failure to take reasonable care[37]—to an approach that places a greater weight on the responsibility of individuals to take reasonable care for themselves (*Boyded Industries Pty Ltd v Canuto* [2004] NSWCA 256 at [4], per Beazley JA).

However, it is difficult to discern a consistent trend in the approach of the High Court to the issue of personal responsibility. For example, in *Manley v Alexander* [2005] HCA 79,[38] the plaintiff sustained injury when he was struck by a tow truck driven by the defendant at about 4 am while lying in the middle of the road. He had consumed twelve stubbies of beer in the preceding eight hours, and had no recollection of how he came to be on the roadway. The defendant testified that while his attention was drawn to the side of the road by the plaintiff's friend, Mr Turner, he maintained a speed of between 55 and 60 kilometres per hour, and veered to the centre of the road, thus running over the plaintiff, whom he did not see. The majority of the High Court (Gummow, Kirby, and Hayne JJ) accepted that the form of the plaintiff was well illuminated by street lights and the defendant had an uninterrupted view of the road ahead. The lights cast by the vehicle headlights extended about sixty metres ahead of the vehicle, providing the defendant with a reasonable time to avoid the plaintiff. Their Honours stated that (at [11]–[12]):

---

36. The factors of knowledge, voluntary conduct and individual responsibility are also central to the defence of voluntary assumption of risk, discussed in Chapter 17.
37. The high-water mark of this approach was the High Court decision in *Nagle v Rottnest Island Authority* (1993) 177 CLR 423.
38. See also: *Thompson v Woolworths (Q'land) Pty Limited* [2005] HCA 19, discussed in Chapter 17.

No doubt the appellant's attention was drawn to the figure of Mr Turner standing at the side of the road and behaving in a way that suggested that he might act in some way that would require the appellant to respond. But recognising one possible source of danger does not mean that a driver can or must give exclusive attention to that danger. Driving requires reasonable attention to all that is happening on and near the roadway that may present a source of danger. And much more often than not, that will require simultaneous attention to, and consideration of, a number of different features of what is already, or may later come to be, ahead of the vehicle's path.[39]

Callinan and Heydon JJ in dissent noted (at [43]) that the decision by the Full Court, which found the defendant negligent:

> assumes that a motorist is not entitled to give attention to a particular and potentially dangerous emergency situation in priority to an apparently benign one. To the appellant the situation on the road itself appeared benign, because it was extremely unlikely that at the time and place in question, a mature adult dressed in dark clothing, whether drunk or sober, would be lying in the centre of a wet roadway, approximately parallel to it, and unable to move, or uninterested in moving, out of the way of a relatively slow moving large motor vehicle with its headlights illuminated.

According to their Honours, in those circumstances it was reasonable for the defendant to concentrate his attention for a time on the peril presented by the risk of Mr Turner, who was clearly inebriated, moving on to the road.

It is questionable whether the majority decision reflects community standards regarding what can reasonably be expected of drivers and pedestrians—or rather, of persons lying in a drunken stupor—on our roads. In any event, there are now statutory provisions in New South Wales, Queensland and Victoria that affect claims by intoxicated plaintiffs. These will be discussed below.

RELEVANCE OF THE OBVIOUS NATURE OF THE RISK

A relevant factor in determining breach is whether the plaintiff failed to exercise reasonable care to avoid an obvious risk of injury. The notion that the duty to take reasonable care might not in some circumstances extend to obvious risks, was first articulated by the High Court of Australia, in *Romeo v Conservation Commission of the Northern Territory* (1998) 192 CLR 431, in relation to public authorities. The majority of the court held that it was not reasonable to require a public authority to provide a warning to persons entering a cliff-top reserve about the risks of walking

---

39. The plaintiff's damages were reduced by 70 per cent for his contributory negligence.

over a cliff or to erect a barrier at the cliff edge, as the dangers were obvious. The authority was entitled to expect that entrants to the cliff would exercise reasonable care for their own safety and would not ignore the obvious dangers posed by the cliffs. Kirby J expressed the principle as follows (at [123], emphasis added):

> While account must be taken of the possibility of inadvertence or negligent conduct on the part of entrants, the occupier is generally entitled to assume that most entrants will take reasonable care for their own safety. For example, it would be neither reasonable nor just to impose upon a body such as the Commission an obligation to erect secure climb-proof fencing along the entire elevated headland of the reserve against the risk of injury suffered by the occasional visitor bent on suicide. ... [T]he scope of the duty of care imposed by the common law will be no more than that of reasonable care. *Where a risk is obvious to a person exercising reasonable care for his or her own safety, the notion that the occupier must warn the entrant about that risk is neither reasonable nor just.*

In *Woods v Multi-Sport Holdings Pty Ltd* (2002) 208 CLR 460 the High Court discussed the relevance of the obviousness of the risk to the breach of duty inquiry. The majority of the court, Gleeson CJ (at [43]–[45]), Hayne J (at [144]), and Callinan J (at [159]), held that the operator of an indoor cricket venue had not breached its duty of care to the plaintiff by failing to warn the plaintiff of the risk of being hit in the eye with a ball while playing the game, because the risk was so obvious that reasonableness did not require a warning. According to Hayne J (at [144]), given the risks involved, it was evident to all participants that any player could suffer all kinds of 'serious injury, even permanent and disabling injury', thus there was no 'reason to single out one form of injury and warn of that'.

These High Court decisions have been applied by lower courts in a variety of contexts to deny liability in situations where the risk should have been apparent to the plaintiff. In *Gillies v Saddington* [2004] NSWCA 110, the plaintiff was walking down the steep slope of the driveway of the defendant's home when she slipped, fell and injured herself. According to Giles JA (Sheller and Ipp JJ agreeing), it would have been obvious to a person of ordinary experience that the driveway would be slippery when wet, and that they would need to take appropriately cautious steps. Consequently, the defendant was not negligent in failing to provide an alternative means of access to his home, such as a flight of stairs.[40] In *Clarke v Coleambally Ski Club Inc* [2004] NSWCA 376 the plaintiff swung across a river on a rope and attempted a backwards somersault into the water, landing feet-first. He misjudged the situation and entered shallow water head first, striking his head on the bottom and becoming a quadriplegic. The ski club, which had effective control over that part of the river was held not to have acted unreasonably in failing to remove the

---

40. See also: *Waterways Authority v Mathews* [2003] NSWCA 330, where the plaintiff, who slipped on wet rocks, was denied a claim as the risk was obvious.

rope or the branch from which it was hanging. Ipp JA (at [23]–[24], Beazley JA agreeing), concluded that the club was entitled to rely on the fact that swinging on a rope and attempting a backwards somersault into the water is 'so obviously dangerous that no person, taking reasonable care for his or her safety, would do such a thing.'

These decisions should not, however, be thought to have created a general principle of common law that there is no duty to warn against or prevent even an obvious risk. In *Woods v Multi-Sport Holdings Pty Ltd* (2002) 208 CLR 460, Kirby J pointed out (at [128]) that:

> Warnings are sometimes required by those in control of situations to alert those who are inattentive, distracted or unlikely in the circumstances to consider the risk, although objectively, and with hindsight, it is 'obvious'.

The approach of the High Court to the issue of obviousness is yet to be crystallised. In such cases as *Brodie v Singleton Shire Council*; *Woods v Multi-Sport Holdings Pty Ltd*; and *Swain v Waverley Municipal Council*,[41] the High Court indicated that the obvious nature of the danger is only one factor to be taken into account in determining the reasonableness of the defendant's response. In *Thompson v Woolworths (Q'Land) Pty Ltd*, [2005] HCA 19, Gleeson CJ, McHugh, Kirby, Hayne and Heydon JJ, in a joint judgment, opined (at [37]) that:

> The factual judgment involved in a decision about what is reasonably to be expected of a person who owes a duty of care to another involves an interplay of considerations. The weight to be given to any one of them is likely to vary according to circumstances. If the obviousness of a risk, and the reasonableness of an expectation that other people will take care for their own safety, were conclusive against liability in every case, there would be little room for a doctrine of contributory negligence. On the other hand, if those considerations were irrelevant, community standards of reasonable behaviour would require radical alteration.

Jurisprudential dilemmas facing the High Court in relation to deciding whether obviousness is a conceptual determinant of the scope of duty of care—or merely one of the factors to be taken into account in relation to the breach of duty—were highlighted in *Vairy v Wyong Shire Council* [2005] HCA 62 and *Mulligan v Coffs Harbour City Council* [2005] HCA 63. These were companion cases heard by the court together. In both cases, the plaintiffs suffered serious spinal injuries as a result of diving into water without first checking the depth. In both cases, the plaintiffs failed to establish a breach of duty by the local authority in control of the swimming

---

41. *Brodie v Singleton Shire Council; Ghantous v Hawkesbury City Council* (2001) 206 CLR 512; *Woods v Multi-Sport Holdings Pty Ltd* (2002) 208 CLR 460; 201 ALR 470; *Swain v Waverley Municipal Council* (2005) 79 ALJR 565; 213 ALR 249.

area for failing to erect a sign warning of the risks of diving, although views differed in the various judgments as to the weight to be given to the 'obviousness factor' as a determinative of breach. In *Vairy*, Gleeson and Kirby JJ considered that the obvious nature of the danger is only one factor to be taken into account in determining whether reasonable care required the avoidance of that obvious danger. Having noted (at [7]) that 'the obviousness of a danger can be important in deciding whether a warning is required', they concluded (at [8]):

> It is impossible to state comprehensively, or by a single formula, the circumstances in which reasonableness requires a warning. The question is not answered by comparing the cost of a warning sign with the seriousness of possible harm to an injured person. Often, the answer will be influenced by the obviousness of the danger, the expectation that persons will take reasonable care for their own safety, and a consideration of the range of hazards naturally involved in recreational pursuits.

Likewise, McHugh J (at [55], [95]), Gummow J (at [95]) and Hayne J (at [162]–[163]) took the view that 'reference to a risk being "obvious" cannot be used as a concept necessarily determinative of questions of breach of duty'. McHugh J (at [46]) (with whom Hayne J (at [162]) agreed), observed that 'The obviousness of the risk goes to the issue of the plaintiff's contributory negligence, rarely to the discharge of the defendant's duty.' Hayne J (at [163]) stressed that since the 'focus of inquiry [at the breach of duty stage] must remain upon the putative tortfeasor, not upon the person who has been injured, and not upon others who may avoid injury': 'the obviousness factor' is not to be elevated into some doctrine or general rule of law.[42]

In contrast, Callinan and Heydon JJ adopted (at [223]) all statements they had expressed in *Mulligan v Coffs Harbour City* when they held:

> obviousness may be of such importance, indeed of such a very high degree of importance as to be overwhelmingly so, and effectively conclusive in some cases.

Having observed (*Mulligan* at [78]) that '[o]bviousness of a risk very much conditions the response, or even the necessity for any response at all to it', their Honours (at [80]) provided the following policy reasons for their approach:

> The imperialism of the law of torts has had many beneficial products. Employers, governments, statutory authorities and others have been forced to exercise their minds in the interests of those who may be injured by their conduct and to

---

42. In *Berrigan Shire Council v Ballerini & Anor* [2005] VSCA 159, a case of diving from a log, Nettle JA (at [54]) echoed this approach, when he said that: 'Obviousness of a risk is one factor to be considered as part of that process. But obviousness of risk is not a principle, and as a proposition of fact it is not of universal validity.' His Honour relied on *Romeo v Conservation Commission of the Northern Territory* (1998) 192 CLR 431 at [123], and *Woods v Multi-Sport Holdings Pty Ltd* (2002) 208 CLR 460 at [45] (per Gleeson CJ), and at [127] (per Kirby J).

improve performance accordingly. Even empires must however have their borders and equally, society should be entitled to expect that people will take elementary precautions at least for their own safety against obvious risks. ... It is only reasonably to be expected that people will conduct themselves according to dictates of common sense, which must include the observation of, and an appropriately careful response to what is obvious. Courts in deciding whether that response has been made are bound to keep in mind that defendants have rights and interests too. A tendency to see cases through the eyes of plaintiffs only is to be avoided.

To summarise the common law position, it is not a universal proposition of law that there can never be a duty to warn of an obvious risk or to take steps to prevent that risk eventuating. The ultimate question in each case is what action a reasonable defendant would have taken in all of the circumstances of the case in response to the foreseeable risk. However, the fact that the danger should have been obvious to the plaintiff will in many circumstances be a significant, perhaps critical, factor in determining the reasonableness of the defendant's conduct.

Statutory provisions

Some jurisdictions have statutory provisions that deny liability in certain contexts where the risk was obvious. Although the definition of an 'obvious risk' varies slightly between the jurisdictions, s 5F of the *Civil Liability Act 2002* (NSW) is representative of these provisions:[43]

(1) For the purposes of this Division, an *obvious risk* to a person who suffers harm is a risk that, in the circumstances, would have been obvious to a reasonable person in the position of that person.
(2) Obvious risks include risks that are patent or a matter of common knowledge.
(3) A risk of something occurring can be an obvious risk even though it has a low probability of occurring.
(4) A risk can be an obvious risk even if the risk (or a condition or circumstance that gives rise to the risk) is not prominent, conspicuous or physically observable.

In all jurisdictions other than the Territories,[44] the legislation raises a presumption of awareness of obvious risk, which reverses the common law burden of proof. For example, *Civil Liability Act 2002* (NSW), s 5G, provides:

---

43. See also: *Civil Liability Act 2003* (Qld), s 13; *Civil Liability Act 1936* (SA), s 36; *Civil Liability Act 2002* (Tas), s 15; *Civil Liability Act 2002* (WA), s 5F; *Wrongs Act 1958* (Vic), s 53.
44. *Civil Liability Act 2002* (NSW), s 5G; *Civil Liability Act 2003* (Qld), s 14; *Civil Liability Act 1936* (SA), s 37; *Civil Liability Act 2002* (Tas), s 16; *Civil Liability Act 2002* (WA), s 5N; *Wrongs Act 1958* (Vic), s 54.

(1) In determining liability for negligence, a person who suffers harm is presumed to have been aware of the risk of harm if it was an obvious risk, unless the person proves on the balance of probabilities that he or she was not aware of the risk.

The risk is defined very broadly:

(2) For the purposes of this section, a person is aware of a risk if the person is aware of the type or kind of risk, even if the person is not aware of the precise nature, extent or manner of occurrence of the risk.

Likewise, legislation in New South Wales, Queensland, South Australia, Tasmania, and Western Australia provides that the defendant does not owe a duty of care to warn the plaintiff of an obvious risk.[45] The effect of these provisions is that the obvious nature of the risk will of itself determine whether the defendant owed a duty to warn of that risk. These provisions, however, do not apply in the following specified circumstances:[46]

(a) the plaintiff has requested advice or information about the risk from the defendant, or

(b) the defendant is required by a written law to warn the plaintiff of the risk, or

(c) the defendant is a professional and the risk is a risk of the death of or personal injury to the plaintiff from the provision of a professional service by the defendant.

New South Wales, Queensland, Tasmania, and Western Australia also have specific provisions relating to dangerous recreational activities. They provide that the defendant is not liable in negligence for harm suffered by the plaintiff as a result of the materialisation of an obvious risk of a dangerous recreational activity engaged in by the plaintiff, whether or not the plaintiff was aware of the risk.[47] A 'dangerous recreational activity' is defined as a recreational activity that involves a significant risk of harm.[48] A 'recreational activity' includes any sport and any pursuit or activity engaged in for enjoyment, relaxation or leisure.[49]

The New South Wales provisions concerning obvious risk were considered by the New South Wales Court of Appeal in *Doubleday v Kelly* [2005] NSWCA 151, the case (discussed above) of the seven-year-old girl who was injured while skating

---

45. *Civil Liability Act 2002* (NSW), s 5H; *Civil Liability Act 2003* (Qld), s 15; *Civil Liability Act 1936* (SA), s 38; *Civil Liability Act 2002* (Tas), s 17;. *Civil Liability Act 2002* (WA), s 5O.
46. Id.
47. *Civil Liability Act 2003* (Qld), s 19; *Civil Liability Act 2002* (NSW), s 5L; *Civil Liability Act 2002* (Tas), s 20; *Civil Liability Act 2002* (WA), s 5H.
48. *Civil Liability Act 2002* (NSW), s 5K; *Civil Liability Act 2003* (Qld), s 18; *Civil Liability Act 2002* (Tas), s 19; *Civil Liability Act 2002* (WA), s 5E.
49. Id.

on top of a trampoline. The issue was whether the risk of falling off the trampoline was 'a risk that, in the circumstances, would have been obvious to a reasonable person in the position of the [plaintiff]' (s 5F). The defendants contended that the full force of this provision applies to children as if they are adults. The fact the plaintiff was a child of seven was said to be irrelevant, as the reference is to a generalised reasonable person. The court rejected that argument, Bryson JA holding that s 5F:

> requires consideration of the position of the person who suffers harm and whatever else is relevant to establishing that position. The characteristics of being a child with no previous experience in the use of trampolines or roller skates, who chose to get up early in the morning and play unsupervised, is part of that position.

As a reasonable seven-year-old would not regard a trampoline as an obvious risk, the obvious risk provisions in the legislation did not apply to the claim. This view reflects the general principle that children are not to be held responsible to the same degree of care as an adult (see below, and Chapter 17).

Intoxicated plaintiffs

In *Manley v Alexander* [2005] HCA 79 (discussed above), the High Court held that a plaintiff who was struck by a car when lying in a drunken stupor in the middle of the road was entitled to recover damages from the driver of the vehicle that struck him. There are now statutory provisions in some jurisdictions that modify the common law approach.[50] For instance, s 14G of the Victorian *Wrongs Act 1958* provides that, in determining whether a defendant has breached a duty of care, Victorian courts must take into consideration whether the plaintiff was intoxicated by alcohol or drugs that were consumed voluntarily, as well as the level of the intoxication. The effect of s 14G is to require courts to consider whether it would be unreasonable to require a defendant to take increased precautions to avoid a foreseeable risk of injury to persons who were intoxicated or acting unlawfully at the time of the injury. In that event, recovery will be denied to a plaintiff who would probably not have suffered injury had he or she been sober and acting lawfully at the time of the injury.

Legislation in New South Wales specifically prohibits an award of damages where it is likely the plaintiff would not have suffered the injury if sober.[51] Legislation in that State and in Queensland also provides that, in determining whether a duty of care arises, it is not relevant to consider the possibility or likelihood that a

---

50. *Civil Liability Act 2002* (Tas), s 5; *Civil Liability Act 2002* (WA), s 5L; *Civil Liability Act 1936* (SA), s 46; *Civil Liability Act 2003* (Qld), s 47; *Civil Liability Act 2002* (NSW), s 50; see also: *Personal Injuries (Liabilities and Damages) Act 2003* (NT), s 14.
51. *Civil Liability Act 2002* (NSW), s 50.

person may be intoxicated or that a person who is intoxicated may be exposed to increased risk because the person's capacity to exercise reasonable care and skill is impaired as a result of being intoxicated.[52] Furthermore, in those jurisdictions, the fact that a person is or may be intoxicated will not of itself increase or otherwise affect the standard of care owed to the person.[53]

Pursuant to these statutory provisions, it is unlikely that a person in the position of the plaintiff in *Manley v Alexander* would be permitted to recover damages in negligence, as he would not have been lying in the middle of the road but for his intoxicated state.

Failure to warn

Ever since *Nagle v Rottnest Island Authority* (1993) 177 CLR 423, plaintiffs in negligence actions have routinely pleaded the failure of a defendant to provide a warning of the foreseeable risk. In *Nagle*, the then 29-year-old plaintiff decided to go for a swim at the Basin on Rottnest Island in Western Australia. He walked up to the Basin, a small, sand-bottomed, U-shaped bathing area surrounded by steep limestone cliffs on all sides except for a flat rock area known as a wave platform, and dived into the water. The bed of the basin was below the low-water mark. At the time, the tide was approximately thirty centimetres above the low-water level, so the wave platform was submerged in about five centimetres of water. The plaintiff's view below the surface of the water could have been impaired by the glitter of sun reflection, but he could see other rocks in the line of rocks adjacent to the wave platform on the eastern perimeter. There were six rocks in this line. Mr Nagle saw rocks 1 and 2 but did not see rock 3, which was the rock onto which he dived. He struck his head on the submerged rock and as a result of his injuries became quadriplegic. The High Court found that the Rottnest Island Board breached its duty of care to the plaintiff by failing to provide warning signs that the ledge from which he dived into a rock pool was unsafe for diving. Although the case seems to have been interpreted as standing for the proposition that there is a duty to warn of hidden risks, the provision of a warning came to be considered a cheap and practical means of avoiding the incident, and therefore the expected 'necessary minimum' response of the defendant. Plaintiffs have often argued that the occupier of recreational premises or the local authority managing recreational area should have erected signs warning of the risks of those activities. However, recently, many of these claims have been unsuccessful as the courts have determined the fact that the risk would have been apparent to a reasonable person in the plaintiff's position

---

52. *Civil Liability Act 2002* (NSW), s 49; *Civil Liability Act 2003* (Qld), s 46.
53. Ibid. Most jurisdictions also exclude claims for damages where the accident happened while the injured person was engaged in conduct that is a serious offence, and that conduct 'contributed materially' to the injury. These provisions will be discussed further in Chapter 17, dealing with defences to negligence.

as a factor indicating that it was not unreasonable for the defendant not to provide a warning. Apart from *Woods v Multi Sport Holdings* (2002) 208 CLR 460, the 'obviousness' factor has been relied upon to hold that a local authority is under no obligation to warn that seaside rocks will be slippery if waves wash over them,[54] and that an employer has no obligation to warn an employee that a glass table might break if sat on,[55] or not to attempt to lift unaided a 65 kilogram refrigerator cabinet.[56] In *The University of Wollongong v Mitchell* [2003] NSWCA 94, the plaintiff was injured when she tried to sit down on a theatre seat that had automatically retracted when she had vacated it a short time previously. Her claim that the defendant was negligent in failing to warn entrants about the need to push the seat down before sitting on it was dismissed on the basis that any danger of not doing so would have been 'glaringly obvious'.[57] Meagher JA (at [10]–[13]) commented that:

> since every object can in some circumstances be dangerous, it would be inconvenient (to say the least) if it had to carry its own warning notice. The surface of the earth would be covered with notices—which, among other things, would distract people from reading any relevant notice. Worse, in these multi-cultural and anti-discriminatory days, each notice would have to be duplicated in each of the one hundred and fifty languages spoken in Australia.

In the course of application for special leave to appeal to the High Court, the following exchange took place between Mr Rayment, Counsel for the plaintiff, and Gleeson CJ:

> Mr Rayment: His Honour [Meagher J] there says that, in effect, there could not be a warning sign put up because, in this multicultural society, you would have to put up hundreds of warning signs in hundreds of different languages …
>
> Gleeson CJ: A warning of hundreds of different risks that we all encounter from the moment we get out of bed in the morning.[58]

The plaintiff's application was refused with costs.

Statutory provisions

In New South Wales, Queensland, South Australia, Tasmania, and Western Australia it is provided that the defendant does not owe a duty of care to warn the plaintiff of an obvious risk. Section 50 of the Victorian *Wrongs Act 1958* emphasises that where

---

54. *Waverley Municipal Council v Lodge* (2001) 117 LGERA 447. See also: *Waterways Authority v Mathews* [2003] NSWCA 330.
55. *Boyded Industries P/L v Canuto* [2004] NSWCA 256.
56. *Australian Traineeship System v Wafta* [2004] NSWCA 230.
57. *The University of Wollongong v Mitchell* [2003] NSWCA 94 at [13], per Meagher JA; see also: [37], per Giles JA.
58. *Mitchell v University of Wollongong* [2004] HCA Trans 181 (28 May 2004).

a defendant does have a duty to warn or provide information in respect of a matter, the defendant will satisfy that duty by taking reasonable care in giving that warning or other information.

PUBLIC AUTHORITIES

The High Court in recent judgments has identified two principles as being particularly important to determining the liability of public authorities for injuries suffered by entrants onto land under the control of the authority. First, the fact that the risk in question should have been obvious to the person injured or was an ordinary risk of engaging in an activity of that kind will often be a significant factor in determining liability. Second, liability will not generally be imposed unless the site where the accident occurred contained a risk of injury that was materially different from similar or greater risks of injury in other areas under the control of the authority. For convenience, the authorities will be grouped under two headings: claims arising from recreational activities, and claims against road authorities.

Recreational injuries

The High Court decision in *Romeo v Conservation Commission (NT)* has been referred to above. The lower courts have followed this decision in a number of cases involving claims for injuries suffered by persons engaging in recreational activities on public land.[59] For instance, in *The Secretary to the Department of Natural Resources and Energy v Harper* [2000] VSCA 36, a majority of the Court of Appeal of Victoria held that a national parks authority was under no obligation to warn visitors to State forests of the risks of being injured by a falling tree during high winds. In dismissing the appeal, Batt JA pointed out (at [47]) that the risk of a tree falling is 'endemic' or 'part and parcel of the recreation of camping, walking and indeed living outdoors in the Australian bush.' His Honour concluded (at [48]) that the authority was entitled to rely on the fact that adults entering the park would know that trees and limbs of trees in forests, reserves, and parks will occasionally fall—at any rate in high winds—and will do so randomly. Furthermore, it was unreasonable to expect that the authority would erect warning signs at every place in every reserve under its control where persons might be likely to camp or walk. Tadgell JA observed (at [6]) that there was no reason to differentiate the particular risk that materialised in this case from the variety of other hazards—'animal, vegetable or mineral'—which face a person who enters a national park.

---

59. See, for instance: *Waverley Municipal Council v Lodge* (2001) 117 LGERA 447; *Waterways Authority v Mathews* [2003] NSWCA 330.

In *Prast v Town of Cottesloe* (2000) 22 WAR 474, the plaintiff became a quadriplegic as a result of being dumped by a wave and hurled against the seabed while bodysurfing. The court held that the local authority did not breach its duty of care by failing to warn of this risk, as it was an inherent risk of swimming in the ocean that was obvious and well known. Special warnings might be required if there were especially dangerous currents or rips or surges peculiar to the particular beach, but in this case the risk to the plaintiff was an ordinary risk of the common, everyday activity of swimming in the sea. The obligation of authorities to warn entrants of risks associated with the pursuit of recreational activities on land controlled by public authorities has been considered by the High Court in *Vairy v Wyong Shire Council* and *Mulligan v Coffs Harbour* (discussed above): Mr Vairy had dived from a rock platform into the sea at a popular beach, and Mr Mulligan had dived forward into a submerged sandform from a standing position in thigh-deep water in a creek. The claims were conducted on the basis that the local authorities controlling and managing the area had breached their duty of care by failing to erect signs warning of the dangers of diving or prohibiting diving. The High Court rejected both claims (by majority in *Vairy* and unanimously in *Mulligan*).

Although there were five separate judgments in each case, and each judgment contains differing emphases (and a disagreement on the facts in *Vairy*), a number of common propositions or themes can be extracted from these cases:

1   The ultimate question is whether the defendant acted reasonably in all of the circumstances in failing to warn of the risk. The fact that the risk should have been obvious to the plaintiff will not of itself lead to a conclusion that the defendant did not owe a duty to warn of that risk, but it will often be an important factor to be considered in determining reasonableness.

2   In determining whether the public authority should have taken precautions to prevent the occurrence of the foreseeable risk, the court must take into account the range of hazards faced by an entrant onto the land and determine whether there was a reason to differentiate the particular hazard that faced the plaintiff from all the other potential risks of injury. The scope of the defendant's duty of care must be assessed against the background of the whole multitude of risks that may crystallise on the land that is the responsibility of the authority, and not just by reference to the risk that eventuated in the particular case.[60] The countryside would be littered with warning signs if the authorities were required to warn of each and every possible danger confronting persons coming upon their land. The relevant principles were formulated by Gleeson CJ and Kirby J in *Vairy* (at [7]) as follows:

---

60. *Vairy v Wyong Shire Council* [2005] HCA 62 at [7], per Gleeson CJ and Kirby; at [89], [94], [96], per Gummow J; at [122]–[124], per Hayne J; at [218], per Callinan and Heydon JJ. This point had previously been made by members of the majority in *Romeo v Conservation Commission (NT)* (1998) 192 CLR 431 at [54], per Toohey and Gummow JJ; at [164]–[165], per Hayne J.

[a] conclusion that a public authority, acting reasonably, ought to have given a warning ordinarily requires a fairly clear idea of the content of the warning, considered in the context of all the potential risks facing an entrant upon the land in question. When a person encounters a particular hazard, suffers injury, and then claims that he or she should have been warned, it may be necessary to ask: why should that particular hazard have been singled out?[61]

Their Honours stated that a duty to warn of all hazards irrespective of their obviousness and 'any reasonable expectation that people would take reasonable care for their own safety' would make the signs 'either so general, or so numerous, as to be practically ineffective'. They then wryly observed that:

> If the owner of a ski resort set up warning signs at every place where someone who failed to take reasonable care might suffer harm, the greatest risk associated with downhill skiing would be that of being impaled on a warning sign.

3 A public authority would generally only be required to take precautions against a potential risk where the accident site possesses features that would differentiate it from other sites that carry a similar risk or which would increase the risk of injury. Relevant features might include encouragement by the local authority to pursue a dangerous recreational activity on its land, a natural feature of the site that makes it more likely to be used for a risky recreational activity or that increases the risk of injury at that particular site, and knowledge by the authority that others have previously used the site for the risky activity in question.

4 A determination in a previous case that a warning was or was not required is of limited precedential value for future cases. A conclusion as to whether it was reasonable to require the defendant to provide a warning will turn upon the circumstances of the particular case before the court.[62] Previous cases where claims for diving injuries against public authorities were successful can be distinguished on the basis either that they should be confined to their own particular facts,[63] or as being jury decisions which should not lightly be interfered with.[64]

The common law principles from *Vairy* and *Mulligan* are modified by legislation in some jurisdictions. (The plaintiffs in *Vairy* and *Mulligan* commenced their actions before the relevant New South Wales reforms came into effect). In

---

61. See also: *Commissioner of Main Roads v Jones* (2005) 214 ALR 249 at 251.
62. *Vairy v Wyong Shire Council* [2005] HCA 62 at [3]–[4], per Gleeson CJ and Kirby J; at [31], per McHugh J; at [118], per Hayne J; at [208], per Callinan and Heydon JJ; *Mulligan v Coffs Harbour City Council* [2005] HCA 63 at [1], per Gleeson CJ and Kirby J.
63. As in *Nagle v Rottnest Island Authority* (1993) 177 CLR 423.
64. As in *Swain v Waverley Municipal Council* (2005) 213 ALR 249.

New South Wales, Queensland, South Australia, Tasmania, Victoria, and Western Australia, the defendant does not owe a duty of care to warn the plaintiff of an obvious risk. Also, as noted above, in these jurisdictions (other than South Australia and Victoria) the defendant is not liable for the materialisation of an obvious risk of a dangerous recreational activity. Therefore, the primary focus of litigation in those States will be whether the risk would have been obvious to a reasonable person in the plaintiff's position, and whether the recreational activity can be construed as 'dangerous', in the sense that it carries a significant risk of harm.

Road authorities

A road authority has a duty to take reasonable care for the safety of road users. It will be liable for the negligent construction and design of a road, as well as for its negligent management of the road environment. Road authorities previously enjoyed immunity from liability in respect of non-feasance, which was overturned by the High Court in 2001 in *Brodie v Singleton Shire Council; Ghantous v Hawkesbury City Council* (2001) 206 CLR 512 (see Chapter 14). Following *Ghantous*, at common law a road authority is required to exercise reasonable care to ensure that roads and abutting footpaths and pavements are maintained in a reasonable state of repair for users. By virtue of statute in most jurisdictions, this duty extends only to faults in the road or pavement of which the authority had *actual* knowledge. In *Brodie* the plaintiff was injured when the bridge over which he drove his truck partially collapsed. The shire council responsible for the bridge was found to have breached its duty of care to safely maintain the bridge. The council knew the bridge was dangerous but had merely carried out piecemeal rectification without addressing the fundamental problem that made the bridge unsafe. The bridge had a superficial appearance of safety, and a number of trucks had crossed it without harm earlier on the day of the accident.

The majority in *Brodie* (at [15]) opined that road authorities were obliged to take reasonable care to ensure that their decision whether or not to exercise their powers does not create a foreseeable risk of harm to road users. At the same time, authorities do not have an obligation to ensure the safety of all road users in all circumstances. In *Commissioner of Main Roads v Jones* [2005] HCA 27, the plaintiff suffered serious injuries when the car he was driving collided with a horse on a stretch of unfenced road on the Great Northern Highway in the Kimberley district of Western Australia. The plaintiff argued that the road authority responsible for controlling the highway had breached its duty of care by failing to erect road signs in the locality warning of the danger of animals on the highway, and/or by failing to impose a speed limit lower than the general limit of 110 kilometres per hour. The High Court held that the road authority had not breached its duty of care. The evidence did not establish an unusual concentration of wild animals near the accident site, or a particular propensity for animals to approach that section of the highway, that could have led to the conclusion that the risk of a car striking an animal was greater than in other areas, so as to warrant the measures for which the plaintiff contended. It would be unreasonable to require the authority to shift warning signs from time to time as animal migration patterns changed.

In *Ghantous* the High Court also stated that road authorities are generally entitled to expect that road users will take reasonable care for their own safety. This is particularly the case where the plaintiff is a pedestrian rather than the driver of a motor vehicle, because generally those persons are in a better position to be able to see and avoid imperfections in the road surface. According to Gaudron, McHugh, and Gummow JJ (at [163]), pedestrians 'ordinarily will be expected to exercise sufficient care by looking where they are going and perceiving obvious hazards, such as uneven paving stones, tree roots or holes'. Although each case will turn on its own facts, ordinarily a pedestrian plaintiff has to establish the danger was not apparent because of inadequate lighting or because the surrounding area created a danger in the nature of a 'trap'.[65] Gleeson CJ (at [7], citing *Littler v Liverpool Corporation* [1986] 2 All ER 343 at 345), pointed out that not all pavements and footpaths are perfectly level, and people are regularly required to walk on uneven surfaces both on public and on private land: a road 'is not to be criticised by the standards of a bowling green'.

These principles have been applied in a large number of lower-court decisions to deny claims where the hazard would have been obvious to a pedestrian keeping a reasonable lookout.[66] As a general rule, the particular characteristics of the adult plaintiff, such as his or her old age or infirmity, are not taken into account when assessing the required standard of care. For example, in *Richmond Valley Council v Standing* [2002] NSWCA 359, the New South Wales Court of Appeal (at [47]) declined to hold that a council owed a duty of care to an elderly pedestrian that was higher than that owed to the ordinary pedestrian. Because the plaintiff was elderly and therefore more vulnerable to falls, she should have exercised a higher degree of vigilance for her own safety.[67] Likewise, the courts have declined to find that a higher duty of care is owed to a pedestrian with weak legs,[68] who is intoxicated,[69] or who is running or jogging.[70] The duty of the authority is to ensure the footpath is reasonably safe for the ordinary, reasonable pedestrian keeping a reasonable

---

65. See Chernov JA in: *Boroondara City Council v Cattanach* [2004] VSCA 139 for a review of a number of cases where the danger would not have been obvious to the reasonable person.
66. For a review of the main authorities, see: Chernov JA in *Boroondara City Council v Cattanach* [2004] VSCA 139 and *Ryde City Council v Saleh* [2004] NSWCA 219.
67. This reasoning was adopted in *Hastings Council v Giese* [2003] NSWCA 178 at [31]. See also: *Moyne Shire Council v Pearce* [2004] VSCA 246.
68. *Roads and Traffic Authority of NSW v McGuinness* [2002] NSWCA 210.
69. *Parsons v Randwick Municipal Council* [2003] NSWCA 171.
70. *Boroondara City Council v Cattanach* [2004] VSCA 139; cf *Newcastle City Council v McShane* [2004] NSWCA 425.

lookout; it is not required to guarantee that it is safe for the wide range of persons who might be using the footpath for a wide range of activities.[71]

However, it will be unreasonable for an authority to fail to repair a defect in a footpath where the defect is concealed or in the nature of a 'trap' that could not be observed with a reasonable lookout. Further, the full circumstances of each case must be considered to determine whether the defect would have been obvious to the particular pedestrian in the particular circumstances of the injury.[72] Under legislation in all jurisdictions[73] other than the Northern Territory and South Australia, which continue with full pre-*Brodie* immunity,[74] the obligation of a road authority to maintain and repair roads extends only to particular risks of harm of which the authority had *actual* knowledge.[75] Thus, it is not sufficient that the authority *ought* to have known of the deterioration of the road or the footpath; the plaintiff must prove that the authority *actually knew* about the deterioration. However, proof of knowledge by the authority of the relevant risk is merely a precondition to liability and does not of itself give rise to liability. The question whether the road authority breached its duty to repair a known hazard has to be determined according to the breach principles discussed in this chapter. In some cases, the courts have been willing to infer knowledge by the authority of the risk. In *Leichhardt Council v Serratore* [2005] NSWCA 406, the plaintiff was injured when her right foot caught on the end of a new sandstone block abutting the existing footpath. In issue was whether the council, which had control over the footpath, had inspected the paving and kerb work and thus had 'an actual knowledge' of the trip hazard (under the *Civil Liability Act 2002* (NSW), s 45, 'an actual knowledge' is a precondition to liability). Although the plaintiff was unable to adduce evidence of the inspection, the trial judge inferred that the council inspected the footpath in accordance with contractual specifications between it and the developer who built the new block. Since the trip hazard was obvious, the trial judge and the Court of Appeal (at [12]) were 'satisfied that the defendant had inspected the footpath before the plaintiff's fall'. Once the court found that it 'had actual knowledge of the particular risk', the council was not protected by the section.

---

71. *Boroondara City Council v Cattanach* [2004] VSCA 139 at [18]; *Greater Shepparton Council v Davis* [2004] VSCA 140 at [37].
72. See, for example: *Leichhardt Council v Serratore* [2005] NSWCA 406 and *Roads and Traffic Authority v McGregor* [2005] NSWCA 388.
73. *Civil Liability Act 2002* (NSW), s 45; *Civil Liability Act 2003* (Qld), s 37; *Civil Liability Act 2002* (Tas), s 42; *Road Management Act 2004* (Vic), s 102; *Civil Liability Act 2002* (WA), s 5Z; *Civil Law (Wrongs) Act 2002* (ACT), s 113.
74. The *Civil Liability Act 1936* (SA), s 42, provides that a road authority is not liable for a failure to maintain, repair or renew a road (which includes footpaths), or to take other action to avoid or reduce the risk of harm that results from a failure to maintain, repair or renew a road.
75. See, for example: *Whittlesea City Council v Merie* [2005] VSCA 199, where the council was found liable for injury occasioned by a fall when the plaintiff tripped on a hole in the footpath. The council knew that by negligently patching the pavement hole it had created a hazard for pedestrians.

Statutory breach factors applying to public authorities

The Australian Capital Territory, New South Wales, Queensland, Tasmania, Victoria, and Western Australia have enacted provisions that direct the courts to consider particular factors in determining whether a public authority has a duty of care or has breached that duty. These factors are in addition to the general principles that would be taken into account in determining breach. The statutory provisions state that in determining the liability of an authority, the court is to have regard to the following principles:[76]

(a) the functions required to be exercised by the authority are limited by the financial and other resources that are reasonably available to the authority for the purpose of exercising those functions;

(b) the general allocation of those resources by the authority is not open to challenge;

(c) the functions required to be exercised by the authority are to be determined by reference to the broad range of its activities (and not merely by reference to the matter to which the proceedings relate);

(d) the authority may rely on evidence of its compliance with the general procedures and applicable standards for the exercise of its functions as evidence of the proper exercise of its functions in the matter to which the proceedings relate.

There exist some dicta of the High Court, particularly in *Crimmins v Stevedoring Industry Finance Committee* (1999) 200 CLR 1,[77] to the effect that the resources of the authority should be taken into account[78] when determining breach of duty of care. However, the reform legislation is much more specific. Paragraph (a) confirms that the courts should properly have regard to the limited resources of public authorities and the array of other competing demands on the funds of those authorities. It will therefore be a relevant consideration that the imposition of liability would require the defendant to expend resources to take similar action in other areas under its control which would necessarily divert resources from other areas of equal or greater priority. Paragraph (b), which is omitted from the Victorian provision, confirms the common law proposition that a policy decision of the authority to allocate a certain amount of resources to a particular activity is not justiciable (*Graham Barclay Oysters Pty Ltd v Ryan* (2002) 211 CLR 540).[79]

---

76. *Civil Law (Wrongs) Act 2002* (ACT), s 110; *Civil Liability Act 2002* (NSW), s 42; *Civil Liability Act 2003* (Qld), s 35; *Civil Liability Act 2002* (Tas), s 38; *Wrongs Act 1958* (Vic), s 83; *Civil Liability Act 2002* (WA), s 5W.
77. Gaudron J at [34]; McHugh J at [79], with whom Gleeson CJ agreed.
78. See also: *Romeo v Conservation Commission (NT)* (1998) 192 CLR 431, per Kirby J; *Pyrenees Shire Council v Day* (1998) 192 CLR 330, per McHugh J; *Brodie v Singleton Shire Council*; *Ghantous v Hawkesbury City Council* (2001) 206 CLR 512 at [162], per Gaudron, McHugh, and Gummow JJ.
79. This principle will be discussed further in the omissions chapter (Chapter 14).

Paragraph (c) requires that when assessing the particular risk that materialised in the particular case, the courts take into account the range of responsibilities and activities of the public authority and the numerous risks that it has the responsibility to manage and control. This factor reflects the common law as enunciated by the High Court in cases such as *Romeo v Conservation Commission (NT)* (1998) 192 CLR 341, *Commissioner of Main Roads v Jones*, *Vairy v Wyong Shire Council* and *Mulligan v Coffs Harbour*. Paragraph (d) is an evidentiary provision, the intent of which appears to be to permit a public authority to rely on evidence as to its 'normal' procedures to establish the course of action that was followed in a specific instance. For example, a local council that has in place a procedure for checking rivers and creeks for concealed obstructions that might injure users can rely on this as evidence that a particular river or creek was checked in accordance with that procedure.

Under New South Wales[80] and Western Australian legislation, to negative the alleged breach of duty of care, the defendant public (or other) authority will need to show that another public or other authority with similar functions—for example, another local Council—would have considered its acts or omissions a reasonable exercise of a function. For example, the *Civil Liability Act 2002* (WA), s 5X states:

> In a claim for damages for harm caused by the fault of a public body or officer arising out of fault in the performance or non-performance of a public function, a policy decision cannot be used to support a finding that the defendant was at fault unless the decision was so unreasonable that no reasonable public body or officer in the defendant's position could have made it.

The courts' approach to determining liability in negligence of statutory authorities is well illustrated in *Dungog Shire Council v Babbage* [2004] NSWCA 160. Erin Babbage, the injured plaintiff, crashed her car into a tree that had fallen during a particularly severe windstorm in the Dungog area. The tree was 20 metres tall, and stood 4 metres from the edge of the road. She sued the Dungog Council as a roadway authority, alleging that the council had negligently failed to take reasonable steps by exercising its powers, within a reasonable time, to address the risk posed by the tree, and to have a 'roadside vegetation maintenance programme'. The trial judge found for the plaintiff on the grounds that removal only of those trees that were identified by motorists, land-owners, or council staff in the course of their duties did not amount to a proper (proactive rather than merely reactive) system of checking and maintaining the safety of roadside trees. On appeal, the Court of Appeal asked:

---

80. *Civil Liability Act 2002* (NSW), s 43A(3).

(a) Whether reasonable steps would have revealed a latent danger that this tree would fall; either from observation in the ordinary course of road maintenance work or by way of a feasible system of inspection of roadside trees?

(b) Would reasonable steps have called for the removal of the tree on the basis that the latent danger from that tree would be so identified?

Having considered the expense, difficulty and inconvenience to the authority in taking the steps to alleviate the danger in the light of the financial and other resources that were reasonably available to the Council, the Court of Appeal found (at [65]):

> the danger or risk of a tree falling upon the road and causing injury could never be eliminated, more especially with the prevalence of windstorms. No council could practicably inspect 760 kilometres of local roads within the Shire ... in order to identify every tree that might fall upon the road.

The scale of the task of identifying and removing trees at risk of falling was well outside the resources of a small council like Dungog. The cost of employing an arborist was beyond the financial capacity of a sparsely populated country shire, and it was impracticable to expect council employees to identify sick and potentially vulnerable trees while they were traveling through the hundreds of kilometres of shire roads. The claimants were unable to nominate any council with a formalised documented 'roadside vegetation maintenance programme'. The court concluded (at [81]) that on any application of the *Wyong Shire Council v Shirt* calculus, it was simply not feasible or reasonable in cost or manpower terms to set up such a system for identifying and removing sick trees over the vast network of roads within the shire.

INDUSTRY STANDARDS

It is for the *court* to determine whether or not, in all of the circumstances, the defendant acted reasonably in response to the foreseeable risk of harm. While the custom or practice of the industry in which the defendant operates will be of some evidentiary value, it will not ordinarily be determinative of the question of breach. This is because the industry custom or practice might itself be negligent (*Mercer v Commissioner for Road Transport and Tramways* (1936) 56 CLR 148). As McHugh J pointed out in *Woods v Multi-Sport Holdings Pty Ltd* (2002) 208 CLR 460, at [73]:

> Industry custom and practice can guide but cannot determine whether a person is in breach of a common law duty of care. They are often a good indication of what is reasonable in the conduct of a particular trade, business, profession or activity. But when the risk of injury is high, the effect of injury likely to serious and the cost of eliminating the risk of the injury small, it is unlikely that industry custom or practice will negate a finding of negligence.

In the well-known case of *O'Dwyer v Leo Buring Pty Ltd* [1966] WAR 67, the plaintiff suffered an eye injury when a plastic stopper ejected spontaneously from a bottle of sparkling wine that he was opening, as it was designed to do. The plaintiff, who did not normally drink wine, argued that the bottle of wine should have carried a warning and appropriate directions on the label. The evidence showed that the defendant marketed its wine in the same manner as other manufacturers, and that it was not industry practice to provide a warning about the stopper. Four million bottles of sparkling wine had been sold annually for the previous decade without any similar accident being recorded. Nevertheless, Hale J in the Supreme Court of Western Australia found that the defendant was liable for failure to include a warning on the bottle, as the dangers would not have been obvious to a person who was not familiar with this type of sealing of bottles, and the provision of a warning would have been simple and inexpensive.

Conversely, common practice might in some circumstances be accepted as evidence that the defendant acted reasonably in ignoring the risk. In *Woods v Multi-Sport Holdings Pty Ltd*, cited above, the defendant organised the game of indoor cricket and provided the equipment used by the players, which did not include protective helmets. The plaintiff, who was injured when struck in the eye with the ball, claimed, *inter alia*, that the defendant had breached its duty of care by failing to provide him with a protective helmet. In rejecting the claim, the majority (Gleeson CJ, Hayne and Callinan JJ) relied on evidence that it was not customary to wear helmets in the game; in fact, the Australian Indoor Cricket Federation discouraged the use of helmets and a player needed special permission to wear one.

PROFESSIONAL STANDARDS

Medical professionals

The inquiry into the standard of care required of a medical practitioner tends to arise in two forensic contexts: breach of duty of care in relation to examination, diagnosis, and treatment—including prescription of medication, medical and surgical procedures—on the one hand, and the provision of information about the treatment and the risks it might entail on the other. The common and statutory laws of negligence differentiate between these two categories and therefore they will be discussed separately.

Examination, diagnosis and treatment

Until 1992, determining the standard of medical practice used to form an exception to the general rule that the court has the final say on what is the appropriate standard of care. Under the test articulated by McNair J in the English case of

Bolam v Friern Hospital Management Committee [1957] 1 WLR 582 (the '*Bolam* rule'), the determinative factor in establishing the normative standard of reasonable care in relation to medical diagnosis and treatment is the opinion on that matter held by a responsible body of medical practitioners. McNair J (at 587) said:

> A doctor is not in breach of his duty in the matter of diagnosis and treatment if he acts in accordance with a practice accepted at the time as proper by a reasonable body of medical opinion even though other doctors may adopt a different practice.

Thus, instead of a judicially imposed determination regarding the appropriate standard, the opinion of a reasonable body of medical experts determined whether a practice employed by the defendant doctor reached the required standard diagnosis and treatment.

In *Sidaway v Governors of Bethlem Royal Hospital* [1985] AC 871, the majority of the House of Lords extended the original *Bolam* test to include provision of medical information and advice.

The practical effect of the *Bolam* test was that where the plaintiff's and the defendant's expert witnesses disagree, but both opinions are accepted as proper by a responsible body of medical profession, then the defendant doctor's conduct will not be deemed negligent. This rule was modified in *Bolitho v City and Hackney Health Authority* [1997] UKHL 46; [1998] AC 232. The House of Lords unanimously determined (at 243, Lord Browne-Wilkinson delivering the leading judgment) that in cases:

> where there are questions of assessment of the relative risks and benefits of adopting a particular medical practice, a reasonable view necessarily presupposes that the relative risks and benefits have been weighed by the experts in forming their opinions. But if, in a rare case, it can be demonstrated that the professional opinion is not capable of withstanding logical analysis, the judge is entitled to hold that the body of opinion is not reasonable or responsible.

His Lordship then added (at 243):

> I emphasise that in my view it will very seldom be right for a judge to reach the conclusion that views genuinely held by a competent medical expert are unreasonable. The assessment of medical risks and benefits is a matter of clinical judgment which a judge would not normally be able to make without expert evidence. As the quotation from Lord Scarman makes clear, it would be wrong to allow such assessment to deteriorate into seeking to persuade the judge to prefer one of two views both of which are capable of being logically supported. It is only where a judge can be satisfied that the body of expert opinion cannot be logically supported at all that such opinion will not provide the benchmark by reference to which the defendant's conduct falls to be assessed.

In Australia, however, the High Court in *Rogers v Whitaker* (1992) 175 CLR 479, at 489 (Mason CJ, Brennan, Dawson, Toohey, and McHugh JJ in a joint judgment), rejected the *Bolam* test, and declared that in relation to the duty to advise, the opinion held by a responsible body of medical practitioners will have 'an influential, often decisive, role to play' in determining the required standard of care, but the court should always have the final say. This rule was implicitly extended to diagnosis and treatment in *Naxakis v Western General Hospital* (1999) 197 CLR 269.[81] In *Naxakis*, the High Court held that a neurosurgeon could be held negligent in failing to perform an angiogram on a young child, even though the opinion of all medical expert witnesses but one was that, given the circumstances and the risks associated with angiograms in 1980, a competent medical practitioner would not have undertaken this procedure.[82]

The *Rogers v Whitaker* rule was considered a trigger for the explosion of medico-legal litigation, because to prove the breach of duty of care, the plaintiff only needed to produce one persuasive expert witness to enable the court to exercise judicial discretion to substitute its own lay judgment in disregard of the opinion of a responsible body of medical practitioners.[83] The Ipp Panel was persuaded that this situation was unsatisfactory, and recommended adoption of the *Bolitho* test.

Statutory provisions

Pursuant to the Ipp Panel's recommendation,[84] the *Bolitho* test, with some variations, has now been legislatively enacted in a number of jurisdictions, including New South Wales, Queensland, South Australia, Tasmania, Victoria, and Western Australia.[85] It generally applies to all professionals, not just medical practitioners. Victorian[86] and South Australian[87] legislation distinguishes between persons who

---

81. At [20], per Gaudron J; at [47], per McHugh J; at [81], per Kirby J.
82. The *Naxakis* case was sent back for retrial, however, following Hedigan J's decision in *Naxakis v Western & General Hospital & Anor* [1999] VSC 389 (15 October 1999) on the issue of loss of chance, the case was settled out of court.
83. For example, in *Woods v Lowns & Anor* (1995) 36 NSWLR 344, the trial judge, Badgery-Parker J, disregarded the evidence of the Australian neurologists specialising in childhood epilepsy who, as medical expert witnesses, testified that proper care of children with the plaintiff's condition did not involve informing the parents of the availability and advisability of rectal diazepam to control the *grand mal*. Instead, the judge relied upon evidence provided by a single expert witness brought by the plaintiffs from England in finding that the second defendant, Dr Procopis, a paediatric neurologist, had been negligent. Although the finding of negligence against Dr Procopis was reversed on appeal in *Lowns & Anor v Woods & Ors* [1996] Aust Torts Reps ¶81–376, the Court of Appeal determined that the plaintiff's injury should be attributed to Dr Lowns (the first defendant) for failure to administer the rectal diazepam, even though this drug has never been registered for use in Australia under the *Therapeutic Goods Administration Act* 1989 (Cth).
84. *Ipp Report*, paras 3.18, 3.19.
85. *Civil Liability Act 2002* (NSW), ss 5O, 5P; *Civil Liability Act 2003* (Qld), s 22; *Civil Liability Act 1936* (SA), s 41; *Wrongs Act 1958* (Vic), ss 59, 60.
86. *Wrongs Act 1958* (Vic), ss 57, 58.
87. *Civil Liability Act 1936* (SA), ss 40, 41.

hold out as possessing a particular skill and professionals. In Victoria, a 'professional' is defined with perfect circularity as 'an individual practising a profession'.[88] The courts will need to give meaning to this term by reference to the general understanding in the community as to the types of occupational groups that would now be considered 'professional'. Lawyers, medical practitioners, accountants, and engineers are all examples of persons who are traditionally regarded as being 'professionals'. However, persons engaged in manual work (such as construction and factory workers) or service jobs (such as staff engaged in the hospitality industry) would probably not fall with this definition. The *Civil Liability Act 2002* (WA), s 5PA, refers to 'health professionals', such as medical practitioners, dentists, pharmacists, physiotherapists and psychologists.

The structure and wording of the provisions differs from jurisdiction to jurisdiction, however in each case the objective is the same. The main features of these provisions are as follows.

In all States of Australia[89] (though not in the Territories),[90] professionals, including medical practitioners, are not liable in negligence if they act in a manner that is widely accepted in Australia by peer professional opinion as competent professional practice. Courts will not intervene with the peer opinion, unless it is 'irrational'[91] (in Victoria and Western Australia the threshold for the court's intervention is 'unreasonable' practice).[92] The legislation also provides that 'widely accepted' peer professional opinions can differ, and 'do not have to be universally accepted to be considered widely accepted'.[93]

Once a court accepts that the practice is widely accepted, it must apply that practice as the appropriate standard of care. The statutory test of 'widely accepted'

---

88. *Wrongs Act 1958* (Vic), s 57.
89. *Civil Liability Act 2002* (NSW), s 5O(1): 'A person practising a profession (a professional) does not incur a liability in negligence arising from the provision of a professional service if it is established that the professional acted in a manner that (at the time the service was provided) was widely accepted in Australia by peer professional opinion as competent professional practice.' See also: *Civil Liability Act 2002* (Tas), s 22(1); *Wrongs Act 1958* (Vic), s 59(1); *Wrongs Act 1936* (SA), s 41(1); *Civil Liability Act 2002* (WA), s 5PB(1); *Civil Liability Act 2003* (Qld), s 22(1).
90. The Northern Territory is yet to undertake partial codification of negligence principles, and the Australian Capital Territory has legislation regarding standard of care but not specifically regarding professionals. Thus, both Territories are governed by the common law as stated in *Rogers v Whitaker* (1992) 175 CLR 479 at 487 and *Naxakis v Western General Hospital* (1999) 197 CLR 269.
91. *Civil Liability Act 2002* (Tas), s 22(2); *Civil Liability Act 2002* (NSW), s 5O(2); *Civil Liability Act 2003* (Qld), s 22(2); *Wrongs Act 1936* (SA), s 41(2).
92. Under the *Wrongs Act 1958* (Vic), s 59(2), the court will not rely on peer professional opinion, if it considers the opinion 'unreasonable'. By virtue of s 59(5) and (6), the reasons for a determination that peer professional opinion is unreasonable must be given in writing, unless it is a jury case. Under the *Civil Liability Act 2002* (WA), s 5PB(4), the court will intervene in circumstances where 'the health professional acted or omitted to do something which is, in the circumstances of the particular case, so unreasonable that no reasonable health professional in the health professional's position could have acted or omitted to do something in accordance with that practice'.
93. *Civil Liability Act 2002* (Tas), s 22(3) and (4); *Civil Liability Act 2002* (NSW), s 5O(3) and (4); *Civil Liability Act 2003* (Qld), s 22(3) and (4); *Wrongs Act 1936* (SA), s 41(3) and (4); *Wrongs Act 1958* (Vic), s 59(3) and (4); *Civil Liability Act 2002* (WA), s 5PB(3) and (5).

professional opinion overcomes *Naxakis*. For, although an opinion held by a minority of respected practitioners will satisfy the test of 'widely accepted' opinion, an opinion held by a single medical expert witness that is contrary to the opinion expressed by a 'significant number' of his or her peers will not. Procedurally, where there are two opposing 'widely accepted' equally reasonable opinions, the plaintiff will loose.

Just as importantly, the legislation stresses that professional opinion must relate to the 'time the service was provided'. In *Naxakis*, for example, Dr Klug, the lone expert who said that he would have performed an angiogram, implied that he would do so in 1998 (the year of trial) not 1980 (the time when the plaintiff underwent the treatment)—a fact disregarded by the High Court.

Provision of information

The distinction between diagnosis and treatment on the one hand, and the provision of information and advice on the other, was articulated by the High Court of Australia in *Rogers v Whitaker* (1992) 175 CLR 479. According to the joint judgment, diagnosis of a condition and recommendations for its treatment is a matter of the medical expertise of the doctor; the contribution of the patient is limited to the narration of symptoms and relevant history. However, except in cases of emergency, the choice as to whether to proceed with medical treatment is to be made by the patient on the basis of the information provided by the medical practitioner. The majority reasoned (at [14]) that an important implication of the patient's legal right to give or withhold consent is that the opinions of medical practitioners should not be the sole—or even the primary—means of setting the standard of care about what information ought to be given to patients. Consequently, in *Rogers v Whitaker*, the court held that a patient can only make a proper choice to undergo treatment where informed of all the material risks associated with the procedure. The duty of a medical practitioner is therefore to warn the patient of the material risks inherent in the proposed treatment or procedure. A risk is a 'material risk' if, in the circumstances of the case, a reasonable person in the patient's position, if warned of the risk, would be likely to attach significance to it, or if the medical practitioner is or should have been aware that the particular patient would be likely to attach significance to it (at [16]). It was a matter for the court to determine whether the medical practitioner provided adequate information and advice as to material risks.

In *Rogers v Whitaker*, the defendant, ophthalmic surgeon Dr Rogers, performed surgery upon the plaintiff, Mrs Whitaker, who had lost vision in her right eye at the age of nine. She had retained normal vision in her left eye. In 1984, at the age of forty-seven, she went to Dr Rogers to surgically improve the appearance of the right eye by removing scar tissue. It was also hoped that the operation would restore significant sight to that eye and assist in managing the plaintiff's early glaucoma. Mrs Whitaker was apparently very nervous and 'keenly interested' to know of possible complications of the operation. Dr Rogers told her about some risks, but failed to mention the possibility of the admittedly remote risk (one in 14 000) of sympathetic ophthalmia occurring in her left eye. Mrs Whitaker agreed to the operation, which was carried out without negligence. Nevertheless, she did develop sympathetic ophthalmia in her left eye, and as a result became virtually blind in 1986. She sued Dr Rogers for a negligent failure to respond to her questions about possible complications by failing to warn her of the risk, albeit remote, of sympathetic ophthalmia. The court held that he was liable. Applied to the facts, a reasonable person in the plaintiff's position—with only one good eye—was likely to attach significance to a possibility that it might be affected by an elective procedure. But in any event, the evidence disclosed that the defendant should have realised that the risk was material to this particular patient. The plaintiff had 'incessantly' questioned the doctor about possible complications and shown a particular concern about unintended or accidental interference with her 'good' left eye. There was evidence of a body of opinion in the profession at the time which considered that given the rarity of the condition and the remoteness of the risk, patients should not be advised about the risk of sympathetic ophthalmia unless they specifically asked about it. However, the court determined that it was unreasonable in the circumstances for the defendant to withhold information about sympathetic ophthalmia simply because the plaintiff had not asked the precise question. It was sufficient that she had demonstrated a clear concern that no injury should befall her one good eye.[94]

In *Rogers v Whitaker*, the court recognised that the duty of the medical practitioner to disclose material risks is subject to a 'therapeutic privilege'. The concept of therapeutic privilege allows the physician discretion in respect of whether or not, and if so, when, to disclose disturbing information directly to the patient. Therapeutic privilege operates in those cases where there is a particular danger that the provision of all relevant information will harm an unusually nervous, disturbed or volatile patient. The disclosure in such situations is usually made to a relative or a close associate who is regularly attending the patient.

The approach in *Rogers v Whitaker* relating to the duty of medical practitioners to warn of material risks has been embodied in legislation in Queensland and Tasmania. Under s 21 of the *Civil Liability Act 2003*(Qld):

(1) A doctor does not breach a duty owed to a patient to warn of risk, before the patient undergoes any medical treatment (or at the time of being given medical advice) that will involve a risk of personal injury to the patient, unless the doctor at that time fails to give or arrange to be given to the patient the following information about the risk—
   (a) information that a reasonable person in the patient's position would, in the circumstances, require to enable the person to make a reasonably

---

94. *Rogers v Whitaker* (1992) 175 CLR 479 at [17]–[18].

informed decision about whether to undergo the treatment or follow the advice

(b) information that the doctor knows or ought reasonably to know the patient wants to be given before making the decision about whether to undergo the treatment or follow the advice.

The Tasmanian provisions (*Civil Liability Act 2002* (Tas), s 21) are identical, except that they refer to a 'medical practitioner' rather than 'doctor'.

In other jurisdictions, the rule in *Rogers v Whitaker* regarding the duty to provide adequate information and warn of risks has been extended to provision of any professional service.[95] With regard to the duty to warn and advise, the court determines whether the failure to warn or inform was reasonable. Thus, the statutory test will apply to determine the standard of care of a solicitor in formulating the provisions of a will, as well as to the provision by that solicitor of advice to a client regarding the need for or effect of those provisions.

To sum up, it appears that broadly, the new statutory paradigm requires the following analysis for professional negligence:

1 What was the content of the defendant's duty of care in relation to the injured plaintiff?
2 Was the risk of injury 'not insignificant', when analysed in terms of foreseeability *before* the harmful event occurred?
3 How would a reasonable person in the shoes of the defendant have responded to the risk that materialised, in terms of the statutory calculus of negligence? It is at this stage that the *Bolitho* test of widely accepted peer professional opinion of what is considered competent professional practice becomes relevant.
4 Judicial determination of whether the plaintiff has established on the balance of probabilities[96] that:
    (a) in the opinion his or her peers, the defendant's conduct was not considered competent professional practice;
    (b) the peer opinion supporting the conduct in question was not widely accepted by a respectable body of relevant professionals; or
    (c) the peer opinion supporting the conduct in question though widely accepted by a respectable body of relevant professionals was 'unreasonable' (in Victoria and Western Australia) or 'irrational' (in all other jurisdictions), and therefore not determinative.

---

95. *Wrongs Act 1958* (Vic), s 60; *Civil Liability Act 2002* (NSW), s 5P. The New South Wales provision is specifically limited to situations of a failure to provide a warning, advice or information in respect of *the risk of death or injury* to a person, but the other provisions are not so limited.
96. See, for example: *Civil Liability Act 2002* (WA), s 5PB(6): 'the plaintiff always bears the onus of proving, on the balance of probabilities, that the applicable standard of care (whether under this section or any other law) was breached by the defendant.'

STANDARD OF CARE: THE REASONABLE PERSON

The central inquiry in a negligence action is whether a *reasonable person* would have adopted precautions to avoid a foreseeable risk of injury to the plaintiff. The way in which the reasonable person in the circumstances of the case would have responded to a reasonably foreseeable risk determines the issue of whether the standard of care has been breached. The general proposition is that the reasonableness of the defendant's conduct will be judged against the objective standard of the 'prudent and reasonable' person in the defendant's position: unless the plaintiff has had notice, the particular defendant's intelligence, maturity, personality or level of experience is not considered when the normative standard is determined. A defendant who engages in an activity that carries a risk of harm to others must meet the standard of care expected of a person with ordinary intelligence and experience. Thus, for instance, the inexperience of the defendant will generally not be taken into account. A driver of a motor vehicle, even if only a learner, is generally expected to exercise the degree of skill that could reasonably be expected of an experienced and competent driver;[97] medical practitioners, even those only one day out of medical school, are expected to exercise the degree of skill that could reasonably be expected of experienced and competent medical practitioners.[98] Nor will the physical characteristics of the defendant ordinarily be taken into account. Thus, an elderly person who drives a motor vehicle will be held to the standard of a reasonable driver, and no concession will be made for the fact that the defendant's reactions might be slower because of age. In the same way, a surgeon with Parkinson's disease will be held to the standard of the reasonable surgeon, and no dispensation will be made for his or her illness.

Legislation in the Australian Capital Territory and South Australia provides that the standard of care required of the defendant is that of a reasonable person in the defendant's position who was in possession of all information that the defendant had or ought reasonably to have had at the relevant time.[99]

Modification of the standard of care

Having created the hypothetical 'reasonable' person and imbued this creature with 'ordinary intelligence and experience', the courts still had to grapple with the obvious fact that not all people—even reasonable people—are the same. In some cases, it is necessary to endow the hypothetical reasonable person with at least some characteristics of the defendant.

---

97. *Nettleship v Weston* [1971] 2 QB 691.
98. *Wilsher v Essex Area Health Authority* [1987] QB 730.
99. *Civil Law (Wrongs) Act 2002* (ACT), s 42; *Civil Liability Act 1936* (SA), s 31; see also: *Wrongs Act 1958* (Vic), s 58.

Children

Young children are not expected to exercise the same degree of care as adults, at least where they are engaging in childlike activities, such as playing games. The standard of care must be lowered to that which could reasonably be expected of a child of like age. This proposition was established by the High Court in *McHale v Watson* (1966) 115 CLR 199 (discussed in Chapter 9). Barry Watson, a twelve-year-old boy, threw a sharpened steel rod at a tree; however, it glanced off the tree and struck the plaintiff, a nine-year-old girl, in the eye. The plaintiff claimed in negligence against Barry and his parents. The High Court held that Barry should not be held to the standard of care of an adult, but to the standard of a reasonable child of twelve. The capacity of children to exercise foresight and prudence is quite different from that of adults, and therefore a child's liability should be assessed in accordance with the standards expected of the ordinary child of comparable age. Barry's actions were not negligent because unlike an adult, a twelve-year-old child would not have foreseen that the rod aimed at striking a tree, might be deflected at a tangent, and hit a person instead.

Kitto J emphasised that the standard to be applied is one to which children of like age, intelligence and experience would be expected to conform (at 215). In that sense, the standard is objective. His Honour stated the principle as follows:

> a defendant does not escape liability by proving that he is abnormal in some respects which reduces his capacity for foresight and prudence. The principle is of course applicable to a child. The standard of care being objective, it is no answer for him, any more than it is for an adult, to say that the harm he caused was due to his being abnormally slow-witted, quick-tempered, absent-minded or inexperienced.

In *McHale v Watson*, the defendant was playing a game at the time of the incident. There is, however, authority that a child who is engaging in an adult activity (for example driving a car) should be held to the standard of care expected of the normal adult—at least in relation to other road users who do not know of the youth of the driver: *Tucker v Tucker* [1956] SASR 297.

It is apposite to point out that most children do not carry third-party insurance and do not have substantial assets. Consequently, where a minor has caused damage to a third party, it is his or her parents who are usually sued. Their liability is personal, not vicarious, and it sounds in negligence. In *Smith v Leurs & Ors* (1945) 70 CLR 256, the High Court affirmed that a person who, as a parent, has the control of a child, may be liable in negligence for failure to exercise a reasonable control over the child, if as a result such failure a third party suffers an injury. The basis of the action is that parents ought to exercise sufficient control to restrain their child from doing something that is fraught with an unreasonable degree of risk to a third party. If a child injures a third party, the question arises whether the child's parents failed to take reasonable control measures to prevent the injurious conduct. In some cases, the standard for parental control will be satisfied by a warning given to the child regarding the risks involved in the particular activity;[100] in others, more proactive conduct will be required.[101]

Consensual relationships and inexperience

Driving a motor vehicle is a skilled operation. Motorists on the highway must trust other drivers to perform at a reasonable level of competency. How then do the courts approach the issue of inexperience?

This question was discussed by the High Court in *Cook v Cook* (1986) 162 CLR 376. In that case, the plaintiff, Mrs Irene Cook, persuaded her sister-in-law, Mrs Margaret Cook, the defendant, to drive a car. Irene knew that Margaret was inexperienced, and did not hold even a driver's permit. While driving, Margaret attempted to avoid a collision with a stationary car. Instead, she put her foot on the accelerator, swerved, and hit an electricity pole. Irene sustained serious injuries as a result of the collision, and sued Margaret.

The trial judge dismissed Irene's claim. The Full Court of South Australia allowed the appeal by the plaintiff, but reduced her damages by 70 per cent. The High Court dismissed Margaret's appeal. In a joint judgment, Mason, Wilson, Deane, and Dawson JJ said that in general, the skill or characteristics of an individual driver are not directly relevant to the standard of the duty of care owed by the driver to the passenger. In the ordinary case, the standard of care will not be modified, even if the passenger is aware that the driver has some physical disability, or below-average expertise, or is commonly careless—as these factors may be compensated for, and even careless drivers can take care. However, special and exceptional facts may transform the relationship between the driver and the passenger to such an extent that it would be unreal to regard the relevant relationship as simply that of the ordinary driver and passenger, and unreasonable to measure the standard of care required of that driver by reference to the skill and care reasonably to be expected of an experienced and competent driver. Of course, the standard of care can only be modified in relation to those persons with knowledge of the inexperience or impairment who could be said to have voluntarily assumed the risk of that

---

100. In *Smith v Leurs & Ors* (1945) 70 CLR 256, the High Court held that the parents satisfied the requisite standard of care by warning their thirteen-year-old son of risks posed by a shanghai (catapult). The boy fired a stone from a shanghai, which was a gift from his parents, and hit the plaintiff in the eye, seriously damaging his sight.
101. *Curmi v McLennan* [1993] Aust Torts Reports ¶81–254. Curmi allowed his seventeen-year-old son to invite a group of friends of similar age to spend a week on his houseboat. He was found liable in negligence after one guest shot another in the eye with an airgun, which Curmi had left in an unlocked cupboard on the boat.

inexperience or impairment: the normal standard of care would still be owed to other users of the highway such as other drivers and pedestrians.

Applying these principles to the facts, the court held that the ordinary standard of care—the objective standard of a reasonable person—had to be modified because of the extraordinary circumstances of this case, where Margaret's incompetence and inexperience as a driver were known to Irene, who had voluntarily undertaken to supervise her sister-in-law's driving efforts. The situation was analogous to that of a professional driving instructor and a pupil having his or her first lesson, and accordingly, the standard of care to be expected of the defendant was that of an unqualified and inexperienced learner driver. Nevertheless, and notwithstanding the modification of the standard of care, Margaret was found to have fallen below the modified standard by deliberately accelerating and driving faster in circumstances that required braking and driving more slowly. The court also held that the defence of voluntary assumption of risk was not applicable; its scope did not extend to exonerate the defendant from her failure to observe the *modified* standard of care: the care reasonably expected of an unqualified and inexperienced driver.

This latter point regarding the application of the defence of voluntary assumption of risk needs to be re-examined in light of the civil liability legislation. Pursuant to provisions that exist in most jurisdictions, such as s 54 of the Victorian *Wrongs Act 1958*, if a defence of voluntary assumption of risk is raised, and the risk of harm is obvious, the person who suffered harm is presumed to have been aware of the risk in the absence of proof, on the balance of probabilities, that he or she was not aware of the risk. These provisions would be applicable if it should have been obvious to a person in the position of the plaintiff that the defendant could not comply with the normal standard of care of the ordinary reasonable learner driver, as arguably was the case in *Cook v Cook*.

Disability and mental illness

The primary aim of the law of torts is to compensate the plaintiff who has suffered damage. Therefore, while the courts differentiate between the standard of care expected of a child and that expected of an adult, abnormalities that reduce the defendant's capacity for foresight or prudence are not considered when determining the standard of a reasonable person in the defendant's position.

Neither old age nor physical incapacity of the particular defendant will be relevant to the objective standard of care. To escape liability the defendant would need to establish that he or she was either unconscious or in a state of automatism at the time of the accident. Thus, in *Roberts & Ors v Ramsbottom* (1980) 1 All ER 7, the plaintiff and her daughter were injured when a car driven by a seventy-three-year-old defendant collided with their car. The defendant argued that he should not be found liable in negligence because, some twenty minutes before the collision, he had suffered a stroke that had rendered him incapable of driving properly, or of realising that he was not driving properly. The medical evidence showed that the defendant was not unconscious, but that 'his mind was impaired or clouded.' The court held the defendant liable in negligence because he continued to drive although aware of his disabling symptoms, if not of their proper significance. Since he maintained some control over the car, he was liable for breaching the standard of care of a reasonable person. Also, in *Leahy v Beaumont* (1981) 27 SASR 290, the plaintiff was held liable for an accident caused when he became unconscious from a coughing fit, as he did have a reasonable period of time—albeit small—to pull off the road before becoming unconscious.

A defendant who is in a state of automatism or is otherwise unaware of his or her actions—for example, through suddenly lapsing into unconsciousness—will not be held to the normal standard of care. This principle has a particular application to the drivers of motor vehicles whose ability to drive is suddenly impaired without advance warning. In *Waugh v James K Allan Ltd* [1964] SC (HL) 102, the driver of a motor vehicle suffered a heart attack and died. The House of Lords considered that the important question in such a case is whether the driver could reasonably be expected to have recognised the onset of symptoms and pulled over. Where there is no advance warning of impairment, the driver will not be liable in negligence.

The concept of standard of care has to be considered in light of the primary object of torts, which is to compensate wrongfully injured claimants. Consequently, as between the injured and the injurer, the law of torts operates for the benefit of those who are wrongfully injured, even if the injurer is morally blameless. Therefore, while the courts differentiate between the standard of care expected of a child and that expected of an adult, conditions that reduce the defendant's capacity for foresight or prudence are not considered when determining the standard of a reasonable person in the defendant's position. Mental illness is irrelevant to the objective standard of care.

Unless the injured party was aware of the fact that the defendant was suffering from a mental illness at the time of the accident, the standard of care will not be reduced. If the defendant was aware of the nature of his or her actions, the ordinary standard will apply even though, because of the mental illness, the defendant was deluded as to the reasons for engaging in those actions. This principle is illustrated by *Adamson v Motor Vehicle Insurance Trust* (1957) 58 WALR 56. The plaintiff was run over by a car when crossing the road at a signalled intersection. The car had been driven by Burt, who was mentally ill. Burt knew he was entering the intersection against the signal, and that he had run down the plaintiff, but the reason for his actions was his delusional fear that his workmates were pursuing him in order to murder him. It was held that Burt was responsible in negligence when he hit the plaintiff, as he was aware he was driving the car. His insanity was not a defence because he was not in a state of automatism.

The *Adamson* case was followed in *Carrier v Bonham* [2001] QCA 234 (discussed in Chapter 6), concerning a mentally ill defendant who, while trying to commit suicide, threw himself at or under a bus. He sustained physical injuries, but as a result of his action the plaintiff bus driver also suffered a psychiatric illness. The Court of Appeal held that Mr Bonham was liable in negligence despite his mental illness. McMurdo P observed (at [7]–[8]) that the plaintiff:

> intentionally jumped in front of the bus, intending to harm himself but did not turn his mind to the reasonably foreseeable potential effect of his actions on others. Impulsive acts of suicide or attempted suicide are common amongst those, like the appellant, who are diagnosed as suffering from chronic schizophrenia.

McPherson JA (at [35]) noted that it is impossible to devise a normative standard by which persons of unsound mind could be judged as a class, because there is 'no such thing as a "normal" condition of unsound mind in those who suffer that affliction'.

Special skills

The general public is not in a position to check the qualifications of everyone who performs skilled tasks. Accordingly, a defendant who has held him or herself out as having special skills will be required to exercise the degree of skill and care expected of a person with those special skills (*Rogers v Whitaker* (1992) 175 CLR 479 at 483). For example, medical practitioners who hold themselves out as being specialists in a particular field will be required to exercise the level of care and skill that would ordinarily be exercised by specialists in that field, rather than by general practitioners. The common law rule regarding the standard of care of persons professing to have particular skills is codified in Victoria and South Australia. Section 40 of the *Civil Liability Act 1936* (SA) provides that in a case involving an allegation of negligence, when determining whether the defendant acted with due care and skill, the court has to consider '(a) what could reasonably be expected of a person professing that skill; and (b) the relevant circumstances as at the date of the alleged negligence and not a later date.'[102]

In the absence of representations of special skill or professional qualifications, the required standard of care is that of the ordinary competent person in the defendant's position. For instance, a general practitioner will not be held to the standard of care of a neurosurgeon, which he or she does not profess to be. In *Dovuro Pty Ltd v Wilkins* (2003) 215 CLR 317, the defendant sold canola seeds to the plaintiff containing weeds that were later declared to be prohibited. Hayne and Callinan JJ declared (at [163]) that 'the usual knowledge of an agricultural scientist cannot set the standard of care to be observed by a seed merchant.'

---

102. In Victoria, s 58 of the *Wrongs Act 1958* (Vic) is identical.

It has long been settled that a plaintiff who employs someone to perform a particular service will (in the absence of representations as to special skills) be owed only that standard of care which might be reasonably expected from the type of person hired. In *Phillips v William Whitely Ltd* [1938] 1 All ER 566 the plaintiff had her ears pierced by a jeweller. She later developed an abscess on her neck and sued for damages. Evidence was given that the man who pierced her ears had performed a similar service at least 150 times over a ten-year period. He would heat the needle over a flame and wash his hands, but did not actually sterilise his instruments. Goddard J held that the standard of care required of a person who pierced ears in a jewellery store was not as high as that expected of a surgeon. If one wanted to have one's ears pierced at the level of skill and expertise of a Fellow of the Royal Australian College of Surgeons, one should go to a surgeon. Given the plaintiff's choice of a jeweller to perform the ear piercing, the normative standard required by law will be that of a competent jeweller who is required to observe basic hygiene such as washing hands and using disinfected instruments, but not more. However, while this standard was appropriate for the 1930s, today, even a jeweller is required to take adequate precautions against the risk of HIV infection.

When a person who is not an expert in a field chooses to perform a task in circumstances where a reasonable person would think it necessary to call in an expert, the standard of care and the degree of foreseeability expected may be of the level of an expert. For example, in the case of *Smith v Tabain & Anor* [1985] Aust Torts Reports ¶80–716, a tenant complained to his landlord that the powerlines on the property he was leasing were insecurely attached. The landlord came to the house and attempted to re-secure the lines. However, a few days later a fire broke out because of the defective connection and the house was destroyed.[103] The court held the landlord liable in negligence. Once he chose to interfere in an area calling for technical skill, the standard required of him was that of a trained electrician. In Victoria and South Australia, this rule has been codified in the *Wrongs Act 1958* (Vic), s 58, and in the *Civil Liability Act 1936* (SA), s 40, respectively.

THE NATURE OF INFERENCE IN LAW

The plaintiff has the onus of proving, on the balance of probabilities, that the defendant was in breach of the duty of care. This means the plaintiff has to show that the defendant failed to do what a reasonable person would have done. Sometimes, particularly in motor vehicle collisions, there are no independent witnesses, and the parties involved are either unable or unwilling to recall what happened. In such situations, the court has to rely on *inferences* drawn from circumstantial evidence

---

103. See also: *Papatonakis v Australian Telecommunications Commission & Anor* (1985) 156 CLR 7.

when deciding whether the defendant breached the duty of care owed to the plaintiff. It is not sufficient for the plaintiff to prove that the possibilities were equally open; the inference of negligence must be more probable than not. In *Holloway v McFeeters* (1956) 94 CLR 470, the plaintiff's husband, Mr McFeeters, died when he was struck by a car at night: his body was found lying on the road. The driver had not stopped, and was never identified, and there were no eyewitnesses. The evidence suggested that Mr McFeeters was at about the centre of the road when he was struck by a vehicle, the brakes of which were applied at about the moment of impact. There was no reason why Mr McFeeters should not have seen the vehicle approaching, and no reason why the driver should not have seen Mr McFeeters, for although it was dark, visibility in the area was good. The plaintiff commenced a claim against the nominal defendant. According to the majority, on the facts, an inference arose that it was more probable than not that the driver was driving in a negligent manner at the time of the accident. The visibility was good, and the headlights should have provided the driver with satisfactory vision in front of and to the side of the car. There was also evidence from which it was possible to infer that the car had been travelling at an excessive speed at the moment of impact, particularly as the car had pushed the plaintiff's body for a considerable distance from the place of impact.

In *Jones v Dunkel* (1959) 101 CLR 298, at 304, Dixon CJ pointed out that the law 'does not authorise a court to choose between guesses, where the possibilities are not unlimited, on the ground that one guess seems more likely than another or the others. The facts proved must form a reasonable basis for a definite conclusion affirmatively drawn of the truth of which the tribunal of fact may reasonably be satisfied.'

TNT Management Pty Ltd v Brooks (1979) 23 ALR 345 involved a head-on collision between an unladen pantechnicon (furniture van) travelling south and a loaded semi-trailer travelling north. Both drivers were killed in the crash, and there were no witnesses. According to the evidence, the cabins of both vehicles were torn from their bodies and forced together on the western side of the road; the semi-trailer was to the south on the western side of the road, pointing north, and the pantechnicon body was further north on the eastern side, and pointing east. The question was whether the driver of the pantechnicon was negligent. Gibbs J, with whom Stephen, Mason, and Aickin JJ agreed (Murphy J dissenting), held (at 350) that a reasonable inference could be drawn from the post-collision position and state of the vehicles that on the balance of probabilities, the pantechnicon was, to some extent at least, on the incorrect side of the roadway at the time the collision occurred. If that was so, it should further be concluded that its driver was guilty of negligence which caused, or contributed to, the collision.

Gibbs J, who delivered the leading judgment, stated (at 349–50) that the applicable principle was that articulated in *Bradshaw v McEwans Pty Ltd* (unreported, High Court of Australia, 27 April 1951) and cited in *Luxton v Vines* (1952) 85 CLR 352, at 358 (it was also relied upon in *Holloway v McFeeters* and in *Jones v Dunkel*).

The rule is based on a distinction between the significance of circumstantial evidence in criminal and civil cases. Civil cases are:

> concerned with probabilities, not with possibilities. The difference between the criminal standard of proof in its application to circumstantial evidence and the civil is that in the former the facts must be such as to exclude reasonable hypotheses consistent with innocence, while in the latter you need only circumstances raising a more probable inference in favour of what is alleged. In questions of this sort, where direct proof is not available, it is enough if the circumstances appearing in evidence give rise to a reasonable and definite inference: they must do more than give rise to conflicting inferences of equal degrees of probability so that the choice between them is mere matter of conjecture. ... But if circumstances are proved in which it is reasonable to find a balance of probabilities in favour of the conclusion sought then, though the conclusion may fall short of certainty, it is not to be regarded as a mere conjecture or surmise.

In *Viet Hong Lieng v Harold Delvers* [2002] NSWCA 170, the plaintiff, driving along the centre lane of a three-lane highway, decided to make a left-hand turn across lane 2 into the lane closest to the kerb. While executing this manoeuvre, he was hit by the defendant's car. The defendant did not give evidence. The court noted that no inference of negligence could be drawn from the facts of the case because the defendant, who was driving at 50 kilometres per hour in a 60-kilometre zone, could not have been expected to observe the gap in the lane 2 traffic or the presence of the plaintiff across it. The defendant's vision would have been obscured by two very large trucks to the left of the plaintiff in such a way that it was not readily apparent that the plaintiff was moving into the incorrect lane.

'SLIPPING' CASES

Decisions based on inferences regarding the defendant's standard of care used to feature in the so-called 'slipping cases'. For example, in *Kocis v SE Dickens Pty Ltd (t/as Coles New World Supermarket)* (1996) Aust Torts Reports ¶81–382, the plaintiff, while shopping in the defendant's supermarket, slipped on a pool of disinfectant and fell; when she tried to get up, she slipped and fell again, injuring her back. The evidence established that the defendant had a system of inspection which involved, if necessary, cleaning of floors at intervals of about thirty minutes throughout the day. However, the plaintiff claimed that this system was not in operation on the morning in question. She alleged the relevant spill was there for at least thirty minutes, yet was not noticed and removed. The defendant claimed that the spillage had been on the floor for five minutes. The trial judge found for the defendant, but the Court of Appeal allowed the plaintiff's appeal, and ordered a new trial.

Hayne JA (at 63,311) defined the extent of occupiers' duty:

> It is clear that an occupier of premises is no insurer of those who enter the premises. All that is required of an occupier is that reasonable care be exercised. It follows that the occupier is not to be held liable if a person entering the premises slips upon something which the occupier could not, by the exercise of reasonable care, be expected to have cleared away.

In order to succeed, the plaintiff has first to establish that the presence of slippery substances on the floor was to be expected in the area where the accident occurred, and that the defendant had a duty to clear them away expeditiously. In *Griffin v Coles Myer Ltd* (1991) Aust Torts Reports ¶81–109; 2 Qd R 478, the plaintiff slipped on pink icing, probably from a coffee roll, in a dress department at a Myer store. There was no evidence as to how the icing came to be on the floor in this area of the department store and how long it had been there—it could have been dropped only moments before the plaintiff slipped on it. The court found that since this area of the store was not 'inherently' likely to contain slippery material, the system of cleaning in operation at the time was appropriate to a dress department.

Phillips JA said in *Kocis* (at 63,305), that the evidence of the length of time the material on the floor has been present before the plaintiff slipped on it is not a 'necessary prerequisite to the plaintiff's success'.[104] Knowing the time during which the slippery matter was on the floor may aid the case of either the defendant or the plaintiff. However, Hayne JA stressed in *Kocis* (at 63,311) that:

> the most important factors that will determine whether or not the requisite standard of care has been established involve the 'inherent' likelihood that the floor would become slippery, and the effectiveness of the system of cleaning adopted by the defendant to protect the safety of customers and lawful visitors.

Hayne JA then quoted the statement of McHugh JA in *Brady v Girvan Bros Pty Ltd* (1986) 7 NSWLR 241 (at 254), who observed that each case will have to be determined on its own facts, taking into consideration:

> The number of people who use the premises, the frequency with which spillages occur, the gravity of the danger, and the area to be supervised are also relevant circumstances in determining what standard of care is reasonably required to avoid risk of injury.

Statutory principles relating to obvious and inherent risks, and the doctrine in *Ghantous v Hawkesbury City Council* (2001) 206 CLR 512 (at [163]), that

---

104. See also: *Brady v Girvan Bros Pty Ltd* (1986) 7 NSWLR 241; *Allcorp Cleaning Services Pty Ltd v Fairweather & Anor* (Matter No CA 40148/96 NSWSC 291, 29 June 1998; Mason P, Priestley, and Stein JJA).

pedestrians 'ordinarily will be expected to exercise sufficient care by looking where they are going and perceiving obvious hazards, such as uneven paving stones, tree roots or holes', will probably have the effect of reinforcing the established rules in this area of the law.[105]

The doctrine of *res ipsa loquitur* will be discussed in Chapter 12.

FURTHER READING

Atiyah PS, 'The Legacy of Holmes through English Eyes' (1983) *Boston University Law Review* 341.

Fleming J, *The Law Of Torts*, 9th edn, The Law Book Company, Sydney, 1998, Ch 7.

Honoré T, *Responsibility and Fault*, Hart Publishing, Oxford, 1999.

Ipp DA, Cane P, Sheldon D & Macintosh I, *Review of the Law of Negligence Report (Ipp Report)* <http://www.revofneg.treasury.gov.au/content/reports.asp>

Posner RA, 'A Theory of Negligence' (1972) *Journal of Legal Studies* 29.

Wright, RW, 'Justice and Reasonable Care in Negligence Law' (2002) 47 *The American Journal of Jurisprudence* 243.

---

105. See: *Ragnelli v David Jones (Adelaide) Pty Ltd* (2004) 90 SASR 233.

Causation and Res Ipsa Loquitur

12

INTRODUCTION

Logically, causation should have been the first and the main element of the tort of negligence. The reasons for its position within the paradigm are strictly historical. When the duty of care under the custom of the realm developed in the fourteenth century, liability in tort was essentially strict, so the issue of causation was either irrelevant or of secondary concern. Common law became preoccupied with legal causation as an element of the cause of action in negligence at the beginning of the nineteenth century, when Lawrence J, in *Flower v Adam* (1810) 127 ER 1098, determined that 'the immediate and proximate cause [of the accident was] the unskilfulness of the driver'.[1]

Causation, as a general concept, is concerned with the consequential relationship between two occurrences, one of which is claimed to have brought about the other. However, legal causation differs from philosophical and scientific concepts of causation, which focus on causes in the physical sense.[2] For example, in medicine, causation is seen in terms of the underlying conditions that lead to or result in one or more signs and symptoms, which are the subject of the diagnosis. Thus, hypertension (high blood pressure) may be caused by a number of medical conditions including kidney disease and uraemia or other toxic conditions; endocrine disorders such as hyperthyroidism and acromegaly; artery disease, which reduces elasticity;

---

1. Cf Smith J, 'Legal Cause in Actions of Tort' (1912) 25 *Harvard Law Review* at 103–128; 223–252; 303–27; *Coyle or Brown v John Watson Ltd* [1915] AC 1; *Weld-Blundell v Stephens* [1920] AC 956.
2. The Aristotelian approach to causation identifies four kinds of causes: material, formal, efficient and final. John Stuart Mill (1806–73) explained that, from a philosophical point of view, the cause of an event is the sum total of the conditions which combined to produce the event. See: Mendelson D, 'Aspects of Causation in Hippocratic Medicine and Roman Law of Delict', in Freckleton I & Mendelson D (eds), *Causation in Law and Medicine*, Ashgate, Dartmouth, 2002, pp 58–83.

and tumours of the central portion (medulla) of the adrenal gland.[3] However, there is also a condition known as primary or 'essential' hypertension, which has no apparent specific organic cause. If a known organic cause cannot be found, the diagnosis will be of primary hypertension or essential hypertension.

By contrast, as a general rule, to establish tortious responsibility, the claimant has to prove the causal connection between the defendant's breach of duty of care and his or her harm.[4] Thus, Windeyer J, in *Timbu Kolian v The Queen* (1968) 119 CLR 47 (at 69), explained that in ascribing effects to causes, and in seeking the cause of an event, the purpose of law, civil and criminal, is to attribute legal responsibility to some person—'to fix liability on some responsible person'.

The common law judiciary has been concerned that the legal approach to the issue of causation should not be too intricate or 'metaphysical'.[5] Yet, causative links are often complex. In cases where indirect harm and unintentional conduct are in issue, plaintiffs have often experienced difficulties in establishing a causal connection between the defendant's fault and their injury. Professor Tony Honoré has explained that in order to understand the legal principles of causation, it is useful to distinguish between the concepts of causation, responsibility and legal liability:

> The concept of cause dominates our inquiries into the processes by which things happen, or have happened. Responsibility for good or bad outcomes of human conduct forms the link between causation and legal liability. It is central to the assessment of people's lives and doings, their successes and failures. But both causation and responsibility, though important in law, are concepts drawn from everyday life. The third topic is specific to law. It concerns the conditions that, in the interests of fairness, limit the extent to which people can be made liable for causing harm.[6]

In other words, Professor Honoré emphasises the distinction between responsibility—as we understand it through our common experience of the world in terms of matter, space, and time—and liability to pay damages, which is based on legal theories of justice. The principles developed through jurisprudential theories give rise to legal tests.

This is because legal causation will not be established unless: (1) human responsibility can be ascribed to the physical, physiological or psychological causes

---

3. Memmler RL, Cohen BJ & Wood DL, *The Human Body in Health and Disease*, JB Lippincott Co, New York, 1992, p 228.
4. Hart HLA & Honoré T, *Causation in the Law*, 2nd edn, Clarendon Press, Oxford, 1985, p 133.
5. See, for example: *Alphacell Ltd v Woodward* [1972] AC 824 at 847, per Lord Salmon; *Bennett v Minister for Community Welfare* (1992) 176 CLR 408 at 412–13, per Mason CJ, Deane and Toohey JJ; *Allianz Australia Insurance Ltd v GSF Australia Pty* [2005] HCA 26 at [54], per McHugh J.
6. Honoré T, 'Principles and Values Underlying the Concept of Causation in Law', in Freckelton & Mendelson, above n 2, p 3.

of a harmful event; and (2) the plaintiff can establish that the person responsible for causing the harm was under a duty to avoid it. Or, as Professor Honoré elegantly observed:

> The law approaches the questions of the cause of the injurious outcome and the responsibility for this outcome by reference to our common experience of the world in terms of matter, space and time on the one hand, and by policy considerations based on the notion of fairness and public or community interest on the other.[7]

Thus, there are two aspects to the legal determination of causation in civil cases: one involves an inquiry into 'the cause-in-fact', meaning who or what actually 'did' the damage, while the other requires a determination of who should pay for the harm. The phrase 'attribution of responsibility' refers to the 'who-should-pay' decision, for it involves an inquiry into the scope of the defendant's liability, and is frequently based on policy considerations, and thus, questions of law.[8]

It is a fundamental rule of negligence that the defendant's acts or omissions must be specifically wrongful and causally related to the plaintiff's injury.[9] The fact that the defendant's conduct was wrongful or morally reprehensible in *general* may not be sufficient for attribution of legal responsibility. For, as Lord Hoffmann pointed out in *Fairchild v Glenhaven Funeral Services Ltd* [2002] UKHL 22; [2003] 1 AC 32, at [56]:

> the purpose of the causal requirement rules is to produce a just result by delimiting the scope of liability in a way which relates to the reasons why liability for the conduct in question exists in the first place.

GENERAL COMMON LAW RULES FOR ATTRIBUTING LEGAL LIABILITY

Nomenclature

The phrase 'necessary condition' refers to a condition without which the harm would not have materialised. It tends to be used in the legal context to distinguish 'necessary conditions' from 'sufficient causes'. The latter refers to a situation where two or more acts or events occur, each of which would be sufficient to bring about the plaintiff's injury.

---

7. Id, p 3.
8. Vinson K, 'Proximate Cause Should Be Barred from Wandering Outside Negligence Law' (1985) 13 *Fla St UL Rev* 215.
9. Hart HLA & Honoré T, *Causation in the Law*, 2nd edn, Clarendon Press, Oxford, 1985.

Common law principles of causation

One of the seminal cases on causation in Australia is *Haber v Walker* [1963] VR 339. In that case, a man suffered brain injury as a result of a motor accident caused by the negligent driving of the defendant. He was hospitalised for ten weeks and attended an outpatient clinic for another five months. He was then diagnosed as suffering from depression and severe anxiety, and was referred for psychiatric assessment. However, his psychiatric condition continued to deteriorate, and he committed suicide nearly eighteen months after the accident. His wife and eight children sued the defendant under the *Wrongs Act 1958* (Vic). There were two issues before the court: the first was whether the suicide was caused by the defendant's negligence; the second, concerning remoteness of damage, was whether the husband's death was foreseeable. The court found for the plaintiff on both issues.

In his judgment, Smith J (at 357–8) summed up the traditional principles of legal causation in the following way:

> In the first place a wrongful act or omission cannot ordinarily be held to have been a cause of subsequent harm unless that harm would not have occurred without the act or omission having previously occurred with such of its incidents as to render it wrongful. Exceptions to this first principle are narrowly confined.

This principle is sometimes known as the 'but for' test, the *causa sine qua non* or 'proximate cause' test of causation. In 1991, Mason CJ pointed out in *March v Stramare* (1991) 171 CLR 506, at 516, that the 'but for' test eliminates matters that could not have been the necessary cause of the plaintiff's damage.

Smith J in *Haber v Walker* (at 358) also discussed the concept of multiple sufficient causes:

> Secondly, where the requirements of this first principle are satisfied, the act or omission is to be regarded as a cause of the harm unless there intervenes between the act or omission an occurrence which is necessary for the production of the harm and is sufficient in law to sever the causal connection.

His Honour referred to circumstances where the defendant's conduct, which was wrongful, may be considered but one factor, condition or cause among others, all of which constitute multiple sufficient causes productive of harm of which the plaintiff is complaining.

Smith J (at 358) explained the doctrine of *novus actus interveniens* in the following way:

> And, finally, the intervening occurrence, if it is to be sufficient to sever the connection, must ordinarily be either—
>
> (a) human action that is properly to be regarded as voluntary, or
> (b) a causally independent event the conjunction of which with the wrongful act or omission is by ordinary standards so extremely unlikely as to be termed a coincidence.

The following discussion analyses common law tests for attributing legal responsibility for the plaintiff's injury, as Smith J has described them, in turn.

The 'but for' test

The 'but for' test determines the presence or absence of a single 'necessary condition' providing the nexus between the defendant's breach of duty and the plaintiff's damage by posing a question: would the plaintiff's damage have happened but for the wrongful act?

Where there is only one act amounting to a breach of the standard of care, the defendant's wrongful conduct will be regarded as the effective (necessary) cause of the damage, if the damage would not have happened but for the wrongful act. In applying the 'but for' test, the court has to determine the answer to a hypothetical question: What would have happened had the defendant *not* been negligent in an identical set of circumstances? Had the lifeguard been present, would the toddler have been saved from drowning?

It must be more probable than not, that in such a hypothetical set of circumstances, the plaintiff would not have been injured. For example:

- If the plaintiff would probably still have been injured, the defendant will not usually be held to have caused the plaintiff's injury.
- However, if the plaintiff probably would not have suffered the injury, a prima facie causal connection between the wrongful conduct and the plaintiff's harm is established.

Test of value judgment based on common sense and experience

The 'but for' test 'as a negative criterion of causation'[10] is useful in eliminating non-causes; however, the formula is not sufficiently nuanced to test legal causation in circumstances where there is more than one necessary cause, or in the exceptional situations of multiple sufficient causes. In *Bennett v Minister for Community Welfare* (1992) 176 CLR 408, at 412–13, Mason CJ, Deane and Toohey JJ said:

> The inadequacy of the 'but for' test has emerged in cases in which a superseding cause, amounting to a *novus actus interveniens*, has been held to break the chain of causation which would have otherwise resulted from an earlier wrongful act or omission. In those cases, though the earlier wrongful act or omission may have amounted to an essential condition of the occurrence of the ultimate harm, it was not the true cause or a true cause of that harm.

---

10. *Bennett v Minister for Community Welfare* (1992) 176 CLR 408 at 412.

The case of *March v E & MH Stramare* (1991) 171 CLR 506 involved two necessary conditions of the ultimate harm. March sued Stramare to recover damages for personal injuries which he sustained when, at about 1 am, he struck a truck owned by Stramare. The truck was parked along the centre lane of a six-lane street in Adelaide. The trial judge found that March's driving ability was impaired through intoxication; this meant that one necessary condition of the accident was March's own carelessness due to inebriation, while the other necessary condition was the defendant's negligence in parking the truck in the middle of the street.[11]

On the 'but for' test alone, the plaintiff would not have been able to establish causation; however, the majority of the High Court (Mason CJ, Deane, Toohey, and Gaudron JJ) determined that the 'but for' test should not be an *exclusive* test of causation. Since the question of causation in negligence is essentially a question of fact, it should be answered by reference to common sense and experience, in which considerations of policy and value judgments, including 'the infusion of policy considerations' play a part (Mason CJ at 515, 516). Deane J (at 522) thus formulated the test:

> For the purposes of the law of negligence, the question of causation arises in the context of the attribution of fault or responsibility: whether the identified negligent act or omission of the defendant was so connected with the plaintiff's loss or injury that, as a matter of ordinary common sense and experience, it should be regarded as a cause of it.

The test of common sense based on 'value judgment involving ordinary notions of language and common sense' was used in cases where:

- there were two or more acts or events which would each be sufficient to bring about the plaintiff's injury; or
- the defendant claimed that a superseding event provided a break in the chain of causation of the injury, which would otherwise have resulted from an earlier wrongful act.[12]

Professor Harold Luntz explained the reasoning of the majority in *March v Stramare* thus:

> The 'but for' test is mostly very easy to satisfy—too easy, since it can take one back to Adam and Eve. That is one reason why the majority in *March v Stramare* rejected it as an *exclusive* test of causation. They recognised that it could play a useful exclusionary role in eliminating non-causes ('as a negative criterion of causation') in all except the exceptional situations of multiple sufficient causes (with which they were not faced in that case and which are very rare). It still leaves many necessary conditions in play and that is where 'policy and value'

---

11. The court apportioned the liability as 70 per cent against March and 30 per cent against Stramare.
12. *March v E & MH Stramare* (1991) 171 CLR 506 at 509, per Mason CJ.

judgments enter into it, ie in choosing from the many necessary conditions the ones to attribute legal responsibility to. The case is important also in telling judges that they don't have to choose only one such condition for this purpose, but may choose more than one.[13]

Critique of the 'value judgment and common sense' test of causation

Initially, the function of the 'common sense' test was to circumscribe the scope of the inquiry into factual causation. In practice, however, the appeal to common sense allowed the courts to conflate factual causation inquiry with what Honoré refers to as 'notions of fairness and other relevant considerations'. In *Environment Agency v Empress Car Co (Abertillery) Ltd* [1999] 2 AC 22, at 29, Lord Hoffmann criticised the opaqueness inherent in the 'common sense' test:

> The first point to emphasise is that common sense answers to questions of causation will differ according to the purpose for which the question is asked. Questions of causation often arise for the purpose of attributing responsibility to someone, for example, so as to blame him for something which has happened ... one cannot give a common sense answer to a question of causation for the purpose of attributing responsibility under some rule without knowing the purpose and scope of the rule.[14]

In law, the issue is not what caused the result complained of, but whether the defendant caused it. Drawing on the arguments of Hart and Honoré, Lord Hoffmann (at 30) illustrated the relationship between the 'common sense' test and the purpose for which we use it with the example of:

> the man who forgets to take the radio out of his car and during the night someone breaks the quarterlight, enters the car and steals it. What caused the damage? If the thief is on trial, so that the question is whether he is criminally responsible, then obviously the answer is that he caused the damage. It is no answer for him to say that it was caused by the owner carelessly leaving the radio inside. On the other hand, the owner's wife, irritated at the third such occurrence in a year, might well say that it was his fault. In the context of an inquiry into the owner's blameworthiness under a non-legal, common sense duty to take reasonable care of one's own possessions, one would say that his carelessness caused the loss of the radio.

Kirby J, citing McHugh J (who dissented in *March v Stramare*), observed in *Chappel v Hart* (1998) 195 CLR 232, at 269, that the 'reference to "commonsense",

---

13. Luntz H, Personal communication, 27 August 2004.
14. In *Chappel v Hart* (1998) 195 CLR 232, Gummow J referred to Lord Hoffmann's judgment in *Environment Agency v Empress Car Co (Abertillery) Ltd* at [63]–[65]; Kirby J at [96]; and Hayne J at [122].

[is] at best an uncertain guide involving "subjective, unexpressed and undefined extra-legal values" varying from one decision-maker to another'.[15]

The test of common sense and value judgments was reconsidered in *Allianz Australia Insurance Ltd v GSF Australia Pty* [2005] HCA 26 and in *Travel Compensation Fund v Robert Tambree t/as R Tambree and Associates* [2005] HCA 69.

In *Allianz*, Mr Oliver worked as a technician. However, he was called by his employer to help another employee with unloading containers from a truck when it transpired that the truck's motorised T-bar, which activated a set of rollers enabling the containers to be more easily loaded and unloaded from it, was inoperative. Mr Oliver was instructed to insert a crowbar between the rollers on the floor of the trailer so as to lever the containers along the rollers. He was injured while implementing this procedure. In issue was whether he should be indemnified under the *Workers Compensation Act 1987* (NSW) or the *Motor Accidents Act 1988* (NSW), or both. The answer to this question depended on the court's determination whether the harm suffered by Mr Oliver fell within the definition of 'injury' for the purposes of the *Motor Accidents Act 1988* (NSW) (as amended by the *Motor Accidents Amendment Act 1995* (NSW)). The High Court found that it did not, because Mr Oliver's injury was not caused by a defective vehicle but by an unsafe system of work created by his employer.

In the *Travel Compensation Fund* case, the court had to determine whether part of a loss claimed by trustees of the Travel Compensation Fund (TCF) should be attributed to the negligence of the defendants or to the illegal conduct of a third party. The defendants were an accountant and an auditor who, in November 1998, negligently supplied TCF with false and misleading statements about the financial position of Travel Shop International (TSI) for the years ended 30 June 1997 and 30 June 1998. The trial judge found that the defendants had engaged in misleading conduct in contravention of s 42 of the *Fair Trading Act 1987* (NSW),[16] which enabled TSI to trade for a much longer period than otherwise would have been the case. TSI was operated by Ms Fry, who, at her own request, ceased to be a participant of the TCF on 23 February 1999, thus losing her travel agent's licence. She nevertheless continued to trade illegally for another four weeks, until 20 April 1999. The High Court determined that the defendants were responsible for compensation paid by the TCF to customers who made deposits and other payments for services they did not receive in the period of illegal trading.[17]

---

15. In *Chappel v Hart* (1998) 195 CLR 232, four out of five Justices regarded the 'but for' test as a prerequisite to finding liability in causation, and all Justices determined the question of causation by the 'common sense and experience' approach. Yet the majority reached a conclusion that was diametrically opposed to that of the minority.
16. This provision essentially mirrors s 52 of the *Trade Practices Act 1974* (Cth).
17. The defendants' responsibility for the loss sustained by the TCF in the period leading to 23 February 1999 was not in dispute.

In *Allianz*, Gummow, Hayne, and Heydon JJ, in a joint judgment, refused to rely on the *March v Stramare* test of common sense. Instead, their Honours endorsed Lord Hoffmann's concept—in *Environment Agency v Empress Car Co (Abertillery) Ltd* [1999] 2 AC 22—that causation in the sense of attributing legal (as against social or moral) responsibility to someone has to be specifically linked to the purpose and scope of the particular cause of action, and if applicable, to the purpose and scope of the statutory enactment under which the issue of causation arises. Gummow, Hayne, and Heydon JJ (at [96]) agreed with Santow JA of the New South Wales Court of Appeal[18] 'that the question of causality [is] not at large or to be answered by "common sense" alone; rather, the starting point is to identify the purpose to which the question is directed.'[19] Then, in the *Travel Compensation Fund* case, Gummow and Hayne JJ[20] (at [45]) stated:

> As was recently emphasised in *Allianz Australia Insurance Ltd v GSF Australia Pty Ltd* ... it is doubtful whether there is any 'common sense' notion of causation which can provide a useful, still less universal, legal norm. There are, therefore, cases in which the answer to a question of causation will require examination of the purpose of a particular cause of action, or the nature and scope of the defendant's obligation in the particular circumstances.[21]

Gleeson CJ did not refer to the 'common sense' test. At the same time, while acknowledging (at [29]) that 'in appropriate circumstances, normative considerations have a role to play in judgments about issues of causation', he rejected the notion that judges should 'engage in value judgments at large'. According to his Honour (at [30]), the answer to the question of causation is to be found by examining the purpose of the relevant legislation as related to the circumstances of a particular case—and presumably, where applicable, the purpose of the common law cause of action.

Naturally, judges have often looked at purpose for the imposition of common law or statutory duty when determining causation.[22] The difference of the purpose-oriented approach lies in its emphasis on a close examination of the objectives and the intended effects of the relevant statutory scheme or common law as indicia of causation.

---

18. *Allianz Australia Insurance Limited & Ors v General Cologne Re Australia Limited* (2003) 57 NSWLR 321 at 330. Determination of causation in *Allianz* was predicated on statutory interpretation of 'injury' for the purposes of the *Motor Accidents Act 1988* (NSW).
19. In *Allianz Australia Insurance Ltd v GSF Australia Pty*, at [97], Gummow, Hayne, and Heydon JJ approved the statements of McHugh J, who in his dissenting judgment in *March v (E & M H Stramare)*, 'doubted whether there is any consistent commonsense notion of what constitutes a "cause".'
20. Heydon J was not a member of the bench in *Travel Compensation Fund*.
21. *Kuwait Airways Corpn v Iraqi Airways Co (Nos 4 and 5)* [2002] 2 AC 883 at 1091 [70]-[71], per Lord Nicholls of Birkenhead.
22. See, for example: Mason CJ in *March v Stramare* at 519: 'The purpose of imposing the common law duty on the second respondent [Stramare] was to protect motorists from the very risk of injury that befell the appellant [March].'

In contradistinction, two members of the bench in the *Travel Compensation Fund* case mounted a vigorous defence of the 'value judgment and common sense' test. Callinan J observed (at [80]):

> It would be a delusion to think that a disputed question of causation can be resolved according to an invariable scientific formula, and without acknowledgment that common sense, that is, the sum of the tribunal's experience as a tribunal, its constituents' knowledge and understanding of human affairs, its knowledge of other cases and its assessment of the ways in which notional fair minded people might view the relevant events, is likely to influence the result. Of course it is possible to say, sometimes with force, that tribunals may on occasions tend to become remote from the community and its values, indeed that there is not a community value as such, but a multiplicity of community values, themselves shifting from time to time, and that one person's common sense may sometimes be another's nonsense. ... But tribunals of fact have to do the best they can. And that which has to be done is better done with candour, and candour demands the acknowledgment by any tribunal or any judge called upon to resolve a matter, of the use of his or her common sense in determining causation. Value judgments may sometimes be inescapably involved, but that they may, does not justify the division of the question into a 'but for' test and a further inquiry whether a defendant should in law be held responsible for a plaintiff's damage.

Kirby J (at [63]), without agreeing with Callinan J's reasoning, concurred with his remark that in deciding cases such as the present, tribunals of fact cannot resort to 'an invariable scientific formula'. They must draw on commonsense, experience, understanding, a multiplicity of community values and their own judgment. They should explain their reasoning 'with candour' which 'demands the acknowledgment ... of the use of ... common sense in determining causation [questions]'.

STATUTORY DEFINITION OF LEGAL CAUSATION

Reflecting the current common law jurisprudence on causation, the *Review of the Law of Negligence Report*[23] proposed a two-limb definition of causation, which has been adopted in New South Wales,[24] Queensland,[25] Tasmania,[26] the Australian

---

23. Ipp D, Cane P, Sheldon D & Macintosh I, *Review of the Law of Negligence Report*, 2 October 2002; <http://www.revofneg.treasury.gov.au/content/reports.asp>.
24. *Civil Liability Act 2002* (NSW), s 5D(1).
25. *Civil Liability Act 2003* (Qld), s 11(1).
26. *Civil Liability Act 2002* (Tas), s 13(1).

Capital Territory,[27] Western Australia,[28] South Australia,[29] and Victoria.[30] The legislation provides that:

> A determination that negligence caused particular harm comprises the following elements—
> (a) that the negligence was a necessary condition of the occurrence of the harm (*factual causation*); and
> (b) that it is appropriate for the scope of the negligent person's liability to extend to the harm so caused (*scope of liability*).

In New South Wales, South Australia, the Australian Capital Territory, and Victoria, the term 'negligence' has been statutorily defined as 'failure to exercise reasonable care and skill'.[31] These jurisdictions have identical provisions relating to factual causation. The Queensland and Tasmanian provisions do not define 'negligence', but instead refer to a causative nexus between 'breach of duty' and the harm suffered by the plaintiff,[32] while Western Australia focuses on 'fault' as the 'necessary condition' of the occurrence of the harm.[33] Whether these semantic differences will influence judicial interpretation of the tests for determining 'factual causation' is yet to be seen.

Factual causation

At law, conceptually, factual causation ('the cause-in-fact of the damage'), which forms the first limb of the statutory definition of causation, requires the plaintiff to establish on the balance of probabilities that the defendant's negligence (fault—breach of duty) caused or materially contributed to the alleged injury. In the process of attributing responsibility for the injury, the law has regard both to conduct causing the harm itself, and to conduct creating opportunities by 'enabling others (or other things) to do harm'.[34] The process of establishing factual causation is retrospective, and involves examination of past events through the prism of testimony by the parties to the litigation, witnesses and expert opinions. However, as Lord Hoffmann's car radio example in the *Environment Agency* case illustrates,

---

27. *Civil Law (Wrongs) Amendment Act 2003* (ACT), s 45(1).
28. *Civil Liability Amendment Act 2003* (WA).
29. *Civil Liability Act 1936* (SA), s 34(1).
30. *Wrongs Act 1958* (Vic), s 51(1).
31. *Wrongs Act 2003* (Vic), Pt X, s 3 ('failure to exercise reasonable care'); *Civil Liability Act 2002* (NSW), s 5 ('failure to exercise reasonable skill and care'); *Civil Liability (Wrongs) Act 2002* (ACT), s 40 ('failure to exercise reasonable care and skill'); *Civil Liability Act 1936* (SA), s 3 ('failure to exercise reasonable care and skill, and includes breach of a tortious, contractual or statutory duty of care').
32. *Civil Liability Act 2003* (Qld), s 11(1); *Civil Liability Act 2002* (Tas), s 13(1).
33. *Civil Liability Act 2002* (WA), s 5C(1). The Northern Territory legislation contains no provisions on causation.
34. Hart HLA and Honoré T, *Causation in the Law*, 2nd edn, Clarendon Press, Oxford, 1985, p 133.

depending on how the question of causality is posed, the same set of facts may render quite different answers.

In *Fairchild v Glenhaven Funeral Services Ltd* [2002] UKHL 22; [2003] 1 AC 32, Lord Hoffmann (at [52]) thus explained the question, in what sense is causation a question of fact?

The question of fact is whether the causal requirements which the law lays down for that particular liability have been satisfied. But those requirements exist by virtue of rules of law. Before one can answer the question of fact, one must first formulate the question. This involves deciding what, in the circumstances of the particular case, the law's requirements are.

For,

> Unless one pays attention to the need to determine this preliminary question, the proposition that causation is a question of fact may be misleading. It may suggest that one somehow knows instinctively what the question is or that the question is always the same … this is not the case. The causal requirements for liability often vary, sometimes quite subtly, from case to case. And since the causal requirements for liability are always a matter of law, these variations represent legal differences, driven by the recognition that the just solution to different kinds of case may require different causal requirement rules.

His Lordship then stated (at [54]) that 'one is never simply liable, one is always liable *for* something—to make compensation for damage, the nature and extent of which is delimited by the law.' This involves the second element of statutory causation—the 'scope of liability'.

Scope of liability

Scope of liability, for the purposes of causation, refers to an inquiry 'whether the loss to the plaintiff (in the history of which the defendant's tortious conduct played a role) *should* be held to be within the *appropriate* scope of liability for consequences of the tortious conduct'.[35] Ultimately, the answer requires determinations of policy, and therefore is a question of law.

The High Court is yet to judicially define the meaning and the nature of either element of statutory causation. However, it appears that the majority may not employ their value judgment and 'common sense' as criteria for determining the

---

35. Stapleton J, 'Scientific and Legal Approaches to Causation', in Freckelton I & Mendelson D, *Causation in Law and Medicine*, Ashgate, Dartmouth, 2002, p 30. See also: Stapleton J, 'Cause-in-Fact and the Scope of Liability for Consequences' (2003) 119 *LQR* 388.

scope of defendants' liability.[36] Professor Dieter Giesen[37] has criticised the concept of 'scope of liability' in the context of causation, on the basis that it confers on the courts a very wide 'discretion in judging what forms of harm are within the scope of the legal rule violated' using such vague criteria as 'legal policy' or 'sense of justice'. A purpose-oriented approach to determining the scope of liability in each case may help to make the process of judicial reasoning more transparent than the 'value judgment and common sense' tests.

When judges embark on interpretation of the statutory test of causation, they might consider the following observation of Callinan J in *Allianz* (at [105]–[106]):

> As well as a question of causation this appeal raises a question whether courts may bring to the construction and application of amending legislation an inclination to read it as intended to produce a result that the legislature has fairly and clearly eschewed, and with a view to effecting a form of justice according to a judge's, or judges' particular perceptions of moral responsibilities or to who happens to be the longer-pocketed defendant.
>
> It is understandable that legislators become exasperated with courts that fail to give effect to the manifest intention of legislation, especially legislation enacted to arrest judicial trends that have become entrenched over the years.

TESTS FOR ATTRIBUTING LEGAL LIABILITY IN EXCEPTIONAL CASES OF 'EVIDENTIAL GAPS'

The problem of 'evidential gap' tends to arise in the following three circumstances:

1. Where there is one defendant, and the claimant's injury was caused by 'cumulative operation'[38] of an identified single causative agent, which emanated from two or more sources (either concurrently or consecutively); only one source is due to or created by the defendant's negligence, but scientific evidence cannot determine the exact contribution of each source (*Bonnington Castings Ltd v Wardlaw* (1956) AC 613).

2. Where there is one defendant, and the claimant's injury was caused by cumulative operation of several causative agents, only one of which was due to

---

36. For example, the Hon Mr Carr in his Second Reading Speech on the *Civil Liability Amendment (Personal Responsibility) Bill*, NSW Legislative Assembly, *Hansard*, 23 October 2002, p 5764, stated that: 'Its intention is to guide the courts as they apply a commonsense approach.'
37. Giesen D, *International Medical Malpractice Law*, JCB Mohr (Paul Siebeck), Tubingen; Martinus Nijhoff Publishers, Dordrecht, 1988, p 169.
38. Ipp D, Cane P, Sheldon D & Macintosh I, *Review of the Law of Negligence Report*, 2 October 2002 at [3.325] <http://www.revofneg.treasury.gov.au/content/reports.asp>, Second Report—released on 2 October 2002.

the defendant's negligence (*Wilsher v Essex Area Health Authority* [1988] AC 1074).

3   Where the claimant's injury was caused by cumulative operation of an identified single causative agent, but there are several defendants, and the scientific evidence cannot determine the exact contribution of each defendant (*Fairchild v Glenhaven Funeral Services Ltd* [2003] 1 AC 32).

These three English cases, as well as *McGhee v National Coal Board* (1973) 1 WLR 1, have exerted very significant influence both on the common law and on the codification of negligence in Australia. Consequently, they will be discussed at some length.

Bonnington Castings Ltd v Wardlaw: origins of the test of 'material contribution'

The test of 'material contribution' was developed to alleviate the problem of plaintiffs like Mr Wardlaw in *Bonnington Castings Ltd v Wardlaw* (1956) AC 613. Mr Wardlaw worked at a dressing workshop of the Bonnington Castings foundry, and while employed there he contracted pneumoconiosis, which was caused by a gradual accumulation in his lungs of minute particles of silica inhaled over a period of eight years. At work, he was exposed to silica dust emanating from the pneumatic hammer and swing grinders. No dust extraction plant was known or practicable for use with the hammer; however, a considerable quantity of dust also escaped into the air of the workshop from the swing grinders. The defendant admitted that the dust-extraction plant for these grinders was not kept free from obstruction as it should have been. Mr Wardlaw's disease was caused by the whole of the noxious material he inhaled, but that material came from two sources, one 'innocent' (the pneumatic hammer, from which dust could not be extracted) and the 'guilty' source (the swing grinders, which should have been made dust-free). In the leading judgment,[39] Lord Reid (at 621) acknowledged that it was impossible to wholly attribute the cause of the disease to material from one source or the other. His Lordship then said:

> It appears to me that the source of his disease was the dust from both sources, and the real question is whether the dust from the swing grinders materially contributed to the disease. What is a material contribution must be a question of degree. A contribution which comes within the exception *de minimis non curat lex* [law is not concerned with insignificant matters] is not material, but I think that any contribution which does not fall within that exception must be material. I do not see how there can be something too large to come within the de minimis principle but yet too small to be material.

---

39. Viscount Simonds, Lord Tucker, Lord Keith of Avonholm and Lord Somervell of Harrow in broad agreement.

Lord Reid concluded (at 623) that the swing grinders contributed 'a quota of silica dust which was not negligible to the [claimant's] lungs and therefore did help to produce the disease.'

McHugh J, in *Henville v Walker* [2001] HCA 52, at [106], described the function of 'material contribution' thus:

> If the defendant's breach has 'materially contributed' to the loss or damage suffered, it will be regarded as a cause of the loss or damage, despite other factors or conditions having played an even more significant role in producing the loss or damage. As long as the breach materially contributed to the damage, a causal connection will ordinarily exist even though the breach without more would not have brought about the damage. In exceptional cases, where an abnormal event intervenes between the breach and damage, it may be right as a matter of common sense to hold that the breach was not a cause of damage. But such cases are exceptional.

The test of 'material contribution' was devised in the 1940s and 1950s to deal with specific conditions of industrial health and safety before stronger general legislation was introduced to protect workers from harmful dust diseases.[40] This was the primary policy reason for allowing recovery on the modified basis of 'material contribution' in the controversial case of *McGhee v National Coal Board* (1973) 1 WLR 1. In that case, the plaintiff's job was to clean brick kilns. He was thus exposed during work hours (eight hours) to brick dust, which carried the risk of dermatitis. The employer did not provide after-work showers for employees, so the plaintiff was unable to remove the brick dust until he arrived home, fifteen minutes later. The experts could not estimate the relative contributions to total risk of each of three possible physical causes:

(a) exposure at work (an 'innocent' cause);
(b) exposure to the dust on the way home due to wrongful failure of the defendant to provide showers;
(c) the possibility that the plaintiff was predisposed to dermatitis.

The facts in *McGhee* differed from *Bonnington Castings*, in so far as in *McGhee* the causative agent was the same, but the contribution from the two sources could be clearly identified and measured: the 'innocent' exposure of eight hours of work and the 'guilty' exposure during the fifteen minutes of riding home while covered with the brick dust. In this situation, if the House of Lords had applied the 'but for' test, the plaintiff's claim would have failed. Lord Wilberforce, who delivered the leading judgment in *McGhee* (at 7), acknowledged as much when he said:

---

40. See: *Vyner v Waldenberg Brothers Ltd* [1946] KB 50 at 55; *Betts v Whittingslowe* (1945) 71 CLR 637; *Nicholson v Atlas Steel Foundry and Engineering Co Ltd* [1957] 1 WLR 613.

the default here consisted not in adding a material quantity to the accumulation of injurious particles but by failure to take a step which materially increased the risk that the dust already present would cause injury. And I must say that, at least in the present case, to bridge the evidential gap by inference seems to me something of a fiction, since it was precisely this inference which the medical expert declined to make.

Nevertheless, the plaintiff succeeded on the basis that in the special circumstances of evidential gap, the fact that the defendant's fault materially increased *the risk of the injury* was sufficient to raise an *inference* of cumulative causation from a single source. Since the plaintiff's dermatitis was physically caused by the brick dust, the only question was whether its continued presence on the plaintiff's skin after the time that he should have been provided with a shower caused or materially contributed to the dermatitis. According to Lord Wilberforce, in the absence of any other evidence regarding the causative agent (apart from the brick dust), a common sense *inference* could be drawn, that on the balance of probabilities, the employer's failure to take precaution materially caused or contributed to the dermatitis.

In *Wilsher v Essex Area Health Authority* [1988] AC 1074, at 1088, Lord Bridge of Harwich explained Lord Wilberforce's reasoning in *McGhee* as follows:

> where the layman is told by the doctors that the longer the brick dust remains on the body, the greater the risk of dermatitis, although the doctors cannot identify the process of causation scientifically, there seems to be nothing irrational in drawing the inference, as a matter of common sense, that the consecutive periods when brick dust remained on the body probably contributed cumulatively to the causation of the dermatitis.

The controversial aspect of the case involved Lord Wilberforce's proposition that once the plaintiff established breach of duty of care, an inference of an increase in risk from one cause should be sufficient for attribution of fault to this cause rather than to others. His Lordship reasoned that in many industrial cases, medical opinion cannot segregate the causes of an illness between compound causes. In such situations, according to Lord Wilberforce (at 6): 'where a person has, by breach of a duty of care, created a risk, and injury occurs within the area of that risk, the loss should be borne by him unless he shows that it had some other cause.'[41] This is because from the evidential point of view, a worker 'who is able to show that his employer should have taken certain precautions, because without them there is a risk, or an added risk, of injury or disease, and who in fact sustains exactly that

---

41. Referring to the *McGhee* case, in *Bennett v Minister of Community Welfare* (1992) 176 CLR 408, at 416, Mason CJ, Deane and Toohey JJ left open the question of whether or not a real distinction exists between breach of duty and causation, ie, whether once the plaintiff has established on balance of probabilities the breach of duty of care, the evidentiary onus of proof should shift onto the defendant. See also: Gaudron J at 420–1.

injury or disease', should not have to assume the burden of proving more: namely, 'that it was the addition to the risk, caused by the breach of duty, which caused or materially contributed to the injury'. Lord Wilberforce (at 6–7) provided the following policy reason for his approach:

> if one asks which of the parties, the workman or the employers, should suffer from this inherent evidential difficulty, the answer as a matter of policy or justice should be that it is the creator of the risk who, *ex hypothesi* must be taken to have foreseen the possibility of damage, who should bear its consequences.

The policy reasons that underpin this reasoning are pertinent to injuries that occur in industrial settings where the issues of an imbalance of power and control between employers and employees may be relevant. Yet, in Australia, the test has been applied indiscriminately in many legal contexts.[42] For example, the 'material contribution' test was used in *Chappel v Hart* (1998) 195 CLR 232,[43] a case which is generally credited with opening the floodgates of medical malpractice litigation for failure to warn about potential risks, including theoretical risks inherent in the proposed surgical procedure. The Ipp Panel (at [3.326]) noted:

> the term 'material contribution to harm' is often used not in the sense in which it was used in *Bonnington Castings v Wardlaw*, but merely to express the idea that a person whose negligent conduct was a necessary condition of harm may be held liable for that harm even though some other person's conduct was also a necessary condition of that harm.[44]

Fairchild v Glenhaven Funeral Services: modified 'material contribution' test

Like Mr Wardlaw in *Bonnington*, and Mr McGhee in *McGhee*, the claimants[45] in *Fairchild v Glenhaven Funeral Services Ltd* [2003] 1 AC 32 were also workers who suffered injury (mesothelioma) by inhaling heavily polluted air (asbestos dust) while at work. They too, suffered harm as a result of cumulative operation of an identified single causative agent, asbestos dust, which occurred over a number of years. However, unlike Mr Wardlaw and Mr McGhee, they worked for several employers (the defendants). Each of these defendants, while admitting a breach of duty to protect the workers from the risk of contracting mesothelioma, claimed that it was the 'other' employer(s) who materially contributed to the injury. The workers,

---

42. See, for example: *Kavanagh v Akhtar* (1998) 45 NSWLR 588.
43. At 239–40, per Gaudron J; at 244–5, 250, 251, per McHugh J (dissenting); and at 273–4, per Kirby J. Gaudron, McHugh and Kirby JJ all discussed material contribution. Other Justices referred to the 'but for' test tempered by various 'additional factors'.
44. The *Ipp Report* at [3.326] concluded: 'In this sense, both joint and concurrent tortfeasors materially contribute to the harm resulting from their respective conduct.'
45. The House of Lords determined three appeals, which were heard together.

therefore, encountered 'evidential gap' because the scientific evidence was not able to determine the exact contribution of each defendant.

Lord Bingham of Cornhill (at [2]) thus summarised the issues in *Fairchild*:[46]

- the plaintiff was employed at different times by both A and B, and both employers had a duty to prevent C inhaling asbestos dust because it was known to cause mesothelioma
- both A and B breached their respective duties with the result that C inhaled asbestos dust during both periods of employment
- C suffered from mesothelioma; and
- any cause of C's mesothelioma other than the inhalation of asbestos dust at work could be ruled out.

However, because of the limits of science, C could not prove, on the balance of probabilities, that he contracted mesothelioma as a result of inhaling asbestos during his employment by A or during his employment by B or during his employment by A and B taken together. The question before the court was whether C was entitled to recover damages against either A *or* B, or against A *and* B.

The House of Lords unanimously determined that C was entitled to recover damages against both A and B, despite being unable to pass the 'but for' test, on the basis that: 'in the special circumstances of such a case, principle, authority or policy requires or justifies a modified approach to proof of causation' (at [2]). According to the modified test, in exceptional cases, the claimants can establish causation if they can show, on the balance of probabilities that each defendant's wrongdoing had materially increased their *risk* of contracting the disease.

Their Lordships held that the *McGhee* case provided the correct basis for determining causation in cases of multiple tortfeasors where there is no way of identifying, even on a balance of probabilities, the source of the causative agent (the fibre or fibres), which initiated the genetic process that culminated in the injury (mesothelioma). The leading judgment was given by Lord Bingham of Cornhill, who interpreted (at [21]) the *McGhee* case thus:

> it was expressly held by three members of the House [in *McGhee*] (Lord Reid at p 5, Lord Simon at p 8 and Lord Salmon at pp 12–13) that in the circumstances no distinction was to be drawn between making a *material contribution to causing* the disease and *materially increasing the risk* of the pursuer contracting it. [emphasis added]

Lord Hoffmann, conscious of the jurisprudential implications of the modified test if it were to be used as a general test of causation, identified (at [64]) the following five factors, which were present in both cases:

---

46. Discussed in the *Ipp Report* at [3.327].

1   the employer was under a duty specifically intended to protect employees against being unnecessarily exposed to the risk of a particular disease
2   the duty was one intended to create a civil right to compensation for injury relevantly connected with its breach
3   it was established that the longer the workman worked in the polluted work environment, the greater was the risk of his contracting the disease
4   the mechanism by which dust caused the disease was unknown, so that medical science was unable to prove the exact timing and proportions of the harmful effects of the dust. All that could be said was that the absence of facilities added materially to the risk that he would contract the disease
5   the employee contracted the disease against which he should have been protected.

His Lordship then concluded (at [67]) that when (and only when) the above five factors are present, 'the law should treat a material increase in risk as sufficient to satisfy the causal requirements for liability.' This will be so, irrespective of whether the case concerns just one defendant employer (*McGhee*), or multiple employers (*Fairchild*), providing each employer was in breach of the duty to provide safe conditions of work, including protection from known harmful environmental pollutants. The exception should only apply to 'conduct which only increased the chances of the employee contracting the disease.'[47]

On the particular facts of this case, the outcome in *Fairchild*—allowing the recovery—was undoubtedly just. Yet it is arguable that the *McGhee* and *Fairchild* approach of broadening the *Bonnington v Wardlaw* test from the harm-based theory of causation to 'the risk of harm' theory stands the classic paradigm of negligence on its head. This is because, within the paradigm, the inquiry into the defendant's liability in negligence for the plaintiff's harm operates on descending levels of abstraction. At the duty of care stage, 'the defendant and plaintiff are so placed in relation to each other that it is reasonably foreseeable as a possibility that careless conduct of any kind on the part of the former may result in damage of some kind to the person or property of the latter'.[48] The scope of the defendant's duty at this stage is restricted by the requirement that the *risk* of harm be reasonably foreseeable. The issue of violation of duty at the breach stage is correspondingly restricted—with the inquiry focusing on the nature of the foreseeable *risk* of *some* kind of harm that the *particular* kind of carelessness charged against the defendant might cause. Classically, at the stage of causation, the plaintiff is required to establish a factual and legal connection between the defendant's specific violation of duty and the *actual* harm which constitutes the claim for damages.

---

47. *Gregg v Scott* [2005] UKHL 2 at [78], per Lord Hoffmann.
48. *Minister Administering the Environmental Planning and Assessment Act 1979 v San Sebastian Pty Ltd* [1983] 2 NSWLR 268 at 295–6, per Glass JA.

Treating 'an increase in risk as equivalent to a material contribution' (*Fairchild* ar [32], per Lord Bingham of Cornhill), does not sit easily with the fundamental principle of compensation that a person is not compensated for tortiously inflicted physical injury, but for the loss and needs created as a result of that injury (as against the risk thereof).

Hotson v East Berkshire Area Health Authority: pre-existing condition

What happens in a case where, because of a pre-existing condition, the plaintiff would have suffered the same effects whether or not the tortious event had occurred?

In *Malec v JC Hutton Pty Ltd* (1990) 169 CLR 638, which was discussed in Chapter 2, the High Court stated that past events, when established on the balance of probabilities, are treated as certainty. Therefore, historically, once it is accepted that the plaintiff suffers from a pre-existing condition, he or she will bear the legal onus of proving what proportion of that disabling condition should be ascribed to the defendant's supervening negligence. Unless the plaintiff can discharge this onus on the balance of probabilities, the causal responsibility will be attributed to the pre-existing condition rather than to the wrongful act of the defendant. The defendant will not be liable for the effects of the pre-existing condition.

Hotson v East Berkshire Area Health Authority [1987] 1 AC 750 illustrates this principle. In *Hotson*, the plaintiff, Stephen Hotson, then aged thirteen, injured his hip joint, which was irreparably damaged by the loss of blood supply to its cartilage in a fall. This kind of injury carried with it a high risk of avascular necrosis developing later. Stephen suffered excruciating pain, due to negligence at the hospital to which he was taken, and where his condition was wrongly diagnosed. It was not until five days later that he received appropriate emergency treatment. The delay meant that the risk Stephen had faced before being admitted to the hospital had been increased, and at the time of the trial, he was suffering from symptoms of necrosis. The trial judge assessed the risk the plaintiff had faced immediately following the fall at 75 per cent, and the risk added by the negligent medical treatment at 25 per cent. The plaintiff argued that while it was possible that an immediate surgical intervention would have produced the same result, the hospital's negligence turned the risk of an adverse outcome into a certainty. In other words, Stephen's argument was that the defendant's negligence deprived him of a 25 per cent chance of good recovery.

The House of Lords accepted the trial judge's finding that 'immediately after the fall, that is before admission to hospital and therefore *before* the duty was imposed upon the defendants properly to diagnose and treat, the epiphysis [hip joint] was doomed' (emphasis in original).[49] Therefore, on the balance of probabilities, the

---

49. At 792, per Lord Ackner.

plaintiff had failed to show a causal connection between the negligence and the necrosis, for even before he entered the hospital, he was 'doomed' in the sense that the probability of developing the condition was 75 per cent. It was therefore more probable than not that he would have developed necrosis, regardless of quick and appropriate medical attention. Thus, his initial fall was the sole cause of the necrosis.

The test of legal causation in *Hotson* was determined on the balance of probabilities. The test of balance of probabilities requires the plaintiff to establish that it was more probable than not that the tortious conduct caused the injury. Thus, the plaintiff must establish his case with at least 51 per cent of probability. If the plaintiff can only establish the case as equally likely or unlikely—at 50 per cent—his case will fail, because the test requires not some probability of causation, but that in the circumstances of the case the alleged wrongful cause be more probable than not.

Their Lordships declared that in the circumstances of the *Hotson* case, it was not correct to say, as the trial judge did (upheld by the Court of Appeal), that on arrival at the hospital, on the balance of probabilities, Stephen had more than an even chance of recovery. His chance of recovery at that stage was estimated at only 25 per cent. Consequently, on the balance of probabilities, the plaintiff never did have any chance of a better outcome, and the hospital's negligence did not cause him the loss of any such chance. Lord Ackner (at 793) explained:

> Once liability is established, on the balance of probabilities, the loss which the plaintiff has sustained is payable in full. It is not discounted by reducing his claim by the extent to which he has failed to prove his case with 100 per cent certainty.

Likewise, according to Lord Bridge (at 783):

> But if the plaintiff had proved on a balance of probabilities that the authority's negligent failure to diagnose and treat his injury promptly had materially contributed to the development of avascular necrosis, I know of no principle of English law which would have entitled the authority to a discount from the full measure of damage to reflect the chance that, even given prompt treatment, avascular necrosis might well still have developed.

Wilsher v Essex Area Health Authority: several causative agents

In non-industrial personal injury cases, the problem of evidential gap due to cumulative causation may arise where there is one defendant, but the claimant's injury was caused by cumulative operation of several different causative agents, only one of which was due to the defendant's negligence. This happened in *Wilsher v Essex Area Health Authority* [1988] AC 1074. The plaintiff, a three-months premature baby who was at risk of death or serious brain damage by reason of incompletely developed lungs, was placed in the defendant hospital's special care unit. Due to his prematurity and undeveloped retina, he also faced the well-known hazard of blindness through retrolental fibroplasia. A junior doctor inserted an umbilical catheter into the baby's umbilical vein instead of artery, with the effect of saturating the plaintiff in oxygen. This mistake was undetected for eight hours. The plaintiff claimed damages from the defendants for negligent medical treatment which, he argued, materially increased the risk of the retrolental fibroplasia that he developed some three weeks later, and which resulted in his blindness. The plaintiff only succeeded in establishing that the excessive oxygen was administered; however, he was not able to establish, on the balance of probabilities, that this raised the partial pressure of oxygen (O_2) in the plaintiff's arterial blood to a sufficiently high level for a sufficient length of time to play any part in the causation of the retrolental fibroplasia. Administration of excessive oxygen was merely one of a number of possible causes of the plaintiff's condition, which included apnoea, hypercarbia, intraventricular haemorrhage, and patent ductus arteriosus. The plaintiff suffered from each of these conditions. No causal mechanisms linking these conditions with the development of the retrolental fibroplasia were positively identified, but neither was the excess of oxygen.

Lord Bridge of Harwich, delivering the leading judgment,[50] adopted the approach of Sir Nicolas Browne-Wilkinson V-C (who dissented when the case was heard in the Court of Appeal) and held (at 1091) that 'A failure to take preventative measures against one out of five possible causes is no evidence as to which of those five caused the injury.'

Thus, the House of Lords determined that, where a number of different factors were capable of causing the condition, there could be no presumption that it was the excess oxygen, rather than one of the other four factors, which caused the plaintiff's blindness. The plaintiff's condition was simply a risk faced by virtue of being born prematurely, and it was impossible to say whether, in this case, the excess oxygen caused or contributed to the condition. In other words, the House of Lords held that the 'but for' test as a prerequisite of causation was not satisfied by mere increase in a pre-existent risk of harm due to negligence. Their Lordships sent the case back for retrial of causation in accordance with the test of material contribution.

Burden of proof in causation

In *McGhee*, Lord Wilberforce suggested that in certain cases, once the plaintiff has established on the balance of probabilities the breach of duty of care, the evidentiary onus of proof should shift to the defendant. Lord Bridge in *Wilsher*, in his critique

---

50. Lord Fraser of Tullybelton, Lord Lowry, Lord Griffiths, and Lord Ackner agreeing.

of the *McGhee* approach, rejected the notion of shifting the burden of proof in causation.

In *Fairchild*, while Lord Bingham of Cornhill criticised Lord Bridge's rejection of *McGhee*'s extension to the material contribution test (equating material contribution to the damage with materially increasing the risk of damage) in *Wilsher*, he accepted the correctness of *Wilsher*, in particular the rule that the plaintiff bears the substantive burden of proving causation. Lord Hutton (in dissent, at [103]) said:

> *McGhee* is not now, and never was, authority for the legally adventurous proposition that if a breach of duty is shown, and damage is proven within the area of risk that brought about the duty, and if the breach of duty materially increases the risk of damage of that type, then the onus of proof shifts from the plaintiff to the defendant to disprove the causal connection. That proposition could be derived only from the speech of Lord Wilberforce and it is now clear that it was never a binding principle emerging from the *McGhee* case.

In Australia, in *Bennett v Minister of Community Welfare* (1992) 176 CLR 408, at 416,[51] Mason CJ, Deane and Toohey JJ left open the question of whether or not a real distinction exists between breach of duty and causation: ie, whether once the plaintiff has established on balance of probabilities the breach of duty of care, the evidentiary onus of proof should shift onto the defendant. Gaudron J (at 420–1), referring to *McGhee*, said in a somewhat obscure passage:

> in the case of a positive act, questions of causation are answered by reference to what, in fact, happened. In the case of an omission, they are answered by reference to what would or would not have happened had the act occurred. In that exercise, ... the issue is approached on the basis that 'when there is a duty to take a precaution against damage occurring to others through the default of third parties or through accident, breach of the duty may be regarded as materially causing or materially contributing to that damage', should it occur, subject of course to the question whether performance of the duty would have averted the harm.

However, in *Chappel v Hart* (1998) 195 CLR 232 (discussed below), Kirby J (at [93(viii)]) found Lord Wilberforce's reasoning regarding the shift in burden of proof 'compelling'. His Honour stated that:

> Once a plaintiff demonstrates that a breach of duty has occurred which is closely followed by damage, a prima facie causal connection will have been established. It is then for the defendant to show, by evidence and argument, that the patient should not recover damages.

---

51. See also: Gaudron J at 420–1.

Although, in *Chappel v Hart*, Kirby J was a member of the majority, regarding the liability of the defendant, his Honour's position on this point was not supported, and thus cannot be taken as representing the majority view. Mason P, in *Bendix Mintex Pty Ltd v Barnes* (1997) 42 NSWLR 307 and *TC by his tutor Sabatino v The State of New South Wales & Ors* [2001] NSWCA 380, interpreted the position of Lord Wilberforce, Gaudron, and Kirby JJ as standing for the proposition that in certain cases of omissions, the evidentiary onus may shift to the defendant. His Honour, however, observed (at [59]) that: 'Australian law has not adopted a formal reversal of onus of proof of causation in negligence, even negligence involving breach by omission.'

The principle of non-reversal of the onus of proof is now statutorily entrenched in identical form[52] in Victoria, Queensland, New South Wales, Tasmania, the Australian Capital Territory, and Western Australia. It reads:

> In deciding liability for negligence, the plaintiff always bears the burden of proving, on the balance of probabilities, any fact relevant to the issue of causation.[53]

The 'loss of chance' doctrine

In *Hotson*, the House of Lords rejected the applicability of the 'loss of chance' doctrine in claims of medical negligence. Likewise, in *Wilsher*, the House of Lords reversed the Court of Appeal's award of damages for the reduction in the chance of a favourable outcome. However, in *Fairchild*, which was not a medico-legal case, their Lordships imposed liability for conduct which merely increased the chances (risk) of the employee contracting the disease.

In *Gregg v Scott* [2005] UKHL 2, the majority of the House of Lords (Lord Hoffmann, Lord Phillips of Worth Matravers, and Baroness Hale of Richmond; Lord Nicholls of Birkenhead and Lord Hope of Craighead dissenting) refused to 'introduce into the law of clinical negligence the right of a patient who has suffered an adverse event to recover damages for the loss of a chance of a more favourable outcome'.[54] On 22 November 1994 Mr Gregg consulted Dr Scott, his general practitioner, about a lump under his arm. Dr Scott diagnosed it as a lipoma (a benign collection of fatty tissue). On 22 August 1995, Mr Gregg told another general practitioner that over the past year, the lump had gradually enlarged. This doctor also thought that it was a lipoma, but referred Mr Gregg, on a non-urgent basis, for an investigation. On 2 November 1995, Mr Gregg was examined by a surgeon who diagnosed a non-Hodgkin's lymphoma. The trial judge found that Dr Scott was

---

52. The principle that 'the onus of proof of any fact relevant to causation always rests on the plaintiff' follows Recommendation 29(a) of the *Ipp Report*.
53. *Wrongs Act 1958* (Vic), s 52; *Civil Liability Act 2003* (Qld), s 12; *Civil Liability Act 2002* (NSW), s 5E; *Civil Liability Act 2002* (Tas), s 14; *Civil Law (Wrongs) Act 2002* (ACT), s 46; *Wrongs Act 1936* (SA), s 35; *Civil Liability Act 2002* (WA), s 5D.
54. At [125], per Lord Phillips of Worth Matravers.

negligent in excluding the possibility that the growth might not be benign, and not referring Mr Gregg to a specialist following the original consultation. Although the trial and appeals were run on the basis that Mr Gregg had poor chances of survival, he was still alive in 2005, some nine years after the commencement of his treatment (survival for more than ten years is considered a cure). The question before the House of Lords was whether the likely premature death of Mr Gregg should be attributable to the wrongful act of the defendant medical practitioner.[55]

In this case—as in most pleas involving loss of chance—the plaintiff relied on statistical evidence to establish that early treatment would probably have produced a remission. According to the experts, a study had shown that the delay in diagnosis reduced Mr Gregg's chances of survival for more than ten years from 42 per cent to 25 per cent. There were two distinct approaches to this statistical evidence. Lord Nicholls of Birkenhead (at [3]) essentially transposed the general findings for the cohort, and applied them to Mr Gregg as an individual, stating that to provide a remedy in cases where the claimant had suffered a 55 per cent loss of prospect of recovery, but deny damages in cases where the loss of recovery is 45 per cent 'would be irrational and indefensible', because in both cases the patient was worse off due to the doctor's breach of duty.

However, this approach does not properly reflect the nature of statistical studies of cohorts, which examine multiple potential consequences for a given potential risk factor.[56] In their separate judgments, Lord Hoffman and Lord Phillips of Worth Matravers (at [153]) pointed out that experts merely established statistically the likely fate of the cohort under study. Statistics gave 'no indication of the factors that would determine what would befall an individual member of that cohort.' Therefore, according to the majority, the statistical reduction in the prospect of a favourable outcome ('loss of chance') is not a recoverable head of damage.

In rejecting the plaintiff's submission that 'the exceptional rule in *Fairchild* should be generalised and damages awarded in all cases in which the defendant may have caused an injury and has increased the likelihood of the injury being suffered' (at [84]), Lord Hoffmann stated (at [80]):

> the progress of Mr Gregg's disease had a determinate cause. It may have been inherent in his genetic make-up at the time when he saw Mr Scott, as *Hotson's* fate was determined by what happened to his thigh when he fell out of the tree. Or it may, ... have been affected by subsequent events and behaviour for which Dr Scott was not responsible. Medical science does not enable us to say. But the outcome was not random; it was governed by laws of causality [in physical as against legal sense] ...

---

55. The trial judge held that Mr Gregg had failed to prove, on balance of probabilities, that the delay in commencing his treatment had adversely affected his clinical experience or expectation of life (at [129]).
56. For a general discussion, see: Senn SJ, *Dicing with Death*, Cambridge University Press, Cambridge, 2003.

Likewise, Baroness Hale of Richmond observed (at [203]):

> Doctors do not cause the presenting disease. If they negligently fail to diagnose and treat it, it is not enough to show that a claimant's disease has got worse during the period of delay. It has to be shown that treating it earlier would have prevented that happening, at least for the time being.

In the 1980s, some United States jurisdictions adopted the controversial 'loss of chance' doctrine of causation whereby plaintiffs needed only to establish, by a preponderance of the evidence, that the defendant's negligence denied them a chance for a better result, for example that a negligent delay in treatment lessened the effectiveness of the medical therapy (*Herskovits v Group Health Coop* 99 Wash 2d 609, 664 P2d 474 (1983)).[57] The concept has been discussed—sometimes with less than perfect understanding[58]—in a number of Australian courts.[59] However, in *Naxakis v Western General Hospital & Anor* (1999) 197 CLR 269, Gaudron J (at [35]) pointed out difficulties in allowing damages for the loss of a chance in personal injury cases, noting that:

> Assessment of the value of the chance must depend either on speculation or statistical analysis. And in the case of statistics, there is the difficulty that a statistical chance is not the same as a personal chance.

Although other members of the High Court have also generally commented on the question of loss of chance in *Chappel v Hart* (1998) 195 CLR 232 and *Rosenberg v Percival* (2001) 205 CLR 434, the High Court is still to determine this issue.

In *Gregg v Scott*, Baroness Hale of Richmond was highly critical of *Rufo v Hosking* [2004] NSWCA 391, in which Hodgson and Santow JJA, and Campbell AJA allowed damages for loss of a less than 50 per cent chance of avoiding spinal microfractures, which the claimant suffered while being treated for lupus with heavy dosages of corticosteroids. Hodgson JA, agreeing with Campbell AJA, held (at [3]) that although the plaintiff could not establish on the balance of probabilities that, but for the defendant paediatrician's negligence, the harm (spinal microfractures) suffered by her would not have occurred, or that the negligence materially contributed

---

57. For example, *Reardon v Bonutti Orthopaedic Services Ltd* 316 Ill App 3d 699 at 710; 737 NE2d 309 at 317–8; 249 Ill Dec 919 (2000) involved an allegation that the chances of saving the plaintiff's foot would have been greater had the defendant physician physically examined his foot. The court held that 'the plaintiff must prove, by a preponderance of the evidence, that the doctor's negligence cost him a chance for a better result. Negligent delay or treatment that lessens the effectiveness of treatment is sufficient to prove proximate cause under the "loss of chance" doctrine.' However, the sole citation to this case has been *Gee v Treece* Ill. App (April 27, 2006), in which a differently constituted Appellate Court of Illinois (at [*12]) interpreted *Reardon* as standing for the proposition that that the standard of care a physician owes to a patient is an element that a plaintiff must prove.
58. *Sullivan v Micallef* (1994) Aust Torts Reps ¶81–308 (NSW CA).
59. *Locher v Turner* [1995] Aust Torts Reps ¶81–336; *Gavalas v Singh* [2001] VSCA 23 (22 March 2001); *Board of Management of Royal Perth Hospital v Frost* (unreported, WA FC, 26 February 1997); *Rufo v Hosking* [2004] NSWCA 391 (1 November 2004).

to the harm, the defendant 'materially increased a risk, which was otherwise very substantial, that fractures would occur; and that the occurrence of the fractures was a realisation of this total risk (as distinct from the increment to the risk created by the negligence).' The plaintiff was thus 'entitled to be compensated for the loss of the chance that, but for the negligence, the fractures would not have occurred (or would not have occurred at the time or with the severity of their actual occurrence).'[60]

Baroness Hale (at [214]) quoted the following passage from Campbell AJA's judgment:[61]

> adopting a robust and pragmatic approach to the primary facts of this case ... it seems to me that more probably than not the excess of corticosteroid consumed after 10 June 1992 in the context of the osteoporotic and vulnerable state of the appellant's spine caused the loss of a chance that the appellant would have suffered less spinal damage than she in fact did.

Her Ladyship then commented (at [215]):

> This conclusion comes after many paragraphs of dense and careful analysis of the evidence before the trial judge. But in the end the appeal is to common sense. And common sense will often suggest that the chances of a better outcome would have been better if the doctor had done what he should have done: for why else should he have done it but to improve the patient's chances? Reformulating the damage in this way could lead to some liability in almost every case.

STATUTORY APPROACH TO 'EVIDENTIAL GAPS'

The legislators in South Australia and the Australian Capital Territory addressed the *Fairchild* problem of 'evidential gaps' by providing a very specific exception to the 'but for' test. The *Civil Liability Act 1936* (SA), s 34(2), provides:

> if a person (the plaintiff) has been negligently exposed to a similar risk of harm by a number of different people (the defendants) and it is not possible to assign responsibility for causing the harm to any one or more of them:
>
> (a) the court may continue to apply the established common law principle under which the responsibility may be assigned to the defendants for causing the harm,[1] but
>
> (b) the court must consider the position of each defendant individually and state reasons for bringing the defendant within the scope of liability.

[1] See *Fairchild v Glenhaven Funeral Services Ltd* [2002] 3 WLR 89.

---

60. The New South Wales Court of Appeal has followed *Rufo v Hosking* in *New South Wales v Burton*; [2006] NSWCA 12. However, the Queensland Court of Appeal did not follow *Rufo v Hosking* in *Moore v Queensland* [2005] QCA 299.
61. Campbell AJA gave the leading judgment in the Court of Appeal at [405].

The *Civil Law (Wrongs) Act 2002* (ACT), s 45(2), is identical, but does not refer specifically to *Fairchild v Glenhaven*.

Both provisions use the phrase 'negligently exposed to a similar risk of harm by a number of different people (the defendants)', which makes this exception very narrow. Its focus on multiple tortfeasors, rather than multiple causative factors, precludes the risk that the provision will be used to overcome or pre-empt the principle in *Wilsher v Essex Area Health Authority*.

Section 5D(2) of the *Civil Liability Act 2002* (NSW) addresses the problem of evidential gaps as follows:

> In determining in an exceptional case, in accordance with established principles, whether negligence that cannot be established as a necessary condition of the occurrence of harm should be accepted as establishing factual causation, the court is to consider (amongst other relevant things) whether or not and why responsibility for the harm should be imposed on the negligent party.

The wording of this provision is ambiguous and open to different interpretations. The Victorian provision[62] is similar in its substance to the New South Wales s 5D(2), but is designed to expand defendants' liability even further, for it allows the courts in 'appropriate'—rather than 'exceptional'—cases to eliminate the 'but for' requirement of factual causation. The Western Australian Parliament in its *Civil Liability Act 2002* (WA), s 5C(2), adopted the Victorian wording, which provides:

> In determining in an appropriate case, in accordance with established principles, whether a fault that cannot be established as a necessary condition of the occurrence of harm should be taken to establish factual causation, the court is to consider (amongst other relevant things): (a) whether and why responsibility for the harm should or should not be imposed on the tortfeasor; and (b) whether and why the harm should be left to lie where it fell.

The provision in clause (b) directs that in determining liability in cases where the plaintiff is unable to establish factual causation, the court should consider not only reasons for the imposition or otherwise of liability, but also 'whether and why the harm should be left to lie where it fell'. The final clause may be interpreted as signalling that courts are expected to take into account social and economic consequences (costs of the loss-shifting) of the ultimate decision when determining the 'appropriate' cases.

In New South Wales, Victoria, and Western Australia, where the defendant has been found to be in breach of a duty of care to the plaintiff, but the latter cannot establish the causal link between the breach and the plaintiff's injury, the court may still attribute the legal liability to the defendant, providing it considers, among other relevant things, 'whether or not and why responsibility for the harm should

---

62. *Wrongs Act 1958* (Vic), s 51(2).

be imposed on the party in breach' (and the loss-shifting, in Western Australia). However, the wording linking the breach with the injury is unclear and leaves open the possibility that the defendant's breach of duty need not relate specifically to the plaintiff's harm for causation to be established. This is precisely the kind of open-ended approach to liability in negligence that the common law has guarded against since *Palsgraf v Long Island Railroad Co* 162 NE 99 (1928), where Cardozo CJ said that the fact that the defendant owes a duty of care not to injure one person does not mean that the duty of care is owed equally to another. The 'reasonable foreseeability of harm' test establishing the defendant's duty of care and its breach must be applied separately to each particular plaintiff who suffers harm as a result of the defendant's conduct. Moreover, the wording of Victorian, New South Wales, and Western Australian provisions does not direct the judiciary to follow, or even consider, Lord Hoffmann's five limiting factors in *Fairchild* (discussed above). By the same token, nor does the legislation prevent such approach.

No doubt cognisant of the danger of inadvertently introducing a statutory scheme of strict liability in general negligence, the Queensland and Tasmanian provisions acknowledge that the claimant must establish some breach of duty towards the plaintiff:

> In deciding in an exceptional case, in accordance with established principles, whether a breach of duty—being a breach of duty that is established but which cannot be established as satisfying subsection (1)(a)—should be accepted as satisfying subsection (1)(a), the court is to consider (among other relevant things) whether or not and why responsibility for the harm should be imposed on the party in breach.[63]

The provisions governing 'exceptional' or 'appropriate' cases state that the courts should decide these cases 'in accordance with established principles' of the common law. Unfortunately, the legislation does not provide any statutory criteria for determining whether and when a common law principle should be regarded as 'established'.[64]

The problem is compounded by the fact that with the exception of South Australia and the Australian Capital Territory, all jurisdictions exclude dust and/or asbestos disease-related cases from the statutory regime.[65] Yet they are precisely

---

63. *Civil Liability Act 2003* (Qld), s 11(2); *Civil Liability Act 2003* (Tas), s 13(2).
64. It is unclear whether the 'established principles' are supposed to be those extant at the time of the reforms (2002–03) or the ones developed in the future (contemporaneous with the time of hearing).
65. *Civil Liability Act 2003* (Qld), s 5(b) and (c); *Personal Injuries Proceedings Act 2002* (Qld), s 6(3)(b); *Civil Liability Act 2002* (NSW), s 3B(b) and (c); *Wrongs Act 1958* (Vic), s 45(1)(e) and (f); *Personal Injuries (Liabilities And Damages) Act 2003* (NT), s 4(3)(c); *Civil Liability Act 2002* (WA), ss 3A(4) (smoking and other use of tobacco products) and 6(4) (asbestos-related diseases); *Civil Liability Act 2002* (Tas), s 3B(1)(b) (smoking and other use of tobacco products).

the kinds of cases to which the House of Lords in *McGhee* and *Fairchild* wished to confine the modified test of causation.

Likewise, with the exception of South Australia and the Australian Capital Territory, the legislation does not prevent the court adopting the loss of chance doctrine. Though, as Baroness Hale pointed out in *Gregg v Scott*, reformulating the damage in terms of chance, 'could lead to some liability in almost every case' (at [215]).

In Western Australia, but not necessarily in New South Wales, Victoria, Queensland, or Tasmania, the courts would at least have to consider the economic and social impact of introducing the loss of chance doctrine.

ATTRIBUTING LEGAL LIABILITY IN CASES OF FAILURE TO ADVISE

Another issue of factual causation arises in cases of negligent failure to warn about inherent material risks, where the hypothetical question is: what would have been the decision of the plaintiff had he or she been provided with the warning?

The causal problems in claims about negligent failure to warn are well illustrated in the following scenario outlined by Lord Hoffmann in *Banque Bruxelles Lambert SA v Eagle Star Insurance Co Ltd* [1997] AC 191 (at 213):

> A mountaineer about to undertake a difficult climb is concerned about the fitness of his knee. He goes to a doctor who negligently makes a superficial examination and pronounces the knee fit. The climber goes on the expedition, which he would not have undertaken if the doctor had told him the true state of his knee. He suffers an injury which is an entirely foreseeable consequence of mountaineering but has nothing to do with his knee.

Should the doctor be liable for the mountaineer's injury?

Unlike the hypothetical 'but for' test in cases involving established past events, where the 'but for' test is applied in cases of failure to warn or inform, the answer, which determines the issue of factual causation, is not provided by the court but by the plaintiff. When answering this question, the plaintiff, by definition, has the benefit of hindsight and a self-serving interest in denying knowledge or awareness of the risk.

In Australia, the two major High Court cases on negligent failure to warn of inherent risks arose in the context of medico-legal litigation. In response, a number of reforming jurisdictions enacted legislation intended to modify the common law. They are discussed in turn.

Chappel v Hart

In *Chappel v Hart* (1998) 195 CLR 232, Mrs Hart, a senior teacher and librarian with the New South Wales Education Department, had a wide-necked pharyngeal diverticulum (oesophageal pouch) which measured 3 cm by 1.5 cm.[66] Due to this condition small scraps of food which she swallowed would collect in the pouch, causing infection and inflammation. Mrs Hart's condition was stressful, 'relentlessly progressive' and surgery provided the only cure.[67] She was referred to Mr Chappel, an ear, nose, and throat (ENT) surgeon, who advised that she should have the oesophageal pouch surgically removed. Critical to Mrs Hart's success in this case was the determination of what was said at the initial consultation, for, under the rule in *Rogers v Whitaker* (1992) 175 CLR 479, the more inquisitive the patient the broader is the medical duty to warn. Mrs Hart claimed to have had the prescience to refer to the safety of her voice, and the court, on questionable grounds (see below), accepted her evidence on this issue. This meant that the defendant had a duty to disclose to her all of the relevant risks inherent in the procedure. Perforation of the oesophagus is a well recognised complication of the removal of an oesophageal pouch. The court accepted that perforations can and do occur without any negligence on the part of the surgeon. Mr Chappel advised Mrs Hart about the risk of oesophageal perforation. In the great majority of cases, the perforation will have no lasting adverse effects. However, on rare occasions, bacteria may be present in the oesophagus. Such presence occurs at random. If this happens, there is a risk that the bacteria may escape through the perforation into the mediastinum and cause inflammation of the tissues of the mediastinum (mediastinitis). Mediastinitis may in turn lead to a number of further complications, including inflammation of laryngeal nerves, which may, on a rare occasion, cause a loss of function in a vocal cord.[68]

The surgeon failed to warn the plaintiff about the risk of mediastinitis and its possible complications. The operation was performed competently, but subsequent mediastinitis resulted in temporary paralysis of the plaintiff's laryngeal nerve, which left her unable to shout. As a result of her disability, Mrs Hart resigned from work.

Mrs Hart's sole claim was that Dr Chappell did not warn her of the remote risk of vocal damage posed by the surgery. Mrs Hart admitted that she would have undergone the surgery in any event,[69] but submitted that, had she been warned of the risk of vocal damage, she would have deferred the operation, and probably had the operation later, at the hands of the most experienced surgeon.

The question before the High Court was whether the defendant's failure to warn of the risk of mediastinitis and potential paralysis of the laryngeal nerve was

---

66. 'Professional Negligence: Medical Practitioners and Hospitals', (1991) *Australian Torts Reporter* ¶36–950.
67. *Chappel v Hart* (unreported, SC(CA) NSW, Mahoney P, Handley JA, Cohen AJA, No 40438/94, 24 December 1996), at [3], per Handley JA.
68. Though theoretically known, until it actually occurred in Mrs Hart's case, this particular complication was apparently so rare that it was not described in medical textbooks. In his evidence, Professor Benjamin, the leading expert on pharyngeal diverticulum appearing for the plaintiff, deposed that he had never encountered mediastinitis leading to the kind of injury sustained by Mrs Hart.
69. Even though the procedure performed by the defendant had reduced the severity of Mrs Hart's symptoms, in February 1985, a grape stuck in her throat and had to be surgically removed. In June 1985, she once again submitted to the procedure to remove the oesophageal pouch.

the *cause* of plaintiff's physical injury. The High Court determined by majority of three (Gaudron, Gummow, and Kirby JJ) to two (McHugh and Hayne JJ) that Dr Chappel's failure to warn the plaintiff about the risk to vocal damage constituted a breach of duty of care, which caused Mrs Hart's injury.

No evidence was led during the trial about the hierarchy of skill and care required for the oesophageal perforation to occur once in forty procedures as against once in twenty interventions.[70] Nevertheless, Gaudron J said, and Kirby J concurred, that had the defendant surgeon informed Mrs Hart about a more experienced surgeon, the nature of the risk would have remained the same, but the degree of risk would have been diminished. According to Gaudron J (at [10]):

> If the foreseeable risk to Mrs Hart was the loss of an opportunity to undergo surgery at the hands of a more experienced surgeon, the duty would have been a duty to inform her that there were more experienced surgeons practising in the field.

McHugh J disagreed. His Honour (at [40]) stressed the pure coincidence of the bacteria moving up from the stomach to the oesophagus at the time of the operation, and its role as the causative agent of mediastinitis: 'the random chance of bacteria being present in the oesophagus when the perforation occurs' and concluded (at [45]) that

> it is also close to a certainty that neither mediastinitis nor damage to the laryngeal nerve would have occurred if the defendant had performed the operation on some other day or even at some different hour on that day. He was not as experienced a surgeon as Professor Benjamin but he had performed the operation successfully on previous occasions. If reasonable care is exercised, there is only a remote possibility that damage to a laryngeal nerve resulting from mediastinitis will lead to paralysis of the vocal cords, as happened with the plaintiff, irrespective of which surgeon performs the procedure. Moreover, given the plaintiff's abandonment of any claim that the defendant had performed the operation negligently, he must be taken to have exercised reasonable skill and care on this occasion. His performance on this occasion was differentiated from that of others only by the eventuation of a risk that is inherent in the procedure whoever performs it.

McHugh J (at [47]) also pointed out that the correct factual causation question in the failure to warn cases is whether the negligent omission caused the defendant to *do* something that resulted or materially contributed to the plaintiff's injury. In *Chappel v Hart*, the correct question should have been:

> Did the defendant's failure to warn cause or materially contribute to him perforating the defendant's oesophagus?

---

70. *Chappel v Hart* (1998) 195 CLR 232, 9 at [39]–[43], per McHugh J; see also: Mendelson D, 'The Breach of the Medical Duty to Warn and Causation: *Chappel v Hart* and the Necessity to Reconsider Some Aspects of *Rogers v Whitaker*' (1998) 5 *Journal of Law and Medicine* 312–319.

In the scenario presented by Lord Hoffmann in *Banque Bruxelles Lambert SA v Eagle Star Insurance Co Ltd* [1997] AC 191, at 213, the factual causation question should be whether the medical practitioner's negligent failure to disclose *caused the doctor to injure* (or materially contributed to the doctor injuring) the mountaineer.

Retrospectivity

Chappel v Hart was a deeply flawed case. Mrs Hart consulted Dr Chappel and was operated on by him in 1983. But it was only in 1992 that, in *Rogers v Whitaker*, the High Court established the rule that doctors—and all professional practitioners—have a duty to inform their patients (or clients, in case of other professionals) about material risks. This novel duty was applied retrospectively to events which occurred some nine years before. By way of contrast, in *Bonello by his tutor Warren Frank Bonello v Lotzof* (unreported, Supreme Court of New South Wales, Grove J 23 September 1997), Grove J, when determining the issue of breach of duty of care with respect of events that took place in 1978, averred to the principles in *Rogers v Whitaker*, but was careful to apply the legal standards relating to the exercise of professional skills as they operated in 1978, rather than norms introduced some two decades later. The reform legislation (discussed below) has confirmed Grove J's approach.

Hindsight bias

In *Chappel v Hart*, at trial, some eleven years after the events, the determinative issue of fact involved a conflict regarding what was said in the course of the initial consultation between Mr Chappel and Mrs Hart. Mrs Hart asserted that she had raised the question of the safety of her voice with Mr Chappel, when she made 'a throwaway' remark: 'I don't want to wind up like Neville Wran.'[71] Mr Chappel denied the Neville Wran comment was ever made. The trial judge, Donovan AJ, found that although Mrs Hart was inaccurate in most of the matters in contest, her evidence on this issue should be accepted, for the reason that:

> The plaintiff is in a situation where she not only has a memory of saying those words but she also has a memory of what was in her mind at the time and of what her concerns were. Dr Chappel, on the other hand, could only observe and have a recollection through what he heard, that is, by hearing the words used. He could not have the matter in his mind in any other way. In my view it is more likely that the words and the issue would remain in the plaintiff's memory, in the forefront of her memory, than they would in the defendant's memory.[72]

---

71. Hon Neville Wran, Premier of New South Wales (1976–86). His vocal cords were damaged following an operation that was totally unrelated to the procedure which Mrs Hart was going to undergo.
72. *Chappel v Hart* (unreported, SC(CA) NSW, Mahoney P, Handley JA, Cohen AJA, No 40438/94, 24 December 1996), quoted by Mahoney P at [10].

What the learned judge did not consider is that when people examine past decisions they are inclined 'to highlight data that were consistent with the final outcome and de-emphasise data that were contradictory or ambiguous'.[73] The issue of causal responsibility turned on a contested 'throwaway' remark, which gave raise to a hypothetical decision Mrs Hart would have reached, if the defendant had not been in breach of the duty of care to warn. In the Court of Appeal, Mahoney P commented that:

> There is something of unreality in a law which (if I may adapt a metaphor) hazards the whole of the damage suffered by a plaintiff upon the hazard that the plaintiff may be able to recollect, and to recollect accurately, a conversation or remark of this kind.[74]

Under Australian common law, the test for the plaintiff's hypothetical decision is subjective.[75] An unqualified test of subjective causation in cases involving failure to warn of a risk that materialises will invariably lead to a finding of liability, because with the benefit of hindsight, plaintiffs like Mrs Hart in *Chappel v Hart*—having experienced the adverse outcome—are predisposed to believe that they would never have agreed to the procedure.

Rosenberg v Percival and the hindsight bias

In *Rosenberg v Percival* (2001) 205 CLR 434, the plaintiff, Dr Percival, a qualified nurse with longstanding experience and a PhD in nursing, having considered three different treatment options for correction of severe malocclusion due to an underdeveloped jaw, underwent an elective bilateral sagittal split osteotomy. Post-operatively, Dr Percival developed a painful temporomandibular joint disorder. The plaintiff was not warned of the inherent risk of temporomandibular disorders, and claimed that had she been alerted to this risk, she would not have consented to undergo the procedure. The possibility of temporomandibular disorders following an osteotomy was known, but experts were divided in their opinion on the degree of remoteness of the contingency, and the need to warn about it. The High Court, in separate judgments, unanimously upheld the trial judge's finding that the plaintiff failed to prove her claim that, if warned of the risk, she would not have proceeded with the surgery.

Gummow J (at [86]) stated that in cases where the allegation concerns negligent medical advice, causation requires satisfaction of two criteria:

---

73. Redelmeier DA, Rozin P & Kahneman D, 'Understanding Patients' Decisions: Cognitive and Emotional Perspectives' (1993) 270 (1) *JAMA* 72 at 73.
74. *Chappel v Hart* (unreported, SC(CA) NSW, Mahoney P, Handley JA, Cohen AJA, No 40438/94, 24 December 1996) at [20].
75. *Rosenberg v Percival* (2001) 205 CLR 434 at 443, 449, per McHugh J; at 484–5, per Kirby J.

The first criterion is a breach of the duty to warn of a material risk, that risk having eventuated and caused, in the physical sense, injury to the plaintiff. The second criterion is that, had the warning been given, the injury would have been averted, in the sense that the relevant patient would not have had the treatment in question.

All Justices emphasised that in Australia, in cases where failure to warn is in issue, causation has to be established by the subjective test of whether the particular patient–plaintiff's state of mind was such that, if told of the risk, he or she would have refused to undergo the procedure. Gleeson CJ (at [16]) identified the evidentiary problem raised by the subjective test of causation:

> In the way in which litigation proceeds, the conduct of the parties is seen through the prism of hindsight. A foreseeable risk has eventuated, and harm has resulted. The particular risk becomes the focus of attention. But at the time of the allegedly tortious conduct, there may have been no reason to single it out from a number of adverse contingencies, or to attach to it the significance it later assumed. Recent judgments in this Court have drawn attention to the danger of a failure, after the event, to take account of the context, before or at the time of the event, in which a contingency was to be evaluated.[76]

Gleeson CJ's comments also reflect expressions of judicial concern regarding the problem of hindsight reasoning, encapsulated in the popular nineteenth century dictum that: 'nothing is so easy as to be wise after the event' (Bramwell B in *Cornman v The Eastern Counties Railway Co* (1859) 4 H & N 781 at 786). Such phrases as the 'prism of hindsight' or 'hindsight bias' refer to a well-known psychological phenomenon whereby people, while retrospectively considering the occurrence of a past event, 'tend to exaggerate the extent to which it could have been correctly predicted beforehand.'[77] Baruch Fischoff in his pioneering empirical study,[78] observed that even those who are aware that knowing the outcome would affect their perceptions 'still face the unenviable task of reconstructing their foresightful state of mind'. The task is difficult because in reconstructing the past, people often are 'unable to adequately *unanchor* themselves from the perspective of hindsight' (at 297; emphasis added).

Thus, through the prism of hindsight, once the undisclosed risk has materialised, medical practitioners appear negligent, even if in foresight that would not have been the case. The statement by the trial judge, Donovan AJ, in *Chappel v Hart* is not an

---

76. Referring to *Jones v Bartlett* (2000) 205 CLR 166 and *Modbury Triangle Shopping Centre Pty Ltd v Anzil* (2000) 205 CLR 254.
77. Arkes HR and Schipiani CA, 'Medical Malpractice v the Business Judgment Rule: Differences in Hindsight Bias' (1994) 94 *Or L Rev* 587 at 588.
78. Hindsight≠Foresight: the Effect of Outcome Knowledge on Judgment under Uncertainty', (1975) 1 *J Experimental Psycho Hum Perception and Performance* 288 at 297. Rachlinski JJ in 'A Positive Psychological Theory of Judging in Hindsight', (1998) 65 *U Chicago L Rev* 571, at 606 has estimated that in the assessment of reasonable foreseeability, the hindsight bias provides an average of a 15 per cent 'boost' to the assessed probability in foresight, sufficient 'to enable the plaintiff to surmount the 50 per cent threshold needed to establish liability in a close case'.

unusual example of failure to factor in the hindsight bias when determining legal causation in cases of negligent omission to warn. In the High Court, Gaudron J did not consider the hindsight effect when she stated (at 239):

> If that evidence is to the effect that the injured person would have acted to avoid or minimise the risk of injury, it is to apply sophistry rather than common sense to say that, *although the risk of physical injury which came about called the duty of care into existence*, breach of that duty did not cause or contribute to that injury, but simply resulted in the loss of an opportunity to pursue a different course of action' (emphasis added).

To counter some of the most unfair aspects of hindsight bias, in *Rosenberg v Percival*, McHugh J (at [45]) provided a two-step approach to the plaintiffs' testimony regarding failure to disclose risks. It involves assessment of the plaintiff's mental state at the time of receiving advice and his or her decision regarding the course of action (whether or not to undergo the procedure). In relation to plaintiffs' credibility as witnesses when they assert that if warned of the risk they would not have proceeded with the surgery, while upholding the discretion of the trial judge to believe or disbelieve a plaintiff's claim, the High Court[79] suggested a number of objective factors that have a role in the assessment of the plaintiff's state of mind at the time of electing to have the procedure. These factors include:

- the need for the procedure as established by the plaintiff's medical history and medical opinion;
- the knowledge of treatment options;
- the plaintiff's willingness to undergo the general risks of the procedure (for example, a general anaesthetic);
- the plaintiff's professional background;
- the plaintiff's questioning or failure to ask about the specific risk;
- the nature of the risk and its likelihood of materialising (in *Rosenberg*, the court accepted that if the warning were given, it would have been characterised as 'very slight'; in *Chappel v Hart*, the specific risk at the time of advice would have been theoretical); and
- the plaintiff's personality and demeanour, which determine the issue of credibility.[80]

Unfortunately, it is unclear from the judgment which of these factors, apart from 'personality and demeanour',[81] is a mandatory prerequisite for the determination of subjective causation.

---

79. Gleeson CJ at 581 [17]; McHugh J at 585 [33]; Kirby J at 592 [64], 595 [80].
80. *Rosenberg v Percival* (2001) 205 CLR 434, at [30]: McHugh J noted that the assessment of the witness's credibility should not be influenced by determining the cause or causes of the lack of credibility, be they psychological or physical consequences of the unfortunate event or the desire to win the case.
81. *Devries v Australian National Railways Commission* (1993) 177 CLR 472 at 482–3.

STATUTORY APPROACHES TO HINDSIGHT BIAS

The Ipp Panel accepted the subjective test of causation, but went one step further than the High Court in *Rosenberg* and recommended that plaintiffs' testimony about what they would have done if the warning had been provided should be inadmissible:

> the Panel is ... of the view that the question of what the plaintiff would have done if the defendant had not been negligent should be decided on the basis of the circumstances of the case and without regard to the plaintiff's own testimony about what they would have done. The enormous difficulty of counteracting hindsight bias in this context undermines the value of such testimony. In practice, the judge's view of the plaintiff's credibility is likely to be determinative, regardless of relevant circumstantial evidence. As a result, such decisions tend to be very difficult to challenge successfully on appeal. We therefore recommend that in determining causation, any statement by the plaintiff about what they would have done if the negligence had not occurred should be inadmissible.[82]

New South Wales, Queensland, Western Australia, and Tasmania adopted this recommendation as a remedy for the mischief of relying solely on the plaintiff's assertions in *Chappel v Hart* in determining subjective causation. For example, s 11(3) of the *Civil Liability Act 2003* (Qld) states:

> If it is relevant to deciding factual causation to decide what the person who suffered harm would have done if the person who was in breach of the duty had not been so in breach—
> (a) the matter is to be decided subjectively in the light of all relevant circumstances, subject to paragraph (b); and
> (b) any statement made by the person after suffering the harm about what he or she would have done is inadmissible except to the extent (if any) that the statement is against his or her interest.

The wording of the Tasmanian and New South Wales provisions is very similar;[83] as is s 5C(3)(b) of the *Civil Liability Amendment Act 2003* (WA), though in this provision, the bar on the claimants' testimony of what they would have done is more absolute, namely: 'evidence of the injured person as to what he or she would have done if the tortfeasor had not been at fault is inadmissible.'[84]

---

82. *Ipp Report* at [3.3]. The authors added: 'This recommendation could be extended to cover any case in which the issue of causation depends on what a person—whether the plaintiff or a third party—would have done if the defendant had not been negligent.'
83. *Civil Liability Act 2002* (Tas), s 13(3); *Civil Liability Act 2002* (NSW), s 5D(3).
84. The text of the *Civil Liability Act 2003* (WA), s 5C(3), follows more closely *Ipp Report* Recommendation 29(g)(i): 'For the purposes of sub-paragraph (ii) of this paragraph, the plaintiff's own testimony, about what he or she would have done if the defendant had not been negligent, is inadmissible.'

Victoria has decided to entrench the subjective test of causation without adopting the clause of inadmissibility:

> If it is relevant to the determination of factual causation to determine what the person who suffered harm (the injured person) would have done if the negligent person had not been negligent, the matter is to be determined subjectively in the light of all relevant circumstances.[85]

In so doing, Victoria has preserved the common law position in relation to the subjective test of causation, but left the issue of hindsight bias unresolved.

The phrase 'the matter is to be determined subjectively in the light of all relevant circumstances', which is present in all provisions, may be interpreted as involving the two-tier analysis suggested by McHugh J in *Rosenberg v Percival* (2001) 205 CLR 434, at 449. His Honour distinguished between claimants' states of mind at the time of receiving (or not receiving) the advice in issue, and their decisions regarding subsequent course of action:

> In terms of causation theory, the critical fact is whether the patient would have taken action—refusing to have the operation—that would have avoided the harm suffered. But that fact can only be determined by making an anterior finding as to what the patient would have decided to do, if given the relevant warning. It is not possible to find what the patient would have done without deciding, expressly or by necessary implication, what decision the patient would have made, if the proper warning had been given. If the court finds that the patient would have decided not to have the operation, it concludes that he or she would not have had the operation. What the patient would have decided and what the patient would have done are hypothetical questions. But one relates to a hypothetical mental state and the other to a hypothetical course of action.

The question of the claimant's mental state, in the sense of anxiety, inquisitiveness, determination, etc, by definition has to be determined subjectively, while objective circumstances and influential factors can be considered when the full assessment is made of the claimant's state of mind at the time of electing to have the procedure. However, at least in Victoria, it is by no means certain that the courts would adopt a two-tier approach. It is unlikely, but not impossible, that the phrase 'all relevant circumstances' might be interpreted as referring to the subjective circumstances of the plaintiff, as did the majority in *Chappel v Hart*, who accepted Mrs Hart's claim that had she been warned of the risk of damage to her laryngeal nerve, she would have consulted a more experienced surgeon.

In Victoria, South Australia, the Australian Capital Territory, and the Northern Territory, the issue of hindsight bias is governed by the High Court's approach in *Rosenberg v Percival*.

---

85. *Wrongs Act 1958* (Vic), s 51(3).

NOVUS ACTUS INTERVENIENS

Even where the 'but for' test is satisfied, the defendant may be able to escape liability if he or she can show that the causal link was severed by unforeseeable tortious conduct or an unforeseeable set of independent events or conditions which amount to a 'sufficient cause'.

Thus, central to the success of the plea of *novus actus interveniens* is the question of foreseeability of the intervening event: did the intervening act pose a risk of injury in respect of which the defendant had a duty of care? This question brings the analysis back to the content of the *Donoghue v Stevenson* duty of care principle with its reference to the reasonable foreseeability of risk towards one's neighbour in law.

If the defendant's duty extends to the risk of injury from the intervening act, then the chain of causation cannot be broken by the intervention. As Mason CJ said in *March v Stramare* (1991) 171 CLR 506, at 518–9:

> As a matter of both logic and common sense, it makes no sense to regard the negligence of the plaintiff or a third party as a superseding cause or *novus actus interveniens* when the defendant's wrongful conduct has generated the very risk of injury resulting from the negligence of the plaintiff or a third party and that injury occurs in the ordinary course of things.

In *March v Stramare*, the defendant had created a situation involving a foreseeable risk of collision due to the carelessness of an inebriated driver.

Following the Torts Reforms, the common law approach may be affected by 'obvious risks' provisions.[86]

Intervening action of the plaintiff

In *Nominal Defendant v Gardikiotis* (1996) 186 CLR 49, at 55, relying upon academic authorities as well as case law,[87] McHugh J stated that:

> Under the common law theory of common sense causation, a free, informed and voluntary act of the plaintiff or a third party, which builds on a situation resulting from the defendant's tort and causes loss or damage to the plaintiff, negatives any causal connection between that tort and the loss or damage. That is so even though the act of the plaintiff or third party would not have occurred but for the defendant's tort.

---

86. *Wrongs Act 1958* (Vic), s 53.
87. Hart HLA & Honoré T, *Causation in the Law*, 2nd edn, Clarendon Press, Oxford, 1985, p 136; Luntz H, *Assessment of Damages for Personal Injury and Death*, 3rd edn, Butterworths, Sydney, 1995, p 121; *Haber v Walker* [1963] VR 339 at 358.

However, there may be circumstances where even a deliberate action by the plaintiff will not negate the duty of care of the defendant. Generally, in cases where the intervening cause responsible for the injury is the conduct of the plaintiff, then the court will adopt a two-tier approach. It will ask first whether the intervening cause was reasonably foreseeable. Providing the answer to the first question is affirmative, the court will ask a second question: was the plaintiff's conduct truly voluntary? Only if the conduct in issue is truly voluntary will it be held to have broken the chain of causation. For example, in *Caterson v Commissioner for Railways* (1973) 128 CLR 99, the High Court of Australia held that the plaintiff's conduct in jumping from an express train which started to move without warning was not truly voluntary, but was brought about by the pressure of circumstances created by the wrongful act of the defendant.

The plea of *novus actus interveniens* may be raised by the defendant not only at the stage of establishing the element of causation, but also at other stages, such as remoteness of damage. For instance, *Medlin v State Government Insurance Commission* (1994) 182 CLR 1 concerned a claim by the plaintiff, Professor Medlin, who was seriously injured in a motor vehicle collision at the age of fifty-six. His university tenure would have allowed him to continue as a Professor of Philosophy at Flinders University until he turned sixty-five. However, he retired voluntarily at sixty on the grounds that the effects of his injuries including 'pain, fatigue and loss of intellectual energy' had led to a situation where discharge of his administrative and teaching duties precluded him from doing the research and creative work which he would otherwise have been able to do. The plaintiff claimed damages for diminished earning capacity resulting in the loss of four-and-a-half years of salary and long service leave entitlements due to the early retirement. The defendant established that the injured plaintiff would not have been dismissed. Consequently, the defence argued that the loss of his earning capacity was caused not by the accident but the voluntary decision of Professor Medlin to take early retirement.

The majority in the High Court of Australia disagreed, and decided that causation is not necessarily negated by the intervention of some act or decision of the plaintiff or a third party, which constitutes a more immediate cause of the loss or damage than the defendant's negligence. This is particularly so: 'in cases where the negligent act or omission was itself a *direct* or *indirect* contributing cause of the intervening act or decision' (emphasis in original). According to Deane, Dawson, Toohey, and Gaudron JJ (at 6):

> the ultimate question must ... always be whether, notwithstanding the intervention of the subsequent decision, the defendant's wrongful act or omission is, as between the plaintiff and the defendant and as a matter of common sense and experience, properly to be seen as having caused the relevant loss of damage.

The premature termination of his employment was the consequence of wrongfully occasioned injuries suffered by Professor Medlin in the motor vehicle accident, even though it was brought about by his own decision to accept voluntary retirement. Hence, the intervening decision of the plaintiff to accept premature retirement did not break the chain of causation between the defendant's negligence and the plaintiff's loss of earning capacity. The majority (at 69) noted that the question of *reasonableness* should not be framed in abstract of terms of whether the plaintiff's decision to retire was 'reasonable'; rather, the issue was whether Professor Medlin, suffering injuries for which the defendant was found responsible, 'acted reasonably or unreasonably in resigning from his post'.

In *March v Stramare*, the defendant's scope of duty extended to reasonably foreseeable conduct of the plaintiff, which was unintentional if careless. In *Kavanagh v Akhtar* (1998) 45 NSWLR 588, the scope of duty based on reasonable foreseeability was extended to intentional risk-creating actions of the plaintiff. In that case, Mrs Akhtar, who was thirty-nine at the time, sustained injury to the left shoulder, left arm and jaw when, due to the admitted negligence of the defendant, a heavy box containing perfume bottles fell on her. As a result, she had difficulty in taking care of her extremely long hair, and some months after the accident she had it cut short, against the wishes of her husband and the Imam (the family were devout Indian Muslims). Her husband reacted with hostility, and consequently left the marital home. Mrs Akhtar sustained psychiatric injury as a result of the failure of the marriage. Although she was not working at the time of the accident, the court accepted that but for the injury, she would have found work either as a cashier or as a cleaner.[88]

Defence counsel argued that the plaintiff's own decision to cut her hair, against her husband's express wishes, amounted to a *novus actus interveniens*. Relying on *Medlin* and *Chappel*, Mason P (Priestley and Handley JJA agreeing) determined (at 98) that the decision, while voluntary in one sense, 'was nevertheless the product of the tortiously-created pain and discomfort under which she was labouring. And that led to the psychiatric illness in consequence of the stress placed on the marriage'. It is yet to be seen whether the statutory 'obvious risk' provisions will modify this approach, in so far as the court would now have to consider whether, given the husband's explicit threat to end the marriage on the one hand, and the painful but transient (the physical injuries healed by the time of the trial) problems associated with caring for her hair on the other, a reasonable person in Mrs Akhtar's position would have ignored an obvious risk of a marital break up and its consequences.

In England, in *Reeves v Commissioner of Police of the Metropolis* [1999] 3 WLR 363, the House of Lords held that the theory of *novus actus interveniens* did not apply in a case where a prisoner hanged himself in his cell in a police station. While

---

88. The court awarded Mrs Akhtar damages of $265 691, including past general damages for injury to the left shoulder, left arm and jaw of $52 500, and future general damages of $62 500; *Griffiths v Kerkemeyer* damages of $90 000; past economic loss: $10 000; future economic loss: $34 500; superannuation loss: $10 000; out-of-pocket expenses of $1191, and $5000 interest.

in custody for fraud, he had made two attempts at suicide, with the second occurring on the morning of his death. After the second incident, he was seen by a doctor, who found no evidence of any psychiatric disorder or clinical depression, but gave instructions that, as a suicide risk, he should be frequently observed. An hour later, while the policeman was not looking, the prisoner used his shirt as a ligature to hang himself by pushing it through the wicket hatch and securing it to the door.

The House of Lords held that those entrusted with the custody of prisoners have a duty to take reasonable care for their safety while in custody. The duty arises from the complete control which the police or prison authorities have over a prisoner, and the well-known risk of the special danger of people in prison taking their own lives. Consequently, the prisoner's deliberate and informed act, intended to exploit a situation created by the defendant, did not nullify causation where the defendant was in breach of a specific duty imposed by law to guard against that very act. This was so, irrespective of whether the prisoner was of sound or unsound mind—for, as Lord Hoffmann noted (at 367), such distinction was 'inadequate to deal with the complexities of human psychology in the context of the stresses caused by imprisonment'. Accordingly, since the defendant was admittedly in breach of duty, the deceased's act in taking his own life did not break the chain of causation.

Intervening action of a third party

Mahony v J Kruschich (Demolitions) Pty Ltd & Anor (1985) 156 CLR 522[89] provides perhaps the best explication of the principle that legal responsibility will be attributed to the person whose original wrongdoing has made the plaintiff more vulnerable to negligent acts of others. In that case, Branko Glogovic, the plaintiff, sued his employer, J Kruschich (Demolitions) Pty Ltd for personal injury, which he alleged to have suffered in the course of his employment. The injury required medical treatment. In a cross-claim, the defendant employer sought indemnity or contribution from the plaintiff's medical practitioner, Dr Mahony. The employer alleged that Dr Mahony's negligent treatment had caused or contributed to the continuing injuries and incapacities for which the plaintiff was suing the employer.[90]

Gibbs CJ, Mason, Wilson, Brennan, and Dawson JJ, in a joint judgment, stated (at 528) that liability of a negligent wrongdoer for the consequences of a plaintiff's subsequent tortiously inflicted injury will depend 'on whether or not the subsequent tort and its consequences are themselves properly to be regarded as foreseeable

---

89. The *Mahony* case was decided on the pleadings.
90. The High Court held (at 530) that the cross-claim should not be struck out, because if it were proved at the trial that an aspect of the plaintiff's condition was properly to be regarded as a foreseeable consequence of both Kruschich's negligence and Dr Mahony's negligence, Kruschich would 'be entitled to seek contribution ... from Dr Mahony in respect of so much of the damages awarded against it as relates to that aspect.'

consequences of the first tortfeasor's negligence'. Their Honours noted that 'A line marking the boundary of the damage for which a tortfeasor is liable in negligence may be drawn either because the relevant injury is not reasonably foreseeable or because the chain of causation is broken by a novus actus interveniens.'

However, in cases:

> where it is not possible to draw a clear line, the first tortfeasor may be liable in negligence for a subsequent injury and its consequences although the act or omission of another tortfeasor is the more immediate cause of that injury. [at 529]

According to the High Court (at 529), as a general rule, in cases where the original injury is exacerbated by negligent medical treatment, such exacerbation will be regarded as a foreseeable consequence for which the first tortfeasor is liable, if the plaintiff acts reasonably in seeking or accepting the treatment. In these cases, 'The original injury can be regarded as carrying some risk that medical treatment might be negligently given'. The only exceptions to this rule are cases where:

> the original injury does not carry the risk of medical treatment or advice that is 'inexcusably bad', or 'completely outside the bounds of what any reputable medical practitioner might prescribe' or 'so obviously unnecessary or improper that it is in the nature of a gratuitous aggravation of the injury' or 'extravagant from the point of view of medical practice or hospital routine'. [at 530]

In such cases, the exacerbation of a plaintiff's condition will be attributed to the 'inexcusably bad' or completely inappropriate negligent medical treatment or advice, and the chain of causation broken.

Mahony v J Kruschich involved an allegation of *negligent* tortious conduct by a third party; however, the original negligent tortfeasor might not avoid liability for the consequences of *intentionally* inflicted subsequent injury if the later tort and its consequences are foreseeable consequences of the first tortfeasor's negligence. For example, in *Curmi v McLennan* [1993] Aust Torts Reports ¶81–254, the court held that the defendant breached his duty towards the plaintiff by allowing unsupervised access to an airgun to boys under eighteen years of age, of whom the plaintiff was one. The intentional firing of the gun by one of the boys, Peter Mobilia, did not sever the causal link between the defendant's breach and the plaintiff's injury because the defendant was under a duty not to expose the plaintiff to the risk of under-age boys with little or no shooting skills using an airgun. The defendant's negligent conduct created the very risk which, it could be said, occurred 'in the ordinary course of things' within the context of the risky situation.[91]

---

91. At 62,658. See also: *Kavanagh v Akhtar* (1998) 45 NSWLR 588 (discussed above), where Mason P noted (at 601) that the husband's ending the marriage as a response to Mrs Akhtar's haircut was also a reasonably foreseeable voluntary conduct by a third person.

Conversely, in *Rickards v Lothian* [1913] AC 263, someone maliciously turned a lavatory basin water tap on full and plugged up (with nails, soap, penholders, and like) the waste-pipe on the top floor of the defendant's building. The water overflowed damaging the plaintiff's goods. The Privy Council advised that the defendant was not responsible unless either he instigated the act or the jury had found that he ought reasonably to have prevented it; and that although he was bound to exercise all reasonable care he was not responsible for damage not due to his own default, whether caused by inevitable accident or the wrongful acts of third persons. The case was distinguished in *Mahony v J Kruschich* at 529.

ATTRIBUTION OF LIABILITY FOR UNRELATED SUBSEQUENT EVENTS

Unrelated subsequent tortious events

Attribution of liability for wrongfully inflicted personal injuries that are aggravated or exacerbated by subsequent tortious events causally unrelated to the initial wrongful conduct is illustrated by *Baker v Willoughby* [1970] AC 467. In that case, the plaintiff's ankle was damaged as a result of a car collision, and became stiff. He suffered pain, loss of amenities, and loss of earning capacity, but obtained a job sorting scrap metal. Before the trial relating to the car accident, and while he was at work, a second defendant shot him in the injured leg during a robbery. His leg had to be amputated and an artificial limb fitted.

In *Baker v Willoughby* (at 493), Lord Reid said that plaintiff's loss:

> is not in having a stiff leg; it is in his inability to lead full life, his inability to enjoy those amenities which depend on the freedom of movement and his inability to earn as much as he used to earn or could have earned, if there had been no accident. In this case the second injury did not diminish any of these. So why should it be regarded as having obliterated or superseded them?

His Lordship continued:

> the wrongdoer must take the plaintiff (or his property) as he finds him; that may be to his advantage or disadvantage. In the present case the robber is not responsible or liable for the damage caused by the respondent [1st tortfeasor]; he would only have to pay for additional loss to the appellant [plaintiff] by reason of his now having an artificial leg instead of the stiff leg.

Discussing attribution of liability and apportionment of damages, Lord Pearson said that when injuries are caused by two or more successive and independent tortious acts, it is necessary to ensure that the plaintiff is fully compensated for the aggregate effects of *all* the injuries. This means that where the supervening injury is inflicted by another tortfeasor, the computation begins with the assessment of the plaintiff's total loss. The second tortfeasor's award is then deducted from the plaintiff's total loss, with the balance being awarded against the first tortfeasor.[92]

The court assesses the aggregate quantum before apportioning liability between the first and the second tortfeasor to ensure that the second tortfeasor pays for all additional disabilities and injuries suffered by the plaintiff as a result of the second tort. Unless this is done, the result will be unjust. For example, in *Rogers v Whitaker* (1992) 175 CLR 479 (for discussion of this case, see Chapter 11), the defendant surgeon would have been able to argue thus:

> I only failed to advise Mrs Whitaker about the rare possibility that she might become blind in the right eye: I should only be responsible for damage to that eye; the kid who pocked the stick into her left eye when she was eight, should be responsible for that injury.

The fact that Mrs Whitaker was now totally blind would not have been taken into account.

Moreover, it is also unfair to treat the plaintiff as 'devalued' when assessing damages for the second injury on the basis that the injured person is already partially incapacitated.

Attribution of liability for subsequent non-tortious injury

There are also cases where a tortiously injured plaintiff suffers further injury from an innocent cause, due to the 'vicissitudes of life'. If these occur prior to the trial, the court must take them into account when assessing damages. For example, in *Jobling v Associated Dairies* [1982] AC 794, the plaintiff suffered a slipped disc in 1973 due to the defendant employer's negligence. From that time, he could do only light work. Three years later, he suffered from cervical myelopathy, a condition unrelated to the accident, which totally incapacitated him before the trial in 1979.

The House of Lords held that a supervening illness is regarded in law as an ordinary vicissitude of life. The fact that it would have occurred in any event has to be taken into account when compensation to the plaintiff is calculated. Damages should be reduced correspondingly.

Lord Keith at 815 summed up the principles related to compensation in the face of supervening harmful events in the following way:

(a) In cases where the plaintiff who has been tortiously injured, suffers greater injury as a result of a supervening tortious event, the computation should start from the assessment of the plaintiff's total loss. The second tortfeasor's award should be computed on the basis that the plaintiff, whom he or she has injured, was already to some extent incapacitated. The second tortfeasor's award, so

---

92. *Jobling v Associated Dairies* (1982) AC 794; (1981) 2 All ER 752, per Lord Keith.

calculated, is then deducted from the plaintiff's total loss, with the balance being awarded against the first tortfeasor.
(b) Where a tortious act is followed by a wholly unrelated, non-tortious supervening event which exacerbates the harm caused by the tort, the principle of vicissitudes of life will be applicable.

In *Faulkner v Keffalinos* (1970) 45 ALJR 80, the plaintiff was injured in a motor vehicle collision in 1968, caused by the defendant's negligence, as a result of which he could do only light work. In 1969, while driving his car, he ran into another vehicle and suffered further injuries. The second collision was apparently the plaintiff's own fault. It decreased the plaintiff's earning capacity much more seriously than the first accident had, and he became totally incapacitated and suffered cumulative psychological and physical effects.

Windeyer J determined that without the second accident, the defendant would have had to compensate the plaintiff for the loss of full earning capacity until the age of sixty-five. However, since after the second collision the plaintiff lost all capacity to earn money, the defendant had to pay compensation only until 1969.

ATTRIBUTION OF LIABILITY FOR PROPERTY DAMAGE

Attribution of responsibility for personal injury is governed by different principles to those applied in attributing causation for property damage.

In circumstances of multiple sufficient causes of property damage, where one or more of the causes is innocent, causal responsibility will be attributed to the innocent cause, provided the damage from the wrongful cause is 'submerged within' the damage from the innocent event. For example, in *Carslogie Steamship Co Ltd v Royal Norwegian Government* [1952] AC 292, the ship the *Carslogie* was solely responsible for a collision with the *Heingar*. Having undergone temporary repairs in the United Kingdom, the *Heingar* sailed to the United States for main repairs. During the voyage, it was further damaged by bad weather. Repairs necessitated both by wrongful and by innocent causes, and unrelated modifications, were carried out simultaneously, taking fifty days. Time taken to repair damage from the collision was assessed at ten days, with repairs for the weather damage assessed at thirty days. The House of Lords held that the plaintiff suffered no loss from non-utilisation of the *Heingar* for ten days because the ship would have been unavailable during that time in any case. The defendants were not liable for the demurrage fees—and, therefore, by inference, for damage caused by their wrongful act—because the damage from the collision had been submerged in the need to repair the damage caused by the weather.

The doctrine that in circumstances where two or more acts are wrongful, causal liability will be attributed to the first event in time, provided that the first event caused at least as much damage as the subsequent events, was established in *Performance Cars Ltd v Abraham* [1962] 1 QB 33. In that case, the plaintiff's Rolls-Royce had been damaged in a collision. The damage necessitated the respraying of the whole of the lower body of the car. The plaintiff was awarded £75 against the driver, who accepted full responsibility, but was unable to pay the damages. Before the respraying of the car could be carried out, the second defendant collided with the Rolls-Royce. This collision did less damage, but also necessitated the respraying of the whole lower body. The Court of Appeal held that second tortfeasor was not liable.

Although it is arguable that each tortfeasor, whether consecutive or not, should be liable to the plaintiff for the damage he or she caused, the approach adopted in *Performance Cars Ltd v Abraham* is reflected in the statutory proportionate liability legislation (discussed in Chapter 22).

Application of the maxim of *res ipsa loquitur*

Finally, sometimes the very fact of the injury raises an inference that it was caused by the defendant's negligence. For instance, a patient in otherwise excellent condition is admitted to a hospital for a knee operation. If, after the anaesthetic wears off, she finds she has a broken arm, the patient may argue that very fact of the broken arm raises an inference of negligence by the hospital staff. Thus, she may raise a plea based on the approach reflected in the Latin maxim of *res ipsa loquitur* (literally, 'the thing speaks for itself') whereby the court may infer negligence as causal explanation for her otherwise unexplained injury. The maxim of *res ipsa loquitur* is essentially a summation of the principle applicable in cases where it is clear that the plaintiff had suffered damage, but the question is: who breached the duty which caused the damage? In other words, the maxim essentially reverses the order of reasoning by allowing the plaintiff to argue from causation to the breach of the duty of care.[93]

According to Gleeson CJ and McHugh J in *Schellenberg v Tunnel Holdings Pty Ltd* (2000) 200 CLR 121, at 132 [20], the term *res ipsa loquitur* was apparently first used in a negligence context during argument in *Byrne v Boadle* (1863) 2 H & C 722; 159 ER 299. The plaintiff who was walking past the defendant's shop, when a barrel of flour fell upon him from a window above the shop and injured him. These facts were held to provide sufficient primâ facie evidence of negligence for the jury, to cast on the defendant the onus of proving that the accident was not caused by his negligence. The maxim was articulated by Erle CJ speaking for the majority of the Court of Exchequer in *Scott v London & St Katherine Docks Co* [1865] 3 H & C

---

93. In Canada, the use of *res ipsa loquitur* has been abandoned: *Fontaine v British Columbia (Official Administrator)* [1998] 1 SCR 424.

596 at 601; 159 ER 665 at 667, which also involved a claim by the plaintiff that he was injured when a barrel rolled from the defendant's warehouse:

> There must be reasonable evidence of negligence. But where the thing is shewn to be under management of the defendant or his servants, and the accident is such as in the ordinary course of things does not happen, if those who have management use proper care, it affords reasonable evidence, in the absence of the explanation by the defendants, that the accident arose from want of care.

The maxim is not a substantive rule of law, but a method of reasoning about matters of proof designed to ameliorate the difficulties that arise from a lack of evidence as to the specific cause of an accident. In Australia, the plaintiff will satisfy the burden of proof as long as an inference of negligence can be drawn from the circumstantial evidence, but will fail if this evidence merely leads to conjecture. For example, in the case of *Mummery v Irvings Pty Ltd* (1956) 96 CLR 99, the plaintiff, pleading *res ipsa loquitur*, alleged that he entered the defendant's timber shed to buy some timber. Apparently, as he started moving towards the foreman, who was working at a circular saw, he was struck in the face by a piece of wood 'flying through the air', which caused him a severe injury. The defendant provided no evidence. The High Court held that the plea failed because, although the plaintiff explained the physical cause of the accident, he produced no evidence from which a positive inference could be drawn that the injury was due to the defendant's negligence.[94]

Windeyer J, in *Anchor Products Ltd v Hedges* (1966) 115 CLR 493, at 500, pointed out that:

> for Australian courts the phrase *res ipsa loquitur* denotes a fact from which, if it be unexplained, it is permissible to infer negligence: but that the onus in the primary sense—that is the burden of proving the case against the defendant—remains with the plaintiff. To say that an accident speaks for itself does not mean that if no evidence is given for the defendant the plaintiff is entitled in law to a verdict in his favour. The occurrence speaks of negligence, but how clearly and convincingly it speaks depends upon its circumstances.

In *Schellenberg v Tunnel Holdings Pty Ltd* (2000) 200 CLR 121, at 149 [76], Gleeson CJ and McHugh J noted that being part of the law of causation, the maxim 'is concerned with whether an event was caused by the negligence of the defendant, not with its physical cause'. This means that to succeed in the plea of *res ipsa loquitur* the plaintiff has to establish a positive inference of the lack of care on the part of the defendant as the probable cause of the harmful occurrence.[95] Referring to academic

---

94. See also: *Schellenberg v Tunnel Holdings Pty Ltd* (2000) 200 CLR 121 at 134 [24], 147 [70]. See also: *Franklin v Victorian Railways Commissioners* (1959) 101 CLR 197 at 201; *Government Insurance Office of NSW v Fredrichberg* (1968) 118 CLR 403 at 413–4, per Barwick CJ.
95. *Piening v Wanless* (1968) 117 CLR 498 at 507.

authorities,[96] Gleeson CJ and McHugh J (at 134 [25]) and Kirby J (at 162 [107]) said that to find for the plaintiff, the tribunal of fact has to conclude that:

1. there is an 'absence of explanation' of the occurrence that caused the injury;
2. the occurrence was of such a kind that it does not ordinarily occur without negligence; and
3. the instrument or agency that caused the injury was under the management and control of the defendant.

In *Schellenberg v Tunnel Holdings Pty Ltd*, the plaintiff was employed as a mechanical foreman, responsible for the supervision of the air pressure system and hoses in a workshop supplying and servicing of pumps and valves. While he was working with a tool powered by a compressed air hose, the hose became detached from its coupling. The escaping compressed air caused the hose to swing uncontrollably, and it struck him in the face. To avoid being hit again, the plaintiff twisted his body sharply, injuring his back.

Mr Schellenberg was unable to show that the coupling was defective or damaged, or that any other part of the equipment was badly maintained. In other words, he pointed out the physical cause of his injury—the detached hose—but failed to explain it in terms of legal causation.

In both *Schellenberg* and *Mummery* the respective plaintiffs could show that they had suffered an injury: a circumstantial cause-in-fact. However, they did not provide sufficient technical and managerial evidence to draw an inference that the accidents were caused by the defendants' breach of duty of care to them.

Thus, to succeed on a plea of *res ipsa loquitur*, the plaintiff's counsel must bring in precise and detailed evidence to define the immediate cause of the occurrence as being of a class that does not ordinarily happen if those who have the management use proper care, while at the same time disprove neutral evidence, or evidence which suggests that the plaintiff was at fault. If the lawyer leaves it to the *res* to speak for itself, without any lateral arguments or evidence, the plaintiff will probably fail. However, what is good for the goose is good for the gander—in some cases, unless the defendant's lawyers do their homework, and provide a credible cause for the accident that does not involve negligence on the part of the defendant, the plaintiff will win by default.

For example, in *Smith v Retirement Benefits Fund Investment Trust* [1994] Aust Torts Reports ¶81–286, sixty-five-year-old Mrs Smith went to a shopping centre owned and operated by the defendant. Mrs Smith approached the automatic sliding doors, at an angle—walking along the side of the building rather than towards it. She saw the doors open as another person left the building, and then begin to close.

---

96. Balkin RP & Davis JLR, *Law of Torts*, 2nd edn, Butterworths, Sydney, 1996, pp 287–296; and Fleming JG, *The Law of Torts*, 9th edn, The Law Book Company, Sydney, 1998, pp 353–359.

Believing the doors would re-open as she passed through, she proceeded to enter. However, the doors continued to close and trapped her. After some minutes of struggling, she managed to 'squeeze' herself out. But the force exerted by the doors, and her attempts to extricate herself, caused her injury.

She sued, pleading *res ipsa loquitur*. The defendant submitted that there was no case to answer, contending there was no evidence that would entitle a jury to find it negligent. Neither side adduced evidence relating to the nature of the door mechanism, nor led expert evidence to explain causes of the accident. Zeeman J of the Tasmanian Full Court gave the following reasons for holding (by majority) that it was open to the jury to decide on issues of breach and causation:

(a) a reasonable person in the defendant's position would have foreseen that automatic doors involved risk of failure. The jury would therefore have been entitled to conclude on foreseeability of the risk of serious injury due to such failure;

(b) the actual injuries suffered and the inherent danger involved in two doors closing from opposite directions on a person could have led the jury to conclude that there was a significant risk of injury to such a person; and

(c) in the absence of evidence regarding the likelihood of injury from mechanism failure, the jury was entitled to view the matter as a real risk, rather than a fanciful one.

FURTHER READING

Fleming JG, *The Law of Torts*, 9th edn, The Law Book Company, Sydney, 1998, Ch 9.

Freckelton I & Mendelson D (eds), *Causation in Law and Medicine*, Ashgate, Dartmouth, 2002 (The International Library of Medicine, Ethics and Law Series).

Hart HLA & Honoré T, *Causation in the Law*, 2nd edn, Clarendon Press, Oxford, 1985.

Honoré T, 'Causation and Disclosure of Medical Risks' (1998) 114 *Law Quarterly Review* 52.

Luntz H, 'Loss of Chance', in Freckelton I & Mendelson D (eds), *Causation in Law and Medicine*, Ashgate, Dartmouth, 2002 (The International Library of Medicine, Ethics and Law Series) pp 152–98.

Mendelson D, 'The Breach of the Medical Duty to Warn and Causation: *Chappel v Hart* and the Necessity to Reconsider Some Aspects of *Rogers v Whitaker*' (1998) 5 *Journal of Law and Medicine* 312–319.

Mendelson D, '*Quo Iure?* Defendants' Liability to Rescuers in the Tort of Negligence' (2001) 9 *Torts Law Review* 130–164.

Mendelson D, 'Australian Tort Law Reform: Statutory Causation and the Common Law' (2004) 11 *Journal of Law and Medicine* 492–510.

Stapleton J, 'Scientific and Legal Approaches to Causation', in Freckelton I & Mendelson D (eds), *Causation in Law and Medicine*, Ashgate, Dartmouth, 2002 (The International Library of Medicine, Ethics and Law Series) pp 14–38.

Zeeman WP, 'Contributory Negligence' (1994) 2 *Torts Law Journal* 16.

Remoteness of Damage   13

INTRODUCTION

Having established that the defendant's negligent conduct was legally responsible for the plaintiff's injury, the plaintiff has to show also that the injury was not too remote. The injury will not be deemed too remote if the plaintiff can prove that the damage was a reasonably foreseeable consequence of the defendant's negligent conduct. In the United States, this is a part of an inquiry into proximate cause. Anglo-Australian jurisprudence has traditionally distinguished the question whether the legal cause for the plaintiff's harm should be attributed to the defendant's fault from the question whether the damage so caused was reasonably foreseeable. Unlike the duty and causation requirements of the tort of negligence, common law principles governing remoteness of damage have not been affected by the reform legislation.

THE MEANING OF 'REASONABLE FORESEEABILITY'

Meaning and function of the reasonable foreseeability test in negligence

The test for remoteness of damage is based on the reasonable foreseeability of the injury occurring as a consequence of negligent conduct. Reasonable foreseeability is a means of determining the boundaries of duty—unforeseeable plaintiffs (as individuals or a class), and unforeseeable risks are outside the scope of duty of care. However, foreseeability is also the reference point for the content of duty of care in breach, the scope of duty in causation (whether the duty extends to intervening events in the chain of causation), and the scope of duty in remoteness of damage (whether its ambit encompasses the nature or the extent of the plaintiff's damage).

It is helpful to discuss the function and nature of the 'reasonable foreseeability' test as it applies to each element of the tort of negligence.

Duty of care

The test of reasonable foreseeability at the stage of duty of care focuses on the sphere of foreseeable risks that the defendant's conduct might create within a legal neighbourhood (people foreseeable as individuals or a class); it delineates the ambit of duty owed by defendants to those who are their neighbours in law. The function of the test at this stage is to lay a foundation for the determination of the content of the defendant's duty of care. This content will be defined at the standard of care stage, where the question is how a reasonable person in the circumstances of the defendant would respond to a foreseeable real risk of injury.

Standard of care

To use the terminology introduced by Glass JA in *Minister for Environmental Planning and Assessment Act 1979 v San Sebastian Pty Ltd* (1983) 2 NSWLR 268 (CA), at 295–6, at the breach of duty stage, the analysis focuses on examining the nature of the foreseeable risk of *some* kind of damage that the *particular* kind of carelessness charged against the defendant might cause. This involves an assessment of the risk: was the risk of harm sufficiently substantial ('not insignificant') or merely trivial? And, most importantly, how should the defendant react to such a risk?

Causation (*novus actus interveniens*)

At the stage of causation, the test of reasonable foreseeability is only applied in those cases where the defendant claims that causal liability should be attributed to a *novus actus interveniens*—in the sense that liability for the plaintiff's injury should be attributed to the intervening events or actions. To rebut the defendant's claim, the plaintiff has to show that the intervening act or occurrence constituted a reasonably foreseeable risk falling within the defendant's sphere of duty of care. Mason CJ in *March v E & MH Stramare* (1991) 171 CLR 506, at 518–19, said that jury is asked whether

> the defendant's wrongful conduct has generated the very risk of injury resulting from the negligence of the plaintiff or a third party and that injury occurs in the ordinary course of things.

Thus, reasonable foreseeability for *novus actus interveniens* relates to the foreseeability of the causes of the alleged damage. *Chapman v Hearse* (1961) 106 CLR 112 illustrates how the test for foreseeability at the stage of duty and the foreseeability test for the purposes of the *novus actus interveniens* both deal with the ambit or scope of risks, and thus are conceptually intertwined.

Remoteness of damage

Under the doctrine in *Overseas Tankship (UK) Ltd v Morts Dock & Engineering Co Ltd (The Wagon Mound (No 1))* [1961] AC 388, reasonable foreseeability at the remoteness stage concerns the nature of the damage sustained by the plaintiff; its function is twofold: (1) to ascertain whether the kind of damage caused by the defendant's negligence was foreseeable, and hence compensable; and (2) to determine the foreseeability of the extent of such damage for the purpose of compensation.

Therefore, at this stage, the plaintiff must establish that the kind of damage suffered was foreseeable as a possible outcome of the actual negligence already proven.

Even where the plaintiff can prove that the type of damage suffered was reasonably foreseeable, the defendant may counter that although the original or primary damage was reasonably foreseeable, its *extent* was unforeseeable due to external factors. The test of reasonable foreseeability will be used to determine the foreseeability of external factors which have aggravated, exacerbated, or prolonged the original damage.

Reasonable foreseeability at the remoteness of injury stage has two distinct temporal foci:

(a) before the initial injury was sustained (tortiously or non-tortiously), including predisposition; and
(b) the medical, psychiatric, and economic consequences of this injury.

Denning LJ in *Roe v Ministry of Health* [1954] 2 All ER 131, at 138, noted that 'the three questions, duty, causation and remoteness, run continually into one another. It seems ... they are simply different ways of looking at one and the same question which is this: is the consequence fairly to be regarded as within the risk created by the negligence?'

THE CONCEPT OF REMOTENESS OF DAMAGE

Brief history of tests for remoteness of damage

Historically, the test for remoteness of damage that governed intentional torts held the wrongdoer liable for all probable direct (flowing naturally from) consequences of an intentional wrongful act, whether or not these consequences were foreseeable. With the development of the tort of negligence, this test was questioned by Chief Baron Pollock of the Court of Exchequer in *Rigby v Hewitt* (1850) 5 Ex 240, at 243, and in *Greenland v Chaplin* (1850) 5 Ex 243, at 248. Speaking for himself, rather than the court, his Lordship expressed:

> considerable doubt, whether a person who is guilty of negligence is responsible for all the consequences which may under any circumstances arise, and in respect

of mischief which could by no possibility have been foreseen, and which no reasonable person would have anticipated ...

Nevertheless, the courts continued to consider reasonable foresight to be irrelevant to the question whether the consequences of the defendant's breach of duty were too remote.[1] Thus, in *Re Polemis and Fyrness, Withy & Co, Ltd* [1921] 3 KB 560, the Court of Appeal held that the direct test of remoteness of damage also applied to unintentional torts. In that case, the ship's cargo contained a quantity of cases filled with tins of benzine and petrol. Some of the tins leaked, and petrol vapour collected in the hold of the ship. At a port of call, while some of the benzine tins were being shifted, one of the employees negligently knocked a plank into the hold. The ship immediately burst into flames and was totally destroyed. The defendant charterers were found liable for all direct consequences of the negligence, even though, they were unforeseen.

Until *Donoghue v Stevenson* [1932] AC 562, which established a general duty of care in negligence, a plaintiff who intended to sue for negligence had to show that the defendant's conduct came within an established category of duty to take care. The law would impose a particularised duty based on a pre-existing relationship. The test of direct consequences was oriented towards recovery for the plaintiff on the basis that, as between the innocent victim and those who cause the injury, the latter should bear the loss, if some fault is found on their part. As long as the duty of care itself was limited to a range of particular relationships, the extensive liability that might be imposed by the test of directness upon the defendants was counterbalanced by the fact that the duty was relatively limited. However, in the wake of the *Donoghue v Stevenson* decision, the *Re Polemis* test of remoteness was criticised as being too harsh upon defendants.

The case that changed the test for remoteness of damage was *Overseas Tankship (UK) Ltd v Morts Dock & Engineering Co Ltd (The Wagon Mound (No 1))* [1961] AC 388. On 30 October 1951, the SS *Wagon Mound* was taking in bunkering oil from Caltex Wharf in Sydney Harbour when, due to the carelessness of its engineers, a large quantity of furnace oil overflowed onto the surface of the water and drifted to Sheerlegs Wharf, Morts Bay, where it caught fire. At the time, the plaintiffs, who were the owners of the Sheerlegs Wharf, were carrying out repair work to a ship, including the welding of metal. Molten metal from the plaintiffs' wharf fell onto floating cotton waste which, smouldering, ignited the furnace oil on the water. The plaintiffs' wharf sustained substantial damage by fire. In an action by the plaintiffs for damages for negligence, it was found as a fact that the defendant shipowners did not know, and could not reasonably have been expected to know, that the furnace oil was capable of being set alight when spread on water. On appeal to

---

1. Winfield PH, *Law of Torts* 4th edn, Sweet & Maxwell Ltd, London, 1948, p 66. See also: *Smith v London and South Western Railway Company* (1870) LR 6 CP 14.

the Privy Council, the Judicial Committee discarded the test of directness and, in the words of Viscount Simonds, 'insisted that the essential factor in determining liability is whether the damage is of such a kind as the reasonable man should have foreseen.' Viscount Simonds (at 422) explained the policy reasons underlying the new test:

> it does not seem consonant with current ideas of justice or morality that for an act of negligence, however slight or venial, which results in some trivial foreseeable damage the actor should be liable for all consequences however unforeseeable and however grave, so long as they can be said to be 'direct'.

Viscount Simonds continued (at 422–3):

> a man must be considered to be responsible for the probable consequences of his act. To demand more of him is too harsh a rule, to demand less is to ignore that civilised order requires the observance of a minimum standard of behaviour.

Given the findings of fact, on the application of the reasonable foreseeability of damage test, the Privy Council held that damage to the Sheerlegs Wharf was not reasonably foreseeable.

The fire, which was the result of furnace oil spilt from the *Wagon Mound*, also caused extensive damage to two vessels that were undergoing repairs at Sheerlegs Wharf. In *Overseas Tankship (UK) Ltd v The Miller Steamship Co Ltd (The Wagon Mound (No 2))* [1967] 1 AC 617; [1966] 2 All ER 709, the owners of the two ships sued Overseas Tankship (UK) Ltd for nuisance and negligence. In relation to nuisance, they were successful at the trial; however, in relation to negligence, the trial judge found that the officers of the *Wagon Mound* would have regarded the possibility of furnace oil igniting on water as 'one which would become an actuality only in very exceptional circumstances'. The case eventually was appealed to the Privy Council. Their Lordships applied the *Wagon Mound No 1* test of remoteness of damage and held that damage to the vessels was not too remote, because a reasonable person in the position of the *Wagon Mound* engineer would have foreseen that there was a real risk of fire through a continuing discharge of furnace oil on the water. Lord Reid, who delivered the opinion of the Board (the Judicial Committee), held (at 718–19) that a reasonable person in the position of the engineer would have known that the oil was very difficult to ignite, and that ignition could only happen in very exceptional circumstances; 'but that does not mean that a reasonable man would dismiss such risk from his mind and do nothing when it was so easy to prevent it'.

The new test was based on the principle that neither direct nor indirect damage is too remote if it was foreseeable. In contrast, direct damage may be too remote if it was not foreseeable as an outcome of the defendant's negligence.

In so far as the objective of the new test of reasonable foreseeability in negligence was to ameliorate the harshness and limit the scope of liability of defendants—which was perceived to be the fault of the old test of directness test in *Re Polemis*—it was unsuccessful.

THE TEST FOR REMOTENESS OF DAMAGE

The kind of harm

To be compensable, damage must be of the same kind, class, character, or type as that which was reasonably foreseeable. In other words, while the specific consequences of negligence may not be reasonably foreseeable, they may belong to a class or kind of consequence that is foreseeable. As interpreted by modern courts, only injurious consequences that fall outside a general set or class of foreseeable risks will be deemed too remote. A typical example of this approach is that of a passenger who drowns as a result of a motor car collision after being thrown out of the car and, concussed, lands face-down in a gutter filled with water from a heavy rain. If the question is framed narrowly, and one asks whether *drowning* is a reasonably foreseeable consequence of a motor vehicle collision, the answer will be 'no'. However, if the question is framed in terms of a class or a general kind of damage—namely, is *death* a reasonably foreseeable consequence of a motor vehicle collision—the answer will be 'yes'.

The manner in which foreseeable damage occurs

Once liability for causation has been determined, it does not matter that the *precise manner* in which the harm was occasioned was unforeseeable, so long as the actual harm suffered is of the same kind as that reasonably foreseeable at the duty stage. In *Hughes v Lord Advocate* [1963] AC 837, Lord Reid said the defendant is liable for the claimant's injury as long as it is of a kind that was foreseeable, even if the damage is greater in extent than was foreseeable, or was caused in a way that could not have been foreseen. In this case, workers, having removed the cover of a manhole in the carriageway, erected a tent over the manhole and placed four paraffin lamps in position around it. While no one was around, two boys aged eight and ten entered the tent, taking with them a ladder from the site and one of the paraffin lamps. They went down the manhole, but on their way up the lamp was either knocked or dropped into it and a violent explosion took place. The plaintiff, the eight-year-old boy, suffered extensive burning injuries. An explosion occurred in a manner which, according to the experts, could not have been foreseen.

Relying on the doctrine in *The Wagon Mound (No 1)* the lower court dismissed the plaintiff's claim. The House of Lords, however, reversed that decision, holding that it was not necessary to foresee the exact way in which an accident occurs, as long as one anticipates the general type of consequence that transpires.

Likewise, in the case of *Jolley v Sutton London Borough Council* [2000] 1 WLR 1082, the Council, which negligently failed to remove a decayed cabin cruiser from the grounds of its housing estate, argued that while it was foreseeable that a child might be injured by rotten planking giving way, it was not foreseeable that the plaintiff would sustain injury by the boat falling on him. Lord Hoffman (at 1091) rejected this contention, and having approved of the trial judge's description of the foreseeable risk as being that children would 'meddle with the boat at the risk of some physical injury', said:

> what must have been foreseen is not the precise injury which occurred but injury of a given description. The foreseeability is not as to the particulars but the genus. And the description is formulated by reference to the nature of the risk which ought to have been foreseen.

But how broad should the scope of foreseeable kinds of damage be?

In *British Steel Plc v Simmons* [2004] UKHL 20 HL 553, due to the admitted negligence of the defendant, the plaintiff Mr Simmons, while employed as a steelworks burner, fell from a burning table and hit his head. He was wearing a protective helmet, but nevertheless developed some physical symptoms that lasted several weeks. After the accident he experienced exacerbation of a pre-existing skin condition, psoriasis. Apparently, anger that the accident had happened led to a change in Mr Simmons' personality and resulted in a severe depressive illness that prevented him from returning to work. The House of Lords (at 573–4) held that no distinction should be drawn between a psychiatric condition triggered by the accident itself and the claimant's anger at the happening of the accident:

> Regret, fear for the future, frustration at the slow pace of recovery and anger are all emotions that are likely to arise, unbidden, in the minds of those who suffer injuries in an accident such as befell the pursuer. If, alone or in combination with other factors, any of these emotions results in stress so intense that the victim develops a recognised mental illness, there is no reason in principle why he should not recover damages for that illness.

In *British Steel Plc*, the aggravation of Mr Simmons' psoriasis and the anger which sprang from the accident led to much more serious consequences than the immediate effects of the head injury.

The extent of harm

Thus, in a negligence action, the defendant will be liable for a reasonably foreseeable kind of harm, including harm of a greater extent than reasonably foreseeable, as long as it remains of the same kind. The extent of damage will depend in each individual case upon the physical and psychological characteristics of the plaintiff. For example, in *Baltimore City Pass R Co v Kemp* 61 Md 74 (1884), Mrs Adaline Kemp claimed damages for breast cancer, which her medical experts attributed to a hurt she sustained in a railway carriage accident caused by the defendants. The Court of Appeals of Maryland held (at 82) that it was for the jury to determine from the evidence whether the cancer did result from the injury and, if so, that under the *talem qualem* rule (tortfeasors take their victim as they find them), the defendants were liable, even though they had no reason to anticipate such a result:

> It is not for the defendants to say that, because they did not or could not in fact anticipate such a result of their negligent act, they must therefore be exonerated from liability for such consequences as ensued. They must be taken to know and to contemplate all the natural and proximate consequences, not only that certainly would, but that probably might, flow from their wrongful act.

The liability for the extent of the harm which, due to the plaintiff's pre-existing condition, was much more serious than anticipated is based on the rule that the defendant must 'take the plaintiff as he finds him' (*talem qualem*). This principle of liability is also known as the 'egg-shell skull rule'. The appellation is a reference to the following explanation provided by Kennedy J in *Dulieu v White & Sons* [1901] 2 KB 669. In this case, Mrs Dulieu was standing behind the bar of her husband's public house when a pair-horse van crashed into the premises due to the driver's negligence. As a consequence of the fright caused to her, Mrs Dulieu sustained severe nervous shock, which led to premature delivery of intellectually disabled baby son. The Court of Appeal held that the defendant was liable for all physical damage following reasonably and naturally from shock. Kennedy J (at 681) observed:

> If a man is negligently run over or otherwise negligently injured in his body, it is no answer to the sufferer's claim for damages that he would have suffered less injury or no injury at all, if he had not had an unusually thin skull or an unusually weak heart.[2]

Nader v Urban Transit Authority of NSW (1985) 2 NSWLR 501

Sometimes, the sequelae of the original injury negligently inflicted by the defendant is significantly prolonged or exacerbated by the intervention of the plaintiff or a third party. The case of *Nader v Urban Transit Authority of NSW* (1985) 2 NSWLR 501 illustrates both, the reasoning adopted by the New South Wales Court of Appeal in relation to determining the issue of foreseeability of harm, and liability for harm that was aggraved by the intervention of third parties. In *Nader*, ten-year-old George Nader struck his head on an electricity pole when he jumped off a bus travelling at the time at between 10 and 15 kilometres per hour. The bus driver negligently opened the doors before coming to a full stop. Although the boy sustained only a superficial physical cut to his forehead, and no neurological damage, his father saw a solicitor that very day. Some weeks later, George developed headaches, fits of dizziness, lack of concentration, and then a very rare psychiatric condition known as

---

2. This rule was reaffirmed by the House of Lords in *Smith v Leech Brain & Co Ltd* [1962] 2 QB 405.

Ganser Syndrome.[3] He was eventually hospitalised. Medical and nursing witnesses testified that when his family was not present, George behaved like a normal ten-year-old boy; however, once the family members were with him, he presented all the symptoms of Ganser Syndrome. His family began to stay with him twenty-four hours per day, and refused the request by the team of psychiatrists to have the boy removed for three months to a psychiatric facility away from his family. The case, which went on for six years, involved two main issues relating to the remoteness of damage:

- Was Ganser Syndrome a reasonably foreseeable kind of damage?
- Did the parents' intervention constitute a *novus actus interveniens* which made not the onset, but the continuation of the condition too remote?

In relation to the first question, the Court of Appeal observed that Ganser Syndrome is a very rare condition, but it is a recognised psychiatric illness, and psychiatric illness is a reasonably foreseeable kind of damage that may follow physical injury (McHugh JA, at 536). In the case of George Nader, the kind of damage he originally sustained—headaches, spells of dizziness and lack of concentration—was compensable. Since these signs and symptoms constituted a part of the condition known as Ganser Syndrome, the syndrome itself was held to be in the class of reasonably foreseeable risks, and thus compensable.

In relation to the second issue, the majority decided that the parents' intervention did not make the damage too remote. McHugh JA found an analogy between the parental intervention in the *Nader* case and tetanus spores in a wrongfully inflicted physical wound. According to his Honour, where reasonably foreseeable damage caused by the defendant, such as an open wound, combines with another cause, such as tetanus spores, to produce further damage in the form of tetanus, the defendant will be liable for the damage in its entirety, as long as the consequent damage is not different in kind from the foreseeable damage (the physical injury). Here, apparently, the possible psychiatric reaction to the accident was combined with particular parental attitudes to produce a much more grave and long-lasting psychiatric condition which, however, was not *different in kind* from the foreseeable damage.

These principles were applied by the New South Wales Court of Appeal in *Kavanagh v Akhtar* (1998) 45 NSWLR 588. Mason P (with whom Priestley and Handley JJA agreed) held (at 602) that the psychiatric illness suffered by Mrs

---

3. Ganser Syndrome was first described by Sigbert Ganser in 1898. It is characterised by the patient providing approximate and invariably wrong answers (*vorbeireden*, literally meaning 'talking past the point') to even the simplest of questions. For example, a patient could answer 'three' to a question 'how many legs does a dog have'; 'five' to 'how much is two plus two'. Other symptoms include inattentiveness or drowsiness. The syndrome has been most frequently described in relation to prisoners who claim lack of competency to plead. It is classified in the Diagnostic and Statistical Manual of Mental Disorders (DSM-IV-TR) as one of the dissociative disorders.

Akhtar was a reasonably foreseeable consequence of the physical accident (injury to her left shoulder, left arm and jaw):

> The fact that the [marriage] breakdown occurred in consequence of a perhaps unforeseeable step taken by the respondent (cutting her hair) or the perhaps unforeseeable reaction of her husband is irrelevant in the light of cases such as *Hughes* and *Nader*, so long as psychiatric injury is itself regarded as a foreseeable consequence of the physical injury inflicted on the respondent (see *McLean* [*Commonwealth v McLean* (1996) 41 NSWLR 398]).

Mason P commented (at 601) that although the principle that tortfeasors take their victim as they find them 'is not absolute and unqualified', there is no reason why it should not include the victim's family and its cultural setting (as the court did in *Nader*):

> Equality before the law puts a heavy onus on the person who would argue that the *'unusual'* reaction of an injured plaintiff should be disregarded because a minority religious or cultural situation may not have been foreseeable (cf generally Calabresi, *Ideals, Beliefs, Attitudes and the Law* (1985)). Whether or not the husband's response (with its consequences) was consistent with his marital obligations (and I am not inferring a judgment either way), the unchallenged evidence showed that it was a direct response to the hair-cutting.

His Honour added (at 602):

> the law should, in this area, take *'human nature as it is, with its infirmities, and having regard to the relationship of the parties concerned'* (per Lord Wensleydale in *Lynch v Knight* (1861) 9 HLC 577 at 600, 11 ER 854 at 863). Often in personal injury cases evidence is led that injury has led to strains in marital or other domestic relationships. That evidence is treated as part of the pain and suffering and loss of enjoyment of life which is compensable by general damages. Loss of libido (and the flow-on effects) is a well-established element of compensable damage. The same principles apply *a fortiori* when physical injuries lead not just to pain and discomfort but to psychiatric injuries[4] (emphasis added).

Mason P's approach reflects social and ethical values of a modern multicultural society, though such an open-ended rule of liability may not be followed in other jurisdictions.

---

4. In its conclusion with respect to remoteness of damage, the Court of Appeal relied on the following authorities: *Commonwealth v McLean* (1996) 41 NSWLR 398; *Encev v Encev* (unreported, Supreme Court of Victoria, Ashley J, 24 November 1997); *Hird v Gibson* [1974] Qd R 14; *Hughes v Lord Advocate* [1963] AC 837; *Nader v Urban Transit Authority* (NSW) (1985) 2 NSWLR 501.

The principle of vicissitudes of life

As noted in Chapter 2 and Chapter 12, non-tortious contributory and contemporaneous causal factors (other than the defendant's own negligence) may not eliminate the defendant's liability. Nevertheless, generally, the effect of non-tortious causal factors will be taken into account when the quantum of damages is assessed. For instance, while the principle of the egg-shell skull rule prevents the plaintiff's prior susceptibility being the basis for causal denial of liability, the plaintiff's predisposition to injury will be taken into account by increasing the discount for contingencies.[5]

The egg-shell skull principle involves harm greater than it would otherwise be, due to a pre-existing condition of the plaintiff. Conversely, sometimes the defendant's negligence makes the plaintiff more vulnerable to the negligent acts of others. This was the case in *Mahony v J Kruschich (Demolitions) Pty Ltd* (1985) 156 CLR 522 referred to in Chapter 12. The Full Court of the High Court pointed out that when a negligently caused injury is exacerbated by negligent medical treatment, the exacerbation will generally be regarded as a foreseeable consequence of the original injury, and the original tortfeasor's liability extends to the consequent injury. As a general rule, the only time the original defendant will not be liable for subsequent exacerbation of the plaintiff's condition by medical negligence is if the exacerbation is due solely to outrageously gratuitous aggravation through negligent medical treatment.

FURTHER READING

Dietrich J, 'Critique and Comment Giving Content to General Concepts' (2005) 29 *Melbourne University Law Review* 218.
Fleming JG, *The Law of Torts*, 9th edn, The Law Book Company, Sydney, 1998, Ch 9.
Winfield PH, *Law of Torts*, 4th edn, Sweet & Maxwell Ltd, London, 1948.

---

5. *Western Australia v Watson* [1990] WAR 248 at 312; *Wilson v Peisley* (1975) 50 ALJR 207 at 209.

Part IIIA

PARTICULAR CATEGORIES OF CASE

INTRODUCTION

Between the mid-1930s and mid-1970s there was virtually no expansion in the liability of defendants for negligently occasioned harm beyond the limits established by the *Donoghue v Stevenson* [1932] AC 562 case. However, over the past three decades, the law of torts, especially the law of negligence, has developed new categories of case, dramatically extending the scope of liability. The new categories of case include liability for omissions; for negligent infliction of pure psychiatric harm; for pure economic loss resulting from negligent physical conduct; for negligent advice resulting in economic or physical loss; and for breach of non-delegable duty of care. This categorisation is not ideal because, like negligence *simplex* (the *Donoghue v Stevenson* cause of action), omissions, negligent advice and non-delegable duty of care are differentiated on the basis of the defendant's conduct, whereas pure psychiatric injury and pure economic loss are distinguished on the basis of the injury suffered by the plaintiff—which is inconsistent with the principle that wrongful conduct, not damage, is the basis of tort liability (*Stanley v Powell* [1891] 1 QB 86). Nonetheless, since the mid-1970s, courts have developed distinct principles and doctrines, both substantive and evidentiary, for each of these categories of case, which will be discussed in turn.

Search for tests that would govern the existence of duty of care in novel categories of case

In the 1970s, the judiciary recognised that it was unjust and unfair not to compensate those who suffered personal or economic injury because of others' negligence but were unable to bring themselves within the *Donoghue v Stevenson* writ. The courts, however, were also aware that the *Donoghue v Stevenson* 'neighbour test' of reasonable foreseeability (discussed in Chapter 10) was so wide that if applied as the sole determinant of the existence of a duty of care in novel categories of case that, unless constrained, it could be very harsh on individual defendants. There was a risk that it would open the proverbial floodgates of litigation, lead to fraudulent claims, or have adverse economic, social and other deleterious policy repercussions. For, as John Fleming commented,[1] the major problem with the test of reasonable foreseeability is that it does not make clear whether it is intended to be strictly a test of reasonable foresight, or whether it also allows for other factors to be considered when deciding the existence of a duty or the reasonable foreseeability of a class of plaintiff.

Lord Reid, in *Home Office v Dorset Yacht Club* [1970] AC 1004, signalled a shift in the jurisprudence of duty of care when, referring to Lord Atkin's legal neighbourhood principle, he said (at 1027): 'The time has come when we can and should say that it ought to apply unless there is some justification or valid explanation for its exclusion.'

The need to place limits or controls on the *Donoghue v Stevenson* reasonable foreseeability test when determining duty of care in new categories of case was articulated by Lord Wilberforce in *McLoughlin v O'Brian* [1982] 2 All ER 298; [1983] 1 AC 410, at 420, in the following way:

> foreseeability must be accompanied and limited by the law's judgment as to persons who ought, according to its standards of value or justice, to have been in contemplation. Foreseeability, which involves a hypothetical person, looking with hindsight at an event which has occurred, is a formula adopted by English law not merely for defining, but also for limiting the persons to whom duty may be owed and the consequences for which an actor may be held responsible ... When it is said to result in a duty of care being owed to a person or class, the statement that there is a 'duty of care' denotes a conclusion into the forming of which considerations of policy have entered. That foreseeability does not of itself, and automatically, lead to a duty of care is I think clear.

The question was how to retain the principle of reasonable foresight as a general foundation of the duty of care while also applying negative policy considerations as a control mechanism to limit the scope of the duty in novel categories of negligence. Broadly, the following ways of reasoning were employed in those novel

---

1. *The Law of Torts* 9th edn, The Law Book Company, Sydney, 1998, p 137.

cases where the test of reasonable foreseeability was regarded as insufficient for the imposition of the duty of care:

1   The traditional 'incremental method' of reasoning from analogy and precedent was articulated by Brennan J in *Sutherland Shire Council v Heyman* (1984) 157 CLR 424, at 481:

> It is preferable, in my view, that the law should develop novel categories of negligence incrementally and by analogy with established categories, rather than by a massive extension of a prima facie duty of care restrained only by indefinable 'considerations which ought to negative, or to reduce or limit the scope of the duty or the class of person to whom it is owed'.

2   A special 'notion of proximity' was originally proposed by Stephen J in *Caltex Oil v The Dredge Willemstad* (1976) 136 CLR 529, at 573–4, and then developed by Deane J. The circumstantial relationship between the parties was examined from the perspective of policy considerations, and served as the overriding control mechanism for the existence of a duty of care. In *Jaensch v Coffey* (1984) 155 CLR 549, at 583, Deane J explained the distinction between Atkinian reasonable foreseeability and his own notion of proximity in the following way:

> The essential function of such requirements or limitations [the special notion of proximity] is to confine the existence of a duty to take reasonable care to avoid reasonably foreseeable injury to the circumstances or classes of case in which it is the policy of the law to admit it. Such overriding requirements or limitations shape the frontiers of the common law of negligence.

3   A two-stage test was enunciated by Lord Wilberforce in *Anns v Merton London Borough Council* [1978] AC 728, whereby the existence of the duty of care would be assumed once the reasonable foreseeability of damage through the defendant's want of care was established. This assumption could then be negated (or the scope of the duty limited or reduced) by policy and other considerations.

4   The *Anns v Merton London Borough Council* test was inverted by Lord Bridge of Harwich in *Caparo Industries PLC v Dickman* (1990) AC 605, at 617–18, thus introducing a threefold approach of foreseeability, proximity and reasonableness. This *Caparo* test incorporated the incremental approach, 'starting with situations in which a duty has been held to exist and then asking whether there are considerations of analogy, policy, fairness and justice for extending it to cover a new situation.'[2] According to Lord Bridge (at 617–18):

---

2. Lord Hoffmann in *Stovin v Wise* [1996] AC 923 at 949.

in addition to the foreseeability of damage, necessary ingredients in any situation giving rise to a duty of care are that there should exist between the party owing the duty and the party to whom it is owed a relationship characterised by the law as one of 'proximity' or 'neighbourhood' and that the situation should be one in which the court considers it fair, just and reasonable that the law should impose a duty of a given scope upon the one party for the benefit of the other.

Lord Hoffmann in *Stovin v Wise* [1996] AC 923 (at 949), referring to assumption or non-assumption of existence of duty, observed:

> It can be said that, provided that the considerations of policy etc are properly analysed, it should not matter whether one starts from one end or the other. On the other hand the assumption from which one starts makes a great deal of difference if the analysis is wrong. The trend of authorities has been to discourage the assumption that anyone who suffers loss is prima facie entitled to compensation from a person (preferably insured or a public authority) whose act or omission can be said to have caused it. The default position is that he is not.

This is the general position in the United Kingdom. In Australia, from 1984 until 1997, the High Court considered the special notion of proximity as a 'conceptual determinant' of duty of care in special categories of case (*Burnie Port Authority v General Jones Pty Ltd* (1994) 179 CLR 520 at 543, per Mason CJ, Deane, Dawson, Toohey, and Gaudron JJ in a joint judgment). Brennan J, however, in *Sutherland Shire Council v Heyman* (1985) 157 CLR 424 and subsequent cases, refused to accept this doctrine. In England, Lord Oliver in *Caparo Plc v Dickman* [1990] 2 AC 605, at 633, commented: '"Proximity" is, no doubt, a convenient expression so long as it is realised that it is no more than a label which embraces not a definable concept but merely a description of circumstances from which, pragmatically, the courts conclude that a duty of care exists'. The special notion of proximity was discarded by the High Court in *Hill v Van Erp* (1997) 188 CLR 159, at 189–90; *Perre v Apand Pty Ltd* (1999) 198 CLR 180, at [27]; *Crimmins v Stevedoring Industry Finance Committee* (1999) 200 CLR 1, at [165]; and *Sullivan v Moody; Thompson v Connon* (2001) 207 CLR 562, at [48].

In *Perre v Apand Pty Ltd* (1999) 198 CLR 180, McHugh J (at [76]), having observed that: 'Members of this Court have said that the differences between proximity as a criterion and the incremental approach are to a great extent more apparent than real,'[3] added:

> since the fall of proximity, the Court has not made any authoritative statement as to what is to be the correct approach for determining the duty of care question. Perhaps none is possible. At all events, the differing views of the members of this

---

3. McHugh was referring to Toohey J's judgment in *Hill v Van Erp* (1997) 188 CLR 159.

Court in the present case suggest that the search for a unifying element may be a long one.

Hayne J (at [330]) agreed that: 'to search ... for a single unifying principle lying behind what is described as a relationship of proximity is ... to search for something that is not to be found.'

In *Modbury Triangle Shopping Centre Pty Ltd v Anzil* (2001) 205 CLR 254, Kirby J (at [61]) also referred to 'the failed notion of "proximity" as the universal indicium of the duty of care at common law,' though he noted that:

> as a measure of factors relevant to the degree of physical, circumstantial and causal closeness, proximity is the best notion yet devised by the law to delineate the relationship of 'neighbour'.

Kirby J, in *Pyrenees Shire Council v Day & Ors* (1998) 192 CLR 330 and *Perre v Apand Pty Ltd* (1999) 198 CLR 180, adopted the *Caparo* three-stage test of duty of care, which analyses the relationship between the plaintiff and the defendant focusing on proximity, fairness, and policy considerations. The *Caparo* test is still the governing principle for imposition of duty of care in novel categories of case in the United Kingdom (*JD (FC) v East Berkshire Community Health NHS Trust & Ors* [2005] 2 AC 373; *D v East Berkshire Community Health NHS Trust & Ors* [2005] 2 AC 373; *Brooks v Commissioner of Police of the Metropolis & Ors* [2005] 1 WLR 1495); however, in *Sullivan v Moody* (2001) 207 CLR 562, Gleeson CJ, Gaudron, McHugh, Hayne, and Callinan JJ in a joint judgment (at [49]) rejected the *Caparo* test.

In *Sullivan*, the court (at [50]) noted that 'different classes of case give rise to different problems in determining the existence and nature or scope, of a duty of care.' Their Honours identified a number of issues that should be 'the focus of attention in a judicial evaluation of the factors which tend for or against a conclusion [regarding the existence of duty], to be arrived at as a matter of principle'. These include:

- issues associated with 'the harm suffered by the plaintiff, as, for example, where its direct cause is the criminal conduct of some third party' (as in *Modbury Triangle Shopping Centre Pty Ltd v Anzil* (2000) 176 ALR 411);
- issues, which arise where 'the defendant is the repository of a statutory power or discretion' (as in *Crimmins v Stevedoring Industry Finance Committee* (1999) 200 CLR 1; *Brodie v Singleton Shire Council* (2001) 180 ALR 145);
- issues of indeterminacy involving 'the difficulty of confining the class of persons to whom a duty may be owed within reasonable limits' (as in *Perre v Apand Pty Ltd* (1999) 198 CLR 180); and
- 'the need to preserve the coherence of other legal principles, or of a statutory scheme which governs certain conduct or relationships' (*Hill v Van Erp* (1997) 188 CLR 159 at 231, per Gummow J).

Sullivan itself served as an example of the fourth category: the plaintiffs, *inter alia*, claimed that they suffered pure psychiatric injury as a result of being told by the defendant medical practitioners and child welfare officials that they were under suspicion of child sexual abuse. The court (at [54]) stated that as professionals, the defendants acted out of concern for, and in the interests of, the children to whom they owed a duty of care. To impose upon the defendants a duty of care to avoid psychiatric harm to the plaintiffs would play havoc with the principles of the law of defamation by allowing 'recovery of damages for publishing statements to the discredit of a person where the law of defamation would not'.

The four issues identified by the High Court in *Sullivan* were conceptually quite disparate. The 'plaintiff's harm' problem was closely related to causation; the second problem involved liability of public authorities (the terms 'public' and 'statutory' authority are used interchangeably); the third concerned liability for pure economic loss and pure psychological injury; and the fourth was a question of legal policy and philosophy. Apart of the notion of the coherence of the law, clear principle or test that could form conceptual basis for a reasoned conclusion was not spelt out.

Ever since the end of the twentieth century, when the High Court jettisoned the notion of proximity as the conceptual determinant and a unifying principle applicable across all novel categories of case in negligence, the majority of the High Court, while rejecting the *Caparo* test, has been unable to agree on a common approach to determining the existence of duty of care in non-*Donoghue v Stevenson* categories of case. The failure to adopt a common approach is troubling—for, as Callinan J observed in *D'Orta-Ekenaike v Victoria Legal Aid* [2005] HCA 12, at [358], the law still adheres to the legal fiction whereby 'decisions restating the common law are merely declaratory of it both prospectively and retrospectively'.

In the same case (which, by majority, reaffirmed the doctrine that barristers and solicitors owe no duty of care towards clients in performance of work affecting the conduct of the case in court), his Honour also noted (at [367]) that:

> Although the common law in general changes only incrementally, there have in recent times been changes of a radical and even sudden kind.

These factors have rendered the general scope of liability in negligence uncertain and unpredictable. Perhaps the time has come to develop such special categories of case as omissions, liability for pure mental harm, negligent advice, pure economic loss, and non-delegable duty of care into proper subspecies of negligence, and treat them as discrete causes of action.

Pure Nonfeasance (Pure Omissions)

14

HISTORICAL INTRODUCTION: ACTS AND PURE OMISSIONS

Samuel von Pufendorf—a seventeenth-century writer of the natural law school—noted that the reason for holding people responsible for their acts is that they undertake them of their own will. It is because these positive actions are voluntary that people are commonly held to account before a human court.[1]

The tort of trespass was the main remedy for injury in medieval England. Its object was to suppress violations of the royal peace. This meant that the law only redressed injuries directly caused by positive conduct. In contrast, negligence redresses both misfeasance and certain omissions.

In the context of the law of negligence, the term 'omission' is used in three ways. It refers to:

(a) failure to act in the course of positive conduct where there is an obligation to act with care;
(b) passive inaction when there is no prior duty to act, now termed 'pure' or 'mere' omissions, also called 'pure' or 'mere' nonfeasance; and
(c) non-performance of a statutory duty by public authorities.

An example of the first kind of omission is a failure to apply the brake while driving, thus causing a motor car collision. It is to this kind of omission that Lord Atkin referred in *Donoghue v Stevenson* [1932] AC 562, in his 'neighbour principle'. From the moment you start up the car, you embark on 'positive conduct' or action, and thus have undertaken responsibility—an obligation not to cause harm. You are under a duty of care to avoid acts or omissions that endanger other road users; and

---

1. Pufendorf S, *De Officio Hominis et Civilis* (1682 edn), lib I, cap I, § 10. Translation by Moore FG, Oxford University Press, Oxford, New York, 1927.

if you do negligently omit to act in circumstances when a reasonable driver would have acted, there exists a *prima facie* presumption of responsibility unless your inaction can be excused or justified.

In *Stovin v Wise* [1996] AC 923, at 933, Lord Nicholls of Birkenhead described the problem of liability for pure omissions thus:

> Liability for [pure] omissions gives rise to a problem not present with liability for careless acts. He who wishes to act must act carefully or not at all. ... With liability for [pure] omissions, however, a person is not offered a choice. The law compels him to act when left to himself he might do nothing.

PURE NONFEASANCE AND THE COMMON LAW

Consider a situation where, on the way to a train station, you see that your neighbour's gate is open, and your neighbour's puppy is sitting on the porch and eyeing the open gate—clearly ready to make a dash for the busy street outside. Although you have not been asked, nor voluntarily undertaken to look after it, you know that unless you close the gate, the puppy is likely to run outside and get lost, or be run over by a car. Are you under any legal obligation to close the gate?

You are not, because your conduct falls within the second category of omissions: mere omission or nonfeasance—passive inaction when there is no prior duty to act. As Professor Smith put it in his book *Liability in Negligence*,[2] there exists a distinction between what we morally 'ought' to do and what we have a legal obligation to do. Indeed, the common law historically did not impose an affirmative duty to act, and did not consider people legally responsible for failing to act when not under a legal duty to do so. In *Donoghue v Stevenson*, Lord Atkin implied as much when he said (at 580):

> acts or omissions which any moral code would censure cannot in a practical world be treated so as to give a right to every person injured by them to demand relief. In this way rules of law arise which limit the range of complainants and the extent of their remedy. The rule that you are to love your neighbour becomes in law, you must not injure your neighbour; and the lawyer's question, Who is my neighbour? receives a restricted reply.

Windeyer J in *Hargrave v Goldman* (1963) 110 CLR 40 (at 66) interpreted Lord Atkin's use of the phrase 'love your neighbour'—which refers to the scriptural parable of the Good Samaritan who attended to a wounded stranger—in the context of determination of the existence of a duty of care, thus:

> The priest and the Levite, when they saw the wounded man by the road, passed by on the other side. He obviously was a person whom they had in contemplation

---

2. Sweet & Maxwell, London, 1984, p 30.

and who was closely and directly affected by their action. Yet the common law does not require a man to act as the Samaritan did.

There is, therefore, strict distinction between moral and legal duties. Plaintiffs who claim they were injured as a result of mere nonfeasance must first establish that the defendant was an under an obligation or *duty to act*. But reasons for existence of a *duty to act* are different from reasons for the existence of a *duty to take care when acting*.

Jurisprudential explanation for this distinction is based on concepts of responsibility and obligation. In all cases of causing damage through action there is an element of responsibility which the actor undertakes, and the concomitant obligation not to create risks that may cause harm. In a case where persons negligently cause damage through their action, there is thus a *prima facie* presumption of responsibility, and it is up to the actors to rebut it by providing a legal excuse or justification. Consequently, all cases of causing damage through action fall under a single principle of obligation.

It is, however, exceptional for people to be considered responsible for failing to act when they are not under any prior obligation to take positive steps. In such cases, a *prima facie* presumption is one of no responsibility for the failure to act. In *Smith v Leurs* (1945) 70 CLR 256, Dixon J (as he then was) commented (at 262) that everything else being equal, 'one man is under no duty of controlling another man to prevent his doing damage to a third'. In *Sutherland Shire Council v Heyman* (1985) 157 CLR 424, Deane J (at 501), having examined earlier authorities, extended Dixon J's formulation:

> The common law imposes no prima facie general duty to rescue, safeguard or warn another from or of reasonably foreseeable loss or injury or to take reasonable care to ensure that another does not sustain such loss or injury.[3]

McHugh J in *Pyrenees Shire Council* (1998) 192 CLR 330, at [101], emphasised that the common law does not 'impose any duty on a person to take steps to prevent harm, even very serious harm, befalling another ... The careless or malevolent person, who stands mute and still while another heads for disaster, generally incurs no liability for the damage that the latter suffers'. In *Agar v Hyde; Agar v Worsley* (2000) 201 CLR 552, at 578 [68], Gaudron, McHugh, Gummow, and Hayne JJ summarised the doctrine of pure nonfeasance thus:

> from the earliest times, the common law has drawn a distinction between a positive act causing damage and a failure to act which results in damage. The common law does not ordinarily impose a duty on a person to take action where no positive conduct of that person has created a risk of injury to another person.

---

3. For example, according to the English Court of Appeal in *P Perl (Exporters) Ltd v Camden London Borough Council* [1984] QB 342, at 357–8, 359–60, occupiers do not owe neighbours a duty to prevent thieves gaining access to their own property for the purpose of robbing their neighbour's premises.

In England, Lord Hoffmann in *Stovin v Wise* [1996] AC 923, at 943–4, provided political, moral, and economic reasons for treating omissions in the sense of pure nonfeasance differently from positive conduct. According to his Lordship, 'in political terms it is less of an invasion of an individual's freedom for the law to require him to consider the safety of others in his actions than to impose upon him a duty to rescue or protect'. From a moral point of view, the issue is one of indeterminacy and consequent inequity:

> A duty to prevent harm to others or to render assistance to a person in danger or distress may apply to a large and indeterminate class of people who happen to be able to do something. Why should one be held liable rather than another?

From the economic perspective, the efficient allocation of resources usually requires that an activity should bear its own costs. Any activity that benefits from 'externalities, that is, being able to impose some of its costs on others results in market distortion because the activity appears cheaper than it really is. Consequently:

> liability to pay compensation for loss caused by negligent conduct acts as a deterrent against increasing the cost of the activity to the community and reduces externalities. But there is no similar justification for requiring a person who is not doing anything to spend money on behalf of someone else. Except in special cases (such as marine salvage) English law does not reward someone who voluntarily confers a benefit on another. So there must be some special reason why he should have to put his hand in his pocket.

Lord Hoffmann was referring to expenditure of money rather than physical action because in *Stovin v Wise* the question before the House of Lords was whether the local highway authority should be liable for failure to take steps to remove known danger to road users of a junction from impaired visibility caused by obstruction on an adjoining private land. The facts were as follows: Mr Stovin, was riding a motorcycle along a road when a car driven by Mrs Wise suddenly emerged from a junction into his path, crashing into him. He was severely injured. The trial judge found that Mrs Wise failed to keep a proper look out and was thus 70 per cent responsible for the accident. He held the Norfolk County Council, which Mrs Wise had joined as co-defendant, 30 per cent liable to Mr Stovin on the grounds that, while knowing that the junction was dangerous, it negligently failed to make it safer.

The Norfolk County Council, as the local authority, did not create the obstruction, but it was argued that the duty should be imposed because the Council knew that the probability of the risk of serious injury was high, and the remedial work could be done quickly and effectively for less than £1000. The House of Lords by majority rightly rejected this argument. Considerations that determine the reasonableness of the defendant's response to a reasonably foreseeable risk of harm (the calculus of negligence) are part of the inquiry into the breach of duty of care.

They form the content of the duty of care, and consequently are irrelevant, unless a prior duty of care has been held to exist. It is tempting but wrong-headed to invert the paradigm of negligence and make the existence of the duty of care contingent on the ease (or otherwise) of taking precautions.

To paraphrase McHugh J's statement in *Pyrenees Shire Council v Day & Ors* (1998) 192 CLR 330 (at [102]), a person may only be liable in damages for the failure to act when some special relationship exists between the person harmed and the person who fails to act. His Honour listed:

(a) contracts, which involve an obligation to take positive action to avoid loss or injury to the other party;

(b) fiduciary relationships of trust and confidence, which arise where one party to the relationship assumes an obligation to act in the other's proprietary interests. This kind of trusting relationship is characteristic of partnership, agency, trusteeship, the employment relationship, solicitor and client, as well as companies and directors;[4]

(c) obligations under statute. These may arise under relevant statutory powers, duties, or functions; for example, where duties and functions[5] of an office expressly call for positive action by the holder of office.

Another important exception that imposes an affirmative duty to act to prevent harm to third parties arises out of occupation or possession of property. Under both negligence and the tort of nuisance, occupiers have a positive duty to remove hazards to adjoining land if they have created those risks; however, they may also be under a duty to remove risks of physical harm to the adjacent property which they did not create, but which the previous owner created (*Hargrave v Goldman* (1966) 115 CLR 458). Thus, inherent in the occupation of land or premises is a duty to take positive steps to protect others from harm.

LIABILITY OF PUBLIC AUTHORITIES FOR OMISSIONS AT COMMON LAW

Liability for non-exercise of a power by public authorities

Chapter 11 analysed the common law and statutory principles governing the inquiry into whether a statutory authority breached its duty of care to a person claiming to have suffered an injury as a result of such negligence. However, before the issue of breach can arise, the plaintiff has to establish that the defendant public authority owed him or her duty of care in the first place. When the allegation involves a failure to exercise statutory power, the issues can be very complex.

---

4. Glover J, *Commercial Equity Fiduciary Relationships*, The Law Book Company Ltd, Sydney, 1995, p 6.
5. The term 'function' comes from the Latin *function*, the performance of official and other duties (*fungi*).

As a general rule, actions against the Crown and public authorities for failure to take positive action to prevent foreseeable harm involve consideration of two major issues. The first concerns the circumstances in which a positive duty to exercise its powers to safeguard the safety of individuals may be imposed upon the Crown or statutory authorities. In *Sutherland Shire Council v Heyman* (1985) 157 CLR 424, the High Court declared that to attract liability, the relationship between the individual plaintiff and the defendant statutory body must satisfy additional legal requirements. Various requirements suggested by the High Court will be discussed below.

The second issue involves the tension between duties imposed by private law on the one hand and public law duties arising from statutory powers vested in public bodies on the other. In *Sullivan v Moody*, [2001] HCA 59, at [60], the High Court adopted the reasoning of Lord Browne-Wilkinson in *X (Minors) v Bedfordshire County Council* [1995] 2 AC 633, at 739, who stated that

> a common law duty of care cannot be imposed on a statutory duty if the observance of such common law duty of care would be inconsistent with, or have a tendency to discourage, the due performance by the local authority of its statutory duties.

In other words, the fact that the defendant 'is subject to statutory obligations which constrain the manner in which powers or discretions may be exercised, does not of itself rule out the possibility that a duty of care is owed to a plaintiff', provided the statutory obligations are not irreconcilable with the common law duty (*Sullivan v Moody* [2001] HCA 59, at [60]). Whether or not the statutory and common law duty can be reconciled will depend on the purpose of the statute, the nature of the relevant statutory requirements, as well as powers of discretion vested in the authority.

Thus, in *Sullivan*, the relevant provisions of the *Community Welfare Act 1972* (SA) specified the functions, powers and responsibilities of the various persons and authorities who reported and investigated the suspicions about the plaintiffs' sexual abuse of their children. It was a scheme for the protection of children, requiring the defendants to treat the interests of the children as paramount. The defendants, as legally qualified medical practitioners and employees of agencies that provided health and welfare services to children, were under a statutory duty to notify an officer of the department of a suspicion that an offence had been committed against a child.[6] The court (at [63]) found that

> it would be inconsistent with the proper and effective discharge of those [statutory] responsibilities that they [the defendants] should be subjected to a legal duty, breach of which would sound in damages, to take care to protect persons who were suspected of being the sources of that harm.

---

6. *Community Welfare Act 1972* (SA), s 91(1)(b).

Moreover, unlike individuals, the actions of the Crown and public authorities invariably involve expenditure of public funds, which they have a duty to administer. In *Brodie v Singleton Shire Council; Ghantous v Hawkesbury City Council* (2001) 206 CLR 512, at [295], Hayne J (in dissent) noted that the difficulties with drawing analogies between the position of a private person owing a particular kind of duty and the position of a statutory authority stem from two facts:

(i) public authorities are bodies of limited powers, established for the performance of functions or the provision of services to which all, or large sections, of the community may resort.

(ii) they are bodies of finite financial resources, yet they cannot readily withdraw from their central activity of performing particular functions or providing particular services.

The legal scrutiny of bodies exercising statutory powers is primarily within the province of public law—constitutional, administrative, and criminal law.[7] Furthermore, in many cases, the statute is unclear about the extent of duty imposed upon a public authority. There is thus a question of defining the nature of the legal relationship between the enforcement of public-law duties on the one hand, and the conferral of a private right to sue for damages on the other. For, as Gleeson CJ observed in *Graham Barclay Oysters Pty Ltd v Ryan* (2002) 211 CLR 540 (at [6]):

decisions as to raising revenue, and setting priorities in the allocation of public funds between competing claims on scarce resources, are essentially political.

His Honour added (at [7]) that: 'if the reasonableness of such priorities is a justiciable issue, that can be so only within limits'.

Discretional and operational decisions

In *Anns v Merton London Borough Council* [1978] AC 728, a case which involved a claim against the Council for a negligent failure to inspect foundations of a building, Lord Wilberforce (at 754) distinguished between discretional and operational decisions:

Most, indeed probably all, statutes relating to public authorities or public bodies, contain in them a large area of policy. The courts call this 'discretion' meaning that the decision is one for the authority or body to make, and not for the courts. Many statutes also prescribe or at least presuppose the practical execution of policy decisions: a convenient description of this is to say that in addition to the area of policy or discretion, there is an operational area. Although this distinction between the policy area and the operational area is convenient, and illuminating, it is probably a distinction of degree; many 'operational' powers or duties have in

---

7. See: the discussion in *Stovin v Wise* [1996] AC 923.

them some element of 'discretion.' It can safely be said that the more 'operational' a power or duty may be, the easier it is to superimpose upon it a common law duty of care.

Mason J in *Sutherland Shire Council v Heyman* (1985) 157 CLR 424, at 442, adopted Lord Wilberforce's approach, saying:

> The distinction between the area of policy and the operational area is a logical and convenient one. There is no doubt that a public authority may be liable for the negligent acts of its servants or agents in carrying out their duties, or exercising their powers, within the operational area, although if the performance of their duties or the exercise of their powers involves the exercise of a discretion, an act will not be negligent if it was done in good faith in the exercise of, and within the limits of, the discretion.

His Honour then (at 469) explained why policy decisions are non-justiciable:

> The distinction between policy and operational factors is not easy to formulate, but the dividing line between them will be observed if we recognize that a public authority is under no duty of care in relation to decisions which involve or are dictated by financial, economic, social or political factors or constraints. Thus, budgetary allocations and the constraints which they entail in terms of allocation of resources cannot be made the subject of a duty of care. But it may be otherwise when the courts are called upon to apply a standard of care to action or inaction that is merely the product of administrative direction, expert or professional opinion, technical standards or general standards of reasonableness.

Referring to this passage, Gleeson CJ in *Graham Barclay Oysters v Ryan* (2002) 211 CLR 540, at [13], observed:

> One of the reasons why matters of the first kind [policy decisions] are inappropriate as subjects of curial judgment about reasonableness is that they involve competing public interests in circumstances where, as Lord Diplock put it, 'there is no criterion by which a court can assess where the balance lies between the weight to be given to one interest and that to be given to another'. (*Dorset Yacht Co v Home Office* [1970] AC 1004 at 1067)

In *Stovin v Wise* [1996] AC 923, Lord Hoffmann (at 951) considered the policy-operation distinction inadequate as an analytical tool for determining the existence of the duty of care because 'practically every decision about the provision of ... [public] benefits, no matter how trivial it may seem, affects the budget of the public authority in either timing or amount'.[8]

---

8. In *Stovin v Wise* [1996] AC 923, Lord Goff of Chieveley, Lord Jauncey of Tullichettle and Lord Hoffmann (Lord Slynn of Hadley and Lord Nicholls of Birkenhead dissenting) held that the Council was under no statutory duty to act—it had a discretionary power to decide whether or not anything

Indeed, although jurisprudential dichotomy between policy and operational decisions seems to be entrenched, the law of liability of public authorities for non-feasance is evolving. The approach of the High Court to liability of public (statutory) authorities and reform legislation is discussed in turn.

Sutherland Shire Council v Heyman

In *Sutherland Shire Council v Heyman* (1985) 157 CLR 424, the plaintiff had in 1975 purchased a house from its previous owners, who had it built in 1970. The house was built on steeply sloping land. In 1976, after heavy rains, serious defects appeared and it was found that the foundations were inadequate and unsafe. Repairs were carried out, but they could not adequately address the problem and the house lost value as a result. The loss of, or depreciation in, the market value of the house due to inadequate foundations is regarded as pure economic loss.

A positive negligent action—placing unsafe foundations—was performed by the builder, but the builder could not be found. Therefore, the plaintiff sued the local Sutherland Shire Council for depreciation in the value of the house.

The plaintiff alleged that the defendant council had an obligation under the *Local Government Act 1919* (NSW) to enforce the applicable building regulations, and that it either carelessly inspected, or negligently omitted to inspect, the foundations that had been negligently placed by the builder and resulted in a pure economic loss to the plaintiff.[9] The action proceeded on the assumption that the Council omitted to make the inspection: ie, on the basis of nonfeasance. The question was whether the omission should be regarded as negligent misfeasance or pure ('mere') nonfeasance.

The defendant Council argued that:

(a) it made no representations to the plaintiff regarding the condition of the house before the purchase, and

(b) the plaintiff, as a purchaser, never applied to the Council—as he was entitled to do under the *Local Government Act*—for a certificate indicating that the house was built in compliance with the building regulations.

(c) although under the *Local Government Act* one of its statutory functions was to inspect foundations, the Act did not impose a mandatory duty to perform such inspections.

The High Court determined that the Council did not owe the claimants a duty of care to inspect the foundation but left open the possibility that in appropriate

---

should be done about the junction; consequently, it was not liable to compensate persons who had suffered loss by reason of its non-performance.

9. Wilson J (at 426) observed that the source of the loss was the weakened foundations of the house in ignorance of which the purchasers paid more for it than they would otherwise have done.

circumstances, the liability could extend to the negligent non-exercise of a discretionary power vested in the authority.[10]

The *Sutherland Shire Council* case was the first in which Deane J formulated his special notion of proximity as a prerequisite to a duty of care in particular categories of case, including pure omissions (non-feasance). Although the doctrine of proximity has been abandoned by the High Court, other aspects of his Honour's reasoning are still good law. Deane J distinguished between economic loss and physical injury, and found (at 509) that the Sutherland Shire Council had no obligation to take positive action. For although the relevant Acts and Ordinances conferred upon the Council powers and duties for the purpose of protecting health and preventing injury to persons and property within its jurisdiction, these powers and duties did not include within them a 'general purpose of protecting the owners of premises from sustaining economic loss by reason of defects in buildings which they, or their builders may erect, or which they might purchase after erection'. Reasonable foreseeability of pure economic loss was not a sufficient reason to place the Council under a statutory duty to act. Therefore, the plaintiff was unable to establish that the Council was under a statutory duty to act. Moreover, at common law, there was no relationship between the plaintiff and the defendant that could give rise to a duty of care because:

- There was no contact between the plaintiff and the defendant Council prior to the purchase: thus there was no assumption of responsibility by the Council to inspect foundations of the house.
- At the time of purchase the plaintiff had made no enquiries about the Council's records and certificates of compliance: there was no evidence that the plaintiff relied on the Council to undertake inspections.
- The Council made *no* representation to the plaintiff about the exercise of its statutory powers and functions in respect of the house. Hence there could be no inference of inducing or encouraging the plaintiff's reliance.
- No reliance was placed by the plaintiff upon the Council's actual or assumed exercise of statutory powers and functions.
- The causal relationship between the Council's carelessness in inspecting the foundations and the damage sustained by the plaintiff was indirect. According to Deane J, the failure to properly inspect the foundations on the part of the Council would have been inconsequential, were it not for the builder's negligent construction of the foundations. Since the true cause of the damage to the house was the builder's negligent construction of the foundations, there was no causal nexus between its failure to inspect and the damage.

---

10. Hogg KM, 'The Liability of a Public Authority for the Failure to Carry out a Careful Exercise of its Statutory Powers: The Significance of the High Court's Decision in *Sutherland Shire Council v Heyman*' (1991) 17 *Mon LR* 285.

The final reason provided by Deane J for denying the existence of duty of care in *Heyman* involved policy considerations. His Honour stated (at 511) that there is 'No readily discernible reason in principle, policy or justice why a general body of rate-payers within the area should bear an economic loss sustained by such an owner of land.'

Gibbs CJ confirmed the general rule that public authorities may be liable for damage caused by a negligent failure to act when under a duty to act, or by a negligent failure to consider whether to exercise in the public interest a conferred power. However, his Honour emphasised that a failure to act is not negligent unless there is a duty to act. The duty may arise because of the conduct of the defendant himself or herself, or it may be created by the statute.

Mason J (at 464) introduced a doctrine of 'general' and 'specific' reliance. General reliance or dependence was based on a notion that some public bodies are granted powers of such magnitude or complexity as to create a general expectation on the part of individual members of society that the power will be exercised for their benefit, while on the authority's part, there exists a realisation of this general reliance or dependence on its exercise of power. The doctrine of general reliance was specifically adopted by Dawson J in *Hill v Van Erp* (1997) 188 CLR 159, at 186. However, in *Pyrenees Shire Council v Day & Ors* (1998) 192 CLR 330, the doctrine was criticised by Brennan CJ, Gummow and Kirby JJ. Gummow J (at [163]) described 'general reliance' as a legal fiction[11] that operates 'to reconcile a specific legal outcome or result with a premise or postulate involving unexpressed considerations of social and economic policy'.[12] In *Graham Barclay Oysters Pty Ltd v Ryan* (2002) 211 CLR 540, Callinan J observed (at [310]) that '*Pyrenees* ... sounded its demise on its express disapproval by three of the Justices: Brennan CJ (at [20]), and Gummow and Kirby JJ (at [223]).' In *Brodie v Singleton Shire Council* (2001) 206 CLR 512, Hayne J (at [294]) agreed with Gummow J's description of general reliance in *Pyrenees*, and questioned the usefulness of this concept in determining the existence of a positive duty to exercise power on the part of public authorities. Hayne J noted (at [308]) that many statutory bodies, including highway authorities, are monopolies, and members of the public have no real choice in availing themselves of the services provided by them. This means that neither special dependence (reliance) nor vulnerability[13] are useful tests in deciding whether a statutory authority owes a duty of care. As analytical tools, general reliance and vulnerability are:

---

11. This was also the view of the House of Lords in *Stovin v Wise* [1996] AC 923 at 937–8.
12. Gummow J referred to Fuller LL, *Legal Fictions*, Stanford University Press, Stanford, 1967, p 71, and Harmon L, 'Falling Off the Vine: Legal Fictions and the Doctrine of Substituted Judgment' (1990) 100 *Yale Law Journal* 1 at 14–16.
13. Toohey and McHugh JJ, in dissent, strongly supported the application of the doctrine to situations where individuals are vulnerable to harm from immense dangers, which they can neither control nor understand. In *Crimmins v Stevedoring Industry Finance Committee* (1999) 200 CLR 1, Gaudron J (at [43]) seems to have interpreted the notion of general reliance in terms of vulnerability.

Either ... no more than legal fictions or they are descriptions of the nature of the relationship between a statutory authority and a user of the facility or service it provides which add nothing to the conclusion that statutory authorities provide facilities and services to which the public resort as of course and often as of right.

Nevertheless, a statutory authority not under the common law duty to take positive action may place itself under such a duty if, through its conduct, it has led particular individuals to rely on it with regard to protection of their safety and interests. Where the authority by practice or conduct has created such reliance, it may be obliged to take positive action actually to protect these individuals, or at least to warn them about risks to personal safety or other relevant interests. For example, in *Timbs v Shoalhaven City Council* [2004] NSWCA 81, the owner of the land asked the Council to remove from his land, or authorise a removal of, what he considered to be a dangerous tree. However, the Council's employee opined that the tree was not dangerous, and refused to recommend it for removal, citing the Tree Preservation Order. Acting on its employee's advice, the Council refused permission to cut the tree down. The Council was held liable when the tree fell and killed the owner—on the basis that by electing to proffer an opinion on the particular tree's safety, the Council specifically assumed responsibility in relation to that tree.

The existence of a duty of care was determined in *Nagle v Rottnest Island Authority* (1993) 177 CLR 423 in reliance on Deane J's special notion of proximity. The majority of the High Court found that the Rottnest Island Authority Board was under a statutory duty to control and manage the Rottnest Island reserve for the benefit of the public. The fact that the Board encouraged recreational activities on the island placed it in a special relationship of proximity with the visitors to the reserve, thus giving rise to an affirmative duty to prevent foreseeable risks of injury to them. The act of encouragement, is of course, positive conduct.

Pyrenees Shire Council v Day

Pyrenees Shire Council v Day (1998) 192 CLR 330 concerned specific powers and actions of the Council. In that case, Mr and Mrs Stamatopoulos, through their family company, Eskimo Amber Pty Ltd, tenanted premises in 70 Neill Street in Beaufort, a small township in Victoria. Part of the premises was a fish and chip shop and part was a residence. They went into possession of the property in January 1990 under an assignment of tenancy by Mr and Mrs Tzavaros, the previous tenants. The premises were owned by Mr and Mrs Nakos.

Before going to bed on the night of 22 May 1990, Mr Stamatopoulos had lit a log fire in a fireplace.[14] Shortly after midnight, he woke to discover that there was

---

14. He used a fire screen to prevent the escape of sparks.

a fire. Mr Stamatopoulos succeeded in getting his family out of the premises. The entire premises were destroyed by the fire. The fire also spread to the shop next door, owned by Mr and Mrs Day.

While Mr Stamatopoulos did not know that the chimney of the fireplace was defective, the assignor, Mr Tzavaros, and the Pyrenees Shire Council, knew that it was unsafe to use. This was because two years previously, in August 1988, the Country Fire Authority (the CFA) had been summoned to the premises when Mr Tzavaros' assistant became alarmed by what he thought was a fire in the chimney. The CFA officer who attended the call, saw that there was some mortar missing from the bricks in the back and bottom of the fireplace. He advised the assistant that the fireplace was unsafe to use.

The *Local Government Act 1958* (Vic), particularly s 695(1A), when read with other provisions of that Act, gave the Council power to deal with the specific problem of an unsafe chimney. Therefore, once the CFA notified the Council of the occurrence, the Council's building and scaffolding inspector inspected the premises. The inspector found that the back wall of the fireplace was defective, and that this created a substantial risk of fire. He pointed out the defects to Mr Tzavaros and told him he should not use the fireplace unless it was repaired. On the instructions from the Shire Engineer, the inspector sent a letter addressed to 'P Tsavaros & S Nakos' to 70 Neill Street. In it he wrote, *inter alia*, that it was 'imperative that the fireplaces be not used under any circumstances' unless certain specified repairs were carried out.

However, Mr Tsavaros did not inform Mr or Mrs Stamatopoulos about either the contents of the letter or an earlier verbal warning by the inspector when the parties were negotiating the purchase of the business and the lease of the premises in January 1990.[15] Consequently, when Mr Stamatopoulos lit the fire on 22 May, he had no knowledge of the latent defects in the fireplace.

Eskimo Amber Pty Ltd, Mr and Mrs Stamatopoulos, Mr and Mrs Day and Mr and Mrs Nakos sued Mr Tzavaros and the Council in negligence. Mr and Mrs Day succeeded against both Mr Tzavaros and the Council, but the rest of the plaintiffs were originally unsuccessful against the Council. They appealed to the High Court.

The issue before the High Court concerned liability of a local authority in a situation where the local authority knew of a dangerous situation existing in premises but failed to exercise a discretionary statutory power or powers available to it, which might have prevented damage sustained by the plaintiffs.

The majority of the High Court accepted that the statutory powers were conferred upon a local authority for the purpose of preventing the kind of harm (fire) that befell the plaintiffs. The question therefore was whether these powers were properly exercised. McHugh J in dissent (at 371) pointed out that:

---

15. In reply to Mr Stamatopoulos' enquiry whether the fire place was in use, Mr Tzavaros said that it was.

the fact that the authority owes a common law duty of care because it is invested with a function of power does not mean that the total or partial failure to exercise that function or power constitutes a breach of that duty. Whether it does will depend upon all the circumstances of the case including the terms of the function or power and the competing demands on the authority's resources.

However, the majority said that the authority, in the exercise of powers vested in it, had imposed, but failed to enforce on the occupier of the premises, conditions designed to avert a risk of harm to persons and property that was known to the authority but not to the plaintiffs. The plaintiffs claimed that the exercise by the authority of its enforcement powers might have prevented the fire, and hence, the damage. Those Justices who found the Council liable argued that once the Council embarked upon alleviating the known danger of the unsafe chimney, it brought itself under a duty to follow it through. Gummow J (at 391–2) said that the liability of the authority was to be established by application of the principles of common law negligence:

> A public authority which enters upon the exercise of statutory powers with respect to a particular subject matter may place itself in a relationship to others which imports a common law duty to take care which is to be discharged by the continuation or additional exercise of those powers.

The majority stressed that once the Council took the initial action, further steps to remedy the dangerous situation existing in premises were both permissible and practicable. This was because the relevant statutory power was 'addressed to the special risk of fire which, of its nature, can imperil identifiable life and property.'[16]

Unlike the plaintiffs who sued the Sutherland Shire Council for pure economic loss, all the plaintiffs who sued the Pyrenees Shire Council suffered physical damage. Though the outcome in *Sutherland* was different from that in *Pyrenees*, the reasoning was similar. The general approach taken by the court in *Pyrenees* was consistent with both Deane and Mason JJ's discussion in *Sutherland* of the principle that public authorities can be liable for negligent failure to exercise their powers. However, unless a public authority is under a specific statutory duty to act, it will not be considered responsible for failing to act when it is not under any prior common law obligation so. Neither Council was under a specific statutory or prior common law obligation to act, but while the Council in *Sutherland* by doing nothing fell within the general principle of pure nonfeasance, the *Pyrenees* Council initiated a positive action when on the instructions of the Shire Engineer, it sent a letter about

---

16. Brennan CJ observed that the common law duty of care imposed on a statutory authority was analogous to a public duty. This approach was rejected in *Romeo v Conservation Commission* (1998) 192 CLR 431. In *Romeo*, the majority (Toohey, Gaudron, McHugh, Gummow, Kirby, and Hayne JJ) reaffirmed the principle that liability of a public authority is grounded in common law negligence (at 423 [252], per Kirby J).

the defective chimney to the then occupier of the premises and the owner. The authority by its conduct thus placed itself under an obligation to take care when acting. By failing to follow up the warning letter it breached that duty.

In *Crimmins v Stevedoring Industry Finance Committee* (1999) 200 CLR 1 McHugh J commented (at [166]) that in some cases:

> the powers vested by statute in a public authority may give to it such a significant and special measure of control over the safety of the person or property of the plaintiff as to oblige it to exercise its powers to avert danger or to bring the danger to the knowledge of the plaintiff. The powers of the appellant with respect to fire prevention in *Pyrenees Shire Council v Day* were in this category.[17]

Crimmins v Stevedoring Industry Finance Committee

The question of how to reconcile the principles that impose public law obligations upon statutory authorities with private law rules that underpin the cause of action in negligence was further clarified in *Crimmins v Stevedoring Industry Finance Committee* (1999) 200 CLR 1. In that case, the defendant, the Australian Stevedoring Industry Authority, as it was then constituted, was empowered under s 8 of the *Stevedoring Industry Act 1956* (Cth) to 'perform its functions, and exercise its powers … with view to securing the expeditious, safe and efficient performance of stevedoring operations'. Registered waterside workers were assigned for work by the Authority in accordance with the needs of registered employers. Once assigned, the worker became subject to the authority and directions of the employer. Mr Crimmins was employed as a waterside worker in the Port of Melbourne from 1961 to 1965. His work involved unloading asbestos cargoes packed in loosely woven hessian bags. He and other waterside workers were required to work in clouds of airborne asbestos dust without any protective clothing or equipment. No one warned them about the dangers of inhaling asbestos dust. In 1997, Mr Crimmins was diagnosed as suffering from mesothelioma caused by inhalation of asbestos fibres. Before his death from mesothelioma in 1998, he sued several defendants, alleging that his condition had been caused by their negligence. All but one of those claims were settled while he was still alive. The action that survived[18] was against the Stevedoring Industry Finance Committee (SIFC), a successor to the Australian Stevedoring Industry Authority (ASIA).

Both SIFC and ASIA were creatures of statute. Their powers and functions were derived entirely from statute, and the duty of care imposed upon them was strictly a duty of care related to the exercise of statutory powers.[19]

---

17. *Crimmins v Stevedoring Industry Finance Committee* (1999) 200 CLR 1, at 32 [166].
18. Survival of actions under the *Administration and Probate Act 1958* (Vic), s 29(1).
19. *CLT v Connon & Ors* (2000) 77 SASR 449 at 454 [36], per Doyle CJ.

In *Crimmins*, there were seven separate judgments. Gleeson CJ, Gaudron, McHugh, Kirby, and Callinan JJ (Gummow and Hayne JJ dissenting) held that the Authority owed the plaintiff a common law duty to take reasonable care to protect him from reasonably foreseeable risks of injury arising from his employment by his then employers. However, Gleeson CJ pointed out that finding that a statutory authority may owe a duty of care to the plaintiff is only the first step in an evaluation of the authority's conduct for the purpose of determining tortious liability: His Honour (at [5]) reiterated that a legislative grant of power to protect the general public does not ordinarily give rise to a duty owed to an individual or to the members of a particular class:

> In some cases, the difficulty of formulating the practical content of a duty to take reasonable steps to avoid foreseeable risks of harm, for the purpose of measuring the performance of an authority against such a duty, may be a reason for denying the duty. In other cases, of which the present is an example, recognition of the existence of a duty is consistent with the need, when dealing with the question of breach, to take account of complex considerations, perhaps including matters of policy, resources, and industrial relations.

In the *Crimmins* case, however, the majority (Gleeson CJ, Gaudron, McHugh, and Callinan JJ) found that the Authority had or should have had knowledge of the special risks that members of the class which included Mr Crimmins were subject. It was in a position to control or minimise those risks by the exercise of its statutory powers. In contrast, Mr Crimmins, along with other wharf labourers, was vulnerable to injury because of the casual and hazardous nature of his employment. Finally, nothing in the legislation governing the Authority's powers and functions negatived the existence of a common law duty of care by taking steps to eliminate, so far as was reasonably practicable, the risk of harm to waterside workers. Indeed, the relevant statute recognised the employer-employee relationship between workers and the stevedoring companies, and encouraged 'safe working in stevedoring operations'.[20]

Determination of whether such a duty of care has been breached must involve consideration of matters of policy and competing demands on the resources of the authority. According to McHugh J (at [79]):

> Common law courts have long been cautious in imposing affirmative common law duties of care on statutory authorities. Public authorities are often charged with responsibility for a number of statutory objects and given an array of powers to accomplish them. Performing their functions with limited budgetary resources often requires the making of difficult policy choices and discretionary judgments. Negligence law is often an inapposite vehicle for examining those choices and judgments. Situations which might call for the imposition of a duty

---

20. *Crimmins v Stevedoring Industry Finance Committee* (1999) 74 ALR 1 at 65 [359], [360].

of care where a private individual was concerned may not call for one where a statutory authority is involved. This does not mean that statutory authorities are above the law. But it does mean that there may be special factors applicable to a statutory authority which negative a duty of care that a private individual would owe in apparently similar circumstances. In many cases involving routine events, the statutory authority will be in no different position from ordinary citizens. But where the authority is alleged to have failed to exercise a power or function, more difficult questions arise.

Graham Barclay Oysters P/L v Ryan

Graham Barclay Oysters P/L v Ryan (2002) 211 CLR 540 involved an issue of whether the producer, distributors, the Council and the State should be liable to the plaintiff who suffered injury as a result of eating oysters contaminated with hepatitis A. Graham Barclay Oysters Pty Ltd (the company) had cultivated oysters in Wallis Lake in New South Wales since the early twentieth century without a mishap. When, in the period 22–25 November 1996, heavy rain in the vicinity of Wallis Lake increased the risk of viral contamination, the company ceased harvesting its oysters until 26 November 1996. Sample oysters tested by the company and its distributor between 26 November 1996 and 9 January 2003 were found to be negative for *E coli* bacteria, suggesting, but not establishing, that the oysters were free from viral contamination. During that period, oysters were harvested, depurated with clean water, disinfected by ultraviolet radiation, and supplied for sale. Some were consumed by Grant Ryan and other claimants, all of whom fell ill with hepatitis A. Mr Ryan brought a representative action in the Federal Court of Australia on behalf of a group of consumers who had contracted hepatitis, alleging that the company, the distributor of the oysters, the local council for the area in which Wallis Lake was located, and the New South Wales Government were liable in negligence for the harm suffered. In relation to the company and its distributor, he alleged breach of duty of care, but in relation to the government and the Council, the allegation was not that they were careless in the exercise of their respective statutory powers, but that they omitted to do so.

The majority determined that the company (and its distributor) did not breach its duty of care to the plaintiff,[21] and that the Council and the State did not owe

---

21. The majority found that the only alternative for the company to avoid an increased risk of viral contamination from the heavy rainfall, was to cease harvesting and selling oysters for an unspecified, and potentially indefinite, period, or to relocate its business at some unspecified waterway isolated from human beings. Each alternative represented action in alleviating the risk of harm to consumers of the most expensive and inconvenient type. The bare possibility of a known risk of a hepatitis A outbreak which, until the 1996–97 oyster harvest season, had never eventuated, did not constitute a magnitude of risk warranting such alleviating action. Accordingly, the company, by temporarily ceasing harvesting, and by testing sample oysters for *E coli* bacteria, had taken reasonable care to ensure that its oysters were safe for human consumption.

Mr Ryan the relevant duty of care. In relation to the State, the majority held that government decisions about the proper extent of regulation of private or commercial behaviour, or of a particular industry, are policy decisions that are inappropriate for judicial review (they are non-justiciable). Gleeson CJ said (at [32]) that powers to protect public and 'similar powers, covering a wide range of activities, are given to Ministers and government authorities in the interests of public health and safety. A legislative grant of power to protect the general public does not ordinarily give rise to a duty owed to an individual or to the members of a particular class.'

In relation to the Council, the High Court held that although it had powers in respect of some or most of the sources of the oyster contaminant, it did not at any stage exercise control over the risk of the harm that materialised. Like the powers of the State, the powers of the Council were conferred for the benefit of the public generally, not for the protection of a specific class of persons. Therefore, according to Gleeson CJ (at [39]):

> there is nothing in the relevant statutory provisions, or in the circumstances concerning the relationship between the Council and oyster consumers, to justify a conclusion that the Council's powers were given for the protection of oyster consumers, or any other particular class.

Gummow and Hayne JJ (at [192]) emphasised the rule against hindsight—that is, 'formulating a duty of care retrospectively as an obligation purely to avoid the particular act or omission said to have caused loss, or to avert the particular harm that in fact eventuated' applied across all actions in negligence. This is because such formulation is 'likely to obscure the proper inquiry as to breach', which involves 'identifying, with some precision, what a reasonable person in the position of the defendant would do by way of response to the reasonably foreseeable risk.'

The court noted that the governing test of the reasonable person's response should be the calculus of negligence as set out by Mason J in *Wyong Shire Council v Shirt* (1980) 146 CLR 40, at 47–8.

New South Wales v Bujdoso

In *New South Wales v Bujdoso* [2005] HCA 76 Gleeson CJ, Gummow, Kirby, Hayne, Callinan, and Heydon JJ, in a joint judgment, determined that statutory authorities should be liable for failure to take affirmative action to protect those under their control and care. Mr Bujdoso, while in Silverwater Prison in New South Wales serving a prison sentence for sexual assaults on male persons under the age of eighteen, was attacked in his cell by assailants wearing balaclavas, and severely injured. The prison authorities had actual knowledge that Mr Bujdoso was being verbally abused by other inmates and that there existed 'expressly threatened' risk of considerable physical injury to him. Nevertheless, those in control of the prison took no steps to protect Mr Bujdoso. Among a number of American and English authorities, their Honours (at [45]) quoted with approval the following passage from §320 of the *Restatement of Torts*:[22]

> One who is required by law to take or who voluntarily takes the custody of another under circumstances such as to deprive the other of his normal power of self-protection or to subject him to association with persons likely to harm him, is under a duty to exercise reasonable care so to control the conduct of third persons as to prevent them from intentionally harming the other or so conducting themselves as to create an unreasonable risk of harm to him, if the actor
> (a) knows or has reason to know that he has the ability to control the conduct of the third persons, and
> (b) knows or should know of the necessity and opportunity for exercising such control.

A similar affirmative obligation to use care to control the conduct of others may also apply to relationships *in loco parentis* (in place of a parent).[23]

General principles for determining the existence of the duty of public authorities as well as principles governing the inquiry into the breach of duty as articulated by the High Court in *Graham Barclay Oysters* and *New South Wales v Bujdoso* will underpin the statutory regime relating to liability of public authorities.

Notably, Western Australia, Tasmania, Victoria, New South Wales, and the Australian Capital Territory[24] have enacted identically worded provisions that reflect the common law principle that 'the fact that a public or other authority exercises or decides to exercise a function does not of itself indicate that the authority is under a duty to exercise the function or that the function should be exercised in particular circumstances or in a particular way'.

LIABILITY OF HIGHWAY AUTHORITIES

Callinan J, in *D'Orta-Ekenaike v Victoria Legal Aid* [2005] HCA 12 (at [358]), provided two examples of the High Court's decisions that were 'of a radical and even sudden kind'. One of them was *Lange v Australian Broadcasting Corporation* (1997) 189 CLR 520, discussed in Chapter 20, and the other was *Brodie v Singleton Shire Council; Ghantous v Hawkesbury City Council* (2001) 206 CLR 512. Highway authorities were immune from a suit in negligence with regard to a failure to inspect, discover and repair defects on public works such as roads, pavements, and bridges

---

22. *Restatement of Torts*, 2d, Vol 2, Div 2, 'Negligence', Ch 12, 'General Principles' (1965).
23. Harper FV, James F & Gray OS, *The Law of Torts*, 2nd edn, Aspen Law & Business, Gaithersburg, 1986, Vol 3 at §18.7, cited with approval in *New South Wales v Bujdoso* [2005] HCA 76 at [45].
24. *Civil Liability Act 2002* (WA), s 5AA; *Civil Liability Act 2002* (Tas), s 43; *Wrongs Act 1958* (Vic), 85; *Civil Liability Act 2002* (NSW), s 46; *Civil Law (Wrongs) Act 2002* (ACT), s 114.

under their jurisdiction because such failure was not considered an actionable misfeasance. In *Buckle v Bayswater Road Board* (1937) 57 CLR 259 (at 283), Dixon J (as he then was) expressed this rule thus:

> a road authority owes to the members of the public using a highway no duty to undertake active measures whether of maintenance, repair, construction or lighting in order to safeguard them from its condition.

Since the rule was formulated in terms of 'tortious liability', the immunity extended to negligence and nuisance. However, in *Brodie v Singleton Shire Council*, the majority of the High Court determined that the rule exempting highway authorities from liability for pure nonfeasance should not be followed.[25] Instead, when determining liability of highway authorities in relation to the exercise, or failure to exercise, their powers with respect to the construction and maintenance of roads, the courts should apply the ordinary principles of negligence and nuisance that govern other statutory bodies.[26] Gaudron, McHugh and Gummow JJ, in a joint judgment forming part of the majority, stated (at [150]):

> Where the state of a roadway, whether from design, construction, works or non-repair, poses a risk to that class of persons, then, to discharge its duty of care, an authority with power to remedy the risk is obliged to take reasonable steps by the exercise of its powers within a reasonable time to address the risk. If the risk be unknown to the authority or latent and only discoverable by inspection, then to discharge its duty of care an authority having power to inspect is obliged to take reasonable steps to ascertain the existence of latent dangers which might reasonably be suspected to exist.

Adapting the test for determining the breach of the duty of care articulated by Mason J in *Wyong Shire Council v Shirt* (1980) 146 CLR 40, at 47–8, their Honours declared (at [151]) that the inquiry into the question whether the public authority took reasonable steps to remove the danger should include:

> a consideration of various matters; in particular, the magnitude of the risk and the degree of probability that it will occur, the expense, difficulty and inconvenience to the authority in taking the steps described above to alleviate the danger, and any other competing or conflicting responsibility or commitments of the authority.

This meant that in cases involving pure nonfeasance, the burden was on the defendant authority to prove that its conduct of not acting to eliminate a foreseeable

---

25. Gaudron, McHugh, and Gummow JJ at [55], [137]; Kirby J at [226].
26. Gleeson CJ, Hayne and Callinan JJ considered that the changes to the common law doctrine should be left to the Parliament. In England, the highway immunity rule was abolished by the *Highways (Miscellaneous Provisions) Act 1961* (UK), s 1(1).

risk was reasonable in the context of its 'competing or conflicting responsibility or commitments'.[27]

Brodie but not *Ghantous* (see: pp 301 and 302) has been specifically overcome by (differently drafted) legislation in Tasmania, Queensland, Victoria, New South Wales, the Australian Capital Territory, and Western Australia, which provides special nonfeasance protection for public or other authorities responsible for carrying out road works and the like.[28] Under New South Wales, the *Civil Liability Act 2002*, (NSW) s 45(1) provides that a roads authority is not liable for harm arising from a failure of the authority to carry out road work, or to consider carrying out road work, unless at the time of the alleged failure the authority had actual knowledge of the particular risk the materialisation of which resulted in the harm. However, s 45(2) states that s 45(1) 'does not operate (a) to create a duty of care in respect of a risk merely because a roads authority has actual knowledge of the risk, or (2) to affect any standard of care that would otherwise be applicable in respect of a risk'. In other words, actual knowledge of the risk of itself is not sufficient to impose liability; other considerations such as the expense, difficulty and inconvenience to the authority in taking the steps to alleviate the danger must also be considered.

In South Australia, the *Civil Liability Act 1936*, s 42, provides that a road authority is not liable for a failure to maintain, repair or renew a road (which includes footpaths, laneways, bridges and carparks); or to take other action to avoid or reduce the risk of harm that results from a failure to maintain, repair or renew a road.

ENTITIES VESTED WITH REGULATION-MAKING POWER

The question whether law-making institutions should be liable for failure to make regulations, rules, and laws that would make a particular enterprise, environment, or activity safer was discussed in *Agar v Hyde; Agar v Worsley* (2000) 201 CLR 552. In that case, two rugby players who were injured in the course of rugby union matches sued the International Rugby Football Board (IRFB) in negligence. The plaintiffs alleged that the IRFB as the effective 'law-giver for the sport of rugby' had failed to amend the Laws of the Game of Rugby Football in order to make the game safer. The High Court determined that since members of the IRFB did nothing to create

---

27. *Civil Liability Act 2002* (NSW), s 45; *Civil Liability Act 2003* (Qld), s 37; *Civil Liability Act 2002* (Tas), s 42; *Road Management Act 2004* (Vic), s 102; *Civil Liability Act 2002* (WA), s 5Z; *Civil Law (Wrongs) Act 2002* (ACT), s 113.
28. *Civil Liability Act 2002* (NSW), s 45; *Civil Liability Act 2003* (Qld), s 37; *Civil Liability Act 2002* (Tas), s 42; *Road Management Act 2004* (Vic), s 102; *Civil Liability Act 2002* (WA), s 5Z; *Civil Law (Wrongs) Act 2002* (ACT), s 113.

or increase the risk of harm to either one of the plaintiffs, they did not owe them a duty of care. As Gaudron, McHugh, Gummow, and Hayne JJ (at 578 [69]) put it:

> The complaint is that they [IRFB] failed to alter the status quo, failed to alter the rules under which the [plaintiffs] voluntarily played the game. In our view, they no more owed a duty of care to each rugby player to alter the laws of rugby than parliamentarians owe a duty of care to factory workers to amend the factories legislation.

In the Australian Capital Territory, New South Wales and Tasmania,[29] similarly worded legislation provides that public or other authorities are not liable for failure to exercise regulatory functions to the extent that the claim is based on the failure of the authority to exercise or to consider exercising any function of the authority to prohibit or regulate an activity, 'if the authority could not have been required to exercise the function in proceedings instituted by the claimant.' For the purposes of these provisions, the scope of the function to regulate includes 'a function to issue a licence, permit or other authority in respect of an activity, or to register or otherwise authorise a person in connection with an activity'.

FURTHER READING

Cane P & Stapleton J (eds), *The Law of Obligations: Essays in Celebration of John Fleming*, Clarendon Press, Oxford, 1997.

Honoré AM, 'Are Omissions Less Culpable?', in Cane P & Stapleton J (eds) *Essays for Patrick Atiyah*, Clarendon Press, Oxford, 1991, p 31.

Kortmann J, *Altruism in Private Law*, Oxford University Press, Oxford, 2005.

Simester AP, 'Why Omissions Are Special' (1995) 1 *Legal Theory* 311–335.

Markesinis B, 'Plaintiff's Tort Law or Defendant's Tort Law? Is the House of Lords Moving Towards a Synthesis?' (2001) 9 *Torts Law Journal* 168.

Trindade F & Cane P, *The Law of Torts in Australia*, 3rd edn, Oxford University Press, Melbourne, 1999, pp 400–411.

---

29. *Civil Law (Wrongs) Act 2002* (ACT), s 112; *Civil Liability Act 2002* (NSW), s 44; *Civil Liability Act 2002* (Tas), s 41.

Mental Harm: Liability for Negligently Occasioned Pure Psychiatric Injury*

INTRODUCTION

The concept of emotional injury is very old. All countries whose laws of delict (tort) are derived from the Roman cause of action for *iniuria* (*actio iniuriarum*) recognise a head of damages for emotional injury and anguish suffered by the members of the family of an unlawfully killed or seriously injured person. In Scottish law, which was strongly influenced by Roman legal tradition, the law of *assythment* entitled the family of a person who was wrongfully killed to be indemnified by the wrongdoer for the pecuniary loss and the suffering occasioned by the death. The Scottish law also adopted the civil law concept of compensation for *solatium* to mark or acknowledge 'the grief and sorrow needlessly inflicted on the surviving relative.'[1] In the nineteenth century, the law of *assythment*, and with it the doctrine of *solatium*, was repudiated by the English and Australian common law.[2] However, South Australia and the Northern Territory have created independent statutory causes of action for *solatium*,[3] whereby the spouse and children of a person who died as a result of negligence or misconduct of the wrongdoer can claim compensation for mental suffering occasioned by the wrongful death. A number of jurisdictions also

---

* This chapter is partly based on an article by Mendelson D, 'The Modern Australian Law of Mental Harm: Parochialism Triumphant' (2005) 12 *Journal of Law and Medicine* 402–412.
1. *Quin v Greenock Tramways* [1926] SC 544 at 547.
2. *Blake v Midland Ry Co* (1852) 21 LJ QB 233 at 237. Coleridge J said that 'the Scottish law of assythment is wholly alien to the common law of England'. See also: discussion of the Canadian civil law concept of 'solatium doloris' in *Augustus v Gosset* [1996] 3 SCR 268.
3. *Civil Liability Act 1936* (SA), ss 28, 29; *Compensation (Fatal Injuries) Act 1974* (NT), s 10. See also: *Civil Liability Act 1961* (Ire), s 49; *Fatal Accidents Act 1976* (UK), s 1A (1982 amendment).

allow statutory claims for psychiatric injury and pure nervous shock under their criminal injuries compensation schemes.[4]

At common law, compensatory damages are awarded for any emotional disturbance—including fright, humiliation, embarrassment, and grief, as well as psychiatric injury—that results from intentional wrongs. Torts such as false imprisonment or assault need not involve physical contact, but must satisfy the requirements of directness and intention. The tort in *Wilkinson v Downton* [1897] 2 QB 57 (action on the case for intentional infliction of nervous shock) allows compensation for intentionally inflicted pure nervous shock in the form of a recognised psychiatric disorder.[5]

Under the common law of negligence, a psychiatric disorder that was a result of an unintentionally occasioned wrongful physical impact or injury has been compensable under the *Donoghue v Stevenson* [1932] AC 562 cause of action. In fact, the plaintiff in *Donoghue v Stevenson*, Mrs Donoghue, who drank ginger beer out an opaque bottle that also contained a decomposed snail, was awarded damages both for severe gastroenteritis and for nervous shock. Another example is that of *Malec v JC Hutton Pty Ltd* (1990) CLR 638, where damages were awarded for a psychiatric disorder Mr Malec developed as a consequence of brucellosis, which he contracted as a result of the defendant's negligence.

The modern law of compensation for psychiatric disorders occasioned by wrongful conduct is very complex. In Australia, the law of psychiatric injury is a patchwork of codified law and common law that varies from jurisdiction to jurisdiction. Assorted State and Commonwealth statutory schemes relating to workers, motor accidents, and compensation for criminal injuries have provisions relating to recovery for nervous shock or psychiatric injury.[6] In addition, compensability and assessment of damages for a claim involving psychiatric disorder is determined by whether the injury is a result of an intentional wrong, nuisance or negligence. In 2002–03 most jurisdictions enacted statutory rules governing private actions for negligently occasioned psychiatric injury. However, these rules are not uniform.

Nomenclature

The phrase 'nervous shock' was introduced into legal usage from medicine in the 1860s.[7] Nervous shock was considered a head of compensable damage for secondary symptoms of what was thought to be an organic but not demonstrable

---

4. *Victims Support and Rehabilitation Act 1996* (NSW), Sch 1, cl 5(a).
5. See: Chapter 6.
6. *Victims Rights Act 1996* (NSW), s 5.
7. Mendelson D, *Interfaces of Medicine and Law: The History of Liability for Negligently Caused Psychiatric Injury (Nervous Shock)*, Ashgate International, Aldershot, 1998, p 6.

injury occasioned by railway accidents.[8] In the 1880s, medicine reconceptualised nervous shock as a functional disorder, denoting a bodily dysfunction without any apparent lesion, produced as a consequence of fear and alarm triggered by the shock of an accident.[9] In the nineteenth century, lawyers used the term 'mental shock' to refer to such painful but transitory emotional experiences as anxiety, anguish, or grief—which, it was then thought, were not productive of any appreciable injury to the organism. Where mental shock or mental suffering was the sole harm arising from negligent conduct, it was not compensable.[10] Once nervous shock came to be regarded as a functional disorder, 'mental shock' and 'nervous shock' were sometimes used interchangeably.

With the development of modern psychiatry, the term 'nervous shock' was jettisoned from medical nomenclature, but the law retained it as a label for a discrete head of damage. In *Jaensch v Coffey* (1984) 155 CLR 549, the High Court expressed a preference for the phrase 'psychiatric injury'.[11] Brennan J noted (at 560) that:

> The term 'nervous shock' is useful ... as a term of art to indicate the aetiology of a psychiatric illness for which damages are recoverable in an action on the Case when the other elements of the cause of action are present.[12]

Since the 1980s the term 'psychiatric injury' has often been used in preference to 'nervous shock'. In *Jaensch v Coffey*, Deane J (at 593) also defined the phrase 'mere psychiatric injury' as denoting 'psychoneurosis and mental illness which is not the adjunct of ordinary bodily injury to the person affected'.[13]

Jurisdictions that have codified rules governing compensation for negligently occasioned psychiatric injury refer to mental harm (rather than nervous shock) as a general head of damages, which is divided into:

- 'consequential mental harm', which follows on physical injury—as where depression is suffered as a result of an injury to the body; and
- the 'stand alone harm' or 'pure mental harm'—as where a person suffers anxiety as a result of witnessing traumatic events.

In *Morris v KLM Royal Dutch Airlines* [2002] 2 AC 628, one of the plaintiffs brought an action for damages against the defendant airline for clinical depression,

---

8. Erichsen JE, *On Railway and Other Injuries of the Nervous System*, Walton & Maberly, London, 1866, p 64–67.
9. Page HW, *Injuries of the Spine and Spinal Cord Without Apparent Mechanical Lesion and Nervous Shock in Their Surgical and Medical Aspects*, J & A Churchill, London, 1883, p 148.
10. Beven T, *Principles of the Law of Negligence*, Stevens and Haynes, London, 1889.
11. For a more recent critique of terminology associated with claims for psychiatric injury, see: *Morris v KLM Royal Dutch Airlines* [2002] 2 AC 628, the judgment of Lord Hobhouse of Woodborough.
12. See also: *Jaensch v Coffey* (1984) 155 CLR 549 at 551, 552, per Gibbs CJ.
13. See also: Mullany NJ & Handford PR, *Tort Liability for Psychiatric Damage: The Law of 'Nervous Shock'*, The Law Book Company Ltd, Sydney, 1993.

which was a result of an indecent assault by a male passenger in the adjoining seat when, at the age of fifteen, she was flying from Kuala Lumpur to Amsterdam. While discussing whether psychiatric illness can qualify as 'bodily injury' (*lésion corporelle*) for the purposes of Article 17 of the Warsaw Convention, Lord Hobhouse of Woodborough pointed out (at 682 [157]) that reference to 'mental' injury or harm evokes the concept of body–mind dualism articulated by Rene Descartes in 1649,[14] and nowadays discarded as unscientific. According to his Lordship:

> The adjective *mental* means relating to the mind. The mind is a metaphysical concept associated with the self-consciousness of human beings. The word can be used in a descriptive but not a substantive sense. One can have a mental illness or disorder just as one can have a respiratory illness or disorder. But one cannot usefully refer to having a *mental* injury.

The same observation is applicable to 'mental harm'.

The *Ipp Report*[15] recommended (at [3.42]) a change from the traditional appellation of 'nervous shock' to 'mental harm', which in New South Wales, Tasmania, Western Australia, the Australian Capital Territory, and South Australia, has been defined as 'impairment of the person's mental condition'.[16] In Victoria, the definition of 'mental harm' is less circular, namely: 'psychological or psychiatric injury' (no explanation is provided for the distinction between psychological and psychiatric injury).[17]

Lord Hobhouse of Woodborough also commented on the confusion of psychiatry with psychology, which, as the reform provisions demonstrate, seems prevalent among lawyers.[18] Hampel J drew a useful, if not exhaustive, distinction between these two disciplines in *R v David Joel Whitbread* (unreported, Supreme Court of Victoria, Appeal Division, 14 March 1995). His Honour characterised psychology as 'a branch of science which deals with mind and mental processes'.[19] Psychologists are generally graduates of arts or science faculties, who, according to Hampel J, are trained in the 'science of nature, functioning and development of human mind and the study of the behaviour of the mind'. His Honour then defined psychiatry as 'a medical treatment of mental illness, emotional disturbance and

---

14. Descartes R, 'The Passions of the Soul' (1649), in *The Philosophical Works*, Haladane ES & Ross DRT, Dover, New York, 1955, Vol 1.
15. Ipp D, Cane P, Sheldon D & Macintosh I, *Review of the Law of Negligence Report*, 2 October 2002; <http://www.revofneg.treasury.gov.au/content/reports.asp> Second Report—released 2 October 2002.
16. *Civil Law (Wrongs) Act 2002* (ACT), s 32; *Civil Liability Act 2002* (NSW), s 27; *Civil Liability Act 2002* (Tas), s 29; *Civil Liability Act 2002* (WA), 5Q; *Civil Liability Act 1936* (SA), s 3.
17. *Wrongs Act 1958* (Vic), s 67.
18. For a discussion of this issue, see: Mendelson D, 'Damages for Nervous Shock: *Coates & Coates v Government Insurance Office of New South Wales*' (1995) 3 *Journal of Law and Medicine* 8–10.
19. Id.

abnormal behaviour'.[20] Psychiatrists graduate in medicine before undertaking postgraduate medical training in psychiatry. Only psychiatrists have the professional competence to diagnose psychiatric pathology and treat psychiatric disorders, which for the purposes of the law of torts form the content of psychiatric injury or damage.[21]

Recognised psychiatric illness

A recognised psychiatric illness or disorder is the prerequisite to recovery for negligently occasioned psychiatric injury.[22] For, unlike the law in the United States, Anglo-Australian law distinguishes mere 'emotional injury'—such as normal grief, anxiety, humiliation, and anguish—from psychiatric conditions or disorders.

The distinction is important, and has been discussed in a number of recent cases. However, it is surprising that even at the level of the High Court some Justices use the term 'recognisable' psychiatric illness—how does one recognise a psychiatric illness?—rather than 'recognised' psychiatric illness.[23]

In the *Review of the Law of Negligence Report*,[24] the Ipp Panel, noting that 'the concept of illness is, to some extent, a social construction, and the catalogue of mental illnesses is not closed,'[25] recommended (at [3.47]; Recommendation 3) that:

> a panel of experts, including experts in forensic psychiatry and psychology, be appointed to develop a set of guidelines, for use in legal contexts, for assessing whether a person has suffered a recognised psychiatric illness. These guidelines should be given formally-recognised status.[26]

The recommended guidelines are yet to be developed.

---

20. *R v David Joel Whitbread* (unreported, Supreme Court of Victoria, Appeal Division, 14 March 1995).
21. The clinical instruction of medical students includes the study of nosology—the theory and classification of diseases—which, together with the knowledge of such parts of medicine as anatomy, physiology, neurology, pathology, aetiology, treatment and prognosis, provides the basis for diagnosis of the patient's complaint: Laor N & Agassi J, *Episteme 15. Diagnosis: Philosophical and Medical Perspectives*, Kluwer Academic Publishers, Dordrecht, 1990.
22. *Hinz v Berry* [1970] 2 QB 40 at 42–3, per Lord Denning MR; *Mount Isa Mines Ltd v Pusey* (1970) 125 CLR 383 at 394, per Windeyer J.
23. See, for example: the judgments of Gleeson CJ, Gaudron, Gummow, and Kirby JJ in *Tame v New South Wales*; *Annetts v Australian Stations Pty Ltd* [2002] HCA 35; (2002) 211 CLR 317; and the judgments of Gleeson CJ, Gummow and Kirby JJ in *Gifford v Strang Patrick Stevedoring Pty Ltd* [2003] HCA 33; (2003) 214 CLR 269.
24. Ipp D, Cane P, Sheldon D & Macintosh I, *Review of the Law of Negligence Report*, 2 October 2002; <http://www.revofneg.treasury.gov.au/content/reports.asp> Second Report—released 2 October 2002.
25. Ipp D, Cane P, Sheldon D & Macintosh I, *Review of the Law of Negligence Report*, id. The Panel reiterated Hayne J's concerns in *Tame v New South Wales* [2002] HCA 35 at [285]–[297] about the use for forensic purposes of the *Diagnostic and Statistical Manual of Mental Disorders* (DSM-IV-TR).
26. Ipp D, Cane P, Sheldon D & Macintosh I, *Review of the Law of Negligence Report*, id, at [3.47]; Recommendation 3.

In *Morris v KLM Royal Dutch Airlines* [2002] 2 AC 628, Lord Hobhouse of Woodborough, wrote (at 679 [153]):

> Psychiatry (the science of mental illness) has been able to develop a more reliable classification and aetiology enabling better diagnoses to be made and more reliable opinions to be given as to the probable causation of observed disorders.

There are two major classifications of psychiatric disorders: the *International Classification of Diseases* (ICD), which is produced by the World Health Organization and is widely used in Europe; and the *Diagnostic and Statistical Manual of Mental Disorders* (DSM-IV-TR), often used by psychiatrists who practise in common law countries. The *Diagnostic and Statistical Manual of Mental Disorders* (DSM III) was developed in the 1970s by the Task Force on Nomenclature and Statistics for the Council on Research and Development of the American Psychiatric Association. The DSM in its various iterations was intended as a classificatory tool for use by psychiatrists in clinical contexts, and by researchers undertaking large-scale epidemiological studies of disorders.[27]

Consequential nature of the injury

The concept of 'consequential mental harm' has to be distinguished from the consequential nature of claims for pure psychiatric injury.[28] Persons who claim compensation for 'pure nervous shock' or 'pure mental harm' are sometimes called 'secondary victims' (*victimes par ricochet* in French). The essence of their claim is that a specific event, resulting from the defendant's tortious action, has caused them a recognised psychiatric disorder. Historically, shock was an essential element of all common law claims for pure nervous shock. The basis for recovery was not the emotional shock itself, but, as Windeyer J explained in *Mount Isa Mines Ltd v Pusey* (1971) 125 CLR 383, at 394, the recognised psychiatric condition consequent upon it:

> Sorrow does not sound in damages. A plaintiff in an action in negligence cannot recover damages for a 'shock', however grievous, which was no more than an immediate emotional response to a distressing experience sudden, severe and saddening. It is, however, today a known medical fact that severe emotional distress can be a starting point of a lasting disorder of mind and body, some form of psychoneurosis or a psychosomatic illness. For that, if it be the result of

---

27. For the historical background of DSM, and in particular controversies relating to inclusion of post-traumatic stress disorder (PTSD), see: Mendelson D, *Interfaces of Medicine and Law: The History of the Liability for Negligently Caused Psychiatric Injury (Nervous Shock)*, Ashgate International, Aldershot, 1998, pp 183–187.
28. Mendelson D, 'English Medical Experts and the Claims for Shock Occasioned by Railway Collisions in the 1860s: Issues of Law and Ethics and Medicine' (2002) 25(4) *International Journal of Law and Psychiatry* 303–329.

Chapter 15: Mental Harm: Liability for Negligently Occasioned Pure Psychiatric Injury

a tortious act, damages may be had. It is in that consequential sense that the term 'nervous shock' has come into law.

Today, the emphasis is placed on the damage—psychiatric injury—rather than the particular manner in which it was occasioned—by way of a single shock.

As a general rule, the law identifies three kinds of events that may produce compensable psychiatric injury:

1. negligently inflicted physical harm resulting in a recognised psychiatric condition;
2. presence at the scene where another person has been killed, injured or put in peril, if the traumatic experience of witnessing the events results in a recognised psychiatric disorder; and
3. negligently occasioned death, injury or imperilment of the claimant's relatives by the defendant where the claimant, although not present at the scene of the accident, develops a recognised psychiatric disorder.

EVOLUTION OF LIABILITY FOR NEGLIGENTLY OCCASIONED PURE PSYCHIATRIC INJURY

The history of compensation for psychiatric injury is vital to the understanding of the intricacies and nuances of this jurisprudence. For more than any other area of the law, the modern law of psychiatric injury has been shaped by its history. An examination of the five most important Australian cases will be followed by analysis of statutory reforms.

Coultas v The Victorian Railway Commissioners

The first reported case of damages claimed for nervous shock triggered by non-physical-impact trauma was *Coultas et uxor v The Victorian Railway Commissioners* (1886) 12 VLR 895. In the late evening in May 1886, Mr and Mrs Coultas, together with Mrs Coultas' brother, were driving home in a horse-drawn carriage from Melbourne to Hawthorn. The gates at the railway level crossing in Swan Street, East Richmond, were closed. However, the gate-keeper, employed by the Victorian Railways Commissioners, opened the near gate and indicated that they should proceed to cross the line. They had just passed over one set of rails when a train came past. Frightened by the train, Mrs Coultas fainted and shortly afterwards suffered a miscarriage; she was ill for several months. Medical evidence indicated she had suffered a 'severe nervous shock from the fright, and that the illness from which she afterwards suffered was the consequence of the fright'.

The jury found for the plaintiffs. The Full Bench of the Supreme Court of Victoria decided Mrs Coultas could recover for 'mental and physical injuries' resulting from nervous shock caused by the defendants' negligence. The Victorian Railways Commissioners appealed to the Privy Council. The Privy Council in *Victorian Railway Commissioners v James Coultas and Mary Coultas* (1888) 13 AC 222 advised that recovery for negligently caused nervous shock not accompanied by physical impact should be denied on the grounds that this kind of injury was too remote. The Privy Council's advice not to impose liability for negligently caused nervous shock was motivated by suspicion that absence of actual physical impact or demonstrable physical lesion may lead to fraudulent and unsubstantiated claims that would open the 'floodgates of litigation'.

For many decades, judges who allowed recovery for unintentionally caused nervous shock would distinguish the *Coultas* decision on the facts rather than the principle.[29] Moreover, since the *Coultas* case, recovery of damages for negligently occasioned pure psychiatric injury has been determined by the nature of the injury and the way it was caused rather than the conduct of the defendant.

Chester v The Council of the Municipality of Waverley

In the early twentieth century, the majority of Australian jurisdictions enacted legislation specifying that: 'in any action for injury to the person the plaintiff shall not be debarred from recovering damages merely because the injury complained of arose wholly or in part from mental or nervous shock.'[30] These provisions, however, merely confirmed that pure psychiatric injury may sound in damages. Thus, in *Chester v The Council of the Municipality of Waverley* (1939–40) 62 CLR 1, the majority of the High Court (with a powerful dissent by Evatt J) determined that claimants suffering from negligently occasioned pure psychiatric injury could not recover damages unless their psychiatric illness resulted from a direct sensory perception of the actual accident in which a close relative was killed, injured, or threatened with grave injury. The case concerned a mother who sought recovery for severe psychiatric illness suffered as a result of seeing her seven-year-old son Max's body taken out of a water-filled trench. The defendant admitted negligence in leaving the seven-foot-deep, rain-filled trench unattended. The trench was protected only by a railing under which children could easily pass to play with white sand on the edge. The court held that plaintiff's action should fail because Mrs Chester was not physically present at the scene and did not witness Max's drowning. Consequently, the Council did not owe her a duty of care.

---

29. Mendelson D, *Interfaces of Medicine and Law: The History of Liability for Negligently Caused Psychiatric Injury (Nervous Shock)*, Ashgate International, Aldershot, 1998, pp 75–115.
30. *Wrongs Act 1958* (Vic), s 23. See also: *Law Reform (Miscellaneous Provisions) Act 1944* (NSW), s 3, now *Civil Liability Act 2002* (NSW), s 29; *Civil Law (Wrongs) Act 2002* (ACT), s 33; *Law Reform (Miscellaneous Provisions) Act 1956* (NT), s 24(1); *Civil Liability Act 2002* (Tas), s 31; *Wrongs Act Amendment Act 1939* (SA), s 28.

In issue were both the nature and the content of the duty of care, for it was regarded a pivotal principle of negligence that:

> The victim [of negligence] does not sue derivatively, or by right of subrogation, to vindicate an interest invaded in the person of another ... he sues for breach of a duty owing to himself.[31]

This meant that claimants suing for pure psychiatric injury had to establish not only that their injury was foreseeable, but also that the defendant breached a duty of care, owed to them personally, by negligently injuring or killing another person. If, in the *Chester* case, a duty of care were imposed on the Waverley Council, the court would have had to determine the standard of care the Council owed not to Max but to Mrs Chester. By refusing to impose a duty of care on the Council, the High Court, was relieved of having to devise an appropriate test for the standard of care required in cases of pure psychiatric injury.

The decision in the *Chester* case was controversial.[32] Primarily in response to the *Chester* case, New South Wales[33] created, in 1944, a statutory cause of action for nervous shock; it provided that a member of the family of a person killed, injured, or put in peril by the negligence of a defendant may bring an action for nervous shock if the person was within the sight or hearing of such member of the family. Thus, the statutory independent cause of action for nervous or mental shock made it unnecessary—at least for a close relative—to establish, as a foundation of the action, both duty of care and its breach. It was effectively sufficient to establish the required kind of damage and causation (nervous or mental shock). Similar provisions were adopted in 1955 by the Northern Territory and the Australian Capital Territory.[34]

Mount Isa Mines Ltd v Pusey

In other jurisdictions, however, *Coultas* was the ruling precedent with respect to the remoteness of damage, and *Chester* denied a duty of care to all those who did not directly perceive the actual accident with their own senses. The High Court reversed the *Coultas* doctrine in *Mount Isa Mines Ltd v Pusey* (1970) 125 CLR 383. The court accepted (at 393) the trial judge's findings that in the context of an employer's duty to provide a safe working environment, the plaintiff's action

---

31. *Palsgraf v Long Island Railroad Co* 162 NE 99 at 101, per Cardozo J (1928); this issue was also discussed by the House of Lords in *Bourhill v Young* [1943] AC 92.
32. Mendelson D, *Interfaces of Medicine and Law: The History of Liability for Negligently Caused Psychiatric Injury (Nervous Shock)*, Ashgate International, Aldershot, 1998, pp 138–144; 149–151.
33. Section 4 of the *Law Reform (Miscellaneous Provisions) Act 1944* (NSW). Section 4, together with s 3, was repealed in part by the *Civil Liability Amendment (Personal Responsibility) Act 2002* (NSW) and replaced by the *Civil Liability Act 2002* (NSW), Pt 3.
34. *Law Reform (Miscellaneous Provisions) Act 1955* (ACT), s 24(1). This provision has been repealed and a modified version is now contained in the *Civil Law (Wrongs) Act 2002* (ACT), s 36. See also: *Law Reform (Miscellaneous Provisions) Act 1956* (NT), s 25.

of providing the assistance to his fellow workers, and 'the possibility of shock and some form of mental illness' were reasonably foreseeable, and hence not too remote. Mr Pusey recovered damages for an acute schizophrenic episode and depression, rendering him unemployable, which he suffered after assisting two co-workers who were severely burnt in an explosion. Mr Pusey heard the explosion, but he neither witnessed the accident nor knew the victims. The High Court overcame *Coultas* by recognising that to ground liability it is sufficient that a recognised class of mental disorders, rather than a particular type of injury, be a foreseeable consequence of the defendant's conduct (at 402).

Employees and rescuers

In *Pusey*, Windeyer J discussed the intertwined nature of employers' duty in the employee–rescuer cases. He pointed out (at 403) that imposition of a duty of care upon defendants for pure nervous shock was historically regarded as exceptional, and limited to close relatives. His Honour noted, however, that in England, Donovan J in *Dooley v Cammell Laird & Co* [1951] 1 Lloyd's Rep 271[35] and Waller J in *Chadwick v British Railways Board* [1967] 1 WLR 912[36] had allowed recovery of damages to rescuers. Windeyer J (at 403–4) concluded that Australian courts should follow the reasoning in these two cases. In *Pusey*, the duty of care was based not only on the principle of foreseeability of injury by shock, but also on employers' legal duty to provide safe working conditions for employees (at 405). Thus, the High Court recognised that, while some injured rescuers could only sue defendants for pure psychiatric injury under general principles of negligence, others could also bring actions under special rules relating to employer–employee relationships.[37]

Jaensch v Coffey

The *Chester* requirement that in circumstances other than *Pusey*, a duty of care will not arise unless the claimant was present at the scene and experienced the shocking event with his or her own 'unaided senses' was overcome in the early 1980s by the High Court in *Jaensch v Coffey* (1984) 155 CLR 549. The court unanimously

---

35. In *Dooley*, the defendant's negligence led to the breaking of the rope of a crane, so that its load fell into the hold of a ship where men were working. The plaintiff who operated the crane was in no personal danger, but he was awarded damages for the psychiatric injury he suffered from the shock of perceiving the danger to the men in the hold. By chance, none of the workers was injured.
36. In *Chadwick*, the plaintiff, who lived near the scene of the accident, provided succour to the victims of a railway collision in Lewisham, in which ninety people were killed and well over 200 were injured. As a result of this experience he became 'psychoneurotic' and spent six months in a psychiatric hospital.
37. See: *Walker v Northumberland County Council* [1995] 1 All ER 737; *Gillespie v Commonwealth* (1991) 105 FLR 196; *New South Wales v Seedsman* [2000] NSWCA 119; Handford P, 'Psychiatric Injury in the Workplace' (1999) 7 *Tort L Rev* 126.

allowed recovery for pure nervous shock to Mrs Coffey, who was at home when her husband was severely injured in a vehicle collision. The court determined that Mrs Coffey could recover damages for pure nervous shock, because, though not present at the scene of the accident, she came to the hospital during the period of the immediate post-accident treatment of her injured husband, which was defined as the 'aftermath' of an accident. The decision extended the scope of the defendant's duty of care to persons in a 'close and intimate' relationship (Gibbs CJ at 555), usually a close relative—or a fellow employee, where the plaintiff was a rescuer. Damages became recoverable for a recognised psychiatric illness that was a result of a shock occasioned by the death or injury of a loved one, even though the plaintiffs were not present at the scene of the accident, if they experienced the 'immediate aftermath' of the event 'with their own unaided senses' (at 560).[38] The plaintiff's sensory perception of the accident could be either visual or auditory, or both.[39]

In *Jaensch v Coffey*, the High Court followed the decision of the House of Lords in *McLoughlin v O'Brian* [1983] 1 AC 410. In that case, damages for pure psychiatric injury were awarded to a plaintiff who was at home, away from the scene of the accident in which a negligently driven lorry severely injured her husband and children. When she arrived at the hospital some two hours later, Mrs McLoughlin was told that one of her daughters was dead; she heard her son screaming before he lapsed into unconsciousness; and she saw her husband distressed and mumbling incomprehensibly. While in *McLoughlin v O'Brian* and *Jaensch v Coffey* the English and Australian law of nervous shock converged, it since has developed in opposite directions. In a series of cases beginning with *Alcock v Chief Constable* [1992] 1 AC 310; through *Page v Smith* [1996] 1 AC 155; *White (or Frost) v Chief Constable of South Yorkshire Police* [1999] 2 AC 455; and *W v Essex County Council* [2000] 2 WLR 601 among others, the House of Lords has progressively narrowed the scope of the defendants' liability for pure nervous shock. The Australian approach has been much more expansive.

Jaensch v Coffey: prerequisites to recovery

Exceptions to duty of care

In *Jaensch v Coffey*, the High Court—while skipping over the breach of duty—modified the elements of duty of care and causation for the purposes of recovery of

---

38. See also: *Campbelltown City Council v Mackay* (1989) 15 NSWLR 501.
39. In *Petrie v Dowling* [1989] Aust Torts Reports ¶80–263, the court awarded compensation for nervous shock to a mother who collapsed with grief upon being informed at the hospital that her young daughter was killed in a collision caused by the defendant's negligence.

damages for pure psychiatric injury. In relation to the duty of care,[40] bystanders in the sense of officious intermeddlers, curious onlookers and involuntary onlookers who were strangers to the primary victims of the accident were excluded. Also excluded were claimants who sustained psychiatric injury as a result of concern for the defendant who died, or was injured or imperilled by his or her wrongful conduct.[41] This exception has been criticised on the grounds that there is no reason in principle to deny recovery to primary victims who suffer psychiatric injury as a result of being involved in an accident occasioned by the tortfeasor whose own shocking death triggers the disorder. For example, in *Shipard v Motor Accident Commission* (1997) 70 SASR 240, Mr Shipard was driving a prime mover when Mr Young, riding his motorcycle, collided with the prime mover and was decapitated. Mr Shipard successfully claimed damages for nervous shock and post-traumatic stress disorder, which he suffered as a result of the collision that was due to Mr Young's negligence. See also: *FAI General Insurance Co Ltd v Lucre* (2000) 32 MVR 540, in which a car driver was wholly responsible for collision with a truck. The car and its driver were crushed under the truck. The truck driver, though not physically injured, successfully claimed damages for post-traumatic stress disorder occasioned by the crash. The court held that he was an immediate victim to whom the deceased owed a duty of care.

Causation

The *Jaensch v Coffey* test of causation was specific to the pure psychiatric injury category of case. It required the psychiatric illness to be induced by single 'shock'.[42] Psychiatric injury caused by bereavement—unless it amounted to 'pathological grief'[43]—or prolonged and constant association and care of a seriously injured relative subsequent to immediate post-accident treatment was not compensable (Brennan J, at 565). Moreover, the subjective test of causation[44] was qualified by the prerequisite of 'normal fortitude'.

---

40. Deane J held that in addition to the general test of reasonable foreseeability, the claimants must establish the existence of special proximity between the parties The notion of proximity as a 'conceptual determinant for the existence of duty of care' overarching the test of reasonable foreseeability was developed by Deane J, with whom all Justices of the High Court, except Brennan J, eventually agreed. However, Deane J's notion of proximity has since been abandoned: *Sullivan v Moody; Thompson v Connon* [2001] HCA 59 at [42].
41. *Jaensch v Coffey* (1984) 155 CLR 549 at 604, per Deane J. This exception was first formulated by Lord Robertson in *Bourhill v Young* [1943] 1 AC 92.
42. See also: *Campbelltown City Council v Mackay* (1989) 15 NSWLR 501.
43. *Swan v Williams (Demolition) Pty Ltd* [1987] Aust Torts Reports 68, 656 at ¶80–104; 9 NSWLR 172.
44. *Rosenberg v Percival* [2001] HCA 18, McHugh J at [24], [44], [45]; Gummow J at [87]; Kirby J at [153], [154].

Normal fortitude

The requirement of 'normal predisposition' or 'normal fortitude' was originally imposed by Wright J in *Wilkinson v Downton* [1897] 2 QB 57, at 59, who, when imputing to the defendant the intention to produce the physical harm that Mrs Wilkinson suffered as a result of nervous shock triggered by his practical joke, observed that 'the effect was produced on a person proved to be in ordinary state of health and mind'. This observation was transformed into a rule when the courts began to require claimants to show that a person of 'normal fortitude' would have suffered pure psychiatric injury as a result of the defendant's negligent act or omission.[45] This requirement has been criticised. In *Mount Isa Mines Ltd v Pusey* Windeyer J (at 405) commented that:

> The idea of a man of normal emotional fibre, as distinct from a man sensitive, susceptible and more easily disturbed emotionally and mentally, is I think imprecise and scientifically inexact.

In *Jaensch v Coffey*, however, the High Court ignored Windeyer J's observation and assumed that in order to be recoverable, nervous shock must be produced on a person of 'normal fortitude', 'normal disposition', or 'normal standard of susceptibility'. Gibbs CJ (at 556) said:

> It may be assumed (without deciding) that injury for nervous shock is not recoverable unless an ordinary person of normal fortitude in the position of the plaintiff would have suffered some shock.

The criterion of 'normal fortitude' did not apply where the defendant had prior knowledge of the plaintiff's susceptibility to psychiatric illness (*Jaensch v Coffey* at 565).

Remoteness of damage

With respect to the remoteness of damage, once breach and causation were established, the 'take your victim as you find him' rule would apply to extend the duty to any exacerbation of any condition that was due to the victim's psychological vulnerability.[46]

---

45. *Bunyan v Jordan* (1936) 36 SR(NSW) 350; (1936–37) 57 CLR 1; *Barnes v Commonwealth* (1937) 37 SR(NSW) 511; *Levi v Colgate-Palmolive Pty Ltd* (1941) 41 SR(NSW) 48; *Bourhill v Young* [1943] AC 92; *Mount Isa Mines Ltd v Pusey* (1971) 125 CLR 383; *Jaensch v Coffey* (1984) 155 CLR 549; *Woodrow v Commonwealth of Australia* (1993) 45 FCR 52.
46. *Nader v Urban Transit Authority of NSW* (1985) 2 NSWLR 501; *Havenaar v Havenaar* [1982] 1 NSWLR 626, *Commonwealth v McLean* (1996) 41 NSWLR 389.

Tame v New South Wales; Annetts v Australian Stations Pty Ltd

The High Court's decision in *Tame v New South Wales; Annetts v Australian Stations Pty Ltd* (2002) 211 CLR 317 was, in some respects, revolutionary. The two cases were heard together,[47] and involved reconsideration of three questions of law, which Gaudron J (at [45]) described as the 'sudden shock rule'; the 'normal fortitude rule'; and the 'direct perception rule'. The High Court jettisoned the special prerequisites that had been considered by many to be arbitrary and based on fear rather than principle.[48]

In *Tame*, Acting Sergeant Beardsley, in the course of investigating a motor car collision between Mrs Tame and another driver, transposed the latter's blood-alcohol reading of 0.14 and her own, which was nil. Mrs Tame, who sustained some physical injuries in the collision, sued the negligent motorist under the *Donoghue v Stevenson* cause of action and was compensated. Although Beardsley's mistake was subsequently corrected, and no one had acted on the erroneous information, Mrs Tame sued the police (the State of New South Wales) for pure nervous shock. She claimed that she developed a psychotic depressive illness—not as a result of shock of the collision, but when her solicitor told her of the incorrect entry. The High Court determined that Beardsley, and hence New South Wales, did not owe Mrs Tame a duty to take reasonable care to avoid causing her injury of the kind she suffered.

According to the High Court, it was not reasonably foreseeable that upon being informed of a clerical mistake, a person of 'normal fortitude' would have developed such an 'extreme and idiosyncratic' reaction as claimed by Mrs Tame (Gummow and Kirby JJ at [233]). Gleeson CJ reaffirmed the doctrine in *Sullivan v Moody; Thompson v Connon* [2001] HCA 59, at [60],[49] which held that as a matter of policy, no duty should be imposed on the defendant to take care to protect from possible psychiatric illness a person whose conduct is the subject of investigation and report, where such duty would be inconsistent with the defendant's other professional or statutory duties. The court also invoked the theory of the consistency of law. Gleeson CJ stated (at [28]) that if a duty were to be imposed to protect Mrs Tame, as the person under investigation, from pure nervous shock, such duty would play havoc with the principles of the law of defamation. The imposition of duty in those

---

47. Appeal from *Morgan v Tame* (2000) 49 NSWLR 21 (affirmed); appeal from *Annetts v Australian Stations Pty Ltd* (2000) 23 WAR 35 (reversed).
48. Mendelson D, 'The Defendants' Liability for Negligently Caused Nervous Shock in Australia—Quo Vadis?' (1992) 18 *Monash Law Review* 16–70.
49. In this case, the plaintiffs claimed that they suffered pure psychiatric injury as a result of being informed by the defendant medical practitioners and child welfare officials that they were under suspicion of sexually abusing their children.

circumstances would allow 'recovery of damages for publishing statements to the discredit of a person where the law of defamation would not' (at [54]).

In *Annetts*, sixteen-year-old James Annetts from New South Wales worked as a jackaroo on the defendant's cattle station in Western Australia. Prior to his undertaking the job, the defendant employer assured James' parents in a telephone conversation that their son would be safe, working under constant supervision. This did not occur; instead James was sent to work alone as a caretaker at a remote location 100 kilometres away from the station. After seven weeks, a police officer notified James' parents that their son and another teenager employed by the defendant on another station were missing. Mr Annetts collapsed on hearing the news. Subsequently, James' parents visited the station several times in search of further information. Their son's remains were found nearly five months after his death. According to the coroner's report, after their four-wheel-drive became bogged in the Western Australian desert, James died of dehydration and Simon, the other jackaroo, of a rifle wound. Allowing recovery, the High Court determined by a majority that ordinary principles of negligence should govern the case 'unhindered by artificial constrictions based on the circumstance that the illness for which redress was sought was purely psychiatric' (Gummow and Kirby JJ at [236]).

In *Annetts*, the damage suffered by James' parents was pure psychiatric injury; however, because of the telephone conversation, the relationship between them and the defendant employer was based on a pre-existing relationship. Historically, until the adoption of the reasonable foreseeability test in *Donoghue v Stevenson* as a determinant of the duty of care in negligence, duty of care was based upon personal responsibility in negligence. The court would examine each case on its own merits. The duty would be invariably imposed upon the defendant if the plaintiff could show either a pre-existing relationship (be it contractual, proprietary, equitable, statutory, etc), or physical contact between the parties. Consequently, Mr Annetts' psychiatric injury would have been compensable under the general principle that duty of care arises in situations where there exists a prior undertaking. McHugh J (at [144]) noted that the plaintiffs could have sued in contract or for breach of fiduciary duty, as well as negligence because:

> the assurance of the employer gave rise to a duty, the breach of which entitled Mr and Mrs Annetts to sue for any damage suffered that was reasonably foreseeable in a general way. It might be expenditure incurred in paying for medical treatment for their son or in searching for him if he became lost. Or it might be injury—personal or psychiatric—suffered by themselves.

Nevertheless, the court, using the pre-existing relationship merely as an evidentiary factor, enunciated rules applicable to mere psychiatric injury in cases where there was no pre-existing relationship between the parties.

Elements of action for negligently occasioned pure psychiatric injury at common law

In *Tame* and *Annetts*, the High Court recast the substantive aspects of this cause of action in terms of 'reasonable foreseeability'; 'normal fortitude'; 'sudden shock' and 'direct perception' factors; 'mere knowledge'; and the nature of the relationship between the parties. Each of these requirements will be discussed in turn.

Reasonable foreseeability

The court held that reasonable foreseeability should be the fundamental test for the imposition of a duty of care in pure psychiatric injury cases. Consequently, at common law there is now no difference between cases of physical injury and those of psychiatric injury; in both, reasonable foresight of risk of harm will prima facie determine the existence of duty of care. However, McHugh J (at [105]) noted that:

> What is foreseeable is a question of fact—prediction, if you like. But reasonableness is a value. At least in some situations, policy issues may be relevant to the issue of reasonable foresight because reasonableness requires a value judgment.

Moreover, the risk of the plaintiff developing psychiatric injury must be reasonably foreseeable at the time when the wrong was occasioned. For example, in *Koehler v Cerebos (Australia) Ltd* [2005] HCA 15, the claimant, Nuha Jamil Koehler, accepted an offer of employment as a part-time merchandising representative. Soon after acceptance of the offer, Ms Koehler found the performance of duties to which she had agreed more arduous than she anticipated. Over a period of some six months, the plaintiff made a number of oral and written complaints about her workload. Ms Koehler sued her employer, alleging that *Cerebos* so negligently overloaded her with work that through stress she suffered a severe depressive injury disabling her from working. The High Court held that the employer could not reasonably have foreseen that the claimant was exposed to a risk of psychiatric injury as a consequence of her duties at work, because (at [36]):

> the employer engaging an employee to perform stated duties is entitled to assume, in the absence of evident signs warning of the possibility of psychiatric injury, that the employee considers that he or she is able to do the job.

McHugh, Gummow, Hayne, and Heydon JJ, in a joint judgment (Callinan J concurring in a separate judgment), found (at [28]) that none of the complaints made by the plaintiff expressed any fear of danger to her health, and thus: 'did not *at the time* bear the significance which hindsight may now attribute to them. What was said did not convey at *that* time any reason to suspect the possibility of future psychiatric injury' (emphasis in original).

The 'normal fortitude' test

In *Tame* and *Annetts*, the majority held that 'normal fortitude' is a relevant consideration but not an independent test or a precondition of liability for negligently infliction of psychiatric injury.[50] Gummow and Kirby JJ said (at [189]) that 'normal fortitude' should be factored into the court's assessment 'at the stage of breach, of the reasonable foreseeability of the risk of psychiatric harm'. McHugh J (at [110]) dissented on this point and observed that foreseeability of risk in pure psychiatric illness cases should not 'be anchored by reference to the most vulnerable person in the community' as this 'would place an undue burden on social action and communication', and 'would seriously interfere with the individual's freedom of action and communication.' His Honour concluded that to:

> require the actor to take steps to avoid potential damage to the peculiarly vulnerable would impose an intolerable burden on the autonomy of individuals. Ordinary people are entitled to act on the basis that there will be a normal reaction to their conduct.

In *Koehler v Cerebos*, Callinan J (at [55]) interpreted the majority judgment in *Tame* as standing for the doctrine that:

> foreseeability is not to be assessed by reference to a notional person of normal fortitude, but on the basis of the impression created by, and the other overt or foreseeable sensitivities of the actual person affected. The fact however that a psychiatrist placed in the same position as an employer might have foreseen a risk of psychiatric injury, does not mean that a reasonable employer should be regarded as likely to form the same view.

This test of foreseeability imposes two singularly subjective criteria for determining employers' legal liability for failure to foresee and alleviate the risk of psychiatric harm to an employee, namely: 'the impression created by, and the other overt or foreseeable sensitivities of the actual person affected'. Thus, on the one hand, the employers are to be guided in their assessment of the risk by their 'impression'—a feeling, a vague notion or belief created as a consequence of experience; and on the other hand, the affected employees need to make 'overt or foreseeable' their 'sensitivities'—a quality of being sensitive or capacity to respond to stimulation. Though commendable as a call for more personalised relationships between employers and employees, the test does little to provide normative standards for safeguarding workers from negligently occasioned psychiatric harm.

---

50. See also: *Koehler v Cerebos (Australia) Ltd* [2005] HCA 15 at [33].

The 'sudden shock' and 'direct perception' factors

In *Tame v New South Wales*, Gleeson CJ (at [18]), agreeing with Gummow and Kirby JJ)[51] declared that the common law:

> should not and does not, limit liability for damages for psychiatric injury to cases where the injury is caused by a sudden shock, or to cases where a plaintiff has directly perceived a distressing phenomenon or its immediate aftermath.

His Honour went on to say (at [18]) that 'sudden shock' and 'direct perception' are factual considerations pertinent to:

> the question whether it is reasonable to require one person to have in contemplation injury of the kind that has been suffered by another and to take reasonable care to guard against such injury. In particular, they may be relevant to the nature of the relationship between plaintiff and defendant, and to the making of a judgment as to whether the relationship is such as to import such a requirement.

In other words, in *Tame* and *Annetts*, the 'sudden shock' and 'direct perception' control mechanisms were removed from the category of prerequisites or preconditions to the recovery of damages for negligently inflicted pure psychiatric injury, and became factors to be considered in determining the nature of the relationship between the parties. According to Gummow and Kirby JJ (at [225]):

> Distance in time and space from a distressing phenomenon, and means of communication or acquisition of knowledge concerning that phenomenon, may be relevant to assessing reasonable foreseeability, causation and remoteness of damage in a common law action for negligently inflicted psychiatric illness. But they are not themselves decisive of liability.

Gaudron J (at [66]) observed that 'in many cases, the risk of psychological or psychiatric injury will not be foreseeable in the absence of a sudden shock.' Gummow and Kirby JJ (at [210]) commented that cases of 'protracted suffering'—presumably caused by a series of distressing events, as opposed to 'sudden shock'—should be considered at the stage of causation and remoteness of damage rather than the duty of care.

Mere knowledge

The 'mere knowledge' rule in relation to tortfeasors was thus defined by Windeyer J in *Mount Isa Mines Ltd v Pusey* (1971) 125 CLR 383 (at 407):

> If the sole cause of shock be what is told or read of some happening then, ... unless there be an intention to cause a nervous shock, no action lies against ... the person who caused the event of which they tell.

---

51. Gummow and Kirby JJ at [189], [213], [214], [225]. See also: Gaudron J at [51], [66]; Hayne J at [267].

Once distance in time and space ceased to be a barrier to imposition of the common law duty of care for pure psychiatric injury, the 'mere knowledge' rule is no longer good law.

However, the rule still applies to the messengers. Windeyer J in *Pusey* (at 407) concluded that: 'There is no duty in law to break bad news gently or to do nothing which creates bad news.'

This aspect of the rule was reaffirmed by the High Court in *Sullivan v Moody; Thompson v Connon* [2001] HCA 59; and in *Tame* and *Annetts*, Gummow and Kirby JJ (at [230]) observed that when the identifiable tortfeasor and the messenger are different parties, the tortfeasor should not be sheltered from liability as distinct from the messenger who conveys information about the distressing consequences of the tortfeasor's conduct.

The nature of the relationship

The holdings relating to foreseeability and direct perception in *Tame* and *Annetts* were applied and elaborated on in *Gifford v Strang Patrick Stevedoring Pty Ltd* (2003) 214 CLR 269. In *Gifford*, Mr Barry Gifford was crushed to death by a forklift vehicle as a result of the admitted negligence of the defendant employer. His children, who were teenagers at the time of the accident, sued the defendant for psychiatric injury each of them suffered as a consequence of learning about the death of their father. They did not live with the deceased, but maintained a close and loving relationship with him. The claimants did not witness the accident. The High Court determined that the lack of direct perception by the children of the death of their father was 'not fatal' to their action in negligence for nervous shock (Gummow and Kirby JJ at [65]). Gleeson CJ (at [10]) stated that at common law:

> If it is reasonable to require any person to have in contemplation the risk of psychiatric injury to another, then it is reasonable to require an employer to have in contemplation the children of an employee.

McHugh J (at [27]) observed that the logical conclusion stemming from the reasoning in *Tame* and *Annetts*, which dispensed with the requirement of 'direct perception' is that:

> An employer owes a duty to take care to protect from psychiatric harm all those persons that it knows or ought to know are in a close and loving relationship with its employee. It is not a condition of that duty that such persons should be present when the employee suffers harm or that they should see the injury to the employee.

His Honour also noted (at [48]) that: 'the relationship between two friends who have lived together for many years may be closer and more loving than that of two siblings'. Therefore, the determining factor in reasonable foreseeability of psychiatric injury, and hence duty of care, should be: 'the closeness and affection of the relationship—rather than the legal status of the relationship' (at [48]). Thus, according to McHugh J (at [51]):

> The test is, would a reasonable person in the defendant's position, who knew or ought to know of that particular relationship, consider that the third party was so closely and directly affected by the conduct that it was reasonable to have that person in contemplation as being affected by that conduct?

Employer–employee relationship

In *Koehler v Cerebos (Australia) Ltd* [2005] HCA 15, McHugh, Gummow, Hayne, and Heydon JJ stated (at [21]) that in cases where there exists an employer–employee relationship, the employer owes the duty to each employee. However, the duty to avoid psychiatric injury will be engaged only 'if psychiatric injury to the *particular* employee is reasonably foreseeable' (at [35]; emphasis in the original). In order to determine the content of this duty, an account must be taken of:

> the obligations which the parties owe one another under the contract of employment, the obligations arising from that relationship which equity would enforce and, of course, any applicable statutory provisions. (This last class may require particular reference not only to industrial instruments but also to statutes of general application such as anti-discrimination legislation.)[52]

Their Honours, having noted (at [36]) 'that obligations of the parties are fixed at the time of the contract unless and until they are varied,' concluded (at [29]):

> An employer may not be liable for psychiatric injury to an employee brought about by the employee's performance of the duties originally stipulated in the contract of employment. In such a case, notions of 'overwork', 'excessive work', or the like, have meaning only if they appeal to some external standard. ... Yet the parties have made a contract of employment that, by hypothesis, departs from that standard. Insistence upon performance of a contract cannot be in breach of a duty of care.

Recognised psychiatric illness or condition

Reference to a 'recognised' psychiatric illness, disease, or disorder implies a condition that has been identified and classified by an authoritative specialist body for research and clinical use by qualified psychiatrists. It appears that both relatively transient and pre-existing conditions can qualify. For example, following the decision of the High Court in *Gifford v Strang Patrick Stevedoring*, the case was remitted to

---

52. *Koehler v Cerebos (Australia) Ltd* [2005] HCA 15 at [21].

the New South Wales District Court for assessment of damages. Puckeridge J found that each of Mr Gifford's children—Darren, Matthew, and Kelly—suffered stress-related psychiatric conditions. Darren, who had epilepsy, recovered $46 504.36 for 'unresolved grief reaction' and post-traumatic stress disorder, with an additional $4880.00 for medical and out-of-pocket expenses. Darren testified that some six to twelve months after his father's death he became a heavy drinker and marijuana smoker. His medication regimen was affected by drinking and he shifted from one job to another. Apparently he was continually plagued by memories of his father, and in 1999 was diagnosed as having depression and other symptoms consistent with 'pathological grief reaction'. Matthew Gifford, too, began to drink heavily and lost interest in many things, including football training. He was diagnosed in March 1998 as suffering from a long-term depressive illness. There was evidence that his skin condition was exacerbated by the stress caused by his father's death. The judge awarded Matthew $49 504.36 for 'an abnormal continuing grief ... attributable to psychological depressive illness', and $9627.86 to cover medical expenses. Kelly Gifford also recovered $39 504.36 for 'an abnormal grief reaction following the death of her father.' She suffered bouts of bulimia and showed symptoms of serious long-term stress.

Causation

In *Tame* and *Annetts*, the High Court did not discuss the applicable causation test, which, given that shock is no longer a prerequisite of liability for pure psychiatric injury at common law, will need to be reformulated.

In *Cubbon v Roads and Traffic Authority of NSW* [2004] NSWCA 326, the New South Wales Court of Appeal (Sheller JA; Handley and Tobias JJA agreeing), applied the 'material contribution' test of causation. In that case, Geoffrey and Kenneth Cubbon, together with Lynda Bates, sued the defendant Roads and Traffic Authority (RTA) for nervous shock[53] caused by the death of their mother and sister in a car accident for which RTA admitted negligence. In March 1997, when the accident happened, they were adults, but they all enjoyed a close and loving relationship with their mother and sister. None of the claimants witnessed the accident, though Geoffrey went to the morgue to identify the bodies; he and his sister Lynda also saw the bodies in the hospital.[54] Geoffrey lived at home and worked as a mechanic. His grief reaction was deep. He had problems with sleeping and lost interest in various sporting activities following the accident. In September 1997, strife in the family home developed over his father's activities involving other women. Geoffrey also became determined to establish the responsibility

---

53. The action was under *Law Reform (Miscellaneous Provisions) Act 1944* (NSW) as amended.
54. A few days later, they all went to the police holding yard at Belmont, apparently to retrieve some jewellery from the car wreck. They found this to be a disturbing experience.

of the RTA for the deaths of his mother and sister, and at the time, this activity adversely impacted on his work performance. He was treated for clinical depression, from which he substantially recovered in 2000. The New South Wales Court of Appeal (at [78]) applied the test 'whether the RTA's negligence, resulting in the deaths of Mrs Cubbon and Maree, caused or materially contributed to the major depression from which Geoffrey suffered.' The same test was applied to the claims by Kenneth[55] and Lynda.[56]

The 'material contribution' test of causation was devised by Lord Reid in *Bonnington Castings Ltd v Wardlaw* (1956) AC 613 to cover circumstances where the same causative harmful agent (silica dust, in the case of Mr Wardlaw), had emanated from two different sources, only one of which was wrongful, but where it was impossible to determine the actual proportions of their respective contributions to the plaintiff's injury. This test does not provide the most appropriate analysis for determining causation in cases of 'pure psychiatric injury' where both the sources and the causative agents are complex and varied.

Rescuers

In general, rescuers do not know the victims of an accident, and they often come onto the scene after the injurious event. Nevertheless, ever since *Mount Isa Mines Ltd v Pusey* (1971) 125 CLR 383, at 386, rescuers who were not at the scene of the accident, and thus did not directly perceive it, but who developed a psychiatric disorder as a result of the rescue effort in the immediate aftermath, have been able to recover damages. The *Tame* and *Annetts* decisions have reinforced this approach. In the United Kingdom, however, the House of Lords in *White v Chief Constable of South Yorkshire Police)* [1999] 2 AC 455 determined that rescuers cannot recover damages for pure psychiatric injury unless they personally were within the range of foreseeable physical injury.

---

55. Kenneth had suffered a nervous breakdown at the age of fourteen and received treatment by way of psychotherapy at that time. In 1979 he was convicted of armed robbery and served a prison term of three years for this offence. He was addicted to alcohol, heroin and other illegal substances. He had never been employed. At the time of the accident he was living alone, and was taking anti-depressant medication. In July 1997, while visiting his Social Security Department caseworker he collapsed in a trance, and received treatment. Following the accident, he too clashed with his father, and stopped visiting him.
56. Lynda left the family home in 1979 when she married. Her marriage ended in 1996, and she raised four children as a sole parent. In October 1996, Lynda had difficulties in coping with the behaviour of her eldest daughter, and was prescribed anti-depressant medication. Following the March 1997 accident, Lynda was further prescribed anti-depressant medication, which she was continuing to take at the time of the trial. She experienced disturbing dreams, and claimed to have considered suicide.

CODIFICATION OF THE LAW OF PSYCHIATRIC INJURY IN AUSTRALIA

In 2002–03, six jurisdictions—New South Wales, Tasmania, the Australian Capital Territory, South Australia, Western Australia, and Victoria—codified, to a greater or lesser extent, the law of psychiatric injury. Some jurisdictions followed recommendations contained in the Ipp Panel's *Review of the Law of Negligence Report*.[57] The Northern Territory has retained provisions that allow recovery where close relatives of the person killed, injured, or put in peril sustain injury arising wholly or in part from mental or nervous shock.[58] In Queensland, actions for negligently caused psychiatric illness are entirely governed by common law and the general negligence provisions contained in the *Civil Liability Act 2003* (Qld).

For reasons rather difficult to discern, among the jurisdictions that adopted the Ipp Panel's recommendations there are small but not insignificant differences in wording.

STATUTORY PARADIGM FOR RECOVERY OF DAMAGES FOR NEGLIGENTLY CAUSED MENTAL HARM

The scope of statutory provisions

New South Wales, Tasmania, Western Australia, and Victoria exclude various statutes or particular provisions from the operation of statutory civil liability for mental harm.[59] The four jurisdictions also exclude cases where the injury or death concerned 'resulted from smoking or other use of tobacco products.'[60] These cases are governed by common law. For example, the exclusion would apply to smokers who sue tobacco companies in negligence for a recognised psychiatric illness they developed through worrying about lung cancer, as well as close relatives of a smoker who suffer a recognisable psychiatric illness from nursing the smoker with cancer.[61]

In Victoria, s 69(2) of the *Wrongs Act 1958* states: 'A claim for damages referred to in subsection (1)(e) [dust-related condition] or (1)(f) [smoking or other use of tobacco products] does not include a claim for damages that relates to the provision

---

57. Ipp D, Cane P, Sheldon D & Macintosh I, *Review of the Law of Negligence Report*, 2 October 2002; <http://ww.revofneg.treasury.gov.au/content/reports.asp> Second Report—released 2 October 2002.
58. *Law Reform (Miscellaneous Provisions) Act 1956* (NT), s 25.
59. *Civil Liability Act 2002* (NSW), 3B(1); *Civil Liability Act 2002* (Tas), s 3B(1); *Civil Liability Act 2002* (WA), s 3A(1); *Wrongs Act 1958* (Vic), s 69(1).
60. *Civil Liability Act 2002* (NSW), 3B(1)(c); *Civil Liability Act 2002* (Tas), s 3B(1)(b); *Civil Liability Act 2002* (WA), s 3A(1); *Wrongs Act 1958* (Vic), s 69(1)(f).
61. The examples were provided by Luntz H, 'Recovery of Damages for Negligently Inflicted Psychiatric Injury: Where Are We Now?' delivered to the Forensic Psychiatry Association, 16 August 2004.

of or the failure to provide a health service.' Presumably, this means that statutory provisions govern claims for mental harm by patients who sue doctors for failure to make a timely diagnosis of a smoking-related lung cancer.

Threshold requirement of requisite injury

Victoria, New South Wales, Tasmania, the Australian Capital Territory, South Australia, and Western Australia adopted the *Ipp Report's* distinction between 'consequential mental harm' and 'pure mental harm'. In each jurisdiction, legislation provides that:

- damages may only be awarded for *pure mental harm* if the harm consists of a recognised psychiatric illness; and
- damages may only be awarded for economic loss resulting from *consequential mental harm* if the harm consists of a recognised psychiatric illness.[62]

Therefore, just as at common law, in order to recover damages for pure mental harm or economic damages for consequential mental harm, plaintiffs have to establish that they suffer or have suffered 'a recognised psychiatric illness'.

Moreover, in all jurisdictions apart from the Australian Capital Territory, patients have to meet statutory thresholds before they can recover damages for non-economic loss.[63]

Elements of liability

The reforming jurisdictions accepted the *Tame* and *Annetts* doctrine that the reasonable foreseeability should be the touchstone for the existence of duty of care in psychiatric injury cases. They were rather less certain that the test should dispense with the 'normal fortitude' requirement. Consequently, in New South Wales,[64] Tasmania,[65] Western Australia,[66] and the Australian Capital Territory,[67] the legislation provides that:

---

62. *Civil Liability Act 1936* (SA), s 53(2) and (3); *Civil Law (Wrongs) Act 2002* (ACT), s 35(1) and (2); *Civil Liability Act 2002* (Tas), ss 33, 35; *Wrongs Act 1958* (Vic), ss 72(1), 75; *Civil Liability Act 2002* (NSW), ss 31, 33; *Civil Liability Act 2002* (WA), ss 5S(1), 5T.
63. *Trade Practices Act 1974* (Cth), ss 87P–87S; *Civil Liability Act 2002* (NSW), s 16; *Civil Liability Act 1936* (SA), s 52; *Civil Liability Act 2003* (Qld), ss 61, 62; *Wrongs Act 1958* (Vic), ss 28LB, 28LE, 28LF; *Personal Injuries (Liabilities and Damages) Act 2003* (NT), Div 4, ss 22–28; *Civil Liability Act 2002* (Tas), s 27; *Civil Liability Act 2002* (WA), ss 9, 10. For a detailed discussion of thresholds to personal injury litigation, see Chapter 2.
64. *Civil Liability Act 2002* (NSW), s 32(1).
65. *Civil Liability Act 2002* (Tas), s 34(1).
66. *Civil Liability Act 2002* (WA), s 5S (1).
67. *Civil Law (Wrongs) Act 2002* (ACT), s 34(1).

A person (the defendant) does not owe a duty to another person (the plaintiff) to take care not to cause the plaintiff mental harm unless a reasonable person in the defendant's position would have foreseen that a person of normal fortitude in the plaintiff's position might, in the circumstances of the case, suffer a recognised psychiatric illness if reasonable care were not taken.[68]

The reference to 'mental harm' means that in four jurisdictions, the statutory test for the existence of duty of care applies both to consequential and to pure mental harm. In Victoria,[69] the definition is identical, except that it only applies to 'pure mental harm', thus excluding consequential mental harm. The Victorian legislation is a more accurate reflection of the common law, which historically has treated consequential mental harm in the same way as any physical injury and its medical complications.

The legislation provides that a duty of care is imposed in the circumstances of the case where the defendant ought to have foreseen 'that a person of normal fortitude *might* ... suffer a recognised psychiatric illness'. The use of the modal verb 'might' as a determinant for the imposition of duty of care is baffling. The term 'might' is defined as 'expressing a possibility based on an unfulfilled condition',[70] and is usually interpreted as referring to a mere chance or contingency. The statutory test for the imposition of a duty to take reasonable care based on a possibility or chance of harm differs profoundly from the common law approach. It is much more onerous on the defendant than the statutory test for duty of care in general negligence, which grounds the duty on foreseeability of 'not an insignificant risk'.[71] Depending on how far the judges are willing to extend the scope of liability for mental harm, it is always possible to speculate that the defendant ought to have foreseen a chance that a person of normal fortitude might suffer such an injury. However, speculation as a basis for imposition of liability does not necessarily make a good law.

If the statutory test were applied literally in *Tame*, Mrs Tame would have succeeded in her action—as she did at the first instance. For, there is always a chance that a person of 'normal fortitude' might have responded to the police

---

68. The statutory duty of care is subject to an exception, which codifies the common law principle that knowledge of the plaintiff's vulnerability imposes upon the defendant duty to take greater care. See: *Civil Liability Act 2002* (Tas), s 34(4); *Civil Liability Act 2002* (NSW), s 32(4); *Civil Liability Act 2002* (WA), s 5S(4): 'This section does not require the court to disregard what the defendant knew or ought to have known about the fortitude of the plaintiff'; *Civil Law (Wrongs) Act 2002* (ACT), s 34(4) and *Wrongs Act 1958* (Vic), s 72(3): 'This section does not affect the duty of care of a person (the defendant) to another (the plaintiff) if the defendant knows, or ought to know, that the plaintiff is a person of less than normal fortitude.'
69. *Wrongs Act 1958* (Vic), s 72(1).
70. Soames C & Stevenson A (eds), *The Concise Oxford English Dictionary*, Oxford University Press, Oxford, 2004; *Oxford Reference Online*, Oxford University Press, Deakin University, 1 May 2005, <http://www.oxfordreference.com/views/ENTRY.html?subview=Main&entry=t23.e35332>.
71. *Civil Law (Wrongs) Act 2002* (ACT), s 43(3); *Wrongs Act 1958* (Vic), s 48(3); *Civil Liability Act 2002* (NSW), s 5B(3); *Civil Liability Act 2002* (Tas), s 11(3); *Civil Liability Act 2002* (WA), 5B(3).

officer's clerical mistake in the same manner as she did. To ensure consistency of the reasonable foreseeability test for duty of care in negligence, the courts will need to interpret the mental harm foreseeability test in terms of the *risk* that a person of normal fortitude *would* suffer a recognised psychiatric illness if reasonable care were not taken.[72] Presumably, that risk would be a 'not insignificant' risk.

Perhaps inadvertently, the statutory definition of requirements for the existence of duty in cases of mental harm ('pure mental harm' in Victoria) has effectively created a distinct category of case, which prescribes tests that are additional to the general statutory and common law principles governing breach of duty and causation.

The conjunction 'unless' makes the imposition of duty of care for mental harm ('pure mental harm' in Victoria) exceptional, in the sense that it is contingent upon the plaintiff having to establish on the balance of probabilities three elements:

1   *Duty of care*: the court has to be persuaded of the reasonable foreseeability of a recognised psychiatric illness that might be suffered by a person of 'normal fortitude', based on the objective test of 'a reasonable person in the defendant's position' in the 'circumstances of the case'.
2   *Breach (or content) of duty:* the defendant failed to take 'reasonable care' to avoid such harm. In issue will be the standard of response to be ascribed to the reasonable person placed in the defendant's position at the time of the allegedly wrongful event. The breach is to be determined in accordance with statutory principles of the 'calculus of negligence'.[73]
3   *Causation*: the court has to be persuaded that 'a person of normal fortitude' in the plaintiff's position might, in the circumstances of the case, have suffered a recognised psychiatric illness. This will involve establishing both factual causation and scope of liability.[74]

The expression 'normal fortitude' is not defined in the legislation, and will be governed by the common law understanding of this notion. The statutory tests leave little room for the reasoning employed in cases like *Nader v Urban Transit Authority of NSW* (1985) 2 NSWLR 501[75] or *Kavanagh v Akhtar* (1998) 45

---

72. The test is expressed in normative terms: what the defendant ought to have foreseen, and thus is a question of law.
73. *Civil Law (Wrongs) Act 2002* (ACT), s 43(2); *Wrongs Act 1958* (Vic), s 48(2); *Civil Liability Act 2002* (NSW), s 5B(2); *Civil Liability Act 2002* (Tas), s 11(2); *Civil Liability Act 2002* (WA), 5B(2).
74. *Civil Law (Wrongs) Act 2002* (ACT), s 45; *Wrongs Act 1958* (Vic), s 51; *Civil Liability Act 2002* (NSW), s 5D; *Civil Liability Act 2002* (Tas), s 13; *Civil Liability Act 2002* (WA), s 5C.
75. In this case, at the age on ten the plaintiff developed Ganser's Syndrome (a factitious disorder, also known as nonsense syndrome, pseudodementia or prison psychosis, whereby the person provides nonsensical or wrong answers to questions, and does things incorrectly) some three weeks after bumping his head against an electricity pole when he jumped out of a bus whose driver negligently opened the doors before coming to a stop. The plaintiff needed three stitches on his forehead but suffered no neurological damage.

NSWLR 588,[76] in which the issue of foreseeability of the particular mental harm was established by analogy with foreseeability of a psychiatric illness as a consequence of a bodily injury.

In New South Wales, Tasmania, Western Australia, and the Australian Capital Territory, as well as in Victoria, the test of normal fortitude might serve as a limitation on claims for pure mental harm.

The 'circumstances of the case'

The reference to the 'circumstances of the case' in the definition of the duty of care indicates that the 'circumstances', as specified in the legislation, form an element of the cause of action, at least in relation to pure mental harm. In all five jurisdictions,[77] the 'circumstances of the case' in relation to pure mental harm are defined as including:

- whether or not the mental harm was suffered as the result of a sudden shock;
- whether the plaintiff witnessed, at the scene, a person being killed, injured or put in danger;
- the nature of the relationship between the plaintiff and any person killed, injured or put in danger; and
- whether or not there was a pre-existing relationship between the plaintiff and the defendant.

It is not clear whether the four factors comprising the statutory 'circumstances of the case' are merely factors that the court must consider, but having done so, may disregard. Judicial discretion in relation to the statutory 'circumstances of the case' will be vital to determining the scope of liability.

The first two factors or considerations were drafted in response to the *Tame* and *Annetts* refusal to limit the liability for damages for pure mental harm 'to cases where the injury is caused by a sudden shock, or to cases where the plaintiff has directly perceived a distressing phenomenon or its immediate aftermath'.[78] However, the first factor relating to 'whether or not the mental harm was suffered as the result of a sudden shock' is ambiguous. Historically, 'sudden shock' was always a special legal requirement of, or control mechanism for, the existence of duty of care in relation to pure nervous shock. It was jettisoned in *Tame* and *Annetts*, though the High Court observed that it may be relevant to other issues such as causation

---

76. Due to the defendant's negligence, Mrs Akhtar sustained an injury to her left shoulder, arm and jaw. Unable to properly look after her long hair, Mrs Akhtar cut it, despite her husband's warning that he would leave her if she did so. When her husband left the marital home, Mrs Akhtar developed psychiatric illness for which she recovered damages from the defendant.
77. *Civil Liability Act 2002* (NSW), s 32(2); *Civil Liability Act 2002* (Tas), s 34(2); *Civil Liability Act 2002* (WA), s 5S (2); *Civil Law (Wrongs) Act 2002* (ACT), s 34(2); *Wrongs Act 1958* (Vic), s 72(2).
78. *Tame v New South Wales* [2002] HCA 35 at [18], per Gleeson CJ.

and remoteness of damage. The phrase is expressed in the singular, and therefore precludes a series of gradual shocks (as was the case in *Annetts*).

The second factor, while imposing the requirement of the claimant witnessing, 'at the scene, a person being killed, injured or put in danger', actually broadens the scope of liability, for it allows bystanders (strangers) who suffer pure mental harm as a result of such circumstances to recover damages. This requirement will probably be interpreted narrowly, and will not include the *Jaensch v Coffey* notion of an 'immediate aftermath' of the accident. For example, in *Burke v State of New South Wales & Ors* [2004] NSWSC 725, the claimant alleged that he suffered psychiatric injury following a landslide in the immediate vicinity of two ski lodges that destroyed both buildings and killed eighteen people on 30 July 1997. Master Malpass found that the claimant did not meet the threshold requirement for recovery of damages for pure mental harm because at the time he was some 500 metres away, and did not witness either the landslide or the destruction of the lodge in which one of his friends died.

The interpretation of the third consideration, which refers to 'the nature of the relationship between the plaintiff and any person killed, injured or put in danger' is open to interpretation. Apart from family members, it might also include close ('affectionate') friendships, collegiate relationships, and co-workers, as well as rescuers.

The fourth factor, involving the presence of 'a pre-existing relationship between the plaintiff and the defendant' reflects the common law—which, as a general rule, tends to impose a duty of care on parties in pre-existing relationships.

The four factors are not cumulative, and presumably, the plaintiff will need to satisfy only one or two of them in order to fulfil the requirement of the 'circumstances of the case'.

Victoria, New South Wales, and Tasmania[79] impose two further threshold requirements in relation to pure mental harm. The legislation prohibits recovery for pure mental harm 'arising wholly or partly from mental or nervous shock in connection with another person (*the victim*) being killed, injured or put in peril by the act or omission of the defendant' unless the plaintiff 'witnessed, at the scene, the victim being killed, injured or put in danger; or is or was a close member of the family of the victim.'[80]

In South Australia, the *Civil Liability Act 1936*, s 53(1), provides:

> damages may only be awarded for mental harm if the injured person:
> (a) was physically injured in the accident or was present at the scene of the accident when the accident occurred; or

---

79. *Wrongs Act 1958* (Vic), s 73(2); *Civil Liability Act 2002* (NSW), s 30; *Civil Liability Act 2002* (Tas), s 32.
80. *Wrongs Act 1958* (Vic), s 73(2)(b); *Civil Liability Act 2002* (NSW), s 30(2)(b); *Civil Liability Act 2002* (Tas), s 32(3): includes children, step-children, siblings, and a spouse of the victim (including de facto spouse).

(b) is a parent, spouse or child of a person killed, injured or endangered in the accident.

In these four jurisdictions, the legislation thus entrenches the right of bystanders present at the scene to recover for 'mental or nervous shock' if they can establish the statutory requirements for existence of the defendant's duty of care. The legislation also confirms that close family members do not need to be present at the scene of the accident in order to recover damages for pure mental harm.

Section 36 of the *Civil Law (Wrongs) Act 2002* (ACT) is narrower in scope than provisions in other jurisdictions. It imposes:

> liability in relation to an injury caused by a wrongful act or omission by which someone else (A) is killed, injured or put in danger includes liability for injury arising completely or partly from mental or nervous shock received by—
>
> (a) a parent of A; or
> (b) a domestic partner of A; or
> (c) another family member of A, if A was killed, injured or put in danger within the sight or hearing of the other family member.

As noted above the Northern Territory has retained its existing statutory cause of action for nervous shock (*Law Reform (Miscellaneous Provisions) Act* 1956 (NT), s 25).

None of the statutes define the term 'mental or nervous shock'. This suggests that the legislatures wished to retain—or were unable to improve upon—its historic, common law meaning as defined in *Mount Isa Mines v Pusey* and *Jaensch v Coffey*, with its emphasis on sudden experience that traumatises the mind or emotions.

There is a lot of uncertainty about the meaning and operation of the new statutory provisions and their interaction with the existing legislation and the common law. Thus the Torts Reform, instead of having a harmonising effect has led to fragmentation of the law of 'mental harm' along jurisdictional divisions.

FURTHER READING

Handford P, 'Compensation for Psychiatric Injury: the Limits of Liability' (1995) 2 *Psychiatry, Psychology and Law* 37–52.

Handford P, 'Psychiatric Injury in the Workplace' (1999) 7 *Torts Law Review* 126.

Mendelson D, 'The Defendants' Liability for Negligently Caused Nervous Shock in Australia—Quo Vadis?' (1992) 18 *Monash Law Review* 16–70.

Mendelson D, *Interfaces of Medicine and Law: The History of the Liability for Negligently Caused Psychiatric Injury (Nervous Shock)*, Ashgate International Publishing (Dartmouth Medico-Legal Series), Aldershot, 1998.

Mendelson D, '*Quo Iure*? Defendants' Liability to Rescuers in the Tort of Negligence' (2001) 9 *Torts Law Review* 130.

Mendelson D, 'The Modern Australian Law of Mental Harm: Parochialism Triumphant' (2005) 13 *Journal of Law and Medicine* 64–72.

Mullany NJ & Handford PR, *Tort Liability for Psychiatric Damage: The Law of 'Nervous Shock'*, The Law Book Company, Sydney, 1993.

Trindade F & Cane P, *The Law of Torts in Australia*, 3rd edn, Oxford University Press, Melbourne, 1999, pp 357–369.

Pure Economic Loss 16

NEGLIGENTLY OCCASIONED PURE ECONOMIC LOSS

Introduction

Compensation for negligently occasioned psychiatric injury is predicated on a distinction between 'primary' victims, who suffer psychiatric injury that follows upon an actual or threatened physical injury, and 'secondary' victims, whose injury is 'pure' in the sense that it is consequential upon emotional shock. The law relating to economic loss also distinguishes between 'primary' and 'secondary' or 'pure' economic loss.

The term 'primary economic loss' refers to economic harm that is a direct effect of the actual physical damage to the plaintiff's person or property caused by the defendant's negligent conduct.

Secondary economic loss can be occasioned in two ways:

- as an indirect consequence of a negligently inflicted physical damage to property, for example, loss of value due to an underlying defect in a chattel, dwelling, or land which was caused by the wrongdoer's acts or omissions; and
- as a result of negligent misstatement.

Historically, while compensation for wrongfully occasioned primary loss was always allowed, the common law, with few exceptions,[1] precluded recovery for secondary economic loss not directly consequential on physical injury to person or property. For example, in *Cattle v Stockton Waterworks* (1875) LR 10 QB 453, the plaintiff had a contract to build a tunnel through an embankment that had been saturated by a burst water main, the property of the defendant waterworks

---

1. One of these exceptions, which dates back to medieval England was the action per *quod servitium amisit*, which permitted the employer to recover damages for loss of services from a person who injured his servant. See: Brett P, 'Consortium and Servitium: A History and Some Proposals,' (1955) 29 *ALJ* 321 at 389, 428; Jones GH, 'Per Quod Servitium Amisit,' (1958) 74 *LQR* 39.

company. The flooding of the land had been caused by the defendant's negligence. The inundated embankment was harder to tunnel, and made the undertaking much less profitable. Blackburn J refused to compensate the plaintiff for loss of profit.[2]

The tension between defendants' contractual obligations and their duties of care to the third parties as well as the problem of potentially infinite extension of liability was discussed in an American case, *Moch Co Inc v Rensselaer Water Co* 247 NY 160 (1928). In *Moch*, the defendant, a waterworks company, had a contract with a municipality for the provision of water, including supply of water to fire hydrants. The plaintiff, whose warehouse building and its contents were destroyed by fire, alleged that insufficient water pressure at the fire hydrant was the legal cause of the destruction, and his consequent economic loss. In rejecting the plaintiff's claim, Cardozo CJ of the Appeals Court of New York stated (at 168):

> The plaintiff would have us hold that the defendant, when once it entered upon the performance of its contract with the city, was brought into such a relationship with everyone who might potentially be benefited through the supply of water at the hydrants as to give to negligent performance without reasonable notice of a refusal to continue, the quality of a tort ... We are satisfied that liability would be unduly and indeed indefinitely extended by this enlargement of the zone of duty ... Everyone making a promise having the quality of a contract will be under a duty to the promisee by virtue of a promise, but under another duty, apart from the contract to an indefinite number of potential beneficiaries when performance has begun. The assumption of one relation will mean the involuntary assumption of a series of new relations, inescapably hooked together.

Liability for negligent misstatements (as against deceit and fraud) was rejected in *Derry v Peek* (1889) 14 App Cas 337. In that case, Sir Henry Peek claimed that he was misled when he bought shares in the Plymouth, Devonport and District Tramways Company on the strength of a prospectus issued by its directors. The prospectus negligently stated that the company was permitted by statute to use steam-powered trams, when in fact the corporations of Plymouth and Devonport withheld such permission. The House of Lords refused to award damages. The decision was interpreted as standing for the notion that the tort of negligence should be confined entirely to deeds, and no duty of care should exist for careless words.[3] In the later case of *Ultramares Corporation v Touche* 255 NY 170; 174 NE 441 (1931), the question of where to draw the line if liability is extended to cover pure economic loss occasioned by negligent misstatement—imposing on professionals

---

2. Blackburn J's decision was approved by the House of Lords in *Simpson v Thompson* (1877) 3 AC 279.
3. See, for example: *Le Lievre v Gould* [1893] 1 QB 491. The decision in *Peek v Derry* was reversed by the *Directors' Liability Act 1890* (UK), which provided that directors are liable for untrue statements in a prospectus unless they prove that they had reasonable ground to believe and did believe that the statements were true.

liability for economic loss suffered by third parties—was posed by Cardozo J (at 179; 444) in the following terms:

> If liability for negligence exists, a thoughtless slip or blunder, the failure to detect a theft or forgery beneath the cover of deceptive entries, may expose accountants to a liability in an indeterminate amount for an indeterminate time to an indeterminate class.

Ultramares Corporation v Touche involved an action for damages by Mr Touche, who suffered financial loss when he advanced money to the Stern Company in reliance on its balance sheet. The defendant firm of accountants negligently certified the balance sheet, which misrepresented the Stern Company's position by showing surplus when in fact the corporation was unable to pay its debts as and when they fell due. There was no contract between the plaintiff and the defendant.

Referring to Cardozo CJ's judgment in *Bryan v Maloney* (1995) 182 CLR 609 (discussed on pp 469–471), Brennan J in his dissenting judgment (at 632) commented:

> If liability were to be imposed for the doing of anything which caused pure economic loss that was foreseeable, the tort of negligence would destroy commercial competition (per Lord Reid in *Dorset Yacht Co v Home Office* [1970] AC 1004 at 1027), sterilize many contracts and, in the well-known dictum of Chief Judge Cardozo,[4] expose defendants to potential liability 'in an indeterminate amount for an indeterminate time to an indeterminate class'.

In turn, Gleeson CJ, Gummow, Hayne and Heydon JJ specifically approved Brennan J's statement in *Woolcock St Invest v CDG Pty Ltd* (2004) 216 CLR 515, at [21].

Arguments for and against denial of compensation

Three major arguments have been used to justify denial of recovery for pure economic loss:

1   Impossibility of foreseeing pure economic loss: as a general rule, neither the nature nor the incidence of pure economic loss can reasonably be predetermined. For example, in *Cattle v Stockton Waterworks*, the court noted that the defendant could not reasonably have foreseen that the person whose land he had flooded might have had a contractual relationship with a third party whose profits would be adversely affected.
2   Where the loss is foreseeable, it is usually impossible to determine its extent and impact; thus there is a danger that the defendant might be liable for an indeterminate number of claims of indeterminate size.

---

4.   *Ultramares Corporation v Touche* 255 NY 170 at 179; 174 NE 441 at 444 (1931).

3   Even where the issue of foreseeability and indeterminacy is overcome, there is a jurisprudential question of the role of the law of negligence in protecting competent adults from pure economic loss.

Discussing the first two arguments, Jane Stapleton, in 'Duty of Care and Economic Loss: A Wider Agenda',[5] pointed out that in relation to the indeterminate number of claimants, the objection is *not* that there might be large numbers of claims for pure economic loss. Rather, it is that the volume cannot be determined beforehand because of the 'ripple' effect, not unlike that in the *Cattle v Stockton Waterworks* case, where the defendant could not have foreseen the landowner's contractual relationship with a third party whose profits were reduced by his negligent flooding of neighbouring property. Alternatively, the ripple effect could be created by a carelessly caused power cut leading to a plaintiff's fish stocks to go bad, and consequent loss of profits resulting in his bankruptcy. If the plaintiff cannot pay the supplier, he, in turn, cannot pay the fisherman, who then cannot pay the lease instalments on his boat, and so on. Reiterating Professor Stapleton's approach, McHugh J in *Perre v Apand Pty Ltd* (1999) 198 CLR 180 (discussed below), stated (at [112]) that as a general rule, 'No duty will be owed to those who suffer loss as part of a ripple effect.' This is because one cannot insure against liability in cases where it is impossible to determine beforehand the number and the quantum of claims.

Physical injuries differ in so far as the volume of potential 'first-victim' claims is usually reasonably foreseeable, even if large. Great numbers of people may be physically injured in a train crash, aeroplane disaster, accidental release of harmful fumes, and so on. These primary victims, their dependants, and rescuers, can all recover under the *Donoghue v Stevenson* principle. Physical injuries rarely have a legal ripple effect, except for cases of pure psychiatric injury and rescuers.

Moreover, the quantum of pure economic loss claims, especially for loss of profits, is a problem. How can defendants foresee the commercial expectations of people with whom they have had no prior relationship?

Lord Denning illustrated the problem of indeterminacy of pure economic loss in *Spartan Steel v Martin & Co* [1973] QB 27, at 38:

> If claims for economic loss were permitted for this particular hazard [a carelessly caused power cut], there would be no end of claims. Some might be genuine, but many might be inflated, or even false. A machine might not have been in use anyway, but it would be easy to put it down to the cut in supply ... If there was economic loss on one day, did the claimant do its best to mitigate it by working harder the next day?

---

5.   (1991) 107 *The Law Quarterly Review* 249–297.

In *Spartan Steel*, the defendants were doing roadwork repairs. They were given plans showing the position of cables, mains, and the like. Despite this, they damaged the electricity cable that supplied the plaintiff's factory. The plant was at that time working round the clock, and the power was cut off for fourteen hours. At the time of the accident, metal which was being melted for ingots was in an arc furnace. This batch was spoiled and the plaintiff lost metal worth £368. Had that particular melt been properly completed, the plaintiff would have made a profit of £400. Further, during the time when the power was off, the plaintiff could have put four more melts through the furnace—by being unable to do so, he lost a profit of £1767.

The Court of Appeal held that the plaintiff could recover for the physical damage to the first melt (£368), and the loss of profit on that melt (£400), but *not* for loss of profit on the other four melts, as this was pure economic loss; due to the nature of the damage—cutting off power—there was a danger of the indeterminacy of claims, and fraud.

The problem of jurisprudential tension between respect for the principle of freedom of action within the limits of the law on the one hand, and recovery of damages for pure economic loss on the other, was thus set out by McHugh J In *Hill v Van Erp* (1997) CLR 159 at 211:

> Anglo–Australian law has never accepted the proposition that a person owes a duty of care to another person merely because the first person knows that his or her careless act may cause economic loss to the latter person. Social and commercial life would be very different if it did. Indeed, leaving aside the intentional tort cases of wrongful interference with another person's legal rights (inducing breach of contract, intimidation and conspiracy, for example) a person will generally owe no duty to prevent economic loss to another person even though the first person intends to cause economic loss to another person. In our free enterprise society, no one questions the right of the trader to increase its advertising or cut its prices even though that action is done with the intention of taking the market share of its rivals.

In *Perre v Apand Pty Ltd* (1999) 198 CLR 180,[6] at [115], McHugh J commented:

> The immunity from liability referred to in that passage is a consequence of the common law's concern for the autonomy of the individual and its desire to give effect to the choices of the individual by not burdening his or her freedom of action. Nor is the immunity confined to traders. As long as a person is legitimately protecting or pursuing his or her social or business interests, the common law will not require that person to be concerned with the effect of his or her conduct

---

6. Both *Hill v Van Erp* (1997) 188 CLR 159 and *Perre v Apand Pty Ltd* (1999) 198 CLR 180 are discussed below.

on the economic interests of other persons. And that is so even when that person knows that his or her actions will cause loss to a specific individual.

Yet, since the 1960s, the courts have recognised that there are circumstances in which the three objections are not applicable. The development of defendants' liability for pure economic loss has been incremental. Chronologically, recovery for pure economic loss resulting from negligent misstatement was allowed somewhat earlier than damages for pure economic loss occasioned by wrongful physical actions. These two categories of case are discussed in turn.

NEGLIGENT MISSTATEMENT

The cause of action for negligent misstatement or negligent advice relates to situations where the plaintiff acts to his or her financial detriment in reliance upon a statement or advice proffered by the defendant. According to the High Court in *San Sebastian v The Minister Administering the Environmental Planning and Assessment Act 1979* (1986) 162 CLR 341, at 353, it is not the words of the negligent defendant, but the conduct of the plaintiff, in reliance on those words, that causes the financial loss:

> damage flows, not immediately from the defendant's act in making a statement but from the plaintiff's reliance on the statement and his action or inaction which produces consequential loss.

Therefore, the damage suffered is pure economic loss because it is at least once removed from the actual negligence. In *San Sebastian*, the High Court noted that negligent misstatement cases are concerned with the nature of the negligent conduct—the way in which the damage was caused (through words), as well as the consequent type of loss suffered (pure economic loss).

In *Hedley Byrne v Heller & Partners* [1964] AC 465, the House of Lords overruled *Derry v Peek* (1889) 14 AC 337, and recognised that in certain circumstances involving negligent misstatement, a duty of care might exist in regard to pure economic loss. Hedley Byrne, the plaintiff, wished to know whether it could safely extend credit to a client company, Easipower Ltd. For this purpose, the plaintiff asked its own bank to approach the defendants, Heller & Partners, bankers to Easipower Ltd, to assess its viability. The plaintiff's bank approached Heller & Partners on the basis that the financial standing of Easipower Ltd would be disclosed 'in confidence and without responsibility' (on the part of the defendants). Heller & Partners gave, without making any charge for it, a reference which was so carelessly phrased that it led Hedley Byrne to believe that Easipower Ltd was creditworthy, when in fact it was not. The defendants attached a disclaimer of liability to the reference. Hedley Byrne extended credit to Easipower Ltd, and suffered loss when the company went into liquidation. The plaintiff was neither a customer nor a potential customer of Heller & Partners, but it sued the bank for damages in negligence.

In *Hedley Byrne*, the House of Lords proceeded on the basis of a clear distinction between negligent acts and negligent words. All the judgments in *Hedley Byrne* were based on the assumption that a claim for pure economic loss was not very different from one for physical damage. The difference lay in the source of this loss: the negligent misstatement. This meant that their Lordships concentrated on the *way* in which the loss was caused, and whether a duty of care should apply to loss caused this way. The focus on the nature of the conduct—negligent words—brought to the fore the risk of an indeterminate volume of claims for financial loss which could result from a single misleading statement broadcast through the mass media. It was this inherent potential of words to cause vast economic damage that led the House of Lords to place strict limits upon the duty of care for negligent misstatement. Their Lordships agreed that the legal status of the relationship (contractual, fiduciary or confidential) was not the sole determinant of the existence of duty; liability for negligent misstatement could be imposed if the following factors were present:

- voluntary undertaking by the defendant of responsibility for the statements (discussed by Lord Devlin);
- reasonable reliance by the plaintiff on the negligent misstatement (discussed by Lord Reid); and
- circumstances and the nature of the transaction (discussed by Lord Pearce).

According to Lord Devlin (at 529), to recover for negligent misstatement, unless the plaintiff is in a fiduciary or contractual relationship, he or she must show that the parties were in a relationship equivalent to contract: 'that is, where there is an assumption of responsibility in circumstances in which, but for the absence of consideration, there would be a contract'. His Lordship determined that 'wherever there is a relationship equivalent to contract, there is a duty of care'. Such a relationship, which may either be general (for instance solicitors, bankers, financial advisers, and their clients), or specific to a particular transaction, gives rise to a duty of care to be careful when proffering advice or making statements. This is so, irrespective of the absence of consideration (at 532). Moreover, according to Lord Devlin (at 528):

> It cannot matter [once the responsibility is voluntarily accepted or undertaken] whether the information consists of fact or of opinion or is a mixture of both, nor whether it was obtained as a result of special inquiries or comes direct from facts already in the defendant's possession or from his general store of professional knowledge. One cannot ... distinguish in this respect between a duty to inquire and a duty to state.

The assumption of responsibility on the part of the person making the statement can be either express or implied. Lord Devlin found, however, that the disclaimer of responsibility negatived any undertaking of the responsibility for the reference.

The notion of 'reasonable reliance'

Lord Reid (at 502–3) introduced the principle of *reasonable reliance* in relation to recovery for negligent statements thus:

> My Lords, I consider that it follows and that it should now be regarded as settled that if someone possessed of a special skill undertakes, quite irrespective of contract, to apply that skill for the assistance of another person who relies upon such skill, a duty of care will arise. The fact that the service is to be given by means of or by the instrumentality of words can make no difference. Furthermore, if in a sphere in which a person is so placed that others could reasonably rely upon his judgment or his skill or upon his ability to make careful inquiry, a person takes it upon himself to give information or advice to, or allows his information or advice to be passed on to, another person who, as he knows or should know, will place reliance upon it, then a duty of care will arise.

Where such duty of care exists, pure economic loss may be recoverable. In this case, given the disclaimer, the plaintiff's reliance on the reference was not reasonable.

Lord Pearce said (at 539) that for the imposition on the defendants of a duty of care to the plaintiffs in relation to inquiries and advice, there has to exist 'a special relationship'. The existence of the requisite relationship 'depends on the circumstances of the transaction':

> If, for instance, they disclosed a casual social approach to the inquiry, no such special relationship or duty of care would be assumed. To import such a duty the representation must normally, ... concern a business or professional transaction whose nature makes clear the gravity of the inquiry and the importance and influence attached to the answer.

Lord Pearce concluded (at 539–40), that in *Hedley Byrne*, 'a most important circumstance ... [was] the form of the inquiry and of the answer. Both were here plainly stated to be without liability'.

The *Hedley Byrne* principle of voluntary assumption of responsibility and reasonable reliance as the essential prerequisite for recovery of damages for pure economic loss was subsequently adopted in a modified form by the High Court in *Mutual Life and Citizens' Assurance Co Ltd v Evatt* (1968) 122 CLR 556, at 572–3, in which Barwick CJ stated:

whenever a person gives information or advice to another upon a serious matter in circumstances where the speaker realises, or ought to realise, that he is being trusted to give the best of his information or advice as a basis for action on the part of the other party and it is reasonable in the circumstances for the other party to act on that information or advice, the speaker comes under a duty to exercise reasonable care in the provision of the information or advice he chooses to give.

In *Mutual Life and Citizens' Assurance Co Ltd v Evatt* (known as *MLC v Evatt*), Mr Evatt, a policy holder in an insurance company, asked this company to provide him with advice concerning the financial stability of Palmer Pty Ltd. Both the insurance company and Palmer Pty Ltd were subsidiaries of MLC. The insurance company knew that Mr Evatt intended to make investment decisions regarding Palmer Pty Ltd but it incorrectly informed Mr Evatt that Palmer Pty Ltd was financially stable and that it would be safe to make a further investment in it. There was no disclaimer of responsibility attached. In reliance on the information and advice, Mr Evatt kept his shares in Palmer Pty Ltd and invested further sums. Subsequently, he lost the value of the investment together with interest.

MLC claimed that whereas Lord Reid made the defendant's 'skill and judgement' in the area in which the advice was being requested a precondition to reasonable reliance, it was not in the business of giving investment advice. The High Court rejected this argument and found for Mr Evatt. Barwick CJ (at 572–3) said:

> In my opinion, the elements of the special relationship to which I have referred do not require either actual possession of skill or judgement on the part of the speaker or any profession by him to possess the same. His willingness to proffer the information or advice in the relationship which I have described is, in my opinion, sufficient.

In a controversial decision the Privy Council ([1971] AC 793)[7] by majority (with strong dissent from Lord Reid and Lord Morris of Borth-y-Gest) allowed the appeal, holding that the defendant insurance company did not owe the plaintiff a duty of care, because it did not have, and did not profess to have, special skill in giving investment advice. Barwick CJ's wider formulation of duty was accepted by the High Court in *Esanda Finance Corporation Limited v Peat Marwick Hungerfords* (1997) 188 CLR 159.[8] Thus, special skill, though important, is not determinative in deciding whether the plaintiff's reliance on the defendant's statement was reasonable. The speaker does not need to know the precise use to which the information will be put. It is enough if the defendant knows, or ought to know, that the inquirer is requesting it for a serious purpose, proposes to act upon it, and may suffer loss if it proves inaccurate (*Hill v Van Erp* (1997) 188 CLR 159).

---

7. See, for example: *Spring v Guardian Assurance plc* [1995] 2 AC 296 at 320, per Lord Goff of Chieveley.
8. See also: dicta of Mason and Aickin JJ in *L Shaddock & Ass v Parramatta City Council* (1980–81) 150 CLR 225 at 234.

Nomenclature

As noted above, negligent misstatement cases are instances of pure economic loss because damage is consequential, and loss flows not from the defendant's statement (information, advice, warning), but from the conduct the plaintiff embarks upon in reliance on that statement. The reference to negligent conduct in this category of case includes both incorrect statements as well as a failure to make a statement in circumstances in which the making of the statement would have avoided the consequent injury.

In *Hawkins v Clayton Utz* (1988) 164 CLR 539, Gaudron J (at 596) noted that in such cases, the plaintiff would plead either 'reasonable reliance' or 'reasonable expectation'. However, the jurisprudential significance of these concepts, as well as that of 'assumption of responsibility', is somewhat ambiguous. In *Hill v Van Erp* (1997) 188 CLR 159, at 228–31, Gummow J observed that the meaning of such terms as 'assumption of responsibility' and 'reliance' was imprecise. In *Esanda Finance Corporation Ltd v Peat Marwick Hungerfords* (1997) 188 CLR 241, at 298, he commented that 'emphasis upon them in a real sense reflects the quest for an alternative to consideration'. McHugh J, in *Perre v Apand Pty Ltd* (1999) 198 CLR 180, at [124], pointed out that neither the concept of reliance nor the concept of voluntary assumption of responsibility 'represents a necessary or a sufficient criterion for determination of a duty of care',[9] though:

> commonly, but not necessarily, a duty will arise in cases which 'involve an identified element of known reliance (or dependence) or the assumption of responsibility or a combination of the two'.

McHugh J concluded (at [125]):

> In my view, reliance and assumption of responsibility are merely indicators of the plaintiff's vulnerability to harm from the defendant's conduct, and it is the concept of vulnerability rather than these evidentiary indicators which is the relevant criterion for determining whether a duty of care exists. The most explicit recognition of vulnerability as a possible common theme in cases of pure economic loss is found in the judgment of Toohey and Gaudron JJ in *Esanda Finance Corporation Ltd v Peat Marwick Hungerfords* (1997) 188 CLR 241 at 263–4.

In *Woolcock St Invest v CDG Pty Ltd* (2004) 216 CLR 515, Gleeson CJ, Gummow, Hayne, and Heydon JJ, at [23], have also embraced the concept of vulnerability as 'an important requirement in cases where a duty of care to avoid economic loss has been held to have been owed'.

---

9. McHugh J referred to Gummow J's criticism of 'reasonable reliance' and 'assumption of responsibility' in *Esanda Finance Corporation Ltd v Peat Marwick Hungerfords* (1997) 188 CLR 241 at 298–9.

Prerequisites to recovery for negligent misstatement

In *L Shaddock v Parramatta CC* (1980–81) 150 CLR 225, the High Court stated that subject to the loss being reasonably foreseeable, the amount of money recoverable for negligent misstatement is the amount necessary to restore the plaintiff to the position he or she was in before the statement was made.

To recover damages for pure economic loss occasioned by negligent misstatement the plaintiff has to establish a number of elements.

Defendant's duty of care

In *Tepko Pty Limited v Water Board* (2001) 178 ALR 634, at 650 [74], Gaudron J noted that in relation to negligent misstatement:

> the circumstances which attract a duty of care have been identified as 'known' reliance (or dependence) or the assumption of responsibility or a combination of the two. In that context, the word 'known' includes circumstances in which reliance or dependence ought to be known.

Thus, apart from relationships which are, broadly speaking, either contractual or equivalent to contract (*Hedley Byrne v Heller & Partners* [1964] AC 465), the duty may arise in the following situations.

Professional relationships

Hill v Van Erp (1997) 188 CLR 159 is an example of a category of case where assumption of responsibility through a professional relationship with one party is deemed to extend to third parties. Legally, there is no contractual or fiduciary relationship between a testator's solicitors and the intended beneficiaries of the will. However, Mrs Van Erp successfully sued a solicitor, Mrs Hill, for loss of a testamentary gift. The solicitor allowed Mrs Van Erp's husband to sign as witness to the will, under which she was a beneficiary. Mr Van Erp's signing of the will attracted the operation of s 15(1) of the *Succession Act 1981* (Qld), which made the disposition null and void. All the members of the court, apart from Gaudron J, agreed that the loss of testamentary gift was a pure economic loss. The High Court (Brennan CJ, Dawson, Toohey, Gaudron, and Gummow JJ; McHugh J dissenting) held that the solicitor was in breach of a duty of care owed to the intended beneficiary and hence was liable in damages for the value of the intended disposition. Dawson J, with whom Toohey J agreed, said (at 185):

> when a solicitor accepts responsibility for carrying out a client's testamentary intentions, he or she cannot, in my view, be regarded as being devoid of any responsibility to an intended beneficiary. The responsibility is not contractual but arises from the solicitor's undertaking that the duty of ensuring that the testator's

intention of conferring a benefit upon a beneficiary is realised. In a factual, if not a legal sense, that may be seen as assuming a responsibility not only to the testatrix but also to the intended beneficiary.

His Honour referred to Lord Browne-Wilkinson's judgment in *White v Jones* [1995] 2 AC 207, at 273–4, a case in which a solicitor who, though instructed to prepare a will, delayed carrying out the instructions, and was found to have breached a duty of care to the intended beneficiary.[10]

The High Court emphasised that liability in *Hill v Van Erp* for purely economic loss was to an identified person, rather than to an indeterminate number of plaintiffs, and the loss was a fixed sum rather than an indeterminate amount.

Assumption of responsibility by the defendant

In situations outside contract where the defendant assumes responsibility, a causal connection between the defendant's statements and the injury sustained by the plaintiff may be established. According to Barwick CJ in *MLC v Evatt* (1968) 122 CLR 556, at 572–3:

> whenever a person gives information or advice to another upon a serious matter in circumstances where the speaker realises, or ought to realise, that he is being trusted to give the best of his information or advice as a basis for action on the part of the other party and it is reasonable in the circumstances for the other party to act on that information or advice, the speaker comes under a duty to exercise reasonable care in the provision of the information or advice he chooses to give.

Practice of supplying information by public authorities

Duty of care may also extend to public bodies that follow the practice of supplying information. For example in *L Shaddock & Ass v Parramatta CC* (1981) 150 CLR 225, a solicitor acting for a redevelopment company applied to the Council of the City of Parramatta, by a form in common use, for a certificate under the *Local Government Act 1919* (NSW). On the form, he asked whether the property that the company intended to purchase was affected by any road-widening proposals, and indicated that the purpose for which he sought the information was 'conveyancing'. It was the Council's practice, when it received such requests for information regarding road-widening proposals, to refer to the proposal, if there was one, at the foot of the certificate. No fee was payable for providing the information. Before completion of the purchase, the solicitor received a certificate which did not

---

10. See also: *Gorham v British Telecommunications plc* [2000] 1 WLR 2129, in which the negligence of the defendant company in drafting an insurance policy resulted in loss of benefits to the widow and children of the deceased, who was the company's client. The company knew of the client's intention to make provision for dependants in event of his death, and the court held that the disappointed beneficiaries under the policy could recover damages from the insurance company.

mention any road-widening proposals. Relying upon the certificate, the purchasers completed the contract. In fact, proposals affecting the land had been approved by the Council and, as a result, the company suffered economic loss. The company sued the Council. The High Court held that once it undertook to issue the certificate, the Council placed itself under a duty to the purchasers to take reasonable care that the information given in the certificate was correct. The failure to mention the road-widening proposals on the certificate amounted to an erroneous statement that none existed, which breached its duty.

Employment contracts
In the United Kingdom, duty of care has been imposed under an implied term of an employment contract. For example, an employer who gives a reference in respect of an employee (both past and present) owes that employee a duty to take reasonable care in its preparation and can be liable to him or her in negligence if it fails to do so and the employee thereby suffers economic damage: *Spring v Guardian Assurance plc* [1995] 2 AC 296. The existence of a duty to take care in such cases will be determined by considering the law of defamation and competing interests of the parties, including other responsibilities imposed on the defendant in relation to the matter (*Sullivan v Moody* (2001) 207 CLR 562 at [54]–[55]).

Policy considerations may include balancing public interest issues arising from circumstances before the court (*Sullivan v Moody*).

Scope of the duty of care: knowledge and vulnerability

According to the majority of the High Court in *Tepko Pty Limited v Water Board* (2001) 206 CLR 1, in cases of negligent misstatement, for the liability to attach, the provider of negligent advice must have had specific knowledge or foresight of the purpose for which the plaintiff intended to use and used the information. In *Tepko*, a developer was advised that the land he wished to subdivide could be rezoned from rural to rural–residential, if the Water Board agreed to connect its water supply system to the land. In a response to an inquiry by the Minister for Natural Resources, the Water Board negligently stated that the provisional cost of such connection would be a 'ball park' figure of $2 500 000 (as against $1 700 000). This negligent information was supplied to the Minister for his use, though the defendant knew that it would eventually be passed on to the plaintiff.

The court found for the Water Board on three grounds:

1   The knowledge was not sufficient to satisfy the test of specific knowledge or foresight; for although the Water Board was aware that the plaintiff would rely on this information in his decision whether to proceed with the proposed development, it lacked the necessary 'knowledge', in the sense that it was not apprised of the plaintiff's actual economic and business circumstances.

2   The plaintiff was not a 'vulnerable' person within the terms of the definition—he could have approached the Water Board himself rather than through the offices of the Minister.
3   It was unreasonable for him to rely on the 'ball park' figure, which was only provisional, and by its very nature had an implication of a disclaimer. Gaudron J (at [76]) noted that '"Reliance" as the test for the existence of a relationship that will call a duty of care into existence is not actual reliance, but reasonable reliance.'

Breach of duty by way of negligent misstatement

As noted above, the term 'misstatement' encompasses a wide range of negligent communications. Making a prediction or representations may give rise to a duty of care, and a failure to make a statement may also be regarded in some cases as negligent misstatement. For example, in *Hawkins v Clayton Utz* (1988) 164 CLR 539, Clayton Utz, a firm of Sydney solicitors, had drawn up, executed and retained custody of the last will of their client. Upon being notified of her death, the firm undertook certain actions on behalf of the estate, including a search for any later will. However, the firm failed for six years to notify the plaintiff, who was named as executor and the principal beneficiary in the will, either of the death of the testatrix or of the existence of the will. The plaintiff, a former tenant, was not a member of the testatrix's family, but he lived in Sydney, and his name and address were in the telephone book. As a result of the defendant's failure to notify and appoint the executor, the estate incurred a fine for late lodgement of a return form for death duty. Unattended and uninhabited, in the course of six years, the testatrix's house fell into disrepair, and all its antique furniture was stolen.

In the High Court, the majority held that Clayton Utz having had custody of their client's will was liable for economic loss resulting from its failure, on the death of the testatrix, to inform the nominated executor and residuary beneficiary of his interest under the will. Deane J, with whom Mason CJ and Wilson J agreed, said that the relationship of solicitor and client is a relationship that ordinarily gives rise to a duty requiring the solicitor to take positive steps that prevent the client from suffering foreseeable economic loss. In this case, the relationship between Clayton Utz and the testatrix extended to notification and appointment of an executor. Consequently, the testatrix's solicitors owed a duty of care to the plaintiff in his representative capacity as executor of the will (but not in his personal capacity as a beneficiary). They breached this duty by failing to inform the executor of the existence of the will, thus preventing him from entering upon administration of the estate.

However, the plaintiff must not only show a duty to make a careful and considered representation, but also establish that a negligent representation was actually made. For example, in *San Sebastian Properties Pty Ltd v Minister Administering the*

Environment Planning and Assessment Act 1979 (1986) 162 CLR 341, a property developer, Mr Baker, saw in the Sydney Town Hall an exhibition of proposals for the redevelopment of Woolloomooloo. The State Planning Authority and the Sydney City Council had prepared the proposals, which were embodied in a redevelopment study, development proposals, and a brochure. Relying on this information, Mr Baker and his partners purchased large parcels of land at Woolloomooloo. After the redevelopment plan was found unworkable and abandoned, the plaintiffs suffered serious financial loss when their land was sold or compulsorily acquired.

Mr Baker and his partners sued for damages for financial loss caused by negligent preparation and publication of a redevelopment plan, and failure to warn them that the plan was to be abandoned. They alleged that they relied, to their detriment, on the information contained in the study documents when they purchased the land. According to the plaintiffs' argument, since the documents appeared to present expert research in a 'proper and workmanlike manner', based on sound town planning principles, they amounted to a representation made with the intention of inducing developers to rely on that representation.

The High Court found the inference that the documents embodied expert research and were prepared in 'workmanlike manner' to be irrelevant, because they contained no statement, express or implied, that would amount to an invitation to developers to rely on the contents as a basis for acquisition and development of properties in the area. The High Court therefore concluded that the statements allegedly relied upon by the plaintiffs were not made: the proposals could not be construed as inducements to purchase land. Consequently, the defendant had no case to answer.

Generally, where a defendant is under a duty to protect the plaintiff's economic interest, the breach may take the form of negligent omission to issue timely summons; ensure that relevant signatures are provided; obtain competent advice for the client; obtain consent order from the court of an otherwise limited jurisdiction to exercise unlimited jurisdiction (*Berryman v Joslyn & Anor; Wentworth Shire Council v Joslyn & Anor* [2001] NSWCA 95); include exclusion of liability clauses in commercial contracts (*Astley & Ors v Austrust Ltd* (1999) 197 CLR 1);[11] or delete clauses prejudicial to the client's interest.

The statement must be made negligently

The defendant's duty of care must be capable of being discharged solely by the statement to the plaintiff.

In *Hill v Van Erp* (1997) 188 CLR 159, the reasoning of at least two Justices (Gaudron and Gummow JJ) suggests that in the category of case for negligent misstatement, the concept of reliance will be supplemented by the requirement of

---

11. In *Astley & Ors v Austrust Ltd*, the High Court determined that in the case of solicitors, the liability is concurrent in contract and in tort.

proof that at the time of the alleged negligent conduct the defendant had, or ought to have had, knowledge or control of the information contained in the statement or lack thereof. In *Hill v Van Erp*, the defendant solicitor had control over legal procedures that were necessary for the realisation of the testamentary intentions of the testatrix, whereas the potential beneficiaries had no knowledge of the law of wills.

As a general rule, in allegations of negligent misstatement, to establish breach of duty of care, the plaintiff has to show:

1. that the defendant knew or ought to have known that the plaintiff would rely on the representation (*Tepko Pty Limited v Water Board* (2001) 206 CLR 1; *Hill v Van Erp* (1997) 188 CLR 159);
2. that the representation was actually made (*San Sebastian Properties Pty Ltd v Minister Administering the Environment Planning and Assessment Act 1979* (1986) 162 CLR 341); and
3. that the representation was made negligently because the defendant:
   (a) did not provide information (*Hawkins v Clayton Utz* (1988) 164 CLR 539; *L Shaddock & Ass v Parramatta CC* (1981) 150 CLR 225);
   (b) gave information that was incomplete or inaccurate (*Hedley Byrne v Heller & Partners* [1964] AC 465);
   (c) did not qualify the information so as to negative reliance: provide a disclaimer, or warning that the statement was not conclusive, or by directing the plaintiff to another source of information (*Butcher v Lachlan Elder Realty P/L* (2004) 218 CLR 592); or
   (d) failed to provide additional information.

Norris & Anor v Sibberas & Ors [1990] VR 161

If the alleged representation was oral, the court will make its own determination of what was actually said, and then decide: (i) whether the plaintiff's reliance upon the statement was reasonable, and (ii) whether the damage was caused by reliance upon the advice or representation.

In cases where the actual words have not been recorded, each party—usually many years after the event—relies on recollections that are inevitably affected by hindsight bias. The outcomes of these cases turn on which party's version the court ultimately accepts. For although, in theory, the common law forensic process is dialectical in nature, concomitant with the acceptance by the court of a particular version of the facts is the adoption of that version's perspective.

Norris & Anor v Sibberas & Ors [1990] VR 161 illustrates these issues. In that case, the plaintiffs, Mr and Mrs Sibberas, contacted the defendant estate agent, Mrs Norris, and told her that they wished to purchase a motel. The Sibberases had no previous business experience but they attended a seminar on the running of motels. Mrs Norris told them that she had owned motels herself, and was experienced in motel management. She found a motel with a milk bar attached to it at Bonnie Doon near Mansfield, in Victoria. The motel was newly built by the vendors and had operated for a mere eleven weeks at the time of the sale. The business was operating at a loss, and the outlook was not propitious: 1983 was a year of a disastrous drought and a bad snow season. However, all figures were disclosed to the plaintiffs, and the price of the goodwill was low.[12] According to the trial judge, Mrs Norris told them that 'the business was a great opportunity at a bargain price and that it was a gold mine with a good all year trade.' The Sibberases pleaded that they had relied on these representations. Mrs Norris agreed that she made a number of statements and forecasts about the business, but she claimed to have qualified them on the basis that the success would depend on diligence and hard work as well as good management by the operators.

The plaintiffs also consulted an accountant experienced in motel businesses, Mr Bell, who was recommended to them by Mrs Norris. Despite meeting with Mr Bell and providing him with details of their financial position, the plaintiffs signed the contract of purchase before receiving a written report on the financial viability of the business from him. In the three months during which they operated the motel business, it remained unprofitable, and the Sibberases were forced to sell at loss.

The Sibberases sued Mrs Norris and Mr Bell for damages for negligent misstatement. At the trial their claim against Mr Bell failed, but they were successful against Mrs Norris. In issue before the Appeal Division of the Supreme Court of Victoria was the exact phrase used by Mrs Norris in relation to the 'gold mine'. Marks J (Murphy and Beach JJ agreeing) reversed the trial judge's decision.[13] Marks J found:

1. Mrs Norris did not make the particular statements, because she did not tell the plaintiffs that the business '*was* a gold mine'; rather, she made a prediction that that 'once you get going it will be a gold mine'.
2. The statements about the potential of the business to flourish were correct, even if, in the circumstances—drought, bad snow season, and the fact that the Sibberrases supplied $40 000 of their own money, borrowed $70 000 at 19 per cent interest, and were required to pay $673 per week in rent for six months—it would have been over a long period of time.
3. Once the court accepted that Mrs Norris's statements were only about the potential profitability of the business, the plaintiffs were unable to establish

---

12. The plaintiffs also paid $94 000 for chattels, which accorded with the genuine value of these items.
13. *Norris & Anor v Sibberas & Ors* [1990] VR 161 was decided before the High Court (Brennan CJ, Toohey, McHugh, Gummow, and Kirby JJ in a joint judgment) in *Zuvela v Cosmarnan Concrete Pty Ltd* (1996) 140 ALR 227, at 230, determined that in cases where the verbal exchange between the parties has not been recorded, and the issue is how the person to whom the words were addressed understood them, the correct question for appellate courts is whether the words were reasonably understood by the person to bear the meaning that the trial judge attributed to them.

the breach of duty of care. For, although the evidence showed that at the time the tourist trade was down (the plaintiffs knew of this fact before the purchase), Mrs Norris had ascertained, and provided Mr Bell with, details of the takings of another motel, in the picturesque tourist town of Mansfield, which had enjoyed full occupancy during the preceding two ski seasons.

Causation and vulnerability

Vulnerability

The outcome of the *Norris* case would have been the same—the plaintiffs would have lost—if the court were to apply the subsequently developed requirement of vulnerability. In *Woolcock St Invest v CDG Pty Ltd* (2004) 216 CLR 515 (discussed below), Gleeson CJ, Gummow, Hayne, and Heydon JJ (at [23]) stated:

> 'Vulnerability', [in the context of pure economic loss] is not to be understood as meaning only that the plaintiff was likely to suffer damage if reasonable care was not taken. Rather, 'vulnerability' is to be understood as a reference to the plaintiff's inability to protect itself from the consequences of a defendant's want of reasonable care, either entirely or at least in a way which would cast the consequences of loss on the defendant.[14]

McHugh J, in a separate concurring judgment in *Woolcock St Invest*, defined 'vulnerability' as follows (at [80]):

> Whether or not the plaintiff was vulnerable to the risk of injury from the defendant's conduct is a key issue in determining whether the defendant owed a duty of care to the plaintiff ... In this context, vulnerability to risk means not that the plaintiff was exposed to risk but that by reason of ignorance or social, political or economic constraints, the plaintiff was not able to protect him or herself from the risk of injury.

In *Norris v Sibberas*, even if it were held that Mrs Norris said that the business *was* a gold mine, the plaintiffs could have protected themselves against the risk of economic loss consequent upon such statement by waiting for Mr Bell to provide them with professional advice before purchasing the business.

In *Woolcock St Invest v CDG Pty Ltd* (2004) 216 CLR 515, Gleeson CJ, Gummow, Hayne, and Heydon JJ referred to *Perre v Apand Pty Ltd* (1999) 198 CLR 180 (discussed below), *Hill v Van Erp*, and *Esanda Finance Corporation Ltd v Peat Marwick Hungerfords* (1997) 188 CLR 241 as examples of cases in which the requirement of vulnerability was applicable. Their Honours added (at [24]):

---

14. Their Honours referred to Stapleton J, 'Comparative Economic Loss: Lessons from Case-law-focused "Middle Theory"' (2002) 50 *University of California Los Angeles Law Review* 531 at 558–559.

In other cases of pure economic loss (*Bryan v Maloney* [(1995) 182 CLR 609] is an example) reference has been made to notions of assumption of responsibility and known reliance. The negligent misstatement cases like *Mutual Life & Citizens' Assurance Co Ltd v Evatt* [(1971) AC 793] and *Shaddock & Associates Pty Ltd v Parramatta City Council [No 1]* [(1980–81) 150 CLR 225] can be seen as cases in which a central plank in the plaintiff's allegation that the defendant owed it a duty of care is the contention that the defendant knew that the plaintiff would rely on the accuracy of the information the defendant provided. And it may be, as Professor Stapleton has suggested,[15] that these cases, too, can be explained by reference to notions of vulnerability … It is not necessary in this case, however, to attempt to identify or articulate the breadth of any general proposition about the importance of vulnerability.

The final sentence leaves it unclear whether the court determined that the requirement of reasonable reliance is now superseded by the requirement of vulnerability. It is arguable that where the requirement of vulnerability is absent, the elements of reasonable reliance also cannot be satisfied. For, in order to establish causal reliance, the plaintiff must show:

1   That he or she had actually relied on the defendant's representation (a subjective test). For example, in *Rosenberg v Percival* (2001) 205 CLR 434, the court found that Dr Percival did not rely solely on the defendant's representations when she decided to undergo the operation—she obtained two other opinions, and did her own research on the internet, thus the issue of vulnerability did not arise.
2   That the reliance was reasonable in the circumstances. It would not be reasonable for the plaintiff to act on advice or information given casually on some social or informal occasion. For example, if a guest at a dinner party asks an eminent lawyer about the tax implications of a million-dollar investment and then acts to her detriment on that off-the-cuff, gratuitous advice, a court is likely to conclude that her reliance was not reasonable, and that she was well able to protect herself from the consequences of the lawyer's want of reasonable care by paying for that—or another—lawyer's professional services.
3   That the defendant had reasonably foreseen, or ought reasonably to have foreseen, such reliance on the part of the plaintiff. In *Hill v Van Erp* (1997) 188 CLR 159, the solicitor should have foreseen that the testatrix, and Mr and Mrs van Erp, depended entirely on her expertise in drafting and executing the will: they were vulnerable because they could do nothing to ensure that the solicitor was acting properly (it was reasonable for them to rely on the solicitor's advice).

---

15. Ibid.

4   That the defendant induced or encouraged such reliance. For example, in *San Sebastian Properties Pty Ltd v Minister Administering the Environment Planning and Assessment Act 1979* (1986) 162 CLR, the defendant council did not encourage large property developers to purchase vast amounts of land in reliance on redevelopment proposals which were published for the purpose of public discussion. The developers were not vulnerable—they could easily have ascertained that 'green paper' proposals are by their nature discretionary and impermanent, both in content and implementation.

Remoteness of damage

The test of remoteness of damage in negligent misstatement cases is narrowly interpreted. In *Henville v Walker* [2001] HCA 52, at [103], McHugh J thus explained the process of determining remoteness of damage in cases where the plaintiff has acted to his or her detriment by reason of, or following, the defendant's statement, suggestion, act, or omission:

> [the damage] will not be regarded as causally connected with the detriment if it provides no more than the reason why the person acted to his or her detriment. If the defendant intended the person suffering a detriment to act in the general way that he or she did, the common law will invariably hold that a causal connection existed between the conduct and the detriment. But if the conduct merely provides the reason why the person acted, it will not be sufficient to establish a causal connection unless the purpose of the legal norm that the defendant has breached is to prevent persons suffering detriment in circumstances of the kind that occurred. If a broker negligently advises a client to retain shares because they are a good investment, the broker will be liable for the loss sustained in retaining those shares. But if, having received that advice, the client decides to buy more shares, the broker will not be liable for the further losses unless the terms of the original retainer imposed a duty on the broker to advise in respect of further purchases.

Remedies

Depending on the circumstances, negligent statements may also amount to false or misleading conduct in contravention of s 52 or s 53 of the *Trade Practices Act 1974* (Cth), and relevant State or Territory legislation, for instance, s 11 or s 13 of the *Fair Trading Act 1985* (Vic). If these causes of action are established, the court may rescind the contract and award damages. For instance, in *Krakowski & Anor v Eurolynx Properties Ltd & Anor* (1995) 130 ALR 1, the High Court declared the appellants were induced to enter the contract of sale by conduct that was fraudulent and, in terms of s 52 of the *Trade Practices Act*, misleading.

Negligent advice and physical harm

There exists a conceptually and jurisprudentially confusing distinction between physical and pure economic loss occasioned by negligent advice. Historically, categorisation of torts has reflected the defendant's conduct, not the type of damage brought about by the wrongful conduct. Consequently, the split between negligent advice which results in physical damage to the plaintiff and negligent advice occasioning mere economic loss is anomalous. In *Rogers v Whitaker* (1992) 175 CLR 479, a medical practitioner negligently failed to advise his patient about risks inherent an eye operation. The operation was performed with the required skill. However, the patient was rendered blind. Using the reasoning of consequential and primary loss, it is arguable that the patient's decision to undergo the operation caused her damage, and that this decision was consequential upon the insufficient advice provided by the medical practitioner. Conceptually, the situation of Mrs Whitaker was not unlike that of Hedley Byrne Co, because the damage suffered in both cases was not an inevitable consequence of the defendant's wrongful conduct. Rather, it came about as a consequence of each plaintiff's own decision. Mrs Whitaker decided to undergo the operation, and Hedley Byrne Co decided to extend credit. Mrs Whitaker's choice or consent was considered 'meaningless' because she had insufficient information. Hedley Byrne Co's decision was also arguably 'meaningless', since it was made on the basis of insufficient and inaccurate advice. Yet, in the case of negligent medical advice, the cause of action is argued under ordinary *Donoghue v Stevenson* principles, whereas negligent advice regarding financial matters is treated as a separate category of case with its own prerequisite of reasonable reliance. There is no discernible reason for treating conduct involving negligent advice as falling into a particular category of case purely on the basis of the type of damage suffered by the plaintiff.

PURE ECONOMIC LOSS CAUSED THROUGH NEGLIGENT PHYSICAL CONDUCT

The first case in Australia to modify the strict rule that pure economic loss caused by physical conduct does not sound in damages was *Caltex Oil v The Dredge Willemstad* (1976) 136 CLR 529. In *Caltex*, Australian Oil Refining Pty Ltd (AOR) owned an oil refinery at Kurnell, in Sydney. It also owned a connecting pipeline that had been laid on the bed of Botany Bay. Caltex Oil owned a terminal at Banksmeadow. By agreement between Caltex and AOR, Caltex supplied crude oil to the refinery for processing, and the refined products were delivered to the Caltex terminal by pipeline. When the dredge *Willemstad* fractured AOR's pipeline, the Caltex production cycle was disrupted. Caltex was unable to distribute and sell petrol from its terminal, and lost profits. The crew of the *Willemstad* knew of the pipeline, because a detailed map of this part of Botany Bay's topography was supplied to them.

The High Court (Gibbs, Stephen, Mason, Jacobs, and Murphy JJ) allowed Caltex to recover for loss of benefit that resulted from damage to AOR's pipeline. The court determined that economic loss not consequential upon property damage may be recoverable from those who negligently occasion the loss if they (the defendants) could reasonably foresee that a specific plaintiff—as against a general class of plaintiffs—will suffer loss as a consequence of their negligence.

Their Honours relied extensively on the reasoning of Lord Devlin in *Hedley Byrne v Heller*; Stephen J (at 558) interpreted his Lordship's decision as standing for the principle that 'purely economic loss will be recoverable if there is sufficient proximity between the parties to give rise to a special duty relationship'. His Honour explained (at 573) that 'the need, in cases of purely economic loss, for some further control of liability apart from that offered by the concept of reasonable foreseeability' arises because:

> in cases of physical injury to person or property, the concept has been given a very far-reaching operation, far more extensive than may be thought to have been conveyed by Lord Atkin's reference to that which one 'can reasonably foresee would be likely to injure' a person in the relationship of neighbour.

He added (at 574), that the control mechanism on liability, additional to the test of reasonable foreseeability should be:

> based upon notions of proximity between tortious act and resultant detriment ... Its precise nature and the extent to which it should restrict recovery for purely economic loss must depend upon policy considerations.

It was this notion of proximity that Deane J later developed in *Jaensch v Coffey* (1984) 155 CLR 549 and *Sutherland Shire Council v Heyman* (1985) 157 CLR 424 (discussed in Chapter 14).

In the *Caltex Oil* case, Stephen J referred (at 576) to a number of 'salient features' that together established a sufficient proximity to entitle the plaintiff to recover its reasonably foreseeable economic loss. These included knowledge of the pipelines and their inherent value and nature as productive equipment to the plaintiffs by the owners of the dredge. For, as his Honour observed, the defendants also knew, or had means of knowing, that the pipelines were connected with the plaintiff's refinery, 'leading to the quite obvious inference that their use was to convey refined products from the refinery to the terminal'.

The *Caltex Oil* test, which allows recovery in cases where the defendant has knowledge or the means of knowledge that a particular person, not merely as a member of an unascertained class, will be likely to suffer economic loss as a consequence of his negligence, was been criticised by the Privy Council as capricious and arbitrary in *Candelwood Navigation Corp v Mitsui Osk Lines (The Mineral Transporter)* [1986] AC 1. Nevertheless, in Australia, the *Caltex Oil* test has governed the existence of the duty of care in relation to pure economic loss in circumstances analogous to the facts in that case. For example, in *Minister for Environment and Planning v San Sebastian* (1983) 2 NSWLR 268, Hutley and Glass JJA in the Court of Appeal, New South Wales, relied on *Caltex Oil* when they concluded that the State Planning Authority and the Sydney City Council owed no duty of care to the plaintiff developers in respect of the financial loss the latter suffered, because at the time of preparing the proposals the defendants had no knowledge of the plaintiffs as specific individuals. The planning proposals were merely directed to a general class of developers—the plaintiffs being undifferentiated members of that general class.

More recently, in *Woolcock Street Investments Pty Ltd v CDG Pty Ltd* (2004) 216 CLR 515 (discussed below), Gleeson CJ, Gummow, Hayne, and Heydon JJ, in a joint judgment, interpreted *Caltex Oil* in terms of control and vulnerability. Their Honours noted (at [24]):

> the reference in *Caltex Oil* to economic loss being 'inherently likely' can also be seen as consistent with the importance of notions of vulnerability.

The defendants knew—or should have known—of the pipeline, and were in control of the dredging operations.

Pure economic loss occasioned by negligent supply of a defective product

In *Perre v Apand Pty Ltd* (1999) 198 CLR 180, the defendant, Apand Pty Ltd, had negligently supplied experimental seed potatoes to a farmer in South Australia for a trial planting. The seed was infected, and introduced a bacterial wilt disease onto the farmer's land. The plaintiffs, the Perres, collectively owned, or had other interests in, land which was in the neighbourhood (within a 20 kilometre zone) of land directly affected by Apand's negligent conduct. They were growing potatoes for export to Western Australia. No property belonging to, or used by, the Perres suffered any physical harm. However, they suffered financial harm through the loss of the Western Australian market, because Western Australian regulations imposed a five-year prohibition on the importation into that State of potatoes not only grown on land known to be affected by the disease, but also of those grown on land within 20 kilometres of the affected land.

The trial judge found that Apand had never heard of the particular plaintiff companies and their operations, but was aware that some farmers in the area supplied potatoes to Western Australian. The issue before the High Court was whether Apand owed a duty of care to the Perres in relation to pure economic loss, in the circumstances where Apand knew:

- the risks associated with bacterial wilt;
- the vulnerability of potato growers to the effects of the disease; and
- the regulations governing access to the Western Australian potato market and the exports of potatoes from South Australia.

The majority held that Apand knew of the special requirements of the Western Australian law with respect to the importation of potatoes grown in the adjoining areas to those where there was an outbreak of the disease. Apand also knew, or ought to have known, that farmers like the Perres grew commercial potato crops within a 20 kilometre radius. The majority held that the defendant owed a duty of care to all claimants. McHugh J limited the duty to the claimants who grew potatoes for the Western Australian market (Warruga), or owned land on which they were grown; and Hayne J determined that the duty was owed to plaintiffs who grew potatoes for direct sale into the Western Australian market and those who processed such potatoes.

Each of the seven judges in *Perre* approached the issue of duty in a different way. In the process, McHugh J was critical of Gaudron J's approach; Gummow J was not persuaded by the reasoning of either McHugh J or Gleeson CJ; while McHugh and Hayne JJ were opposed to the methodology for establishing the duty of care proposed by Kirby J. However, it seems that the common thread in reasoning present in *Burnie Port Authority v General Jones Pty Ltd* (1994) 179 CLR 520 and *Pyrenees Shire Council v Day & Ors* (1998) 192 CLR 330 (discussed in Chapter 14) relating to control, knowledge, and vulnerability as factors in determining the existence of duty of care, was generally followed. The question whether Apand owed a duty of care to the Perres in relation to pure economic loss was decided by focusing on Apand's knowledge and the Perres' vulnerability. The court found that at the time when it supplied the seed for the trial, Apand knew of:

- the risks associated with bacterial wilt;
- the vulnerability of potato growers to the effects of the disease;
- the Western Australia market, which was lucrative for South Australian potato growers;
- the Western Australian law with respect to the importation of potatoes grown in the adjoining areas to those where there was an outbreak of the disease; and
- the vulnerability of the class of potato growers within the 20 kilometre zone to pure economic loss.

Thus, Apand could reasonably have foreseen that potato growers within the 20 kilometre buffer zone would be adversely affected by contamination of potatoes on one of its client's farms. In contrast, the Perres had no way of appreciating the existence of the risk to which they were exposed by the trial of the seed, and had no means of protecting themselves against such risk.

Dovuro Pty Ltd v Wilkins (2003) 215 CLR 317 also concerned a claim for pure economic loss against seed suppliers. Dovuro Pty Ltd, a distributor of canola seed produced in New Zealand, was aware that the seed packages contained small quantities of weeds, which at the time of the importation were not prohibited under either federal or State legislation. However, a month after the plaintiffs bought and planted one tonne of the seed, the Western Australian Government declared the weeds a prohibited species. The plaintiffs did not suffer any actual harm to the crop, or their land. Their financial loss resulted from the fact that the declaration required them to take certain precautionary measures. The plaintiffs were an ascertainable and limited class of purchasers of the seeds. As such, they were owed a duty of care to avoid causing pure economic loss. In issue was whether Dovuro breached that duty. The majority—McHugh, Gummow, Hayne, Callinan, and Heydon JJ (Gleeson CJ and Kirby J dissenting)—held that Dovuro did not breach a duty of care for pure economic loss because at the time the seed was imported and sold in Western Australia, the weed was not known to be harmful, and it had not been prohibited.[16] Hence it was not reasonably foreseeable that buyers of the seed would suffer economic damage due to a subsequent decision to declare the weed a prohibited plant.

Defective buildings occasioning pure economic loss

As a general rule, concerns relating to indeterminate number and quantum of claims do not apply to pure economic loss (loss of value) consequent upon negligently constructed buildings. Both the class of potential purchasers and the diminution in the value of a defective property can readily be foreseen by the original builder or developer. In *Sutherland Shire Council v Heyman*, for example, there was just one claimant who bought a defective house and as a result suffered loss in the value of his asset.

These factors were considered by the High Court in *Bryan v Maloney* (1995) 182 CLR 609. Mrs Maloney was the third owner of a defective house. She sued the builder of the house for pure economic loss in the form of money expended on repairs to the foundations, the inadequacy of which became apparent through cracks in the wall.[17] The cracks appeared when the house was seven years old, and the repairs to the footings were intended to prevent future damage. Mrs Maloney's

---

16. McHugh J and Gummow J applied the calculus of negligence (*Wyong Shire Council v Shirt* (1980) 146 CLR 40 at 47).
17. The contract between the builder and the original owner of the house was 'non-detailed'—it did not contain exclusion or limitation of liability. This meant that there was an implied warranty of the house being free of defects. This warranty passed on to the subsequent purchasers: *Bryan v Maloney* (1995) 182 CLR 609 at 622.

damages were assessed by the trial judge at $34 440, representing the cost of underpinning the footings and repairing the cracks.

This financial outlay (like that in *Sutherland Shire Council v Heyman*, discussed in Chapter 14), was regarded as pure economic loss because the defects made the affected buildings less valuable, without posing physical danger to person or property. Had the owners waited until the defects caused an injury, the repair expense would have been considered specific damage recoverable under the *Donoghue v Stevenson* principles. This is because the law of torts is reactive rather than proactive: it offers remedies once injury has accrued or crystallised into an enforceable claim. At that point, the law may provide compensation—or, sometimes, injunctive relief to prevent repetition of the injury-causing conduct. However, it is very rare for torts law to act prophylactically to prevent potential risks of injury from developing. This was one of the arguments in Brennan J's dissenting judgment in *Bryan v Maloney*. Having distinguished between defects that pose physical danger to person or property and defects that affect the quality of construction occasioning mere economic loss, his Honour reasoned that, unless the faults are physically dangerous, a defectively constructed house should be placed in the same category as defectively manufactured products.

The majority in *Bryan v Maloney* held, however, that the duty owed by the builder of a dwelling house to the original owner may be owed to subsequent purchasers who equally rely on his skill to protect them from reasonably foreseeable decreases in value resulting from latent defects in the house. Mason CJ, Deane and Gaudron JJ in a joint judgment noted (at 618) that 'the field of liability for mere economic loss is a comparatively new and developing area of the law of negligence'. Therefore, to recover damages, the plaintiff had to establish a 'special' requisite relationship of proximity between the parties—which in this case involved an assumption of responsibility by the builder and known reliance on the builder's expertise and care by the building owner. This, according to the joint judgment (at 624), was sufficient to satisfy the requirement of causal proximity between the two parties, and the consequent duty of care in respect of pure economic loss. While the notion of special requirement of causal proximity has since been abandoned, such factors as assumption of responsibility and vulnerability are still considered essential to establishing liability for pure economic loss.

Bryan v Maloney, which involved a subsequent purchaser of a family residence, was interpreted by a number of appellate courts as holding that those who build or design commercial buildings do not owe any duty of care to subsequent purchasers.[18] However, in *Woolcock St Invest v CDG Pty Ltd* (2004) 216 CLR 515, Gleeson CJ, Gummow, Hayne, and Heydon JJ in a joint judgment (at [17]) stated that without

---

18. *Fangrove Pty Ltd v Todd Group Holdings Pty Ltd* [1999] 2 Qd R 236; *Woollahra Municipal Council v Sved* (1996) 40 NSWLR 101; *Zumpano v Montagnese* (1997) 2 VR 525; *Woolcock St Investments* [2002] Aust Torts Reports ¶81–660.

the 'overriding requirement of a relationship of proximity', 'it may be doubted that the decision in *Bryan v Maloney* should be understood as depending upon drawing a bright line between cases concerning the construction of dwellings and cases concerning the construction of other buildings'. Their Honours noted that:

> some buildings are used for mixed purposes: shop and dwelling; dwelling and commercial art gallery; general practitioner's surgery and residence. Some high-rise apartment blocks are built in ways not very different from high-rise office towers. The original owner of a high-rise apartment block may be a large commercial enterprise. The list of difficulties in distinguishing between dwellings and other buildings could be extended.

Vulnerability

According to Gleeson CJ, Gummow, Hayne, and Heydon JJ (at [23]), the better approach is to focus on the element of vulnerability. When applied to the facts in *Woolcock Street Investments*, their Honours concluded that the claimant was not vulnerable to the economic consequences of any negligence of the engineers in their design of the foundations for the building. For, although it was established that Woolcock Street Investments had bought the building not knowing that the foundations were inadequate, the company was unable to establish that the defects could not have been discovered at the time of purchase (at [32]). For example, the company sought and obtained from the relevant local authority a certificate that the building complied with the *Building Act 1975* (Qld) and some subordinate legislation. But it could have also undertaken other investigations. Moreover, as McHugh J, in a separate concurring judgment, pointed out (at [94]–[96]): 'The first owners and subsequent purchasers of commercial premises are usually sophisticated and often wealthy investors who are advised by competent solicitors, accountants, architects, engineers and valuers'. The company could have protected itself against the pure economic loss by incorporating appropriate clauses into the contract of purchase.

McHugh J said (at [80]) that: 'the purchaser's vulnerability to economic loss is the critical issue in determining whether those involved in the construction of commercial premises owe a duty of care to the purchaser'. His Honour found that the company did not establish the requirement of vulnerability, and (at [114]) arrived at the following conclusion:

> The failure of Woolcock Street Investments to take reasonable steps that were open to it is not a ground for holding that the respondents owed it a duty to take care in respect of pure economic losses arising from the defects in the foundations of the building. No doubt if Woolcock had insisted on contractual protection from its vendor, it may have had to pay a higher price for the building. But that only shows that, in this area, contract rather than tort is a better, more just and probably more efficient way of dealing with the problem of pure economic

losses arising from defective construction. The price of a commercial building almost invariably reflects the inherent and other risks—including the risk of latent defects—of buying the building.

It appears that in cases of pure economic loss, the High Court is taking an incremental approach to the particular circumstances. It is yet to develop general principles or tests to govern this area of the law. The requirements and factors considered relevant to recovery include:

- the defendant's knowledge or means of knowledge of the plaintiff as a specific individual or member of a specific class as opposed to a member of an unascertained class;
- control by the defendant in terms of knowledge and conduct;
- vulnerability of the plaintiff to pure economic loss;
- policy factors generally; and
- where relevant, the interposition of a contract of sale between the party to whom the defendant owed a duty of care and the plaintiff; particularly where the relevant damage is not latent.[19]

FURTHER READING

Baron A, 'The "Mystery" of Negligence and Economic Loss: When is a Duty of Care Owed?' (2000) 19 *Australian Bar Review* 167.

Cane P, 'The Blight of Economic Loss: Is There Life After *Perre v Apand*?' (2000) 8 *Torts Law Journal* 246.

Erbacher S, 'Builders' Liability for the Negligent Construction of Dwelling Houses: The Tort-Contract Demarcation Dispute' (1996) *University of Tasmania Law Review* 105–130.

Katter NA, '"Ball Park" Figures and the Ambit of Duty of Care for Negligent Misstatement' (2001) 75 *The Australian Law Journal* 427.

Lobban M, 'Nineteenth Century Frauds in Company Formation: Derry v Peek in Context' (1996) 112 *Law Quarterly Review* 287–334.

Stapleton J, 'Duty of Care and Economic Loss: A Wider Agenda' (1991) 107 *The Law Quarterly Review* 249–297.

Stapleton J, 'Comparative Economic Loss: Lessons from Case-law-focused "Middle Theory"' (2002) 50 *University of California Los Angeles Law Review* 531.

Warne S, 'Legal Professional Liability: Part 1' (2000) 8 *Torts Law Journal* 283.

---

19. *Seas Sapfor v Electricity Trust of South Australia* (unreported, Full Court of the Supreme Court of South Australia, 9 August 1996).

Defences to Negligence

INTRODUCTION

Once the plaintiff establishes prima facie negligence, the burden of proof shifts to the defendant, who will usually seek to raise common law and statutory defences to negligence.

The notion that 'if anyone incurs loss, which is his own fault, he is not regarded as incurring loss', goes back to the dictum of the classical Roman jurist, Sextus Pomponius: *'quod quis ex culpa sua damnum sentit, non intelligitur damnum sentire'* (D 50.17.203).[1] In Roman law, the dictum and its variations[2] was the basis for the plea of contributory negligence in delictual actions under *lex Aquilia* and analogous actions.[3] These actions allowed owners to sue for financial loss (*damnum*) when their property, including slaves, was damaged or destroyed by a third party. If the plaintiff's slave was killed through failure to take care for his own safety, the cause of death would be attributed to the slave's own fault, and the complete defence of contributory negligence would apply—the slave's owner could not recover damages. However, whenever the killing of the slave was deliberate, the *Aquilian* action for damages would lie, irrespective of the slave's contributory negligence.[4]

At common law, the rule was adopted in relation to plaintiffs suing defendants for their own personal injuries. From an economic or Roman law perspective, it is

---

1. *The Digest of Justinian* (Watson A, trans, ed) University of Pennsylvania Press, Philadelphia, 1998, Vol 2.
2. See, for example: Ulpian, referring to a slave whose throat was cut, by jerking of the razor when the barber's hand was knocked: '... if someone entrust himself to a barber who has his chair in a dangerous place he has only himself to blame for his misfortune': *The Digest of Justinian*, ibid, D.0.2.11.
3. *Lex Aquilia* was a *plebiscite*, which was eventually incorporated into *Corpus Juris Civilis*. The statute contained three chapters. Chapters I and III dealt with remedies for wrongfully caused *(damnum iniuria datum)* financial loss and damage to property. Chapter II, which became obsolete after the beginning of the second century CE, provided a remedy for stipulators who were victims of fraud. For a discussion of the origins and nature of *lex Aquilia*, see: Zimmerman R, *The Law of Obligations*, Clarendon Press, Oxford, 1996, pp 955–957.
4. *The Digest of Justinian*, above n 1, D.9.2.9.4.

arguable that defendants should only pay for the loss that is directly attributable to their wrongful conduct. Loss attributable to injuries occasioned by the plaintiff's own negligence should be borne by him or her alone. However, while this approach makes sense in the context of unintentionally occasioned economic loss, its application to the tort of negligence in relation to personal injuries is more problematic. For, before the defences of contributory negligence and voluntary assumption of risk become relevant, the defendant's breach of duty of care, causation and remoteness of damage would have been established on the balance of probabilities. Moreover, although a denial or reduction of damages to reflect the plaintiff's contribution to his or her injury is in harmony with the deterrence aspects of the tort, it is less compatible with the needs-based theory of compensation. Denial or apportionment of damages for contributory negligence or voluntary assumption of risk in effect punishes the wrongfully injured person by denying him or her compensation, or a portion thereof, for loss manifested by the needs that would not otherwise exist.[5] Yet the needs that stem from physical and psychiatric disabilities created by a wrongfully inflicted injury are not diminished by the fact that the plaintiff failed to take care for his or her safety.

Ultimately, in our society the cost of injuries—whether wrongfully occasioned by defendants or by plaintiffs—is borne by the community. In jurisdictions which do not operate no-fault work and motor vehicle compensation schemes,[6] if the plaintiffs are successful, the ratepayers fund the payouts by councils; and contributors to insurance and professional indemnity funds pay for damages awards through higher premiums. When injured plaintiffs are unsuccessful, or their damages are reduced for contributory negligence, they usually have to rely on taxpayer-funded medical and social security benefit schemes. The lives of these people, already blighted by the injury, are often made harsher by poverty and the lack of proper nursing care, the unwelcome companion of disability. It is with these considerations in mind that judges make decisions in relation to defences of contributory negligence, voluntary assumption of risk, and illegality.

This approach, in turn, leads to other questions—including whether the role of torts law should be confined to fair resolution of disputes in accordance with legal rules, or whether it should also exercise the political and social function of providing a social and medical safety net irrespective of fault.

---

5. The contributory negligence defence only becomes relevant after the defendant's duty, breach, causation and remoteness of damage have been established on the balance of probabilities.
6. In Victoria, the no-fault compensation schemes for workplace and transport accidents—the *Transport Accident Act 1986* (Vic), *Accident Compensation Act 1985* (Vic) and *Accident Compensation (WorkCover Insurance) Act 1993* (Vic)—have been in operation for twenty years. They have provided benefits, support and rehabilitation for injured claimants without any discernible negative impact on the financial viability of the State of Victoria.

HISTORICAL BACKGROUND

The common law origins of defences of contributory negligence and voluntary assumption of risk go back to the fourteenth century and the imposition of strict liability of common innkeepers. For example, in a 1372 case, an Aylesbury innkeeper successfully established that having told the plaintiff about the ruinous state of the inn (and that it was not a common inn), he refused to lodge him unless the plaintiff accepted the risk.[7] In another case, from 1374, the defendant innkeeper pleaded both assumption of risk by a plaintiff whose horse had been stolen while he was lodging at the inn, and what today would be called contributory negligence. The defendant claimed that he informed the plaintiff about the incomplete inclosure of the inn, and made him assume the risk. He also gave the plaintiff a room with a key. The plaintiff and his horse stayed in the room, but the plaintiff neglected to lock the door. The defendant was successful on the legal point, but lost on the facts before the jury.[8]

However, it was only at the end of the eighteenth century and the beginning of the nineteenth, as the courts were developing the tort of negligence, that they also fashioned defences to this action. The first recorded case of an employee seeking compensation from his employer in negligence was *Priestly v Fowler* (1837) 3 M & W 1. In this case, the judiciary also created the doctrine of common employment.

In *Priestly v Fowler*, the plaintiff, who was employed by the defendant as a butcher, was injured by the collapse of the defendant's goods wagon. The wagon collapsed when the defendant's apprentices negligently overloaded the van with mutton. At the trial at Assizes before Park J, the jury returned a verdict of £100 (equivalent to several years' wages) for the employee. However, on appeal to the Court of Exchequer, the jury's verdict was overturned. Abinger CB held that the contract of employment between the plaintiff and his employer contained an implied term that the employee would not hold his employer liable for an injury due to the negligence of a fellow servant. The Chief Baron observed (at 308) that allowing this action 'would be an encouragement to the servant to omit that diligence and caution which he is in duty bound to exercise on behalf of his master', and which offers much better protection against injuries 'than any recourse against his master for damages could possibly afford'.[9]

---

7. Discussed in Palmer RC, *English Law in the Age of the Black Death 1348–1381*, The University of North Carolina Press, Chapel Hill and London, 1993, p 258. According to the custom of England, while common inns were under a duty to receive travellers, they also had the corresponding privilege of lien and obligation to insure the safety of the guest's goods. See: *Daniel v Hotel Pacific* [1953] ALR 1043, Sholl J's judgment.
8. Id.
9. For a discussion of this case see: Stein MA, '*Priestly v Fowler* (1837) and the Emerging Tort of Negligence' (2003) 44 *Boston College L Rev* 689.

In the first part of the nineteenth century, propelled by the use of steam engine power, rapid and unbridled industrialisation contributed to the growing rate of tragic accidents on the highways, the railways, in unsafe factories, and in the mines. In 1815, Robert Dale Owen toured some of the largest factories of Great Britain with his father. In his 1854 book *Threading My Way* (p 102), he recalled that 'in some large factories from one-fourth to one-fifth of the children were either cripples or otherwise deformed, or permanently injured by excessive toil, sometimes by brutal abuse.'[10] In some industries, such as the cotton mills, the rate of injury among the child labourers through loss of fingers, crushing, or severe laceration of hands may have exceeded 50 per cent of those employed. According to Friedrich Engels, in 1843 the Manchester Infirmary treated 2426 cases of accidental injury, of which 962 were caused by machinery. This amounted to a serious accident rate of approximately 2.5 per cent per annum.[11]

Yet, as *Priestly v Fowler* illustrates, very few injured workers recovered damages in negligence against employers. There were both social and legal impediments to compensation for negligently occasioned harm.

The position of the law underlying the development of negligence in the nineteenth century was well summarised by John Fleming[12] when he said:

> At this crucial stage of social and economic transformation, the courts responded to the call for a new pattern of loss adjustment by fastening on the concept of negligence. The axiom 'no liability without fault' was quickly raised to a dogmatic postulate of justice, because it was best calculated to serve the interests of expanding industry and the entrepreneurial class, in relieving them from the hampering burden of strict (merely causal) liability and conducing to that freedom of individual will and enterprise which was at the forefront of contemporary aspirations.

Prevailing community standards set by courts favoured employers. Very few workers could afford expensive litigation. Peter WJ Bartrip and Sandra B Burman in *The Wounded Soldiers of Industry*[13] write that although actions *in forma pauperis*—whereby poor plaintiffs received free legal counsel in all courts of record—had been available since 1495, the procedure was so difficult that in the twenty-three years from 1859 to 1882, total applications averaged less than five per year. According to Bartrip and Burman,[14] by the 1880s there had developed a black market in legal aid, whereby trade societies, for example, would conduct cases on a commission basis, payment being a proportion of the amount recovered. There was sometimes

---

10. Quoted in Bartrip PWJ & Burman SB, *The Wounded Soldiers of Industry*, Clarendon Press, Oxford, 1983, p 9.
11. Id, pp 10, 13.
12. Fleming J, *The Law of Torts*, 9th edn, Sydney, The Law Book Company Ltd, 1998, at 114.
13. Bartrip PWJ & Burman SB, *The Wounded Soldiers of Industry*, Clarendon Press, Oxford, 1983, p 26.
14. Id, p 27.

a requirement that the plaintiff undertake to pay back money spent on the case—a precursor to modern contingency fees. Despite attempts by the Law Society in England to stamp out such practices, some solicitors also adopted this system.[15] It was only in the 1890s that qualified professional advice became available as charity provided by solicitors and barristers who belonged to the Poor Man's Lawyers' Society.

However, by that time, largely in response to the reluctance of the common law to provide redress to injured workers, statutory Workers' Compensation Schemes were enacted, in particular, the *Workmen's Compensation Act 1897* (UK), which replaced the more limited *Employers' Liability Act 1880*. Originally, only workers in dangerous occupations—coal miners, factory employees, and railway construction workers—came within statutory protection. Eventually, however, when a substantially revised Act was re-enacted in 1906, it extended to all workers. By the end of the first decade of the twentieth century, similar legislation had been enacted in almost all Australian States.[16]

Many nineteenth-century English parliamentarians, such as Lord Ashley, realised that even if an injured worker got to court, the odds were against the plaintiff. The judges made sure of it. Three defences, known as the 'unholy Trinity', originally supplemented the two major elements of the negligence designed to limit defendants' liability—duty of care and remoteness of damage. These defences were:

- the doctrine of common employment;
- contributory negligence; and
- the doctrine of voluntary assumption of risk.

The defence of common employment, which absolved the employer of legal responsibility if the employee's injury was due to the careless conduct of another employee, was abolished by the United Kingdom Parliament in the *Employer's Liability Act 1880* 43 & 44 Vict, c 42. The legislation was enacted in the face of fierce judicial opposition.[17] In 1897, in the House of Commons during a debate on workers' compensation, the Secretary for Ireland would observe that the doctrine of common employment was planted by Lord Abinger CB in *Priestly v Fowler*, 'Baron Alderson watered it, and the Devil gave it increase'.[18] The other two defences, however, survive, though in modified form. These defences and that of illegality are discussed below.

---

15. Abel-Smith B & Stevens R, *Lawyers and the Courts. A Sociological Study of the English Legal System*, Heinemann, London, 1967, pp 138–139, referring to (1883) 28 *The Law Journal* 384; quoted in Bartrip PWJ & Burman SB, *The Wounded Soldiers of Industry*, Clarendon Press, Oxford, 1983, pp 26–27.
16. Hill EF & Bingeman JB, *Principles of the Law of Workers Compensation*, The Law Book Company Ltd, Sydney, 1981.
17. Bartrip PWJ & Burman SB, *The Wounded Soldiers of Industry*, op cit, p 197.
18. Friedman LM & Ladinsky J, 'Social Change and the Law of Industrial Accidents' (1967) 67 *Columbia Law Review* 50.

CONTRIBUTORY NEGLIGENCE

Evolution of the defence of contributory negligence

Butterfield v Forrester (1809) 11 East 60; 103 ER 926 was the first recorded case in which a successful plea of contributory negligence defeated the plaintiff's claim entirely. In this case, the defendant wrongly obstructed a road by placing a pole across it. The plaintiff, who was riding 'violently' on the road in the dusk, did not see the pole, and his horse ran into it. He was thrown off and injured. The evidence established that the pole was visible from 100 yards away. Bayley J (at 61) found for the defendant, saying that 'If he [the plaintiff] had used ordinary care he must have seen the obstruction; so that the accident appeared to happen entirely from his own fault.' Parke B of the Court of Exchequer in *Bridge v Grand Junction Railway Company* (1838) 3 M & W 244 adopted this rule, and expressed it (at 248) in terms of standard of care:

> although there may have been negligence on the part of the plaintiff, yet *unless* he might, by the exercise of ordinary care, have avoided the consequences of the defendant's negligence, he is entitled to recover; if by ordinary care he might have avoided them, he is the author of his own wrong.

In *Tuff v Warman* (1858) 5 CBNS 573, the courts determined that the plaintiff's failure to take care should be the cause of his or her harm. In that case, Wightman J (at 585) articulated the rule of contributory negligence thus:

> It appears to us that the proper question for the jury in this case, and indeed others of the like kind, is, whether the damage was occasioned entirely by the negligence or improper conduct of the defendant, or whether the plaintiff himself so far contributed to the misfortune by his own negligence or want of ordinary and common care and caution, that, but for such negligence or want of ordinary care and caution on his part, the misfortune would not have happened. In the first place the plaintiff would be entitled to recover, in the latter not; as, but for his own fault, the misfortune would not have happened. Mere negligence or want of caution would not, however, disentitle him to recover, unless it were such, that, but for that negligence or want of ordinary care the misfortune *could* [also reported as *would*] not have happened (emphasis added).

The problem with this rule was its vagueness about the requisite standard of negligence or 'want of ordinary care'. Soon, even the slightest negligence on the part of the injured person, if directly or proximately connected with or contributory to the accident, would disentitle the plaintiff from recovery (*Dowell v General Steam Navigation Co* (1855) 5 E & B 195).

To ameliorate the harshness of this defence, the courts created the doctrine of 'last opportunity', under which the plaintiff could recover if, notwithstanding his own negligence, the defendant could have avoided injuring him by taking reasonable care. For example, in *Davies v Mann* (1842) 10 M & W 546; 152 ER 588, the defendant, driving a wagon at 'a smartish pace' (faster than he ought to have done), ran down the plaintiff's donkey, whose forefeet the plaintiff had illegally fettered before leaving it on the highway. Though both parties were at fault, the court found no contributory negligence, because the animal was in full view of the defendant, who had the 'last opportunity' to avoid the accident but failed to do so. The doctrine of 'last opportunity' precluded the use of the defence of contributory negligence in relation to intentional torts, for in these cases, tortfeasors would invariably have the last say on whether or not to take advantage of the plaintiff's negligence.

Lindley LJ in *The Bernina (No 2)*; *Mills v Armstrong* (1887) 12 PD 58,[19] at 89, summarised the nineteenth-century law of contributory negligence as follows:

[If:]
(1) A without fault of his own is injured by the negligence of B, then B is liable to A.
(2) A by his own fault is injured by B without fault on his part, then B is not liable to A.
(3) A is injured by B by the fault more or less of both combined, then the following further distinctions have to be made:
   (a) if, notwithstanding B's negligence, A with reasonable care could have avoided the injury, he cannot sue B: *Butterfield v Forrester* [1809] 11 East 60; *Bridge v Grand Junction Railway Company* [1838] 3 M & W 244; *Dowell v General Steam Navigation Company* [1855] 5 E & B 195;
   (b) if, notwithstanding A's negligence, B with reasonable care could have avoided injuring A, A can sue B: *Tuff v Warman*, 5 CB (NS) 573; *Radley v London and North Western Railway Company* [1876] 1 App Cas 754; *Davies v Mann* [1842] 10 M & W 546;
   (c) if there has been as much want of reasonable care on A's part as on B's, or, in other words, if the proximate cause of the injury is the want of reasonable care on both sides, A cannot sue B. In such a case A cannot with truth say that he has been injured by B's negligence, he can only with truth say that he has been injured by his own carelessness and B's negligence, and the two combined give no cause of action at common law. This follows from the two sets of decisions already referred to. But why in such a case the damages should not be apportioned, I do not profess to understand. However, as already stated, the law on this point is settled and not open to judicial discussion.

---

19. The case arose out of a collision in 1884 between the steamships *Bushire* and *Bernina*, caused by the negligence of both masters. As a result, Mr Armstrong and three other persons were drowned.

The law was indeed settled—for, as the Law Revision Committee in its *Report on Contributory Negligence* (Cmd 6032, June 1939) explained (p 4),[20] the origins of the rule that contributory negligence was a complete defence:

> are to be found in the historical development of the English Law. Until comparatively recent times the question which arose when a plaintiff sued a defendant was not 'Has the defendant broken any duty which he owed to the plaintiff?' but 'Has the plaintiff any form of action against the defendant, and if so what form?'. Most forms of action in tort began in trespass and developed through trespass on the case and an action on the case. To such a writ the proper plea in the defence was 'not guilty'. Under such a plea the defendant must be found guilty or not guilty; it was not possible for him to be partly guilty and partly not guilty, and therefore there was no method by which liability could be divided between plaintiff and defendant. It was all or nothing—the plaintiff must wholly succeed or wholly fail.

Apportionment legislation

The 1939 Report recommended apportionment in cases of contributory negligence. However, the Second World War intervened, and it was only in 1945 that the English Parliament enacted the *Law Reform (Contributory Negligence) Act 1945*, s 1, which overcame the common law rule by providing that:

> (1) Where any person suffers damage as the result partly of his own fault and partly of the fault of any other person or persons, a claim in respect of that damage shall not be defeated by reason of the fault of the person suffering the damage, but the damages recoverable in respect thereof shall be reduced to such extent as the court thinks just and equitable having regard to the claimant's share in the responsibility for the damage ...

Persons injured partly through their own negligence can still recover, though the quantum of damages will be reduced. The English provisions were adopted in the late 1940s and mid-1950s in New Zealand[21] and in most Australian jurisdictions.[22] New South Wales, however, retained contributory negligence as a complete defence until 1965, which meant that the courts in that jurisdiction used every possible argument and creative doctrine to find injured plaintiffs not guilty of contributory

---

20. For a full discussion in the context of contributory negligence in deceit, see: *Standard Chartered Bank v Pakistan National Shipping Corporation, Seaways Maritime Limited, SGS United Kingdom Limited, Oakprime International Limited, Arvind Mehra* [2000] 3 WLR 1692 at [49]–[56], per Aldous LJ.
21. *Contributory Negligence Act 1947* (NZ).
22. *Wrongs (Contributory Negligence) Act 1951* (Vic); *Law Reform (Tortfeasors Contribution, Contributory Negligence and Division of Chattels) Act 1952* (Qld); *Law Reform (Miscellaneous Provisions) Act 1965* (NSW); *Tortfeasors and Contributory Negligence Act 1954* (Tas), s 4; *Law Reform (Miscellaneous Provisions) Act 1955* (ACT); *Law Reform (Miscellaneous Provisions) Act 1955* (NT).

negligence.[23] The wording of the Western Australian *Law Reform (Contributory Negligence and Tortfeasors' Contribution) Act 1947*, s 4, is different from that of other jurisdictions. It incorporates the 'last opportunity' doctrine,[24] and, thus refers to the plaintiff's contributory negligence in relation to 'the happening of the event which caused the damage' rather than 'the claimant's share in the responsibility for the damage'. This difference in formulation used to have significant implications for deciding causation in contributory negligence.[25] However, in *Motor Vehicle Insurance Trust v Wilson* [1976] WAR 175, the Full Court of the Western Australian Supreme Court determined that failure to take precautions to lessen injury may amount to contributory negligence[26]—thus aligning the common law in Western Australia with the rest of the Australian jurisdictions.

As noted above in the introduction to this chapter, according to the High Court in *Griffiths v Kerkemeyer* (1977) 139 CLR 161 (discussed in Chapter 2), the modern justification of the defence of contributory negligence is that the tortfeasor must pay compensation for any economic and non-economic loss created by his or her wrongful conduct. Conversely, where the economic and non-economic loss caused by injury or death is not attributable to the defendant's wrongful conduct, it should not be compensable in tort.

'Apportionment of 100 per cent'

As part of the Torts reforms, four jurisdictions have overcome the common law rule preventing an apportionment of 100 per cent responsibility to one party. The common law approach was articulated in *Wynbergen v The Hoyts Corporation Pty Ltd* (1997) 149 ALR 25, at 29, by Hayne J who, speaking for the court (Gaudron, McHugh, Gummow and Kirby JJ agreeing), said that once causation was established whereby the cause of the plaintiff's injury was attributed to the defendant's negligence, the apportionment legislation did not permit the exclusion of defendant's responsibility on the basis of contributory negligence. His Honour noted that:

> There may be cases in which a defendant may be shown to have failed to exercise reasonable care for the plaintiff, but the plaintiff is, in all the circumstances, judged

---

23. See: Mason J's discussion of this issue in *March v E & MH Stramare Pty Ltd* (1991) 171 CLR 506.
24. *Law Reform (Contributory Negligence and Tortfeasors' Contribution) Act 1947*, s 4(1): 'Whenever in any claim for damages founded on an allegation of negligence the Court is satisfied that the defendant was guilty of an act of negligence conducing to the happening of the event which caused the damage then notwithstanding that the plaintiff had the last opportunity of avoiding or could by the exercise of reasonable care, have avoided the consequences of the defendant's act or might otherwise be held guilty of contributory negligence, the defendant shall not for that reason be entitled to judgment, but the Court shall reduce the damages which would be recoverable by the plaintiff if the happening of the event which caused the damage had been solely due to the negligence of the defendant to such extent as the Court thinks just in accordance with the degree of negligence attributable to the plaintiff.'
25. *Taggart v Rose* [1975] WAR 41.
26. *Richards v Mills* (2003) 27 WAR 200 at [26].

to have been the sole author of the misfortune of which that plaintiff complains. But that is to conclude that the defendant's want of reasonable care was not a cause of the plaintiff's damage; it is to deny that the fault of both plaintiff and defendant contributed to that damage.

Nonetheless, New South Wales, Victoria, Queensland, and the Australian Capital Territory now provide, in identical terms, that contributory negligence can defeat a claim.[27] For example, by virtue of s 24 of the *Civil Liability Act 2003* (Qld):

> In deciding the extent of a reduction in damages by reason of contributory negligence, a court may decide a reduction of 100 per cent if the court considers it just and equitable to do so, with the result that the claim for damages is defeated.

Thus, the law has turned full circle, though the finding of the plaintiff's failure to care for his or her own safety would have to be such as to overwhelm the defendant's negligent contribution to the harm in issue and, as Hayne J pointed out, determine the issue of causation in the defendant's favour.

The scope of the defence

Contributory negligence is a legal defence and must be specifically raised by the defendant.[28] Apart from Western Australia[29] and (in part) South Australia (see below), all other jurisdictions retained the wording of s 1 of the *Law Reform (Contributory Negligence) Act 1945* (UK), except that instead of 'fault', the legislation refers to a 'wrong' or 'wrongful act'.[30] Thus, the *Civil Law (Wrongs) Act 2002* (ACT), s 101(1), provides that:

> If a person (the *claimant*) suffers damage partly because of the claimant's failure to take reasonable care (*contributory negligence*) and partly because of someone else's wrong—
> (a) a claim for the damage is not defeated because of the claimant's contributory negligence; and
> (b) the damages recoverable for the wrong are to be reduced to the extent the court deciding the claim considers just and equitable having regard to the claimant's share in the responsibility for the damage.

---

27. *Civil Liability Act 2002* (NSW), s 5S; *Civil Law (Wrongs) Act 2002* (ACT), s 47; *Wrongs Act 1958* (Vic), s 63.
28. Leave to amend pleadings will usually be granted when evidence discloses contributory negligence in the course of the proceedings: *Christie v Bridgestone Australia Pty Ltd* (1983) 33 SASR 177.
29. *Law Reform (Contributory Negligence and Tortfeasors' Contribution) Act 1947* (WA), s 4(1).
30. *Wrongs Act 1958* (Vic), s 26(1); *Law Reform (Miscellaneous Provisions) Act 1965* (NSW), s 9(1); *Law Reform Act 1995* (Qld), s 10(1); *Law Reform (Miscellaneous Provisions) Act 2001* (NT), s 16(1); *Civil Law (Wrongs) Act 2002* (ACT), s 102(1); *Wrongs Act 1954* (Tas), s 4: 'Where a person suffers damage as the result partly of that person's wrongful act …';. *Law Reform (Contributory Negligence and Apportionment of Liability) Act 2001* (SA), s 7(2): 'If a claimant's harm is caused partly by another's negligent wrongdoing negligent wrongdoing …'.

The term 'wrong' is defined as 'an act or omission' that:

(a) gives rise to a liability in tort in respect of which a defence of contributory negligence is available at common law; or
(b) amounts to a breach of a contractual duty of care that is concurrent and co-extensive with a duty of care in tort.[31]

The definition of 'wrong' confirms the applicability of the defence of contributory negligence to all torts (not just negligence), except those for which this defence is not available at common law. For example, in Victoria, in *Horkin v North Melbourne Football Club Social Club* [1983] 1 VR 153, Brooking J determined that at common law, contributory negligence was not a defence in an action for intentional battery;[32] therefore, given the wording of the provision, it was not a defence under the legislation.[33]

In South Australia, the *Law Reform (Contributory Negligence and Apportionment of Liability) Act 2001*, s 7(1), focuses on the causative nexus between contributory negligence and the harm: 'If contributory negligence contributes to (but is not the sole cause of) the harm for which a claimant seeks damages, the claim is not to be defeated on the ground of the contributory negligence'.

In Western Australia, s 4(3) of the *Law Reform (Contributory Negligence and Tortfeasors' Contribution) Act 1947* includes breach of statutory duty in its definition of 'negligence'. The Australian Capital Territory is the only jurisdiction that excludes contributory negligence as a defence to the action for breach of statutory duty.[34]

Following *Astley & Ors v Austrust Ltd* (1999) 197 CLR 1, in which the majority of the High Court determined that the defence of contributory negligence did not apply to claims founded on a breach of a contractual duty of care, all Australian jurisdictions enacted legislation to overcome this part of the decision. The statutory rule now provides that the apportionment legislation does not operate to defeat any defence arising under a contract.[35]

---

31. *Law Reform Act 1995* (Qld), s 5; *Wrongs Act 1958* (Vic), s 25(1); *Law Reform (Miscellaneous Provisions) Act 2001* (NT), s 15(1); *Civil Law (Wrongs) Act 2002* (ACT), ss 19, 101(1); *Law Reform (Miscellaneous Provisions) Act 1965* (NSW), s 8; *Civil Liability Act 1936* (SA), s 3: definition of negligence includes: 'failure to exercise reasonable care and skill, and includes a breach of a tortious, contractual or statutory duty of care'.
32. Luntz H & Hambly D, *Torts Cases and Commentary*, 5th edn, Butterworths, Sydney, 2002, p 761.
33. See also: *Harper v Ashtons Circus Pty Ltd* [1972] 2 NSWLR 395; *Australian Guarantee Corporation Ltd v Commissioners of State Bank of Victoria* (1989) VR 617; *Venning v Chin* (1974) 10 SASR 299; *Wilton v Commonwealth Trading Bank of Australia* [1973] 2 NSWLR 644.
34. *Civil Law (Wrongs) Act 2002* (ACT), s 102(2).
35. *Civil Law (Wrongs) Act 2002* (ACT), s 102(1)(a); *Law Reform (Miscellaneous Provisions) Act 2001* (NT), s 16(2); *Law Reform (Miscellaneous Provisions) Act 1965* (NSW), s 9(2); *Law Reform Act 1995* (Qld), s 10(2); *Wrongs Act 1954* (Tas), s 4(1)(a); *Wrongs Act 1958* (Vic), s 25(1A); *Law Reform (Contributory Negligence and Tortfeasors' Contribution) Act 1947* (WA), s 4(1)(a); *Civil Liability Act 1936* (SA), s 3: definition of negligence includes 'a breach of a tortious, contractual or statutory duty of care'.

Plaintiff's standard of care

To succeed in the plea of contributory negligence, the defendant must prove that the person who suffered harm has failed 'to exercise reasonable care and skill for his or her own protection, or for the protection of his or her own interests',[36] in circumstances where a reasonable person would have done so.

While determination of liability in negligence concentrates on the defendant's response to a foreseeable risk, the plaintiff's conduct is at the centre of the inquiry into contributory negligence. In *Astley & Ors v Austrust Ltd* (1999) 197 CLR 1,[37] Gleeson CJ, McHugh, Gummow, and Hayne JJ pointed out (at [29]–[30]) that:

> Contributory negligence focuses on the conduct of the plaintiff. The duty owed by the defendant, although relevant, is one only of the many factors that must be weighed in determining whether the plaintiff has so conducted itself that it failed to take reasonable care for the safety of its person or property.

Nevertheless, according to their Honours (at [29]–[30]), the scope of the defendant's duties and responsibilities will be critical to determining whether contributory negligence exists and, if so, to what degree. That said, when pleading the defence, defendants do not need to show that the plaintiff's conduct involved reasonably foreseeable risk of harm to anyone else. For the gist of the defence is that the plaintiffs failed to reasonably foresee the risk of injury to themselves, whereas defendants are charged with negligently failing to foresee an injury to others. These two objects of foreseeability are quite distinct. In particular, as a general rule, unlike harming others, self-harm or a failure to avoid self-harm is legally permissible, if not always morally approved, or socially costless. Consequently, under common law, the standard of care of a reasonable person in the injured plaintiff's circumstances was not expected to be as high as that of a reasonable person in the shoes of the defendant.[38]

Employer–employee relationship

The judiciary has been very conscious that the effect of contributory negligence, initially as a full defence and even under apportionment legislation, was particularly severe on employees injured in industrial accidents. In *Sungravure Pty Ltd v Meani* (1964) 110 CLR 24, the plaintiff, an employee at a printing works, was told by the factory foreman, some two hours before the accident, to apply manual pressure to steady the motion of a 'bumpy reel' of newsprint, which was being unwound on a

---

36. *Civil Liability Act 1936* (SA), s 3; see also: *Civil Liability Act 2002* (WA), s 5K(2).
37. *Astley & Ors v Austrust Ltd* (1999) 197 CLR 1. Please note that although the *Astley's* majority's finding on the issue of non-availability of contributory negligence in relation to a breach of contract has been legislatively reversed, a number of other formulations of principle in this case are valid as a precedent at common law.
38. *Pennington v Norris* (1956) 96 CLR 10 at 16.

spindle in a machine called a spider. The plaintiff was not given any instructions how to apply the manual pressure, so he devised his own method, which included placing his hand at the end of the reel. This method carried the risk that if his sleeve were caught by the reel, the momentum would be great enough to draw him between it and the spider. He momentarily lost concentration, the risk materialised, and his forearm was badly crushed. The defendant pleaded contributory negligence; however, the High Court described the plaintiff's conduct as mere inadvertence or thoughtlessness that did not necessarily constitute contributory negligence. Windeyer J referred with approval to Lord Wright's statement in *Caswell v Powell Duffryn Associated Collieries Ltd* [1940] AC 152, at 178–9, who said that:

> What is all important is to adopt the standard of what is negligence to the facts, and to give due regard to the actual conditions under which men work in the factory or mine, to the long hours and fatigue, to the slacking of attention, which naturally comes from the constant repetition of the same operation, to the noise and confusion in which the man works, to his preoccupation in what he is actually doing at the cost perhaps of some inattention to his own safety.

According to the High Court in *Smith v Broken Hill Pty Co Ltd* (1957) 97 CLR 337, at 342–3, and *Da Costa v Cockburn Salvage and Trading Pty Ltd* (1970) 124 CLR 192, at 218, in circumstances where work is repetitive and involves physical strain, the employer is required to anticipate possible inadvertence or carelessness by employees. Jacobs J in *Commissioner for Railways v Halley* (1978) 20 ALR 409, at 415, observed that:

> If an employee is required by the nature of his employment to expose himself to some dangers but not to others, the employee is not shown to be guilty of contributory negligence simply by exposing himself to a situation which he knew or ought to have known was dangerous, or even highly dangerous. It must also be shown that he knew or ought to have known that it was not expected of him that he would expose himself to that danger.

Jacobs J imposed on the employers a duty to warn employees of risks associated with their working environment, or the execution of their job. Mason, Wilson, Brennan, and Dawson JJ in *McLean v Tedman* (1984) 155 CLR 306 (discussed in Chapter 11) went further. Noting (at 311) that 'the standard of care expected of the reasonable man requires him to take account of the possibility of inadvertent and negligent conduct on the part of others', their Honours (at 312–13) extended the employers' duty to provide a safe system of work to encompass the risk of their employees being negligent:

> If there is a foreseeable risk of injury arising from the employee's *negligence* in carrying out his duties then this is a factor which the employer must take into account. [emphasis added]

When *McLean v Tedman* was applied in another industrial injury case, *Podrebersek v Australian Iron and Steel Pty Ltd* (1985) 59 ALR 529, the High Court (Gibbs CJ, Mason, Wilson, Brennan, and Deane JJ in a joint judgment) retreated somewhat from the extension of the employer's duty to guard against the risk of injuries sustained as a result of the employee's own negligence. Their Honours stated (at 531) that when the employer pleads contributory negligence, the question is whether in the particular circumstances and under the conditions in which the injured worker was required to work, his or her conduct 'amounted to mere inadvertence, inattention or misjudgment, or to negligence'. In *Czatyrko v Edith Cowan University* [2005] HCA 14 (discussed in Chapter 11), Gleeson CJ, McHugh, Hayne, Callinan, and Heydon JJ (at [12]) reiterated the rule that when devising safe methods of operation or providing adequate safeguards to eliminate real risks of injury in a workplace, the 'employer must take into account the possibility of thoughtlessness, or inadvertence, or carelessness' on part of the employees, particularly if they are engaged in repetitive work'. Although, in *Czatyrko*, the High Court referred to *McLean v Tedman* only indirectly,[39] it is the latter case that appears to set the standard for the scope of employers' duty of care in relation to employees' contributory negligence.

In *Liftronic Pty Limited v Unver* (2001) 179 ALR 321, the High Court reaffirmed the rule in *Commissioner for Railways v Halley*, holding that contributory negligence will be established if the evidence shows that the injury was caused by an act done against the employer's instructions, which were aimed at safeguarding the safety of the employee. In *Liftronic*, the plaintiff, a lift mechanic of seventeen years' experience, sustained an injury to his back when he did not comply with the defendant employer's system of work. The employer's system was designed to eliminate or minimise the physical effort of lifting heavy metal rails. Instead of doing what he was instructed to do, the plaintiff introduced his own, unauthorised, system. Within some ten minutes after adopting this new procedure, the plaintiff complained of severe pain and discomfort in his back. The main difference between using the employer's system and the method devised by the plaintiff was that the former required that the body be held straight, whereas the latter involved bending over and picking up rails.

The issue before the High Court involved the question of whether the New South Wales Court of Appeal erred in setting aside the jury's apportionment of fault. Gummow and Callinan JJ observed (at [60]) that the jury's:

---

39. Through a reference to Kirby J' statement in *Woods v Multi-Sport Holdings Pty Ltd* (2002) 208 CLR 460, at [128], that employers 'must warn employees of risks, taking into account possibilities of "inadvertence or carelessness" on the part of the employee'. Kirby J had cited *McLean v Tedman* (1984) 155 CLR 306, at 313, as the authority for this proposition. See also: Ashley J in *Victorian WorkCover Authority v Carrier Air Conditioning Pty Ltd* [2006] VSCA 63 at [10].

collective knowledge and experience of the workplace were unlikely to be inferior to those of judges. The different view of the majority of the Court of Appeal from the jury's view is probably indicative of too ready a judicial inclination to absolve people in the workplace from the duty that they have to look out for their own safety which will often depend more, or as much, upon their own prudence and compliance with directions, as upon any measures that a careful employer may introduce and seek to maintain.

Their Honours' comments were equally pertinent to the judicial attitudes, particularly by the lower-instance courts, towards the responsibilities of patients in doctor–patient relationships, and of inebriated drivers and so on.[40]

In the *Ipp Report*,[41] at [3.10] and [3.11], the Ipp Panel observed that on this point the judiciary was at odds with community values:

> there is in the Australian community today a widely-held expectation that, in general, people will take as much care for themselves as they expect others to take for them. This is an application of the fundamental idea that people should take responsibility for their own lives and safety, and it provides powerful support for the principle that the standard of care for negligence and contributory negligence should be the same.
>
> There is a perception (which may reflect the reality) that many lower courts are more indulgent to plaintiffs than to defendants. In some cases judges have expressly applied a lower standard of care for contributory negligence.[42] This may result, for example, in motorists being required to keep a better lookout than pedestrians. In the Panel's view, this approach should not be supported. ...

The members of the Panel (at [3.11] and [3.13]) concluded that:

> In the view of the Panel, a legislative statement setting out the approach to be followed in dealing with the issue of contributory negligence, emphasising that contributory negligence is to be measured against an objective standard of reasonable conduct, stating that the standard of care applicable to negligence and contributory negligence is the same, and establishing the negligence calculus as a suitable basis for considering contributory negligence, could discourage the tendency of courts to be overly indulgent to plaintiffs when apportioning damages for contributory negligence.

---

40. See, for example: *O'Shea v Sullivan* (1994) Aust Torts Reports ¶81–273; *Kalokerinos v Burnett* [1995] (unreported, New South Wales Court of Appeal, Kirby P, Clarke and Powell JJA, 1 November 1995).
41. Available at <http://revofneg.treasury.gov.au/content/review2.asp>.
42. *Commissioner of Railways v Ruprecht* (1979) 142 CLR 563 at 577–8, per Murphy J; *Cocks v Sheppard* (1979) 25 ALR 325; *Watt v Bretag* (1982) 56 ALJR 760; *Pollard v Ensor* [1969] SASR 57; *Evers v Bennett* (1982) 31 SASR 228.

Statutory reforms

What amounts to 'reasonable care' in safeguarding one's own interests is a question of fact: *Sibley v Kais* (1967) 118 CLR 424, at 427. In *Joslyn v Berryman* (2003) 214 CLR 552, McHugh J (at [35]), citing *Glasgow Corporation v Muir* [1943] AC 448 (at 457), emphasised both the objective nature of the test and the inherent similarity between the party's standard of care for the purpose of negligence and contributory negligence:

> Contributory negligence, like negligence, eliminates the personal equation and is independent of the idiosyncrasies of the particular person whose conduct is in question.

Tasmania, South Australia, New South Wales, Western Australia, Queensland, and Victoria have adopted the *Ipp Report's* Recommendation 3 and enacted legislation that directs courts to apply general principles relating to the breach of duty of care in the context of determining contributory negligence. The Tasmanian[43] and South Australian[44] provisions simply state that:

> The principles that are applicable in determining whether a person has been negligent also apply in determining whether a person who suffered harm (the *plaintiff*) has been contributorily negligent.

The legislation in New South Wales, Western Australia, Queensland, and Victoria,[45] is virtually identical but more elaborate. For example, the *Civil Liability Act 2003* (Qld), s 23, provides as follows:

> (1) The principles that are applicable in deciding whether a person has breached a duty also apply in deciding whether the person who suffered harm has been guilty of contributory negligence in failing to take precautions against the risk of that harm.
>
> (2) For that purpose—
>   (a) the standard of care required of the person who suffered harm is that of a reasonable person in the position of that person; and
>   (b) the matter is to be decided on the basis of what that person knew or ought reasonably to have known at the time.

The wording of the provision suggests that in determining whether the plaintiff's conduct fell below the objective standard for his or her own safety, the courts will apply the statutory calculus of negligence to assess the reasonable person's response to the risks posed by the defendant's negligence. The final

---

43. *Civil Liability Act 2002* (Tas), s 23(1).
44. *Civil Liability Act 1936* (SA), s 44(1).
45. *Civil Liability Act 2002* (NSW), s 5R; *Civil Liability Act 2002* (WA), s 5K; *Civil Liability Act 2003* (Qld), s 23; *Wrongs Act 1958* (Vic), s 62.

clause, relating to the particular plaintiff's knowledge, codifies the common law, and in particular the statement of McHugh J in *Joslyn v Berryman* (2003) 214 CLR 552, at [37], who observed that the courts should consider not only the facts and circumstances which were actually known to the injured person, but 'take into account as a matter of course those facts and circumstances that the plaintiff could have discovered by the exercise of reasonable care.'

In *Thompson v Woolworths (Q'land) Pty Limited* [2005] HCA 19, Gleeson CJ, McHugh, Kirby, Hayne, and Heydon JJ, in a joint judgment (at [37]), cautioned that that 'the obviousness of a risk, and the reasonableness of an expectation that other people will take care for their own safety' should always be considered as relevant, but not automatically conclusive of liability.

The joint judgment in *Thompson v Woolworths* (discussed in Chapter 10) found the defendant liable for the failure to ensure that the system of managing rubbish bins at the back of its supermarket did not expose women of small stature (who wished to move them) to an unreasonable risk of injury. However, it is not entirely clear whether the liability was imposed upon the defendant as an occupier in relation to entrants on its land, or as a principal under a non-delegable duty of care for injuries sustained by its independent contractors. Mrs Thompson's damages were reduced by one-third to take account of her contributory negligence. Mrs Thompson knew of her recent back injury, and 'was aware of the risk involved in moving the bins herself. She had recorded in her diary that they were too heavy for her. She and her husband had complained about the matter' (at [39]). Yet, rather than waiting for her husband or the defendant's storeman to help her, she decided to move the bin herself, thus sustaining a further injury to her back. In a joint judgment, their Honours made a vague comment (at [40]) that 'different considerations arise in the case of contributory negligence on the part of employees'. Since the 'different considerations' have not been articulated, it is impossible to decide whether Mrs Thompson would or would not have been found to be contributorily negligent if she were an employee.

The legislation provides that the matter of contributory negligence 'is to be decided on the basis of what that person knew or ought reasonably to have known at the time'.[46] In other words, the plaintiff's knowledge of the risk of harm is to be measured by objective and normative standards: the courts have to consider what the plaintiff 'ought reasonably to have known' at the time. This was the case with Mrs Thompson, and her knowledge of the risk was independent of her status as an independent contractor, a lawful entrant on the land, or an employee.

At present, only in the Australian Capital Territory and the Northern Territory is the standard of care for contributory negligence governed by common law.

---

46. *Civil Liability Act 2002* (NSW), s 5R(2)(b); *Civil Liability Act 2002* (WA), s 5K(2)(b); *Civil Liability Act 2003* (Qld), s 23(2)(b); *Wrongs Act 1958* (Vic), s 62(2)(b).

Nevertheless, in all jurisdictions some common law doctrines relating to standard of care in contributory negligence cases are still relevant.

Foreseeing or knowing that others may be careless

We are expected to take reasonable steps to protect ourselves against the carelessness of others. In *Jones v Livox Quarries Ltd* [1952] 2 QB 608, the plaintiff was riding on the towbar of a traxcavator, which was coming to a halt. While he was still standing on the towbar, another vehicle negligently ran into him from behind, and he was crushed between the two vehicles. Lord Denning MR pointed out that a person will be held liable under the doctrine of contributory negligence if he ought to have foreseen that if he did not act as a reasonable and prudent man, he might hurt himself. In his reckoning, he must take into account the possibility of others being careless.

Mere compliance by the plaintiff with regulations or statutory rules may not negate contributory negligence. The High Court in *Sibley v Kais* (1967) 118 CLR 424, at 427, observed that:

> The failure to take reasonable care in given circumstances is not necessarily answered by reliance upon the expected performance by the driver of the give way vehicle of his obligations under the regulations; for there is no general rule that in all circumstances a driver can rely upon the performance by others of their duties, whether derived from statutory sources or from the common law. Whether or not in particular circumstances it is reasonable to act upon the assumption that another will act in some particular way, as for example by performing his duty under a regulation, must remain a question of fact to be judged in all the particular circumstances of the case.

Although the rule was expressed in relation to motor vehicles, it has a general application. For example, in *Chandley v Roberts* [2005] VSCA 273, the plaintiff, Mr Roberts, fell four metres from a scaffold plank when the ladder supporting the scaffolding moved because of Mr Chandley's failure to properly secure it. The court rejected the defence submission that Mr Roberts' damages should be reduced for failure to check that the ladder was secure. The court noted that over some thirty years of working together on building sites, the two men had established a long-standing system of work in relation to the use of scaffolding for plaster work. This system included a specific method of securing the ladder, which on the particular occasion was undertaken by Mr Chandley. The risk posed by an unsecured ladder was obvious, and Mr Roberts had no reason to doubt Mr Chandley's competence or reliability. Therefore, (at [26]) the plaintiff's failure to check that the defendant had completed the task he undertook in the usual and expected way did not amount to a failure to take any, or any proper, care for Mr Roberts' own safety.

Causation

The two main elements of contributory negligence are fault and causation. The inquiry into the plaintiff's standard of care is essential for the purpose of apportionment whereby a comparison is made between the two parties at fault; however, for the purposes of compensation, the central focus of contributory negligence is causation. The injured plaintiffs' negligence (failure to take reasonable care of themselves or their interests) is only relevant if it contributed to the damage or harm (in Western Australia, 'the happening of the event which caused the damage').

At common law, the plaintiff's negligence need only contribute to his or her own injuries, and need not cause, or even contribute to, the accident. For example, in *Froom v Butcher* [1976] QB 286, the plaintiff, Mr Froom, suffered a broken rib, bruises to his chest, abrasions to his head, and a broken finger when his car was struck head-on by a negligent driver. At the time in the United Kingdom, the wearing of seat belts was not compulsory. Although the car was fitted with seat belts, Mr Froom was not wearing one. The defendant argued that all the plaintiff's injuries, save the broken finger, would have been prevented had he worn the seat belt. Lord Denning held the plaintiff guilty of contributory negligence. His Lordship said (at 291) that the 'the question is not what was the cause of the accident. It is rather what was the cause of the damage'.

However, there must be evidence to show that wearing of a seat belt would have prevented the damage. Thus, in *Woodward v Porteous* [1971] Tas SR 386,[47] Burbury CJ held that the defendant did not show that plaintiff's failure to wear a seat belt caused, or materially contributed to, his eye damage. Since it is not always possible to unpick the events so as to trace the plaintiff's specific breach of duty to the specific consequence solely attributable to that breach,[48] the material contribution test of causation (discussed in detail in Chapter 12) tends to be applied. For example, in *Richards v Mills* (2004) 27 WAR 200, Ms Mills attempted to merge into the right traffic lane without sufficient clearance. In the event, the right-hand rear corner of her vehicle made contact with the left-hand front corner of the Richards' vehicle, and went out of control. She was not wearing a seat belt. Flung from the vehicle, Ms Mills sustained damage to the spinal cord, which rendered her paraplegic. Anderson J (Parker J concurring) upheld (at [27]) the trial judge's finding that Ms Mills' failure to wear a seat belt increased the likelihood of spinal injury of the kind she suffered. There was, however, uncontradicted medical evidence to the effect that even with a seat belt on, she might have sustained the spinal injuries in question.[49]

---

47. See also: *Guidera v Government Insurance Office (NSW)* [1990] Aust Torts Reports ¶81–040 (NSW).
48. See, for example: Cosgrove J discussing this point in *Smedley v Smedley* (1984) Tas R 49 at 51.
49. Anderson J also considered that Ms Mills was careless in attempting to weave into the right lane without allowing sufficient clearance. Her failure to ascertain that it was quite safe to proceed with the manoeuvre heightened the risk of contact between the two vehicles. Ms Mills' damages were reduced by 55 per cent to account for her contributory negligence.

Intoxication

In *Joslyn v Berryman; Wentworth Shire Council v Berryman* (2003) 214 CLR 552, Kirby J summed up the pre-reform common law relating to intoxication, when he observed (at [102]) that 'the judicial reluctance to find contributory negligence against intoxicated drivers and passengers ... ultimately provoked Parliament to enact the statutory law.'[50]

Joslyn v Berryman; Wentworth Shire Council v Berryman (2003) 214 CLR 552

Joslyn v Berryman illustrates a range of judicial attitudes towards passengers and drivers whose decision-making or driving ability at the time of the accident was impaired as a consequence of alcohol- or drug-induced intoxication.

One Sunday morning in October 1996, following thirty-six hours of binge drinking, Sally Joslyn and Allan Berryman, then aged twenty-two, decided to drive in Berryman's utility from Dareton, New South Wales, to Mildura for breakfast. Berryman drove to Mildura, but on the way back, while at the wheel, he began to doze off, so Joslyn took over as a driver. Berryman claimed that he allowed Joslyn to drive because she appeared sober, though the evidence established that she had been drinking for hours (she was seen at 4.30 am 'quite drunk and staggering about'). Berryman also knew that Joslyn had lost her driving licence after being convicted of driving with a blood alcohol content of 0.15g/100ml, and had last driven a vehicle three years earlier. Having driven about one kilometre, Joslyn passed a sign for a T-junction without noticing it, and lost control of the vehicle while negotiating a curve in the road.[51] She testified that: 'It was just there all of a sudden and it turned really sharply and the car wouldn't go round the bend.' The vehicle overturned, and as a result, Berryman suffered serious injuries. He sued Joslyn and the Wentworth Shire Council for damages, claiming that she had driven negligently and that the Council was negligent in failing to provide proper warning signs.

The case was tried in the District Court of New South Wales in 1999. The defendants pleaded contributory negligence (under the *Motor Accidents Act 1988* (NSW), s 74) and 'joint illegal activity'.[52] The trial judge, Boyd-Boland ADCJ, held that Joslyn and the Council were both liable in negligence. With respect to the Council, the learned judge found that:

> it was the Council who erected a sign which was inadequate and misleading, and failed to erect signs which were proper, given the nature of the curve, I find, in

---

50. His Honour was referring to s 74 of the *Motor Accidents Act 1988* (NSW).
51. Joslyn did not know what speed she was travelling when the accident occurred because the speedometer of the vehicle was broken. She was also unaware that the utility had a tendency to roll.
52. The defence of voluntary assumption of risk in relation to motor vehicles was abolished in New South Wales: *Motor Accidents Act 1988* (NSW), s 76.

this instance, the Council carried out that work without due care and skill for the safety of the road users. The work which Council performed was not carried out in accordance with the standard at the time ...[53]

Boyd-Boland ADCJ also found that at the time of the accident (8.45 am): 'Joslyn exhibited none of the obvious signs of intoxication which one would expect to be present', but determined that Berryman was 25 per cent contributorily negligent.[54] He assessed that the damages payable by Joslyn in the sum of $1 995 086 should be reduced to $1 496 314.[55] Having assessed the damages payable by the Council in the sum of $2 505 311, his Honour entered judgment for $750 000, which was then the limit of the District Court's jurisdiction (Berryman's lawyers had failed to take procedural steps[56] to increase the court's jurisdiction).[57]

On appeal, Meagher JA of the New South Wales Court of Appeal[58] who delivered the leading judgment, overturned this finding and determined that Berryman was not contributorily negligent because:

> although at the time of the accident the blood alcohol levels of Miss Joslyn and Mr Berryman were estimated as being 0.138g/100ml and 0.19g/100ml respectively, there is no evidence that either of them were drunk at the time, and certainly no evidence that at the time Mr Berryman had any reason to think that Miss Joslyn was affected by intoxication. Indeed, quite to the contrary. ... it seems quite impossible to justify his Honour's conclusion on contributory negligence. I would be in favour of reducing it from 25% to 0%.[59]

The Council's appeal against Joslyn was dismissed with costs.[60] The Council's defence of 'joint illegal activity' asserted against Berryman and Joslyn was also rejected (this defence will be discussed below).

The High Court allowed the appeal, holding that in determining contributory negligence relating to intoxication, all the circumstances must be taken into account, not just the appearance of the driver. McHugh J (at [16]) stated that:

---

53. *Joslyn v Berryman; Wentworth Shire Council v Berryman* [2003] HCA 34 at [61]. Given that Joslyn admitted that she ignored the sign, it is difficult to identify the grounds on which causation was established in this case.
54. *Berryman v Joslyn;Wentworth Shire Council v Joslyn* [2004] NSWCA 121 at [4].
55. Calculated according to the *Motor Accidents Act 1988* (NSW).
56. Under the *District Court Act 1973* (NSW), s 55.
57. See: *Berryman v Joslyn;Wentworth Shire Council v Joslyn* [2004] NSWCA 121 at [4], per Tobias JA (Mason P and Baezely JA agreeing).
58. *Berryman v Joslyn & Anor;Wentworth Shire Council v Joslyn & Anor* [2001] NSWCA 95 (Priestley JA, and Ipp AJA agreeing) at [21].
59. The Court of Appeal entered judgment of $1 995 086.36 and $750 000 against Joslyn and the Council respectively.
60. The Court of Appeal held that the maintenance and control of the road resided in the Council: accordingly there was no basis for a review of the trial judge's finding of negligence against the Council for failing to erect adequate signage.

in principle, any fact or circumstance which a reasonable person would know or ought to know and which tends to suggest a foreseeable risk of injury in accepting a lift from an intoxicated driver, is relevant in determining whether the passenger was guilty of contributory negligence in accepting the lift.

In assessing whether Berryman ought to have been aware of Joslyn's capacity to drive, the court should consider the events in which they had participated over the preceding thirty-six or so hours before the accident. The High Court also held that it was just and equitable for the Council's liability to be reduced by the plaintiff's contributory negligence. When the case was remitted to the New South Wales Court of Appeal for determination, *inter alia*,[61] Tobias JA—applying the objective test of a reasonable sober person in the circumstances of the case—assessed Berryman's contributory negligence at 60 per cent.[62]

Statutory reforms

Every jurisdiction now has statutorily entrenched rules relating to intoxication. Some statutory regimes are much more elaborate and prescriptive than others. Apart from Victoria,[63] all jurisdictions reverse the onus of proof by imposing a presumption of contributory negligence in cases where:

> it is established that the person whose death, injury or damage is the subject of proceedings for the recovery of damages was, at the time of the act or omission that caused the death, injury or damage, intoxicated to the extent that the person's capacity to exercise due care and skill was impaired.[64]

However, there are significant differences in tests imposed upon the party under the onus of rebuttal. In Tasmania, New South Wales, and Western Australia, to rebut the presumption of contributory negligence, the court must be 'satisfied that the person's intoxication did not contribute in *any way* to the cause of the

---

61. The High Court found that the Court of Appeal erred in failing to consider s 74 of the *Motor Accidents Act 1988* (NSW).
62. This meant that the judgment against Joslyn was reduced from $1 496 314 to $798 034.44. However, the sum of $750 000 against the Council remained undisturbed because, given that the original judgment was for $2 505 311, any further reduction would have required a finding of contributory negligence on the part of Berryman at or greater than 70 per cent: *Berryman v Joslyn; Wentworth Shire Council v Joslyn (2)* [2004] NSWCA 239 at [4].
63. The *Wrongs Act 1958* (Vic), s 14G(2), has a very vague provision stating that 'in determining whether the plaintiff has established a breach of the duty of care owed by the defendant, the court must consider, among other things: (a) whether the plaintiff was intoxicated by alcohol or drugs voluntarily consumed and the level of intoxication; (b) whether the plaintiff was engaged in an illegal activity'. A similar provision forms part of the *Wrongs Act 1958* (Vic), Pt IIA (Occupier's liability), s 14B(4)(fa) and (fb).
64. For example, *Civil Liability Act 2002* (Tas), s 5(1).

death, injury or damage'.[65] South Australia, the Australian Capital Territory, and the Northern Territory[66] impose on the injured persons the onus of establishing on the balance of probabilities that 'the intoxication did not contribute to *the accident*'.[67] Unlike the other six jurisdictions, which mandate that the injured plaintiffs rebut the causative link between their intoxication and injury, Queensland's *Civil Liability Act 2003*, s 47(3)(a), requires the rebuttal of the link between intoxication and the plaintiff's standard of care. It provides that 'the person may only rebut the presumption by establishing on the balance of probabilities (a) that the intoxication *did not contribute to the breach of duty*'. This is a more literal approach to the concept of contributory negligence in so far as its aim is to determine whether, in the circumstances, a plaintiff's intoxication amounts to a failure to take care for his or her own safety. Once such failure is established, the defendant does not need to show that the plaintiff caused or contributed to the accident or the injury.

In both Queensland[68] and New South Wales,[69] the test for rebuttal of contributory negligence through intoxication needs to be read in the context of surrounding provisions, which:

- provide that 'a person is not owed a duty of care merely because the person is intoxicated';
- exclude from the scope of duty of care 'the possibility or likelihood that a person may be intoxicated or that a person who is intoxicated may be exposed to increased risk because the person's capacity to exercise reasonable care and skill is impaired as a result of being intoxicated'; and
- declare that 'the fact that a person is or may be intoxicated does not of itself increase or otherwise affect the standard of care owed to the person'.

Consequently, an intoxicated person who fell into a hole in a driveway and suffered serious injury would first have to establish that the hole posed a not-insignificant risk of injury to a reasonable sober person in the plaintiff's position. Once the defendant's negligence is established, the injured plaintiff (in New South Wales) will then have to rebut the onerous presumption that her or his 'intoxication did not contribute in *any way* to the cause of the *death, injury or damage*'; in Queensland the presumption would be virtually irrebuttable. All seven jurisdictions

---

65. *Civil Liability Act 2002* (Tas), s 5(1); *Civil Liability Act 2002* (NSW), s 50(3). Section 5L(3) of the *Civil Liability Act 2002* (WA) provides: 'If this section applies, it is to be presumed that the person was contributorily negligent unless the plaintiff establishes, on the balance of probabilities, that the person's intoxication did not contribute in any way to the cause of the harm'.
66. In the *Personal Injuries (Liabilities and Damages) Act 2003* (NT), s 14(2)(a), the phrase is: 'did not materially contribute to the *incident*'.
67. *Civil Law (Wrongs) Act 2002* (ACT), s 95(2)(a); *Civil Liability Act 1936* (SA), s 46(a).
68. *Civil Liability Act 2003* (Qld), s 46.
69. *Civil Liability Act 2002* (NSW), s 49.

exempt cases where the 'intoxication was not self-induced' from the operation of the presumption.[70]

Tasmania and South Australia have special provisions relating to intoxication by use of medicines. In Tasmania, the *Civil Liability Act 2002* (Tas), s 5(6), provides that where intoxication is attributable to drugs 'taken for a medicinal purpose', the injured person has to satisfy the court that he or she was not aware of the effect of the drug taken. In South Australia, under s 47(c) of the *Civil Liability Act 1936* (SA), injured persons have the burden of proving both (i) that their 'intoxication is wholly attributable to the use of drugs in accordance with the prescription or instructions of a medical practitioner'; and (ii) that they were 'complying with the instructions and recommendations of the medical practitioner and the manufacturer of the drugs as to what he or she should do, or avoid doing, while under the influence of the drugs'.

The test of intoxication is whether the injured person was intoxicated to the extent that his or her 'capacity to exercise reasonable care and skill was impaired' (Australian Capital Territory, Tasmania, New South Wales, Western Australia, the Northern Territory, and Queensland).[71] The statutory test of intoxication reflects the modern scientific understanding of interactions between driver skill level and the effects of alcohol or other intoxicants, in relation to reduction in driving precision, sleepiness and other effects.[72] The legislation refocuses the attention on the injured party's own intoxicated state and its effects. For example, if the *Joslyn v Berryman; Wentworth Shire Council v Berryman* (2003) 214 CLR 552 case were litigated under a statutory regime, a claimant in Berryman's position would have been unable to rebut the presumption of contributory negligence. Joslyn took over as a driver only because Berryman's own 'capacity to exercise reasonable care and skill was impaired' by intoxication—he was falling asleep at the wheel. Since the reason for the driver change-over was the effect of his own intoxication, it would be difficult to

---

70. *Civil Liability Act 2002* (Tas), s 5(4); *Civil Law (Wrongs) Act 2002* (ACT), s 95(1)(b); *Civil Liability Act 1936* (SA), s 46(2)(b); *Civil Liability Act 2002* (NSW), s 50(5); *Civil Liability Act 2002* (WA), s 5L(2); *Civil Liability Act 2003* (Qld), s 47(3)(b); *Personal Injuries (Liabilities and Damages) Act 2003* (NT), s 14(2)(b): 'was involuntary'.
71. *Civil Law (Wrongs) Act 2002* (ACT), s 92; *Civil Liability Act 2002* (Tas), s 5(1); *Civil Liability Act 2002* (NSW), s 50(1); *Civil Liability Act 2002* (WA), s 5L(4); *Personal Injuries (Liabilities and Damages) Act 2003* (NT), s 3; *Civil Liability Act 2003* (Qld), s 47 Sch 2 Dictionary. The *Civil Liability Act 1936* (SA), s 48(2), is narrower, referring to a person who 'was at or about the time of an accident so much under the influence of alcohol or a drug as to be unable to exercise effective control of a motor vehicle'.
72. Harrison EL & Fillmore MT, 'Are bad drivers more impaired by alcohol? Sober driving precision predicts impairment from alcohol in a simulated driving task' (2005) 37(5) *Accident; Analysis and Prevention* 882–889; Barrett PR, Horne JA & Reyner LA, 'Alcohol Continues to Affect Sleepiness Related Driving Impairment, When Breath Alcohol Levels have Fallen to Near-zero' (2004) 19 *Human Psychopharmacology* 421–423. See also: Connor J, Norton R, Ameratunga S, & Jackson R, 'The Contribution of Alcohol to Serious Car Crash Injuries' (2004) 15(3) *Epidemiology* 337–344 and Paljärvi T, Mäkelä P & Poikolainen K, 'Pattern of Drinking and Fatal Injury: A Population-based Follow-up Study of Finnish Men' (2005) 100 *Addiction* 1851–1859, which suggest that alcohol tolerance does not lower the risk of injuries (including fatal injuries) among frequent heavy drinkers.

persuade the court that this fact 'did not contribute in *any way* to the cause of' his injury (New South Wales, Tasmania, Western Australia), or to the accident (South Australia, the Australian Capital Territory, and the Northern Territory), or to the breach of duty of care for his own safety (Queensland).

In Victoria, the *Wrongs Act* 1958 (Vic), s 14G(2)(a), provides that 'In determining whether the plaintiff has established a breach of the duty of care owed by the defendant, the court must consider, among other things (a) whether the plaintiff was intoxicated by alcohol or drugs voluntarily consumed and the level of intoxication.' It is unclear whether 'level of intoxication' refers strictly to the blood alcohol level or to the pathological state (psychological and physiological effects) produced by alcohol or some other drug, or both.[73]

Some jurisdictions have special evidentiary provisions relating to the levels of intoxication. Thus, in South Australia and the Northern Territory, where the court finds that 'at or about the time of an accident' ('incident' in the Northern Territory), the person had 'present in his or her blood a concentration of alcohol of .08 or more grams in 100 millilitres of blood', this finding is to be accepted as 'conclusive evidence' of those facts and that the person was intoxicated at the time. The wording suggests that this evidentiary provision applies not only to motor vehicle accidents, but in all cases where contributory negligence is pleaded.[74]

In South Australia, Queensland, the Northern Territory, and Tasmania, damages to which the person would be entitled in the absence of contributory negligence must be 'reduced on account of contributory negligence by 25 per cent or a greater percentage determined by the court to be appropriate in the circumstances of the case'.[75]

In Queensland and South Australia, additional evidentiary provisions mandate that where the injured person was the driver of a motor vehicle involved in the accident and the evidence establishes that (a) the concentration of alcohol in the driver's blood was 150mg (.15g) or more of alcohol in 100mL of blood;[76] or (b) 'the driver was so much under the influence of alcohol or a drug as to be incapable of exercising effective control of the vehicle'; the minimum reduction [for contributory negligence] 'is increased to 50 per cent'.[77]

---

73. Brookhuis KA, De Waard D, Fairclough SH, 'Criteria for Driver Impairment' (2003) 46 *Ergonomics* 433–445.
74. *Civil Liability Act 1936* (SA), s 48(1); *Personal Injuries (Liabilities and Damages) Act 2003* (NT), s 16.
75. *Civil Liability Act 1936* (SA), s 46 (3); *Civil Liability Act 2003* (Qld), s 47(4) *Personal Injuries (Liabilities and Damages) Act 2003* (NT), s 17. The *Civil Liability Act 2002* (Tas), s 5(2), provides for a '25% or a greater or lesser percentage', with s 5(3) placing 'the onus of satisfying the court that damages ought to be reduced on account of contributory negligence by a percentage of less than 25% ... on the person whose death, injury or damage is the subject of the proceedings for the recovery of damages'.
76. 150mg or more of alcohol in 100mL blood is the equivalent of .15g per cent.
77. *Civil Liability Act 1936* (SA), s 46(4).

South Australia, Queensland, the Northern Territory, and (in part) the Australian Capital Territory[78] have enacted identical provisions, which impose a presumption of contributory negligence where an injured person 'of or above the age of sixteen' relies on care and skill of person known to be intoxicated.[79] Unless the presumption is rebutted,[80] the court must apply a fixed statutory reduction of 25 per cent in the assessment of damages.[81] In relation to assessment of damages for injuries occasioned by motor vehicle accidents, in South Australia and Queensland (but not the Northern Territory), the fixed statutory reduction is increased to 50 per cent if evidence establishes that (a) 'the concentration of alcohol in the driver's blood was .15 grams or more in 100 millilitres of blood'; or (b) 'the driver was so much under the influence of intoxicating liquor or a drug as to be incapable of exercising effective control of the vehicle'.[82]

Three jurisdictions have included statutory provisions specifically relating to failure to wear a seat belt or safety helmet. Thus, in the Australian Capital Territory and South Australia, the legislation imposes a rebuttable statutory presumption of contributory negligence (with a fixed 25 per cent reduction of damages in South Australia) on injured persons who, at the age of sixteen or above, were not wearing a seat belt or a safety helmet at the time of a motor vehicle accident.[83]

South Australia, the Australian Capital Territory, and Queensland exclude the operation of the common law defence of *volenti non fit injuria* from cases where the person who suffered harm relied on care and skill of an intoxicated person.[84] In other jurisdictions, however, the defendants may be able to plead that the conduct of plaintiffs who drive while intoxicated, or who are voluntary passengers in a vehicle driven by an intoxicated driver, amounts to a voluntary assumption of 'obvious risk' (discussed below).

In some instances, consumption of intoxicants (alcohol and/or drugs) *after* the accident may be considered contributory negligence, if it exacerbates the claimant's injury: *Commonwealth v McLean* (1996) 41 NSWLR 389, at 398.

As noted at the beginning of this chapter, from the defendant's perspective, proportionate reduction of the quantum of damages for contributory negligence reflects the reality of the event where both parties contributed to the plaintiff's

---

78. *Civil Liability Act 1936* (SA), s 47(1); *Civil Liability Act 2003* (Qld), s 48(1); *Personal Injuries (Liabilities and Damages) Act 2003* (NT), s 15(1).
79. *Civil Law (Wrongs) Act 2002* (ACT), ss 96, 97(1).
80. Under the *Civil Liability Act 1936* (SA), s 47(2), and *Civil Liability Act* 2003 (Qld), s 48(3), the presumption of contributory negligence can be rebutted only if the injured claimant can establish that (a) the intoxication did not contribute to the accident; or (b) the injured person could not reasonably be expected to have avoided the risk.
81. *Civil Liability Act 1936* (SA), s 47(4) and (5); *Civil Liability Act 2003* (Qld), ss 48(4) and 49(2); *Personal Injuries (Liabilities and Damages) Act 2003* (NT), s 15(2).
82. *Civil Liability Act 1936* (SA), s 47(5); *Civil Liability Act 2003* (Qld), s 49(2).
83. *Civil Law (Wrongs) Act 2002* (ACT), s 97; *Civil Liability Act 1936* (SA), s 49.
84. *Civil Liability Act 1936* (SA), s 47(6); *Civil Law (Wrongs) Act 2002* (ACT), s 96(5); *Civil Liability Act 2003* (Qld), s 48(5).

injury. However, from the plaintiff's point of view, the picture is more complex, particularly in cases of catastrophic injury. Passengers who fail to protect themselves by refusing a lift from a drunken driver, and as a result of a crash become brain-damaged or suffer paraplegia, will 'pay' for their contributory negligence for the rest of their lives. Should they also be deprived of the care they need as a result of their wrongfully occasioned injury through reduction in damages?

Children

Can children be guilty of contributory negligence? At least in relation to being a passenger in a vehicle driven by an intoxicated driver, legislation in South Australia, Queensland, the Australian Capital Territory, and the Northern Territory provides that the presumption of contributory negligence does not apply to persons under sixteen years of age.

However, in other cases and jurisdictions, as McHugh J observed in *Joslyn v Berryman* (2003) 214 CLR 552, at [35]:

> Ever since *Lynch v Nurdin*, common law courts have accepted that, in determining whether a child is guilty of contributory negligence, the relevant standard of care is that to be expected of an ordinary child of the same age.[85]

The New South Wales Court of Appeal in *Doubleday & Anor v Kelly* [2005] NSWCA 151 (discussed in Chapter 11) examined the applicability to children of the codified principle of contributory negligence, which provides that the 'standard of care required of the person who suffered harm is that of a reasonable person in the position of that person'.[86] Bryson JA (at [26], Young CJ in Eq and Hunt AJA agreeing) interpreted the provision as implying that in relation to seven-year-old Bianca, who suffered injury when, unsupervised, she attempted to roller-skate on a trampoline, 'The characteristics of a reasonable person in the position of the person who suffered harm include the characteristics of being a child of seven years.'

When assessing a child's contributory negligence, the court will consider the nature of the danger created by the defendant, including its duration. In *Sainsbury v Great Southern Energy Pty Ltd* [2000] NSWSC 479, Barr J found that a twelve-year-old plaintiff who received electrical burns when he climbed to the top of a power pole (having previously climbed only halfway for fear of electrocution) was contributorily negligent because 'an ordinary twelve year old boy in the plaintiff's position and knowing what he knew would not have climbed the pole.'

---

85. See also: *McHale v Watson* (1966) 115 CLR 199 at 214–15, per Kitto J, and at 204, per McTiernan ACJ.
86. *Civil Liability Act 2002* (NSW), s 5R(2)(a). This provision is identical to the *Civil Liability Act 2002* (WA), s 5K; *Civil Liability Act 2003* (Qld), s 23; *Wrongs Act 1958* (Vic), s 62.

Thus, the plaintiff's careless conduct contributed 10 per cent to his own injury. In his determination of contributory negligence, his Honour referred to *Kelly v Bega Valley County Council* (unreported, New South Wales Court of Appeal, 13 September 1982),[87] in which Glass JA identified such factors as the nature of danger created by the defendant, its duration, and whether or not the defendant's default constituted 'an allurement which in a real sense provoked and facilitated the default of the plaintiff.'[88]

Intentional conduct on the part of the plaintiff

In *Reeves v Commissioner of Police of the Metropolis* [2000] 1 AC 360, the House of Lords said the defence of contributory negligence applied to the suicide of a man, detained in police custody, who had previously attempted to commit suicide following his arrest and detention. The House of Lords determined that contributory negligence could include intentional acts as well as negligence. Having noted that 'intention is a different state of mind from negligence', Lord Hoffmann (at 369–70) reasoned that since the legal test of causation in contributory negligence is whether the injury was caused by the plaintiff's failure to take care for his or her own safety, a plaintiff who intended to injure himself would fall within the scope of the test. In view of the fact that the defendant Commissioner of Police in this case owed a duty to prevent, or take reasonable care to prevent, the plaintiff from deliberately causing injury to himself, there was no break in causal connection between any prior breach of duty by the defendant and the damage suffered by the plaintiff.[89] At the same time, the deceased had responsibility for his own life and his intentional act, while he was of sound mind, was a substantial cause of his death. Their Lordships apportioned the responsibility for the suicide equally between the deceased and the Commissioner of Police.

Doctrine of alternative danger

When reading early cases involving the defence of contributory negligence, it is useful to keep in mind that the judges' approach to the issues was coloured by the devastating effect the full defence could have for an injured plaintiff. Of the

---

87. This case also involved an eleven-year-old boy who was severely burned as a result of climbing an electricity pole.
88. See also: *Gerick v Municipality of Peterborough* [1984] Aust Torts Reports 80–605, in which an eleven-year-old plaintiff climbed up a wooden platform supporting an electricity transformer on a public street. He slipped and, trying to avoid falling, grabbed the electric wires which were not insulated. He was badly burned. The South Australian Supreme Court found the defendant liable in negligence because the structure was not fenced and there was no notice warning of the danger. Since the plaintiff had no knowledge of the danger, and a boy of his age would not know of it, he was not contributorily negligent.
89. See also: Williams G, *Joint Torts and Contributory Negligence*, Stevens, London, 1951, p 199.

many doctrines developed to ameliorate the harshness of this defence, the theory of 'alternative danger' has been the most enduring. Generally, as the High Court noted in *March v Stramare*, even where the defendant creates a dangerous situation, a reasonable person in the plaintiff's position is expected to take steps to avoid or minimise his or her injury, or face liability for contributory negligence.

However, both at common law and under statute, the plaintiff's conduct will be judged by reference to all the circumstances. This will be particularly so where the plaintiff was placed by the defendant's negligence in a position of choice between two dangers. In such cases, the reasonableness of the plaintiff's acts is judged by weighing the degree of inconvenience and risk to which the plaintiff was subjected through the defendant's negligence, against the risk the plaintiff took to escape it.

This balancing of externally imposed risks and the plaintiff's response to them is known as the 'doctrine of alternative danger', the 'sudden emergency doctrine', or the 'rule in *The Bywell Castle*' [1879] 4 PD 219. In *The Bywell Castle*, the English Court of Appeal said that where one ship has by wrong manoeuvres placed another ship in imminent danger of collision, the other ship will not be held contributorily negligent for failing to manoeuvre with perfect skill and presence of mind. Although determined under Admiralty law, *The Bywell Castle* has been cited as an authority in civil cases.

The 'sudden emergency' doctrine is nicely illustrated in *Caterson v Commissioner for Railways* (1973) 128 CLR 99. The plaintiff was seeing a friend off at a railway station. He carried the friend's luggage into a carriage and was about to leave when the train started to move without warning. The plaintiff's fourteen-year-old son was left alone on the platform, some forty miles from home. The next station was eighty miles away. There was probably a communication cord on the train, but the plaintiff did not think of it. He jumped from the train and was injured. In the circumstances of this case, the High Court rejected the plea of contributory negligence.

However, the law distinguishes between a plaintiff who, having been placed in a position of risk, merely fails to anticipate danger, and a person who actually creates it. The latter cannot rely on the sudden emergency doctrine. For instance, in *Municipal Tramways Trust v Ashby* [1951] SASR 61, the plaintiff was injured when he overtook a tram in a narrow lane. Intending to turn left, but finding the road blocked, he stopped in the tram's path. Napier CJ (at 63–4) observed:

> there is no warrant for making special allowance for the difficulties of a situation which the plaintiff courted either deliberately or through the failure to exercise reasonable foresight ... It is unreasonable—where there is no necessity for it—to cut things so fine as to allow no margin of safety for the mistakes or thoughtlessness of other people.

The application of contributory negligence in relation to breach of statutory duty will be discussed in Chapter 22.

Assessment of damages

In all jurisdictions, the legislation provides that:

> the damages recoverable in respect of the wrong must be reduced to such extent as the court thinks just and equitable having regard to the claimant's share in the responsibility for the damage.[90]

The phrase 'having regard to the claimant's share in the responsibility for the damage' has been traditionally interpreted by the courts in terms of apportionment of responsibility for the damage, and reduction of the quantum of damages in proportion to each party's departure from the standard expected of a reasonable person in the circumstances.

In *Podrebersek v Australian Iron and Steel Pty Ltd* (1985) 59 ALR 529, at 532, Gibbs CJ, Mason, Wilson, Brennan, and Deane JJ stated that when the tribunal of fact makes an apportionment of responsibility for the injury to be borne by the plaintiff and defendant respectively, it does so by comparing the whole conduct of each negligent party in relation to the circumstances of the accident. In other words, as Hayne J put it in *Wynbergen v Hoyts Corporation Pty Ltd* (1997) 149 ALR 25, at 29, put it, the plaintiff's share of responsibility is assessed against the totality of the defendant's negligence, with the judge having to balance the 'relative importance of the acts of the parties in causing the damage'. In *Podrebersek v Australian Iron and Steel Pty Ltd* (at 532), the joint judgment cited with approval Lord Wright's statement in *British Fame (Owners) v Macgregor (Owners)* [1943] AC 197 (at 201) that a finding of apportionment is:

> [a] question, not of principle or of positive findings of fact or law, but of proportion, of balance and relative emphasis, and of weighing different considerations. It involves an individual choice or discretion, as to which there may well be differences of opinion by different minds.

Apportionment of damages involves both:

- comparison of culpability in the degree of respective departures by each party from the standard of the reasonable person (*Pennington v Norris* (1956) 96 CLR 10 at 16); and
- comparison of the relative importance of their respective acts in causing the actual damage (*Podrebersek v Australian Iron and Steel Pty Ltd* [1985] ALR 529 at 534). The court assesses 'the whole conduct of each negligent party in relation to the circumstances of the accident which must be subjected to

---

90. *Wrongs Act 1958* (Vic), s 26(1)(b); *Wrongs Act 1954* (Tas), s 4(1); *Civil Law (Wrongs) Act 2002* (ACT), s 102(1)(b); *Law Reform (Contributory Negligence and Apportionment of Liability) Act* 2001 (SA), s 7(2)(b); *Civil Liability Act 2002* (NSW), s 9(1)(b); *Law Reform (Contributory Negligence and Tortfeasors' Contribution) Act 1947* (WA), s 4(1); *Personal Injuries (Liabilities and Damages) Act 2003* (NT), s 16(1)(b); *Law Reform Act 1995* (Qld), s 10(1)(b).

comparative examination' (*Wynbergen v Hoyts Corporation Pty Ltd* (1997) 149 ALR 25, at 29).

In *March v Stramare*, the court determined that the plaintiff was 70 per cent responsible for his own injuries, so the defendant bore responsibility for 30 per cent. In *Liftronic Pty Limited v Unver* (2001) 179 ALR 32, the plaintiff's responsibility was apportioned at 60 per cent. If both the plaintiff and the defendant are equally responsible for the plaintiff's injuries, the damages of each will be reduced by 50 per cent.

'Just and equitable'

In *Joslyn v Berryman* [2003] 214 CLR 552, Kirby J said (at [144]):

> The mere fact that, at the time Ms Joslyn took the keys and accepted Mr Berryman's express or implied invitation to drive his vehicle, she did not appear to be affected by alcohol intoxication is much less significant in this case than it might be in other factual circumstances. If, for example, a passenger without knowledge of a driver's insobriety, accepted an invitation to travel in a vehicle, the initial appearances of the driver could be very important to the statutory question of what was 'just and equitable in the circumstances of the case'. Similarly, it could be important to what a court thinks is 'just and equitable having regard to the claimant's share in the responsibility for the damage'.
>
> In so far as law reflects standards and attitudes prevalent at a given time in a society it governs, it also reflects the values—and with them, moral considerations—of the judiciary. The defence of contributory negligence poses difficult questions of justice, compassion, and social policy in relation to personal injury claimants who, through their carelessness, intoxication, impulsiveness, or sheer stupidity have contributed to their own injury, with the consequences of which they have to live for the rest of their lives.

VOLUNTARY ASSUMPTION OF RISK

The defence of contributory negligence re-examines the elements of breach of duty of care and causation from the defendant's perspective, analysing the plaintiff's conduct and its contribution to the injury. The plea of voluntary assumption of risk, which is 'only available when the plaintiff freely and voluntarily with full knowledge of the nature and extent of the risk, impliedly agreed to incur it',[91] focuses on the existence and scope of the duty of care.

---

91. *Burnett v British Waterways Board* [1973] 1 WLR 700 at 705, per Lord Denning, MR at 705. His Lordship referred to *Letang v Ottawa Electric Railway Co* [1926] AC 725 at 731 and *Nettleship v Weston* [1971] 2 QB 691 at 701.

The defence of voluntary assumption of risk of being injured by the defendant's negligent conduct is based on the notion that as part of the principle of personal autonomy, a person should be able to waive his or her legal rights not to be injured by the defendant's negligence. It is both similar to and different from the defence of consent as applicable to intentional torts (see below). Sir Donaldson MR in *Freeman v Home Office (No 2)* [1984] Q.B. 524, at 557, pointed out that the maxim *volenti non fit injuria* provides merely a bar to enforcing a cause of action; it does not negative the cause of action itself.

A successful defence effectively denies injured persons the right to sue in negligence on the ground that they had agreed to take personal responsibility for the risks that materialised. Although in *Cole v Sth Tweed Heads Rugby Club* (2004) 217 CLR 469 (discussed in Chapter 10), the defence of voluntary assumption of risk was not pleaded, Gleeson CJ and Callinan J, in separate judgments, held that the defendant rugby club did not owe a general duty to take reasonable care to protect adult patrons against risks of physical injury resulting from voluntary consumption of alcohol. Callinan J observed (at [121]) that 'the voluntary act of drinking until intoxicated should be regarded as a deliberate act taken by a person exercising autonomy for which that person should carry personal responsibility in law.'

However, the principle of personal responsibility, though it underpins the defence of voluntary assumption of risk, is not of itself determinative. At common law, for the plea to succeed, the plaintiff must perceive, understand and appreciate the full extent of both the risk of an injury and the legal consequences of the 'waiver of the duty of care'.

The case which set out the test for the defence was *Smith v Charles Baker & Sons* [1891] AC 325. In that case, a worker employed as a driller in a tunnel-building enterprise suffered serious injury when a stone that was being slung above him fell from its sling and hit his head. The employer argued that the employee assumed the risk of injury because he knew that he was engaged to perform a dangerous job, and was told to be aware of stones that were being slung. The House of Lords, by a majority, held that the plaintiff received no warning about the particular stone that had hit him, even though other workers moved out of the way, and therefore (at 336, per Lord Halsbury LC):

> did not consent at all. His attention was fixed upon a drill, and while, therefore, he was unable to take precautions himself, a stone was negligently slung over his head without due precautions against it being permitted to fall.

In relation to the maxim *volenti non fit injuria*, Lord Herschell stated (at 360): 'The maxim is founded on good sense and justice. One who has invited or assented to an act being done towards him cannot, when he suffers from it, complain of it as a wrong.'

Smith v Charles Baker & Sons has been interpreted as standing for the following propositions:

- Voluntary assumption of risk 'cannot be imputed to a plaintiff merely because he encountered a known hazard and thereby consented to the risk of being hurt'.[92]
- The defendant has the burden of proving that 'the injured person assumed not merely the *physical* but also the *legal* risk of injury'.[93]
- The defendant must show that the plaintiff has agreed to a particular, rather than a general, risk.

The High Court in *Roggenkamp v Bennett* (1950) 80 CLR 292, at 300, affirmed the rule that voluntary assumption of the risk of being injured by the defendant's negligence without legal recourse is a complete defence, which must be pleaded and proved by the defendant.

Consent

This defence is based on implied agreement,[94] whereby plaintiffs must effectively agree to absolve the defendant from the duty of care otherwise owed to them, with the result that the defendant's carelessness will not be regarded as a breach of the duty of care. What are the similarities and differences between the defence of voluntary assumption of risk and the defence of consent?

1   This defence of consent, like that of voluntary assumption of risk, is a complete defence. The first applies to intentional torts, the second to negligence.
2   The plaintiff's consent makes lawful what would otherwise be unlawful conduct by the defendant. Voluntary assumption of risk by the plaintiff relieves the defendant of the duty of care to guard against, eliminate, or minimise the foreseeable risk that may injure the plaintiff.
3   In intentional torts, the plaintiff agrees to the infringement of his or her dignitary rights: the right to personal self-determination; the right to an untarnished reputation; the right to free motion and locomotion; the right to undisturbed possession of and title to goods; the right to peaceful occupation and enjoyment of land; and, possibly, the right to privacy. In voluntary assumption of risk, the plaintiff assumes the risk of being physically or psychiatrically injured by the defendant's negligent conduct.
4   Consent as a defence to intentional torts applies only to positive conduct. Voluntary assumption of risk applies to negligent misfeasance as well as negligent omissions.

---

92. Fleming JG, *Law of Torts*, 9th edn, The Law Book Company Ltd, Sydney, 1998, p 333.
93. Ibid. Emphasis added.
94. *Burnett v British Waterways Board* [1973] 1 WLR 700 at 705.

5   To be valid, consent has to be free and informed: duress and misrepresentation or fraud will invalidate the defence of consent. This is true for the voluntary assumption of the risk of harm.

6   The major exception to the defence of informed and voluntary consent is consent given 'not for a good cause', such as sado-masochistic activities and perpetration of fraud—for instance, maiming plaintiffs at their request to obtain and share compensation. Voluntary assumption of the risk of being negligently injured by the defendant for the purposes of fraud or crime would fall into the category of joint illegal enterprise, which is also a complete defence.

In New South Wales, the defence of voluntary assumption of risk has been abolished in relation to motor accidents (except motor car racing), and the workers' compensation scheme; there is a reduction of damages where the defence would otherwise be available.[95] The *Wrongs Act 1936* (SA), s 35A(4), has abolished the defence of *volenti non fit injuria* 'where—(a) the injured person was, at the time of the accident, a voluntary passenger in or on a motor vehicle; and (b) the driver's ability to drive the motor vehicle was impaired in consequence of the consumption of alcohol or a drug and the injured person was aware, or ought to have been aware, of the impairment.' The defence, however, has been retained in all other States.

The elements of the voluntary assumption of risk defence

Given its harsh consequences and wide ambit, in the second part of the twentieth century the courts endeavoured to narrow the parameters of this defence.

In *Scanlon v American Cigarette Company (Overseas) Pty Ltd (No 3)* [1987] VR 289, the plaintiff sued a cigarette company in negligence, alleging that she had started smoking in 1963 at the age of fifteen, and continued to smoke twenty cigarettes per day until 1985, when she developed lung cancer. The defendant company raised the plea of voluntary assumption of risk. The court had to determine the definition of the voluntary assumption of risk defence. Drawing upon earlier authorities, Nicholson J indicated that there were three elements of the defence:

- the plaintiff has to know of the facts constituting the danger;
- the plaintiff must appreciate the danger inherent in the particular situation; and
- the plaintiff must freely and willingly agree to encounter the danger.

An inference of voluntariness may be drawn in cases where the defendant can establish that:

- the risk of danger was apparent (*Insurance Commissioner v Joyce* (1948) 77 CLR 39); or

---

95. *Motor Accident Act 1988* (NSW), s 76; *Workers' Compensation Act 1987* (NSW), s 151O.

- proper warning was given of it (*Imperial Chemical Industries Ltd v Shatwell* [1956] AC 656); and
- there was nothing to indicate coercion or obligation to accept the risk (the defendant must show that the plaintiff freely and willingly agreed to encounter the particular danger and to absolve the defendant); and
- the plaintiff must have fully accepted the risk of the very occurrence which eventuated: acceptance of one risk is not necessarily acceptance of all risks (*Rootes v Shelton* (1967) 116 CLR 383); and further
- the risk accepted must be the legal risk of exonerating the defendant from the duty of care, so that the plaintiff forgoes the right to compensation (*Wilkinson v Joyceman* [1985] 1 Qd R 567).

In contrast, the element of voluntariness will not be made out where:

- the plaintiff had knowledge of danger but not full comprehension of its extent (*Randwick City Council v Muzic* [2006] NSWCA 66 (at [47–50]); or
- while taking an ordinary and reasonable course, the plaintiff was not given an adequate opportunity to choose whether to accept or reject the risk (see below).

The classic case on the issue of voluntariness is *Burnett v British Waterways Board* [1973] 1 WLR 700. The plaintiff, Mr Burnett, was working as a lighterman on a barge being warped into a lock when,[96] due to the British Waterways Board's negligence, a defective rope snapped and hit him, causing an injury. The defendant claimed protection through an exclusion notice posted at the entrance to the dock addressed to 'To Lightermen & Others', which stated that they brought their craft into the dock 'at their own risk and upon the understanding that no liability whatever shall attach to the British Waterways Board or its servants for any loss, damage or injury from whatever cause ... to ... any person ... on board'. Mr Burnett admitted that he had read the notice as an apprentice, many years before the accident. Lord Denning MR distinguished cases where persons who have notice of the risk are in a position to voluntarily agree to it, and those, like Mr Burnett, who have no freedom of choice. His Lordship (at 705) cited the following passage from the judgment of the trial judge, Waller J:[97]

> The plaintiff was not somebody arriving on his own at the entrance to this dock and saying: 'Well, I will not go in because of this notice.' He was an employee on a barge, part of a train of barges, and by the time he had got to the dock it was certainly beyond his ability to make a choice and not go in.

---

96. The mooring and warping equipment of canallers is specially arranged for maneuvering the vessel through the canal locks, where the clearance in many vessels is only a few inches.
97. *Burnett v British Waterways Board* [1972] 1 WLR 1329 at 1334.

Consequently, the English Court of Appeal held that the defence of *volenti non fit injuria* did not apply, for although the wording of the notice was sufficiently broad to cover the plaintiff's accident, the plaintiff was not bound by the notice because in the circumstances he had not expressly or impliedly agreed to be bound by its terms and had had no choice in the matter.

Employer–employee relationship

Ever since the rule in *Smith v Charles Baker & Sons*, and the principle that the plaintiff must have a real choice in waiving the protection of the duty owed to him or her by the defendant, it is only on very rare occasions that the defence of voluntary assumption of risk will be successful when pleaded by an employer. To amount to *volenti*, the injury must be self-inflicted by a deliberate conduct.

For example, in *Imperial Chemical Industries v Shatwell* [1965] AC 656, two brothers, who were qualified shot firers, were seriously injured in an explosion that occurred due to their use of an unsafe method in testing explosives. This particular method of checking for defective detonators was prohibited by their employer and by statute. The plaintiffs were warned by the employer about its dangers, and had received instructions about safe practices. The House of Lords determined that the brothers' deliberate conduct was not mere carelessness or negligence, but a voluntary assumption of risk made with full knowledge of the risk of injury.

Risks accepted by the plaintiff

As a general rule, a person does not voluntarily assume the risk of negligence on the part of another merely by engaging in a sport or pastime, even if the sport or pastime is inherently dangerous. The common law defence is based on a subjective standard. It focuses on the plaintiff's actual knowledge when he or she decided to voluntarily accept the risk in question, including its legal consequences. For example, in *Kent v Scattini* [1961] WAR 74, the plaintiff, a sixteen-year-old girl, together with a group of others, was sprayed with water by means of a bicycle pump by a group of other youths driving a car. The plaintiff's group then armed themselves with a similar pump and set off in a car in pursuit of the first car. They were travelling at about 50 miles per hour when due to Scattini's negligent driving, the car failed to take a bend, and the plaintiff was injured in the subsequent crash. The defendant argued that the plaintiff was part of a risky venture and her injuries were a consequence of the risk to which she had consented. The court held that the plaintiff consented to getting wet, but *not* to Scattini's breach of the duty of care through speeding around the bend. For the defence to succeed, the defendant must show that the injured plaintiff accepted the very risk which had materialised; the acceptance of one risk is not necessarily the acceptance of all risks.

Likewise, in *Rootes v Shelton* (1967) 116 CLR 383, the High Court held that by engaging in a sport or pastime, a person might be held on occasion to have accepted risks which are inherent in that sport or pastime. However, the defendant has to show that the injured plaintiff had voluntarily assumed the specific risk relating to his or her negligent conduct that has materialised.

These general principles have been qualified by the reform legislation.

Statutory reforms

Under common law, the defence of voluntary assumption of the risk of harm is very narrow. The defendant has the burden of proof to establish that the plaintiff agreed to take the responsibility for the particular risk that had materialised. Following the Ipp Panel's Recommendation 11, statutory reforms in six State jurisdictions have created a rebuttable statutory presumption that injured persons are aware of, and therefore assume responsibility for 'obvious risks'. The statutory concept of an 'obvious risk' is more broadly defined. The notion is relevant to the assessment of the defendant's standard of care, particularly in relation to the duty to warn (discussed in Chapter 11); the defence of contributory negligence (discussed above); determination of the scope of the duty of care; and, in some jurisdictions, the defence of voluntary assumption of risk.

Definition of an 'obvious risk'

All six State jurisdictions define the term 'obvious risk' in very similar terms.[98] For example, according to s 5F of the *Civil Liability Act 2002* (NSW), 'obvious risk' is 'a risk that, in the circumstances, would have been obvious to a reasonable person in the position of that person'. Included within the definition of obvious risks are 'risks that are patent or a matter of common knowledge', even though they have 'a low probability of occurring', and 'even if the risk (or a condition or circumstance that gives rise to the risk) is not prominent, conspicuous or physically observable'.

Victoria[99] and Queensland[100] add that 'a risk from a thing, including a living thing, is not an obvious risk if the risk is created because of a failure on the part of a person to properly operate, maintain, replace, prepare or care for the thing, unless the failure itself is an obvious risk'.

---

98. *Civil Liability Act 2003* (Qld), s 13; *Civil Liability Act 1936* (SA), s 36; *Civil Liability Act 2002* (Tas), s 15; *Civil Liability Act 2002* (WA), s 5F; *Wrongs Act 1958* (Vic), s 53.
99. *Wrongs Act 1958* (Vic), s 53(5).
100. *Civil Liability Act 2003* (Qld), s 13(5). Two statutory illustrations of the application of s 13(5) are provided: '(1) A motorised go-cart that appears to be in good condition may create a risk to a user of the go-cart that is not an obvious risk if its frame has been damaged or cracked in a way that is not obvious. (2) A bungee cord that appears to be in good condition may create a risk to a user of the bungee cord that is not an obvious risk if it is used after the time the manufacturer of the bungee cord recommends its replacement or it is used in circumstances contrary to the manufacturer's recommendation'.

The relevant risk has to be obvious 'to a reasonable person in the position of that person' (presumably meaning a reasonable person standing, as it were, in the shoes of the injured person), in the particular circumstances of the event. Thus, the obviousness of the risk must be assessed objectively, though viewed from the perspective of the reasonable person in the position of the claimant, not the defendant.

The burden of proof

Defendants have the burden persuading the court that the risk in issue was 'obvious' within the terms of the statute. However, once the defendant has discharged this burden, a statutory presumption will arise that the plaintiff was aware of the risk of harm. To displace this presumption, plaintiffs must prove on the balance of probabilities that they were not aware of it.[101]

The injured party's burden of disproving awareness of the obvious risk is very onerous because the notion of 'awareness' is a much more vague concept than the common law requirement of actual (not constructive) knowledge. Furthermore, unlike the common law—which requires the defendant to establish that the plaintiff agreed to the particular risk that materialised—in Western Australia, South Australia, New South Wales, Tasmania, and Queensland, the statutory presumption merely requires that the injured person was 'aware of the type or kind of risk, even if the person is not aware of the precise nature, extent or manner of occurrence of the risk'.[102]

In Western Australia, New South Wales, South Australia, Tasmania, and Queensland,[103] the plaintiff's awareness of an obvious risk relieves the defendant from the duty to warn unless (a) the plaintiff has requested advice or information about the risk from the defendant; or (b) there is a requirement 'by a written law to warn the plaintiff of the risk'; or (c) 'the defendant is a professional and the risk is a risk of harm to the plaintiff from the provision of a professional service by the defendant'.[104] Additionally, four jurisdictions[105] stipulate that the risk, which places

---

101. Under the *Civil Liability Act 1936* (SA), s 37(1), plaintiffs have to prove that they were 'not *actually* aware of the risk' (emphasis added).
102. *Civil Liability Act 2002* (WA); *Civil Liability Act 1936* (SA), s 37(2); *Civil Liability Act 2002* (NSW), ss 5N(2), 5G(2); *Civil Liability Act 2002* (Tas), s 16(2); *Civil Liability Act 2003* (Qld), s 14(2). The wording of this definition superficially echoes the rule for remoteness of damage. However, in the remoteness of damage rule, the focus is on the foreseeability of damage as a kind or type, and the manner in which it occurred. As Gummow J expressed it in *Rosenberg v Percival* (2001) 205 CLR 434, at [64], 'the precise and particular character of the injury or the precise sequence of events leading to the injury need not be foreseeable. It is sufficient if the kind or type of injury was foreseeable, even if the extent of the injury was greater than expected.'
103. *Civil Liability Act 2002* (WA), s 5O(2).
104. *Civil Liability Act 2002* (WA), s 5O(2).
105. *Civil Liability Act 2002* (NSW), s 5H(2)(c); see also: *Civil Liability Act 1936* (SA), s 38(2)(c), which does not refer to professionals; *Civil Liability Act 2002* (Tas), s 17(c) and *Civil Liability Act 2003* (Qld), s15(1)(c), which apply to professionals 'other than' doctors.

a professional under a duty to warn, has to relate to 'the death of or personal injury to the plaintiff from the provision of a professional service by the defendant'. The plaintiff has the onus of proving the existence of one or more of these conditions.

The nature of the 'obvious risk' plea

In *Clarke v Coleambally Ski Club Inc* [2004] NSWCA 376, Young CJ in Exchequer observed (at [96]) that at common law, the plea of *volenti* concerns the duty of care, whereas the plea of 'obviousness of risk' concerns the breach of duty of care:

A successful plea of *volenti* amounts to waver of duty of care, while a plea of obviousness of risk is a factor that the court will consider when assessing the scope of defendant's duty of care. It may lead to the determination by the court that there was no breach of duty because the defendant was entitled to assume that people will not injure themselves through obvious risk.

The difference between the two pleas is semantic rather than substantive. Both involve the scope of the duty of care, though in voluntary assumption of risk, the defendant's scope of duty is limited by the waiver, whereas in the plea of obvious risk, this type or kind of risk is excluded from the ambit of the duty, except as provided by the statute.

Technically, the plea of obvious risk is a defence, in so far as the initial burden of proving obviousness is on the defendant. Tasmania, Victoria, Queensland, and South Australia[106] explicitly refer to the defence of voluntary assumption of risk (*volenti non fit injuria*), stating that where a defence of voluntary assumption of risk is raised 'and the risk of harm is an obvious risk, the person who suffered harm is presumed to have been aware of the risk, unless the person proves on the balance of probabilities that the person was not aware of the risk'.

Additionally, in South Australia, 'in order to establish a defence of voluntary assumption of risk, it is necessary to establish that the risk was such that a reasonable person in the plaintiff's position would have taken steps (which the plaintiff did not in fact take) to avoid it'.[107] In other words, for the defence to succeed, defendants must first establish both the limitation of their scope of the duty of care (obviousness of risk—which raises a rebuttable presumption that the plaintiff was aware of the obvious risk) and the plaintiff's own breach of duty (failure to avoid the obvious risk, in circumstances where a reasonable person would have done so).

In Victoria,[108] the statutory defence of voluntary assumption of risk does not apply to:

---

106. *Civil Liability Act 2002* (Tas), s 16(1) *Civil Liability Act 2003* (Qld), s 14(1); *Wrongs Act 1958* (Vic), s 54(1); *Civil Liability Act 1936* (SA), s 37.
107. *Civil Liability Act 1936* (SA), s 37(3).
108. *Wrongs Act 1958* (Vic), s 54(2).

(a) a proceeding on a claim for damages relating to the provision of, or the failure to provide, a professional service or health service; this exception encompasses proceedings for malpractice against lawyers, architects, engineers, accountants, medical practitioners and other professionals as well as providers of 'health services' such as personal trainers, masseurs, or chiropractors; or
(b) a proceeding on a claim for damages in respect of risks associated with work done by one person for another; this exception may include employer–employee relationships (including harm occasioned to employees by independent contractors hired by their employer), contractors and subcontractors, principals and agents, as well as professional–client relationships.

These cases are governed by the common law defence of voluntary assumption of risk: the defendant must show that the plaintiff had actual knowledge of the existence, nature, and extent of the risk, and voluntarily accepted personal responsibility if it materialised.

Obvious risks and dangerous recreational activities

To complicate matter further, four jurisdictions exclude liability for harm suffered from the materialisation of obvious risks relating to dangerous recreational activities,[109] whether or not the plaintiff was aware of the risk.[110] In Tasmania and Queensland, the distinguishing factor between 'recreational' activity and 'dangerous activity' is 'a significant degree of risk of physical harm to a person'.[111] In contrast, Western Australia and New South Wales have created yet another category of risk by defining 'dangerous recreational activity' as 'a recreational activity that involves a *significant risk* of physical harm' (emphasis added).[112] Provisions governing liability for dangerous recreational services refer to 'obvious risk' as defined for the purposes of assumption of risk (discussed above).

In the case of *Fallas v Mourlas* [2006] NSWCA 32, two friends, Morulas and Fallas were 'spotlighting'—shooting kangaroos at night with the aid of a spotlight on a vehicle. Morulas, who at the time of the accident was inside the vehicle, asked

---

109. *Civil Liability Act 2002* (WA), s 5E; *Civil Liability Act 2002* (NSW), s 5K; *Civil Liability Act 2002* (Tas), s 19. The *Civil Liability Act 2003* (Qld), s 18, provides a broader definition: '*dangerous recreational activity* means an activity engaged in for enjoyment, relaxation or leisure that involves a significant degree of risk of physical harm to a person'.
110. The *Civil Liability Act 2003* (Qld), s 19(1); *Civil Liability Act 2002* (NSW), s 5L(1); and *Civil Liability Act 2002* (Tas), s 20(1), have identical wording: 'A person is not liable in negligence for harm suffered by another person as a result of the materialisation of an obvious risk of a dangerous recreational activity engaged in by the person suffering harm'. *Civil Liability Act 2002* (WA), s 5H(1), is more specific, providing that the defendant is not liable for harm caused by the defendant's fault suffered by the plaintiff 'while the plaintiff engaged in a dangerous recreational activity if the harm is the result of the occurrence of something that is an obvious risk of that activity'.
111. *Civil Liability Act 2003* (Qld), s 19(2); *Civil Liability Act 2002* (Tas), s 20(2).
112. *Civil Liability Act 2002* (WA), s 5H(2); *Civil Liability Act 2002* (NSW), s 5L(2).

Fallas not to enter the vehicle with a loaded gun. Fallas assured him that the gun was not loaded and that it was safe for him to enter. Once inside the vehicle, Fallas, contrary to Morulas' request, while attempting to to un-jam the gun, pointed it in the direction of his friend. The gun accidentally discharged, injuring Morulas in the leg. The learned Justices, Ipp and Basten JJA of the New South Wales Court of Appeal (Tobias JA dissenting), in separate judgments, determined that the risk that materialised (shooting the plaintiff in the leg), did not constitute an 'obvious risk' for dangerous recreational activity as defined in s 5F of the *Civil Liability Act 2002* (NSW).

In the course of discussing the nature of the statutory 'obvious risk', Ipp J (at [52]) re-introduced into the common law of negligence the concept of 'gross negligence':

> Negligence comes in an infinite number of forms and the degrees of negligent conduct are infinite. The term 'gross negligence' is nowadays not often used but courts from time to time still consider its meaning and application.[113] It is sufficient, for the purposes of these reasons, to say that gross negligence is negligence to an extreme degree.

Having observed (at [53]) that 'while a person might accept the risk of harm caused by another's negligent conduct, that person is less likely to accept the risk of a person being grossly negligent', his Honour thus opined (at [54]):

> In my view, when considering whether there has been a materialisation of an obvious risk, a distinction may have to be drawn between a risk of negligent conduct on the part of another and conduct that is grossly negligent. In some circumstances, it may not be sufficient merely to ask whether the risk of harm caused by a person being negligent was obvious. If the conduct that caused the risk amounted to gross negligence, it would be necessary, in my opinion, to determine whether the risk of harm caused by gross negligence of the kind in question was obvious. Otherwise, if—for the purposes of s 5L [of the *Civil Liability Act 2002* (NSW)]—the 'risk of negligence' is to be regarded as a descriptive catch-all for the risks of any kind of careless conduct, no matter how extreme, harm caused by grossly negligent conduct could be held to be an obvious risk where in fact such a risk was not obvious at all.

The problem with Ipp J's application of a 'gross negligence' test to determine the existence of an 'obvious risk' is that it stands in direct contrast to the statement

---

113. In support of his statement, Ipp J relied relied on *R v De'Zilwa* (2002) 5 VR 408, *R v Leusenkamp* (2003) 40 MVR 108, *Etna v Arif* [1999] VR 353 at 383, and *Re Bendeich (No 2)* (1994) 53 FCR 422 at 427 as examples of courts utilising the concept of 'gross negligence'. However, none of these cases relates to the tort of negligence. *R v Leusenkamp* and *R v De'Zilwa* concerned interpretation of s 318(2)(b) of the *Crimes Act 1958* (Vic), pertaining to persons charged with culpable driving, while *Etna v Arif* and *Re Bendeich* involved interpretation of the wording contained in the relevant rules of civil procedure.

by Taylor J in *Fitzgerald v Penn* (1954) 91 CLR 268, at 283–4, which has not, since then, been contradicted or repudiated by the High Court, or other appellate courts. Taylor J, having observed that there are 'no grades or degrees of negligence', and no rule that plaintiffs are 'prevented from recovering by "mild" negligence', and can only recover for damage caused by 'gross' negligence, stated:

> Generally speaking in civil cases 'gross' negligence has no more effect than negligence without an opprobrious epithet. Negligence is the breach of that duty to take care, which the law requires, either in regard to another's person or his property, or where contributory negligence is in question, of the man's own person or property. The degree of want of care which constitutes negligence must vary with the circumstances. What that degree is, is a question for the jury or the Court in lieu of a jury.

Drunken drivers and the defence of voluntary assumption of risk

For more than forty years, the courts have followed the High Court's decision in *Roggenkamp v Bennett* (1950) 80 CLR 292, allowing the defendant to successfully plead voluntary assumption of risk even when the plaintiff was too drunk to fully appreciate the risk involved. However, in the 1990s, in such cases as *Spicer v Coppins* (1991) 56 SASR 175, *Radford v Ward* (1990) 11 MVR 509 at 515, *Suncorp Insurance and Finance Ltd v Blakeney* (1993) 18 MVR 361 at 368, and *McPherson v Whitfield & Anor* [1995] QCA 62 (unreported, Queensland Court of Appeal, 15 March 1995), the courts have tended to reduce the drunken plaintiff's damages under the doctrine of contributory negligence rather than apply the defence of voluntary assumption of risk in drinking cases. Legislation relating specifically to intoxicated and drunken drivers (discussed above), as well as the concept of 'obvious risk', may modify this trend.

Exclusion of liability clauses

Nicholson J in *Scanlon v American Cigarette Company (Overseas) Pty Ltd (No 3)* [1987] VR 289 adopted a distinction (articulated by Francis Trindade and Peter Cane in their *The Law of Torts in Australia*)[114] between exclusion of liability by way of exemption clauses and the defence of voluntary assumption of risk.

Two competing public policy interests underpin the exclusion of liability clauses that exculpate the defendant from tortious liability. There is the public policy interest of respect for the sanctity of contract and the autonomy of contracting

---

114. Oxford University Press, Melbourne, 1985.

parties on the one hand, and the public interest in compensating those who have been tortiously injured, on the other.[115] Behind the public interest in contractual autonomy lies the notion that the major role of contract law is the encouragement of economically efficient transactions. The principles of contract are designed to facilitate commercial transactions by ensuring that parties are held to the bargain they struck.[116] The major concern of the law of torts is compensation for the wrongfully injured. Exclusion clauses effectively import contractual doctrines into the substantive law of torts. The courts have long held that where the duty of care between plaintiff and defendant arises from a consensual relationship, the defendant is free to define the terms of the relationship. The plaintiff has a reciprocal freedom to decline. By agreeing to enter into a contractual relationship, the plaintiff consents to the conditions, providing the defendant has taken reasonable steps to draw them to the plaintiff's attention. For example, in *Toll (FGCT) Pty Ltd v Alphapharm Pty Ltd* [2004] 219 CLR 165, an officer of a corporation was authorised to contract on behalf of the plaintiff corporation. He signed a document governing the storage and transportation of some goods. On the reverse side of this document, under the title *Conditions of Contract*, were exclusion clauses. He failed to read these clauses. The High Court concluded that the exclusion clauses on the reverse of the document were clearly spelt out and hence formed binding part of the contract.

Thus, just like the statutory defence for voluntary assumption of obvious risk—and unlike the common law defence of voluntary assumption of risk—the test for the defence of exclusion of liability clauses is objective. In conformity with the rule that rights and liabilities of the parties to a contract are determined by the principle of objectivity,[117] the court will examine the facts to determine whether in the circumstances of the case:

- the plaintiff knew or ought to have known of the exclusion clause; and
- the plaintiff accepted the stipulation in the exclusion clause that the defendant should not be liable if a risk, whatever it might be, does materialise.

The courts consider that as a general rule, the conduct of signing a contract or any legal document 'would convey to a reasonable person that the signatory either has read and approved the contents of the document or is willing to take the chance of being bound by those contents. It is immaterial whether the party who signed it has read the document.'[118] *Gowan v Hardy* (unreported, CA 40531/89, 8 November 1991) is a case in point. The plaintiff was a pupil of a parachuting

---

115. For a further discussion of this issue, see: Radcliffe RA, 'When Should the Trier of Fact Determine the Validity of Personal Injury Releases?' (1988) 63 *Washington Law Review* 749.
116. Id at 757.
117. *Toll (FGCT) Pty Ltd v Alphapharm Pty Ltd* [2004] 219 CLR 165 at [40]; *Pacific Carriers Ltd v BNP Paribas* (2004) 78 ALJR 1045; 208 ALR 213.
118. *Toll (FGCT) Pty Ltd v Alphapharm Pty Ltd* (2004) 219 CLR 165 at [47].

school. She sued, *inter alia*, the pilot of her drop plane, because he came in to land too close to the landing zone. The plaintiff had to swerve out of the way, and as a result landed badly, breaking her leg. Before joining the program, the plaintiff had signed a form that excluded negligence and was expressed to be for the benefit of instructors, servants, and agents of the school. The trial judge and the Court of Appeal found that although the pilot was negligent, he did not have to pay damages, because he was 'a servant of the school' and therefore his negligence was covered by the exclusion clause.

Even where the plaintiff reads but misunderstands the exclusion clause, it may still be binding. For example, in *Neill v Fallon* [1995] Aust Torts Reports ¶81–321, the plaintiff signed a membership agreement with the defendants, who owned and operated the Body Shape Fitness Centre. The agreement stated:

> I acknowledge that during all such times whilst on the premises both my property and my person shall be at my own risk and I will not hold Body Shape Fitness Centre or instructors liable for any personal injury or loss of property whether caused by Body Shape Fitness Centre, its servants or agents.

The defendant explained that the clause was to cover silly accidents such as dropping a weight on the plaintiff's foot. The plaintiff, who had previously injured his back, was advised by the defendants to undertake a body-building program, which included doing squats that were inappropriate for his back condition. The plaintiff told the defendants that the squats gave him back trouble, but they did not follow this issue up, and he eventually suffered a serious back injury requiring surgery. At the trial, the defendants argued that they were protected by the exclusion clause. The Queensland Court of Appeal agreed. As a general rule, in relation to recreational activities, the courts have considered that persons intending to engage in such pastimes should take out insurance.

The courts, however, distinguish cases of unsigned documents where contract terms and conditions, including exclusion clauses, appear in a notice or a ticket. In such cases, the onus of proof is on the party relying on the exclusionary terms to prove that the injured party was aware, or ought to have been aware, of its terms and conditions (*L'Estrange v Graucob* [1934] 2 KB 394 at 402–3). For example, in *Vine v Waltham Forest London Borough Council* [2000] 1 WLR 2383, while driving home from a hospital in a distressed state after being told by doctors that she required an urgent operation, Mrs Vine, the plaintiff, experienced pain and violent nausea. She parked her car in a private parking space within sight of a notice, which read: 'Any vehicle left unattended is liable to be towed away or wheel clamped. Recoverable by payment of a fine of £105'. Evidence established that the plaintiff did not see the notice when she left her car to vomit by the roadside. When she returned, Mrs Vine found her car clamped by a contractor employed by the defendant council and was forced to pay £105, plus a £3.68 fee for using a credit card, to secure its release. She was successful in recovering £108.68.

In relation to notices, Waller LJ observed (at 2393):

> absent unusual circumstances, if it is established that a car driver saw a notice and if it is established that he appreciated that it contained terms in relation to the basis on which he was to come onto another's land, but did not read the notice, and thus fully understood the precise terms, he will not be able to say that he did not consent to, and willingly assume the risk of being clamped.

The burden of proof is on the defendant to show both that the driver actually did see the notice, and that he or she appreciated the terms contained therein. In relation to the question whether particular terms have been incorporated into contracts for the parking of motor cars, or other kinds of notice excluding liability, Waller LJ cited the statement of Lord Denning MR in *Mendelssohn v Normand Ltd* [1970] 1 QB 177, at 182, who determined that such terms are 'not imported into the contract unless it is brought home to the party so prominently that he must be taken to have known of it and agreed to it …'

This approach, which places a high onus on the party relying on an exclusionary term in a contract or notice, is particularly pertinent to reform legislation permitting 'self assumption of risk'[119] by consumers of recreational services.

Statutory reforms

Western Australia, New South Wales, Victoria, South Australia, and the Northern Territory have followed the Commonwealth in enacting legislation allowing suppliers of recreational services to validly include waiver clauses in contracts for such services. The waiver clauses can exclude, restrict or modify liability for the breach of an express or implied warranty that the services will be provided with reasonable care and skill.

Under the *Trade Practices Act 1974* (Cth), s 74(1) and (2) respectively imply into contracts for the supply of services by a corporation to a consumer in the course of a business an implied warranty that the services will be rendered with due care and skill, and an implied warranty that the services will be reasonably fit for their intended purpose. By virtue of s 68, any term of a contract that purports to exclude or restrict the warranties implied by s 74 is void. In 2002, the Commonwealth enacted the *Trade Practices Amendment (Liability for Recreational Services) Act 2002*, creating s 68B, which provides that: 'a term of a contract for the supply by a corporation of recreational services is not void under s 68 by reason only that the term excludes, restricts or modifies, or has the effect of excluding, restricting or modifying': (a) the application of, or (b) consumer rights conferred

---

119. According to the Explanatory Memorandum to the *Trade Practices Amendment (Liability for Recreational Services) Act 2002* (Cth) circulated by authority of the Minister for Revenue and Assistant Treasurer, Senator the Hon Helen Coonan.

by, or (c) any liability of the supplier of the recreational services for a breach of statutory warranties in relation to the supply of services under s 74, as long as (d) the exclusion, restriction or modification is limited to liability for death or personal injury.[120]

Section 68A of the *Consumer Affairs and Fair Trading Act 1996* (NT) (as in force in 2005) essentially replicates the Commonwealth provisions in relation to exclusionary terms in contracts for the supply of recreational services, though it mandates that these terms must be disclosed (verbally or in writing) to the person entering into the contract for the recreational services, so that the consumer is 'aware of the general effect' of the exemption clause(s); and 'has a reasonable opportunity to consider whether or not to enter into the contract on that basis'.

Western Australia[121] and New South Wales[122] have very similar waiver provisions which, in rather convoluted language, provide that a term of a contract for the supply of recreational services to the effect that the customer engages in a recreational activity at his or her own risk shall operate to exclude liability for the breach of an express or implied warranty that the services will be rendered with reasonable care and skill. The statutory definition of 'recreational activity' is very wide; it includes: '(a) any sport (whether or not the sport is an organised activity); (b) any pursuit or activity engaged in for enjoyment, relaxation or leisure; and (c) any pursuit or activity engaged in for enjoyment, relaxation or leisure at a place (such as a beach, park or other public open space) where people ordinarily engage in sport or in any pursuit or activity for enjoyment, relaxation or leisure'.[123] Services supplied 'for the purposes of, in connection with or incidental to the pursuit' of a recreational activity are defined as 'recreational services'. There are two major exceptions to the scope of statutorily protected exclusion of liability. One relates to contravention of a law 'that establishes specific practices or procedures for the protection of personal safety', while the other concerns harm that has 'resulted from an act done or omission made with reckless disregard, with or without consciousness, for the consequences of the act or omission'.

Rule 5 of the *Fair Trading (Recreational Services) Regulations 2004* (Vic) enables suppliers of recreational services to obtain express or implied consent from

---

120. According to the Explanatory Memorandum to the *Trade Practices Amendment (Liability for Recreational Services) Act 2002* (Cth) circulated by authority of the Minister for Revenue and Assistant Treasurer, Senator the Hon Helen Coonan, 'the contractual rights which consumers have by virtue of the TPA [*Trade Practices Act*] were not enacted with any specific intention that they might be used to provide remedies where consumers died or were injured as a result of a breach of a condition or warranty implied by the Act. The purpose of this Bill is to ensure that the object of the TPA is not subverted for an improper purpose.'
121. *Civil Liability Act 2002* (WA), s 5J.
122. *Civil Liability Act 2002* (NSW), s 5N.
123. *Civil Liability Act 2002* (WA), s 5E; *Civil Liability Act 2002* (NSW), s 5K. See also: *Trade Practices Act 1974* (Cth), s 68B; *Consumer Affairs and Fair Trading Act 1996* (NT) (as in force in 2005), s 68A(3); *Recreational Services (Limitation of Liability) Act* 2002 (SA), s 3.

customers to waive their rights under the *Fair Trading Act 1999* (Vic) by including an exclusionary term on a sign displayed at the place at which the recreational services are being supplied; in a notice given to the purchaser; or by a signed waiver form. In each case, the waiver must be accompanied by the following statutory warning: 'If you participate in these activities your rights to sue the supplier under the *Fair Trading Act 1999* if you are killed or injured because the activities were not supplied with due care and skill or were not reasonably fit for their purpose, are excluded, restricted or modified in the way set out in or on this *sign/*notice'. The warning must be accompanied by a note that 'the change to the customer's rights does not apply if the death or injury is due to gross negligence on the supplier's part'. Rule 4 defines 'gross negligence' as 'the act or omission ... done or omitted to be done with reckless disregard, with or without consciousness, for the consequences of the act or omission'.

The *Recreational Services (Limitation of Liability) Act 2002* (SA) has created a different regime, whereby under s 4 providers of recreational services need to register with the Minister an undertaking to comply with a registered code governing particular recreational services, before they can 'enter into a contract with a consumer modifying the duty of care owed by the provider to the consumer so that the duty of care is governed by the registered code' (s 6).

Exclusionary clauses relating to the provision of recreational services in Tasmania, Queensland, and the Australian Capital Territory are governed by common law and by the *Trade Practices Act 1974* (Cth).

In his Second Reading Speech, introducing the Bill to amend the *Trade Practices Act 1974* (Cth),[124] Mr Peter Slipper, MP, said:

> In allowing people to voluntarily waive their right to sue, it is important to achieve a balance between protecting consumers and allowing them to take responsibility for themselves. This bill seeks to achieve that balance in a way that will benefit consumers and the many small businesses that are involved in recreational activities.

These statutory provisions will certainly benefit many small and big businesses; it is more difficult to envisage how exactly they are going to benefit the consumers injured by negligent provision of recreational services. It is unclear whether parents, guardians, or persons *in loco parentis* can validly agree on behalf of children to contractual arrangements that exclude liability of the providers as contemplated under the legislation. In determining the issue, the courts will, no doubt, examine the objective context of the purported agreement to establish that the parent entered it voluntarily: *Macleay Pty Ltd v Moore* [1991] Aust Torts Reports ¶81–151.

---

124. House of Representatives, *Hansard*, 27 June 2002, p 4543.

The enforceability of waivers against minors will presumably depend on whether the defendant can establish on the balance of probabilities that at the time of accepting the exclusion or modification of his or her right to sue the provider for failure to take reasonable care and skill in providing recreational services, the minor understood the legal consequences of the waiver (or the waiver itself).[125]

DEFENCE OF JOINT ILLEGAL ENTERPRISE AND THE NATURE OF ILLEGALITY

The fact that, at the time of sustaining wrongfully inflicted injury, the plaintiff was involved in an illegal activity may be a consideration in determining the defendant's standard of care;[126] give rise to the defence of contributory negligence (discussed above); or give rise to the defence of joint illegal enterprise.

The defence of a joint illegal enterprise generally arises in cases where the conduct of the parties at the time of injury is either criminal—for example, an armed robber accidentally shooting one of his associates instead of the intended victim—or is considered to be illegal because of its criminal context—for example, driving is generally not illegal, but driving a get-away car from the crime scene is.[127] In *Fabre v Arenales* (1992) 27 NSWLR 437, the New South Wales Court of Appeal held that the driver of a stolen car being pursued by the police did not owe a duty of care to his passenger, who was injured when the vehicle crashed as a result of the driver's error. Another often-quoted example is that of using explosives for demolition purposes, as against using them to blow up a bank safe for the purpose of robbing it.

In *Smith v Jenkins* (1970) 119 CLR 397, the plaintiff and defendant assaulted and robbed the owner of a motor vehicle, and then unlawfully took it for a ride. The plaintiff was injured when, some hours later, while being driven at very high speed, the car left the road and hit a tree. Windeyer J (at 422) observed:

> If two or more persons participate in the commission of a crime, each takes the risk of the negligence of the other or others in the actual performance of the criminal act. That formulation can be regarded as founded on the negation of duty, or on some extension of the rule *volenti non fit injuria*, or simply on the refusal of the courts to aid wrongdoers. How it be analysed and explained matters not.

Kitto J (at 403) stated that 'persons who intentionally engage in criminal conduct cannot avail themselves of legal redress in order to receive a benefit as the direct result of criminal activities'.

---

125. See also: *Minors (Property and Contracts) Act 1970* (NSW); *Minors Contracts (Miscellaneous Provisions) Act 1979* (SA); *Minors Contracts Act 1988* (Tas).
126. See, for example: *Wrongs Act 1958* (Vic), s 14G.
127. *Holland v Tarlinton* (1989) 10 MVR 129 (NSW CA).

In general, the conduct of the parties has to be such that a court will decline, for public policy reasons, to grant relief.

The denial of relief for joint illegal enterprise is related to the illegality of the enterprise and the hazards inherent in its execution. The plaintiff would fail only if the appropriate standard of care for the defendant's conduct could not be determined without reference to the illegal nature of the activity. Thus, in *Jackson v. Harrison* (1978) 138 CLR 438, the plaintiff and the defendant, despite knowing that each had been suspended from driving, set out to drive from Adelaide to Port Augusta and back, in a car belonging to one of them. The plaintiff was injured when the car overturned due to negligent driving by the defendant driver. Mason, Jacobs, Murphy, and Aickin JJ held that the plaintiff should be allowed to recover damages. Mason, Jacobs and Aickin JJ (in separate judgments) found that the joint illegal activity of driving without a licence was a traffic offence, and had no bearing on the standard of care reasonably expected of a driver. Barwick CJ dissented on policy grounds. His Honour pointed out (at 451) that: 'a motor car on a public road in unqualified or irresponsible hands can be a lethal instrument', and that as a matter of public policy, where in issue is 'the disqualification of a person to drive a car because of lack of skill or because of irresponsible tendencies is a means whereby the safety and health of the community is secured', the seriousness of the offence should not be minimised. Referring to *Smith v Jenkins*, Barwick CJ observed (at 451):

> I cannot accept that the protection of property or possession of a motor vehicle is of more consequence to the community than the safety and health of its citizens: that the principle of *Smith v Jenkins* extends to theft or its equivalent but not to conduct endangering health or life.

In contrast, Mason J (at 453) noted that where the defence of joint illegal enterprise is applied inflexibly, its effect is 'too Draconian to command acceptance', for:

> There is nothing inherent in the character of an unlicensed driver which is inconsistent with his owing a duty of care to other road users and to his passengers who happen to be engaged in unlawful activity. However, it is said that if the passenger acquiesces or participates in the illegal use of the car no such duty is owed.

Mason J also commented that the passenger's acquiescence should not be used to find the defence of joint illegal enterprise 'when the facts fall short of *volenti*, a defence which might otherwise be thought to be appropriate'.

In *Gala & Ors v Preston* (1991) 172 CLR 243, the High Court approached the issue of joint illegal enterprise as one involving the denial of the duty of care. Gala, Preston, and two others, having drunk some forty or so scotches each, stole a car. While 'joy riding' they consumed more alcohol (at the time of the accident, their blood alcohol concentration was in excess of .2 per cent). Gala was driving the car when Preston went to sleep in the back seat. Soon afterwards, the vehicle left the roadway and struck a tree. One of the passengers was killed and Preston dislocated his right hip and suffered some other minor injuries by being thrown from the car. He sued Gala for damages. The High Court determined that Gala did not owe Preston a duty of care, on the basis that public policy considerations precluded the existence of legal proximity[128] between the plaintiff and the defendant. Mason CJ, Deane, Gaudron, and McHugh JJ, in a joint judgment, commented (at 253) that in cases where parties are involved in a joint criminal activity, the court has to consider 'the appropriateness and feasibility of seeking to define the content of a relevant duty of care'. Their Honours stated (at 255) that in the circumstances of the case, to conclude that Gala 'should have observed the ordinary standard of care to be expected of a competent driver would be to disregard the actual relationship between the parties', and 'to seek to define a more limited duty of care by reference to the exigencies of the particular case would involve a weighing and adjusting of the conflicting demands of the joint criminal activity and the safety of the participants in which it would be neither appropriate nor feasible for the courts to engage'.

Statutory reforms

Four jurisdictions have enacted legislation that excludes civil liability for injuries sustained in the course of criminal conduct. In New South Wales[129] and Tasmania,[130] damages are not to be awarded if the court is satisfied that at the time of the person's death, injury, or loss, he or she was engaged in conduct that the court finds, on the balance of probabilities, to constitute a 'serious offence', and that this conduct 'contributed materially to the death, injury or damage or to the risk of death, injury or damage'.[131] In both jurisdictions, statutory exclusion of liability 'operates whether or not a person whose conduct is alleged to constitute an offence has been, will be or is capable of being proceeded against or convicted of any offence concerned.' The 'serious offence' is defined to mean 'an offence punishable by imprisonment for 6 months or more'.

Queensland's provisions are similar,[132] but they refer to the court being satisfied on the balance of probabilities that (a) 'the breach of duty from which civil liability would arise, apart from this section, happened while the person who suffered

---

128. The term 'legal proximity' refers to the now discarded notion of proximity as a general determinant of the categories of case in the developing areas of the law of negligence.
129. *Civil Liability Act 2002* (NSW), s 54.
130. *Civil Liability Act 2002* (Tas), s 6(1).
131. The *Civil Liability Act 2002* (NSW), s 54(2), provides that the exclusion of liability 'does not apply to an award of damages against a defendant if the conduct of the defendant that caused the death, injury or damage concerned constitutes an offence (whether or not a serious offence)'.
132. *Civil Liability Act 2003* (Qld), s 45.

harm was engaged in conduct that is an indictable offence', and (b) 'the person's conduct contributed materially to the risk of the harm'. Just as in New South Wales and Tasmania, 'it does not matter whether the person whose conduct is alleged to constitute an indictable offence has been, will be or is or was capable of being proceeded against or convicted of an indictable offence'.[133] The legislation provides for an exception, allowing the court to award damages 'in a particular case if satisfied that in the circumstances of the case, the statutory exclusion of liability 'would operate harshly and unjustly'. However, in such exceptional cases damages to which the injured person would be otherwise entitled are to be reduced by 25 per cent or a greater percentage as decided by the court, by reason of the injured person's conduct.

The South Australian regime under the *Civil Liability Act 1936* (SA), s 43(1), is different in so far as it effectively bifurcates the proceeding by mandating that liability for damages can only be excluded if the court:

(a) is satisfied *beyond reasonable doubt* that the accident occurred while the injured person was engaged in conduct constituting an indictable offence; and
(b) is satisfied on the *balance of probabilities* that the injured person's conduct contributed materially to the risk of injury.' [emphasis added]

For the purposes of subsection (1)(a), a relevant conviction or acquittal is to be accepted as conclusive evidence of guilt or innocence of the offence to which it relates.

Section 45(2) provides for an exception to the exclusionary rule on the grounds of harsh and unjust operation; however, unlike the Queensland legislation, it does not direct the court to reduce damages in consideration of the criminal conduct.

Section 45(4)(c) of the *Civil Liability Act 1936* (SA) specifically provides that the statutory exclusion of liability 'does not affect the operation of a rule of law relating to joint illegal enterprises'.

There is nothing in the wording of the relevant provisions in the other three jurisdictions to suggest that they intend to oust the common law defence of joint illegal enterprise.

Breach of statutory prohibition

What happens when persons are injured by a negligent defendant, in circumstances where their own conduct was in breach of a statutory prohibition?

As a general rule, at common law, a person engaged in an unlawful conduct, providing he or she is not engaged in a joint illegal enterprise, will not be barred

---

133. *Civil Liability Act 2003* (Qld), s 45(2).

from bringing an action in negligence against the negligent tortfeasor. This rule was articulated by the High Court in *Henwood v Municipal Tramways Trust (SA)* (1938) 60 CLR 438. In this case, the plaintiff, a twelve-year-old boy, was travelling on a tram when he became sick. He leaned out of the window to vomit but his head fatally struck against an electricity pole placed very close to the tram tracks. There was a statutory prohibition against passengers leaning out of tram windows. A warning notice was placed inside tram carriages. The danger arose because the defendants had purchased tram carriages too wide for the tram tracks. The defendants were aware of four previous serious accidents due to the width of the trams, yet did nothing to prevent this clearly foreseeable harm, apart from posting the warning notice. The defendants argued that the plaintiff breached the statute and was therefore engaged in an illegal activity when the accident happened.

Latham CJ (at 446) held that the law does not deny liability for negligence on the ground that the plaintiff at the relevant time was breaking some provision of the law. Breach of a statutory provision does not prevent the plaintiff from recovering for deliberate or negligently occasioned injury. His Honour gave examples of a child injured in a motor car accident while playing truant from school; a burglar on his way to a professional engagement; and an employee absent from work in breach of contract—stating that 'none of these facts is relevant for the purpose of deciding the existence or defining the content of the obligation of a motor driver not to injure them'.

The issue that needs to be examined is whether the law in question was designed to protect the plaintiff or the defendant. If the law was designed to protect the plaintiff, the plaintiff invariably will have a civil remedy. Even where the regulation or prohibition was designed to protect the defendant, a civil remedy will still lie, unless the statute expressly and clearly provides that someone doing the prohibited act is disentitled from complaining of the other party's negligence. This might happen in certain circumstances where the court determines that the risk was 'obvious'.

But what if both the plaintiff and the defendant are in breach of a statutory prohibition? This question was explored in *Progress Properties Ltd v Craft* (1976) 135 CLR 651. The plaintiff was a plumber working on a twenty-five-storey building being constructed at Darling Point in Sydney. On an outside face of the construction there was a hoist for raising bricks. The operation was controlled from ground level by an operator. There was an internal lift for workers, but it only went to the twelfth floor, whereas the plaintiff had to work on the twentieth floor. The plaintiff and other workers were being taken to the top of the building in the hoist when the operator's foot slipped off the pedal of the brake. The hoist plummeted to the ground, severely injuring the plaintiff. Statutory regulation made it an offence to ride on the hoist or to permit another person to do so. The defendants claimed that since both the plaintiff and the hoist operator were in breach of the statutory prohibition, they were jointly engaged in an illegal activity, and thus should come within the ambit of the defence of illegality.

Jacobs J, with whom Stephen, Mason, and Murphy JJ agreed (Barwick CJ dissenting), ruled (at 669) that the defence of illegality and consequent denial of duty could not succeed in this case, because the defence of joint illegal enterprise is wholly inapplicable to the circumstances of regulations designed to enforce a high specific duty to ensure the safety of the participants.

His Honour also noted at (at 688) that:

> A duty of care arises out of the relationship of particular persons one to another. ... Where there is a joint illegal activity the actual act of which the plaintiff in a civil action may be complaining as done without care may itself be a criminal act of a kind in respect of which a court is not prepared to hear evidence for the purpose of establishing the standard of care which was reasonable in the circumstances. A court will not hear evidence nor will it determine the standard of care owing by a safe blower to his accomplice in respect of an explosive device.

In the case of the joint illegal activity of the injured plumber and the hoist operator, the court did not have to examine the illegality itself when deciding upon the reasonable standard of care the operator owed to the plumber. Therefore, the illegality could not absolve the operator from the duty of care to operate the hoist with due care for the plumber's safety.

FURTHER READING

Abel-Smith B & Stevens R, *Lawyers and the Courts: A Sociological Study of the English Legal System*, Heinemann, London, 1967.

Bartrip PWJ & Burman SB, *The Wounded Soldiers of Industry*, Clarendon Press, Oxford, 1983.

Fleming J, *The Law of Torts*, 9th edn, The Law Book Company Ltd, Sydney, 1998.

Friedman LM & Ladinsky J, 'Social Change and the Law of Industrial Accidents' (1967) 67 *Columbia Law Review* 50.

Luntz H & Hambly D, *Torts Cases and Commentary*, 5th edn, Butterworths, Sydney, 2002.

Palmer RC, *English Law in the Age of the Black Death 1348–1381*, The University of North Carolina Press, Chapel Hill and London, 1993.

Radcliffe RA, 'When Should the Trier of Fact Determine the Validity of Personal Injury Releases?' (1988) 63 *Washington Law Review* 749.

Simons KW, 'Assumption of Risk and Consent in the Law of Torts: A Theory of Full Preference' (1987) 97 *Boston University Law Review* 213.

Stein MA, 'Priestley v Fowler (1837) and the Emerging Tort of Negligence' (2003) 44 *Boston College Law Review* 689.

Williams G, *Joint Torts and Contributory Negligence*, Stevens, London, 1951.

Zimmerman R, *The Law of Obligations*, Clarendon Press, Oxford, 1996.

Part IV

STRICT-LIABILITY TORTS

Part III analysed the most important cause of action which evolved from the original writ of action on the case, namely the tort of negligence. Part IV examines the strict-liability torts of private nuisance and breach of statutory duty, as well as defamation and vicarious liability.

Private Nuisance 18

INTRODUCTION

Nuisance is one of the oldest and most important torts. The writ of assize of nuisance dates back to 1166 and was probably a subgenus of the assize of novel disseisin.[1] The writ of nuisance was also specifically mentioned in the *Statute of Westminster II, In Consimili Casu 1285* Stat 1 13 Edw I c 24. The tort of nuisance protected a freeholder from damage to land and interference with its enjoyment by offensive conduct taking place outside its boundaries. The assize was only available in cases where both the plaintiff and the defendant were freeholders. Thus, there was no remedy for or against leaseholders. Originally, the interference with the plaintiff's right to enjoyment of possession of the land had to be occasioned directly by human action. Consequently, the assize of nuisance did not lie against pollution of a watercourse, or failure to repair a ditch. The assize of nuisance went into abeyance with the end of the feudal era and its system of vassalage. In the late sixteenth century, nuisance on the case effectively replaced the assize of nuisance.

Due to its historical origins in medieval property law, the tort of private nuisance is a proprietary cause of action related to land—yet, being a species of action on the case, it is quite distinct from trespass to land. The distinction was illuminated in *Hales' Case* (*c* 1560),[2] where it was argued that 'if one who hath a horrible sickness be in my house, and will not depart, an action will lie against him; and yet he taketh not any air from me, but infecteth that which I have.' The remaining on the land constituted trespass, but the infection was a nuisance.

Private nuisance differs from trespass in that it is concerned with *indirect* harm. Nuisance often arises upon an indirect and unreasonable interference with the rights of another to use and enjoy land. As *Hales' Case* illustrates, the tort is frequently

---

1. Baker JH, *An Introduction to English Legal History*, 2nd edn, Butterworths, London, 1981, p 352.
2. Published as *A Briefe Declaration for What Manner of Speciall Nusance ... a Man May Have His Remedy* (1636), per Mounson J; quoted in Baker JH, *An Introduction to English Legal History*, 2nd edn, Butterworths, London, 1981, p 357.

concerned with tangible and intangible pollutants emanating from neighbouring properties. In this sense, private nuisance can be described as an environmental tort, though probably the most efficient remedies against pollution are well-drafted public health and environment statutes.

LEGAL SPECIES OF NUISANCE

There are four legal species of nuisance:

- the statutory tort of nuisance;
- the tort of public nuisance;
- the crime of public nuisance; and
- private nuisance.

Each is dealt with in turn below.

Statutory tort of nuisance

Statutory nuisance, as the name suggests, is governed by various environmental, zoning, and public health and safety laws.[3] Some statutes provide criminal penalties, as well as temporary or permanent licence cancellation for breach of prohibition against statutory nuisance. In cases of loss, destruction, or damage to property, an order for compensation may be made.[4] For example, s 32(1) of the *Domestic (Feral and Nuisance) Animals Act 1994* (Vic)[5] provides that the occupier of any premises where a dog or cat is kept or permitted to remain must not allow that animal to be a nuisance, with one penalty unit for breach. Under s 32(2), 'A dog or cat is to be regarded as a nuisance if (a) it injures or endangers the health of any person'; or (b) 'creates a noise, by barking or otherwise, which persistently occurs or continues to such a degree or extent that it unreasonably interferes with the peace, comfort or convenience of any person in any other premises'. Clause (a) of the prohibition

---

3. *Health Act 1958* (Vic), Pt III (Nuisance); *Summary Offences Act 1966* (Vic), ss 4, 5, 7, 8; Pt V (Clean Water), Pt VI (Clean Air), Pt VII (Control of Solid Wastes and Pollution of Land), Pt VIII (Control of Noise) and ss 62–65A (Abatement and Cost Recovery and Compensation). *Environment Protection Act 1970* (Vic), s 48A and *Environment Protection (Residential Noise) Regulations 1997* (Vic); *Local Government Act 1989* (Vic), s 111 and Sch 1 (Functions of Councils), Sch 10; *Building Act 1993* (Vic), Pt 7 (Protection of Adjoining Property) and the *Building Regulations 1994*; *Crimes Act 1958* (Vic), s 320; *Residential Tenancies Act 1997* (Vic), s 60; *Domestic (Feral and Nuisance) Animals Act 1994* (Vic), s 32; *Marine Act 1988* (Vic), s 38; *Pollution of Waters by Oil and Noxious Substances Act 1986* (Vic).
4. *Sentencing Act 1991* (Vic), s 86; see also: the *Environment Protection Act 1970* (Vic), s 65A (includes the reasonable costs or estimated costs of a clean up).
5. See also: the *Domestic Animals Act 2000* (ACT), s 109, which provides that 'For this Part, animal nuisance exists if the keeping or behaviour of an animal causes a condition, state or activity that constitutes (a) damage to property owned by a person other than the keeper; or (b) excessive disturbance to a person other than the keeper because of noise; or (c) danger to the health of an animal or a person other than the keeper.'

refers to 'physical harm', whereas clause (b) concerns 'non-physical harm'; both kinds of actionable nuisance will be discussed below.

By virtue of s 32(3), 'If a person is convicted of an offence against this section, the court may order the convicted person to take that action (if any) to abate the nuisance which is specified in the order.' Penalty for breach of s 32(3) is three penalty units.[6]

The crime of public nuisance and the tort of public nuisance

The crime of public nuisance, which in medieval times was prosecuted in courts leet (manorial criminal courts for the punishment of small offences) safeguarded the public from inconvenience such as diversion of watercourses, razing of dykes, narrowing or blocking of roads, placing filth on the street, and so on.

In *Overseas Tankship (UK) Ltd v Miller Steamship Co Pty (The Wagon Mound No 2)* (1967) 40 ALJR 165 (PC), at 168, Lord Reid defined the crime of common or public nuisance as unlawful conduct which endangers the lives, safety, health, property or comfort of the public, or which has the effect of obstructing the public in the exercise or enjoyment of any common law rights.

Since public nuisance is a crime, the creator of the nuisance can be prosecuted. However, the crime of public nuisance may also be civilly actionable as public nuisance at the suit of an individual who suffers particular harm or damage by its commission.[7]

Private and public nuisance are quite distinct causes of action. The purpose of an action in private nuisance has always been to protect the right to use and enjoy land; the purpose of public nuisance is to safeguard the public from nuisance on, or emanating from, the defendant's land.[8] In some circumstances, there is an overlap between private and public nuisance—the same act or omission can constitute both. For example, in *Brodie v Singleton Shire Council; Ghantous v Hawkesbury City Council* (2001) 206 CLR 512, the case of *Brodie* involved a partial collapse of an old bridge in Tasmania, which injured the plaintiff. He sued in private nuisance; however, in a joint judgment, Gaudron, McHugh, and Gummow JJ were cognisant of the fact that since the bridge formed part of a public road, an action for public nuisance would also lie against the defendant Council.[9]

The scope of the tort of public nuisance has always been much wider than that of private nuisance. It included the wrong of storing gunpowder in a dangerous place, the keeping of a dovecote, and, in *R v Hall* (1671) 1 Vent 169, the wrong of

---

6. See also: *Domestic (Feral and Nuisance) Animals Regulations 2005 No 151* (Vic).
7. Newark FH, 'The Boundaries of Nuisance' (1949) 5 *Law Quarterly R* 480.
8. This is why public nuisance principles applicable to nuisance on the highway do not extend to private roads: *Murley Bros v Grove* (1882) 46 JP 360.
9. *Walsh v Ervin* [1952] VLR 361; [1952] ALR 650.

blocking the highway and encouraging apprentices to leave their shops to stand and gape at the defendant performing a trapeze act. In this case, a rope-dancer was convicted of creating a public nuisance by judges who, while en route to the courts at Westminster, saw him performing in London's Strand.

The Attorney-General can ask the court, in the public interest, for an injunction to restrain public nuisance either in a *relator* action, at the request of an individual affected by the nuisance, or *ex officio*, on his or her own motion. This happened in *Attorney-General v Tod Heatley* [1897] 1 Ch 560, in which the defendant was the owner and occupier of some vacant land in London. He surrounded it with a hoarding, 'but people threw filth and refuse over the hoarding and broke it down', so that the condition of the land and the use to which it was put constituted a public nuisance. The Attorney-General, representing the public, brought proceedings. Lindley LJ (at 568) said that 'It is the common law duty of the owner to prevent this piece of land from being a nuisance', and held that the defendant owner should clean up the land at his own expense, even though it was other people who polluted it. In *Hargrave v Goldman* (1963) 110 CLR 40, at 59, Windeyer J commented that the tort of public nuisance is something—for example, an overhanging tree branch—that 'currently and continuously interferes with the safe enjoyment of a public right of way'.

Indeed, interference with the highway is one of most frequent reasons for invoking the remedy of public nuisance. In the English case of *Railtrack plc v Wandsworth London Borough Council, The Times*, 2 August 2001; [2001] EWCA Civ 1236, the Wandsworth London Borough Council, as the local highway authority, sued in public nuisance Railtrack plc, which was the owner of a railway bridge. Droppings of wild pigeons, which were allowed to roost on the underside of the railway bridge, soiled the clothing of pedestrians and the pavements, making them slippery. The English Court of Appeal held that the infestation by pigeons constituted a public nuisance, and granted a declaration that the defendants were liable to abate the nuisance and pay damages of £10 000.

The distinguishing characteristic of the tort of public nuisance is that once the plaintiff establishes the existence of a public nuisance on the defendant's land, the issue whether it was created by the defendant or some third party, or by natural causes, is irrelevant. The tort consists of four elements:

1   the defendant has to have possessory interest in the land;
2   the defendant must have knowledge of the nuisance to the public;
3   the defendant must have the means to abate it; and
4   the defendant must fail to take appropriate means to abate it.

The option of having the Attorney-General taking on the role of a plaintiff in the public interest makes the tort of public nuisance more affordable for the affected individuals or community than an action in negligence. Moreover, the tort of public nuisance is much easier to establish than the tort of negligence.

The status of the tort of public nuisance as a discrete tort in Australian common law was questioned in *Brodie v Singleton Shire Council; Ghantous v Hawkesbury City Council* (2001) 206 CLR 512, which, by majority, abolished the rule exempting highway authorities from liability in nuisance in relation to injuries caused to members of the public through the want of repair. The High Court held (at [50]) that public authorities in which are vested statutory powers for the construction, maintenance and repair of public roads, including bridges, culverts and footpaths, can be liable in nuisance to injured members of the public if they fail to inspect, reasonably maintain and repair these amenities, irrespective of whether they have created them.

In the course of a joint judgment, Gaudron, McHugh, and Gummow JJ (at [55] and [129]) stated that: 'the tort of public nuisance in highway cases has been subsumed by the law of negligence'. Their Honours did not provide jurisprudential or any other reasons why the tort of public nuisance in highway cases should be subsumed by the law of negligence. This radical statement—which would have the effect of creating a profound change in law—was not discussed, let alone supported by other Justices. Hayne J observed (at 237 [335]) that in relation to the highway authorities' duty to repair:

> No different result should follow from casting the claim as a claim in nuisance rather than negligence. There is much to be said for the view that nuisance should be confined to claims alleging interference with a plaintiff's enjoyment of rights over land, and not applied to secure enforcement of public duties ... No action for nuisance should lie where the plaintiff's complaint is founded upon the failure of a statutory authority to exercise its powers and an action for breach of statutory duty or negligence would not lie.

It is unclear whether his Honour was referring to private nuisance or public nuisance.

Gaudron, McHugh, and Gummow JJ did not elaborate on the question whether the liability of highway authorities for public nuisance in negligence in relation to the exercise of their road duties[10] constitutes a discrete exception—meaning that other defendants, both private and statutory, will remain liable under public nuisance.

---

10. As a general rule, a road authority may be liable in public nuisance when it exercises, within a highway, statutory functions other than road functions, for example, as non-road drainage. However, liability of all statutory authorities is now subject to legal tests set out in: *Wrongs Act 1958* (Vic), Pt XII: (Liability of Public Authorities); *Road Management Act 2004* (Vic), Pt 6 (Civil Liability); *Civil Law (Wrongs) Act 2002* (ACT), Ch 8 (Liability of Public and Other Authorities); *Civil Liability Act 1936* (SA), Div 5 (Liability of Road Authorities); *Civil Liability Act 2002* (NSW), Pt 5 (Liability of Public and Other Authorities); *Civil Liability Act 2002* (Tas), Pt 9 (Liability of Public and Other Authorities); *Civil Liability Act 2002* (WA), s 5Z (Special Protection for Road Authorities); *Civil Liability Act 2003* (Qld), Pt 3 (Liability of Public and Other Authorities). At the time of writing, the Northern Territory is considering the form and content of its legislation in the area of civil liability reforms arising from the *Ipp Report*, and common law principles still apply.

Nearly every Australian Parliament has enacted legislation either to overcome, or to substantially modify, the imposition in *Brodie* of the common law liability in negligence and nuisance on highway authorities exercising their road duties.[11]

In general, statutory reforms to the law governing liability in negligence of public and other authorities will impact on the liability of these bodies in public and private nuisance.

Private nuisance

Private nuisance is distinct from both public nuisance and statutory nuisance. This chapter will focus on private nuisance (referred to as 'nuisance').

DEFINITION OF THE TORT OF PRIVATE NUISANCE

The nature of the tort of nuisance

Goldman v Hargrave (1966) 115 CLR 458; [1967] 1 AC 645 (Privy Council), is one of the seminal Australian cases in nuisance and negligence.[12] On Saturday, 25 February 1961, during an electrical storm, lightning struck a red gum tree that stood at about the centre of Mr Goldman's grazing property near Gidgegannup in Western Australia. The lightning started a fire in the fork of the tree, more than eighty feet above the ground. Mr Goldman called for the fire brigade, and the tree was cut down, but as it fell sparks ignited another tree, which then also fell. As a result, there were two logs burning on the ground. Mr Goldman cleared the area in the vicinity of the tree of all readily combustible material, and sprayed the surrounding area with water so as to minimise the risk of the fire escaping. Apparently thinking that the logs could then safely be left to burn themselves out, he did not hose the smouldering logs with water. During the subsequent heat-wave, a strong, hot wind whipped up the fire, which, having burnt Mr Goldman's homestead, travelled across to the adjoining land of Mr Hargrave, destroying his house and property. Both the High Court and the Privy Council found that Mr Goldman as the occupier, was liable both in negligence and in nuisance.

In the High Court (*Hargrave v Goldman* (1963) 110 CLR 40), at 59, Windeyer J defined the tort of private nuisance as 'an unlawful interference with [the occupier's] use or enjoyment of land, or of some right over, or in connection with it'. His Honour went on to say (at 62):

---

11. Id.
12. It was in *Goldman v Hargrave* (1966) that a duty was imposed on occupiers to act with reasonable care to alleviate risks to neighbouring properties posed by hazards present on their land, which they did not create.

In nuisance liability is founded upon a state of affairs, created, adopted or continued by one person (otherwise than in the reasonable and convenient use by him of his own land) which, to a substantial degree, harms another person (an owner or occupier of land) in his enjoyment of his land.

In *Gartner v Kidman* (1962) 108 CLR 12, Windeyer J (at 21) stated that private nuisance safeguards against unlawful interferences not only with possessory rights in land that a person has by virtue of lawful occupation, but also rights that one may possess over another person's land. These rights may include easements and reversions, *profits á prendre*,[13] and riparian rights.[14]

Types of harm resulting from nuisance

Non-physical and physical harm

Historically, nuisance was a remedy for damage to rights in land, rather than personal injury. However, in the nineteenth century, the distinction became rather fuzzy. The tort protects persons with land interests against both physical and non-physical damage. Non-physical damage includes harm occasioned by fumes, smell and noise, as well as psychological discomfort caused by harassing phone calls, vibrations, or fear for one's safety or health. Physical damage to land arises from flooding, fire, dust, tree roots and the like.

However, the scope of the tort is limited. The House of Lords in *Hunter v Canary Wharf Ltd; Hunter v London Docklands Development Corp* [1997] AC 655 held that private nuisance does not protect an interest in having an unobstructed view from one's windows,[15] or being able to enjoy television reception without interference. Moreover, as John Fleming pointed out in *The Law of Torts*,[16] infringement of privacy whereby the person's home is being spied on from beyond the boundary does not amount to actionable in nuisance, unless the actions constitute watching and besetting.

Undermining the support of land

Interference with the natural right to support of land, but not of buildings,[17] is actionable in nuisance.

---

13. The right to take soil, minerals, or produce (such as wood, turf, or fish) from another's land (the servient tenement) or to graze animals on it. These rights are also referred to as 'servitudes': Martin EA (ed), *A Dictionary of Law*, Oxford University Press, Oxford, 2002; *Oxford Reference Online*, Oxford University Press, Deakin University, 22 May 2005, <http://www.oxfordreference.com/views/ENTRY.html?subview=Main&entry=t49.e2865>.
14. Possessory rights that proprietors of the banks—'ripa'—of a river or a stream have, to take and use the water.
15. *Newcastle City Council v Shortland Management Services* (2003) 57 NSWLR 173.
16. Fleming JG, *The Law of Torts*, 9th edn, The Law Book Company Ltd, Sydney, 1998, p 466.
17. *Kebewar Pty Ltd v Harkin* (1987) 9 NSWLR 738.

A landowner has a common law right to the preservation of support provided to his land by adjoining lands or by the subsoil of adjoining lands. A person whose conduct has the effect of undermining my property by withdrawal of its lateral support is strictly liable in nuisance for any subsidence, and for any consequential damage caused by it. However, the owner's right under common law is limited to the land being supported while in its natural state. Therefore, where the land which subsides is supporting buildings or walls, or has been filled, or even simply covered with topsoil, the court will ask whether the land would have subsided if it had not been covered or built on. If it would, the neighbour will be liable in nuisance for subsidence, including the damage to the land, buildings, and other structures (*Walker v Corporation of the City of Adelaide* [2004] SASC 98 at [256]–[259]). However, McHugh JA (relying on the rule in *Dalton v Henry Angus* (1881) 6 App Cas 740), noted in *Kebewar Pty Ltd v Harkin* (1987) 9 NSWLR 738 that if the land would not have subsided *but for* the additional weight of buildings, there will be no liability in nuisance.[18]

INTERFERENCE WITH THE USE AND ENJOYMENT OF PROPERTY RIGHTS

To establish liability for private nuisance, plaintiffs must show that the defendant's interference with their right to use of the land—in the sense of personal comfort—was serious and unreasonable. However, plaintiffs only have to establish unreasonable interference with their rights in the land. It is not for the plaintiff to allege or prove unnatural or unreasonable use of the land by the defendant. Therefore, unreasonable use is not an element of the cause of action in nuisance.[19]

The law protects a possessor of an interest in land not only from a single, serious and unreasonable interference, but also from repeated or continuous ones. This rule was established in *Tenant v Goldwin* (1704) 2 Ld Raym 1089; 3 Ld Raym 324; 6 Mod Rep 311, where the defendant failed to repair his 'privy house of office' (toilet). When the wall collapsed, the excrement flowed into the plaintiff's cellar, contaminating his beer and coal supply.

What constitutes 'serious' and 'unreasonable' interference with use and enjoyment of property rights depends on the individual facts in each case. The court must balance the plaintiff's desire to enjoy property rights without unreasonable interference against the desire of others to undertake interfering activity. As Bramwell B put it in *Bamford v Turnley* (1862) 3 B & S 62, at 83–4, it is a test of 'common sense', based on the notion that neighbours must expect to 'give and take, live and let live' in the course of normal and reasonable use of property.

---

18. See also: *Torette House Pty Ltd v Berkman* (1940) 62 CLR 637; *Lamb v Camden Council* [1981] QB 625.
19. *Corbertt v Pallas* (1995) Aust Torts Reps ¶81–329 at 62,241, per Priestley JA.

The neighbourhood principle

The 'give and take' rule whereby 'as between neighbouring occupiers of land', under which 'those acts necessary for the common and ordinary use and occupation of land and houses may be done, if conveniently done, without subjecting those who do them to an action' was articulated by Baron Bramwell in 1862 in *Bamford v Turnley* (1862) 3 B & S 66 (Ex CH). The facts in *Bamford* are a testimony to the kind of human interactions that result in augmenting the nuisance jurisprudence. The defendant decided to construct his own house. For this purpose, he built temporary kilns to make bricks from the clay on his land. The temporary kilns were as far removed from the plaintiff's property as possible. The plaintiff sued the defendant in nuisance, alleging the kilns produced 'unwholesome vapours, smoke, fumes, stinks and stenches' that 'entered in, spread and diffuse[d] themselves over, upon, into, through and about' the plaintiff's house. These pollutants were 'corrupted, offensive, unwholesome, unhealthy and uncomfortable' to the plaintiff, his family and servants. Bramwell B said (at 83) that acts necessary for 'the common and ordinary use and occupation of land and houses' will not be subject to liability in nuisance. However, although it might be reasonable to burn bricks in the vicinity of convenient deposits of clay, it is unreasonable to inflict the consequences upon the occupants of nearby houses.

In *Southwark London Borough Council v Tanner & Ors* [2001] 1 AC 1, tenants in a block of flats complained that due to lack of sound insulation, they could hear all the sounds made by their neighbours, including noises from television sets, babies crying, sounds of cooking and cleaning, quarrels, and love-making. The neighbours were not unreasonably noisy, but the lack of privacy caused tension and distress.[20] The House of Lords determined that there was no actionable nuisance.

Lord Millet (at 20)[21] commented that in relation to nuisance, when determining whether the use of land is reasonable, the court considers the issue not only from the users' point of view, but also from the perspective of their neighbours. The test is:

> What is reasonable from the point of view of one party may be completely unreasonable from the point of view of the other. It is not enough for a landowner to act reasonably in his own interest. He must also be considerate of the interest of his neighbour. The governing principle is good neighbourliness, and this involves reciprocity.

His Lordship then discussed Bramwell B's judgment in *Bamford v Turnley*, and concluded (at 21) that under the neighbourhood principle, activities which

---

20. At 7, per Lord Hoffmann.
21. Lord Millet adopted Sir George Jessel MR's approach in *Broder v Saillard* [1876] 2 Ch D 692 at 701–2.

would otherwise be actionable will be exempted from liability in nuisance, if the acts complained of are shown by the defendant to be:

- 'necessary for the common and ordinary use and occupation of land and houses'; and
- 'done with proper consideration for the interests of neighbouring occupiers'.

Seriousness or gravity of harm

In *Halsey v Esso Petroleum Co Ltd* [1961] 1 WLR 683; 2 All ER 145, the acid smuts containing sulphate or sulphuric acid emitted from the Esso depôt's chimney damaged Mr Hasley's clothing left out to dry on a clothesline. Finding the defendant liable, Veale J pointed out that as long as damage is 'not trivial', liability for nuisance will be established on proof of damage caused by the deposits on the property. The plaintiff's car was also damaged by the smuts while it was standing on the public highway. The damage to the car was therefore considered public nuisance.

Nuisance and negligence

In cases where the defendant has been responsible for the creation of a nuisance, liability focuses on the extent of the harm actually caused by the defendant's unreasonable use of land.[22] In contrast, the notion of 'unreasonable risk' in negligence focuses on the standard of conduct expected of a reasonable person to avoid a foreseeable risk of harm. According to Professor Fleming:[23]

> 'duty' not to expose one's neighbours to a nuisance is not primarily discharged by exercising reasonable care or even all possible care. In that sense, therefore, liability is strict.

Moreover, unlike the classic paradigm of negligence where the plaintiff has the burden of proving duty, breach, causation and remoteness, in nuisance, once the plaintiff has shown a prima facie infringement, the burden of establishing that the impeached land usage was 'natural' and not 'unreasonable' shifts to the defendant. Thus, tortious negligence is not an essential element of liability in nuisance.

Fault

Negligence and nuisance are both species of action on the case. Consequently, nuisance, like negligence, is fault-based. However, according to Lord Reid in

---

22. *Cambridge Water Co v Eastern Counties Leather PLC* [1994] 2 AC 264 at 299, per Lord Goff of Chieveley.
23. Fleming JG, *The Law of Torts*, 9th edn, The Law Book Company Ltd, Sydney, 1998, p 473.

Overseas Tankship (UK) Ltd v The Miller Steamship Co Ltd (The Wagon Mound No 2) [1967] 1 AC 617, at 639, unlike negligence, which requires failure to foresee a real risk of harm together with wrongful conduct, the fault in nuisance lies solely in the failure by the defendant to foresee damage to the plaintiffs' proprietary rights in their land. Thus, as a general rule, in order to recover damages in private nuisance, plaintiffs must show that interference with their actual use of the property, or an adverse effect on their comfort and pleasure derived from occupancy of the land, was reasonably foreseeable. Lord Reid (at 639) noted that for the purposes of nuisance: 'the fault is in failing to abate the nuisance of the existence of which the defender is or ought to be aware as likely to cause damage to his neighbour'.

Reasonable foreseeability of damage or serious interference

Plaintiffs have the burden of showing that physical damage to, or serious interference with, their land was reasonably foreseeable. In *Cambridge Water Co v Eastern Counties Leather PLC* [1994] 2 AC 264, the defendant leather manufacturers used a chlorinated solvent in degreasing pelts at their tannery, which was situated some 1.3 miles from the Cambridge Water Co borehole which used its water for supply to some 275 000 people in the Cambridge area for domestic purposes. In the 1970s, small quantities of solvent would sometimes spill, but instead of evaporating as one would expect, it seeped into the ground below the defendants' premises whence it was conveyed in percolating water in the direction of the borehole, thus making it unfit for human consumption. The plaintiffs brought an action for damages on three alternative grounds,[24] including nuisance. The House of Lords determined that 'the storage of substantial quantities of chemicals on industrial premises should be regarded as an almost classic case of non-natural use' for the purposes of nuisance.[25] However, the plaintiffs lost because their Lordships also held that foreseeability of harm of the relevant type by the defendants is a prerequisite of the recovery of damages in nuisance; and the pollution of bore water supply by the solvent was in the circumstances not foreseeable.

Likewise, in *Arscott v The Coal Authority* [2004] EWCA (Civ) 892 (CA), the local council owned a large recreation area that was susceptible to flooding. In 1972, the coal waste from an adjacent tip was deposited onto the recreation area in order to raise its level and create a playground. In October 1998, a river overflowed and caused damage to a number of residential properties in the vicinity. The English Court of Appeal accepted that the raised level of the recreation area was a material cause of the damage. Nevertheless, their Honours determined that the plaintiff

---

24. The other two grounds were negligence and the rule in *Rylands v Fletcher* (1866) LR 1 Ex 265.
25. *Cambridge Water Co v Eastern Counties Leather PLC* [1994] 2 AC 264 at 309, per Lord Goff of Chieveley.

could not succeed in nuisance because the flood damage had not been reasonably foreseeable at the time the works were carried out. The court also held that the 'common enemy' doctrine was applicable in this instance. Under that doctrine, occupiers of land are entitled to use or develop their land so as to prevent flood waters coming on to the land, and are not liable in nuisance if flood occurs despite their efforts.

The requirement of fault based on foreseeability of the risk of harm means that where the defendant's unreasonable interference causes physical damage to land, there is now almost a complete overlap between negligence and nuisance. However, there will be many instances where nuisance will lie but negligence will not. This will be particularly so in cases of nuisance where the infringement causes non-physical damage—for example, bad smells or noises.

Unusually sensitive plaintiff

The test of determining whether the defendant's use of land was 'unreasonable' is objective. This means that unless an unusually sensitive plaintiff can show that a 'normal' person would also find the alleged interference serious and unreasonable, she or he may not be protected.

For instance, in the Canadian case of *McKinnon Industries v Walker* [1951] 3 DLR 577, the plaintiff complained that sulphur dioxide from the defendant's premises caused damage to orchids he was growing commercially in his nursery. The Privy Council advised that sulphur dioxide emissions constituted nuisance, since even those of normal sensitivity would regard them as unreasonable. The plaintiff was therefore granted an injunction to restrain the defendant from causing the damage to the orchids, although the damage exceeded that which a normally sensitive person would suffer in the circumstances.

Factors taken into account in actionable nuisance

The law strives to strike a fair balance between the plaintiff's right to undisturbed enjoyment of land, and the defendant's right to lawfully use his or her property.[26] In striking a balance between what constitutes unreasonable interference and the discomfort a plaintiff may be expected to endure, the court will take into account:

- the location in which the interference occurs;
- its frequency and extent;
- the sensitivity of the person affected; and
- malice (if any) by the defendant.

Each factor will be considered in turn.

---

26. *Halsey v Esso Petroleum Co Ltd* [1961] 1 WLR 683.

Locality

Locality is an important but not determinative factor in deciding the level of discomfort the plaintiff can be expected to endure. As Lord Millet pointed out *Southwark London Borough Council v Tanner & Ors*, we all have to endure noises and other interferences that constitute the ordinary incidents of life in our particular locality. However, it is all a question of degree. Some established activities will be regarded as unreasonably interfering with the enjoyment of land by others if they go beyond what an ordinary person should have to put up with in that locality. For example, in *Halsey v Esso Petroleum Co Ltd* [1961] 1 WLR 683, Mr Hasley was the owner and occupier of a terrace house in a street in a residential area, which abutted busy industrial development, including the defendants' oil storage and issuing depot. There was also a boiler house containing two steam boilers with metal chimney stacks from which, from time to time, noxious acid smuts were emitted.

When the defendants introduced a night shift at the depot from 10 pm till 6 am, the noise (which at its peak reached 63 decibels) from the boilers went on throughout the night despite efforts made by the defendants to minimise it. Oil tankers and other vehicles, sometimes in convoy, came and went every night. The defendants denied nuisance, claiming that given the nature of the locality, their activities were reasonable. Vale J disagreed, and held that the environmental pollution created by the defendant was so heavy that the 'character of the locality' was not relevant.

Nuisance and other community values

It is no defence for the defendant to say that the plaintiff chose to be close to the defendant's pre-existing noxious activities. Also, if the plaintiff can show that the defendant's activity is an actionable nuisance, it will be actionable regardless of its utility.

This does not necessarily mean that noxious industrial activity must cease altogether. Rather, courts have insisted that it be carried out in such places and in such a manner as to avoid harming individual landowners' rights to enjoyment of their land. Thus, in the case of *Jones v Powell* (1629) Palm 536; Hutton 135, Jones J said that a brewhouse was acceptable in Newgate (a slum area of London) but not in Cheapside. Likewise, while building construction, with its attendant noise and vibrations, will rarely be banned altogether, its hours of operation may well be restricted. Thus, in *Halsey v Esso Petroleum Co Ltd*, Vale J granted an injunction to restrain the defendants from operating their plant at the depot and from driving their vehicles at night between 10 pm and 6 am.

In determining whether usage amounts to a nuisance, courts have regard to prevailing community standards and values. For example, in the English case of *Miller v Jackson* [1973] QB 966, a cricket ground previously surrounded by fields was, by 1970, adjacent to a row of houses built on its boundary. Despite high walls, cricket balls would fall into the rear gardens of these houses. The inhabitants sued in nuisance for an injunction to force the cricket club to move. The Court of Appeal held that the defendant could not plead that the plaintiffs came to the nuisance, but refused the injunction, and instead awarded a small sum for damages to cover all past and future loss.

The English decision may be contrasted with the Australian case of *Lester-Travers v City of Frankston* [1970] VR 2. The plaintiff owned and occupied a house behind which was the defendants' practice fairway. Across the road in front of the house were two holes of the golf links. The plaintiff picked up at least thirty-six golf balls in the space of twelve months. Golfers would wander into her garden to retrieve lost balls. A window in the plaintiff's house had been damaged, and a hole had been made in her roof, which caused water to get in and the ceiling to sag. She feared for her personal safety and the security of her property. She was handicapped when entertaining friends. The value of her property had diminished as well. The defendant erected a wire screen near one of the tees in front of the house, but this proved ineffective.

The defendant claimed the interference was reasonable, and that the plaintiff's refusal to tolerate the interference was itself an interference with the golfers' enjoyment; that the plaintiff was unduly sensitive and had failed to take obvious steps for her own safety by staying indoors while golf was played. In the Victorian Supreme Court, Anderson J, however, noted that 'errant golf balls do not arrive by appointment', and granted an injunction, stating that it was not imperative that golf be carried on in the locality in question. If it could not be played without inconvenience and danger of personal injury and property damage, it ought not to be played there at all.

Likewise, in *Campbelltown Golf Club Limited v Winton & Anor* [1998] NSWSC 257, the plaintiffs bought vacant land adjacent to the golf course, and built a house on it. The plaintiffs established that for the period from 1 January 1995 to 17 May 1995 alone, 421 balls came onto their property, damaging their home and garden as well as posing a threat to their physical safety. The court rejected the golf club's argument that a plaintiff who had come to a nuisance might suffer a reduction in damages because of having come to it. The court noted that apart from 'some exceptional cases', defendants sued in nuisance cannot rely on the defence of contributory negligence. The club was obliged to remedy the nuisance and pay the plaintiffs $26 214.80 in damages.[27]

---

27. On nuisance created by golf courses, see: *Ryde-Parramatta Golf Club* (unreported, Supreme Court of New South Wales, Helsham CJ, 23 February 1978); *Campbelltown Golf Club Ltd v Winton* (unreported, New South Wales Court of Appeal, Sheller, after CJ, Powell JJA and Sheppard AJA, 23 June 1998); *Champagne View Pty Ltd v Shearwater Resort Management Pty Ltd* (unreported, Supreme Court of Victoria, Gillard J, 25 May 2000).

Smells, fumes, emissions, and noise

Smells

Liability for emission of offensive smells was established in 1610, in *Aldred v Benton* (1610) 9 Co Rep 57. The plaintiff complained that his home was made uninhabitable by unhealthy odours that flowed through his hall from a pigsty that the defendant had erected. The defendant argued that pigs were necessary as food, and that the plaintiff should not have such a delicate nose. The court, however, held the defendant liable for putrefying the air. In early cases, liability in nuisance for offensive smells probably had less to do with distaste for odours than with concern that health may be endangered through 'infectious smells'.[28]

Some 300 years on, the English Court of Appeal found liability in nuisance on very similar facts. In *Bone v Seale* (1975) 1 All ER 787, the defendant operated a pig farm. The plaintiffs, owners of neighbouring properties, sought to restrain the defendant from creating smells by storing pig manure and boiling pig swill. The injunction was granted. The court also awarded £1000 to each plaintiff as compensation for offensive smells.

In *Domachuk v Feiner* (unreported, New South Wales Court of Appeal, 28 November 1996), the court, in upholding a restraining order against the defendant mushroom grower, stated that an agricultural zoning permit did not protect the defendant from actions in private nuisance for creating offensive smells by keeping quantities of compost largely made up of stable straw saturated with urine and mixed with horse manure. Each neighbour was also awarded $7500 in damages.

The emissions need not be injurious to health and property to constitute nuisance, but if they are inherently harmful, both an injunction and damages will be granted.

Noise

In Victoria, in *Munro v Southern Dairies Ltd* [1955] VLR 332, the defendant company conducted a dairy in the then-outlying Melbourne suburb of Mentone. In the 1950s, horse-drawn vehicles were widely used for milk deliveries in Melbourne, and suburban stables for dairy horses were quite common. The plaintiff–neighbour sued the defendant in nuisance, claiming that the horses were noisy, and the smell from their manure and urine attracted flies.

Sholl J granted an injunction restraining the keeping of horses on the premises. His Honour held that the loss of a single night's sleep from the noise of the dairy could amount to a substantial interference.

---

28. Baker JH, *An Introduction to English History*, 2nd edn, Butterworths, London, 1981, pp 357–358.

The law insists that it is not an answer to nuisance to claim that the noxious activity benefits the wider public. Private nuisance is oriented towards protection of the local neighbourhood, and defendants who interfere with neighbours' use and enjoyment of land cannot plead the importance of their activities to others who live out of physical range of these activities.

The fact that the creator of a nuisance is doing something for the public interest will be a factor in assessing the reasonableness of the user, but it is simply unfair to make certain innocent individuals suffer for the greater public good. Professor John Fleming wryly noted that 'If the public be interested let the public as such bear the costs.'[29]

Balancing private and public interests can involve complex policy considerations. In *Dennis v Ministry of Defence* [2003] EWHC 793 (QB), Mr and Mrs Dennis, owners of Walcot Hall Estate which was built in 1678 in the English countryside, sued the Royal Flying Corps for nuisance occasioned by Harrier fighter squadrons flying over their land in the course of pilot training. The experts testified that the noise levels were sufficiently high as to cause disturbance to the occupants of Walcot Hall and material interference with their normal domestic and business activities. Buckley J (at [47]) recognised that maintaining the training programme for Harrier pilots was in the public interest, however, he ruled that 'selected individuals should not bear the cost of the public benefit'.

The judge did not grant an injunction, holding that the public interest in maintaining the training programme at the RAF station was greater than the plaintiffs' individual private interests. Nevertheless, common fairness demanded that they should be compensated. The plaintiffs were awarded £650 000 for past and future loss of amenity, past and future loss of use, and £300 000 for loss of capital value to their home (pure economic loss).

Interference with reception of electronic signals

In cases where the unreasonable interference with the plaintiff's use and enjoyment of land is *not* caused by negligent or unreasonable conduct of the defendant, the court will have to balance two reasonable—albeit conflicting—desires to exercise the same right: the right to use and enjoy one's land as one pleases without interference, and the right to conduct lawful trade, construct buildings, manufacture or industry. This is why the House of Lords in *Hunter & Ors v Canary Wharf Ltd; London Docklands Corporation v Hunter & Ors* [1997] AC 655 held that interference with television reception caused by construction of a building—which complied with

---

29. Fleming JG, *The Law of Torts*, 9th edn, The Law Book Company Ltd, Sydney, p 471, citing Bohlen *Studies in the Law of Torts*, Bobbs-Merrill Co, Indianapolis, c 1926, 429.

building regulations—on neighbouring land was not capable of constituting an actionable nuisance.[30]

The *Canary Wharf* litigation involved claims of interference with enjoyment of television programs in private premises rather than transmission of electronic signals for commercial purposes. Nowadays, however, the mobile phone is an integral part of the mobile office paradigm, and outside interference with a mobile phone network may compromise a person's ability to do business and result in loss of income. The conflicting rights that need to be balanced in such a situation are different; it remains to be seen whether the courts will extend principles of nuisance to claims by persons who suffer damage as a result of having their wired network unreasonably interfered with or affected by, for example, a building construction.

ACTIVITIES THAT OFFEND SENSIBILITIES OF NEIGHBOURING OCCUPIERS

In the colourful English case of *Thompson-Schwab v Costaki* [1956] 1 WLR 335, the defendants owned a property that they used for the purposes of (at 336–7):

> carrying on their practices as prostitutes; they were ... walking for the purpose of solicitation towards Curzon Street, returning to the house with the men whom they had solicited, and then the men would leave the house and the women would leave after them.

The neighbouring landowners alleged that activities carried out on the defendants' property amounted to private nuisance. The court granted an injunction, despite the defendants' argument that there was no material physical interference with the plaintiffs' land or their use of it. Lord Evershed MR (at 339) said that the alleged nuisance could be inferred because:

> The perambulations of the prostitutes and of their customers is something which is obvious, which is blatant, and which, as I think, the first plaintiff has shown prima facie to constitute not a mere hurt of his sensibilities as a fastidious man, but so as to constitute a sensible interference with the comfortable and convenient enjoyment of his residence.

Duration and time

The duration, time of day, frequency and extent of the interference will be relevant in determining whether it is unreasonable. A serious interference for a short period

---

30. Likewise, interference with view is not actionable under nuisance (*Newcastle City Council v Shortland Management Services* [2003] NSWCA 156).

of time may still be held to be unreasonable: for instance, according to *Andreae v Selfridge & Co Ltd* [1938] Ch 1; [1937] 3 All ER 255, noise made by drilling and excavating machines on a construction site, even if only for an hour or two, will be held to be unreasonable where it occurs at night or in the early morning in a residential area. Excavating noise will also be regarded unreasonable if it occurs during office hours in a business district.

Improper motive

Agricultural activities involving the discharging of a gun, general activities such as telephoning people, or domestic use of pots and pans, would normally be regarded as ordinary incidents of the use and enjoyment of land. However, Baron Bramwell pointed out in *Bamford v Turnley* (1862) 3 B & S 66 (Ex CH) at 83 that ordinary activities 'done wantonly or maliciously' for the purpose of causing stress and annoyance to the plaintiff's use and enjoyment of land, form an exception to the 'give and take' principle.

For instance, in *Stoakes v Brydges* [1958] QWN 5, the plaintiffs were directors of Pauls Icecream and Milk Ltd. The defendant, a milk vendor, was very unhappy with noise made by the company's servants. In revenge, he telephoned the plaintiffs during the night so as to disturb their sleep. Townley J granted a permanent injunction to restrain the defendant's activities, which he held to be a substantial interference with the ordinary enjoyment by the plaintiffs of their premises. Townley J said that although conventional use of a telephone was not tortious, its deliberate use to interfere materially with the health or comfort of others in the ordinary enjoyment of their premises, including their sleep, was an actionable nuisance.

Likewise, unreasonable and malicious use of lights, including floodlights, may amount to private nuisance. In *Raciti v Hughes* (unreported, Supreme Court of New South Wales, Young J, 19 October 1995); NSW LEXIS 10736, Hughes, the defendant, installed on his land floodlights and camera surveillance equipment. The floodlights and the surveillance equipment were so positioned that they illuminated the neighbours'—the Racitis'—backyard and recorded on video tape everything that occurred there. Any movement or noise on the plaintiffs' land would activate the floodlight system through a sensor, and the camera would then film what was happening in their backyard, day or night. The plaintiffs, who previously used the backyard for hanging up their clothes, doing gardening, and recreation, became distressed and suffered health problems. Young J found that the continued illumination of the plaintiffs' land amounted to actionable nuisance.

Conduct characterised as harassment, watching, and besetting also has an element of improper motive. In *Raciti v Hughes*, Young J considered that the surveillance and accompanying recording by video camera of the plaintiffs' backyard was a 'deliberate attempt to snoop on the privacy of a neighbour and to record that on video tape'. The defendant's conduct was akin to 'watching and besetting' and could constitute private nuisance.

'Watching and besetting'

Picketing or gathering in front of someone's premises will not of themselves amount to nuisance. Such activities only become a nuisance if they constitute an unreasonable and substantial interference with the use and enjoyment—including commercial enjoyment—of land. Nuisance will generally be made out where the object of the defendants' conduct is to compel a person on the premises, or a potential customer, or a guest, or a person intending to enter, to act against his or her will. In *J Lyons & Sons v Wilkins* [1899] 1 Ch 255, at 267–8, Lindley MR said that where such conduct is established:

> Proof that the nuisance was 'peaceably to persuade other people' would afford no defence to such action. Persons may be peaceably persuaded provided the method to persuade is not a nuisance to other people.

In Australia, according to Mason JA in *Sid Ross Agency Pty Ltd v Actors and Announcers Equity Association of Australia* (1971) 1 NSWLR 760, at 767:

> At common law, picketing is not necessarily a nuisance and unlawful as such, but it becomes so if it involves obstruction and besetting.

Where the premises sustain a loss of business as a result of picketing, and where legitimate alternative methods of making the point are available, even peaceful picketing may be considered a substantial and unreasonable interference amounting to nuisance. For example, in *Dollar Sweets Pty Ltd v Federated Confectioners Association of Australia* [1986] VR 383, the plaintiff, a confectionery manufacturer and distributor, was involved in an industrial dispute with members of the Federated Confectioners Association (FCA). A number of members of the FCA formed a picket line outside the premises of the plaintiff's factory, preventing delivery and despatch of goods to and from the premises. Members of the picket line directed violence and threats of violence to persons attempting to deliver and carry away goods. As a result of these activities, the plaintiff's business was seriously disrupted. The loss of profits, if continued, would have forced the plaintiff to cease trading. The plaintiff asked for an interlocutory injunction, which was granted. Murphy J (at 388–9) defined 'besetting' as:

> a term applied to the occupation of a roadway or passageway through which persons wish to travel, so as to cause those persons to hesitate through fear to proceed or if they do proceed to do so only with fear for their safety or the safety of their property.

His Honour found that:

> the acts of all the defendants which have now been repeatedly performed over many months cannot be considered to be a lawful form of picketing, but amount to a nuisance involving, as they do, obstruction, harassment and besetting ... the latter meaning, in this context, to set about or surround with hostile intent.

The case of *Animal Liberation (Vic) Inc v Gasser* [1991] 1 VR 51, at 58, involved picketing by members of Animal Liberation (Vic) Inc. The Animal Liberation activists sought to intimidate and dissuade patrons from attending the plaintiff's circus by forcing them to 'run the gauntlet' between lines of shouting and placard-waving demonstrators. The Victorian Full Court (Crockett, Fullagar, and Nathan JJ), in a joint judgment, decided that the conduct of members of Animal Liberation (Vic) Inc constituted 'harassment and besetting' and thus was actionable as private nuisance. The court observed that 'a besetting includes a surrounding with hostile demeanour so as to put in fear of safety'. Their Honours noted that it will take less to intimidate the elderly and the young.

However, ultimately the question whether a protest or a picket amounts to besetting is a matter of degree. Relying, *inter alia*, on judgments in the *Dollar Sweets* and *Animal Liberation* cases, Jones J in *McCoy Constructions Pty Ltd v Aleko Dabrowski* [2000] QSC 385 refused a grant of injunction. The plaintiff wished to prevent the defendant, Aleko Dabrowski, from sitting on the footpath between 10 am and 5.30 pm at the entrance to the display home area owned by McCoy Constructions, and speaking to intending visitors to those homes. McCoy Constructions and Mr Dabrowski were in dispute over the quality of the home built by the former. The defendant's actions, carried on over a period of four days, were intended to dissuade potential customers from visiting the display homes. His Honour found (at [22]) that although Mr Dabrowski's conduct was no doubt annoying and potentially commercially disruptive to the company, he did not 'watch and beset' intending visitors. There was no evidence that any of the visitors approached by the defendant 'suffered either emotionally or physically as a result of their interaction with him.' Moreover, there was no evidence that Mr Dabrowski's action dissuaded any visitors from dealing with the applicant thus causing a decrease in sales for McCoy Constructions.

Wrongfully watching and besetting a place is also a crime.[31] Stalking, too, may amount to both crime and private nuisance. Stalking has been defined as involving, *inter alia*, telephoning, sending electronic messages to, or otherwise contacting, the victim; entering or loitering outside or near the victim's place of residence or of business or any other place frequented by the victim or the other person; or keeping

---

31. *Crimes Act 1900* (NSW), s 545B; *Criminal Code 1899* (Qld), s 534 (limited to industrial context); *Criminal Law Consolidation Act 1935* (SA), s 19AA; *Criminal Code 1913* (WA), s 338D; *Criminal Code 1924* (Tas), s 192; *Criminal Code Act 1983* (NT), s 189; *Crimes Act 1900* (ACT), s 34A.

the victim or any other person under surveillance. The requisite intention must be to cause 'physical or mental harm to the victim or of arousing apprehension or fear in the victim for his or her own safety or that of any other person and the course of conduct engaged in actually did have that result'.[32]

Under the *Trade Practices Act 1974* (Cth), corporations and natural persons engaged in overseas or interstate trade and commerce may seek an injunction under s 80, or damages under s 82, against those contravening s 45D(1), which prohibits secondary boycotts that lessen competition by an alliance which hinders or prevents the supply of goods or services by another to a business. Moreover, s 60 of the *Trade Practices Act* provides that 'A corporation shall not use physical force or undue harassment or coercion in connection with the supply or possible supply of goods or services to a consumer for the payment for goods or services by a consumer.'

TITLE TO SUE

Nuisance is a proprietary wrong. Therefore, generally, standing to sue in private nuisance is dependent on the actual possession of the affected land. Proprietors of the banks of a stream or a river may possess riparian rights to use the water and fish therefrom. They have the right to sue in nuisance if the defendant's activities have the effect of polluting the water, so that it cannot be used for farming, irrigation, or to pasture cattle on the plaintiff's land.

Reversionary owners can only sue in nuisance for permanent impairment to the utility of the land—for example, subsidence or other structural damage to the land.

A licensee without possession, such as a lodger or an invitee, cannot maintain an action in nuisance. The House of Lords, in *Hunter v Canary Wharf Ltd* [1997] AC 655, stated that the law of nuisance does not protect those without a proprietary interest in land. Their Lordships there overruled the nuisance aspect of the English Court of Appeal's decision in *Khorasandjian v Bush* [1993] QB 727, which allowed a sixteen-year-old girl living in her parents' house to sue in private nuisance, despite the fact that she was a 'mere licensee'.

In Australia, the High Court has not finally determined the issue of standing in nuisance. However, in at least two jurisdictions, an interference with the plaintiff's rights arising out of his or her lawful occupation of the land will be sufficient to allow the plaintiff to sue in nuisance. This would include any persons in actual possession of the land affected—not only as a freeholder or tenant, but also as a licensee with exclusive possession. Thus, in *Animal Liberation (Vic) Inc v Gasser* [1991] 1 VR 51, the Appeal Division of the Victorian Supreme Court granted an injunction to

---

32. *Crimes Act 1958* (Vic), s 21A; *Criminal Code 1924* (Tas), s 192; see: *Allen v Tasmania Police* [2004] TASSC 30.

restrain picketing by members of Animal Liberation, who sought to obstruct and intimidate patrons attending the plaintiff's circus, even though the plaintiff had no more than a licence to conduct a circus on the land. Likewise, in *Deasy Investments Pty Ltd & Anor v Monrest Pty Ltd* [1996] QCA 466, the Queensland Court of Appeal determined that a person in possession of premises as a mere licensee could sue for private nuisance. Admittedly, Pincus JA, who delivered the leading judgment in *Deasy*, relied, among other authorities, on the English Court of Appeal decision in *Khorasandjian v Bush* [1993] QB 727.[33] The House of Lords disapproved of *Khorasandjian* in *Hunter v Canary Wharf Ltd* [1997] AC 655.

WHO MAY BE SUED?

In a great majority of cases, nuisance would emanate from the land of the defendant. However, in *Hargrave v Goldman* (1963) 110 CLR 40, at 60, Windeyer J stated that creators of nuisance may be liable even where they are not in occupation or control of the land on which they commit the acts of nuisance. Moreover, defendants may be liable for committing nuisance on land occupied by or under the control of the plaintiff. This is particularly so in cases of watching and besetting.[34]

Occupier's liability

In certain circumstances, an occupier may be responsible for a nuisance created by third parties, including licensees, independent contractors, predecessors in title, or by natural causes, providing that:

1. The occupier is or ought to be aware of it. The issue of knowledge of nuisance was discussed in *Montana Hotels Pty Ltd v Fasson Pty Ltd* (1986) 69 ALR 258; [1987] Aust Torts Reports ¶80–109.[35] In April 1981, water was discovered in the cellar of the Montana's Laird O'Cockpen Hotel in Collingwood, Victoria. It was traced to a faulty downpipe on the adjoining building, which had been erected some six months before by the defendant, Fasson. In November 1981, the Supreme Court of Victoria granted an injunction directing Fasson to prevent the further flow of water from its building to the hotel. In December, Fasson replaced the downpipe and the faucet, and thereafter no further water was observed entering the hotel. However, the changed moisture content of

---

33. See also: *Stockwell v State of Victoria* [2001] VSC 497 at [241].
34. *Animal Liberation (Victoria) Inc & Anor v Gasser & Anor* [1991] VR 51; *Hooper v Rogers* [1975] Ch 43 at 50, per Scarman CJ; *Wilson & Ors v New South Wales Land and Housing Corporation* (unreported, Supreme Court of New South Wales, Harrison M, 18 March 1998), 1998 NSW LEXIS 477.
35. See also: *Cartwright v McLaine and Long Pty Ltd* (1979) 143 CLR 549; *Torette Howe Pty Ltd v Berkman* (1940) 62 CLR 637.

the soil beneath the hotel continued to cause damage. The tribunal of fact (the Planning Appeals Board) found that Fasson did not know of the defect, was not at fault up to the stage when the problem was identified, and thereafter acted promptly to remedy the situation. On appeal, the Privy Council, Lord Ackner delivering the advice of their Lordships' Board reiterated (at 262), that, 'the liability for nuisance is not, at least in modern law, a strict or absolute liability.' Occupiers are not *prima facie* responsible for a nuisance created without their knowledge and consent. If they are to be liable, a further condition is necessary, namely, that they 'knew or should have known of the nuisance in time to correct it and obviate its mischievous effects.'

2   Once it is established that the occupier knew or should have known of the nuisance, liability will attach if he or she either adopts the nuisance or passively permits it to continue by failing to abate it within reasonable time.[36] An example of failure to abate nuisance in a timely fashion is the Queensland case of *Challen v The McLeod Country Golf Club* [2004] QCA 358. Mrs Challen owned and lived with her family at the house adjacent to the fairway of the twelfth hole of the McLeod Country Golf Club since 1988. In 1991, she sent the first of a series of letters to the golf club containing accounts or receipts in relation to damage caused by golf balls to her roof tiles, windows and garage doors. On 8 November 1994, Mrs Challen wrote to the club informing it that she continued 'to get between twelve and twenty golf balls' in her back yard each week. The defendants paid for most of the damage, but did nothing to rectify the problem. In March 2001, Mrs Challen's solicitors requested that the golf club redesign the twelfth hole in order to eliminate the nuisance of golf balls intruding onto their client's property. This was done; however, between two and three balls a week were still landing on the property.[37] Mullins J (McPherson and Davies JJA agreeing) awarded Mrs Challen damages, holding (at [38]) that the club was on notice of the nuisance from the receipt of the letter of 8 November 1994. Consequently, according to his Honour, 'the steps taken to address the problem in late 2001 and early 2002 could not amount to a reasonable response in all the circumstances to abate the nuisance.'

3   The knowledge of nuisance will be imputed to the occupier if the claimant can establish that the occupier's employees were aware of it. Thus, in *Sedleigh-Denfield v O'Callaghan* [1940] AC 880, the local authority laid a pipeline in a ditch on the defendants' land. The purpose of the pipeline was to carry off rainwater; however, the authority placed a grate on it so inadequately that over a period of three years it became blocked and the water flooded the adjacent

---

36. *White v Jameson* (1874) 18 LR Eq 303.
37. Mullins J observed (at [39]) that even two or three balls per week regularly coming onto the claimant's property with the risk of physical harm or damage to persons or property on the premises is a material interference with the enjoyment of his or her property.

premises of the plaintiffs. The defendant occupiers never authorised the construction of the pipe. Nevertheless, they were found liable for 'continuing nuisance' because they knew, through their employee, who was in charge of cleaning the ditch, both about the existence of the pipe and about its dangerous condition. The House of Lords held that the knowledge of a responsible servant should be imputed to the occupier. The defendants ought thus to have foreseen the risk of flooding. In addition, it was found that the defendants 'adopted the nuisance' because they used the pipeline to remove water from their own property without taking steps to abate the risk of flooding the neighbouring one.

The law of nuisance is still developing. In *Fennell v Robson Excavations Pty Ltd* [1977] 2 NSWLR 486, at 491–2, Glass JA observed:

> Although there appears to be no direct authority fastening liability on a complete stranger to the occupier of land upon which the nuisance is created, the weight of authority, it seems to me, attaches liability to any person who creates a nuisance while present on land with the authority of its occupier.[38]

Nuisance emanating from the defendant occupier's land

Thompson-Schwab v Costaki [1956] 1 WLR 335, in which the streetwalkers were found liable in private nuisance, stands for the proposition that an occupier of land may be liable in nuisance for activities of his or her licensees that take place off her land.

A landowner may also be liable for trespassers who are allowed to stay on his or her land, but who commit nuisance on the land occupied by, or under the control of, the plaintiff. In *Lippiatt & Anor v South Gloucestershire Council* [2000] QB 51 (CA), the defendant Council allowed and facilitated trespassers' presence on its land between 1991 and 1994 (when they were evicted). The trespassers used the Council's land as a base for unlawful activities on the plaintiffs' land. The English Court of Appeal held that the Council knew that the trespassers had 'shown a disposition to commit acts of vandalism and worse on the land of the plaintiffs'. The Council never relinquished its control of the land, and was in a position to evict them earlier. It could therefore be liable in nuisance for the acts of trespassers.

Landlords may be liable if they specifically authorise others to commit nuisance.[39] Moreover, the lessor of the premises from which the nuisance emanates may be liable for nuisance created by the lessee where it is the natural and necessary result of the purpose for which the premises were let.[40] In *De Jager v Payneham and*

---

38. Cited with approval in *Casley-Smith v FS Evans & Sons Pty Ltd [No 5]* [1989] Aust Torts Reports 68,351 (¶80–227), where it was noted that such a proposition is consistent with *Attorney-General v Stone* (1895) 12 TLR 76 and *White v Jameson* (1874) LR 18 Eq 303.
39. See: *Smith v Scott* [1973] Ch 314; *London Borough of Southwark & Anor v Mills & Ors; Baxter v Mayor etc of the London Borough of Camden* [1999] 3 WLR 939; 4 All ER 449.
40. *De Jager v Payneham & Magill Lodges Hall Inc* (1984) 36 SASR 498.

Magill Lodges Hall Inc (1984) 36 SASR 498, the owner of a suburban hall hired the hall out for functions. The plaintiff, who was a tenant in neighbouring premises, successfully sued the owner in nuisance caused by excessively loud music and other noise made by the people to whom the hall was hired. King CJ (with whom the other members of the court agreed), determined (at 502) that:

> An occupier of premises who hires the premises out for a particular purpose, which involves a special danger of nuisance, is liable for any nuisance caused by the hirer in carrying out that purpose.

Nuisance created by natural causes

When is the occupier liable for nuisance created by natural causes?

In *Goldman v Hargrave* (1966) 115 CLR 458 (in the Privy Council: [1967] 1 AC 645), Lord Wilberforce, delivering the opinion of the Privy Council, stated that where the nuisance is created by natural causes, as a general rule, the existence of a duty to abate nuisance will be based upon the defendant occupier's knowledge of the hazard, his or her 'ability to foresee the consequences of not checking or removing it, and the ability to abate it.'

Where a nuisance has been created by natural causes without the actions, omissions, authority or permission of the occupier of land, the occupier is liable if he or she:

- knows or ought to know of the existence of the nuisance;
- omits to remedy it within a reasonable time after he or she became aware, or ought to have become aware, of it;[41] and
- it is foreseeable that damage could occur.

For instance in *Stockwell v State of Victoria* [2001] VSC 497, the plaintiff, a former farmer, recovered $60 047.56 in damages for nuisance created by marauding wild dogs from the State reserve. The wild dogs killed and maimed his sheep, caused loss to the value of his wool clip, and decreased the market value of his property. Damages were also awarded for the plaintiff's expenses associated with attempts to abate the nuisance, inconvenience, upset and anxiety.

Likewise, in *Leakey v National Trust for Places of Historic Interest or Natural Beauty* [1980] QB 485, the plaintiffs were neighbours of the defendants' land, upon which was situated a large mound of soil and rubble that was liable to crack and slip as a result of weathering. Rubble from the hillside property used to fall on to the plaintiffs' land. The defendants were aware of the instability of the land. After the dry summer of 1976, a crack opened up in the mound. The plaintiffs requested that the defendants attend to the danger of a major landslip but the defendants refused

---

41. *Goldman v Hargrave* (1966) 115 CLR 458, per Taylor and Owen JJ.

to do anything about it. Some weeks later, a large quantity of earth and tree stumps fell on the plaintiffs' land. The Court of Queen's Bench held that the defendants were liable in nuisance because even though the landslip had been caused by natural processes, they were at fault by failing in their duty to take reasonable steps to avert the danger of which they had been made aware.

Megaw LJ in *Leakey* (at 522) observed that with regard to parklands and urban reserves, a council, as an occupier of a park, may be liable in nuisance even though it did not plant the trees whose roots now encroach on the plaintiff's property and cause damage to walls, paving, or drains. However, because, strictly speaking, the nuisance—in the form of expanding roots—was not brought about by human agency, the council's liability as an occupier will not arise until it acquires, or ought to have acquired, knowledge of the growth and the danger created by the roots. Thus, in *City of Richmond v Scantelbury* [1991] 2 VR 38, the complaint involved damage to the plaintiffs' house caused by the encroachment of roots from two elm trees, which grew in the adjacent parkland. The defendant Council had control and management of the park. The elm trees were over a hundred years old when, in 1986, the plaintiffs informed the defendant Council that damage to their home had been caused by the elms' roots. Kaye J held (at 44) that even before 1986 Council's officers ought to have known that the elms' canopy was overhanging the plaintiff's home. Since elm tree roots extend for a distance of 1.5 times the tree's height, they were likely to have encroached under the property. The Council should have taken reasonable precautions to prevent or minimise the risk of damage by constructing a concrete barrier along the boundary of the plaintiffs' property.

REMEDIES

The main remedies for nuisance are self-help, damages, and injunctions. Remedies in nuisance are based on a different principle from negligence: both damages and injunction are awarded in response to the harm done—not, as in negligence, to the culpability of the defendant. Statutory remedies under various environmental and zoning laws, as well as public health and safety laws, are also available.

Self-help

Self-help permits an occupier to take necessary steps to abate an existing or threatened nuisance. Self-help is a common remedy in cases where roots or branches of trees from a neighbouring property encroach upon the occupier's land. An occupier may lop them and then hand back the off-cuts to the owner.

However, this must be done without committing trespass to land. In *Gazzard & Anor v Hutchesson* [1995] Aust Torts Reports ¶81–337, the defendants told the plaintiffs that the overhanging branches of their poplar trees were 'a problem'. Soon afterwards, knowing that the plaintiffs were absent, the defendants employed a tree lopper to cut the poplar trees. The tree lopper cut not only the overhanging branches, but also branches growing on the plaintiffs' land. Bollen J of the South Australian Supreme Court found that, although the defendants were entitled to cut the branches that overhung their property, they committed trespass to land by severely and substantially cutting back other branches. The plaintiffs' claim of trespass to land was therefore made out, irrespective of whether or not the tree lopper actually stepped onto their land during lopping. Bollen J (at 62,360) explained this principle by providing the following example:

> If I put a stepladder near my dividing fence, mount it, lean over the fence and cut my neighbour's roses down, I have committed a trespass. Perhaps it is a trespass to land done with my arm and hand against flora growing on my neighbour's land. Perhaps it is a trespass simply to the roses or, in the present case, to the trees.

Consequently, except in an emergency when the doctrine of necessity affords a defence to trespass, entry onto the neighbour's land to abate a nuisance must be preceded by notification of the existence or threat of nuisance, and a request for permission to enter to abate it.

Where damage is only threatened and the affected landholder cuts encroaching roots and boughs to obviate damage, he or she will not have an action in nuisance to recover costs of abatement. Costs of abatement may only be recovered where actual damage has occurred and the abatement constituted a reasonable mitigation of damage.

Damages

Compensation for property damage in nuisance is based on reasonable foreseeability of damage. Damages aim to restore the plaintiffs to the position they would have been in if their property had not been damaged. This includes damages for diminution in value of the plaintiffs' property.

Nuisance is a continuing tort, and each substantial interference with the plaintiff's right to enjoyment of land creates a fresh cause of action. In *Stockwell v State of Victoria* [2001] VSC 497, Gillard J held (at [492–3]):

> So long as the nuisance exists and continues to cause loss, there is a separate cause of action established each time a loss is suffered ... The devaluation continued each time there was a dog attack. If the relevant employees [of the defendant] had performed their duty [by fencing off the area or eliminating the wild dogs], the value of the land in the hands of the plaintiff would have been restored to what it should have been if the nuisance did not exist ... In my opinion, the plaintiff is entitled to recover the loss which crystallised on the sale. The loss was continuing.

The defendant may be liable if he or she fails to take new precautions when they become available. Moreover, as a general rule, it is not up to the plaintiff to tell the defendant about appropriate precautions.

With respect to claims for unlawful interference with use and enjoyment of land, the court endeavours to award reasonable and fair compensation, taking into consideration such factors as the rights of both parties.

Consequential financial losses, such as loss of profits resulting from disruption of business activities, are compensable in private nuisance.

In *Gazzard v Hutchesson*, by the time the case was tried some twelve months later, the branches of the poplar trees had regrown. Nonetheless, damages were assessed at $100 per tree. Additionally, the defendants were required to pay $3000 in punitive damages because they acted 'with contumelious disrespect for the rights of enjoyment' by the plaintiffs of the trees (at 62, 353).

Injunctions

Injunctions are a discretionary remedy. Mandatory injunctions require the defendant to remove the nuisance. It is also possible to obtain a *quia timet* ('because he fears') injunction before an actual tort is committed. The *quia timet* injunction is granted in cases where the plaintiff proves that unless the defendant is made to desist, there is a real probability of substantial damage to the plaintiff's land or comfort. In *Khorasandjian v Bush* [1993] QB 727, the court granted such an injunction to restrain harassment by way of telephone calls.

In exceptional circumstances, as in *Dennis v Ministry of Defence* [2003] EWHC 793 (QB), the plaintiff may be forced to accept damages for future loss in lieu of an injunction. In such cases, the defendant must show that damages would be an adequate remedy, and that an injunction would be unfair to the defendant.

Both damages and injunction may be appropriate where the defendant's activities cause ongoing flooding, or repeated emissions of fumes, smells, and noises.

DEFENCES

The main defences to nuisance are consent, statutory authority, and prescriptive right to commit nuisance.

Consent

Historically, consent tended to be implied in circumstances where the plaintiff's premises form part of the defendant's building.[42] However, the majority in *Burnie Port Authority v General Jones Pty Ltd* (1994) CLR 520 suggested that the mere fact that the plaintiff's premises form part of the defendant's building will not necessarily imply that the former voluntarily assumed risks created by the defendant (the issue of nuisance was not pleaded on appeal to the High Court in *Burnie*).

---

42. *Lyttleton Times Co Ltd v Warners Ltd* [1907] AC 476 (PC); *Clarey v Principal and Council of the Women's College* (1953) 90 CLR 170.

However, an adjoining owner can acquire the right to have the additional weight of buildings or other improvements such as filling on his land supported by grant, by easement or by prescription.[43]

Statutory authority

In the absence of negligence, an unambiguous statutory authorisation of the activity that constitutes nuisance will be regarded as a full defence to nuisance, if the defendant—and the burden of proof is on the defendant—can show that:

- the legislation imposed a duty upon him or her; and
- the nuisance was an inevitable consequence of performance of the statutory duty or exercise of power. 'Inevitable consequence' means that there was no reasonable way the function could be performed without causing damage (*York Brothers v Commissioner for Main Roads* [1983] 1 NSWLR 391).

The defendant can also plead the defence of statutory authority where the legislation, while conferring an authority to act, also provides for a specific method or location, and nuisance is an inevitable consequence of doing the act authorised in that way or in that location.

Young J in *Lawrence v Kempsey Shire Council* [1995] Aust Torts Reports ¶81–344 observed that what the defendant must show is that it acted having all reasonable regard and care for the interests of others.

Statutory authorisation only extends to acts expressly authorised or conduct necessarily incidental to such acts; and even then there is an implied obligation to perform them in a careful manner. According to Barwick CJ in *Benning v Wong* (1969) 122 CLR 249, at 256, this implication can only be displaced by the plainest of language which allows for the careless execution of an authorised act.

The defence of statutory authorisation is subject to the fundamental principle of statutory interpretation that legislation is presumed *not* to derogate from common law rights unless it specifically so provides. Therefore it is not sufficient that the activity complained of be authorised by an Act. The creation of a nuisance in the performance of the authorised conduct must also be expressly or impliedly authorised.

Consequently, the defence will fail where:

- the activity is not, as a matter of construction, authorised by the statute;
- the nuisance is created by failure to take reasonable care in performing an authorised activity in the specified place and manner; or
- the authorised activity could reasonably be undertaken in some other place or manner without creating a nuisance. Thus, in *Lester-Travers v City of Frankston*

---

43. *Walker v Corporation of the City of Adelaide* [2004] SASC 98 at [265], per Perry J.

[1970] VR 2, although the construction of the golf course was authorised by statute, the legislation did not require it to be built in that precise location.

The case of *Lawrence v Kempsey Shire Council* [1995] Aust Torts Reports ¶81–344 is a case in point. In 1976, the Kempsey Shire Council constructed a channel to pass effluent from a Kempsey sewage treatment plant into Christmas Creek. In 1985, the Council deepened the creek. The plaintiff, the owner of land abutting Christmas Creek, sued the Council in nuisance, claiming that the channel forced nutrient-enriched water into the creek. This resulted in the growth of water hyacinth and smartweed, which effectively choked the creek and led to the spread of smartweed over native pasture land, adversely affecting the plaintiff's proprietary interests. The defendant Council relied on the defence of statutory authority. However, Young J of the New South Wales Supreme Court held that the Council had failed to demonstrate that the damage was an inevitable consequence of the operation of the sewerage works and discharge of the effluent into the creek. The statutory function could have been carried out in ways that involved less interference with the plaintiff's land.

Reasonable use

To establish nuisance, the plaintiff must show that the defendant's 'unnatural' or not 'ordinary' use of land created 'unreasonable' interference with their enjoyment of proprietary rights. Whether the defendant's use of land is 'natural' and reasonable will be determined having regard to all the circumstances, including the purposes for which the land is being used.

Today the construction of a swimming pool is considered to be a natural use of land. However, when the flow of water is diverted and it floods the plaintiff's land as a consequence of such construction, it will be regarded as an 'unnatural use'. For example, in *Corbertt v Pallas* [1995] Aust Torts Reports ¶81–329, Mrs Corbertt engaged a builder to build a swimming pool in her backyard. While the final work on her pool was in progress, there was a period of heavy rains during which water flowed from her land into her neighbour's land and house. Following expert advice, the neighbour, Mr Pallas, decided to build a retaining wall between the properties. Before building the wall, he asked Mrs Corbertt to allow his builder to build the wall. Mrs Corbertt refused to comply with this request, and with a further request for costs of the retaining wall. Mr Pallas built the retaining wall, and sued Mrs Corbertt in nuisance.

Priestley JA (at 62,241) found that while construction of the swimming pool in itself was reasonable, the consequential diversion and concentration of stormwater runoff was unreasonable. The cause of the flooding was the installation of the swimming pool without any drainage measures to deal with the changed drainage position. This was not a 'natural and reasonable' use of the land. Therefore, Mrs Corbertt, who created the nuisance, was responsible for the damage caused to Mr Pallas's land.

Conformation of land

In *Kraemers v Attorney-General (Tas)* [1966] Tas SR 113, the Tasmanian Supreme Court held (at 118) that, in actions for material damage brought about by water, it will be sufficient for the plaintiff to allege and prove material damage to his or her property resulting from an increase in the flow or percolation of surface water due to the defendant's altering of the conformation of land. Therefore, the defendant may plead, as a distinct defence, that his or her activity did not alter the conformation of land.

Prescriptive right to commit private nuisance

A prescriptive right to commit private nuisance may be acquired by the defendant upon proving that over a period of twenty years the plaintiff, or a predecessor in title, could have taken action to abate, or sue for, a constant and uniform actionable nuisance, but has failed to do so. Under the doctrine in *Sturgess v Bridgman* (1879) 11 Ch D 852, a prescriptive right to continue the interference arises where actions amount to an easement by prescription. This right can be claimed in several jurisdictions.[44] As a general rule the defendant has to establish that:

- the interference is of a kind that can constitute the subject-matter of a grant of an easement from the owner of the land affected; for instance, it is possible to acquire by prescription the right to pollute a stream (*Carlyon v Lovering* (1857) 1 H & H 784; 156 ER 1417), or to have sewerage and drainage systems emptying into a soakaway on another's land (*Robin v Tupman* [1993] 15 EG 145);
- the interference has continued for more than twenty years or a period prescribed by statute granting easement, without any variation in the degree or extent of that interference; and
- the plaintiff could have prevented the interference or sued in nuisance during the twenty-year period, but elected to refrain from acting, thus authorising the interference.

FURTHER READING

Buckley RA, *The Law of Nuisance*, Butterworths, London, 1996.
Ibbetson DJ, *A Historical Introduction to the Law of Obligations*, Oxford University Press, Oxford, 1999.
Brenner JF, 'Nuisance Law and the Industrial Revolution' (1974) 3 *The Journal of Legal Studies* 403.
Wightman J, 'Nuisance—the Environmental Tort? *Hunter v Canary Wharf* in the House of Lords' (1998) 61 *Modern Law Review* 870.

---

44. See for example: Re State Electricity Commission of Victoria & Joshua's Contract [1940] VLR 121; Conveyancing Act 1919 (NSW); Water Administration Act 1986 (NSW); Property Law Act 1974 (QLD); Law of Property Act 1936 (SA); Prescription Act 1934 (TAS) repealed by Land Titles Amendment (Law Reform) Act 2001 (TAS); Property Law Act 1958 (VIC); Property Law Act 1969 (WA).

19 Breach of Statutory Duty

HISTORICAL INTRODUCTION

A private law cause of action for breach of statutory duty will arise 'if it can be shown that the statutory duty was imposed for the protection of a limited class of the public, and Parliament intended members of that class to have a private right of action for breach of that duty.'[1]

When Parliament imposes a statutory duty, that duty—particularly if there are specified penalties for breach—has the character of a public duty. In some cases, the statute will also allow a private person injured through a breach of statutory duty to have an action for damages.

In the fourteenth century, an action for violation of statutes such as the *Statute of Labourers 1351* 23 Edw III, m 87 d[2] was 'trespass on the statute'. Originally referred to as 'contempt and trespass', in the sixteenth century these statutory actions were treated as actions on the case. By the eighteenth century, Giles Jacob in his *New Law Dictionary*,[3] referring to Sir Edward Coke's commentaries in Volume 2 of the *Institutes of the Laws of England* (published in 1642, pp 55, 74, 131, 163), wrote:

> Every Statute made against an Injury, gives a Remedy by Action, expressly or implicitly. And besides an Action upon the Statute, as the Subject's private Remedy; the Offender may be punished for Contempt at the King's suit, by Fine, &c.

Like the tort of negligence, the modern action for breach of statutory duty developed its main elements in the nineteenth century. However, the two causes of action have quite different jurisprudential underpinnings. As McHugh and Gummow JJ stated in *Byrne v Australian Airlines Ltd* (1995) 185 CLR 410, at 459, from the early 1800s, successive Parliaments enacted private Acts enabling private involvement in construction of railways, modernisation of roads, supply of water

---

1. *X (Minors) v Bedfordshire County Council* [1995] 2 AC 633.
2. Discussed in Kiralfy AK, *The Action on the Case*, Sweet & Maxwell Ltd, London, 1951, p 133.
3. Seventh edn, Henry Lintot, Savoy, 1756; entry under 'Statute'.

and gas, as well as other infrastructure projects. Since, according to Maxwell's *On the Interpretation of Statutes*,[4] these statues 'invested private persons or bodies, for their own benefit or profit, with privileges and powers interfering with the rights of others', it was only fair that they should be construed more strictly than other enactments:

> A private Act partook of the nature of a compact, as a contract between the promoters, or the portion of the public directly interested in it, and the legislature.

In *Byrne*, McHugh and Gummow JJ stated (at 459–61):

> The modern Australian counterpart [of the old private Acts] is legislation which adopts or otherwise gives effect to agreements between governments or public authorities and trading or financial corporations, often in connection with asset sales or resource development.

Legislative intention

The question of whether the plaintiff has a right to institute a private action for breach of statutory duty rests upon legislative discretion. However, once such a right is established, Maxwell's *On the Interpretation of Statutes*[5] should be followed, and the language of the statute:

> treated as the language of [its] promoters, who asked the Legislature to confer exceptional powers on them; and when doubt arises as to the construction of the language ... The benefit of the doubt is to be given to those who might be prejudiced by the exercise of the powers which the enactment grants, and against those who claim to exercise them.

It is therefore inappropriate to transpose to the tort of negligence principles regarding duty, breach, and causation that have been developed by breach of statutory duty jurisprudence.

In *X (Minors) v Bedfordshire County Council* [1995] 2 AC 633, at 730H, Lord Browne-Wilkinson, who delivered the leading judgment, found that private law claims for damages in relation to breach of statutory duty involve:

- actions for breach of statutory duty *simpliciter* (ie, irrespective of whether the breach was occasioned through carelessness or otherwise);
- actions based on a common law duty of care, arising from either the imposition of the statutory duty or the performance of it; or

---

4. First edn, W Maxwell & Son, London, 1875, pp 268–269; quoted in *Byrne v Australian Airlines Ltd* (1995) 185 CLR 410 at 460.
5. Ibid.

- misfeasance in public office (ie, the failure to exercise, or the exercise of, statutory powers either with the intention to injure the plaintiff or in the knowledge that the conduct is unlawful).

His lordship stated that the careless performance of a statutory duty does not in itself give rise to any cause of action in the absence of either a statutory right of action, or a common law duty of care.

Damages for harm occasioned by breach of statutory duty as well as injunctions to prevent and apprehend breach of statutory duty are available.

NATURE OF PRIVATE ACTION FOR BREACH OF STATUTORY DUTY

In *Pyrenees Shire Council v Day* (1998) 192 CLR 330, at 342, Brennan CJ reaffirmed the doctrine that the cause of action for breach of statutory duty is distinct from, and independent of, common law actions for damages in negligence, nuisance, trespass, or misfeasance in public office. An action for breach of statutory duty must be pleaded separately and specifically, though it can be pleaded concurrently with negligence, or with any other tort arising from the facts. Mason J noted, in *Sutherland Shire Council v Heyman* (1984) 157 CLR 424, that breach of statutory duty may also provide evidence in other tortious actions, particularly negligence and nuisance.

A private action for breach of statutory duty is generally based on strict liability in the sense that once all the elements are proven, the only complete defence is to show that the breach of statute was occasioned *solely* by the plaintiff's conduct, without any independent fault on the part of the defendant.

The right to sue for breach of statutory duty

Unlike negligence, where duty is imposed by common law, a private action for breach of statutory duty does not arise automatically from imposition of a statutory duty, but is a matter of the legislation conferring a right on the injured person to have the duty performed.

Very few statutes that impose a duty of care also explicitly grant the right to a private action in damages for breach of that statutory duty by those who have suffered harm as a result of such breach (although plaintiffs might have a separate action in, for example, negligence or nuisance). Consequently, the existence or otherwise of such a right must be inferred from the legislative intention, which involves statutory interpretation. In *Byrne v Australian Airlines Ltd* (1995) 185 CLR 410, at [16], Brennan CJ, Dawson and Toohey JJ, referring to *Sovar v Henry Lane Pty Ltd* (1967) 116 CLR 397 at 404–5, stated that a plaintiff will establish a cause of action for damages for breach of statutory duty only:

where a statute which imposes an obligation for the protection or benefit of a particular class of persons is, upon its proper construction, intended to provide a ground of civil liability when the breach of the obligation causes injury or damage of a kind against which the statute was designed to afford protection.

In *Crimmins v Stevedoring Industry Finance Committee* [1999] 200 CLR 1, at 58 [158], Gummow J, referring to the American cases of *Touche Ross & Co v Redington* Trustee 442 US 560 (1979) and *Karahalios v National Federation of Federal Employees* Local 1263 489 US 527 (1989),[6] stressed that in jurisdictions which adhere to the separation of judicial and legislative powers, the statute can only form a foundation for the common law duty if the Parliament has intended to create private rights of action.

His Honour (at 58 [157]) summed up the position as follows:

1   The relevant statutory duty must be attended by a sanction for non-performance.

2   'There is no action for breach of statutory duty unless the legislation confers a right on the injured person to have the duty performed' (*Northern Territory v Mengel* (1995) 185 CLR 307, at 343–4); and, as Dixon J pointed out in *O'Connor v SP Bray Ltd* (1937) 56 CLR 464, at 477–8, the legislation will rarely yield the necessary implication positively giving a civil remedy.

3   As indicated by McHugh and Gummow JJ in *Byrne v Australian Airlines Ltd* (1995) 185 CLR 410, at 458, where the legislation is a law of the Commonwealth, and the question is one respecting the creation of new rights and liabilities to engage Ch III of the Constitution, it is to be expected that the Parliament will clearly state its will.

Earlier, in *Byrne v Australian Airlines Ltd* (1995) 185 CLR 410, McHugh and Gummow JJ (at 459 [104]) wrote:

In Australia, the proposition that the courts give effect to 'the intention of the legislature' tends to disguise the compromises between contradictory positions which may be involved in obtaining the passage of legislation, particularly through a bicameral and federal legislature. To plumb the intent of the particular body which enacted the law in question may be an illusory quest … The task of the court, aided by such provisions as s 15AB of the *Acts Interpretation Act 1901* (Cth), is to give effect to the will of the legislature but as it has been expressed in the law and by ascertaining the meaning of the terms of the law.

---

6.   See also: *Salahuddin v Alaji* 232 F3d 305; 2000 US App (2000), in which the United States Court of Appeals for the Second Circuit dismissed a civil claim under the *Child Support Recovery Act 1992* 18 USCS § 228, on the basis that the legislation did not provide aggrieved parties a civil remedy and such a right could not be inferred from the Act's legislative history.

More recently, in *Travel Compensation Fund v Robert Tambree t/as R Tambree and Associates* [2005] HCA 69, which involved interpretation of statute for the purpose of establishing whether the defendants' conduct was the cause of the claimant's loss, Callinan J (at [78]) emphasised that in a cause of action conferred by statute 'the scope and objects of the relevant enactment are critically important'.

Statutory interpretation

In relation to interpretation of the relevant provisions, Gleeson CJ in *Singh v Commonwealth of Australia* [2004] HCA 43, at [19], observed that:

> a principle of interpretation, referred to by this Court in several recent judgments, is that courts do not impute to the legislature an intention to abrogate or curtail fundamental rights or freedoms unless such an intention is clearly manifested by unmistakable and unambiguous language.[7]

These 'fundamental rights' would include the right to sue for damages at common law. Gleeson CJ went on to say:

> where a statute imposes a duty, the question whether a breach of the duty will give rise to an action for damages at the suit of an injured victim 'depends upon the intention to be extracted from the statute when read as a whole, having regard to its general scope and purview as well as to its particular provisions'.[8] In *Sovar v Henry Lane Pty Ltd* [(1967) 116 CLR 397 at 405], Kitto J warned that the intention that such a private right shall exist is not conjured up by judges to give effect to their own ideas of policy, and then imputed to Parliament.

His Honour then provided the following warning:

> The danger to be avoided in references to legislative intention is that they might suggest an exercise in psychoanalysis of individuals involved in the legislative process; the value of references to legislative intention is that they express the constitutional relationship between courts and the legislature. As Kitto J said, references to intention must not divert attention from the text, for it is through the meaning of the text, understood in the light of background, purpose and object, and surrounding circumstances, that the legislature expresses its intention, and it is from the text, read in that light, that intention is inferred.

---

7. His Honour referred to *Coco v The Queen* (1994) 179 CLR 427 at 437; *Plaintiff S157/2002 v Commonwealth* (2003) 211 CLR 476 at 492 [30].
8. The reference is to *Martin v Western District of the Australasian Coal and Shale Employees' Federation Workers' Industrial Union of Australia (Mining Department)* (1934) 34 SR (NSW) 593 at 596, per Jordan CJ, citing *Pasmore v Oswaldtwistle Urban Council* [1898] AC 387 at 394.

The preliminary question to be asked is: did the statute create a right of private action, or did it merely impose upon a statutory authority a duty vis-à-vis the State to exercise its powers and to undertake responsibilities?

According to Kitto J in *Sovar v Henry Lane Pty Ltd* (1967) 116 CLR 397, at 405, the courts will determine whether such inference arises by balancing

> the nature, scope and terms of the statute, including the nature of the evil against which it is directed, the nature of the conduct prescribed, the pre-existing state of the law, and, generally, the whole range of circumstances relevant upon a question of statutory interpretation.

Where a regulation is in issue, the plaintiff must rebut any claim that the regulation was not validly made.

ELEMENTS OF THE ACTION FOR BREACH OF STATUTORY DUTY

The plaintiff who is successful in an action for breach of statutory duty can recover damages for personal injury, or can obtain an injunction to restrain its apprehended breach. However, the equitable remedy of injunction is discretionary.

To succeed in a private action for breach of statutory duty, the plaintiff must establish on the balance of probabilities the following elements:

- that the right to have the defendant perform the statutory duty, which has been imposed upon him or her, is enforceable by a private action in tort;
- that the plaintiff belongs to the class of persons the statute intended to protect;
- that the harm suffered by the plaintiff was of the kind the statute intended to prevent;
- breach of duty;
- statutory provisions governing breach of duty by statutory authorities; and
- causation: that the plaintiff's injury was caused by the defendant's breach.

Enforceability of the statutory breach as a private action in tort

The plaintiff must show that the statute created a right enforceable through a private action for breach of statutory duty, rather than imposing a criminal penalty on the tortfeasor or establishing a system for complaints to the Minister or Ombudsman, or to an appropriate administrative tribunal.

Where the statute provides a criminal penalty for breach, the question of whether a private right of action will arise will depend on whether the object of the statute was to punish the offender exclusively by the criminal sanction, or whether it also intended to compensate the plaintiff for injury.

Two contrasting rules of interpretation come into play where the statute prescribes a criminal penalty, such as a fine, for breach of statutory duty. There is a rule of construction that legislation creating an offence must be strictly (narrowly) construed. Dixon J (as he then was) in *O'Connor v SP Bray Ltd* (1937) 56 CLR 464, at 477–8, said that in these circumstances, the legislation will rarely yield the necessary implication positively giving a civil remedy. However, Kitto J, in *Sovar v Henry Lane Pty Ltd* (1967) 116 CLR 397, at 406, pointed out that the wording and the legislative context of each provision has to be examined before determining that the statute has exempted the defendant from civil liability for its contravention.

In general, legislation furthering industrial safety tends to be construed broadly so as to give the fullest relief allowed by a fair meaning of the words of the provision. In *Waugh v Kippen* (1986) 160 CLR 156, at 164, Gibbs CJ, Mason, Wilson, and Dawson JJ, in a joint judgment, said:

> the court must proceed with its primary task of extracting the intention of the legislature from the fair meaning of words by which it has expressed intention, remembering that it is a remedial measure posed for the protection of the worker. It should not be construed strictly as to deprive the worker of the protection which parliament intended that he should have.

South Australia and Queensland allow injured employees to sue their employers for statutory breaches of health and safety regulations. However, the Commonwealth, New South Wales, Victoria, the Australian Capital Territory, and the Northern Territory have occupational and health safety legislation that specifically excludes common law action for breach of provisions that impose general standards on employers for health and safety of the workplace.[9]

In non-industrial cases, the test was stated by Atkin LJ in *Phillips v Britannia Hygienic Laundry Co* [1923] 2 KB 832, at 842, as follows:

> the question is whether these regulations, viewed in the circumstances in which they were made and to which they relate, were intended to impose a duty which is a public duty only or whether they were intended, in addition to the public duty, to impose a duty enforceable by an individual aggrieved.

In *Phillips v Britannia Hygienic Laundry Co*, a wheel of the defendants' motor lorry came off while the lorry was being driven on a public highway, and damaged the plaintiff's van. The accident happened because of a defect in the axle. Two days before the accident, the defendants had received the lorry back from the makers, a

---

9. *Occupational Health and Safety (Commonwealth Employment) Act 1991* (Cth), s 79; *Occupational Health and Safety Act 1983* (NSW), s 22; *Occupational Health and Safety Act 1985* (Vic), s 28; *Occupational Health and Safety Act 1989* (ACT), s 95; *Work Health Act 1986* (NT), s 34.

firm of known competence, to whom it had been sent to be overhauled and repaired. The plaintiff sued in negligence and breach of statutory duty, relying on a provision contained in the Motor Cars (Use and Construction) Order 1904, which required a motor car and all its fittings to be 'in such a condition as not to cause, or be likely to cause, danger to any person on the motor car or on any highway', and imposed 'a duty enforceable by individuals injured, but a public duty only, the sole remedy for which is the remedy provided by way of a fine'.

Section 32 of the *Domestic (Feral and Nuisance) Animals Act 1994* (Vic), set out in Chapter 18, enables prosecution of dog owners, in cases where the animal 'injures or endangers the health of any person', and imposes a fine of one penalty unit. The legislation does not grant the injured person the right to sue the owner for breach of the statutory duty. However, depending on the circumstances, the injured person may have an action in negligence, private nuisance, or action on the case for intentional infliction of physical harm.

The relevant statute must impose a duty on the defendant

The plaintiff must show that the statutory duty was imposed on the defendant; for the action will only lie against the person upon whom the duty is imposed. In general, unless the legislation provides otherwise, a defendant cannot discharge a duty imposed by delegating its performance to another. Employers cannot avoid liability for breach of duty when it is cast on them, by showing that the breach was due to the act of an employee, or an independent contractor. In the past, the obverse effect of this rule has been to preclude employer's liability where one employee is injured through breach of the statutory duty cast on the offending employee. In other words, an employer would not be liable under statute for an employee's breach of statutory duty where the duty was cast solely upon that employee. Thus, in *Darling Island Stevedoring and Lighterage Co Ltd v Long* (1957) 97 CLR 36, the High Court held that a regulation which imposed a statutory duty upon 'a person in charge' to take certain precautions was directed to a supervisor or a foreman, but not to the employer. As a result, an injured employee had a private right of action for breach of statutory duty against a fellow stevedore, but not against his employer. Likewise, a principal is not vicariously liable for breach of statutory duty where the duty was imposed upon his or her servant or agent. In the context of employment, the *Darling Island Stevedoring* decision, which has some resemblance to the old defence of common employment, is incompatible with the doctrine of non-delegable duty to provide a safe system of work. The 1957 decision has been bypassed in a number of subsequent cases, including *Progress Properties Ltd v Craft* (1976) 135 CLR 651.

In *Progress Properties* (discussed in Chapter 17), the plaintiff, a plumber, sustained a severe injury when a hoist used for raising bricks, which he had to use to access the upper stories of a twenty-five-storey building under construction, plummeted to the ground at a speed that exceeded 600 feet per minute. Riding on such a hoist was prohibited by statutory regulation, which made it an offence to ride on the hoist, or to permit a person to do so. Moreover, r 139(7) of the *Scaffolding and Lifts Regulations 1912* (NSW) provided that 'The speed at which any load is raised or lowered shall not exceed 600 feet per minute'. Jacobs J, with whom Stephen, Mason, and Murphy JJ agreed, observed (at 670) that there:

> was nothing in the sub-regulation or its context to suggest that there should be no right of civil action as a consequence of its breach by the person carrying out building work or by a person for whose acts the builder is vicariously liable.

Jacobs J (at 671) affirmed the holding of the New South Wales Court of Appeal that the plaintiff was injured as a result of the hoist operator's breach of r 139(7).

Plaintiff must be within the protected class

To have standing to sue for breach of statutory duty, plaintiffs must be within the protected class. In *Pyrenees Shire Council v Day* (1998) 192 CLR 330, at 347, Brennan CJ said that one must look to see whether the statute gives a remedy to people in the situation of the plaintiff if the statutory duty is not fulfilled. He then said (at [26]):

> No duty breach of which sounds in damages can be imposed when the power is intended to be exercised for the benefit of the public generally and not for the protection of the person or property of members of a particular class.

Thus, no action for breach of the statutory duty will lie with respect to traffic regulations, because the public as a whole is not a 'class' of persons.

Earlier, in *Byrne v Australian Airlines Ltd* (1995) 185 CLR 410, at 424 [16], Brennan CJ, Dawson and Toohey JJ, referring to *O'Connor v SP Bray Ltd* (1937) 56 CLR 464, at 478, said:

> One generalisation that can be made is that where the persons upon whom the statutory obligation is imposed are under an existing common law duty of care towards the persons whom the statute is intended to benefit or protect, the statutory prescription of a higher or more specific standard of care may, in the absence of any indication of a contrary intention, properly be construed as creating a private right.

Their Honours provided an example of legislation designed to protect the health and safety of employees in the particular workplace, which has been held to impose statutory duties the breach of which would give rise to a right to sue for damages. In Victoria, South Australia, the Northern Territory, and New South Wales, as well as under Commonwealth legislation, workers' compensation provisions abrogate or limit common law actions, including action for breach of the statutory duty by workers or deceased workers' dependants entitled to compensation under workers' compensation schemes.

An example of a statutorily protected class is *Onus & Anor v Alcoa of Australia Ltd* (1981) CLR 27. Aboriginal persons claiming to be custodians of their tribe's relics sought an injunction restraining Alcoa from carrying out works which would interfere with these relics. Aboriginal relics were protected by Victorian legislation, which made it an offence to wilfully or negligently deface a relic, or to carry out an act likely to endanger a relic. The injunction was granted on the ground that the plaintiffs would be more particularly affected than any other member of the community by the apprehended breach.

The harm suffered must be within the scope of the risks contemplated by the legislation

Sutherland Shire Council v Heyman (1985) 157 CLR 424 illustrates the principle that, even though the plaintiff might have been in contemplation of the statute, the private action for breach of the statutory duty will fail if the injury was outside the scope of risks at which the legislation was directed. Likewise, in *Kebewar Pty Ltd v Harkin* [1987] Aust Torts Reports ¶80–123, action for breach of the statutory duty based upon legislation regulating excavations, retaining walls and the protection of adjoining properties failed, because the injury complained of—withdrawal of support of land—was held not to have been within the contemplation of the statute.

Breach of the duty

There is no general standard of care governing the breach of statutory duty—the content of the statutory duty depends upon the wording of the legislation. In cases where the statute provides for the particular standard of care, the question of breach is always a matter of statutory interpretation.

Public authorities and the Torts reforms

Under Torts Reform legislation, in a proceeding for breach of statutory duty, 'the fact that a public authority exercises or decides to exercise a function does not of itself indicate that the authority is under a duty to exercise the function or that the function should be exercised in particular circumstances or in a particular way.'[10]

---

10. See, for example: *Wrongs Act 1958* (Vic), s 85.

Exercise of discretionary functions

In *X (Minors) v Bedfordshire County Council* [1995] 2 AC 633, the House of Lords determined that where a decision complained of as being in breach of statutory authority falls within the ambit of a statutory discretion, it cannot be actionable in common law unless it is so unreasonable as to fall outside the ambit of the discretion conferred.[11]

The *Ipp Report*, in its Recommendation 39, proposed a broader principle that would relate to actions in negligence as well as for breach of statutory duty:

> In any claim for damages for personal injury or death arising out of negligent performance or non-performance of a public function, a policy decision (that is, a decision based substantially on financial, economic, political or social factors or constraints) cannot be used to support a finding that the defendant was negligent unless it was so unreasonable that no reasonable public functionary in the defendant's position could have made it.[12]

All jurisdictions[13] except the Northern Territory and South Australia have adopted this principle in relation to breach of statutory duty. For example, the *Civil Liability Act 2003* (Qld), s 36, provides that in a proceeding based on an alleged wrongful exercise of, or failure to exercise, a function of a public or other authority:

> For the purposes of the proceeding, an act or omission of the authority does not constitute a wrongful exercise or failure unless the act or omission was in the circumstances so unreasonable that no public or other authority having the functions of the authority in question could properly consider the act or omission to be a reasonable exercise of its functions.

Thus, in six jurisdictions, to negative the alleged breach of statutory duty, the defendant authority will need to show that one 'public (or other) authority' with similar functions—for example, another local council—would have considered that the acts or omissions in issue were a reasonable exercise of a function.

There is also a wider limitation on liability of statutory authorities under s 84(3) of the *Wrongs Act 1958* (Vic), which states:

> For the purpose of the proceeding [for breach of statutory duty] the public authority is not liable for damages caused by the wrongful exercise of or failure

---

11. Per Lord Browne-Wilkinson.
12. The phrase 'public functionary' was defined as referring to both corporate bodies and natural persons (Recommendation 40), and the Report noted (at [10.28]) that the policy defence embodied in Recommendation 39 should be 'available only in cases where a public functionary has made a [policy] decision about the performance or non-performance of a public function. The defence would not be available in a case where the functionary did not consider whether or not to perform the function.'
13. *Civil Liability Act 2003* (Qld), s 36; *Wrongs Act 1958* (Vic), s 84; *Civil Liability Act 2002* (WA), s 5X; *Civil Law (Wrongs) Act 2002* (ACT), s 111(2); *Civil Liability Act 2002* (NSW), s 43(2); *Civil Liability Act 2002* (Tas), s 40.

to exercise a function of the authority unless the provisions and policy of the enactment in which the duty to exercise the function is created are compatible with the existence of that liability.

Under common law, alleged wrongful conduct of statutory authorities that involves a decision whether or not to exercise a function based on policy considerations is not justiciable, for 'the court cannot adjudicate on such policy matters and accordingly a common law duty of care in relation to the taking of decisions involving policy matters cannot exist.'[14] Consequently, the plaintiff suing a statutory authority for breach of statutory duty, in circumstances where the legislative policy is a factor in the exercise or failure to exercise a function, will have to persuade the court that the matter is justiciable.

Limitations on duty of statutory authorities relating to the reasonableness and policy considerations do not apply to the statutory duty which is imposed as an absolute duty on the public authority to do or not to do a particular thing.[15] For example, where the statute includes safety regulations that provide instructions on how the safety precautions are to be achieved, such regulations tend to be interpreted as imposing an absolute duty. Plaintiffs who can establish that they fall within the class of statutorily protected persons may succeed with respect to the issue of breach of such safety provisions by pleading *res ipsa loquitur* (*Galashiels Gas Co Ltd v O'Donnell* [1949] AC 275).

Betts v Whittingslowe (1945) 71 CLR 637 is one of the seminal Australian cases on breach of statutory duty. Derek Betts, at fourteen years of age, was employed by Whittingslowe to operate a fast-moving power press, which included a moving ram highly dangerous to the hands of an operator. The machine was equipped with a guard fencing the front of the ram, which had to be raised every time a small piece of metal was inserted between the dies. The guard did not extend to the right or left side of the ram. On his second day at work, Derek's right hand was crushed by the press and seriously injured. The trial judge was not really persuaded by any evidence as to how the accident happened; however, he found the explanation that the plaintiff had put his hand around and behind the guard the least improbable. The *Industrial Code 1920–36* (SA), s 321, provided that: 'The occupier of a factory shall securely fence or safeguard ... all dangerous parts of the machinery therein' and 'cause all fencing and safeguards to be constantly maintained in an efficient state while the parts required to be fenced or safeguards ... are in motion or use for the purpose of any manufacturing process.' The High Court found that Whittingslowe was in breach of an absolute obligation imposed by the statute to securely fence or safeguard all dangerous part or parts of his machinery.[16]

---

14. *X (Minors) v Bedfordshire County Council* [1995] 2 AC 633; *Graham Barclay Oysters Pty Ltd v Ryan; Ryan v Great Lakes Council; State of New South Wales v Ryan* [2002] HCA 54.
15. *Wrongs Act 1958* (Vic), s 84(4);
16. See also: *Piro v W Foster & Co Ltd* (1943) 68 CLR 313.

Dixon J (at 649) determined that:

> the breach of duty coupled with an accident of the kind that might thereby be caused is enough to justify an inference, in the absence of any sufficient reason to the contrary, that in fact the accident did occur owing to the act or omission amounting to the breach of statutory duty. In the circumstances of this case that proposition is enough. For, in my opinion, the facts warrant no other inference inconsistent with liability on the part of the defendant.

Causation

In *Travel Compensation Fund v Robert Tambree t/as R Tambree and Associates* [2005] HCA 69, Gummow and Hayne JJ (at [49]) reiterated the statement of Gummow, Hayne, and Heydon JJ in *Allianz Australia Insurance Ltd v GSF Australia Pty Ltd* [2005] HCA 26, at [99], that in relation to statutory claims, 'notions of "cause" as involved in [that] statutory regime are to be understood by reference to the statutory subject, scope and purpose.'

In non-industrial cases, the plaintiff must establish a causal connection between the breach of statutory duty by the defendant and the injury complained of. In *Henville v Walker* [2001] HCA 52, at [102], McHugh J discussed the following two cases in which the object of the statutory duty—and consequently, the causative nexus—was very narrowly interpreted. McHugh J wrote:

> in *Gorris v Scott* (1874) LR 9 Ex 125, in the course of a voyage on the defendant's ship, the plaintiff's sheep were washed overboard because the defendant neglected his statutory duty to provide pens on the deck of the ship. The action was dismissed because the statute was aimed at preventing disease and was not directed to the events that had happened. Thus, in spite of the existence of a breach of duty that resulted in damage to the plaintiff, there was no relevant causal connection because the damage was outside the contemplation of the statute. Similarly, in *Close v Steel Company of Wales Ltd* [1962] AC 367, the defendant, in breach of its duty, had failed to fence a dangerous drilling machine. The plaintiff was injured when the drill bit fragmented. His action failed because the House of Lords held that the duty to fence was limited to keeping the worker from coming into contact with the dangerous machinery and did not extend to protecting the worker from injury caused by ejected pieces of the machine.[17]

However, in some cases a presumption of causation may arise. This is particularly so where the statute is framed in such a way as to indicate that its intention is to prevent injury from incompetence. The intention of the statute may provide the foundation for a prima facie presumption of causation where it can be inferred

---

17. McHugh J noted the comment of Lord Simonds in *Nicholls v F Austin (Leyton) Ltd* [1946] AC 493 at 505: 'The fence is intended to keep the worker out, not to keep the machine or its product in.'

from the facts that the injury was in fact caused by incompetence. In *John Pfeiffer Pty Ltd v Canny* (1981) 148 CLR 218, a worker was shot in the head by the explosive-powered 'Ramset' gun used for firing a steel pin, while it was being used by a fellow worker who was not qualified to use the gun. The fellow worker was in breach of a regulation that prohibited use of this tool by an unqualified person. The High Court held that, where a tool caused damage, the person who allowed the operator to use it in contravention of the regulation was liable without need for further proof of causation. At the same time, a breach of statutory duty consisting of a person failing to hold a required certificate or licence will not of itself establish causation.

In other cases, it will be sufficient for the plaintiff to show that the breach had materially contributed to the injury. This doctrine was established in *Bonnington Castings Ltd v Wardlaw* [1956] AC 613 (discussed in Chapter 12), where Mr Wardlaw, a steel dresser, contracted pneumoconiosis after being exposed for eight years to silica dust emanating from the pneumatic hammer at which he worked and also from swing grinders. No dust extraction plant was known or practicable for use with the hammer but, though the swing grinders were fitted with such equipment, they were not kept free from obstruction, and in this respect the factory owners were in breach of their statutory duty under r 1 of the *Grinding of Metals (Miscellaneous Industries) Regulations 1925* (UK). The House of Lords held that the failure of the employer to keep the ducts designed to carry away the noxious silica dust from the swing grinders clear of obstruction was a material contributing cause of the plaintiff's illness.

DEFENCES

Plaintiff's conduct

Where the statute casts a duty in the same terms on both employer and employee, the defendant employer will escape liability in an action for breach of the statutory duty only if he or she can show that the plaintiff employee's conduct was the *sole* reason for the breach, ie that there was no independent 'fault' on the part of the defendant.

In the case of *Nicol v Allyacht Spars Pty Ltd* (1987) 163 CLR 611, the plaintiff Mr Nicol was both an employee and a director of a small company, Allyacht Spars, which manufactured flag poles without installing them. Mr Nicol was injured when he attempted to replace a banner on a flag pole supplied by the company. He used an unsafe work system that was devised and agreed to beforehand by all directors, including the plaintiff. He sued for breach of an employer's statutory duty to provide a safe system of work as well as in negligence for breach of the employer's non-delegable duty of care to provide a safe system of work.

Mason CJ, Toohey and Gaudron JJ of the High Court held (at 618) that Mr Nicol was not disabled from complaining of the failure to provide a safe system of work on the ground that the system had been devised by him because it was not solely his fault:

> It was in part his fault in acquiescing in the use of the system and helping to put it into operation. But it was also very much the fault of those who devised the system.

The majority, with Dawson J dissenting on the facts, held that Mr Nicol was 40 per cent liable for contributory negligence in acquiescing in the use of the system and helping to put it into operation.

Dawson J noted (at 625) that:

> An employee cannot succeed in an action against his employer for breach of statutory duty where the conduct which is at fault and upon which the action is based is that of the employee notwithstanding that the same conduct puts the employer in breach of his statutory duty. It is said to offend ordinary sensibilities that an employer should be liable to an employee for his own wrongdoing. The application of the principle is, however, limited to those occasions when the wrongful conduct is that of the employee alone and no fault can otherwise be attributed to the employer.

Thus, according to Dawson J, some contributory negligence on the part of the employee may not vitiate the cause of action for breach of statutory duty, for, as his Honour put it (at 625):

> it does not seem to me that the duty of an employer and an employee in such regard [breach of statutory duty] can ever be co-extensive or co-terminous. The duty is that of the employer and even if the employee is entrusted with its performance it remains an independent obligation of the employer of a more comprehensive kind to ensure that reasonable care is taken.

Gleeson CJ, McHugh, Gummow, Hayne, and Heydon JJ, in a joint judgment in *Andar Transport Pty Ltd v Brambles Ltd* [2004] HCA 28, at [44],[18] specifically agreed with this statement of the law, and stated (at [39]) that 'the reasoning of Dawson J in his dissenting judgment in *Nicol* should be preferred'.

---

18. Brambles Ltd outsourced to Andar Transport Pty Ltd the provision of laundry delivery services to a number of hospitals, which involved, amongst other things, the delivery by truck of large trolleys of clean linen. The plaintiff, Mr Daryl Wail was employed by Andar as well as being one of the two directors and shareholders in the company. Mr Wail was injured when he attempted to pull free one of the trolleys which was jammed against another trolley. Mr Wail sued Brambles and Andar for failure to ensure that the trolleys could be manoeuvred without risk of injury and a failure by Brambles to ensure that the trolleys could be manoeuvred having regard to their excessive weight when fully laden. In issue was contribution between tortfeasors; however, the High Court also discussed contributory negligence in relation to breach of statutory duty.

However, there are cases in which the employee acts foolishly despite the employer's efforts to fulfil the independent obligation to ensure that reasonable care is taken. For instance, in *Millington v Wilkie t/as Max Wilkie Plumbing Services & Anor* [2005] NSWCA 45, Mr Wilkie employed the plaintiff Mr Millington, an experienced plumber, to relocate a pipe at a height of seven metres. Mr Wilkie twice instructed Mr Millington not to use a ladder that was too short, and to wait for a longer ladder to be brought. Nevertheless, Mr Millington placed the ladder, unsecured at both top and bottom, against a column of the bridge and ascended about two metres. The ladder then slipped out and the plaintiff fell, sustaining severe injuries. Mr Millington sued, *inter alia*, for breaches of statutory duties under rr 73(2), 80 and 141 of the regulations under the *Construction Safety Act 1912* (NSW). The New South Wales Court of Appeal (Giles, Hodgson, and Ipp JJA) held that the absence of any fault of Mr Wilkie precluded Mr Millington from succeeding on the basis of breach of any of the regulations under the Act. The court stated that:

> Where an employer is put in breach of statutory duty by reason of conduct of an employee, and nothing done or omitted by the employer contributes to the breach, the employee is excluded from the class of persons for whose benefit the statutory duty was imposed and so has no cause of action for breach of duty (*HC Buckman & Son Pty Limited v Flannagan* (1974) 133 CLR 422, *Nicol v Allyacht Spars Pty Ltd* (1987) 163 CLR 611 at 624, *Andar Transport Pty Ltd v Brambles Ltd* [2004] HCA 28 at [39] to [42]).

Contributory negligence and voluntary assumption of risk

In *Bourke v Butterfield and Lewis* (1926) 38 CLR 354, the High Court decided that, as a matter of principle, contributory negligence did not apply to breach of statutory duty actions. However, in *Piro v W Foster & Co Ltd* (1943) 68 CLR 313, the court followed the precedent set by the House of Lords' decision in *Caswell v Powell Duffryn Associated Collieries Ltd* [1940] AC 152 and, overruling *Bourke v Butterfield*, held that the defence was applicable to breach of the statutory duty. In *Nicol v Allyacht Spars Pty Ltd* (1987) 163 CLR 611 at 618, the majority declared that while plaintiffs could not succeed if their injuries were caused solely by their own fault, their claim was subject to apportionment where the injuries were caused partly by their own fault and partly by the fault of other employees. Dowson J, in dissent stated (at 626) where the employer was at fault in failing to provide adequate equipment and devise safe system of work, the plaintiff-employee could not be guilty of contributory negligence even if the manner in which he carried out his task 'was manifestly dangerous'.

In *Astley & Ors v Austrust Ltd* (1999) 197 CLR 1, the specific issue before the court was the interpretation of the now repealed s 27A of the *Wrongs Act 1936* (SA), which defined 'fault' as including 'negligence, breach of statutory duty or other act or omission'. Nevertheless, Gleeson CJ, McHugh, Gummow, and Hayne JJ noted (at 15 [31]):

> Thus, it is now settled that a plaintiff may be guilty of contributory negligence even though he or she is injured as the result of a breach of a statutory duty whose very purpose was to prevent that type of injury. In *Davies v Adelaide Chemical and Fertilizer Co Ltd* (1946) 74 CLR 541 this Court ... accepted that, in Australia also, a plaintiff could be guilty of contributory negligence where the defendant had breached a statutory duty even if the purpose of the statute was to prevent the very damage or accident which occurred.

The Commonwealth Law Reform Commission Report (ACT) on *Contributory Negligence*[19] recommended in paragraph 14 that the defence of contributory negligence should be abolished in breach of statutory duty cases because:

1. Breach of statutory duty is a cause of action created by Parliament applying to those in charge of dangerous operations as a standard of safety to ensure, as far as possible, that accidents do not happen even if people are careless. Therefore, a reduction of compensation for breach of such a duty on the grounds of contributory negligence is contrary to the very purpose of the imposition of a statutory duty designed to protect workers against their own inadvertence.
2. Since an action for breach of statutory duty is not a negligence action, it is the legislation that determines the nature of the obligation and negligence may have nothing to do with its breach. Consequently, the courts should not intrude into the province of legislature and 'apply standards of negligence to the injured person when those same standards may not apply in determining whether an employer has breached a statutory duty'.
3. Statutory duty tends to be imposed on the employer as the person in the best position, in terms of resources and knowledge, to make sure that the enterprise is safe. Moreover, employers are required to take out insurance against compensation claims; hence, they are generally in a better position to pay than an uninsured worker.

The defence of contributory negligence applies to breach of statutory duty cases in the Northern Territory, Queensland, Western Australia, South Australia, Tasmania, and New South Wales.[20] In the Australian Capital Territory, the *Civil Law*

---

19. Commonwealth Law Reform Commission, *Contributory Negligence*, Report 3, Australian Capital Territory, June 1991.
20. *Law Reform (Miscellaneous Provisions) Act 1956* (NT), s 16(1); *Law Reform (Contributory Negligence) Amendment Act 2001* (Qld), s 5; *Law Reform (Contributory Negligence and Tortfeasors' Contribution) Act 1947* (WA), s 3; *Law Reform (Contributory Negligence and Apportionment of Liability) Act 2001* (SA), 3; *Tortfeasors and Contributory Negligence Amendment Act 2000* (Tas), s 2(c); *Law Reform (Miscellaneous Provisions) Act 1965* (NSW), s 9.

(Wrongs) Act 2002 (ACT), s 102(2), provides that: 'if the claimant suffered personal injury and the wrong was a breach of statutory duty, the damages recoverable by the claimant for the personal injury must not be reduced because of the claimant's contributory negligence'.

Victoria is governed by common law as set out in *Nicol v Allyacht Spars Pty Ltd* (1987) 163 CLR 611, *Astley & Ors v Austrust Ltd* (1999) 197 CLR 1, at 15 [31], and *Andar Transport Pty Ltd v Brambles Ltd* [2004] HCA 28, at [44].

Generally, voluntary assumption of risk is not a defence in cases where a private action for breach of statutory duty is made out. However, in *Imperial Chemical Industries v Shatwell* [1965] AC 656, the House of Lords held that voluntary assumption of risk was a complete defence if the employer was not at fault and was only vicariously liable for the acts of a servant.

Given the difficulties involved in establishing the right to sue (and, following the Torts reforms, the breach of duty of care by public authorities), it is relatively rare for plaintiffs to pursue actions for breach of statutory duty in jurisdictions that have no-fault workers' compensation schemes. However, in *Brodie v Singleton Shire Council* (2001) 180 ALR 145, at 160 [58], Gaudron, McHugh, and Gummow JJ noted:

> To say of a statute that it does not create a cause of action for breach of the norms it imposes is not necessarily to say that there is no room for the operation of the principles of negligence.

FURTHER READING

Balkin RP & Davis JLR, *Law of Torts*, 2nd edn, Butterworths, Sydney, 1996, Ch 16.

Johnstone R, 'Paradigm Crossed? The Statutory Occupational Health and Safety Obligations of the Business Undertaking' (1999) 12 *Australian Journal of Labour Law* 73.

Markensis BS, Auby J-B, Coester-Waltjen & Dakin SF, *Tortious Liability of Statutory Bodies* Hart Publishing, Oxford 1999.

Raday F, 'Privatising Human Rights and the Abuse of Power' (2000) 3 *Canadian Journal of Law and Jurisprudence* 103.

20 Establishing Defamation*

INTRODUCTION

The tort of defamation protects a person's reputation. Broadly speaking, defamation laws confer a cause of action against another for publication of matter that tends to lower the plaintiff in the estimation of ordinary persons, expose the plaintiff to ridicule or derision, or exclude the plaintiff from society. Defamation liability encompasses not only disparagement of an individual's personal character, but also disparagements of an individual's or corporation's reputation in trade, business, profession, or office.[1] Defamation is a tort of strict liability. Provided defendants have the requisite intention to publish the defamatory matter—or could reasonably anticipate publication—they do not escape liability by establishing that they had no intention to injure the plaintiff's reputation, or otherwise acted without fault.

The objective of the law of defamation is to strike a balance between two competing interests: the private interest of protection of reputation and the public interest in freedom of expression.[2] As we will see, it is relatively simple for a plaintiff to establish a prima facie case in defamation; the defences therefore play a critical role in reconciling these interests—more so than in any other area of torts law. A number of defences to defamation actions permit publication of defamatory matter where it is true, a matter of fair comment, or spoken on an occasion of privilege. These defences are considered in detail in the following chapter. In particular, it is not necessary to establish a *prima facie claim* in defamation to prove that the statement was false. The truth of the matter is, rather, the subject-matter of a defence (the defence of justification).

---

*   This chapter was written by Sharon Erbacher.
1.   *Random House Australia Pty Ltd v Abbott & Ors* (1999) 94 FCR 296 at 306.
2.   *Lange v Australian Broadcasting Corporation* (1997) 189 CLR 520 at 568; *Chakravarti v Advertiser Newspapers Ltd* (1998) 193 CLR 519 at 575, per Kirby J.

Defamation and privacy

The true motivation for a defamation action is often a desire by the plaintiff to protect his or her privacy, or to obtain compensation for an invasion of privacy. However, the law of defamation is concerned with the protection of interests in reputation, not privacy, and hence its ability to safeguard privacy is limited.[3] The publication of matter that would expose the plaintiff to scorn or ridicule—such as nude photographs of the plaintiff[4]—might be actionable in defamation. Outside this limited circumstance, however, defamation law is not well equipped to prevent the dissemination of private and confidential information regarding the plaintiff. The common law defence of justification requires merely that the matter be true. This defence protects the publication of personal and confidential details of the plaintiff's life—provided those details are accurate—even though it could not be said that members of the public have a legitimate interest in receiving that information.

In some jurisdictions, there has until recently been a requirement to prove that, in addition to the matter being true, publication was in the 'public interest' (Queensland, Tasmania, and the Australian Capital Territory) or for the 'public benefit' (New South Wales). The imposition of this added requirement had the effect of limiting the publication of defamatory matter relating to a person's private life where there was no wider public interest or benefit in publication, but did not prevent the publication of merely embarrassing, but non-defamatory, matter. However, these jurisdictions are soon to abolish the added requirement of public benefit or interest. Each Australian jurisdiction has agreed to adopt uniform defamation laws (discussed below), under which the defence of justification will be based on general law principles where truth alone will constitute a defence. These uniform laws will impose no significant limitations on the publication of intimate facts having no relevance to public affairs or the public conduct of the subject, provided those facts are true.

A national law of defamation

Australian defamation law has for many decades comprised a confusing and complex hotchpotch of common law and State and Territory legislation. Queensland and Tasmania codified defamation law.[5] New South Wales partially codified defamation law, particularly in relation to defences.[6] In the other jurisdictions, defamation law was primarily based on the common law, but that foundation was overlaid by various

---

3. Nor is there a tort of breach of privacy in Australia, although there are indications that the High Court might be amenable to development of such a tort: *Australian Broadcasting Corporation v Lenah Game Meats Pty Ltd* (2001) 208 CLR 199.
4. *Ettingshausen v Australian Consolidated Press Ltd* (1991) 23 NSWLR 443.
5. *Defamation Act 1889* (Qld); *Defamation Act 1957* (Tas).
6. *Defamation Act 1974* (NSW).

statutory provisions.[7] These jurisdictional differences have created considerable uncertainty for national media organisations publishing in multiple jurisdictions. They have also led to increased costs of defending a defamation claim. The plaintiff is entitled to commence separate actions in multiple jurisdictions,[8] or bring one cause of action in a single jurisdiction but plead separate causes of action for each State and Territory in which the matter is published. If pleading separate causes of action for each jurisdiction, the defendant will be required to plead a defence to each cause of action, and the judge and jury will be required to apply a different law for each jurisdiction. This adds considerably to the length, complexity and cost of the trial.[9]

The Australian Law Reform Commission in 1979 recognised these problems and recommended that uniform defamation laws be adopted across all States and Territories.[10] However, no great progress was made toward establishing a national defamation law for nearly twenty-five years as the Attorneys-General of the various States and Territories were unable to agree on the content of such a law. The development of national media organisations reaching national audiences, and the vast increase of communications across borders made possible by technological developments such as the internet and email, have provided even greater impetus for change over the last decade.[11] Recognising that the argument for uniform laws had become compelling, the Commonwealth Attorney-General's Department released a discussion paper and draft Bill in 2004.[12] Following the release of that discussion paper, the Standing Committee of the Attorneys-General (comprising the Attorneys-General from each State and Territory) agreed to adopt a national uniform law. In late 2005 and early 2006 the six states have passed legislation enacting the model provisions agreed to by the Attorneys-General.[13] It is expected that the two Territories will also enact these uniform laws. The principal features of the uniform laws are:

(a) the adoption (though with modifications) of the common law principles to determine defamation liability;
(b) the abolition of the distinction between libel and slander;
(c) the enactment of provisions to facilitate resolution of disputes without litigation;

---

7. *Civil Law (Wrongs) Act 2002* (ACT), Ch 9; *Defamation Act 1938* (NT); *Wrongs Act 1958* (Vic); *Civil Liability Act 1936* (SA), Pt 2; *Criminal Code 1913* (WA), Ch 35.
8. *Dow Jones Inc v Gutnick* (2002) 210 CLR 575. This is discussed further below.
9. Australian Law Reform Commission, *Unfair Publication: Defamation and Privacy*, Report No 11, 1979, pp 25–27.
10. Australian Law Reform Commission, *Unfair Publication: Defamation and Privacy*, Report No 11, 1979.
11. Commonwealth, Attorney-General's Department, *Revised Outline of a Possible National Defamation Law*, July 2004, Canberra, ACT, p 9.
12. Commonwealth, Attorney-General's Department, *Revised Outline of a Possible National Defamation Law*, July 2004, Canberra, ACT.
13. Civil Law (Wrongs) Act 2006 (ACT) Ch 9; Defamation Act 2005 (NSW); Defamation Act 2006 (NT); Defamation Act 2005 (QLD); Defamation Act 2005 (SA); Defamation Act 2005 (Tas); Defamation Act 2005 (VIC); Defamation Act 2005 (WA).

(d) the reform of damages principles by abolishing exemplary damages and imposing a cap on the amount of damages for economic loss that can be awarded;
(e) the adoption of truth alone as a defence;
(f) the establishment of a qualified privilege defence based on s 22 of the *Defamation Act 1974* (NSW);
(g) the creation of a new limitation period of one year in most cases; and
(h) the specification of the respective roles of juries and judges in defamation trials.

Reference will be made throughout this and the following chapter to the uniform laws, as applicable. It should be noted that the common law of defamation will continue to apply except to the extent otherwise provided in the uniform laws.

LIBEL AND SLANDER

The traditional significance of the distinction

The distinction between libel and slander was abolished some years ago in all jurisdictions except Victoria, South Australia, and Western Australia. With the adoption of the uniform laws in those three states, the significance of the distinction will soon become a matter of purely historical interest. For that reason, the following discussion of libel and slander will be brief.

Broadly speaking, libel is defamatory matter in a permanent form (such as the written word), whereas slander is defamatory matter in a transient form (such as the spoken word). At common law, libel is actionable *per se*, whereas slander is not generally actionable without proof of special damage.[14] The reasons why libel is treated more seriously than slander are partly historical,[15] and partly based on the fact that libellous matter tends to be more enduring than slanderous statements and to have the potential to be more widely propagated. Also, it is thought that greater significance is attached to the written rather than the spoken word, and that written words suggest a calculated intention to injure the plaintiff, whereas the spoken word could have resulted from a spontaneous outburst.[16]

Although the general rule is that slander is only actionable upon proof of special damage, some exceptional categories of slander are actionable *per se*. Actual damage does not need to be shown where the imputation is that the plaintiff had committed a crime, has a contagious or infectious disease, is unchaste (in the case

---

14. *Chakravarti v Advertiser Newspapers Ltd* (1998) 193 CLR 519 at 558. Special damage refers to pecuniary loss capable of precise estimation, such as the loss of a job promotion.
15. Libel originated as a crime whereas slander had civil origins.
16. Fleming JG, *The Law of Torts*, 9th edn, The Law Book Company Ltd, Sydney, 1998, pp 601–602.

of females), or is unprofessional or unfit to hold his or her office.[17] Damage is presumed in these situations, as the imputations were considered likely to lead to social shunning and ostracism.

Under the uniform laws all defamatory matter will be actionable without proof of special damage, regardless of whether it would be classified as libel or slander at common law: s 7. It is unlikely that this reform will result in a significant increase in defamation litigation for slanderous statements, as it will be a defence under s 33 for the defendant to prove that the defamation was trivial, in the sense that the circumstances of the publication were such that the plaintiff was unlikely to sustain harm. Accordingly, defamatory matter spoken to a small number of people will often not be actionable. The defence of triviality will be discussed in further detail in the next chapter.

CAUSE OF ACTION FOR PUBLICATION OF DEFAMATORY MATTER

A single cause of action

At common law, a person has one cause of action for a publication of defamatory matter, regardless of the number of defamatory imputations (meanings) arising from the matter.[18] Legislation in some jurisdictions provided that a separate cause of action arose for the publication of each separate defamatory imputation, but there was considerable criticism of this approach, on the basis that it led to complex interlocutory proceedings and placed too much emphasis on the ingenuity and expertise of the pleader in drafting the imputations.[19] The uniform laws adopt the common law position, so that there will be a single cause of action for the publication of the defamatory matter, irrespective of the number of imputations contained in the matter: s 8.

Who can bring a cause of action?

Deceased persons

The rule is that a dead person cannot be defamed. A defamation action is considered to be personal to the person defamed, and as such the estate of a deceased person is not permitted to sue for defamation of the deceased—which explains why

---

17. This category included a slander related to the conduct of the plaintiff's business: *D & L Caterers Ltd v D'Ajou* [1945] KB 210 at 215; *Feo & Anor v Pioneer Concrete (Vic) Pty Ltd* [1999] VSCA 180 at [57]; *Middendorp Electric Co Pty Ltd v Sonneveld* [2001] VSC 312 at [260].
18. *Herald & Weekly Times Ltd v Popovic* [2003] VSCA 161 at [284]–[311], per Gillard AJA (Winnecke ACJ and Warren AJA agreeing).
19. *Chakravarti v Advertiser Newspapers Ltd* (1998) 193 CLR 519 at 578, per Kirby J.

allegations are often made about persons only once they have died. The arguments normally advanced in favour of preventing a cause of action by a deceased estate are that the dead do not have a reputation to protect; the death of the person defamed makes it impossible to establish the truth of the matter through cross-examination; and that contemporary historical writing would be inhibited.[20]

Furthermore, except in Tasmania,[21] the defamation cause of action is considered personal to the parties and thus dies with the parties. This means that the plaintiff's estate cannot continue with the action after the death of the plaintiff, nor can a plaintiff commence, continue, or enforce an action against a defendant if the defendant dies. The justifications for these principles essentially mirror those put forward for the rule that the dead cannot be defamed.

Despite a recommendation in the discussion paper released by the Commonwealth Attorney-General's Department for a relaxation of these rules, the uniform laws maintain the current common law position.[22] Section 10 provides that a personal representative of a deceased person cannot commence, continue, or enforce a defamation action in relation to the publication of defamatory matter about a deceased person, whenever the matter was published, nor can a defamation action be commenced, continued, or enforced against a person who has died since publication.

Corporations

Any entity with a separate legal personality is entitled to sue in defamation at common law. This includes trading corporations, which are entitled to bring an action for statements affecting their trading or business reputations.[23] In what became the longest-running trial in United Kingdom history, the McDonald's Corporation commenced defamation proceedings against two Greenpeace activists who were critical of certain aspects of McDonald's activities. The litigation has been colloquially dubbed the 'McLibel' litigation. The defendants had distributed leaflets accusing McDonald's of being responsible for starvation in the Third World, of destroying vast areas of Central American rainforest, of lying about the use of recycled paper, of serving unhealthy food with a real risk of causing heart disease, bowel and breast cancer, and food poisoning, of exploiting children with its advertising and marketing, of cruelty to animals, and of treating its employees badly. McDonald's was ultimately successful in establishing defamation in relation to the accusations that its food caused cancer and food poisoning, that it was responsible

---

20. Commonwealth, Attorney-General's Department, *Revised Outline of a Possible National Defamation Law*, July 2004, Canberra, ACT, p 13.
21. *Administration and Probate Act 1935* (Tas), s 27.
22. Commonwealth, Attorney-General's Department, *Revised Outline of a Possible National Defamation Law*, July 2004, Canberra, ACT, pp 13–14.
23. *Australian Broadcasting Corporation v Comalco Ltd* (1986) 12 FCR 510.

for Third World starvation, that it had destroyed rainforests, and that it had lied about using recycled paper.[24] It was awarded £40 000 in damages, which were never paid and which it did not seek to recover. In the Court of Appeal the defendants (appellants) argued that McDonald's should not have the right to maintain an action for defamation because it was a multinational public corporation, which must always be open to unfettered scrutiny and criticism, particularly on issues of public interest. The Court of Appeal rejected this argument, recognising that it is an entrenched right of all corporations to sue to for damage done to their trading reputations, regardless of size. There was no principled basis upon which a line could be drawn between powerful corporations—which on the appellants' argument would not be able to sue—and weaker corporations, which would be permitted to maintain the cause of action.

In New South Wales, the Parliament was prompted by arguments such as those of the appellants in the 'McLibel' litigation to restrict the right of large corporations to sue in defamation.[25] These arguments now appear to have gained support in other States and Territories. Despite the recommendation in the Federal Attorney-General's discussion paper that the common law position should be maintained,[26] s 9 of the uniform laws provides that a corporation cannot maintain an action in defamation unless it is a not-for-profit organisation, or it employs fewer than ten persons and is not related to another corporation (ie, it is not part of a bigger group of companies). In assessing the number of employees of a corporation, part-time employees are to be taken into account as an appropriate fraction of a full-time equivalent: s 9(3).

Section 9 will not affect any cause of action that would otherwise be available to individuals associated with the corporation, such as managers and directors.[27]

Elected government bodies

Elected government bodies, such as local authorities, are not entitled to maintain an action in defamation. In *Ballina Shire Council v Ringland* (1994) 33 NSWLR 680, the New South Wales Court of Appeal followed the English House of Lords in *Derbyshire County Council v Times Newspapers* [1993] AC 534, and held that the conduct of an elected government body should be subject to public criticism and debate unrestrained by the threat of civil liability for defamation. In *Ballina Shire Council*, Gleeson CJ (at 691) said in this regard:

---

24. *McDonald's Corporation v Steel & Morris* [1997] EWHC QB 366; *Steel and Morris v McDonald's Corporation* [1999] EWCA Civ 1144.
25. *Defamation Act 1974* (NSW), s 8A (a corporation cannot sue if it has more than ten employees or has subsidiaries).
26. Commonwealth, Attorney-General's Department, *Revised Outline of a Possible National Defamation Law*, July 2004, Canberra, ACT, pp 38–39.
27. Ibid.

The idea of a democracy is that people are encouraged to express their criticisms, even their wrong-headed criticisms, of elected governmental institutions, in the expectation that this process will improve the quality of the government. The fact that the institutions are democratically elected is supposed to mean that, through a process of political debate and decision, the citizens in a community govern themselves. To treat governmental institutions as having a 'governing reputation' which the common law will protect against criticism on the part of citizens is, to my mind, incongruous … [T]o maintain that an elected governmental institution has a right to a reputation as a governing body is to contend for the existence of something that is incompatible with the very process to which the body owes its existence.

The uniform laws maintain this common law position. Section 9 puts it beyond doubt that a 'public body', defined as a local government body or other governmental or public authority, is not entitled to bring an action, even if it would otherwise fall within the definition of a corporation that can sue.

ELEMENTS OF THE CAUSE OF ACTION

A prima facie cause of action arises in defamation where the defendant communicates, to a third party, defamatory matter relating to the plaintiff. The three elements of the defamation action are:[28]

1. the matter conveys a defamatory imputation or imputations;
2. the matter identifies, or is capable of identifying, the plaintiff as the person defamed; and
3. the matter has been published by the defendant to at least one person other than the plaintiff.

The onus then shifts to the defendant to prove a defence, such as justification, fair comment or privilege (see Chapter 21).

The uniform laws adopt the common law principles relating to each of these three elements of the prima facie claim: s 6. Accordingly, with the exception of the abolition of the distinction between libel and slander (discussed above), common law principles existing before the enactment of the laws will continue to determine whether the plaintiff has a good prima facie claim.

---

28. *Consolidated Trust Co Ltd v Browne* (1948) 49 SR (NSW) 86 at 88.

ELEMENT 1: THE MATTER CONVEYS A DEFAMATORY IMPUTATION OR IMPUTATIONS

Overview

There are two steps to determining whether matter is defamatory:

1. identification of the potentially defamatory meanings (imputations) that are conveyed by the matter; and
2. determination of whether the matter is in fact defamatory of the plaintiff.

Where the defamation action is being heard before a judge and jury, the judge will determine as a preliminary question of law whether the imputations are reasonably capable of being drawn from the impugned matter.[29] The judge will reject those meanings 'which can only emerge as the product of some strained, or forced, or utterly unreasonable interpretation'.[30] The imputations that are reasonably capable of being drawn will be put to the jury, which must determine whether they are in fact conveyed by the matter, and whether they are in fact defamatory of the plaintiff.

Identification of defamatory imputations

It is irrelevant whether the defendant intended the matter to convey meanings defamatory of the plaintiff.[31] It is the meanings that the hypothetical referee would reasonably understand to be drawn from the matter that will be relevant.[32] There is no one definition of the hypothetical referee; it has been variously described as the 'reasonable person'[33] or 'right thinking members of society generally'[34] or as an ordinary person 'not avid for scandal'.[35] The hypothetical referee is a person who draws on normal knowledge and experience of human affairs to interpret the matter. It is not a person in whom the publication excites emotional feelings of animosity or prejudice that would add defamatory sting to the matter.[36]

The alleged defamatory meanings might be conveyed by the plain, literal meaning of the matter, such as where the plaintiff is called a liar, a thief or a

---

29. *Jones v Skelton* [1964] NSWR 485.
30. Ibid. at 491; *Favell v Queensland Newspapers Pty Ltd* [2005] HCA 52 at [9].
31. *Chakravarti v Advertiser Newspapers Ltd* (1998) 193 CLR 519 at 545, per Gaudron and Gummow JJ.
32. *Chakravarti v Advertiser Newspapers Ltd* (1998) 193 CLR 519 at 573, per Kirby J; *Random House Australia Pty Ltd v Abbott & Ors* (1999) 94 FCR 296 at 304, per Beaumont J.
33. *Jones v Skelton* (1963) 63 SR (NSW) 644 at 650–1.
34. *Sim v Stretch* (1936) 52 TLR 669 at 671.
35. *Lewis v Daily Telegraph* [1964] AC 234 at 260. The use by the courts of a 'hypothetical referee' has recently been criticised: *Favell v Queensland Newspapers Pty Ltd* [2005] HCA 52 at [23]–[26], per Kirby J.
36. *Mirror Newspapers Ltd v Harrison* (1982) 149 CLR 293 at 301.

murderer.³⁷ However, the courts must not only consider imputations evident on the face of the matter but also any insinuations or innuendoes that can reasonably be read into the natural, ordinary meanings of the words.³⁸ The ordinary person is not a lawyer, and will approach the material impressionistically, and with an increased tendency to draw inferences and read between the lines:

> The ordinary man does not live in an ivory tower and he is not inhibited by a knowledge of the rules of construction. So he can and does read between the lines in the light of his general knowledge and experience of worldly affairs.³⁹

There are in fact two different types of innuendoes on which the plaintiff can rely: 'popular' or 'false' innuendos, and 'legal' or 'true' innuendos.

'Popular' or 'false' innuendos

A 'popular' or 'false' innuendo refers to a meaning that ordinary people would understand or infer from the words used, without the need to rely on extrinsic facts or details to support the meaning.⁴⁰ A popular innuendo might be drawn from the secondary meaning of a word. Examples of words that have acquired secondary meanings are 'queer', 'gay', 'junkie', 'loopy', 'cow' and 'sad'. In *Murphy v Plasterers Society* [1949] SASR 98, the defendant, during the course of a strike, referred to the plaintiff as a 'scab'. It was recognised that this word had popularly acquired a secondary meaning of a worker who is treacherous and disloyal to striking fellow workers. In *Bjelke-Peterson v Warburton* [1987] 2 Qd R 465, a statement that the ministers in the Queensland Government had their 'hands in the till' was popularly understood to convey an allegation of corruption and dishonest appropriation to the ministers of property properly belonging to the State of Queensland.

Alternatively, a popular innuendo might be drawn by inference from the matter; ie, by 'reading between the lines'. In *Reader's Digest Services Pty Ltd v Lamb* (1982) CLR 500, the defendant published a book that included a chapter about the abduction and subsequent murder of Muriel McKay. The chapter included a reference to Lamb, the plaintiff, who was the editor of the *Sun* newspaper, noting that he had been a longstanding friend of the victim's husband, Mr McKay. It said that Mr McKay had called for Lamb when his wife went missing, but that the trouble was: 'Lamb is a newspaperman through and through and he has a

---

37. *Lewis v Daily Telegraph* [1964] AC 234 at 258; *Chakravarti v Advertiser Newspapers Ltd* (1998) 193 CLR 519 at 531, per Brennan CJ and McHugh J; *Random House Australia Pty Ltd v Abbott & Ors* (1999) 94 FCR 296 at 304–5, per Beaumont J.
38. *Lewis v Daily Telegraph* [1964] AC 234 at 280; *John Fairfax Publications Pty Ltd v Rivkin* (2003) 201 ALR 77 at 82, per McHugh J.
39. *Lewis v Daily Telegraph* [1964] AC 234 at 258, per Lord Reid. See also: *Favell v Queensland Newspapers Pty Ltd* [2005] HCA 52 at [10].
40. *Chakravarti v Advertiser Newspapers Ltd* (1998) 193 CLR 519 at 531, per Brennan CJ and McHugh J; *Random House Australia Pty Ltd v Abbott & Ors* (1999) 94 FCR 296 at 304–5, per Beaumont J.

nose for a story, and that's how the wires started humming and word got around that Muriel McKay is missing'. The defamatory imputation that was reasonably capable of being inferred from this passage was that the plaintiff, in order to secure a sensational newspaper story, had exploited the tragedy that had befallen an old friend.

In *Random House Australia Pty Ltd v Abbott & Ors* (1999) 94 FCR 296, two Commonwealth Government ministers and their spouses claimed they were defamed by a passage contained in a book published by the defendant. The impugned passage stated:

> they're both in the Right Wing of the Labor Party till the one woman [had sexual relations with] both of them and married one of them and inducted them into the Young Liberals.

The ministers were successful in establishing that this passage conveyed a number of defamatory imputations: that they lacked personal integrity because they were prepared to change political allegiances in return for sexual favours; that their political commitment was so shallow that they would abandon their principles in return for sex; and that they were of a weak and unreliable character who allowed political decisions to be dictated by their wives. All three imputations were found to a fair paraphrase of the central thrust of the passage, which was that the political commitment of the men was shallow and that they would change beliefs, not on a matter of principle, but for nothing more important than the opportunity of a sexual liaison.

The reference to the 'woman' in the passage was sufficiently imprecise as to also permit both wives to sue. Both were successful in establishing that the matter conveyed defamatory imputations that they had engaged in sexual misconduct by using sex to induce men to join the Liberal Party; that they were political manipulators who used sex in order to recruit Labor Party members into the Liberal Party; and that they were of low morality in behaving in these ways. However, they were ultimately unsuccessful in establishing an imputation that they were sexually promiscuous. That term imports indiscriminate, casual sexual behaviour,[41] whereas the material merely suggested isolated incidents of pre-marital sex. They were also unsuccessful in establishing an imputation that 'they were so lacking in respect for their husbands that even being married to them did not stop them trying to subvert their husband's political beliefs'. This pleaded imputation was rejected on the basis that it was not clear from the passage whether the alleged defection preceded or followed the marriage.[42]

---

41. *Random House Australia Pty Ltd v Abbott & Ors* (1999) 94 FCR 296 at 309–10, per Beaumont J.
42. Ibid at 311, per Beaumont J; at 335, per Drummond J (Miles J agreeing).

Reports of criminal investigations

Material that merely reports that the plaintiff is accused or suspected of a crime, or was investigated in relation to a crime, is not actionable as there is a legitimate public interest in the receipt of such facts.[43] However, a defendant who reports that the plaintiff has been accused of a crime or is being investigated for a crime must take particular care to ensure that the report would not impute to the reasonable person that the plaintiff has actually committed the crime, or that there is a reasonable basis for the accusation against the plaintiff or for the investigations into his or her conduct.[44] In *Mirror Newspapers Ltd v Harrison* (1982) 149 CLR 293, the plaintiff had complained of an article stating that three men had been arrested in connection with the bashing of a State Member of Parliament who had made allegations of infiltration of the Labor Party by organised crime groups. The arrests were said to follow a month of 'intensive investigation' by a special squad of detectives who had 'worked around the clock' to ensure the culprits would be found. The plaintiff's photograph appeared in the article as one of the men arrested. In the leading judgment, Mason J held that the article was not defamatory of the plaintiff. A bare report that the plaintiff has been arrested and charged with a criminal offence is not of itself capable of bearing the imputation that the plaintiff is guilty of that offence. The reasonable reader would be mindful of the presumption of innocence and that persons are not infrequently acquitted of crimes with which they are charged. Although the reader would view the plaintiff with some suspicion, this did not warrant the conclusion that the defendant was imputing guilt (at 301).

The High Court has recently affirmed in *Favell v Queensland Newspapers Pty Ltd* [2005] HCA 52 that a *mere* statement that a person is under investigation, or that a person has been charged, may not be enough to impute guilt. However, it held that the position is different if that statement is accompanied by an account of the suspicious circumstances that have aroused the interest of the authorities, and that point toward a likelihood of guilt (at [12]). In *Favell*, a newspaper owned by the defendant had carried a story that the plaintiffs' home had been destroyed by fire. The article stated that the plaintiffs had applied to develop the site as a five-storey block of units, and that the application had caused quite a controversy in the local community. It then went on to say that the police investigation into the cause of the fire was continuing, and quoted a police officer as saying: 'All fires are treated as suspicious until otherwise disproved and we will follow all lines of inquiry'. The plaintiffs pleaded a number of imputations as being reasonably conveyed by the article, the most important of which were:

---

43. *Mirror Newspapers Ltd v Harrison* (1982) 149 CLR 293 at 300–1.
44. *Chakravati v Advertiser Newspapers Ltd* (1998) 193 CLR 519.

(a) they had committed the crime of arson;
(b) they were reasonably suspected by the police of committing the crime of arson; and
(c) the second plaintiff, Mrs Favell, had lied about neighbourhood reactions to the proposed development of the plaintiffs' property.

The third imputation was based on the juxtaposition of a quote from Mrs Favell to the effect that the neighbours had been fine about the development application with statements from neighbours that they were in fact unhappy about the application.

At an interlocutory hearing, Helman J held that none of the three imputations was reasonably capable of being conveyed by the material as the article went no further than to state that the police were investigating the fire. The plaintiffs appealed to the Queensland Court of Appeal, which held that an imputation similar to imputation (b) as pleaded by the plaintiff was supported by the material. On appeal to the High Court it was held that all three imputations could reasonably be drawn. In a joint judgment, Gleeson CJ, McHugh, Gummow, and Heydon JJ held that a prominent feature of the article was the link drawn between the house fire and the controversial development application. It implied that the destruction of the house facilitated the redevelopment, thus suggesting that the plaintiffs had a motive to burn down their house. The statement that the police were treating the fire as suspicious, when coupled with the implications about motive, imputed that there were reasonable grounds for suspecting that the plaintiffs were guilty of arson (imputation (b)) and that these suspicions were well-founded (imputation (a)). Their Honours also found that imputation (c) was reasonably capable of being conveyed by the material. A report that Mrs Favell had given a different account of the reaction to the development application to her neighbours, standing alone, would be construed as merely reporting two different points of view. However, when that report was published in the context of an account of a suspicious fire, the grounds for suspicion being based on the development proposal, a different impression could be created: that Mrs Favell had lied about the neighbourhood reaction.

'Legal' or 'true' innuendos

A 'legal' or 'true' innuendo refers to a meaning that would be conveyed only to persons who have extrinsic information. For a legal innuendo to be actionable, the plaintiff must show that the matter was published to at least one person with the relevant extrinsic information. It is not, however, necessary to prove that the publisher was aware of the additional facts that would convey a defamatory meaning.[45] An often-cited example of a legal innuendo is that given by Lord Devlin

---

45. *Cassidy v Daily Mirror Newspapers Ltd* (1929) 2 KB 331.

in *Lewis v Daily Telegraph Ltd* (1964 AC) 234, at 258. If the defendant publishes information that the plaintiff was seen to enter a particular address to a recipient with knowledge of the extrinsic fact that a brothel was conducted at that address, that recipient would infer that the defendant was intending to state that the plaintiff was visiting a brothel. It is irrelevant that the defendant did not so intend.

A legal innuendo might arise because the recipient of the publication possesses knowledge of an earlier publication which, together with a subsequent publication, conveys the defamatory meaning,[46] or because the recipient has knowledge of a special meaning of a word that might not be known to other persons. Likewise, a statement that is innocent on its face might convey a discreditable meaning to persons with special knowledge of the plaintiff's circumstances. In a well-known defamation action, the former Federal Treasurer, Jim Cairns, and his personal assistant, Juni Morosi, brought a defamation action against a newspaper which published an account of an interview referring to Morosi as Cairns' 'girlfriend'. The plaintiffs (both married to other persons) pleaded an imputation that they were improperly involved in a romantic or sexual association contrary to their marital obligations. The trial judge held that this amounted to a true innuendo,[47] as it would only be conveyed to persons with knowledge that both plaintiffs were married and that Cairns employed Morosi as his personal assistant, and who knew of previous media speculation as to the nature of their relationship. In *Cassidy v Daily Mirror* (1929) 2 KB 331, the defendant published a photograph of a man and a woman with the caption: 'Mr M Corrigan, the racehorse owner and "Miss X" whose engagement has been announced'. The man in the photograph was in fact lawfully married to the plaintiff. The plaintiff was successful in establishing a true innuendo, conveyed to those readers who knew she was living with the man in the photograph, that she was an immoral woman who had cohabited with a man who was not her husband.[48] And in *Mirror Newspapers Ltd v Fitzpatrick* [1984] 1 NSWLR 643, the defendant published a news report stating (inaccurately) that the plaintiff, a prominent actress, had attended a televised award ceremony. This report was capable of conveying, to those who knew that the plaintiff earlier that day had claimed she was too sick to work on a film production, that the plaintiff had lied about her health and avoided her legal obligations so that she could prepare to attend the awards.

The relevant extrinsic information might lead a recipient to infer that the plaintiff has acted unprofessionally or is not fit to hold a particular office. Thus,

---

46. A true innuendo was pleaded on this basis in *John Fairfax Publications Pty Ltd v Rivkin* (2003) 201 ALR 77, though ultimately was not successful.
47. See, on appeal: *Cairns v John Fairfax & Sons Ltd* (1983) 2 NSWLR 708.
48. This decision was followed by the Court of Appeal in *Hough v London Express Newspaper Ltd* [1940] 2 KB 502, however it has been criticised on the basis that the innuendo was not based on a fact published by the defendant but on further conclusions drawn by the readers: see Hunt J in *Anderson v Mirror Newspapers Ltd* (1986) 6 NSWLR 99 at 107–11.

in *Ettingshausen v Australian Consolidated Press Ltd* (1991) 23 NSWLR 443, a magazine published a nude photograph of the plaintiff, a well-known rugby league star. The plaintiff pleaded, *inter alia*, an imputation that he was unfit to be a schools promotions officer for the NSW Rugby League as he had deliberately allowed a nude photograph to be taken for the purpose of publication in a magazine. This was a true innuendo as it rested upon knowledge of the extrinsic fact that the plaintiff was employed as a schools promotions officer.

Context and mode of the publication

The meaning of a publication is to be ascertained by viewing the publication as a whole.[49] There will be situations where something defamatory is said of the plaintiff in one part of the publication, but the 'sting' is neutralised by the remainder of the article. In this situation, both the 'bane' and the 'antidote' should be taken together when determining whether defamatory imputations are reasonably capable of being drawn from the material. In *Bik v Mirror Newspapers Ltd* [1979] 2 NSWLR 679, the plaintiff complained about a report of parliamentary proceedings. He claimed the report had defamed him by disclosing allegations made at a coronial inquiry to the effect that he had designed a faulty crane that led to the death of a worker. The New South Wales Court of Appeal held that the report was not defamatory of the plaintiff when read as a whole, as it had gone on to state that the relevant minister had 'completely cleared' the plaintiff. In *Charleston v News Group Newspapers Ltd* [1995] 2 AC 65, the plaintiffs were actors in the long-running television series 'Neighbours'. The defendant's newspaper published photographs showing the plaintiffs' faces superimposed on the near-naked bodies of models in pornographic poses. These photographs were contained in an article with the prominent headlines: 'Strewth! What's our Harold up to with our Madge?', and 'Porn Shockers for Neighbours stars'. The text of the article made it clear that the photographs had been produced by the makers of a pornographic computer game without the knowledge or consent of the plaintiffs, and it castigated the makers of the game. The plaintiffs claimed that the publication conveyed the imputations that the plaintiffs had been willing participants in the production of the photographs by posing for them personally—or, alternatively, by agreeing to allow their faces to be superimposed on the bodies of others—and/or were willing to participate in the making of pornographic films. The plaintiffs conceded that no reader who read beyond the first paragraph would draw those inferences, but argued that a 'significant proportion' of the readership would have done no more than read the headlines and look at the photographs. The House of Lords reaffirmed two basic principles: namely that the publication must be read as a whole in determining its

---

49. *Australian Broadcasting Corporation v Comalco Ltd* (1986) 12 FCR 510 at 516, 571–2, 590. See also: *Charleston v News Group Newspapers Ltd* [1995] 2 AC 65 at 71.

meaning, and that the court must arrive at a single meaning which the publication conveyed to the notional reasonable reader.[50] The plaintiffs' claim failed as the ordinary, reasonable reader would read the text of the article, which in this case clearly neutralised any defamatory implication.[51]

The *Charleston* decision has not escaped criticism, however, on the basis that tabloid newspapers deliberately present material in a sensationalist way with no expectation or intention that the normal reader will read the whole article carefully. In *Chakravarti v Advertiser Newspapers Ltd* (1998) 193 CLR 519, Kirby J (at 574) expressed doubt about the *Charleston* decision, and continued:[52]

> In my view [*Charleston*] ignores the realities of the way in which ordinary people receive, and are intended to receive, communications of this kind. It ignores changes in media technology and presentation. It removes remedies from people whose reputation may be greatly damaged by casual or superficial perception of such publications ... The ordinary reader will draw conclusions from general impressions. He or she will not re-read or review the matter complained of. Such a reader will tend to be specially influenced by headlines, bylines, graphics and the other techniques by which the mass media seek to communicate their principal messages to a mass audience. In a society increasingly used to the immediacy of 'channel surfing' with remote controls and accessing the Internet with computers, publishers must take special care with prominently published matter. This obligation clearly applies to headlines, captions, photographs, pictures and their digital equivalents—where such material may diminish the reputations of those affected. [footnotes omitted]

The medium of the publication can also be important. A radio or television broadcast is generally not the subject of careful scrutiny and attention.[53] The transient nature of the broadcast material, and the short time the viewer has to assess the assertions, counter-assertions, pictures, and images will lead to the formation of overall impressions rather than carefully considered conclusions.[54] Newspaper and magazine articles, particularly where presented in a sensationalist way, might also lead to a certain amount of loose thinking.[55] On the other hand, a book would generally be subjected to more careful attention and analysis.[56]

---

50. *Charleston v News Group Newspapers Ltd* [1995] 2 AC 65 at 71.
51. Ibid at 72–3.
52. McHugh J made similar comments about the impact of sensational headlines in *John Fairfax Publications Pty Ltd v Rivkin* (2003) 201 ALR 77 at 83.
53. *Amalgamated Television Services Pty Ltd v Marsden* (1998) 43 NSWLR 158 at 165–6; *Carleton v Australian Broadcasting Corporation* (2002) 172 FLR 398 at 414.
54. *Australian Broadcasting Corporation v Comalco Ltd* (1986) 12 FCR 510 at 515–16, per Smithers J; *Henry v TVW Enterprises* (1990) Aust Torts Rep 81–031 at 67,911.
55. *Chakravarti v Advertiser Newspapers Ltd* (1998) 193 CLR 519 at 574.
56. *Farquhar v Bottom* [1980] 2 NSWLR 380 at 386.

Determination that material is in fact defamatory

Material is defamatory where it has the tendency to lower the plaintiff's reputation in the estimation of the ordinary reasonable person, expose the plaintiff to ridicule, or cause others to shun or avoid the plaintiff.[57] It is also defamatory to discredit the plaintiff in his or her trade, profession, or business.

The essence of the defamation action is matter that disparages or discredits the plaintiff's reputation. It is defamatory to impute that the plaintiff is a hypocrite;[58] is treacherous and disloyal;[59] has committed a crime;[60] or has associated with known criminal and underworld figures[61]. It is also defamatory to disparage the plaintiff's trade, professional, official or business reputation—for example, by imputing that the plaintiff is not of an appropriate character to hold a particular public office;[62] is not a fit and proper person to remain as an executive of a corporation by reason of misconduct;[63] is lacking in professionalism;[64] or that the plaintiff's business is responsible for the destruction of rainforests and Third World starvation.[65]

The orthodox view is that whether matter is defamatory is to be decided by reference to a hypothetical referee, variously described as the 'ordinary reasonable person' or the 'right-minded person'.[66] The tribunal of fact must determine whether the matter is defamatory by applying a common social or moral standard held by the community as a whole.[67] However, in recognition of the diversity of beliefs and attitudes in modern Australian communities, it has sometimes been suggested that it is impossible to find one single community standard, and that the test should be whether 'an appreciable and reputable section of the community' would think less of the plaintiff.[68] However, most Australian decisions still refer to a single community standard as the determinant of the defamatory nature of the material, and it is yet to be seen whether the courts will embrace the enlarged definition. What is clear is that a publication will not be considered defamatory where only a small, prejudicial minority would consider the plaintiff's reputation to be lowered. For example, it is not defamatory to refer to someone as a police informant, as right-thinking people

---

57. *Chakravarti v Advertiser Newspapers Ltd* (1998) 193 CLR 519 at 545; *Defamation Act 1957* (Tas), s 5.
58. *Thorley v Lord Kerry* (1812) 4 Taunt 355.
59. *Murphy v Plasterers Society* [1949] SASR 98.
60. *Chakravarti v Advertiser Newspapers Ltd* (1998) 193 CLR 519.
61. *Hawke v Tamworth Newspapers* [1983] 1 NSWLR 699.
62. *Hawke v Tamworth Newspapers* [1983] 1 NSWLR 699.
63. *Chakravati v Advertiser Newspapers Ltd* (1998) 193 CLR 519.
64. *Carleton v Australian Broadcasting Corporation* (2002) 172 FLR 398.
65. *Steel and Morris v McDonald's Corporation* [1999] EWCA Civ 1144.
66. *Chakravarti v Advertiser Newspapers Ltd* (1998) 193 CLR 519 at 573, per Kirby J; *Random House Australia Pty Ltd v Abbott* (1999) 94 FCR 296 at 304, per Beaumont J.
67. *Reader's Digest Services Pty Ltd v Lamb* (1982) CLR 500 at 505–6; *Random House Australia Pty Ltd v Abbott & Ors* (1999) 94 FCR 296.
68. *Hepburn v TCN Channel 9 Pty Ltd* [1983] 2 NSWLR 682 at 694. See also: *Krahe v TCN Channel Nine Pty Ltd* (1986) 4 NSWLR 536.

would not consider that it was disparaging of someone to say that they are providing information to the police (*Byrne v Dean* [1937] 1 KB 818).

Community attitudes and beliefs will of course change over time, and the defamatory nature of material must be judged according to the prevailing views and beliefs of the community.[69] Until relatively recent times, it would have been defamatory to say of a man that he is a homosexual or has engaged in a homosexual act (*R v Bishop* [1975] QB 274); however, this probably is no longer the case.[70] Something more would be required, such as allegations of hypocrisy, infidelity, predatory behaviour, or the abuse of a position of power and trust.[71] Damages have also been recovered where the imputation was that the plaintiff had slept with one of his young employees as this suggested an abuse of power and exploitative and predatory behaviour;[72] and similarly, where the imputation was that the plaintiff had engaged in sex with underage boys.[73]

Likewise, community attitudes toward pre-marital and extra-marital sex have become more permissive over time. It is probably no longer defamatory *per se* to suggest that the plaintiff engaged in pre-marital sex[74] or had an adulterous affair.[75] In 1983, in *Cairns v John Fairfax & Sons Ltd* (1983) 2 NSWLR 708, the majority of the New South Wales Court of Appeal (Hutley and Mahoney JJA, Samuels JA dissenting) held that it was not perverse of the jury to find that the Federal Treasurer and his assistant (both married to other people) had not been defamed by a report that they were engaged in an adulterous relationship. Community attitudes to sexual relationships had changed, and it was open to the jury to find that a sexual association between the plaintiffs did not lower their standing.[76] This approach would apply *a fortiori* in the twenty-first century. However, it would still be defamatory of a female plaintiff to impute that she is sexually promiscuous, in the sense that she has engaged in indiscriminate sexual behaviour, or that she has engaged in sexually manipulative behaviour.[77]

---

69. *Middendorp Electric Co Pty Ltd v Sonneveld* [2001] VSC 312 at [190].
70. *Rivkin v Amalgamated Television Services Pty Ltd* [2001] NSWSC 432; *Quilty v Windsor* (1999) SLT 346 at 354, per Lord Kingarth.
71. *Rivkin v Amalgamated Television Services Pty Ltd* [2001] NSWSC 432.
72. Rivkin, ibid. The flamboyant stockbroker and businessman Renee Rivkin successfully recovered damages for imputations made to this effect on Channel 7's 'Witness' program.
73. *Amalgamated Television Services Pty Ltd v Marsden* [2002] NSWCA 419. In this case Channel 7 was found to have defamed the plaintiff (the former president of the NSW Law Society) by the broadcast of two current affairs programs containing various imputations of sex with underage boys.
74. *Random House Australia Pty Ltd v Abbott & Ors* (1999) 94 FCR 296.
75. In 1999 Jeff Kennett (the then Premier of Victoria) lost a defamation action in a jury trial against the *Australian* newspaper for a suggestion that he had cheated on his wife. See: Lobez S, 'The Law Report', Radio National Transcripts, Tuesday, March 16, 1999 http://www.abc.net.au/rn/talks/8.30/lawrpt/lstories/lr990316.htm (accessed on 3 August 2006).
76. Hutley JA (at 710) noted that attitudes regarding the affairs of the glamorous and powerful could 'transcend middle-class morality', and took the view that the jury might even have considered that the plaintiffs' reputations were actually *enhanced* by the allegation of an affair with each other.
77. *Random House Australia Pty Ltd v Abbott & Ors* (1999) 94 FCR 296 at 331–4, per Drummond J (Miles J agreeing).

Requirement that the statement disparage the plaintiff

At common law, matter is only defamatory if it is disparaging of the plaintiff by imputing matters about the plaintiff's private character, or professional reputation, for which the plaintiff is responsible. Persons can be defamed by disparaging statements about their character, such as their honesty, integrity or fidelity. But they cannot be defamed by statements about personal characteristics over which they have no control—such as personal appearance or ethnic background—because no blame can be attributed to a person for these things. For instance, it would not be defamatory to call a person a 'wog' or an 'arab', or to suggest that a person is overweight or unattractive (at least when unaccompanied by a suggestion that the weight gain or lack of attractiveness resulted from a lack of discipline or from 'letting oneself go'). Nor is it ordinarily defamatory to impute that the plaintiff is unwell or has an illness, although it might be different if the further imputation was made that the plaintiff is a hypochondriac or malingerer. The same reasoning means that it will not ordinarily be defamatory to impute that the plaintiff has been an innocent victim of a crime, as again this is a matter outside the plaintiff's control.

The same principles are applied to statements about the plaintiff's trading, professional, official or business reputations. Accordingly, it would not at common law be defamatory of the plaintiff's business to state falsely that it had been acquired by another company and had ceased to trade,[78] or that it had gone into bankruptcy—at least where there is no suggestion that this had occurred because of poor business skills.[79] Nor would it be defamatory to impute that a horse stud farm had been forced to close because of a virus,[80] or that an airline was the innocent victim of a terrorist hijacking.[81] The basic proposition, expressed by Stephen J in *Sungravure Pty Ltd v Middle East Airlines Airliban SAL* (1975) 134 CLR 1, at 13, is:

> However much a statement may tend to injure a man in the way of his office, profession or trade it will only be defamatory at common law if it involves some reflection upon his personal character or upon the mode in which he carries on his business, his business reputation.

In Queensland and Tasmania, legislation included a statutory definition of defamatory matter that was held to be sufficiently broad to encompass statements that injured a business even though they were not disparaging.[82] However, the law of these states will be brought back into line with other jurisdictions with the

---

78. *Hall-Gibbs Mercantile Agency Ltd v Dun* (1910) 12 CLR 84, although an action in injurious falsehood might be available.
79. *Mirror Newspapers Ltd v World Hosts Pty Ltd* (1979) 141 CLR 632 at 638–9.
80. *Dawson Bloodstock Agency Pty Ltd v Mirror Newspapers Ltd* [1979] 1 NSWLR 16.
81. *Sungravure Pty Ltd v Middle East Airlines Airliban SAL* (1975) 134 CLR 1 at 13, per Stephen J.
82. *Hall-Gibbs Mercantile Agency Ltd v Dun* (1910) 12 CLR 84; *Sungravure Pty Ltd v Middle East Airlines Airliban SAL* (1975) 134 CLR 1; *Mirror Newspapers Ltd v World Hosts Pty Ltd* (1979) 141 CLR 632.

introduction of the uniform laws. The uniform laws adopt the common law principles regarding defamatory matter, and as such, the general rule in all jurisdictions will be that a matter is generally actionable only when it disparages the plaintiff by attributing characteristics to the plaintiff for which the plaintiff is responsible or to blame. There are, however, two exceptional situations where the common law does not require blameworthiness, which would continue to apply under the uniform laws. These are where the imputation casts the plaintiff in a 'ridiculous light', or where it has the tendency to cause people to 'shun or avoid' the plaintiff.[83]

The first exception—in a ridiculous light—is still to be tested in the High Court. However, there is authority for the principle that to hold a plaintiff up to ridicule or contempt, even in the absence of blameworthiness or discredit, is actionable in defamation.[84] This proposition applies where the matter conveys the impression that the plaintiff is ridiculous, in the sense of deserving to be laughed at, or absurd.[85] The imputation will often carry a disparaging connotation, but it is not always necessary to prove disparagement. In *Boyd v Mirror Newspapers Ltd* [1980] 2 NSWLR 449, the plaintiff, a professional rugby league player, was described in a newspaper article as 'slow, fat and predictable' and as having 'waddled' onto the field. The article went on to state that the main reason Boyd was overweight was because of injury. Hunt J of the New South Wales Supreme Court ruled that this material supported an imputation that Boyd was so fat that he appeared ridiculous as he entered the field to play. His Honour rejected the argument that an imputation is only actionable where it suggests that the plaintiff is at fault or to blame for the condition. An imputation would also be actionable where it ridiculed the plaintiff— as by expressing incredulity as to the appearance of the plaintiff.[86] In the later case of *Ettingshausen v Australian Consolidated Press Ltd* (1991) 23 NSWLR 443, Hunt J found that the publication of a nude photograph of Andrew Ettingshausen, another rugby league footballer, taken in the shower without Ettinghausen's permission, was capable of being defamatory as casting him in a ridiculous light. This imputation was not dependent on an inference that the plaintiff had deliberately allowed a nude photograph to be taken of him for publication.[87] A similar principle has been recognised in England. In *Berkoff v Burchill* [1996] 4 All ER 1008, two articles were published about the plaintiff, a well-known actor, director, and writer, containing statements that would be understood as meaning that he was 'hideously ugly'. The

---

83. For a detailed discussion of these exceptions, refer to Watterson R, 'What is Defamatory Today?' (1993) *Australian Law Journal* 811.
84. *Boyd v Mirror Newspapers Limited* [1980] 2 NSWLR 449; *Ettingshausen v Australian Consolidated Press Limited* (1991) 23 NSWLR 443 at 449; *Brander v Ryan and Messenger Press Pty Ltd* [2000] SASC 446 at [79]; *Berkoff v Burchill* [1996] 4 All ER 1008 at 1018.
85. Ibid.
86. Hunt J also found that the material conveyed the disparaging imputation that the plaintiff was responsible for allowing his fitness to deteriorate to the point that he had become a hopeless player.
87. Although the jury did find that such a disparaging imputation arose, and awarded damages on that basis.

majority of the Court of Appeal held that these remarks were capable of defaming the plaintiff. The remarks gave the impression that he was not merely physically unattractive in appearance, but 'actually repulsive'. The plaintiff, who was in the public eye and who, at least in part, made a living as an actor, would by virtue of the remarks be cast as an object of ridicule, scorn or derision. According to Neill J (at 1018), it did not matter that the remarks imputed neither discreditable conduct to the plaintiff nor any lack of skill or efficiency in his profession.

The second exception—causing people to shun and avoid—is well established, and applies to imputations that would tend to cause persons to avoid the plaintiff, such as imputations that the plaintiff has a psychiatric disorder (*Morgan v Lingen* (1863) 8 LT (ICS) 800); has been the victim of a rape (*Youssoupoff v Metro-Goldwyn Mayer Pictures Ltd* (1934) 50 TLR 581); or has an infectious disease. Although the ordinary reasonable person should not think less of a person in these unfortunate circumstances, it is said that these imputations tend to affect a person's standing in society due to people's irrational prejudices. The unfortunate reality is that they can lead to a degree of social isolation or exclusion.[88]

ELEMENT 2: THE MATTER IDENTIFIES, OR IS CAPABLE OF IDENTIFYING, THE PLAINTIFF AS THE PERSON DEFAMED

Reference to the plaintiff

The plaintiff can sue in relation to defamatory imputations if he or she was identified or reasonably *identifiable* from the material. In most cases, identification will not be an issue as the plaintiff will have been expressly referred to by name in the matter. However, if not expressly named, or if the imputations could be identified as relating to more than one person, the question is whether the ordinary, reasonable reader, viewer, or listener would identify the plaintiff as the person referred to in the matter. The intention of the defendant is once again irrelevant. In *Lee v Wilson* (1934) 51 CLR 276, a newspaper report of evidence given at an inquiry into allegations that members of the Victorian police force had accepted bribes referred to a 'Detective Lee' as one of the police officers involved. There were in fact three policemen by the name of Lee in the force. The plaintiffs were two of the policemen named Lee, neither of them being the 'Lee' referred to in the report. The High Court held that the plaintiffs were entitled to maintain an action in defamation. Dixon J considered that if defamatory words are capable of relating to more than one person and are found actually to defame each of them among the respective groups in the

---

88. *Sungravure Pty Ltd v Middle East Airlines Airliban SAL* (1975) 134 CLR 1 at 23–4, per Mason J.

community that knows them, they can all maintain actions, notwithstanding that the intention was to refer to a completely different person.[89]

Even a work of fiction that creates 'fictional' characters can be found to have defamed a plaintiff if ordinary readers would reasonably identify the plaintiff as the person referred to. In *Hulton & Co v Jones* (1910) AC 20, the defendant published a story regarding a fictional character called 'Artemus Jones'. A barrister of the same name was entitled to bring defamation proceedings as readers could reasonably understand that the story was referring to him. It was irrelevant that the author could prove that he had never heard of the plaintiff and had intended to create a purely fictitious character.

Where the identity of the plaintiff would only be known to certain persons or groups with special extrinsic knowledge, the plaintiff must establish that the matter was published to at least one person with that knowledge who identified the plaintiff as the person referred to.[90] In *Consolidated Trust Co Ltd v Browne* (1948) 49 SR (NSW) 86, the plaintiffs were unsuccessful in suing on a report defaming the owners of two buildings without expressly naming the plaintiffs as the owners. The plaintiffs' identity was not a matter of general knowledge, and they had failed to call evidence that the report was published to persons who would know who the owners were. However, the relevant evidence as to publication was present in *Henry v TVW Enterprises* (1990) Aust Torts Reports ¶81–031. A current affairs program, 'Hinch', carried a story about a dentist who had hepatitis B but was still practising, and had not informed his patients of his disease. During the story, it was stated that the program was restrained from showing footage of the dentist or from naming him. At various places throughout the story footage was shown of the plaintiff dentist's distinctive surgery, green gloves and pink nurses' uniforms. The plaintiff was not the dentist to whom the story was referring, but nevertheless he was able to bring a claim in defamation as evidence was given by a number of his patients and acquaintances, as well as by other dentists, that they had identified him from the story. The plaintiff was successful in recovering damages for the defamatory imputations that he had deliberately exposed his patients to the risk of contracting a contagious and dangerous disease and that he had acted in breach of his professional obligations in failing to warn his patients of his condition.

The requirement from *Consolidated Trust Co Ltd v Browne* of proof that that matter is published to at least one person who can identify the plaintiff does not apply where the plaintiff's identity is a matter of general notoriety. For example, it would not be necessary to call witnesses to give evidence that they knew the identity of 'the Prime Minister of Australia' (*Consolidated Trust Co Ltd v Browne*).

---

89. *Lee v Wilson* (1934) 51 CLR 276 at 295.
90. *Mirror Newspapers Ltd v World Hosts Pty Ltd* (1979) 141 CLR at 638–9, per Mason and Jacobs JJ (Gibbs and Stephens JJ agreeing); at 644, 645, per Aickin J.

Defamation of a group

A member of a group can sue if the defamatory statements can reasonably be understood as referring to the plaintiff as an individual within the group, or as referring to each member of a small, determinative group. In *Bjelke-Petersen v Warburton* [1987] 2 Qd R 465, the Queensland Premier and the other members of the Queensland Cabinet (18 in total) were all held to have standing to bring a defamation action over an imputation by the Deputy Leader of the Opposition that the Queensland Government was corrupt and that the ministers had their 'hands in the till'. The reference to 'the Government' could reasonably be understood as a reference to the ministerial members, particularly when coupled with the subsequent specific reference to the ministers. The ministers formed a small, determinate class, and the allegation of corruption could reasonably said to refer to each of them.

The position might be different if the allegation is not capable of imputing that *each* member of the group had engaged in the relevant behaviour. In *McCormick v John Fairfax & Sons Ltd* (1989) 16 NSWLR 485, allegations that one of the partners in a firm of private investigators was involved in corrupt activities was not actionable by the plaintiff (one of the three partners in the firm) as the imputation could only be taken to refer to one of the partners.[91] This case was distinguished in *Vitale v Bednall* [2000] WASC 207, in relation to an allegation that a group of students had engaged in vandalism. The allegation was being made of each member of the group, and the plaintiff would reasonably be identified to be such a member.

A generalised and extravagant allegation about a large or indeterminate number of persons is not actionable in defamation by an individual member of that class.[92] So a statement that 'all lawyers are thieves' or 'all Muslims are terrorists' does not, without more, give rise to an action in defamation law.[93] This is apparently not because such statements are not defamatory in nature, but because they are 'so intemperate and generalised as to be unlikely to damage the reputation of any individual [within the group]'.[94] Generalisations usually permit exceptions. Thus, in *Mann v The Medicine Group* (1992) 38 FCR 400, defamatory statements made about all bulk-billing doctors in Australia were not actionable by the plaintiff (a bulk-billing doctor) as they were not capable of being understood as referring to him as an individual.

---

91. Though contrast: *Random House Australia Pty Ltd v Abbott & Ors* (1999) 94 FCR 296.
92. *Knupfler v London Express* [1944] AC 116 at 122.
93. *Mann v The Medicine Group* (1992) 38 FCR 400 at 401.
94. Ibid.

ELEMENT 3: THE MATTER HAS BEEN PUBLISHED BY THE DEFENDANT TO AT LEAST ONE PERSON OTHER THAN THE PLAINTIFF

Publication to a third party

Defamatory matter concerning the plaintiff will be actionable only where the matter has been published in a comprehensible form to at least one person other than the plaintiff. The conveyance of the matter to the third person might take a variety of forms, such as the written word, the spoken word or audible sounds, gestures, signals or facial expressions.

Publication by the defendant to his or her spouse is not a publication to another person for defamation purposes, on the basis of the policy interest in preserving privacy of communications within the family.[95] Accordingly, communications between a defendant and spouse would be protected by a form of absolute privilege. In contrast, publication to the *plaintiff's* spouse is publication to a third party.[96]

Publication to the plaintiff's agent, including an employee, will suffice as publication.[97] This position is straightforward where the plaintiff is a natural person or another non-corporate entity such as a sole trader or partnership, but more contentious where the plaintiff is a corporation. There is authority that communication to an employee of the plaintiff corporation will be sufficient to show publication.[98] For example, in *Traztand Pty Ltd v Government Insurance Office of New South Wales* (1984) 2 NSWLR 598, defamatory remarks made to two employees of a car repair company about the quality of repair to some cars were held by Hunt J to be third-party publications. However, the New South Wales Court of Appeal expressed doubt about this decision in *State Bank of New South Wales Ltd v Currabubula Holdings Pty Ltd* [2001] NSWCA 47. Giles JA (with whom Heydon JA and Ipp AJA agreed) emphasised that a company can only act through human agents. Accordingly, publication to employees of a plaintiff company who receive the communication in the ordinary course of business is not publication to a third party. In that case, defamatory bank documents faxed to the office of the plaintiff were not published for the purposes of defamation law merely because they were received by natural persons whose business it was to receive those statements.[99] The court further held that publication made to a member of the governing body

---

95. *Wenhak v Morgan* (1880) 20 QBD 637; *Gatley on Libel and Slander*, P Milmo & WVH Rogers (Eds) 10th edn, Sweet & Maxwell, London, 2004, para 6.6.
96. *Wenman v Ash* (1853) 13 CB 536; *Howard v Howard* (1885) 2 WN (NSW) 5.
97. *Pullman v Walter Hill & Co* [1891] 1 QB 185.
98. This has been held to even be the case where the communication is an internal communication from one employee to another, and is not published to an outside person: *Riddick v Thames Board Mills* [1977] QB 893.
99. The position might have been different had there been evidence that the fax machine was positioned in a place that persons with no business looking at the bank documents would be able to see them.

of the corporation (a director, the managing director, or the company secretary) would never constitute publication to a third party. Such persons should be viewed as representing the corporation, in the sense of being its alter ego, and therefore would be 'the corporation' for the purposes of defamation law. On this view, it would appear that communication to such authorised persons would not be publication for defamation law purposes even if made outside of the ordinary course of business.

Where the imputation is raised as a matter of legal innuendo, or where the plaintiff is not expressly named in the matter, the plaintiff must show that the matter has been published to at least one person with the relevant extrinsic information or who would identify the plaintiff.[100]

Unintentional publication

The publisher will be liable be for all publications that were intended or authorised. The publisher will also be liable for unintentional publications, where publication was the natural and probable consequence of its actions.[101] In *Pullman v Walter Hill & Co* [1891] 1 QB 185, the defendant sent a letter defamatory of two members of a partnership in an envelope addressed to the firm. A clerk of the firm opened the letter in the ordinary course of business, and it was also read by two other clerks. The defendant was liable for the publication to the clerks as it had allowed the letter to leave its control without taking sufficient steps to ensure that it was only opened by the plaintiffs. The letter was not directed to the plaintiffs in their private capacities, nor did the envelope indicate that the letter was private and confidential; the probable consequence was that the letter would be opened by a clerk.[102] In contrast, there would normally be a presumption that a letter addressed privately to the plaintiff will only be opened by the plaintiff.[103] However, all of the circumstances must be considered. In *Theaker v Richardson* [1962] 1 WLR 151, a letter defamatory of the plaintiff was opened by her husband. The defendant was found liable for the publication to the husband as the envelope in which the letter was placed was similar in appearance to an election notice. In that circumstance, the defendant should reasonably have anticipated that another member of the household might open the letter, not realising that it was a private communication.

---

100. *Henry v TVW Enterprises* (1990) Aust Torts Rep 81–031; *Consolidated Trust Co Ltd v Browne* (1948) 49 SR (NSW) 86.
101. *Theaker v Richardson* [1962] 1 WLR 151.
102. *Pullman v Walter Hill & Co* [1891] 1 QB 185 at 528, per Lord Esher MR; at 529, per Lopes LJ.
103. *Powell v Gelston* [1916] 2 KB 615 (defendant not liable for publication to father who opened his son's correspondence); *Huth v Huth* [1915] 3 KB 32 (defendant not liable for publication to a butler who opened and read the letter purely as a matter of curiosity).

Republication or repetition of defamatory matter

Every person who has taken part in the publication of the defamatory matter is prima facie liable in defamation (see below). The defendant cannot use as an excuse the fact that it is merely repeating or reporting statements made by a third party. This will be the case even if the defendant expressly states that it is doing no more than repeating the statements of a third party and has no personal knowledge of the matter. As McHugh J said in *John Fairfax Publications Pty Ltd v Rivkin* (2003) 201 ALR 77, at 83:

> The general rule is that a person who publishes the defamatory statement of a third party adopts the statement and has the same liability as if the statement originated from the publisher. Accordingly, it is not the law that a person reporting the defamatory statement of another is only liable if he or she adopts the statement or reaffirms it.

The same principles that apply to unintentional publications of matter (discussed above) apply equally to unintended republications of the matter. The defendant will be liable for a re-publication where it was intended or authorised, or where it was the natural and probable consequence of the defendant's actions.[104] In *Sims v Wran* [1984] 1 NSWLR 317, the Premier of New South Wales made certain defamatory statements about the plaintiff journalist during a press conference; the statements imputed that the plaintiff was not objective and was affected by personal malice. These comments were subsequently widely broadcast throughout Australia on radio and television and in the press. Hunt J of the New South Wales Supreme Court found that Premier Wran was liable for the subsequent broadcasts and re-publications of his statement. The natural and probable consequence of such a statement being made by a prominent politician such as the Premier at a press conference was undoubtedly that the remarks would be repeated by the media (at 320).

Who is liable?

Subject to the defence of innocent dissemination discussed below, any person who is involved in the publication of defamatory matter is prima facie liable. For example, in respect of a defamatory broadcast by a radio or television station, the journalist, producer and proprietors will all prima facie be liable for the publication.[105] In respect of a defamatory newspaper article, the journalist, editor, proprietor, printer, and newsagent will all prima facie be liable.[106] The proprietor of a radio or television

---

104. *Selecta Homes and Building Co Pty Ltd v Advertiser-Weekend Publishing Co Pty Ltd* (2001) 79 SASR 451 at 462, per Lander J; at 476, per Gray J.
105. See, for example: *Carleton v Australian Broadcasting Corporation* (2002) 172 FLR 398.
106. *Goldsmith v Sperrings Ltd* [1977] 2 All ER 566.

station or of a newspaper will be prima facie liable not just for defamatory statements made by employees (for which they would be vicariously liable), but also for the comments of guests, interviewees, and talkback callers (in the case of broadcasters) and for letters to the editors and articles by freelance journalists (in the case of newspapers). It is no defence merely that the statements were made by a third party, not the defendant.[107]

The 'innocent dissemination' defence

The defence of 'innocent dissemination' will in some circumstances protect persons who were merely involved in the mechanics of the publication. The uniform laws contain an innocent dissemination defence; however, the common law principles will briefly be discussed first to provide the necessary background.

The innocent dissemination defence is available to 'secondary' or 'subordinate' distributors who were not the main publishers of the matter: newsagents, libraries, bookshops, and printers, for example. At common law, a defendant who is a subordinate distributor is able to take advantage of this defence where it can establish the following elements:

(a) it did not know that the publication contained defamatory information;
(b) it was not negligent in failing to realise that the publication contained defamatory information; and
(c) it did not know, nor ought it to have known, that the publication was of such a character that it was likely to contain defamatory matter.

These elements were established in the seminal cases of *Emmens v Pottle* (1885) 16 QBD 354 and *Vizetelly v Mudie's Select Library* [1900] 2 QB 170. In the former case, a newspaper vendor was protected from liability as it did not know, and should not have known, that the newspaper contained defamatory matter. Bowen LJ (at 358) rather colourfully commented that:

> A newspaper is not like a fire; a man may carry it about without being bound to suppose that it is likely to do an injury.

In *Vizetelly*, a library was found to be a secondary distributor within the meaning of the defence. However, the defence failed, as the library had ignored a trade circular notifying recipients that the book in question contained defamatory matter and requesting the return of the book so the particular page could be withdrawn.

---

107. Although the fair comment defence might be available (see following chapter).

The uniform laws contain a statutory defence of innocent dissemination that is intended to be largely reflective of these common law principles. Section 32[108] provides that it will be a defence for the defendant to prove that it:

(a) published the matter merely in the capacity of a subordinate distributor (or as an employee or agent thereof);
(b) neither knew, nor ought reasonably to have known, that the matter was defamatory; and
(c) was not negligent in failing to know that the matter was defamatory.

A 'subordinate distributor' is defined as a person who was not the first or primary distributor of the matter, was not the author or originator of the matter, and did not have any capacity to exercise control over the content or publication of the matter before it was published: s 32(2). The provision specifically provides that persons such as printers, newsagents, news vendors, booksellers, and other retailers and wholesalers are not primary distributors of the matter merely because they are involved in its publication: s 32(3). The provision also seeks to clarify the position of ISPs and other providers of electronic and communication services.[109] A provider of these services will be treated as being a subordinate distributor for the purposes of the defence, unless it can be shown that it was the author or originator of the matter or had the capacity to exercise effective control over it: s 32(3)(g). For instance, the service provider will be considered to be a subordinate distributor where the defamatory matter was contained in an email sent using the service, or in a website merely hosted by the service—but not where the defamatory matter is contained in a website created by the service provider itself selling its goods and services.

Section 32 also regulates the position of radio and television broadcasters. It provides that a broadcaster of a live radio or television program is not a primary distributor where it has no effective control over the person who makes the statements. The provision does not contain a definition of 'effective control', although presumably the object is to override the decision in *Thompson v Australian Capital Television* (1996) 186 CLR 574. In that case, the High Court held that a television station that had broadcast live to viewers a current affairs program produced by another station was not a subordinate distributor. The program by its nature carried a high risk of defamatory statements, and the station had the ability to control, supervise and monitor the material that it televised. It was no answer that the program was broadcast near-instantaneously, as doing so was the decision of the television station.[110] It was within the control of the station to delay the broadcast

---

108. Section 30 in South Australia.
109. The position of ISPs at common law has been uncertain, although there is authority that an ISP is an innocent disseminator for the purposes of the defence: *Godfrey v Demon Internet Ltd* [1999] 4 All ER 342. See also: *Thompson v Australian Capital Television* (1996) 186 CLR 574 at 589.
110. Ibid at 590.

to monitor it for defamatory content. It is arguable that the mere power to delay the transmission would not be construed as 'effective control' over the person who makes the statements for the purposes of s 32, and that therefore broadcasters will be able to rely on s 32 to avoid liability in this situation.

PROCEDURAL MATTERS

Role of the judge and jury in defamation trials

Jury trials have previously been permitted in all jurisdictions except the Australian Capital Territory and South Australia,[111] although in some jurisdictions a court order was necessary.[112] Pursuant to the uniform laws, a jury trial will be available at the election of either party unless the court otherwise orders: s 21.[113] However, the South Australian Parliament has not adopted those provisions relating to jury trials in its model legislation,[114] therefore jury trials will continue to be prohibited in that jurisdiction.

Pursuant to s 21 of the uniform laws, the jury will determine whether the defendant has published defamatory matter about the plaintiff and whether any defences apply. However, this is subject to the qualification that the jury will not determine any issue that at general law is an issue to be determined by the judge: s 22(5). Examples of issues that at general law are issues for the judge include whether a matter has been published on an occasion of absolute or qualified privilege for the purposes of a defence.[115] Whether the material is reasonably capable of bearing the imputations pleaded would presumably also fall within this qualification.[116]

Pursuant to these reforms, the jury will also have no role in determining the amount of damages to be awarded in a successful case; this can only be done by the judge.

Choice of jurisdiction in which to sue

Before discussing the provisions in the uniform laws relating to choice of law, it is important to provide the common law background.

---

111. *Juries Act 1927* (SA), s 5; *Supreme Court Act 1933* (ACT), s 22.
112. In the Northern Territory (*Juries Act 1962* (NT), s 7(1)) and in the Federal Court.
113. Section 21 anticipates that a judge will order a trial without jury where the trial would require a prolonged examination of records or technical, scientific or other issues that could not be conveniently resolved by a jury: s 21(3).
114. *Defamation Act 2005* (SA).
115. *Rajski v Carson* (1988) 15 NSWLR 84 at 100–1.
116. *Jones v Skelton* (1963) 63 SR (NSW) 644 at 650–1.

The common law rule is that the plaintiff has a cause of action for each publication of the defamatory matter.[117] Accordingly, if publication occurred in more than one State or Territory, the plaintiff can commence separate proceedings in each of those jurisdictions.[118] Alternatively, the plaintiff can choose to sue in one jurisdiction and recover one damages award for all of the publications, including those in other States and Territories. As discussed above, this practice requires the court to consider and apply the law from each jurisdiction in which the plaintiff is claiming damages.[119] Whichever course the plaintiff adopts, the cost and complexity of the trial or trials will be considerable. Despite significant criticism of these principles,[120] they have recently been affirmed and applied by the High Court to internet publications in *Dow Jones & Co Inc v Gutnick* (2002) 210 CLR 575. The plaintiff, a resident of Victoria, sued the defendant, a corporation based in the United States, for defamation. The claim related to material that the defendant uploaded onto the internet in New Jersey. The material was contained in a business news service made available for downloading to subscribers. There were more than 500 000 subscribers, of whom approximately 1700 were in Australia. The plaintiff claimed that he had been defamed by the publication in Victoria of the material, which had been downloaded there by subscribers. The defendant disputed that the plaintiff was entitled to bring a cause of action in Victoria. It argued that the proper jurisdiction in which to sue was New Jersey, as that was where the material had been placed on the web server, and therefore where publication had occurred. Relying largely on policy considerations, it argued that there should be one single law governing the conduct of a person who chooses to make material available on the internet so that publishers can be certain in predicting the law that will govern their conduct, and in this case this single law should be the law of New Jersey where the material was uploaded. In a joint judgment, Gleeson CJ, McHugh, Gummow, and Hayne JJ affirmed the general law principle that a defamation action can be commenced in any jurisdiction in which publication occurs. In the case of material published over the internet, this meant that as a general rule, the plaintiff would have a good cause of action in each jurisdiction in which the internet material is downloaded. Although recognising the inconvenience that this could cause to publishers, their Honours held that this inconvenience had to be balanced against an individual's interest in protecting his or reputation from unwarranted slur or

---

117. *Australian Broadcasting Corporation v Waterhouse* (1991) 25 NSWLR 519 at 535; *Dow Jones & Co Inc v Gutnick* (2002) 210 CLR 575 at 600.
118. The principles of res judicata and issue estoppel might result in separate proceedings being stayed in some circumstances: *Dow Jones & Co Inc v Gutnick* at 604.
119. See: *Australian Broadcasting Corporation v Waterhouse* (1991) 25 NSWLR 519
120. See: Australian Law Reform Commission, *Unfair Publication: Defamation and Privacy*, Report No 11, 1979, pp 25–7.

damage. The harm to reputation occurs where defamatory matter is published in a comprehensible form, and accordingly the tort of defamation is committed in each jurisdiction where this occurs. In the case of material on the internet, it is not available in a comprehensible form until downloaded onto a computer using a web browser. It is in the place (or places) where the material is downloaded that the publication occurs and that the damage to reputation may be done. Accordingly, it is that place (or places) where the tort of defamation is committed. On these facts, the material regarding the plaintiff was downloaded in Victoria by subscribers to the news service, and therefore the tort of defamation was committed in Victoria.

The court clearly felt uncomfortable with the fact that the natural consequence of its decision was that a plaintiff could potentially commence actions in multiple jurisdictions around the world. However, it suggested that well-established rules relating to abuse of process and powers to stay proceedings could be used to prevent multiplicity of claims in appropriate situations.

Once all Australian jurisdictions have enacted the uniform laws, there will be a single law of defamation in this country and therefore there should be no substantive advantage in choosing to sue in one jurisdiction over another. However, the uniform laws will not affect a publication that occurs overseas which is litigated in an Australian court. In those circumstances, Australian courts would apply the law of the place where publication occurred, which potentially could be a number of overseas jurisdictions.

Limitation periods

The limitation periods for defamation actions have previously varied significantly between jurisdictions. In New South Wales and the Australian Capital Territory, the limitation period was one year, with a provision for extension in some circumstances.[121] In South Australia and Western Australia, the limitation period was two years for slander actions, but six years for libel actions.[122] In other jurisdictions, the limitation period was six years for all defamation actions.

The uniform laws will introduce into each jurisdiction a basic limitation period of one year from the date of publication of which the plaintiff is complaining: s 47. However, a court is required to extend the period to up to three years from the date of publication if satisfied that it was not reasonable for the plaintiff to commence proceedings in the shorter time period: s 48.

---

121. *Limitation Act 1985* (ACT), s 21B; *Limitation Act 1969* (NSW), ss 14B, 56A.
122. *Limitation of Actions Act 1937* (SA), s 37; *Limitation Act 1935* (WA), s 38.

NON-LITIGIOUS MEANS OF RESOLVING DISPUTES

Offers to make amends

One of the main objects of the uniform laws is to resolve defamation disputes without litigation. The laws contain provisions enabling a publisher to offer to make amends for material that is, or may be, defamatory.[123] In essence, an 'offer to make amends' is a written offer to publish a reasonable correction of the matter, or at least of particular specified imputations, and to meet the aggrieved person's reasonable expenses incurred before the offer was made and in considering the offer. It might also include an offer to pay compensation in a stated amount, an amount to be agreed, or an amount to be determined by a court or an arbitrator. If the offer of amends is accepted, and provided the publisher carries out its terms, the aggrieved person cannot commence or continue an action (even if the offer was limited to particular imputations.) If the offer of amends is not accepted, the publisher will have a defence in a defamation action where it can establish that the offer had been made as soon as practicable after it became aware that the matter in question was or might have been defamatory, it was willing to carry out the terms of the offer, and that the offer was reasonable in the circumstances.

The effect of an apology on liability

Section 20 of the uniform laws provides that an apology by or on behalf of the publisher will not constitute an admission of liability and will not be relevant to the determination of fault or liability on a defamation claim. The object of this provision is clear: to encourage publishers to issue an apology as soon as possible in order to lessen the plaintiff's feelings of grievance. The provision of an apology is a factor that can be taken into account in mitigation of damages: s 38. This will be discussed in the next chapter.

FURTHER READING

Australian Law Reform Commission, *Unfair Publication: Defamation and Privacy*, Report No 11, 1979.
Baker R, 'Defining the Moral Community: The "Ordinary Reasonable Person" in Defamation Law' in *Submission for the Communications Research Forum*, Communications Law Centre, University of New South Wales, 2003.
Commonwealth, Attorney-General's Department, *Revised Outline of a Possible National Defamation Law*, July 2004, Canberra, ACT.

---

123. These provisions are contained in Pt 3, Div 1.

21 Defences and Remedies in Defamation Law*

INTRODUCTION

Once the plaintiff has established a prima facie case of liability, the onus will shift to the defendant to prove a defence. The defences in defamation law seek to strike an appropriate balance between the protection of the plaintiff's reputation and freedom of speech.

At common law, it is a defence to establish that the matter is true in substance, the subject of honest comment, or published on an occasion of absolute or qualified privilege. These defences will be retained with modifications under the uniform defamation laws enacted in each of the States and Territories in 2006.[1] The uniform laws also contain specific defences relating to the publication of public documents and fair reports of proceedings of public concern, as well as a defence of 'triviality'. The defences contained in the uniform laws are in addition to those established at common law and will not of themselves vitiate, limit, or abrogate another common law defence: s 24.

The main remedy for defamation is damages to provide consolation to the plaintiff for the harm to reputation and to vindicate the plaintiff's reputation.

JUSTIFICATION

Introduction

At common law, it is a defence to establish that the defamatory imputations are true in substance. It follows that a defendant is in effect liable for defamatory matter only

---

* This chapter was written by Sharon Erbacher.
1. See the preceding chapter for further discussion of the introduction of the uniform laws and p 580 for the list of relevant legislation.

where it is *false*—or, more accurately, where the defendant is unable to prove that it is true. The truth of the matter constitutes a defence because:[2]

> no wrong is done to [a person] by telling the truth about him. The presumption is that, by telling the truth about a man, his reputation is not lowered beyond its proper level, but is merely brought down to it …

The defence of justification is complete upon proof of the substantial truth of the matter; unlike the defences of honest comment and qualified privilege, it will not be defeated by malice or proof the defendant knew the facts to be false. However, it is a defence that must be used with caution, as the defendant might be liable for aggravated damages if the defence fails.[3]

Public interest or benefit

The uniform laws have adopted the common law defence of justification (where truth alone constitutes the defence) in preference to the formerly existing laws in some jurisdictions, where the defendant was required to prove in addition that the material was published for the public benefit (Australian Capital Territory,[4] Queensland,[5] and Tasmania)[6] or in the public interest (New South Wales).[7] The extra condition of public benefit or public interest imposed some limitation on the ability of media organisations to publish intimate details about the plaintiff's private life. In contrast, under the uniform laws (as at common law) defamation law will be only of limited utility in protecting privacy. The publication of embarrassing and private details of a person's life will be permitted, provided they are accurately portrayed, even though there might be no wider public interest or benefit in the receipt of those details.

Truth in substance

Section 25[8] of the uniform laws provides that it is a defence if the defendant proves that the defamatory imputations carried by the impugned matter are substantially true. The term 'substantially true' is defined in s 4 as meaning 'true in substance or not materially different from the truth'. As at common law, the test is not whether the matter is literally true, but whether the defendant can justify the 'sting' or 'gist' of the matter In *Howden v 'Truth' and 'Sportsman' Ltd* (1937) 58 CLR 416, the defendant

---

2. *Rofe v Smith Newspapers* (1924) 25 SR (NSW) 4 at 21–2, per Street ACJ.
3. *Coyne v Citizen Finance Ltd* (1991) 172 CLR 211 at 237, per Toohey J.
4. *Civil Law (Wrongs) Act 2002*, s 127.
5. *Defamation Act 1889* (Qld), s 15.
6. *Defamation Act 1957* (Tas), s 15.
7. *Defamation Act 1974* (NSW), s 15.
8. In South Australia the justification defence is contained in s 23.

published a statement to the effect that the plaintiff had been convicted of the crime of conspiracy to defraud and had been sentenced to a term of imprisonment of fifteen months. That conviction and sentence had indeed been imposed, but the conviction had been quashed before the date of the publication. The High Court held that the defence of justification was not available to the defendant. The sting of the defamatory matter was that the defendant had been found guilty of the crime of conspiracy to defraud and served a substantial term of imprisonment. This was not true, as both the conviction and sentence had been quashed.[9]

Similarly, if the defendant imputes that the plaintiff, who is being investigated for a crime, is guilty of the crime or that there are reasonable grounds for the investigation, the defendant must prove guilt in order to justify the statement.[10] On the other hand, it will not defeat the defence that the publication contains minor inaccuracies. The defence is not defeated by immaterial or trivial errors or mistakes that do not alter the defamatory sting of the matter.[11] For example, an erroneous statement that the plaintiff was sentenced to twenty years' imprisonment for murder might be able to be justified even though the sentence of imprisonment was actually nineteen years.[12] The gist of the statement is that a substantial term of imprisonment was imposed for a serious offence, which is true.

The defendant cannot justify a statement merely on the basis that it is an accurate repetition of what others have published,[13] or that the defendant honestly believed in the truth of the matter; the defendant must show that the substance of the statement is true.[14] Likewise, a defendant cannot escape liability by qualifying a statement as only being a rumour that might not be true.[15]

The general rule is that the defendant must justify the statement by reference to facts that existed at the time of the publication. However, this will depend on the nature of the statement: a general statement about the plaintiff's character—for example, 'the plaintiff is a liar'—might be justified by events occurring both before and after publication that show the defendant to be a liar.[16]

The defendant must justify each imputation pleaded by the plaintiff, unless it can be established that the imputations were not separate or distinct but, as a whole, carried a 'common sting'. In that eventuality, it is sufficient for the defendant to prove that the common sting (the collective imputation) is true. For example, matter that carries a common sting of sexual promiscuity might be justified by

---

9. Ibid at 419, per Starke J; at 421, per Dixon J; at 423, per Evatt J.
10. *Mirror Newspapers Ltd v Harrison* (1982) 149 CLR 293; *Favell v Queensland Newspapers Pty Ltd* [2005] HCA 52.
11. *Herald & Weekly Times Ltd v Popovic* [2003] VSCA 161 at [306], per Gillard AJA (Winneke ACJ and Warren AJA agreeing).
12. See, by analogy: *Alexander v NE Rwy* (1865) 6 B&S 340.
13. *John Fairfax Publications Pty Ltd v Rivkin* (2003) 201 ALR 77 at 83, per McHugh J.
14. *Stern v Piper* [1997] QB 123.
15. *Rivkin v Amalgamated Television Services Pty Ltd* [2001] NSWSC 432.
16. *Maisel v Financial Times Ltd* [1915] 3 KB 336.

proof of several extra-marital affairs—even though the truth of the allegation of the specific affair about which the plaintiff chose to sue could not be proved.[17] On the other hand, imputations that are severable and distinct from the common sting must be separately justified from the common sting. For example, assume the matter conveys imputations that the plaintiff (a politician) betrayed his party leader, 'ratted' on his party, was a drunk, and used to beat his wife.[18] The first two imputations arguably carry a common sting of disloyalty and treachery which could be justified collectively; however, the imputations that the plaintiff was a drunk and a wife-beater are separate and distinct imputations, and each would need to be severally justified.

These principles, which were laid down in the English case of *Polly Peck plc v Trelford* [1986] QB 1000, have been widely applied in Australia.[19]

Contextual truth

Section 26 of the uniform laws provides for a defence of contextual truth.[20] To understand this defence (which does not exist at common law) it is necessary to set out the common law background. The principles from the case of *Polly Peck* have been discussed above. It has become a widely accepted practice following this case that the plaintiff is permitted to cherry-pick those imputations about which to complain. The plaintiff can decide to plead only a selection of the imputations and ignore others that are at risk of being justified, provided the pleaded imputations are separate and distinct from those not pleaded.[21] Where the plaintiff chooses to complain about only some of the imputations, the defendant will be prevented from leading evidence that would justify other imputations about which there is no complaint.[22] In *Cruise and Kidman v Express Newspaper plc* [1998] QB 931, statements about the characters of the plaintiffs, who were well-known actors—including that they were arrogant, and dishonest about the true state of their marriage—were considered to be separate and distinct from statements about their adherence to the Church of Scientology, about which they did not complain. Accordingly, the English Court of Appeal held that the trial judge was correct in preventing the defendant from leading evidence that would justify statements about

---

17. *Khashoggi v IPC Magazines Ltd* [1986] 3 All ER 577.
18. These are the facts of *Mutch v Sleeman* (1928) 29 SR (NSW) 125.
19. See, for example: *Hore-Lacy v David Syme & Co Ltd* [1998] VSC 96 at [18]; *Carrey v ACP Publishing Pty Ltd* [1999] 1 VR 875 at 885–6; *Whelan v John Fairfax Publications Pty Ltd* [2002] NSWSC 1028; *Herald & Weekly Times Ltd v Popovic* [2003] VSCA 161 at [302].
20. In South Australia this defence will be contained in s 24.
21. *Herald & Weekly Times Ltd v Popovic* [2003] VSCA 161 at [305], [345], per Gillard AJA (Winnecke ACJ and Warren AJA agreeing).
22. *Anderson v Nationwide News Pty Ltd* [2001] 3 VR 619 at 634; *Herald & Weekly Times Ltd v Popovic* [2003] VSCA 161 at [323], per Gillard AJA (Winnecke ACJ and Warren AJA agreeing).

their membership of that Church. Brooke LJ (with whom Knox LJ and Stuart-Smith LJ agreed) commented (at 954):

> It is no defence to a charge that 'you called me A' to say 'Yes, but I also called you B on the same occasion, and that was true', if the second charge was separate and distinct from the first.

The *Polly Peck* practice of permitting a plaintiff to choose which parts of a publication to sue upon has been criticised as leading to situations where the plaintiff artificially confines the dispute to a relatively minor matter which, in context, does not harm the plaintiff's reputation:[23]

> assume a publication makes two claims: the plaintiff is a murderer (which happens to be true) and they stole some raffle tickets (which is false). The plaintiff could decide to sue only on the claim that they stole some raffle tickets and so avoid dealing with the more serious charge ... [T]he result might be that the defendant is forced to pay damages for defamation when the charge of theft does no additional harm to the plaintiff because of the truth of the other charge. [footnotes omitted]

To address this problem, the uniform laws will contain a defence of contextual truth in s 26. This defence will apply where the plaintiff has chosen to proceed with one or more, but not all, of the defamatory imputations carried by the matter. In that circumstance, the defendant may rely on the defence of contextual truth by proving that:

(a) the matter conveyed, in addition to the imputations of which the plaintiff complains, one or more other imputations (contextual imputations) that are substantially true; and
(b) the imputations of which the plaintiff complains do not further harm the reputation of the plaintiff because of the substantial truth of the contextual imputations.

In essence, this defence will be available where the defendant can prove that the publication, when taken as a whole, is substantially true, and that the specific false imputation or imputations relied on by the plaintiff have caused no further harm to the plaintiff's reputation. In other words, the defendant must establish, when looking at the material as a whole, that the matters proved to be true in the publication were at least equal in terms of their effect on the plaintiff's reputation to the false imputations on which the plaintiff relies.[24] The defence will apply even

---

23. Commonwealth, Attorney-General's Department, *Revised Outline of a Possible National Defamation Law*, July 2004, Canberra, ACT, p 16.
24. See: *John Fairfax Publications Pty Ltd v Blake* (2001) 53 NSWLR 541 (interpreting a similar provision in New South Wales).

if the contextual imputations are separate and distinct from those of which the plaintiff complains.[25]

The defence of contextual truth has existed for some years in legislation in New South Wales,[26] and a similar defence also exists in the United Kingdom.[27] The United Kingdom provision was applied in *Irving v Penguin Books Ltd* [2000] EWHC QB 115, involving a defamation claim brought by the controversial historian and Holocaust denier, David Irving. The trial judge (Gray J) held that a number of defamatory charges against the plaintiff were substantially true, including that he had for his own ideological reasons persistently and deliberately misrepresented historical evidence regarding the treatment of Jewish people by the Nazi regime in the Second World War; that he was an active Holocaust denier; that he had portrayed Hitler in an unwarrantedly favourable light; that he was anti-semitic and racist; and that he associated with right wing neo-Nazi extremists. These true charges were of such gravity that no further damage would be done to the plaintiff's reputation by publication of other specific matters not proven to be true, such as that he had attended a conference which was also attended by various representatives of terrorist organisations and that he had a self-portrait by Hitler hanging over his desk (at [13.167]).[28]

The defence of contextual truth will be rejected where the contextual imputations that have been proven to be true would not have caused the same amount of damage to the plaintiff's reputation as the false imputations pleaded by the plaintiff. Thus, in *John Fairfax Publications Pty Ltd v Blake* (2001) 53 NSWLR 541, the plaintiff had pleaded that the matter was capable of conveying the false imputation that he had been convicted of causing actual bodily harm to a child. The defendant sought to justify these charges by pleading true contextual imputations to the effect that the plaintiff had threatened a child with harm and possessed a dangerous weapon that was capable of inflicting physical harm. The New South Wales Court of Appeal struck out the defence of contextual truth on the basis that a charge that the plaintiff had caused actual harm to a child, or had been convicted of harming a child, would cause further harm to the plaintiff's reputation than a charge merely that he *threatened* harm to a child and possessed the means to do so.

---

25. Although it might be expected a false imputation, that is separate and distinct from the other imputations and that relates to different aspects of the plaintiff's reputation, is generally likely to cause further harm to the plaintiff's reputation and to be amenable to a damages award. Thus, an imputation that the plaintiff politician is a wife-beater is likely to cause damage to his personal reputation quite separately from the damage caused to his professional reputation by an imputation of political disloyalty (see the facts of *Mutch v Sleeman* (1928) 29 SR (NSW) 125, above).
26. *Defamation Act 1974* (NSW), s 16.
27. *Defamation Act 1952* (UK), s 5.
28. This reasoning was upheld by the Court of Appeal: *Irving v Penguin Books Ltd* [2001] EWCA Civ 1197 at [100].

HONEST OPINION (FAIR COMMENT)

Introduction

At common law, it is a defence that the impugned matter is an honestly held statement of opinion on a matter of public interest. The objective of the defence is to permit commentary, opinion, analysis, critical reviews, and editorials on matters of legitimate interest to the public.

A defence of honest opinion is contained in s 31[29] of the uniform laws. This statutory defence retains the essence of the common law defence, though it differs from it in some respects, as will be discussed. The statutory defence does not abrogate or exclude the common law defence: s 24. Accordingly, defendants could, if they chose, rely on the common law defence as an alternative to the statutory defence.

The common law defence will be examined first, followed by a discussion of the new statutory defence.

Fair comment at common law

The elements of the common law defence of fair comment are:[30]

(a) the matter is a statement of opinion rather than fact;
(b) it is on a matter of public interest;
(c) the facts on which the opinion is based are true or privileged; and
(d) the opinion is one which an honest person could reasonably draw from the material.

The defence will be lost if the plaintiff can establish that the defendant acted maliciously.

Statement of opinion

The defence protects statements of opinion, not fact. Furthermore, the statement must be objectively recognisable by the ordinary, reasonable recipient as a statement of opinion rather than fact.[31] The material must be phrased and presented in such a way that it would reasonably be understood to be a commentary, analysis, conclusion, inference, observation, or criticism rather than a factual statement. The

---

29. Section 29 in South Australia.
30. *Peterson v Advertiser Newspapers* (1995) 54 SASR 152 at 190; *Herald & Weekly Times Ltd v Popovic* [2003] VSCA 161 at [259].
31. *Hawke v Tamworth Newspaper Co Ltd* [1983] 1 NSWLR 699 at 716, 720; *Radio 2UE Sydney Pty Ltd v Parker* (1992) 29 NSWLR 448; *Orion Pet Products v RSPCA* (2002) 120 FCR 191 at 233.

test is not what the defendant intended, but the objective construction that would be placed on the material by the reasonable recipient.[32]

In construing a statement as opinion rather than fact, both the context of the statement and the language used will be important factors:[33]

> the general context of the communication will influence whether the statements are properly regarded as factual or not. Statements made in a work of fiction, for example, should be presumptively construed as opinion. In contrast, a 'news' story should be presumptively construed as factual. However the emphasis in all instances should be on the overall context of the communication and on how the statements were reasonably understood in that context. [Also] the use of qualifying language such as 'In my opinion', or a disclaimer may suggest that a statement is opinion rather than fact.

A statement made without reference to the facts on which it is based will generally be construed as a statement of fact. It is a requirement of the defence that the matter must state or indicate a sufficient factual substratum, or that the factual substratum must constitute a matter of general notoriety or contemporaneous history, so as to enable recipients to identify the statement as an opinion drawn from these facts and to ascertain whether they agree with the opinion.[34] Bare inferences or allegations without reference to the factual basis (or notorious facts) are at risk of being treated as statements of fact, not opinion. Thus, it is a statement of fact to state that a person's conduct has been disgraceful without stating what that conduct was, but a statement of comment to accurately refer to the conduct of a person and then assert that that conduct is disgraceful.[35] *Hawke v Tamworth Newspapers* [1983] 1 NSWLR 699 involved a defamation action by the then Prime Minister of Australia in respect of alleged defamatory matter contained in a letter to the editor published in a country newspaper before his election to Federal Parliament. The letter said that 'Ironically, I could have [Hawke] banned from this or any other election quite easily, but I'm not saying how'. The defence of fair comment was rejected on the basis that this statement was not capable of being construed as comment. The statement would be construed by the reasonable recipient as a statement of fact due to the failure of the writer to include the factual basis for the statement or to identify from contemporary history or from general knowledge or notoriety any conduct of the plaintiff that could possibly base a comment that he was unfit to be a member of parliament.

---

32. *Pervan v North Queensland Newspaper Co Ltd* (1993) 178 CLR 309 at 329; *Radio 2UE Sydney Pty Ltd v Parker* (1992) 29 NSWLR 448 at 466–7.
33. Commonwealth, Attorney-General's Department, *Revised Outline of a Possible National Defamation Law*, July 2004, Canberra, ACT, p 18.
34. *Goldsborough v John Fairfax & Sons Ltd* (1934) 34 SR (NSW) 524 at 331–2; *Hawke v Tamworth Newspaper Co Ltd* [1983] 1 NSWLR 699 at 704.
35. *Kemsley v Foot* [1952] AC 345 at 356.

Where the criticism is of a movie, book, or other artistic work such as a painting, it would of course be impossible for the critic to reproduce the work. As it will usually be apparent from the context that it is a criticism or review (and therefore a statement of opinion),[36] it will generally be sufficient that the critic sufficiently identifies the work so that members of the public have the opportunity to ascertain for themselves the subject-matter on which the comment is based and to determine whether they agree with the opinion.[37]

The comment must be based on material that existed at the time the comment was made.[38] This is because it is central to the defence that the recipients must be able to judge for themselves whether they agree with the published comment upon the material.[39] Accordingly, the defendant is not entitled to rely upon material which comes into existence subsequent to the comment, although in appropriate circumstances the subsequent facts might be admissible to prove that the material relied upon did exist at the relevant time.[40]

Public interest

The comment must be on a matter of public interest,[41] in the sense of being of legitimate interest to the public. It must 'affect "people at large" so that they may be legitimately interested in, or concerned at, what is going on.'[42] It is not sufficient merely that the public is interested or curious to know of the matter. Subject-matter that is in the public interest includes the views and conduct of former, current or aspiring public officials, such as politicians;[43] the conduct of those serving on public bodies;[44] the public activities of large corporations;[45] the conduct of members of the media and of media proprietors;[46] and the conduct of entertainers[47] and sportspersons.[48]

Generally, the comment must pertain to the public views and conduct of the public figure; comment on the private affairs of a person, no matter how well known, would not usually be in the public interest. It is different, however, if the private conduct impacts on or is relevant to that person's public conduct—for instance, by

---

36. *Gardiner v John Fairfax & Sons Pty Ltd* (1942) 42 SR (NSW) 171 at 174, 175, per Jordan CJ.
37. *Kemsley v Foot* [1952] AC 345 at 355.
38. *Cohen v Daily Telegraph Ltd* [1968] 1 WLR 916; *Hawke v Tamworth Newspaper Co Ltd* [1983] 1 NSWLR 699 at 704.
39. *Peterson v Advertiser Newspapers* (1995) 54 SASR 152 at 192.
40. *Hawke v Tamworth Newspaper Co Ltd* [1983] 1 NSWLR 699.
41. *London Artists Ltd v Littler* [1969] 2 QB 375.
42. *Orion Pet Products v RSPCA* (2002) 120 FCR 191 at 234, citing *London Artists Ltd v Littler* [1969] 2 QB 375 at 391.
43. *Pervan v North Queensland Newspaper Co Ltd* (1993) 178 CLR 309; *Peterson v Advertiser Newspapers Ltd* (1995) SASR 152.
44. *Radio 2UE Sydney Pty Ltd v Parker* (1992) 29 NSWLR 448.
45. *Australian Broadcasting Corporation v Comalco Ltd* (1986) 12 FCR 510.
46. *Kemsley v Foot* [1952] AC 345.
47. *London Artists Ltd v Littler* [1969] 2 QB 375.
48. *Lloyd v David Syme & Co Ltd* (1985) 3 NSWLR 728.

suggesting qualities that would impact on fitness or ability to perform the public role. As an example, if a member of parliament who was well known for advocating family values was criticised as being a hypocrite because he had an illegitimate child as a result of an adulterous affair, such a matter could be said to impact on his conduct as a member of parliament, and therefore to be a matter in the public interest.

Literary and other artistic works submitted to the public for appraisal are also of public interest. Thus, the defence extends to comments made by critics in the course of reviewing works such as movies, plays, television shows, artistic pieces, and books. However, a personal attack on the character of the author or artist would not generally be within the defence.[49]

Basis in true or privileged facts

The opinion must be based on facts that are substantially true or privileged.[50] An opinion will not be protected where it is based on facts that are untrue or patently distorted,[51] unless those facts are otherwise protected under the defence of privilege. In *Herald & Weekly Times Ltd v Popovic* [2003] VSCA 161, the plaintiff, a Victorian magistrate, brought defamation proceedings over an article in a newspaper that contained various imputations defamatory of her, including that she had subverted the law by prejudging a case, behaved outrageously by bullying the police prosecutor for simply arguing the law, and so misconducted herself as to warrant removal as a magistrate. The article reported part only of an exchange between the plaintiff and the prosecutor, did not refer to the context of the exchange, and did not mention that the hearing was a preliminary hearing rather than the final hearing of the charge. The Victorian Court of Appeal held that the article was not protected by fair comment as it provided a selective and distorted account of the facts that could not be justified.

The comment identified by the defendant for the purposes of this defence must pertain to a meaning of the article on which the plaintiff relies, rather than a severable meaning of which the plaintiff has no complaint. In *Anderson v Nationwide News Pty Ltd (No 2)* (2001) 3 VR 639, the plaintiff was the managing director of BHP Ltd. He claimed that an article published by the defendant's newspaper concerning a merger of BHP with another company bore the defamatory imputation that he had supported the merger for ulterior personal purposes. The defendant argued that the article was fair comment on a matter of public interest. The substance of the comment as formulated by the defendant was that the plaintiff was supporting a merger on terms which were not favourable to BHP shareholders.

---

49. *Gardiner v John Fairfax & Sons Pty Ltd* (1942) 42 SR (NSW) 171 at 174, per Jordan CJ.
50. *London Artists Ltd v Littler* [1969] 2 QB 375; *Goldsborough v John Fairfax & Sons Ltd* (1934) 34 SR (NSW) 524 at 534.
51. *Peterson v Advertiser Newspapers* (1995) 54 SASR 152 at 193.

Bongiorno J in the Victorian Supreme Court struck out the defence on the basis that the comment went only to a defamatory charge of a lack of business judgment and did not meet the sting of the plaintiff's pleaded imputation, which was that of ulterior motives (at 642).[52]

The opinion could be held by an honest person

A statement of opinion will be protected no matter how unfair, exaggerated, prejudiced, or biased the statement of opinion might be: 'The basis of our public life is that the crank, the enthusiast, may say what he honestly thinks just as much as the reasonable man or woman'.[53] The unfair comment is protected provided that the facts founding the comment are stated or indicated in the matter, so that recipients can determine its merits for themselves.

There has been considerable controversy about whether this requirement is subjective or objective. Must the defendant prove that he or she honestly held the opinion (a subjective belief), or is it sufficient that objectively an honest person could hold the opinion conveyed? The clear weight of authority in Australia supports the view that the test is objective.[54] The defendant discharges his or her onus of proof on this issue by proving that the comment is one which an honest person, however biased or prejudiced, could have drawn from the facts.[55] It is questionable whether the objective element of fairness adds anything of substance to the application of the defence. As some commentators have pointed out,[56] any comment whatever could be attributed to an honest person if they are allowed to be as exaggerated, prejudiced and emotional as they like. For example, describing a medical practitioner who terminated pregnancies as guilty of 'genocide' and 'murder' was within the protection of the defence, notwithstanding that it was a highly emotive comment.[57] Therefore, this element does not appear to impose a significant limitation on the operation of the defence.

Abuse of the defence: malice

The defence will be lost if the plaintiff can establish that the defendant was motivated by malice, in the sense that the comment was actuated by ill will or personal

---

52. Bongiorno J followed a decision of Ashley J in earlier strike-out proceedings: *Anderson v Nationwide News Pty Ltd* (2001) 3 VR 619.
53. *Silkin v Beaverbrook Newspapers Ltd* [1958] All ER 516.
54. *Pervan v North Queensland Newspaper Co Ltd* (1993) 178 CLR 309 at 329; *Hawke v Tamworth Newspaper Co Ltd* [1983] 1 NSWLR 699 at 716, 720; *Peterson v Advertiser Newspapers* (1995) 54 SASR 152 at 190–1.
55. *Hawke v Tamworth Newspaper Co Ltd* [1983] 1 NSWLR.
56. Irish Law Reform Commission, *Consultation Paper on the Civil Law of Defamation*, 1991, p 274; Commonwealth, Attorney-General's Department, *Revised Outline of a Possible National Defamation Law*, July 2004, Canberra, ACT, p 17.
57. *Grundemann v Georgeson* [1996] Aust Torts Rep 63–500.

hostility.[58] It is not sufficient merely that malice existed; the plaintiff must prove that the defendant *acted because of* the malice. Just because, for example, there is personal enmity between the plaintiff and defendant does not mean the defendant loses the defence of fair comment, provided that it cannot be shown that the defendant's judgement was distorted because of the enmity.[59] To establish malice it would be necessary to show that the malice has informed the opinion in the sense that the defendant was primarily motivated by a desire to harm the plaintiff.[60] Proof by the plaintiff that the defendant did not honestly hold the opinion will be almost conclusive proof of malice.[61]

Media organisations regularly publish opinions of persons unconnected with that organisation, such as opinions of interviewees, talkback callers and writers of letters to the editor. An issue has arisen whether a media organisation that publishes an opinion by a third party loses the protection of the defence unless it can establish that it honestly agreed with the comment of the third party. The preferred view in Australia is that this is not necessary.[62] The defendant publisher can take advantage of the defence where the comment is objectively fair, provided it did not adopt the opinion as its own and was not motivated by malice.[63] It is fundamental to a democracy that a media organisation be permitted to publish a wide range of different opinions on a matter of public interest. Freedom of speech would be unduly inhibited if a media organisation were allowed only to publish statements with which it agreed.[64]

Statutory defence of honest opinion

The statutory defence of honest opinion contained in s 31 of the uniform laws provides that it is a defence for the defendant to prove:

(a) the matter was an expression of opinion of the defendant [or an employee or agent] of the defendant rather than a statement of fact;

(b) the opinion related to a matter of public interest; and

(c) the opinion is based on proper material.

---

58. *Gardiner v John Fairfax & Sons Pty Ltd* (1942) 42 SR (NSW) 171 at 173, per Jordan CJ; *Renouf v Federal Capital Press of Australia Pty Ltd* (1977) 17 ACTR 35 at 54, per Blackbury J.
59. *Gardiner v John Fairfax & Sons Ltd* (1942) 42 SR (NSW) 171.
60. *Renouf v Federal Capital Press of Australia Ltd* (1977) 17 ACTR 35.
61. *Roberts v Bass* [2002] 212 CLR 1; *Peterson v Advertiser Newspapers* (1995) 54 SASR 152 at 189.
62. The same approach has been adopted in England: *Telnikoff v Matusevitch* [1992] 2 AC 343. However in Canada the defence is lost unless the defendant publisher can show that it honestly held the opinion: *Cherneskey v Armadale Publishers Ltd* (1978) 90 DLR (3d) 321.
63. *Pervan v North Queensland Newspaper Co Ltd* (1993) 178 CLR 309; *Hawke v Tamworth Newspaper Co Ltd* [1983] 1 NSWLR; *Australian Broadcasting Corporation v Comalco Ltd* (1986) 12 FCR 510 at 559, per Smithers J.
64. Ibid. This would be a particular problem in regional areas where there is only one local newspaper.

The defence will be defeated if, and only if, the plaintiff proves that the defendant did not honestly hold the opinion expressed—or did not honestly believe the opinion was held by the employee or agent—at the time of the publication of the defamatory matter: s 31(4).

If the opinion is that of a third-party commentator, as in a letter to the editor or a call on talkback radio, the defendant has a defence if the defendant proves that that matter was an expression of opinion of the commentator on a matter of public interest and based on proper material. The onus will then be on the plaintiff to prove the defendant had reasonable grounds to believe that the opinion was not honestly held by the commentator at the time of publication: s 31(3) and (4).

For the purposes of the section, an opinion is based on 'proper material' if based on material that is substantially true or privileged—whether at common law or under the uniform laws—or is otherwise protected under the provisions of the uniform laws: s 31(5).

This defence is intended largely to reflect common law principles. However, it differs from the common law defence in some respects:

(a) It will no longer be a requirement for the defendant to establish as an element of the defence that the comment was objectively fair, in the sense that it was an opinion that an honest commentator could draw from the material. The omission of this element will probably have no substantial impact on the application of fair comment. As discussed above, the common law element was so broadly formulated that even the most emotive, exaggerated, and unreasonable comments would be protected.

(b) The definition of 'proper material' that can be used to found the defence makes it clear that not every fact must be true or privileged, or otherwise protected, in order for the defence to apply. It is enough to prove that there is sufficient material that is true or otherwise protected that can provide a reasonable basis for the comment. This provision resolves a debate at common law as to whether the defendant must justify *every* fact on which the comment is based.[65] The section will make it clear that it is not necessary to justify every fact; it will be enough that the opinion might reasonably be based on such facts that are proven to be true or protected. As at common law, the defence will be lost if based on facts that are distorted or misrepresented.[66]

(c) The statutory defence will be defeated if the plaintiff can prove that the opinion was not honestly held by the defendant (or the employee or agent responsible for publishing the comment). This clarifies that the 'malice' required to defeat the defence is the lack of an honest belief by the defendant in the truth of the

---

65. See, for example, the differences of opinion as to the requirement that facts be justified in: *Australian Broadcasting Corporation v Comalco Ltd* (1986) 12 FCR 510.
66. See: the previous discussion of *Herald & Weekly Times Ltd v Popovic* [2003] VSCA 161.

opinion. As at common law, however, it will be irrelevant that the opinion is unfair, exaggerated or prejudiced; it is sufficient that it is honestly held.

(d) The statutory defence will adopt the common law principle that a defendant who publishes an opinion of a third-party commentator is not required to prove that it agreed with the opinion expressed. However, s 31 provides that the defence will be defeated if the plaintiff can prove the defendant did not have reasonable grounds to believe the opinion was not honestly held by the commentator. That aspect of the defence probably represents a modification to common law principles. At common law, the defendant publisher loses the defence if it acted with malice. Knowledge by the publisher that the third party did not honestly hold the opinion is presumptive evidence of malice; however, a lack of reasonable grounds for believing the opinion was held by the commentator would not generally constitute malice.

ABSOLUTE PRIVILEGE

There are occasions where the free expression of ideas is considered to be so important that absolute protection should be granted to defamatory matter even if the defendant knew the statements to be false and published them with the express intention of harming the plaintiff. The main occasions of absolute privilege are parliamentary proceedings, judicial and quasi-judicial proceedings, and ministerial communications. The unifying rationale for these categories is that they relate to communications that are essential for the effective discharge of the public functions and duties of the legislative, executive, and judicial branches of government.[67] The application of the privilege in a particular circumstance will therefore depend upon whether its application is necessary for the effective discharge of these functions.[68] The privilege is viewed as exceptional, and courts generally are unsympathetic to its expansion.[69]

A defence of absolute privilege is enacted in s 27 of the uniform laws.[70] The section contains a non-exhaustive list of certain publications of matter that are published on occasions of qualified privilege. These categories will be discussed below. Section 27 will also permit additional circumstances of absolute privilege to be specified in Schedule 1,[71] and provides that if the publication would be absolutely privileged in one jurisdiction if published there, it will also be absolutely privileged

---

67. *Mann v O'Neill* (1997) 191 CLR 204 at 213–214, per Brennan CJ, Dawson, Toohey and Gaudron JJ; at 239, per Gummow J; at 264, per Kirby J.
68. *Gibbons v Duffell* (1932) 47 CLR 520 at 528, per Duffy CJ, Rich and Dixon JJ; *Mann v O'Neill* (1997) 191 CLR 204.
69. Ibid.
70. In South Australia this defence will be contained in s 25.
71. This provision is not contained in the South Australian legislation.

in each other jurisdiction: s 27(2)(c) and (d). These provisions ensure that if a State or Territory includes a publication in its equivalent of Schedule 1, then that publication will likewise have the benefit of absolute privilege in all other States and Territories that enact the uniform laws.[72]

Parliamentary proceedings

This is a well-established category of absolute privilege, conferring immunity on members of parliament for anything said or done in the course of parliamentary proceedings.

Section 27 of the uniform laws contains a defence of parliamentary absolute privilege. The section provides that absolute privilege attaches to matter published in the course of the proceedings of a parliamentary body including, but not limited to, the publication of a document by order or under the authority of the body; the publication of debates and proceedings of the body and matter contained in evidence given before the body or while presenting or submitting a document to the body.

The privilege does not, however, extend to statements that are repeated outside of parliament;[73] hence members of parliament are often challenged to 'take it outside'.

Judicial proceedings

At general law, absolute privilege attaches to all statements made in the course of judicial and quasi-judicial[74] proceedings, including statements by witnesses, parties, legal representatives, judicial officers, and members of the jury.[75] The absolute privilege also extends to pleadings, other documents filed in the proceedings, documents tendered as evidence, and other documents properly published as incident to the proceedings.[76]

Section 27 of the uniform laws now provides that matter is published on an occasion of absolute privilege where it is published in the course of the proceedings of an Australian court or tribunal, including in documents lodged or filed in the proceedings, in testimony or evidence given before the court or tribunal, or in any judgment order or other determination of the court or tribunal. This is a non-exhaustive definition of the scope of the privilege and is not intended to cut down

---

72. The New South Wales legislature has specified in Schedule 1 a number of additional publications to which absolute privilege applies, such as matters relating to the Ombudsman or Legal Aid.
73. *Beitzel v Crabb* [1992] 2 VR 121.
74. This is a reference to proceedings of tribunals which act in a manner similar to a court, such as disciplinary tribunals, boards of inquiry and military courts: *Mann v O'Neill* (1997) 191 CLR 204 at 212 (fn 36), 214–15.
75. *Mann v O'Neill* (1997) 191 CLR 204; *Gibbons v Duffell* (1932) 47 CLR 520 at 525; *Cabassi v Vila* (1940) 64 CLR 130; *D'Orta-Ekenaike v Victoria Legal Aid* [2005] HCA 12 at [30].
76. *Mann v O'Neill* (1997) 191 CLR 204 at 211–12.

the scope of the existing privilege enumerated in cases such as *Mann v O'Neill* (1997) 191 CLR 204. The defendant was an unsuccessful litigant in two actions in the Small Claims Court of the Australian Capital Territory. He wrote to the Commonwealth Attorney-General and the Chief Magistrate questioning the mental fitness of the special magistrate who had heard the actions, suggesting that he be suspended while an examination of his fitness to sit was examined. The defendant's letter also requested a rehearing of one of the actions. The defendant subsequently again questioned the mental capacity of the magistrate in a letter to the Minister of Justice. There was no formal procedure for the making of complaints, requesting a rehearing, or the removal or suspension of special magistrates. The defendant relied on the defence of absolute privilege in a defamation action commenced by the magistrate. In the High Court, Brennan CJ with Dawson, Toohey, and Gaudron JJ held that the letters were not published on an occasion of absolute privilege. The rationale for absolute privilege attaching to statements made in the course of judicial proceedings (and also parliamentary proceedings) is that it is necessary for the effective performance of the judicial process (at 213). Persons involved in judicial proceedings—whether witnesses, judges, jury, legal representatives, or litigants—must be able to discharge their duties freely and without fear of civil action for anything said by them in the course of the proceedings. The administration of justice and inquiry into truth would be jeopardised if civil liability were to attach to their statements. The letters in this case were not published on an occasion of absolute privilege, as it was not necessary for the proper administration of justice that they be protected. The sending of the letters did not constitute a further step in the proceedings before the special magistrate, nor were they seeking to initiate an appeal. The letters were 'wholly outside and foreign to the judicial process' (at 214).

Ministerial communications

Absolute privilege attaches to communications between persons holding high executive office in the course of performing their official duties.[77] The privilege unquestionably attaches to ministers (State or federal), and to other high executive officers analogous to ministers,[78] but does not apply to other members of the public service.[79] There is no express provision in the uniform laws dealing with this form of privilege; however, it is clear from s 27 that existing forms of absolute privilege will continue.

---

77. *Catterton v Secretary of State for India* [1895] 2 QB 189; *Mann v O'Neill* (1997) 191 CLR 204 at 258, per Kirby J.
78. See: *Isaacs & Sons Ltd v Cook* [1925] 2 KB 391.
79. *Gibbons v Duffell* (1932) 47 CLR 520 (privilege held not to apply to a report made by a police inspector to his superior officer).

PUBLIC DOCUMENTS

The common law defence of qualified privilege protects the publication of some types of public documents, such as extracts of documents held on a public register and open to public inspection.[80] However, the classes of documents protected at common law have necessarily been developed on an ad hoc basis. Also, the statutory provisions governing the publication of public documents have differed significantly in their ambit, giving rise to considerable confusion.

Section 28 of the uniform laws provides a much-needed comprehensive and nationwide defence for the publication of public documents. Section 28 provides a defence if the defendant proves the matter was published in a public document or a fair copy thereof, or in a fair summary or extract of a public document.[81] The defence will be defeated if the plaintiff proves 'that the defamatory matter was not published honestly for the information of the public or the advancement of education': s 28(3). Section 28 is akin to a qualified privilege defence (discussed below).

Section 28 contains a comprehensive, but not exhaustive, list of documents that fall within its ambit. The definition of 'public document' includes (s 28(4)):

(a) any report or paper published by a parliamentary body,[82] or any record of votes, debates or other proceedings relating to a parliamentary body published under its authority;

(b) any judgment, order or determination of a court or tribunal of any country in civil proceedings, including any record kept by the court or tribunal or report by it of the judgment, order or determination and the reasons for it;

(c) any report or other document that under the law of any country is authorised to be published or required to be presented or tabled before a parliamentary body;

(d) any document issued by the government (including a local authority) of a country, or by an officer, employee or agency of the government, for the information of the public; or

(e) any record or other document open to inspection by the public that is kept by an Australian jurisdiction or under the legislative authority thereof or by an Australian court.

The legislature can specify, in Schedule 2, particular documents or classes of documents that will be treated as public documents.[83] This provision ensures

---

80. *John Jones & Sons Ltd v Financial Times Ltd* (1909) 25 TLR 677.
81. A document does not lose protection as a public document merely because it does not strictly comply with formalities regarding content, layout or time frames: s 28(2).
82. Defined as including parliaments or legislatures, or a committee thereof, of any country: s 5.
83. The South Australian draft legislation does not make provision for Schedule 2.

that documents specified in Schedule 2 by one State or Territory will also have the benefit of the defence in all other jurisdictions that enact the model provisions.[84]

Some of the public documents referred to—such as the votes and proceedings of a parliamentary body under its authority, and judgments of courts and tribunals—will also fall within the absolute privilege defence in s 27 or at common law, and therefore will be absolutely protected (not affected by proof of malice). Section 28 extends protection to publications of these documents or fair extracts or summaries of them by third parties, provided the defendant was not acting with malice. For example, the section would protect the publication of a fair summary or extract from a public document for teaching purposes, such as where a law lecturer summarises a case for students. It would also allow the publication of judicial decisions on legal databases such as Austlii as well as the publication of the case in the hard-copy reports, and also the headnote, provided it is a fair summary of the case.

REPORTS OF PROCEEDINGS OF PUBLIC CONCERN

At common law, fair and accurate reports of parliamentary[85] and judicial proceedings[86] attract qualified privilege. For instance, a newspaper or television report providing a fair and accurate summary of a parliamentary debate, or of civil or criminal proceedings, would be privileged provided it was not published with malice. The privilege might also attach to reports of proceedings of other public bodies where such reports are in the public interest, as determined on a case-by-case basis.[87] The defence of qualified privilege is discussed below.

The common law privilege regarding fair reports was enacted in legislation in each Australian jurisdiction, but the different defences varied considerably in terms of the proceedings to which they related and the limitations to which they were subject. The uniform defamation laws provide much-needed clarity. Section 29[88] provides a defence to the publication of defamatory matter if the defendant proves that the matter was, or was contained in, a fair report of any proceedings of public concern. It will also be a defence if the matter was contained in an earlier published report of proceedings of public concern and the defendant can prove that its publication was a fair copy, summary, or extract from the earlier published report, and that it had no knowledge that would reasonably have made it aware that the

---

84. There is a number of documents included in Schedule 2 of the New South Wales legislation, including documents relating to medical and legal disciplinary tribunals, documents arising under workers compensation legislation, and documents relating to special commissions of inquiry and administrative tribunal decisions.
85. *Wason v Walter* (1968) LR 4 QB 73.
86. *Kimber v Press Association Ltd* [1893] 1 QB 65.
87. See the discussion by Brennan J in: *Stephens v West Australian Newspapers Ltd* (1994) 182 CLR 211 at 247–9.
88. Section 27 in South Australia.

earlier published report was not fair: s 29(2). The defence will be defeated if (and only if) the plaintiff proves 'that the defamatory matter was not published honestly for the information of the public or the advancement of education': s 29(3).

There is a comprehensive and exhaustive definition of 'proceedings of public concern' in s 29(4). That definition includes:

(a) public proceedings of a parliamentary body;[89]
(b) public proceedings of a local government body of any Australian jurisdiction;
(c) public proceedings of the governments or international organisations of any country and of any international conference at which governments of any country are represented;
(d) public proceedings of a court or arbitral tribunal of any country and of international courts or tribunals;
(e) public proceedings of an inquiry held under legislative or governmental authority of any country;
(f) proceedings of a learned society, sport or recreation association or trade association to the extent the proceedings related to a decision or adjudication made in Australia about members of the association or subject to legal control by the association;
(g) proceedings of a public meeting of shareholders of an Australian public corporation held anywhere in Australia;
(h) proceedings of an ombudsman of any country if the proceedings related to a report of the ombudsman; and
(i) public proceedings of a law reform body of any country.

The section will make provision for the specification of further classes of proceedings of public concern in Schedule 3, and ensure that if one jurisdiction includes a class of proceedings in Schedule 3, then those proceedings will also have the benefit of the defence in all other States and Territories that enact the model provisions.

There is no definition in the section of what constitutes a 'fair report'; therefore, this must be determined by reference to common law principles. According to the authorities, to be 'fair' the report must be an accurate summary of the proceedings which does not distort the facts or provide a misleading impression.[90] The critical issue is whether the report 'substantially records what was said and done'.[91] A report will not be fair where the defamatory sting is added by the journalist rather than by a repetition or summary of what occurred in the proceedings.[92] The

---

89. Defined as including parliaments or legislatures, or a committee thereof, of any country: s 5.
90. *Jones v Fairfax* (1986) 4 NSWLR 466.
91. *Waterhouse v Broadcasting Station 2GB Pty Ltd* (1985) 1 NSWLR 58 at 65, endorsed in *Cornwall v Rowan* (2004) 90 SASR 269 at 405.
92. *Rogers v Nationwide News Ltd* 216 CLR 327 at 338, per Gleeson CJ and Gummow J.

publication in question must also bear the character of a 'report'. A mere repetition of information obtained from proceedings might not be sufficient to give the document the character of a 'report'; it must constitute the journalist's account of the events as they happened.[93] A 'report' cannot 'properly include the independent comments or opinions of the reporter',[94] nor can a debate between two antagonists generally be construed as a 'report'.[95]

COMMON LAW QUALIFIED PRIVILEGE

Introduction

It is a defence at common law that the matter was published in good faith on an occasion of qualified privilege. The defence has been developed on the basis of a broad general principle that the 'common convenience and welfare of society'[96] demands that communications published on particular occasions be privileged. The privilege is 'qualified' because it will be lost if the plaintiff proves that the defendant was actuated by ill will or other improper motive.

It is critical to the defence that there exists a reciprocity of duty or interest between the publisher and the recipient.[97] The publisher must have a legitimate interest or duty in publishing the information to the recipient, who must have a corresponding legitimate interest or duty in receiving this information.[98] In this context, 'duty' is not limited to a legal duty, but also refers to occasions where the defendant has a 'social or moral' duty to communicate the matter. In *Stuart v Bell* [1891] 2 QB 341,[99] Lindley LJ (at 350) stated that a 'social or moral' duty refers to a duty 'recognised by … people of ordinary intelligence and moral principle'. The test is: 'Would the great mass of right-minded people in the position of the defendant have considered it their duty, under the circumstances, to make the communication?'

The privilege will be lost if publication is made too broadly; publication must be limited to those to whom the defendant has a legitimate interest or duty in communicating the information and who in turn have a legitimate interest or duty in receiving that information.[100] It follows that, putting to one side the extended qualified privilege relating to political and governmental communications, communications made by the media to the public at large will generally exceed the

---

93. *Rogers v Nationwide News Ltd* 216 CLR 327 at 338.
94. *Burchett v Kane* [1980] 2 NSWLR 266.
95. *Cornwall v Rowan* (2004) 90 SASR 269 at 406.
96. *Toogood v Spyring* (1834) 1 CM&R 181 at 193; 149 ER 1044 at 1049–50.
97. Ibid.
98. *Adam v Ward* [1917] AC 309 at 334, per Parke B.
99. [1891] 2 QB 341. See also *Australian Broadcasting Corporation v Comalco* (1986) 12 FCR 510 at 533–4, per Smithers J.
100. *Mowlds v Fergusson* (1939) 40 SR (NSW) 311 at 318, per Jordan CJ.

limits of privilege.[101] This is because not every member of the public will have a legitimate interest or duty to receive the information. It is not sufficient merely that the members of the public are 'interested in' that material, as explained by Brennan J in *Stephens v West Australian Newspapers Limited* (1994) 182 CLR 211, at 242–3:

> When a publication is said to have been made in discharge of a social or moral duty, the occasion is privileged only if it be in 'the interest of the community', 'for the welfare of society' or 'for the good of society in general'—these phrases being synonyms for Baron Parke's [in *Toogood v Spyring* (1834) 1 CM&R 181; 149 ER 1044] 'for the common convenience and welfare of society'. When it is said that a publication is privileged because it is made in the public interest, 'interest' is not to be equated with curiosity. It is used in a non-technical sense to mean that the publication is made for the welfare of society. As [*Telegraph Newspaper Co Ltd v Beford*] illustrates, a publication defamatory of the plaintiff is not made on an occasion of qualified privilege merely because the person or persons to whom it is made—in that case, the readers of the newspaper—were interested in the subject matter. And, if the publication is made to protect an interest of the person making the defamatory statement, the publication is protected only if it be made to 'a person who, if the defamatory matter be true, may reasonably be expected to be of service in the protection of the interest'. The common law places a higher value on the protection of personal reputation than on the satisfaction of curiosity or on the dissemination of defamatory material which is not reasonably calculated to be of service in the protection of the interests of the person making the defamatory statement. [footnotes omitted]

The categories of qualified privilege are not closed,[102] and can be adapted or extended from time to time meet the 'the varying conditions of society'.[103] For the purposes of this chapter, the occasions of common law privilege are grouped under three main headings: first, public interest; second, protection of an interest of the publisher or recipient, or a common interest of both the publisher and recipient; and third, political and governmental communications.

Public interest

The publication of defamatory matter will be protected where it 'is of information on a subject of legitimate public interest of such a nature that for the convenience

---

101. *Stephens v West Australian Newspapers Ltd*(1994) 182 CLR 211 at 243–6, per Brennan J; at 261, per McHugh J; *Lange v Australian Broadcasting Corporation* (1997) 189 CLR 520 at 570–2; *Australian Broadcasting Corporation v Comalco* (1986) 12 FCR 510.
102. *London Association for Protection of Trade v Greenlands Ltd* [1916] 2 AC 15 at 23; *Herald & Weekly Times Ltd v Popovic* [2003] VSCA 161 at [69].
103. *Wason v Walter* (1968) LR 4 QB 73 at 93; *Stephens v West Australian Newspapers Ltd* (1994) 182 CLR 211 at 240, per Brennan J.

and benefit of society there is a duty in the publisher to publish.'[104] Matters that are a legitimate subject of public interest have been held to include discussion of the views, performance and suitability for office of members of parliament and those seeking election to parliament;[105] alleged misconduct by senior army officers;[106] and fair reports of parliamentary and judicial proceedings.[107] The privilege will only attach however where the publication is restricted to those persons who have a legitimate interest in knowing the matter. As previously discussed, this requirement greatly reduces the ability of the media to rely on this defence to protect a communication made to the public at large—for example, to the national audience of a television consumer affairs program.[108] As discussed above, it is necessary to distinguish between matters that are in the public interest and those that are merely of interest to the public. The public must not merely be interested in the matter as a matter of gossip or curiosity, but as a matter of substance.[109] Accordingly, there is no privilege for a media organisation to publish a report containing defamatory matter merely because it is of general interest to its audience. It follows that the mass publication of defamatory matter by national media organisations will not ordinarily be privileged because not every viewer, listener, or reader—or even the great majority of them—will have a legitimate interest in receiving that information, as opposed to being curious about it.[110] Thus, in *Australian Broadcasting Corporation v Comalco* (1986) 12 FCR 510, the broadcast by a national current affairs program of matter derogating the treatment of Aboriginal communities in Weipa by a mining corporation was not privileged as members of the public generally did not have a legitimate interest in receipt of this information, and therefore the ABC did not have a legitimate duty or interest to publish it to them. This was so even though the treatment of Aboriginal people was an important matter of public concern.

There might be limited instances where publication to a mass audience is protected—for example, publication of information issued by the government to ensure that the public is not deceived,[111] and publication of warnings to the public about potential dangers such as unsafe products or contaminated food[112]—at least in circumstances where publication in the media is the 'only reasonable mode

---

104. *Australian Broadcasting Corporation v Comalco* (1986) 12 FCR 510 at 534, per Smithers J.
105. *Roberts v Bass* [2002] 212 CLR 1.
106. *Adam v Ward* [1917] AC 309.
107. Section 29 of the uniform laws now provides a defence in respect of fair reports of proceedings of public concern. This is discussed below.
108. *Stephens v West Australian Newspapers Ltd* (1994) 182 CLR 211 at 249, per Brennan J; *Australian Broadcasting Corporation v Comalco* (1986) 12 FCR 510.
109. *Stephens v West Australian Newspapers Ltd* (1994) 182 CLR 211 at 244–5, per Brennan J; *Howe v Lees* (1910) 11 CLR 361 at 398, per Higgins J.
110. *Stephens v West Australian Newspapers Ltd* (1994) 182 CLR 211 at 243–6, per Brennan J; at 261, per McHugh J; *Lange v Australian Broadcasting Corporation* (1997) 189 CLR 520 at 570, 572.
111. *Dunford Publicity Studios Ltd v News Media Ownership Ltd* [1971] NZLR 961.
112. *Camporese v Parton* (1983) 150 DLR (3d) 208.

of communication'.[113] However, in most situations, mass publication will not be privileged. Thus, while a newspaper in possession of information that a medical practitioner is practising without a licence would be protected in communicating that information to the proper State and professional authorities, it would not be protected for a mass publication of that information to its general readership.[114] The strictness of the requirement for reciprocity has been justified on the basis that:[115]

> If the law were different ... it would be a charter for scandal-mongering. Personal reputations could be destroyed by any person who honestly believed the scandal for, in that event, the possibility of vindication would be denied. The massive power of the modern media would be free both to define the subjects of public debate and to feed those debates with information having no more substantial provenance than the publisher's own belief in its truth.

The limitations on the ability of media organisations to publish matter to the public at large led to the establishment of an extended category of political and governmental qualified privilege in *Lange v Australian Broadcasting Corporation* (1997) 189 CLR 520. This defence is discussed below.

Protection of an interest of the publisher, of the recipient, or both

There are other occasions where defamatory communications 'fairly warranted by any reasonable occasion or exigency, and honestly made ... are protected for the common convenience and welfare of society'.[116] Broadly speaking, those occasions fall within three limbs: response to an attack on the publisher (self-defence); defence of the interests of the recipient and protection of the common interest of the publisher and recipient.

Self-defence

A defamatory communication is made on an occasion of privilege where it is published by way of a response to an attack on the defendant's reputation and in vindication of that reputation. The defendant is entitled to publish the defence to those who might be of service in vindicating his or her reputation and others with a legitimate interest in receiving that information.[117] In this respect, the courts have shown a willingness to take a broad approach to determining those persons with a legitimate interest in knowing of the response. In *Mowlds v Fergusson* (1940) 64

---

113. *Stephens v West Australian Newspapers Ltd* (1994) 182 CLR 211 at 263, per McHugh J.
114. *Smith's Newspapers Ltd v Becker* (1932) 47 CLR 279.
115. *Stephens v West Australian Newspapers Ltd* (1994) 182 CLR 211 at 245–6, per Brennan J.
116. *Toogood v Spyring* (1834) 1 CM&R 181.
117. *Mowlds v Fergusson* (1940) 64 CLR 206 at 215, per Dixon J.

CLR 206, the defendant, a senior police officer, was severely criticised by a Royal Commissioner in respect of a report he had made in a matter involving the conduct of the plaintiff. Later, at the request of the New South Wales Premier, the defendant made a further report on the same matter, seeking to justify the earlier report. The later report contained matter defamatory of the plaintiff. The defendant showed his second report to Childs, who had been Commissioner of Police at the time the first report was made, but who had since resigned. The plaintiff argued that the publication to Childs was not privileged as Childs, no longer being Commissioner of Police, had no more than curiosity in the subject-matter of the report. The High Court found that the report was published to Childs on an occasion of privilege as the required reciprocity of interest or duty was present. The defendant had a legitimate interest in defending his professional reputation to his former chief and in seeking his assistance and support, and Childs had a legitimate interest in his own prior administration of the service and in knowing that his former trusted subordinate had not deceived him (Starke J at 212, Williams J agreeing):

> The law does not allow idle curiosity in the concerns of others, but the [defendant] had a duty or interest, moral or social, to justify himself to his former chief and his former chief had a duty or interest, moral or social, to hear his answer to the comments made upon him or his apologia.[118]

If the attack on the defendant's reputation is made publicly, the defendant is entitled to publish the response to members of the public who would have become aware of it as those members of the public should be taken to have an interest in receiving the response.[119]

Protection of the interests of the recipient

The publication of defamatory matter will be privileged where required to protect a legitimate interest of the recipient and where the defendant has a legal or moral duty or interest to make it. Accordingly, a character reference by an employer to another person considering engaging the employee would be privileged;[120] the employer has a social duty to give the reference and the recipient has a commercial interest in receiving it. Accusations made about the plaintiff to the police who are investigating the commission of a crime would also be privileged under this limb,[121] as would the communication of suspicions about the character of a person employed by the recipient.[122]

---

118. See also: at 215–16, per Dixon J.
119. *Coward v Wellington* (1836) 7 Car & P 531; 173 ER 234; *Adam v Ward* [1917] AC 309; *Mowlds v Fergusson* (1940) 64 CLR 206 at 219, per Williams J.
120. *Kelly v Partington* (1833) 4 B&Ad 700; 110 ER 619; *Phelps v Kemsley* (1942) 168 LT 18.
121. *Kine v Sekwell* (1838) 3 M&W 297.
122. *Stuart v Bell* [1891] 2 QB 341.

Furtherance of a 'community of interest' between the publisher and recipient

A defamatory communication will be protected where the publication is made to further a 'community of interest' between the publisher and recipient in having the matter known. In *Switzerland Australia Health Fund Pty Ltd v Shaw* (1988) 81 ALR 111, the plaintiff was a small health insurance fund which had newly entered the Victorian market. The defendant was a large and well-established fund with a significant market share in Victoria. The plaintiff approached the Private Hospital Association of Victoria (PHAV) offering to reduce the gap between benefits and hospital expenses for its members if PHAV would endorse its action and publish an advertisement congratulating the plaintiff on this action. This proposal was agreed to at a regular meeting of the executive of PHAV and an advertisement was duly issued in the daily newspapers congratulating the plaintiff and urging the other health funds to take similar action. The defendant's general manager subsequently sent a letter to each of the eighty-two members of PHAV stating, *inter alia*, that PHAV had decided to endorse a small health fund which 'is badly perceived by the public'. This statement imputed that the plaintiff's fund was held in poor regard by, or had a bad reputation with, the general public, and it was therefore defamatory. Woodward J in the Federal Court rejected the defendant's argument that the matter was privileged as having been made on occasion of self-defence. The advertisement did not constitute an occasion of attack on the defendant such as to justify such a vigorous and defamatory response. Nevertheless, the letter was privileged on the basis that it was made on a subject of common interest of both the publisher and recipients. The executive body of PHAV had sided with one of two business competitors in a way that could potentially give that competitor a significant commercial advantage. In those circumstances, the defendant had a legitimate business interest in putting its case to the members of the body that had acted against its interests, and the members of the body had a legitimate interest in knowing whether PHAV was acting inappropriately in endorsing the plaintiff's fund.

Extended qualified privilege: political and governmental communications

In a groundbreaking decision, the High Court in *Lange v Australian Broadcasting Corporation* (1997) 189 CLR 520 unanimously expanded common law qualified privilege by extending protection to communications of 'political and governmental matters' made to the public at large. The court held that the freedom of the public to discuss, argue, and inform itself on matters of government and politics is an indispensable element of the system of representative and responsible government as created by the Constitution. It is therefore crucial in a representative democracy that information about governmental and political matters be communicated to the widest possible audience. Members of the public must be free to communicate with each other on matters that could affect their voting choices or that could throw light on the performance of ministers and the conduct of the executive branch of government. The court considered that the existing law relating to qualified privilege unreasonably impaired that freedom as it was only in exceptional circumstances that it would permit mass communication to the public at large. The law of qualified privilege had to be expanded to ensure that the constitutional freedom of political and governmental debate was not unduly restricted. Accordingly, the court declared (at 571):

> each member in the Australian community has an interest in disseminating and receiving information, opinions and arguments concerning government and political matters that affect the people of Australia. The duty to disseminate such information is simply the correlative of the interest in receiving it. The common convenience and welfare of Australian society are advanced by discussion—the giving and receiving of information—about government and political matters. The interest that each member of the Australian community has in such a discussion extends the categories of qualified privilege. Consequently, those categories now must be recognised as protecting a communication made to the public on a government or political matter.

To establish the defence the defendant must establish two elements:

(a) the defamatory publication concerns political or governmental matters; and
(b) the publication was reasonable in all the circumstances.

As with the other categories of common law privilege, the defence will be defeated if the plaintiff can establish the defendant was motivated by malice.

It should be noted that the expanded version of the defence does not exhaustively define the circumstances where political and governmental communications are privileged. The conventional forms of the defence discussed above continue to apply to restricted publication of political and governmental matter where the required reciprocity of interest or duty is present.[123] It will usually only be necessary to rely on the *Lange* defence where the publication was made to the general public.

Matters of political or governmental discussion

This expanded version of the qualified privilege defence will be available only where the matter complained of has a sufficient nexus with political and governmental matters. What is encompassed within the conception of political and government matters will depend on the circumstances of each case.[124] At the core of the privilege

---

123. *Roberts v Bass* (2002) 212 CLR 1 at 29.
124. *Herald & Weekly Times Ltd v Popovic* [2003] VSCA 161 at [241, per Gillard J. See also: Winneke ACJ at [7], [9].

are criticism, discussion, argument, and provision of information regarding the views, performance and capacity of members of parliament or candidates for election, and of their suitability for public office. Also central to the defence will be discussions relating to the executive arm of government as well as the views, performances and suitability for office of those in the executive government. Accordingly, discussion of the policies and actions of government departments and the relevant minister will be within the defence, as would discussions about the public conduct of senior public servants and their fitness for office. The defence should also extend to the performance and policies of statutory authorities and other statutory bodies such as Medicare and CentreLink. It is clear that the defence is not limited to a discussion of federal politics or government but also to politics at a State, Territory, and local government level. In *Lange* it was said (at 571–2):

> discussion of government or politics at State or Territory level and even at local government level is amenable to protection by the extended category of qualified privilege, whether or not it bears on matters at the federal level. Of course, the discussion of matters at State, Territory or local level might bear on the choice that the people have to make in federal elections or in voting to amend the Constitution, and on their evaluation of the performance of federal Ministers and their departments. The existence of national political parties operating at federal, State, Territory and local government levels, the financial dependence of State, Territory and local governments on federal funding and policies, and the increasing integration of social, economic and political matters in Australia make this conclusion inevitable.

A discussion of the private conduct of a member of parliament or of the executive government would not normally be covered by the defence, although it will be different if that conduct impacts upon his or her performance in, or suitability for, office. Thus, hypothetically, a revelation that a leader of a major political party appears to have a drinking problem which is impacting upon his performance as a member of parliament and political leader would arguably constitute a matter of political discussion.

While it is clear that criticism and discussion of the public views, conduct, and fitness for office of members of the political and executive branches of government fall within the defence, it is more controversial whether discussions concerning members of the judiciary will fall within it. In a case preceding *Lange*,[125] the High Court had stated in obiter that the defence might apply to members of the judiciary. This issue subsequently arose directly for consideration by the Victorian Court of Appeal in *Herald & Weekly Times Ltd v Popovic* [2003] VSCA 161. One of the issues before the court was whether criticism of the conduct of a magistrate in a particular

---

125. *Theophanous v Herald & Weekly Times Ltd* (1994) 182 CLR 104 at 123–34.

case would be a political and governmental matter. A majority of the court held that that it was not. Winneke ACJ (at [9]) stated the following:

> I do not consider that a criticism of the performance of a magistrate in the management of an isolated proceeding in his or her court is a discussion of political or government matters in the sense that such discussion is necessary for the effective operation of representative and responsible government. Quite apart from the fact that—as Spigelman CJ pointed out (in a different context) in *John Fairfax Pty Ltd v Attorney-General (NSW)* (2000) 181 ALR 694 at 709—the conduct of courts 'is not, of itself, a manifestation of any of the provisions relating to representative government upon which the freedom is based', the conduct of individual judicial officers is carried out independently of the legislative and executive branches of government, and is not to be described, in my view, as an exercise of power at a government or administrative level. It can be conceded that judicial officers are 'public figures' appointed, or recommended for appointment, by the executive branch of government. It can also be conceded that the executive branch of government has a strong interest in the due administration of justice. However those concessions, at least to my mind, do not carry with them the implication that a discussion about the discharge by a judicial officer of his or her function in a particular case is a discussion concerning political or government matters in the relevant sense.

Winneke ACJ recognised that discussion about a particular judicial officer might be a matter of political or governmental discussion where the discussion involves the actions or failure to act by the executive arm of government to appoint or remove a judge. However, discussion of the manner in which a judicial officer discharged his or her functions in an individual case was of a different nature, not falling within the ambit of political or governmental discussion, even where it involved an expression of opinion that the judicial officer was not fit for office (at [10]). Warren AJA also held that the defence does not extend to discussions concerning judicial officers as the judiciary is a separate organ of government. On the other hand, Gillard AJA expressed the provisional view that discussion of the conduct of a magistrate in a particular case could amount to a matter of political or governmental discussion. A judicial officer, although independent of government, is a servant of the public performing a very important public task entrusted to it by the government. Judicial officers are appointed by the government and paid out of public funds. Furthermore, the administration of justice is a vital and essential ingredient in the system of government. Accordingly, the conduct of judicial officers and their fitness for office are matters that every member of the Victorian community has a real and legitimate interest in knowing about (at [248]–[252]).

Notwithstanding the wider view of Gillard AJA, it follows from the views of the majority that on the current state of the law a discussion of the judiciary will constitute a political or governmental matter only where it intersects with the parliamentary or executive government—for example, because it involves a matter of governmental policy or the exercise or failure to exercise powers by the executive to appoint members of the judiciary. Similar views have also been expressed by members of the New South Wales Court of Appeal.[126]

The extent to which the notion of political and governmental discussion would extend to discussion of the public views and conduct of persons who are engaged in the wider political process—trade union leaders, Aboriginal political leaders, environmental activists, political lobby groups, religious leaders, and political and economic commentators and the like—is also presently unclear. In *Theophanous v Herald & Weekly Times Ltd* (1994) 182 CLR 104, a decision of the High Court preceding *Lange*,[127] Mason CJ, with Gaudron and Toohey JJ, considered that such matters would be 'political or governmental' in nature, endorsing the idea that 'political speech' encompasses all discussion relevant to the development of public opinion on the range of issues on which citizens should inform themselves (at 124). However, the current state of authority suggests that *Lange* has adopted a narrower conception of political and governmental matters that would protect only those communications that have a direct nexus to voting choices.[128] It is not enough that the defamatory matter relates to a matter of public interest or debate. In *Conservation Council of SA Inc v Chapman* (2003) 87 SASR 62, the Full Court of the Supreme Court of South Australia held that the mere fact that the defamatory statements relate to or contribute to ongoing public comment and debate on a matter of public concern does not mean those statements are political or governmental in nature. In that case, the defamatory statements related to the ongoing public controversy over the construction of a bridge to Hindmarsh Island in South Australia. The plaintiffs were property developers, planning a development on Hindmarsh Island, who claimed they were defamed by a number of publications by the Conservation Council and its officers in the course of a campaign against building the bridge. The plaintiffs complained that the publications imputed they had commenced court proceedings for the purpose of suppressing freedom of speech and stifling debate over the bridge issue. A majority, Doyle CJ and Besanko J, held that the defamatory matter did not fall within the *Lange* defence. Discussion of the conduct and motivations of a private individual in commencing court proceedings is not a political or governmental matter, and the mere fact that the conduct had occurred

---

126. *John Fairfax Publications Pty Ltd v Attorney-General (NSW)* (2000) 181 ALR 694 at 709, per Spigelman CJ (Priestley JA agreeing); *John Fairfax Publications Pty Ltd v O'Shane* [2005] NSWCA 164 at [250] ff, per Young CJ.
127. The court in *Theophanous* recognised an implied constitutional defence concerning political and governmental discussion, however this was rejected in *Lange* in favour of extending the doctrine of qualified privilege.
128. Meagher D, 'What is Political Communication? The Rationale and Scope of the Implied Freedom of Political Communication' [2004] *Melbourne University Law Review* 14; Kenyon AT, '*Lange* and *Reynolds* Qualified Privilege: Australian and English Defamation Law and Practice' [2004] *Melbourne University Law Review* 14.

in the course of an important public debate about the impact of the bridge on the environment and Aboriginal interests was not sufficient to characterise it in this way.[129] For the *Lange* defence to apply, the discussion must pertain to the conduct of a public officer and not merely that of a private individual.[130]

Reasonableness of publication

The High Court, in *Lange v Australian Broadcasting Corporation* (1997) 189 CLR 520, at 573, incorporated into the expanded political and governmental form of the defence an additional condition of 'reasonableness of publication'. This additional requirement applies only where the defendant has sought to invoke the expanded category of qualified privilege to protect a publication which otherwise would be held to have been to too wide an audience. Whether the defendant's conduct in publishing the matter was reasonable must be judged in all the circumstances of each case; however, the court in *Lange* stated (at 573) that generally the defendant's conduct will not be reasonable unless the defendant establishes that it was unaware of the falsity of the matter and did not act recklessly in making the publication. In addition, under the *Lange* doctrine (at 574), the defendant would also generally need to prove that it:

(a) had reasonable grounds for believing the imputation was true;
(b) took reasonable steps to verify the accuracy of the material and did not believe it to be untrue; and
(c) where practicable, had sought a response from the person defamed and published the response.

These factors direct attention to considerations such as the reliability and integrity of the defendant's source, whether the defendant has published the substance of the plaintiff's side of the story, and whether the defendant conducted investigations into the truth of the allegations that were adequate, taking into account the seriousness of the allegations.

The degree of accuracy of the facts on which the communication is based will be an important factor in determining reasonableness. In *Herald & Weekly Times Ltd v Popovic* [2003] VSCA 161, the Victorian Court of Appeal emphasised that a judge should be very cautious to find that a publication was reasonable where it is based on facts that have been proved to be untrue. In that case (the facts of which are stated above) the publisher's conduct was judged unreasonable as it had distorted

---

129. *Conservation Council of SA Inc v Chapman* (2003) 87 SASR 62 at 71, per Doyle CJ; at 128–9, per Besanko J. See also: *Orion Pet Products Pty Ltd v RSPCA* (2002) 120 FCR 191.
130. Cf *Cornwall v Rowan* (2004) 90 SASR 269 (discussions whether a government minister had acted correctly in withdrawing funding for a women's refuge were political or governmental in nature).

the facts that were central to the article.[131] It was said that it would be in a 'very rare case'[132] that publishers could be found to have acted reasonably where they had failed to provide a fair and accurate account of the facts. The defence of qualified privilege should not be used to protect 'slipshod' journalism.[133]

The publication of material is not reasonable where the publisher's conclusions do not logically follow from the material obtained. In *John Fairfax Publications Pty Ltd v O'Shane* [2005] NSWCA 164, the defendant publisher was found by the New South Wales Court of Appeal to have acted unreasonably in making generalised statements regarding the impartiality and fitness for office of the plaintiff magistrate, where the views in question could not reasonably follow from the material obtained by the journalist during the course of researching the story.

The factors enumerated in the new statutory defence of qualified privilege in s 30 of the uniform laws (based on s 22 of the *Defamation Act 1974* (NSW)) provide additional guidance as to relevant factors going to reasonableness of publication for the purposes of the *Lange* defence.[134] These factors, which are set out in full below, include the extent to which the matter distinguishes between suspicions, allegations and proven facts; the nature of the business environment in which the defendant operates; and whether it is in the public interest in the circumstances for the matter to be published expeditiously.

As stated previously, the requirement of reasonableness applies only where the defendant seeks to rely on the extended qualified privilege defence relating to political and governmental communications to the public at large. It does not apply where the conventional forms of the defence are invoked. A defendant who has restricted the communication of political or governmental information to a restricted group of persons with a legitimate interest in receiving that information will not need to prove the additional reasonableness element. For instance, a member of the public who makes a complaint to a minister concerning the administration of his or her government department can rely on the conventional form of the defence, and therefore the reasonableness of his or her conduct will not be in issue.[135] Likewise, the communication of views about the conduct of a candidate for election published only to members of the relevant electorate would be privileged on conventional principles, and therefore the defendant would once again not be required to prove reasonableness.[136]

---

131. *Herald & Weekly Times Ltd v Popovic* [2003] VSCA 161 at [12], per Winneke ACJ; at [221], per Gillard AJA (Warren AJA agreeing).
132. Ibid at [221].
133. Ibid at [12], [14], per Winneke ACJ; see also: *Austin v Mirror Newspapers Ltd* [1986] 1 AC 299 at 313, 317. The defendant journalist also acted unreasonably in failing to seek a response from the plaintiff magistrate.
134. *John Fairfax Publications Pty Ltd v O'Shane* [2005] NSWCA 164 at [308], per Young CJ.
135. *Lange v Australian Broadcasting Corporation* (1997) 189 CLR 520 at 573.
136. *Roberts v Bass* [2002] 212 CLR 1 at 27–8, 59.

Malice and qualified privilege

The defence of qualified privilege (including the expanded category of privilege concerning political and governmental communications) is lost if the plaintiff can prove that the defendant had been motivated by malice. Malice is established where the defendant in making the publication was predominantly motivated by an improper purpose in making the publication.[137] A defendant loses the protection of the privilege where the dominant purpose[138] for defaming the plaintiff was one that was foreign to the privileged occasion, such as a desire to injure the plaintiff because of ill will or spite. For instance, a complaint to an employer about a fellow employee's performance will lose the protection of privilege if the complainant was primarily motivated by feelings of hatred toward the fellow employee, rather than because of a genuine desire to protect the employer's interests. It is not sufficient for the plaintiff to prove merely that malice existed (for example, that the defendant felt ill will toward the plaintiff); the plaintiff must prove that the defendant was *actuated* to make the publication because of the improper motive.[139]

The High Court has examined the concept of malice at some length in *Roberts v Bass* [2002] 212 CLR 1. The facts were that Rodney Bass sued Geoffrey Roberts and Kenneth Case for defamation in respect of a number of publications issued during the course of Bass' campaign for election to a seat in the South Australian Parliament. When the publications were made, Bass was the sitting member in the relevant seat and Roberts and Case were electors in that electorate and an adjoining electorate respectively. Bass commenced defamation proceedings against Roberts in respect of three publications prepared by Roberts. The first two publications were a mock postcard and an election pamphlet sent to all households in the electorate in which Bass was portrayed as a 'frequent flyer' and which included a mock-up of a frequent flyer statement containing information fabricated by Roberts. The third was a 'How to Vote' card distributed at polling booths on election day. Bass commenced defamation proceedings against Case for distributing the publications. Each of the three publications contained defamatory imputations that Bass had misused public moneys for his own personal benefit to the detriment of his constituents, including that he had taken advantage of his position as a member of parliament to obtain a free holiday in Nauru and to accrue frequent flyer points for his and family's use and benefit.

The main judgment was a joint judgment of Gaudron, McHugh, and Gummow JJ. Kirby J agreed in substance with the discussion of malice in the joint judgment—at least in so far as it related to political and governmental communications. The main issue on the appeal was whether Roberts and Case published

---

137. *Horrocks v Lowe* [1975] AC 30; *Roberts v Bass* (2002) 212 CLR 1 at 11–12, per Gleeson CJ; at 30, per Gaudron, McHugh and Gummow JJ.
138. *Roberts v Bass* [2002] 212 CLR 1 at 41.
139. Ibid.

the matter with malice so as to lose the protection of the defence. The joint judgment made a number of important statements about the nature of malice in the context of the defence of qualified privilege:[140]

1. Malice will be established where the statement was predominantly motivated by an improper purpose, ie, a purpose foreign to the duty or interest that protects the making of the statement. Proof merely that the defendant held ill will or animosity toward the plaintiff is not sufficient to establish malice; it is necessary to prove that the ill will or animosity was the predominant motivation for making the publication.
2. Knowledge of the falsity of the defamatory matter is not an independent head of malice, nor is proof of knowledge of falsity in itself sufficient to establish malice. The motive of the publisher in publishing the defamatory matter is paramount. However, proof that the defendant knew the defamatory matter to be false is *almost invariably conclusive evidence* that the publication was actuated by an improper motive. There will be exceptional cases where the defendant can establish that, despite knowledge of falsity, he or she was motivated by a proper purpose, however this will be a difficult evidentiary onus to discharge.
3. In exceptional cases, sheer recklessness by the defendant in making the defamatory statement might justify a finding of malice. This will be the situation where the defendant's recklessness was so gross as to constitute wilful blindness, in the sense that the defendant has deliberately refrained from making enquires because he or she prefers not to know the truth. The law will treat wilful blindness as equivalent to knowledge of falsity.
4. A mere lack of belief in the truth of the matter is not to be treated as equivalent to knowledge of falsity and therefore as almost conclusive proof of malice. It is not enough to establish malice that the defendant did not have a positive belief in the truth of the matter, for example where the defendant merely assumed that the matter was true or did not turn his or her mind to the question of truth (unless amounting to wilful blindness).
5. Mere carelessness in making the statement or in failing to reasonably investigate the matter never provides a ground for inferring malice. The law of qualified privilege requires the defendant to use the occasion for a proper purpose, but imposes no obligation on the defendant to act carefully: 'even irrationality, stupidity or refusal to face facts concerning the plaintiff'[141] does not constitute malice.
6. A failure by the defendant to apologise or correct the false material when discovered is not evidence of malice.

---

140. *Roberts v Bass* [2002] 212 CLR 1 at 30–41.
141. Ibid at 41.

Where the defamatory publication concerns the public views and conduct of a member of parliament or candidate for election, their Honours endorsed the view in *Lange*[142] that the mere fact the defendant is motivated to cause political damage to the plaintiff is not an improper motive that would amount to malice.[143] The publication of matter with the intention of harming a candidate's political reputation so as to cause an electoral defeat is at the core of the electoral and democratic system. There is nothing improper about such a motive, so long as the defendant is using the occasion to express views regarding the political views or fitness for office of the candidate, however vigorously. The privilege is lost only where the publication was made for a purpose inconsistent with the occasion of the privilege; ie, for a purpose other than the communication of information, arguments, facts, and opinions concerning the views and policies of the plaintiff politician.

Applying these principles to the facts, it was held that Roberts and Case were not guilty of malice merely because they had sought to injure the political reputation of Bass and cause him to lose office. The imputations made against Bass concerned the performance of his duties as a parliamentarian, and were aimed at lowering his reputation as a politician and parliamentarian; they were not directed to matters foreign to his political or parliamentary reputation. A majority of the court gave judgment for Case on the basis that there was evidence that he held a strong belief in the truth of the statements on the 'How to Vote' card. It was irrelevant that he had failed to make reasonable enquiries into the truth of the statements. The majority held that the protection given to a volunteer handing out election material would not ordinarily be lost even in circumstances where the volunteer did not have a positive belief in the truth of the material as the Australian electoral process can only work effectively with the assistance of such volunteers.[144]

A majority of the court ordered that there should be a new trial of the action against Roberts on the question of malice. Roberts had fabricated material, and although his knowledge of the falsity of the material was not by itself proof of an improper motive, it was almost conclusive evidence of it. The majority sent the matter back to the trial judge to make a finding on whether Roberts was using the occasion to provide the electors with information concerning Bass, or for some other unidentified purpose, foreign to the occasion of the qualified.

The principles from *Roberts v Bass* were applied in *Conservation Council of SA Inc v Chapman* (2003) 87 SASR 62. As discussed above, the defendant made defamatory imputations about the plaintiff property developers in the course of a vigorous and sustained campaign against the construction of a bridge to Hindmarsh Island in South Australia. The trial judge found that the defendant had acted with malice, however this was overturned on appeal. The plaintiffs had

---

142. *Lange v Australian Broadcasting Corporation* (1997) 189 CLR 520 at 571.
143. *Roberts v Bass* [2002] 212 CLR 1 at 28–42.
144. Ibid at 40–1.

not proven that the defendant had acted with the dominant purpose of injuring the plaintiff. Although the inevitable result of a successful campaign to stop the bridge would be that the plaintiffs would suffer economic loss, this consequence had to be distinguished from the defendant's purpose in making the defamatory statements. That purpose was to gather public support for the campaign against the bridge. A public campaign of this kind will often involve reliance on the pressure of public opinion and public disapproval of the plaintiff's actions, but this is part of the ordinary process of public debate. A court should be careful about making inferences of malice in this situation.[145]

The principle that knowledge of falsity of the material is almost conclusive evidence of malice does not apply where the defendant was under a legal duty to publish the defamation. This qualification, recognised in *Roberts v Bass* [2002] 212 CLR 1, was relevant in the later South Australian case of *Cornwall v Rowan* (2004) 90 SASR 269. A public review committee was convened by a government minister to investigate the administration by the plaintiff of a women's shelter. The report provided by the committee to the minister contained various defamatory imputations of the plaintiff's financial management of the shelter and personal misconduct. One of the issues was whether the committee had acted with malice because some members knew that some of the allegations in the report were not substantiated. The Full Court of the Supreme Court of South Australia followed *Roberts v Bass* and held that knowledge of falsity of some of the matters raised in the report were not sufficient in itself to establish malice. Furthermore, the defendants were under a legal duty to publish the report to the minister—in which case, the principle that knowledge of falsity is almost conclusive proof of malice would no longer apply. The minister had convened the committee, determined its terms of reference and directed the committee to include the unsubstantiated allegations for his own political purposes. The committee was required to comply with that direction. Nor was there sufficient evidence of other factors, such as personal animosity toward the plaintiff, which could found an improper motive; the members of the committee had sought the advice of the minister whether to include the unsubstantiated allegations, indicating a desire to include defamatory material only where directed to do so by the minister.

STATUTORY QUALIFIED PRIVILEGE

The uniform laws contain a statutory defence of qualified privilege in s 30. This defence will not replace the existing common law defences, but will be available to the defendant in addition to the common law defences discussed above.[146] The defence in s 30 (s 28 in South Australia) is in the following terms:

---

145. *Conservation Council of SA Inc v Chapman* (2003) 87 SASR 62, see in particular: Doyle CJ at 71–2.
146. Section 24.

30 Defence of qualified privilege for provision of certain information

(1) There is a defence of qualified privilege for the publication of defamatory matter to a person (the recipient) if the defendant proves that:
   (a) the recipient has an interest or apparent interest in having information on some subject, and
   (b) the matter is published to the recipient in the course of giving to the recipient information on that subject, and
   (c) the conduct of the defendant in publishing that matter is reasonable in the circumstances.

(2) For the purposes of subsection (1), a recipient has an apparent interest in having information on some subject if, and only if, at the time of the publication in question, the defendant believes on reasonable grounds that the recipient has that interest.

(3) In determining for the purposes of subsection (1) whether the conduct of the defendant in publishing matter about a person is reasonable in the circumstances, a court may take into account:
   (a) the extent to which the matter published is of public interest, and
   (b) the extent to which the matter published relates to the performance of the public functions or activities of the person, and
   (c) the seriousness of any defamatory imputation carried by the matter published, and
   (d) the extent to which the matter published distinguishes between suspicions, allegations and proven facts, and
   (e) whether it was in the public interest in the circumstances for the matter published to be published expeditiously, and
   (f) the nature of the business environment in which the defendant operates, and
   (g) the sources of the information in the matter published and the integrity of those sources, and
   (h) whether the matter published contained the substance of the person's side of the story and, if not, whether a reasonable attempt was made by the defendant to obtain and publish a response from the person, and
   (i) any other steps taken to verify the information in the matter published, and
   (j) any other circumstances that the court considers relevant.

(4) For the avoidance of doubt, a defence of qualified privilege under subsection (1) is defeated if the plaintiff proves that the publication of the defamatory matter was actuated by malice.

(5) However, a defence of qualified privilege under subsection (1) is not defeated merely because the defamatory matter was published for reward.

This defence is based on s 22 of the *Defamation Act 1974* (NSW) (now replaced by s 30 *Defamation Act 2005* (NSW)). The defence is broader than common law qualified privilege because it is unnecessary for the defendant to show a reciprocity of interest or duty. The term 'interest' in s 22 has been interpreted liberally and in its 'broadest popular sense'[147] to mean an interest of substance in the subject-matter. A wide range of matters have been held to be of interest to the general public, and therefore justifying general publication. These include criticism of the competence of a business consultant to a public telecommunications company;[148] the conduct of the Australian Taxation Office relating to the assessment of taxation of damages for personal injuries;[149] and the training methods of a rugby league coach.[150] However, notwithstanding this broad approach to the question of interest or apparent interest, very few cases have in fact succeeded under s 22. This is because the defendant has generally failed meet the further requirement that the publication of untrue material was reasonable in the circumstances.[151] There is no reason for confidence that a defendant would fare better in establishing this element under s 30.

Section 30 lists a number of factors to be taken into account in determining whether the defendant's publication was reasonable in the circumstances, which largely replicate those contained in s 22. However, these factors are not exhaustive and a court may also take into account any other relevant circumstance: s 30(3)(j). Other factors that might be taken into account that are not explicitly referred to in s 30 are whether the defendant's conclusions followed logically, fairly and reasonably from the information obtained,[152] and whether legal advice was sought before publishing.[153]

The relevant considerations that will determine whether a publisher has acted reasonably will vary with the circumstances of each individual case,[154] but of particular importance will be the steps taken by the defendant to verify the accuracy of the information. It has been said that a court should not lightly find that it was reasonable for a defendant to publish material without first making reasonable enquiries whether it is true.[155] In *Rogers v Nationwide News Pty Ltd* (2003) 216 CLR 327, the defendant newspaper published an article about a court decision

---

147. *Barbaro v Amalgamated Television Services Pty Ltd* (1985) 1 NSWLR 30 at 40.
148. *Morgan v John Fairfax & Sons Ltd [No 2]* (1991) 23 NSWLR 374.
149. This was held to be a matter of general public interest at first instance in *Rogers v Nationwide News Pty Ltd* (2003) 216 CLR 327. This issue was not discussed by the High Court.
150. *Austin v Mirror Newspapers Ltd* [1986] AC 299 at 313.
151. *Nagle v Chulov* [2001] NSWSC 9 at [53].
152. *Morgan v John Fairfax & Sons Ltd [No 2]* (1991) 23 NSWLR 374 at 388, per Hunt AJA; *John Fairfax Publications Pty Ltd v O'Shane* [2005] NSW CA 164.
153. *Rogers v Nationwide News Pty Ltd* (2003) 216 CLR 327 at 347, per Hayne J; at 379, per Heydon J.
154. Ibid at 339, per Gleeson CJ and Gummow J; *Austin v Mirror Newspapers Ltd* [1986] AC 299 at 313.
155. *Austin v Mirror Newspapers* [1986] AC 299 at 317; *Herald & Weekly Times Ltd v Popovic* [2003] VSCA 161 at [12], [101].

concerning the taxation of the damages that had been awarded to a patient of the plaintiff surgeon in a prior medical negligence case.[156] The article imputed that the plaintiff surgeon had negligently blinded his patient as a result of an eye operation he performed on her. This was an incorrect and misleading characterisation of the negligence case, in which the plaintiff had been found negligent for failing to warn his patient of an extremely low risk of the occurrence of an inherent risk sympathetic ophthalmia. The defendant relied solely on the judgment in the taxation case as the source of information about the facts of the medical negligence case and did not check the earlier decision even though this would have been quite easy to do. Furthermore there was nothing in the taxation judgment which suggested that the plaintiff had blinded his patient by operating on her negligently. That was the journalist's own contribution to the story, and it was this addition of an untrue fact which gave the article its defamatory sting. In that circumstance it could not be said that the defendant had acted reasonably in publishing the article.[157]

Section 30 makes specific reference to the nature of the business environment in which the defendant operates as a factor to be considered in determining reasonableness. However, the weight the courts will give to this factor is in doubt. In *Rogers v Nationwide News*, Gleeson CJ and Gummow J conceded that newspapers are published in a competitive environment but went on to say that (at 340):

> The legitimate commercial interests of the respondent are entitled to due consideration. But reasonableness is not determined solely, or even mainly, by those commercial interests. The respondent carries on its business with a view to making profits for the benefit of its shareholders. All business entails risk. Profit is the reward for taking risks. From the point of view of the success of the respondent's enterprise it might be rational to take a risk of damaging someone's reputation, and of being found liable to pay damages. A publisher may calculate that it is worthwhile to risk defaming somebody, or perhaps even to set out deliberately to defame somebody. From the point of view of its internal management, such conduct may be economically rational. That does not mean it is reasonable for the purposes of s 22(1)(c).

The defence in s 30 will only apply where the matter is published 'in the course of giving to the recipient information on the subject' of interest or apparent interest. This requirement will not be met where the defendant publishes extraneous information that is not reasonably necessary to communicate the subject-matter of interest to the recipient. In *Rogers v Nationwide News*, Hayne and Heydon JJ held that the provision of information by the journalist regarding how the defendant's patient became blind and what role the defendant might have to play in that outcome did

---

156. The well-known case of *Rogers v Whitaker* (1992) 175 CLR 479 (discussed in Chapter 11).
157. *Rogers v Nationwide News Pty Ltd* (2003) 216 CLR 327 at 338–9, per Gleeson CJ and Gummow J; at 368, per Callinan J.

not have a sufficient connection to the subject in which the readers may have had a relevant interest. That subject concerned the activities of the Australian Taxation Office, not the activities of the defendant.[158]

Section 30(4) makes it clear that the defence will be defeated if the plaintiff proves that the publication was actuated by malice. The general law principles as discussed above will apply to determine whether the defendant was motivated by malice: s 24(2).

TRIVIALITY

The uniform laws contains a defence to safeguard against trivial claims. Section 33 provides that it is a defence to the publication of defamatory matter if the defendant proves that the circumstances of the publication were such that the plaintiff was unlikely to sustain any harm. This section is designed to prevent claims in limited circumstances where the defendant is unlikely to suffer damage, such as where publication is made to a small group of people who are already aware of the allegation, or who are well acquainted with the plaintiff and able themselves to make a judgment as to the likelihood that there is any substance in the imputation conveyed.[159] It will also potentially have application where the publication would not be taken seriously by the recipients, as 'where a slightly defamatory statement in made in jocular circumstances to a few people in a private home'.[160]

REMEDIES

Damages

Three categories of damages can be awarded at common law: compensatory, aggravated, and exemplary damages. The first two categories will remain available under the uniform laws, but exemplary damages will not.

Compensatory damages

The purpose of a damages award in defamation is to compensate the plaintiff for the damage to reputation. An individual plaintiff is entitled to an award of damages for non-economic loss as well as special damages for actual pecuniary harm suffered that can be precisely quantified. A corporate plaintiff can only recover special damages and damages for injury to its business or trading reputation. It cannot

---

158. Ibid at 347, per Hayne J; at 379, per Heydon J.
159. *Perkins v NSW Aboriginal Land Council* (unreported, Supreme Court of New South Wales, Badgery-Parker J, 15 August 1997) at 27.
160. *Morosi v Mirror Newspapers Ltd* [1977] 2 NSWLR 749 at 800.

recover anything by way of consolation to hurt feelings, as it has no feelings that can be injured.[161]

The majority of the High Court in *Carson v John Fairfax & Sons Ltd* (1993) 178 CLR 44, at 60–1, indicated that the purpose of an award is threefold: (a) consolation for the personal distress and hurt to the plaintiff; (b) reparation for harm done to the plaintiff's personal or professional reputation; and (c) vindication of the plaintiff's reputation. The first two factors constitute consolation for the wrong done to the plaintiff, and include matters such as the plaintiff's hurt, anxiety, loss of self-esteem, sense of indignity and sense of outrage.[162] The third factor looks to the attitude of others to the plaintiff, and requires a court to award a sum that will vindicate the plaintiff's reputation in the public eye—considering matters such as the seriousness of the defamation and the social standing of the plaintiff.

Section 34 of the uniform laws provides that a court, in determining the amount of damages in a defamation case, must ensure that there is 'an appropriate and rational relationship' between the harm sustained by the plaintiff and the amount of damages awarded.[163] This provision directs the courts to ensure that an award of damages in defamation reflects the subjective impact of the particular defamation on the individual plaintiff. It is the harm to that particular plaintiff that must be assessed. Furthermore, it would appear[164] that one of the purposes of s 34 is to ensure that the courts make comparisons with personal injury damages awards when determining the proper level of a defamation damages award. This is a reflection of existing common law principles that require the courts to maintain a proper and appropriate relationship between damages awards in defamation cases and damages awards in personal injury cases.[165] The proposition is that the courts should be mindful of the fact that a person's reputation should not generally be valued more highly than loss of life or limb.[166] Thus, it is has been said that 'If an award of damages for defamation is greater than the amount that would be allowed for the non-economic consequences of the most serious physical injuries with permanently disabling consequences, it may be evident that the amount awarded for defamation is manifestly excessive'.[167] A court is therefore required to ensure that any defamation award is consistent with the general trend of damages awards for non-economic loss personal injury case.[168]

---

161. *Australian Broadcasting Corporation v Comalco Ltd* (1986) 12 FCR 510 at 586, 602.
162. *Carson v John Fairfax & Sons Ltd* (1993) 178 CLR 44 at 71, per Brennan J; *Random House Australia Pty Ltd v Abbott* (1999) 94 FCR 296 at 318–20, per Miles J.
163. This provision previously existed as s 46A of the *Defamation Act 1974* (NSW).
164. The section admittedly does not specifically direct a court to make such a comparison (contrast s 46A of the *Defamation Act 1974* (NSW)), however the common law background would suggest that this was one of the objectives of the provision.
165. *Coyne v Citizen Finance Ltd* (1991) 172 CLR 211 at 221; *Carson v John Fairfax & Sons Ltd* (1993) 178 CLR 44 at 56–60.
166. *Theophanous v Herald and Weekly Times Ltd* (1994) 182 CLR 104 at 132.
167. *Rogers v Nationwide News Pty Ltd* (2003) 216 CLR 327 at 351, per Hayne J (Gleeson CJ and Gummow J agreeing).
168. Ibid.

A damages award for non-economic loss in defamation cases must not in any event exceed the prescribed limit in s 35 of the uniform laws. This limit is currently set at $250 000, although this is subject to indexation. A court will not be permitted to order a defendant to pay damages that exceed the maximum limit unless it is satisfied that the circumstances of the publication of the matter warrant an award of aggravated damages.

In addition to damages for non-economic loss, the plaintiff is also entitled to claim special damages for any actual pecuniary loss suffered as a result of the defamation, such as loss or refusal of employment, loss or refusal of business, reduced employment and/or business prospects, or a demotion.[169]

Mitigation

Section 38 of the uniform laws provides that evidence of the following factors can be taken into account in mitigation of damages:

(a) an apology by the defendant to the plaintiff about the publication;
(b) a publication by the defendant of a correction; and
(c) recovery by the plaintiff of damages or a settlement amount in relation to any other publication of matter having the same meaning or effect as the defamatory matter, or commencement by the plaintiff of proceedings for such damages.

The factors in mitigation that can be taken into account are not limited to these factors (s 38(2)). One further important mitigating factor that the courts take into account is evidence of a prior tarnished reputation in relation to that aspect of character that has been defamed.[170]

Aggravated and exemplary damages

An aggravated damages award is made where the defendant's conduct has aggravated the plaintiff's loss by augmenting the hurt, indignity, and humiliation suffered by the plaintiff. An aggravated damages award is made in addition to ordinary compensatory damages for hurt feelings.[171] Circumstances of aggravation include the sensationalist and exaggerated manner of publication,[172] the gravity of the defamation,[173] the failure to give a sufficient apology, and the circumstances surrounding an apology.[174] At

---

169. *Chakravarti v Advertiser Newspapers Ltd* (1998) 193 CLR 519; *Middendorp Electric Co Pty Ltd v Sonneveld* [2001] VSC 312 at [234].
170. *Chappell v Mirror Newspapers Ltd* (1984) Aust Torts Rep 80–691.
171. *Uren v John Fairfax & Sons* (1966) 117 CLR 118.
172. *Rogers v Nationwide News*(2003) 216 CLR 327 at 340–1; *Waterhouse v Broadcasting Station 2GB Pty Ltd* (1985) Aust Torts Rep 80–728.
173. *Rogers v Nationwide News*(2003) 216 CLR 327.
174. Ibid at 370; *Random House Australia Pty Ltd v Abbott* (1999) 94 FCR 296 at 322, 340.

common law, malice by the defendant could give rise to an aggravated damages award;[175] however, this has been criticised on the basis that the defendant's state of mind or motivations would not necessarily have an impact on the effect of the defamation on the plaintiff.[176] Section 36 of the uniform laws provides that in determining damages for defamation the court is to disregard the malice or other state of mind of the defendant at the time of the publication, except to the extent that the malice or other state of mind affects the harm sustained by the plaintiff. This provision has the effect of generally ruling out malice as the basis of an aggravated damages award unless, for instance, the plaintiff can show that the hurt or distress suffered was augmented by the knowledge that the defendant was acting out of ill will and spite.

The prescribed maximum amount of damages for non-economic loss that can be awarded under s 35 (currently $250 000) does not apply where the court is satisfied that the circumstances of the publication warrant an award of aggravated damages: s 35(2).

Exemplary damages are available at common law where the plaintiff has shown a callous disregard for the rights of the plaintiff. However, the uniform laws will prohibit an award of exemplary damages to a plaintiff for defamation: s 37.

Injunction

An interim injunction to prevent the publication of material alleged to be defamatory is only granted in exceptional cases so as not to fetter freedom of speech and the public exchange of ideas.[177] An interim injunction will only be granted where it is clear that the matter is defamatory and that no defences apply.[178]

FURTHER READING

Australian Law Reform Commission, *Unfair Publication: Defamation and Privacy*, Report No 11, 1979.

Barendt E, 'Interests in Freedom of Speech: Theory and Practice', in Sin KF (ed), *Legal Explorations: Essays in Honour of Professor Michael Chesterman*, The Lawbook Company Ltd, Sydney, 2003, Ch 4.

Chesterman M, *Freedom of Speech in Australian Law: A Delicate Plant*, Ashgate, 2000, Ch 4.

Commonwealth, Attorney-General's Department, *Revised outline of a possible national defamation law*, July 2004, Canberra, ACT.

---

175. *Uren v John Fairfax & Sons* (1966) 117 CLR 118 at 150.
176. Ibid.
177. *National Mutual Life Association of Australasia Ltd v GTV Corporation Pty Ltd* (1989) VR 747 at 754; *Bonnard v Perryman* [1891] 2 Ch 269 at 284.
178. *Bonnard v Perryman* [1891] 2 Ch 269; *Khashoggi v IPC Magazines Ltd* [1963] 3 All ER 577 at 581.

22 Vicarious Liability and Non-Delegable Duty of Care: Types of Liability

INTRODUCTION

This chapter discusses the different forms of liability whereby the law compels others to take responsibility for damage caused by the tortfeasor.

Vicarious liability has been defined as 'liability imposed on one person for the wrongful act of another on the basis of the legal relationship between them'.[1] In *New South Wales v Lepore; Samin v Queensland; Rich v Queensland* (2003) 212 CLR 511 Gummow and Hayne JJ, at [199], observed that vicarious liability:

> is imposed regardless of the fault of the party who is held vicariously responsible, it is imposed regardless of the capacity of that party to avoid the harm that occurs.

Non-delegable duty of care is a discrete category of case in negligence. It was developed in the nineteenth century as a response to the exclusion from the scope of vicarious liability of torts committed by independent contractors. Non-delegable duty of care imposes liability on the person under such duty to take care for the negligence of another to whom the former has delegated the performance of some task within the ambit of duty.

According to the *Ipp Report's* Recommendation 16, liability for breach of a non-delegable duty should be 'treated as equivalent in all respects to vicarious liability for the negligence of the person to whom the doing of the relevant work was entrusted by the person held liable for breach of the non-delegable duty'. Only Victoria and

---

1. Nygh PE & Butt P, *Australian Legal Dictionary*, Butterworths, Sydney, 1997, p 1244.

New South Wales have followed this recommendation, enacting provisions, which are virtually identical. Thus, s 61(1) of the *Wrongs Act 1958* (Vic) provides:

> The extent of liability in tort of a person (the defendant) for breach of a non-delegable duty to ensure that reasonable care is taken by a person in the carrying out of any work or task delegated or otherwise entrusted to the person by the defendant is to be determined as if the defendant were vicariously liable for the *negligence* of the person in connection with the performance of the work or task[2] (emphasis added).

Under the South Australian statutory regime, both vicarious liability and non-delegable duty of care are treated as 'derivative liability'.[3]

This chapter will discuss vicarious liability and non-delegable duty of care, liability of joint and several tortfeasors, and of several concurrent tortfeasors, as well as rules governing solidary and proportionate liability.

VICARIOUS LIABILITY

Historical note

The cause of action in *master's liability* was one of the earliest writs issued by Chancery. According to Professor John Fleming in *The Law of Torts*,[4] its origins lay in the Roman system of noxal liability (*Justinian's Institutes* 4.8), which imposed legal responsibility upon the head of the household (*pater familias*) for the conduct of his *familia*, including the family servants.[5] Under common law, however, vicarious liability has never been imposed on parents for the torts of their children.

The concept of vicarious liability was used in the context of the master–servant relationship. In the fourteenth century, under the custom of the realm, common innkeepers were liable to lodgers whose goods were stolen, irrespective of whether

---

2. *Civil Liability Act 2002* (NSW), s 5Q(1): 'The extent of liability in tort of a person (*the defendant*) for breach of a non-delegable duty to ensure that reasonable care is taken by a person in the carrying out of any work or task delegated or otherwise entrusted to the person by the defendant is to be determined as if the liability were the vicarious liability of the defendant for the negligence of the person in connection with the performance of the work or task.'
3. *Law Reform (Contributory Negligence and Apportionment of Liability) Act 2001* (SA), s 3(1): 'derivative liability means: (a) a vicarious liability (including a partner's liability for the act or omission of another member of the partnership); or (b) a liability of a person who is subject to a non-delegable duty of care for the act or omission of another that places the person in breach of the non-delegable duty; or (c) if an insurer or indemnifier is directly liable to a person who has suffered harm for the act or omission of a person who is insured or indemnified against the risk of causing the harm—the liability of the insurer or indemnifier; or (d) a liability as nominal defendant under a statutory scheme of third-party motor vehicle insurance.'
4. Ninth edn, The Law Book Company Ltd, Sydney, 1998, p 409.
5. Originally, under noxal actions (or noxal surrender) a master who was sued for acts of a slave, or a parent sued for the acts of a child, could hand over the slave or child to the plaintiff, either to be sold for compensation or to suffer private vengeance.

they or a complete stranger committed the theft.[6] Initially, a master was responsible for all torts committed by his servants;[7] then, master's liability was narrowed to actions which he directly commanded, and which were regarded as immediate extensions of his will. In the seventeenth century, Holt CJ of the Court of King's Bench adopted the approach of the specialised Merchants' Court and the Court of Admiralty whereby vicarious liability lay for the servant's acts either ordered or ratified by the employer.[8] In the case of *Boson v Sandford* (1691) 91 ER 382, owners of cargo that was damaged while under the supervision of the ship's master sued the ship's owners. The owners of the ship pleaded that they were not liable, because they had not personally undertaken to ship the goods; however, Lord Holt held (at 382) that 'whoever employs another is answerable for him, and undertakes for his care to all that make use of him'.

Liability was originally based on the theory of representation: masters were personally liable 'because they were acting through their servants'.[9] Thus, in *Tuberville v Stampe* (1697) 1 Ld Raym 264; 92 ER 944, a fire, which had started on the defendant's heath, escaped onto the plaintiff's land and burned his furze shrubs,[10] to the value of £40. Lord Holt (at 264) elaborated on the nature of vicarious liability thus:

> if the defendant's servant kindled the fire in the way of husbandry, and proper for his employment, though he had no express command of his master, yet his master shall be liable to an action for damage done to another by fire; for it shall be intended that the servant has authority from his master, it being for his master's benefit.

Modern doctrine of vicarious liability

Holt CJ appears to have grounded the theory of vicarious liability on the principle of agency, which is part of contract. With the separation of torts from contract and the evolution of the tort of negligence, this theory became too narrow to encompass new developments. No particularly convincing theory has emerged since.[11] In the nineteenth century, the imposition of vicarious liability was justified on the grounds

---

6. *Navenby v Lassels and Stanford* (1367) KB 27/428, m 73, in Baker JH & Milsom SFC, *Sources of English History: Private Law to 1750*, Butterworths, London, 1986, p 552.
7. For example, liability attached to a person whose servants negligently burned down a house in which he was lodging: *Brainton v Pinn* (1290), discussed in Palmer RC, *English Law in the Age of the Black Death 1348–1381*, The University of North Carolina Press, Chapel Hill and London, 1993, p 275.
8. *Lane v Cotton* (1701) 11 Mod 12; 88 ER 853; *Jones v Hart* (1698) 2 Salk 441; 91 ER 382; *Tuberville v Stampe* (1697) 1 Ld Raym 264; 92 ER 944.
9. Ibbetson D, *A Historical Introduction to the Law of Obligations*, Oxford University Press, Oxford, 1999, p 70.
10. Furze or gorse are evergreen plants used as hedges, fodder for animals and yellow dye.
11. See: *Hollis v Vabu Pty Ltd* (2001) 207 CLR 21 at [35], per Gleeson CJ, Gaudron, Gummow, Kirby, and Hayne JJ.

that such liability works as a deterrent and encourages employers to take great care in selecting, training and supervising employees.[12] Furthermore, it is said that since employers receive the benefits of the business activities, it is only just and fair they should also bear its burdens. These are, of course, considerations of policy.

Likewise, both policy and expediency are involved in the recognition that there is a greater chance of employers—as against the employees—having insurance against third-party liability. It is this 'deep pocket' institution of insurance that enables injured plaintiffs to actually receive compensation, rather than empty vindication of their rights to compensation. Professor Glanville Williams in 'Vicarious Liability and Master's Indemnity'[13] wrote that, essentially, the modern doctrine of vicarious liability:

> owes its explanation, if not its justification, to the search for a solvent defendant. It is commonly felt that when a person is injured ... he ought to be able to obtain recompense from someone; and if the immediate tortfeasor cannot afford to pay, then he is justified in looking around for the nearest person of substance who can plausibly be identified with the disaster. Where there is no immediate tortfeasor at all, the same sentiment works itself out through the rules of strict liability.

More recently, in *Hollis v Vabu Pty Ltd* (2001) 207 CLR 21, at [42], Gleeson CJ, Gaudron, Gummow, Kirby, and Hayne JJ quoted with approval Friendly J's statement in *Ira S Bushey & Sons, Inc v United States* 398 F 2d 167 at 171 (1968) that the doctrine of *respondeat superior* (vicarious liability) rests:

> in a deeply rooted sentiment that a business enterprise cannot justly disclaim responsibility for accidents which may fairly be said to be characteristic of its activities.

In *Hollis v Vabu Pty Ltd*, Vabu Pty Ltd conducted a business, called 'Crisis Couriers', of delivering parcels and documents. In December 1994, it had about twenty-five or thirty people working as bicycle couriers, and a number of others on motorcycles and in motor vehicles. Mr Hollis suffered a serious injury to his knee when he was struck by an unidentified cyclist. The cyclist, who was wearing a green jacket, on the front and back of which, in gold lettering, there appeared the words 'Crisis Couriers', said 'Sorry mate' and left the scene, pushing his bicycle.

Gleeson CJ, Gaudron, Gummow, Kirby, and Hayne JJ, found (at [61]) that as an employer, Vabu was vicariously liable for the consequences of the courier's

---

12. Pollock F, *Essays in Jurisprudence and Ethics*, Macmillan and Co, London, 1882, discussed by Gummow and Hayne JJ in *New South Wales v Lepore; Samin v Queensland; Rich v Queensland* 212 CLR 511 at [198]–[202].
13. Williams G, 'Vicarious Liability and Master's Indemnity' (1957) 20 *The Modern Law Review* 220 at 232.

negligent performance of his work. The Vabu bicycle courier injured Mr Hollis while in pursuit of his employer's interests. Their Honours stated (at [42]):

> In general, under contemporary Australian conditions, the conduct by the defendant of an enterprise in which persons are identified as representing that enterprise should carry an obligation to third persons to bear the cost of injury or damage to them which may fairly be said to be characteristic of the conduct of that enterprise.

However, in *Sweeney v Boylan Nominees Pty Limited* [2006] HCA 19, Gleeson CJ and Gummow, Hayne, Heydon and Crennan JJ, in a joint judgment (at [15]), imposed limitations of the concept of representation for the purposes of vicarious liability. Their Honours distinguished between the notion of a 'representative'— indicating a relationship in which one person stands 'in the shoes of, or acts on behalf of, another'—and the transitive verb 'represent', which denotes 'the conveying of information or the inducing of a belief in another'. According to the majority, the doctrine of vicarious liability is limited to cases where the tortfeasor has acted in right of the principal (in the sense of acting in execution of the principal's authority), rather than in his or her own independent capacity. In contradistinction, Kirby J stated (at [36]) that 'Now is not the time to reverse recognition of the fact that, in specified circumstances, a principal is liable for the acts done by its "representative" in the world at large.'

Three main categories of vicarious liability

1. Vicarious liability of principals for wrongs committed by their agents

Historically, principals were held vicariously liable for the tort of their agents where:

(a) the agent has acted within the scope of his or her actual authority, either express or implied; or
(b) the principal has later ratified the tortious act, which must have been done for the 'purposes' or the 'benefit' of the principal.

In *Colonial Mutual Life Assurance Society Ltd v Producers and Citizens Co-operative Assurance Co of Australia Ltd* (1931) 46 CLR 41, Ridley, while a canvasser and agent for the Colonial Mutual Life Assurance Society (CMLAS), made defamatory statements about the Producers and Citizens Co-operative Assurance Co, which were in breach of his terms of agreement with the CMLAS.[14] Although

---

14. According to *Colonial Mutual Life Assurance Society Ltd v Producers and Citizens Co-operative Assurance Co of Australia Ltd* (1931) 46 CLR 41, at 42, the 'terms of this agreement were as follows: "(1) That the agent will not in any circumstances whatsoever use language or write anything respecting any person or institution which may have the effect of reflecting upon the character, integrity or conduct of such person or institution, or which may tend to bring the same into disrepute or discredit."'

Ridley was not a servant of CMLAS, the Society was found vicariously liable for his statements because he made them while acting as its agent. In *Sweeney v Boylan Nominees Pty Ltd* [2006] HCA 19, Gleeson CJ and Gummow, Hayne, Heydon, and Crennan JJ, in a joint judgment (at [22]), interpreted the *CMLAS* decision as establishing the rule:

> that if an independent contractor is engaged to solicit the bringing about of legal relations between the principal who engages the contractor and third parties, the principal will be held liable for slanders uttered to persuade the third party to make an agreement with the principal.

Their Honours noted (at [22] and [24]) that in such cases, vicarious liability will only arise where the independent contractor is engaged as the agent of the principal to bring about legal relations between the principal and third parties, and the tortious conduct is 'undertaken in the course of, and for the purpose of, executing that agency'.

In *Sweeney v Boylan Nominees Pty Ltd* [2006] HCA19, Mrs Sweeney was injured while opening a refrigerator door in a convenience store. The door, which came off and hit Mrs Sweeney on the head, neck, and hand, was negligently attended to earlier that day by a mechanic, Nick Comninos, who was sent by Boylan Nominees, the lessors of the refrigerator, in response to a service call. The majority noted (at [3]) that the claimant would have succeeded in an action against Comninos; however, for unexplained reasons, he was not made a party to the proceedings. In issue before the High Court was whether Boylan Nominees should be vicariously liable for the mechanic's negligence. The majority (Kirby J dissenting) determined that vicarious liability did not apply, because Comninos was neither an employee nor an agent of the defendants. He conducted his own business through his own company, which had workers' compensation and public liability insurance. Although Comninos was engaged from time to time as a contractor to perform maintenance work for Boylan Nominees, he 'was not presented to the public as an emanation' of Boylan Nominees (at [32]).

Kirby J (at [77]) adopted the statement of Dixon J in *CMLAS*, who observed (at 48–9) that while an independent contractor carries out his work, not as a representative but as a principal:

> a difficulty arises when the function entrusted is that of representing the person who requests its performance in a transaction with others, so that the very service to be performed consists in standing in his place and assuming to act in his right and not in an independent capacity.

His Honour then commented (at [78]) that 'the emergence of new "hybrid" forms of "employment"' make the principle stated by Dixon J in *CMLAS* 'one especially apt for the relationships with business enterprises in contemporary Australia'. Accordingly, the notion of representation should be interpreted more broadly because 'the proliferation of independent contracts in place of employment' means that there will be cases where the tortfeasor contractors are uninsured or cannot be identified, or where it is impossible to establish 'which of several contractors was responsible for causing the damage'. In such cases, his Honour pointed out, 'the law of vicarious liability may ... make the difference between recovery and non-recovery. Accordingly, this is an important area of law and justice' (at [106]).

In the area of personal injuries, the issue of vicarious liability on the basis of agency used to arise mostly in relation to motor vehicles. Nowadays, the majority of Australian jurisdictions as a prerequisite of registration require compulsory insurance covering the owner and the driver—whether the latter is driving with the authority of the owner or not—against liability for personal injury. Furthermore, various motor vehicle accident compensation schemes contain a provision that deems the driver of a motor vehicle, driving with or without the authority of the owner, to be the agent of the driver for the purposes of the legislation.[15] In these jurisdictions, where insurance is not taken out by the owner, the injured person has recourse against a statutory fund.

Outside the legislative schemes, for vicarious liability to arise at common law, the relationship between the owner or bailee of a motor vehicle and the driver must be that of agency. According to *Scott v Davis* (2000) 204 CLR 333,[16] which involved negligent flying of a two-seater aeroplane, the owners or bailees of motor vehicles will be liable only if they are in the vehicle or are otherwise in a position to assert control over the driver, whom they must have appointed to drive it. This rule also applies to other vehicles: for example, railway trains, motor boats, sailing vessels, aeroplanes, or horse-drawn carriages.

2. Vicarious liability in partnership

At common law and under the *Partnership Acts*, which codify the law of partnership throughout Australia,[17] every partner of a firm is jointly and severally liable for any tort, fraud, misapplication of money or property received into the custody of the firm. However, the partnership will be liable only if the partner was acting within the scope of his or her authority.

---

15. Liability with respect to Commonwealth-owned cars is governed by the *Commonwealth Motor Vehicles (Liability) Act 1959* (Cth), s 5.
16. Affirming *Soblusky v Egan* (1960) 103 CLR 215, but confining this case to motor vehicles. See also: *Samson v Aitchison* (1960) 103 CLR 215 at 231, per Dixon CJ, Kitto and Windeyer JJ; *Mako v Land* [1956] NZLR 624 at 627, per Turner J; *Scarsbrook v Mason* [1961] 3 All ER 767, per Glyn-Jones J; *Morgans v Launchbury* [1973] AC 127; *Greenwood v Commonwealth of Australia* [1975] VR 859 (FC) at 865, per Gillard J.
17. See, for example: *Partnership Act 1892* (NSW), s 10; *Partnership Act 1958* (Vic), s 14.

3. Vicarious liability of employers

Traditionally, at common law,[18] vicarious liability was generally attributed to the employer, provided the wrongful acts of the employee were carried out during the course of his or her employment and within the scope of the employee's authority, or reasonably incidental to it.

In *Hollis v Vabu Pty Ltd*, the High Court endorsed the concept of 'enterprise risk' as the test for vicarious liability. This test was introduced by McLachlin J (as she then was), speaking for the Supreme Court of Canada in *Bazley v Curry* [1999] 2 SCR 534, a case of sexual assault of a teacher on a pupil. The test (at 548–9), links the employee's wrongful conduct with the nature of the employer's enterprise:

> where the employee's conduct is closely tied to a risk that the employer's enterprise has placed in the community, the employer may justly be held vicariously liable for the employee's wrong.

Under the 'enterprise risk' test, the court has to consider whether the risks created by the employer's enterprise were sufficiently connected to the employee's misconduct. If the connection between the employer's enterprise and the employee's misconduct is sufficiently strong, vicarious liability will be attributed to the employer. In *Hollis v Vabu*, the very nature of a courier delivery enterprise created risks of vehicular collisions like the one that injured Mr Hollis.

New South Wales v Lepore; Samin v Queensland; Rich v Queensland (2003) 212 CLR 511 were heard together. In *Lepore*, the plaintiff, Angelo Lepore, sued the State of New South Wales and his former primary school teacher for damages, claiming that the teacher, having accused him of misbehaviour, would send him to a storeroom, where he smacked and touched him indecently. In separate proceedings, the teacher pleaded guilty to common assault, and was fined and placed under deferred sentence; however, the High Court held that his employer, the State of New South Wales, was not vicariously liable for his conduct. In *Samin* and *Rich*, the plaintiffs were the victims of gross sexual misconduct by a teacher at a one-teacher school in Queensland.

In *Lepore*, Gaudron J and Kirby J expressed doubts regarding the 'course of employment' test and relied on the following formulation of the test by Lord Steyn in *Lister v Hesley Hall Ltd* [2002] 1 AC 215, at [28]:

> The question is whether the ... torts were so closely connected with his employment that it would be fair and just to hold the employers vicariously liable.

---

18. The *Civil Liability Act 1936* (SA), s 59, provides that where an employee commits a tort for which his employer is vicariously liable the employee shall not be liable to indemnify the employer in respect of the vicarious liability incurred by the employer; and unless the employee is otherwise entitled to indemnity in respect of his liability, the employer shall be liable to indemnify the employee in respect of liability incurred by the employee in respect of the tort, unless the employee commits serious and wilful misconduct in the course of his employment and that misconduct constitutes the tort in issue.

Kirby J (at [315]) defined the content of the 'connection' thus:

> a sufficiently close connection between the employer's enterprise and the acts alleged to constitute wrongdoing of the employee. The expression 'connection' potentially connotes either a causal or temporal connection, or both, between those acts and the employment.[19]

Gummow and Hayne JJ, in a joint judgment, also examined the concept of the 'course of employment', and concluded (at [239]) that vicarious liability, in the case of an intentional tort of an employee, should at present be confined to two kinds of case:

> first, where the conduct of which complaint is made was done in the intended pursuit of the employer's interests or in the intended performance of the contract of employment or, secondly, where the conduct of which complaint is made was done in the ostensible pursuit of the employer's business or the apparent execution of the authority which the employer held out the employee as having.

The employee's conduct, whether tortious or criminal, has to be sufficiently connected with the tortfeasor's responsibilities to fall within the scope of his or her employment. This is a question both of policy and of fact. For example, in *Samin v Queensland; Rich v Queensland* (2003) 212 CLR 511, Gummow and Hayne JJ held (at [242]) that sexual assaults on pupils by teachers employed in State schools amounted to a clearly deliberate and criminal conduct, which was so grossly outside their scope of employment as teachers that, as a matter of policy, the State should not be vicariously liable for their criminal conduct:

> The rules governing vicarious liability exhibit the difficulty they do because they have been extended and applied as a matter of policy rather than principle. In the present cases the chief reason for holding the State responsible would be to give the appellants a deep-pocket defendant to sue. That is not reason enough in a case where the conduct of which they complain was contrary to a core element of the teacher's contract of employment. So to hold would strip any content from the concept of course of employment and replace it with a simple requirement that the wrongful act be committed by an employee.

The determination whether the wrongful act had sufficiently close connection with employment will also depend on whether the act of intentional wrongdoing was (a) solely for the benefit of the employer or (b) the employee outside of the scope of the employment. In *Samin v Queensland; Rich v Queensland* (2003) 212

---

19. Likewise, Gaudron J (at [131]) stated that: 'A person will ordinarily not be estopped from denying that another was acting as his or her servant, agent or representative unless there is a close connection between what was done and what the person was engaged to do.'

CLR 511, Gummow and Hayne JJ determined (at [243]) that the sexual assaults committed by the teachers were not acts:

> done in the intended pursuit of the interests of the State in conducting the particular school or the education system more generally. They were not done in intended performance of the contract of employment. Nor were they done in the ostensible pursuit of the interests of the State in conducting the school or the education system. Though the acts were, no doubt, done in abuse of the teacher's authority over the appellants, they were not done in the apparent execution of any authority he had. He had no authority to assault the appellants. What was done was not in the guise of any conduct in which a teacher might be thought to be authorised to engage.

Likewise, in the seminal case of *Deatons Pty Ltd v Flew* (1949) 79 CLR 370, the High Court held that the conduct of a barmaid who threw a glass of beer in the plaintiff's face, as a result of which he lost the sight of one eye, was outside her scope of employment. According to Dixon J (at 382):

> The truth is that it was an act of passion and resentment done neither in furtherance of the master's interests nor under his express or implied authority nor as an incident to or in consequence of anything the barmaid was employed to do. It was a spontaneous act of retributive justice. The occasion for administering it and the form it took may have arisen from the fact that she was a barmaid but retribution was not within the course of her employment as a barmaid.

The narrow operation of *Deatons Pty Ltd v Flew* can have very harsh consequences. For example, in *Gordon v Tamworth Jockey Club Inc* [2003] NSWCA 82, Sheller JA held (Beazley and Giles JJA agreeing) that the Tamworth Jockey Club Inc was not vicariously liable for actions of its employee in the following circumstances. The plaintiff, Ms Gordon, was helping—no remuneration or terms of employment were discussed—her friends with the catering at the Tamworth Races, when a drunken cleaner employed by the club seized her around her neck from behind and held her in a strong grip for between five and ten minutes. He then pushed her and her chair backwards, causing her to hit her head on the concrete, causing an injury. Ms Gordon was awarded $63 729.70 in damages against the insolvent drunken cleaner; however the court determined that the cleaner's actions were not within the scope of his authority, and were neither within a mode of doing the authorised work, nor incidental to his employment.[20]

---

20. The Tamworth Jockey Club Inc was not liable as an occupier of the land, because under *Modbury Triangle Shopping Centre Pty Ltd v Anzil* (2000) 205 CLR 254, its duty did not extend to taking reasonable care to hinder or prevent criminal conduct of an employee that would injure persons lawfully on their premises in the absence of any indication that the employee in question proposed to commit a criminal act.

Canterbury Bankstown Rugby League Football Club Ltd v Rogers; Bugden v Rogers

The employer can be vicariously liable for prohibited conduct of the employee, which falls within the latter's scope of employment. For example, in *Canterbury Bankstown Rugby League Football Club Ltd v Rogers; Bugden v Rogers* (1993) Aust Torts Reports ¶81-246 (discussed in Chapter 4), the plaintiff, Rogers, was a professional rugby player with the Cronulla club. The defendant, Bugden, was a professional player with the Canterbury Bankstown club. During a match, Bugden deliberately, and with intention to hurt, struck Rogers on the face, breaking his jaw. He sued Bugden and his employer, the Canterbury Bankstown club.

Bugden's contract included the requirement that he would play the rugby game in a sportsmanlike manner and in accordance with its rules, which allow for striking in the chest and shoulders, but prohibit tackles on the head. Nevertheless, the Canterbury Bankstown club was found vicariously liable for compensatory damages because grappling with Rogers, in order to stop him and bring him to the ground, was merely an unauthorised or improper mode of carrying out authorised tasks within the scope of Bugden's employment with the club (at 62,543):

> what Bugden did was to do the head, what he was authorised to do to the body, and he did it for the purpose for which he was employed by the club.

In other words, the employer will be ordinarily liable if the employee does in an illegitimate way something that he or she has been employed to do in a legitimate way.

The club was also held vicariously liable for aggravated damages because the court found that the coach of the club 'revved up' the members of the team, including Bugden, and gave them to understand that they should do whatever was necessary to 'stop' three top Cronulla players, one of whom was Rogers. In determining vicarious liability of the club, Mahoney JA (at 62,544) took judicial notice of 'motivation' to win techniques. His Honour noted that there is a line between what is permitted and what is not. If the employer encourages action, which is close to the line, he may have to bear the consequences of action over the line:

> If the employee, in seeking to win, uses means which are legitimate in one area but not in another, and the employer, by his attitude to winning and his motivation of or instructions to the employee, creates a real risk that the employee will act illegitimately, that may assist the finding that the employer is liable for what happened.

However, since it was not established that the club 'condoned, encouraged or incited the illegal play by Bugden',[21] the player, but not his employer, was mulcted for exemplary damages.

---

21. *Canterbury Bankstown Rugby League Football Club Ltd v Rogers; Bugden v Rogers* (1993) Aust Torts Reports ¶81-246 at 62,555, per Giles AJA.

Generally, an employer cannot seek a contribution or an indemnity from his employee unless the latter's wrongful act amounts to serious or wilful misconduct.[22]

Police officers

Under common law, police officers are deemed to exercise independent authority and discretion, and as such they are personally liable for their torts. Consequently, at common law, the Crown was not vicariously liable for the actions of members of police. This rule has been statutorily abrogated in every Australian jurisdiction, making the Crown in the right of each State or Territory liable for certain torts committed by police officers in the performance of or incidental to their service.[23] At the same time, with the exception of the Commonwealth, the Northern Territory, and the Australian Capital Territory,[24] all other jurisdictions exempt from liability in tort acts and omissions of members of their respective police forces done in 'good faith'[25] or 'without corruption or malice'[26] in the course of their duty. Additionally, the Northern Territory, Queensland, Western Australia, and the Commonwealth[27] exclude vicarious liability (or liability as a concurrent tortfeasor) to pay punitive damages.

INDEPENDENT CONTRACTORS

At common law, with few exceptions, vicarious liability does not extend to torts committed by independent contractors.

In *Humberstone v Northern Timber Mills* (1949) 79 CLR 389, Dixon J (as he then was) said (at 404–5) that for the purposes of vicarious liability, an employee is a person engaged under a contract *of* service, and 'the essence of a contract of service is the supply of the work and skill of a man'.

---

22. See, for example: *Civil Liability Act 1936* (SA), s 59.
23. *Police Administration Amendment (Powers and Liability) Act 2005* (NT) s 148C (1); *Police Service Administration Act 1990* (Qld) s 5.15(a) (Crown to be treated as joint tortfeasor); s 10.5(1) and (1A); *Police Act 1998* (SA), s 65(2); *Police Service Act 2003* (Tas), s 84(2); *Police Regulation Act 1958* (Vic), s 123(2); *Police Act 1892* (WA), s 137(5); *Police Act 1990* (NSW), s 212; *Australian Federal Police Act 1979* (Cth), s 64B(1) and (2); *Police Offences (Amendment) Act 1991* (ACT).
24. The Australian Capital Territory does not have an independent police force; it relies upon the Australian Federal Police for policing services.
25. *Police Regulation Act 1958* (Vic), s 123(1); *Police Act 1990* (NSW), s 213; *Police Service Act 2003* (Tas), s 84(1); *Police Act 1998* (SA), s 65(1): 'honest act or omission in the exercise or discharge, or purported exercise or discharge, of a power, function or duty'.
26. *Police Act 1892* (WA), s 137(3).
27. *Police Administration Amendment (Powers and Liability) Act 2005* (NT), s 148C(3); *Police Service Administration Act 1990* (Qld), s 10.5(2), 10.6(1); *Police Act 1892* (WA), s 137(6); *Australian Federal Police Act 1979* (Cth), s 64B.

According to Dixon J in *CMLAS Pty Ltd v Producers and Citizens Co-operative Assurance Co* (1931) 46 CLR 41, at 48, an independent contractor for the purposes of vicarious liability is a person engaged under a contract *for* services. Parties to a contract for services are regarded as principals in their own right. Hence, even though work undertaken by an independent contractor is done for the benefit of the party who has contracted out this work, it is considered different from the situation where the party obtaining the benefit does so by having a representative standing in his or her place either as an employee, an agent or a partner. In *Marshall v Whittaker's Building Supply Co* (1963) 109 CLR 210, at 217, Windeyer J said that the distinction between an employee and an independent contractor is:

> rooted fundamentally in the difference between a person who serves his employer in his, the employer's, business, and a person who carries on a trade or business of his own.

In *Northern Sandblasting Pty Ltd v Harris* (1997) 188 CLR 313, at 366, McHugh J explained:

> The rationale for excluding liability for independent contractors is that the work which the contractor has agreed to do is not done as the representative of the employer.[28]

Consequently, according to *Stevens v Brodribb Sawmilling Co Pty* (1986) 160 CLR 16, an independent contractor is generally regarded as another principal, and is thus liable for his or her own wrongful acts.

There are two exceptions to the rule that the hiring principal is not liable for torts committed by the independent contractor:

- where the hiring principal directly authorises the doing of the tortious act; and
- where the hiring principal who is under a duty of care to a third party or his or her employees engages the independent contractor to perform a task within the scope of this duty, and the independent contractor fails to perform it.[29]

In *Stevens v Brodribb Sawmilling Co Pty Ltd* (1986) 160 CLR 16, the High Court stated that when determining whether the wrongdoer was an employee or an independent contractor, the relationship between the parties should be examined in its totality, with the traditional control test being merely one of the relevant factors (referred to as the 'classic test').[30] These factors should include:

---

28. Cited with approval in *Hollis v Vabu Pty Ltd* (2001) 181 ALR 263 at [40].
29. *Smith v Lewis* (1945) 70 CLR 256; *Dorset Yacht Co Ltd v Home Office* [1970] AC 1004; *Colonial Mutual Life Assurance Society Ltd v Producers & Citizens Co-operative Assurance Co of Australia Ltd* (1931) 46 CLR 41; *Kondis v State Transport Authority* (1984) 154 CLR 672; *Stevens v Brodribb Sawmilling Co Pty Ltd* (1986) 160 CLR 16.
30. If adopted, a taxation test that deems a person who derives 80 per cent of his or her income from one source to be an employee would be consistent with the reasoning in *Hollis v Vabu*; and the 'classic tests' in *Stevens v Brodribb*.

- the person's ability to negotiate the level of payment and the mode of remuneration (fees, salary and benefits);
- the provision and maintenance of equipment;
- the required mode of working (subordination to detailed orders);
- the hours of work and provision for holidays;
- deduction of income tax;
- the power to delegate;
- the way in which the parties see their relationship (as one of employee–employer relationship or as contract between an independent contractor and a principal); and
- the power of dismissal.

The problem is that nowadays, in a deregulated labour market, where employers frequently subcontract or contract out work that used to be performed by employees, it is often very difficult to identify any meaningful distinction between an employee and an independent contractor. For example, in *Hollis v Vabu Pty Ltd* (2001) 207 CLR 21, the majority of the High Court (at [61]) found that the relationship between Vabu and the bicycle courier who struck down Mr Hollis was that of employer and employee. The majority emphasised, however, that while the employer–employee relationship applied to couriers who provided their own bicycles, it may not apply to couriers who provide other vehicles.

In the same case, McHugh J (at [68]) agreed with the majority that a bicycle courier was not an independent contractor 'in the sense of someone who acts as an independent principal, exercising an independent discretion in carrying out a task for his own business interest and who is retained simply to produce a result.' However his Honour found that on the 'classic tests' (*Stevens v Brodribb*) the relationship between Vabu and the couriers was not strictly that of employer and employee. Instead, McHugh J held that that Vabu's relationship with the couriers was one of a principal and its agents. Couriers were subject to Vabu's general direction and control and acted within the scope of the authority conferred on them. Thus, when the courier negligently injured Mr Hollis, he was acting as Vabu's representative in carrying out the task of delivering documents that Vabu had agreed to perform.

NON-DELEGABLE DUTY OF CARE

The doctrine of personal non-delegable duty of care was developed by English judiciary in the nineteenth century primarily in order to circumvent the exclusion of torts committed by independent contractors entrusted with the performance of the task from the ambit of vicarious liability.

The doctrine of non-delegable duty of care involved imposition of a special duty of care, and was therefore an aspect or a category of case within the tort of negligence. The difference lay in the fact that it imposed personal liability in relation to a non-personal fault.

In *Kondis v State Transport Authority* (1984) 154 CLR 672, Mason J noted (at 678) that the concept of personal duty departs from the basic principles of liability in negligence because it substitutes the duty to take reasonable care with a more stringent duty: namely, a duty to *ensure* that reasonable care is taken by third parties. In *New South Wales v Lepore; Samin v Queensland; Rich v Queensland* (2003) 212 CLR 511, Gummow and Hayne JJ (at [255]) observed that: 'A duty to ensure that reasonable care is taken is a strict liability'.[31]

Historical note

Pickard v Smith (1861) 10 CB (NS) 470; 142 ER 535 was one of the first cases in which the Court of Common Pleas imposed upon occupiers a duty to take reasonable care to ensure that visitors were not injured—rather than taking reasonable care not to injure a visitor—either by their employees or by independent contractors.[32] In this case, the plaintiff fell through a trapdoor of a coal cellar underneath a railway platform left open by a coal merchant who delivered the coal to the defendant occupier. According to Williams J (at 480, 539), the act of opening the trap door:

> was the act of the employer, though done through the agency of the coal-merchant; and the defendant, having thereby caused danger, was bound to take reasonable means to prevent mischief. The performance of this duty he omitted; and the fact of his having intrusted it to a person who also neglected it, furnishes no excuse, either in good sense or law.

Occupiers were also held to be liable for the negligence of their independent contractors under non-delegable duty of care to avoid undermining support for adjoining walls (*Dalton v Angus* (1881) 6 AC 740). The tort in *Rylands v Fletcher* (1866) LR 1 Ex 265, affirmed at (1868) LR 3 HL 330, was a variant of non-delegable duty of care, which imposed strict liability on an occupier of land for injury caused by the escape of a dangerous substance. In Australia, this tort has been subsumed into negligence (*Burnie Port Authority v General Jones Pty Ltd* (1994) 179 CLR 520, discussed below). Beyond duties imposed upon occupiers, persons under a statutory duty of care were made responsible for independent contractors who failed in their performance of the duty (*Hole v Sittingbourne and Sheerness Railway Co* (1861) 6 H & N 488).

---

31. Reiterating Gummow J's statement in *Scott v Davis* [2000] 175 ALR 217, at [248], that: 'the characterisation of a duty as non-delegable involves, in effect, the imposition of strict liability upon the defendant who owes that duty'.
32. For discussion, see: Ibbetson D, *A Historical Introduction to the Law of Obligations*, Oxford University Press, Oxford, 1999, p 183.

The doctrine was extended to employers in *Wilsons and Clyde Coal Co v English*, where the court held that employers had a duty to provide competent staff, adequate material, and a proper system of effective supervision. The application of a non-delegable duty of care to employer–employee relationships was partly a response to the defence of common employment (*Priestly v Fowler* (1837) 3 M & W 1; 150 ER 1030), which was a full defence for an employer in cases where one employee injured another in the course of 'common employment', and partly to the inadequacy of vicarious liability to cover wrongs committed by independent contractors.[33] The English legislature responded to this problem by enacting 'no-fault' Workers' Compensations Schemes[34]—which, however, did not become compulsory until 1946.

In Australia, liability in negligence under non-delegable duty of care was affirmed by the High Court in *Commonwealth of Australia v Introvigne* (1982) 150 CLR 258, in the context of a school–pupil relationship. The doctrine extended to liability for intentional torts occasioned by employees or independent contractors.[35] However, in *New South Wales v Lepore*, Gleeson CJ, Gummow, Kirby, Hayne, and Callinan JJ held that the liability of a school authority under its non-delegable duty of care owed to pupils does not extend to intentional criminal conduct against a pupil by a teacher employed by the authority. Presumably, liability for criminal conduct is also excluded from other relationships involving non-delegable duty of care.

Non delegable duty of employers

Kondis v State Transport Authority (1984) 154 CLR 673 was the first case in which the High Court of Australia imposed upon employers a personal, non-delegable duty of care to provide safe working conditions for their employees. In *Kondis*, the defendant, the Victorian State Transport Authority, employed Kondis as part of a team engaged in dismantling a large metal structure. To this end, the Transport Authority hired a crane, owned by Clissold. Clissold was hired as an independent contractor, and the crane was operated by one of its employees. Kondis was injured through the negligence of Clissold's employee. The High Court found that an employer's duty to provide a safe system of work was non-delegable, and this

---

33. The defence of common employment was abolished in the United Kingdom and Australia. See: *Law Reform (Personal Injuries) Act 1948* (UK), s 1; *Navigation Act 1912* (Cth), s 59A; *Law Reform (Miscellaneous Provisions) Act 1955* (ACT), s 21; *Law Reform (Miscellaneous Provisions) Act 1956* (NT), s 22; *Workers' Compensation Act 1926* (NSW), (repealed) s 65; *Workers Compensation Act 1987* (NSW), s 151AA; *Law Reform Act 1995* (Qld), s 3 (previously *Law Reform (Abolition of the Rule of Common Employment) Act 1951* (Qld); *Wrongs Act 1936* (SA), s 30; *Employers' Liability Act 1943* (Tas), s 5; *Employers and Employees Act 1958* (Vic), (repealed) s 34; *Law Reform (Common Employment) Act 1951* (WA), s 3.
34. *Workmen's Compensation Act 1897* 60 & 61 Vict c 37 (Eng). Australian schemes are discussed in Chapter 3.
35. See: *Australian Capital Schools Authority v El Sheik* [2000] FCA 931.

encompassed liability for negligence by its independent contractor who failed to adopt a safe system of work.

The court held that the employer's duty to provide a safe system of work extends to ensuring that employees as well as independent contractors do not injure others who are employed in the course of employment.[36] This means that in a situation where an employer contracts the services of an independent contractor, and this independent contractor injures any of the employer's own employees, the latter will be personally liable for breach of a non-delegable duty of care to provide a safe system of work. Non-delegable duty may also include provision of suitable plant and equipment as well as warnings (*Czatyrko v Edith Cowan University* [2005] HCA 14).

The High Court emphasised that in cases of non-delegable duty to provide a safe system of work, the question of vicarious liability does not arise: the person engaging the independent contractor is personally liable in negligence, whether or not the contractor is also liable.

Brennan CJ in *Northern Sandblasting Pty Ltd v Harris* (1997) 188 CLR 313, at 330–1, suggested that imposition of such duty *cum* strict liability may be justified in cases where defendants authorise an independent contractor to perform a task involving inherent risks to persons to whom they owe a duty of care. In such cases, if:

> the risk eventuates and causes such damage, the employer [of the independent contractor] may be liable even though the independent contractor exercised reasonable care in doing what he was employed to do, because the employer authorised the running of the risk and the employer may be in breach of his own duty for failing to take the necessary steps to avoid the risk which he authorised.

However, his Honour's explanation (at 330–1) of the distinction between vicarious liability and non-delegable duty of care is not very convincing:

> if the defendant is under a personal duty of care owed to the plaintiff and engages an independent contractor to discharge it, a negligent failure by the independent contractor to discharge the duty leaves the defendant liable for its breach. The defendant's liability is not a vicarious liability for the independent contractor's negligence but liability for the defendant's failure to discharge his own duty. The duty in such a case is often called a 'non-delegable duty'.[37]

---

36. The principle of the employer's non-delegable duty of care has now been given legislative force under occupational health and safety legislation. See: *National Occupational Health and Safety Commission Act 1985* (Cth); *Occupational Health and Safety (Commonwealth Employment) Act 1991* (Cth); *Occupational Health and Safety Act 1983* (NSW); *Occupational Health and Safety Act 1985* (Vic); *Occupational Health and Safety Act 1989* (ACT); *Occupational Health and Safety and Welfare Act 1986* (SA); *Occupational Safety and Health Act 1984* (WA); *Workplace Health and Safety Act 1989* (Qld); *Industrial Safety, Health and Welfare Act 1977* (Tas); *Work Health Act 1986* (NT).
37. His Honour referred to *Voli v Inglewood Shire Council* (1963) 110 CLR 74 at 95.

Burnie Port Authority v General Jones: non-delegable duty of occupiers

In *Burnie Port Authority v General Jones* (1994) 179 CLR 520, the High Court set out the requirements that determine the existence of non-delegable duty. The joint judgment of Mason CJ, Deane, Dawson, Toohey, and Gaudron JJ (Brennan and McHugh JJ dissenting) is complicated by the fact that its *ratio decidendi* was based on the notion of legal proximity as an overriding control mechanism for determining the existence of the duty of care in special categories of case. This concept has now been abandoned; however, the elements of control, vulnerability and dependence—which, according to the majority, were required to determine the existence of duty of care in special categories of case—are still considered valid.

Moreover, the court changed the existing law in two areas by holding that:

(1) the *ignis suus* rule contained in the *Fires Prevention (Metropolis) Act 1774* 14 Geo 111 c 78 and its Australian equivalents, which excluded the liability of any person for the spread of fire that accidentally began on their premises, does not survive in Australia; and
(2) the tort in *Rylands v Fletcher* (1868) LR 3 HL 330 should be replaced by liability in negligence. The rule in *Rylands v Fletcher* imposed strict liability for dangerous substances (substances creating an abnormal risk of harm), accumulated on the defendant's land, that escaped and caused damage. Unlike general negligence, where liability is based on fault, and flows from a breach of a duty owed by the defendant to the plaintiff, the tort in *Rylands v Fletcher* was based on 'strict liability' in the sense that it could arise without personal fault. The court determined that situations to which the tort in *Rylands v Fletcher* was applicable in the past can be accommodated within the doctrine of non-delegable duty, which also allows for liability without fault.[38]

In *Burnie Port Authority*, the defendant, the Burnie Port Authority, was the occupier in control of the building in which the plaintiff, General Jones Pty Ltd, warehoused its frozen vegetables. The Authority allowed its independent contractors to carry out welding in the part of the building where thirty cardboard cartons containing expanded polystyrene (EPS) were also stored.[39] Through the negligence of the welders, a spark from the welding gun fell on one of the cartons; the ensuing fire destroyed the warehouse holding the stocks of frozen foodstuffs. The independent contractors admitted negligence, but were insolvent. Mason CJ, Deane, Dawson, Toohey, and Gaudron JJ in a joint judgment (Brennan and McHugh JJ dissenting) said (at 551–2) that non-delegable duty of care will arise where the occupier in control of the land:

---

38. Neither the United Kingdom nor Canada has followed or adopted the Australian position.
39. Expanded polystyrene is an insulating material which, when ignited, dissolves into a liquid fire.

- introduces or allows others to introduce or retain on the land a dangerous substance; or
- undertakes or allows others to undertake a dangerous activity on its land or premises.

This is because:

> a person, outside the premises and without control over what occurs therein, whose person or property is thereby exposed to a foreseeable risk of danger. In such a case, the person outside the premises is obviously in a position of special vulnerability and dependence. He or she is specially vulnerable to danger if reasonable precautions are not taken in relation to what is done on the premises. He or she is specially dependent upon the person in control of the premises to ensure that such reasonable precautions are in fact taken. Commonly, he or she will have neither the right nor the opportunity to exercise control over, or even to have foreknowledge of, what is done or allowed by the other party within the premises.

In contrast, the occupier in control is 'so placed in relation to [that other] person or his property as to assume a particular responsibility for his or its safety'.

In *Burnie Port Authority*, the Authority as the occupier was in control of the premises and thus in a position to insist that reasonable care be taken on its premises. Yet, having authorised or allowed stockpiling of a dangerous substance in the form of the EPS cartons, the Authority also allowed its independent contractor to do the welding on the site. Strictly speaking, EPS is not an inherently dangerous substance, nor is welding an inherently dangerous activity. The court held, however, that the combination of negligent welding and the particular characteristic of EPS created a dangerous environment, which exposed a neighbouring occupier to a foreseeable risk of harm. Thus, according to the majority judgment, in view of the magnitude of the risk of an accident and the seriousness of potential damage if it did occur (the calculus of negligence), the Authority's non-delegable duty of care included a duty to ensure that its independent contractor undertook such special precautions as were necessary to prevent the EPS being set alight as a result of the welding. Since the contractor failed to take reasonable care, the Authority was in breach of its personal duty of care to General Jones, and liable to it for all reasonably foreseeable damage.

Their Honours emphasised (at 551) that the existence of the central element of control, as well as the position of vulnerability and dependence is to be viewed from the perspective of the person to whom the duty is owed. Since the test is subjective, the party in control of the premises onto which dangerous substances are brought or stored, or where a dangerous activity is taking place, need not be aware of the specific dangers to attract liability.

The court also considered the fact that General Jones, as the occupier of neighbouring premises, was vulnerable to the risk of danger, yet had no right and no opportunity to exercise control over what occurred on the Authority's premises, and was thus dependent for the safety of its premises on the party in control. The Authority, therefore, was held to have assumed a particular responsibility for the vulnerable plaintiff's safety, which amounted to a non-delegable duty of care. The concept of vulnerability is really a rewording of the Atkinian definition of the foreseeable plaintiff—we owe a duty of care to persons who are rendered vulnerable as a result of our risky conduct. However, the concept is very broad and prone to retrospective validation.

Non-delegable duty of care is owed by occupiers of dangerous premises (either because of substances stored therein or activities) not only to occupiers of neighbouring premises but to such persons as:

- lawful entrants on the defendant's land;
- occupiers and invitees;
- owners or occupiers of private premises neighbouring the defendant's land;
- licensees on private land neighbouring the defendant's land;
- persons who have no relationship to the neighbouring land of the defendant apart from being on it at the time of the escape; and
- members of the public on a highway or in a public park.[40]

The specific position of a *trespasser* was reserved by the High Court, with the proviso that such person may not be excluded.[41] The High Court did not have to determine whether an occupier in control of premises onto which dangerous substances have been introduced, or where dangerous activities are taking place, owes a non-delegable duty of care toward a lawful visitor. Nevertheless, the court concluded, *obiter*, that prima facie, such a duty was owed. This is because a person on the premises who has no control over what occurs there is essentially in the same position as a neighbour. Both persons are vulnerable to dangerous activities conducted or hazardous materials stored on the premises, and in each case their safety depends upon the party in control of the premises ensuring that reasonable precautions are taken to prevent injury to them.

To sum up: for the non-delegable duty to arise, there must exist in the relationship between the parties an element of control on the one hand, and an element of dependence or vulnerability on the other. This will usually be so in circumstances where:

- the defendant had undertaken the care, supervision or control of a person or property in a way that, unless special care is taken, the person, activities carried

---

40. *Burnie Port Authority v General Jones Pty Ltd* (1994) 68 ALJR 331 at 343; the High Court has adopted statements of Windeyer J in *Benning v Wong* (1969) 122 CLR at 320.
41. *Australian Safeway Stores Pty Ltd v Zaluzna* (1987) 162 CLR 479 at 484–8.

out or substances stored on the property may adversely affect legally protected interests of the plaintiff; or alternatively
- where defendants were so placed in relation to the plaintiff's person or property as to assume a particular responsibility for his, her or its safety, the plaintiff might reasonably expect that due care will be exercised.

The majority in *Burnie Port Authority* (at 550) designated 'adjoining owners of land in relation to work threatening support of common walls; master and servant in relation to a safe system of work; hospital and patient; school authority and pupils; and (arguably), occupier and invitee' as being in a relationship that would give rise to a non-delegable duty of care.

Calculating combinations of potentially dangerous factors as a basis for identifying a foreseeable risk imposes a very heavy burden on the defendant occupier. As much was acknowledged by the majority, who observed (at 554) that 'depending upon the magnitude of the danger, the standard of "reasonable care" may involve "a degree of diligence so stringent as to amount practically to a guarantee of safety".' This approach to the required standard of care is not in harmony with the concept of reasonable care that is the touchstone of the law of negligence.

The common law non-delegable duty of care operates alongside statutory provisions which govern occupiers' liability in Victoria, Western Australia, South Australia, Queensland, the Australian Capital Territory and the Northern Territory.[42] In *Northern Sandblasting Pty Ltd v Harris* (1977) 188 CLR 313, two judges (Toohey J and McHugh J) found a non-delegable duty of care was owed by landlords in relation to residential tenanted premises. The existence of such a duty was rejected by the majority of the High Court in *Jones v Bartlett* (2000) 75 ALJR 1. In *Bartlett*, Gummow and Hayne JJ noted that whereas patients in hospitals and children in schools manifest a dependence or vulnerability that would be a factor in an imposition of the non-delegable duty, the element of vulnerability may not necessarily be present in the relationship of landlord and tenant.

The scope of non-delegable duty of care

In *Lepore*, the High Court attempted to circumscribe the scope of non-delegable duty of care. Gleeson CJ (at [31]) said a responsibility to take reasonable care for the safety of others and a responsibility to see that reasonable care is taken for the safety of another does not amount to an obligation to prevent any kind of harm. Consequently, to impose upon a school authority a liability for any injury, accidental or intentional, inflicted at school upon a pupil by a teacher would be too broad, and the responsibility too demanding (at [34]).

---

42. *Residential Tenancies Act 1987* (WA), s 42(1); *Residential Tenancies Act 1994* (Qld), s 103; *Residential Tenancies Act 1995* (SA), ss 65, 68; *Residential Tenancies Act 1997* (ACT), ss 67, 68; *Residential Tenancies Act 1997* (Vic), ss 65, 68; *Tenancy Act 1996* (NT), s 55(1).

Likewise, Gummow and Hayne JJ noted (at [261]) that since the duty is focused upon the conduct of third parties (employees or independent contractors) who are employed to perform the duty:

> the person upon whom the duty is cast ... [is not] the insurer of those to whom the duty is owed. The duty that is identified is imposed on a person in relation to a particular kind of activity—employing others in some business or other venture, conducting a school or hospital. The duty concerns the *conduct* of that activity. It is not a duty to preserve against any and every harm that befalls someone while that activity is being conducted (emphasis in the original).

Gaudron J (at [102]) defined the concept of 'safety' as meaning 'free of a foreseeable risk of harm'.

Non-delegable duty of care and vicarious liability

The jurisprudential rationale for non-delegable duty of care has not been very convincing. John Fleming[43] found it difficult to discern a substantial difference between personal non-delegable duty of care and vicarious liability. In *Elliott v Bickerstaff* (1999) 48 NSWLR 214, at 236–8 [77], Giles JA, speaking for the court, said:

> The person who owes the non-delegable duty of care may be liable without fault, whether personal or of a servant or agent. Although conceptually the breach of duty will be a breach of that person's duty of care, the so-called duty of care in truth is not a duty to take care but a mechanism for responsibility for someone else's failure to take care.

Likewise, Mason J, the President of the New South Wales Court of Appeal in *Lepore v State of New South Wales & Anor* [2001] NSWCA 112, at [29], pointed out that:

> The expression 'non-delegable duty' is somewhat misleading. It implies that a person cannot delegate a duty, but the truth is that the person cannot avoid liability by relying on the delegation, even to a competent delegate. A non-delegable duty is said to be personal or direct, rather than vicarious, but even this difference is more semantic than substantial.[44]

It was partly in recognition of the substantive similarity between these two theories of strict liability that Victoria[45] and New South Wales[46] enacted legislation

---

43. Fleming J, *Law of Torts*, 9th edn, The Law Book Company Ltd, Sydney, 1998, p 434.
44. Mason P referred to JP Swanton's 'Non-delegable Duties: Liability for the Negligence of Independent Contractors' (1991) 4 *JCL* 183; (1992) 5 *JCL* 26.
45. *Wrongs Act 1958* (Vic), s 61.
46. *Civil Liability Act 2002* (NSW), s 5Q.

(discussed above) in which liability based on non-delegable duty is to be determined as if the person upon whom the duty is imposed were vicariously liable for the negligence. These provisions apply to any claim for damages in tort, whether or not it is a claim for damages resulting from negligence—ie, including intentional torts.

SOLIDARY AND PROPORTIONATE LIABILITY

The main types of liability relating to multiple tortfeasors include:

- 'joint and several' and 'several concurrent' liability—both also known as 'solidary' liability; and
- proportionate liability.

Solidary liability

'Joint and several' liability refers to a case where two or more tortfeasors are jointly responsible for the same tort. 'Joint' liability will be imputed to multiple tortfeasors in the following instances:

- agency, where the agent commits a tort on behalf of the principal;
- vicarious liability, where the employee commits a tort in the course of employment;
- breach of duty, in cases where a number of persons breach a joint duty; and
- concerted action.

The classic example of concerted action is the seventeenth-century case of *Smithson v Garth* (1691) 3 Lev 324; 83 ER 711, in which three thugs were held responsible for the entire damage inflicted on the plaintiff, even though one committed battery, another false imprisonment, and the last stole the plaintiff's silver buttons.

According to *Thompson v ACT Television Pty Ltd* (1996) 141 ALR 1, publication of a book or article, or a broadcast on radio or television, is usually a joint venture; for example, between a writer or journalist, a printer, publisher, distributor, radio or television station. If original material is found to be defamatory, all involved will be deemed to have acted in concert in committing the tort, and consequently all will be liable as joint tortfeasors.

Solidary liability (the term is probably derived from the Roman law *actiones solidae*—actions for the whole debt) is based on the theory of collective responsibility for the whole harm suffered by the plaintiff. It enables the plaintiff to sue all defendants in one action, and does not require him or her to prove which defendant was responsible for which particular injury. The plaintiff can recover compensatory damages from one or several joint tortfeasors, though some defendants may be liable for exemplary damages while others may not.[47] Exemplary damages for negligence can only be awarded in jurisdictions that have retained them (Chapter 2).

Where the plaintiff takes action against one of joint tortfeasors, the latter can join others; and where the plaintiff receives full compensation from one of the joint defendants, the latter can seek to recover a share of the damages from the others. Solidary liability is based on the principle that 'because the wrongful conduct of each of the wrongdoers was a necessary condition of the harm suffered by the plaintiff, it should not be open to any of the wrongdoers to resist—as against the plaintiff—the imposition of liability for the whole of the harm suffered'.[48]

'Several' or 'concurrent' liability refers to a case where two or more tortfeasors commit independent torts, but are responsible for the same damage.[49] Where concurrent tortfeasors are liable for the same damage, the plaintiff may join several tortfeasors as co-defendants in the same action, although he or she would also have separate causes of action against them. In cases where several concurrent causes of action are combined, the plaintiff may need to identify the individual contributions of each wrongdoer to the total injury. Devlin LJ in *Dingle v Associated Newspapers Ltd* [1961] 2 QB 162, at 189, explained:

> If four men, acting severally and not in concert, strike the plaintiff one after another and as a result of his injuries he suffers shock and is detained in hospital and loses a month's wages, each wrongdoer is liable to compensate for the whole loss of his earnings. If there were four distinct physical injuries each man would be liable only for the consequences peculiar to the injury he inflicted, but in the example I have given the loss of earnings is one injury caused in part by all four defendants.

Gummow J in *Thompson v ACT Television Pty Ltd* (1996) 141 ALR 1, at 25, noted that that the entry of judgment in an action: 'against a concurrent tortfeasor does not prevent the plaintiff obtaining judgment against another concurrent tortfeasor liable in respect of the same damage for the reason that, whilst there is only one damage, there are separate injuries for which each concurrent tortfeasor is liable'.

However, his Honour reiterated that once the loss is fully recouped, the plaintiff cannot thereafter pursue any other concurrent tortfeasor regarding the same damage. This rule is based on the doctrine that a plaintiff cannot recover more than full

---

47. *Law Reform (Miscellaneous Provisions) Act 1946* (NSW), s 5(1). See also: *XL Petroleum (NSW) Pty Ltd v Caltex Oil (Australia) Pty Ltd* (1985) 155 CLR 448.
48. Ipp D, Cane P, Sheldon D and Macintosh I, *Review of the Law of Negligence Report* at [3.154] <http://www.revofneg.treasury.gov.au/content/reports.asp> (accessed on 17 February 2006).
49. *The Koursk* [1924] P 140 at 159–60 is the authority for the proposition that joint tortfeasors will be regarded as such in law if there was 'a concurrence in the act or acts causing damage, not merely a coincidence of separate acts which by their conjoined effect cause damage'.

compensation in respect of a particular wrong suffered.[50] Where several tortfeasors are sued as co-defendants, a prudent plaintiff who is settling an action against one would reserve his or her rights to continue the action against the others.

Proportionate liability

The Ipp Panel, in its *Review of the Law of Negligence*, was required to consider and make recommendation in relation to the replacement of 'joint and several' liability for negligently caused personal injury and death with a system of proportionate liability.[51] The Ipp Panel strongly recommended against reforming the personal injury law by the introduction of a system of proportionate liability. The Panel at [3.155]–[3.156] provided the following reasons for its conclusion:

> The most important practical consequence of solidary liability is that the risk that one or more of the multiple wrongdoers will not be available to be sued or will not be able to pay the damages awarded, rests on the other wrongdoers rather than on the plaintiff. The justification for this is that as between the various wrongdoers and an innocent plaintiff, it is unfair that the risk that one or more of the wrongdoers will be unavailable to be sued or will be insolvent should rest on the plaintiff.
>
> ... contrasted with solidary liability is proportionate liability. Under a regime of proportionate liability, liability for the harm caused (jointly or concurrently) by the multiple wrongdoers is divided (or 'apportioned') between them according to their respective shares of responsibility. A plaintiff can recover from any particular wrongdoer only the proportion of the total damages awarded for which that wrongdoer is held liable ... The main practical effect of proportionate liability is that the risk that one or more of the multiple wrongdoers will be unavailable to be sued, or will be insolvent, rests on the person who suffers the harm.

The practical distinction between the two kinds of liability is important, for in the complex world of local and global outsourcing, it is often very expensive for the harmed claimant to trace all wrongdoers. The joint and several liability rules are plaintiff-oriented. They ensure that even in cases where a court finds that several tortfeasors have jointly or separately caused the plaintiff's loss, he or she needs to identify only one against whom a case can be proved. That tortfeasor is then potentially liable for all the damages payable to the claimant. He or she can join others as co-defendants or, once the damages are paid, trace the other contributing

---

50. See also: *XL Petroleum (NSW) Pty Ltd v Caltex Oil (Australia) Pty Ltd* (1985) 155 CLR 448 at 466–7, per Brennan J; followed in *Boyle v State Rail Authority* (NSW) [1997] NSWDDT 3 (4 March 1997); (1997) 14 NSWCCR 374.
51. Ipp D, Cane P, Sheldon D and Macintosh I, *Review of the Law of Negligence Report* at [3.150] <http://www.revofneg.treasury.gov.au/content/reports.asp> (accessed on 17 February 2006).

wrongdoers, and bring the action against them for contribution. Thus, the solidary liability rule protects claimants by allowing them to recover from at least one of the tortfeasors a full compensation for the damage they have suffered.

Proportionate liability legislation

The solidary rule has been considered to be unfair to tortfeasors because of the tendency to pursue and hold liable the 'deep-pocket' financially viable or insured tortfeasors, regardless of how slight their contribution.[52] Consequently, while the Ipp Panel's recommendation regarding personal injury claims was followed, as part of the Torts reforms, all Australian jurisdictions have enacted legislation providing for proportionate liability of concurrent tortfeasors for pure economic loss and property damage.[53] With the exception of South Australia, which has developed its own scheme,[54] all other jurisdictions have, with some variations, adopted the model prepared by the officers' committee of the Standing Committee of Attorneys-General.

The legislation specifically excludes application of proportionate liability to personal injury.[55] Thus, solidary liability has been retained in all actions for personal injury and death irrespective of whether the tortfeasors' liability is 'joint and several' or 'concurrent and several', and regardless of whether such injury was occasioned by intentional torts, negligence, nuisance, breach of statutory duty, or under vicarious liability.

In relation to claims for pure economic loss (ie, not resulting from a personal injury), and for loss arising from property damage, the legislation, with the exception of South Australia,[56] has abolished the distinction between 'joint and several' and 'concurrent and several' tortfeasors by defining a *'concurrent wrongdoer'* as:

---

52. Dr Toyne (Justice and Attorney-General), Second Reading Speech, *Proportionate Liability Bill*, Legislative Assembly of the Northern Territory, *Hansard*, 17 February 2005.
53. *Audit Reform Disclosure Act 2004* (Cth); *Civil Law (Wrongs) Act 2002* (ACT), Ch 7A; *Proportionate Liability Act 2005* (NT); *Civil Liability Act 2002* (NSW), Pt IV; *Civil Liability Act 2003* (Qld), Pt 2; *Civil Liability Act 2002* (Tas), Pt 9A; *Civil Liability Act 2002* (WA), Pt 3; *Wrongs Act 1958* (Vic), Pt IVAA; *Law Reform (Contributory Negligence and Apportionment of Liability) (Proportionate Liability) Amendment Act 2005* (SA), Part 3.
54. *Law Reform (Contributory Negligence and Apportionment of Liability) Act 2001* (SA).
55. *Civil Law (Wrongs) Act 2002* (ACT), s 107B(3)(a); *Civil Liability Act 2003* (Qld), s 28(3)(a); *Civil Liability Act 2002* (NSW), s 34(1)(a); *Civil Liability Act 2002* (Tas) s 43A(1)(a); *Civil Liability Act 2002* (WA), s 5AI(1)(a); *Civil Liability Act 2003* (Qld), s 28(3)(a); *Proportionate Liability Act 2005* (NT), s 3; *Wrongs Act 1958* (Vic), s 24AG. Some jurisdictions (see, for example: the *Civil Law (Wrongs) Act 2002* (ACT), s 107B(3)(b), and *Civil Liability Act 2003* (Qld), s 28(3)(b)) also exclude consumer claims relating to goods and services for personal, domestic or household use or consumption.
56. The *Law Reform (Contributory Negligence and Apportionment of Liability) Act 2001* (SA), s 3(2), provides that 'a liability is an *apportionable liability* if the following conditions are satisfied: (b) 2 or more wrongdoers (who were not acting jointly) committed wrongdoing from which the harm arose'.

a person who is one of two or more persons whose acts or omissions (or act or omission) caused, independently of each other or jointly, the damage or loss that is the subject of the claim.[57]

Proportionate liability applies to claims against concurrent wrongdoers 'in an action for damages—whether in tort, in contract, under statute or otherwise—arising from a failure to take reasonable care'.[58] Proportionate liability also applies to claims for economic loss or damage to property under specified parts of the State and Territory *Fair Trading Acts* (unfair practices).[59] The Commonwealth legislation provides for apportionability of claims between tortfeasors responsible for economic loss caused by misleading or deceptive conduct, providing the economic loss, or the damage to property, was not caused intentionally or fraudulently.[60]

In most jurisdictions, proceedings relating to proportionate liability are to be determined as if in relation to a single claim, even if the proceedings involve more than one cause of action, of the same or a different kind.[61] Liability then is apportioned to concurrent wrongdoers according to their respective shares of responsibility:[62]

> the liability of a defendant who is a concurrent wrongdoer for an apportionable claim is limited to an amount reflecting that proportion of the damage or loss claimed that the court considers just having regard to the extent of the defendant's responsibility for the damage or loss.

---

57. *Civil Liability Act 2002* (NSW), s 34(2); *Civil Law (Wrongs) Act 2002* (ACT), s 107D(1); *Civil Liability Act 2002* (Tas), s 43A(2); *Civil Liability Act 2002* (WA), s 5AI(b); *Proportionate Liability Act 2005* (NT), s 6(1); *Civil Liability Act 2003* (Qld), s 30(1); *Wrongs Act 1958* (Vic), s 24AH(1). The *Law Reform (Contributory Negligence and Apportionment of Liability) Act 2001* (SA), s 3, defines a 'wrongdoer' as 'a person who has a derivative liability for harm resulting from the act or omission of someone else'.
58. *Wrongs Act 1958* (Vic), s 24AF(1)(a); *Civil Law (Wrongs) Act 2002* (ACT), s 107B(1)(a); *Civil Liability Act 2002* (NSW), s 34(1)(a); *Civil Liability Act 2002*, (Tas), s 43A(1)(a); *Civil Liability Act 2002* (WA), s 5AI(1)(a); *Civil Liability Act 2003* (Qld), s 28(1)(a); *Proportionate Liability Act 2005* (NT), s 4(2)(a). The *Law Reform (Contributory Negligence and Apportionment of Liability) Act 2001* (SA), s 3(2), provides that 'liability is an apportionable liability if the following conditions are satisfied: (a) the liability is a liability for harm (but not derivative harm) consisting of—(i) economic loss (but not economic loss consequent on personal injury); or (ii) loss of, or damage to, property; (b) 2 or more wrongdoers (who were not acting jointly) committed wrongdoing from which the harm arose; (c) the liability is the liability of a wrongdoer whose wrongdoing was negligent or innocent'.
59. *Civil Law (Wrongs) Act 2002* (ACT), s 107B(2)(b); *Civil Liability Act 2002* (NSW), s 34(1)(b); *Civil Liability Act 2002* (Tas), s 43A(1)(b); *Civil Liability Act 2002* (WA), s 5AI(1)(b); *Civil Liability Act 2003* (Qld), s 28(1)(b); *Proportionate Liability Act 2005* (NT), s 4(2)(b); *Wrongs Act 1958* (Vic), s 24AF(1)(b); *Law Reform (Contributory Negligence and Apportionment of Liability) Act 2001* (SA), s 3(2) (Example).
60. *ASIC Act 2001* (Cth), s 12GF; *Corporations Act 2001* (Cth), s 1041I; *Trade Practices Act 1974* (Cth), s 82.
61. *Wrongs Act 1958* (Vic), 24AF (2); *Civil Law (Wrongs) Act 2002* (ACT), s 107B(6); *Civil Liability Act 2002* (NSW), s 34(1A); *Civil Liability Act 2002* (Tas), s 43A(9); *Civil Liability Act 2002* (WA), s 5AJ(4); *Civil Liability Act 2003* (Qld), s 28(2); *Proportionate Liability Act 2005* (NT), s 8; see also: *Law Reform (Contributory Negligence and Apportionment of Liability) Act 2001* (SA), s 11.
62. *Wrongs Act 1958* (Vic), s 24AI(1); *Civil Law (Wrongs) Act 2002* (ACT), s 107F(1); *Civil Liability Act 2002* (NSW), s 35(1); *Civil Liability Act 2002* (Tas), s 43B(1); *Proportionate Liability Act 2005* (NT), s 13(1)(a) and (b); *Civil Liability Act 2002* (WA), s 5AK(1); *Civil Liability Act 2003* (Qld), s 31(1); *Law Reform (Contributory Negligence and Apportionment of Liability) Act 2001* (SA), s 8(4): 'in relation to each defendant whose liability is limited under this section, a proportion of the plaintiff's notional damages equivalent to the percentage representing the extent of that defendant's liability'.

Judgment must not be given against the defendant for more than that amount in relation to that claim.

Since it is irrelevant for apportionment purposes whether a concurrent wrongdoer is insolvent, is being wound up, has ceased to exist or has died, the plaintiff must bear the loss of non-payment in such cases.

Vicarious liability

The statutory scheme also provides that persons (employers, partners and principals) can be vicariously liable for a proportion of any apportionable claim for which the concurrent tortfeasor has been found liable.[63] In other words, an apportionable claim will be assessed on the basis of the concurrent wrongdoer's share of responsibilities in the loss, but then the rules governing vicarious liability will take over. For example, if a concurrent tortfeasor was a partner who committed the tort while acting within the scope of her authority, the partnership will be vicariously liable for her share of damages.

Contributory negligence

Each concurrent wrongdoer can raise the defence of contributory negligence. If established on the balance of probabilities, the plaintiff's contributory negligence will be assessed in relation to the particular concurrent wrongdoers.[64] In apportioning responsibility as between concurrent wrongdoers, the court will then exclude the proportion of the damage or loss in relation to which the plaintiff was found to be contributorily negligent.

Exclusions

As noted above, claims relating to compensation for death and personal injury are excluded from the operation of the proportionate liability legislation. Victoria, South Australia, and Queensland specifically provide that liability to pay exemplary or punitive damages rests on individual wrongdoers (they are not apportionable).[65]

---

63. *Wrongs Act 1958* (Vic), s 24AP; *Civil Law (Wrongs) Act 2002* (ACT), s 107K; *Civil Liability Act 2002* (NSW), s 39; *Civil Liability Act 2002* (Tas), s 43G; *Civil Liability Act 2002* (WA), s 5AO; *Civil Liability Act 2003* (Qld), s 32I; *Proportionate Liability Act 2005* (NT), s 14.
64. *Civil Law (Wrongs) Act 2002* (ACT), s107F(2)(a); *Law Reform (Contributory Negligence and Apportionment of Liability) Act 2001* (SA), s 8; *Civil Liability Act 2002* (NSW), s 35(3)(a); *Civil Liability Act 2002* (Tas), s 43B(3)(a); *Civil Liability Act 2002* (WA), s 5AK(3)(a); *Civil Liability Act 2003* (Qld), s 31(3); *Proportionate Liability Act 2005* (NT), s 13(2); *Wrongs Act 1958* (Vic), s 24AN.
65. *Wrongs Act 1958* (Vic), s 24AP(d); *Law Reform (Contributory Negligence and Apportionment of Liability) Act 2001* (SA), ss 3(3), 8(6); *Civil Liability Act 2003* (Qld), s 32I(d).

As a general rule, the liability of concurrent wrongdoers who intended to or fraudulently caused pure economic loss or damage to property that is the subject of the claim are excluded from the proportionate liability scheme (ie, they are liable severally).[66] The wording is obscure. The exclusion seems to apply to a cause of action involving 'a failure to take reasonable care',[67] in which the court finds that the particular concurrent wrongdoer 'intended to cause, or fraudulently caused' the relevant loss. The prase 'a failure to take reasonable care' may be interpreted strictly, as referring to the breach of duty of care in negligence and breach of statutory duty, or it might be read broadly as referring to carelessness. The latter interpretation would include all intentional torts, both trespassory (trespass to land, trespass to goods) and actions on the case (conversion, detinue, deceit, injurious falsehood, defamation, malicious prosecution, collateral abuse of process, misfeasance in public office), relating to pure economic and property loss.

Given the requirement that under proportionate liability schemes all causes of action are to be treated as a single claim, a better view is that once damages are calculated, concurrent wrongdoers liable for intentional torts as well as those who are found to have 'intended to cause, or fraudulently caused' pure economic and property loss are meant to be excluded from the benefit of apportionable claims.

The South Australian *Law Reform (Contributory Negligence and Apportionment of Liability) Act 2001*, s 8(4), may be adapted to provide a general model for assessment of damages in cases involving apportionable liability. Under this model, the court is required to proceed as follows:

(a) determine the total amount of the damages to which the plaintiff is notionally entitled;
(b) give judgment against any defendant whose liability is not subject to proportionate liability; this will include defendants found liable for intentional torts and fraud, as well as defendants liable for exemplary damages;
(c) separate the amount assessed under paragraph (b), and then determine, in relation to each defendant whose liability is limited under proportionate liability, a proportion of the rest of the plaintiff's notional damages equivalent to the percentage representing the extent of that defendant's liability;

---

66. *Civil Liability Act 2002* (NSW), s 34A(1)(a) and (b); *Proportionate Liability Act 2005* (NT), s 7; *Civil Liability Act 2002* (Tas), s 43A(5)(a) and (b); *Civil Liability Act 2002* (WA), s 5AJA(1)(a) and (b); *Civil Liability Act 2003* (Qld), s 32F (specifically excludes contravention of the *Fair Trading Act 1989* (Qld), s 38 [misleading and deceptive conduct]); *Wrongs Act 1958* (Vic), s 24AM; *Civil Law (Wrongs) Act 2002* (ACT), s 107E(1); *Law Reform (Contributory Negligence and Apportionment of Liability) Act 2001* (SA), s 3(2) (Example).
67. *Wrongs Act 1958* (Vic), s 24AF(1)(a); *Civil Law (Wrongs) Act 2002* (ACT), s 107B(1)(a); *Civil Liability Act 2002* (NSW), s 34(1)(a); *Civil Liability Act 2002* (Tas), s 43A(1)(a); *Civil Liability Act 2002* (WA), s 5AI(1)(a); *Civil Liability Act 2003* (Qld), s 28(1)(a); *Proportionate Liability Act 2005* (NT), s 4(2)(a). The *Law Reform (Contributory Negligence and Apportionment of Liability) Act 2001* (SA), s 3(2)(c), refers to 'the liability of a wrongdoer whose wrongdoing was negligent or innocent'.

(d) give judgment against each such defendant based on the assessment made under paragraph (b), having deducted any loss due to the plaintiff's contributory negligence or contractual arrangements in relation to any of the apportionable claims; and finally
(e) determine issues of vicarious liability.

The *Law Reform (Contributory Negligence and Apportionment of Liability) Act 2001* (SA), s 8(4), provides the following example to illustrate the process of assessment:

> A Ltd (which runs a forestry business) has engaged B (an independent contractor) to protect its forest from fire. C (an arsonist) sets the forest on fire. B is negligent in failing to detect and stop C's malicious act. A Ltd sues B and C for damages. In this case, B would be entitled to a limitation of liability under … [proportionate liability] but C would not. In working out the amounts for which judgment should be given, the court would determine first the amount of damages necessary to cover the damage caused by the fire. Judgment for that amount would be given against C. In determining the amount for which judgment should be given against B, responsibility for the damage would be divided between B and C on essentially the same basis as would formerly have been applicable to an action for contribution between them. Judgment would be given against B for an amount reflecting the proportionate responsibility assigned to B on that basis.

FURTHER READING

Cohen Z, 'Directors' Negligence Liability to Creditors: A Comparative and Critical View' (2001) 26 *Iowa Journal of Corporation Law* 351–391.

Collins H, 'Independent Contractors and the Challenge of Vertical Disintegration to Employment Protection Laws' (1990) 10 *Oxford Journal of Legal Studies* 353.

Handford P, 'Trimming the Wings of Vicarious Liability' (2001) 9(2) *The Tort Law Review* 97–101.

Luntz H & Hambly D, *Torts: Cases and Commentary*, Butterworths, Sydney, 1995, Ch 17 and 18.

McKendrick E, 'Vicarious Liability and Independent Contractors: A Re-examination' (1990) 53 *The Modern Law Review* 770–784.

Phegan C, 'Employers' Liability for Independent Contractors in Tort Law' (2000) 4 *The Judicial Review* 395.

Schwartz GT, 'Corporate Tort Liability Symposium: The Hidden and Fundamental Issue of Employer Vicarious Liability' (1996) 69 *Southern California Law Review* 1739

White S & Orr G, 'Precarious liability: The High Court in *Lepore*, *Samin* and *Rich* on School Responsibility for Assaults by Teachers' (2003) 11 *Torts Law Journal* 101.

Index

Absolute privilege
  defamation defence 623–5
  judicial proceedings 624
  ministerial communications 625
  parliamentary proceedings 624
Abuse of process *see* Collateral abuse of process
Action *in personam* 89–90
Action *in rem* 89–90
Action on the case 7, 8, 128–56
  history 128–9
Agent
  vicarious liability of principal 656–8
Aggravated damages 28, 39–45
  assault and battery 94
  deceit 166
  defamation 650
  personal injury or death 42
  trespass to land 123
  trespass to the person 94
Aircraft
  trespass to land 122–3
Alternative dispute resolution 5
Animals
  breach of statutory duty by owners 567
  cattle trespass 8
  scienter, writ of 14
Arbitration 5
Asbestos-related injuries
  survivor action 70
Assault 6, 99–104
  aggravated damages 94
  alarming words 104
  apprehension of impending contact 101
  conditional threats 103
  criminal prosecution 94
  damages, nature of 93–4
  definition 100
  direct physical threat 102
  elements of 101–3
  exemplary damages 94
  felonious tort rule 94
  history of tort 99–100
  intentional tort 7, 91

  police, by 45
  reasonableness of apprehension 101
  rights protected 6
  state of mind of victim 101–2
  trespass to the person 8, 91
Assessment of damages 31, 58–67
  average weekly earnings 63
  'buffer' damages 64
  contributory negligence 502–3
  discount
    future contingencies 64–6
    lump sum, statutory rate 65
    outgoings 66–7
  future contingencies, discounting for 64–6
  future economic loss 60
  future events 58–61
  loss of earning capacity 61–4, 75
  past events 58–9
  potential events 58–61
  survivor actions 70
  vicissitudes of life, discounting for 64–6
  wrongful death 75
Assumpsit, writ of 14, 242
Assythment 415

Bailment 171–3
  conversion 198–9
  detinue 180
Battery 6, 95–9
  aggravated damages 94
  criminal prosecution 94
  damages, nature of 93–4
  defences
    consent *see* Consent
    defence of property 223
    good samaritans 220–2
    insanity 225
    lawful arrest 226–7
    legal authority 226–7
    necessity 218–20
    self-defence 223–4
    volunteers 222
  definition 95–6

direct act resulting in contact with other person 98
elements of 97–9
exemplary damages 94
felonious tort rule 94
good samaritans 220–2
history of tort 95
intention 97
intentional tort 7, 91
knowledge of contact 99
medical treatment 96, 207
  consent *see* Consent
  defence of legal authority 226
non-consensual touching 217
police, by 45
positive and affirmative action 97
protection of life 96
rights protected 6
trespass to the person 8, 91
voluntary act 98
volunteers 222
Bracton, Henry 15
Breach of confidence 152–6
  action on the case 155
  history of tort 153–5
  misuse of private information 155
  requirements 155
Breach of duty of care *see* Negligence
Breach of promise to marry
  survivor action 70
Breach of statutory duty 7, 560–77
  breach of duty 569
  causation 572–3
  criminal penalty imposed 565, 566
  defences
    contributory negligence 575–7
    plaintiff's conduct 573–5
    voluntary assumption of risk 577
  discretionary functions, exercise of 570–2
  duty imposed on defendant 567–8
  elements of action 565
  employer 566
  enforceability of right as private action in tort 565–7
  harm within scope contemplated by legislation 569
  history of tort 560
  legislative intention 561
  nature of action for 562–5
  private action for 562–5
  protected class 568–9
  public authorities 569
    absolute duties 571
    exercise of discretionary functions 570–2
  res ipsa loquitur 571
  right to sue for 562–3
  rights protected 6
  standard of care 569
  statutory interpretation 564–5

statutory tort 8
strict liability tort 527
unintentional tort 7
Burden of proof *see* Onus of proof

Calculus of negligence 275–80, 396
Cattle trespass 8
Causation
  balance of probabilities 346, 347
  breach of statutory duty 572–3
  'but for' test 328, 329, 330
    statutory exception 351–4
  causa sine qua non 328
  common law principles 327–34
  common sense test 329–34
  contributory negligence 483, 491
  deceit 165
  definition, statutory 334–7
  dust-related disease 341–4, 353–4
  evidential gaps 337–51
    statutory approach 351–4
  factual causation 335–6
  failure to warn cases 354–60
    hindsight bias 357–62
    retrospectivity 357
  general concept 325
  hindsight bias 357–62
    statutory approach 361–2
  'loss of chance' doctrine 348–51, 354
  'material contribution' test 338–44, 347, 435, 436
    contributory negligence 491
  misfeasance in public office 151
  'necessary condition' 327, 329
  negligence, element of 238, 325–74
  negligent misstatement 463
  non-tortious causal factor 385
  novus actus interveniens 328, 363–8
    plaintiff's intervening act 363–6
    reasonable foreseeability test 376
    third party's intervening act 366–8
  onus of proof 346–8
  pre-existing condition 344–5, 385
  property damage 370–1
  'proximate cause' test 328
  pure psychiatric injury 426, 435–6, 440
    'material contribution' test 435, 436
    statutory provisions 440
  question of fact 151
  reasonable foreseeability test 376
  res ipsa loquitur 371–4
  scope of liability 336
  several causative agents 345–6
  'sufficient cause' 327, 363
  tortious liability, establishing 326
  unrelated subsequent events 368–70
    attribution of liability 368–70
    non-tortious injury 369–70
    tortious events 368–9

684 *Index*

Causation (*cont.*)
  value judgment based on common sense and experience 329–34
  wrongful death 73–4
Chattels
  bailment 171–3
  conversion *see* Conversion
  definition 171
  detinue *see* Detinue
  intentional interference with 171
  recaption, privilege of 5, 231
  torts protecting right of possession 6, 171
  trespass *see* Trespass to goods
Child
  consent to medical treatment 211–15
    blood transfusion 214–15
    lifesaving treatment 212
    non-therapeutic purposes 213, 214
    parens patriae jurisdiction 211, 212
    sterilisation 211, 213
    unborn child 210
  contributory negligence 499
  duty to control 262, 315
  limitation of actions 232
  personal liability of parents 315
  standard of care 315
  unborn *see* Unborn child
Civil Liability Acts 22–6
  implementation 23–5
  scope 25–6
Classification of torts 5–8
Collateral abuse of process 6, 139–42
  action on the case 8, 128
  elements of 140–2
  history of tort 139
  indirect intentional tort 7
  intention 141–2
  manifestation of improper purpose 141–2
  nature of tort 140
  proceedings, abuse of 140
  rights protected 6
Common law 3
  compensation, law of 27, 28
Compensation
  criminal injuries *see* Criminal injuries compensation
  damages *see* Damages
  history 29–31
  law of 27–67
  liability, evolution of 29–31
  motor accident 80–3
  object of torts law 4, 27
  personal injury and death 77–8
  rights and duties 32–3
  statutory schemes 77–87
  terminology 32
  workers' *see* Workers' compensation
Conciliation 5
Confidentiality
  breach of confidence 152–6
  personal information protection 156
  privacy distinguished 152
  protection of 153, 156
Consent
  acquiescence distinguished 216
  breach of the peace 216
  defence to intentional torts 205–18
  duress 215–16
  exigencies of everyday life 217–18
  false imprisonment defence 227
  fraud, obtained by 215
  implied 216–17
  medical procedures 206–15
    adult 206–8
    incompetent person 211–15
    lifesaving treatment 208–10
    minor 211–15
    unborn child 210
  nuisance defence 556–7
  onus of proof 206
  sadomasochistic practices 216
  valid 207
  voluntary assumption of risk distinguished 217, 505–6
Conspiracy 6, 7
Contemptuous damages 39
Contributory negligence
  alternative danger, doctrine of 500–1
  application to all torts 483
  apportionment 502
    legislation 480–2
    100 per cent 481–2
  assessment of damages 502–3
  breach of statutory duty defence 575–7
  burden of proof 239
  carelessness of others, foreseeability 490
  causation 483, 491
  children 499
  circumstances of case 501
  compliance with regulations or rules 490
  conduct of plaintiff 484
  conversion defence 201
  creation of danger 501
  deceit defence 166
  employees 484–7
  employer's instructions, acting against 486
  evolution of defence 478–80
  failure to anticipate danger 501
  fault element 480, 491
  history 478–80
  inadvertence distinguished 485
  intentional conduct 500
  intoxication 492–9
    common law 492
    evidentiary provisions 497
    extent of impairment of skill 496
    joint illegal activity 492, 493
    medicines 496
    rebuttable presumption 494–5
    statutory reduction of damages 498

Index

statutory reforms 494–9
voluntary assumption of risk 498
joint illegal activity 492, 493, 520
'just and equitable' damages 503
knowledge of risk 489
material contribution test 491
motor accident compensation 81
negligence defence 239, 478–503
objective test 488
obviousness of risk 489
personal responsibility 487
proportionate liability 679
reduction of damages 498, 502–3
scope of defence 482–3
seat belt, failure to wear 491, 498
standard of care of plaintiff 484
statutory reforms 22, 488–90
sudden emergency doctrine 501
workers' compensation 80, 484–7
wrongful death 77
Conversion 6, 182–201
action on the case 8
bailment for use 198–9
changing nature of goods 193
conduct amounting to 193–5
consequential damages 200
contributory negligence 201
copyright 186, 198
criminal investigations, property seized in 188, 192
Crown treasure trove 191–2
damages 199–201
defendant not at fault 183
defendant's conduct 192
definition 182
denial of ownership 188
denial of possessory rights 188
discretion as to restitution 200
economic tort 7
electronic commerce 198
exemplary damages 200
fault 183
finders 189–91
foreseeability of distress or damage 199
general damages 199
goods that may be converted 197–8
history of tort 182–3
intangible rights 198
intent to exercise control 192
intentional tort 7
major interference with title 186
mistake 192
occupier of land/building, possessory rights 191
physical possession 188
plaintiff's possessory rights 187
positive misfeasance 195–6
possession 186–9
purpose of goods 200
reckless intent 192
refusal to deliver 193, 195

rights protected 6
serious misuse 193
specific restitution 200
subject 197–8
title to goods 186
trespass to goods compared 183–5
trover 182–4
unauthorised movement 193
warrant, article seized under 189
wrongful dealing 193–5
wrongful interference 192
Copyright
conversion 186, 198
Corporations
defamation 583–4
Court of Chancery 3, 13
Court of Common Pleas 12, 13
Court of Exchequer 12
Court of King's Bench 12, 13, 15
Court of Nisi Prius 13
Covenant, writ of 14
Criminal injuries compensation 83–7
Australian Capital Territory 86
counselling services 86
funeral expenses 86
New South Wales 84, 86
New Zealand 83
Northern Territory 86
other remedies, right to 84
pain and suffering 86
Queensland 86
South Australia 86
subrogation of rights 85
Tasmania 85
Victoria 84, 86
Western Australia 84, 87

Damages 4–5
aggravated *See* Aggravated damages
assault/battery 93–4
assessment *see* Assessment of damages
'buffer' 64
capping 23, 28, 48
classification 38–53
common law 27, 28, 33–4
compensatory 45
compromise of claim 38
contemptuous 39
conversion 199–201
criminal injuries 83–7
damage distinguished 31
deceit 165
defamation 648–51
definition 31
detinue 181
disability, definition 32
disfigurement 47, 49
exemplary *see* Exemplary damages
general 30, 46
gratuitous services 31, 53–8

Damages (*cont.*)
   Griffiths v Kerkemeyer 31, 53–8
   hospital/medical expenses 31, 46, 70
   impairment, definition 32
   law of compensation 27–67
   liability, evolution of 29–31
   loss of capacity to care for others 57
   loss of earning capacity 61–4, 75
   lump sum 35, 36
   mental harm *see* Pure psychiatric injury
   nominal 38, 94, 123
   non-economic loss 47–53
      thresholds 48–53
   nursing services 31
   object of torts law 4, 27
   'once for all' rule 35, 36
   out-of-court settlement 33, 38
   out-of-pocket expenses 46
   pain and suffering 47–50
      criminal injuries 86
      survivor actions 70
      victims of crime 84
   personal injury *see* Personal injury
   private nuisance 555–6
   proportionate liability *see* Proportionate liability
   psychiatric injury 51, 58
   punitive *see* Exemplary damages
   pure economic loss *see* Pure economic loss
   pure psychiatric injury *see* Pure psychiatric injury
   reduction 36
      contributory negligence *see* Contributory negligence
   restitutio in integrum 30
   social function 5
   solatium 74–7, 415
   special 46
   statutory limitations 28
   structured settlements 23, 37–8
   Sullivan v Gordon 57
   trespass to land 123–4
   trespass to the person 93–4
   victims of crime 83–7
   wrongful life 264–9
Dangerous activities
   obvious risk 294, 512–14
Dangerous premises
   occupier's duty of care 671
Dangerous substances
   occupier's duty of care 669
De Legibus et Consuetudinibus Angliae 15
Death
   aggravated/exemplary damages 42
   criminal injuries *see* Criminal injuries compensation
   defamation of deceased person 582
   defendant 69
   motor accident compensation 80
   plaintiff 69–71
   proportionate liability, exclusion 679
   statutory compensation schemes 77–8
   survival of causes of action 68–71
   wrongful *see* Wrongful death
Debt, writ of 14
Deceit 7, 158–66
   action on the case 8
   aggravated damages 166
   ambiguity 162
   causation 165
   contributory negligence 166
   damages 165
   economic loss as result 165
   elements of 159
   exemplary damages 166
   false representation 160–1
   fraudulent representation 161–3
   history of tort 158
   indirect intentional tort 7
   injurious falsehood distinguished 159
   intention that plaintiff rely on representation 163–4
   knowledge of falsity 161–2
   motive irrelevant 162
   negligent misstatement distinguished 162, 166
   non-disclosure 160
   partial disclosure 160
   plaintiff induced to rely on representation 164
   reasonable foreseeability of loss 165
   remedies 165
   rights protected 6
   s 52 *Trade Practices Act* compared 157–8
   subsequent change in circumstances 161
   subsequent discovery of falsity 161
Defamation 7, 167, 578–651
   action on the case 8
   aggravated damages 650
   apology, effect of 609
   choice of jurisdiction 606–8
   community standards 594
   context of publication 592
   corporations 583–4
   criminal investigation reports 589–90, 612
   damages 648–51
      aggravated 650
      compensatory 648–50
      exemplary 651
      mitigation 650
   deceased persons 582–3
   defamatory imputation 586–98
      identification of 586–93
   defamatory material 594–8
   defences *see* Defences to defamation
   disparaging statements 596–8
   elements of 585
   exemplary damages 651
   false innuendo 587–90
   freedom of speech 170
   government bodies 584–5
   group 600

identification of plaintiff 598–600
injunction 651
injurious falsehood distinguished 167
innocent dissemination 603, 604–6
innuendo 587
  criminal investigation reports 589–90
  legal/true 590–2
  popular/false 587–90
intentional tort 7
judge, role of 606
jury trial 606
legal innuendo 590–2, 602
liability 610
  apology, effect on 609
  defences see Defences to defamation
  unintentional publication 603
libel/slander distinction 581–2
limitation of actions 608
local authorities 584–5
'McLibel' case 583–4
mitigating factors 650
mode of publication 593
national law 579–81
objective of law 578
offer to make amends 609
onus of proof 585
overview 578
popular innuendo 587–90
prima facie claim 578, 585
privacy protection 579
proceedings for 606–8
  choice of jurisdiction 606–8
  jury trial 606
  limitation period 608
  multiple jurisdictions 580, 607
proof of damage not required 167
publication of defamatory matter 582–5
publication to third party 601–6
qualified privilege see Qualified privilege
reasonable person test 586, 594
reference to plaintiff 598–600
remedies 648–51
repetition of defamatory matter 603
republication of defamatory matter 603
reputation, protection of 578, 579
'ridiculous light', casting in 597
right-minded person test 586, 594
rights protected 6, 579
single cause of action 582
slander/libel distinction 581–2
social/moral standards 594
subordinate distributor 605
true innuendo 590–2
uniform law 579–81
unintentional publication 602–6
  innocent dissemination defence 603, 604–6
  liability 603
  republication 603
who can sue 582–5

Defective buildings
  duty of care to subsequent purchasers 470
  negligently constructed 469
  pure economic loss 469–71
  vulnerability of claimant 471
Defective product
  negligently supplied 467–9
  pure economic loss 467–9
  vulnerability of claimant 468
Defences to breach of statutory duty
  contributory negligence 575–7
  plaintiff's conduct 573–5
  voluntary assumption of risk 577
Defences to defamation
  absolute privilege 623–5
    judicial proceedings 624
    ministerial communications 625
    parliamentary proceedings 624
  contextual truth 613–15
  fair and accurate report 627–9
  fair comment (common law defence) 616–21
    basis in true or privileged facts 619–20
    elements of defence 616
    honest person could hold opinion 620
    malice 620–1
    public interest 618
    statement of opinion 616–18
    statutory defence distinguished 622
  honest opinion (statutory defence) 616, 621–3
    common law defence distinguished 622
    elements of defence 621
    proper material 621, 622
    public interest 621
  innocent dissemination 603, 604–6
  justification 610–15
  proceedings of public concern, reports of 627–9
  public documents 626–7
  public interest or benefit 579, 611, 618, 630–2
  qualified privilege see Qualified privilege
  self-defence 632–3
  triviality 648
  true or privileged facts, based on 619–20
  truth in substance 611–13
Defences to intentional torts 204–33
  abatement of nuisance 230, 555
  automatism 225
  battery defences 218–27
  certification of psychiatric patient 228
  consent see Consent
  contributory negligence see Contributory negligence
  Crown powers of entry 229
  defence of others 223–4
  defence of property 223, 230
  false imprisonment defences 227–9
  good samaritans 220–2
  illegality 25
  insanity 225

688 *Index*

Defences to intentional torts (*cont.*)
  involuntary treatment 226
  jus tertii 177
  lawful arrest 226–7
  lawful imprisonment 227
  legal authority 226–7
  limitation of actions 231–2
  mistake 232
  mistaken self-defence 232
  necessity 218–20
  non-voluntary treatment 226
  quarantine 228
  recaption of chattels 231
  re-entry on land 230
  self-defence 223–4, 232
  serious offence 25
  statutory policy 23
  trespass to land defences 229–31
  volenti non fit injuria 217–18
  volunteers 222
Defences to negligence 238, 473–525
  automatism 317, 318
  breach of statutory prohibition 523–5
  common employment 477
  contributory negligence *see* Contributory negligence
  exclusion of liability clauses 514–20
    recreational services 517–9
  history 475–7
  illegality 238, 520–3
  insanity 318
  joint illegal activity 492, 493, 520
  limitation of actions 239
  obvious risk *see* Obvious risk
  overview 473–4
  unconsciousness 317, 318
  unlawful conduct 523–5
  voluntary assumption of risk *see* Voluntary assumption of risk
Defences to nuisance 556–9
  conformation of land 559
  consent 556
  prescriptive right 559
  reasonable use 558
  statutory authority 557–8
Definition of tort 4
Detinue 6, 178–82
  action on the case 8
  bailment 180
  damages 181
  definition 178
  demand 179
  economic tort 7
  elements of 179
  exemplary damages 181–2
  history of tort 178
  intentional tort 7
  lawful detention 178–9
  possession requirement 179
  qualified refusal 180
  refusal to deliver 180
  replevin 178
  rights protected 6
  specific restitution 181
  standing to sue 179
Disability
  definition 32
  person under
    limitation of actions 232
    standard of care 317
Disfigurement
  damages for 47, 49
Domestic services
  damages for 31, 53–8
  loss of capacity to provide, damages for 57
Donoghue v Stevenson 250–1, 387, 388, 393
Duress
  consent obtained by 215–16
  economic tort 7
  intentional tort 7
  rights protected 6
Dust-related disease
  causation 341–4, 353–4
  exclusion from Civil Liability Acts 25, 353
  survivor actions 70
Duty of care
  breach *see* Negligence
  Caparo test 389–92
  definition 246
  Donoghue v Stevenson 250–1, 387, 388, 393
  element of negligence 238
  employers 240, 262, 424
    non-delegable 667–8
  evolution of requirement 249–51
  general limitations 251–6
  history 241–5
  landlord 256–8
  nature of foreseeable risk 255–6
  neighbour principle 251, 252, 388, 393
  non-delegable *see* Non-delegable duty of care
  novel categories of case 388–92
  occupier 258–63
    non-delegable 666, 669–72
  personal responsibility and 246–7, 287–9
  police 248
  proximity 251, 252, 389–2
  reasonable foreseeability 238, 250, 376, 388–92
    plaintiff as person to whom duty owed 252, 388
    risk of injury to others 255
    test 376
  reasonableness, concept of 245–6
  rescuers, to 253, 424
  scope 246–9
  standard of care *see* Standard of care
  unborn child, to 263–9
  unforeseeable plaintiff 253–4

Economic integrity 4
Economic loss
 primary 445
 secondary *see* Pure economic loss
Egg-shell skull rule 382, 385
Ejectment 8
Employees
 contributory negligence 484–7
 duty to control 262
 voluntary assumption of risk 508
Employers
 breach of statutory duty 566
 duty of care 240, 424, 457, 485, 486
  non-delegable 667–8
  providing safe system of work 486, 668
 duty to control employees 262
 duty to warn employees of risks 485
 negligent misstatement 457
 non-delegable duty of care 667–8
 vicarious liability 659–63
English courts
 historical 3, 12–13
 precedent, doctrine of 15–17
 writ system 13–14
 Year Books 16
Evidence
 intentional or negligent destruction of 202–3
 negligence, of
  causation, evidential gaps 337–54
  circumstantial 322
  inference 320–2
Exclusion of liability clauses 514–20
 burden of proof 517
 defence to negligence 514–20
 misunderstood by plaintiff 516
 objective test 515
 public policy interests 514
 recreational services contracts 517–19
 statutory reforms 517–20
 unsigned documents 516
 void under Trade Practices Act 517
 voluntary assumption of risk compared 515
Exemplary damages 28, 39–45
 assault and battery 94
 conversion 200
 deceit 166
 defamation 651
 detinue 181–2
 history 40
 personal injury or death 42
 proportionate liability, exclusion 679
 survivor actions, excluded 70
 tobacco-related injuries 42
 trespass to land 124
 trespass to the person 94

Fair comment
 defamation defence 616–21
 honest person could hold opinion 620
 malice 620–1
 public interest 618
 statement of opinion 616–18
 statutory defence distinguished 622
 true or privileged facts, based on 619–20
False imprisonment 6, 105–13
 burden of proof 106
 damages, nature of 93–4
 defences 227–9
  certification of psychiatric patient 228
  consent 227 *see also* Consent
  quarantine 228
  treatment of infectious disease 228
 definition 106
 direct act of restraint 109–11
 elements of 106–7
 failure to act 111–12
 history of tort 105–6
 immigration detention 106, 152
 intentional tort 7, 91
 judge or magistrate's order 110
 knowledge of 113
 malice 112
 misapprehension of law 228
 motive 112
 origins of tort 91–4
 place of restraint 109
 police, by 45, 108–9
  false allegations, acting on 110
 psychological coercion 108
 rights protected 6
 total restraint of liberty 107
 trespass to the person 8, 91
 unreasoning prejudice 112
 voluntary conduct 111
Fault
 contributory negligence, element of 480, 491
 conversion 183
 intentional torts 204–5
 negligence action based on 238
 private nuisance 538
Federal/State powers 24
Felonious tort rule 94
Foetus *see* Unborn child
Food donors
 exclusion of liability in negligence 249
Foreseeability *see* Reasonable foreseeability
Freedom of belief and opinion 6
Freedom of social and commercial exchange 6
Funeral expenses
 survivor action 70
 victims of crime 86

Good samaritan protection 23
 battery 220–2
 negligence 248
Goods
 bailment 171–3
 conversion *see* Conversion

Goods (*cont.*)
   detinue *see* Detinue
   intentional damage to 201
   intentional interference with 171
   torts protecting right of possession 6, 171
   trespass *see* Trespass to goods
Gratuitous services
   damages for 31, 53–8
   loss of capacity to provide, damages for 57
   survivor action 70
Griffiths v Kerkemeyer damages 31, 53–8

Harassment 135, 546
Hearing loss damages 51
Highway
   authorities *see* Road authorities
   negligence 533
   public nuisance 532–3
HIH collapse 20
History of torts law 9–26
   action on the case 128–9
   compensation 29–31
   courts 12–13
   customary law 9
   English law adopted in Australia 18–19
   liability, evolution of 29–31
   negligence 241–5
   oaths 10
   ordeals 10
   precedent, doctrine of 15–17
   trial by battle 11
   writ system 13–14
Hospital/medical expenses
   liability for 30
   special damages 46
   survivor action 70

Illegality
   contributory negligence 492, 493
   defence to intentional torts 25
   defence to negligence 238, 520–3
   joint illegal activity 492, 493, 520–3
Immigration
   false imprisonment 106, 152
   misfeasance in public office 152
Impairment
   definition 32
   non-economic damages 47–53
Independent contractor
   employer's liability for 667–8
   non-delegable duty of care in relation to 665–8
   occupier's liability for 666
   vicarious liability for 657, 663–5
Inference of negligence 320–2
Injunction
   defamation 651
   injurious falsehood 170
   nuisance 46, 541, 542, 543, 547, 550, 554, 556
   quia timet 556
   trespass to land 122
Injurious falsehood 7, 159, 166–70
   action on the case 8
   actual damage caused 167, 169
   classic case 166
   damages 170
   deceit distinguished 159
   defamation distinguished 167
   economic tort 7
   elements of 168
   goods, business or profession, statement about 168
   history of tort 166
   injunction 170
   intentional tort 7
   malice 168
   proof of actual damage 167, 169
   remedies 170
   s 52 *Trade Practices Act* compared 157–8
Innominate torts 4
Innuendo *see* Defamation
Insanity defence
   intentional tort 225
   negligence 318
Insurance crisis 20–1
Intentional damage to goods 201
   action on the case 201
   limitation of actions 201
Intentional infliction of nervous shock 6, 130–5
   action on the case 8, 128
   cases 131–2
   damage 132, 134
   definition 130
   elements of 132–4
   harassment 134–5
   indirect intentional tort 7
   intention 132–4
   nature of injury 134
   psychiatric illness 131, 134
   purely mental distress 134
   rights protected 6
   stalking 135
   suicide 133
   Wilkinson v Downton 4, 6, 131–5
Intentional infliction of physical harm 6, 129–30
   action on the case 8, 128, 129
   damage, requirement of 130
   definition 129
   elements of 130
   indirect intentional tort 7
   intention 130
   rights protected 6
Intentional torts 7, 89
   common law 28
   consent defence *see* Consent
   defences *see* Defences to intentional torts
   fault, concept of 204–5
   intentional/negligent conduct overlap 28

Interference with contractual relations 7, 8
Internet
  wrongful interference with websites 127
Intoxication
  contributory negligence 492–9
    common law 492
    evidentiary provisions 497
    extent of impairment of skill 496
    joint illegal activity 492, 493
    medicines 496
    rebuttable presumption 494–5
    statutory reduction of damages 498
    statutory reforms 494–9
  drunk driving 492, 493, 514
  plaintiff in negligence action 295–6, 302
  voluntary assumption of risk 498, 504, 514
Ipp Report 22, 24, 275, 309, 341, 419, 437, 488, 652
Ius commune 15

Joint and several liability 674–6
Judge
  defamation trial 606
  false imprisonment on order of 110
  role of trial judge 11
Jury 12
  defamation trial 606

Land, trespass to *see* Trespass to land
Landlord
  duty of care 256–8
  nuisance, liability for 552
  standard of care 320
  trespass to land 118
Law of torts
  Civil Liability Acts 22–6
  history *see* History of torts law
  implementation of reforms 23–5, 27
  object of 4
  origins 9–17
  precedent, doctrine of 15–17
  reforms 2002–03 19–27, 239–40
  rights protected by 5–6
Lex loci delicti 26
Libel *see* Defamation
Lifetime Care and Support Authority (NSW) 82
Limitation of actions
  children 232
  date of discoverability 232
  defamation 608
  defence to intentional torts 231–2
  defence to negligence 239
  defendant's estate, action against 69
  disability, person under 232
  intentional damage to goods 201
  personal injury actions 232
  surviving actions 69
  wrongful death 72
Listening devices 126
Locus standi see Standing to sue

Lord Campbell's Act 71
Loss of earning capacity
  assessment of damages 61–4, 75
  wrongful death action 75–6
Loss of services
  action on the case 8
  survivor action 70

Maintenance and champerty 8
Malicious prosecution 6, 135–9
  action on the case 8, 128
  damages 138–9
  elements of 136–8
  history of tort 135
  indirect intentional tort 7
  instrumentality 137–8
  malice 137, 138
  principles 136
  rights protected 6
  risk to personal security 136–7
  risk to reputation 136
  risk to security of property 137
Mediation 5
Medical negligence
  Bolam test 308
  Bolitho test 308, 309, 313
  defamation 647
  failure to warn and advise 311–13
    causation 354–60
    hindsight bias 357–62
    retrospectivity 357
  hindsight bias 357–62
    statutory approach 361–2
  information, provision of 311–13
  inherent risks 287
  Ipp Report recommendations 309
  'loss of chance' doctrine 348–51
  professional standards 307–13
    accepted practice 310
    examination, diagnosis and treatment 307–11
    provision of information 311–3
    statutory provisions 309–11
  therapeutic privilege 312
  warning of risk 311–3
Medical treatment
  battery 96, 207
    defence of legal authority 226
  child, consent 211–15
    blood transfusion 214–15
    lifesaving treatment 212
    non-therapeutic purposes 213, 214
    parens patriae jurisdiction 211, 212
    sterilisation 211, 213
  consent 206–15
    adult 206–8
    incompetent person 211–15
    lifesaving treatment 208–10, 212
    minor 211–15
    unborn child 210

Medical treatment (cont.)
  infectious diseases 228
  involuntary treatment 226
  necessity 218–20
  non-voluntary treatment 226
  professional standards 307–13
  quarantine 228
  right to refuse treatment
    child 212
    lifesaving or life-sustaining 208–10
    viable foetus 210
  sterilisation of intellectually disabled person
    child 211, 213
    necessity 218
  trespass to the person 207
Mental harm *see* Psychiatric injury
Mental illness *see also* Psychiatric illness
  standard of care 317–9
Mental integrity, freedom from interference with 6
Misfeasance in public office 6, 143–52
  action on the case 8, 128
  bad faith 145, 149
  bank 143
  boundaries of tort 151
  causation 145, 151
  damage 151
  definition 143
  elements of 145
  government department 144
  history of tort 143
  honesty or dishonesty 147
  indirect intentional tort 7
  intention 148
  invalid or unauthorised act 145, 147
  knowledge of lack of power 145, 150
  legal practitioners 146
  malice 145, 148–50
  police 146
  policy considerations 151
  public officer 145–7
  rationale of tort 143
  reckless indifference 145, 149, 150
  remoteness of damage 151
  rights protected 6
  standing to sue 150
  targeted malice 145, 148
  untargeted malice 145, 149, 151
  visa cancellation 152
Misleading or deceptive conduct 157
  deceit compared 157–8
  injurious falsehood compared 157–8
  remedies 157
  s 52 *Trade Practices Act* 157–8
  strict liability 157
Misrepresentation 6, 7
Mistake
  conversion 192
  defence to intentional torts 232
  mistaken self-defence 232
  trespass to goods 177
Misuse of power *see* Misfeasance in public office
Motor accident compensation
  contributory negligence 81
  New South Wales 82–3
  'no fault' scheme 81
  Northern Territory 81
  pecuniary loss 81
  personal injury or death 80
  serious injury 80
  statutory schemes 80–3
  Tasmania 81
  Victoria 80–1

Necessity defence 218–20
Negligence 235–385
  action on the case 8, 236
  breach of duty of care 270–324
    general principles 272–84
    onus of proof 320
  calculus of 275–80, 396
  causation *see* Causation
  cause of action 237–40
  circumstantial evidence 322
  community standards 289
  compensable damage 236
  contributory *see* Contributory negligence
  damage requirement 236
  defences *see* Defence to negligence
  duty of care *see* Duty of care
  elements of 238, 239
  failure to warn 296–7
    causation 354–60
    obvious risk 297
  fault-based cause of action 238
  general principles 272–84
  hindsight bias 357–62, 410
    statutory approach 361–2
  history of tort 241–5
  industry standards 306–7
  inference 320–2
  inherent risks 286–7, 323
  intoxication of plaintiff 295–6, 302
  knowledge of plaintiff's vulnerability 280
  law reform 19–26, 239–40
  'loss of chance' doctrine 348–51
  medical *see* Medical negligence
  not insignificant risk of harm 274–5
  novus actus interveniens 328, 363–8
  nuisance compared 538
  obvious risk *see* Obvious risk
  onus of proof 320
  overlap of intentional and negligent conduct 28
  overview 235–40
  personal responsibility and 246–7, 287–9
  police, immunity from suit 248
  probability of harm 276, 279
  professional standards 307–13

property damage 370–1
proportionate liability *see* Proportionate liability
public authorities 298–306
　recreational activities 294, 298–301
　statutory breach factors 304–6
rationale for tort 236, 270
reasonable foreseeability 238, 250, 375–7, 388–92
reasonable precautions to avoid risk 275–80
　burden of taking 281–2
　considerations in determining 275–6
　onus of proof 283
　subsequent safer precautions adopted 282
recreational activities 294, 298–301
remoteness of damage *see* Remoteness of damage
res ipsa loquitur 371–4
retrospective nature of inquiry 271–2
rights protected 6
road authorities 301–3
seriousness of harm 276, 279
slipping cases 322–4
social utility of activity creating risk 276, 284–5
standard of care *see* Standard of care
tests of foreseeability 22, 273, 274
time for assessing risk 285–7
unintentional tort 7
unrelated subsequent events 368–70
voluntary assumption of risk *see* Voluntary assumption of risk
Negligent misstatement 450–65
　assumption of responsibility 454, 456
　breach of duty 458–9
　causal reliance 463
　cause of action 450
　damages 464
　deceit distinguished 162, 166
　denial of compensation 446, 447–9
　duty of care 455–8
　duty to protect economic interests 459
　employer 457
　estate agent 460
　failure to make statement 454
　foreseeable reliance 463
　incorrect statement 454
　knowledge of intended use of information 457
　negligence requirement 459–60
　negligent words distinguished from negligent acts 451
　nomenclature 454
　physical damage 465
　prerequisites to recovery for 455–62
　professional relationship 455
　public authorities 456
　pure economic loss 446, 450–65
　　physical damage distinguished 465
　reasonable expectation 454
　reasonable reliance 452–4, 463
　relationship of parties 451, 455
　remedies 464
　remoteness of damage 464
　rescission of contract 464
　solicitors 455, 458
　special skill 453
　vulnerability 454, 457, 462–3
Negligent physical conduct
　defective buildings 469–71
　defective product 467–9
　denial of compensation 447–50
　proximity of parties 466
　pure economic loss 445, 465–72
　reasonable foreseeability 466
　vulnerability 468, 471–2
Negligent trespass 104–5
Nervous shock
　compensable damage in negligence 236, 239, 416
　definition 130, 416
　intentional infliction *see* Intentional infliction of nervous shock
　pure psychiatric injury *see* Pure psychiatric injury
Nominal damages 38
　trespass to goods 178
　trespass to land 123
　trespass to the person 94
Nominate torts 4
Non-delegable duty of care 652, 665–74
　employers 667–8
　history 666
　igni suus rule 669
　independent contractor, to 665–8
　occupiers 666, 669–72
　　dangerous premises 671
　　dangerous substances 669
　　trespasser 671
　overview 652
　Rylands v Fletcher, rule in 669
　scope 672–3
　vicarious liability distinguished 668, 673
Non-economic damages 47–53
　Australian Capital Territory 52
　caps 48
　Commonwealth 48
　disfigurement 47, 49
　extreme cases 49
　future pecuniary needs 53
　hearing loss 51
　judicial discretion 49
　New South Wales 48
　Northern Territory 50
　pain and suffering 47–50
　psychiatric injury 51
　Queensland 50
　significant injury 50–1
　South Australia 49, 50
　Tasmania 52
　thresholds 48–53
　Victoria 50
　Western Australia 52

694 *Index*

Nonfeasance *see* Pure nonfeasance
Novus actus interveniens 328, 363–8
   negligent tortious conduct 367
   obvious risk 363
   plaintiff's intervening act 363–6
   reasonable foreseeability test 376
   reasonableness 365
   third party's intervening act 366–8
   two-tier approach 364
Nuisance 7
   action on the case 8
   history of tort 529
   legal species of 530–4
   private *see* Private nuisance
   public 531–4
   rights protected 6
   statutory tort 530–1

Obvious risk 22, 289–98, 509–14
   breach of duty of care 289–98
   burden of proof 510, 511
   dangerous recreational activities 294, 512–14
   defence to negligence 509–14
   definition 293, 509
   failure to warn 296–7
   gross negligence test 513–14
   intoxication of plaintiff 295–6
   nature of plea 511–12
   reasonable care to avoid 289–98
   reasonable person in circumstances 510
   slipping cases 323
   statutory provisions 293–5, 297, 509
   volenti defence compared 511
Occupiers' liability 258–63
   criminal conduct of third parties 260
   independent contractors, for torts of 666
   non-delegable duty of care 666, 669–72
      dangerous premises 671
      dangerous substances 669
      trespasser 671
   nuisance 550–2
   private land 259
   public land 258
   recreation, land used for 260
   slipping cases 322–4
   status of entrant 258
   status of land 258
   third parties
      criminal conduct of 260
      duty to control 261–3
Omissions *see* Pure nonfeasance
Onus of proof
   breach of duty of care 320
   causation 346–8
   consent 206
   defamation 585
   false imprisonment 106
   obvious risk defence 510, 511
   reasonable precautions to avoid risk 283

Parens patriae 91
   consent to medical treatment 211, 212
Passing off 7, 8
Personal injury
   aggravated/exemplary damages 42
   caps on damages 23
   common law damages 33–4
   limitation of actions 232
   motor accident compensation 80–3
   proportionate liability, exclusion 679
   statutory compensation schemes 77–87
   victims of crime 83–7
Personal liberty, right to 6
Physical harm, intentional infliction of *see*
      Intentional infliction of physical harm
Physical integrity, right to 5
Pleadings 33
Police
   assault and battery 45
   duty of care in investigations 248
   exemplary damages 45
   false imprisonment by 45, 108–9
      false allegations, acting on 110
   immunity from suit in negligence 248
   misfeasance in public office 146
   personal liability 663
   vicarious liability 663
Precedent, doctrine of 15–17, 25
   English precedents followed in Australia 18
   ratio decidendi 17, 18, 19
   stare decisis 18, 19, 25
Prison
   duty of care to prisoners 366
   duty to control prisoners 261, 262, 411
   nonfeasance by authorities 410
   suicide 365–6
Privacy
   confidentiality distinguished 152
   defamation and 579
   listening devices 126
   misuse of private information 152–6
   personal information protection 156
   right to 6
   tort protecting 6
   trespass to land, whether protected by 124–7
   websites, interference with 127
Private nuisance 7, 534–59
   abatement by self-help 5, 554–5
      trespass 230, 554, 555
   action on the case 8, 538
   community values 541
   continuing tort 555
   damages 555–6
   defences 556–9
      conformation of land 559
      consent 556
      prescriptive right 559
      reasonable use 558
      statutory authority 557–8

definition   534
duration   545
emissions   543
factors taken into account   540
fault   538
frequency   545
golf course   542
harassment   546
history of tort   529
improper motive   546
injunction   46, 541, 542, 543, 547, 550, 554, 556
interference with use and enjoyment of land   536–45
landlord's liability   552
licensee, title to sue   549
lights   546
locality   541
natural causes   553–4
nature of tort   534
negligence compared   538
neighbourhood principle   537
noise   543, 553
non-physical harm   535
occupier's liability   550–4
   knowledge of nuisance   550–2
   natural causes   553–4
   neighbouring premises   552
offending sensibilities of neighbours   545–9
physical harm   535
picketing   547–8
pre-existing noxious activities   541–2
proprietary rights   535, 549
prostitutes   545
public interest   544
public nuisance distinguished   531
quia timet injunction   556
reasonable foreseeability of harm   539–40
remedies   554–6
reversionary owners, title to sue   549
rights protected   6, 535, 536
secondary boycott   549
self-help, abatement by   5, 554–5
   trespass   230, 554, 555
serious and unreasonable interference   536, 540
seriousness of harm   538
smells   543
stalking   548
standing to sue   549–50
strict liability tort   527
surveillance   546, 549
television reception, interference with   544–5
time of day   545
types of harm resulting from   535–6
undermining support of land   535–6
unreasonable interference   536, 540
unusually sensitive plaintiff   540
watching and besetting   547–9, 550
who may be sued   550–4
Private vs public wrongs   27

Professional indemnity insurance   21
Property damage
   attribution of liability   370–1
   nuisance   542
Property rights   6
Proportionate liability   676–81
   assessment   681
   concurrent wrongdoers   677–8
   contributory negligence   679
   exclusions   679
   exemplary damages excluded   679
   legislation   677–9
   personal injury or death damages excluded   679
   vicarious liability   679
Psychiatric illness
   bodily injury, whether   418
   causation   328
   certification of psychiatric patient   228
   classifications   420
   compensable damage for purpose of negligence   236
   foreseeability   383–4
   nervous shock, constituting   131, 134
Psychiatric injury
   causation   365
   compensable   236, 239, 417, 421
   damages   51, 58
      pure psychiatric injury *see* Pure psychiatric injury
   egg-shell skull rule   382
   nervous shock   130, 416, 417
   nomenclature   416–9
   secondary victims *see* Pure psychiatric injury
   solatium   74–7, 415
Public authorities
   breach of statutory duty   569–72
      absolute duty   571
      exercise of discretionary functions   570–2
      res ipsa loquitur   571
   defamation   584–5
   liability in negligence   298–306
      failure to warn   296–9
      obvious risk   296–7
      reasonable precautions   299
      recreational activities   298–301
      road authorities   301–3
      statutory breach factors   304–6
   negligent misstatement   456
   omissions, liability for   397–411
      discretional/operational decisions   399–414
      duty of care, existence of   402–3
      duty to control others   411
      general reliance doctrine   403
      hindsight, rule against   410
      non-exercise of power   397–9
      private vs public law duties   398, 407
   road authorities *see* Road authorities
   statutory policy defence   23

696 *Index*

Public nuisance 531–4
  crime 531
  elements of tort 532
  highway cases 532–3
  private nuisance distinguished 531
  scope of tort 531
Public officer
  definition 145
  misfeasance *see* Misfeasance in public office
Punitive damages *see* Exemplary damages
Pure economic loss
  damages for 240, 445–72
  defective buildings 469–71
  defective product negligently supplied 467–9
  denial of compensation 447–50
  negligent misstatement *see* Negligent misstatement
  negligent physical conduct 445, 465–72
  negligently occasioned 445–72
  overview 445–7
  secondary economic loss 445
  vulnerability element 454, 457, 462–3, 468, 471–2
Pure nonfeasance 394–414
  common law 394–7
  legal obligation to act 394–7
  moral and legal duties distinguished 395
  omission, meaning 393
  public authorities 397–411
    discretional/operational decisions 399–414
    duty of care, existence of 402–3
    general reliance doctrine 403
    hindsight, rule against 410
    non-exercise of power 397–9
    private law vs public law duties 398, 407
  regulation-making power, entities with 413–14
  road authorities 411–13
Pure psychiatric injury
  absence from accident scene 422–5
  breach of duty 440
  bystanders 426, 442, 443
  causation 426, 435–6, 440
    'material contribution' test 435, 436
    statutory provisions 440
  circumstances of the case 441–3
  codification of law 437
  compensable 417, 421
  consequential mental harm 417, 420–1, 438
  damages for 22, 134, 417, 420–36
  direct perception of accident 422, 432
  duty of care 423, 425, 440
  elements 430–4, 438–41
  employer's duty 424, 431, 434
  exceptions to duty of care 425–6
  history 420–36
  Ipp Report recommendations 437, 438
  mental harm 417, 418
  mere knowledge 432
  nature of relationship 425, 433, 442, 443

  negligence of primary victim 426
  negligently occasioned 415–43
  nervous shock 416, 417
  nomenclature 416–19
  'normal fortitude' 426, 427, 428, 431
  post-traumatic stress disorder 426
  pre-existing relationship 429, 442
  prerequisites to recovery 425–9
  presence at accident scene 422, 442
  reasonable foreseeability 423, 429, 430
  recognised psychiatric illness 419–20, 434–5, 438
  remoteness of damage 427–9
  rescuers 424, 436
  secondary victims 420
  solatium 74–7, 415
  statutory provisions 437–43
    circumstances of the case 441–3
    elements of liability 438–41
    scope 437
    threshold requirement 438
    tobacco-related injury or death excluded 437
  'sudden shock' 432, 441
  vulnerability of victim 427

Qualified privilege
  business environment 647
  common law 627–44
  'community of interest', furtherance of 634
  defamation defence 626–5
  failure to investigate 642, 646
  fair and accurate report 627
  governmental communications 634–40
    reasonableness of publication 639–40
  judicial proceedings 627
  knowledge of falsity 642
  limited publication 629
  malice 641–3
  overview 629–30
  parliamentary proceedings 627
  political communications 634–40
    reasonableness of publication 639–40
  political discussion 635–40
  proceedings of public concern, reports of 627–9
  protection of common interests 634
  protection of publisher's interests 632
  protection of recipient's interests 633
  public documents 626–7
  public interest 630–2
  public views of politician 643
  reasonable inquiries as to truth 642, 646
  s 30 of uniform law 645
  self-defence 632–3
  statutory 644–8
Quarantine 228

Ratio decidendi 17, 18, 19
Reasonable foreseeability
  conversion, distress or damage caused by 199

deceit, loss caused by   165
duty of care   376, 388–92
negligent misstatement, reliance on   463
novel categories of case   388–92
novus actus interveniens   376
nuisance, harm caused by   539–40
pure psychiatric injury   423, 429, 430
remoteness of damage *see* Remoteness of damage
tests   238, 250, 375–7, 388–92, 430
wrongful death   74
Recreational activities
  dangerous   294, 512–14
  exclusion of liability clauses   517–19
  implied consent to being struck   216–17
  obvious risk   294, 512–14
  occupier's liability   260
  public authorities, liability   298–301
Remedies   4–5
  damages *see* Damages
  injunction *see* Injunction
  litigation   4
  non-judicial   5
  object of torts law   4
  restitutionary   5
Remoteness of damage
  egg-shell skull rule   382, 385
  extent of harm   381–4
  history of tests for   377–9
  kind of harm   380
  manner in which damage occurs   380–1
  misfeasance in public office   151
  negligent misstatement   464
  non-tortious causal factor   385
  pre-existing condition   385
  pure psychiatric injury   427–9
  reasonable foreseeability test   375–7
  talem qualem rule   382
  test for   380–5
  vicissitudes of life principle   385
  vulnerability of victim   382, 427
Replevin   178
  writ of   14
Res ipsa loquitur   371–4, 571
Rescuers
  duty of care to   253, 424
  pure psychiatric injury damages   424, 436
Restitutio in integrum   30
Rights protected by torts law   5–6
Road authorities
  liability in negligence   301–3
    actual knowledge of defects   303
    duty to maintain roads and footpaths   303
    standard of care   302
  omissions, liability for   411–13
  public nuisance   533
Rylands v Fletcher, rule in   669

Scienter, writ of   14, 243
Secondary boycott   549
Self-defence
  battery defence   223–4
  defamation defence   632–3
  mistaken   232
  reasonable proportionality   224
Slander *see* Defamation
Solatium damages   74–7, 415
Solidary liability   674–6
Spoilation of evidence   202–3
Sport *see* Recreational activities
Stalking   135, 548
Standard of care   314–20
  children   315
  community standards   289
  consensual relationships   316
  disability   317
  industry standards   306–7
  inexperience   316–17
  medical practitioners   307–13, 314
    accepted practice   310
    examination, diagnosis and treatment   307–11
    provision of information   311–13
    statutory provisions   309–11
  mental illness   317–19
  modification   314
  plaintiff in negligence action   484
  professionals   22, 307–13, 319
  reasonable foreseeability test   376
  reasonable person   314
  special skills   319–20
Standard of proof   34
Standing to sue
  breach of statutory duty   562–3
  detinue   179
  misfeasance in public office   150
  nuisance   549–50
  trespass to goods   175
  trespass to land   120
Stare decisis   18, 19, 25
Statutory tort   8
  breach of statutory duty *see* Breach of statutory duty
  nuisance   530–1
Strict liability torts   527
Structured settlements   23, 37–8
Suicide
  causation   328, 365
  intentional infliction of nervous shock   133
  mental illness and standard of care   319
Sullivan v Gordon damages   57
Summons   14
Survival of causes of action   68–71
  defendant, death of   69
  dust-related disease   70
  exemplary damages excluded   71
  limitation of actions   69
  pain and suffering damages   70
  plaintiff, death of   69–71

Talem qualem rule 382
Tobacco-related injuries
  aggravated/exemplary damages 42
  exclusion from Civil Liability Acts 25
  pure psychiatric injury damages, exclusion 437–8
  voluntary assumption of risk 506
Tort
  classification 5–8
  definition 4
Trespass 7, 8
  ab initio 119
  de bonis asportatis 173, 176
  goods *see* Trespass to goods
  intentional tort 7, 89
  land *see* Trespass to land
  meaning 91
  person *see* Trespass to the person
  vi et armis 242
  writ of 92, 128, 177
Trespass to goods 6, 173–8
  actual damage 174
  constructive possession 175
  conversion compared 183–5
  damages 177
  definition 173
  direct interference 176
  electronic trespass 175, 177
  elements of 175
  history of tort 173–4
  intention 177
  jus tertii defence 177
  mistake 177
  nature of damage 174
  nominal damage 178
  possession requirement 175–6
  rights protected 6
  standing to sue 175
  trespass *de bonis asportatis* 173, 176
  trover as alternative 183–5
  unauthorised use 174
  voluntary act 177
  wrongful intention 177
Trespass to land 6, 114–27
  above surface of land 121
  actionable *per se* 117
  adverse possessors 120–1
  affirmative action 118
  aggravated damages 123–4
  aircraft 122–3
  below surface of land 121
  continuing trespass 120
  damages 123–4
  defences 229–31
    abatement of nuisance 230, 555
    Crown powers 229
    defence of property 230
    recaption of chattels 231
    re-entry on land 230
  direct interference with land 117
  elements of 117–19
  exemplary damages 124
  history of tort 114–17
  injunction 122
  intentional tort 7, 89
  landlords 118
  liability 122–3
  limitations of tort 124–5
  listening devices 126
  possessory interests 120
  privacy, whether protected by 124–7
  projecting objects 122
  remedies 122
  rights protected 6, 114
  standing to sue 120
  trespass *ab initio* 119
  voluntary conduct 118
  ways of committing 118
  websites, interference with 127
Trespass to the person 6, 91–113
  assault *see* Assault
  battery *see* Battery
  conceptual basis 92–3
  damages, nature of 93–4
  false imprisonment *see* False imprisonment
  fault 205
  historical overview 91–2
  medical treatment *see* Medical treatment
  negligent trespass 104–5
  origins of tort 91–4
  proof of actual damage 92
  reasonable chastisement 93
  reckless or deliberate intent 93
  rights protected 6
Trover 182–4
  see also Conversion

Unborn child
  duty of care to 263–9
  medical treatment, mother's consent 210
  mother's duty of care 263
  no rights at law 263
  wrongful life 264–9
Unfair competition
  action on the case 8
  economic tort 7
  intentional tort 7
Unintentional torts 7

Vicarious liability
  agents, torts by 656–8
  categories 656–63
  definition 652
  employers 659–63
  history 653–4
  independent contractors, torts by 657, 663–5
  modern doctrine 654–6

non-delegable duty of care distinguished 668, 673
overview 652
partners 658
police, torts by 663
principals 656–8
proportionate liability 679
Victims of crime *see* Criminal injuries compensation
Volenti non fit injuria see Voluntary assumption of risk
Voluntary assumption of risk
  acceptance of specific risks 508
  actual knowledge of risks 508
  availability of defence 503
  breach of statutory duty defence 577
  burden of proof 511
  common law defence 503–9
  consent distinguished 217, 505–6
  drunk driving 514
  elements of defence 506–8
  employment relationship 508
  exclusion notice, implied acceptance 507
  exclusion of liability clause distinguished 515
  implied agreement 505
  intentional tort defence 217–18
  intoxication 498, 504, 514
  legal risk, assumption of 505
  negligence defence 22, 238, 477, 503–14
  obvious risk *see* Obvious risk
  personal autonomy principle 504
  propositions 505
  smoking 506
  statutory defence *see* Obvious risk
  statutory reforms 509
  volenti non fit injuria maxim 217, 504
  waiver of duty of care 511
Volunteer protection 23

battery 222
negligence 249

Wilkinson v Downton, tort of 4, 6, 131–5
Workers' compensation
  common employment defence 477
  contributory negligence 80, 484–7
  duty to warn employees of risks 485
  exclusion from Civil Liability Acts 25
  'no fault' schemes 78, 667
  non-delegable duty of care 667
  preconditions for payment 79
  statutory schemes 78–80
Writs
  assumpsit 14, 242
  covenant 14
  debt 14
  historical 13–14
  replevin 14
  scienter 14, 243
  summons 14
  trespass 92, 128, 177
Wrongful death 71–7
  assessment of damages 75
  assythment 415
  causation 73–4
  contributory negligence 77
  deceased's right of action 74
  foreseeable loss 74
  history 71–2
  limitation of actions 72
  Lord Campbell's Act 71
  loss of earning capacity 75–6
  requirements for establishing 73–5
  scope of legislation 73
  solatium damages 74–7, 415
Wrongful life 264–9